THE SAGE HANDBOOK OF

COUNSELLING AND PSYCHOTHERAPY

Sara Miller McCune founded SAGE Publishing in 1965 to support the dissemination of usable knowledge and educate a global community. SAGE publishes more than 1000 journals and over 800 new books each year, spanning a wide range of subject areas. Our growing selection of library products includes archives, data, case studies and video. SAGE remains majority owned by our founder and after her lifetime will become owned by a charitable trust that secures the company's continued independence.

Los Angeles | London | New Delhi | Singapore | Washington DC | Melbourne

CONTENTS

PART IV: PROFESSIONAL ISSUES   113

PART V: THEORY AND APPROACHES   173

LIST OF FIGURES AND TABLES

FIGURES

TABLES

ABOUT THE EDITORS AND CONTRIBUTORS

Colin Feltham is Emeritus Professor of Critical Counselling Studies, Sheffield Hallam University. He teaches counselling psychology at the University of Southern Denmark and also runs experiential skills workshops in Denmark. He speaks and examines at various UK universities as well as internationally. His many publications include *Counselling and Counselling Psychology: A Critical Examination* (PCCS Books, 2013), *Keeping Ourselves in the Dark* (Nine-Banded Books, 2015) and *Depressive Realism* (Routledge, 2017). In addition to counselling, the topics he writes on include failure, humanistic psychology, evolutionary psychology, anthropathology, and death.

Dr Terry Hanley, CPsychol, AFBPsS, is the Programme Director for the Doctorate in Counselling Psychology at the University of Manchester. He is a Fellow of the Higher Education Academy, an Associate Fellow of the British Psychological Society and was Editor of *Counselling Psychology Review* between the years 2009 and 2015. He has a keen interest in training therapists in research skills and is a co-author of *Introducing Counselling and Psychotherapy Research* (Sage, 2013). Additionally, his own therapeutic practice and research has primarily focused around work with young people and young adults, a topic on which he is also lead editor of the text *Adolescent Counselling Psychology* (Routledge, 2013). He is an HCPC-registered Counselling Psychologist and presently works as a therapist with the organisation Freedom from Torture providing psychological support to a football therapy project. Follow him on twitter @drterryhanley.

Dr Laura Anne Winter, CPsychol, is an HCPC-registered Counselling Psychologist and Lecturer in Education and Counselling Psychology based at the University of Manchester. Her research interests include social justice, and in particular the impact of economic and relational inequality on wellbeing and education. Previous research has included exploring social justice within counselling and educational psychology, the impact of welfare reform on families, and the way in which schools are supporting emotional wellbeing in the context of austerity. Her clinical practice has predominantly been based within NHS Primary Care settings, working with individuals who have been diagnosed with 'moderate' and 'severe' 'mental health problems'.

Kate Adam, BSc (Hons), PostGrad Dip, Reg. MBACP, MSc, Post MSc Dip, CPsychol, AFBPsS, Reg. HCPC, RAPPS, is a Chartered Consultant Counselling Psychologist, Applied Practice Supervisor and Associate Fellow of the British Psychological Society. She works as the Head of Psychology in a senior leadership position at ABL Health Ltd, a community health-care provider and in private practice. Kate is experienced in providing a range of clinical interventions, across the life span in a variety of settings. Her specialist interests include: long-term health conditions, eating disorders, personality disorders, psychological trauma, supervision and service development. She has an active interest in evidencing best practice and the application of models in therapy, including positive psychology, behaviour change and mindfulness.

Zubeida Ali is a BACP-accredited Counsellor and Professional Lead for Counselling for a large IAPT service in the north of England. She held the post of Chair of BACP's Healthcare Division from 2012 until 2016, having served on the Healthcare Executive for a number of years prior to this. Zubeida also serves on the North West Psychological Professions Network (NWPPN) Steering Committee and chairs the NWPPN Counsellors Working in the NHS Network.

Dr India Amos is a lecturer in Counselling and Psychotherapy at the University of Salford and HCPC registered Counselling Psychologist. Her research interests include qualitative research methodologies, particularly the aesthetic dimension of qualitative description. India is particularly interested in how we can engage individuals in an embodied way with research findings to aid deeper empathic understanding of human experience.

Dr Kate Anthony, FBACP, is an expert in the field of technology in mental health. She is CEO and co-founder of the Online Therapy Institute, a company specialising in training mental health and coaching practitioners to use technological tools in their services. She is a Fellow of the British Association for Counselling and Psychotherapy (BACP), awarded for her outstanding services to the profession, and Past-President and Fellow of the International Society for Mental Health Online (ISMHO).

Lionel Bailly is a Practising Analyst of the Association Lacanienne Internationale (Paris) and an Academic Associate of the British Psychoanalytical Society. He is Honorary Senior Lecturer at University College London Psychoanalysis Unit where he is particularly involved in the doctoral school. He trained in medicine and psychiatry at the Salpêtrière Hospital in Paris and before moving to the UK was head of the Child and Adolescent Bio-Psychopathology Unit of the Henri Rouselle Centre at St Anne Hospital (Paris). He is the author of *Lacan* in the Beginner's Guide Series (One World Press, 2009).

Clark Baim is a Senior Trainer in Psychodrama Psychotherapy and the Co-Director of the Birmingham Institute for Psychodrama, Birmingham, England. From 2000 to 2012, he was the Co-Lead National Trainer for the Probation Service's Sexual Offending Groupwork Programmes in England and Wales. In 1987 he established and was the Founder Director of Geese Theatre UK, a company focusing on rehabilitative work in criminal justice. In 2007 he received the David Kipper Scholar's Award from the American Society of Group Psychotherapy and Psychodrama.

Liz Ballinger is a BACP Senior Accredited Counsellor. She is a lecturer at the University of Manchester. She acts as Programme Director for the MA in Counselling, alongside supervising doctorate and masters students' research and providing input on the counselling and educational psychology doctorate programmes. Her doctoral thesis focused on tutors' experience of counsellor training. Her belief in the importance of the social context in the shaping of human experience has led her to an ongoing critique of therapy, and a related interest in the relationship of both gender and social class to therapeutic processes and outcomes.

Jill Balmont has worked as a Chartered Clinical Psychologist in the NHS for over 30 years. She specialises in the field of HIV and sexual health for both Nottinghamshire and Derbyshire Healthcare NHS Foundation Trusts, and she has regularly taught on the Doctorate in Clinical Psychology Course at Hull University. She is grateful to Dr Janet Garley, Consultant in Genito-urinary Medicine, for her comments on the medical aspects of her chapter.

Dr Sara Bardsley qualified as a Clinical Psychologist in 2016 from the University of Manchester, having completed specialist training in Psychodynamic Interpersonal Therapy.

Rowan Bayne is Emeritus Professor of Psychology and Counselling at the University of East London where he was a core tutor on the postgraduate diploma in counselling and psychotherapy for 32 years. His recent books include: *Psychology for Social Work Theory and Practice* (with Paula Nicolson, Palgrave Macmillan, 4th ed., 2014); *Applied Psychology: Research, Training and Practice* (edited with Gordon Jinks, Sage, 2nd ed., 2013); and *The Counsellor's Guide to Personality: Understanding Preferences, Motives and Life Stories* (Palgrave Macmillan, 2013).

Professor Jenny Bimrose, based at the Institute for Employment Research, University of Warwick, has over 30 years of experience teaching at postgraduate level in counselling, researching and managing in higher education. Many of her research projects have focused on the theory and practice of counselling and on the career development of women. International comparative research into older women's career progression across nine countries, on which Jenny led, was recently completed and published.

Tim Bond is an Emeritus Professor at the University of Bristol and a Visiting Professor to the University of Malta and a registered member of BACP. He researches and writes about ethical and legal issues for the talking therapies and is a consultant to BACP on the *Ethical Framework for the Counselling Professions*.

John Boorman, DClinPsych, is a Clinical Psychologist for South London and Maudsley NHS Trust and Co-director of Greenheart Psychological Services, an ACT and contextual-based therapy provider. He is also Visiting Lecturer in the University of Hertfordshire's Clinical Psychology Department. John regularly delivers Acceptance and Commitment Therapy (ACT) training for a range of National Health Service, University and private organisations. He is currently on the committee board for the British Association of Behavioural and Cognitive Psychotherapies (BABCP) ACT Special Interest Group, which promotes the dissemination and training of ACT throughout the UK. His research interests include using ACT and contextual behavioural approaches with children, young people and their families.

Jude Boyles iis a BACP Senior Accredited Psychological Therapist. She has been practising as a Therapist for the last 24 years. Prior to qualifying, Jude worked in a Rape Crisis centre and in Women's Aid refuges. Jude qualified as a therapist and worked in a Mental Health Crisis service for 11 years before establishing the Freedom from Torture Centre in Manchester in 2003. Jude managed the centre for 14 years, and carried a caseload of torture survivors during that time. Jude starts a new role in August 2017 as a Psychological Therapist with Syrians resettled to the UK via the Syrian Vulnerable Persons Resettlement Programme.

Dr Richard J. Brown is Senior Lecturer in Clinical Psychology and Programme Director for the Clinical Psychology Doctorate at the University of Manchester. He is also Honorary Consultant Clinical Psychologist with Greater Manchester Mental Health NHS Foundation Trust where he runs the Functional Neurological Disorders (FuND) Service. He delivers therapy, training and supervision in Psychodynamic Interpersonal Therapy (PIT), co-developed PIT skills training for Psychological Wellbeing Practitioners and co-authored the PIT treatment manual for psychogenic non-epileptic seizures. He is a founding member of the Psychodynamic Interpersonal Therapy Special Interest Group UK.

Jo Cooper has been involved with NLP since the 1980s and was certified by Richard Bandler as a master trainer in the mid-1990s. She was a partner in an NLP training company for 10 years and now works as a freelance trainer and consultant. She has a private practice in which much of her work is with equestrians, specialising in confidence coaching, performance enhancement and trauma recovery. She has a special interest in working systemically with the mind–body system which is especially relevant when working with sports people.

Mick Cooper is a Professor of Counselling Psychology at the University of Roehampton and a Chartered Counselling Psychologist. Mick is author and editor of a range of texts on person-centred, existential, and relational approaches to therapy, including *Existential Therapies* (Sage, 2nd ed., 2017), *Working at Relational Depth in Counselling and Psychotherapy* (with Dave Mearns, Sage, 2005), and *Pluralistic Counselling and Psychotherapy* (with John McLeod, Sage, 2011). Mick has also led a range of research studies exploring the process and outcomes of humanistic counselling with young people. Mick's latest book is *Existential Psychotherapy and Counselling: Contributions to a Pluralistic Practice* (Sage, 2015).

Alex Coren initially trained as a psychiatric social worker working in both adult mental health and in child and family guidance clinics. After training as a psychoanalytic psychotherapist he worked as a psychotherapist in a variety of clinical settings and contexts, including both secondary and tertiary education, predominantly at King's College London and Oxford University. He was Director of Psychodynamic Studies in the Department for Continuing Education at Oxford University and has written extensively in the field of education and short-term therapy. His books include *A Psychodynamic Approach to Education* (Sheldon Press, 1997) and *Short-term Psychotherapy* (Palgrave, 2010).

Olivier Cormier-Otaño is a BACP-accredited counsellor, a psychosexual therapist and a supervisor in private practice for over 10 years. He volunteered for over five years for LGBT charities as an assessor and a counsellor. He practises in English, French and Spanish, and has a particular interest in the intersections of language, cultures and narratives in therapy and has run a therapeutic group for Gay male asylum seekers and refugees. Olivier facilitates various training events and teaches on various diplomas for Pink Therapy, the Centre for Psychosexual Health (CPH), Beeleaf Institute and independently. Olivier has contributed to articles and presented in conferences on the subject of asexuality.

Dr Mary Creaner is Course Director for the MSc Clinical Supervision, and Assistant Professor with the Doctorate in Counselling Psychology, Trinity College Dublin. She is an accredited therapist/supervisor with the Irish Association for Counselling and Psychotherapy, a member of the American Psychological Association and also acts as a supervision consultant and trainer to statutory and voluntary agencies. Among her publications is the book, *Getting the Best out of Supervision in Counselling and Therapy* (Sage, 2014) and she was guest editor for a special section on 'Current trends in clinical supervision' (2014) with the *Counselling Psychology Quarterly* journal.

Rudi Dallos is Professor and Research Director on the Doctorate in Clinical Psychology training programme in Plymouth University, UK. He has worked as a family therapist in a variety of contexts for over 35 years with a specialism in work with children and adolescents. He has recently developed a programme of attachment and family therapy intervention (SAFE) for families with a child diagnosed with autism which has gained research funding. He has published several books, including: *An Introduction to Family Therapy* (4th ed., Open University Press, 2010), *Systemic Therapy and Attachment Narratives*, (Routledge, 2009) and *Formulation in Psychotherapy and Counselling* (Taylor and Francis, 2006).

Dominic Davies is the Founder and CEO of Pink Therapy (www.pinktherapy.com). He is a Fellow of the British Association for Counselling and Psychotherapy and the National Counselling Society. He is a Senior Accredited Psychotherapist with the National Council of Psychotherapists and a member of the World Professional Association for Transgender Health. Dominic is co-editor (with Charles Neal) of the *Pink Therapy* trilogy, which were the first British textbooks for therapists working with lesbian, gay, bisexual and transgender clients. He works as a therapist, supervisor, mentor and international training consultant on gender sexuality and relationship diversity issues.

Gill Donohoe is a clinical lead for cognitive behavioural psychotherapy within the Improving Access to Psychological Therapies Service (Sheffield IAPT), Sheffield Health & Social Care NHS Foundation Trust. She is a trained mental health nurse and a BABCP-accredited clinician, supervisor and trainer. Gill helped to establish and teach on the Postgraduate Diploma in High Intensity Psychological Interventions at the University of Sheffield from 2008 to 2016. Her interests include large group psychological interventions, mindfulness-based cognitive group therapy and self-practice and self-reflection (SPSR). She is current chair of Yorkshire BABCP branch.

Windy Dryden is Emeritus Professor of Psychotherapeutic Studies at Goldsmiths University of London, and is a Fellow of the British Psychological Society. He has authored or edited more than 220 books and edits 20 book series in the area of counselling and psychotherapy. His major interests are in rational emotive behavior therapy and CBT; single session interventions; the interface between counselling and coaching; pluralism in counselling and psychotherapy; writing short, accessible self-help books for the general public; and demonstrating therapy live in front of an audience.

Dr Christine Dunkley is a Consultant Psychotherapist with 30 years' NHS experience, first as a medical social worker and then as a BACP senior accredited therapist. As a Senior Trainer with the British Isles Dialectical Behaviour Therapy training team, she helps clinicians implement the therapy in the UK and internationally through training events, site visits and regular consultations. She has published widely on DBT, mindfulness, emotional pain and supervision. She is an honorary lecturer for Bangor University and has consulted on a large NHS trial on DBT at the University of Southampton. She co-founded the Society for DBT in 2012.

Graham Dyson, PhD, DClinPsy, is an HCPC-registered Clinical Psychologist currently working in a Health Psychology setting. He has recently worked in the area of psychological trauma within independent practice and also as a Senior Lecturer on the Doctorate in Clinical Psychology programme at Teesside University, where he was responsible for recruitment and personal professional development. He worked as a Clinical Psychologist in the National Health Service for six years post qualification, primarily with adults in a low security setting. He completed his Interpersonal Therapy training in 2005 and has since been engaged in teaching and supervision within the Durham and Teesside areas.

Michael Ellis, MA, is a UKCP Registered Psychotherapist. He is a Director of the Gestalt Centre London and a tutor on the MA Programme in Psychotherapy. He has a private practice working with individuals and couples, is a supervisor, and works with organisations as a trainer and organisational consultant.

Gail Evans is a trainer and educator in counselling and psychotherapy and has worked in the field for over 30 years. She had a background in social work and worked for many years for Relate as couple counsellor, psychosexual therapist, trainer and clinical supervisor. Formerly Head of the Counselling Studies Unit, Sheffield Hallam University (SHU), Gail is currently Programme Director at The Academy: SPACE, which she founded with SHU's blessing in 2010 when they discontinued professional counselling courses. She also co-founded, in 2006, a thriving Counselling and Therapy Centre in Sheffield.

The late **Fay Fransella** was Emeritus Reader in Clinical Psychology at the University of London and Visiting Professor of Personal Construct Psychology at the University of Hertfordshire. After retiring from her University of London post, she established the Centre for Personal Construct Psychology in London, eventually transferring it to the University of Hertfordshire, together with the Fransella Collection of personal construct psychology resources. She was a Fellow of the British Psychological Society, and was one of 12 psychologists invited to contribute their reminiscences in a book marking the Society's centenary. She authored or edited over 100 publications.

Kevin Friery is a Counsellor and Psychotherapist with a background in behavioural psychology. Having worked for many years in the NHS, he moved into the world of workplace counselling in 2001 and since then has been clinical head of a major Employee Assistance Provider. While maintaining a small private therapy practice, he also works as a consultant to organisations seeking to resolve complex interpersonal situations and is often called on to provide training in mental health in the workplace.

Antony Froggett is a UKCP registered Psychotherapist. He is a training analyst and supervisor with the Institute of Group Analysis (IGA). He is the owner of Thinking Space Consultancy, which provides consultation and training about leadership and teamwork. He is also a senior lecturer at Birmingham University, where he is employed on the Elizabeth Garrett Anderson Masters programme in Leadership, organised on behalf of the NHS Leadership Academy.

David Geldard had extensive experience in working as a counselling psychologist with troubled children and their families. He worked in mental health and community health settings, and also in private practice. Together with his wife Kathryn he was heavily involved in training counsellors, social workers and psychologists, in ways to use media and activity when counselling children. Additionally he showed a keen interest in training workers in the use of experiential counselling methods and in family therapy. He and Kathryn are the authors of several counselling texts published internationally and translated into several languages.

Dr Kathryn Geldard is Adjunct Senior Lecturer in Counselling at the University of the Sunshine Coast (USC), Australia. Her role includes programme leadership of the Counselling programme and development of postgraduate Master of Counselling degrees. Her research interests include adolescent peer counselling, and counsellor training, assessment and effectiveness. Additionally, Kathryn conducted research with Australian Aboriginal adolescents focused on developing a culturally sensitive peer support programme. She is the author of a number of textbooks founded on her extensive counselling background with children, young people and their families and has several years' experience in supervising and training counsellors.

Dr Sobhi Girgis, MMedSci, MRCPsych LLM (Mental Health Law), is a Consultant Psychiatrist and Associate Medical Director with Sheffield Health and Social Care NHS Foundation Trust and Honorary Senior Clinical Lecturer at Sheffield University. He is trained in both General Adult and Forensic Psychiatry. He is the Co-Chair of the Mental Health Act Committee in his NHS Trust. He organises and teaches on induction and refresher training courses, approved by the North of England Approval Panel, for S12 (2) and Approved Clinicians.

Dr David Goss is a Chartered Counselling Psychologist. He is a lecturer in counselling and psychology at Staffordshire University and director of Zence Psychology in the UK. Clinically, he has his own private practice and has spent a number of years as clinical lead for a neurological charity counselling service. His research interests involve integrating humanistic qualitative research with neuroscientific quantitative research, to continually develop our understanding and support of human mental health. He is particularly interested in understanding consciousness and self, decision making and intuition, and the psychology of spectating sport.

Dr Stephen Goss, MBACP, BA, LFHCfSS, is Principal Lecturer on the DPsych (Professional Studies) at the Metanoia Institute, London. He is Research Director at the Online Therapy Institute and co-Editor (Counselling) for the *British Journal of Guidance and Counselling*. He is a clinical supervisor for counselling and psychotherapy and an international consultant in the development of support services and the uses of technology in the delivery of counselling, psychotherapy and mental health care. His recent publications include *Making Research Matter* (Routledge, 2016) and *Technology in Mental Health: Applications for Practice, Supervision and Training* (CC Thomas, 2nd ed., 2016).

Andrew Guppy is Professor of Applied Psychology at the University of Bedfordshire and is a Health Psychologist and an Occupational Psychologist registered with the Health and Care Professions Council. He has been involved in the provision and evaluation of counselling and other interventions in the stress, alcohol and drug fields for over 25 years.

Dr Claudia Herbert is a Chartered Consultant Clinical Psychologist, CBT Psychotherapist, EMDR Consultant, Schema Therapist, Psychological Practice Supervisor and Director of the Oxford Development Centre, the longest established, ongoing independent psychological trauma treatment service in England. She is an internationally recognised trauma specialist and, among other publications, she wrote the first psychological self-help book published on trauma in the United Kingdom.

Dr Vanessa Herbert qualified as a Clinical Psychologist in 2016 from the University of Manchester, having completed specialist training in Psychodynamic Interpersonal Therapy.

Nick Hodge is Professor of Inclusive Practice at The Autism Centre, Sheffield Hallam University. Nick's research interests focus on all issues that impact on the education and wellbeing of disabled children and young people and their families. Much of his work has involved challenging deficit-led models of disability that mark children and young people as disordered and other.

Sarah Hovington is a Senior Practitioner for a large IAPT service in the north of England. She is a BACP-accredited counsellor and a BABCP-accredited CBT therapist and also holds a qualification in primary care mental health. Sarah has served on the Executive Committee of BACP Healthcare and is the former editor of its journal.

Dr Chris Irons is a Clinical Psychologist. He is a Director of Balanced Minds, a London-based organisation offering compassion-focused services (e.g., therapy, supervision, coaching, training and teaching). He is a board member of the Compassionate Mind Foundation (www.compassionatemind.co.uk), the charity that sits behind CFT. He is a nationally and internationally recognised trainer and supervisor in CFT.

Peter Jenkins is a registered counsellor, trainer, supervisor and researcher. He has been a member of both the BACP Professional Conduct Committee and the UKCP Ethics Committee. He has written extensively on legal, ethical and professional aspects of counselling and psychotherapy, including *Counselling, Psychotherapy and the Law* (2nd ed., Sage, 2007) and, with Debbie Daniels, *Therapy with Children: Children's Rights, Confidentiality and the Law* (2nd ed., Sage, 2010).

Dr Lucy Johnstone is a Consultant Clinical Psychologist, author of *Users and Abusers of Psychiatry* (2nd ed., Routledge, 2000), co-editor of *Formulation in Psychology and Psychotherapy: Making Sense of People's Problems* (2nd ed., Routledge, 2013) and author of *A Straight-talking Introduction to Psychiatric Diagnosis* (PCCS Books, 2014). She is the former Programme Director of the Bristol Clinical Psychology Doctorate and was lead author of the *Good Practice Guidelines on the Use of Psychological Formulation* (Division of Clinical Psychology, 2011.) She has many years of clinical experience in adult mental health settings, and is an experienced conference speaker, lecturer and trainer.

Dr Elaine Kasket, CPsychol, is an HCPC registered Counselling Psychologist, an Associate Fellow of the British Psychological Society, a UKCP-registered and BACP-accredited Psychotherapist, and Programme Director of the DPsych in Counselling Psychology at Regent's University London. In her areas of research and scholarship, she has contributed to pre-recorded programmes for BBC Radio 4, has featured on numerous live national and regional radio broadcasts, and has appeared on the BBC, ITN Channel 4 News, the Discovery Channel, the Canadian Broadcasting Company, and America's Health Network. She has also authored or contributed to articles in national and international magazines, newspapers and online news sources.

Catherine Kerr, CPsychol, MBACP (Snr. Accred), EMDR Europe Approved Consultant, has many years' experience of working with a wide range of people, and specialises in working with post traumatic stress disorder. Cath has a Master's degree in Psychological Trauma and has worked in a variety of settings such as the private sector, community colleges, women's refuges and the voluntary sector. She is currently a Director of KRTS International Ltd. She co-authored *Integrating EMDR into Your Practice* with Liz Royle, and provides training and clinical supervision to practitioners who are working with psychological trauma.

Dr Naoko Kishita, PhD, completed a Clinical Psychology training programme and qualified as a Clinical Psychologist in 2012 in Tokyo, Japan. She has maintained active research activities in cognitive and behavioural psychotherapies since her doctoral training. She joined the Department of Clinical Psychology at the University of East Anglia in July 2014. Since then she has broadened her expertise in clinical psychology, especially cutting-edge expertise in Cognitive Behaviour Therapy with older people under the mentorship of Professor Laidlaw. Her current research interests are in evidence-based psychological treatments for older people and their carers.

Dr Konstantina Kolonia, BA (Hons), MSc, DPsych, CPsychol, SchemaAdvCert, is a Chartered Counselling Psychologist and an Advanced Schema Therapist, and Supervisor specialising in personality disorders and trauma. She is a member of the International Society of Schema Therapy (ISST) and an affiliate of the Schema Therapy UK. Over the last 14 years Konstantina has worked extensively in various adult mental health settings in the NHS, as well as the forensic and voluntary sectors. Konstantina is currently working in community settings in West London with patients experiencing severe and enduring mental health difficulties.

Dr Helen Kyritsi, BSc (Hons) Psychology, DClinPsy, is a Principal Clinical Psychologist and an Advanced Schema Therapist and Supervisor. She has been working in community mental health teams for over 10 years in West London, specialising in the provision of evidence-based psychological therapies for clients with severe and enduring mental health problems. She has developed a specialist interest in the treatment of personality disorders and complex trauma. Helen is a member of the International Society for Schema Therapy and also an affiliate of the Schema Therapy UK.

Dr Sunil Lad is a Counselling Psychologist employed by Northamptonshire Healthcare Foundation Trust. He works in several services that offer supervision, therapy and support to people in contact with the Criminal Justice System with mental health difficulties, including prisons, probation and liaison and diversion in the Midlands where he provides input and therapy.

Professor Ken Laidlaw, PhD, is Head of Department of Clinical Psychology and Programme Director of the ClinPsyD Clinical Psychology Training Programme at the Norwich Medical School, University of East Anglia. He is also Honorary Consultant Clinical Psychologist with Norfolk and Suffolk NHS Trust, having for many years served as Professional Lead of an Older Adult Clinical Psychology Service. He maintains ongoing research activity in cognitive behaviour therapy (CBT) for late life depression and anxiety, especially with complex, chronic and comorbid conditions. He was the Principal Investigator on the first UK randomised controlled trial of CBT for late life depression.

Mark Linington is an Attachment-based Psychoanalytic Psychotherapist and Child Psychotherapist (UKCP registered). He trained with The Bowlby Centre, where he is the Chair of the Executive Committee, a Training Therapist and a Training Supervisor. He worked for 12 years in the NHS as a Psychotherapist with people with intellectual disabilities who have experienced trauma and abuse. He currently works as a Consultant Psychotherapist and Supervisor with the Clinic for Dissociative Studies, at a secondary school in London for young people with complex special needs, and in private practice with children, families and adults.

Dr Linda Machin trained as a Medical Social Worker. She went on to specialise in work in bereavement and established a service for bereaved people in North Staffordshire. Linda moved into academia, lecturing in social work and counselling and is now an Honorary Research Fellow in the Research Institute for Primary Care and Health Sciences at Keele University. She is engaged in ongoing research arising from her development of the Range of Response to Loss model and the Adult Attitude to Grief scale and works as a freelance trainer and counselling consultant.

Dr David Mair, Senior Accredited Member of BACP, is the Head of the Counselling and Wellbeing Service at the University of Birmingham. His doctoral research focused on attempts among gay, bisexual and queer male students to construct meaningful, unified life-narratives from their lived experience as members of multiple communities. He has edited a book about short-term counselling in higher education (Routledge, 2016) and is editor of the BACP journal *University and College Counselling*.

Doireann Mangan is an Irish trainee counselling psychologist currently studying for a doctorate at the University of Manchester. Completing a Master's in Contemporary Migration and Diaspora Studies, along with travelling and working in a wide variety of settings, has brought her into contact with many different cultures and influenced her work and research. To date, her research has mainly centred on issues to do with cultural diversity, education and mental health. As well as counselling psychology, other areas of professional interest include reflexive practice, feminist and social justice perspectives, and refugee issues.

Brian Martindale is a Consultant Psychiatrist, Psychoanalyst and Psychotherapist now working in private practice. Between 2005 and 2012 he was a Consultant Psychiatrist in Early Intervention in Psychosis for Northumberland, Tyne and Wear NHS Foundation Trust. He is past Chair of the International Society for Psychological and Social Approaches to Psychosis (ISPS) and was Editor of the ISPS book series. He is Honorary President of the European Federation of Psychoanalytic Psychotherapy and represented Western Europe to the World Psychiatric Association for six years. In 2009 he was winner of the British Psychoanalytic Council Award for Outstanding Professional Leadership.

Rosaleen McElvaney, PhD, is a Clinical Psychologist/Psychotherapist with over 20 years' experience working in the field of child sexual abuse. She is Chair of the Doctorate in Psychotherapy programme in Dublin City University and is author of *Finding the Words: Talking Children Through the Tough Times (Veritas, 2015), How Children Tell: Containing the Secret of Child Sexual Abuse* (Lambert Academic Publishers, 2015), and *Helping Children to Tell About Sexual Abuse: Guidance for Helpers* (Jessica Kingsley, 2016). She is a Fellow of the Psychological Society of Ireland.

John McLeod is Visiting Professor at the Department of Psychology, University of Oslo, and the Institute of Integrative Counselling and Psychotherapy, Dublin. He has published widely on a range of topics in counselling and psychotherapy, with a particular interest in the development of flexible, collaborative approaches to therapy that are informed by cultural awareness and relevant research evidence.

DeeAnna Merz Nagel, MEd, LMHC, BCC is a Psychotherapist and wellness coach. She is a counsellor and coach educator specialising in the use of technology. In addition to delivering online coaching services, she teaches the ethical integration of alternative approaches in practice. She is co-founder of the Online Therapy Institute as well as founder of Havana Wellness Studio located in Havana, Florida.

Anthea Millar is a Psychotherapist, Trainer and Supervisor working in independent practice and with organisations in the UK and abroad. She coordinated the four-year Adlerian counselling training in Cambridge for 26 years and is co-founder of Cambridge Supervision Training (www.cambridgesupervisiontraining.com). Anthea is on the training committee of the UK Adlerian Society and co-editor of their journal. She is a co-author of *Practical Supervision: How to Become a Supervisor for the Helping Professions* (Jessica Kingsley Publishers, 2014).

Dr Barbara Mitchels, PhD, is a Psychotherapist working in Devon. A retired solicitor, Barbara combines her legal and therapy practice experience in writing, workshops and providing a web-based consultancy service for therapists at www.therapylaw. co.uk. Her publications, research and workshops include topics related to post-traumatic stress, conflict resolution, therapy, confidentiality and the court process, children and the application of law and ethics to therapy practice.

Eric Morris, PhD, works as the Director of the La Trobe University Psychology Clinic, in Melbourne, Australia. He is a clinical psychologist and researcher with a long-term interest in Acceptance and Commitment Therapy and contextual behavioural science. Eric researches ACT as an intervention for people with serious mental illness, caregivers, and in the workplace. He is the co-author of *ACTivate Your Life: Using Acceptance & Mindfulness to Build a Life that is Rich, Fulfilling and Fun* (with Jon Hill and Joe Oliver, Robinson, 2015), and a co-editor of *Acceptance and Commitment Therapy and Mindfulness for Psychosis* (with Louise Johns and Joe Oliver, Wiley-Blackwell, 2013).

Jill Mytton, MSc, CPsychol, DPsych is a Chartered Counselling Psychologist. She is a Visiting Lecturer at the New School of Psychotherapy and Counselling, London. She is listed on the British Psychological Society media list for Cults and Thought Reform, has been involved in several television broadcasts and has presented at international conferences. Her primary research interest is the mental health of Second Generation Adults, i.e., those born or raised in cultic groups. Now retired from academic work, she is an independent researcher and has a small private practice.

Julia Noble is a Chartered Counselling Psychologist based in Manchester, working in the National Health Service and private health care with individuals with complex and enduring difficulties. Julia has a keen research interest in the use of outcome measures, and the areas of personality disorders and self-harm, maintaining a critical perspective towards diagnosis and interventions. She also lectures on the University of Manchester Counselling Psychology doctorate.

Dr Denis O'Hara is Professor of Counselling and Psychotherapy at the Australian College of Applied Psychology, Brisbane. Dr O'Hara is a Chartered Psychologist with the British Psychological Society, and member of the British Association of Counselling and Psychotherapy as well as the Psychotherapist and Counsellors Federation of Australia. He is a keen researcher and author in counselling and psychotherapy. Some of his research interests include hope, self-differentiation, chronic problems of the self, and psychotherapy integration. Dr O'Hara enjoys providing professional development and supervision.

Joe Oliver, PhD, is a Consultant Clinical Psychologist and Director for Contextual Consulting, an ACT-based consultancy in the UK. He is joint-Director for the University College London Cognitive Behavioural Therapy in Psychosis Postgraduate Diploma, while also holding a post within the NHS. He is a peer-review ACBS ACT trainer and regularly trains professionals both nationally and internationally. His research interests are in the use of contextual CBTs to enhance workplace wellbeing and also with people with distressing psychosis. Joe is co-editor of the textbook, *Acceptance and Commitment Therapy and Mindfulness for Psychosis* (with Louise Johns and Eric Morris, Wiley-Blackwell, 2013) and co-author of the ACT self-help book, *ACTivate Your Life: Using Acceptance & Mindfulness to Build a Life that is Rich, Fulfilling and Fun* (with Jon Hill and Eric Morris, Robinson, 2015).

Stephen Palmer is Director of the Centre for Stress Management, Visiting Professor of Work Based Learning and Stress Management, Middlesex University, and Adjunct Professor of Coaching Psychology, Aalborg University, Denmark. He has received awards for his contributions to both counselling psychology and coaching psyology. He has authored/edited over 50 books, including the *Handbook of Coaching Psychology* (with Alison Whybrow, Routledge, 2007) and *The Beginner's Guide to Counselling and Psychotherapy* (Sage, 2015).

Simon Parritt, CPsychol, AFBPsS, MSc, BSc (Hons), BA, CPsSC, is a Chartered Counselling Psychologist specialising in psychosexual and relationship therapy and disability in addition to his general work as a Counselling Psychologist. The former Director of SPOD (Association to Aid the Sexual & Personal Relationships of People with a Disability), he has worked in geriatric medicine at St George's Hospital Medical School, primary care and the voluntary sector. Currently, he is also Visiting Lecturer on disability and diversity at Surrey University Doctorate in Psychotherapeutic and Counselling Psychology. He has been a disabled person since the age of five.

Stephen Paul is a Psychotherapist and Group Therapist. He is co-editor of *The Therapeutic Relationship Handbook* (McGraw Hill, 2014) and co-author of *An Introduction to the Therapeutic Relationship* (with Divine Charura, Sage, 2015). In the mid 1970s he introduced group therapy to a Liverpool psychiatric hospital. He was later head of a group therapy unit at West Middlesex Hospital and then head of a therapeutic school in Newcastle. He was Director of The Centre for Psychological Therapies at Leeds Metropolitan University until 2012 where he taught group therapy for 19 years. Stephen now writes, practises therapy, supervision and coaching, and provides training.

Claire Pollitt is a Chartered Clinical Psychologist currently working within a primary care psychology service for complex cases, based in South Manchester. Claire qualified as a Cognitive Analytic Therapy (CAT) Practitioner in February 2015 and she routinely uses this as a therapeutic model within her work. She also has a keen interest in compassion-focused therapy, and finds that the imagery work and focus on compassionate behaviours complement the revision stage of CAT, when the client is seeking to form more positive and helpful ways of relating to themselves and others.

Dr Andrew Reeves is a Senior Lecturer and a BACP Senior Accredited Counsellor/Psychotherapist with 30 years' experience of working in a range of settings. His original professional background was in social work and, over the years, his research and writing has focused on psychotherapeutic interventions with people who present a suicide risk or who self-injure. He is author of *An Introduction to Counselling and Psychotherapy: From Theory to Practice* (SAGE, 2012), has edited other texts and is a previous Editor of *Counselling and Psychotherapy Research* journal.

Tom Ricketts, PhD, is a BABCP-accredited cognitive-behavioural psychotherapist and nurse consultant working in the NHS. He has developed and taught both qualifying courses for cognitive-behavioural psychotherapists and introductory courses for non-specialists. He has a particular interest in widening access to cognitive-behavioural therapy through the use of self-management approaches and the training of health professionals.

Dr Elizabeth Robinson, a psychiatric nurse by background, received her Interpersonal Psychotherapy (IPT) training in 1997 from Professor John Markowitz and Kathleen Clougherty (both trained by Gerald Klerman, the originator of IPT). She was the principal IPT research therapist for two clinical studies; the latter, a brain imaging study of IPT in treatment-resistant depression, was for her PhD at Durham University. She works part-time in private clinical practice and as an IPT trainer/supervisor as part of the government initiative Improving Access to Psychological Therapies for IPT training for adults, and IPT A for adolescents (Northumbria University).

Chris Rose is a psychotherapist, supervisor and consultant working in private practice and higher education, with extensive experience in counselling and psychotherapy training. She has had a long involvement with both group work and Professional and Personal Development (PPD) and is the author of *The Personal Development Group: The Student's Guide* (Karnac, 2008) and editor of *Self Awareness and Personal Development: Resources for Psychotherapists and Counsellors* (Palgrave Macmillan, 2012). She writes regularly for *Therapy Today* and is an accredited member of BACP and UKCP.

Maxine Rosenfield has 25 years' experience as a counsellor, supervisor and trainer. She pioneered telephone counselling in the UK, writing *Counselling by Telephone* (Sage, 1997), and *Telephone Counselling: A Handbook for Practitioners* (Palgrave Macmillan, 2013), and has contributed to counselling and social work texts in the UK and the USA. Now based in Sydney, Australia, she continues counselling, supervising, training and writing. An educator at the Australian College of Applied Psychology, Maxine has private practices in two Sydney locations and works by phone and Skype with clients and supervisees throughout Australia and internationally. Maxine is currently a member of the Psychotherapy and Counselling Federation of Australia's (PACFA) Ethics Committee as well as the PACFA Professional Standards Committee and is a Board member of the Australasian Association for Supervision.

Liz Royle, PhD, MA, MBACP (Accred.) EMDR Europe Approved Consultant, has published and presented internationally on the subject of Eye Movement Desensitisation Reprocessing (EMDR) and psychological trauma. She specialises in working with the emergency services and lead the Uniformed Services task force for the European Society of Traumatic Stress Studies from 2008 to 2015. Liz has used EMDR in her clinical practice for nearly 20 years, working with a range of presentations from recent events through to complex trauma and dissociative disorders. She was a founder member of the UK Psychological Trauma Society and is now a Director of KRTS International Ltd.

Anja Rutten is an experienced and practicing therapist, psychologist and academic. Anja's research interests are in therapeutic experiences of clients with Asperger Syndrome, and in person-centred/experiential counselling for this client group. Anja currently works for the Sherwood Psychotherapy Training Institute (SPTI) as Head of Training.

Bernie Ryan completed her Masters in Counselling and postgraduate certificate in Supervision in Counselling and the Helping Professions at the University of Manchester. Bernie worked at the St Mary's Sexual Assault Referral Centre (SARC) in Manchester, as a counsellor and latterly as Centre Manager before taking early retirement in 2016. She now provides independent consultancy and supervision and works as a training and development manager for a sexual violence organisation. She has provided training and consultancy nationally and internationally. Bernie was awarded an OBE in the Queen's 2016 New Year's Honours for services to supporting victims of sexual violence.

Christiane Sanderson is a Senior Lecturer in Psychology at the University of Roehampton with 28 years' experience working with survivors of child sexual abuse, domestic abuse and complex trauma. She has delivered consultancy and training to voluntary and statutory agencies, including the Metropolitan Police Service and the NSPCC. She is a trustee of the charity One in Four and the author of a number of books, including *Counselling Skills for Working with Shame* (Jessica Kingsley Publishers, 2015), *Counselling Skills for Working with Trauma* (Jessica Kingsley Publishers, 2013), *Counselling Skills for Working with Survivors of Domestic Abuse* (Jessica Kingsley Publishers, 2008), *Counselling Adult Survivors of Child Sexual Abuse* (Jessica Kingsley Publishers, 2006) and *The Warrior Within* (One in Four, 2010).

Dr Adam J. Scott is a Chartered Counselling Psychologist and works as a manager, therapist and supervisor. He is currently the Assistant Head of Psychology at ABL Health, a community health-care provider based in the North of England, and a Trauma-Focused Therapist at Survivors Manchester. Adam is experienced in working therapeutically with clients with long-term health conditions, eating disorders and psychological trauma. He has an active interest in the application of mindfulness, positive psychology and behavioural change to his therapeutic practice.

Julia Segal is a Fellow of BACP. She trained with Relate and since 1983 has been counselling people with physical illnesses or disabilities and their families, using the ideas of Melanie Klein to understand and illuminate everyday experience. She is interested in the effects on health-care professionals of working with people who have neurological conditions. She has written extensively on the effects of illness on relationships. Julia is best known for her books, which include *Phantasy in Everyday Life* (Penguin, 1985; Karnac, 1995), *Melanie Klein: Key Figures in Counselling and Psychotherapy* (Sage, 1992) and *Helping Children with Ill or Disabled Parents* (Jessica Kingsley Publishers, 1996).

Heather Sequeira, CPsychol PhD, is a Chartered Counselling Psychologist. Heather is a visiting Lecturer at the University of Birmingham and runs PTSD Trauma Workshops, specialising in Trauma-Focused CBT for psychologists and other mental health professionals. Heather sits on the British Psychological Society committee for Crisis, Disaster and Trauma. She has published widely and consults on trauma, OCD and CBT with universities, businesses and individuals. She continues to work in a specialist capacity for the NHS. In previous years Heather held the editorship of the journal *Counselling Psychology Review* and the post of Clinical Research Fellow at the University of London.

Victoria Settle is an Attachment-based Psychoanalytic Psychotherapist at The Bowlby Centre in London, where she is a teacher and supervisor. She chairs the Clinical Training Committee, which oversees the registration of members on the four-year attachment-based psychoanalytic course, and she also sits on the Executive. Victoria has a private practice based in East London and has a long-standing interest in how attachment theory can be used to work with people who are suffering from more serious mental health difficulties. She is also a massage practitioner.

Guy Shennan is a registered social worker in the UK who works as an independent consultant, teaching, using and writing about solution-focused approaches. In 2014 Guy completed his Master's degree in philosophy, focusing in his dissertation on implications of embodied and extended cognition for personal identity. He is now considering the implications of these for solution-focused brief therapy. Also in 2014, Guy's book, *Solution-Focused Practice*, was published by Palgrave Macmillan. Guy is the current chair of the British Association of Social Workers.

Helen Sieroda has been involved in training and supervising counsellors, psychotherapists and coaches in the UK and Scandinavia for over 25 years. Helen is an UKCP-registered psychotherapist, holds an MSc in Responsibility in Business Practice and a BA in Comparative Religion. Founder and director of Wise Goose Limited, partner at Gameshift Limited and co-chair of the Psychosynthesis and Education Trust, she has a long-standing interest in developing leaders who are able to meet the complex challenges of our times.

Charlotte Sills, MA, MSc (Psychotherapy) is a Psychotherapist and Supervisor in private practice and Visiting Professor at Middlesex University and at Ashridge Business School. She is a qualified TA Clinician and a Teaching and Supervising

Transactional Analyst. She is a member of faculty at Metanoia Institute, London, teaching on the MSc in TA Psychotherapy and MSc in Humanistic Psychotherapy. She is also a member of faculty on Ashridge's MSc in Coaching and Diploma in Coaching and Consulting Supervision. Among her publications are *An Introduction to Transactional Analysis* (with Phil Lapworth, Sage, 2011), *Transactional Analysis: A Relational Perspective* (with Helena Hargaden, Routledge, 2002) and *Relational TA: Principles in Practice* (edited with Heather Fowlie, Karnac, 2011).

Jonathan Smith is an Associate Lecturer in Psychology at Birkbeck College, University of London, where he teaches psychology to groups of adult students. He is also an accredited Gestalt Psychotherapist and supervisor with a private practice in London. He works as a trainer on the MA programme at the Gestalt Centre, London, and for the Music Therapy Master's course at the Guildhall School of Music and Drama.

William B. Stiles is Professor Emeritus of Psychology at Miami University, Oxford, Ohio, USA, and Adjunct Professor of Psychology at Appalachian State University, Boone, North Carolina, USA. He received his PhD from UCLA in 1972. He has been President of Division 29 (Psychotherapy) of the American Psychological Association and of the Society for Psychotherapy Research. He has served as Editor of *Psychotherapy Research* and *Person-Centered and Experiential Psychotherapies*. He has published more than 300 journal articles and book chapters, most dealing with psychotherapy, verbal interaction, and research methods.

Léonie Sugarman, PhD, is a Chartered Psychologist and Emeritus Professor of Applied Psychology at the University of Cumbria. She is an Honorary Fellow and former Vice President of the British Association for Counselling and Psychotherapy. She has published in the area of life-span development, including *Counselling and the Life Course* (Sage, 2004) and *Occupational Therapy and Life Course Development* (with Ruth Wright, Wiley, 2009). Now retired, for many years she held editorial roles with the *British Journal of Guidance and Counselling*.

Michaela Swales, PhD, is a Consultant Clinical Psychologist with Betsi Cadwaladr University Health Board and Reader in Clinical Psychology on the North Wales Clinical Psychology Programme, Bangor University. She became Director of the British Isles DBT Training Team in 2002 and in this role has trained more than a thousand professionals in Dialectical Behaviour Therapy, seeding over 400 programmes in the UK, Ireland and Norway. She is the author, with Heidi Heard, PhD, of *Dialectical Behaviour Therapy: Distinctive Features* (Routledge, 2009) and *Changing Behavior in DBT: Problem-Solving in Action* (Guilford, 2015). Dr Swales is President of the Society for DBT in the UK and Ireland.

Digby Tantam, MA, MPH, PhD, FRCPsych, AFBPsS, FBACP, FUKCP, FHEA, is Emeritus Professor of Psychiatry at the University of Sheffield, Visiting Professor at Middlesex University, and a Director of the Septimus Group of Companies, including the New School of Psychotherapy and Counselling, where he currently teaches existential counselling psychology and psychotherapy. He directs three online courses: an MSc in Psychotherapy Studies, an MSc in Autism and Neurodevelopmental Disorders and an MA in Working with Diversity (subject to validation). He also works in Dilemma Consultancy as a Consultant Psychotherapist and Psychiatrist, providing both psychotherapy supervision and assessments of people with Autism Spectrum Disorders. He is author or co-author of 171 scientific publications and author or editor of 12 books. His most recent book is *Emotional Well-being and Mental Health: A Guide for Counsellors & Psychotherapists* (Sage, 2014) and *The Interbrain* (Jessica Kingsley Publishers, 2017).

Ladislav Timulak, PhD, is Course Director of the Doctorate in Counselling Psychology, Trinity College, Dublin. He is involved in the training of counselling psychologists and psychotherapists. He has written several books and over 60 peer-reviewed papers and chapters. His most recent books include *Research in Psychotherapy and Counselling* (Sage, 2008), *Developing Your Counselling and Psychotherapy Skills and Practice* (Sage, 2011) and *Transforming Emotional Pain in Psychotherapy* (Routledge, 2015). He maintains a part-time private practice.

Nick Totton is a therapist and trainer with over 30 years' experience. Originally a Reichian body therapist, his approach has become broad based and open to the spontaneous and unexpected. He is deeply involved with ecopsychology and addressing climate change. He has a grown-up daughter. Nick has written or edited 14 books so far, most relevantly *Wild Therapy* (PCCS Books, 2011) and *Vital Signs* (edited with Mary-Jayne Rust, Karnac Books, 2012). He lives in Cornwall with his partner and grows vegetables. He has a website at www.nicktotton.net.

Professor Rachel Tribe is Professor of Applied Psychological Practice at the School of Psychology, University of East London. In 2014 she obtained the British Psychological Society Award for Challenging Social Inequalities in Psychology. She is a Fellow of the British Psychological Society and active in national and international consultancy and training work. She is a member of the BPS Presidential Task Force on Refugees and Asylum Seekers. She co-produced a DVD and guidance notes on Working with Interpreters in Mental Health for the Department of Health. Her latest book is *The Handbook of Professional and Ethical Practice for Psychologists, Counsellors and Psychotherapists* (Routledge, 2015).

Keith Tudor is Professor of Psychotherapy and currently Head of the School of Public Health & Psychosocial Studies at Auckland University of Technology, Aotearoa, New Zealand, and is a Teaching and Supervising Transactional Analyst (with the International Transactional Analysis Association). He also has a long and strong association with the person-centred approach, identifies both as a transactional analyst and a person-centred therapist, and has published extensively about both approaches. His latest books are: *Co-creative Transactional Analysis: Papers, Dialogues, Responses, and Developments* (with Graeme Summers, Karnac, 2014); *Conscience and Critic: The Selected Works of Keith Tudor* (Routledge, 2017); and *Psychotherapy: A Critical Examination* (PCCS Books, 2018).

Dr Aneta D. Tunariu is a Chartered Psychologist with the British Psychological Society, Senior Lecturer in Psychology with specialism in the Psychology of Relationships, and the Head of Subject for Psychological Interventions in the School of Psychology at the University of East London. Her applied practice, academic expertise, and research are closely informed by concepts from social psychology, existential positive psychology, coaching psychology, developmental psychoanalytic theory and psychotherapy. Dr Tunariu offers practitioner-development workshops, keynote lectures and research presentations in both national and international settings, and is regularly commissioned to deliver bespoke psychological interventions across the private and public sectors.

Zsófia Anna Utry , MSc, is a Coaching Psychologist, studied at the University of East London following her psychological studies at the University of Glasgow. She is a full member of the International Society for Coaching Psychology and the Hungarian Association for Coaching Psychology. She is involved in the development of a pluralistic approach to coaching and also coordinates the research group in the Hungarian Association for Coaching Psychology, where they are interested in advanced case study methods.

Emmy van Deurzen is a Philosopher, Counselling Psychologist and Existential Psychotherapist who founded the School of Psychotherapy and Counselling at Regent's University, the Society for Existential Analysis, the New School of Psychotherapy and Counselling and the Existential Academy. Her application of philosophical ideas to psychology, psychotherapy, counselling and coaching has been instrumental in establishing the existential paradigm firmly in the UK and elsewhere in Europe. Her books have been translated into many languages. She is Visiting Professor with Middlesex University. Among her books are *Existential Psychotherapy and Counselling in Practice* (3rd ed., Sage, 2012), *Psychotherapy and the Quest for Happiness* (Sage, 2009), *Everyday Mysteries* (2nd ed., Routledge, 2010) and *Paradox and Passion in Psychotherapy* (2nd ed., Wiley, 2015).

Dr Biljana van Rijn is a Transactional Analysis Psychotherapist and a Counselling Psychologist. She is a Faculty Head of Applied Research and Clinical Practice at Metanoia Institute in London, where she manages a large community clinic. Biljana leads a psychotherapy research centre at Metanoia Institute and has authored a number of publications. Her latest book on assessment is *Assessment and Case Formulation in Counselling and Psychotherapy* (SAGE, 2015).

Richard Velleman is both a clinical and an academic Psychologist, has worked in the addictions and mental health fields in the UK for almost 40 years, and has always held dual posts in universities and the health service. He is a leading authority on substance misuse, and is an Emeritus Professor at the University of Bath and a Senior Research Fellow with the Sangath Community Health NGO, Goa, India. He has been awarded grants of more than £8,500,000 over his research career to date, and published over 200 items, including 15 books, and many chapters and scientific journal papers.

Caroline Vermes is Director of Oakwood Psychology Services, a social sector NHS partner organisation. Caroline has specialised in the psychotherapeutic care of people with eating and weight distress since 1994, providing individual, family and group therapies for adults and children in hospital and community settings in USA and UK. She has led psychological programmes and treatment teams for health services since 2006. She has been involved with the development of local and regional NHS care pathways for adults and children with eating disorders in Greater Manchester. Her research interests include the role of social connections in mental health.

Ida Waksberg, AFBPsS, has worked for over 12 years as a Chartered and HCPC-registered Counselling Psychologist in HIV and Sexual Health Services for Derbyshire Healthcare NHS Foundation Trust. Her other clinical interests are working with trauma and with refugees, and she is an experienced Psychodynamic Psychotherapist.

Professor William West is a Visiting Professor to the University of Chester and Honorary Reader in Counselling Studies at the University of Manchester, where he was most noted for his interest in counselling and spirituality and for his work with PhD students. William has published 32 academic papers, 19 book chapters and 25 professional articles. He has written/edited six books, the most recent one being *Therapy, Culture and Spirituality: Developing Therapeutic Practice* (co-edited with Greg Nolan, Palgrave, 2015).

Christine Wilding, Charted MCIPD, BACP Accr., holds a Postgraduate Diploma in Cognitive Behavioural Therapy. She works in private practice as a CBT therapist and is the author of several books, including *How to Deal with Low Self Esteem* (Hodder, 2015).

Gareth Williams has been working in the field of mental health since 1997. He has studied a wide range of psychotherapies, worked with children, adults and families, and is currently a visiting teacher on the Doctorate in Counselling Psychology at Manchester University. Special interests include creativity, ecotherapy, spirituality, and the benefits of mindfulness and self-compassion for people suffering with anxiety. In 2015 he left a six-year position as a senior practitioner with Mind to develop a private practice as a counsellor, supervisor and mindfulness teacher.

Ruth Williams gained an MA in Jungian and Post-Jungian Studies at the Centre for Psychoanalytic Studies, University of Essex. She is a Jungian Analyst-Analytical Psychologist, Integrative Psychotherapist and Supervisor based in London. She is Chair of the Confederation for Analytical Psychology for whom she runs a series on Jung and Film. She is a Training Analyst for the Association of Jungian Analysts, London, and member of the International Association for Analytical Psychology based in Zurich. She has a particular interest in working with dreams and the imagination. She has been in private practice for 25 years. For publications, see www.RuthWilliams.org.uk.

Dr Emma Williamson, Principal Clinical Psychologist and Clinical Lead at South London and Maudsley NHS Foundation Trust, has for the past five years been working in partnership to develop innovative mental health and support services for homeless people in Lambeth using a 'Psychologically Informed Environments' framework. Emma formerly worked at Tavistock and Portman NHS Foundation Trust and has a personal interest in contributing to the evidence base for applied psychoanalytic ways of working with socially excluded and complex needs populations. Emma also works in private practice and teaches on the Clinical Psychology Doctorate at the Institute of Psychiatry.

David Winter is Professor Emeritus of Clinical Psychology at the University of Hertfordshire. He was previously Programme Director of the University's Doctorate in Clinical Psychology, and spent most of his working life practising as a Clinical Psychologist and Personal Construct Psychotherapist in the English National Health Service. He has held visiting positions at various universities, including Visiting Professor at the University of Padua, Brotherton Fellow at the University of Melbourne, and Visiting Scholar at the University of Wollongong. He is a Fellow of the British Psychological Society, and has over 170 publications, primarily on personal construct psychology and psychotherapy research.

Sally Woods is Joint Programme Coordinator for the MSc Drug Use and Addiction at Liverpool John Moores University. She also lectures on the undergraduate Applied Psychology degree course and is a member of BPS.

Val Wosket has worked as a therapist, supervisor and trainer in university and private practice settings for over 25 years and is a past teaching faculty member of the International Society for the Study of Trauma and Dissociation. She is author of *The Therapeutic Use of Self: Counselling Practice, Research and Supervision* (Classic Edition, Routledge, 2017), *Supervising the Counsellor and Psychotherapist: A Cyclical Model* (with Steve Page, Routledge, 2015) and *Egan's Skilled Helper Model: Developments and Applications in Counselling* (Routledge, 2006).

Jessica Yakeley is Consultant Psychiatrist in Forensic Psychotherapy at the Portman Clinic and Director of Medical Education and Associate Medical Director, Tavistock and Portman NHS Foundation Trust. She is also a Fellow of the British Psychoanalytical

Society. She has published widely on topics including psychodynamic approaches to medical education, violence, risk assessment, prison health, and antisocial personality disorder, is the author of *Working with Violence: A Contemporary Psychoanalytic Approach* (Palgrave, 2009) and is Editor of the journal *Psychoanalytic Psychotherapy*. She is currently Research Lead for the Royal College of Psychiatrists Psychotherapy Faculty and for the British Psychoanalytic Council.

Rebecca Yin Foo is an Educational and Developmental Psychologist who is experienced in providing support for children with developmental disabilities and their families at the Cerebral Palsy League. She currently works in private practice in Brisbane, Australia. Prior to obtaining her Honours degree in Psychology and Master's degree in Educational and Developmental Psychology, she completed a Bachelor of Medical Engineering. She has published a number of journal articles and presented conference papers nationally and internationally in relation to her studies in Engineering and Psychology. She is the co-author, with David Geldard and Kathryn Geldard, of the books *Counselling Children* (SAGE, 2017), *Counselling Adolescents* (SAGE, 2016) and *Basic Personal Counselling* (Cengage, 2017).

Dr Daniel Zahl is a Consultant Clinical Psychologist, having gained undergraduate and graduate degrees at Oxford. He works across medical specialities at the teaching hospital in Oxford. He leads a multidisciplinary chronic fatigue treatment service, and is involved in teaching and service-related research. He also works in private practice, where he sees patients with medically unexplained symptoms. He has extensive experience working in primary care and is an accredited CBT Therapist.

PREFACE TO THE FOURTH EDITION

COLIN FELTHAM

The most obvious change in this edition is the retirement of Ian Horton, who brought enormous experience and authority to the conception of this book and its editorship, and welcoming Terry Hanley and Laura Winter on board. Terry and Laura are prominent, energetic and well connected among the next generation of therapists and trainers, and they will take this well-received text ahead when I retire quite soon. The first edition appeared in 2000 and it is quite natural that not only relevant world events and professional developments have had an impact on counselling and psychotherapy but also that personnel will change.

We have studied and learned from the feedback of our readers and made due alterations to some of the topics in this edition, as well as to authorship where necessary, and format. We very much hope these changes fairly and helpfully reflect significant changes in the field and in the needs of readers.

Since the previous edition, the British Association for Counselling and Psychotherapy (BACP) and United Kingdom Council for Psychotherapy (UKCP) Voluntary Registers have been established. The fifth edition of the *DSM* appeared. Significant work has been done on evidence-based guidelines, and modifications and innovations introduced accordingly. The BACP *Ethical Framework for the Counselling Professions* has been updated and (at the time of writing) the UKCP *Ethical Principles and Code of Professional Conduct* is being revised. Statutory provision of counselling and Cognitive Behavioural Therapy has been developed. Indeed, ceaseless activity can be witnessed throughout the field. At the same time, no one would claim that those responsible for professional progress have got everything right, and a duly critical eye on developments is one of the features in this edition of the *Sage Handbook*.

A hundred years ago psychoanalysis was being energetically consolidated. Almost 80 years ago the British National Health Service was established and today remains a massive, treasured project, but is worryingly under-funded. BACP was formally established 40 years ago (with earlier roots in 1970) at a time when counselling was still received quite sceptically by a large section of the British public. Most of the major founding figures in the counselling and psychotherapy field are, sadly, now dead. During the twentieth century and the early part of the twenty-first, Europe has experienced dramatic social and political upheavals and most recently we have seen large demographic changes, which arguably challenge the apolitical assumptions and economic naivety of the original counselling movement.

It usually proves foolhardy to make predictions, but it is not unreasonable to declare informed desires for the future of the field. Work is still awaited on integrative inroads on the problematic proliferation of therapeutic models. Similarly, although some attention is being paid to the politics of therapy, much more is needed; and opportunities exist to demonstrate the potential of therapeutic insights to be applied educationally to knowledge of interpersonal relationships, community building, and cooperation in addressing social cohesion needs. Counselling and psychotherapy are naturally pitched at the level of individual and family interventions and are sought in times of trouble. A new generation of psychologically minded practitioners is needed who can help proactively to bridge the gaps between individual, community and international needs.

TERRY HANLEY AND LAURA WINTER

As the incoming editors to *The SAGE Handbook of Counselling and Psychotherapy*, we begin by saying welcome to this new edition. Taking on such a task is a mammoth endeavour. With 113 chapters it has taken a huge amount of effort to commission, review and liaise with so many authors. It has, however, also been a privilege to be immersed into the worlds of so many esteemed colleagues and to engage proactively with the work that they do. We are sure you will find a great deal of useful and interesting content in the pages that follow.

As you will no doubt be aware, this handbook has not been conceived afresh. It is entering its fourth edition, after being a stalwart on the reading lists of counselling and psychotherapy programmes within the United Kingdom and beyond for approximately 17 years, with the first edition appearing in 2000, the second edition in 2006 and the third edition in 2012. The legacy of Colin Feltham and Ian Horton is therefore a difficult one to follow and we are indebted to both Colin and Ian for the firm foundations that they have already set for this textbook as we move into a new era. Further, we would both note that it has been a pleasure to work alongside Colin in pulling this edition together – the good-humoured support has been invaluable.

As Colin has alluded to in his preface above, a lot has changed in the world of counselling and psychotherapy in recent years. The political nature of the work that therapists do is inescapable and numerous changes have occurred during the lifespan of this textbook – changes that will have direct impacts upon both those who choose to read it, and those that readers find themselves working with. As a consequence, it is important to keep the contents of a handbook such as this fresh and up to date. Thus, it is with this in mind that we have been proactive in revising the contents of the book, with our own observations of the changing landscape, along with comments solicited from the previous edition, leading to changes to both the content and the format of the book. We briefly comment on these changes in turn.

If you compare the contents list of this edition with that of the previous edition you will see a number of updates have been made. Although we do not want to outline the specifics of these changes, in summary:

Part 1: *Counselling and Psychotherapy in Context* has been reframed to explicitly answer fundamental questions related to the field of counselling and psychotherapy.

Part 2: *Socio-cultural Perspectives* has been thoroughly revised and updated.

Part 3: *Therapeutic Skills and Clinical Practice* has been updated and restructured to focus more directly upon the different stages of the therapeutic endeavour.

Part 4: *Professional Issues* has been expanded and revised to cover additional professional issues that practitioners will encounter in their work outside the therapeutic encounter.

Part 5: *Theory and Approaches* retains the wide breadth of content but has been revised and updated to reflect new and developing trends in the field of counselling and psychotherapy.

Part 6: *Client Presenting Problems* has been expanded and each chapter has been presented using a consistent frame so that the reader can easily reflect upon different issues being considered.

Part 7: *Therapeutic Specialisms* has been reordered and includes reference to new trends that have emerged in the field.

ACKNOWLEDGEMENTS

COLIN FELTHAM

To Terry and Laura for taking over the editorship of this *Handbook*. Also thanks to Susannah from Sage for supporting the process and helping out when needed.

TERRY HANLEY

To Becky for being supportive throughout this process and my children for all of the distractions – Arthur, for the conversations about football boots; Matilda, for the nights reading Harry Potter; and Wilfred, for demonstrating that you shouldn't give up on a goal if you desire it enough (and even if that is to sit on your fringe).

Thanks to colleagues at the University of Manchester, trainees on the Doctorate in Counselling Psychology, and the football group at Freedom from Torture. You've all helped to keep me motivated to finish this project.

Thanks to Colin, Laura and the people at Sage. Colin for entrusting Laura and I with the future of the *Handbook*, Laura for agreeing to be involved, and the people at Sage for the guiding nudges when needed.

LAURA WINTER

Thank you to my fellow editors and colleagues at Sage for the support, and for making what has been such a mammoth and sometimes overwhelming task enjoyable. Also to Jack and to Bump (who became Rosa during the process of completing this book): thanks for everything.

PART I

COUNSELLING AND PSYCHOTHERAPY IN CONTEXT

1.1 WHAT ARE COUNSELLING AND PSYCHOTHERAPY?

COLIN FELTHAM AND TERRY HANLEY

OVERVIEW AND KEY POINTS

When starting a book such as this, it is important to set some parameters for content that follows. This chapter therefore begins by providing a working definition of what is meant by the use of the terms 'counselling' and 'psychotherapy'. The chapter then:

- provides a brief overview of the historical developments related to psychotherapy and counselling within the United Kingdom (UK);
- introduces the major counselling and psychotherapy professional bodies in the UK;
- discusses how counselling and psychotherapy relate to a variety of allied professions, such as health interventions (psychiatry, psychology and mental health nursing), complementary medicines and other core professions;
- reflects upon the values that psychotherapists and counsellors commonly hold onto within the UK. These are discussed in relation to some core issues, such as professionalisation and evidence-based practice.

DEFINITIONS AND AIMS

It may seem odd that a profession cannot clearly define its central activity, but no consensually agreed definition of either counselling or psychotherapy exists in spite of many attempts across the decades in Britain, North America and elsewhere to arrive at one. The question of pinning down crucial distinctions arose in concrete terms in the UK in the first decade of the twenty-first century when the Health Professions Council (HPC: now the Health and Care Professions Council (HCPC)) initiated preliminary steps towards the legal protection of the titles 'counsellor' and 'psychotherapist'. This proved incredibly contentious, with attempts to load the former with wellbeing-associated tasks and the latter with competencies in addressing more severe psychological problems soon breaking down.

For the purposes of this book, the following working definition is used as a starting point:

Counselling and psychotherapy are mainly, though not exclusively, listening-and-talking-based methods of addressing psychological and sometimes psychosomatic problems, including deep and prolonged human suffering, situational dilemmas, crises and developmental needs, and aspirations towards the realization of human potential. In contrast to biomedical approaches, the psychological therapies operate largely without medication or other physical interventions and may be concerned not only with mental health but with spiritual, philosophical, social and other aspects of living. Professional forms of counselling and psychotherapy are based on formal training which encompasses attention to pertinent theory, research skills, clinical and/or micro-skills development, the personal development/therapy of the trainee, and supervised practice.

A brief definition of this kind offers some parameters but omits mention of the many, ever-expanding and often competing schools of therapy, the arenas, and the several professions in which they are practised. The contention advanced by this book's editors is that counselling and psychotherapy, in spite of partly different historical roots and affiliations, have much more in common than they have serious and demonstrable differences and that practitioners and the public stand to gain more from the assumption of commonality than from spurious or infinitesimal distinctions. It is often acknowledged that 'British counselling' much more closely resembles psychotherapy as practised in the United States of America and parts of Europe than it does the various kinds of guidance and mentoring that it is often confused with. The term 'psychotherapeutic counselling' adopted by the United Kingdom Council for Psychotherapy (UKCP) acknowledges this.

Practitioners in this field work with many different types of goal and expectation (see Feltham and Hanley – Chapter 1.2, this volume), implicit and explicit, each of which may call for the use of somewhat different skills, but arguably little is to be gained practically from further controversy about professional titles and distinctions. Optimal clarity about services for those seeking them should however be an overriding aim.

DEVELOPMENT OF PSYCHOTHERAPY AND COUNSELLING IN THE UK

Sigmund Freud was developing psychoanalysis – often considered the grandparent of most of the diverse schools in existence today – in Austria in the late nineteenth and early twentieth centuries. He lived the last year of his life in London. Before Freud there were many kinds of psychologically oriented therapies and many had already used the concept of an unconscious. However, Freud has come to mark the historical pivot when previous centuries of religious, philosophical and pseudo-scientific theories and methods (from religious propitiation to shamanism, sleeping cures, magnetism, hypnotism, etc.) were challenged by serious aspirations to establish psychotherapy as a scientific discipline. Psychoanalysis is perched curiously between being perceived as a challenge to previous faith in reason (the Enlightenment) and as the new grand narrative capable of rationally explaining all the psychological ills of humanity. Freud is often (although not by all) ranked with Darwin and Marx as one of the most significant scientific thinkers at the dawn of the twentieth century.

Psychoanalysis moved through Europe and North America in the first few decades of the twentieth century, the International Psychoanalytical Association being established in 1910 and the British Psychoanalytic Society in 1924. The British Association of Psychotherapists (originally the Association of Psychotherapists) was founded in 1951. In spite of much public and medical resistance to psychoanalysis (which was originally radically counter-cultural), interest and support grew, partly in connection with the two world wars and the search for remedies for 'shell shock' (the predecessor of post-traumatic stress disorder (PTSD)) and other problems experienced by military personnel. Concern about scientology led in 1971 to the Foster Report, which had implications for psychotherapy, and in 1978 to the publication of the Sieghart Report on the statutory regulation of psychotherapists. During the 1980s conferences regularly held at Rugby (organized by the British Association for Counselling (BAC)) led eventually, in 1993, to the now United Kingdom Council for Psychotherapy (UKCP). The British Psychoanalytic Council (BPC) represents training institutions with a psychoanalytic affiliation. The UKCP, containing member organizations from humanistic, cognitive-behavioural, integrative and other traditions, was established in 1991. In recent years it has extended its membership categories to include 'psychotherapeutic counsellor' and more flexible routes to membership.

The development of counselling is harder to trace, there being no single dominant figure like Freud, or monolithic theory like psychoanalysis. Hans Hoxter may, however, be credited as one outstanding individual for his part in creating the counselling movement, including bringing American training ideas to Britain. Further relevant historical information is available in Aldridge (2014). It is usually agreed that early American vocational guidance projects and associations (for example, Frank Parsons' Vocation Bureau in Boston in 1908) laid the foundations of counselling, and guidance, for the young. This certainly features in the early career of Carl Rogers, who is probably the closest to being the 'founder' of (non-directive) counselling in the 1940s. Another player is perhaps Rollo May, who, influenced by Alfred Adler, wrote what many consider to be the first counselling text in the 1920s (May, 1992). In the United States of America (USA) counselling was also originally closely linked with personnel management and the workplace. In general, it is true to say that counselling has *historical* roots in practical guidance and problem-solving issues, and was often agency-based rather than associated with private practice. However, it is now mainly characterized as distinctly other than advice giving and as having a primarily client-centred, facilitative and therapeutic function.

Seminal events in the UK included the establishment of the National Marriage Guidance Council in 1938, the import of counselling training methods from the USA to the Universities of Reading and Keele in 1966 (to serve the pastoral needs of students), and the establishment of the Westminster Pastoral Foundation in 1969. The Standing Conference for the Advancement of Counselling in 1970 led to the formation of the British Association for Counselling in 1977, renamed the British Association for Counselling and Psychotherapy (BACP) in 2000. The BACP is by far the largest such body in the UK. It should be said that a great deal of cross-fertilization between these developments and others in psychotherapy was taking place and the emergence of psychodynamic counselling, for example, demonstrates these close links.

Another significant development to consider in the therapeutic landscape of the UK is the growth of counselling psychology. Much as counselling and psychotherapy developed along different paths, counselling and psychology also appear to have run relatively parallel trajectories. Counselling psychology in the UK has therefore grown with the view of explicitly bringing together these different bodies of work (Strawbridge and Woolfe, 2010). Its home has primarily been the Division of Counselling Psychology, which was created in 1994 within the British Psychological Society (BPS) after emerging as a special section in 1982 (Orlans and Van Scoyoc, 2009). Despite counselling psychology being a relative newcomer to the applied psychologies within the UK, the BPS itself being created in 1901, it has quickly emerged as a popular training option. Although, in theory, practice and research, there are many overlaps between the work of counsellors and psychotherapists (see Feltham (2013a) for a critical review of this territory), counselling psychology was regulated separately by the HCPC along with the other applied psychologies (e.g., clinical psychology and educational psychology) in 2009. The title Counselling Psychologist is therefore now a protected title, with only those approved by the HCPC being eligible to use it.

Alongside these developments we should also note pertinent developments elsewhere. Originally the Association of Medical Officers of Asylums and Hospitals for the Insane (AMOAHI, founded 1841), the Royal College of Psychiatrists was so named in 1971. Significant mutual aid and voluntary organizations such as Alcoholics Anonymous (1935), the Samaritans (1953) and Cruse (1959) should also be included in this brief portrait, as should the parallel existence of the personal social services and its casework tradition, which closely mirrored developments in counselling and psychotherapy.

Theoretically, psychotherapy and counselling develop continuously, some might say all too prolifically, with significant departures from psychoanalytic theory and practice observable from its earliest days. Jung and Adler were among the earliest to break away from Freud, and similar schisms, factions and developments are in evidence throughout psychotherapeutic history. Hence there resulted the growth of what is still thought to be the more than 500 schools (also known as theoretical orientations, approaches, brand names) of therapy we have today. The question of whether such proliferation is desirable and in clients' interests, or not, must be faced by thoughtful practitioners, and indeed the integrationist movement stemming from the 1980s represents shared concern for convergence (Cooper and McLeod, 2010). In addition to eclectic, integrative and pluralistic developments, attempts have been made at a comprehensive unification of psychotherapies (Magnavita and Anchin, 2013).

In contrast to the moves towards the integration of approaches, early twenty-first century tensions regarding statutory regulation sometimes appeared to be pushing the psychoanalytic, humanistic and cognitive-behavioural therapy (CBT) camps further apart (see House and Loewenthal, 2008; Parker and Revelli, 2008; Weatherill, 2004). But much of this was fuelled by professionalization pressures, economic demands highlighting the advantages of time-limited models, and government requirements for evidence-based practice.

A summary of some of the key points of this necessarily succinct history of events is provided in Table 1.1.1. Readers may also like to consult Aldridge (2014), Dryden (1997), Ellenberger (1970) and Feltham (2013a).

Table 1.1.1 Key historical developments

Year	Birth/growth of institutions and professional organizations	Significant events	Appearance of schools (approximate dates)
1900		Freud's *Interpretation of Dreams* published	Psychoanalysis (Freud)
1907	British Psychological Society (BPS) Vienna Psychoanalytic Society		
1908		First (careers) counselling center, Boston, USA (Frank Parsons)	
1910	International Psychoanalytical Association		
1913	National Vocational Guidance Association (USA) London Psychoanalytic Society		Analytical psychology (Jung)
1919	Institute of Psycho-analysis		
1920	Tavistock Clinic		Behavioural psychology

Year	Birth/growth of institutions and professional organizations	Significant events	Appearance of schools (approximate dates)
1921			Psychodrama
1924	British Psychoanalytic Society		
1926	London Clinic of Psychoanalysis		
	Medico-Psychological Association (MPA; previously AMOAH I, originally 1841)		
1935	Alcoholics Anonymous		
1936	Society of Analytical Psychology		
1937		Death of Adler	
1938	National Marriage Guidance Council (now Relate)		
1939		Death of Freud	
1940			Client/person-centred approach
1948		British National Health Service T groups	
		First student counselling service (University College Leicester)	
1950	International Association for Vocational and Educational Guidance (IAVEG)		Gestalt therapy
1951			Rogers's client-centred therapy
1952	Group Analytical Society	*Diagnostic and Statistical Manual (DSM)* 1st ed.	
	American Association for Counseling and Development (AACD)		
	American Counseling Association (ACA; originally NVCA)		
1953	Samaritans		
1955			Rational emotive behaviour therapy (originally RT then RET)
			Personal construct therapy
1957			Transactional analysis
1958			Behaviour therapy
1959	Cruse		
	Scottish Pastoral Association		
1960		First fee-charging counsellor in private practice in UK	
		Death of Melanie Klein	
1961		Death of Jung	
		J.D. Frank's *Persuasion and Healing*	

(Continued)

Table 1.1.1 (Continued)

Year	Birth/growth of institutions and professional organizations	Significant events	Appearance of schools (approximate dates)
1962			Cognitive therapy
1965		Halmos's *The Faith of the Counsellors*	
1966		Counselling training at Universities of Reading and Keele	
1969	Westminster Pastoral Foundation		
	Association of Humanistic Psychology (USA 1962, UK 1969)		
1970	First Standing Conference for the Advancement of Counselling (annual)	Death of Perls and Berne	
	MPA becomes Royal College of Psychiatrists		
1971		*Foster Report* on Scientology	
1974		*BPS Code of Professional Conduct* (the ethical code) approved.	
1975	National Association of Young People's Counselling and Advisory Services (later Youth Access)		Neuro-linguistic programming
1976		The Medical Section of the BPS is renamed the Section of Medical Psychology and Psychotherapy (later changed to the Psychotherapy Section in 1988)	
1977	British Association for Counselling (BAC)		
1978		*Sieghart Report* on statutory regulation of psychotherapists	
1980	Association of Humanistic Psychology Practitioners (AHPP)	Smith et al. *The Benefits of Psychotherapy*	
1982		Rugby Psychotherapy Conference (set up by BAC)	Acceptance and Commitment Therapy
		Counselling Psychology Section formed in the BPS	
1983	Society for the Exploration of Psychotherapy Integration (SEPI)	First BAC accreditation scheme	Solution-focused Therapy
1987		Death of Carl Rogers	
1989	United Kingdom Standing Conference on Psychotherapy (UKSCP)	Death of R.D. Laing	Eye Movement Desensitization and Reprocessing
1990		Death of John Bowlby	Cognitive Analytic Therapy
1991	British Confederation of Psychotherapists		
1992	European Association for Counselling	BPS Charter of Counselling Psychologists	
		First UK Chair of Counselling (Windy Dryden)	

Year	Birth/growth of institutions and professional organizations	Significant events	Appearance of schools (approximate dates)
1993	United Kingdom Council for Psychotherapy (UKCP, originally UKSCP): advice, guidance, counselling and psychotherapy lead body		Dialectical Behaviour Therapy Ecotherapy
1994	Independent Practitioners' Network UKCP Register of Psychotherapists	BPS Division of Counselling Psychology	
1995		BCP Register NHS Psychotherapy Services in England Review	
1996	United Kingdom Register of Counsellors (UKRC) (individuals) World Council for Psychotherapy	NHS Psychotherapy Services in England, Department of Health (DoH) Strategic Policy Review	
1997		Death of Viktor Frankl	Emotion Focused Therapy
1998	Association of Counsellors and Psychotherapists in Primary Care (CPC) UKRC (organizations)	Data Protection Act	
1999	National Institute for Clinical Excellence (NICE) developed National Counselling Society		
2000	BAC renamed British Association for Counselling and Psychotherapy (BACP) Universities Psychotherapy Association (UPA) adds 'Counselling' to its title, becoming UPCA	BACP's *Ethical Framework for Good Practice in Counselling and Psychotherapy*	
2001		Lord Alderdice's Psychotherapy Bill *Treatment Choice in Psychological Therapies and Counselling: Evidence-Based Clinical Practice Guidelines* (DoH) BACP's *Guidelines for Online Counselling and Psychotherapy*	
2002	Health Professions Council (HPC) is identified as the regulatory body for all health professions, including counselling and psychotherapy ('talking therapies')	BPS creates Special Group in Coaching Psychology	Mindfulness Based Cognitive Therapy
2003		UKCP establishes its Psychotherapeutic Counselling Section BACP Service Accreditation Scheme Telephone counselling (contractual) is accepted by BACP for accreditation hours	
2004	College of Psychoanalysts British Psychoanalytic Council	Graduate mental health workers in primary care British Confederation of Psychotherapists (BCP) renamed British Psychoanalytic Council (BPC)	

(Continued)

Table 1.1.1 (Continued)

Year	Birth/growth of institutions and professional organizations	Significant events	Appearance of schools (approximate dates)
2005	NICE renamed National Institute for Health and Clinical Excellence (still NICE)		
2006		Improving Access to Psychological Therapies	
		BPS *Code of Ethics and Conduct* revised	
2007		Death of Albert Ellis	
2008		BACP represented on HPC's Professional Liaison Group	Dynamic Interpersonal Therapy
		National Occupational Standards: Psychoanalytic/ dynamic Competencies Framework	
2009		HPC Register for Practitioner Psychologists opened	Compassion Focused Therapy
		HPC *Standards of Proficiency* published for practitioner psychologists	
		UKCP *Ethical principles and Code of Professional Conduct* published	
2011		Statutory regulation plans abandoned by BACP	The Pluralistic Framework
2012	BACP/Professional Standards Authority for Health & Social Care	Initiation of Accredited Voluntary Register for Counsellors & Psychotherapists	
	HPC renamed Health and Care Professions Council (HCPC)		
2013	UKCP/Professional Standards Authority for Health & Social Care	Initiation of Accredited Voluntary Register for Psychotherapists	
	NICE renamed National Institute for Health and Care Excellence (still NICE)	*DSM V* published	
2014		*Counselling for Depression: A Person Centred and Experiential Approach to Practice* published.	
		Death of David Smail	
2015	Formation of the Counselling & Psychotherapy Union	Death of Harold Searles	
		Death of Sheila Ernst	
		HCPC *Standards of Proficiency* revised and published	
		World Confederation for Existential Therapy founding congress, London	
2016		BACP *Ethical Framework for the Counselling Professions* published	
		HCPC *Standards of Conduct, performance and ethics* revised.	

ALLIED PROFESSIONS

Most agree that counselling and psychotherapy – in so far as they *are* professions or emerging professions – are part of the health professions. Freud battled to have psychoanalysis recognized as separate from medicine and Rogers similarly battled with psychiatric and psychological colleagues, but the psychological therapies today concern themselves largely with mental health promotion and mental illness reduction even where these terms are not used and where additional or different aims are espoused, such as personal growth and development, psycho-education, psychopractice, etc. (see Brown and Mowbray, 2002). Counsellors are therefore often found in health and social care settings along with psychotherapists, clinical and counselling psychologists, psychiatrists and mental health nurses. A second group of related professionals includes social workers, probation officers, welfare officers, human resources personnel, career guidance workers, occupational therapists, speech and communication therapists, occupational and health psychologists, and so on. Teachers, nurses, priests and others in caring roles may have some closely related functions. Members of the above groups, sometimes known as the 'core professions', have been considered good candidates for counselling and psychotherapy training, and typical intakes to courses include members of all these groups.

Each professional group has its own professional body, history and traditions of training and supervision. Each has designated tasks that differ from those of others, depending on context and client group. Counselling and psychotherapeutic skills are used to degrees in all these professions and, where individual workers possess dual or multiple qualifications (for example, a social worker may be trained in family and systemic therapy), they may formally provide therapeutic services. However, BACP and other clinically-oriented bodies strive to emphasize a distinction between casual, informal or untrained, and uncontracted use of *counselling skills*, and disciplined, contracted, ethically protected, formal counselling or psychotherapy.

The above-mentioned groups are also related to those involved in practising the so-called complementary therapies (often regarding their work as holistic or mind–body integrated), including acupuncture, homeopathy, reflexology, aromatherapy, Alexander technique, spiritual healing, osteopathy, naturopathy, Bach flower remedies, etc. Again, practitioners may sometimes have dual qualifications and practise both psychological therapy and somatic or sensual therapies alternately or simultaneously, having due regard for appropriate contracting (Sills, 2006). Debates about the rights of certain of these groups to aspire to professional status cannot be ignored, but nor can public scepticism. In relation to distinctions between the titles of those engaged in closely related therapeutic professions, and their putatively distinctive skills and effectiveness, see Cheshire and Pilgrim (2004), Gask (2004), James and Palmer (1996) and Milton et al. (2011). Offering resistance to the professionalizing trend, particularly via the HCPC, which is sometimes perceived as unnecessarily bureaucratizing and distorting therapy, is the Independent Practitioners' Network (IPN) (see House, 2003; Postle, 2011) and the Alliance for Counselling and Psychotherapy (see also Parker and Revelli, 2008). A loose coalition of anti-psychiatric, critical psychology and humanistic therapy practitioners continues to critique any further governmental or pharmaceutical appropriation of or distortion of understanding human distress.

A BRIEF OVERVIEW OF THE VALUES OF COUNSELLING AND PSYCHOTHERAPY

The overarching values, and the professional ethics that stem from these, of counselling and psychotherapy were summed up in the concepts of integrity, impartiality and respect (Bond, 2010). These have been developed and related by BACP (2016) to tenets of moral philosophy: fidelity (honouring the trust placed in the practitioner); autonomy (the client's right to be self-governing); beneficence (concern for the greatest good); non-maleficence (to cause least harm); justice (concern for fairness); accountability and candour; and the practitioner's self-respect (self-knowledge and care of self). Such principles are not without problems, however, since in practice there sometimes are conflicts between, for example, the wishes of a client and possible damaging consequences. Also, it is sometimes the case that what may be professionally ethical and desirable will be challenged as socially undesirable or questionable by others. Hence, the goals of individual autonomy and self-actualization, which are held by many writers as central values in psychotherapy (e.g., Hinshelwood, Holmes and Lindley., 1998), have been criticized by some sociologists as leading to an 'autonomy obsession', an undermining of social responsibility and a cultural insensitivity. It is therefore important to bear in mind that what we often call *professional ethics* (as advocated in professional codes) are not necessarily always coterminous with *social ethics*.

It follows from basic principles that counsellors and psychotherapists value non-judgementalism *vis-à-vis* clients, that they owe a duty of care to clients while remaining necessarily detached to varying degrees, and that their aim is the ultimate good of the client balanced by respect for the client's own choices. Due to the weight placed on respect for self-determination, most therapists are opposed to people being coerced into therapy and into remaining in therapy when they wish to leave, and actively support the principle of informed consent to therapeutic procedures.

All professional bodies in this field have their own codes of ethics and practice – BACP's *Ethical Framework for the Counselling Professions* (2016) being a mature example – usually addressing issues of safety, contracting, relationship-building, competence, confidentiality, boundaries, law, advertising, complaints, care of the self, and so on. Other examples include the UKCP's (2009) *Ethical Principles and Code of Professional Conduct*, the HCPC's (2016) *Standards of Conduct, Performance and Ethics* and the BPS's (2009) *Code of Ethics and Conduct*. Fewer specific prohibitions now exist than historically, although sexual contact with clients, exploitation of clients and breach of confidentiality are prohibitions shared by all professional bodies. Nevertheless, often genuine and valid differences in values do exist between members of different professional bodies (and networks, such as the IPN, which oppose professionalization) and different theoretical affiliations.

Understanding and elaboration of the foundational philosophical assumptions of therapists is an area of theory and training that is taking a long time to mature (Bennett, 2005; Erwin, 1997; Feltham, 2010; Howard,

2000). Recent growth has been seen, however, in connections between psychotherapy and neuroscience, evolutionary science, and socio-economic and ecological disciplines. Advances have also been made in how counselling and psychotherapy are delivered, most clearly in technological media. Such developments continue to push the parameters of what might constitute the traditional value base(s) of counselling and psychotherapy and raise numerous questions for those working in this arena.

A final area that warrants special mention is the push for evidence-based practice (EBP). Despite the clear tension between many therapists' holistic positioning and the reductive nature of the methodologies commonly adopted in efficacy and effectiveness research, the EBP movement continues to gather momentum. Issues such as cost-effectiveness and clinical effectiveness are becoming increasingly commonplace and, in many practice settings, counsellors and psychotherapists have to understand the implications of such concepts upon their work. For those who are challenged by such a position, this can involve opting out of certain services all together, for others it can involve working pragmatically so as to embed 'evidence' into their ways of working (e.g., Hanley, Cutts, Gordon and Scott, 2013). Whatever an individuals' perspective, EBP has become a core area that therapists need to be aware of, with accrediting bodies incorporating research into syllabi and supporting the development of textbooks (e.g., Cooper, 2008; Midgely, Hayes and Cooper, 2017).

Despite counselling and psychotherapy having a presence in the UK for almost a century, they are still relatively new professions (if we are to use that term).

REFERENCES

Aldridge, S. (2014). *A Short Introduction to Counselling*. London: Sage.
BACP (2016) *Ethical Framework for the Counselling Professions*. Rugby: British Association for Counselling and Psychotherapy.
Bennett, M. (2005) *The Purpose of Counselling and Psychotherapy*. Basingstoke: Palgrave.
Bond, T. (2010) *Standards and Ethics for Counselling in Action* (3rd ed.). London: Sage.
BPS (2009) *Code of Ethics and Conduct*. Leicester: British Psychological Society.
Brown, J. and Mowbray, R. (2002) Visionary deep personal growth. In C. Feltham (Ed.), *What's the Good of Counselling and Psychotherapy? The Benefits Explained*. London: Sage.

Cheshire, K. and Pilgrim, D. (2004) *A Short Introduction to Clinical Psychology*. London: Sage.

Cooper, M. (2008) *Essential Research Findings in Counselling and Psychotherapy: The Facts are Friendly*. London: Sage.

Cooper, M. and McLeod, J. (2010) *Pluralistic Counselling and Psychotherapy*. London: Sage.

Department of Health (2001) *Treatment Choice in Psychological Therapies and Counelling: Evidence-based Clinical Practice Guidelines*. London: Department of Health.

Dryden, W. (Ed.) (1997) *Developments in Psychotherapy: Historical Perspectives*. London: Sage.

Ellenberger, H.F. (1970) *The Discovery of the Unconscious*. New York: Basic Books.

Erwin, E. (1997) *Philosophy and Psychotherapy*. London: Sage.

Feltham, C. (2010) *Critical Thinking in Counselling and Psychotherapy*. London: Sage.

Feltham, C. (2013a) *Counselling and Counselling Psychology: A Critical Examination*. Ross-on-Wye: PCCS Books.

Feltham, C. (2013b) The cultural context of British psychotherapy. In W. Dryden and A. Reeves (Eds), *The Handbook of Individual Therapy* (6th ed.). London: Sage.

Gask, L. (2004) *A Short Introduction to Psychiatry*. London: Sage.

Hanley, T., Cutts, L., Gordon, R. and Scott, A. (2013). A research-informed approach to counselling psychology. In G. Davey (Ed.), *Applied Psychology*. London: Wiley.

HCPC (2016) *Standards of Conduct, Performance and Ethics*. London: Health and Care Professions Council.

Hinshelwood, R.D., Holmes, J. and Lindley, R. (1998) *The Values of Psychotherapy* (2nd ed.). London: Karnac.

House, R. (2003) *Therapy beyond Modernity: Deconstructing and Transcending Profession-Centred Therapy*. London: Karnac.

House, R. and Loewenthal, D. (Eds) (2008) *Against and for CBT: Towards a Constructive Dialogue?* Ross-on-Wye: PCCS Books.

Howard, A. (2000) *Philosophy for Counselling and Psychotherapy: Pythagoras to Post-modernism*. Basingstoke: Palgrave.

James, I. and Palmer, S. (Eds) (1996) *Professional Therapeutic Titles: Myths and Realities*. Leicester: British Psychological Society.

Magnavita, J.J. and Anchin, J.C. (2013) *Unifying Psychotherapy: Principles, Methods, and Evidence from Clinical Science*. New York: Springer.

May, R. (1992) *The Art of Counselling*. London: Souvenir.

Midgely, N., Hayes, J. and Cooper, M. (2017) *Essential Research Findings in Child and Adolescent Counselling and Psychotherapy*. London: Sage.

Milton, J., Polmear, C. and Fabricius, J. (2011) *A Short Introduction to Psychoanalysis* (2nd ed.). London: Sage.

Orlans, V. and Van Scoyac, S. (2009) *A Short Introduction to Counselling Psychology*. London: Sage.

Parker, I. and Revelli, S. (Eds) (2008) *Psychoanalytic Practice and State Regulation*. London: Karnac.

Postle, D. (2011) *Therapy Futures: Obstacles and Opportunities*. London: WLR/ipnosis.

Sandler, J. and Dreher, A.U. (1996) *What Do Psychoanalysts Want? The Problem of Aims in Psychoanalytic Therapy*. London: Routledge/Institute of Psycho-Analysis.

Sills, C. (Ed.) (2006) *Contracts in Counselling* (2nd ed.). London: Sage.

Strawbridge, S. and Woolfe, R. (2010) Counselling psychology: origins, developments and challenges. In R. Woolfe, S. Strawbridge, B. Douglas and W. Dryden (Eds), *Handbook of Counselling Psychology* (3rd ed., pp. 3–22). London: Sage.

UKCP (2009) *Ethical Principles and Code of Professional Conduct*. London: United Kingdom Council for Psychotherapy.

Weatherill, R. (2004) *Our Last Great Illusion: A Radical Psychoanalytic Critique of Therapy Culture*. Exeter: Academic.

1.2 WHAT DO PEOPLE COME TO COUNSELLING AND PSYCHOTHERAPY FOR?

COLIN FELTHAM AND TERRY HANLEY

OVERVIEW AND KEY POINTS

People attend counselling and psychotherapy for a wide variety of reasons. These vary from person to person and invariably mean that therapy will differ from relationship to relationship. In complicating things further, many therapeutic approaches, and the settings in which they are offered, have their own understanding of the purpose of therapy. As such, therapy can take on a multitude of forms and address a variety of goals. With this in mind, this chapter:

- provides a non-partisan range of therapeutic goals that people might have when they attend therapy;
- offers a reflection on how different theoretical models and approaches (such as those presented in Part 5 of this book) might influence the therapeutic work engaged in;
- offers a reflection on how different presenting issues (such as those presented in Part 6 of this book) might influence the therapeutic work engaged in;
- reflects upon how different organizational settings (e.g., those emphasizing short-term or long-term work) might influence the type of therapeutic work engaged in.

Counselling and psychotherapy in the United Kingdom have developed organically and according to path dependency principles (Aldridge, 2011). Some critics have said they have flowed almost promiscuously into many areas of our lives, so that exactly what they are *for*, what their goals are, is not always clear. It is possible to state that the overall goal of therapy is to facilitate clients' own resourcefulness, insight, problem-solving capacities, happiness, and so on, but critics are entitled to question such global terms. As Sandler and Dreher (1996) convey well, it is far from clear to many psychoanalytic practitioners exactly what the legitimate scope and aims of their work are and should be. Freud himself expressed various aims for psychoanalysis at different times, such as symptom removal, making the unconscious conscious, restoring the capacity to love and work, helping clients to move from neurotic misery to ordinary unhappiness, and conducting research into the human psyche. Each of the contemporary 'schools' of therapy has its characteristic and sometimes conflicting aims – some being altogether wary of 'aim attachment' and some being explicitly goal-oriented and driven to reach and demonstrate successful outcomes. Currently, a broad distinction may be seen between short-term outcome-focused therapy (such as is found in Improving Access to Psychological Therapies (IAPT) programmes) and open-ended process-oriented therapy. Here we look at some of the range of actual and possible goals.

SUPPORT

The term 'supportive therapy' suggests that some clients may primarily need and benefit from a form of therapy that upholds current ego strength and/or coping skills and does not seek to challenge or uncover. Some may need long-term supportive therapy, while others require short-term support in crises. Support may be in the form of warm, non-judgemental listening and encouragement and, although most therapy does not become advocacy, on occasion supportive therapy or counselling may also lean in this direction. Such supportive work remains disciplined and professional and distinct from befriending or friendship. Its aim is to support the person through a difficult time and/or towards a position of independence or readiness for more challenging therapy.

PSYCHO-EDUCATIONAL GUIDANCE

A wide range of psychologically informed practices is to be found under this umbrella term. Appropriate information giving, administering of questionnaires, coaching, mentoring, provision of social skills, lifeskills training, assertiveness and relaxation training, marriage enrichment programmes, parent effectiveness training, relapse prevention programmes, stress inoculation training, emotional intelligence and positive psychology training, are all examples. All aim to identify improvable behaviour and to teach personal skills in various areas of life. The goal is not to uncover presumed psychopathology but to directly enhance cognitive, behavioural and interpersonal functioning, to assist clients in meeting developmental challenges and to equip them with concrete coping techniques and philosophies. Coaching in particular has grown in recent years.

ADJUSTMENT AND RESOURCE PROVISION

The idea that people may be helped simply to adjust to their circumstances has usually been severely criticized by counsellors and psychotherapists. However, it is probably a fact in at least some therapy settings (e.g., employee assistance programmes (EAPs)) that clients seek short-term adjustment-oriented help that may include elements of supportive therapy, problem-solving skills, assertiveness training, brainstorming solutions, *plus* the provision of contextual information (e.g., how an organization works, how to complain about your boss harassing you, etc.) and other welfare-oriented information, such as that relating to welfare benefits, housing, childcare, pensions, etc. In such contexts, therapists may act *both* as non-directive facilitators *and* as providers of relevant information and in some cases as brokers between individual client and organizations.

CRISIS INTERVENTION AND MANAGEMENT

These terms are used broadly here to include the intervention and support of professionals in the aftermath of large-scale (e.g., plane crash, bombing incident), small-group (e.g., bank raid) or personal disasters (e.g., road traffic accidents). Survivors and witnesses of critical incidents or breakdowns of many kinds are often offered immediate help which includes debriefing, support, practical and active-directive help, referral to specialist resources, and gradual restoration of normal functioning. The aim is to provide sensitive, non-intrusive, psychologically strengthening help in the first instance, avoiding connotations of psychopathology. Crisis intervention is concerned primarily with restoration of the level of functioning that existed prior to the crisis.

PROBLEM SOLVING AND DECISION MAKING

For a certain proportion of clients, the purpose of entering counselling or psychotherapy is to examine a life situation or dilemma and come to a (probably quite early) resolution or decision. How to cope with nuisance neighbours and difficult relationships, whether to have a termination of pregnancy, when to retire and whether to live in sheltered accommodation, whether or not to have optional surgery, are some examples. The aim is to facilitate exploration of issues, feelings and practicalities; addressing anxiety and loss may be part of the process. In some approaches, a philosophy and techniques of problem solving may be imparted as a proactive tool for living.

SYMPTOM AMELIORATION

A symptom is a usually distressing or troublesome change of condition which manifests in a crisis, inability to function as normal, or apparently inexplicable somatic phenomena. A majority of people who seek or are referred to therapy for the first time want their symptoms to go away; they wish to return to their normal mode of functioning and self-image. Sometimes their goals are hazy or implicit; a depressed client may, for example, obviously want to be simply less (or not) depressed. Probably one of the greatest mismatches between clients' and (many) therapists' goals is that while the former seek symptom amelioration or elimination, the latter often have more ambitious agendas based on the belief in presenting problems as merely the tip of an iceberg, as 'defence mechanisms' masking underlying, unconscious conflicts. Exceptions to this tend to be cognitive-behavioural therapists, whose main aim is the identification of problematic behaviour and its reduction or elimination in the most efficient time span; and practitioners who strive to respond to consumers' stated needs and stages of change (e.g., Hanley, Sefi and Ersahin, 2016; Burton, 1998; Elton Wilson, 1996).

INSIGHT AND UNDERSTANDING

Some clients, and many therapists, have as their primary goals the investigation of causes of problematic feelings, thoughts and behaviour. Both client and therapist may wish to pursue the search for historical causes and the reasons for persistently counterproductive behaviour in current life circumstances. ('Why did this happen to me? Why am I like this? *Aha! – now I see where this comes from.*') For some practitioners and clients, the goal of therapy may be the attainment of deeper and deeper insights or a state of continuous understanding of self, of how conflicts arise, of motivations, etc.

CURE

Almost all psychotherapists and counsellors avoid use of the term 'cure' and any client expectations that therapy will result in final and dramatic removal of suffering. This may be due to (1) clinical experience, as clients are very seldom dramatically, comprehensively or resolutely cured; (2) dislike of medical connotations, by which suffering, problems in living, are not regarded as biological disturbances to be treated with medical interventions; or (3) resistance to engendering hopes of unrealistic outcomes (and perhaps the disappointment and even litigation that might accompany such expectations). However, at least one approach, primal therapy, conceptualizes human problems in unitary terms as *neurosis* (a psychobiological state) for which it possesses *the cure*. Increasingly, too, the pressure from the evidence-based practice lobby and the influence of the National Institute for Health and Care Excellence (NICE) lead practitioners to speak explicitly in terms of specifically outcome-focused work.

SELF-ACTUALIZATION

Under this heading may be included all aims towards becoming a better person, having greater self-awareness or self-knowledge, and attaining a state of fully functioning personhood. The range of goals subsumed here may include, for example, anything from 'I want to be more assertive/risk-taking/happy' to 'I want to try out everything life has to offer, I want to overcome all obstacles in my life and find the real me.' Concepts of individuation, maturation, finding the real self, being true to oneself and increasing self-awareness fit here. Most observers accept that the concept of an end-point – the fully functioning person – is somewhat mythical; self-actualization suggests a continuous process, a valuing of the journey more than a need to reach a goal; and some are highly critical of this aim altogether (Weatherill, 2004).

PERSONALITY CHANGE

Eschewed by the more cognitive-behavioural and short-term approaches, hints at least of the possibility of quite far-reaching personality change are either found in or projected into certain forms of therapy. At an illusory level, the rather retiring, somewhat unattractive and untalented person may fantasize that therapy will compensatorily convert him or her into everything that he or she is not. However, a number of client claims and testimonies based on dramatic disappearance of distressing symptoms or limitations ('Therapy completely changed/saved my life') have suggested major life changes as a desired outcome for some clients. Many, particularly humanistic, psychotherapists regard their work as 'life-transforming therapy'. This goal raises questions about the nature of the concept of 'personality' and what actually constitutes personality change.

DISCOVERY OF MEANING AND TRANSCENDENTAL EXPERIENCE

Particularly in the wake of the relative decline of formal religion and loss of spiritual and moral leaders and mentors, it seems that therapy has become for many an avenue for the exploration of existential, spiritual or metaphysical meaning and transcendental experience. The existential, humanistic and transpersonal approaches lend themselves most explicitly to such aspirations. This 'movement' has been gathering momentum in recent years and may well change the nature of at least some therapy practice (West, 2011).

SYSTEMIC, ORGANIZATIONAL OR SOCIAL CHANGE

In some forms of therapy, change within domestic partnerships, families, task groups and other groupings is clearly a goal. But counselling and psychotherapeutic skills as human relations skills (sometimes based on an understanding of unconscious conflicts, sometimes not) are also applied to conflict resolution within and between organizations. Experimentation with group counselling and therapy where more than a dozen or so participants are involved, and sometimes hundreds of members participate, has often had goals of conflict resolution and other aspects of social change.

Clients may change their goals over time, and the aims of therapy negotiated between therapist and client may change. It is not unusual for some clients to begin with modest goals and to find further, more ambitious or deeper aims to work on. It has been said that some therapists may be satisfied with the client *feeling better* as an aim, when a more enduring aim might be to *get better*. It has also to be remembered that the types of goal previously identified refer to avowed types of goal. We know that there are also 'shadow goals': some clients may wish to be in a 'sick role', to prove how incapable they are, to maintain a therapist's attention, etc.; some therapists may primarily wish to prove something to themselves, to hold power, to perpetuate a livelihood, to find vicarious intimacy. In spite of ethical codes or frameworks, requirements for training therapy, supervision and other safeguards, unhealthy covert goals cannot be eliminated altogether.

REFERENCES

Aldridge, S. (2011) Counselling: An Insecure Profession? A Sociological and Historical Analysis. Unpublished PhD thesis, University of Leicester.

Burton, M.V. (1998) *Psychotherapy, Counselling and Primary Health Care: Assessment for Brief or Longer-term Treatment*. Chichester: Wiley.

Elton Wilson, J. (1996) *Time-Conscious Psychological Therapy*. London: Routledge.

Hanley, T., Sefi, A. and Ersahin, Z. (2016). From goals to tasks and methods. In M. Cooper and W. Dryden (Eds), *The Handbook of Pluralistic Counselling and Psychotherapy* (pp. 28–41). London: Sage.

Sandler, J. and Dreher, A.U. (1996) *What Do Psychoanalysts Want? The Problem of Aims in Psychoanalytic Therapy*. London: Routledge/Institute of Psycho-Analysis.

Weatherill, R. (2004) *Our Last Great Illusion: A Radical Psychoanalytic Critique of Therapy Culture*. Exeter: Academic.

West, W. (Ed.) (2011) *Exploring Therapy, Spirituality and Healing*. Basingstoke: Palgrave.

RECOMMENDED READING

The websites of key organisations (e.g., the British Association for Counselling and Psychotherapy, the United Kingdom Council for Psychotherapy and the National Health Service) provide overviews of the type of issues people present with in counselling and psychotherapy. Many of these issues are also introduced in Part 6 of this text.

Hanley, T., Sefi, A. and Ersahin, Z. (2016). From goals to tasks and methods. In M. Cooper and W. Dryden (Eds), *The Handbook of Pluralistic Counselling and Psychotherapy* (pp. 28–41). London: Sage.

This chapter reflects upon how therapists might work with the different types of goals that clients present with. It specifically discusses how professionals might use the goals articulated by clients to guide the therapeutic approach adopted. A video of Terry Hanley reflecting upon the goals of humanistic therapy can be found at http://serious-science. org/counselling-psychology-5975

Feltham, C. (2010) *Critical Thinking in Counselling and Psychotherapy*. London: Sage.

A book that encourages counsellors and psychotherapists to critically reflect upon all aspects of their work. This includes considering questions such as 'Are there limits to personal change in therapy?' and 'Does the client know best?'

1.3 WHAT ARE THE TRAINING ROUTES IN COUNSELLING AND PSYCHOTHERAPY?

LAURA ANNE WINTER AND TERRY HANLEY

OVERVIEW AND KEY POINTS

This chapter provides a reflection on how individuals train in counselling and psychotherapy, and considers the various possible routes and some of the issues to think about along the way. Counselling and psychotherapy are considered separately, with reference made to both the similarities and differences in the training routes, as well as a short mention of training in allied disciplines. The main points covered in the chapter are as follows:

- Starting training in any therapeutic field is a big decision and has significant implications which should be considered prior to starting a course. These include reflecting on your personal and emotional readiness, as well as considerations around how training and subsequent work in a therapeutic field would work in your life financially and in terms of the time required.
- Training in counselling can be done in a variety of settings, but increasingly takes place within universities on a full- or part-time basis. Courses usually incorporate both a professional and an academic training component, and can be completed at undergraduate or postgraduate level.
- Training in psychotherapy is also completed in a variety of settings, and is typically done part-time over a number of years. Similar to counselling, this will usually involve completion of supervised therapeutic practice, personal therapy hours, theoretical training and academic assignments.
- Individuals might also choose to train in allied disciplines, for example counselling psychology, or as a Psychological Wellbeing Practitioner or High Intensity Cognitive Behaviour Therapist for the National Health Service Improving Access to Psychological Therapy (IAPT) Programme.

BEFORE EMBARKING ON TRAINING

Beginning training in a new career is a big step, and becoming a counsellor or psychotherapist involves significant investment both in terms of time and money, as well as the emotional energy required. Reeves (2013: 29–30) suggests that when considering beginning training in counselling or psychotherapy it may be useful to reflect on the following questions:

1. Does counselling or psychotherapy training fit into your existing set of skills or employment?
2. If not, are counselling and psychotherapy skills likely to enhance your work? If so, how?
3. Have you ever been a client for counselling or psychotherapy? If so, was this a positive experience (and what was particularly helpful)?
4. Have you ever thought of seeking counselling or psychotherapy for yourself but decided against it? If so, why?
5. Is there a danger that you are considering counselling or psychotherapy training instead of actually going to receive counselling or psychotherapy yourself?
6. Do you know what counselling and psychotherapy is? Have you done some research to find out more?
7. Are you at a point in your life where you want or need a change in direction? Have you thought that being a counsellor or psychotherapist would be 'worthwhile'?
8. Have you looked into the career prospects for counsellors and psychotherapists?
9. Do you understand the different types of counselling and psychotherapy, and have you thought about the ones that might interest you the most?

It is also important to spend some time considering any practical issues in making the decision about if and where to train in counselling or psychotherapy. For example, it might be useful to think about costs and how the training will be paid for, as well as managing how time can be managed if studying alongside work, family, or other commitments. Furthermore, many individuals find that they have a desire to become a 'therapist' or 'to help people' rather than having initial ambitions more specific than this. If this is the case, there are choices to be made about what specific therapeutic profession to train in. The sections which follow give a brief introduction to training in counselling, psychotherapy and two allied professions in turn.

COUNSELLING TRAINING

Traditionally, counselling training was structured around several stages of development as a counsellor, and students studied at first at introduction, then at skills and finally diploma level in order to qualify. Training programmes were mostly found in Further Education (FE) establishments, independent providers and charities, or voluntary organisations. Increasingly, however, there has been a move to locate training programmes in Higher Education (HE) providers such as universities, and many courses moved to postgraduate level (either postgraduate diploma, or masters). Both of these training routes are still available, and there are also increasingly courses at undergraduate level based in HE. Further, there are options to complete undergraduate degrees which combine teaching on both 'psychology' as an academic discipline and practice in counselling skills (Smith, 2016). Reeves (2013: 31) suggests that the move towards degree or masters level training in counselling represents a shift 'towards the professionalization of counselling'. He also raises the argument that increasing the academic requirements of training to be a counsellor may lose potentially talented therapists who have no academic background or ambition, and some of the more relational quality at the core of counselling. However, some might argue that increasing the academic emphasis of training will increase the knowledge base and therefore skill of the counselling workforce. The shift towards university training may therefore be viewed as a positive or a negative thing, depending on who you speak to, but this clear change in training has significant implications for those wanting to become therapists. For example, the costs of training are likely to be much higher at university level. Training in counselling has typically been part-time over two or three years: structured across a day or evening per week, or at weekends. Some courses now run full-time, however, and undergraduate programmes are mostly full-time.

The particular content of the course will vary, as counselling programmes will adopt different core models of therapy: for example, some may be focused on a single approach such as the person-centred model (see Tudor – Chapter 5.20, this volume), while others may be focused on training individuals to be 'integrative' in their practice. Such courses typically use a particular integrative approach to harness the training, for example Egan's Skilled Helper Model (see Wosket and Jenkins – Chapter 5.32, this volume) or more recently McLeod and Cooper's Pluralistic Framework (McLeod and Cooper – Chapter 5.30, this volume). Most programmes, however, will include the following aspects.

THEORETICAL TRAINING

This will vary depending on the approach, but students will often be required to attend classes or seminars, and will need to engage in some self-directed study, such as reading books or articles on the theory behind the practice of counselling.

TRAINING IN THE PRACTICE OF COUNSELLING

This is typically done through observation of tutor-led demonstrations and triad work (Smith, 2016), where one student will act in the role of 'client', one as 'counsellor' and one as 'observer'.

SUPERVISED PLACEMENT WORK

Typically, counselling courses require that students complete 100 or 150 hours of supervised therapeutic practice. Placements can be located in various settings, including health care, education and the voluntary sector.

PERSONAL DEVELOPMENT WORK

This varies across programmes but will often involve taking part in a 'personal development group' and engaging in your own personal therapy, as well as taking part in experiential group activities on the course (Donati and Watts, 2005).

Assessments of work might include a mixture of academic written work, videoed skills work, or feedback from placement supervisors. In addition to the four areas noted above, courses which are completed at postgraduate level will typically involve conducting a research project in the final year (see Hanley, Lennie and West (2013) for an introductory research text which includes examples of students' experiences of research).

A final consideration to note is whether or not the programme is 'accredited', and if so, with which professional organisation. In the UK organisations such as the British Association for Counselling and Psychotherapy (BACP), the United Kingdom Council for Psychotherapy (UKCP), Counselling and Psychotherapy in Scotland (COSCA) or the British Association for Behavioural and Cognitive Psychotherapy (BABCP) all accredit training courses. Accreditation means that the organisation has deemed that the course meets their requirements in terms of curriculum and training.

PSYCHOTHERAPY TRAINING

There are many similarities between counselling training and training in psychotherapy, and therefore much of what was said above applies here. For example, psychotherapy training courses will involve teaching in theory, training in the practice of psychotherapy, and will include both supervised placement work and personal development work of some kind. Training in psychotherapy will usually involve completing a significantly greater number of hours of personal therapy (which necessarily comes with increased costs). Often training in psychotherapy is a longer process than in counselling, and courses will take four years or more. In contrast to counselling, there are fewer psychotherapy training programmes in the UK. Similarly, though, they are provided by a range of organisations, including privately owned providers, or FE/HE institutions. It also operates typically on a part-time basis and can sometimes be quite flexible in terms of students being able to plan their own learning. Therefore, training can sometimes take much longer than structured programmes based in HE, but can also fit around other commitments perhaps more easily.

All psychotherapy training in the UK is affiliated to a college of the UKCP. These colleges vary in terms of their model of therapy (e.g., there is a college for 'Humanistic and Integrative Psychotherapy' and one for 'Family, Couple and Systemic Therapists'). Therefore, just as with counselling training, those interested in training in psychotherapy have an initial decision of what model of therapy they wish to be trained to deliver. Interested readers are referred to Part 5 of this book which gives a brief introduction to a wide range of therapeutic theories and models.

TRAINING IN ALLIED PROFESSIONS

Outside the specific disciplines of counselling and psychotherapy, there are a number of 'allied professions' which involve similar work. Two of these are briefly discussed here.

Many individuals in England are now training as psychological therapists within the National Health Service Improving Access to Psychological Therapy Programme (IAPT). IAPT is a government-funded initiative which aims to respond to the need for greater access for talking therapies for common mental health problems in order to improve people's wellbeing and reduce the costs of poor

wellbeing (Clark, 2012). As well as employing some counsellors to provide humanistic counselling (see Winter, Feltham and Hanley – Chapter 1.4, this volume), IAPT has their own training path for 'Psychological Wellbeing Practitioners' (PWPs) and 'High Intensity Cognitive Behavioural Therapists'. Training programmes are run at various UK universities and students' time is split between teaching at the university and time on supervised placements. The training for PWPs is focused on providing cognitive-behavioural interventions for individuals who are diagnosed with anxiety or depression and are typically classed as having a 'mild to moderate' presentation. Qualified High Intensity CBT therapists provide interventions for individuals who are classed as having moderate to severe anxiety or depression. The training for both roles involves one-year postgraduate diplomas, and you will need to qualify and work as a PWP prior to progressing to the High Intensity CBT course.

The profession of 'counselling psychology' is a branch of applied psychology which combines the fields of psychology and counselling, and thus tries to bring together ideas around the use of scientific research as applied to practice (from psychology) and the emphasis on humanistic values and viewing the individual in a holistic way (from counselling) (Hanley, Sefi, Cutts and Lennie, 2013). Woolfe (2016: 6) reflects on the difference between counselling and psychotherapy and counselling psychology and describes it as a '…minefield of complexity. The difference between these two activities, if it exists, is not at all clear'. Nevertheless, an important difference exists between training pathways. In order to become a qualified counselling psychologist you need to have an academic background in psychology, a requirement which is typically met by an undergraduate degree in Psychology accredited by the British Psychological Society (BPS), or a postgraduate conversion programme if your first degree wasn't in Psychology. You will then need to train to doctorate level or its equivalent in counselling psychology (Jones Nielson and Nicholas, 2016). This is typically a three-year, full-time route, or a longer part-time programme based in a HE institution, which involves completing a doctoral level research project as well as training in counselling psychology theory and practice. Courses also require that trainees engage in personal development, similar to courses in counselling and psychotherapy. Programmes need to be accredited by the Health and Care Professions Council in order that graduates can use the protected title of 'counselling psychologist', and they are also often accredited by the BPS. An alternative training path run by the BPS is possible, called the 'Qualification in Counselling Psychology' (QCoP) (see Galbraith, 2016).

FINAL WORDS AND CONCLUSION

This chapter has given a brief introduction to the large area of training in counselling and psychotherapy. Training in a therapeutic field can be time-consuming and emotionally draining, and requires both a personal and a professional commitment. Training is often very busy and can be quite difficult, as you are required to develop your skills and knowledge in theory and practice, all alongside developing on a personal level (and sometimes doing research too!). Alongside all this work, hopefully training in counselling and psychotherapy is a rewarding process which leads to qualification and then satisfaction in subsequent employment!

REFERENCES

Clark, D.M. (2012). The English Improving Access to Psychological Therapies (IAPT) Program: history and progress. In R.K. McHugh and D.H. Barlow (Eds), *Dissemination and Implementation of Evidence-based Psychological Interventions.* (pp. 61–77). Oxford: Oxford University Press.

Donati, M. and Watts, M. (2005). Personal development in counsellor training: towards a clarification of inter-related concepts. *British Journal of Guidance and Counselling, 33*(4), 475–484.

Galbraith, V.E. (2016). Engaging with academia and training programmes. In B. Douglas, R. Woolfe, S. Strawbridge, E. Kasket and V. Galbraith (Eds), *The Handbook of Counselling Psychology* (4th ed.) (pp. 74–92). London: Sage.

Hanley, T., Lennie, C. and West, W. (2013). *Introducing Counselling and Psychotherapy Research*. London: Sage.

Hanley, T., Sefi, A., Cutts, L. and Lennie, C. (2013). Historical context. In T. Hanley, N. Humphrey and C. Lennie (Eds), *Adolescent Counselling Psychology: Theory, Research and Practice*. London: Routledge.

Jones Nielson, J.D. and Nicholas, H. (2016). Counselling psychology in the United Kingdom. *Counselling Psychology Quarterly, 29*(2), 206–215.

Reeves, A. (2013). *An Introduction to Counselling and Psychotherapy: From Theory to Practice*. London: Sage.

Smith, K. (2016). Learning from triads: training undergraduates in counselling skills. *Counselling and Psychotherapy Research, 16*(2), 123–131.

Woolfe, R. (2016). Mapping the world of helping: the place of counselling psychology. In B. Douglas, R. Woolfe, S. Strawbridge, E. Kasket and V. Galbraith (Eds), *The Handbook of Counselling Psychology* (4th ed.) (pp. 5–19). London: Sage.

RECOMMENDED READING

Each of the major professional counselling and psychotherapy organisations has syllabi that courses need to comply with to retain continued accreditation. These can be found on the different organisations' websites (e.g., the BACP at www.bacp.co.uk, the UKCP at www.psychotherapy.org.uk). Similar documents can be found for those working in IAPT services (developed by the NHS) and counselling psychologists (developed by the HCPC and BPS). These documents, although not riveting reads, provide a useful overview of what programmes cover.

Bor, R. and Watts, M. (2017). *The Trainee Handbook: A Guide for Counselling and Psychotherapy Trainees*. London: Sage.

This is a useful resource for the trainee counsellor or psychotherapist. It provides introductory chapters about starting a training programme, reflections on the skills needed while on a programme and consideration of what happens after training has been completed.

Galbraith, V.E. (2016). Engaging with academia and training programmes. In B. Douglas, R. Woolfe, S. Strawbridge, E. Kasket and V. Galbraith (Eds), *The Handbook of Counselling Psychology* (4th ed.) (pp. 74–92). London: Sage.

For those who are interested in allied professions, this chapter reflects on the process of training in counselling psychology.

1.4 WHERE DO COUNSELLORS AND PSYCHOTHERAPISTS WORK?

LAURA ANNE WINTER, COLIN FELTHAM AND TERRY HANLEY

OVERVIEW AND KEY POINTS

Within the final chapter in this section we address the question 'where do counsellors and psychotherapists work?' In doing so, we provide some brief background and context to a discussion regarding employment contexts within counselling and psychotherapy. Following this, we discuss several different potential areas for work, including voluntary agencies, educational settings, the National Health Service (NHS), private practice and workplace settings. The key points covered within the chapter are as follows:

- Counsellors and psychotherapists find employment in a variety of settings and often will have a number of different roles rather than one role as a therapist.
- Areas of growth in terms of employment in counselling and psychotherapy include educational and workplace settings.
- A large proportion of counsellors and psychotherapists in the United Kingdom (UK) work in the NHS, including within Improving Access to Psychological Therapies (IAPT) services.
- Seeing clients in private practice continues to be a common element of the workload of a counsellor.

INTRODUCTION AND CONTEXT

Within this chapter we take a brief look at the types of potential employment for trainees and those developing a career in counselling. We have chosen to include this because the subject of employment, although of obvious interest to both those wishing to enter the profession and those already trained, is often not touched upon in textbooks. It is perhaps an open secret that, in spite of the huge growth of interest in counselling and therapy and the expansion of their training markets, it remains the case that relatively few full-time jobs exist.

It has been variously estimated that the UK counselling workforce may be up to 70,000 or even that employees using counselling skills make up about 1.7% of total employment (half a million workers) (Aldridge, 2011). The British Association for Counselling and Psychotherapy conducted an Employment Survey of 4,537 of their members in 2014 and found that just under half of those asked had multiple job roles as a therapist (48%) and only 52% had just one role as a therapist. Of the therapists who responded, 29% stated that their main role was in paid employment, with 27% in private practice, 24% working as a volunteer and 18% were self-employed (British Association for Counselling and Psychotherapy (BACP), personal communication).

The reasons for this mixed picture of employment are not easy to specify but no doubt include: (1) the fact that much counselling stems from and remains attached to the voluntary sector and a great deal of counselling is still provided as an unpaid service; (2) the continuing emergence of counselling and therapy as valid and evidence-based forms of professional service deserving of some but limited statutory funding; and (3) their relatively 'soft' image in competition with the work of, for example, psychiatrists (Gask, 2004) and clinical psychologists (Cheshire and Pilgrim, 2004). Alongside the number of relatively few full-time jobs, as reflected in the BACP survey, there are of course patterns of part-time and sessional (hourly paid) opportunities, private practice, counselling/therapy-related work (e.g., supervision, training/lecturing, consultancy, writing) and the use of counselling and therapeutic skills in other roles (e.g., social work, mentoring). Indeed, there is a growing literature on the use of counselling skills in professions outside counselling (McLeod and McLeod, 2015). In the sections which follow we discuss several specific areas of work for counsellors and psychotherapists.

VOLUNTARY AGENCIES AND THIRD SECTOR SETTINGS

These settings include those national organisations such as Relate, Samaritans, Cruse, Victim Support, Mind, and Turning Point, as well as local third-sector or charitable/voluntary agencies. Provision of local women's therapy centres, rape crisis centres, HIV/AIDS agencies, and family-oriented drug- and alcohol-related services is widespread. Many of these rely on a mixture of statutory funding, voluntary fundraising and donations. Some will concentrate on a specific client group – for example, there are agencies supporting those who have been impacted by cancer, or individuals with eating disorders – while others will have a more generic or broad remit for their work. Voluntary agencies and third-sector organisations often employ counsellors and psychotherapists in a mixture of voluntary and paid positions. The services are sometimes offered free at the point of access, or on a donation or sliding scale of fees basis. Typically, services will now offer a mixture of online, telephone and face-to-face individual or group support. Therefore, the work is not always purely or solely counselling or psychotherapy, but may include telephone helplines, befriending, advocacy, information and advice giving, awareness raising, and so on.

EDUCATIONAL SETTINGS

Schools, further and higher education and special educational projects are some of the longest-established settings in which forms of counselling and therapy take place. Primary and secondary schools in the UK offer counselling services, although not consistently. Across the UK the provision varies, with Wales and Northern Ireland presently committed to having counsellors in all secondary schools and England and Scotland having between 61% and 85% counsellors within schools (Hanley, Noble and Toor, 2017).

There is a developing interest in school-based counselling and opportunities for employment, as well as a large amount of research focused on evaluating the effectiveness of the services on students' psychological wellbeing and educational outcomes (Cooper, 2013). With recent UK government reports highlighting the need for mental-health support and integrated services in education (Carter, 2015; Department of Health, 2015), this is a trend which, at least in the short term, is likely to increase. In addition to specific counselling services, schools also continue to offer therapeutic work and pastoral support by educational psychologists, behaviour support workers, mentors and teachers.

Counsellors and psychotherapists also work in Further Education (FE) and Higher Education (HE) settings. This is an example of a setting in which counselling has been offered successfully for decades. In the transitional and vulnerable period between adolescence and adulthood, issues of career uncertainty, susceptibility to emotional, interpersonal and sexual problems, drugs and alcohol, homesickness, and educational and financial pressures require sensitive help. Student counsellors may have relatively high caseloads of self-referred clients presenting a wide range of personal concerns. Turnover is often high since the work is often crisis-oriented and determined by the pressures of the academic calendar. Student counsellors (and those with psychotherapy training may be found as much as those from a counselling background) work in one of the few areas with a relatively good, clear structure of pay, conditions and progression prospects (see also Reeves – Chapter 7.10, this volume).

COUNSELLING IN THE NATIONAL HEALTH SERVICE (NHS)

Counsellors and psychotherapists might be employed within a variety of settings within the NHS, including:

- Primary care, where a single professional is responsible for the care of the individual, for example in General Practice (GP) surgeries, or dedicated mental health primary care settings (see also Hovington and Ali – Chapter 7.14, this volume).
- Specialist services, for example services directed specifically at women or men, at people with specific physical health problems, or with a dual diagnosis of a mental health disorder and a drug or alcohol dependency.
- Secondary care, where a team of professionals are responsible for the care of the individual, for example in community mental health teams or inpatient services.
- Improving Access to Psychological Therapy (IAPT) services. This is a government-funded initiative in England which started in 2008, initially serving only adults and then extended to include a children and adolescent service in 2010. This initiative aimed to respond to the need for greater access for talking therapies for common mental health problems in order to improve people's wellbeing and reduce the costs of poor wellbeing (such as welfare benefits and medical costs) (Clark, 2012). IAPT employees the equivalent of just over 5,500 full-time therapists to work within a 'stepped care' system implementing evidence-based psychological therapies recommended by the National Institute for Health and Care Excellence (NICE) for common mental health problems such as depression and anxiety (Improving Access to Psychological Therapies, 2015). Counsellors and psychotherapists are often

found at step 2 or 3 of IAPT services, offering low or high intensity Cognitive Behavioural Therapy (CBT) or humanistic counselling.

In recent years the NHS has undergone significant changes as a result of political forces (particularly since the 2010–2015 Coalition Government of Conservatives and Liberal Democrats). Often NHS services are now provided by non-statutory providers, such as private health care companies and third-sector organisations who compete to win the contracts for services. Furthermore, given the climate of 'austerity' in the UK, there have been significant cuts to health services, which necessarily impacts the potential for employment within the sector.

PRIVATE PRACTICE

Private practice is traditionally the location for most long-term counselling and psychotherapy and is based typically in practitioners' own homes, and sometimes in purpose-rented offices and group premises (see also Williams – Chapter 7.13, this volume). North American texts have been issuing warnings for some years that this is the practice sector most under threat from 'managed care' and from consumers' greater sophistication, awareness of outcome research and precarious personal finances. On the other hand, some now believe that NHS waiting lists, time-limited and often CBT-oriented treatment may encourage more people to use the services of independent practitioners. Small private practices probably compose an element of many counsellors' and psychotherapists' workloads, quite typically supplementing part-time incomes in other settings (Clark, 2002; Syme, 1994; Thistle, 1998). Apostolopoulou (2013) reflects on the tensions raised by countries' economic problems for counsellors and psychotherapists in private practice, noting that while psychological distress and need may have increased, people's ability to pay for therapy may have decreased.

EMPLOYEE COUNSELLING IN THE WORKPLACE

Increasingly, this has been the site of developments in counselling and opportunities for employment (see also Friery – Chapter 7.16, this volume). Employee counselling, established in the United States of America (USA) for decades, has also grown considerably in Britain. Just as student retention is one of the motives behind provision of student counselling, so prevention of absenteeism is a motive behind employee counselling services.

The therapy provided is typically short term and time-limited. Employers' concerns include drug and alcohol abuse, stress at work, employee relations, management of change, redundancy, accidents in the workplace, etc. Many large companies provide their own in-house counselling and coaching provision, sometimes as part of occupational health; some refer out to individual counsellors or group practices; many contract the services of external employee assistance programme (EAP) providers. These EAP providers are private companies who will manage the counselling service for the organisation, by receiving referrals and providing therapists to conduct assessments and therapeutic interventions. A systematic review of the research literature indicated that counselling in the workplace is generally effective at reducing psychological distress and has a significant impact on absence from work (McLeod, 2010). It did, however, note several methodological weaknesses in the research synthesised.

FINAL WORDS AND CONCLUSION

It is clear that such a short chapter can only provide an introduction to answering the question 'where do counsellors and psychotherapists work?' In addition to the settings mentioned above, therapy may be offered in a range of further statutory services, such as social and probation services, police services and prisons; private health care organisations; and religious and pastoral organisations, e.g., Jewish Care's Shalvata (Holocaust Survivors' Centre), Catholic Marriage Advisory Centres, etc. As mentioned earlier, while relatively few full-time salaried posts exist, many of these offer reasonable pay levels. Some statutory employers pay well, and EAP providers – where they offer more than occasional sessional (hourly) work – can offer relatively high remuneration. Otherwise, pecuniary rewards run from nothing (particularly for trainees and those working as volunteers in community agencies) to modest hourly pay, to average wages for caring professionals. In private practice, some practitioners have been known to generate quite high incomes, but a trend towards a probable relative decline in clients being seen predictably from twice to five times a week (as in traditional psychoanalysis) for some years, and the growth in short-term therapies, is likely to undercut high incomes for all but a very few. As can be seen from this chapter, however, there are significant opportunities for counsellors and psychotherapists in a range of diverse settings. These opportunities and settings will undoubtedly shift over time and new avenues open alongside some possibilities narrowing.

REFERENCES

Aldridge, S. (2011). Counselling: An Insecure Profession? A Sociological and Historical Analysis. Unpublished PhD thesis, University of Leicester.

Apostolopoulou, A. (2013). The impact of the economic crisis on the private practice of counselling and psychotherapy: How much are clients and therapists 'worth'? *European Journal of Psychotherapy & Counselling, 15*(4), 311–329.

Carter, A. (2015). *Carter Review of Initial Teacher Training (ITT)*. London: Department for Education.

Cheshire, K. and Pilgrim, D. (2004). *A Short Introduction to Clinical Psychology*. London: Sage.

Clark, D.M. (2012). The English Improving Access to Psychological Therapies (IAPT) Program: History and progress. In R.K. McHugh and D.H. Barlow (Eds), *Dissemination and Implementation of Evidence-Based Psychological Interventions*. (pp. 61–77). Oxford: Oxford University Press.

Clark, J. (Ed.) (2002). *Freelance Counselling and Psychotherapy*. London: Brunner-Routledge.

Cooper, M. (2013). *School-based Counselling in UK Secondary Schools: A Review and Critical Evaluation*. Glasgow: University of Strathclyde.

Department of Health (2015). *Future in Mind: Promoting, Protecting and Improving Our Children and Young People's Mental Health and Wellbeing*. London: NHS England.

Gask, L. (2004). *A Short Introduction to Psychiatry*. London: Sage.

Hanley, T., Noble, J. and Toor, N. (2017). Policy, policy research on school-based counseling in United Kingdom. In J. Carey, B. Harris, S.M. Lee and J. Mushaandja (Eds), *International Handbook for Policy Research in School-Based Counseling*. Switzerland: Springer.

Improving Access to Psychological Therapies (2015). *2014 Adult IAPT Workforce Census Report*. (www.iapt.nhs.uk/silo/files/2014-adult-iapt-workforce-census-report.pdf).

McLeod, J. (2010). The effectiveness of workplace counselling: A systematic review. *Counselling and Psychotherapy Research, 10*(4), 238–248.

McLeod, J. and McLeod, Julia (2015). Research on embedded counselling: An emerging topic of potential importance for the future of counselling psychology. *Counselling Psychology Quarterly, 28*(1), 27–43.

Syme, G. (1994). *Counselling in Independent Practice*. Buckingham: Open University Press.

Thistle, R. (1998). *Counselling and Psychotherapy in Private Practice*. London: Sage.

RECOMMENDED READING

See Parts 6 and 7 of this handbook.

These sections provide introductions to a wide range of therapeutic contexts. These discuss common presenting issues that people attend therapy for (and thus begin to introduce problem-specific contexts – e.g., eating disorder services) and further specialisms that therapists might focus on. The latter section has numerous chapters that explicitly look at different settings that therapists might find themselves working in.

The jobs pages on the websites associated with the major professional organisations (e.g., the BACP, UKCP and BPS).

Each of these regularly provide updated posting of jobs available to counsellors, psychotherapists and psychologists. Reviewing these, and the specifications related to the different roles, can be incredibly helpful in gaining a view of the employment landscape for therapists.

McLeod, J. and McLeod, Julia (2015). Research on embedded counselling: An emerging topic of potential importance for the future of counselling psychology. *Counselling Psychology Quarterly, 28*(1), 27–43.

This is an interesting and useful paper reflecting on the developing use of counselling skills by professions outside counselling and psychotherapy.

PART II

SOCIO-CULTURAL PERSPECTIVES

2.1 INTRODUCING SOCIO-CULTURAL PERSPECTIVES: SOCIAL JUSTICE AND INTERSECTIONALITY

LAURA ANNE WINTER

OVERVIEW OF THIS SECTION

Part II of this *Handbook* takes our focus outside the therapy room to the social, political and cultural contexts in which counselling and psychotherapy are situated. In this introductory chapter, I aim to give a brief overview of the chapters which are included in this part of the book. In addition to this, however, I also hope to illustrate the importance of issues of diversity and difference in counselling and psychotherapy, and in the following section I briefly introduce the reader to issues of 'social justice'. Finally, I leave readers with three questions to consider which relate to socio-cultural perspectives in counselling and psychotherapy.

This section of the book, covering 'socio-cultural perspectives', has seven chapters, each covering a broad area of 'diversity and difference'. In the following section I reflect further on the terms 'diversity and difference' and how we might understand them. Specifically, the section includes chapters on gender, disability, age, social class, sexuality, religion and spirituality, and race, culture and ethnicity. Importantly, while considered separately for ease of reference, these are clearly not to be considered in isolation. The theory of 'intersectionality' brings our attention to the way in which these dimensions of difference interact, and the 'meaning and consequences of multiple categories of social group membership' (Cole, 2009: 170). For example, I am not just White; I am a White female. Writings drawing on intersectionality have focused attention on the consideration of multiple inequalities, and the impacts of belonging to multiple social groups which are in some way oppressed (Walby, Armstrong and Strid, 2012). Equality, power, privilege and oppression are all important issues to consider throughout this section of the book, as I discuss below. I would therefore urge the reader to consider the ways in which the issues raised in the separate chapters overlap and intersect in important and significant ways, rather than viewing them as discreet and separate issues.

Each chapter within the section is structured slightly differently according to the particular content, but all include a number of key headings: *History and Context* and *Relevance to Counselling and Psychotherapy*. This will hopefully serve to navigate the reader to the topic, but also ensure that our key focus in these brief contributions is on the applicability of these ideas within counselling and psychotherapy. As with all chapters in this *Handbook*, authors have also provided an *Overview* and some *Key Points*, as well as *References* and *Recommended Reading*.

SOCIAL JUSTICE IN COUNSELLING AND PSYCHOTHERAPY

So why is it important to consider socio-cultural perspectives in counselling and psychotherapy? As noted above, what we are considering when we talk about 'socio-cultural perspectives' are issues of diversity and difference. One reason it might be important to think about diversity and difference relates to our ethical and our professional responsibilities. The British Association for Counselling and Psychotherapy's (BACP) *Ethical Framework* (BACP, 2016) outlines six Ethical Principles of Counselling and Psychotherapy. One of these is 'Justice' which relates to 'the fair and impartial treatment of all clients and the provision of adequate services' (p. 2). This explicitly speaks of equality of opportunity, avoiding discrimination and ensuring a fair provision of counselling and psychotherapy services for all members of society. Similarly, the United Kingdom Council for Psychotherapy's (UKCP) *Ethical Principles and Code of Professional Conduct* (UKCP, 2009) speaks of 'diversity and equality' and psychotherapists are required to 'actively consider issues of diversity and equalities as these affect all aspects of their work' (p. 4), and must not allow prejudice to impact their relationships with clients. Statements can also be found in both the Health and Care Professions Council's (HCPC, 2016) and British Psychological Society's (BPS, 2009) ethical guidance documentation (see Winter, 2015, for a discussion of these issues in applied psychology ethical codes). A further reason for the importance of diversity and difference in counselling and psychotherapy might relate to legal requirements. The Equality Act 2010 legally protects people from discrimination on the basis of a number of 'protected characteristics' which relate to diversity and difference (age, disability, gender reassignment, marriage or civil partnership, pregnancy and maternity, race, religion or belief, sex, and sexual orientation). Clients might therefore be able to make complaints of discrimination under the Equality Act should issues arise in the service they receive.

Professional or ethical responsibilities and legal requirements are both very good reasons for considering diversity and difference. Nevertheless, it is also important to recognise that no discussion of these issues is complete without reference to issues of power, oppression and privilege in our society. It is commonly argued that in order to fully reflect on diversity and difference, and sociocultural contexts in psychotherapy and counselling, we need to consider issues of social justice. Social justice can be defined as being

> …both a goal of action and the process of action itself, which involves an emphasis on equity or equality for individuals in society in terms of access to a number of different resources and opportunities, the right to self-determination or autonomy and participation in decision-marking, freedom from oppression, and a balancing of power across society. (Cutts, 2013: 9–10)

Within counselling and psychotherapy, a social justice perspective relates to viewing individuals in their wider social and political contexts rather than in isolation. It encourages a consideration of the numerous potential social factors which might impact upon individuals and trigger distress (rather than a consideration solely of the individual psychological factors). It also urges practitioners to work towards actively challenging and addressing inequality on micro (individual), meso (group or community) and macro (political and societal) levels (Chung and Bemak, 2012; Cutts, 2013; Winter, Guo, Wilk and Hanley, 2016). If we come back to the issue of sociocultural perspectives in counselling and psychotherapy and how we understand 'diversity and difference' we can see that 'when considered from … [a] social justice perspective, diversity and difference becomes about recognition of power differentials, oppression and inequalities in society' (Winter, Guo et al., 2016: 277). Individuals differ in many ways, but talking about diversity generally involves talking about differences relating to value or status. 'Difference' is determined by the majority cultures which hold the greater amount of social power and resources (Lago, 2011).

A critical approach within counselling, psychotherapy and psychology has a long history (Fox and Prilleltensky, 1997; Proctor, Cooper, Sanders and Malcom, 2006; Smail, 1987), and more recently a 'social justice agenda' has been developing momentum across these fields (Chung and Bemak, 2012; Cutts, 2013; Toporek, Gernstein, Fouad, Roysircar and Israel, 2006). Counselling has been critiqued as taking an overly individualistic approach which neglects the importance of wider social forces, and therefore potentially maintains inequalities and discrimination in our society (Smail, 1987). While some have described social justice as one of the foundational values of mental health professionals (Aldarondo, 2007), others see these discussions as unwelcome invasions of values and politics into counselling and psychotherapy. Nevertheless, research has clearly documented a link between mental health and social and political factors. For an excellent example we can turn to the work of Wilkinson and Pickett, who, in their 2009 book *The Spirit Level*, argued that mental health problems are much more common in more unequal societies (Wilkinson and Pickett, 2009). If psychological wellness is so related to, and impacted by, fairness in our societies, it seems to follow that social justice is an issue of utmost importance for those in the helping professions (Prilleltensky, 2013). An ecological perspective encourages us to see individuals as embedded in, and potentially inseparable from, their social and political contexts (Bronfenbrenner, 1979; Winter, Burman, Hanley, Kalambouka and McCoy, 2016).

I therefore encourage you to read the chapters which follow in this section on 'socio-cultural perspectives' through the 'social justice' lens I have briefly outlined here. The authors who have contributed chapters each introduce you to what could be considered to be one area of 'diversity and difference'. It is important to remember that with these factors, whether ethnicity, age, gender, disability, sexuality, social class or religion, often comes histories of oppression, marginalisation and discrimination for particular groups of society. Understood as part of an ecological framework, we can see how these issues may impact our clients, ourselves, and the communities within which we are situated. As I noted above, these areas also do not stand alone, but instead are intertwined and interact with each other and doubtless many other factors. An awareness of these issues allows counsellors and psychotherapists to potentially challenge some of the inequality and discrimination in our society, rather than to ignore, maintain (or at worst contribute to) such differences in their work.

QUESTIONS

1. Consider an individual, couple, family or group you have worked with in a supportive capacity (either as a counsellor/psychotherapist or another role utilising counselling skills). In what ways were you similar to or different from them? How do you think this impacted your relationship with them?
2. Consider how you define yourself in terms of gender, disability, age, social class, sexuality, religion and spirituality, and race, culture and ethnicity. What kinds of perceived benefits and disadvantages do you think you might experience as a result of defining yourself in these ways in the society in which you live?
3. Do you think counselling and psychotherapy can, or should, be apolitical and value free? In either case, what are your reasons for thinking this?

REFERENCES

Aldarondo, E. (2007). Rekindling the reformist spirit in the mental health professions. In E. Aldarondo (Ed.), *Advancing Social Justice through Clinical Practice* (pp. 3–17). Englewood Cliffs, NJ: Lawrence Erlbaum Associates.

British Association for Counselling and Psychotherapy (2016). *Ethical Framework for the Counselling Professions.* Lutterworth, Leicestershire: BACP.

British Psychological Society (2009). *Code of Ethics and Conduct.* Guidance Published by the British Psychological Society. Leicester: BPS.

Bronfenbrenner, U. (1979). *The Ecology of Human Development: Experiments by Nature and Design.* Cambridge, MA, and London: Harvard University Press.

Chung, R.C.-Y. and Bemak, F.P. (2012). Social Justice Counseling: The Next Steps beyond Multiculturalism. London: Sage.

Cole, E.R. (2009). Intersectionality and research in psychology. *American Psychologist, 64*(3), 170–180.

Cutts, L.A. (2013). Considering a social justice agenda for counselling psychology in the United Kingdom. *Counselling Psychology Review, 28*(2), 8–16.

Fox, D. and Prilleltensky, I. (Eds) (1997). *Critical Psychology: An Introduction.* London: Sage.

Health and Care Professions Council (2016). *Standards of Conduct, Performance and Ethics.* London: HCPC.

Lago, C. (2011). Diversity, oppression, and society: Implications for person-centered therapists. *Person-Centered & Experiential Psychotherapy, 10*(4), 235–247.

Prilleltensky, I. (2013). Wellness without fairness: The missing link in psychology. *South African Journal of Psychology, 43*(2), 147–155.

Proctor, G., Cooper, M., Sanders, P. and Malcolm, B. (2006). *Politicizing the Person-centred Approach: An Agenda for Social Change.* Ross-on-Wye: PCCS Books.

Smail, D. (1987). *Taking Care: An Alternative to Therapy.* London: Constable.

Torporek, R.L., Gerstein, L.H., Fouad, N.A., Roysircar, G. and Israel, T. (Eds) (2006). *Handbook for Social Justice in Counseling Psychology: Leadership, Vision, and Action.* Thousand Oaks, CA: Sage.

UK Council for Psychotherapy (2009). *Ethical Principles and Code of Professional Conduct.* London: UKCP.

Walby, S., Armstrong, J. and Strid, S. (2012). Intersectionality: Multiple inequalities in social theory. *Sociology, 46*(2), 224–240.

Wilkinson, R. and Pickett, K. (2009). *The Spirit Level: Why Equality is Better for Everyone.* London: Penguin.

Winter, L.A. (2015). The presence of social justice principles within professional and ethical guidelines in international psychology. *Psychotherapy and Politics International, 13*(1), 55–66.

Winter, L.A., Burman, E., Hanley, T., Kalambouka, A. and McCoy, L. (2016). Education, welfare reform and psychological wellbeing: A critical psychology perspective. *British Journal of Educational Studies*, DOI: 10.1080/00071005.2016.1171823.

Winter, L.A., Guo, F., Wilk, K. and Hanley, T. (2016). Difference and diversity in pluralistic therapy. In M. Cooper and W. Dryden (Eds), *The Handbook of Pluralistic Counselling and Psychotherapy.* London: Sage.

2.2 GENERAL GENDER

JENNY BIMROSE

OVERVIEW AND KEY POINTS

The gender of an individual refers to their membership of a particular social category, masculine or feminine, which aligns more or less to the two sexes. It is, however, different from sex, sexual orientation, sexual preference and from other categories or descriptions that relate to various behaviours and identities associated with the sexes. Gender is defined by reference to those attributes associated with 'being female' and 'being male'. These attributes are not, however, fixed. They differ between cultures or societies during any one period in history and change within the same culture or society over time. Such changes are bound up with role changes and are linked to subtle changes in social attitudes and values. Gender, then, is socially constructed, defined by societies, and highlights the ways in which 'being male' and 'being female' are valued differently – different and not equal. This chapter will:

- review the depth and breadth of gender inequalities, nationally and internationally;
- reflect on some implications for counselling and psychotherapeutic practice;
- present selected approaches to help counsellors respond more effectively to gender differences in counselling and psychotherapy.

HISTORY AND CONTEXT

A study of gender focuses attention on the profound and persistent inequalities suffered by women and girls. The World Economic Forum (2015) recently confirmed the magnitude of current national gender gaps, acknowledging that these are the result of the subtle interplay of various socio-economic, political and cultural variables. They argue that:

> People and their talents are among the core drivers of sustainable, long-term economic growth. If half of these talents are underdeveloped or underutilized, growth and sustainability will be compromised. Moreover, there is a compelling and fundamental values case for empowering women: women represent one half of the global population – they deserve equal access to health, education, earning power and political representation. (World Economic Forum, 2015: v)

The majority of the world's poor are women and their lack of access to financial resources has a negative impact on their overall wellbeing. While there is progress in some areas, this is slow. In the United Kingdom (UK), the gender pay gap has fallen to 13.9%. This is in line with international trends, where it has narrowed from 23 percentage points (ppts) in 1990 to 13ppts in 2012 (ILO-IMF-OECD-WBG, 2014). Yet, for older women (Bimrose, 2015), some black and minority ethnic (BME) women, women in certain occupations (e.g., skilled trades) and women on higher earnings in the UK, the pay gap is wider (Fawcett Society, 2015). A female UK graduate, for example, can expect to earn 20% less, on average, over her lifetime than a male graduate (Business in the Community, 2015). Women continue to be more likely to have low-paid, low-status, precarious jobs, with limited or no social protection or basic rights (United Nations, 2016a). They continue to have disproportionate responsibility for unpaid work, such as caregiving, which limits their full participation in education, the labour market and public life (United Nations, 2016a). Undoubtedly, social changes have heralded increasing levels of freedom for women regarding their reproductive functions, their relationship to the marriage contract and their financial affairs. However, alongside these types of positive lifestyle changes, many inequalities and injustices continue that have to be routinely confronted by women across a whole range of areas in their daily lives. Perhaps the most shocking relates to the statistics on violence. Violence against girls and women is described as a pandemic (United Nations, 2016b). It is estimated that 35% of women worldwide have experienced either physical and/or sexual intimate partner violence or sexual violence by a non-partner at some point in their lives, with some national studies showing that up to 70% of women have experienced physical and/or sexual violence from an intimate partner in their lifetime. Although data are hard to collect and difficult to compare, existing evidence shows a high prevalence rate of psychological violence. In the 28 European Union Member States, 43% of women have experienced some form of psychological violence by an intimate partner in their lifetime (United Nations, 2016b).

The increased educational achievement of girls and women, however, does represent a real success story. Despite the well-documented progress made in this area (e.g., Unterhalter, North, Arnot, Lloyd, Moletsane, Murphy-Graham, Parkes and Saito, 2014), with girls now performing as well, or better, than boys at all stages of the National Curriculum assessments in England, gendered practices in education continue. For example, both teaching methods and the curricula continue to be plagued by gendered stereotypes, with girls and women consequently excluded and marginalized in the curriculum, content and practices of education, particularly prevalent in science, technology, engineering and mathematics (Organization for Economic Co-operation and Development (OECD), 2015). With the significant gains in girls' educational achievement has, however, come concern over 'new gaps in educational achievement' (OECD, 2015: 13), referring to boys' (relative) under-achievement. However, this focus on boys' under-achievement can shift attention away from the fact that large numbers of girls are also low attainers and that the gendered subject choices made by girls have a negative impact in terms of their subsequent career choices (Bimrose, 2008; Department for Education and Skills, 2007).

Evidence of gender inequality can be found in many other domains, such as health care, legal rights, housing, training and welfare. Further, where different social, biological and cultural categories coincide with gender, like age, socio-economic status, ethnicity/race, intersectionality is a useful concept for understanding the complexity of the layers of disadvantage often evident (Bimrose, McMahone and Watson, 2015). Consequently, important questions for counsellors and psychotherapists are: to what extent and in what ways should the extent and depth of these inequalities be taken into account in their practice, and how?

RELEVANCE TO COUNSELLING AND PSYCHOTHERAPY

The suggestion that gender represents a dimension in the therapeutic relationship that deserves special consideration can be contentious among professionals. Resistance to this suggestion can relate to many issues, for example, concern about stereotyping clients – because grouping clients within a grand category, such as gender, risks generalizations and detracts from the uniqueness of individuals. One other concern relates to any suggestion that women (and girls) are more deserving of special attention or consideration in counselling

than men (and boys). Despite a level of resistance from the field, gender is increasingly attracting the attention of researchers, writers and practitioners, who argue that counsellors and therapists need to be ready to adapt their approach when working with women, who often suffer psychological distress as victims of social injustice, including discrimination and prejudice (Fischer and Holz, 2007). Counsellors may need to review, fundamentally, the adequacy of traditional theories of assessment and treatment that underpin their practice for work with all clients who are systematically disadvantaged, including women (Coogan and Chen, 2007; Eriksen and Kress, 2008; McLeod and Machin, 1998). The integration of new approaches is indicated, which takes account of context:

> it is often forgotten that the roots of women's so-called psychological problems have frequently been social and political rather than the individual and intrapsychic in origin. (Eriksen and Kress, 2008: 152)

Examples of integrated approaches include multicultural combined with a social justice approach (Comstock, Hammer and Strentzsh, 2008) and multicultural with feminist and social justice elements (Crethar, Rivera and Nash, 2008).

A useful framework for reviewing existing contributions comes from multicultural counselling and therapy (MCT) (Bimrose, 1996). The multicultural literature has now matured and established itself within counselling psychology (Bimrose, 1998; Worthington, Soth-McNett and Moreno, 2007). It is not, however, without critics (Worthington et al., 2007) and its introduction into professional training programmes and practice has been contentious (Comstock et al., 2008). Despite possible shortcomings, a particular strength is the way it helps clients understand how problems they are confronting may emanate from their ethnicity, gender, age, disability or socio-economic status, rather than internalizing problems as individual deficits for which they have to take responsibility (Constantine, Hage, Kindaichie and Bryant, 2007; Ivey, Ivey and Simek-Morgan, 1997). One other attractive feature of this approach is the explication of what multicultural skills and competencies are required for practice. Even qualified and experienced practitioners have reported feelings of inadequacy around working with clients who are different from themselves in some respect, especially regarding gender and ethnicity (Bimrose and Bayne, 1995). Thus a competency framework provides a practical means of developing expertise and confidence.

The multicultural standards and competencies that define the multiculturally competent counsellor (Sue, Arrendondo and McDavis, 1995: 625) are presented in a three-by-three matrix. The three basic dimensions of this matrix are defined as: therapist awareness, understanding and skills. It is within these dimensions that approaches to gender in therapy will now be considered.

Gender-aware therapy (GAT) is one approach that specifically encourages therapists to explore gender-related experiences with both women and men (Good, Gilber and Scher, 1990). If adopted, the principles of GAT would enhance all three dimensions of multicultural competence in practice. Five are identified: (1) gender issues must be integrated into counselling and therapy equally with women and men (for example, problems related to childcare are discussed with men in the same way as with women); (2) problems which arise in counselling must, where relevant, be linked clearly to their social origins (for example, stress and anxiety which are created by a lack of availability of quality childcare provision should be related to systems failure in the provision of this service); (3) collusion with gender stereotypical solutions to problems must be avoided (for example, women experiencing stress and anxiety because of a lack of quality childcare provision should *not* be encouraged to give up work or to work part-time); (4) collaborative therapeutic relationships must be developed in preference to an expert therapist role; (5) and most important, clients' freedom to choose must be respected, rather than a value position being imposed. Overall, an important goal of GAT is to help clients learn to act in new ways that will allow them to develop in a manner not constrained by stereotypical gender assumptions.

Applying Sue et al.'s (1995) multicultural competency framework, the second GAT principle implies increased knowledge and understanding about the precise nature and extent of gender inequalities within all aspects of society, together with their consequences. The third GAT principle implies the need for all therapists to increase their own self-awareness about gender issues as well as their awareness of gender stereotypes which operate generally. The first, fourth and fifth GAT principles imply particular skills and techniques which should be adopted by therapists in practice. For example, the first would require a conscious exploration of issues with men in therapy which relate to matters often associated only with women.

Feminist counselling approaches gender in a similar way to gender-aware therapy, highlighting the destructive potential of gender, since it limits role expectations and relegates half the population to second-class status. This issue is explored in depth in Chapter 7.4 (Ballinger – this volume) so will not be dealt with in any depth here. It is concerned with inequality generally, not just that associated with gender, and is eclectic in approach, so it can be used with any other approaches to therapy.

Applying the framework for multicultural competence to feminist counselling, the approach emphasizes increased counsellor self-awareness of gender inequality together with knowledge about, and understanding of, the dimensions of social inequality. Such knowledge would be used beyond individual counselling sessions to influence, even change, structures and systems that create and maintain gender inequalities. This resonates with the social justice and advocacy movement which is gaining ground in counselling psychology (Arrendondo, Tovar-Blank and Parham, 2008; Lee and Rodgers, 2009; Lopez-Baez and Paylo, 2009; Roysircar, 2009; Toporek, Lewis and Crethar, 2009; Toporek and Liu, 2001), where intervening on behalf of clients and/or taking a more active community role may be necessary to achieve the change that makes the difference to the life chances of women.

Gendered approaches to therapy are still being developed. They represent a serious and reflective attempt to address issues raised by gender in therapy. Ivey et al., (1997: 175) discuss how feminist therapy can be combined with multicultural counselling and therapy, highlighting the value that can be derived when therapists work beyond the level of the individual to, for example, the community. Culture-infused counselling, proposed by Collins and Arthur (2010), focuses on the working alliance between counsellors and their clients. They argue that the concept of a working alliance goes beyond theoretical frameworks to provide a more robust structure for competency frameworks. Indeed, a conscious approach to gender can be particularly valuable when working cross-culturally, where cultures and value systems define strongly marked gender roles.

CONCLUSION

The extent of continuing gender discrimination, inequality and injustice is shocking, especially since legislation has been enacted in many countries to make this illegal. Often difficult to separate from other types of disadvantage (such as that associated with ethnicity/race, age, or socio-economic status), it can be subtle and hard to detect. Yet it is destructive in its impact on the individual, as well as on society.

Here, it has been argued that gender represents a legitimate challenge for counselling and psychotherapy practice. Should clients be assisted to return to the very systems and contexts which damaged them? Or should it seek to influence those systems and contexts, as well as reflecting upon and changing those values and practices inherently discriminatory in practice itself? Gender-aware therapy, feminist counselling, multicultural counselling and psychotherapy, combined with social justice approaches, are all attempts to address gender-related issues. They are still evolving, but do represent a serious and constructive attempt to pose legitimate questions about practice and incorporate new and different ways of responding to clients.

REFERENCES

Arrendondo, P., Tovar-Blank, Z.G. and Parham, A. (2008) Challenges and promises of becoming a culturally competent counselor in a sociopolitical era of change and empowerment. *Journal of Counseling & Development*, 86 (3): 261–268.

Bimrose, J. (1996) Multiculturalism. In R. Bayne, I. Horton and J. Bimrose (eds), *New Directions in Counselling* (pp. 237–247). London: Routledge.

Bimrose, J. (1998) Increasing multicultural competence. In R. Bayne, P. Nicolson and I. Horton (eds), *Counselling and Communication Skills for Medical and Health Practitioners* (pp. 88–102). Leicester: British Psychological Association.

Bimrose, J. (2008) Guidance with women. In J.A. Athanasou and R.V. Esbroeck (eds), *International Handbook of Career Guidance* (pp. 375–404). Dordrecht: Springer.

Bimrose, J. (2015) Voices of older women from England. In J. Bimrose, M. McMahon and M. Watson (eds), *Women's Career Development throughout the Lifespan: An International Exploration* (pp. 139–151). London and New York: Routledge.

Bimrose, J. and Bayne, R. (1995) The multicultural framework in counsellor training. *British Journal of Guidance and Counselling*, 23 (2): 259–265.

Bimrose, J., McMahon, M. and Watson, M. (2015) Introduction. In J. Bimrose, M. McMahon and M. Watson (eds), *Women's Career Development throughout the Lifespan: An International Exploration* (pp. 1–7). London and New York: Routledge.

Business in the Community (2015) International Women's Day Factsheet. Women and Work. (http://gender.bitc.org.uk/sites/default/files/kcfinder/files/Opportunity%20Now/Women%20and%20Work%20The%20Facts.pdf).

Collins, S. and Arthur, N. (2010) Culture-infused counselling: a fresh look at a classic framework of multicultural counselling competencies. *Counselling Psychology Quarterly*, 23 (2): 203–216.

Comstock, D.L., Hammer, T.R. and Strentzsh, J. (2008) Relational-cultural theory: a framework for bridging relational, multicultural, and social justice competencies. *Journal of Counseling & Development*, 86 (3): 279–287.

Constantine, M.G., Hage, S.M., Kindaichie, M.M. and Bryant, R.M. (2007) Social justice and multicultural issues: implications for the practice and training of counselors and counseling psychologists. *Journal of Counseling & Development*, 85 (4): 24–29.

Coogan, P.A. and Chen, C.P. (2007) Career development and counselling for women: connecting theories to practice. *Counselling Psychology Quarterly*, 20 (2): 191–204.

Crethar, H.C., Rivera, E.T. and Nash, S. (2008) In search of common threads: linking multicultural, feminist, and social justice counseling paradigms. *Journal of Counseling & Development*, 86 (3): 269–278.

Department for Education and Skills (2007) *Gender and Education: The Evidence on Pupils in England*. (http://webarchive.nationalarchives.gov.uk/20130401151715/www.education.gov.uk/publications/eOrderingDownload/00389-2007BKT-EN.pdf).

Ericksen, J.A. and Kress, V.E. (2008) Gender and diagnosis: struggles and suggestions for counselors. *Journal of Counseling & Development*, 86 (2): 152–162.

Fawcett Society (2015) *Fawcett's Equal Pay Day Briefing (2015)*. (www.fawcettsociety.org.uk/wp-content/uploads/2016/03/Gender-Pay-Gap-Briefing-2016.pdf).

Fischer, A.R. and Holz, K.B. (2007) Perceived discrimination and women's psychological distress: the roles of collective and personal self-esteem. *Journal of Counseling Psychology*, 54 (2): 154–164.

Good, G.E., Gilber, L.A. and Scher, M. (1990) Gender aware therapy: a synthesis of feminist therapy and knowledge about gender. *Journal of Counseling and Development*, 68: 376–380.

ILO-IMF-OECD-WBG (2014) *Achieving Stronger Growth by Promoting a More Gender Balanced Economy*. (www.oecd.org/g20/topics/employment-and-social-policy/ILO-IMF-OECD-WBG-Achieving-stronger-growth-by-promoting-a-more-gender-balanced-economy-G20.pdf).

Ivey, A.E., Ivey, M.B. and Simek-Morgan, L. (1997) *Counseling and Psychotherapy: A Multicultural Perspective* (4th ed.). Needham Heights, MA: Allyn and Bacon.

Lee, C.C. and Rodgers, R.A. (2009) Counselor advocacy: affecting systemic change. *Journal of Counseling & Development*, 87 (3): 284–287.

Lopez-Baez, S.I. and Paylo, M.J. (2009) Social justice advocacy: community collaboration and systems advocacy. *Journal of Counseling & Development*, 87 (3): 276–283.

McLeod, J. and Machin, L. (1998) The context of counselling: a neglected dimension of training, research and practice. *British Journal of Guidance & Counselling*, 26 (3): 325–336.

OECD (2015) *The ABC of Gender Equality in Education: Aptitude, Behaviour, Confidence*. (www.oecd.org/pisa/key-findings/pisa-2012-results-gender-eng.pdf).

Roysircar, G. (2009) The big picture of advocacy: counselor, heal society and thyself. *Journal of Counseling & Development*, 87 (3): 288–294.

Sue, D.W., Arrendondo, P. and McDavis, R.J. (1995) Multicultural counseling competencies and standards: a call to the profession. In J.G. Ponterotto, J.M. Casas, L.A. Suzuki and C.M. Alexander (eds), *Handbook of Multicultural Counseling*. Thousand Oaks, CA: Sage.

Toporek, R.L., Lewis, J.A. and Crethar, H.C. (2009) Promoting systemic change through the ACA competencies. *Journal of Counseling & Development*, 87 (3): 260–269.

Toporek, R.L. and Liu, E.M. (2001) Advocacy in counseling: addressing race, class and gender oppression. In D.B. Pope-Davies and H.L.K. Coleman (eds), *The Intersection of Race, Class, and Gender in Multicultural Counseling*. Thousand Oaks, CA: Sage.

United Nations (2016a) *UN Women: Economic Empowerment. Facts and Figures*. (www.unwomen.org/en/what-we-do/economic-empowerment/facts-and-figures).

United Nations (2016b) *UN Women: Ending Violence against Women. Facts and Figures*. www.unwomen.org/en/what-we-do/ending-violence-against-women/facts-and-figures.

Unterhalter E., North A., Arnot M., Lloyd C., Moletsane L., Murphy-Graham E., Parkes J. and Saito, M. (2014) *Interventions to Enhance Girls' Education and Gender Equality. Education Rigorous Literature Review*. London: Department for International Development. (www.gov.uk/government/uploads/system/uploads/attachment_data/file/326205/Girls__Education_Literature_Review_2014_Unterhalter.pdf).

World Economic Forum (2015) *The Global Gender Gap Report*. Insight Report, 10th Anniversary Edition. Geneva: WEF. Available from: (www3.weforum.org/docs/GGGR2015/cover.pdf).

Worthington, R.L., Soth-McNett, A.M. and Moreno, M.V. (2007) Multicultural counseling competencies research: a 20 year content analysis. *Journal of Counseling Psychology*, 54 (4): 351–361.

RECOMMENDED READING

1.   Collins, S. and Arthur, N. (2010). Culture-infused counselling: a fresh look at a classic framework of multicultural counselling competencies. *Counselling Psychology Quarterly*, 23 (2): 203–216.

Argues for a more inclusive definition of culture, as a means of integrating additional domains of practice, and for a shift away from the narrow focus on strategies and techniques. A new model of culture-infused counselling is proposed, with the potential to accommodate gender, which focuses on the working alliance between counsellors and clients.

2.   Comstock, D.L., Hammer, T.R. and Strentzsh, J. (2008) Relational-cultural theory: a framework for bridging relational, multicultural, and social justice competencies. *Journal of Counseling & Development*, 86 (3): 279–287.

(Continued)

Discusses the concept of the fourth force in counselling and psychotherapy, presenting seven self-reflective questions that are designed to support the development of new relational and multicultural/social justice counselling competencies, to enable professionals to work more effectively as change agents/social justice advocates.

3. Ivey, A.E., Ivey, M.B. and Simek-Morgan, L. (1997) *Counseling and Psychotherapy: A Multicultural Perspective* (4th ed.). Needham Heights, MA: Allyn and Bacon.

A comprehensive reference text for early career counselling professionals and for experienced counsellors wishing to update their knowledge/understanding. It foregrounds the issues of diversity and disadvantage. It provides summaries of a wide range of theoretical orientations, together with strategies and techniques, as well as consideration of broader issues, such as ethical practice and supervision from a multicultural perspective.

2.3 DISABILITY

SIMON PARRITT

OVERVIEW AND KEY POINTS

Definitions of disability and a disabled person have become increasingly diverse and often contentious over recent years. This chapter will attempt to outline the main socio-cultural issues and developments around disability, as they relate to counsellors and psychotherapists working with disabled people and issues that arise in various practice contexts. Exploring the historical and socio-cultural roots will help to highlight the tensions between the medical and social models of disability and address the complications, confusion and misunderstandings between disability, illness and impairment. Key points include:

- An understanding of the concept of disability and how disability is defined and conceptualised within the current socio-cultural and political context is important both in and outside the therapy room.
- Being aware of the historical and cultural background in which disability is experienced every day, by the disabled client and by the counsellor or psychotherapist, is fundamental to working with disability within a therapeutic relationship.

- The context in which counselling services are delivered influences both the model, limits and scope of the therapeutic relationship, as well as the experience and expectations of the disabled client.
- Understanding the relative dynamics that disability, impairment and illness play in a number of overlapping identities and experiences is an essential task for both therapist and disabled client.

HISTORY AND CONTEXT

Historically, disability was associated with disease and contamination posing a real threat to community survival and so avoidance of disabled people was triggered by cues such as 'physical disabilities, facial disfigurements, and other unusual morphological characteristics even though these features may be objectively unrelated to contagious disease' (Park, Faulkner and Schalle, 2003: 69). Disability and illness was also seen as divine retribution or punishment for past deeds, placing it within the realm of magic, religion and traditional beliefs. By the late nineteenth century, Victorian society began a shift in attitudes towards dealing with the 'aged and infirm'. As Barnes states, '…the nineteenth-century was also significant for an upsurge of Christian charity and "humanitarian" values among the Victorian middle and upper classes. As a consequence several charities controlled and run by non-disabled people for disabled people were founded during this period' (Barnes, 1997: 18). In addition, the growth of a biomedical and scientific paradigm and the separation of the physical from the spiritual, advances in, as well as the kudos of, modern medicine began to alter and improved disabled people's lives. Nevertheless, older archaic beliefs and superstitions persist at some level within most societies and cultures, where disability is still perceived as inherently bad or deviant. Today, medical and social interventions have been aimed at altering disabled individuals physically, or psychologically, to meet a non-disabled social norm. Faced with inevitably falling short of this, responses and strategies to cope with being seen as 'less than', or where possible 'pass as' non-disabled, can cause psychological distress. 'Nearly all disabled people confront, often routinely, the choice of hiding their disability or drawing attention to it and the question of what to do when others overlook it' (Brune, 2003: 1).

DISTRIBUTION AND PREVALENCE

The *World Report on Disability* (World Health Organisation (WHO), 2011) estimates that some one billion people in the world experience disabilities of various types and degrees and 200 million experience considerable difficulties in functioning. While around 80 per cent of disabled people live in the developing world, the United Kingdom (UK) estimate is 12.9 million (Department of Work and Pensions, 2016). Moreover, disabled people are not evenly distributed across society, as those from economic, social and educationally deprived environments are more likely to fall within a definition of disabled.

DEFINITIONS OF DISABILITY

Problems arise when estimating the prevalence of disability, as there is an ongoing debate and controversy over how it is defined. In 1980, WHO defined disability as the deficits in performance of activities resulting from physical impairment, where physical impairment is the deficit in structure or functioning of some part of the body (World Health Organisation, 1980). It was later extended to include all forms of impairment. The problem of such international classifications and definitions is that this medical approach can be seen as lacking the individual and social experience as it has 'been based upon

able-bodied assumptions of disability' (Lin, 2003: 21). The social model of disability, on the other hand, differentiates between impairment and disability, where the impairment may be sensory or mobility but disability itself is seen as socially constructed by lack of access to buildings, services and society. Therefore, the social model conceptualises the problem as being created by lack of social inclusion and access, as a result of the attitudes of a non-disabled society. Disability as a social construct has given rise to the United Nations (UN) Convention on the Rights of Persons with Disabilities, which came into force in 2008 and is a legally binding international treaty and has 160 signatories being ratified by the European Union on 23 December 2010 (United Nations, 2010).

However disability is defined, prevalence increases with age and with an increasingly ageing population in the UK (Office for National Statistics, 2014) it follows that people who identify themselves, or are classified, as disabled will increase over time. Hence, policies encouraging older people to remain economically active impact most upon disabled people, who are more excluded and less able to participate in work and society. In March 2013, of all unemployed people of working age, 50 per cent were disabled (The Papworth Trust, 2016).

Disabled people differ from other minority and disadvantaged groups, as a person can become disabled at any point in their life. Indeed, only 17 per cent of disabled people were born with impairments (Regan and Stanley, 2003: 60) and the vast majority will acquire impairments during their lifetime, whether or not they chose to identify as disabled. Despite, or because of this, therapists can unconsciously distance themselves, seeing disability as something that happens to others. To see disability as 'other' is perhaps an inevitable consequence of society's fear and denial, but not to reflect upon one's own relationship to disability, chronic illness and impairment is a flawed strategy for those of us who are counsellors and psychotherapists.

RELEVANCE TO COUNSELLING AND PSYCHOTHERAPY

Counselling and psychotherapy have traditionally taken an individualistic approach to distress, tending to marginalise socio-cultural issues such as social exclusion and societal attitudes. One consequence of this is that some disabled clients struggle with feeling isolated and rejected, seeing the cause of feeling marginalised, different or 'worth less' as residing in themselves and their impairments. The degree to which this is the reality of society and its policies towards disabled people, and how much is reflected and reinforced within a client's own belief systems and attitudes to disability, are important considerations.

At the end of the twentieth century, policies and practices promoting the social model, self-determination and empowerment had increased. However, funding of counselling services increasingly relies on outcomes that prioritise economic over social benefits and recent support for these aspirations in employment, entertainment, transport, sex and relationships have come under economic scrutiny. While accepting the reality of this, therapists must avoid adopting this narrow framework in the therapy room itself and look to employ a wider pluralist approach. Indeed, '[h]ow we experience and work with difference when we encounter the "other" is fundamental to working in a modern pluralistic and culturally diverse society' (Parritt, 2016: 199). During times of economic decline, enabling disabled people's lives comes under increasing scrutiny, both financially and socially, which can lead to a socio-cultural shift in how disability is defined and portrayed, with a danger of returning to a view of disability which resonates with the older, nineteenth-century view of the disabled as either deserving or undeserving. Therefore, while recognising access in terms of economic and physical barriers, it is also important to reflect upon the philosophy which underpins a particular service.

DISABILITY COUNSELLING SERVICES

Over the past 30 years, charities have struggled with the legacy of being organisations run for disabled people by the non-disabled, rather than by disabled people themselves. There has been genuine progress incorporating aspects of the social model, but progress has recently slowed, due partly to the socio-economic climate in which not-for-profit organisations and charities need to restructure within a business model, in order to obtain funding and ensure continued existence.

Also, while a disability charity can offer a disabled person counselling from its own particular knowledge base, it should deliver the same high standard as might be expected from any professional counselling service. Empathy, while essential, is not sufficient and quality counselling services are expensive, requiring expert training, supervision and staffing. The solution is, increasingly, to contract out, or refer to agencies that may not encompass disability or the social model within their core training and are often staffed by less experienced counsellors or trainees.

The reality is that '...there are a few counselling agencies which specialise in working with disabled clients, but these are not available to the vast majority of disabled people' (Reeve, 2014: 258).

General counselling services need to address access beyond the basic issues, such as hearing loops and wheelchair access. Missed or late appointments due to illness, fatigue or the unpredictability of accessible transport and carers are all factors that need to be assessed within a wider social context. Without proactive and flexible policies acknowledging this reality, disabled people will be notable by their invisibility or absence. Therapists need to reflect on how these issues are relevant in their ways of working, from a philosophical and ethical standpoint, in respect of each client, their life stage, socio-cultural background and the context in which they work.

DISABILITY, DIVERSITY AND DIFFERENCE

Placing disability within the wider context of diversity and difference provides a body of theory and research that can underpin and position it alongside others, such as women, Black and Ethnic Minorities (BME) and Lesbian, Gay, Bisexual, Trans, and/or Intersex (LGBTI) groups. Within these groups, the value of training addressing the fundamentals of diversity and difference offers counsellors and psychotherapists an approach to disability within a relevant socio-cultural framework.

Counsellors and psychotherapists should also be aware of the diversity of cultural beliefs that surround disability, at a community, family and individual level. For example, a disabled client may be expected to adopt a dependent role within the family, not to work, nor be sexual, or form their own family. Such attitudes can be rationalised within a particular cultural and historical context but are forms of oppression and disempowerment that pervade disabled people's lives, echoing the experiences of oppressed minority groups across the world. Therapists, while being sensitive to clients' everyday reality, must also be courageous enough to help clients explore and challenge oppressive and disablist attitudes, beliefs and practices both within themselves and their community.

CHRONIC ILLNESS AND DISABILITY

Why do fewer clients actually present as disabled? A factor may be the widening description and overlap with illness, chronic illness and the long-term sick. Therapists may have many clients with long-term impairments, such as heart disease, epilepsy and rheumatoid arthritis, but do not conceptualise or record them as being 'disabled'. With the introduction of the Improving Access to Psychological Therapies (IAPT) programme within the National Health Service (NHS), many clients with depression and other mental health issues have been offered therapy, often Cognitive Behaviour Therapy (CBT). These clients may or may not be identified as disabled, but given the co-morbidity between anxiety and depression and long-term impairment, it would seem likely that many are subsumed within this cohort of clients who do not identify as disabled. The reason behind this 'denial' or 'invisibility' of disability is complex and therapists need to become aware of the underlying socio-cultural and psychological issues. Clients may be reluctant to be associated with a stigmatised group, preferring to be ill, as this is open to treatment or cure, rather than adopting the more permanent negative identity of disabled. As with many minority disadvantaged and stigmatised groups, internalised oppression can also play a role within disabled people, who may be harbouring 'inside ourselves the pain and the memories, the fears and the confusions, the negative self-images and the low expectations, turning them into weapons with which to re-injure ourselves, every day of our lives' (Mason, 1992: 27). As well as understanding the client's own internal attitudes and beliefs, therapists need to reflect upon their own experience and reactions to difference, disability and impairment and how to avoid unconsciously colluding with a negative socio-cultural and historical view of disability

THE SOCIAL MODEL, COUNSELLING AND PSYCHOTHERAPY

Disabled campaigners and writers have attempted to map out an identity which parallels other oppressed minority groups and establish their own unique socio-cultural experience and positive identity. However, problems have arisen in the original social model, as definitions of disability have become more diverse in the last 40 years. Although the fundamentals continue to be relevant to counselling and psychotherapy, the original social model can now be seen to only partly illuminate the lived experience of disabled people. The image of disabled people is still often polarised between the heroic paralympian and the dependent benefit recipient. The truth is never that clear-cut and despite a wheelchair being the international symbol for disability, only around 2 per cent of the UK disabled population are actually wheelchair users. While it is important to be aware of the whole individual and that impairment and disability may not be central to the presenting issues, it would be a mistake to deny that it is a factor for any disabled person living in a non-disabled world.

DIVERSITY WITHIN DISABILITY

There is as much diversity and difference within the disabled community as there is in society at large, and some may also belong to other minority disadvantaged groups, such as the BME and LGBTI communities or being a woman, which will impact upon how disability is perceived and experienced within their society and themselves. There are also differences in how the individual experience may include physical pain and fatigue or restriction due to their impairment, not just as a result of social or physical barriers, and it would be unrealistic and unhelpful to deny this reality. It is important to understand that being disabled is not, in itself, a reason for needing therapy, so reactions such as pity, a concentration on loss or feelings of tragedy can militate against a successful therapeutic alliance. Research has consistently shown that the quality of the therapeutic relationship is more important than other factors, so it is how therapists, non-disabled or disabled, relate to clients that is critical.

Some clients embrace disability as a positive identity for change and growth and, though less common, they do illuminate the impact of embracing the social model as a core belief system. This can be problematic for a therapist who sees disability as 'loss' and 'tragedy', and who works within a model which sees the cause of distress within the individual alone. This approach may make it impossible to form a cooperative therapeutic alliance with a client who refuses to view disability *per se* as negative but refers to the impact of the social context on their lives.

More common are clients who are distressed by their impairments, not because of the disabling environment but because they are in pain of some kind. They may have less energy and be experiencing an ongoing sense of loss, unable to do things that previously defined them as a person. Adopting a position where this is seen as secondary to a 'disabling environment' located outside the individual, in the social environment, would be, of course, equally harmful. Finding the balance between these two positions is perhaps the hardest task and requires the therapist to listen to the client's internal experience, the unfolding therapeutic process and their own inner process. Attempting to place all this within the relevant socio-cultural context is core, and appropriate supervision is therefore of paramount importance.

REFERENCES

Barnes, C. (1997) A legacy of oppression: A history of disability in western culture. In Len Barton and Mike Oliver (eds), *Disability Studies: Past Present and Future* (pp. 3–24). Leeds: The Disability Press.

Brune, J. (2003) Introduction. In Jeffrey Brune and Daniel Wilson (eds), *Disability and Passing: Blurring the Lines of Identity* (pp. 1–12). Philadelphia, PA: Temple University Press.

Department of Work and Pensions (2016) *Family Resources Survey 2014/15*. (www.gov.uk/government/uploads/system/uploads/attachment_data/file/531242/family-resources-survey-2014-15.pdf).

Lin, J.D. (2003) The exploratory study of the definition and classification of disability. *Journal of Medical Science*, 23(1): 19–23.

Mason, M. (1992) Internalized oppression. In Richard Reisner and Micheline Mason (eds), *Disability Equality in the Classroom: A Human Rights Issue* (2nd ed.) (pp. 27–28). London: Disability Equality in Education.

Office for National Statistics (2014) *National Population Projections: 2014-based Statistical Bulletin*. (www.ons.gov.uk/peoplepopulationandcommunity/populationandmigration/populationprojections/bulletins/nationalpopulationprojections/2015-10-29).

Park, H.J., Faulkner, J. and Schalle, M. (2003) Evolved disease-avoidance processes and contemporary anti-social behavior: Prejudical attitudes and avoidance of people with physical disabilities. *Journal of Nonverbal Behavior*, 27(2): 65–87.

Parritt, S. (2016) Working with difference and diversity. In B. Douglas, R. Woolfe, S. Strawbridge, E. Kasket, and V. Galbraith (eds), *Handbook of Counselling Psychology* (4th ed.) (pp. 198–212). London: Sage.

Reeve, D. (2014) Counselling and disabled people: Help or hindrance? In J. Swain SF, C. Barnes and C. Thomas (eds), *Disabling Barriers – Enabling Environments* (3rd ed.) (pp. 255–261). London: Sage.

Regan, S. and Stanley, K. (2003) Work for disabled people. *New Economy*, 10(1): 56–61.

The Papworth Trust (2016) *Disability in the United Kingdom 2016: Facts and Figures* (www.papworthtrust.org.uk/sites/default/files/Disability%20Facts%20and%20Figures%202016.pdf).

United Nations (2010) *Convention on the Rights of Persons with Disabilities*. New York: UN (www.un.org/disabilities/convention/conventionfull.shtml).

World Health Organisation (1980) International Classification of Impairments, Disabilities, and Handicaps: A Manual of Classification relating to the Consequences of Disease. Geneva: World Health Organisation.

World Health Organisation (2011) *World Report on Disability*. Geneva: World Health Organisation and The World Bank.

RECOMMENDED READING

1. Goodley, D. (2011) Disability Studies: An Interdisciplinary Introduction. London: Sage.

An interdisciplinary introduction to disability studies incorporating a broad perspective covering the individual, psychological, social, cultural and educational aspects.

2. Shakespeare, T. (2013) *Disability Rights and Wrongs Revisited*. London: Taylor & Francis/Routledge.

This examines current disability theory and politics across a range of areas while also questioning the basis behind the theories in the real world.

3. Smith, J.L.T. (2015) *Women, Disability and Mental Distress*. London: Taylor & Francis/Routlegde.

A book that explores the issues and service needs of disabled women who also have a mental health condition from both a user and social worker's perspective.

2.4   *AGE*

LÉONIE SUGARMAN

OVERVIEW AND KEY POINTS

The population of the United Kingdom (UK) is ageing, and while counsellors and psychotherapists will increasingly need to engage with this under-represented group of clients, the issue of age has much wider relevance – for clients, therapists and the therapeutic relationship.

Age is an ever-present, but often unspoken, dimension of difference in therapy. Chronological age is frequently used as an expedient index of social age and, despite its ambiguous meaning and significance, is salient throughout life. Our age is used to structure economic, social and political life, and affords us particular rights and obligations. Despite its limitations, we still use age as a guide in accommodating to the behaviour of others, in formulating our self-image, in interpreting our experience and in contemplating our past and our future. Therapists cannot escape age – their clients' or their own. Key points include:

- Age is an often overlooked but nonetheless relevant dimension of difference in counselling and psychotherapy.
- Clients' age will influence, but not totally determine, their needs.
- Clients' and therapists' age will influence their responses to each other.

HISTORY AND CONTEXT

The population of the UK is ageing. In 2014 the median age of UK residents reached 40 for the first time, and in 2015 those aged 65 or over comprised 17.8 per cent of the total (up from 15 per cent in 1984), with the fastest increase being in those aged 85 and over (Office of National Statistics, 2016). It is clear that counsellors and psychotherapists will increasingly need to engage with this under-represented group of clients (Improving Access to Psychological Therapies (IAPT), 2014). However, the issue of age has much wider relevance than this – for clients, therapists and the therapeutic relationship.

The age of the client, the age of the therapist and the difference between them are ever-present, but often unspoken, elements of the socio-cultural context of therapy, and a potentially significant dimension of difference. Age, while seemingly a straightforward personal characteristic indicating time lived since birth, is also a social marker that structures, knowingly or unknowingly, the way we interpret our experience, and organises the ways in which we perceive and interact with each other (Baars, 2012). By dividing the human lifespan into socially meaningful units, we translate calendar time into social time, producing an age-grade system in which life stages such as 'youth', 'midlife' and 'old age' imply not only chronological age, but also a cluster of socially defined rights, responsibilities, developmental tasks and preoccupations that reflect cultural traditions, laws, values and beliefs concerning age-appropriate behaviour (Carney and Gray, 2015).

In the face of uncertainly, age norms and assumptions about ageing can offer a subtle sense of security (Dannefer and Setterson, 2010) and a set of ready-made and compelling life goals against which to assess how well or poorly we are doing 'for our age'. At the same time, age norms and age-related goals can directly or indirectly restrict personal choice and serve as mechanisms of social control. Therapists may need to help clients disentangle whether, in striving for age-related targets, they are 'being themselves' or merely 'acting their age'. While the loosening of age norms is potentially liberating, it can leave us unsupported by social structures and more dependent on personal resources and skills (Wrosch and Freund, 2001). The disorder, discontinuity and uncertainties of a fluid life cycle may propel clients into therapy as much as might the constraints of rigid age restrictions and expectations.

The negative stereotype of old age as a period of loss encompassing declines in physical attributes and mental acuity, increasing dependence on others, absence of role identity and lack of respect from society (Kite and Wagner, 2002) has for some time been counterposed with notions of successful ageing that emphasise independence, productivity and self-maintenance – in effect, an 'anti-ageing' movement. However, this perspective can be criticised for failing to acknowledge the reality of bodily ageing (Clarke and Korotchenko, 2011) and as reflecting Western, neo-liberal cultural values that place a moral obligation on older people to resist ageing through continual efforts at lifestyle maximisation and body optimisation (Lamb, 2014; Rudman, 2006). Such a discourse sustains ageism by promoting perpetual youthfulness as a goal, and draws attention away from the socially constructed nature of disadvantage in later life (Vincent, 2013).

There is a need for theorising about old age that goes beyond the binaries of success and decline. In this vein, Boudiny (2013) proposes strategies for the fostering of adaptability, redefinitions of what is meant by involvement with life, and policies that prioritise the agency of the client in decisions over long-term care. Liang and Luo (2012) seek to emphasie balance based on difference rather than uniformity in their concept of harmonious ageing, while Sandberg (2013) develops the notion of affirmative ageing that construes the changes of ageing in midlife and beyond not as decline, but as the continuous production of difference. From this perspective, the self is seen not as ageless, but as ageful (Andrews, 2000) and, in the same way that difference is celebrated in axes such as race and gender, the importance of age is not ignored. This applies to therapists as much as clients, and is seen, for example, in senior therapists' reflections on their experience of ageing and its impact on their work and professional identity (Geller and Farber, 2015).

RELEVANCE FOR COUNSELLING AND PSYCHOTHERAPY

While universal themes such as attachment, separation, dependency, change and loss will permeate counselling and psychotherapy irrespective of the clients' age or life stage, they take on a different hue according to the psychosocial context of successive life stages (Jacobs, 2012). Clients of different ages and life stages have different psychological, cognitive and sensory capacities. Therapists working with children and young adolescents need to be sensitive to both their level of verbal and cognitive development and their level of emotional maturity, while with clients in late adulthood accommodation may need to be made for decreasing sensory capacity (notably sight and hearing) and/or the declining mobility and cognitive functioning that may – but does not inevitably – accompany the ageing process.

Similarly, some issues will occur more frequently for clients within a particular age range. The design and structure of therapy services may reflect this understanding of life stage, such that, despite anti-discrimination legislation, age may be used as a gateway to therapy-related opportunities and resources. While this is more expedient than individualised assessment of need, age and need are imperfectly correlated, and any presumed correspondence may be based on erroneous assumptions and outmoded patterns of social organisation. As such, age- or life-stage based services encourage the stereotyping of particular age groups as problematic, and inadvertently add to age separation and segregation (Bytheway, 2005). However, to deny differential treatment to particular groups identified primarily by age may be to ignore real differences in capacity, vulnerability and power.

Access to therapy is influenced by money and power (Pilgrim, 1997), and people in early and middle adulthood are most likely to be both economically active and in positions not only to purchase their own therapy, but also to determine who else receives therapy or other mental health services, and for what problems. In this regard, children and older adults are similar since the economic power of the very young and the very old is frequently either minimal or negative – although even here one must exercise caution since the assumption that all older people are inevitably impoverished is itself an ageist myth. Nonetheless, the very young and the very old do frequently lack direct economic power and, as a result, they also lack social power – both of which may be needed to gain access to appropriate counselling and psychotherapy.

Children and frail older adults are less likely to self-refer than those in the more socially powerful and (potentially) more economically active stages of the life course. In addition, it is also more likely that therapists working with these clients will have direct contact with family members or professionals who may well have instigated the referral process. It should always be asked whether the services provided are in the best interest of the clients or, for example, of parents and school teachers in the case of children, or children and health care professionals in the case of vulnerable older clients. While advocacy by others may be a legitimate response to clients' limited capacities, therapists need to be wary of ageism that defines reality on behalf of either the young or the old, and decides for them what interventions are required.

Although both therapists and clients will hold assumptions concerning the ageing process and what it means to be a particular age, there remains relatively little discussion of how such images and assumptions affect the therapeutic relationship (Kessler and Bowen, 2015).

Clients' age will influence how they perceive the therapist. Clients who are significantly older or significantly younger than their therapist may believe that 'the world is different now' and that the therapist, being of a different generation, cannot possibly understand them. Thus, older clients may consider a much younger therapist to be inexperienced and/or presumptive in assuming they have anything to offer, with transference issues reflecting their relationship with their children or grandchildren. Also, older clients may imbibe ageist assumptions that devalue their own lives and experiences and, as a consequence, question whether they are deserving of therapeutic time and resources. Children and adolescents, by contrast, may experience the therapist as an authority figure, and parental transference may be relevant, with clients re-experiencing and re-enacting with the counsellor aspects of the relationship they have or had with their parents.

Younger clients may remind therapists of themselves at that age, or bring therapists' own children to mind, while older clients may remind them of their parents or grandparents (Knight, 2004). Older clients may trigger a deep-seated unease in young and middle-aged therapists, possibly distorting their clinical judgement as they catch glimpses of problems and challenges that may lie ahead both for the therapists themselves and for their parents and grandparents (Semel, 2006). Dysfunctional emotional reactions include threat, disgust, fear, shame and guilt (Knight, 2004), whereby younger, healthy, cognitively alert therapists are threatened by the reminder that one day they too may be older, ill and cognitively impaired. They may experience shame at this reaction, guilt regarding their own youth and health in comparison to that of their clients, and disgust at the indignities of extreme old age.

Therapists will remember something of what it was like to be a child or adolescent, and draw on this experience in developing their relationships with younger clients. Such knowledge can be both a resource and a hindrance. Not only is each individual's experience unique, but we are all not only of our place, but of our time. Every generation or cohort is distinctive, having grown up in a particular economic, political and social environment, with particular shared experiences. This reduces the extent to which our own life experiences can be used as a basis for understanding those in later or earlier generations.

Therapists may identify readily with the issues faced by clients of a similar age to themselves and who present scenarios that mirror issues that they are also addressing. While this can facilitate the development of empathy, therapists need to be wary of over-identifying with clients who seem 'similar to me', or of projecting onto clients their own reactions and interpretations. Also, it cannot be assumed that clients see counsellors of the same age as 'like them'. Similarity of age may reinforce clients' sense of inadequacy – 'how come he/she is coping so well, whereas I need help?'

Therapists, like clients, will be embedded in a network of inter-generational relationships, and need, therefore, to be sensitive to their emotional reactions to clients of different ages, carefully considering their possible impact on the course of therapy (Terry, 2008). While all therapists will have experienced young, and possibly middle, adulthood, fewer will have personal knowledge of late adulthood. This brings the advantage that clients can be faced without interference from the therapist's direct experience of this life stage, but increases the scope for therapists to be prey to unsubstantiated stereotypes and unarticulated assumptions concerning later life. When making the journey into the unknown territory of the life of significantly older or significantly younger clients, therapists need to be wary of unwarranted interference from their own life experience, their stereotypes about different life stages, and the chauvinistic prioritisation of their own current life goals and values.

Ageism – stereotyping, prejudice and discrimination based on chronological age – affects all individuals from birth onwards (Bytheway, 2005). As with other forms of oppression, such as sexism and racism, it involves attributing characteristics to individuals simply by virtue of their membership of a particular group. As with other forms of oppression, it is reinforced by the structures of society, being used to restrict access to services, privileges, entitlements and responsibilities. As a form of oppression it is unique, however, in that its nature and particular impact on an individual fluctuates and changes across the life course.

Ageism is frequently discussed primarily in relation to the lives of older adults (for example, Nelson, 2011). While drawing attention to the prejudice and discrimination experienced by older people, this bias can serve both to obscure ageism directed at other age groups, and also blind us to ageism within ourselves. Seeing the concept of ageism as relevant only to older adults fosters a 'them' and 'us' view of 'the elderly' as a minority group. If older people or, indeed, children are seen as different and separate from the rest of society then this can be used *per se* to justify different and separate treatment.

In sum, I propose that age is an ambiguous concept that in some ways is becoming less significant, but in other ways remains crucial. Age cannot by itself define individual lives (Rogoff, 2002), but therapists should remain mindful of how it can be both crucially important in their therapeutic work and, at the same time, (almost) completely irrelevant.

REFERENCES

Andrews, M. (2000) Ageful and proud. *Aging and Society*, 20(6): 791–5.

Baars, J. (2012) Critical turns of aging, narrative and time. *International Journal of Ageing and Later Life*, 7(2): 143–65.

Boudiny, K. (2013) 'Active ageing': From empty rhetoric to effective policy tool. *Ageing and Society*, 33(6): 1077–98.

Bytheway, B. (2005) Ageism. In M.L. Johnson, V.L. Bengtson, P.G. Coleman and T.B.L. Kirkwood (eds), *The Cambridge Handbook of Age and Ageing*. Cambridge: Cambridge University Press.

Carney, G.M. and Gray, M. (2015) Unmasking the 'elderly mystique': Why it is time to make the personal political in ageing research. *Journal of Aging Studies*, 35(2): 123–34.

Clarke, L.H. and Korotchenko, A. (2011) Aging and the body: A review. *Canadian Journal on Aging/La Revue canadienne du vieillissement*, 30(3): 495–510.

Dannefer, W.D. and Settersten, R.A. (2010) The study of the life course: Implications for social gerontology. In W.D. Dannefer and C. Phillipson (eds), *International Handbook of Social Gerontology*. London: Sage.

Geller, J.D. and Farber, B.A. (2015) Introduction: Reflections of senior therapists. *Journal of Clinical Psychology*, 71(11): 1049–59.

IAPT (2014) *Older People*. (www.iapt.nhs.uk/equalities/older-people/).

Jacobs, M. (2012) The Presenting Past: The Core of Psychodynamic Counselling and Therapy (4th ed.). Buckingham: Open University Press.

Kessler, E.-M. and Bowen, C.E. (2015) Images of aging in the psychotherapeutic context: A conceptual review. *GeroPsych: The Journal of Gerontopsychology and Geriatric Psychiatry*, 28(2): 47–55.

Kite, M.E. and Wagner, L.S. (2002) Attitudes toward older adults. In T.D. Nelson (ed.), *Ageism: Stereotyping and Prejudice against Older Persons*. Cambridge, MA: MIT Press.

Knight, B.G. (2004) *Psychotherapy with Older Adults* (3rd ed.). Thousand Oaks, CA: Sage.

Lamb, S. (2014) Permanent personhood or meaningful decline? Toward a critical anthropology of successful aging. *Journal of Aging Studies*, 29: 41–52.

Liang, J. and Luo, B. (2012) Toward a discourse shift in social gerontology: From successful aging to harmonious aging. *Journal of Aging Studies*, 26: 327–34.

Nelson, T.D. (2011) Ageism: The strange case of prejudice against the older you. In R.L. Wiener and S.L. Wilborn (eds), *Disability and Aging Discrimination: Perspectives in Law and Psychology*. New York: Springer.

Office for National Statistics (2016) *Population Estimates for UK, England and Wales, Scotland and Northern Ireland: Mid-2015*. (www.ons.gov.uk/peoplepopulationandcommunity/populationandmigration/populationestimates/bulletins/annualmidyearpopulationestimates/latest).

Pilgrim, D. (1997) *Psychotherapy and Society*. London: Sage.

Rogoff, B. (2002) How can we study cultural aspects of human development? *Human Development*, 45(4): 209–10.

Rudman, D. L. (2006) Shaping the active, autonomous and responsible modern retiree: An analysis of discursive technologies and their links with neo-liberal political rationality. *Ageing and Society*, 26: 181–201.

Sandberg, L. (2013) Affirmative old age: The ageing body and feminist theories on difference. *International Journal of Ageing and Later Life*, 8(1): 11–40.

Semel, V.G. (2006) Countertransference and ageism: Therapist reactions to older patients. In C.M. Brody and V.G. Semel (eds), *Strategies for Therapy with the Elderly: Living with Hope and Meaning* (2nd ed.). New York: Springer.

Terry, P. (2008) Ageism and projective identification. *Psychodynamic Practice*, 14(2): 155–68.

Vincent, J. (2013) The anti-aging movement: Contemporary cultures and the social construction of old age. In M. Schermer and W. Pixtons (eds), *Ethics, Health Policy and (Anti-) Aging: Mixed Blessings*. New York: Springer.

Wrosch, C. and Freund, A.M. (2001) Self-regulation or normative and non-normative developmental challenges. *Human Development*, 44(5): 264–83.

RECOMMENDED READING

1. Geller, J.D. and Farber, B.A. (2015) Introduction: Reflections of senior therapists. *Journal of Clinical Psychology*, 71(11): 1049–59.

The introduction and opening paper of a special issue on senior therapists' reflections on their experience of ageing and its impact on work and professional identity.

2. Kessler, E.-M. and Bowen, C.E. (2015) Images of aging in the psychotherapeutic context: A conceptual review. *GeroPsych: The Journal of Gerontopsychology and Geriatric Psychiatry*, 28(2): 47–55.

A discussion of images of ageing with specific reference to counselling and psychotherapy.

3. Sugarman, L. (2004) *Counselling and the Life Course*. London: Sage.

Using the framework of the life course, considers both the distinctiveness and commonalities of working with clients at different points in the lifespan. Also encourages readers to reflect on their own life course and life stage.

2.5   SOCIAL CLASS

LIZ BALLINGER

OVERVIEW AND KEY POINTS

This chapter offers a summary of differing views concerning the nature of social class. The questioning of its continuing relevance and a review of evidence pointing to its continued importance are offered. The silence around class within counselling literature is problematised and its salience to the therapeutic endeavour highlighted. Some recommendations are offered for consideration.

-   While social class is a disputed topic, evidence points to its continued significance in areas such as living standards, life chances, lifestyle, sense of self, physical and mental health.
-   The literature points to a middle-class bias in both therapists and the client base.
-   Counselling and psychotherapy have historically neglected the importance of class despite its evident relevance to the counselling process.
-   The development of a class-sensitive approach is necessary to address the middle-class bias of the therapy world and afford it a wider social significance.

HISTORY AND CONTEXT

While Britain continues to be regarded as a peculiarly class-ridden society, paradoxically, its contemporary relevance has become increasingly questioned. The scale and nature of economic, political and social change in the second part of the twentieth century is argued to have led to the demolition of old class barriers and the redundancy of class as a meaningful concept, socially, economically and academically. Its obituaries were written. Cannadine, (2000: 14) wrote of class analysis as being 'consigned to the waste paper basket of history'. Such a context perhaps helps to explain what has been described as the silence around class issues within the therapeutic field (e.g., Appio et al., 2013).

There are, however, some signs of class 'rising from the ashes'. The notion of the classless society began to be punctured by rising levels of inequality from the 1980s and, as we entered the twenty-first century, the divisive effects of economic recession and financial austerity. Important new work in the economic and social sciences highlighted the importance of class and inequality (e.g., Atkinson, 2015; Savage, 2015; Wilkinson and Pickett, 2010). However, its rising profile has not been reflected in a significant increase in the overt attention paid to social class within the United Kingdom (UK) counselling and psychotherapy worlds.

CLASS AS A CONCEPT

Questions of definition and salience surround the issue of social class in contemporary Britain and elsewhere. In terms of definition, it is a complex, multi-layered and somewhat elusive construct. It has attracted a range of different, often competing understandings over time – too many for a comprehensive coverage to be provided here. However, two abiding central matters of concern can be identified: economic structures or material inequality and the social manifestations of inequality. These two dimensions interact with other evident dichotomies, for example the objective and subjective dimensions of class, academic and lay understandings that have coloured its understanding differentially over time.

In terms of material inequality, an important official measure of class continues to be occupation, seen as connected with other potential measures such as income, acquired wealth and vulnerability to poverty. Occupation was central to the 1911 Registrar General's Scale, the first official measure of class. While purportedly an objective measure of economic position, the divide drawn between middle-class non-manual and working-class manual work had manifest cultural overtones of superiority and inferiority. The National Statistics Socio-Economic Classification (NS-SEC), the current official measure, aimed to avoid such pitfalls. While retaining the centrality of occupation, it was designed to provide a more accurate, less culturally loaded classification system (Savage, 2015), and is the bedrock for much current class-related research.

When we turn to an assessment of social dimensions of class, the whole area of subjective lay judgement is opened up, or how a set of 'signs and signals help determine how any one individual regards him-(or her-) self, and how he (or she) is regarded and categorised by others' (Cannadine, 2000: 22). These are said to include, among others: family background, accent, education, dress, housing and lifestyle. Such assessments can be understood as relating to ownership of different forms of capital or 'properties capable of conferring strength, power and consequently profit on their holder' (Bourdieu, 1987: 4). In terms of class, the important forms of capital are economic (income and wealth), social (networks and group membership) and cultural (ownership of valued knowledge and know-how). A fourth category, symbolic

capital, refers to possession of the symbols acknowledged as legitimate expressions of ownership of these different forms of capital – or the accepted 'signs and signals' of class.

Bourdieu's ideas have been influential in recent work on social class in Britain. One high-profile product has been a new model developed on an understanding of class as 'a crystallization of different kinds of capital' rather than on occupation (Savage, 2015: 180). Based on a wide-scale national survey, it identifies seven classes: a wealthy elite; the established middle class: the technical middle class; new affluent workers; traditional working class; emerging sector workers; the precariat.

On a final note here, Bourdieu's notion of habitus, or the socialised norms guiding thinking, feeling, behaviour and practice, has recently been gainfully employed in a small but growing area of study – the lived experience of class. Researchers such as Reay (2005), Savage et al. (2005) and Skeggs (1997, 2004) have explored the continuing impact of social class in shaping self-esteem, self-identity and emotional experiencing, the way we make sense of our world as well as interact with it.

THE CONTEMPORARY SIGNIFICANCE OF CLASS

Despite the so-called 'death of class', evidence of significant inequality across a range of human experience seems to demonstrate its continued power. As mentioned above, there has been rising economic inequality dating back to the so-called 'inequality turn' of the 1980s. Savage (2015: 392) talks of 'new mountains of inequality'. According to the Office for National Statistics (ONS), the mean income of the top 10% of the population in 2015 was nearly ten times as high as that of the lowest 10%. Between 2012 and 2014, the richest 10% of households held 45% of the nation's wealth, while the poorest half owned 8.7%. Such inequality has repercussions across a whole range of measures, such as housing standards, transport, services and material goods. Vulnerability to unemployment and underemployment are patterned by socio-economic status. Reflecting its title, the precariat, as identified by Savage (2015), lives a precarious existence. Making up 15% of the population, members' lives are characterised by low incomes, negligible savings, rented housing, and movement between low paid, insecure work and unemployment. Generally, vulnerability to poverty increases as we descend the income scale, both for those in and out of work. According to the ONS, 33% of the population had experienced relative poverty at least once in the years between 2010 and 2013: 7.8% were in persistent poverty throughout.

Similar inequality characterises the nation's physical health. There is a clear health gradient, with those within the strongest socio-economic positions tending to have the best quality of health and those in the lowest socio-economic positions the worst (Benzeval et al., 2014). Crucially for counselling and psychotherapy, research evidence points to continuing class differences in mental health (Rogers and Pilgrim, 2003). High income and material standard of living are associated with relatively low rates of mental health problems; low income and poor living standards correlate with relatively high rates of mental health issues. It is important to note that simply increasing national income is not the answer. Health and wellbeing appears much more strongly correlated to the level of economic inequality within societies than to their overall wealth (Wilkinson and Pickett, 2010).

While the 'highly unequal distribution of prizes' (Atkinson, 2015: 11) touched on above is important, so is inequality of opportunity. It is now clear that the heralded changes of the second half of the twentieth century provided the illusion rather than the reality of enhanced upward mobility between classes. In relation to children born in 1958, those born in 1970 actually had *less* chance of achieving a higher class status than that of their parents. A major reason was that middle-class children benefited more than working-class children from the opening up of educational opportunities and the expansion of middle-class occupations that characterised the late twentieth century. Social class of origin continues to strongly shape people's educational outcomes and hence impacts on their occupational and economic destinations (Blanden et al., 2005).

A final area of significance comes out of the small amount of research focusing specifically on the lived experience of class, which challenges the notion of the decline of popular class consciousness, cited as one of the features of its increasing irrelevance. Rather than talk of decline, Savage (2015: 365) instead talks of a new 'more muted, individualized and complex set of class identities'. While some studies have demonstrated a general lack of personal identification with class (e.g., Savage et al., 2005; Skeggs, 1997), the same studies and others have demonstrated a recognition of its continuing existence as a system. Savage (2015) also points to the continuation of 'implicit, class-based references' used by people in order to place others and, by extension, themselves socially. Other studies point to the importance of internalised class messages. Reay (2005) talks of a 'psychic landscape of class', populated by notions of inferiority and superiority and lived out in emotions such as envy, pride and shame. Interestingly, despite the focus on current or achieved status in modern class analysis, the importance of class born into, or ascribed status, features heavily in such subjective accounts.

RELEVANCE TO COUNSELLING AND PSYCHOTHERAPY

Consideration of class issues would seem important at a number of levels. Some of the challenges are for counselling and psychotherapy *per se* and their professional organisations. Others are more matters for consideration on the part of individual therapists, counselling organisations and training providers. Some straddle both areas. Here they are briefly addressed under a number of banner headings.

THE VALUE BASE OF COUNSELLING AND PSYCHOTHERAPY

Therapy's so-called 'class-blindness' can be contextualised within a long-running critique of counselling and psychotherapy, that of its rooting of psychological distress within individual psychology rather than social circumstance. This can and does lead to criticisms, from within and without, of political naivety, social irrelevance and, indeed, political and social conservatism. While the setting up of organisations such as Psychotherapists and Counsellors for Social Change (PCSC) has been one result, it can be argued that fundamental change has not ensued. The most active raising of class issues has taken place within the United States (US) (e.g., Liu, 2015). There is thus far an absence of a developed research interest or body of relevant literature concerning the differing dimensions of class and their relevance to counselling within contemporary Britain.

THE CLASS BASE OF COUNSELLORS AND COUNSELLING

While there is a lack of definitive evidence of the class base of counselling and psychotherapy, it is commonly perceived as a middle-class one, leading to therapy 'being worryingly out of touch with the needs, the strengths and struggles of working-class people' (Trevithick, 1998: 116). It can be somewhat of a circular argument: if occupation is the measure, becoming a psychotherapist or counselling psychologist is inevitably an entrée into middle-classness. Indeed, the drive towards the professionalisation of counselling can be viewed as a group attempt to gain middle-class status. While there is actually limited available information about therapists' class background, it can perhaps be inferred from the expense and length of training and the educational qualifications required for entry. On a positive note, some small-scale research did find a strong level of personal identification with 'working-classness' among participating counsellors (Ballinger and Wright, 2007). Generally, however, the whole question of widening access to practice as well as paying attention to the class-awareness of counsellors within training would seem to be important areas for development.

THE CLASS BASE OF CLIENTS

A variety of factors are argued to contribute to a parallel middle-class bias within the client population, despite their reduced likelihood of mental health issues compared to their poorer counterparts. Again, evidence is incomplete here, reflecting in part the diversity of therapeutic settings and perhaps a continued failure to take class seriously. One well-documented setting, however, is the statutory health sector, where clear differences emerge in access to talking therapies. Those on lower incomes are less likely to be offered talking therapies and more likely to be prescribed medication when presenting with mental health issues (Rogers and Pilgrim, 2003). One proffered explanation is bias on the part of referrers, with 'downward classism' or 'marginalization directed to those who are perceived to be in a lower class then the perceiver' (Liu, 2015: 8) evident among referring medics. Other explanations focus on the characteristics of working-class patients, pointing to a lack of assertiveness, a deference to medical authority or, conversely, a level of suspicion or aversion towards counselling. Holman (2014) found four factors in the underuse of therapy by working-class people: therapy's emphasis on the verbalisation of emotions and introspection; reduced expectations of emotional health; the greater deference to medical authority; and the desire for more practical solutions.

THE COUNSELLING RELATIONSHIP AND PROCESS

The middle-class character of the counselling body is regarded as potentially problematic here. It has been argued that social class can have a substantial impact on the quality of the counselling relationship. One area relates to an imbalance of power and status and its repercussions. Working-class clients have reported a sense of discomfort and inferiority when working with counsellors they perceived as middle class (Balmforth, 2009). On a parallel note, unacknowledged classism on the part of counsellors can lead to stereotyping and judgementalism, antithetical to the empathy and positive regard widely seen as fundamental to the counselling endeavour.

THE NATURE OF COUNSELLING ITSELF

The social, economic, cultural and political roots of distress raise questions over therapy's relevance, particularly to disadvantaged members of society. Moreover, Holman (2014) talks of a level of incompatibility between the inherently middle-class counselling habitus and that of working-class clients. One result may be that working-class people may self-exclude. Another may be the shaming experience of feeling negatively judged as inadequate and disempowered (Sayer, 2015). Such classism, albeit unconscious and unintended, can potentially stray into the field of victimisation of society's victims, constituting a form of what Bourdieu labels 'symbolic violence' over working-class lives.

CONCLUSION

The construction of a class-sensitive approach to counselling calls on the addressing of such issues sketched above. Any such approach would need to consider barriers to access, look at ways of drawing therapists from across the social spectrum, widen training to embrace more sociological understandings and promote class awareness. There remains the challenge of developing services tailored to best meet the needs of individuals across the social spectrum. Appio et al. (2013), provide a good starting point, in their injunction to listen to the voices of the poor.

REFERENCES

Appio, L., Chambers, D.-A. and Mao, S. (2013) Listening to the voices of the poor and disrupting the silence about class issues in psychotherapy. *Clinical Psychology*, 69(2), 152–161.

Atkinson, A.B. (2015) *Inequality: What Can Be Done?* Cambridge, MA: Harvard University Press.

Ballinger, L. and Wright, J. (2007) Does class count? Social class and counselling. *Counselling and Psychotherapy Research*, 7(3), 157–163.

Balmforth, J. (2009) 'The weight of class': clients' experience of how perceived differences in social class between counsellor and client affect the therapeutic relationship. *British Journal of Guidance and Counselling*, 37(3), 375–386.

Benzeval, M., Bond, L., Campbell, M., Egan, M., Lorenc, T., Petticrew, M. and Popham, F. (2014) *How Does Money Effect Health*? York: Joseph Rowntree Foundation.

Blanden, J., Gregg, P. and Machin, S. (2005) *Intergenerational Mobility in Europe and North America*. A Report for the Sutton Trust. London: The Centre for Economic Performance.

Bourdieu, P. (1987) What makes a social class? On the theoretical and practical existence of groups. *Berkeley Journal of Sociology*, 32, 1–17.

Cannadine, D. (2000) *Class in Britain*. London: Penguin Books.

Holman, D. (2014) 'What help can you get talking to somebody?' Explaining class differences in the use of talking treatments. *Sociology of Health and Illness*, 36(4), 531–548.

Liu, W.M. (ed.) (2015) *The Oxford Handbook of Social Class and Counseling*. Oxford: Oxford University Press.

Reay, D. (2005) Beyond consciousness? The psychic landscape of social class. *Sociology*, 39(5), 911–928.

Rogers, A. and Pilgrim, D. (2003) *Mental Health and Inequality*. Basingstoke: Palgrave.

Savage, M. (2015) *Social Class in the Twenty-First Century*. London: Penguin Books.

Savage, M., Bagnall, G. and Longhurst, B. (2005) Local habitus and working-class culture. In F. Devine, M. Savage, J. Scott and R. Crompton (eds), *Rethinking Class: Culture, Identities and Lifestyle* (pp. 95–122). Basingstoke: Palgrave Macmillan.

Sayer, A. (2005) *The Moral Significance of Class*. Cambridge: Cambridge University Press.

Skeggs, B. (1997) Formations of Class and Gender: Becoming Respectable. London: Sage.

Skeggs, B. (2004) *Class, Self, Culture*. London: Routledge

Trevithick, P. (1998) Psychotherapy and working class women. In I. Bruna Seu and M. Colleen Heenan (eds), *Feminism and Psychotherapy: Reflections on Contemporary Theories and Practice* (pp. 115–134). London: Sage.

Wilkinson, R. and Pickett, K. (2010) *The Spirit Level: Why Equality is Better for Everyone*. London: Penguin Books.

RECOMMENDED READING

1. Savage, M. (2015) *Social Class in the Twenty-First Century*. London: Penguin Books.

This provides an accessible overview of understandings of social class and the differing dimensions of inequality in contemporary Britain.

2. Kearney, A. (1996) *Counselling, Class & Politics: Undeclared Influences in Therapy*. Ross-on-Wye: PCCS Books.

While this has become somewhat dated, it remains one of the strongest and most accessible introductions to issues of class blindness within counselling in the UK.

3. Liu, W.M. (ed.) (2015) *The Oxford Handbook of Social Class and Counseling*. Oxford: Oxford University Press.

While the focus is class within the USA, this is a superb, comprehensive source for reference across a wide range of counselling issues.

2.6

SEXUALITY

DAVID MAIR

OVERVIEW AND KEY POINTS

Sexuality is an evolving concept which impinges on our own and our clients' lives in various ways. In this chapter I consider:

- the emergence of sexuality as a key personal identifier in Western culture;
- competing narratives which seek to define understandings of sexuality;
- the impact of restraining narratives of 'healthy' sexuality on individuals;
- the possible benefits of postmodern narratives of sexuality for ourselves and our clients.

HISTORY AND CONTEXT

Sexuality is a fundamental part of human experience, but our perceptions of it are by no means universal or uncomplicated. Instead they are shaped by the social attitudes, laws, religious and biological narratives which prevail at a particular time. What we think of as an intensely personal identity and experience is actually constructed within the meaning-making possibilities of the culture and historical age in which we happen to be living. How we express our sexuality and what sexual acts are acceptable and sanctioned are specific to a particular culture. They have evolved over centuries and continue to do so. *Sex* (the 'intertwined practices of pleasure, desire and power', Garton, 2004, p. x) and *sexuality* ('the ways sexual practices are turned into signifiers of a particular type of social identity', Garton, 2004, p. x) are not one and the same. Grasping the difference is essential both to understanding in this area and to its practical application when working with clients. For instance, men have always had sex with other men, and women have always had sex with other women. But men and women who have sex with each other either historically or in the present do not necessarily see such behaviour as indicative of a particular type of *sexuality* (Katz, 1995, 2001). Classical Greek accounts of same-sex encounters between men and youths do not equate to modern understandings of homosexuality. Within

these relationships there appears to have been a complex interplay between ideas about citizenship, power, masculinity, and the symbolic meaning of who penetrates who during sex (Garton, 2004). Sexuality, as understood today, emerged in the West largely after the eighteenth century, through the work of sexologists such as Krafft-Ebing (1894), Ellis (1897–1928) and Kinsey (1948, 1953). They attempted to apply scientific inquiry to sexual experience and they were writing at times of great upheavals in society through urbanisation, industrialisation and the rise of capitalism. Newly created institutions such as asylums enabled populations of particular groups to be observed *en masse*. The categorisation of sexual *types* emerging from sexual *behaviour* has profoundly impacted on how modern individuals perceive themselves: '…before sexuality there were sexual acts not sexual identities' (Padgug, cited in Garton, 2004, p. 23).

So how we view our sexuality is contingent, rather than essential and it is important to note that opinion about what constitutes *healthy* sexuality is disputed. While sex 'experts' tell us that frequent sexual expression (usually meaning genital intercourse) is essential to happiness in personal relationships (Barker, 2013; Barker and Crabb, 2016), we are also warned of the dangers of sex addiction (itself a contested term) and its ability to ruin careers and family life (Hall, 2012). The forms of sexual expression a culture allows not only affect the individual but also shape the very structure of society, its family units, institutions and laws. In recent years, in some countries, a broadened understanding of sexuality has led to a relaxing of restriction. But agreement is far from unanimous even within those countries. The boundaries around sexuality and its expression we inherit and grow up with determine the ideas we individually own about healthy/normal sexuality.

LENSES FOR VIEWING SEXUALITY

Mottier (2008) suggests that there are three principal lenses/narratives through which attitudes towards sexuality are shaped: religion/morality, biology and social construction. All are fluid, have evolved over time, and are likely to go on doing so. As therapists, we need to be aware of these lenses as they shape understandings of sexuality – our own and our clients'.

RELIGION/MORALITY

Sexuality and sexual expression has frequently been the focus of religious and moral codes. In the West, Christianity has had enormous influence over attitudes about sexual behaviour. For example, the powerful myth blaming original sin on female sexual misconduct has led to attempts to control human activity and cleanse it of sexual impurity. It is likely that everyone raised in Western culture is aware of and affected by these influences. Consider the following taboos:

Sex before marriage is wrong.

Contraception is sinful.

Homosexuality is sinful.

Wives are obliged to fulfil the sexual needs of their husbands.

Masturbation is sinful.

Paying for sex is always wrong.

Intellectually we may know that all or some of these beliefs are outdated and illogical. Many Christians would no longer espouse them. But we experience the emotional fall-out from such beliefs throughout society. Much anxiety and guilt stems from moral and religious codes which attempt to direct sexual expression into approved norms which may be impossible for individuals to embody. Christianity is not alone in this; most other faiths have versions of such rules. The impact of religion on sexuality is immense and is beyond the scope of this short chapter to explore in depth. But as therapists we need to be aware of the power of such beliefs, even today. They operate at a deep level in our culture, in ourselves and in our clients. Breaking free from such taboos is never easy, especially if they have been internalised at a young age, and may not even be possible if living within tightly knit faith communities. But where they are causing suffering and restraining a person's life damagingly we need to assert that these codes may not be 'natural' and are by no means universal.

BIOLOGY

Biological narratives of sexuality abound in our modern, scientific world, viewing desires as the result of innate, fixed essences determined by such factors as DNA and chromosomes. In addition, this model of sexuality has largely emerged from a normative framework of gender, with 'opposite sex' desire being the 'normal' result of 'healthy' sexuality. Male bodies, it is claimed, should produce masculine identities, and desire for female bodies; female bodies should produce feminine identities and desire for male bodies (Gauntlett, 2008). Homosexuality, bisexuality, and any other variation are then seen as unnatural, immature, confused or problematical, needing to be explained, and possibly treated. Consider the following views which stem from biological narratives of sexuality:

Men's sexual needs are powerful and cannot be denied.

Women are more drawn to romantic rather than physical expressions of love.

Homosexuality is caused by chromosome abnormality in the womb/brain structures.

These narratives have been used both to oppress and to liberate. Initial biological narratives of homosexuality, for instance, focused on the idea that homosexuality represented a mistake, deviation or perversion from the as-nature-intended, heterosexual norm (Klein, 1932; Skynner and Cleese, 1997). The work of early sexologists was driven, in part, by attempts to identify certain *types* of individual (usually 'effeminate' men or 'mannish' women) who could be identified as homosexual as though they were biologically distinct from heterosexuals. A confusion of gender with sexuality is clear here. Liberation movements later depended, in part, on biological determination as the basis to argue for equality. If gay people are 'born that way', the argument went, oppressing and criminalising them must be wrong because they 'can't help it'. But the search for a gay gene or a gay brain has proved elusive. Any claims that one has been identified have been quickly challenged (The Atlantic, 2015).

Biological narratives of sexuality typically differentiate between male and female sexuality, seeing them as fundamentally different. According to this narrative, men are 'hard-wired' to want as much sex as possible, while women are 'hard-wired' to seek romantic attachments with sex very much a secondary concern (Diamond, 2014).

Biological views have led to populist books such as *Men are from Mars, Women are from Venus* (Gray, 1992). However, despite ostensible scientific credentials, biological accounts of sexuality are not immune to challenge. Too often they have been co-opted into the service of moral judgements about appropriate male and female sexuality and have led to what one writer terms 'neuro-sexism' (Fine, 2010). In the 1960s and 1970s, after the introduction of female contraception, and the feminist challenge to much male science in the field of sexuality, Western women started to have greater freedom to explore and express their sexuality. Some women now have a greater ownership of how they achieve sexual pleasure. This may or may not entail a partner, and a male partner at that. Nevertheless, many women still find themselves living within a narrative of male sexual need which must not be denied, and where their own sexual expression has to be channelled into being a good wife and mother. At worst, female sexuality is seen as dangerous and in need of curtailment, leading to cultural practices such as female genital mutilation.

SOCIAL CONSTRUCTION

Although the biological model of sexuality still holds great sway, it has been widely challenged. Havelock Ellis focused on 'normal' sexual behaviour but found that, rather than fitting into anticipated patterns, it was extremely diverse (Mottier, 2008). Kinsey, working in the 1950s, shocked America with his findings that 37% of his male sample had achieved orgasm with another man (despite most of them describing themselves as heterosexual) (www.kinseyinstitute.org/research/ak-data. html#homosexuality). Freud, with his theory of unconscious drives, and of early 'polymorphous perversity' being channelled through a process of repudiation into what is acceptable in society (Freud, 1986), powerfully advocated that sexuality was not merely a biological issue. Yet even he was not able to break free from societal views of 'the homosexual' as the outcome of defective early relationships (Frosch, 2006).

In recent years, social scientists, feminists and Lesbian, Gay, Bisexual and Transsexual (LGBT) activists have, collectively, mounted a powerful challenge to purely biological narratives of causes of sexuality, and the restraining social and political narratives about individuals' sexual experience and identity that they supported. No longer, they assert, need we be constrained by narrow definitions of who we are sexually. 'Gay', 'lesbian' or 'straight' might all be labels which actually limit our potential sexual pleasure and lived experience. In this sense such labels are fiction rather than reality. Nor should we feel compelled to justify sexuality on biological grounds, provided sexual behaviour and identity are acceptable to all participants, and are non-coercive (Barker, 2013). Identity derived from sexual behaviour becomes a much wider field and we must be free to choose who we want to be. Labels may have served a purpose at some stage, but why hold on to them when they rarely describe the totality of an individual's experience? Thus the proliferation of identities such as *bi-romantic* to better express the experience of someone who might have romantic relationships with people of more than one gender, or *polysexual* as a term to signify the experience of someone who can enjoy sexual attraction and experience with people of more than one gender. Queer theory (Butler, 1990; Sullivan, 2003) challenges all modern identity labels (though possibly introduces another one – queer) and instead brings us to PoMosexuality (Post-modern sexuality). Here all labels are questioned and identity can be fluid and evolving rather than fixed and static. PoMosexuality takes us to a place where the following scenario – though no doubt rare in the range of identities it encompasses – is possible for certain individuals within certain cultures, a place where a:

> …lesbian separatist who becomes a professional dominatrix, then falls in love with a male-to-female transsexual grrl, decides to go through with a sex change, becomes a guy, and realises he's a gay man. (Mottier, 2008, p. 126)

Polish sociologist Zygmunt Bauman might argue that this scenario is the essence what he terms 'liquid modernity' (2000), which reflects an absence of clear social narratives to inform personal identity. Others caution that: 'Beyond a certain point, this liquidity results in borderline personality disorder, when unstable identity causes a constant seesaw of emotions' (Verhaeghe, 2014, Kindle). Just as religious/moral and biological understandings of sexuality generate beliefs about what is possible and permissible, so too does social constructionism. Consider the following points, reflecting queer (i.e., social constructionism, applied to gender and sexuality) theory:

Concepts of 'normality' and 'healthiness' are irrelevant applied to sex and sexuality. The only thing that matters is that people who participate in sex should not be coerced in any way and that people should find fulfilment and meaning in their identities.

For some people an asexual identity is perfectly natural. Gender does not determine object(s) of desire.

There is no need to limit sexual experience by adopting labels. Labels automatically limit possibilities and restrict access to aspects of desire which might otherwise emerge.

RELEVANCE FOR COUNSELLORS AND PSYCHOTHERAPISTS

Because sexuality has emerged within Western culture as a key axis around which self-identity forms, awareness both of the history of sexuality as a concept, and of different lenses through which sexuality may be viewed, is paramount for all therapists. Although Mottier's three lenses may seem to offer competing, mutually exclusive narratives, they may usefully be integrated in a biopsychosocial approach (Denman, 2003) which does not seek to uphold therapeutic 'truth' at the expense of client lived experience. And because sexuality is a rapidly evolving field, this is not an issue which counsellors can ever feel that they have completely mastered. For many clients, sexuality may be a background issue. They may not have thought a great deal about it, though their assumptions about sex/sexuality are impinging on their lived experience more than they realise. For others, it may be an urgent, foreground issue: loss of libido, sexual incompatability, and identity confusion are all possible and frequent presentations to therapists, requiring deep understandings of sex and sexuality. Repression (internal and external) because of restrictive religious/moral codes, denial and oppression (from family and wider society) in the form of homo/bi-phobia, anti-gay laws, so-called reparative therapies, verbal and physical violence, or plain basic ignorance of alternatives to biological understandings of sexuality, are powerful forces which impact on individuals. In order to work compassionately and effectively with people of widely varying experience, therapists need to have transcended their own particular 'natural' understanding of sexuality. This going beyond what has been deemed normal in sex and sexuality is the basis of all effective work with clients, particularly with people who are part of a so-called sexual minority. Self-identification as part of a minority sexual group is often accompanied by the experience of *minority stress* (Meyer, 2003), an additional burden to everyday life-stress which needs to be clearly understood.

And of course, sexuality does not exist in isolation, but intersects with other aspects of identity such as race, age, ability and faith. This intersectionality (Crenshaw, 1989) means that each person's experience of sexuality is unique. The possibility of a therapist missing essential aspects of that experience is high. For instance, as a white, male, middle-aged, Protestant gay man, how attuned am I (can I be?) to the lived experience of a black, bisexual, young, Jewish woman? There are so many junctions at which key aspects of experience converge that it is an extremely delicate task to engage sensitively with clients' lives. We want to facilitate exploration and insight without imposing our own experience or understanding. Good supervision with someone who has also thought through and engaged deeply with intersectional issues of sexuality is essential for all therapy.

REFERENCES

Barker, M. (2013) *Rewriting the Rules: An Integrative Guide to Love, Sex and Relationships. Hove*: Routledge.

Barker, M.J. and Crabb, J. (2016) *The Secrets of Enduring Love: How to Make Relationships Last*. London: Vermillion.

Baumann, Z. (2000) *Liquid Modernity*. Cambridge: Polity Press.

Butler, J. (1990) *Gender Trouble*. New York: Routledge.

Crenshaw, K. (1989) Mapping the margins: intersectionality, identity politics, and violence against women of color. In K. Crenshaw et al. (eds), *Critical Race Theory: The Key Writings that Formed the Movement*. New York: The New Press.

Denman, C. (2003) *Sexuality: A Biopsychosocial Approach*. London: Palgrave Macmillan.

Diamond, S. (2014) The psychology of sexuality: why sex is still such a central issue for psychotherapy. *Psychology Today*, May 10, 2014. (www.psychologytoday.com/blog/evil-deeds/201405/the-psychology-sexuality).

Ellis, H. (1897–1928) *Studies in the Psychology of Sex* (Vols 1–6). (www.gutenberg.org/ebooks/13610).

Fine, C. (2010) Delusions of Gender: The Real Science behind Sex Differences. London: Icon Books.

Freud, S. (1986) The Essentials of Psycho-analysis: The Definitive Collection of Sigmund Freud's Writing. London: Penguin.

Frosch, S. (2006) *For and Against Psychoanalysis* (2nd ed.). Hove: Routledge.

Garton, S. (2004) *Histories of Sexuality: Antiquity to Sexual Revolution*. Abingdon: Routledge.

(Continued)

(Continued)

Gauntlett, D. (2008) *Media, Gender and Identity: An Introduction* (2nd ed.). Abingdon: Routledge.

Gray, J. (1992) *Men are from Mars, Women are from Venus*. New York: HarperCollins.

Hall, P. (2012) *Understanding and Treating Sex Addiction: A Comprehensive Guide for People who Struggle with Sex Addiction and Those Who Want to Help Them*. Abingdon: Routledge.

Katz, J.N. (1995) *The Invention of Heterosexuality*. Chicago, IL: University of Chicago Press.

Katz, J.N. (2001) *Love Stories: Sex between Men before Homosexuality*. Chicago, IL: University of Chicago Press.

Kinsey, A. (1948) *Sexual Behavior in the Human Male*. Philadelphia, PA: W.B. Saunders; Bloomington, IN: Indiana University Press.

Kinsey, A. (1953) *Sexual Behavior in the Human Female*. Philadelphia, PA: W.B. Saunders; Bloomington, IN: Indiana University Press.

Klein, M. (1932) *The Psychoanalysis of Children*. London: The Hogarth Press.

Krafft-Ebing, R. (1894) *Psychopathia Sexualis with especial reference to Contrary Sexual Instinct: A Medico-legal Study*. F.A. Davis Company (translation of 7th German edition by Charles Gilbert) (https://archive.org/details/psychopathiasex00chadgoog).

Meyer, I.H. (2003) Prejudice, social stress, and mental health in lesbian, gay and bisexual populations: conceptual issues and research evidence. *Psychological Bulletin*, 129(5), 674–697.

Mottier, V (2008) *Sexuality: A Very Short Introduction*. Oxford: Oxford University Press.

Padgug, R. (1979) Sexual matters: on conceptualizing sexuality in history. *Radical History Review*, Spring/Summer, 2–23.

Skynner, R. and Cleese, J. (1997) *Families and How to Survive Them*. London: Vermillion.

Sullivan, N. (2003) *A Critical Introduction to Queer Theory*. New York: New York University Press.

The Atlantic (2015) No Scientists have found the 'Gay Gene'. *The Atlantic*. (www.theatlantic.com/science/archive/2015/10/no-scientists-have-not-found-the-gay-gene/410059/).

Verhaeghe, P. (2014) *What about Me? The Struggle for Identity in a Market-based Society*. London: Scribe Publications.

RECOMMENDED READING

1. Mottier, V. (2008) *Sexuality: A Very Short Introduction*. Oxford: Oxford University Press.

A masterly overview of the emergence of sexuality as a concept in Western culture. Her 'three lens' model is more fully expounded, and key figures from the history of sexuality are introduced.

2. Richards, C. and Barker, M. (2013) *Sexuality and Gender for Mental Health Professionals*. London: Sage.

A useful introduction to the meaning of a wide range of terminologies and helpful, probing questions to help therapists clarify their own thoughts/beliefs about sexuality.

3. Killerman, S. (2013) *The Social Justice Advocate's Handbook: A Guide to Gender*. Austin, TX: Impetus Books.

Contains the excellent 'genderbread' model which can be used with clients to help them make sense of biological sex, gender identity, sexual desire, romantic desire, and more, in a fluid, potentially liberating way.

RELIGION AND SPIRITUALITY

WILLIAM WEST

OVERVIEW AND KEY POINTS

Working with clients around issues relating to spirituality or religion presents a range of challenges to counsellors and psychotherapists. It is apparent that clients do not always receive best practice in this important area (Jenkins, 2010). There are issues to face in relation to training, supervision and ethics.

It is important to recognise that:

- Religion and/or spirituality remains an important part of many people's lives today.
- Engaging with spirituality and religion can contribute to people's health and wellbeing.
- Therapists need to be familiar with the main religions and with the challenges and benefits of working with their clients around their relationship with religion and spirituality.

HISTORY AND CONTEXT

It would be true to say that counselling and psychotherapy have an uneasy relationship with religion and spirituality, and vice versa. At first glance this might seem strange since both deal with profound questions relating to the human condition, in particular human suffering – how to make sense of it, how to deal with it, and above all how to avoid or at least minimise it. However, if we reflect on the idea that the origins of modern therapy lie in the Victorian era (McLeod, 2009) and, like modern medicine and psychology, early therapists sought to define their theory and practice as 'scientific'; if we then consider that to be 'scientific', indeed to be 'modern' at that time meant to be non- or in some cases anti-religious, then we see the challenges of putting religious and therapeutic systems alongside one another. Consequently, 'It would be a mistake to imagine that all clients reporting religious, spiritual or mystical beliefs or experiences would be understood or well received by their counsellors' (McLeod, 2009: 490).

The expectation of the decline in religion and spirituality as modernism triumphed in the Western world has not wholly proved to be the case, and indeed the role especially of spirituality remains strong in what many now refer to as our postmodern world. In the 2011 Census:

> Christianity was the largest religious group in England and Wales with 33.2 million people (59 per cent of the population). The second largest religious group were [sic] Muslims with 2.7 million people (5 per cent of the population). The proportion of people who reported that they did not have a religion reached 14.1 million people, a quarter of the population. … This compares with 71.6% identifying as Christian in 2001. (For further details see www.ons.gov.uk/peoplepopulationandcommunity/culturalidentity/religion/articles/fullstorywhatdoesthecensustellusaboutreligionin2011/2013-05-16, accessed 8/7/2016)

More recently, Bullivant (2016) analysed data from British Social Attitudes surveys and concluded that people in England and Wales who say they have no religion now significantly outnumber those who regard themselves as Christians. The non-religious group now makes up 48.5% of the population of the adult England and Wales while Christians make up 43.8%.

Apart from the competing roles in relation to human suffering referred to above, there are tensions in the area of equality and human rights where counselling and psychotherapy accept the dominant British cultural position of legal equality between men and women and moves towards equal rights for gay, lesbian and transgendered people. In contrast, religious groups are very often, in effect, homophobic and in many cases restrict the roles available to women. So, for example, women have only recently been appointed as bishops in the Church of England and very few serve as imams in Muslim mosques. However, religious groups have traditionally, and currently, been involved in social actions on behalf of the poor and dispossessed.

DEFINITIONS

There are a number of definitions particularly of spirituality but also of religion. There seems to be a developing consensus, reflected in most dictionary definitions, that spirituality relates to personal beliefs and religion to the organised group of believers, including places of worships, rituals and creeds. We shall use this distinction here. However, not everyone, especially those of a religious nature, accepts these distinctions and many people, whether religious believers or not, are dismissive of personal spirituality. From the viewpoint of therapeutic practice it is always best to explore what words mean for clients.

In terms of definitions that are useful for therapy, Elkins et al.'s (1988) research into what people mean by 'spirituality' seems especially useful with its focus on experience, John Rowan's (2005) transpersonal work reminds us that spirituality can involve changes in our sense of self, and John Swinton (2001) tells us that it is about connections inside the person, between people and with creation. From his research into spiritual experiences in therapy, Ross (2016) developed categories of spirituality of the senses, of the self and of the sacred. The following points seem to me to be a useful composite description of some of the possible components of spirituality that are particularly relevant to therapy:

1. It is rooted in human experiencing rather than abstract theology, that is, it helps to focus on spirituality as a human experience and what this means to people.
2. It is embodied, that is, spiritual experience often actively involves us as physical beings.
3. It involves feeling strongly connected to other people and the universe at large.
4. It involves non-ordinary consciousness, that is, in altered states of consciousness or trance states.
5. Active engagement with spirituality tends to make people more altruistic, less materialistic and more environmentally aware.
6. It deals with the meaning that people make of their lives.
7. It faces suffering, its causes and potentially its meaning to the individual.
8. It relates to God/Goddesses/divine/ultimate reality: these words are especially rich in meaning, and not always unproblematic.
9. It often uses the word 'soul' or 'higher self': these words often have powerful associations and meanings for people.
10. Techniques such as prayer, meditation, contemplation, mindfulness, yoga and Tai Chi are often used as spiritual practices (this is further explored in West, 2004, 2010).

Many people continue to have experiences that they put the word 'spiritual' to. Other people having the same or similar experience may not use the word 'spiritual'. This use of the word 'spiritual' for a human experience – perhaps feeling one with nature or a profound sense of togetherness with another human being – has many implications. For a start, such experiences may not be welcome or altogether pleasant, and even if they are, they may raise many issues. Such spiritual experiences are common among clients (Allman et al., 1992), inevitably happen to therapists, and sometimes occur within the therapy room (Rogers, 1980; Thorne, 1998).

RELEVANCE TO COUNSELLING AND PSYCHOTHERAPY

Working with clients' religious and spiritual issues can raise questions in relation to the therapist's own attitude to religion and spirituality, including any unresolved countertransference issues (Lannert, 1991). The training of therapists is intended to equip them to deal effectively with almost any issues raised by their clients. Inevitably some of these client issues will raise questions relating to the therapist's own personal life and beliefs. So facing challenges arising from their clients' spiritual and religious beliefs should be par for the course. However, there is enough research around spirituality and therapy to show that a fair few therapists cannot rise to the challenges involved (Jenkins, 2010) and neither can some of their supervisors (West, 2000b). Part of the problem may well be limitations within counsellor training (Jafari, 2016).

It is important with a religious or spiritually minded client to clarify the role of spirituality and religion in their life. Just knowing that a client is Christian or Muslim or Jewish is not enough. There are liberal and traditional groupings in almost all religions. The extent to which a client is an active believer is also important background information, as in any tensions they may be aware of in relation to their religion beliefs and their lifestyle. Any form of client assessment should naturally include questions relating to their religious upbringing and what religious or spiritual practices they have in their current life (Richards and Bergin, 2005; West, 2000a). This not only gives the therapist some very useful information (even finding out how unreligious or anti-religious a client might be is itself important), but also gives the client permission to discuss such issues if they see fit. This implies that therapists need to have a good working knowledge of the main religious traditions, including their beliefs and practices, while at the same time being curious as to their clients' own perspective and also having an understanding of modern spirituality.

There are a number of ways of making sense of religion and spirituality within therapy. A detailed exploration of this topic is beyond the scope of this chapter. A few pointers, however, are in order:

1. Within the person-centred tradition, the work of Brian Thorne (1998, 2002, 2012) is worthy of consideration. He talks of the 'mystical power of person-centred approach' and refers to the person-centred therapist as a 'secular priest'. His writings illuminate the challenges of being present to clients' spirituality. Thorne's work is rather controversial, but there are others who value the depth of working that he suggests without necessarily adopting a religious or spiritual perspective, for example Mearns and Cooper (2005).
2. From a humanistic and transpersonal perspective, John Rowan's (2005) work enables us to think very clearly about how to situate our work with clients within therapeutic and spiritual frameworks, which include a careful exposition and development of Ken Wilber's model (see (3) below). Rowan advocates that all therapists pursue their own spiritual path, which is an interesting challenge to consider.
3. From a transpersonal viewpoint, Ken Wilber (2000) presents a model that integrates Western secular therapy with Eastern ideas of spiritual development. His model has aroused both sufficient criticism and strong support to suggest that it has value, and it challenges us to think beyond a 'one size fits all' approach for psychospiritual practice and to tailor our therapeutic response to the perceived (spiritual) and developmental needs of the individual client.
4. There have been some useful explorations recently of the overlap and differences between counselling and spiritual direction/accompaniment, for example, the work of Gubi (2015), Harborne (2012) and West and Goss (2016). Harborne even argues provocatively that spiritual direction been seen as a branch of psychotherapy.
5. We need to view these questions within a cross-cultural perspective, where the work of Roy Moodley (Moodley, 2006, 2007; Moodley and West, 2005), among others (Laungani, 2007; Moodley et al., 2010), invites us to enlarge our understandings of what makes people suffer and of the creative role cultural factors can play in the relief of suffering.

PRACTICE ISSUES

The following are some largely fictional examples of the kind of religious and spiritual issues that can arise in counselling.

1. Angela is a young white English woman who has recently left a residential Buddhist community that apparently functioned as a religious cult.* Although relieved to be no longer living in the community, Angela is unable to move on. She is struggling with her new life since she has lost contact with her pre-Buddhist friends and is feeling a real sense of loss both for the people and the religious life of the community.
2. James, a young African-Caribbean man, was befriended by an evangelical Christian group at his local college. This group provided him with a real sense of home and helped him find his first job. Always confused about his sexuality, after a recent drunken night out that ended up in sexual encounter with another man, James was beginning to wonder if he was gay and, if so, what could he do? He knew that if he came out to his Christian friends they would want to 'cure' him.

*For a source of useful information on cults contact INFORM at www.inform.ac

It is worth reflecting on each of these examples in turn, especially noticing any strong reactions to any part of the stories presented, as this may well alert us to how similar issues presented in the real world could impact on us.

ETHICS

It is important to acknowledge a number of very crucial ethical issues involved when working with clients around issues to do with religion and spirituality. These include:

1. The respectful acceptance of clients' religious and spiritual beliefs and practices however strange and unsettling they may appear to be.
2. A recognition of the limits of both competence and the therapist's willingness to work in the area of religion and spirituality, which should not be seen as a question of therapist inadequacy but rather a clear boundary.
3. How, when spirituality is experienced in the therapy room, there is sometimes an apparent softening of boundaries between client and therapist and great care is then needed.
4. The fact that self-awareness of the therapist with regard to their spiritual and religious beliefs and their attitudes to the same is an important underpinning of best practice in this area (Wyatt, 2002).

5. The fact that supervision of this part of therapeutic practice is especially important even though some supervisors are reluctant to supervise or welcome therapeutic work around spirituality and religion (West, 2003).

As a further aid to ethical practice in this area it is well worth reading the BACP Information sheet on working with spiritual, faith or religion, written by Harborne (2008).

CONCLUSION

The tensions between those of a religious or spiritual faith and the dominant, arguably secular, modern culture are unlikely to ease. Indeed, as counselling and psychotherapy continues its somewhat tortuous path towards professionalisation and forms of statutory accreditation, it may well embody some of these very tensions. It is unlikely that people will cease to have spiritual experiences (Hay and Hunt, 2000) nor cease to struggle to find the help they might well need in making sense of them. However, counsellors and psychotherapists are now better placed than even 10 years ago to meet this client need, but improvements in training and supervision are still, in my view, necessary before clients receive the help they are due with regards to religion and spirituality.

REFERENCES

Allman, L. S., De Las Rocha, O., Elkins, D. N. and Weathers, R. S. (1992) Psychotherapists' attitudes towards clients report mystical experiences. *Psychotherapy*, 29(4): 654–659.

Bullivant, S. (2016) Contemporary Catholicism in England and Wales: A statistical report based on recent British Social Attitudes survey data, Catholic Research Forum Reports 1. London: St Mary's University.

Elkins, D. N., Hedstorm, J. L., Hughes, L. L., Leaf, J. A. and Saunders, C. (1988) Toward a humanistic-phenomenological spirituality. *Journal of Humanistic Psychology*, 28(4): 5–18.

Gubi, P. M. (Ed.) (2015) *Counselling and Spiritual Accompaniment: Journeying with Psyche and Soul*. London: Jessica Kingsley.

Harborne, L. (2008) *Working with Issues of Spirituality, Faith or Religion*. BACP Information Sheet. Lutterworth: British Association for Counselling and Psychotherapy.

Harborne, L. (2012) *Psychotherapy and Spiritual Direction: Two Languages, One Voice?* London: Karnac.

Hay, D. and Hunt K. (2000) *Understanding the Spirituality of People Who Don't Go To Church*. Nottingham: Centre for the Study of Human Relations, Nottingham University.

Jafari, S. (2016) Religion and spirituality within counselling/clinical psychology training programmes: A systematic review. *British Journal of Guidance and Counselling*, 44(3): 257–276.

Jenkins, C. (2010) When the clients' spirituality is denied in therapy. In W. West (Ed.), *Exploring Therapy, Spirituality and Healing*. Basingstoke: Palgrave.

Lannert, J. (1991) Resistance and countertransference issues with spiritual and religious clients. *Journal of Humanistic Psychology*, 31(4): 68–76.

Laungani, P. (2007) *Understanding Cross-cultural Psychology*. London: Sage.

McLeod, J. (2009) *An Introduction to Counselling* (4th ed.). Maidenhead: Open University Press.

Mearns, D. and Cooper, M. (2005) *Working at Relational Depth in Counselling and Psychotherapy*. London: Sage.

Moodley, R. (2006) Cultural representations and interpretations of 'subjective distress' in ethnic minority patients. In R. Moodley and S. Palmer (Eds.), *Race, Culture and Psychotherapy*. London: Routledge.

Moodley, R. (2007) (Re)placing multiculturalism in counselling and psychotherapy. *British Journal of Guidance & Counselling*, 35(1): 1–22.

Moodley, R., Aanchal R. and Alladin, W. (2010) *Bridging East–West Psychology and Counselling: Exploring the Work of Pittu Laungani*. New Delhi: Sage.

Moodley, R. and West, W. (Eds.) (2005) *Integrating Traditional Healing Practices into Counseling and Psychotherapy*. Thousand Oaks, CA: Sage.

Richards, P. S. and Bergin, A. E. (2005) *A Spiritual Strategy for Counselling and Psychotherapy* (2nd ed.). Washington, DC: American Psychological Association.

Rogers, C. R. (1980) *A Way of Being*. Boston, MA: Houghton Mifflin.

Ross, A. (2016) Identifying the categories of spiritual experience encounter by therapists in their clinical work. *British Journal of Guidance and Counselling*, 44(3): 316–324.

Rowan, J. (2005) *The Transpersonal: Spirituality in Psychotherapy and Counselling* (2nd ed.). London: Routledge.

Swinton, J. (2001) *Spirituality in Mental Health Care*. London: Jessica Kingsley.

Thorne, B. (1998) *Person-Centred Counselling and Christian Spirituality: The Secular and the Holy*. London: Whurr.

Thorne, B. (2002) *The Mystical Path of Person-Centred Therapy: Hope beyond Despair*. London: Whurr.

Thorne, B. (2012) *Counselling and Spiritual Accompaniment: Bridging Faith and Person-centred Therapy*. Chichester: Wiley-Blackwell.

West, W. (2000a) *Psychotherapy and Spirituality: Crossing the Line between Therapy and Religion*. London: Sage.

West, W. (2000b) Supervision difficulties and dilemmas for counsellors and psychotherapists around healing and spirituality. In B. Lawton and C. Feltham (Eds.), *Taking Supervision Forwards: Dilemmas, Insights and Trends*. London: Sage.

West, W. S. (2003) The culture of psychotherapy supervision. *Counselling and Psychotherapy Research*, 3(2): 123–127.

West, W. S. (2004) *Spiritual Issues in Therapy: Relating Experience to Practice*. Basingstoke: Palgrave.

West, W. S. (Ed.) (2010) *Exploring Therapy, Spirituality and Healing*. Basingstoke: Palgrave.

West, W. S. and Goss, P. (2016) Jungian influenced therapists and Buddhists in dialogue. *British Journal of Guidance and Counselling*, 44(3): 297–205.

Wilber, K. (2000) *Integral Psychology: Consciousness, Spirit, Psychology, Therapy*. London: Shambhala.

Wyatt, J. (2002) 'Confronting the Almighty God'? A study of how psychodynamic counsellors respond to clients' expressions of religious faith. *Counselling and Psychotherapy Research*, 2(3): 177–184.

RECOMMENDED READING

1. Thorne, B. (2012) *Counselling and Spiritual Accompaniment: Bridging Faith and Person-centred Therapy*. Chichester: Wiley-Blackwell.

This is an excellent text for understanding the overlaps between personal-centred counselling and religious pastoral care.

2. Rowan, J. (2005) *The Transpersonal: Spirituality in Psychotherapy and Counselling (2nd ed.)*. London: Routledge.

This is a key text on spirituality from a humanistic and transpersonal perspective.

3. Laungani, P. (2007) *Understanding Cross-Cultural Psychology*. London: Sage.

This text helps us understand spirituality and religion within a cross-cultural perspective.

2.8   RACE, CULTURE AND ETHNICITY

DOIREANN MANGAN

OVERVIEW AND KEY POINTS

The United Kingdom (UK) is an increasingly ethnically diverse place to live. Nearly 20% of the population of England and Wales identified as belonging to a white or non-white ethnic minority in the 2011 Census (Office for National Statistics, 2016), with that percentage expected to continue to grow. Yet such diversity appears to be set against a global background of rising levels of tension and intolerance between cultural groups. Issues of race, culture and ethnicity have never been more salient. It is crucial that they be considered in all aspects of counselling and psychotherapy, including in training, throughout the therapy process, and at institutional and policy levels. This chapter first introduces some key points on the topic. The concepts of race, culture and ethnicity are then discussed, followed by a brief outline of the history and context of cross-cultural therapeutic engagements. The last section looks at the relevance of these areas for counselling and psychotherapy and offers practical recommendations for working with cultural and racial difference in therapy.

Some key points are presented for consideration:

- Issues of race, culture and ethnicity are bound up with power relations in society. Minority ethnic groups tend to have reduced access to power compared to majority groups. The impact of such social inequality is connected with discrimination and socio-economic disadvantage, and with them increased stress and mental health problems (Wallace, Nazroo and Bécares, 2016; Wilkinson and Pickett, 2009).
- The socio-cultural contexts of clients' lives need to be taken into account. This involves appreciating and acknowledging that factors to do with race, culture and/or ethnicity will influence their life experiences, their psychological wellbeing, and their experiences of therapy.
- Most counselling and psychotherapy models emerged from a Eurocentric worldview, which subscribes to its own particular norms and is primarily individualistic and secular. Training in any model should interrogate in-built cultural assumptions. How to work sensitively and effectively with a culturally diverse range of clients needs to be prioritised as a fundamental rather than additional aspect of training (Lago, 2006).

WHAT IS MEANT BY THE TERMS RACE, CULTURE AND ETHNICITY?

Dalal (2002) points out that the terms race, culture and ethnicity are used in interchangeable ways. He also observes that the emphasis on difference which they imply is essentially a way of distancing and denying similarity. A simplified definition for each term is that race is primarily about physical appearance, culture is of sociological origin, and ethnicity is psychological because of its connection to the identity of the person (Fernando, 2002). I elaborate on the meanings ascribed to these terms, and suggest some of the many ways they are relevant to the therapeutic context.

Race as a concept, and with it racism, largely stemmed from efforts to justify the oppression and exploitation of certain races, on the grounds of their supposed biological inferiority to other races. It is now understood that there is no scientific biological basis to race; rather, it is a potent social construct. While the emphasis on political correctness in society means racially-motivated attacks are less socially acceptable (though still a reality), many argue that more covert forms of racism, including institutional racism, are still very much alive (e.g., McKenzie-Mavinga, 2016). The potential social and psychological impact of belonging to a historically subjugated race cannot be downplayed. It may manifest in suspicion and hostility towards members of historically dominant races. Another possibility is that of 'internalised racism', whereby negative opinions of one's own race are taken on and turned against the self, resulting in low self-esteem or depression (Thompson-Miller and Feagin, 2007). On the other hand, belonging to a white majority has been associated with feelings of guilt or shame, sometimes leading to denial of racial difference (Goldsmith, 2002; Ryde, 2009). The importance of being ready to explore these sorts of issues in the counselling room is highlighted later in the chapter.

Culture, a much-contested term, could be defined as the beliefs, attitudes, customs and values shared by a social collective. As the lens through which someone registers experience, it influences how they see, understand and respond to events. Culture therefore shapes a person's approach to all areas of life, from gender role expectations, to attitude towards authority, to communication style. Beliefs about what causes mental health issues are informed by cultural understandings. Similarly, culture influences what are considered 'socially acceptable' ways of expressing distress. For instance, in many cultures emotional distress is signalled through somatic complaints (e.g., Bhugra and Mastrogianni, 2003). Failure to recognise the significance of such complaints can mean psychological problems go unnoticed, or are misinterpreted, in assessment and therapy.

Ethnicity is generally taken to mean belonging to a distinctive social group that shares a religion, nationality or language. It tends to be used to denote a combination of race and culture. Like race, significant links have been found between ethnicity and socio-economic status and social mobility, although considerable difference does exist between ethnic minority groups. Poverty is up to twice as likely among those from ethnic minority groups in the UK compared to the white ethnic majority (Department for Work and Pensions, UK, 2016). This appears to be partly due to the prevalence of low paid work among workers from ethnic minorities. An example of an ethnicity-related issue in therapy might concern a client struggling with being perceived by others, due to their appearance, as belonging to a particular ethnic group with which they themselves do not feel any connection. Clearly, as even this example shows, there is crossover between ethnic, racial and cultural issues and this is reflected in my use of the terms throughout this chapter.

HISTORY AND CONTEXT

Differential access to mental health services, along with poor outcomes when treatment is received, has consistently been reported for minority ethnic groups (Fernando, 2002; Williams, Turpin and Hardy, 2006). Rates of diagnosis of schizophrenia, as with rates of detention under the Mental Health Act, are much higher for black people compared to white people (Health and Social Care Information Centre, 2015). While undoubtedly complex, factors cited as contributing to such statistics include a tendency to pathologise rather than try to understand difference, 'difference' being decided by the white ethnic majority (Lago and Thompson, 2003). Another factor is the focus on the individual without taking into account possible social and economic factors, such as racism and poor living conditions, and their impact on a person's mental health. This allows the 'problem' and the need for change to be located within the individual, rather than accept any social or systemic need for change. Services and therapy approaches based on Eurocentric views of mental wellness/illness may clash with a person's own cultural values and understandings, making it hard to engage. So-called 'colour-blind' approaches in mental healthcare, presented as anti-discriminatory, have been criticised as a tool used by the white majority to claim innocence for racial discrimination (Holt Barrett and George, 2005). These examples point to built-in, often subtle, socially sanctioned forms of injustice. They outline how engaging with mental health services can be an invalidating and alienating experience for people from ethnic minorities, only serving to increase distress, widen divides, and ultimately exacerbate social inequality.

CROSS-CULTURAL THERAPY MOVEMENTS

Since the 1960s, various developments have sought to respond to the problems evident in cross-cultural mental health provision. Research in the United States has been at the forefront of this, with cross-cultural therapy even being called the 'fourth force' in counselling there, following psychodynamic, humanistic and cognitive behavioural models (Pederson, 1991). Numerous approaches emerged including UK-based movements such as transcultural psychiatry and anti-oppressive practice (Lago and Smith, 2010). Each is rooted in its own

ideology and foregrounds particular aspects of working with diversity. One of the more prominent models has been the 'multicultural counselling competencies' of Sue, Arredondo and McDavis (1992). These fell under three dimensions: awareness of one's own cultural values and potential biases, recognising differences in worldview between oneself and clients, and the ability to implement culturally appropriate interventions. More recently, Collins and Arthur (2010) built on these but proposed a shift away from the narrow focus on strategies and techniques. They proposed an emphasis instead on developing a culturally sensitive working alliance. The same authors posited that all interactions with clients are, on some level, multicultural, that the definition of culture being used was too narrow, and cultural competencies should not be distinguished from professional competencies. They thus adopted the term 'culture-infused counselling' (Collins and Arthur, 2005). Various approaches inform the points offered in the following section.

RELEVANCE TO COUNSELLING AND PSYCHOTHERAPY

Presented here is a general overview from the broad range of literature on working sensitively, ethically and effectively in cross-cultural settings. Points may apply to training and to organisations which offer counselling and psychotherapy, though the focus is mainly on therapeutic practice.

SELF-AWARENESS

The starting point for working with diversity is self-reflection. This means cultivating awareness of one's own cultural and ethnic identity and values, what they mean to you and to others around you. In the case of white therapists, being white and belonging to an ethnic majority has been problematised in recent years, with Ryde (2009) advising that the privileges of whiteness need to be acknowledged in order to practise effectively as a white therapist in a multicultural society. As well as being included in training, continued commitment to reflexive practice is vital – being on the lookout for one's own biases, prejudices and beliefs, about one's own and other cultures. Supervision from a supervisor experienced in working with cultural diversity is recommended to facilitate this. In some circumstances, being transparent and dialoguing with the client about issues such as biases and prejudices may prove helpful for both parties.

CULTURAL AWARENESS

It is likely that there will be misunderstandings and miscommunications between a client and a therapist with different ethnic backgrounds and life experiences. Curiosity, respect and openness are key to avoiding these resulting in ruptures in therapy, and to building a strong therapeutic alliance. Issues of race or culture may show up in subtle ways, and again supervision helps promote vigilance. Learning about a client's culture, when different from one's own, facilitates developing cultural awareness. Importantly, knowledge should be checked through discussion with the client. This serves to help avoid stereotyping, and any notion that cultural groups are homogeneous. It also helps situate understanding from the client's perspective – they may be fully aware of the cultural norms of their ethnic community but disagree with them or choose to ignore them. Eleftheriadou (2010) makes the crucial point that it is the client's *relationship with* the culture that is of interest, not the culture in and of itself. There is a risk of losing sight of the client and their individuality should therapy become overly focused on issues of culture.

'SAMENESS'

Perceived 'sameness' can be an issue in itself, and similarly needs to be questioned. The British Association for Counselling and Psychotherapy's (BACP) ethical framework reminds us that being respectful means being 'open-minded with clients who ... possess familiar characteristics so that we do not suppress or neglect what is distinctive in their lives' (2016: 6). On this note, many studies have investigated whether ethnic matching of client and therapist has any impact on therapy, but overviews of the findings remain inconclusive (Zhang and Burkard, 2008).

ACKNOWLEDGING AND ADDRESSING DIFFERENCE

Racism does not just happen through overt hatred or violence: 'disavowal of a person's "different" existence is itself a way of not recognising the degree to which this pervasive system operates in groups and in the individual' (Thomas, 1992: 135). The fact is that recognising and openly addressing difference commonly arouses people's anxieties. Lago and Thompson (2003) say this is due to the already unequal power balance in the therapy room, and fear that bringing up race will be experienced as an attack. Greene (2005) suggests the fact that race is a social construct inspires guilt and makes it hard to talk about. What is certain is that discussing race is often actively avoided in cross-cultural therapy, with even experiences of racism being minimised. In its place is sometimes a discourse denying difference and instead emphasising that 'as humans we are all the same' (Goldsmith, 2002). In this context, such a discourse rejects the reality of difference in society and denies a part of an individual's lived experience. It signals that

meaningful discussion of racialised experience is off-limits, and seems contradictory to one of the fundamental values of the BACP, 'facilitating a sense of self that is meaningful to the person(s) concerned within their personal and cultural context' (BACP, 2016: 6).

WORKING WITH DIFFERENCE

With the above in mind, it is important that issues of race, ethnicity and culture be introduced and inquired about from assessment. This communicates that the therapy is a place where cultural and racial aspects of the clients' experiences can be discussed, should they wish. Indeed, discussing ethnic difference within the initial counselling sessions has been associated with higher credibility ratings and a more positive working alliance (Zhang and Burkard, 2008). Ultimately, the interaction between a therapist's and client's own cultural and racial positions creates its own reality in the therapy room, bringing the opportunity for whatever arises to be explored in fruitful ways. It may be helpful to inquire about meanings of psychological and emotional distress in relation to the norms of the client's cultural reference group, as well as cultural expectations of therapy and the therapeutic relationship (Fernando, 2002). According to Eleftheriadou, the challenge of cross-cultural work 'is to have the sensitivity and ability to enter a different world ... and not only understand it, but feel comfortable to challenge it' (2010: 201). Koslofsky and Domenech Rodríguez (2017) outline multiple examples of therapists creatively adapting the skills and tools of their evidence-based practice to working with clients from cultural minorities. Some authors also suggest learning about traditional healing practices of the client's culture, and being open to working alongside these in the therapy (e.g., Sue et al., 1992).

ADDITIONAL CONSIDERATIONS FOR WORKING WITH RACE, CULTURE AND ETHNICITY

The intersectionality of clients' experiences also needs to be kept in mind; in other words, how a client's race interacts with other aspects of their identity, such as gender, religion and language. Thus you might wish to consider issues raised here in relation to other chapters in this book, such as those on working with interpreters, and religion and spirituality. On a service level, community-based and community-consulted provision of therapy services may present solutions to overcome barriers to treatment faced by minority communities (Prilleltensky, 2014). In sum, working with racial, cultural and ethnic difference presents rich opportunities for learning and development, while practitioners are also in a position to challenge discrimination at many levels.

REFERENCES

Bhugra, D. and Mastrogianni, A. (2003). Globalisation and mental disorders: overview with relation to depression. *The British Journal of Psychiatry*, 184(1), 10–20.

British Association for Counselling and Psychotherapy (2016). *Ethical framework for the counselling professions*. Lutterworth: BACP.

Collins, S. and Arthur, N. (2005). Culture-infused counselling: a model for developing multicultural competence. *Counselling Psychology Quarterly*, 23(2), 217–233.

Collins, S. and Arthur, N. (2010). Culture-infused counselling: a fresh look at a classic framework of multicultural counselling competencies. *Counselling Psychology Quarterly*, 23(2), 203–216.

Dalal, F. (2002). *Race, colour and the process of racialization: new perspectives from group analysis, psychoanalysis, and sociology*. New York: Brunner-Routledge.

Department for Work and Pensions, UK (2016). *Households below average income (HBAI)*. London: HMSO. Retrieved from www.jrf.org.uk/data/poverty-rate-ethnicity on 26/01/2016.

Eleftheriadou, Z. (2010). Cross-cultural counselling psychology. In R. Woolfe, S. Strawbridge, B. Douglas and W. Dryden (Eds.), *The handbook of counselling psychology* (3rd ed.). London: Sage.

Fernando, S. (2002). *Mental health, race and culture*. Basingstoke: Palgrave.

Goldsmith, B.L. (2002). Experiences in working with the 'other': barrier or catalyst to the clinical encounter? *Journal of College Student Psychotherapy*, 17(1), 55–62.

Greene, B. (2005). Psychology, diversity and social justice: beyond heterosexism and across the cultural divide. *Counselling Psychology Quarterly*, 18(4), 295–306.

Health and Social Care Information Centre (2015). Inpatients formally detained in hospitals under the Mental Health Act 1983, and patients subject to supervised community treatment uses of the Mental Health Act: Annual Statistics, 2014/15. London: HSCIC. Retrieved from http://content.digital.nhs.uk/catalogue/PUB18803/inp-det-m-h-a-1983-sup-com-eng-14-15-rep.pdf on 25/01/2017.

Holt Barrett, K. and George, W.H. (2005). *Race, culture, psychology and law*. New York: Sage.

Koslofsky, S. and Domenech Rodríguez, M.M. (2017). Cultural adaptations to psychotherapy: real-world applications. *Clinical Case Studies*, 16(1), 3–8.

Lago, C. (2006). *Race, culture and counselling: the ongoing challenge* (2nd ed.). Maidenhead: Open University Press.

Lago, C. and Smith, B. (Eds.) (2010). *Anti-discriminatory practice in counselling and psychotherapy* (2nd ed.). London: Sage.

Lago, C. and Thompson, J. (2003). *Race, culture and counselling*. Maidenhead: Open University Press.

McKenzie-Mavinga, I. (2016). *The challenge of racism in therapeutic practice: engaging with oppression in practice and supervision* (2nd ed.). Basingstoke: Palgrave.

Office for National Statistics (2016). *2011 Census aggregate data*. UK Data Service (Edition: June 2016).

Pedersen, P.B. (1991). Multiculturalism as a generic approach to counseling. *Journal of Counseling and Development*, 70, 6–12.

Prilleltensky, I. (2014). Meaning-making, mattering, and thriving in community psychology: from co-optation to amelioration and transformation. *Psychosocial Intervention*, 23(2), 151–154.

Ryde, J. (2009). *Being white in the helping professions: developing effective intercultural awareness*. London: Jessica Kingsley.

Sue, D.W., Arredondo, P. and McDavis, R.J. (1992). Multicultural counseling competencies and standards: a call to the profession. *Journal of Counseling and Development*, 70, 477–486.

Thomas, L. (1992). Racism and psychotherapy. In J. Kareem and R. Littlewood (Eds.), *Intercultural therapy* (pp. 133–145). Oxford: Blackwell.

Thompson-Miller, R. and Feagin, J.R. (2007). Continuing injuries of racism: counseling in a racist context. *The Counseling Psychologist*, 35(1), 106–115.

Wallace, S., Nazroo, J. and Bécares, L. (2016). Cumulative effect of racial discrimination on the mental health of ethnic minorities in the United Kingdom. *American Journal of Public Health*, 106(7), 1294–1300.

Wilkinson, R. and Pickett, K. (2009). *The spirit level: why more equal societies almost always do better*. London: Allen Lane.

Williams, P.E., Turpin, G. and Hardy, G. (2006). Clinical psychology service provision and ethnic diversity within the UK: a review of the literature. *Clinical Psychology and Psychotherapy*, 13(5), 324–338.

Zhang, N. and Burkard, A.W. (2008). Client and counselor discussions of racial and ethnic differences in counseling: an exploratory investigation. *Journal of Multicultural Counseling and Development*, 36, 77–87.

SUGGESTED READING

1. Lago, C. (2006). *Race, culture and counselling: the ongoing challenge* (2nd ed.). Maidenhead: Open University Press.

This landmark book covers a broad range of perspectives and includes sections on training, supervision, and key issues for white and black practitioners in the UK context.

2. Ryde, J. (2009). *Being white in the helping professions: developing effective intercultural awareness*. London: Jessica Kingsley.

This book aims to stimulate white practitioners to develop awareness of their privilege and assumptions in order to work effectively in multicultural societies. It provides practical guidance in dealing with racial and cultural issues in ways that promote a move towards social justice within mental health systems.

3. McKenzie-Mavinga, I. (2016). *The challenge of racism in therapeutic practice: engaging with oppression in pracand supervision* (2nd ed.). Basingstoke: Palgrave.

In this book the author addresses working with clients from a variety of specific ethnic heritages. Also covered are highly relevant topics of everyday racism and intergenerational race-related trauma, and their impact and management in a therapeutic relationship. These are also considered from a supervisory perspective.

PART III

THERAPEUTIC SKILLS AND CLINICAL PRACTICE

3.1 INTRODUCING THERAPEUTIC SKILLS AND CLINICAL PRACTICE: THE 'BASICS' OF THERAPEUTIC PRACTICE?

LAURA ANNE WINTER

OVERVIEW OF THIS SECTION

After having spent some time considering the broader context for our work in Part II of the *Handbook*, Part III narrows our focus down to the process of direct clinical practice and the skills involved in therapeutic work in counselling and psychotherapy. In this introductory chapter I provide a brief overview of what is included within this section. In addition, I briefly reflect on the skills covered in this chapter as being the building blocks or at the heart of what we do in each therapeutic encounter. I reflect on these issues as the more 'generic' elements or 'common factors' in what we do as counsellors and psychotherapists, as opposed to the specific elements of particular theoretical approaches or 'treatments'. Furthermore, I suggest that the importance of these 'basic' skills cannot be underestimated. Following this short discussion, I leave the readers with three questions to consider which relate to such generic therapeutic skills and clinical practice issues in counselling and psychotherapy.

Part III includes eight chapters which have been structured in order to take the reader through the core elements of the therapeutic process, in some ways from start to finish. We begin with the therapeutic relationship as the starting point underpinning everything which follows, and then progress through the assessment and formulation elements of a therapeutic encounter with a client. The final three chapters introduce the reader to broad overarching issues in beginnings, middles and endings in therapeutic practice. Needless to say these chapters do overlap at times, and viewing 'assessment' or 'endings' in isolation from the rest of our therapeutic encounter is in some ways an arbitrary divide on what, in reality, progresses and flows in unique ways across each different therapeutic relationship we form. Overall though, the aim in this section of the book, as noted above, is to look at the core therapeutic skills which run across the different approaches taken in particular models of therapy (see Part V of this *Handbook* for chapters on such different models and approaches). Nevertheless, some models of therapy may disagree with the labels used,

or have different conceptions or understandings of some of the skills we discuss. For example, a person-centred theoretical approach might consider 'assessment' and 'formulation' to be something quite different from assessment and formulation from within a cognitive-behavioural frame (see for example, Gillon (2013) and Simms (2011) for a discussion around this particular issue). Hopefully this is something readers can reflect upon and question as they go through the various chapters.

In terms of structure, chapters within this section often draw on specific case examples, which bring to life some of the issues discussed. Each contribution progresses in different ways, tailored to the particular topic under scrutiny. But as usual authors have provided an *Overview and Key Points* section, as well as *References* and *Recommended Reading*. We hope that this provides the reader with some consistency and points for departure for further inquiry and learning.

THE 'BASIC' SKILLS OF THERAPEUTIC PRACTICE?

Each therapeutic encounter will have a *beginning, middle* and *ending*, no matter how short the contact, the setting in which the contact takes place, or the therapeutic training or favoured model of the therapist. Even if you meet for a single one-hour session with someone, or three years of sessions of counselling or psychotherapy, there will be a beginning, middle and ending. And within each of these encounters we will, at least, have taken some steps towards forming a *therapeutic relationship* with the individual (or couple, family or group, etc.) we are working with. At some point in that encounter, as therapists we will more than likely make some sort of judgements or '*assessments*' of that particular relationship, and potentially on the issues with which the individual has approached us to speak about, and whether or not we can work with them at that particular time and in that particular setting. Undoubtedly these judgements will have allowed us to come to some sort of understanding, or *formulation*, of that individual and their relationship with us, based on various factors, probably including our own experience (personal and professional) as well as some psychological theory. Further, we will have started to 'make sense' of the encounter we are engaged in. These are therefore the 'generic' elements of practice, which we consider in this section.

Many authors have spoken of things which are generic across different models and approaches to counselling and psychotherapy. For example, some of the ways in which the issue of therapeutic integration has been approached involved such a generic approach, or looking at the micro skills or processes occurring within therapeutic practice. Hill (2014) proposes that there are three components underpinning being a successful 'helper'. These are described as having 'facilitate attitudes', including empathy, compassion, warmth and being nonjudgemental; 'self-awareness', which is having knowledge and awareness of what is going on inside oneself; and 'helping skills', which are learnt behaviours and strategies to support and help others. Such components can be considered core or generic across models. Similarly, Egan (2014) looks at the micro skills underpinning therapeutic encounters, such as visibly tuning in to the client, active listening skills, and empathic responding. Can these generic skills thus be considered to be the 'basics' of counselling and psychotherapy? When our thinking about therapeutic practice takes us beyond these issues to consider issues and processes involved in cognitive distortions, the thwarting of the self-actualising tendency, or defence mechanisms, there may be a temptation to view these generic skills as 'basic' and our model or setting-specific skills as 'complex' or more developed in some way.

Indeed, often these generic elements underpinning our therapeutic encounters are given less time than the theoretical models or approaches we are trained in, or the particular presenting problems we work with. We may spend many years reading and learning about what makes someone anxious according to our Jungian Analytical approach, or what leads to eating disorders from a Schema Therapy point of view. The forming of a therapeutic relationship and the successful management of endings in our work may become simply things which we say 'underpin' our more complex work, or worse, things which we might even take for granted as happening appropriately or well in the course of therapeutic practice. But what the chapters which follow in this section of the book hopefully illustrate is the importance of the things which occur in all therapeutic encounters, and run across work with all of our clients, and in all of our therapeutic models. The 'common factors' literature in counselling and psychotherapy has highlighted the importance of the therapeutic relationship, and the strength of that relationship has been found to correlate with the outcome of our therapeutic endeavours (Horvarth, Del Re, Flückiger and Symonds, 2011). Similarly, research has found that a therapist's management of those micro processes of therapy, such as communicating about their understanding or formulation to a client, and successfully dealing with therapeutic endings, have been found to have an important impact on the way in which our clients experience their work with us (Etherington and Bridges, 2011; Pain, Chadwick and Abba, 2008). From a training point of view, these skills are also often challenging for therapists to master, and can involve a great amount of work to develop.

It seems, therefore, that the skills reflected upon in the chapters in this section of the *Handbook* might not be best described as 'basic', but rather as 'core' to what we do and our day-to-day practice as therapists. As noted earlier, different models will indeed take slightly different approaches to the core elements of therapy, such as presenting a different understanding of what assessment might look like, or what the nature of the therapeutic relationship is. Nevertheless, these processes and skills are fundamental to our work and the importance of the micro processes involved in such elements of therapy should not be downplayed or neglected. Hopefully the chapters which follow will prove useful in focusing attention on these important parts of our work.

QUESTIONS

1. The therapeutic relationship is of significant importance in predicting outcomes in counselling and psychotherapy. What do you think are the key components in a 'good' therapeutic relationship?
2. 'Assessment' and 'formulation' are terms which have sometimes been associated with a more medical or diagnostic approach to human distress. How do you understand these concepts/practices in your work in counselling and psychotherapy?
3. Imagine you are a client coming to therapy for the first time, with no background in psychotherapy or counselling. What would you expect from the first meeting with a therapist? Are there are particular things about the 'process' of counselling you would want to know?

REFERENCES

Egan, G. (2014). *The Skilled Helper: A Problem Management and Opportunity-Development Approach to Helping* (10th ed.). Belmont, CA: Brooks/Cole, Cengage Learning.

Etherington, K. and Bridges, N. (2011). Narrative case study research: On endings and six session reviews. *Counselling and Psychotherapy Research*, 11(1), 11–22.

Gillon, E. (2013). Assessment and formulation. In M. Cooper, M. O'Hara, P.F. Schmid and A. Bohart (Eds.). *The Handbook of Person-centred Psychotherapy and Counselling* (2nd ed.) (pp. 410–421). Basingstoke: Palgrave Macmillan.

Hill, C.E. (2014). *Helping Skills: Facilitating Exploration, Insight, and Action* (4th ed.). Washington, DC: American Psychological Association.

Horvath, A.O., Del Re, A.C., Flückiger, C. and Symonds, D. (2011). Alliance in individual psychotherapy. *Psychotherapy*, 48, 9–16.

Pain, C.M., Chadwick, P. and Abba, N. (2008). Clients' experience of case formulation in cognitive behaviour therapy for psychosis. *British Journal of Clinical Psychology*, 47, 127–138.

Simms, J. (2011). Case formulation within a person-centred framework: An uncomfortable fit? *Counselling Psychology Review*, 26(2), 24–37.

3.2 THE CLIENT–THERAPIST RELATIONSHIP

WILLIAM B. STILES

OVERVIEW AND KEY POINTS

Practitioners and researchers agree that the client–therapist relationship is a core aspect of counselling and psychotherapy. This chapter reviews three conceptual approaches to the relationship: psychodynamic, person-centred, and psychometric.

- Psychodynamic authors suggest the relationship encompasses (a) the real relationship, (b) the transference, and (c) the working alliance.
- Person-centred authors focus on three necessary and sufficient therapist-provided conditions in a healing relationship: (a) genuineness, (b) unconditional positive regard, and (c) accurate empathy.
- Psychometric authors have conceptually and statistically distinguished components of the alliance: (a) the affective bond between client and therapist, (b) agreement on the goals of treatment, and (c) agreement on treatment tasks.

INTRODUCTION

Most practitioners would probably agree that the client–therapist relationship is central to counselling and psychotherapy. It is also one of the most researched and conceptualized aspects of therapy, and the sprawling literature continues to expand (e.g., Muran and Barber, 2010; Norcross, 2011). What follows is a personal selection and understanding.

Research and theory about the relationship takes place in the context of the repeated observation that sharply contrasting treatment techniques and theoretical approaches are similarly effective (Lambert and Ogles, 2004; Wampold and Imel, 2015), or 'Everybody has won and all must have prizes' (The Dodo, quoted by Carroll, 1946 [1865]; applied to comparative psychotherapy outcome research by Rosenzweig in 1936 and since then by many others).

The concept of the therapist–client relationship offers to resolve the paradox. Across diverse treatments and populations, the strength of the relationship has been the most consistent process correlate of treatment outcome (Horvath et al., 2011). If the relationship is a major active ingredient or a necessary condition for progress, as some suggest, then it is understandable that many treatment approaches can be effective.

But what is the client–therapist relationship? I review three illustrative conceptual approaches: psychodynamic, person-centred, and psychometric.

PSYCHODYNAMIC CONCEPTS OF THE RELATIONSHIP

Psychodynamic theorists have focused on a distinction between the real relationship and the transference (Freud, 1958; Zetzel, 1956). Some have further distinguished the working alliance (Gelso and Carter, 1994; Greenson, 1965). Gelso and Carter (1994) offered the following relatively succinct version:

> The real relationship is seen as having two defining features: genuineness and realistic perceptions. Genuineness is defined as the ability and willingness to be what one truly is in the relationship – to be authentic, open, and honest. Realistic perceptions refer to those perceptions that are uncontaminated by transference distortions and other defences. In other words, the therapy participants see each other in an accurate, realistic way. (Gelso and Carter, 1994: 297)

> The transference configuration … consists of both client transference and therapist counter-transference. … Transference is the repetition of past conflicts with significant others, such that feelings, attitudes, and behaviors belonging rightfully in those earlier relationships are displaced onto the therapist; and counter-transference is the therapist's transference to the client's material, both to the transference and the nontransference communications presented by the client. (Gelso and Carter, 1994: 297)

> [The working] alliance may be seen as the alignment or joining of the reasonable self or ego of the client and the therapist's analyzing or 'therapizing' self or ego for the purpose of the work. (Gelso and Carter, 1994: 297)

Psychodynamic interest has focused on interpreting the transference as a way of understanding how past hurts can be manifested as problems in the present. Theoretically, problematic relational patterns that brought the client into treatment may be re-experienced and acted out within the therapeutic relationship. The relationship thus gives the client a safe context to resolve conflicts that have been interfering with daily life outside therapy. Positive feelings for the therapist may also represent transference, and

the analysing positive transference can be an effective path to insight (e.g., Brenner, 1979; see Messer and Wolitsky, 2010). Alternatively, from an object relations perspective: the therapist might serve as good internal object; taking in the therapist in this way might be transformative in ways that do not require insight (Geller and Farber, 1993; Zuroff and Blatt, 2006).

Kohut (1971, 1977) distinguished between mirroring transferences, in which the therapist is experienced as an extension of the self, as a twin, or as an appendage whose function is mainly to support the client's (unrealistically) grandiose views of the self, and idealizing transferences, in which the client draws strength or reassurance from being associated with an idealized therapist's exaggerated virtues. In this view, progress may come when the therapist fails to fulfil these unrealistic expectations. The client's resulting frustration brings the expectations into awareness, making it possible to examine and change them.

Manifestations of the transference in treatment can be dramatic, and observations of transference phenomena have figured centrally in the psychoanalytic literature since Freud's case studies of Anna O. and Dora (Breuer and Freud, 1957; Freud, 1953). Reliable measurement has proved more difficult, however. Probably the most sustained and best-known effort has been the work on the core conflictual relationship theme (CCRT; e.g., Luborsky and Crits-Christoph, 1998; Tishby and Wiseman, 2014). CCRT research assesses patients' stories of relationships, reasoning that a client's stories about relationships in or out of therapy are likely to manifest repeated patterns or themes that reveal the core conflicts.

PERSON-CENTRED CONCEPTS OF THE RELATIONSHIP

Whereas psychodynamic theorists may view the transference as a distorted fragment impinging on a distinct real relationship, person-centred theorists have tended to take a holistic, here-and-now perspective (Rogers, 1957, 1980). Yes, people may transfer attitudes and strong feelings from past relationships to present ones, but to consider these as unreal is to deny or derogate the immediacy of the client's actual experience. Rather than seeking to judge and interpret such experiences, the therapist's job is to understand and accept them. Fully experiencing, acknowledging and stating ('symbolizing') experiences allows them to be considered and re-valued in light of current reality (see Greenberg's (1994) commentary on Gelso and Carter (1994)). The value placed on any particular experience is up to the client, not the therapist or the theory. This conceptualization directs attention not to the historical development of the client's problems but instead to the relationship conditions that the therapist provides within the therapy.

Rogers' (1957: 95) six therapist-provided 'necessary and sufficient conditions of therapeutic personality change' have been popularly reduced to three, which may be stated succinctly (my gloss, not Rogers') as: (1) be yourself; (2) trust the client; and (3) listen. Although these facilitative conditions, or attitudes, can be stated simply, they can be endlessly unpacked. Here is a sample of how Rogers did it:

> The first element [be yourself] could be called genuineness, realness, or congruence. The more the therapist is himself or herself in the relationship, putting up no professional front or personal façade, the greater is the likelihood that the client will change and grow in a constructive manner. This means that the therapist is openly being the feelings and attitudes that are flowing within at the moment.
>
> The second attitude of importance in creating a climate for change [trust the client] is acceptance, or caring, or prizing – what I have called 'unconditional positive regard.' When the therapist is experiencing a positive, acceptant attitude toward whatever the client is at that moment, therapeutic movement or change is more likely to occur.
>
> The third facilitative aspect of the relationship [listen] is empathic understanding. This means that the therapist senses accurately the feelings and personal meanings that the client is experiencing and communicates this understanding to the client. (Rogers, 1980: 115–116)

Easy to say, hard to do. From a practitioner's perspective, being genuine (and distinguishing this from self-serving disclosure), accepting the client (who may hold beliefs or engage in practices contrary to your personal principles), and understanding empathically (when the client tells endless bland stories) can be difficult and taxing. Furthermore, under some circumstances, the conditions can be contradictory. For example, if I disapprove (suicide, child molesters, etc.), can I listen empathically, and does being genuine demand that I disclose it? Fortunately, the theory suggests that perfect adherence is not required. Beneficial effects can be expected to the degree that the conditions are fulfilled.

From the perspective of a therapist or a supervisor, the three conditions may seem distinct and even contradictory, but from the perspective of an external observer, they often seem to merge. Although early attempts to measure therapist congruence, unconditional positive regard, and accurate empathy seemed promising, reviewers of the research found fault (Lambert et al., 1978; Mitchell et al., 1977). Nevertheless, research on these three core conditions continues to accumulate (Elliott et al., 2011; Farber and Doolin, 2011; Kolden et al., 2011).

Some person-centred authors have described fully encountering the client as therapeutic work at *relational depth* (Knox et al., 2013; Mearns and Cooper, 2005; Mearns and Schmid, 2006; Schmid and Mearns, 2006). They suggest that therapy's power to transform proceeds from the therapist's ability to 'to engage the client at a more fundamental, existential level,' so that clients 'feel met at the deepest levels at which they experience themselves' (Schmid and Mearns, 2006: 178).

PSYCHOMETRIC CONCEPTS OF THE ALLIANCE

In a seminal conceptualization, Bordin (1979) characterized the alliance as multidimensional, encompassing (a) the affective bond between client and therapist, (b) agreement on the goals of treatment, and (c) agreement on treatment tasks, or means of achieving those goals. Subsequent alliance researchers have constructed scales to assess the dimensions, for example, using ratings on items like 'I feel friendly towards my therapist' to measure bond or 'I am clear as to what my therapist wants me to do in these sessions' to measure agreement on tasks. Typically, investigators have administered a pool of such items to clients, therapists or external raters and then grouped the items into scales using factor analysis or related statistical techniques. Results have offered some support for the multidimensional accounts (i.e., the factors often appear to correspond to conceptual dimensions). The factors tend to be substantially intercorrelated, however (see, for example, Agnew-Davies et al., 1998).

Although some have used Bordin's (1979) concepts of bond, agreement on tasks, and agreement on goals (notably Horvath, 1994), researchers have not concurred on the boundaries of the alliance construct or on the number or names of the dimensions. Some have combined or re-labelled Bordin's dimensions, for example, combining agreement on tasks and agreement on goals as working strategy consensus (Gaston, 1991) or partnership (Agnew-Davies et al., 1998). And others have added dimensions, such as patient working capacity and therapist understanding and involvement (Gaston, 1991; Marmar et al., 1989); patient resistance (hostile, defensive), patient motivation (acknowledged problems, wanted to overcome them), and therapist intrusiveness (fostered dependency, imposed own values) (Hartley and Strupp, 1983); confident collaboration (Hatcher and Barends, 1996); or openness and client initiative (Agnew-Davies et al., 1998). Each such additional dimension has been defined and measured by a set of self-report items. Research has not consistently supported the differentiation of the varied dimensions, however, and many researchers have ignored the dimensional scores, using a single total or aggregate score to assess the alliance.

The alliance has sustained intense interest from researchers because of its replicated positive correlations with measures of psychotherapy outcome (Horvath et al., 2011; Leahy, 2008). Moreover, there is growing evidence that the often-observed differences in the effectiveness of different therapists may be attributable to their differing ability to form strong alliances (Baldwin et al., 2007; Crits-Christoph et al., 2009; Stiles and Horvath, 2017).

Obtaining differentiated measurements of the alliance may require observational approaches (see Luborsky, 1976). Ribeiro et al. (2013) have developed an observational measure of the relationship based on the degree to which therapists work within (or outside) the client's therapeutic zone of proximal development, defined as the space between the client's current therapeutic developmental level and their potential therapeutic developmental level that can be reached in collaboration with the therapist. Observational coding systems have also been developed to provide more differentiated assessments of the alliance in family therapy (Escudero et al., 2010) and child therapy (McLeod and Weisz, 2005).

Training therapists to improve relationships forces therapists and trainers to confront and enact the complexities. Crits-Christoph et al. (2006) have shown that therapists can be trained to improve alliances, with likely positive influences on outcomes. Safran and Muran (2000) designed a successful treatment around improving relationships (see, for example, Safran et al., 2014).

Some significant short-term fluctuations in the alliance have been described as *rupture–repair sequences* (Eubanks-Carter et al., 2010; Safran and Muran, 2000). Ruptures may occur when previously hidden negative feelings emerge or when the therapist makes a mistake or fails to act as the client expects or wishes. If the therapist recognizes the rupture, it may offer an opportunity for therapeutic interpersonal learning, as ruptures in the therapy relationship may recapitulate the client's relationship difficulties outside therapy. More generally, recognizing, acknowledging and overcoming relational difficulties can provide valuable experiential learning in the here-and-now of the session.

REFERENCES

Agnew-Davies, R., Stiles, W.B., Hardy, G.E., Barkham, M. and Shapiro, D.A. (1998) Alliance structure assessed by the Agnew Relationship Measure (ARM). *British Journal of Clinical Psychology*, 37: 155–172.

Baldwin, S.A., Wampold, B.E. and Imel, Z.E. (2007) Untangling the alliance–outcome correlation: Exploring the relative importance of therapist and patient variability in the alliance. *Journal of Consulting and Clinical Psychology*, 75: 842–852.

Bordin, E.S. (1979) The generalizability of the psychoanalytic concept of working alliance. *Psychotherapy: Theory, Research, and Practice*, 16: 252–260.

Brenner, C. (1979) Working alliance, therapeutic alliance, and transference. *Journal of the American Psychoanalytic Association*, 27 (supplement): 137–157.

Breuer, J. and Freud, S. (1957) *Studies on Hysteria*. New York: Basic Books.

Carroll, L. (1946 [1865]) *Alice's Adventures in Wonderland*. New York: Random House.

Crits-Christoph, P., Gallop, R., Temes, C.M., Woody, G., Ball, S.A., Martino, S. and Carroll, K.M. (2009) The alliance in motivational enhancement therapy and counseling as usual for substance use problems. *Journal of Consulting and Clinical Psychology*, 77: 1125–1135.

Crits-Christoph, P., Gibbons, M.B.C., Crits-Christoph, K., Narducci, J., Schamberger, M. and Gallop, R. (2006) Can therapists be trained to improve their alliances? A preliminary study of alliance-fostering psychotherapy, *Psychotherapy Research*, 16: 268–281.

Elliott, R., Bohart, A.C., Watson, J.C. and Greenberg, L.S. (2011) Empathy. *Psychotherapy*, 48: 43–49.

Escudero, V., Heatherington, L. and Friedlander, M.L. (2010) Therapeutic alliances and alliance building in family therapy. In J.C. Muran and J.P. Barber (eds), *The Therapeutic Alliance: An Evidence-based Approach to Practice and Training* (pp. 240–262). New York: Guilford Press.

Eubanks-Carter, C., Muran, J.C. and Safran, J.D. (2010) Alliance ruptures and resolution. In J.C. Muran and J.P. Barber (eds), *The Therapeutic Alliance: An Evidence-based Approach to Practice and Training* (pp. 74–94). New York: Guilford Press.

(Continued)

(Continued)

Farber, B.A. and Doolin, E.M. (2011) Positive regard and affirmation. *Psychotherapy*, 48: 58–64.

Freud, S. (1953) Fragments of an analysis of a case of hysteria. In J. Strachey (ed. and trans.), *The Standard Edition of the Complete Psychological Works of Sigmund Freud* (Vol. 7, pp. 3–122). London: Hogarth Press (original work published 1905).

Freud, S. (1958) The dynamics of transference. In J. Strachey (ed. and trans.), *The Standard Edition of the Complete Psychological Works of Sigmund Freud* (Vol. 12, pp. 99–108). London: Hogarth Press (original work published 1912).

Gaston, L. (1991) Reliability and criterion-related validity of the California Psychotherapy Alliance Scales – patient version. *Psychological Assessment*, 3: 68–74.

Geller, J.D. and Farber, B.A. (1993) Factors influencing the process of internalization in psychotherapy. *Psychotherapy Research*, 3: 166–180.

Gelso, C.J. and Carter, J.A. (1994) Components of the psychotherapy relationship: Their interaction and unfolding during treatment. *Journal of Counseling Psychology*, 41: 296–306.

Greenberg, L.S. (1994) What is 'real' in the relationship? Comment on Gelso and Carter (1994). *Journal of Counseling Psychology*, 41: 307–309.

Greenson, R.R. (1965) The working alliance and the transference neuroses. *Psychoanalysis Quarterly*, 34: 155–181.

Hartley, D.E. and Strupp, H.H. (1983) The therapeutic alliance: Its relationship to outcome in brief psychotherapy. In J. Masling (ed.), *Empirical Studies of psychoanalytic Theories* (Vol. 1, pp. 1–37). Hillsdale, NJ: Erlbaum.

Hatcher, R.L. and Barends, A.W. (1996) Patients' view of the alliance in psychotherapy: Exploratory factor analysis of three alliance measures. *Journal of Consulting and Clinical Psychology*, 64: 1326–1336.

Horvath, A.O. (1994) Empirical validation of Bordin's pantheoretical model of the alliance: The Working Alliance Inventory perspective. In A.O. Horvath and L.S. Greenberg (eds), *The Working Alliance: Theory, Research and Practice* (pp. 109–128). New York: Wiley.

Horvath, A.O., Del Re, A.C., Flückiger, C. and Symonds, D. (2011) Alliance in individual psychotherapy. *Psychotherapy*, 48: 9–16.

Knox, R., Murphy, D., Wiggins, S. and Cooper, M. (2013) *Relational Depth: New Persepctives and Developments*. London: Palgrave Macmillan.

Kohut, M. (1971) *The Analysis of the Self*. New York: International Universities Press.

Kohut, M. (1977) *The Restoration of the Self*. New York: International Universities Press.

Kolden, G.G., Klein, M.H., Wang, C.-C. and Austin, S.B. (2011) Congruence/genuineness. *Psychotherapy*, 48: 65–71.

Lambert, M.J., DeJulio, S.S. and Stein, D.M. (1978) Therapist interpersonal skills: Process, outcome, methodological considerations, and recommendations for future research. *Psychological Bulletin*, 85: 467–489.

Lambert, M.J. and Ogles, B.M. (2004) The efficacy and effectiveness of psychotherapy. In M.J. Lambert (ed.), *Bergin and Garfield's Handbook of Psychotherapy and Behavior Change* (5th ed.). New York: Wiley.

Leahy, R.L. (2008) The therapeutic relationship in cognitive behavioural therapy. *Behavioural and Cognitive Psychotherapy*, 36: 769–777.

Luborsky, L. (1976) Helping alliances in psychotherapy: The groundwork for a study of their relationship to its outcome. In J.L. Claghorn (ed.), *Successful Psychotherapy* (pp. 92–116). New York: Brunner/Mazel.

Luborsky, L. and Crits-Christoph, P. (1998) *Understanding Transference: The Core-Conflictual Relationship Theme Method* (2nd ed.). Washington, DC: American Psychological Association.

Marmar, C.R., Weiss, D.S. and Gaston, L. (1989) Towards the validation of the California Therapeutic Alliance Rating System. *Psychological Assessment*, 1: 46–52.

McLeod, B.D. and Weisz, J.R. (2005) The therapy process observational coding system-alliance scale: Measure characteristics and prediction of outcome in usual clinical practice. *Journal of Consulting and Clinical Psychology*, 73: 323–333.

Mearns, D. and Cooper, M. (2005) *Working at Relational Depth in Counselling and Psychotherapy*. London: Sage.

Mearns, D. and Schmid, P.F. (2006) Being-with and being-counter. Relational depth: The challenge of fully meeting the client. *Person-Centered and Experiential Psychotherapies*, 5: 255–265.

Messer, S.B. and Wolitsky, D.L. (2010) A psychodynamic perspective on the therapeutic alliance. In J.C. Muran and J.P. Barber (eds), *The Therapeutic Alliance: An Evidence-based Approach to Practice and Training* (pp. 97–122). New York: Guilford Press.

Mitchell, K.M., Bozarth, J.D. and Krauft, C.C. (1977) A reappraisal of the therapeutic effectiveness of accurate empathy, non-possessive warmth and genuineness. In A.S. Gurman and A.M. Razin (eds), *Effective Psychotherapy: A Handbook of Research* (pp. 482–502). New York: Pergamon Press.

Muran, J.C. and Barber, J.P. (eds) (2010) *The Therapeutic Alliance: An Evidence-based Approach to Practice and Training*. New York: Guilford Press.

Norcross, J.C. (ed.) (2011) *Psychotherapy Relationships that Work: Evidence-based Responsiveness* (2nd ed.). New York: Oxford University Press.

Ribeiro, E.M., Ribeiro, A.P., Gonçalves, M.M., Horvath, A.O. and Stiles, W.B. (2013) How collaboration in therapy becomes therapeutic: The Therapeutic Collaboration Coding System. *Psychology and Psychotherapy: Theory, Research, and Practice*, 86: 294–314.

Rogers, C.R. (1957) The necessary and sufficient conditions of therapeutic personality change. *Journal of Consulting Psychology*, 21: 95–103.

Rogers, C.R. (1980) *A Way of Being*. Boston, MA: Houghton Mifflin.

Rosenzweig, S. (1936) Some implicit common factors in diverse methods of psychotherapy. *American Journal of Orthopsychiatry*, 6: 412–415.

Safran, J.D. and Muran, J.C. (2000) *Negotiating the Therapeutic Alliance: A Relational Treatment Guide*. New York: Guilford Press.

Safran, J., Muran, J.C., Demaria, A., Boutwell, C., Eubanks-Carter, C. and Winston, A. (2014) Investigating the impact of alliance-focused training on interpersonal process and therapists' capacity for experiential reflection. *Psychotherapy Research*, 24: 269–285.

Schmid, P.F. and Mearns, D. (2006) Being-with and being-counter: Person-centered therapy as an in-depth co-creative process of personalization. *Person-Centered and Experiential Psychotherapies*, 5: 174–190.

Stiles, W.B. and Horvath, A.O. (2017) Appropriate responsiveness as a contribution to therapist effects. In L. Castonguay and C.E. Hill (eds), *How and why are some therapists better than others? Understanding therapist effects* (pp. 71–84). Washington, DC: American Psychological Association.

Tishby, O. and Wiseman, H. (2014) Types of countertransference dynamics: An exploration of their impact on the client–therapist relationship. *Psychotherapy Research*, 24, 360–375.

Wampold, B.E. and Imel, Z.E. (2015) *The Great Psychotherapy Debate: Research Evidence for What Works in Psychotherapy* (2nd ed.). New York: Routledge.

Zetzel, E.R. (1956) Current concepts of transference. *International Journal of Psychoanalysis*, 37: 369–376.

Zuroff, D.C. and Blatt, S.J. (2006) The therapeutic relationship in brief treatment of depression: Contributions to clinical improvement and enhanced adaptive capacities. *Journal of Consulting and Clinical Psychology*, 74, 130–140.

RECOMMENDED READING

1. Norcross, J.C. (ed.) (2011) *Psychotherapy Relationships that Work: Evidence-based Responsiveness* (2nd ed.). New York: Oxford University Press.

A compilation of relationship elements that have demonstrated effectiveness.

2. Muran, J.C. and Barber, J.P. (eds) (2010) *The Therapeutic Alliance: An Evidence-based Approach to Practice and Training*. New York: Guilford Press.

Summaries of clinical and scientific thinking about the therapist–client relationship by authors active in the field.

3. Rogers, C.R. (1957) The necessary and sufficient conditions of therapeutic personality change. *Journal of Consulting Psychology*, 21: 95–103.

The classic description of the necessary and sufficient therapist-provided relationship conditions for successful psychotherapy from a person-centred perspective.

ASSESSMENT

BILJANA VAN RIJN

OVERVIEW AND KEY POINTS

The aim of this chapter is to introduce and begin to explore the assessment process in counselling and psychotherapy. As well as suggesting a definition and aims of assessment, we will also consider a possible structure and ways of conducting the sessions, and revisit some of the ethical values and principles underlying it. I see assessment as a collaborative and reflective process, which at the beginning of therapy has a purpose of ensuring beneficence and integrity of the therapeutic engagement. I will illustrate different aspects of assessment by giving clinical vignettes for your reflection. They are based on my experience as a psychotherapist and the work of a large community clinic at Metanoia Institute in London, where I teach and supervise clinical assessors. My aim is to engage you in a dialogue and reflection on your clinical practice and assist you in developing a style and structure of assessment that most suits your own practice and work environment.

The following are the chapter summary points:

- Assessment is a therapeutic process which is usually the most focused at the beginning of counselling and leads to a decision by the client and the counsellor about engaging in the counselling process. Its main aim is to ensure, as far as possible, that a client is entering into a counselling process that can be beneficial for them.
- An assessment session usually has a focus and a degree of structure. It contains some information gathering, clarification of the main issues the client is bringing to therapy, and beginnings of the therapeutic agreement and formulation.
- Counselling contexts have implications for assessments decision and outcomes. Establishing personal or organisational limitations of the service and professional competence need to be a part of making decisions about assessment outcomes.
- The therapeutic relationship starts to take shape within the assessment process. Reflection on its process and experience could be valuable within the session and a source of information about the future working alliance.
- Risk assessment needs to start with a recognition of the areas and the severity of risk, as well as protective factors, in a client's life. Risk issues could involve: risk of suicide and self-harm; risk of violence and harm to others; safeguarding of vulnerable adults and child protection; and mental health issues and crises.

WHAT IS ASSESSMENT?

Assessment is a therapeutic process which, at the beginning of counselling, leads to a specific outcome, a decision by the client and the counsellor about engaging in the counselling process. This usually gives a particular intensity to the initial sessions and highlights the importance of structure and focus, to best support the client at the time when they are potentially entering into an unknown.

Malan (1979) defined assessment in relation to its tasks of **finding out what the problem is, how it developed** and **what should be done about it**. This definition summarises the focus of the initial sessions and links assessment to formulation and treatment planning.

Historically, there has been an uneasy relationship between humanistic counselling and the idea of assessment, and concern that it would lead to labelling and taking power away from the client. These are legitimate considerations and ethical issues of sharing power, transparency and collaboration are essential in underpinning the assessment process.

WHY DO WE ASSESS?

The primary aims of assessment are linked to ensuring, as far as possible, that a client is entering into a counselling process that can be of benefit to them. That means that a counsellor needs to be able to develop an understanding of the core and the presenting issues for the client and make a decision about their ability to meet those needs. For this reason, an assessment session involves some gathering of information about the client and their circumstances.

CASE STUDY

Ellie is a woman in her late twenties. She recently had Cognitive Behaviour Therapy (CBT) at her local Improving Access to Psychological Therapy (IAPT) service. She found it helpful to talk to someone and is now looking for longer-term therapy. She described herself as 'a worrier', but this had recently got out of hand. She described becoming so anxious that she burst into tears at work and had to leave the office. Her job as a Personal Assistant in a demanding environment was relatively recent and she wanted to show that she was able to cope with it. Ellie has been off sick since that day and felt worried about going back to work. She was frequently thinking about dying and imagining her own funeral. She has been feeling very low in this period and spent most of the days sleeping. Ellie has a support network of friends and family, but she hasn't been using them. She lives alone and has avoided social contact while she was off sick. She also found it difficult to care for herself. Her General Practitioner (GP) has prescribed anti-depressants.

In this case study, Ellies's current circumstances seem to show that depression and anxiety were her primary issues. However, in order to understand her experience better, we might also want to find out how these problems developed and whether they have any resonances in her history.

CASE STUDY (CONTINUED)

Ellie's father was a gambler. He left home when she was two years old and her mother ended up with a lot of his debt. They became homeless for a while and then had to move several times. Although Ellie doesn't remember much of that period, she remembers her mother's struggle to make ends meet. Ellie worried about her mum and tried to be a good daughter for her. She always did her best and worked hard at home and at school. Ellie didn't get on with her sister, whom she described as 'wild' when she was a teenager. Her mother and her sister both live nearby.

Ellie's history suggests early roots to her anxiety and an adaptive strategy of working hard to maintain psychological security. It seemed that at this stage in her life and career, that strategy was breaking down.

If this was your case, you might wish to consider how much support you or your service could provide for Ellie, and whether you might need to have contact with her GP if her depression intensified.

An assessment session is also a beginning of a counselling relationship. If a counsellor is assessing her own clients, an assessment session will be a process by which some of the groundwork for the working alliance will be established.

CASE STUDY (CONTINUED)

Ellie seemed quiet in the assessment session. She responded to questions but did not elaborate on them. She seemed very polite and pleasant. The counsellor liked Ellie, but found it difficult to engage with her and started to feel very drowsy during the session. However, she felt able to work with her and thought that her own drowsiness related to Ellie's depression and psychological withdrawal. She thought that Ellie's internal world was probably very different from the face she presented to the world and that they needed to build trust and safety to allow her to express herself. She agreed with Ellie about the importance of working for a longer period.

HOW TO CONDUCT AN ASSESSMENT SESSION?

An assessment session usually needs to have a focus and a degree of structure and contain a certain amount of information gathering. However, the session itself is not expected to follow a particular format, but can be facilitated by the counsellor to meet these aims while providing space for the client to tell their story. In a previous publication (Bager-Charleson and Van Rijn, 2011) I have suggested that a useful therapeutic stance during assessment would involve:

- a balance between attentive listening and enquiry in order to both explore the relevant issues and gain information;
- a focus on core issues, without going too deeply into the painful emotional content, at the time when the therapeutic relationship is not established;
- establishing a therapeutic frame and boundaries.

It is often helpful to have a template for the assessment notes. You can use it to make notes during the session, or as a background to support you in structuring the session. A number of templates are currently available and in print, or you can create your own. Figure 3.3.1 is an abbreviated assessment form at Metanoia Counselling and Psychotherapy Service (MCPS), with a brief rationale for each category and prompts (see Figure 3.3.1).

In considering how to structure an assessment session in your own practice, you need to consider your work context, experience and the therapeutic approach.

ASSESSMENT CONTEXTS

Counselling assessments take place in different working environments and therapeutic contexts. Counsellors work in organisations where they might assess their own clients,

---

Date of assessment:

Reference number:

Name:

Address and contact details:

DOB:

GP details:

Notes: *Make a note if the client was not taken into the service, signposting to other services.*

PRESENTING ISSUES AND CURRENT CIRCUMSTANCES:

Rationale: *To understand the main focus for counselling, client's motivation, functioning and social support.*

Prompts:

What brings the client into therapy at this stage in their life?

How is the client functioning in social situations and work?

What is their support network like?

FAMILY BACKGROUND AND PERSONAL HISTORY:

Rationale: *Historical and developmental issues that could have an impact on counselling, such as trauma, attachment issues and developmental difficulties.*

Prompts:

Factual information: who was around, order of birth in the family, broadly based personal history, relationship history.

COUNSELLING/PSYCHOTHERAPY HISTORY:

Rationale: *Finding out how the client's previous experience of counselling might impact on the new relationship.*

Prompts:

Where? How long for? Was it helpful?

Give information if the client is new to therapy.

Answer queries.

```
┌─────────────────────────────────────────────────────────────────────────────┐
│  AIMS STATED:                                                                 │
│                                                                               │
│  Rationale: Beginning to formulate the counselling agreement.                 │
│  Prompts: What does the client want to achieve/focus on in counselling?       │
│                                                                               │
│  STATE OF HEALTH:                                                             │
│                                                                               │
│  Health/medication:                                                           │
│  Alcohol intake:                                                              │
│  Smoking:                                                                      │
│  Use of drugs:                                                                │
│  Other:                                                                        │
│  Rationale: Information about medical history, medication, and addictive behaviours. │
│  Prompts: Enquire about the details and any recent changes.                   │
└─────────────────────────────────────────────────────────────────────────────┘
```

Figure 3.3.1 An abbreviated assessment form at Metanoia Counselling and Psychotherapy Service (MCPS)

or conduct assessments in order to make referrals to other therapists within the service.

In organisational contexts, the expectations of an assessment session(s) are often more clearly defined and linked to the available services. Clients often have less choice about the type of counselling or counsellor they might see. The power imbalance could be perceived to be more in favour of the organisation.

If you are conducting an assessment within an organisation, it is important to be familiar with the scope and the limitations of the service. This often relates to the length of therapy, sessional fees, and experience and qualifications of the counsellors.

The scope of the service has implications for the clients who can be accepted by the service. The exclusion criteria, for example, might involve clients with addictions, with severe mental health issues such as psychosis, etc.

Assessments also take place in private practice, although they are often less formal and focus more on a mutual assessment between the therapist and the client. The power and the choice could be seen to be more in favour of the clients.

However, in this context it is also important for a counsellor to ask themselves similar questions about what they are able to provide and their limitations. This could relate to personal limitations that might become an obstacle to establishing a working alliance, such as a counsellor's unresolved personal issues. Limitations could also be professional, such as insufficient training or experience.

In both organisational and private practice settings, it is important to be familiar with mental health and emergency services, their provision and access requirements.

ASSESSMENT AND THE THERAPEUTIC RELATIONSHIP

The therapeutic alliance (Bordin, 1979) is an aspect of the therapeutic relationship related to collaboration between the therapist and the client, and their emotional connection. It has been widely researched as one of the common factors that is essential for successful outcomes (Lambert and Barley, 2002). As in any other relationship, both parties contribute to it, and research shows that clients are active in shaping the relationship (Bohart and Greaves Wade, 2013), as are the therapists (Baldwin, Wampold et al., 2007). This process starts during the assessment when the newness and the intensity of the first meeting often highlight both the client's and the therapist's habitual ways of relating. Reflection on this process can support the establishment of a good working alliance.

Some interventions during an assessment can assist the therapist and the client in thinking about how they experience each other and their expectations of the therapeutic process. The Pluralistic approach to therapy developed by Cooper and McLeod (2011) suggests that a meta-therapeutic dialogue would engage clients in talking about their expectations and preferences about directiveness, self-disclosure, focus of therapy, the amount of challenge, etc.

In an assessment session, as in any other time in counselling, we need to consider that a therapeutic relationship involves both individuals, their preferences and histories. The counsellor and the client bring to it all of who they are, including our broad cultural contexts, personal background and attachment styles (Bowlby, 1982). Our personal context as well as the cultural field will impact both the assessment session and the future therapeutic process.

ASSESSMENT OF RISK

Generally, the risk issues that therapists might come across include:

- a risk of the client's suicide and self-harm;
- violence and harm to others;
- safeguarding of vulnerable adults and child protection;
- mental health and crisis.

In the assessment session, the therapist usually starts with the recognition of the areas of risk and their potential severity, as well as the client's strengths or the protective factors in their life.

Assessing risk is an important part of ethical practice and continues throughout the work with the client. Reeves (2015) reflects on the complexity of these issues and suggests five different contexts for thinking about them. These are linked to: situations and events, the therapeutic relationship, the context in which therapy takes place, professional issues, and risks linked to the wellbeing of the practitioner.

This significantly widens the concept of risk assessment and places it within the context of the therapeutic process. We don't only need to reflect on the severity of risk the client presents with, but also the therapeutic relationship, our work environment and psychological readiness to take on a client (see also Reeves – Chapter 3.4, this volume).

WHAT DO YOU THINK ARE THE ISSUES OF RISK SIAN PRESENTS WITH?

Sian talked about her history of suicide attempts, but also self-harm through alcohol and food, and potentially putting herself in risky situations (for example, taking care of her physical safety when she drinks). Could there be a risk of aggression and violence in the 'heated arguments'?

WOULD YOU BE ABLE TO WORK WITH HER IN YOUR PROFESSIONAL CONTEXT?

Sian has already used her GP, who is aware of some of the issues. It might be beneficial to make contact with the GP to give her access to additional services that might be available, to help her manage the issues with eating and alcohol abuse, alongside therapy. Would you have sufficient resources to deal with all the risk issues she presents in your professional context?

WHAT MIGHT BE THE IMPLICATIONS FOR THE THERAPEUTIC RELATIONSHIP?

Sian has a pattern of interrupted relationships and has 'heated arguments' with the only person she is close to. This style of relating might have implications for the therapeutic relationship. How would you take care of yourself, as well as her, at times of conflict and disruption? It might be helpful to consider talking about managing these times during an assessment. You might also need to consider your own safety and support.

USING QUESTIONNAIRES IN ASSESSMENT

There is an increasing use of questionnaires for evaluation and monitoring of outcomes in current therapeutic practice.

This is the case within the health services, but also within other organisations that provide counselling and psychotherapy. In my experience of running a service which routinely evaluates practice, clients are often more enthusiastic about their use than practitioners. In ongoing counselling, questionnaires can be used for feedback as well as supporting clients in monitoring their own wellbeing. Questionnaires in assessment can help practitioners develop an overview about the level of the client's distress (CORE Information Management Systems Ltd., 2007), or recognise symptoms of mental health issues such as anxiety (Spitzer, Kroenke et al., 2006) and depression (Kroenke, Spitzer et al., 2001). These questionnaires can support us in developing an awareness of risk, which clients often initially disclose in questionnaires. Therapists often have misgivings about a questionnaire format and structure, and it may take a while to feel at ease with integrating them into your own assessment practice.

I have found it useful to think about questionnaires as one of the many ways clients can use to communicate their personal experience, and I engage with them in the same way as any other aspect of our dialogue. It might be helpful to reflect on how you might approach using them in your assessments.

ETHICAL ISSUES

Ethical issues in the assessment process follow the general counselling principles and values reflected in the British Association for Counselling and Psychotherapy (BACP) *Ethical Framework for the Counselling Professions* (BACP, 2016) and the United Kingdom Council for Psychotherapy (UKCP) *Ethical Principles and Code of Professional Conduct* (UKCP, 2009). Ethical considerations are at the heart of how we arrive at assessment decisions, issues of beneficence, therapist competence, and dealing with risk.

REFERENCES

BACP (2016). *Ethical Framework for the Counselling Professions*. Lutterworth: British Association for Counselling and Psychotherapy.

Bager-Charleson, S. and Van Rijn, B. (2011). *Understanding Assessment in Counselling and Psychotherapy*. London: Learning Matters.

Baldwin, S. A., Wampold, B. E., et al. (2007). Untangling the Alliance-Outcome Correlation: Exploring the Relative Importance of Therapist and Patient Variability in the Alliance. *Journal of Consulting & Clinical Psychology*, 75(6): 842–852.

Bohart, A. C. and Greaves Wade, A. (2013). The Client in Psychotherapy. In M. Lambert. *Bergin and Garfield's Handbook of Psychotherapy and Behaviour Change* (pp. 219–257). Hoboken, NJ: John Wiley & Sons.

Bordin, E. S. (1979). The Generalizability of the Psychoanalytic Concept of the Working Alliance. *Psychotherapy: Theory, Research, Practice*, 16(3): 252–260.

(Continued)

Bowlby, J. (1982). *Attachment and Loss. Vol. 1. Attachment*. London: Hogarth Press and the Institute of Psycho Analysis.

Cooper, M. and McLeod, J. (2011). *Pluralistic Counselling and Psychotherapy*. London: Sage.

CORE Information Management Systems Ltd. (2007). *CORE Net* (www.coreims-online.co.uk).

Kroenke, K., Spitzer, R. L., et al. (2001). The PHQ-9: Validity of a Brief Depression Severity Measure. *Journal of General and Internal Medicine*, 16: 606–613.

Lambert, M. J. and Barley, E. D. (2002). Research Summary on the Therapeutic Relationship and Psychotherapy Outcome. In J. C. Norcross (Ed.), *Psychotherapy Relationships that Work: Therapist Contributions and Responsiveness to Patients* (pp. 17–32). Oxford: Oxford University Press.

Malan, D. H. (1979). *Individual Psychotherapy and the Science of Psychodynamics*. [S.l.]. London: Butterworths.

Reeves, A. (2015). *Working with Risk in Counselling and Psychotherapy*. London: Sage.

Spitzer, R. L., Kroenke, R., et al. (2006). A Brief Measure for Assessing Generalized Anxiety Disorder: the GAD-7. *Archives of Internal Medicine*, 166: 1092–1097.

UKCP (2009). *UK Council for Psychotherapy, Ethical Principles and Code of Professional Conduct*. (www.psychotherapy.org.uk/code_of_ethics.html).

RECOMMENDED READING

1. Reeves, A. (2015). *Working with Risk in Counselling and Psychotherapy*. London: Sage.

This book recognises the importance of risk assessment for counsellors and psychotherapists. It gives information about different areas of risk and suggests ways of working with them.

2. Cooper, M. and McLeod, J. (2011). *Pluralistic Counselling and Psychotherapy*. London: Sage.

This book proposes an ethical and empowering therapeutic stance for practitioners of different orientations, which has a potential to develop therapists' responsiveness. Meta-therapeutic dialogue about the process of therapy is of particular relevance for assessments.

3. Van Rijn, B. (2015). *Assessment and Case Formulation in Counselling and Psychotherapy*. London: Sage.

This book presents ways of working with assessments, diagnosis and formulation in reflective therapeutic practice and within different theoretical orientations.

3.4 RISK: ASSESSMENT, EXPLORATION AND MITIGATION

ANDREW REEVES

OVERVIEW AND KEY POINTS

Risk is present in all work we undertake as therapists: from risks about harm to the client, or others, through to risk of unhelpful therapy with poor outcome for the client. Much of the literature, however, talks about risk from a binary perspective: risk is present, or it is not. In reality, of course, the task is not to determine whether risk is present or not, but rather to identify risks pertinent for that particular client and their situation and to find ways, collaboratively with the client in the context in which therapy is taking place, to work with it effectively. This chapter will consider risk from a number of different perspectives and explore ways in which it can be successfully engaged with.

- Risk, in different forms, is present in all therapeutic interactions and the task of the therapist is to identify those risks and work with them proactively, collaboratively with the client.
- While risk to 'self and others' is most commonly thought about by therapists in their work, other risks are present too. Risk can be considered from five primary perspectives: situational, relational, contextual, professional and personal. All need the full attention of therapists during the process of therapy.
- The identification and management of risk has been subject to much consideration, with the development of a large number of quantitative approaches to determine the presence and extent of risk. These are typically called 'risk assessment questionnaires', or similar.
- However, very few risk assessment tools have any meaningful efficacy in determining the extent of risk as it applies to the individual client. Rather, the imperative is for therapists to confidently and openly engage in a dialogue about risk with their clients.
- Working with risk, therefore, is always a collaborative process (assuming the client has capacity to engage in dialogue about their risk).

INTRODUCTION

Therapists learn about risk in their earliest training experiences. When introduced to the concept of contracting in therapy we are told that the contract not only informs and supports the therapeutic process, but also limits aspects of it too. Specifically, the contract is used to outline to clients the limits of confidentiality we are able to offer, typically limited by the potential for the client's suicide, or of harm to another, or through a statutory requirement, for example, terrorism. The term 'risk management' has seeped into popular parlance and is used in a variety of settings and contexts. However, in therapy, the notion of risk management implicitly seems to place the therapist in the position of *doing to* the client, as opposed to *doing with*. This chapter will explore the subtleties of risk, drawing together key practical considerations to help therapists work with risk confidently and effectively.

WHAT DO WE MEAN BY 'RISK'?

Too often in practice risk is viewed as a binary construct: a client is either at risk, or is not. This is clearly a simplistic view of risk that does not pay attention to the multifaceted and dynamic processes that underpin it. Likewise, risk is almost always associated with harm whereas, in many instances, it might also talk of opportunity for change. If we consider the *Oxford English Dictionary* (OED, 2016) definition of risk as 'exposure to the possibility of loss, injury, or other adverse of unwelcome circumstance', that synonymous relationship with harm is clear; the second definition offered, however, says risk can also be 'bold or daring'.

The meaning of risk is often rooted in the perception of it rather than the actuality. For example, were I minded to undertake an ascent of Mount Everest, those around me might perceive the risk to be of loss, injury or even death, whereas for me it might be challenge, opportunity and a life-changing experience. Or, if I were struggling with an intensely painful, chronic health condition and were contemplating suicide, those around me might perceive my risk of suicide to be dangerous, to be avoided and prevented, whereas suicide might for me mean escape, relief and the end of pain. As each individual projects onto the risk situation their own experience of it, society does the same and we might all think of how attitudes to risk change over time.

Previously (Reeves, 2015) I have defined risk across five primary parameters: situational, relational, contextual, professional and personal.

- *Situational risks*: those that often relate to client presentation, such as risk of suicide, self-injury, violence to others, terrorism.
- *Relational Risks*: those that typically refer to dynamics between therapist and client, such as sexual attraction, financial exploitation, unacknowledged or mismanaged transferential or countertransferential dynamics.
- *Contextual risks*: those that relate to the context in which therapy is located, such as an inconsistent or unequitable delivery of therapy, lack of clear ethical position, procedures of working practices inconsistent with the underpinning ethical principles of therapy.
- *Professional risks*: those that relate to the behaviour or actions of the therapist both inside and outside therapy, such as criminal prosecution, adverse publicity, therapist actions and behaviour while using social media.

- *Personal risks*: those that relate to the impact on the therapist of their work, such as vicarious trauma, relationship or family difficulties, meeting own needs in therapy as opposed to those of the client.

Using these parameters, as well as others, we can see how risk is a multilayered presence in our work that includes risk of harm to the client, but not exclusively. Clearly, different therapeutic scenarios might bring with them different types of risk. For example, consider Lesley.

LESLEY

Lesley is a 30-year-old female client. She sees a therapist working in private practice. She has a history of self-injury, although has not injured herself for several months. She talks of 'wanting to go to sleep but not wake up', but is clear that it is not her intention to act on her suicidal ideation. She has approached this particular therapist on a personal recommendation and has found them attentive, empathic and warm. On a couple of occasions Lesley has been unable to pay the agreed fee for therapy and her therapist has said it 'doesn't matter'. She sees this as evidence of her therapist's possible attraction to her.

There are a number of risks identified in this brief scenario:

- *Situational*: previous history of self-injury; expressed suicidal ideation (albeit without intent);
- *Relational*: unexpressed sexual attraction to the therapist, and particularly in the context of other contracted boundaries not being adhered to, e.g., payment;
- *Contextual*: therapy located in private practice (perhaps without written procedures for responding to client risk, etc.); vague contract in relation to payment (and potentially other factors);
- *Professional*: the therapist's failure to manage issues of fee appropriately and the danger of what might be communicated to and experienced by the client; unacknowledged client attraction to the therapist;
- *Personal*: currently possible rather than actual, but the mismanagement of the other four areas of risk has the potential to be personally damaging to the therapist at some point in the future.

The situation with Lesley demonstrates how risks can present in different forms, all with the potential for harm to either the client or the therapist. As such, we need to be mindful that risks can be present in a variety of ways and always be attentive to their presence.

PRESENTING RISKS IN THERAPY

Space does not allow for a comprehensive discussion of risks across all five parameters outlined. For the purposes of this chapter we will focus on situational risks. There are

a number of situational risks that most commonly present in therapy: risk of suicide, dangers associated with self-harm/injury, risk of harm to others, safeguarding and child protection, and mental health crisis.

RISK OF SUICIDE

See Chapter 6.21 (this volume) for a fuller discussion of working with risk of suicide. The potential for suicide is possibly the risk associated with the greatest degree of fear and anxiety for practitioners (Kottler, 2010; Panove, 1994; Reeves, 2010). Many organisations have in place procedural guidelines to support therapeutic work with suicidal clients. The reality is, and this is perhaps where the greatest degree of anxiety sits, that working with suicide risk is an inherently unpredictable endeavour and such procedural guidelines often fail in the face of such unpredictability, or at least do not provide the certainty that anxious practitioners or organisations go in search of.

DANGERS OF SELF-HARM/INJURY

See Chapter 6.21 (this volume) for a fuller discussion of working with self-harm/injury. While self-injury (cutting, burning, hair pulling, scratching, biting, etc.) and self-harm (eating disorders, reckless driving, over work, over exercise, lack of self-care) are typically conceptualised as ways in which clients (or indeed ourselves) cope with adversity and emotional turmoil, often when it has proved impossible to find alternative means of expression or the rights words to articulate distress, the perceived danger can sit heavily on therapists' shoulders. It is important to determine the line between self-harm/injury as a mechanism for self-support, and where it becomes potentially life-threatening, albeit in an unknown way to the client themselves.

RISK OF HARM TO OTHERS

The majority of therapists contract with their clients to act in the event of concern of harm, often meaning child protection. However, the risk of violence to others beyond child protection concerns is very present in therapy but one, I suspect, for which we receive little training to determine. A look at the available literature identifies some information from psychiatry and clinical psychology, but there is very little literature for therapists in helping them to determine levels of risk of violence and indicators for concern. If there were a 'poor relation' in the hierarchy of risk and the attention and thought it attracts, it would be this. I have offered some thoughts previously on this (Reeves, 2015: 72–85).

CHILD PROTECTION AND SAFEGUARDING

Unlike the wider risk of violence to others, child protection and safeguarding concern attract a great deal more attention and supportive literature. It is important to stress that the terms 'child protection' and 'safeguarding' are often used synonymously but are, in fact, distinct. Child protection is an important aspect of safeguarding but safeguarding itself is a wider term that encompasses a broader consideration, such as sexual, physical and emotional health. Additionally, there is provision in much of United Kingdom (UK) law for the safeguarding of vulnerable adults, defined in a 1997 consultation paper (Department of Health (DoH) and Home Office, 2000: 8–9) as:

> A person who may be in need of community care services by reason of mental or other disability, age or illness; and who is or may be unable to take of him or herself, or unable to protect him or herself against significant harm or exploitation.

A range of potential harm to vulnerable adults was also outlined:

- physical abuse
- sexual abuse
- psychological abuse
- financial or material abuse
- neglect or acts of omission
- discriminatory abuse (including racism, sexism, based on disability, etc.).

While not all working procedures or therapeutic contracts will make explicit reference to breaking confidentiality to safeguard vulnerable adults, most will limit confidentiality when there is evidence of child protection concerns.

MENTAL HEALTH CRISIS

It is difficult to define clearly what is meant by a 'mental health crisis' as it could include many presentations that would not, in and of themselves, present an immediate cause for concern in therapy. For example, high levels of distress, as a consequence of anxiety or depression, might not be uncommon for many practitioners. However, some presentations are more likely to cause concern and be perceived as a risk for the client, such as an emerging psychosis, or where there is evidence the client is in such distress they are unable, temporarily, to take responsibility for their own actions and wellbeing. In such situations many therapists would deem it appropriate to seek the input of other specialist services or, in extreme situations, may require that a statutory assessment under the Mental Health Act be undertaken.

RISK ASSESSMENT: QUANTITATIVE APPROACHES

In defining what we mean by risk and outlining some of the primary situational risks that might present in therapy, we are left with the core dilemma for many therapists: how to determine the *level* of risk and what action, subsequently, may be required. If an another invention is indicated, whether the client is able to consent to that intervention and, if not, how best to act while continuing to respect their autonomy, independence and wellbeing; finally, if another invention is indicated and the client is able to consent but refuses to do so, how the therapist should act then.

Many quantitative risk assessment tools have been developed to help apply science, and thus objectivity, to this process. That ultimately is the aim of such tools: the rigorous application of an evidence-based tool to help determine, objectively, the likelihood of the risk occurring (Surgenor, 2015). Due to the plethora of such tools developed by the risk assessment industry, there are too many to detail here. However, they draw on the research evidence that details risk factors (factors that make the risk more likely), while also working to identify protective factors (factors that make the risk less likely).

Such tools can be extremely helpful in providing the practitioner with a structure within which to formulate an understanding of the situation. However, the problem lies not in the tools themselves, but in how they are perceived by practitioners and organisations alike. The confidence vested in their ability to objectively and 'scientifically' judge a human situation is generally higher than the actuality of their ability of being able to do so. In other words, they are not quite as good at their job as we wish they were.

The National Institute for Health and Care Excellence (NICE, 2011: 29) says of such tools: 'The sensitivity and specificity of these scales are, at best, modest.'

It is important therefore, to use such tools as a means of informing decision-making processes and judgements about risk, but not to allow them to direct such judgements. Additionally, such tools can be extremely helpful in both structuring our thinking about risk and finding a way of beginning a discussion with our client about risk, particularly if we feel anxious about doing so.

RISK EXPLORATION: DISCOURSE-BASED APPROACHES

It is hard to overstress the importance of an open, transparent, honest and respectful dialogue with clients about risk. This can trigger anxieties in professionals who fear that a discussion about risk, such as a question about suicide, might appear clumsy, insensitive or, at worst, increase risk by putting the thought of harm into the client's mind when it was not there before. The unacknowledged countertransference (Leenaars, 2004) of working with risk is an important therapeutic consideration for therapists to attend to, in supervision, in therapy, with their manager and in their own self-reflections. Our philosophical position in relation to risk – our views and perspectives – can be powerfully informing in the work we do.

There are, of course, many ways in which such dialogues might be facilitated. Practitioners often look for a blueprint – a ready-made script – they can draw on at times of difficulty in sessions. This is impossible to provide, however, as a relational process is informed by the therapeutic relationship itself: the context in which that relationship is located, the nature of the therapist, the nature of the client, and the ways in which therapy-talk has been constructed between the two. The principle to follow, regardless of the risk being explored, is to be prepared to 'go there' and, as one therapist once described it, 'be brave'.

RISK MITIGATION: RESPONDING TO CONCERNS

Risk mitigation does not necessarily mean the eradication of risk, but rather for risk to be lessened sufficiently so that the threat of harm is reduced and the opportunity for change increased. As we have explored, times of risk can sometimes also present times of opportunity for change, and it is important these are identified and worked with too. The nature of the risk will profoundly inform the response needed. Some situational risks, in virtue of working policy or legislation, will require action on behalf of the therapist. For example, child protection concerns might require a referral to social care agencies because of a child protection policy in place in the organisation, while concerns about the potential for a terrorist act will require a confidential referral to the police, in virtue of the legislative requirements in the UK: some risks demand certain actions.

However, other situational risks allow for a greater scope of response. Making use of quantitative tools, opening a discussion about the presenting risk itself and exploring the meaning for the client and their hoped-for outcome can provide an important opportunity for the client to gain a greater sense of their distress. Interventions should focus on the client's capacity and willingness to take responsibility for their own safety and wellbeing so that, between sessions, they can practise ways in which they can respond to distress differently and more proactively. Indications that a client is unable or unwilling to take such steps might point to a situation where additional or different interventions are required.

COLLABORATIVE POSITIVE RISK-TAKING

Unless a client is deemed temporarily not to have capacity to make informed decisions about their wellbeing, perhaps through high levels of distress or underlying or emerging mental health distress (e.g., psychosis), we need to work with the agency of the client to help safeguard their, and others', wellbeing. The reality is that for most clients with capacity, it will not be the therapist who keeps the client safe, or others safe, but the actions and willingness of the client to act to self-support when away from sessions.

I outline the value of crisis plans – or 'keep safe' plans – in Chapter 6.21 (this volume) in relation to working with suicide and self-harm/injury. These plans can be used in response to other risks too, particularly the risk of violence to others. The same principles would apply in that the plan would be carefully negotiated and agreed in the session with the aim being to help the client take responsibility for their emotional wellbeing and actions, initially between sessions (where the plan can then be reviewed), but also thereafter once the therapy has finished. It is important to keep a number of therapeutic considerations in mind when working with clients collaboratively around risk (Reeves, 2015: 145):

- The client has the capacity to understand the nature and extent of the risk as it presents.
- The client is willing and able to work collaboratively with the therapist around risk.
- The therapist understands the nature and extent of the risk as it presents.

- The therapist is willing and able to work collaboratively with the client around risk.
- Any actions and agreements are made within the context of any contract in place for therapy, or variations are clearly negotiated and agreed to beforehand and remain ethically informed.
- No expectations or agreements should disregard any existing policy or practice expectation around how to respond to risk situations.
- Any actions or agreements are regularly reviewed and fully explored in supervision and line management discussions, if appropriate.
- All actions and agreements are recorded, in writing or in a format accessible to the client, while respecting their confidentiality.

Such crisis plans relate to the wellbeing of the client, or to support them in managing potential violence to others. However, the wellbeing of others is also critical and plans should not be used without careful consideration of the likely impact on other people. For example, therapists should not use plans as a means of managing child protection concerns or where violence is actual and ongoing. In such situations, therapists should act in accordance with their working policies and agreements made at the outset of therapy. In most circumstances, child protection concerns are likely to be raised with safeguarding leads (if working with children and young people) or social care departments. It is difficult to be too definitive with respect to actual or ongoing violence, as some settings would have a policy of breaking confidentiality to the police, whereas others would hold the client's confidentiality. It is important to be clear as to the organisation's expectations in such situations, or to have clearly thought about your own position if working independently.

If practitioners are able to support themselves – their anxieties and fears of 'getting it wrong' – in their work, they can also provide a safe and facilitative opportunity for clients not only to understand the nature of the risk they find themselves in more fully, but to use those opportunities to make important changes.

REFERENCES

Kottler, J. A. (2010). *On Being a Therapist* (4th ed.). San Francisco, CA: Jossey-Bass.
Leenaars, A. A. (2004). *Psychotherapy with Suicidal People: A Person-centred Approach.* Chichester: Wiley.
Lord Chancellor's Office (1997). *Who Decides? Making decisions on behalf of mentally incapacitated adults. A consultation paper issued by the Lord Chancellor's Department.* The National Archive Available at http://webarchive.nationalarchives.gov.uk/+/http://www.dca.gov.uk/menincap/meninfr.htm (accessed 9 May 2017).
National Institute for Health and Care Excellence (2011). *Self-harm in over 8s: Long-term Management.* London: NICE.
Oxford University Press (2016) *Oxford English Dictionary.* Oxford: Oxford University Press.
Panove, E. (1994). Treating suicidal patients: What therapists feel when their patients make suicidal threats. Unpublished thesis, University of Columbia.
Reeves, A. (2010). *Counselling Suicidal Clients.* London: Sage.
Reeves, A. (2015). *Working with Risk in Counselling and Psychotherapy.* London: Sage.
Surgenor, P. W. G. (2015). Promoting recovery from suicidal ideation through the development of protective factors. *Counselling and Psychotherapy Research*, 15(3), 207–216.

RECOMMENDED READING

1. Reeves, A. (2015). *Working with Risk in Counselling and Psychotherapy.* London: Sage.

A text that considers a range of risks in therapy, including exploring the issue of positive risk-taking as well as using supervision to support practice.

(Continued)

(Continued)

2. Niolon, R. (2006). *Dangerous Clients: Assessment and Work Resources for Student and Professionals.* (www.psychpage.com/learning/library/counseling/danger.htm).

A short, online summary of key factors to consider when assessing the risk of violence in clients.

3. Van Rijn, B. (2015). *Assessment and Case Formulation in Counselling and Psychotherapy*. London: Sage.

A helpful introductory text that discusses the key principles surrounding assessment and case formulation in practice.

3.5   FORMULATION

LUCY JOHNSTONE

OVERVIEW AND KEY POINTS

Formulation is a rapidly growing area of interest and practice within mental health, therapy and counselling. A formulation can be defined as an evidence-based summary, hypothesis or narrative that informs the intervention. Formulations can draw on a number of different therapeutic modalities, including integrative ones, and can be used in teams as well as in individual and family work. A number of best practice principles for formulation have been developed, and the relatively limited research to date suggests that it has many potential functions and benefits. The issue of how formulation relates to psychiatric diagnosis is a complex one. However, in the wake of controversy about diagnostic categories, we can expect formulation to play an increasingly central role in therapeutic activity across all settings.

- A formulation is a hypothesis about the reasons for a person's difficulties.
- Formulations can draw from a number of different therapeutic modalities.
- Team formulation is a popular and growing area of practice.
- Formulation is relevant to current debates about the validity of psychiatric diagnosis.

FORMULATION IN PRACTICE

Formulation is a core skill of the profession of clinical psychology, and also appears in the regulatory requirements for clinical, counselling, educational, health, forensic, occupational, sports and exercise psychologists (Health and Care Professions Council, 2009), as well as psychiatrists (Royal College of Psychiatrists, 2010) and mental health nurses (Nursing and Midwifery Council, 2010). The United Kingdom Council for Psychotherapy (UKCP) *Professional Occupational Standards* for cognitive, systemic and constructivist therapists also include formulation (UKCP, n.d). It is also the subject of a growing number of books and articles (Corrie and Lane, 2010; Johnstone and Dallos, 2013). The Division of Clinical Psychology (DCP) of the British Psychological Society (BPS) has issued *Good Practice Guidelines on the Use of Psychological Formulation* outlining criteria for best practice use with individuals, couples, families and teams across a range of settings and specialties (Division of Clinical Psychology, 2011).

The structure, content and emphasis of a formulation vary somewhat according to therapeutic modality (Johnstone and Dallos, 2013). Some traditions – for example, person-centred – do not use explicit formulations at all. This chapter will focus on the features that are common to formulations from all theoretical backgrounds. In this broad sense, a formulation can be defined as 'the tool used by clinicians to relate theory to practice' (Butler, 1998: 2); an evidence-based hypothesis or 'best guess' about the reasons for someone's difficulties that is used to inform the intervention and suggest ways forward. It provides a structure for developing a shared understanding or narrative which draws on two equally important kinds of evidence. The therapist or clinician brings knowledge derived from theory, research and clinical experience, while the client brings expertise about their own life and the meaning and impact of their relationships and circumstances. The core assumption underpinning the co-construction of a formulation is that '...at some level it all makes sense' (Butler, 1998: 2). This exploration of personal meaning within a trusting relationship is at the heart of formulation-based practice.

The term 'formulation' can be used in several senses. Formulation as an event, 'thing' or noun, in other words a specific summary, can be presented in a variety of different ways, from the 'reformulation' letters of Cognitive Analytic Therapy (CAT) to the diagrams favoured in Cognitive Behaviour Therapy (CBT). This is the form in which formulation is encountered by trainees and students. There are times and purposes for which a summary – a formulation as an event – may be useful, such as at the start and end of contact with counselling or mental health services. Appropriately adapted versions can be used for communication with other professionals, in letters to referrers, and so on. However, it is important to remember that any such summary arises out of formulation as a process; in other words, out of a conversation within a relationship. This is captured in the definition 'a process of ongoing collaborative sense-making' (Harper and Moss, 2003: 8). While it may be useful at some point, and for some purposes, to produce a written version, this is only a snapshot of an evolving story which is never complete and always open to revision.

In an even wider sense, formulation can be seen as an entire approach to mental health and therapeutic work. For most clinical psychologists, formulation is not just a specific activity or skill but a whole way of thinking about people's distress and difficulties. All clinical and therapeutic encounters will be approached from the formulation-based assumption that even the most extreme expressions of confusion, despair and distress are, ultimately, meaningful communications about relationships and adversities.

A fictitious example of a formulation that might be developed in collaboration with a client over a period of weeks or months is offered below. The client, 'Matthew', aged 25, is experiencing feelings of low mood and desperation after the ending of a short-term relationship.

You are currently feeling very low, stuck and hopeless because after a number of years of struggling against various difficulties, you seem to have reached a dead end in your life. When your girlfriend left, it seemed to confirm your deepest fear that no one would ever accept and love you, however hard you try.

In our conversations, we have traced back the roots of your despair. Your early life was dominated by your father's violence and abuse towards your mother. This, along with his harsh parenting of you, meant that you were not able to develop a sense of security and self-worth. Although your parents eventually separated, and you are close to your mother, it is not surprising that you have been left with anxieties about relationships. You find it particularly difficult to deal with anger and conflict, because of your dread of turning out like your father.

As a child, you were so pre-occupied with events at home that you found it hard to make friends, and some of your classmates took advantage of your lack of confidence by bullying you. Hating school, despite your academic ability, you truanted and started using cannabis to cope with your fears and loneliness. This has left you unqualified for anything but low-paid jobs, which in turn leaves you short of money and lacking in purpose in your life. You feel excluded from society and conscious that you have not fulfilled your mother's hopes for you. In this context, you have come to see having a relationship as the only answer to your problems. When your last attempt did not work out, you were overwhelmed with self-hatred and hopelessness. In constantly telling yourself that you are a useless failure, you seem to be re-playing your father's harsh criticisms, and being as hard on yourself as he was on you. Your childhood has left you with a deep need to be emotionally close to someone, and when this seems to be out of reach, you are once again overwhelmed by those earlier feelings of loneliness and hopelessness.

Despite all this, you have many strengths. You are intelligent, and have a talent for music. You are sensitive and self-aware, with a good understanding of how you have come to be in this situation. You generally get on well with your mother, and you now have quite a few friends. You have shown great determination in surviving your very difficult early life, and you have already started to take steps towards overcoming your difficulties.

We can see that the formulation is personal to Matthew, while drawing on a body of evidence about the impact of bullying and witnessing domestic violence. The various factors are integrated into a coherent narrative through the central thread of their meaning to Matthew himself. The formulation suggests an individual pathway forward, which will include building on the trusting relationship with a therapist, understanding the impact of his particular life events, and processing the feelings from the past. We would hope that the formulation helps him to feel that his experiences are understandable, that he has many strengths and that, with support, he can eventually overcome his difficulties.

Formulation can have other uses and benefits, including: clarifying hypotheses and questions, providing an overall picture or map, noticing what is missing, prioritising issues and problems, selecting and planning interventions, minimising bias by making choices and decisions explicit, framing medical interventions, predicting responses to interventions, thinking about lack of progress, and ensuring that a cultural perspective is incorporated (Division of Clinical Psychology, 2011: 8). It can also be seen as an intervention in itself. Sensitively developed and shared, it can help the client to feel understood and contained, and strengthen the therapeutic alliance (Division of Clinical Psychology, 2011: 8). The meta-message of a formulation is: 'You are having a normal response to an abnormal situation. Anyone else who had been through the same experiences might well have ended up feeling the same. You too can recover.'

BEST PRACTICE FORMULATION

As well as having potential uses and benefits, formulation can, like any other clinical activity, be carried out badly or unhelpfully. The *Guidelines* (Division of Clinical Psychology, 2011) list a number of criteria which are designed to reduce this risk. In keeping with the distinction between formulation as an event and formulation as a process, the criteria relate to content (for example, expressed in accessible language; culturally aware; non-blaming; inclusive of strengths and achievements) and also to process (for example, collaborative; respectful of the client's views about accuracy and helpfulness) (Division of Clinical Psychology, 2011: 29–30). Therapists are expected to take a reflective stance which helps to avoid formulating in insensitive, non-consenting or disempowering ways (Division of Clinical Psychology, 2011: 21).

Three additional best practice criteria deserve consideration. The first is that formulation should consider 'the possible role of trauma and abuse' (Division of Clinical Psychology, 2011: 29). 'Trauma' here is defined, in keeping with the literature on trauma-informed practice, as including a wide range of adversities such as sexual, physical and emotional abuse, neglect, bullying, witnessing or being a victim of domestic violence, and so on. A large and growing body of research confirms that a range of traumas and adversities play a causal role across all mental health presentations, including anxiety, low mood, eating distress, mood swings and 'psychosis' (Read and Bentall, 2012). Trauma-informed formulations help to ensure that this knowledge is integrated into interventions.

A trauma-informed approach recognises that services may be not only unhelpful but retraumatising through disempowering and coercive practices (Fallot and Harris, 2009). This leads to the principle that formulations developed within service settings should consider the 'possible role of services in compounding the difficulties' (Division of Clinical Psychology, 2011: 29).

A third principle is the requirement to include 'a critical awareness of the wider societal context within which formulation takes place' (Division of Clinical Psychology, 2011: 20). The intention is to minimise the individualising tendency of medical and (some) psychotherapeutic models, which, by locating the difficulties primarily within the person, implicitly convey a message of blame and deficit (Johnstone, 2014).

FORMULATION AND DIAGNOSIS

Formulation is used in many health settings to place diagnoses of cancer, learning disability, stroke, dementia, and so on within a holistic context. The use of diagnosis raises different issues in psychiatry, where the debate about the validity of categories such as 'schizophrenia', 'personality disorder' and 'bipolar disorder' is heated and ongoing. This raises the question of whether, in mental health work, formulation should be used as an addition to, or an alternative to, psychiatric diagnosis. The DCP *Guidelines* (2011: 17) state that 'best practice formulations ... are not premised on psychiatric diagnosis. Rather, the experiences that may have led to a psychiatric diagnosis (low mood, unusual beliefs, etc.) are themselves formulated'. The argument is that if a psychosocial formulation can provide a reasonably complete explanation for the experiences that have led to a psychiatric diagnosis, then there is no place or need for a competing hypothesis that says 'and by the way, it is also because she has schizophrenia.' A comprehensive, evidence-based formulation makes the diagnosis redundant. This contrasts with the training curriculum for psychiatrists, who are required to 'demonstrate the ability to construct formulations of patients' problems that include appropriate differential diagnoses' (Royal College of Psychiatrists, 2010: 25).

It is important to distinguish between psychiatric formulation – an addition to diagnosis – and psychological formulation – an alternative to diagnosis. They look different and have different implications in practice. In the case of Matthew, the contrast is between something like 'Clinical depression triggered by the breakup of a relationship' as opposed to 'Experiencing a loss which has brought earlier unresolved hurts and rejections to the surface'. While both versions can be seen as a welcome widening of the gaze of the biomedical model of distress, the first may simply facilitate a main focus on the 'illness' that the life events have apparently 'triggered', along with medication as the main or only intervention. Only the second fully conveys the message that: 'Your problems are a meaningful and understandable emotional response to your life circumstances.'

FORMULATION IN TEAMS

Team formulation is the process of facilitating a group or team of staff to develop a shared formulation about a service user (Johnstone, 2013). This is now common practice in mental health services and also in many older adult (Dexter-Smith, 2015), learning difficulty (Ingham, 2015), child and adolescent (Milson and Phillips, 2015), forensic (Lewis-Morton et al., 2015) and health (Cole, 2013) settings. Ideally these meetings are a standard feature in the weekly timetable across all parts of the service. The facilitator's role is to reflect, summarise, clarify and encourage creativity and free-thinking about the service user under discussion, not to provide solutions. In this way, the team can develop a shared formulation about the service user's difficulties and any 'stuck points' in their work with them.

While there will be considerable overlap with the content of the individual formulation, the team version typically places a greater focus on staff reactions and counter-transference. For example, if Matthew ended up having a psychiatric admission, the team version of his formulation might include reactions such as 'Some staff find themselves feeling irritated by Matthew's constant self-blame. We can now understand why he does this, and we are aware that we need to avoid repeating his experience with his father by adding to his sense of being criticised.' Since team formulation can be seen as a kind of consultation or supervision, these counter-transference aspects will not necessarily be shared in totality with the service user, although there will be careful discussion about whether and how to feed back the staff perspectives to Matthew in the most helpful way.

Clinicians have reported that team formulations can bring additional benefits such as achieving a consistent approach, dealing with core issues, minimising disagreement, increasing empathy and reflectiveness (Division of Clinical Psychology, 2011), and over time, promoting culture change towards more psychosocial perspectives (British Psychological Society, 2007; Kennedy, Smalley and Harris, 2003).

FORMULATION AND RESEARCH

At present, practice has outstripped research. The evidence for formulation as a specific intervention is limited (Cole, Wood and Spendelow, 2015), although there is extensive research into the theoretical content and psychological principles on which it is typically based (e.g., attachment theory, developmental psychology, CBT, and so on). The questions of whether or not formulation, either in its individual or its team versions, promotes recovery, improves outcomes, reduces the need for medication and admissions, and so on, remain open. Other things being equal, we can assume that clinical practice based on an explicit, shared and agreed hypothesis is likely to be more effective than the alternative. However, more investigation is needed to establish the most effective ways of developing, using and sharing these co-constructed 'best guesses'.

Service user and client reports about individual formulation are mixed. Some describe it as increasing understanding and trust, as empowering, as a relief, and as enabling them to move forward ('It just all made sense. I got it because … it was true'; 'It was bang on, so I trusted that she understood'; 'I think if you know the reason something's happening it automatically becomes more controllable') (Redhead, Johnstone and Nightingale, 2015: 7, 10). Others have reported experiencing it as saddening, frightening or overwhelming (Chadwick, Williams and Mackenzie, 2003; Morberg Pain, Chadwick and Abba, 2008). It is not clear whether these immediate reactions were, in the long term, succeeded by more positive perspectives. Clearly, however, sharing a formulation is a potentially powerful experience that should be carried out thoughtfully and sensitively. The small number of studies into staff perceptions of team formulation suggest that it is highly valued by multidisciplinary teams (Cole et al., 2015; Hollingworth and Johnstone, 2014).

FUTURE DIRECTIONS IN FORMULATION

In the last few years, formulation has grown from a relatively specialised professional term to become common currency within statutory services and therapeutic training and practice. It is no coincidence that this is happening in the wider context of the controversy about psychiatric diagnosis, which is the foundation of mental health theory and practice. In the face of this potential threat, formulation, in its psychiatric version, is increasingly being promoted as an answer to the shortcomings of diagnosis. If diagnosis is 'insufficient in conceptualising psychopathology in any individual patient', formulation can be co-opted to fill the gaps (Craddock and Mynors-Wallis, 2014). It should be noted that views about diagnosis in relation to formulation do not align in any simple way with professional background or discipline, and psychiatrist members of the Critical Psychiatry Network have joined with clinical psychologists to urge us to 'Drop the language of disorder' in favour of a narrative or formulation-based approach (e.g., Kinderman et al., 2013).

Psychological formulation is, essentially, about listening to someone's story. As such, every counsellor or therapist will already be 'formulating', or co-constructing meanings, since this is the heart of all good practice. However, reflecting on this evolving story in an explicit shared form can be a powerfully validating and transformative experience for client and therapist, as well as for teams. Only time will tell whether formulation practice will also bring about a much-needed shift away from primarily biomedical to psychosocial models in mental health services as a whole.

REFERENCES

British Psychological Society (2007). *New ways of working for applied psychologists in health and social care: Working psychologically in teams*. Leicester: British Psychological Society.

Butler, G. (1998). Clinical formulation. In A. S. Bellack and M. Hersen (Eds.), *Comprehensive clinical psychology* (pp. 1–23). Oxford: Pergamon.

Chadwick, P., Williams, C. and Mackenzie, J. (2003). Impact of case formulation in cognitive behaviour therapy for psychosis. *Behaviour Research and Therapy*, 14(6), 671–680.

Cole, S. (2013). Using integrative formulation in health settings. In L. Johnstone and R. Dallos (Eds.) (2013). *Formulation in psychology and psychotherapy: Making sense of people's problems* (2nd ed., pp. 243–259). London: Routledge.

Cole, S., Wood, K. and Spendelow, J. (2015). Team formulation: A critical evaluation of current literature and future research directions. *Clinical Psychology Forum*, 275, 13–19.

Corrie, S. and Lane, D.A. (2010). *Constructing stories, telling tales: A guide to formulation in applied psychology*. London: Karnac.

Craddock, N. and Mynors-Wallis, L. (2014). Psychiatric diagnosis: Impersonal, imperfect and important. *British Journal of Psychiatry*, 204, 93–95.

Critical Psychiatry Network (2013). *Blog post*. (www.criticalpsychiatry.co.uk/index.php?option=com_content&view=section&layout=blog&id=1&Itemid=55&limitstart=15).

Dexter-Smith, S. (2015). Implementing psychological formulations service-wide. *Clinical Psychology Forum*, 275, 43–47.

Division of Clinical Psychology (2011). *Good practice guidelines on the use of psychological formulation*. Leicester: British Psychological Society (downloadable from www.bpsshop.org.uk/Good-Practice-Guidelines-on-the-use-of-psychological-formulation-P1653.aspx).

Fallot, R.D. and Harris, M. (2009). *Creating cultures of trauma-informed care*. Washington, DC: Community Connections.

Harper, D. and Moss, D. (2003). A different chemistry? Re-formulating formulation. *Clinical Psychology*, 25, 6–10.

Health and Care Professions Council (2009). *Standards of proficiency: Practitioner psychologists*. London: Health Professions Council.

Hollingworth, P. and Johnstone, L. (2014). Team formulation: What are the staff views? *Clinical Psychology Forum*, 257, 28–34.

Ingham, B. (2015). Team formulation within a learning disabilities setting. *Clinical Psychology Forum*, 275, 33–37.

Johnstone, L. (2013). Using formulation in teams. In L. Johnstone and R. Dallos (Eds.), *Formulation in psychology and psychotherapy: Making sense of people's problems* (2nd ed., pp. 216–242). London: Routledge.

Johnstone, L. (2014). *A straight-talking introduction to psychiatric diagnosis*. Ross-on-Wye: PCCS Books.

Johnstone, L. and Dallos, R. (Eds.) (2013). *Formulation in psychology and psychotherapy: Making sense of people's problems* (2nd ed.) London: Routledge.

Kennedy, F., Smalley, M. and Harris, T. (2003). Clinical psychology for inpatient settings: Principles for development and practice. *Clinical Psychology Forum*, 30, 21–24.

Kinderman, P., Read, J., Moncrieff, J. and Bentall, R.P. (2013). Drop the language of disorder. *Evidence-based Mental Health*, 16(1), 2–3.

Lewis-Morton, R., James, L., Brown, K. and Hider, A. (2015). Team formulation in a secure setting: Challenges, rewards and service-user involvement. *Clinical Psychology Forum*, 275, online supplement.

Milson, G. and Phillips, K. (2015). Formulation meetings in a Tier 4 CAMHS inpatient unit. *Clinical Psychology Forum*, 275, online supplement.

Morberg Pain, C., Chadwick, P. and Abba, N. (2008). Clients' experience of case formulation in CBT for psychosis. *British Journal of Clinical Psychology*, 47(2), 127–138.

Nursing and Midwifery Council (2010). *Standards for competence for Registered Nurses*. London: NMC.

Read, J. and Bentall, R.B. (2012). Negative childhood experiences and mental health: Theoretical, clinical and primary prevention implications. *British Journal of Psychiatry*, 200, 89–91.

Redhead, S., Johnstone, L. and Nightingale, J. (2015). Clients' experiences of formulation. *Psychology and Psychotherapy: Theory, Research and Practice*, 88(4), 453–467.

Royal College of Psychiatrists (2010). *A competency-based curriculum for specialist core training*. (www.rcpsych.ac.uk/training/curriculum2010.aspx).

United Kingdom Council for Psychotherapy (n.d). *Professional occupational standards: For the information of commissioners, trainers and practitioners*. London: UKCP.

RECOMMENDED READING

1. Corrie, S. and Lane, D.A. (2010). *Constructing stories, telling tales: A guide to formulation in applied psychology.* London: Karnac.

The authors discuss formulation and its relationship to narrative and story-telling, both within and beyond therapeutic settings.

2. Johnstone, L. and Dallos, R. (Eds.) (2013). *Formulation in psychology and psychotherapy: Making sense of people's problems* (2nd ed.) London: Routledge.

The editors give a comprehensive overview of definitions, principles, practice and debates, illustrated by formulating two case histories from a range of therapeutic perspectives.

3. Division of Clinical Psychology (2011). *Good practice guidelines on the use of psychological formulation.* Leicester: British Psychological Society.

These are useful guidelines for formulation produced by the British Psychological Society and freely available online.

OVERVIEW AND KEY POINTS

Outcome and process measures are increasingly becoming a routine part of counselling and psychotherapy services. This chapter provides an overview of this topic by answering the following questions: what are outcome and process measures? Who might want to use them? When can we use them? And how can we implement them into practice?

- Outcome and process measures can be useful for practitioners, services and research.
- Consideration of which measures to use and how they can be implemented may enhance the usefulness of the information gathered.
- Brief measures may be one way of making measures a routine part of practice.
- Organisations have been set up to provide guidance to practitioners wishing to use these approaches in their work.

WHAT ARE OUTCOME AND PROCESS MEASURES?

OUTCOME MEASURES

Outcome measures in counselling and psychotherapy aim to systematically assess one or more aspects of client functioning. There are different types of outcome measure, such as global outcome measures, symptom checklists and diagnostic and screening instruments. Global outcome measures measure general wellbeing and are applicable to all clients regardless of clinical setting, mode of therapy or specific problems. Symptom checklists, diagnostic and screening instruments look for the presence of particular symptoms or conditions (Barkham, Evans, Margison and McGrath, 1998).

PROCESS MEASURES

Process measures are a way of monitoring how a client experiences therapy. There is substantial evidence that the relationship between practitioner and client contributes significantly to outcome, regardless of the model of therapy (Lambert, 2007). These measures aim to frequently track the therapeutic alliance as therapy progresses. This information can then be used as feedback to increase collaborative working (Miller, Duncan, Brown, Sorrell and Chalk, 2006).

GOAL-BASED OUTCOME MEASURES

Goal-based outcome measures are a way of recording at the beginning of therapy what the client and practitioner want to achieve from therapy and thereafter tracking progress towards these goals (Law, 2013). The idea here is that, unlike many measures which adopt an external viewpoint to consider distress, the most important outcome measures are the ones clients have decided on themselves (Hanley, Sefi and Ersahin, 2016).

WHO MIGHT BE INTERESTED IN PROCESS AND OUTCOME MEASURES?

COUNSELLORS AND PSYCHOTHERAPISTS

As part of normal clinical practice therapists routinely assess the progress of their clients. For the most part, therapists assess outcomes in an informal manner based on client reports and clinical judgement (Hatfield and Ogles, 2004). However, it is increasingly recognised that the use of formal assessment can provide additional validation for clinical judgement (Hannan et al., 2005). Research has shown process and outcome measures can actually improve outcomes in therapy, and monitoring client-based outcomes in combination with feedback from the therapist has been observed to increase the effectiveness of therapy by 65% in clinical settings (Duncan, Sparks, Miller, Bohanske and Claud, 2006).

Organisations representing counselling and psychotherapists advocate the use of these measures, with the British Association for Counselling and Psychotherapy (BACP) recommending that 'outcome measures should be used as part of routine therapy, rather than as an adjunct to it; in a manner in which they are of benefit to each client and enrichment of each clinical practice' (BACP, 2010). Research has shown that some of the benefits of such an approach for clinicians include: facilitating a dialogue with clients; reducing the likelihood of dropout; improving the speed with which good outcomes are achieved; improving the quality of information gained by covering potential gaps in assessment and/or review; and improving identification of worsening symptoms (Bickman, Kelley, Breda, de Andrade and Riemer, 2011; Lambert and Shimokawa, 2011; Lambert et al., 2003; Noble, 2016).

COMMISSIONING SERVICES

Other stakeholders with an interest in the results from process and outcome measures are those in charge of commissioning services. The nature of therapy is that it takes place behind closed doors and this can mean it is difficult for organisations to assess its impact. In the current climate, whereby there are limited resources available for counselling and mental health services, services have to find ways of justifying their worth to continue their existence or face being side-lined. Using measures is one of many ways to assess service quality. Naturally, this could make some practitioners a little nervous, feeling their practice might be scrutinised, or that the application of measures is reductionist and thus opposed to the philosophy of more humanistically oriented therapies. These are valid concerns. However, research has shown that by collecting outcome and process measure information on a service level, improvements to services can be made (Simon, Lambert, Harris, Busath and Vazquez, 2012), arguably, thereby making services more secure and less likely to be decommissioned.

EVIDENCE-BASED PRACTICE AND RESEARCH

Measures are also valuable to inform research and create an evidence base for our work. Both outcome and process measures can be used to help answer the question 'what works for whom?' They can objectively assess the client's progress by collecting data systematically throughout the client's duration in therapy. If these data are collected for a large number of clients then researchers can apply statistical tests to analyse the data and look to see if there are general patterns which may inform practice, for example, whether particular modalities (humanistic, psychodynamic, cognitive behavioural therapy) are more effective with certain client groups, whether clients continue to improve after therapy has finished, or identify effective therapy components across modalities.

WHEN DO WE USE OUTCOME AND PROCESS MEASURES?

One valid question is, having decided to use measures, what considerations might need to be made before implementing

them with clients? The BACP, which actively encourages individual practitioners to use measures with clients, emphasises the importance of obtaining *informed consent* from clients and advocates looking at the *validity* and *reliability* of the tool you are intending to use before implementing the measure with clients (Roth, 2010). An explanation of these concepts is given below.

INFORMED CONSENT

Informed consent is a concept most practitioners will be familiar with due to its application to therapy more generally, but it also applies to using measures specifically. The BACP guidance on using measures in practice states that data gathering and measuring must be conducted in the full knowledge of the client (BACP, 2010). This includes explaining how long the data will be kept and its purpose, and who has access to the data. If clients refuse, then it should be made clear that this will not affect their therapy. It is considered best practice to obtain written consent.

VALIDITY AND RELIABILITY

When selecting an outcome measure it is important that it has been validated for its intended purpose, as a poor measure can provide inaccurate information about symptom severity and client progress. By this, we mean it was developed and tested with the intended client group in mind. For example, has it been used with the same age group or cultural demographics as the intended recipient of the measure? If it has not, the tool might be measuring some other factor instead. Furthermore, the concept of reliability is important. Some measures are intended for one-off use only, whereas others are designed for repeated application. Practitioners can check the reliability and validity of a measure by obtaining the reference journal paper (often widely available by searching online). These papers outline the research upon which the measure was based, and include information about the population it was designed for and its conditions of use.

AT WHAT POINTS DURING THERAPY DO WE USE MEASURES?

To answer this question, Law (2014) recommends reflecting on what useful information might be gained from measures from the perspective of both the practitioner and the client. In general, assessment measures may be used to gain a better understanding of the presenting problem, and the goals or aims of therapy. During therapy, measures can be used to gain more information on the client's level of engagement, the therapeutic alliance, and track symptoms and goals. At the end of therapy, measures can help to assess whether further support is needed, evaluate the overall experience and benchmark client's progress over time. The application of a chosen measure should correspond to generating the information you are interested in finding out.

HOW OFTEN SHOULD WE USE MEASURES?

The balance between getting enough useful information through the measure process and not drowning a client in paperwork needs to be carefully considered. Barkham, Stiles, Connell and Mellor-Clark (2012) found that clients do not complete all therapy measures in real-world settings. This can pose a challenge to understanding the effectiveness of an intervention, as typically those clients who complete measures have better attendance and are more motivated in therapy, which can bias its reported effectiveness. Therefore, to get the clearest picture possible, the BACP recommends completing measures at every session (although it is acknowledged this is not always practically possible). By this approach, in the event of an unplanned ending there are pre- and post-measures for comparison. As a consequence of following this guideline, it is recommended by the BACP that measures are selected that are brief and quick to administer and score (Roth, 2010).

HOW CAN OUTCOME AND PROCESS MEASURES BE IMPLEMENTED INTO PRACTICE?

Research has looked at some of the barriers reported by practitioners to implementing measures and found therapists think the process may interfere with therapy by taking time away from the session, lack confidence in administering measures, or feel measures generate unnecessary paperwork (Hatfield and Ogles, 2004). Law and Wolpert (2014) therefore recommend using the Plan, Do, Study, Act cycle (Langley, Nolan, Nolan, Norman and Provost, 2009) as a process template to begin to implement measures into practice (see Figure 3.6.1).

Law and Wolpert (2014) also provide encouragement for practitioners starting out using measures, noting if the process seems unnatural at first or does not go to plan, do not despair, and remember that all change takes time. Groark and Mccall (2011) estimate it takes three years to embed a new practice. Once the process is established, Figure 3.6.2 (modified from Law and Wolpert (2014)) provides some suggestions for good practice when using measures routinely.

WHAT OUTCOME OR PROCESS MEASURES SHOULD I USE?

There is no universally accepted measure of outcome, and there is a vast array of outcome measures, at last count 1,430 were identified (Froyd, Lambert and Froyd, 1996). It is generally accepted that it is helpful if there is some consistency across measures, to enable meaningful interpretation across individuals and services. As a result, numerous organisations including the BACP, the Improving Access to Psychological Therapies (IAPT) initiative based throughout the United Kingdom, and the Child Outcomes Research Consortium (CORC+) offer guidance on recommended measures to use in practice (see Figure 3.6.3 and recommended reading at the end of the chapter).

In recent years, ultra-brief measures have been developed after research suggesting that the majority of clinicians do not consider any measure taking longer than five minutes to complete, score and interpret to be practical (Brown, Dreis and Nace, 1999). Short measures

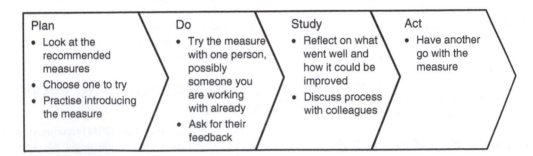

Figure 3.6.1 The Plan, Do, Study, Act cycle for measures

Adapted from Langley G. L., Nolan K. M., Nolan T. W., Norman C. L. and Provost, L.P. (2009). The Improvement Guide: A Practical Approach to Enhancing Organizational Performance (2 ed.). San Francisco: Jossey Bass.

Do	Make sure you have the measures you need ready before the session.
Do	Always explain why you are asking anyone to fill out a measure.
Do	Look at the answers.
Do	Discuss the answers with clients.
Do	Share the information in supervision.
Do	Always use information from the measures in conjunction with other clinical information.
Don't	Give out a measure if you think the person doesn't understand why they are being asked to complete it.
Don't	Use any measure if you don't understand why you are using it.
Don't	Insist on someone filling out measures if they are too distressed.
Don't	See the numbers generated from measures as an absolute fact.
Don't	See your clinical judgement as an absolute fact.

Figure 3.6.2 Some suggested dos and don'ts of using measures

modified from Duncan Law and Miranda Wolpert, *Using Outcomes and Feedback Tools with Children, Young People and Families* (2014), used with permission"

Below are some of the recommended measures (in alphabetical order) by BACP, IAPT and CORC+ which also fulfil criteria of being brief and simple to administer. For more information on measure recommendations check out the organisations' websites.

Outcome measures

Clinical Outcomes in Routine Evaluation (CORE-10) (Barkham et al., 2013).

CORE-10 is designed as a short screening measure of psychological distress where session-by-session change monitoring is required. The 10-item questionnaire includes items covering depression, anxiety, trauma, physical problems and risk. It also assesses general functioning, social functioning, close relationships and the self.

Generalised Anxiety Disorder (GAD-7) (Spitzer, Kroenke, Williams and Löwe, 2006).

The GAD-7 was designed as a seven-item screening tool for generalised anxiety disorder, although it also monitors symptoms of panic disorder, social anxiety and post-traumatic stress disorder.

Outcome Rating Scale (Miller et al., 2003) and Child Outcome Rating Scale (Duncan et al., 2006).

The ORS for ages 13 years and over and the CORS for children under 13 years provide a brief measure of global distress suitable for assessing treatment outcome. These very brief four-item measures take only a few minutes to complete and score.

Patient Health Questionnaire (PHQ-9) (Kroenke, Spitzer and Williams, 2001).

This measure contains nine items and is designed to measure symptoms of depression in primary care. It can be used to monitor changes in symptoms over time and indicates depression severity.

Process measures

Session Rating Scale (SRS) (Duncan et al., 2003) and Child Session Rating Scale (CSRS) (Miller and Duncan, 2004).

The SRS for ages 13 years and over and the CSRS for children aged under 13 years are brief four-item measures. They were developed as a self-report working therapeutic alliance measure designed specifically for every session clinical use.

Figure 3.6.3 Common measures

can be used to provide real-time feedback, and are therefore available for immediate treatment modification to prevent clients dropping out of therapy or suffering a negative outcome (Duncan et al., 2006). By using ultra-brief measures, then, Miller, Duncan, Brown, Sparks and Claud (2003) suggest measure evaluation can become a routine part of therapy.

CONCLUSION

The direction of travel indicates outcome and process measures are fast becoming a requirement at counselling and psychotherapy services. However, Law and Wolpert (2014) point out that there is a danger these measures can be implemented without allowing room for clinical judgement. Researchers have found that when measures are perceived or experienced as part of top-down or tick box culture they may undermine or even harm the therapeutic alliance (Greenhalgh, 2009). However, when implemented with due consideration these measures can be used in ways to improve the therapeutic alliance and learn more about our clients. Law and Wolpert (2014) recommend that these measures are implemented with an ethos of discovering more about the therapeutic process and the client, without neglecting the surrounding context, and that the results of the measures are used collaboratively to enhance shared decision making. Strengths and limitations of measures should be acknowledged as part of this process, and full discussion of these outcomes should take place before any interpretation. The development of brief measures and initiatives by organisations aiming to facilitate consistency in measures and collate large amounts of data, could herald exciting new discoveries for the profession and opportunities for improvement in practice.

REFERENCES

Barkham, M., Bewick, B., Mullin, T., Gilbody, S., Connell, J., Cahill, J., Mellor-Clark, J., Richards, D., Unsworth, G. and Evans, C. (2013). The CORE-10: a short measure of psychological distress for routine use in the psychological therapies. *Counselling and Psychotherapy Research, 13*(1), 3–13.

Barkham, M., Evans, C., Margison, F. and McGrath, G. (1998). The rationale for developing and implementing core outcome batteries for routine use in service settings and psychotherapy outcome research. *Journal of Mental Health, 7*(1), 35–47.

Barkham, M., Stiles, W. B., Connell, J. and Mellor-Clark, J. (2012). Psychological treatment outcomes in routine NHS services: what do we mean by treatment effectiveness? *Psychology and Psychotherapy: Theory, Research and Practice, 85*(1), 1–16.

Bickman, L., Kelley, S. D., Breda, C., de Andrade, A. R. and Riemer, M. (2011). Effects of routine feedback to clinicians on mental health outcomes of youths: results of a randomized trial. *Psychiatric Services, 62*, 1423–1429.

British Association for Counselling and Psychotherapy (2010). *Using routine outcome measures.* (www.bacp.co.uk/research/resources/using-routine-outcome-measures.php).

Brown, J., Dreis, S. and Nace, D. K. (1999). What really makes a difference in psychotherapy outcome? Why does managed care want to know? In M. A. Hubble, B. L. Duncan and S. D. Miller (Eds.), *The heart and soul of change: What works in therapy* (pp. 389–406). Washington, DC: American Psycholoical Association.

Duncan, B., Sparks, J., Miller, S. D., Bohanske, R. and Claud, D. (2006). Giving youth a voice: a preliminary study of the reliability and validity of a brief outcome measure for children, adolescents, and caretakers. *Journal of Brief Therapy, 5*, 66–82.

Duncan, B. L., Miller, S., Sparks, J. A., Claud, D. A., Reynolds, L. R., Brown, J. and Johnson, L. D. (2003). The Session Rating Scale: preliminary psychometric properties of a 'working' alliance measure. *Journal of Brief Therapy, 3*(1), 3–12.

Froyd, M. J., Lambert, M. J. and Froyd, J. E. (1996). A review of practices of psychotherapy outcome measurement. *Journal of Mental Health, 5*(1), 11–16.

Greenhalgh, J. (2009). The applications of PROs in clinical practice: what are they, do they work, and why? *Quality of Life Research, 18*(1), 115–123.

Groark, C. J. and Mccall, R. B. (2011). Implementing changes in institutions to improve young children's development. *Infant Mental Health Journal, 32*(5), 509–525.

Hanley, T., Sefi A. and Ersahin, Z. (2016). From goals to tasks to methods. In M. Cooper and W. Dryden (Eds.), *The handbook of pluralistic counselling and psychotherapy.* London: Sage.

Hannan, C., Lambert, M. J., Harmon, C., Nielsen, S. L., Smart, D. W., Shimokawa, K. and Sutton, S. W. (2005). A lab test and algorithms for identifying clients at risk for treatment failure. *Journal of Clinical Psychology*, *61*(2), 155–163.

Hatfield, D. R. and Ogles, B. M. (2004). The use of outcome measures by psychologists in clinical practice. *Professional Psychology: Research and Practice*, *35*(5), 485.

Kroenke, K., Spitzer, R. K. and Williams, J. B. (2001). PHQ-9: validity of a brief depression severity measure. *Journal of General Internal Medicine*, *16*, 606–613.

Lambert, M. (2007). Presidential address: what we have learned from a decade of research aimed at improving psychotherapy outcome in routine care. *Psychotherapy Research*, *17*(1), 1–14.

Lambert, M. J. and Shimokawa, K. (2011). Collecting client feedback. *Psychotherapy*, *48*(1), 72.

Lambert, M. J., Whipple, J. L., Hawkins, E. J., Vermeersch, D. A., Nielsen, S. L. and Smart, D. W. (2003). Is it time for clinicians to routinely track patient outcome? A meta-analysis. *Clinical Psychology: Science and Practice*, *10*(3), 288–301.

Langley G. L., Nolan K. M., Nolan T. W., Norman C. L. and Provost, L.P. (2009). *The improvement guide: A practical approach to enhancing organizational performance* (2nd ed.). San Francisco, CA: Jossey-Bass.

Law, D. (2013). *Goals and goal-based outcomes (GBOs): Some useful information.* London: CAMHS Press.

Law, D. (2014). General guidance on using forms in therapy. In D. Law and M. Wolpert (Eds.), *Guide to using outcomes and feedback tools with children, young people and families* (pp. 45–52). UK: CORC.

Law, D. and Wolpert, M. (2014). *Guide to using outcomes and feedback tools with children, young people and families.* UK: CORC.

Miller, S. D. and Duncan, B. L. (2004). *The Outcome and Session Rating Scales: Administration and scoring manuals.* Chicago, IL: Author.

Miller, S. D., Duncan, B., Brown, J., Sorrell, R. and Chalk, M. (2006). Using outcome to inform and improve treatment outcomes. *Journal of Brief Therapy*, *5*, 5–22.

Miller, S. D., Duncan, B., Brown, J., Sparks, J. and Claud, D. (2003). The outcome rating scale: a preliminary study of the reliability, validity, and feasibility of a brief visual analog measure. *Journal of brief Therapy*, *2*(2), 91–100.

Noble, J. N. (2016). Evaluating one's own practice while training: a systematic case study design in a further education setting. *Counselling and Psychotherapy*, *16*(4), 235–243.

Roth, T. (2010). *Using measures, and thinking about outcomes.* Lutterworth: British Association for Counselling and Psychotherapy.

Simon, W., Lambert, M. J., Harris, M. W., Busath, G. and Vazquez, A. (2012). Providing patient progress information and clinical support tools to therapists: effects on patients at risk of treatment failure. *Psychotherapy Research*, *22*, 638–647.

Spitzer, R. L., Kroenke, K., Williams, J. B. and Löwe, B. (2006). A brief measure for assessing generalized anxiety disorder: the GAD-7. *Archives of Internal Medicine*, *166*, 1092–1097.

RECOMMENDED READINGS

1. The BACP 'Using Routine Outcome Measures' webpage (www.bacp.co.uk/research/resources/using-routine-outcome-measures.php).

This provides useful guidance and publications about implementing measures into practice.

2. Roth, T. (2010). *Using measures, and thinking about outcomes.* Lutterworth: British Association for Counselling and Psychotherapy.

A short and accessible paper which elaborates on many of the concepts introduced in this chapter.

3. MindEd – the MindEd website project (www.minded.org.uk).

This has produced specific resources to support counsellors and psychotherapists to facilitate integration of process and outcome measures into their practice with children and young people.

3.7

THERAPEUTIC BEGINNINGS

INDIA AMOS

OVERVIEW AND KEY POINTS

For anyone who is interested in the process of therapy, or who has contemplated undertaking a training course in counselling or psychotherapy, the question 'how does therapy unfold?' will have been considered. While it is not possible to predict the course of therapy as it progresses for each individual client, it is assumed that a number of key tasks applicable to the establishment of therapy can be pinpointed and discussed. Although it is acknowledged that different therapeutic approaches may have different priorities, this chapter aims to offer an overview of some of the central elements that may be considered by a therapist at the outset of commencing any type of therapy.

This chapter presents discussion on the following:

- receiving and managing client referrals
- the physical environment; how a therapy room might look and for what purpose
- the establishment of initial psychological contact with the client and therapeutic contracting
- the identification of appropriate therapy goals
- reflexivity in practice.

RECEIVING A REFERRAL

A therapy referral may be received from a General Practitioner (GP) or Consultant Psychiatrist responsible for the client's care. Alternatively, the client may refer her or himself for a therapeutic assessment, or be advised to do so at their place of work. The extent of information contained within a referral can vary. It may include a description of the client's problem, the reason for the referral, relevant risk issues, or it may simply request for the client to be seen. It is the therapist's responsibility to assess the appropriateness of the referral, and whether the form of therapy they offer is suitable in light of the prospective client's psychological problem and goals. An initial assessment session(s) is often arranged with the aim of arriving at a shared understanding of the problems the client hopes to address. It may be that the decision is made not to offer therapy, in which case the client may be referred on.

Within the person-centred counselling tradition the therapist's receipt of prior information regarding a prospective client can be considered problematic (Mearns, Thorne and McLeod, 2013). Client information collected by another practitioner could be considered distracting, even detrimental to the process in which the primary aim is to receive the client with an open mind. In some cases, referral letters or notes might be consulted following the first session with the client. Individual therapists vary in their position on this subject. However, it might be worth considering what client information might be essential to know ahead of your first meeting, if any.

MAKING CONTACT

Therapy can be a challenge. Orienting the client to the nature of the therapeutic process is key. An authentic engagement with emotional material, often at the centre of therapeutic work, is integral to its success. However, commitment to the process can result in the client feeling worse before they feel better. Preparing the client about the 'costs and benefits' of therapy, and the importance of working collaboratively in the process ensures that they are aware of the aims of therapy, and perhaps serves to normalise any fears they may have regarding their role in the relationship. The role of the therapist too should be clarified.

Initial contact with the client can be made through a telephone call, or appointment letter, and it could be said that this is the point where the therapeutic relationship begins. However, for a client who has sought out a therapist online or perhaps via a recommendation, the therapeutic realtionship may have been initiated even before this. On the telephone, the therapist has the opportunity to begin building rapport. Essential information regarding the date, time, location and duration of the session is needed to be imparted to the client, although a warmth and genuineness from the outset can serve to make the client feel understood. Appointment letters commonly specify by what date the client is required to confirm or cancel their first appointment. Explaining to the client what is likely to be expected in the initial session may also be appropriate. For example, the client may be informed of what will occur in the event that they cancel or do not attend the first session.

In order to minimise the potential for the therapist to make assumptions about the client, and instead to enable the therapist to fully appreciate the client as the expert in their own experience of the problem, the establishment and maintenance of a collaborative relationship is paramount. The practitioner seeks to integrate their understanding of the client's social world and, with the client, develops a shared narrative from which to construct meaning (Saha, Beach and Cooper, 2008z); seeking this understanding provides a foundation that makes it possible to tailor interventions to the individual client and their unique socio-cultural experience (Lakes, Lopez and Gallo, 2006).

SETTING UP THE THERAPY ROOM

Miwa and Hanyu (2006: 484) asked 'Can a room environment facilitate counselling, affecting clients' self-disclosure or the interpersonal relationship between a client and a counsellor?' Decisions ranging from the interior design of the therapy room, sources of lighting and arrangement of furniture serve to communicate something to the client. While practical restrictions and financial limitations may play a role in the extent to which the practitioner can prepare their therapy room, the creation of a private and comfortable space is vital. Thoughtful aesthetics can contribute to an atmosphere of safety (Inskipp, 2012). Some therapists may opt to provide the client with a couch rather than a chair, or perhaps offer the client a choice. The classical psychoanalyst, for example, is likely to invite the clients to lie on the couch, with the therapist sitting behind the client so that they are out of sight and therefore less likely to influence the client's thinking. On the other hand, Gestalt therapists consider it essential that therapist and client are face-to-face and in close proximity. Therapeutic orientations vary in their conceptualisation of the physical environment in relation to the purpose, techniques and goals of therapy. Some research suggests that dim lighting induces a positive impression whereas bright lights increase arousal and make people more talkative (Gifford, 1988). The arrangement of furniture may be sparse in order to support the client's introspection, at the same time as containing some more evocative aspects, such as pictures, plants or ornaments. These can have the potential to be used in therapy as helpful metaphors, and have been said to influence levels of client disclosure (Chaikin, Derlega and Miller, 1976).

ESTABLISHING PSYCHOLOGICAL CONTACT

Carl Rogers (1957: 95) proposed that in order for constructive personality change to occur it is necessary that the therapist and client are 'in psychological contact'. Psychological contact is a mutual endeavour, and change on the part of the client only becomes possible when in a relationship with the therapist. The therapist's congruence, empathic understanding and unconditional positive regard for the client are considered vital for the therapist to make a psychological contact with the client, and as a basis for which to develop 'the more profound quality of relationship attained with emotional and subtle contact' (Cameron, 2003: 87).

The first session is likely to include an assessment of what has brought the client to therapy. This may involve an invitation to the client to share their personal story, describe their psychological symptoms, provide information on how they are currently coping, and from where they draw their strength. It may include all or only some of these areas initially. See Van Rijn (Chapter 3.3, this volume) for further details on assessment in therapy.

The concept of therapeutic collaboration is not a new construct and practitioners of all the foremost theoretical orientations subscribe to its significance (Kazantzis and Kellis, 2012).

Working together is the essence of collaboration and this should be modelled from the outset. Putting this ethic into action requires the therapist to recognise and engage with the knowledge their client already possesses, to recognise the shared responsibility for identifying appropriate therapy goals and the active participation of both the client and the therapist in therapy tasks. Frequent reviews of the effectiveness of the work they do collaboratively are also advocated from the start and throughout. The word 'beginning' implies simply that this is the start of developing a therapeutic relationship with the client, which is ongoing throughout the duration of the work. Stiles (Chapter 3.2, this volume) explores the nature of the therapeutic relationship in more depth.

THERAPEUTIC CONTRACTING

Engagement in explicit contracting with the client ahead of their commitment to the therapeutic process ensures the practitioners respect of their client's autonomy (British Association of Counselling and Psychotherapy, 2016; British Psychological Society, 2009). The client's decision to enter into therapy is a significant one, and may feel daunting. Mearns, Thorne and McLeod (2013: 130) encourage practitioners to stay mindful of the question 'what process does the client have to go through to get to me, and what messages does he receive along the way?' Therapists need to provide clients with the information they need in order for them to give their informed consent.

This can include, among other things: informing the client of the limits of confidentiality, the nature and extent of the practitioner's case notes, the therapist's therapeutic orientation and/or training, the alternative therapeutic approaches that are available to the client from other service providers, the length of therapy, the client's right to terminate sessions, and the therapist's fee for sessions. Clients themselves are likely to come to therapy with some preconceptions. Therefore, this discussion can serve to answer any of the client's questions about therapy and dispel any myths. A therapeutic contract refers to the discussion and agreement of the decisions deemed relevant to the progression of therapy, and is used as a way in which to capture and formalise such elements, affording security and clarity for both parties.

CONFIDENTIALITY

The client should be made aware of the limits of confidentiality at the earliest opportunity. Research has demonstrated that such an awareness of the limits of confidentiality also serves to limit the client's therapeutic disclosures in many cases (Miller and Thelen, 1986). While practitioners are encouraged and trained to do everything reasonable to limit the disclosure of confidential material, it is also important, in the spirit of fostering a trusting therapeutic relationship, that therapists take care to inform their clients of where the boundaries lie (Donner, VandeCreek, Gonsiorek and Fisher, 2008).

It may be suitable to provide the client with a therapy leaflet or information sheet to be read outside the session. During the first session a client may not be best positioned to digest some of the information pertaining to issues of confidentiality. Therefore, it can be helpful to provide supporting literature in these cases.

LENGTH OF THERAPY

The length of therapy refers to the number of sessions in which the client engages. Some therapy is open-ended, meaning that the number of sessions can be negotiated and reviewed at any time. This is most commonly the case within private practice (Carey, 2005). Other therapeutic contracts are time-limited and therefore adhere to a specified number of sessions. Short-term therapy is typically between 12 and 25 sessions, with brief therapy being six sessions or less (Shapiro et al., 2003). The term 'therapy duration' can be considered in relation to the 'therapeutic hour' (usually 50 minutes) or the frequency of sessions, which may also need to be negotiated collaboratively with the client (Öst, Alm, Brandberg and Breitholtz, 2001). Typically, therapy sessions are scheduled once a week to maintain continuity, although the circumstances of the

client may not enable this. Within some therapeutic traditions, therapeutic sessions may occur more frequently than once a week. For example, within the psychoanalytic tradition, analysands may attend therapy two or more times per week.

THERAPY FEES

There are a number of ways to approach the issue of payment for therapy. Practitioners can set a fixed fee which is applied to all, or set a variable pay scale, dependent upon the client's financial circumstances. Therapists may choose to provide free therapy or open negotiations with regard to payment. In addition, therapists may or may not accept fees from alternative sources other than the client, often referred to as third-party payment. Whatever approach is incorporated by the practitioner, it is paramount that fee policies are communicated clearly to the client before embarking on therapy. Research in this area presents an interesting picture. Clark and Sims (2014) report how many therapists continue to experience uncertainty around the practice of setting and collecting fees. The literature indicates that practitioners battle with feelings of self-worth (Chandler, 2010), guilt (Pepper, 2004), a desire to help that clashes with the necessity to make a living (Holmes, 1998), ethical concerns about reducing fees for certain clients (Treloar, 2010), and a broad range of countertransference issues (Monger, 1998). While some therapists interpret the exchange of fees as a necessary and straightforward transaction, for others, namely within the psychoanalytic tradition, the exchange of money is ripe with symbolic meaning and therefore may offer relevant information about the client to be utilised in therapy. Fees for missed sessions must also be considered.

The majority of the literature suggests that client fees have little to no impact on therapeutic outcomes; however, it remains a therapist issue permeated with ambiguity. Schonbar and Krueger (1986) encouraged therapists to approach the matter with honesty, forthrightness and a lack of anxiety as it can provide a template for discussing other uncomfortable issues within the therapy setting, potentially serving as a model for the client.

IDENTIFYING THERAPY GOALS

Developing a plan for therapy is a key feature of the initial phase of the process. The therapist may share their understanding of the client's distress or seek clarification on what area the client would like to focus on. The client has arrived with the intention to change something, but this intention may not be fully known or clearly articulated. For some, the establishment of therapy goals ensures the stage is set for effective therapy, thus a 'goal-directedness' approach may be enacted (Dryden and Feltham, 1994). Other therapies seek to pursue intentions and aims without the identification of specific goals (Jacobs, 1999). Often the development of therapy goals is employed with the aim of building a shared sense of therapeutic purpose with the client, translating aims into specific described changes. Throughout the duration of the therapy, there may be the development of short-term, between-session goals, and medium- or long-term goals which ultimately drive the path of therapy. Harris (2009) distinguishes between 'emotional goals', 'insight goals' and 'dead person's goals' in Acceptance and Commitment Therapy (ACT). Treatment goals are designed to be meaningful to the client. For example, the goal of no longer wanting to feel depressed may usefully be translated into a 'living person's goal' by asking the client 'Then what would you do differently? What would you start of do more of? And how would you behave differently with friends and family?' (Harris, 2009: 65). Within ACT, goals which specify what the individual would like to avoid are considered to have far less utility than those goals which the therapist can support the client to move towards. An awareness of the need to balance goal-directed working with the task of creating and maintaining an effective relationship with the client is always required. Inskipp (2012: 79) states that 'competent therapy not only depends on skills but on the capacity of the practitioner to reflect on their use of them'. Integral to the role of the therapist is to consider the rationale for the therapeutic decisions they make as well as allocating time to reflect on their outcome. John Dewey (1933: 78) asserted that 'We do not learn from experience … we learn from reflecting on experience.' Therefore, consideration of what was deemed effective, helpful or a hindrance in the setting up of therapy can be useful for future encounters. Hanley, Sefi and Ersahin (2016) discuss the growing body of research related to goal-oriented therapy approaches. Collaborative goal-setting within the therapeutic relationship can be understood as one way in which to support the notion of the client as an active component in the change process, who is able to identify the appropriate direction of therapy towards their desired goals.

CASE EXAMPLE

Amir is a therapist working in a primary care service. He received a referral asking for client, James, 39 years old, to be contacted for a therapeutic assessment. Attached to the referral was a detailed report from James's General Practitioner (GP) which appeared to extensively outline James's personal history and previous therapy experience. As was routine for Amir, he chose not to consult the referrer's report until after the first session with James, as he was keen not to be influenced by the lens through which another practitioner may have viewed the client. James attended his first scheduled appointment and appeared immediately agitated and restless. Amir found it particularly difficult to aid James's self-disclosure. He wondered whether he was expecting to be asked a list of direct questions in the session, rather than being invited to openly explore his reason for attending therapy. Despite his evident frustration, James tolerated the remainder of the session and Amir agreed to meet James again at the same time the following week for an extended assessment. Shortly after the first session, Amir read the referral report and noticed the depth with which the referrer had detailed James's risk history. The section entitled risk said the following:

James has a significant history of suicide attempts. Aged 15 years, James took a serious overdose which required hospitalisation. Aged 25 years, James was sectioned and admitted to a psychiatric ward following a jump from an 8th floor window, which resulted in both of his legs being broken. James appeared to maintain a stable period of mental health between the ages of 26 and 38. However, four months ago James suffered the death of his brother and consequently took a second overdose, again requiring hospitalisation.

Would Amir have benefitted from knowing this information prior to meeting with James? What impact might it have made if Amir had been aware of James's significant suicide risk history? How might Amir have used the information? See Reeves (Chapter 3.4, this volume) for further discussion of risk assessment and management in therapeutic work.

CONCLUSION

This chapter has offered an overview of some of the central elements that may be considered by a therapist at the outset of commencing therapy. Setting the therapeutic frame is an important stage in the process of therapy. Providing a clear outline of the fixed elements of the therapeutic relationship enhances the possibility for a mutual and collaborative relationship to ensue. In the next chapter considerations for the middle phase of therapy are explored.

REFERENCES

British Association of Counselling and Psychotherapy (BACP) (2016). *Ethical framework for the counselling professions.* Lutterworth: BACP.

British Psychological Society (BPS) (2009). *Code of ethics and conduct.* Leicester: BPS.

Cameron, R. (2003). Psychological contact: basic and cognitive contact. In J. Tolan (Ed.), *Skills in person-centred counselling & psychotherapy.* London: Sage.

Carey, T. A. (2005). Can patients specify treatment parameters? A preliminary investigation. *Clinical Psychology & Psychotherapy, 12*(4): 326–335.

Chaikin, A. L., Derlega, V. J. and Miller, S. J. (1976). Effects of room environment on self-disclosure in a counseling analogue. *Journal of Counseling Psychology, 23*(5): 479.

Chandler, K. (2010). Because you're worth it. *Therapy Today, 21*(5): 7.

Clark, P. and Sims, P. L. (2014). The practice of fee setting and collection: implications for clinical training programs. *The American Journal of Family Therapy, 42*(5): 386–397.

Dewey, J. (1933). *How we think: A restatement of the relation of reflective thinking to the educative process* Lexington, MA: DC Heath and Company.

Donner, M. B., VandeCreek, L., Gonsiorek, J. C. and Fisher, C. B. (2008). Balancing confidentiality: protecting privacy and protecting the public. *Professional Psychology: Research and Practice, 39*(3): 369a.

Dryden, W. and Feltham, C. (1994). *Developing the practice of counselling.* London: Sage.

Gifford, R. (1988). Light, decor, arousal, comfort and communication. *Journal of Environmental Psychology, 8*(3): 177–189.

Hanley, T., Sefi A. and Ersahin, Z. (2016). From goals to tasks to methods. In M. Cooper and W. Dryden (Eds.), *The handbook of pluralistic counselling and psychotherapy.* London: Sage.

Harris, R. (2009). *ACT made simple: An easy-to-read primer on acceptance and commitment therapy.* Oakland, CA: New Harbinger Publications.

Holmes, J. (1998). Money and psychotherapy: Object, metaphor or dream. *International Journal of Psychotherapy, 3*(2), 123.

Inskipp, F. (2012). Generic skills. In Feltham, C., & Horton, I. (Eds.). (2012). *The SAGE Handbook of Counselling and Psychotherapy.* London: Sage.

Jacobs, M. (1999). *Psychodynamic counselling in action.* (3rd ed). London: Sage.

Kazantzis, N. and Kellis, E. (2012). A special feature on collaboration in psychotherapy. *Journal of Clinical Psychology, 68*(2): 133–135.

Lakes, K., López, S. R. and Gallo, L. C. (2006). Cultural competence and psychotherapy: applying anthropologically informed conceptions of culture. *Psychotherapy: Theory, Research, Practice, Training, 43*(4): 380–396.

Mearns, D., Thorne, B. and McLeod, J. (2013). *Person-centred counselling in action.* London: Sage.

Miller, D. J. and Thelen, M. H. (1986). Knowledge and beliefs about confidentiality in psychotherapy. *Professional Psychology: Research and Practice, 17*(1): 15.

Miwa, Y. and Hanyu, K. (2006). The effects of interior design on communication and impressions of a counselor in a counseling room. *Environment and Behavior, 38*(4): 484–502.

Monger, J. (1998). The gap between theory and practice: a consideration of the fee. *Psychodynamic Counselling, 4*: 93–105.

Öst, L.-G., Alm, T., Brandberg, M. and Breitholtz, E. (2001). One vs five sessions of exposure and five sessions of cognitive therapy in the treatment of claustrophobia. *Behaviour Research and Therapy, 39*(2): 167–183.

Pepper, R. (2004). Raising fees in group therapy: some ethical and clinical implications. *Journal of Contemporary Psychotherapy, 34*: 141–152.

Rogers, C. R. (1957). The necessary and sufficient conditions of therapeutic personality change. *Journal of Consulting Psychology, 21*(2): 95.

Saha, S., Beach, M. C. and Cooper, L. A. (2008). Patient centeredness, cultural competence and healthcare quality. *Journal of the National Medical Association, 100*(11): 1275.

Schonbar, A. R. and Krueger, D. W. (1986). *The last taboo: Money as symbol and reality in psychotherapy and psycho-analysis.* New York: Bruner/Mazel.

Shapiro, D. A., Barkham, M., Stiles, W. B., Hardy, G. E., Rees, A., Reynolds, S. and Startup, M. (2003). Times is of the essence: a selective review of the fall and rise of brief therapy research. *Psychology and Psychotherapy: Theory, Research and Practice, 76,* 211–235.

Treloar, H. R. (2010). Financial and ethical considerations for professionals in psychology. *Ethics and Behavior, 20*: 454–465.

RECOMMENDED READING

1.　Hanley, T., Sefi A. and Ersahin, Z. (2016). From goals to tasks to methods. In M. Cooper and W. Dryden (Eds.), *The handbook of pluralistic counselling and psychotherapy.* London: Sage.

Introduces a rationale for the incorporation of goal-setting work in therapy, different types of therapeutic goals as well as practical methods of how goal-setting may be introduced to clients.

2.　Devlin, A. S. and Nasar, J. L. (2012). Impressions of psychotherapists' offices: do therapists and clients agree? *Professional Psychology: Research and Practice, 43*(2): 118–122.

Using photographs portraying a variety of different psychotherapy rooms, this paper investigates psychotherapists' evaluation of the quality of care, comfort in the setting and therapist qualities that they expected clients to experience. Contains recommendations of features likely to create a warm therapeutic office.

3.　Amos, I. and Hanley, T. (2017). The scientist-practitioner and the reflective-practitioner. In V. Galbraith (Ed.), *Topics in applied psychology: Counselling psychology.* London: Wiley.

Provides an overview of two models that have been identified as appropriate for the training and ongoing practice and professional development of practitioner psychologists. Provides a useful insight into the importance of practitioners' development of reflexive knowledge in relation to psychotherapeutic practice and research.

3.8　THERAPEUTIC MIDDLES

INDIA AMOS

OVERVIEW AND KEY POINTS

The process of therapy is a fluid and multidimensional one. It may not be entirely straightforward to pinpoint when exactly the beginning of therapy moves into becoming the middle phase. However, the middle of therapy can be referred to as the 'work phase', and is characterised by those therapy tasks which seek to facilitate the client's psychological change congruent with their identified goals. This chapter presents discussion on the following:

- basic therapeutic skills: managing and maintaining the relationship
- methods of reviewing therapeutic work
- managing attendance
- ruptures and resolutions
- use of the supervisory relationship.

BASIC THERAPEUTIC SKILLS: MANAGING AND MAINTAINING THE RELATIONSHIP

The development of the therapeutic relationship between therapist and client can be said to begin as soon as the first contact with the client is made. It is then ongoing throughout the duration of the work. Importantly, the middle phase of therapy continues its focus on the quality of the therapeutic relationship. The applied nature of this relationship is commonly conceptualised as the working or therapeutic alliance, although it is acknowledged that acceptance of this is far from uniform in the therapeutic literature. Bordin (1979) understood the therapeutic alliance to consist of three elements:

1. agreement between therapist and client on the *goals* of therapy (what therapy is trying to do)
2. agreement on the *tasks* of therapy (how therapy is done)
3. the therapist–client *bond* (consisting of trust and acceptance).

The therapeutic skills covered in this chapter shed light on the ways in which a good therapeutic alliance can be developed and maintained between the therapist and client.

Counselling and psychotherapy can involve the application of a variety of different skills that are understood as being effective for psychological change to occur. Identifying habitual response patterns to distress, improving the client's self-awareness and developing appropriate coping strategies may be considered among the aims of therapy, although the tasks of therapy may differ depending on the therapist's theoretical orientation. While a psychodynamic psychotherapist may focus more explicitly on the transference and countertransference that arises through the relationship, in Cognitive Behavioural Therapy (CBT) the work may be more centred on the client's current problems and what serves to maintain those difficulties in the present. There are chapters in this *Handbook* which are dedicated to the discussion of individual therapeutic orientations, and readers are directed towards those specific chapters for further detail regarding the nature of different types of therapy.

SKILLS: ACTIVE LISTENING AND PARAPHRASING

Active listening and responding appropriately are two of the key skills a counsellor or therapist must possess.

The act of listening may seem like a straightforward one, but it serves a number of important therapeutic purposes that may be easily overlooked. Actively listening to clients offers them a chance to feel heard, which in turn can make clients feel worthy, appreciated and respected. When the therapist offers their client all of their attention, the client may respond positively by interacting on an increasingly authentic level, perhaps becoming more likely to disclose how they are feeling. The practitioner is encouraging the client to continue talking when they are actively listening, at the same time as ensuring their communication remains open. The therapist may also incorporate reflective listening, in which they reflect or restate back to the client what has been said. The therapist may reflect the client's exact words, offering confirmation to the client that they have been heard. Alternatively, the therapist may pick up on the client's feeling and reflect that back to them. For example, 'You are feeling angry about that?', or 'It sounds like the idea of that is scary for you?' Doing this may enable the client to further make sense of what they are saying. Reflecting the feeling of the meaning evident in the client's words can reinforce, to the client, that they have been heard and, perhaps more importantly, understood. When there has been a misunderstanding on the part of the therapist, the technique of reflecting enables the client to clarify what it is they mean.

Paraphrasing can also be a useful tool in addition to reflection (Egan, 2006). Paraphrasing involves the provision of a concise statement of the client's message from the counsellor in an attempt to accurately capture the essence of what the client has disclosed. Again, it can be most effective to use the client's own words when paraphrasing. Words can have a different meaning to each of us, so it is possible that if you sum up what you have heard in entirely your own words you may inadvertently suggest a different meaning from what was said. An example in response to the client saying 'I do not know if lying around in bed all day is good for my mood, but I cannot find any reason to get up and do anything' might be for the therapist to paraphrase by saying 'It sounds like you know what might help with your low mood, but are finding it hard to see the reason to get out of bed at the moment.' As therapists listen they are selecting what to respond to as well as monitoring their own thoughts, feelings, images and bodily sensations. Therapists commonly use their body as an instrument in therapy, continuously drawing on their bodily responses to clients as a way to gain insight into their experience. Clinical psychologist Louise Cozolino (2004) formalised the helpful concept of 'shuttling' to describe the therapist's process of moving their awareness between themselves and their client. The therapist may choose to 'shuttle down' into their bodies in the event that they feel distant or distracted away from their client. Alternatively, they might choose to 'shuttle up' into their minds when feeling confused by client material. This technique may lend itself well to the exploration of why it may be difficult for the therapist to listen to their client effectively.

REVIEWING THE WORK AND MONITORING

Therapeutic practitioners are required by the British Association for Counselling and Psychotherapy (BACP, 2016) to periodically review their therapeutic work with clients. How might the therapist know how the client is experiencing their therapy? Probably the most common way is to ask them. A therapy review may contain a discussion of the client's expectations of therapy, a review of their therapeutic goals, inviting the client to reflect on those aspects of therapy which they have found helpful or unhelpful, or to negotiate the focus of the remainder of the therapy sessions. How therapists may approach conducting a review of therapy can differ. Therapy reviews may be completed via informal or formal methods. Some therapists may prefer to stipulate from the outset that a review session will take place at a specific point in the therapy so the client is aware ahead of time. Others may prefer to informally review the therapeutic process as it develops. Most commonly, this might occur in the event of an impasse or rupture in the relationship (Safran and Muran, 1996). Reviewing therapeutic work with the client can also serve to reinforce the client's learning and change, and has been found to promote therapy attendance (Swift, Greenberg, Whipple and Kominiak, 2012). Therapy reviews serve to maintain the reciprocal and equal relationship necessary between client and therapist. As was indicated in the previous chapter, collaboration in therapy ensures that power is shared within the relationship and reviewing therapeutic work provides an opportunity for the practitioner to 'check out' any assumptions they may have made about the client's experience of the process.

Metacommunication can be defined as communication about communication (Villard and Whipple, 1976). It is the practice of drawing attention to and communciating specifically about the therapist–client interaction and communication. Rennie (1998) identifies four forms or purposes of metacommunication. These include:

- The therapist reveals the purposese of her/his own communication.
- The therapist reveals the impact of the client's communication.
- The therapist enquires into the purposes behind the client's communication.
- The therapist enquires into the impact on the client of the therapist's own communication.

An example of metacommunication may involve the therapist saying 'When I put that to you, how did you find yourself reacting to it? or 'When you said that I found myself feeling...'. These act of metacommunication serve to promote congruence in the therapeutic relationship, as the counsellor is transparent about the intentions of their communication and genuinely curious about the client's reactions. Within pluralistic counselling and psychotherapy (Cooper and McLeod, 2010), client feedback is considered essential in guiding the process. Metacommunication within this form of therapy is integral as it offers the opportunity of an ongoing dialogue between the client and the therapist about what the client is finding helpful or unhelpful about therapeutic sessions. In the context of CBT, Willis and Sanders (2013: 35) refer to metacommunication as 'a type of mindfulness-in-action' as it brings the focus into the here and now and offers the opportunity to reflect on what is occuring in the moment. As a result of these exchanges, helpful insight can be gained that may be used to further inform the client's psychological formulation. Chapter 3.5 (Johnstone – this volume) has discussed the concept of formulation in therapy. Engagement in metacommunication can assist in clarifying, deepening or even modifying the formulation which provisionally seeks to inform the therapeutic work.

REPAIRING RUPTURES TO THE THERAPEUTIC RELATIONSHIP

Ruptures to the therapeutic relationship can offer a suitable opportunity for the therapy to be reviewed. A rupture in the therapeutic alliance can be considered as a moment of interpersonal tension between the therapist and client. Inevitably, in any relationship disturbances or misunderstanding can occur. The therapeutic relationship is no different. Ruptures transpire in all therapies regardless of orientation, although the way they are referred to can differ.

For example, in psychodynamic psychotherapy ruptures may be referred to as transference–countertransference enactments. Ruptures to the therapeutic relationship have been conceptualised as important and critical junctures with the therapy process, and have the potential to occur at any time over the course of therapy. Perhaps they may emerge as a single momentary event, over several sessions, or appear as a recurrent theme throughout the duration. An expanding body of evidence suggests that the repair of ruptures in the therapeutic relationship is related to positive outcomes in therapy (Lingiardi and Colli, 2015). Some even go as far as to say that the negotiation of ruptures in the relationship is at the heart of the change process (Safran and Muran, 2000). Ruptures offer an insight into the interpersonal patterns of the client, which may be a source or maintenance factor in their psychological distress. Experience of a rupture within the therapy can therefore offer moments of potentially productive exploration of interpersonal patterns in sessions (Safran and Segal, 1990). Safran and Muran (1996), two prolific authors in this area, identified two types of rupture that may arise: *withdrawal* ruptures and *confrontation* ruptures. A withdrawal rupture may be indicated by the client offering minimal responses in sessions, or even falling silent completely. Signs of a confrontation rupture may include the direct expression of anger, resentment, frustration or discontent with the therapist or therapeutic process. It is important for the therapist to work constructively with alliance ruptures as the successful resolution or negotiation of alliance ruptures within therapy can foster growth and insight for the client and therapist. The case study offered in this chapter perhaps offers one example of a rupture. How might the scenario presented in the case study be worked with?

An empathic engagement with the client is essential in order to facilitate the client's disclosure and exploration of difficult feelings. Rogers' (1957) core conditions may be considered particularly relevant here as the therapist's unconditional positive regard and empathy can enable the client to work through the challenging terrain of the relationship. This can help clients to experience first-hand that the surfacing of difficult feelings within the context of our relationships does not necessarily destroy them, or indeed destroy ourselves (Safran and Kraus, 2014). Metacommunication skills are implicated again here, as resolving a rupture often can involve self-disclosure on the part of the therapist – sharing their observations and checking out their understanding of the client's experience. This is best communicated in a tentative and exploratory fashion that emphasises the subjectivity of the remarks made.

MANAGING ATTENDANCE

There is an extensive research literature examining the variables that may affect a client's attendance at therapy (Klein, Stone, Hicks and Pritchard, 2003). Clinical severity (Fleury et al., 2012), relationship status (Chen and Rizzo, 2010) and clients' caring responsibilities (Issakidis and Andrews, 2004) have been among the reasons cited for non-attendance. Clients may cancel the therapy session ahead of schedule or not attend on the day without giving notice. This is commonly recorded as the client 'Did Not Attend' (DNA). Some organisations in which counsellors or psychotherapists may work will have cancellation and attendance policies which will indicate how matters of non-attendance must be managed. This can initiate some tension for the therapist, who may be able to see the benefit in continuing therapy with a client who, according to service policy, is required to be discharged. Those practitioners in private practice have to make decisions at their discretion. Fees for missed or cancelled sessions also need to be considered.

Swift, Greenberg, Whipple and Kominiack (2012) concluded that there are six practices that may help to reduce the premature termination of therapy: educating the patient about therapy duration; clarifying the therapist's role; clarifying patterns of change; attending to clients' preferences; strengthening and supporting the client's hope; and assessing the progress of treatment. Indeed, it can be said that the tasks set out in the previous chapter (Amos – Chapter 3.7 this volume), pertaining particularly to the agreement of a therapeutic contract between the therapist and client, should serve to promote the client's attendance. Offering clients their choice of appointment time and providing simple reminders are two effective ways of increasing therapy attendance (Oldham, Kellett, Miles and Sheeran, 2012).

SELF-REFLECTION AND SUPERVISION

There is an ethical obligation for counsellors and psychotherapists to receive supervision support for their therapeutic work. Clinical supervision offers a space for reflection upon therapeutic practice and, as a result, enables the development of skills essential for competent practice. Driscoll (2006) considers the use of experiential learning to develop further knowledge as one function of supervision. In addition, he suggests that the exploration of personal feelings that can surface as a result of client work also serves an important role. With that in mind, reflexive practice can be considered an active process in which the practitioner purposefully explores their experiences

(Amos and Hanley, 2017). They may seek to create possible explanations for their experience, while remaining open to alternative possibilities, even if fundamental beliefs and values are brought into question (Scaife, 2010). A practitioner's reflection on their practice may take place within the context of supervision or on their own. It may be conducted using a structured model aimed at specifically supporting the development of reflexive practice (Mezirow, 1981; Johns, 2004), or it may use no framework at all and simply involve the self-reflection of the therapist to themselves. Regardless of the method, the aim of reflexivity is to draw attention to the ways in which practitioners themselves may influence what emerges within the therapeutic relationship. The case example below highlights the importance of supervision when considering a client's non-attendance at therapy. See Creaner (Chapter 4.3, this volume) for a more in-depth discussion of the forms and purposes of clinical supervision.

CASE EXAMPLE

Verity is a psychotherapist currently engaged in fortnightly supervision with Jasmine. In their last supervisory session, Verity brought one of her current clients to be discussed. Verity used a pseudonym to protect the anonymity of her client when in supervision – she referred to her as Francine. Francine had entered into therapy with signs of mixed anxiety and depression. She had reported having a chaotic childhood, moving to a number of different foster families through her teens. Verity reported how she was becoming increasingly concerned by Francine's sporadic attendance at therapy – she was either turning up late to appointments or not attending at all. Verity reported that their relationship felt increasingly distant and that Francine appeared less and less inclined to explore her psychological distress. This week, in supervision, Verity reports the same thing: Francine was 30 minutes late for their most recent appointment and therefore the only thing they were able to explore in the session was her attendance. Verity confided in Jasmine her consideration over whether to discharge Francine from therapy as she was no longer engaging. Verity reflected on how the situation was making her feel. She expressed feeling irritated by Francine's behaviour, and unsure of why this was occurring week after week as Francine had not opened up about what was preventing her from attending sessions. With support from her supervisor, Verity cast her mind back to the beginning of therapy and the initial six sessions with Francine, all of which she attended. It was only after Verity had to cancel their seventh therapy session at short notice because she needed to attend an urgent hospital appointment that Francine's attendance pattern appeared to change. Jasmine and Verity paused at this point to consider how that event may have impacted Francine, and subsequently how she was presenting in therapy.

Casement (1985) developed the notion of the 'internal supervisor' after noticing how trainees of counselling and psychotherapy would initially rely heavily on their supervisor for guidance in their therapeutic work. Over time trainees would gradually begin to emulate their supervisors, having internalised the qualities they observed. At this point, trainees were said to have developed the capacity to utilise perspectives and insights that are available to them as they work with their clients, both separately and autonomously from their supervisors.

CONCLUSION

The next chapter explores the nature of therapeutic endings, although it is important to note that the ending of therapy is an inferred premise of therapy from the outset, and therefore should be acknowledged and worked with from the very beginning of any therapeutic relationship. In addition, the writing and storing of case notes constitutes an important element of therapeutic engagement and is discussed by Mitchels (Chapter 4.5, this volume). The management of client risk has not been discussed in this chapter. Nevertheless the ongoing management of risk is an integral part of the middle of therapy, as well as the beginning and the end! Readers are referred to Reeves (Chapter 3.4, this volume) for an expanded discussion regarding the management of risk.

REFERENCES

Amos, I., and Hanley, T. (2017). The scientist-practitioner and the reflective-practitioner. In V. Galbraith (Ed.), *Topics in applied psychology: Counselling psychology*. London: Routledge.

Bordin, E. S. (1979). The generalisability of the psychoanalytic concept of the working alliance. *Psychotherapy, 16*: 252–260.

British Association of Counselling and Psychotherapy (BACP) (2016). *Ethical framework for the counselling professions*. Lutterworth: BACP.

Casement, P. (1985). *On learning from the patient London*. London: Tavistock.

Chen, J. and Rizzo, J. (2010). Racial and ethnic disparities in use of psychotherapy: evidence from US national survey data. *Psychiatric Services, 61*(4): 364–372.

Cooper, M. and McLeod, J. (2010). *Pluralistic counselling and psychotherapy*. London: Sage.

Cozolino, L. (2004). *The making of a therapist*. New York: W.W. Norton.

Driscoll, J. (2006). *Practising clinical supervision: A reflective approach for healthcare professionals*. New York: Elsevier Health Sciences.

Egan, G. (2006). *Essentials of skilled helping: Managing problems, developing opportunities*. Belmont, CA: Brooks-Cole.

Fleury, M.-J., Grenier, G., Bamvita, J.-M., Perreault, M., Kestens, Y. and Caron, J. (2012). Comprehensive determinants of health service utilisation for mental health reasons in a Canadian catchment area. *International Journal for Equity in Health, 11*(1): 1–12.

Issakidis, C. and Andrews, G. (2004). Pretreatment attrition and dropout in an outpatient clinic for anxiety disorders. *Acta Psychiatrica Scandnavia, 109*: 426–433.

Johns, C. (2004). *Becoming a reflective practitioner*. Oxford: Wiley-Blackwell.

Klein, E. B., Stone, W. N., Hicks, M. W. and Pritchard, I. L. (2003). Understanding dropouts. *Journal of Mental Health Counseling, 25*(2): 89.

Lingiardi, V. and Colli, A. (2015). Therapeutic alliance and alliance ruptures and resolutions: theoretical definitions, assessment issues and research findings. In O. C. G. Gelo, A. Pritz and B. Rieken (Eds.), *Psychotherapy research: Foundations, process and outcome* (pp. 311–329). New York: Springer.

Mezirow, J. (1981). A critical theory of adult learning and education. *Adult Education Quarterly, 32*(1): 3–24.

Oldham, M., Kellett, S., Miles, E. and Sheeran, P. (2012). Interventions to increase attendance at psychotherapy: a meta-analysis of randomized controlled trials. *Journal of Consulting and Clinical Psychology, 80*(5): 928–939.

Rennie, D. L. (1998) *Person-centred counselling: An experiential approach*. London: Sage.

Rogers, C. R. (1957). The necessary and sufficient conditions of therapeutic personality change. *Journal of Consulting Psychology, 21*(2): 95.

Safran, J. D. and Kraus, J. (2014). Alliance ruptures, impasses, and enactments: a relational perspective. *Psychotherapy, 51*(3): 381.

Safran, J. D. and Muran, J. C. (1996). The resolution of ruptures in the therapeutic alliance. *Journal of Consulting and Clinical Psychology, 64*(3): 447.

Safran, J. D. and Muran, J. C. (2000). Resolving therapeutic alliance ruptures: diversity and integration. *Journal of Clinical Psychology, 56*(2): 233–243.

Safran, J. and Segal, Z. V. (1990). *Interpersonal process in cognitive therapy*. New York: Jason Aronson.

Scaife, J. (2010). *Supervising the reflective practitioner: An essential guide to theory and practice*. London: Routledge.

Swift, J. K., Greenberg, R. P., Whipple, J. L. and Kominiak, N. (2012). Practice recommendations for reducing premature termination in therapy. *Professional Psychology: Research and Practice, 43*(4): 379.

Villard, K. L. and Whipple, L. J. (1976). *Beginnings in relational communication*. New York: Wiley.

Wills, F. and Sanders, D. (2013). *Cognitive behaviour therapy: Foundations for practice*. London: Sage.

RECOMMENDED READING

1.   Clarkson, P. (2003). *The therapeutic relationship* (2nd ed.). London: Whurr.

Explores Clarkson's conceptualisation of five different modalities of client–therapist relationships which may be considered effective in therapy. Presents an integrative principle upon which similarities and differences between therapeutic approaches are considered.

2.   Cooper, M. (2008). *Essential research findings in counselling and psychotherapy: The facts are friendly*. London: Sage.

Provides an introductory overview of important findings related to core issues within therapy research.

3.   Safran, J. D. and Muran, J. C. (2000). *Negotiating the therapeutic alliance: A relational treatment guide*. New York: Guilford Press.

Considers the importance of the therapeutic alliance and its impact on outcome.

3.9   THERAPEUTIC ENDINGS

INDIA AMOS

OVERVIEW AND KEY POINTS

The fact that the therapeutic relationship will end is inevitable from the outset of therapy, and therefore requires specific attention from the counsellor or psychotherapist. Endings have been identified as a fundamental concept within psychotherapy. Whether it is the ending of an individual therapy session or bringing a therapeutic relationship to a final close, the end of therapy can be hugely significant for the client as well as the therapist. In this chapter, the significance of the ending in therapy is elucidated as well as drawing attention to the multiple ways in which therapeutic endings can manifest. The kind of interactions considered relevant to the end of therapy will be discussed, and the question of what constitutes a 'good' ending will be considered.

This chapter presents discussion on the following:

*   Why are therapeutic endings so important?
*   Therapy tasks, including relapse prevention and reviewing therapeutic work.
*   Planned versus unplanned endings.
*   Considering additional referrals.
*   Managing the impact of endings.

Whether the client and therapist have been working together long term or have had engaged in brief therapy, it is likely that the client's relationship with the therapist has played a significant role in his or her efforts to change. Considering the unique and intimate nature of the engagement between the client and therapist over the course of therapy, it is understandable that drawing a therapeutic relationship to a close can evoke a strong emotional reaction for the client as well as for the practitioner. Approaches of how to end (or 'terminate') therapy do not appear vastly different in practice across theoretical orientations and models of therapy. As such, some of the key issues associated with this are reflected in the sections that follow.

PREPARING FOR AN ENDING: TIME LIMITS, THERAPEUTIC PURPOSE AND PATHOLOGY

Providing ample time to prepare for the ending is considered an essential part of the therapeutic process. It is important to begin to prepare clients for termination well before the last session takes place. It is often the case within time-limited therapy that periodic reminders of how many sessions are remaining are offered to the client. In therapy which is open ended, it is important to consider the question of when to end therapy, and this is something to be negotiated between client and therapist. The question of 'what is a good outcome in psychotherapy?' may be relevant here. What does 'getting better' actually look like? There does appear to be agreement among therapeutic approaches of what the therapeutic process strives for. In relation to his objective for clients, Carl Rogers (1961: 171) stated that clients 'seem to move toward more openly being a process, a fluidity, a changing … they are in flux, and seem more content to continue in this flowing current'. The client's self-awareness is sought to be developed as well as their confidence in their own judgement and capacity to manage. An openness to experience internal feelings can be facilitated, and assisting the client's recognition that change and development are an inevitable condition of living can be an important aspect to focus on. Decades of research have demonstrated that a positive alliance, including agreement on goals and tasks in therapy as well as the emotional bond between the therapist and client, is one of the best predictors of outcome (Bordin, 1979; Orlinsky, Rønnestad and Willutzki, 2004). With that in mind, some practitioners may seek to monitor the quality of the developing therapeutic relationship as one way in which to evaluate therapeutic outcome. As research has shown that clinicians are generally poor at gauging their client's experience of the alliance (Norcross, 2010), clinical tools such as the Session Rating Scale (SRS; Johnson, 1995) and Outcome Rating Scale (ORS; Miller and Duncan, 2000) have been developed as a way in which to gain client feedback on their perception of the alliance and their progress in therapy. This serves to empower clients and promote collaboration, as well as to enable the therapist to make the necessary adjustments to therapy in order to enhance outcomes.

FEELINGS ASSOCIATED WITH ENDING: MANAGING CLIENT AND THERAPIST RESPONSES EFFECTIVELY

The prospect of ending therapy can often bring new material to the surface, sometimes related to themes of loss and/or separation (Holmes, 2010). Feelings of abandonment may appear (Salberg, 2010). It is possible that these have already been key themes throughout the therapy so there can be important processing potential at this juncture. In many therapeutic approaches, space is commonly left for the dyad to reflect upon their work together, acknowledge the client's progress in therapy, and to explore his or her feelings about ending the process. Within this period, the gains of ending therapy may also be acknowledged. Time and money which has been invested into the therapeutic process by the client becomes available for alternative ventures, which may serve to help maintain the client's wellbeing.

The therapist too must prepare for the ending, perhaps by reviewing case notes and therapy plans with therapists. Often practitioners seek to have what can be considered an adequate or satisfactory goodbye. This may help the practitioner to recognise the major accomplishments the client has made as well as drawing attention to any specific areas in which the client might benefit from strengthening his or her skills. The therapist's emotional response to completion of therapy work is also important to consider, and may be processed within the context of supervision.

Managing a therapeutic ending effectively can be negotiated in numerous ways. Therapy sessions may become less frequent as the ending moves closer, perhaps moving from weekly to fortnightly (though this is not always the case or possible in some services). Importantly for some, the termination process has been referred to as the resolution to the ultimate alliance rupture (Eubanks-Carter, Muran and Safran, 2010). The therapist may seek to draw the client's attention to their emerging interpersonal pattern, using metacommunication skills, such as the ones discussed in the previous chapter (Amos – Chapter 3.8, this volume). In a research study conducted by Råbu, Binder and Haavind (2013), one of the overarching themes that emerged related to the shared ideal of reaching a consensus between clients and therapists with regards to ending therapy. This agreement seemed to be based largely on an embodied, sensed affect as opposed to the use of arguments or metacommunication exclusively. This study highlighted how both parties within the relationship tended to be careful, considerate and sensitive about the other's feelings and reactions about ending.

THERAPEUTIC TASKS

There are a number of areas which can be explored towards the end of therapy. Assisting clients to integrate their experience of therapy, as well as reinforce positive changes made, is often considered to be one of the primary tasks at this stage. Summarising the work and the client's attainment of goals is also a central task undertaken at the end of therapy (whether articulated as such or not). At the beginning of therapy, specific goals for the client may have been agreed upon. While it is possible that the therapeutic work and the client's goals may have been regularly reviewed throughout the duration of therapy, the impending ending of therapy offers the opportunity to look explicitly at what the client has achieved and why this change has occurred. For many therapists, it is important that clients themselves reflect on their process of change. After all, the client is responsible for any changes made. It is useful to facilitate their recognition of this, as it may go some way in embedding the positive changes observed.

Summarising any new coping strategies or techniques developed can be useful, as well as considering under what circumstances the client might seek to implement these methods in the future. The term 'relapse prevention' refers to the identification and prevention of the return of any old habits, or ways of living, that cause the client psychological distress. In Cognitive Behavioural Therapy (CBT), a more specific structure towards relapse prevention may take place. The last number of sessions may be used specifically to explore, with the client, how they might seek to maintain their progress and manage any setbacks. Of course the client is likely to experience difficult events and painful feelings again in their lives beyond therapy. Helping the client to spot any warning signs related to the return of their difficulties can better equip them to manage any stress which may arise. The therapist may also offer information regarding the support that is available to the client beyond the end of therapy. Often it is recommended that the practitioner make the client aware of the invitation to return or to be re-referred to the service if the need arises (Gelso and Woodhouse, 2002).

Therapists might use specific techniques to encourage discussions related to the client's movement out of therapy. For instance, a goodbye letter to the client from the therapist may include a thoughtful account of the client's original problems and their developing resolution over the course of sessions. Positive achievements may be noted as well as the acknowledgement of difficulties and unresolved feelings. In some therapies, such as Cognitive Analytic Therapy (CAT) (see Pollitt– Chapter 5.27, this volume), letter writing is considered a central feature. Known as a reformulation letter, the therapist writes to the client an account of their life history, drawing attention to personal meanings and emotions, in addition to showing how present ways of living represent the strategies developed to cope with early life. As with all psychological formulations, it is emphasised that the letter is a provisional one and therefore open to revision by clients. Therapeutic letters are intended to extend the work of therapy beyond the sessions themselves, and have been identified by clients as a way to cement the therapeutic relationship (Hamil, Reid and Reynolds, 2008).

Sometimes therapists may offer a follow-up appointment. This may be between six and eight weeks after therapy is finished. The decision to invite the client back after a period of time can reassure the client that the therapeutic relationship, while professional, was genuine, and that a final session to 'check-in' with the client's progression is of interest to the therapist. Holmes (2012) notes how some clients may not opt for a follow-up appointment. Some clients find that following therapy they discover themselves to be much more independent in managing their distress than they may have anticipated. The idea of returning to therapy may be considered as a threat to their new-found freedom, and therefore they may not accept the invitation.

PLANNED VERSUS UNPLANNED ENDINGS

The use of the word 'termination' to describe the ending of therapy, according to Schlesinger (2005: 4), suggests a mutually agreed ending of therapy, associated with the 'opportunity to work through' the thoughts and feelings brought up by the impending end. This description conveys that, for therapists, the ending is an active and integral part of therapy with its own processes and outcomes. Endings that are not mutually agreed have been given various labels. These include 'imposed', 'forced' or 'unplanned' endings. In the event that the therapist changes for the client, the term being 'transferred' may be heard.

It is perhaps idealistic to expect all therapeutic relationships to come to a planned and well-managed ending. In reality, sometimes the end of therapy is forced, meaning it was not foreseen or predicted from the start. An unplanned ending can occur for a variety of reasons. It may be enforced by the client or the therapist. The client may drop out of therapy for an unknown reason, or an adverse event may render the client or therapist unable to continue. Additionally, the client may behave in a manner which is considered incompatible with the requirements of the service. It may be agreed between the client and therapist to end the therapy prematurely, or external factors may influence when it is forced to draw to a close. For example, in the previous chapter (Amos – Chapter 3.8 – this volume) the case example discussed discharging client due to inconsistent attendance to sessions.

Reeves (2010) has written extensively about his experience of an unplanned ending due to his client's suicide. As with any unplanned ending, it is vital that this type of sudden ending be considered, and plans made for the appropriate management in its event. Supervision is of the utmost importance in the event of any ending, unplanned or otherwise. Davis (2008) referred to the potential for therapists to feel anger when a client chooses to end therapy prematurely. A sense of incompleteness to the work may arise. However, it is important for the therapist to remain mindful of his or her own vulnerabilities. Robson (2008) highlights the possible reasons for unexpected endings caused by the therapist, including changes in employment status or personal circumstances or ill-health or death.

CASE EXAMPLE: AN UNPLANNED ENDING

Simon works for a voluntary counselling agency, where policy stipulates that therapists can offer eight sessions to clients. He has been working with client, Alexei, for a month. She had sought therapy after being made redundant and being forced to sell her house. She reported feeling low in mood and less interested in socialising with friends. Therapy appeared to be going well. Their last session together was two weeks ago and since then Alexei has stopped attending sessions and has not contacted the service to explain. Simon reported to a colleague that he was feeling confused about why Alexei had decided to stop coming in and he wondered why she may have chosen this. In line with service protocols, Simon sent Alexei a letter to acknowledge her non-attendance and invite her to contact the service to discuss what action to take. When Alexei did not respond to the letter within the allocated time, or return for sessions, Simon was forced to discharge her from therapy in accordance with the service policy. In supervision Simon reflected on his feeling of sadness that Alexei had not continued with therapy. He expressed a feeling of disappointment in himself, reflecting on the question of 'did I do enough?' With support from his supervisor on the content, Simon chose to write Alexei a therapeutic letter to acknowledge the ending of their therapeutic engagement. The letter summarised the issues they had discussed in therapy, and the progress that was made.

The case example above describes an unplanned ending which occurred as a result of the client's choice. Let's consider a different type of ending which may have occurred for Simon and Alexei.

CASE EXAMPLE: AN IMPOSED ENDING

Alexei and Simon had been seeing each other for seven sessions. In that time, Alexei appeared to have benefitted greatly from exploring the impact of her changing employment status and was feeling more confident about making future career plans. Over the course of sessions Alexei had begun to talk increasingly about her hopes of finding a partner, and the anxiety she felt in relation to dating. Simon considered this to be an important exploration for Alexei within the broader context of her presentation and, despite her original presenting issues already being addressed, could see the advantage of continuing sessions with her. Alexei requested to extend sessions, but this request could not be facilitated by the agency. Simon and Alexei had a final session together before ending therapy.

These examples have offered an insight into two ways in which the therapeutic relationship may come to a close. It may be worth considering what impact either of these scenarios may have on the practitioner and client, and how they might be managed.

MAKING A REFERRAL ONWARDS

In some cases, it might be considered that the client is not yet ready to engage in therapy, and so sessions are brought to an end for that reason. Alternatively, it may be considered that the client requires a different form of therapy, or possibly in a different setting, or of a different type. Or the client may be 'stepped up' to a more intensive course of psychological therapy as a result of a lack of significant gains being achieved within the context of the current treatment.

Dryden (2008) draws attention to the expectation therapists often apply to themselves, thinking that they should be able to work with any client who seeks their help. There can be a pressure on qualified and trainee therapists, who may be seeking client contact hours in order to complete their training or needing to sustain a certain income. Dryden (2008) reminds us, however, of the importance to stay mindful of whether we are able to offer the client the best help possible, or whether another therapist may be a better alternative at that time. Practitioners may, in some cases, not consider themselves the appropriate person to work with the client. Therefore, in this event, they may see the benefit in making onward referrals for clients.

MANAGING THE IMPACT OF THERAPEUTIC ENDINGS

Schlesinger (2005) has argued that therapists tend to have excessively high expectations when it comes to therapeutic endings, that practitioners often imagine endings to be more streamlined than is often possible. Therapists can often be left with a lot of unanswered questions in the event of an unplanned ending, finding it difficult not to know 'the end of the story'. As has been explored in this chapter, when clients do not return to therapy a multitude of thoughts and feelings can surface for the therapist, including worry, guilt, anger, confusion, relief, frustration and sadness. These feelings can be addressed within the context of supervision and, as has been reiterated throughout these last three chapters, approaches to reflexive practice can help practitioners to find optimal ways to support themselves when the end of therapy is prematurely initiated by the client. Endings which are forced due to external factors, like the alternative scenario in the case example detailed above, can also feel like an unsatisfactory ending.

CONCLUSION

This chapter has offered an exploration of the concept of therapeutic endings, as well as demonstrating how endings may be enacted in practice. Endings can be difficult. When the ending is unplanned it can be particularly difficult for the therapist and require some attention within supervision. How we make sense of the ending may depend on our theoretical orientation or worldview. However, it is likely that the aspects of ending discussed in this chapter will resonate with practitioners from across the spectrum of therapeutic approaches. Strategies for anticipating the premature termination of therapy have been explored, with the intention of enabling the appropriate management of these events so that clients do not drop out of therapy before they have experienced the change they initially sought.

REFERENCES

Bordin, E. S. (1979). The generalisability of the psychoanalytic concept of the working alliance. *Psychotherapy*, *16*: 252–260.

Davis, D. (2008). *Terminating therapy: A professional guide to ending on a positive note*. Hoboken, NJ: John Wiley & Sons.

Dryden, W. (2008). Tailoring your counselling approach to different clients. In W. Dryden and A. Reeves (Eds.), *Key issues for counselling in action* (2nd ed.). London: Sage.

Eubanks-Carter, C., Muran, J. C. and Safran, J. D. (2010). Alliance ruptures and resolution. In J. C. Muran and J. P. Barber (Eds.), *The therapeutic alliance: An evidence-based guide to practice*. New York: Guilford Press.

Gelso, C. J. and Woodhouse, S. S. (2002). The termination of psychotherapy: what research tells us about the process of ending treatment. In G. S. Tryon (Ed.), *Counseling based on process research: Applying what we know*. Boston, MA: Allyn & Bacon.

(Continued)

(Continued)

Hamill, M., Ried, M. and Reynolds, S. (2008). Letters in cognitive analytic therapy: the patient's experience. *Psychotherapy Research*, *18*(5): 573–583.

Holmes, J. (2010). Termination in psychoanalytic psychotherapy: an attachment perspective. In J. Salberg (Ed.), *Good enough endings: Breaks, interruptions, and terminations from contemporary relational perspectives* (pp. 63–82). New York and London: Routledge.

Holmes, J. (2012). *Storr's art of psychotherapy* (3rd ed.). Abingdon: Taylor & Francis.

Johnson, L. D. (1995). *Psychotherapy in the age of accountability.* New York: W.W. Norton.

Miller, S. D. and Duncan, B. L. (2000). *The outcome rating scale.* Chicago, IL: Author.

Norcross, J. C. (2010). The therapeutic relationship. In B. L. Duncan, S. D. Miller, B. E. Wampold and M. A. Hubble (Eds.), *The heart and soul of change: Delivering what works in therapy* (2nd ed., pp. 113–141).Washington, DC: American Psychological Association.

Orlinsky, D. E., Rønnestad, M. H. and Willutzki, U. (2004). Fifty years of psychotherapy process-outcome research: continuity and change. In M. J. Lambert (Ed.), *Bergin and Garfield's handbook of psychotherapy and behavior change* (5th ed., pp. 307–389). Hoboken, NJ: John Wiley & Sons.

Råbu, M., Binder, P. E. and Haavind, H. (2013). Negotiating ending: a qualitative study of the process of ending psychotherapy. *European Journal of Psychotherapy & Counselling*, *15*(3): 274–295.

Reeves, A. (2010). *Counselling suicidal clients.* London: Sage.

Robson, M. (2008) Anticipating and working with unplanned endings. In W. Dryden and A. Reeves (Eds.), *Key issues for counselling in action* (2nd ed.). London: Sage.

Rogers, C. (1961) *On becoming a person. A therapist's view of psychotherapy.* Boston, MA: Houghton-Mifflin.

Salberg, J. (2010). Historical overview. In J. Salberg (Ed.), *Good enough endings: Breaks, interruptions, and terminations from contemporary relational perspectives.* New York and London: Routledge.

Schlesinger, H. J. (2005). *Endings and beginnings.* Hillsdale, NJ: The Analytic Press.

RECOMMENDED READING

1. Robson, M. (2008). Anticipating and working with unplanned endings. In W. Dryden and A. Reeves (Eds.), *Key issues for counselling in action* (2nd ed.). London: Sage.

Provides a helpful summary of why therapy may end unexpectedly and the ways in which to manage it.

2. Duncan, B., Miller, S. and Sparks, J. (2004). *The heroic client: A revolutionary way to improve effectiveness through client directed, outcome informed therapy.* San Francisco, CA: Jossey-Bass.

A thought-provoking read which advocates for the client's voice in all aspects of therapy. Includes discussion of the use of formal feedback tools before ending individual therapy sessions as a way in which to guide future interactions.

3. Bolton, G., Howlett, S., Lago, C. and Wright. J. (2004). *Writing cures: An introductory handbook of writing in counselling and therapy.* London: Routledge.

Contains a chapter on the integrative use of writing by clients and therapists in Cognitive Analytic Therapy, which includes reference to goodbye letters.

PART IV

PROFESSIONAL ISSUES

4.1 INTRODUCING PROFESSIONAL ISSUES: THERAPEUTIC SKILLS 'BEYOND THERAPY'

LAURA ANNE WINTER

OVERVIEW OF THIS SECTION

In Part IV of this *Handbook* we take a look at some of the 'Professional Issues' surrounding counselling and psychotherapy. In this introductory chapter I aim to give a brief overview of the chapters which are included in this part of the book. I also briefly discuss what 'Professional Issues' in the fields of psychotherapy and counselling are, and what skills they might require, and reflect on the importance of the work counsellors and psychotherapists do beyond direct client work. I then discuss briefly the implications this has for our training and the broader skill sets we need to work on developing as therapists, suggesting that these skills are potentially different from those required for the application of counselling and psychotherapy theory to practice with clients. Finally, I leave readers to consider three questions which relate to professional issues in counselling and psychotherapy.

This section of the book includes 10 chapters, all of which cover a different element of professional practice issues in counselling and psychotherapy. These include discussions of topics such as research, supervision, leadership, record keeping and note taking. We also include chapters which discuss the legal issues surrounding our work, including therapy and the law more broadly, and, on a more specific level, legal issues connected to mental health law. We have termed these topics 'professional issues' to recognise that, as noted above, these elements of our practice often fall outside the 50-minute therapy hour, or at least outside the application of therapeutic theory to practice in a traditional sense. In contrast to the issues reflected on in the previous parts of the *Handbook*, these chapters focus our attention on the wider skill set and requirements of a therapist's role. As noted in the previous edition of this *Handbook*, the use of the term 'professional issues' may be usefully read against critiques of the *professionalising* trends in counselling and

psychotherapy (see House, 2003). In Chapter 3.1 readers were encouraged to consider the issues discussed in Part III of the book as reflecting on 'core' generic skills which are vital to our practice as counsellors and psychotherapists. It is suggested here that the elements of broader work in therapeutic fields considered in Part IV of the *Handbook* are just as fundamental to work in counselling and psychotherapy, although often taking place outside the therapy room (e.g., supervision and leadership) or only in specific circumstances (e.g., responding to complaints). As I go on to outline, however, they may require a different set of skills or competencies, which any therapist should not neglect to pay attention to in their development.

In terms of the structure of the chapters contained in this section of the *Handbook*, once again each chapter progresses in a different manner depending on the particular context and material covered. As usual, however, authors have provided an *Overview and Key Points* section, as well as *References* and *Recommended Reading*. This will hopefully allow for readers to follow up on any areas of specific interest.

THERAPEUTIC SKILLS 'BEYOND THERAPY'

As aforementioned, in Part III of this book we looked in great detail at the micro processes and overall journey involved in therapy – from building the relationship, meeting the client, right through to endings and finishing our work with clients. Part III therefore got us thinking in close detail about the way we interact with clients in our (typically) 50-minute therapy sessions. This, when combined with our theoretical models and approaches in counselling and psychotherapy, is often what the majority of our initial therapeutic training focuses our attention on, and where we feel most confident in our work as therapists. Training programmes regularly require us to engage in role play and triad-based skills work, and complete a significant amount of placement activities in which we are fundamentally asked to put our therapeutic and psychological theory into practice (Winter and Hanley – Chapter 1.3, this volume). But importantly, counsellors and psychotherapists also spend a good amount of their time (both on such placements and in subsequent employment) doing things which either take place outside the therapy room and have some indirect influence on the therapeutic process, such as research or supervision, or things which bear directly on our therapeutic work but may only occur in specific circumstances, such as writing letters or reports for the courts. We are also required to engage in processes which bear more on the therapist and their development than on any one specific or individual client–therapist relationship: our own personal development. These tasks or roles are not about our direct application of our skills in therapeutic practice and might be considered as skills 'beyond therapy'.

These activities or parts of the job can take up a significant portion of time. Any psychotherapist or counsellor who has worked in the National Health Service, for example, knows how long the record keeping and administrative elements of your role can realistically take, and would not consider this (at least in terms of time spent on the work) as an insignificant part of their job. In our training courses we do talk about and become acquainted with the topics of note taking and record keeping, and often we are taught about ethics and the law and how these impact on our role as a counsellor or psychotherapist. Nevertheless, these professional issues 'beyond therapy' potentially demand very different skills and competencies from what is traditionally viewed as the job of a therapist 'within therapy'. Brown (2006) spoke with counsellors about their experiences of ethical and legal challenges in their work as therapists. She found that there was a wide range of levels of knowledge and confidence in managing such difficulties, and that these issues were given 'highly variable' levels of training in different organisations (2006: 104). Similar findings have emerged when counsellors were asked about processes around information sharing: they had a lack of awareness of policies relating to this area of their practice (Jenkins and Palmer, 2012). These broad professional issues might therefore be areas of work in which counsellors and psychotherapists feel less confident in their own abilities and competence, perhaps because they can sometimes demand a slightly

different skill set and knowledge base. For example, although both require strong communication skills, it seems fair to suggest that one requires a *different* set of communication skills in order to keep appropriate records and write clear reports from the communication skills one requires to practise a particular style of therapy in the room with a client. A counsellor or psychotherapist needs to be able to apply theory to practice and to engage relationally and creatively with the people they work with, but will also potentially be required to apply organisational skills and to be systematic and rigorous when they are asked to conduct research projects or service evaluations.

Some of the professional tasks or roles we consider here might also be viewed as less important by counsellors and psychotherapists, and this can impact how they are engaged with. For example, 'personal development' can be viewed as non-essential and not something individuals want to focus their attention on as a therapist – a distraction from the 'real work'. Wheeler (1991) posed the question of whether personal therapy in counselling training was essential, or whether it was really a 'distraction from focussing on the client'. The notion of potentially being a 'distraction' suggests that this element of our job might actually be taking time away from the core of what we do as therapists, being with clients, rather than supporting such work. Such a question could equally be applied to engaging in research or possessing knowledge and understanding of mental health law. The implication of viewing these professional issues and roles to be non-essential or a distraction is then potentially that we are likely to spend less time on developing the relevant skill set and therefore be less confident in engaging with in them when required.

Hopefully the chapters contained within this section of the *Handbook* will provide some assistance in developing knowledge, confidence and competence in what we have termed the 'professional issues' which make up our therapeutic skills 'beyond therapy'. As noted at the outset of this introductory chapter, the issues reflected upon in the chapters which follow are considered fundamental to the role of the counsellor or psychotherapist, rather than as a 'distraction' or a side-interest. Nevertheless, developing competence in these areas requires a different set of skills, which should not be neglected in our development as therapists.

1. Imagine you are going for a job interview for a post in counselling or psychotherapy. Other than your 'core' therapeutic practice, what skills do you think you need to demonstrate? Why are these important to the role of a therapist?
2. How, if at all, do you think you can train someone to be 'ethical' in their therapeutic practice?
3. How do you think training institutions can best support counsellors and psychotherapists to engage in 'personal development'? What are the alternatives, and why do you think this way is best?

REFERENCES

Brown, A.P. (2006). 'In my agency it's very clear – but I can't tell you what it is': Work settings and ethical challenges. *Counselling and Psychotherapy Research*, 6(2), 100–107.

House, R. (2003). Therapy beyond Modernity: Deconstructing and Transcending Profession-centred Therapy. London: Karnac.

Jenkins, P. and Palmer, J. (2012). 'At risk of harm?' An exploratory survey of school counsellors in the UK, their perceptions of confidentiality, information sharing and risk management. *British Journal of Guidance and Counselling*, 40(5), 545–559.

Wheeler, S. (1991). Personal therapy: An essential aspect of counsellor training, or a distraction from focussing on the client? *International Journal for the Advancement of Counselling*, 14(3), 193–202.

4.2   PERSONAL AND PROFESSIONAL DEVELOPMENT

CHRIS ROSE

OVERVIEW AND KEY POINTS

The contemporary emphasis upon relationality underlines the inextricable link between personal and professional development, making a commitment to self-reflexivity essential for counsellors and psychotherapists. Personal and professional development (PPD) demands emotional engagement, intellectual effort and creativity, challenging complacency, stagnation and burnout. This chapter argues:

- How we conceptualise the nature of both 'self' and 'development' is critical, shaped by socio-political and cultural contexts.

- The training context is particularly important in laying foundations of creative engagement with self and other.
- Learning from the client and from supervision are key elements of PPD.
- Learning styles are varied, and there are many routes to development.

In the context of counselling and psychotherapy, the personal and the professional are inextricably bound together, with no easy distinctions to be made. For every professional decision – which modality to train in, for example – there is a personal story that drives it. In trying to describe the professional therapist, we very quickly use relational qualities such as integrity, compassion, humility and wisdom. Developing personally means developing professionally and vice versa: there is no way to rinse the personal out of a profession that is based upon the ways in which humans relate at depth.

It is now accepted wisdom that the relational qualities of the therapist are more important in determining outcome than any other variable (Rønnestad and Skovholt, 2013; Skovholt and Jennings, 2004). This has assumed even greater significance as our understanding of therapy as a relational process has grown more complex. This has moved from the belief that the therapist could deal with their own difficulties through personal therapy and then provide a clear space to concentrate upon the client, to an acknowledgement that emotions will inevitably transfer from client to therapist and vice versa in the process of therapy, to a recognition that whatever is happening in the room is a joint creation of client and therapist. This appreciation of the co-constructed nature of any therapeutic relationship has meant that self-reflexivity has become increasingly incorporated into training textbooks, with a plethora of 'reflection points' and exercises; an interesting companion to the simultaneous increase in emphasis upon evidence-based practice.

WHAT IS THE SELF THAT WE ARE REFLECTING UPON?

What do we mean by a 'self'? Our seeming obsession with 'self' – self-determination, self-expression, self-awareness, self-sufficiency, self-fulfilment – has arisen in a particular historical, socio-political and economic context. Western society promotes a definition of the self as unitary, capable of autonomous self-willed action to shape individual fortunes. Other cultures, if they are able to withstand the colonising onslaught of globalisation, may hold different views about importance and definition of 'self'. It is important therefore to pause to reflect upon what we mean when we use the word.

Any attempt to interrogate 'oneself' about intimate matters – feelings, desires, dilemmas, for example – reveals a variety of internal views, tensions, conflicts and paradoxes rather than one consistent voice. In addition, it is easy to recognise that our behaviour can radically change according to circumstance. If we attempt to explain this using the concept of 'role', there is the implicit existence of an actor – a 'true self' putting on different emotions, attitudes and behaviours, depending on the performance. In this version of the self, there are costumes to be discarded, layers to be peeled away to reveal the person within. Self-exploration and awareness

here implies a type of archaeological excavation, revealed in phrases such as 'deep down', 'beneath it all' and the 'inner person'. What is concealed deep within becomes reified as 'authentic' whereas the more superficial layers are thought to be the product of social conditioning, and somehow less pure or unchanging.

The 'true self' is a phrase associated with Winnicott (1965), who is perhaps one of the most well-known theorists across all modalities of counselling and psychotherapy. Much of his writing does indeed lend itself to this topographical version of the self, but has also been used to support an intersubjective definition of self – which is a testament both to the subtleties of his work and the complexity of defining a person. His much quoted saying, 'there is no such thing as a baby' states the impossibility of one without the other. There is no self without other, for we are created in interaction. Despite the Western contemporary insistence on autonomy and individuality, people become who they are in the context of others. The social, cultural, political, economic, historical and physical environments shape and give meaning to our lives. The powerful forces of family, class, society, race, religion, age, gender and physical ability teach us how to experience life and what sense to make of it. It is the patterns of responses that we learn in these complex multi-layered experiences that make us who we are.

Rather than a solid core, this version of self is an interpersonal, intrapersonal process. It is created moment to moment in our interactions with others, with past, present and imagined futures, with our internal dialogues. We can move from joy to despair, from compassion to cruelty, persecutor to victim, and so forth. The more we know about ourselves, the more we are able to recognise the paradoxical and sometimes disturbing range of our multiple selves.

It is our capacities to reflect, imagine and create meaning that create the sense of a unitary self. Life is generally chaotic, messy and confused. It is often only in retrospect that we 'understand' what is happening, through selecting and editing the complexity into a coherent narrative. Self-reflection can weave and hold together our multiple selves into a seemingly coherent unity.

Ideas about the self as multiple are well established within counselling and psychotherapy. Configurations of self (Mearns and Thorne, 2007), sub-personalities (Rowan, 1989), the internal society (Hermans, 2014) and the internal group (Rose, 2012) are examples of this way in which the complexity of human experience has been grappled with. Thinking about the self as multiple rather than unitary opens up new avenues for personal development while inviting a more complex appreciation of what development might mean.

WHAT DOES DEVELOPMENT MEAN?

Development as a hopeful vision of constant improvement may have been dismantled intellectually in postmodernism but still colours much of our thinking. We want to be 'more' confident, competent, knowledgeable, authoritative, loveable, wise, compassionate, effective, and so forth. It is important for any counsellor and psychotherapist to have chosen their own list of adjectives – in other words, to have thought seriously about what 'developing' might mean for them.

Psychotherapy and counselling attract clients largely because they offer the possibility of change; perhaps that is what attracts therapists also. Despite the mantra that we all are OK, we are aware that certain ways of living and relating are not. There is a difficult balance between these often less than conscious imperatives to improve and the recognition that as humans we cannot attain perfection. What constitutes 'good enough'?

For many clients, the therapist is the model of psychological health. They are imagined to have successful long-term, loving relationships, to be surrounded by friends and family and bolstered by financial security. The therapist's own self-definition often does not match this image – and may even be tinged with shame that it falls short.

There is, however, the argument that our own struggles are the very stuff that enables us to do the work we do, as expounded, for example, by Jung's archetype of the 'wounded healer' (Jung, 2014). This is part of a widespread discourse across centuries and cultures that links suffering with wisdom. But does personal development require that our own wounds be 'healed' so that we can help others? Or is it the case, as Adams (2014) points out, that there is no such thing as the 'Untroubled Therapist' and personal development involves letting go of any illusion that we can be cleansed and freed from our personal struggles? Just as it is helpful to let go of the idea of a unitary self, so it is important to move away from seeing development as a linear, unidirectional movement. We need more complex, dynamic multidimensional images.

Personal and professional development, I suggest, implies a growth in flexibility and creativity, in the capacity to reflect, and in the tolerance of ambiguity and difference, a widening of what can be seen, heard and understood both cognitively and emotionally. Taking the idea of the 'internal group' as an example, what might this involve?

Using the idea of the self as a group, the driving force of development is identifying, listening to and responding imaginatively to the voices that populate our thoughts.

It means giving a place not only to those more clearly articulated internal voices but also to those in the background, to soma as well as psyche. The more we can discover about our group members, the more it becomes possible to develop a coherent but flexible and creative internal conversation. The internal facilitator, who is a central character in this process of group development, has tough but vital tasks: finding a place for the many voices, however negative or difficult; drawing boundaries; shaping a nuanced and considered group discourse.

This process is fluctuating, uneven, circuitous and rarely smooth. Just as in other groups, the internal group has periods of stagnation, often leading into crisis and instability, which may go on to provide the impetus for genuine change. The relationship between discomfort and growth is an everyday part of therapy. Where are the clients who come into counselling because they are comfortable and think they would like to shake themselves up? Aren't we driven to change by discomfort?

Experiences that disturb both how we feel and how we think can produce long-lasting changes. To learn something new that is not trivial involves a letting go of previous attitudes and ideas. Training courses destabilise and deskill us in the process of expanding our understandings and emotional tolerance. Challenging clients push us into new territories of intellectual and experiential learning. Changes in personal circumstances require us to develop new resources. Personal and professional development, like all worthwhile learning, costs us something before it rewards us.

CONTEXT

We are who we are in the context of the environments that we inhabit – personal, physical, socio-political, environmental, and so forth. The context is not the backdrop to the play, but is seamlessly integrated into who we are and who we might become. It shapes our thoughts, attitudes and emotions and the opportunities that are available to us. Development means struggling wherever possible beyond some of these constraints in order to genuinely hear, see and respect those who are other or different.

The ways in which we have learnt to protect ourselves are parts of the self that all of us are fearful of letting go, even when they have ceased to serve us well. These have been effective in previous contexts, which is why they are so embedded; so much a part of ourselves that there will be aspects that we cannot recognise without the mirror that others hold up to us. Trying to become aware of how we behave, how we relate to others and to the world is a constant challenge for the therapist, and the context within which this challenge is set is always moving. Global movements, political instabilities, climate change, technological advances are part of the larger shifting scene within which changes in personal circumstances and work environments render it impossible to complete the work of PPD.

The end is out of sight, but the beginning is often to be found in the context of training.

TRAINING...

The challenge of self-reflection may be encountered for the first time in the context of training, which in itself presents a dilemma. Training inevitably involves some form of assessment and judgement, in whatever style it is carried out. Students are simultaneously challenged intellectually, exposed to new ideas and theories, and asked to examine their own experiences, attitudes and ways of being. In some instances the combination provides an enormously powerful and effective stimulus to learning, but often the reality of needing to 'pass' constricts these possibilities.

In a context of assessment, it can be difficult for the training course to provide and the student to experience that crucial balance of security and challenge that is needed for meaningful personal learning. Already stretched intellectually and emotionally by theories and practice, it is a step too far for some students to relax their grip on the version of themselves that they are familiar with.

The relationship with authority – being instructed to self-reflect or being required to have personal therapy – can strangle self-exploration and openness, and this often comes at a time before the student has examined the issue of authority in their own lives. This may be compounded by the students' need for guidance and clarity in models and practice to navigate the new ideas and experiences they are encountering. Trainers and supervisors play a highly influential part in the students' development, often with phases of idealisation/denigration.

The counterbalance to all this is the huge potential for personal development that training offers. It has very particular characteristics that may lay down foundations, positive and negative, for future development. Intellectual stimulus in combination with relational challenges and peer support in learning groups and particularly PPD groups (Rose, 2008) provides fertile grounds for self-awareness, as does writing personal and/or learning journals (Wright and Bolton, 2012).

Here it becomes possible for students to identify and work with their core personal issues that they consider to be dominant in their lives. Aponte and Kissil (2016) call

these the 'signature themes' that need identifying in order to understand their impact, real and potential, upon the client work.

...AND BEYOND

Having completed the task of qualification and found work as a therapist, it becomes possible and necessary to take ownership of one's own self-development. There is a continued controversy concerning the value and importance of personal therapy in training, but at least 80 per cent of therapists enter into it at some point and consider it to be valuable (McLeod and McLeod, 2014). The demands of client work bring home the message that no single model can adequately respond to human complexities, and that drawing upon the self is vital.

Whatever is happening in the therapy room is a joint creation, so it is no surprise that learning for the client will involve learning for the therapist also. Evidence from a survey of more than 4,000 psychotherapists from 20 different countries put 'experience in therapy with clients' as the major impact upon their professional development. The supervisory relationship is ranked next in order, demonstrating its central role throughout training and beyond (Orlinsky, Botermans and Rønnestad, 2001, cited in Rønnestad and Skovholt, 2003).

Many other avenues for PPD encountered in training continue to be highly valued by experienced counsellors: further study, learning and PPD groups, journalling, for example. In addition, many find themselves learning through teaching and supervising others.

Any therapist who works over a long time span will experience blows to their own self-worth – clients who fail to attend, to respond, to move on, who attack and denigrate, who self-harm or even kill themselves. How the therapist responds to these experiences is critical.

[A]s practitioners feel more confident and assured as professionals with the passing of time, also they generally see more clearly the limitations in what they can accomplish. Fuelling this process of increased realism are the 'series of humiliations' which therapists experience over time. If these 'blows to the ego' are processed and integrated into the therapists' self-experience, they may contribute to the paradox of increased sense of confidence and competence while also feeling more humble and less powerful as a therapist. (Rønnestad and Skovholt, 2003: 38)

In addition to these 'humiliations', time spent working intimately with the distress and trauma of others takes its toll. Exhaustion and burnout can be avoided or mitigated with space for reflection, along with supportive but challenging supervision and peer relationships (Skovholt and Trotter-Matheson, 2016; Vetere and Stratton, 2016). Donna Orange talks about her own internal support group of writers and philosophers who she values for their sustaining wisdom (Orange, 2016).

HOW

The rationale – the 'why' of PPD – is clearly established. The 'how' is hugely varied, individual, idiosyncratic and, above all, creative. PPD is a particular type of learning, and therapists have different learning styles and ways of engaging and challenging their multiple selves. Groups, journals, art, sport, academic learning, dance, reading, writing, singing, movement, nature and more can all provide rich ground for new learning. The list is extensive, and McLeod and McLeod (2014) offer a comprehensive survey.

The key ingredients in whatever format are curiosity, imagination, reflexivity and an engagement with others. The 'others' might be internal voices, self-dialogues, colleagues, friends, strangers or a sense of the transcendent. A monologue is rarely the vehicle for significant learning. We need interruptions and challenges to enlarge our thinking and experiencing.

CONCLUSION

It has become part of the accepted wisdom that as therapists we can only engage with our clients' worlds to the degree that we can engage with our own. Our own 'signature themes' may never disappear but the more we have acknowledged and explored them, the better able we are to recognise their presence in our client work, use them creatively or, at the very least, mitigate their impact.

With experience it becomes increasingly obvious that the personal and the professional cannot be split apart. Decisions to join a professional organisation, to subscribe to a particular ethical code, to be an active or passive member, are all personal decisions that are open to self-scrutiny and further understanding. The demand for integrity has to be like the lettering in the stick of rock, running throughout the person of the therapist, their practice and their organisation.

Above all, experience brings an increased sensitivity both to the complexities of human experience and to the limits of therapy and the therapist. Any simplistic or reductionist accounts of the human condition are antithetical to personal and professional development. An increased confidence as a therapist is accompanied by the appreciation of the limitations of therapy and therapists. The more we know, the more we realise how little we know.

Intellectual effort, emotional engagement and creativity stand out as the vital qualities that fuel PPD. It is a lifelong process that requires a commitment to learning and self-reflection, and although that might sound dull and worthy, this paradoxically comes hand in hand with an appreciation that we need to take ourselves less seriously! Having fun has got to be somewhere on the list of PPD activities!

REFERENCES

Adams, M. (2014) *The Myth of the Untroubled Therapist*. London and New York: Routledge.

Aponte H.J. and Kissil, K. (eds) (2016) *The Person of the Therapist Training Model: Mastering the Use of Self*. New York: Routledge.

Hermans, H.J.M. (2014) Self as a society of I-positions: a dialogical approach to counselling. *Journal of Humanistic Counselling*, 53:134–159.

Jung, C.G. (2014) *The Practice of Psychotherapy* (2nd ed.). London: Routledge.

McLeod, J. and McLeod, Julia (2014). *Personal and Professional Development for Counsellors, Psychotherapists and Mental Health Practitioners*. *Maidenhead*: Open University Press.

Mearns, D. and Thorne, B. (2007) *Person Centred Counselling in Action* (3rd ed.). London: Sage.

Orange, D. (2016) *Nourishing the Inner Life of Clinicians and Humanitarians*. Abingdon and New York: Routledge.

Rønnestad, M.H. and Skovholt, T.M. (2003) The journey of the counselor and therapist: Research findings and perspectives on professional development. *Journal of Career Development*, 30(1): 5–44.

Rønnestad, M.H. and Skovholt, T.M. (2013) *The Developing Practitioner: Growth and Stagnation of Therapists and Counsellors*. New York: Routledge.

Rose, C. (2008) *The Personal Development Group: The Student's Guide*. London: Karnac.

Rose, C. (ed.) (2012) *Self Awareness and Personal Development: Resources for Psychotherapists and Counsellors*. Basingstoke: Palgrave Macmillan.

Rowan J. (1989) *Subpersonalities: The People Inside Us*. London: Routledge.

Skovholt, T.M. and Jennings, L. (2004) *Master Therapists: Exploring Expertise in Therapy and Counselling*. New York: Allyn and Bacon.

Skovholt, T.M. and Trotter-Matheson, M. (2016) *The Resilient Practitioner: Burnout Prevention and Self-care Strategies for the Helping Professions*. London and New York: Routledge.

Vetere, A. and Stratton, P. (eds) (2016) *Interacting Selves: Systemic Solutions for Personal and Professional Development in Counselling and Psychotherapy*. London and New York: Routledge.

Winnicott, D.W. (1965) *Maturational Processes and the Facilitating Environment*. London: Hogarth Press.

Wright, J. and Bolton, G. (2012) *Reflective Writing in Counselling and Psychotherapy*. London: Sage.

RECOMMENDED READING

1.   McLeod, J. and McLeod, Julia (2014) *Personal and Professional Development for Counsellors, Psychotherapists and Mental Health Practitioners*. Maidenhead: Open University Press.

Comprehensive research-based exploration of the why and hows of PPD, including extensive learning tasks.

2.   Rose, C. (ed.) (2012) *Self Awareness and Personal Development: Resources for Psychotherapists and Counsellors*. Basingstoke: Palgrave Macmillan.

Offers a range of approaches to explore multiple selves including music, the written word, visual imagery, the natural environment, transcendence and embodiment.

3.   Wright, J. and Bolton, G. (2012) *Reflective Writing in Counselling and Psychotherapy*. London: Sage.

Varied ways that reflective writing can be used within different modalities and forms of counselling, with examples and suggestions for self-exploration.

4.3   CLINICAL SUPERVISION

MARY CREANER

OVERVIEW AND KEY POINTS

It is widely accepted that clinical supervision is an essential professional activity in counselling and psychotherapy training (Bernard and Goodyear, 2014). Supervision is also a mandated career-long requirement by the majority of professional organisations for their practising members (e.g., British Association for Counselling and Psychotherapy (BACP). Depending on the professional organisation, various supervision criteria (i.e., ratio of supervision hours to client hours, format and frequency of supervision sessions, etc.) need to be met for accreditation/re-accreditation purposes. Hence, supervision plays a central role in the career-span of the counsellor and therapist. With reference to this background, this chapter provides an overview of the following:

•   The purpose of supervision in counselling and therapy.
•   Negotiating the supervision relationship and working alliance.
•   Feedback and evaluation in supervision.
•   Opportunities and challenges in supervision.

THE PURPOSE OF SUPERVISION IN COUNSELLING AND THERAPY

Historically, supervision in the counselling/therapy tradition was seen as a logical application of the therapy approach being taught, to the supervisee's professional development (Carroll, 2007). As specific supervision models (e.g., Hawkins and Shohet, 2012; Page and Wosket, 2001) inevitably evolved, there has been a shift to understanding supervision as a learning endeavour focused on the practice being undertaken rather than solely on the person of the supervisee (Carroll, 2007). Embedded in many supervision models is what Falender and Shafranske (2004: 3) refer to as the 'pillars' of supervision, namely: the supervisory relationship (the working alliance), inquiry (focus on what is happening in supervision and therapy) and educational praxis (personalised educational interventions to facilitate supervisee learning).

There are many definitions and descriptions of clinical supervision available, due in part to different perspectives arising from the context in which supervision is offered, part to the complexity of the supervision relationship, and part due to the inadequate conceptualisation of supervision (Milne et al., 2008). Nonetheless, most agree that the main purposes are to advance supervisee professional development, safeguard client welfare and provide for gatekeeping in the profession (Bernard and Goodyear, 2014). According to the BACP, supervision may be understood as:

> a specialised form of professional mentoring provided for practitioners responsible for undertaking challenging work with people. Supervision is provided to: ensure standards; enhance quality and creativity; and enable the sustainability and resilience of the work being undertaken. (BACP, 2016: 5)

Within this description, the primary functions of supervision, as outlined by Proctor (1987), are apparent, namely: a normative function which promotes accountability, quality control and ethical best practice; a formative function to facilitate learning and competency development within the profession; and finally, a restorative function to buffer the potential stresses of the work (and training), provide support and foster an attitude of self-care. This framework remains a useful resource for the supervisor in holding the primary foci of supervision in the foreground. It is also an accessible framework for the supervisee to reflect on their learning needs as they prepare for supervision (Creaner, 2014).

Depending on what aspect of practice is brought to supervision for reflection, and the learning goals of the supervisee therein, the emphasis may vary across these three functions at a given time. However, all three functions need to be accommodated within the frame of good supervision. For example, BACP (2016: 11) propose that 'good supervision is much more than case management' and requires attention to the relational circumstance in which it occurs. In contrast, supervisors may be overly supportive or protective of the relationship at the expense of appropriately challenging the supervisee or providing corrective feedback as the need arises (Heckman-Stone, 2004). Hence, there is a need for supervisors to balance between the three functions of supervision and ensure that each is attended to proportionately in the context of the supervision relationship.

NEGOTIATING THE SUPERVISION RELATIONSHIP AND WORKING ALLIANCE

The supervision relationship may be considered as the pivot upon which all supervision endeavours flourish or flounder. Of all of the constructs discussed in relation to supervision, the *relationship* has received considerable attention in the literature (Bernard and Goodyear, 2014). A frequently cited framework within the supervision relationship is that of Bordin's (1983: 37–38) 'working alliance' which comprises 'mutual agreements' between the supervisee and the supervisor with reference to the 'goals' or what is to be accomplished in supervision (e.g., skills development, case conceptualisation); the 'tasks' or methods used for the attainment of the supervision goals (e.g., listening to recordings of client sessions, role play); and the 'bonds' or mutual investment by both the supervisor and supervisee in the supervision process. In other words, setting up a supervision relationship requires teasing out an overall working agreement so that the boundaries of supervision with reference to the relationship, roles, responsibilities and rights of all parties are clear from the outset (see Creaner, 2014, for a learning agreement template).

Agreement on the goals of supervision will naturally be influenced by a variety of factors and the developmental level of the supervisee will elicit particular areas for discussion. For example, in the training situation, the agreement of goals will need to accommodate requirements of the training course (e.g., programme learning outcomes) and their professional accreditation criteria. Similarly, in the case of qualified practitioners, accreditation/re-accreditation criteria will also need to be explicit. Other factors for consideration include the theoretical approach in which the supervisee is training or practising, the context of the client work (e.g., trauma work), the context of the organisation (e.g., a health service), the professional/ethical context (e.g., code of ethics, inclusive practice), and so forth.

With reference to agreement on the tasks of supervision, Bordin (1983) suggests that these are inextricably linked to the specified goals of supervision and the means or methods by which these goals can be facilitated. A variety of methods and interventions (e.g., feedback, critical reflection, monitoring client outcome, etc.) are available and good supervision provides for multiple methods (Milne et al., 2008). Different supervisors will have different styles and, likewise, supervisees will have individual learning preferences. Optimally, the tasks of supervision need to be negotiated and personalised within supervision (see Wallace and Cooper, 2015, *Supervision Personalisation Forms*). Such negotiation and individualisation can contribute to a sense of mutuality in the supervision process and enrich the supervisory bond (Bordin, 1983).

In addition to agreeing on the goals, tasks and bonds of supervision, the agreement should also refer to the practicalities of the work (e.g., frequency and length of supervision sessions, arrangements in the case of emergencies). Clear agreements serve the interests of the supervisor, the supervisee and their client and need to be reviewed regularly as the supervision relationship develops and the learning needs of the supervisee evolve (Bernard and Goodyear, 2014).

THE IMPACT OF THE SUPERVISION RELATIONSHIP

Many positive and negative consequences have been attributed to the quality of the supervisory relationship. On the positive side, good supervision relationships have been seen to contribute to skills development, self-awareness and confidence building (Weaks, 2002; Wheeler and Richards, 2007). In addition, good supervision enhances supervisee satisfaction (Weaks, 2002), encourages the disclosure of practice issues (Sweeney and Creaner, 2014) and promotes culturally sensitive practice (Soheilian, et al., 2014).

Although many studies indicate that the majority of supervisees (both trainee and qualified) experience supervision as useful and growth promoting (e.g., Weaks, 2002; Wheeler and Richards, 2007; Wilson et al., 2015), this is not always the case. Research has demonstrated that negative consequences are frequently experienced by supervisees and the impact of such experiences include decreased disclosure (Sweeney and Creaner, 2014), supervisee distress, feelings of inadequacy and perceived negative impacts upon their clients (Ramos-Sánchez et al., 2002). While negative experiences may also bring the opportunity to openly discuss the difficulty and deepen the supervision alliance, this is unlikely to happen in the absence of a psychologically safe environment (Page and Wosket, 2001).

As discussed by Ellis and colleagues (2014), poor supervision can span a continuum from inadequate to harmful supervision. In the former, inadequate supervision occurs when 'the supervisor fails to provide the minimal level of supervisory care as established by their discipline or profession' (e.g., supervisors not attending to the normative, formative and restorative aspects of supervision) (Ellis et al., 2014: 437). Harmful supervision arises from 'supervisory practices that result in psychological, emotional, and/or physical harm or trauma to the supervisee' (e.g., boundary violations whereby the supervisee feels shamed, pathologised, etc.) (Ellis et al., 2014: 440).

In a recent cross-cultural comparative study (Ellis et al., 2015) between supervisees in the Republic of Ireland (RI) (n=149) and the United States (US) (n=151), the results indicated that, at some point in their career, 92.4% (RI) and 86.4% (US) of the supervisees received inadequate supervision (e.g., no supervision contract, client work not monitored) and that 51.7% (RI) and 39.7% (US) of the supervisees had experienced harmful supervision (e.g., supervisor was abusive). Of further note in this study was that supervisees did not always identify inadequate or harmful supervision as such, indicating that supervisees may need further information on what they have a right to expect from supervision. Considering the negative impact of such experiences on the supervisees, and the unknown impact on their clients, supervisees need to be actively supported in expressing and addressing any difficulties they may encounter, particularly in the training context, where power differentials are salient (Ellis et al., 2015; Wilson et al., 2015).

FEEDBACK AND EVALUATION IN SUPERVISION

Both trainee and qualified supervisees welcome and seek frequent, clear, direct and balanced feedback which offers guidance for further development (Heckman-Stone 2004; Weaks, 2002). Ambiguous feedback and a lack of balance between affirming and corrective feedback are seen as contributing factors to poor supervision (Ramos-Sánchez et al., 2002). From the perspective of a supervisor, providing feedback and evaluation are often seen as challenging tasks, especially if the supervisee demonstrates resistance to receiving feedback (Carroll, 2014). However, as feedback is a key intervention in supervision and a means by which learning is advanced (Milne et al., 2008), supervisors and supervisees need to openly address the challenges that providing feedback may present. Supervisees may also be encouraged to provide regular feedback to their supervisors and seek routine feedback from their clients, optimally through objective outcome measures (see Wheeler et al., 2011).

Within supervision, all feedback is a statement of evaluation, whether formative or summative. Evaluation is what ultimately distinguishes supervision from counselling or therapy and is an essential element of all supervision (Bernard and Goodyear, 2014), whatever the developmental level of the supervisee. Hence, evaluation is intrinsic to reflective supervision 'where review is central to growth' and includes both evaluation of the work done and also planning for continuing development (Carroll, 2014: 53).

While widely endorsed as a necessity in supervision, particularly in training, little is empirically known about the process or effect of evaluation on the supervisees or on outcomes for their clients. Even less is known about the evaluative process with qualified and more experienced practitioners. Although evaluation may not be an explicit feature in the supervision of qualified practitioners (though best practice would suggest that it ought to be explicit in the supervision contract), it is an ever present phenomenon. Beyond training, many professional organisations require reports from supervisors for accreditation and re-accreditation purposes (e.g., BACP).

Evaluation is also linked to the gatekeeping function of supervision, wherein the monitoring of ethical, legal and professional practice for client welfare is a constant responsibility of supervisors across the career-span of supervisees (Bernard and Goodyear, 2014). It is therefore important for supervisors to critically reflect on and make explicit what is being evaluated, when that evaluation will occur, how the evaluation will be delivered and how evaluation of supervision can be elicited. In addition, such criteria need to be explicitly and collaboratively discussed at the outset and form part of the supervision contract (Falender and Shafranske, 2004).

OPPORTUNITIES AND CHALLENGES IN SUPERVISION

SUPERVISOR TRAINING

As mentioned, developments in supervision have contributed to conceptualising supervision as a professional activity in its own right requiring professional competencies which are different from those of the counsellor/therapist (Falender et al., 2004). Along with this understanding, increased focus is being placed on supervisor training. As a consequence, increasingly professional organisations and health services are requiring their supervisors to undertake training and supervision competence frameworks are being developed (e.g., IAPT, 2011; Roth and Pilling, 2009). In addition, professional organisations are providing supervision practice guidelines (e.g., American Psychological Association, 2014), and supervision training curricula (e.g., BACP, 2014). For example, BACP (2014) have devised a detailed 'Counselling Supervision Training Curriculum' in this regard, wherein

they state that the curriculum is intended as a minimum baseline standard for best practice in supervision training. Predicated on Roth and Pilling's (2009) core competencies framework, the BACP (2014: 3) curriculum comprises ten session areas (e.g., building the supervision relationship) and provides an outline of the content, and teaching methods, together with suggested assessment activities provided as flexible guidelines for training institutions.

TECHNOLOGY, SOCIAL MEDIA AND SUPERVISION

The use of technology in clinical supervision is not a new phenomenon (e.g., live supervision, bug-in-ear). As technology and web-based activity has become a facet of everyday life, it is not surprising that it been readily adopted in the supervision domain, as evident in the increasing literature focusing on the use of web technology (e.g., email, video-conferencing) in supervision. This development is partly driven by pragmatic factors (e.g., access to supervisors in rural communities) along with the flexibility and decreased costs of travel that technology provides (Rousmaniere, 2014). However, as with face-to-face counselling and psychotherapy, there are a number of ethical, legal, professional and practical considerations with reference to the use of internet technology in supervision. For example, issues of confidentiality with regard to the security of communication channels; the implications of providing supervision outside one's professional jurisdiction and/or the country of the supervisee; competence in the use of technology for both the supervisor and supervisee (Renfro-Michel et al., 2016). Again, as with other aspects of supervision, the use of technology needs to be accommodated within the supervision contract and also needs to include contingency plans, as relevant, in the event of emergencies, technological breakdowns, and so forth (Rousmaniere, 2014).

Within this arena, the use of social media has also become ubiquitous in recent years and also presents a further area for clarification in supervision with reference to supervisor and supervisee social media presence (Creaner, 2015). This conversation may be included in the initial contract and address such areas as the supervisor's policy on accepting social media 'friend' requests from supervisees, the ethics of online searches for supervisor/supervisee/client information and the ethical implications of social media contact with clients (American Psychological Association, 2014).

SUPERVISION RESEARCH

While the quantity and quality of supervision research has increased in recent decades, there are many gaps in our knowledge and understanding of supervision. For instance, and by no means exhaustive, we need to understand more fully the impact of good and poor supervision on supervisee and client outcomes. In seeking a robust evidence base, we also need to understand more fully how developmental, contextual and cultural factors influence and affect the supervision process. Furthermore, the area of supervisor training, competency development and evaluation are pertinent areas of inquiry.

Considering the multiplicity of variables and factors inherent in the supervision relationship and the counselling/therapy relationship, it is a challenging area of inquiry. Repeatedly, we hear from those who undertake supervision research, particularly systematic reviews (e.g., Wheeler and Richards, 2007) and meta-analysis (e.g., Wilson et al., 2015) of the difficulties concerning the lack of methodological rigour in studies, the lack of a clear conceptualisation of supervision and the diversity of measures employed make it difficult to draw conclusions across studies that could inform practice (Wheeler et al., 2011). Nonetheless, these challenges present many opportunities for further development. Wheeler and colleagues (2011) envisioned a research agenda for supervision being developed, so that a common set of measures are agreed and supervision practitioners and researchers collaborate in the research endeavour.

CONCLUSION

As supervision seeks to collaboratively and critically reflect on practice, an opportunity is also presented to critically reflect on the quality of supervision provided. The fact that there is wide acceptance of its usefulness and effectiveness in counselling and therapy may potentially inhibit critical reflection on the times when it is not experienced as useful or effective. As every encounter between a supervisor and supervisee is a unique experience, each supervisory relationship will also be a unique experience. Hence, the challenge to supervisors is to flexibly engage with the person of the supervisee to facilitate professional development, scaffold and promote best practice, provide support and in light of the inherent hierarchy, work towards a collaborative, growth enhancing and equal relationship.

REFERENCES

American Psychological Association (2014) *Guidelines for Clinical Supervision in Health Service Psychology*. Washington, DC: APA. (www.apa.org/about/policy/guidelines-supervision.pdf; retrieved 18 March 2016).

British Association for Counselling and Psychotherapy (2014) *Counselling Supervision Training Curriculum. BACP Professional Standards*. Lutterworth: BACP. Available at http://www.bacp.co.uk/docs/pdf/15473_13372_supervision-curriculum%20%282%29.pdf (accessed on 19 June 2017)

British Association for Counselling and Psychotherapy (2016) *Ethical Framework for the Counselling Professions: Glossary – Supervision*. Lutterworth: British Association for Counselling and Psychotherapy (www.bacp.co.uk/ethics/glossary.php).

Bernard, J.M. and Goodyear, R.K. (2014) *Fundamentals of Clinical Supervision* (5th ed.). Boston, MA: Pearson.

Bordin, E.S. (1983) A working alliance based model of supervision. *Counseling Psychologist*, 11: 35–41.

Carroll, M. (2007) One more time: what is supervision? *Psychotherapy in Australia*, 13(3): 34–40.

Carroll, M. (2014) *Effective Supervision for the Helping Professions*. London: Sage.

Creaner, M. (2014) *Getting the Best Out of Supervision in Counselling and Psychotherapy: A Guide for the Supervisee*. London: Sage.

Creaner, M. (2015) The role of social media in counselling and psychotherapy. In R. Tribe and J. Morrissey (eds), *Handbook of Professional and Ethical Issues for Psychologists, Counsellors and Psychotherapists* (3rd ed., pp. 158–170). Hove: Routledge.

Ellis, M.V., Berger, L., Hanus, A.E., Ayala, E.E., Swords, B.A. and Siembor, M. (2014) Inadequate and harmful clinical supervision: testing a revised framework and assessing occurrence. *The Counseling Psychologist*, 42: 434–472.

Ellis, M.V., Creaner, M., Hutman, H. and Timulak, L. (2015) A comparative study of clinical supervision in the Republic of Ireland and the United States. *Journal of Counseling Psychology*, 62(4): 621–631.

Falender, C.A., Cornish, J.A.E., Goodyear, R., Hatcher, R., Kaslow, N.J., Leventhal, G., ... Grus, C. (2004) Defining competencies in psychology supervision: a consensus statement. *Journal of Clinical Psychology*, 60: 771–785.

Falender, C.A. and Shafranske, E.P. (2004) *Clinical Supervision: A Competency-based Approach*. Washington, DC: American Psychological Association.

Hawkins, P. and Shohet, R. (2012) *Supervision in the Helping Professions* (4th ed.). Maidenhead: Open University Press.

(Continued)

(Continued)

Heckman-Stone, C. (2004) Trainee preferences for feedback and evaluation in clinical supervision. *The Clinical Supervisor*, 22(1): 21–33.

IAPT (2011) *Guidance for Commissioning IAPT Supervisor Training*. (www.iapt.nhs.uk/silo/files/guidance-for-commissioning-iapt-supervisor-training-revised-2011.pdf).

Milne, D., Aylott, H., Fitzpatrick, H. and Ellis, M.V. (2008) How does clinical supervision work? Using a 'best evidence synthesis' approach to construct a basic model of supervision. *The Clinical Supervisor*, 27(2): 170–190.

Page, S. and Wosket, V. (2001) *Supervising the Counsellor: A Cyclical Model* (2nd ed.). Hove: Brunner-Routledge.

Proctor, B. (1987) Supervision: a co-operative exercise in accountability. In M. Marken and M. Payne (eds), *Enabling and Ensuring: Supervision in Practice* (pp. 21–34). Leicester: National Youth Bureau, Council for Education and Training in Youth and Community Work.

Ramos-Sánchez, L., Esnil, E., Goodwin, A., Riggs, S., Osachy Touster, L., Wright, L.K., Ratanasiripong, P. and Rodolfa, E. (2002) Negative supervisory events: effects on supervision satisfaction and supervisory alliance. *Professional Psychology: Research and Practice*, 33(2): 197–202.

Renfro-Michel, E., Rousmaniere, T. and Spinella, L. (2016) Technological innovations in clinical supervision: promises and challenges. In T. Rousmaniere and E. Renfro-Michel (eds), *Using Technology to Enhance Clinical Supervision* (pp. 3–19). Alexandria, VA: American Counseling Association/Wiley.

Roth, A.D. and Pilling, S. (2009) A competence framework for the supervision of psychological therapies. (www.ucl.ac.uk/pals/research/cehp/research-groups/core/competence-frameworks/Supervision_of_Psychological_Therapies).

Rousmaniere, T.G. (2014) Using technology to enhance clinical supervision and training. In C.E. Watkins and D. Milne (eds), *International Handbook of Clinical Supervision* (pp. 204–237). New York: Wiley.

Soheilian, S., Inman, A.G., Klinger, R., Isenberg, D. and Kulp, L. (2014) Multicultural supervision: supervisees' reflections on culturally competent supervision. *Counselling Psychology Quarterly*, 27(4): 379–392.

Sweeney, J. and Creaner, M. (2014) What's not being said? Recollections of nondisclosure in clinical supervision while in training. *British Journal of Guidance and Counselling*, 42: 211–224.

Wallace, K. and Cooper, M. (2015) Development of supervision personalisation forms: a qualitative study of the dimensions along which supervisors' practices vary. *Counselling and Psychotherapy Research*, 15(1): 31–40.

Weaks, D. (2002) Unlocking the secrets of 'good supervision': a phenomenological exploration of experienced counsellors' perceptions of good supervision. *Counselling and Psychotherapy Research*, 2(1): 33–39.

Wheeler, S., Aveline, M. and Barkham, M. (2011) Practice-based supervision research: a network of researchers using a common toolkit. *Counselling and Psychotherapy Research*, 11(2): 88–96.

Wheeler, S. and Richards, K. (2007) The impact of clinical supervision on counsellors and therapists, their practice and their clients: a systematic review of the literature. *Counselling and Psychotherapy Research*, 7(1): 54–65.

Wilson, H.N., Davies, J.S. and Weatherhead, S. (2015) Trainee therapists' experiences of supervision during training: a meta-synthesis. *Clinical Psychology and Psychotherapy*, doi:10.1002/cpp.1957.

RECOMMENDED READING

1. Bernard, J.M. and Goodyear, R.K. (2014) *Fundamentals of Clinical Supervision* (5th ed.). Boston, MA: Pearson.

This comprehensive text covers all aspects of supervision theory and practice for supervisors.

2. Carroll, M. (2014) *Effective Supervision for the Helping Professions*. London: Sage.

This is an accessible text which considers supervision from the learning, ethical, professional and organisational perspectives.

3. Creaner, M. (2014) *Getting the Best Out of Supervision in Counselling and Psychotherapy: A Guide for the Supervisee*. London: Sage.

Drawing on current supervision research, this book explores the supervisory learning relationship and provides resources for supervisors and supervisees to optimise their supervisory experience.

LEADERSHIP

ANTONY FROGGETT

OVERVIEW AND KEY POINTS

Leadership is popular. Walk into any bookshop at a train station and there will be a selection of books on how to be a leader. A chapter on leadership has even found itself in this new edition of *The Sage Handbook of Counselling and Psychotherapy*! Leadership is associated with professional success, power and esteem, but what do we mean by the term 'leadership' and how might we better understand leadership to become more informed and engaged in our therapeutic work and organisations?

This chapter explores the following questions:

- What do we mean by leadership?
- How is leadership related to management, authority, power and followership?
- What sort of problems require leadership rather than technical management?
- What are the strategies used to solve problems and why do these often not work?
- How are organisations changing, and what are the implications for leadership?
- Are therapists potentially good leaders?

WHAT IS LEADERSHIP?

One definition of leading is, 'to cause (a person or animal) to go with one by holding them by the hand, a halter, a rope, etc., while moving forward' (*Oxford Dictionary of English*, 2010). This definition communicates the idea that leadership is about taking others forward in a chosen direction. We often talk of leaders as providing a vision that will inspire others to follow.

It is common to refer to senior figures in an organisation as 'leaders' regardless of their actions. We might therefore first distinguish between the *position of a post-holder* in a hierarchical structure and the *act of leading* (which might come from different levels within an organisation).

LEADERSHIP VERSUS MANAGEMENT

One common confusion is to use the terms 'leadership' and 'management' as if these were the same thing. Management can be defined as ensuring that an organisation operates efficiently and effectively. Leadership, in contrast, is deciding how to engage with change. Although people often are asked to be leaders, in reality what is being asked for is in fact management, that is, the competence and efficient running of a team within the existing parameters. Ultimately, leadership is a disruptive process.

An example: When Apple launched the iPhone in 2007 it did so without being able to guarantee the success of the new product, but knowing that it would inevitably reduce the sales of the iPod, the product that provided the main revenue for the company. This decision was later described as a 'bet the company risk' by one Apple executive (Haselton, 2013).

Although distinguishing between management and leadership can be useful, Western (2013: 37) cautions us against over-simplistic distinctions – one that often sees leadership as 'sexy' and adventurous, and management as merely technical and following established procedures. He argues that effective organisations need both the efficiency and order provided by management alongside creativity and renewal provided by leadership if they are to function properly.

AUTHORITY

A newly appointed head of a counselling service is full of ideas about how to make improvements. He becomes increasingly frustrated with colleagues who seem suspicious of his intentions. The main figure appears to be the office manager, who has been there for the past 15 years. Staff look up to her and respect her opinions. It appears that nothing happens without her agreement.

In the above example, there is a difference between the formal leadership roles and the reality of how decisions are made within the team. In other words, authority and leadership are not aligned.

Obholzer (1994: 39) refers to authority as the right to make ultimate decisions that are binding on others. He distinguishes between three types of authority:

- authority from above
- authority from below, and
- authority from within.

In the above example, the new manager could appeal to the board of trustees or his own line manager in order to gain authority from above. Alternatively, he could attempt to gain authority from below by establishing relationships with his new team and trying to gain their backing for the changes that he wants to make.

A neglected aspect of leadership is the extent to which our actions are a response to our introjected authority figures (authority from within).

> A supermarket manager tells her coach that she is going to fire one of her staff who has been accused of assaulting a drunken customer. She says that she wants to 'make an example' of the employee. She mentions that when she was a child she was scared of her mother who had a violent temper. She admits that there have been times when she has lost her temper with customers. In the end, she decides that she needs to investigate what happened more thoroughly and that the whole staff team might need additional training in how to deal with difficult customers.

In the above example, the manager was able to see her responses as linked to her experience of a violent parental figure and a wish to deny her own aggressive feelings. By acknowledging these unwanted feelings, she was able to move to a more integrated way of engaging with the problem.

Roberts (1994), in her article 'Is authority a dirty word?', points out that our attitude to authority has changed in the past few decades. Abuse scandals in children's homes and by the clergy have made us more questioning of those in authority, and less likely to assume that they can be trusted.

FOLLOWERSHIP

One neglected aspect of leadership is that it cannot exist without followership. Although many people want to be leaders, few of us want to be followers. There are 629 million search results for the term 'leadership' on the internet. Interestingly, there are only 427,000 search results for the term 'followership', suggesting perhaps that for every person who wants to follow, there are 1,473 people vying to be the one to lead them!

Perhaps one of the consequences of our increased scepticism towards those in authority is that we are less likely to agree to being led. Dynamics of rivalry, competition and envy can also undermine the effective functioning of an organisation. The undermining of the leadership function can take many forms. Obholzer (1994: 44) argues that for counsellors and other helping professionals these envious attacks on leadership can often come in a disguised form, such as a concern with anti-authoritarianism, anti-sexism or anti-racism. These issues can be used as a cover for more destructive impulses that can undermine an organisation.

POWER VERSUS AUTHORITY

Power relates to the control of resources. If authority is something that is conferred by one's role in the organisation, then power is a quality that resides in individuals. There are many different forms of power (such as physical, financial and professional). Problems occur when power and authority are misaligned. If there is authority but no power, then leadership will be weak and ineffectual. If there is power but no authority, then there is dictatorship (Obholzer 1994: 42). In the National Health Service, it is common for managerial responsibilities to be split between a general manager and a clinical lead. This can sometimes result in confusion about who has the ultimate authority to make decisions. It is common for therapists to feel that their clinical decision-making is undermined by ill-informed management processes, and for managers to feel that they are obstructed by therapists who are paid more because of their professional qualifications but who have less organisational responsibility.

TAME AND WICKED PROBLEMS

One of the functions of leaders is to solve our collective problems. Rittel and Webber (1973) made the distinction between tame and wicked problems. Tame problems are problems for which there is an established protocol. The problems might be technically very difficult (such as counting the grains of sand on a beach) but it is possible to agree a procedure for achieving this aim, and it is possible to say when this task has been completed. In contrast, a wicked problem often has no agreed definition or measure of success. The way the problem is understood is dependent upon the values and worldviews of those who are framing the problem. A wicked problem has no 'stopping point'. It can never be ultimately solved but only be made better or worse.

Are the problems that we ask our leaders to solve tame or wicked? For example, in the field of mental health, do we have a clear agreement about what counts as 'health' or how this might be measured? Do we agree about which interventions are effective and which are ineffective? Are the key factors contributing to clients' difficulties within the scope of therapy services to influence?

Sometimes problems that are presented to leaders to solve are entwined with other problems that interact with each other in a way that can appear intractable. Problems such as poverty, addiction, poor mental health, family breakdown and violence often co-exist in a way that is self-reinforcing. It is not unusual for services to see the problems of clients as beyond their remit and therefore for clients to be excluded. In trying to describe the phenomena of multiple, interrelated problems, Ackoff wrote 'Every problem interacts with other problems and is therefore part of a set of interrelated problems, a system of problems. ... I choose to call such a system *a mess*' (1997: 427).

CLUMSY SOLUTIONS

How is a leader meant to act when faced with 'a mess' in which there are disputed understandings of the problem and where there is no clear agreement about the way forward?

Grint (2008) outlines four types of strategies that are used to engage with problems:

1. Egalitarian – these emphasise equality and shared values, the idea that 'we are all in this together'.
2. Hierarchical – these emphasise leadership, expertise and use of rules/the law to implement changes.
3. Individualist – these emphasise choice and self-interest for promoting change.
4. Fatalist – these emphasise acceptance and adaptation to reality, and promoting changing expectations rather than external events.

Strategies for solving a problem are often disputed. For example, it has been argued that introducing minimum unit pricing for alcoholic drinks would reduce alcohol-related harm (hierarchal solution). Others have advocated for better labelling and the promotion of responsible drinking (individualistic solutions). Others still have argued that there is no problem to solve. They point out that the United Kingdom (UK) is ranked 22nd in the amount of alcohol drank in countries in Europe and that countries that drink more than the UK (such as France and Germany) have healthier populations (fatalistic solutions) (World Health Organisation, 2014).

If both the nature of the problem and the solution are contested, it is unlikely that the leader will find many supporters for any proposal. Strategies that work in some contexts may not work when applied to alternative problems or with different groups. Verweij and Thompson (2006) use the concept of 'Clumsy Solutions' to describe the necessity of using multiple solutions, each of which has its own competing perspectives and blind-spots. This may lead to a sense of incoherence and a lack of direction, but may be a more mature way of engaging with the reality of wicked problems.

THE CHANGING ORGANISATION

For many people, organisational life is changing. Some have a 'portfolio' career, perhaps with several part-time jobs or a succession of short-term contracts. This is common in the fields of counselling and psychotherapy. Some people work in multiple teams, across different sites. Others work in 'virtual teams' without an office that 'meet' mainly by Skype. Increasing numbers of people, especially therapists, are self-employed.

Our psychological relationship to work is also slowly, but significantly, changing. Miller (1999) has written about how work no longer meets our needs for security and dependency. Employers no longer feel an obligation to look after us, and we are less likely to feel a sense of commitment to them. This has led Drucker (2007: 17) to comment that increasingly employees have to be managed as if they were volunteers, that is, each employee has to be engaged with the values and vision of the organisation rather than assuming that their behaviour can be directed by management.

If the relationship between the organisation and the individual has become more fluid and contingent, so have the boundaries of the organisation itself. Funding contracts frequently require 'partnership working' with multiple organisations. The changing nature of organisations is captured by Cooper and Dartington (2004), who argue that the traditional, boundaried organisation is being replaced by a network of related groups and organisations. Increasingly, key decisions of an organisation cannot be made in-house by senior management, but must be made in collaboration with partner agencies, stakeholders, commissioners and service-user groups.

Managers are therefore frequently responsible for outcomes over which they have little control. A hospital ward manager, for example, may be chastised for not having a free bed to take a new patient, but is unable to discharge an existing patient because her social care needs (which are the responsibility of the local authority) are not in place for her to be safely allowed to go home.

THERAPISTS AS LEADERS

The demise of traditional organisational structures and assumptions around authority has resulted in the need for a different sort of leadership than the past. Huffington (2004), in her research of female leaders, describes how it is the soft skills that are now key to operating effectively as a leader, such as attending to relationships, establishing a network, engaging and motivating people. Simpson and French (2005) discuss the importance of 'thoughtful leadership', that is, being open to new thoughts and ideas through engagement with the people in the organisation.

In many respects, it is these types of listening and relationship skills that are the core attributes of therapists.

Why then are there not more therapist managers? Discussions about power within the therapeutic relationship are often about the *abuse* of power. Does this experience unconsciously influence the stance of therapists within organisational settings? It may be that the idealism of therapy does not survive the exposure to the dynamics of competition and rivalry within organisational settings. Huffington and Miller, in their article, 'Where angels and mere mortals fear to tread', conclude that 'the fantasy of equality' (2008: 34) can prevent organisations engaging realistically with problems of competition, displacement and fears of annihilation.

The priority of an organisation is ultimately its primary task or purpose, rather than the relationships between colleagues or with clients. This inevitably means a tension between needs of individuals and those of the organisation as a whole. Boydell (2005) uses Jessop's (2003) concept of the 'romantic ironist' to describe a type of stance necessary to be effective as a worker. This involves being able to balance the ideal of creating a better world with a hard-nosed scepticism. This means acknowledging that bosses can make bad decisions and that things sometimes get worse. This approach involves navigating the extremes of idealistic naivety and cynical disengagement.

Shortly before Christmas, a children's ward manager was told that the Christmas tree and decorations must be taken down because of a vomiting bug. She unsuccessfully argued that her ward, which had no vomiting illness, should be exempt from the 'deep clean' that was ordered throughout the hospital. She was told that she would be disciplined if she did not implement hospital policy. In the end she laminated some of the decorations so that they could be wiped clean, and created a detailed spreadsheet (stating when each decoration would be cleaned or removed) which she emailed to her manager. A week later, the vomiting outbreak had subsided. No one came to check whether the decorations were removed and the children's Christmas on the ward was not interrupted.

In the above example, the ward manager avoided taking an idealistic position of arguing on behalf of her patients as she knew this would not be heard above concerns about physical health in the hospital. She also did not give up or retreat into cynicism. Instead she devised an ironic strategy that showed compliance with the directive while focusing on the needs of the children on the ward.

In the end we may not be able to say that therapists make particularly good or bad leaders, but one thing is clear – leadership is not therapy and therapy is not leadership. Although there is an increasing overlap in the skills needed for both roles, we might be wary of attempts to

conflate the two. Using Jessop's terminology, it may be that managers need to become more 'romantic', and that to be successful at operating within organisations therapists need to become more 'ironic'.

CONCLUSION

Leadership is often cited as a panacea for improving public and private organisations. We have, however, perhaps unrealistic expectations of what leadership can do for us. Leadership is like therapy in that it does not provide instant solutions to our problems. The 'lens' of leadership can help us explore and improve how we make decisions, allocate resources and use power. It does not tell us what decisions to make or what the outcome of such decisions will be in advance. Leadership is the conduit for collective decision-making, but it can also be a way of distorting the responsibility for the outcomes of such decisions. We often idolise our leaders (such as Nelson Mandela) or despise them (for example, Tony Blair for the war in Iraq). Sometimes this involves forgetting our own agency. Leaders get to choose but only because they are chosen. The most complex difficulties that we face, such as climate change, need clear leadership, but any solutions will require a level of cooperation, compromise and long-term engagement that leaders by themselves cannot provide. It is only through an engagement with our own responsibilities for leadership and followership that 'wicked problems' can be addressed. This chapter has hopefully encouraged you to explore further the concept of leadership, and prompted you to reflect upon your own relationship to leadership in your organisation and wider society.

REFERENCES

Ackoff, R. (1997) 'Systems messes and interactive planning', in Trist, E., Murray, H. and Emery, F.E. (eds.), *The social engagement of social science*. Volume 3: *A Tavistock anthology – the socio-ecological perspective*. Philadelphia, PA: University of Pennsylvania Press, pp. 417–438.

Boydell, L. (2005) 'The defensive function of interorganisational partnerships', *Organisational and Social Dynamic*, 5(2): 225–241.

Cooper, A. and Dartington, T. (2004) 'The vanishing organisation: organisational containment in a networked world', in Huffington, C., Armstrong, D., Halton, W., Hoyle, L. and Pooley, J. (eds.), *Working below the surface: The emotional life of contemporary organizations*. London: Karnac, pp. 127–150.

Drucker, P. (2007) *Management challenges for the 21st century* (Classic Drucker Collection). London: Routledge.

Grint, K. (2008) 'Wicked problems and clumsy solutions: the role of leadership', *Clinical Leader*, 1(2): 11–15.

Haselton, T. (2013) *IPhone was 'bet the company' risk for apple, exec says*. (www.technobuffalo.com/2013/11/15/iphone-was-bet-the-company-risk-for-apple-exec-says/).

Huffington, C. (2004) 'What women leaders can tell us', in Huffington, C., Armstrong, D., Halton, W., Hoyle, L. and Pooley, J. (eds.), *Working below the surface: The emotional life of contemporary organizations*. London: Karnac, pp. 49–66.

Huffington, C. and Miller, S. (2008) 'Where angels and mere mortals fear to tread: exploring 'sibling' relations in the workplace', *Organisational and Social Dynamics*, 8: 18–37.

Jessop, B. (2003) *Governance and metagovernance: On reflexivity, requisite variety, and requisite irony*. (www.lancaster.ac.uk/fass/resources/sociology-online-papers/papers/jessop-governance-and-metagovernance.pdf).

Miller, E. (1999) 'Dependency, alienation or partnership? The changing relatedness of the individual to the enterprise', in French, R. and Vince, R. (eds.), *Group relations, management and organization*. Oxford: Oxford University Press, pp. 98–111.

Obholzer, A. (1994) 'Authority, power and leadership: contributions from group relations training', in Obholzer, A. and Roberts, V.Z. (eds.), *The unconscious at work: Individual and organizational stress in the human services*. London: Routledge, pp. 39–47.

Oxford Dictionary of English (2010) *Oxford Dictionary of English* (3rd ed.). Oxford: Oxford University Press.

Rittel, H.W.J. and Webber, M.M. (1973) 'Dilemmas in a general theory of planning', *Policy Sciences*, 4(2): 155–169.

Roberts, V.Z. (1994) 'Is authority a dirty word? Some dilemmas in idealistic organisations', *Journal of Social Work Practice*, 8(2): 185–192.

Simpson, P. and French, R. (2005) 'Thoughtful leadership: lessons from Bion', *Organisational and Social Dynamics*, 5(52): 280–297.

Verweij, M. and Thompson, M. (eds.) (2006) *Clumsy solutions for a complex world: Governance, politics and plural perceptions (global issues)*. Basingstoke: Palgrave Macmillan.

Western, S. (2013) *Leadership: A critical text* (2nd ed.). London: Sage.

World Health Organisation (2014) *Global status report on alcohol and health 2014 alcohol*. Geneva: WHO. (www.who.int/substance_abuse/publications/global_alcohol_report/msb_gsr_2014_1.pdf).

RECOMMENDED READING

1. Grint, K. (2010) *Leadership: A very short introduction*. Oxford: Oxford University Press.

A short and accessible introduction to the issue of leadership.

2. Obholzer, A. and Roberts, V.Z. (eds.) (1994) *The unconscious at work: Individual and organizational stress in the human services*. London: Routledge.

A classic book introducing the 'Tavistock approach' (combining systems theory and psychoanalysis) to understanding organisations. Includes interesting examples of consultation work with organisations.

3. Western, S. (2013) *Leadership: A critical text* (2nd ed.). London: Sage.

A critical exploration of the different discourses of leadership, includes the author's own model of 'eco-leadership'.

4.5 CONFIDENTIALITY, NOTE TAKING AND RECORD KEEPING

BARBARA MITCHELS

OVERVIEW AND KEY POINTS

The way in which we make and keep our client notes or records involves both law and ethics. Law provides the rules within which we all have to work, and professional ethical guidance the 'fine tuning' of client and therapist care, in the boundaries of good therapy practice. Making and keeping good records of our work links with the professional duty of confidentiality. Disclosure of records may be required by our clients or others and should only be made in accordance with the law and with ethical practice, so a basic understanding of what is required of us in relation to client confidences is essential. Each practitioner will have their own particular range of clients, work contexts, and professional requirements, so we cannot expect to have a clear 'one size fits all' set of rules that will suit everyone. However, we can, with the help of supervision and an understanding of the law and guidance documents, reflect on the needs of our practice, our clients, and ourselves as practitioners, developing an ethical approach to confidentiality and record keeping appropriate for our work. When practice dilemmas arise, being able to know when help is needed, and where to find it, provides a level of safety and security for therapists and clients.

- Keeping appropriate client records is regarded as a professional responsibility.
- Client notes (records) should be concise, accurate, up to date, and appropriate for the work, and may include all notes identifying or identifiable to the client, correspondence, memos, artefacts and recordings.
- The form and storage of our records may vary with work contexts and legal and ethical requirements.
- The length of time for storing records may vary according to the work context, but clients should be aware of how long their records will be kept.
- Disclosures of client information should only be made in accordance with the law and ethical practice, i.e.,

  o with client consent
  o where the law permits – i.e., where public interest justifies disclosure
  o where the law requires – e.g., statutory requirements or court orders.

For more detailed discussion of the points made in this chapter, see *Confidentiality and record keeping in counselling and psychotherapy* (Bond and Mitchels, 2014).

NOTE TAKING – WHAT MAKES A GOOD RECORD?

It is generally regarded by the courts and professional organisations that our professional responsibilities include making and keeping clear and accurate records of our client work.

Client records act as an aide-memoire for therapy, and also may provide evidence of what happened in a therapy session. They may be protective of both client and therapist if events in a session are later questioned. Notes should be accurate, distinguishing fact from opinion, concise – saying just as much as necessary (i.e., not excessive) – and be respectful of the client, so not intrusive. They should be up to date, and a golden rule is that, although not written for the purpose of evidence, we always need to bear in mind that our notes may one day be required in a court or tribunal and/or that a client may wish to read them.

WHAT DOCUMENTS AND ARTEFACTS MIGHT BE INCLUDED IN A CLIENT RECORD?

The form of our records may vary with work contexts and legal and ethical requirements. Some agencies may have templates or forms for client records, and other practitioners may develop their own way of keeping therapy records.

Records may include:

- all notes and process notes identifying or identifiable to the client (see definition in 'process notes' below)
- correspondence, memos and transcribed text messages
- artefacts (or photographs of artefacts, such as models, sand tray work, etc.)
- any form of recording, e.g., sound, video, etc.

Process notes may become part of the therapy record if they identify the client by name or otherwise, or if they are identifiable to the client (i.e., if the client's circumstances or other factors described in the notes could identify the client to anyone reading them who is familiar with those circumstances). Notes made for supervision purposes may also be included in this definition.

Court orders for production of records: If a court order requires client records to be produced, the order will usually apply to all records in existence at that time which are relevant to that client. Only those process notes or journal reflections which do not identify the client and are in no way identifiable to the client may be regarded as excluded from the client record.

There may be other possible options available to a therapist who is concerned about producing all of their client records in court, such as offering to write a report for the court, or asking the court to accept only the parts of the client record which are relevant to the case (for more on these options, see *Therapists in court* (Bond and Sandhu, 2005).

WHERE AND FOR HOW LONG SHOULD I KEEP MY RECORDS?

Data protection legislation and our duty of care of confidentiality requires that client records are kept 'securely'. This usually means keeping documents in a locked cabinet, in electronic storage on a computer, etc., or uploaded to safe 'cloud' storage, protected by security in the form of encryption or password protection systems. Insurance companies may have specific requirements for secure storage, such as 'a locked metal cabinet', so this is worth checking with the insurer.

The length of time that records are retained may be governed by contract, by the policy of any agency for which the therapist works, or by other relevant professional guidance. In other cases, practitioners may decide for themselves how long they wish to retain their records, with the agreement of their clients. Factors to consider are the time limitations on professional complaints and also for legal actions for professional negligence (see Figure 4.5.1). Clients should be made aware that records are kept, and of any rights of access to them, and the length of time for which the records will be kept.

- Contract – 6 years
- Tort (e.g., professional negligence, breach of duty of care) – 3 years but may be extended in some sexual abuse cases
- Criminal Injury Compensation – 2 years
- Crime – no time limit
- Professional misconduct – check with your professional body (often 3 years from end of contact/complainant's realisation of wrong)

Figure 4.5.1   General time limits for legal matters

WHAT IS CONFIDENTIALITY?

The word 'confide' comes from the Latin, with *con* acting as an intensifier of *fidere* – meaning to trust or put one's faith in. It is probably best translated as 'to strongly trust someone'. Confidentiality occurs when two people decide to restrict the communication of information, keeping it between themselves in order to prevent it being communicated to a third person or to more people. In a professional relationship, 'confidentiality' means protecting information that can only be disclosed at some cost to another's privacy in order to protect that privacy from being compromised any further. The terms of confidentiality should be negotiated and contracted between therapist and client, but note also that:

> A professional (like anyone else) who somehow acquires confidential personal information may be saddled with an obligation of confidentiality toward X, the subject of the information, whether there was a direct, indirect or no contact with X. All that is necessary is that the professional was aware, or a reasonable person in her position would have been aware, that the information is private to X. (Pattenden, 2003: 13)

This means that where a client gives information about others in the course of therapy, our duty of confidentiality will apply to those people as well as to the client.

HOW DOES THE LAW PROTECT CONFIDENTIALITY?

There are different types of law: statute law (i.e., the law made by Parliament) and common law (i.e., the law laid down by court decisions interpreting statute law). Law can cover criminal actions (the criminal law) and the law that protects civil rights and duties and redresses civil wrongs (civil law). If therapists commit criminal acts, for example the sexual assault of clients, they are liable to prosecution under the criminal law. Where therapists breach the duty of confidentiality outside the boundaries allowed by law and ethics, the client may have redress through civil law for acts of professional negligence (breach of the duty of care), for example a breach of confidentiality which was made without appropriate consent, without a court order or one which was clearly not made in the public interest. Civil law also covers the enforcement of contractual rights and duties in therapy contracts. For more detailed discussion of the legal system and how civil law relates to the business of providing therapy, see Mitchels and Bond (2008; see also Jenkins (Chapter 4.9, this volume)). The Data Protection Act 1998, Freedom of Information Act 2000 and the Human Rights Act 1998 may apply both to protect client confidences and provide access to data (see the section on data protection below).

WHEN MAY I DISCLOSE CLIENT INFORMATION?

Client information may lawfully be disclosed by a therapist only when:

(a) The client consents to or requests disclosure.
(b) The law requires disclosure.
(c) The law permits disclosure.

(A) CLIENT CONSENT

If a client consents to disclosure, the duty of non-disclosure ceases to exist. Seeking a client's explicit consent is legally and ethically the most satisfactory way of resolving dilemmas over confidentiality. The consent may be total or, more likely, quite specific in what may be communicated, when and to whom. Anything that is not included in the explicit terms of the client's consent remains protected by an obligation of confidentiality.

A client's consent for disclosures should be obtained wherever possible (see General Medical Council, 2009: 37–39). For discussion of mental capacity, age and consent, see Bond and Mitchels (2014: Chapters 11–12). Where therapists know that they are working in circumstances where they have a specific obligation to pass on information, or they sense that a client is about to give information during therapy that could create an obligation on the therapist to make a disclosure, there is an ethical case for alerting the client to the consequences of their impending disclosure before it is made. This is respectful of client autonomy and trust, and therefore ethically desirable. However, **please note** therapists should exercise caution and/or take appropriate advice before giving such a warning to clients in any situation involving child protection, since this might in some cases adversely affect a child's welfare or compromise a child protection investigation, with potentially serious consequences. Also, alerting a client to the possible need for disclosure of acts in relation to terrorism may be illegal, if it could amount to 'tipping off', which is forbidden (see (B) below).

(B) WHERE THE LAW REQUIRES DISCLOSURE

Court orders: Orders of the court should be obeyed and the penalty for disobedience is punishment for contempt of court. Court orders may be made for a therapist to attend court as a witness, and/or to disclose therapy notes and records, or to provide a report for the court. The therapist may wish to attend a directions hearing to discuss issues of confidentiality of therapy information with the court, and to request appropriate directions. See Bond and Sandhu (2005) for further details of how to handle requests for confidential information by solicitors, which cannot compel disclosure, and court orders, which can. Court orders (sometimes called 'directions') for disclosure of information may be made by civil and criminal courts under a wide range of statutory powers, and are normally issued by the court as a written instruction.

Terrorist activities: There is a general duty to report information which assists in the prevention of terrorist activities. The Terrorism Act 2000, section 38B, makes it a criminal offence (punishable by a fine or imprisonment) for a person to fail to disclose, without reasonable excuse, any information which the person either knows or believes might help prevent another person carrying out an act of terrorism or which might help in bringing a terrorist to justice in the United Kingdom (UK). Professional confidentiality is unlikely to constitute a reasonable excuse.

Section 39 of the Terrorism Act 2000 creates a separate criminal offence popularly known as 'tipping off'. This offence is committed where there is (or is likely to be) a terrorist investigation and a disclosure is made which is likely to prejudice the investigation, or interferes with material which is likely to be relevant to the investigation. Alteration or destruction of therapy notes which may provide potential evidence, or 'tipping off' a client under investigation for terrorist activities might therefore come under this provision.

In addition to (and separate from) the obligations described above under section. 38B of the Terrorism Act 2000, there is a different duty under section. 19 of that Act for all citizens to report to the police any information about specified activities related to money and property used to assist terrorist activities which they have gained through the course of a trade, profession, business or employment (which will therefore include therapy). There is also a separate duty to report information (however arising) about fundraising or the use of money or property for the purposes of terrorism.

See also the 'Prevent' duty in education to counter radicalisation (Department for Education, 2015c).

Drug trafficking and money laundering: Recent developments in the law relating to the reporting of drug trafficking and money laundering for any crime have increased the obligations of people working in legal and financial services. Counselling practitioners are now less likely to acquire the kind of information that is required to be reported under the Drug Trafficking Act 1994, Proceeds of Crime Act 2002, or the Money Laundering Regulations 2007. If in doubt, seek legal advice. In many cases, disclosure of this type of information may be justified on the balance of public interest.

Statutory services and child protection: A statutory duty to report or to provide information to the authorities when requested to do so is more likely to arise when a therapist is working in association with the statutory services. Child protection law and guidance may create obligations with regard to the protection of children, for example an order to disclose to the court the whereabouts of a missing child under section 50 (3) (c) of the Children Act 1989.

Practitioners working with children and young people under the age of 18 should be aware of statutory guidance such as *Working together to safeguard children* (Department for Education, 2015d), which creates a responsibility and clear procedures for disclosure of child protection concerns. It is currently enforceable in certain work contexts, for example schools, the National Health Service (NHS), social care, etc., and to follow it would be regarded by courts as good practice in situations where it is not enforceable. Watch for new law widening the scope of this guidance. A word of caution: child protection needs very careful handling. While in other cases, it is ethically appropriate to discuss and plan a referral or disclosure with a client, in the case of child protection, therapists should exercise caution and wherever possible consult with a supervisor or appropriate professional or legal advisor before warning child clients or others in the child's family in advance of an intention to make a child protection referral or disclosure, because in some cases this could put a child's welfare at risk or compromise a child protection investigation, with potentially serious consequences. For practitioners who do not have an organisational policy and structure for child protection referrals, in urgent cases, the local authority child protection team, Children Panel lawyers, National Society for the Prevention of Cruelty to Children (NSPCC), or Children and Family Courts Advisory and Support Service (CAFCASS) may provide additional sources of information, advice and assistance.

For additional guidance, see *What to do if you are worried that a child is being abused* (Department for Education, 2015a), *Information sharing: Advice for safeguarding practitioners* (Department for Education, 2015b), *Good medical practice* (General Medical Council, 2013), and *Confidentiality* (General Medical Council, 2009).

(C) WHERE THE LAW PERMITS DISCLOSURES IN THE PUBLIC INTEREST (DEFENSIBLE DISCLOSURES)

Circumstances that might justify breaching confidentiality include instances where there is:

- a real risk of serious harm
- the threat appears imminent, and
- disclosure is likely to be effective in limiting or preventing the harm occurring.

Any threat to the life of the client or others inflicting any serious physical harm, rape and child abuse would all be examples of serious harm. The risk of a car accident, accident at work, or the spread of serious disease could also amount to serious harm. The prevention of psychological distress or harm without any associated serious physical injury, criminal activity or child protection issue is best resolved by consent, as it may not necessarily justify a breach of confidentiality in English law, especially for adults and young people who have sufficient understanding, maturity and intelligence to make them capable of giving valid consent. See Bond (2015) for ethical dilemmas, Reeves (2015) for risk assessment and Reeves (2010) for suicide.

RECORDING DISCLOSURES

Disclosures should be communicated on a confidential basis (see the Caldecott Guidelines: Department of Health, 2010), and a record should be made of:

- date of disclosure
- reason for disclosure (nature of risk, seriousness, imminent, etc.)

- person to whom information is given
- content of information disclosed
- method of disclosure
- client consent obtained?
- if no client consent, reason for disclosure without consent.

RECORDS AND DATA PROTECTION

Records may include all client notes (and process notes) identifying or identifiable to the client, memoranda, correspondence, artefacts and recordings. A professional expectation is now that records will be kept. Records should be accurate, concise and appropriate to the service provided. The length of time for retention of records may vary with the practitioner's context of work, and should be made known to clients. The General Data Protection Regulations (GDPR) are new EU legal provisions to come into force on 25 May 2018. The Information Commissioner's office (www.ico.gov. uk) provides guidance on registration and the application of the law, and will also provide guidance on the new provisions.

REFERENCES

Bond, T. (2015) *Standards and ethics for counselling in action* (4th ed.). London: Sage.
Bond, T. and Mitchels, B. (2014) *Confidentiality and record keeping in counselling and psychotherapy* (2nd ed.). London: Sage.
Bond, T. and Sandhu, A. (2005) *Therapists in court: Providing evidence and supporting witnesses*. London: Sage.
Department for Education (2015a) *What to do if you are worried that a child is being abused*. Norwich: The Stationery Office.
Department for Education (2015b) *Information sharing: Advice for safeguarding practitioners*. Norwich: The Stationery Office.
Department for Education (2015c) *The Prevent duty*. Norwich: The Stationery Office. (www.gov.uk/).
Department for Education (2015d) *Working together to safeguard children: A guide to inter-agency working to safeguard and promote the welfare of children*. Norwich: The Stationery Office. (www.dh.gov.uk).
Department of Health (2010) *Caldicott guardian manual, 2010*. London: DoH. (www.dh.gov.uk).
General Medical Council (2009) *Confidentiality*. London: GMC. (www.gmc-uk.org).
General Medical Council (2013) *Good medical practice*. London: GMC. (www.gmc-uk.org).
Mitchels, B. and Bond, T. (2008) *Essential law in counselling and psychotherapy*. London: BACP and Sage.
Mitchels, B. and Bond, T. (2012) *Legal issues across counselling and psychotherapy settings*. London: BACP and Sage.
Pattenden, R. (2003) *The law of professional–client confidentiality: Regulating the disclosure of confidential personal information*. Oxford: Oxford University Press.
Reeves, A. (2010) *Working with suicidal clients*. London: Sage.
Reeves, A. (2015) *Working with risk in counselling and psychotherapy*. London: Sage.

RECOMMENDED READING

1. White, R.H. et al. (eds), (1990) *Clarke Hall and Morrison on children* (looseleaf). London: Lexis Nexis/ Butterworths and Hershman A. and McFarlane, D., *Encyclopaedia of children law and practice* (looseleaf reference volumes). Bristol: Family Law.

Not for reading cover to cover, but for reference, these are the most detailed regularly updated sources of information about the law and child protection practice relating to children and young people under the age of 18.

2. Department of Health (2010) *Caldicott guardian manual, 2010*. London: DoH. (Available at www.dh.gov.uk).

Useful information and guidance on confidentiality and information sharing. See also the linked document Department of Health (2013) *Caldicott review: Information governance in the health care system*. London: DoH. (Available at www.gov.uk).

3. Department of Health (2015) *Mental Health Act 1983: Code of practice*. London: DoH. (Available at www.gov.uk).

New guidance, useful for those working with or alongside the NHS mental health system, which also includes helpful guidance on confidentiality and consent issues for adults and children.

4.6 ETHICAL CODES AND GUIDANCE

TIM BOND

OVERVIEW AND KEY POINTS

This chapter aims to help you make the best use of ethical codes and guidance by considering:

- their purpose
- how guidance is produced
- how to read ethical guidance
- using guidance in ethical problem solving
- the relationship between ethical guidance and the law
- how to use ethical guidance in everyday practice.

THE PURPOSE OF CODES AND GUIDELINES

No one reads codes of ethics for their entertainment value or their poetic beauty. Codes and guidelines about professional ethics are functional documents designed to fulfil many purposes. First and foremost, they are written to offer guidance about what is considered good or bad behaviour by the members of that professional body. The main ethical priorities are the protection of clients' safety

and ensuring that they receive a service based on a reasonable standard of care and competence. As someone who has been involved in writing codes for counsellors and who has taken a wider interest in the codes of the caring professions, I have been frequently consulted about how to use codes or to interpret the potential meanings of a specific ethical statement. This chapter builds on this experience by setting out a series of observations about how to get the best out of codes and guidelines.

Getting the best out of ethical codes and guidance can be harder than it seems at first sight. It can be hard to find a balance between excessive arrogance that tends to ignore the ethical guidance and unquestioning humility that fails to recognize the dangers of blind obedience. The conscientious and competent practitioner seeks a way of reading and engaging with ethical guidance between these two extremes. In practice, this involves preparing yourself in order to thoughtfully ask:

- What does this mean?
- How does it apply to my practice?

- What level of obligation is expected of me?
- What must I do and when am I expected to use my professional judgement to identify good practice?

Generally 'must' or 'will' communicates an overriding duty. 'Should' or 'will normally' offer the practitioner some discretion in how they will achieve the relevant overriding principle.

There is one hazard that frequently gets in the way of understanding ethical guidance accurately. Best practice is to read and re-read the relevant guidance periodically to refresh your memory of its contents well before any difficulties arise. It is almost inevitable that most practitioners will encounter ethical challenges and dilemmas from time to time because of the nature or our work and the unpredictability of clients' circumstances and the issues that trouble them. Even the most experienced practitioners will need to consult the relevant ethical guidance periodically and discuss ethical aspects of their work in supervision or with experienced colleagues.

The greatest difficulties tend to arise where a practitioner is unfamiliar with their ethical guidance and only consults it for the first time in response to an urgent problem. The practitioner's heightened state of anxiety makes it harder to read the ethical guidance in an open-minded and receptive state. Most of us do not feel at our most rational or personally robust in the face of a crisis with a client, a complaint, conflict within an agency, or an impending court case. In any of these circumstances, many therapists turn to their code as a lifeline to rescue them. This is an understandable response. However, these are not the circumstances in which to be considering a code for the first time. The sense of urgency to find a solution may undermine the ability to understand quite complex documents. It is said that drowning people will clutch at straws. In my experience, counsellors in acute ethical difficulty will clutch at clauses that seem to offer them protection. These clauses are often taken out of context. It is a strategy that is seldom successful, because codes need to be read as a whole document. Taken out of context, an individual clause can be deceptive and the interpretation favoured by the therapist is unlikely to stand up to close scrutiny. If you find yourself clutching at clauses, it is better to recognize this as a sign of personal pressure and to seek supportive facilitation in considering the ethical issue that confronts you.

In order to reduce the risk of finding yourself consulting a code for the first time in a crisis, it is better to commit yourself to reading the relevant ethical guidelines in advance of any crisis and periodically revisiting them (see Table 4.6.1 for an overview of some of the key ethical guidance documents in the United Kingdom). Reviewing ethical guidance in supervision or in discussion with colleagues makes regular reviews more rewarding and provides an opportunity to anticipate future challenges by asking yourself 'What if …'. In this way, you will acquire a sense of the totality of the contents and how different provisions are interrelated, as well as some of the strengths and weaknesses of a code for your particular area of work. You will be putting yourself in the best possible position to use codes constructively as a support to your practice.

In the next section I will examine how codes are written to inform your interpretation and application of them to your work.

Table 4.6.1   Sources of ethical guidance

BACP (2016) *Ethical Framework for the Counselling Professions.* Lutterworth: British Association for Counselling and Psychotherapy. www.bacp.co.uk

BPS (2009) *Code of Ethics and Conduct.* Leicester: British Psychological Society. www.bps.org.uk

HCPC (2012) *Standards of Conduct, Performance and Ethics.* London: Health and Care Professions Council. www.hcpc-uk.co.uk

UKCP (2009) *Ethical Principles and Code of Professional Conduct.* London: United Kingdom Council for Psychotherapy. www.ukcp.org.uk

---

DECODING THE ETHICAL INSTRUCTION

Codes and guidelines should be taken seriously. They represent an important version of the collective experience of the organization that produced them. They will also have been subject to scrutiny and debate before gaining the approval by a professional body. However, they are not definitive statements. All organizations find it necessary to publish supplementary guidance and periodically to revise their codes. Some of these changes are due to changes in the law, within the profession or are in response to the challenges of new areas of work. For example, professional bodies concerning therapy have been continually updating their guidance in favour of respecting human diversity and promoting equality and inclusion. This has included opposition to the use of conversion therapy to change people from being gay or lesbian to heterosexual identity and relationships. Over time, all ethical guidance has moved towards requiring that therapists keep accurate records of professional work. The increasing use of digital technology and social media in counselling and psychotherapy have raised new ethical issues that periodically result in additional guidance.

There have been occasions when the publication of a code has provoked controversy about some of its provisions. Some insight into how codes are constructed will explain how these controversies emerge. The creation of codes is always a combination of ethical analysis and political process working towards creating a statement that will at least achieve majority support at its formal adoption. There is usually a consultation with members that informs the development of a code or ethical framework. This process will inevitably evoke a wide range of views on any issue. Those writing the code have to exercise judgement about any minority views that are incompatible with the majority view. The outcome of that judgement is likely to be that a minority view will be:

- ignored – the least desirable outcome
- rejected with clearly articulated reasons to decide the issue or elicit further discussion
- accommodated by 'finessing', that is artfully accommodating the minority view by creating a more inclusive phraseology
- treated as an exception for which special provision is made
- validated as being of sufficient importance to justify reconsidering the majority position and possibly initiating an educational programme.

As codes are designed to cover people working in a wide range of therapeutic orientations with their respective values, ethoses and ethical predispositions and in a wide variety of settings with a variety of established practices and practical constraints, there are always minority issues to be taken into consideration. Depending on their composition, committees may move between actively supporting the ascendancy of a particular section of membership or taking a wider view of being as inclusive as possible of the full range of ethical practice. These are difficult judgements and like all human endeavours are fallible. It is always possible that a specific provision is unduly restrictive and may as a consequence not only be oppressive to an individual or group of counsellors or psychotherapists, but also constrain the future development of psychological therapies. On the other hand, the authors also have to watch for the dangers of being over-cautious and failing to guard against unethical behaviour.

HOW TO READ ETHICAL GUIDANCE

Historically, there have been significant variations between professional bodies representing counsellors, psychotherapists and counselling psychologists. These differences have almost disappeared. There is general consensus around many of the essential behaviours required to be an ethical therapist. The key requirements are:

- having respect for the client, including an emphasis on enhancing the client's self-determination or autonomy and working with client consent
- protecting the client's safety, privacy and confidences
- ensuring clarity about contracting and straightforwardness in dealings with clients
- keeping accurate records
- being competent and working within the limits of competence
- being conscientious in the management of dual relationships and avoiding relationships which can damage clients or undermine the therapeutic relationship
- emphasizing the value of research and that it should be undertaken with integrity
- taking responsibility to keep oneself informed about any law applicable to one's work.

Ethical guidance is an important resource for solving any ethical issues or problems that arise in your work. There are a number of basic tips on how to consult codes and guidelines from professional organizations (see Figure 4.6.1).

- Use the most recent version. Out-of-date versions may be seriously misleading.
- Avoid taking sections out of context by considering the document as a whole.
- Distinguish between statements on obligatory practice and those on recommended practice.
- Interpret supplementary guidance and recommendations by reference to core codes and guidelines.
- Consider the implications for your specific therapy context.

Figure 4.6.1 Tips on consulting codes and guidelines

ETHICAL PROBLEM SOLVING

A useful strategy for problem management is breaking the problem down into its component parts. This helps a problem which is already overwhelming, or has that potential, to become more manageable. Effective ethical problem solving follows this approach. A six-step approach is recommended, as this has proved to be extremely helpful to many practitioners (Bond, 2015: 279–292). Each step builds progressively on the previous step(s) but does not exclude the possibility of creating new insights which might involve some reworking of an earlier step and proceeding again from that earlier point. The steps are as follows.

STEP 1: PRODUCE A BRIEF DESCRIPTION OF THE PROBLEM OR DILEMMA

The aim is to produce a clearer statement of the main elements in the problem. It is very difficult to make progress until the problem can be expressed clearly.

STEP 2: CONSIDER WHO HOLDS RESPONSIBILITY FOR RESOLVING THE PROBLEM

Another way of approaching this step is to ask, 'Whose problem is it anyway?' This is particularly significant in therapy where a great deal of responsibility for the outcome of the therapy rests with the client, for example whether to confront someone, etc. There are occasions when the responsibility rests with the therapist, for example a client has started talking about someone who is already known to you in another context. Sometimes the problem is a shared responsibility and can only be resolved by discussion between therapist and client: for example, the client has selected you as therapist because of her sense of you as a person from knowing you in another context. The therapeutic orientation might determine whether the responsibility would rest with the therapist (more likely in a psychodynamic orientation) or could be resolved by joint exploration of the implications (more likely in humanistic and cognitive-behavioural approaches).

STEP 3: CONSIDER ALL THE RELEVANT ETHICAL AND LEGAL GUIDANCE

The aim of this stage is to identify the goal you are working towards in general terms. It is usually a mistake to race from identifying you have responsibility to solve an ethical problem to choosing a specific action. It is much better to have identified the ethical goal(s) you want to achieve in order to be best placed to select the most suitable actions. One way of achieving this is to consult the ethical guidance of your professional body (see Table 4.6.1) and any directly relevant law to identify what you would most like to achieve ethically. Your most desired outcome becomes your goal.

STEP 4: IDENTIFY ALL POSSIBLE COURSES OF ACTION

It is unusual to find that there is only one possible course of action. Often there is a choice between doing nothing or doing something, which may include saying different things to your client or to someone else, or challenging accepted practice within the profession. Listing all possible courses of action avoids the frequent misconception that because one approach appears to be right, there are no other solutions. Many solutions may be possible from which a selection can be made that best meets your goal.

STEP 5: SELECT THE BEST COURSE OF ACTION

A good test of your level of conviction that you have found an appropriate solution is to test it against three standards first proposed by Holly A. Stadler, a former president of the American Counseling Association:

- Universality
  - Could my chosen course of action be recommended to others?
  - Would I condone my proposed course of action if it was done by someone else?
- Publicity
  - Could I explain my chosen course of actions to other counsellors?
  - Would I be willing to have my actions and rationale exposed to scrutiny in a public forum, e.g. at a workshop, in a professional journal, in a newspaper or on radio/TV?
- Justice
  - Would I do the same for other clients in a similar situation?
  - Would I do the same if the client was well known or influential?

If you find yourself answering 'no' to any of these questions, you may need to reconsider your chosen outcome. A final step in identifying the best course of action may be checking whether the resources are available to implement what is proposed.

STEP 6: EVALUATE THE OUTCOME

After you have implemented your course of action, it is useful to evaluate it in order to learn from the experience and to prepare yourself for any similar situations in the future:

- Was the outcome as you hoped?
- Had you considered all relevant factors, with the result that no new factors emerged after you implemented your chosen course of action?
- Would you do the same again in similar circumstances?

ETHICAL GUIDANCE AND THE LAW

The rule of law is a fundamental principle of any modern democratic society. This principle means that the law ought to apply equally to any citizen regardless of status. Therefore the law overrules any personal or professional ethics or morals where there is conflict between them. This raises two key questions. Why not go straight to the law rather than to ethical guidance issued by your professional body to inform your practice? How ought a professional to respond to situations where the law appears to be unethical or unjust?

The main reason for not going straight to the law for ethical guidance is its complexity and that interpreting the law often requires its own field of technical and professional knowledge held by lawyers. Obtaining legal advice can be expensive for any individual but becomes more manageable when individuals combine their resources through professional bodies to undertake this work on their behalf. Ethical codes, frameworks and guidelines issued by professional bodies have been produced with legal guidance about the application of the law to that area of work. For an overview of key legal issues see Chapter 4.9 (Jenkins, this volume) and Mitchels and Bond (2010). Ethical guidance provides an easily accessible version of the application of the law to how we work.

For most purposes the law and ethics match each other reasonably well. However, it is possible that therapists will encounter situations where what is legal appears unethical, or what is ethical is illegal. In current practice, some therapists report tensions between the law and ethics where the law seems unsupportive of and contributing to the problems experienced by some victims of crime, confused or ineffective responses to problematic drug use and prostitution, and oppressive to refugees and migrants. A commonly encountered issue appears to be the lack of provision or poor quality of some public services, especially with regard to mental health, even in situations where there may be a legal requirement to provide services. How ought a counsellor or psychotherapist respond to such tensions between professional and legal obligations? It would be consistent with professional responsibilities to campaign to draw attention to areas where either the law needs changing or services ought to be provided to meet legal requirements. Such campaigns might be undertaken through a professional body or a special interest or advocacy group.

A much more difficult question is whether it is ever justifiable to break the law for ethical reasons? It is a serious issue for any citizen to break the law because of the risk to personal reputation and the possibility of legal penalties or punishment. The stakes are even higher for professionals because their status and social recognition partly depends on the legal recognition of the role. The Health and Social Care Act 2012 created the legal framework for the statutory regulation of practitioner psychologists, including counselling psychologists, through the Health and Care Professions Council in the UK and for the Accredited Voluntary Registers overseen by the Professional Standards Authority that registers counsellors and psychotherapists through their professional bodies. It could seem hypocritical to claim the benefits of legal protection and recognition based on law while breaking the law on a point of ethical principle. So far as I know, no professional body for talking therapies has had to consider whether actively breaking the law is justifiable by its members. My best guess is that a professional conduct panel or ethics committee considering such a case would want to consider whether:

- the issues at stake are of sufficient legal and ethical significance to justify the actions taken – such as protecting someone's human or civil rights
- other legitimate means of campaigning to resolve the issue at stake have been attempted without success or have little prospect of success
- any illegal actions by the professional(s) do not put members of the public at risk of harm as this would undermine any professional's responsibility to ensure public safety
- the professionals concerned have acted openly, for the benefit of others, and been willing to accept the consequences of their actions – for example, a psychoanalyst who refused to break her client's confidences attended court with a bag packed ready for imprisonment for contempt of court (Bond, 2015: 169–171).

By the very nature of their work, therapists will sometimes be working against widely held social norms that will raise wider legal and ethical questions. It would be a serious matter to break the law – even for the best of ethical motives – which may require consideration by the relevant professional body's professional conduct procedures (for more information, see Bond – Chapter 4.7, this volume).

USING ETHICAL GUIDANCE IN EVERYDAY PRACTICE

This chapter aims to provide some straightforward suggestions about how to make best use of the ethical guidance that applies to your work. It is unlikely to be the most exciting reading you will encounter. However, it is probably some of the most important as it provides the best guide of what is expected of you ethically and legally. The situations that can arise in practice that raise ethical issues will almost certainly grab your full attention. For example, what does your ethical guidance expect of you when:

- an employer of your client phones unexpectedly to ask is that client attending their sessions and for a progress report?
- a client discovers you share the same interests and wants to accompany you on a weekend away?
- a client has a lifestyle that is contrary to your own personal values so you would prefer not to work with that person?
- you realize that you are starting to become sexually attracted to one of your clients?
- you discover that you have accidentally revealed some confidential information about a client through an administrative or computer error?

The answers to some of these questions may be obvious: others less so. Discussing your ethical guidance with colleagues and your supervisor may help to bring the ethical guidance to life.

REFERENCES

Bond, T. (2015) *Standards and Ethics for Counselling in Action* (4th ed.). London: Sage.
Mitchels, B. and Bond, T. (2010) *Essential Law for Counsellors and Psychotherapists*. London: Sage.

RECOMMENDED READING

1. Bond, T. (2015) *Standards and Ethics for Counselling in Action* (4th ed.). London: Sage.

Examines ethical issues and guidance in depth, providing many examples. Supported by online resources.

2. Bond, T. and Mitchels, B. (2015) *Confidentiality and Record Keeping in Counselling and Psychotherapy* (2nd ed.). London: Sage.

Considers some of the most frequently raised ethical issues that occur in the talking therapies, with the relevant legal guidance gathered into one source.

3. Gabriel, L. (2005) *Speaking the Unspeakable: The Ethics of Dual Relationships in Counselling and Psychotherapy*. London: Routledge.

Considers some of the most challenging ethical issues experienced by therapists and clients.

4.7   RESPONDING TO COMPLAINTS

TIM BOND

OVERVIEW AND KEY POINTS

There can be few more emotionally charged experiences for practitioners than being formally complained against and having to appear before professional conduct hearing or disciplinary panels. In this chapter I will consider:

- the range of things that can go wrong;
- ethical expectations of how to respond to things going wrong;
- the key elements to any formal complaints or disciplinary cases;
- some key issues in how to respond to a complaint or in professional conduct procedure;
- the personal and professional impact of being subject to a complaint.

Working as a counsellor or psychotherapist can be an intensely satisfying personal and professional experience. We can experience great joy and satisfaction in helping people to overcome their distress or difficulties. Personal fulfilment often comes from applying our knowledge and expertise to do good and reduce suffering. This is the positive side of our work. However, we also need to be aware that while trying to do good, we may inflict harm on our clients. In most cases this harm will be unintentional. Mistakes happen. The only people who do not make mistakes are those who do nothing. It's what happens next that helps to establish the quality of the service being offered. How we respond immediately to minor mistakes will often determine whether they escalate into something more serious. A quick and fulsome apology and determined effort to rectify the error is usually sufficient. Managed well and with sincerity that is often the end of a minor mistake and therapy may resume.

More serious mistakes may call our professional ability into question and may lead to a suspicion of malpractice, especially if the mistake is not acknowledged or repeated with the same or more clients. For example, arriving late or missing one appointment due to a muddle with a diary is a significant error but can usually be recovered with suitable apology, possibly reimbursing any expenses and ensuring

that it does not happen again. Further difficulties over satisfying appointments with the same client or with other clients may indicate a level of unreliability that suggests unsuitability to work with clients. It creates a suspicion of low commitment to the work, defective self-management skills or some more significant obstacle, such as a mental illness or addiction. Sometimes the problem may not be personal to the practitioner but systemic, for example in an organization, a poorly managed or supported appointment system that frustrates both practitioners and clients. Some mistakes may be so serious that they cross the line from a mistake to an abuse of power, for example misusing the psychological intimacy essential to therapy to seduce clients sexually. Some of the most serious mistakes and abuses that inflict the greatest damage may not be due solely to individual faults but due to collective failure, for example discriminatory practices that are embedded within an organizational culture such as institutional racism, or poor management of resources that leads to overstretched sub-standard services.

There is a lot that can go wrong. Being a professional requires each of us to work above the minimum professional standards for our own work and to know how we will respond when something goes wrong.

THE DUTY OF CANDOUR

What ought to happen following something going wrong in the delivery of a professional service has been the subject of much debate and careful consideration in numerous reports following serious incidents in health and social care. It is also clear that the expectations of service users have changed. In professions with longer histories than counselling and psychotherapy, the dynamic between the professional and client or patient is changing from one of deference and subservience to a partnership working on a more equal basis. This means that old habits of concealing mistakes from clients and patients in order to avoid worrying them are being replaced by an ethical obligation to inform the people concerned in order to empower them to take any corrective action and to make a sincere attempt at preserving their trust in the service being offered. The tipping point in favour of an obligation of candour within the United Kingdom (UK) was the scandal of Mid Staffordshire National Health Service (NHS) Foundation Trust, in which several hundred vulnerable and highly dependent patients are thought to have died prematurely due to serious neglect. There was also an attempt by staff to conceal the cause of death of a young adult patient due to medical error from his relatives and the coroner's court investigating the cause of death. This led to a strong recommendation in the Francis Report 2013 of establishing a duty of candour across health and social care (Francis, 2013).

What does a duty of candour mean for counsellors and psychotherapists? The Good Practice section in the British Association for Counselling and Psychotherapy (BACP) *Ethical Framework for the Counselling Professions* (BACP, 2016) sets out the different elements:

> 47. We will ensure candour by promptly informing our clients of anything important that has gone wrong in our work together, and:
>
> a. take immediate action to prevent or limit any harm
> b. repair any harm caused, so far as possible
> c. offer an apology when this is appropriate
> d. notify and discuss with our supervisor and/or manager what has occurred
> e. investigate and take action to avoid whatever has gone wrong being repeated.

The Health and Care Professions Council (HCPC) (2016) found that 'candour' was insufficiently understood by its registrants and renamed it as being 'open and honest'.

> 8.1 You must be open and honest with the care, treatment or other services that you provide by:
>
> • informing service users, where appropriate, their carers, something has gone wrong;
> • apologising;
> • taking action to put matters right if possible; and
> • making sure that service users or, the appropriate, their carers, receive a full and prompt explanation of what has happened and any likely effects.

When dealing with concerns or complaints:

> 8.2 You must support service users and carers want to raise concerns about the care, treatment or other services they have received.
>
> 8.3 You must give a helpful and honest response to anyone who complains about care, treatment or other services they have received.

The precise circumstances that led to a duty of candour arising from the mistakes in Mid Staffordshire hospitals may not have exact parallels in the talking therapies but we will encounter mistakes that occur from time to time that impact on clients or others at different levels of severity. For example:

• an error in making appointments means a client's appointment cannot be fulfilled because the therapist is not available
• a referral contains inaccurate information that has a significant impact on the therapy being offered
• the therapy being provided is not the most likely to succeed because of an assessment based on incomplete or incorrect information
• an accidental breach of confidentiality
• someone deliberately gaining unauthorized access to confidential client information
• indications that a client is feeling suicidal are overlooked
• the danger a client poses to someone else is seriously underestimated and someone is seriously hurt or killed
• an ending of therapy is managed badly, causing the client additional or avoidable distress
• a significant dual or multiple relationship for either the client or therapist has not been identified or adequately considered at the start of therapy as a potentially complicating or disruptive factor
• a client discloses sexual relationships with a previous therapist
• a therapist is exploiting clients sexually, financially, or in other ways.

Patients and clients who have been the victims of professional mistakes made in good faith frequently only want an acknowledgement that a mistake has occurred and an apology. Escalating the situation to a formal complaint is usually the result of feeling that their concerns are not being acknowledged, they are being exploited, or that they need to act to protect others from repetitions of the same mistake.

PROFESSIONAL CONDUCT PROCEDURES

Professional conduct procedures may take place under a variety of names and may be held by employers as part of their disciplinary procedures or by professional bodies concerning their members. There are legitimate differences in how different bodies organize and run their proceedings. Procedures also change over time. Nonetheless all proceedings are guided by legal requirements under the

Article 6 of the Human Rights Act 1998, the right to a fair trial, and the principles of natural justice to ensure that:

- the proceedings are fair;
- they are held before independent and impartial adjudicators;
- take place within a reasonable time;
- there is presumption of innocence so that the accusers have to establish their case rather the accused establish his or her innocence.

The legal basis for professional conduct hearings differs between bodies like the Health and Care Professions Council (HCPC), which hears cases against counselling psychologists in accordance with the authority granted to them by statute. Hearings by employers and professional bodies like the British Association for Counselling and Psychotherapy (BACP) and the United Kingdom Council for Psychotherapy (UKCP) are based on contract.

The HCPC (2015b) provides examples of the types of complaints and issues that are sufficiently serious to be considered in a formal professional conduct or fitness practice hearing, including when registrants:

- were dishonest, committed fraud or abused someone's trust;
- exploited a vulnerable person;
- failed to respect service users' rights to make choices about their own care;
- have health problems which they have not dealt with, and which may affect the safety of service users;
- hid mistakes or tried to block an investigation;
- had an improper relationship with a service user;
- carried out reckless or deliberately harmful acts;
- seriously or persistently failed to meet standards;
- were involved in sexual misconduct or indecency (including any involvement in child pornography);
- have a substance abuse or misuse problem;
- have been violent or displayed threatening behaviour; or
- carried out other, equally serious, activities which affect public confidence in the profession;
- providing fraudulent or incorrect information to obtain registration.

PROFESSIONAL INVESTIGATION AND ADJUDICATION PROCESS

Although the processes vary in details between organizations, there is a common pattern in how complaints are considered. The typical pattern is:

1. A concern or complaint is made in writing by a named person.
2. The complaint is assessed to decide if it concerns an employee or member of the adjudicating organization and is sufficiently serious to require further investigation.
3. The person complained against is notified about the content of the complaint and the identity of the complainant and given a time-limited opportunity to respond, typically within 21 or 28 days.
4. An assessment panel considers the submitted evidence to decide whether the case ought to proceed to a formal hearing. Cases may be closed at this point, or referred for further investigation or for a full hearing. There may be a right to appeal against this decision.
5. Both the complainant and the person(s) complained against are given full access to all the available evidence in order to prepare for a hearing.
6. The case is heard before a panel of adjudicators.
7. The panel makes a decision and communicates the decision with an explanation of the reasons for that decision to both parties.
8. If the panel has found against the therapist, it can determine a sanction that ranges from no further action, a caution, impose conditions for future working, suspend or remove the practitioner from membership or registration.
9. In the case of BACP and UKCP there are rights of appeal. For HCPC the only right of appeal is to the civil courts – a difficult and expensive process.
10. Any conditions for future working, including retraining or working under supervision, may be formally reviewed to ensure they have been completed satisfactorily or further sanctions may be imposed – typically withdrawal from membership or registration.
11. Decisions against a practitioner may be published on the internet and/or a journal. HCPC publishes all aspects of the process.

In the final sections of this chapter I will consider some key issues associated with responding to a formal complaint.

RESPONDING TO A NOTIFICATION OF A COMPLAINT

Anyone who is notified of a concern or complaint against them is well advised to consult their supervisor, professional indemnity insurers and possibly to obtain relevant specialized advice before deciding how to respond. As the opportunity to respond is always time-limited, it is important to act promptly. Sometimes an honest and straightforward admission, an expression of regret and

Table 4.7.1 Responding to the notification that a complaint or concern has been received by a professional body

1. Make best use of the time available to you. Start promptly by considering how best to respond to the notification of a complaint in consultation with trusted professional advisers. There is typically a time limit in which to make your first response. Doing everything in a rush at the last minute seldom works well.

2. Actively manage the potential tensions between how you may be feeling and the tasks that confront you that require a clear head and rational decision-making.

3. Gather all the available evidence, including your client records, correspondence, email, texts, supervision notes and any other surviving traces of the work.

4. Give careful consideration to what is true and fair in what is alleged against you and what you want to dispute as untrue or unfair. What matters are fully agreed? What is being partially reported in ways that distort what happened? What is completely wrong? It is useful to distinguish between evidence and interpretation. The complainant and you may agree about something occurring – in which case it can be treated as an agreed fact – but you may have very different interpretations of its significance. For example, did your client hear your empathic response, which you intended as an acknowledgement of how she was feeling, as an endorsement to act in a particular way – which was not your intention – and this action has gone badly wrong for them?

5. Draft a response in consultation with your supervisor and any professional or legal advisers. If possible, allow yourself a few days to reflect on your response so that you are as confident in the response as possible. Remember, it is for the complainant to prove the case against you. You are presumed innocent and are not required to disprove their case to establish your innocence. If there are things you got wrong that could justify the complaint against you, it may be better to admit this, make a fulsome apology and state what you have done to prevent any future occurrences. However you respond, this is usually best written in consultation with professional and/or legal advice. It is very hard to evaluate the evidence and make the best judgements on your own behalf.

apology, and an explanation of what has been done to eliminate any repetition may produce the most favourable result. Attempts to delay, mislead or obstruct the professional body usually increase the seriousness of any findings and sanctions against the therapist. The panel will be very interested in knowing whether the therapist has a realistic appreciation of the seriousness of any mistake or wrongdoing and how he or she has responded to this realization.

CONFIDENTIALITY

Most conscientious practitioners worry about how to manage client confidentiality during a professional conduct procedure. It seems strange to be using protected information to contradict a client's allegations. It is important to realize that no professional breach of confidentiality is involved as the client will have waived the right to confidentiality to allow the case to proceed. Where professional conduct procedures are held in public, as with UKCP and HCPC, there are special provisions for matters relating to the private lives of any of the parties involved so that these matters can be heard in private. If in doubt, consult the officials responsible for managing the hearings.

In deciding what to disclose, the test is whether it is relevant to the allegations under consideration. For example, the details of a client's childhood trauma would be irrelevant to whether a practitioner was working to inadequate standards due to an addiction problem. If the circumstances around what the client alleges were erratic or intoxicated behaviour during sessions, then it would be highly relevant.

The degree to which a practitioner attempts to identify what is relevant and restrict disclosures relevant to the complaint will help to inform the panel about the therapist's professionalism. Being over-protective of confidences or willing to disclose confidences too freely, regardless of relevance, can undermine the case in favour of the therapist.

GIVING EVIDENCE AT THE HEARING

It can be very stressful giving evidence on your own behalf. However, it is extremely important to do so and to think about how you will accomplish this. Table 4.7.2 provides some basic tips.

It is usual for witnesses to be cross-examined after giving evidence in their own favour. These questions are likely to be hostile and to try to undermine the evidence already given. It is important to respond to these questions in a carefully considered way as the questions are designed to strengthen your case. It can be helpful to focus on what the panel needs to make a decision between the alternative versions being presented to them.

Table 4.7.2   How to give evidence

- Listen to the question carefully and take time to think about your response.
- Say if you do not understand the question or do not know the answer.
- Answer the questions as directly and clearly as possible.
- Speak to the panel, even if someone else has put the question to you. You may find it helpful to turn to face the panel after a question has been put to you.
- Speak slowly and clearly. Panel members may be taking notes. Pause if you sense a panel member needs more time to finish writing.

ADJUDICATION

After hearing all the evidence, the panel will have to consider whether the allegations are proved against the practitioner concerned to the civil standard or on the balance of probabilities. There are two elements in deciding the case around what has been proved as fact and whether this amounts to a breach of the applicable ethical standards (see Table 4.7.3). The panel's concern is to provide adequate protection for the public rather than to punish misconduct. This means that any sanctions imposed are designed to be protective rather than punitive. Removal of registration is to prevent or, more realistically, to restrict future opportunities to repeat similar causes for concern or complaint that place the public at risk.

Table 4.7.3   The adjudicators' decision-making process

- Whether any allegations have been admitted or proven.
- Whether any admitted or proven allegations are in breach of the relevant code or ethical framework.
- Whether the offences are of sufficient seriousness to remove registration and/or membership or to apply sanctions for less serious offences.

In practice, it is the publication of decisions against a practitioner that the people concerned often find most difficult to bear and may be experienced as shaming and professionally humiliating. However, this is not the purpose of publication. The purpose is to enable the public and others who might be at risk to be empowered to protect themselves and if they choose to work with the therapist concerned, to do so knowingly. The practice of publishing outcomes on the internet makes this far more likely as an outcome than when judgments were restricted to professional journals that were seldom seen by the public. Unfortunately, the ease of access to the internet and to information about identifiable practitioners has compounded the sense of publication as a source of public shame and humiliation.

LIVING THROUGH A PROFESSIONAL CONDUCT PROCESS

Because of my interest in professional ethics I have been approached by or spoken to over thirty people who have been subjected to professional conduct hearings. These informal discussions have left me with a number of clear impressions:

- The process is far more stressful and personally distressing than the therapists had expected so having personal support in place is highly desirable.
- Having a knowledgeable and experienced legal or professional advisor greatly helps.
- Supervisors vary widely in their ability to take an independent view and offer well-informed guidance and support. Some supervisors may be so personally concerned to avoid being implicated that they distance themselves from their supervisee and any involvement. Others may be so supportive to the point of being collusive so that the therapist feels poorly prepared for any difficult issues to be faced in the investigation stages or panel hearing. Some supervisors respond well with an ability to clarify issues constructively through a good balance of challenge and support.
- Making a well-considered first response to the complaint generally helps the therapist to cope better with the challenges of the process. Responding

too quickly out of anxiety or procrastinating and rushing to respond within the time-limit are often regretted.

- Contradictory, deceptive and defensive responses tend to be exposed in the hearing and undermine the confidence of the panel in the integrity and professionalism of the person complained against.

- This is a process that tests personal integrity and resilience to a much greater degree than most other aspects of practice.

- The people who come out of the process best seem to be those who are able to prioritize their sense of integrity and openness over their concern about how others judge them, and are committed to learning from any mistakes they may have made.

REFERENCES

British Association for Counselling and Psychotherapy (2013) *Professional Conduct Procedure: BACP Register of Counsellors and Psychotherapists.* Lutterworth: British Association for Counselling and Psychotherapy.

British Association for Counselling and Psychotherapy (2016) *Ethical Framework for the Counseling Professions.* Lutterworth: British Association for Counselling and Psychotherapy.

Francis, R. (2013) *Report of the Mid Staffordshire NHS Foundation Trust Public Inquiry.* London: Stationary Office.

Health and Care Professions Council (2015a) *The Types of Cases we can Consider.* London: Health and Care Professions Council. (www.hcpc-uk.co.uk/complaints/fitnesstopractise/scope).

Health and Care Professions Council (2015b) *Fitness to Practice* . London: Health and Care Professions Council. (www.hcpc-uk.co.uk/complaints/fitnesstopractise/scope).

Health and Care Professions Council (2016) *Standards of Conduct, Performance and Ethics.* London: Health and Care Professions Council.

United Kingdom Council for Psychotherapy (2016) *The UKCP Complaints and Conduct Process – Guidance for Psychotherapists.* London: United Kingdom Council for Psychotherapy. (www.psychotherapy.org.uk).

RECOMMENDED READING

1. The absolutely essential readings are the professional conduct procedures or fitness to practice procedures alongside the code or ethical framework for your professional body. See references above.

2. British Association for Counselling and Psychotherapy (2016) *Ethical Framework for the Counseling Professions.* Lutterworth: British Association for Counselling and Psychotherapy, and United Kingdom Council for Psychotherapy (2009) *Ethical Principles and Code of Professional Conduct.* London: United Kingdom Council for Psychotherapy.

3. Palmer Barnes, F. (1998) *Complaints and Grievances in Psychotherapy: A Handbook of Ethical Practice.* London: Routledge.

Offers rare insights into the reflections of a panel chair for United Kingdom Council for Psychotherapy (UKCP) and BACP. Outdated in some details.

4.8 CLIENT EXPERIENCES

COLIN FELTHAM

OVERVIEW AND KEY POINTS

Here we are interested in what clients say about their therapy experiences and how we can learn from them. How do they seek help? What anxieties do they experience when first approaching therapists? Common factors are examined, as well as issues of significant power differences. The scope, depth and length of therapy are focused upon. Critical issues of abuse, exploitation, and ineffectiveness receive due attention. What do clients think about payments? How do they express their appreciation of successful therapy? Examined, too, are questions of client-informed feedback and the means of gathering such data.

- We can learn from the ways in which clients seek therapy, and what initially inhibits them.
- Certain commonalities run across all good therapy.
- A proportion of therapy experiences go awry in terms of effectiveness and unprofessional practice.
- Most therapy proceeds well and clients are pleased to report positively.
- Research increasingly shows the benefits of gathering and acting on client feedback.

INTRODUCTION

Therapists are mindful to put each unique client first, to enter the client's inner world, to learn from clients, and to respect the self-determination of the client. But therapy is now a highly overseen enterprise. When therapists meet their clients they are 'armed' with experience, training, theories and a professional infrastructure. The client, however, is more often than not someone in a degree of distress who knows little if anything of the theory of therapy, and their agenda may be quite different from the therapist's. In spite of requirements for therapists to have their own therapy, it is quite likely that such experiences only partially resemble those of distressed clients. For all these reasons – plus an increasing emphasis on accountability generally – this chapter looks at the client's perspective and commends an attitude of raised awareness among therapists about implications for their own practices.

WHAT CLIENTS HAVE SHOWN AND SAID ABOUT THEIR EXPERIENCES OF THERAPY

Presented here is a collated summary of views published unprompted by consumers, formally researched or gleaned from clinical experience.

HELP-SEEKING PATTERNS

It is important to put in perspective the fact that the vast majority of people with problems resolve them themselves or with peer support, and that although up to about 20–25 per cent of the population at any one time may suffer from a diagnosable psychological problem, probably only about 5 per cent receive formal help. A slightly disproportionate number of clients are women, it being speculated that men are less ready to acknowledge personal problems, although this is probably changing too. Many people will have tried other things before turning to professionals almost as a last resort, often waiting months or years before seeking therapy. Many, even after presenting, may wait longer than they would like for a first appointment, and while waiting, up to about 14 per cent resolve their problems to their own satisfaction. Improving Access to Psychological Therapies (IAPT) initiatives have sought to reduce waiting times. Typically, many seek word-of-mouth recommendations to private practitioners, while those eligible for services free at the point of delivery may have quite different experiences of lack of choice, waiting lists, etc. Leong et al. (1995) summarize these and many additional obstacles to effective help for ethnic minority groups. Although clients are sometimes advised to 'shop around' for a service or practitioner with whom they feel comfortable or in whom they have confidence, obviously many feel too distressed to endure such an exercise or are not sufficiently assertive to do so.

SERVICE ANXIETY AND CLIENT FEARS

On top of the 'problem anxiety' that brings clients to therapists, it is common and understandable for them to feel anxious and uncertain about telephoning for an appointment, attending first appointments, knowing what to say and how to behave, and deciding whether what they are receiving is indeed helpful for them. It is quite typical for a power imbalance to exist, especially in counselling or psychotherapy agencies, with the therapist being styled and perceived as the one who is qualified, who knows, who embodies super-sanity, whose powers may apparently border on telepathy, and who may hold the key to an exit from misery. Where discrepancies exist between the status, age, class, race, gender and sexual orientation of therapist and client, an imbalance of power may become all the more problematic and anxiety-engendering. Usually the client must visit the therapist's premises (which could be experienced as frighteningly clinical, for example) and agree to the therapist's conditions, rules and ethos of therapy. Counselling and psychotherapy – we can easily forget – are for many people very strange, counter-cultural experiences: sitting sometimes silently in a room with a stranger, being (or feeling) stared at, and expected to make intimate disclosures. According to some psychoanalytic thinkers, clients are acutely aware of the necessity of consistent physical and business arrangements and will communicate unconsciously to therapists their anxieties about any inconsistencies and subtle abuses.

Service anxiety is discussed by Howe (1989). Additionally, Pipes et al. (1985) detailed some common *client fears*, which are summarized as follows:

- Is therapy what I need?
- Will I
  o be treated as a case?
  o be taken seriously?
  o be made to do things I do not want to do?
  o find out things I don't want to?
  o lose control of myself?
  o be thought of by my friends as crazy?

- Will the therapist
  o share my values?
  o think I'm a bad person?
  o think I'm more disturbed than I am?
  o discover things I don't want him or her to discover?
  o be competent?

Some research (e.g., Le Surf and Lynch, 1999; Setiawan, 2004) shows that although clients know they need help, they do not know enough or are not given enough opportunity to know about what happens in counselling. Additionally, there may be ambivalence about wanting advice and yet not wanting to be controlled.

COMMON FACTORS

Initially surprising to many in the field, but now accepted as highly significant, a majority of clients have expressed the view (or it has been inferred from their accounts) that attention from a socially sanctioned healer in a sanctioned setting plays a large part in setting positive expectations. People are often reassured by appropriate settings, a professional manner, qualifications, and an explicit rationale for therapy. For some, simply being told or reassured by a mental health professional that they are not mad or odd is in itself 'therapeutic', and for some it is all that is required. A large proportion of clients report the importance of being taken seriously; being listened to respectfully and non-judgmentally; being understood; experiencing warmth and genuine concern; feeling contained; being helped to make sense of their otherwise ostensibly chaotic life stories (Howe, 1993). Finding a therapist with whom one can make an optimally therapeutic match is increasingly regarded as significant: this *may* include theoretical orientation but is more likely to involve perceptions of warmth, attractiveness, expertness, personality, and so on (Feltham, 1999).

Most clients appear uninterested in clinical theories or the nomenclature attaching to them, except where this is a vital part of the ongoing therapy (as, for example, in Transactional Analysis or Cognitive Behaviour Therapy (CBT)). Indeed, many clients report that counsellors' and psychotherapists' publicity material is sometimes too jargon-oriented and is not sympathetic to the client's perspective. If this is surprising to readers, it may be because many of us are surrounded by colleagues and friends who are therapeutically involved, whereas a statistical majority of clients, especially first-time clients, seek solutions to distress or confusion, and are rarely fascinated by or steeped in therapeutic theory.

SCOPE, DEPTH AND LENGTH OF THERAPY

It has been a sobering realization for many therapists that clients not only seek crisis resolution and symptom amelioration or removal, but are often satisfied to terminate therapy when these goals have been reached. A discrepancy between the pragmatic, short-term goals of many consumers and the often more ideologically driven goals of in-depth, long-term, psychic exploration and personality overhaul of therapists is something that has to be reckoned with (Strong, 2009). Also, while many clients have appreciated the space for reflection and empathic understanding offered by therapists, they have sometimes been mystified by long, unexplained silences and lack of normal social conversation, for which therapists themselves have rationales (e.g., non-directiveness and therapeutic neutrality). Rather, for some clients, a naturalistic style of therapy is preferred which may include more self-disclosure and simple practical advice than practitioners are willing to give. Related to this is the finding that many clients expect their counselling or therapy to be relatively short term (one estimate has it that therapists typically think therapy will take at least three times longer than clients think it will take) and many clients may prefer an intermittent pattern of attendance as indicated by felt need, rather than a 'once and for all time' model of therapy.

THERAPIST ABUSE, EXPLOITATION, AND INEFFECTIVENESS

Unfortunately, for a significant number of clients, therapy has turned out to be – in spite of therapists' duty of care – a negative and damaging experience (Sands, 2000). Even allowing for media exaggeration, client bias and resistance, and a small proportion of unjustifiably litigation-oriented clients, it is clear that abuse (sexual, emotional, physical) occurs, along with other forms of exploitation and ineffectiveness of therapy. Estimates suggest 5–10 per cent of clients may deteriorate in or after therapy, in response to adverse events, unplanned endings, or ineffective therapists, and some clients with personality disorders are more reactive to therapist errors and ruptures. Up to 20 per cent of clients report not feeling helped.

Sex between clients and therapists is perhaps the most publicized. While it is easy to *understand* how the intimacy of one-to-one therapy can slip into inappropriate sexual contact, accounts of how damaging it usually is for clients have led to its prohibition by all professional bodies. Formalized complaints procedures offer those wronged the opportunity to seek redress, even though this may be rather too late. Emotional abuse (for example, using demeaning language, inappropriate confrontation, engaging in reciprocal emotional entanglements, 'dropping' clients who are regarded as difficult) is reported by some clients. Examples of clients being (or feeling) financially exploited are not so well publicized, but sometimes exist.

The question of whether most clients prefer to pay something for their therapy, and are likely to show more commitment when paying than if they do not, has not been resolved, although increasing clinical experience might suggest that direct payment is not the critical variable in commitment and motivation that it was once assumed to be. The ineffectiveness of some counsellors, psychotherapists and their services gives cause for concern; some clients have reported spending a great deal of time and money in therapy with no discernible results and sometimes experiencing deterioration (Striano, 1988). The extent of this is contradicted by Seligman (1995), but its sting has helped to lead to concern for evidence-based practice (Roth and Fonagy, 2006; Rowland and Goss, 2002). In recent years some client-driven and well-informed websites have appeared which share stories of unhappy therapy experiences and negative views about mental health treatments (see, for example, https://disequilbrium1.wordpress.com). These attest to a growing sophistication among this community of users that therapists cannot afford to ignore.

CLIENT–THERAPIST DIFFERENCES

Although no accurate figures are available, a majority of counsellors and psychotherapists in Britain are white, female, middle-class liberals. Therapeutic theory reflects this bias as well as certain assumptions of secular individualism and, as is pointed out elsewhere in this book, (psychology-saturated) training often marginalizes or neglects the experiences of non-dominant social groups (Palmer, 2002; Shoaib and Peel, 2003). Hence, historically, gay clients have often been assumed to need treatment to reverse their homosexuality (this is no longer permissible); the needs of clients with disabilities have been played down or ignored; women have been assumed to be 'hysterical' (and more recently all to want a career outside the home); older people have been considered too old to benefit from therapy; and different cultural norms pertaining to expressiveness, dress, religion, etc. have been either misinterpreted or ignored. There is now enough evidence from clients' reports to know that therapists can sometimes be ignorant, patronizing, and in some cases dangerous in relation to these factors. The question of *client–therapist matching* is not clear, there being mixed views on whether black people, for example, generally prefer to be seen by black therapists or not. There remains some concern about low awareness of counselling in Asian communities, and more information is needed about the existence and nature of counselling services (Netto et al., 2001; Setiawan, 2004). Client–therapist age difference is a similarly uncharted or disputed area.

Where some trends exist, it is that many women prefer to see a woman therapist when they have a choice, and when they sense that their concerns might be better understood and more sensitively handled by another woman. Similar preferences have been shown to exist among gay and lesbian clients (Liddle, 1996). Often, clients do not want to have to explain matters of daily oppression that are obvious to them. The converse of this picture is that in some cultures it may be the norm to expect mental health professionals to be authorities to be looked up to, and who will duly dispense expert advice. All such cultural differences are mediated by *individual* differences between the parties, adding another layer of complexity. Additionally, factors of emotional distress, transference and counter-transference mean that therapists must be aware of complex interrelationships involving socio-cultural factors (including peer, family and media influences) and individual psychology.

APPRECIATION

The above views need to be balanced by a reminder that many consumers have expressed great satisfaction with their therapy. Client reports and formal research both affirm the overall effectiveness and/or satisfaction levels achieved by therapists (Seligman, 1995). Clients have often said that 'therapy changed my life' or that 'I couldn't have got by without counselling'. Surveys of users of mental health services have confirmed that they overwhelmingly value the talking therapies in preference to medication. Appreciating the common factors mentioned above, clients are often surprisingly unconcerned or forgiving about therapists' occasional mistakes (e.g., clumsy interpretations, forgetting factual details, etc.). Modest changes are often appreciated by clients when therapists are hoping for more radical or dramatic changes. Clients have sometimes reported having 'internalized' the therapist, that is, having a helpful inner (imaginary) dialogue with them between sessions and after therapy has ended. As might be expected, to some extent client evaluations will always represent *some* mixture of the appreciative and the negative (Bates, 2006; Dinnage, 1989; Feltham, 2002).

CLIENT-INFORMED FEEDBACK

Duncan et al. (1992) launched a significant approach now known as client-directed outcome-informed therapy (CDOIT). Reflecting the important work of Lambert, and now led by Miller, this approach involves before- and after-session questions which seek client views on the alliance; process; on their own resources, resilience and strengths. In effect, CDOIT attempts to operationalize the common factors and fully honour client evaluation. An outcome rating scale and session rating scale are used. These developments have American origins and are reflected in UK Client Outcomes in Routine Evaluation (CORE); and in Patient-Reported Outcome Measures (PROMs). Duncan and Miller (2004) took CDOIT forward, stressing the central contribution of the client in the entire enterprise. This work has also led to feedback-informed supervision, which aims to reinforce the client

perspective and keep the therapist focused on what the client needs for positive progress. Anecdotal evidence, however, remains mixed on the compatibility between routine data collection and smoothness of therapeutic process (see also Wolpert, 2014).

Glenys Parry and colleagues at the University of Sheffield have pioneered the AdEPT Project (adept@ sheffield.ac.uk) which collects data from clients about client harm and deterioration, analyses it, and makes recommendations. One such finding concerns the importance of comprehensive case tracking to limit the likelihood of negative outcomes. It has been amply confirmed that inadequate training, variability of effectiveness between therapists, and failure to utilize due theoretical and clinical guidelines may all be responsible for outcome problems.

CONCLUSIONS

It is noteworthy that (1) discrepancies may well exist between the views and goals of therapists and clients; (2) the inherent imbalance of power in the therapeutic relationship can easily lead to forms of abuse, infantilization or insensitive treatment, and their concealment; (3) training analysis or personal therapy/counselling for the trainee is not sufficiently similar to the experience of clients to address the need for understanding; and (4) the complexity and privacy of therapeutic relationships means that clients' views have implications not only for initial training, but for ongoing development, in-session awareness and reflection, and accountability and evaluation. The objection of some therapists that an overly consumerist view of the therapeutic process is unwise must certainly also be factored into our consideration: clients do not *always* know what is best for them, and may *sometimes* unconsciously introduce confusion and revenge-seeking into the enterprise (Sutherland, 1987). Nonetheless there is ongoing interest in the UK in the involvement of consumers in the audit and evaluation of mental health services (Foster, 2007). Procedures for, and satisfactory outcomes of, monitoring and assuring quality are (increasingly) linked to continued funding.

Taking consumers' views seriously has already led to increased concern for *informed consent* (verbal and written explanations and contracts), which extends to publications advising consumers (e.g., Dryden and Feltham, 1995) and better publicized complaints procedures. Mental health agencies such as MIND have long championed users' rights to be heard, for example by taking part in management committees. New evaluation procedures seek consumers' views in order to improve services. Knowledge about the differential effectiveness of therapies in relation to different client issues, now promoted vigorously by NICE, calls for greater awareness of referral issues. Clearly, the overall trend is necessarily towards greater transparency, knowledge sharing, fairness, and constant updating of therapists' knowledge in view of clinical research results and the changing nature of society.

REFERENCES

Bates, Y. (ed.) (2006) *Shouldn't I Be Feeling Better by Now? Client Views of Therapy*. Basingstoke: Palgrave.

Dinnage, R. (1989) *One to One: Experiences of Psychotherapy*. London: Penguin.

Dryden, W. and Feltham, C. (1995) *Counselling and Psychotherapy: A Consumers' Guide*. London: Sheldon.

Duncan, B.L., Miller, S.D. and Sparks, J. (2004) *The Heroic Client: Doing Client-directed Outcome Informed Therapy* (2nd ed). San Francisco, CA: Jossey-Bass.

Duncan, B.L., Solovey, A.D. and Rusk, G.S. (1992) *Changing the Rules: A Client-directed Approach to Therapy*. New York: Guilford Press.

Feltham, C. (ed.) (1999) *Understanding the Counselling Relationship*. London: Sage.

Feltham, C. (2002) Consumers' views of the benefits of counselling and psychotherapy. In C. Feltham (ed.), *What's the Good of Counselling and Psychotherapy? The Benefits Explained*. London: Sage.

Foster, J.L.H. (2007) *Journeys through Mental Illness: Clients' Experiences and Understandings of Mental Distress*. Basingstoke: Palgrave.

Howe, D. (1989) *The Consumer's View of Family Therapy*. Aldershot: Gower.

Howe, D. (1993) *On Being a Client: Understanding the Process of Counselling and Psychotherapy*. London: Sage.

Leong, F.T.L., Wagner, N. and Tata, S.P. (1995) Racial and ethnic variations in help-seeking attitudes. In J.G. Ponterotto, J.M. Casas, L.A. Suzuki and C.M. Alexander (eds), *Handbook of Multicultural Counseling*. Thousand Oaks, CA: Sage.

Le Surf, A. and Lynch, G. (1999) Exploring young people's perceptions relevant to counselling: a qualitative study. *British Journal of Guidance & Counselling*, 27(2): 231–243.

Liddle, B. (1996) Therapist sexual orientation, gender, and counseling practices as they relate to ratings of helpfulness by gay and lesbian clients. *Journal of Counseling Psychology*, 43: 394–401.

Netto, G.S., Thanki, M., Bondi, E. and Munro, M. (2001) Perceptions and experiences of counselling services among Asian people. In G.S. Netto et al., *A Suitable Space: Improving Counselling Services for Asian People*. Bristol: Policy Press and Joseph Rowntree Foundation.

Palmer, S. (ed.) (2002) *Multicultural Counselling: A Reader*. London: Sage.

Pipes, R.B., Schartz, R. and Crouch, P. (1985) Measuring client fears. *Journal of Consulting and Clinical Psychology*, 53(6): 933–934.

Roth, A. and Fonagy, P. (2006) *What Works for Whom? A Critical Review of Psychotherapy Research* (2nd ed.). New York: Guilford Press.

Rowland, N. and Goss, S. (eds) (2002) *Evidence-based Counselling and Psychological Therapies: Research and Applications*. London: Routledge.

Sands, A. (2000) *Falling for Therapy: Psychotherapy from a Client's Point of View*. Basingstoke: Palgrave Macmillan.

Seligman, M. (1995) The effectiveness of psychotherapy: the Consumer Reports Study. *American Psychologist*, 50: 96–104.

Setiawan, J.L. (2004) Indonesian Undergraduates' Attitudes to Counselling: A Study of Areas of Concern, Perceptions Relevant to Counselling, Willingness to Seek Help and Sources of Help. PhD thesis, University of Nottingham.

Shoaib, K. and Peel, J. (2003) Kashmiri women's perceptions of their emotional and psychological needs, and access to counselling. *Counselling and Psychotherapy Research*, 3(2): 87–94.

Striano, J. (1988) *Can Psychotherapists Harm You?* Santa Barbara, CA: Professional.

Strong, T. (2009) Collaborative goal-setting: counsellors and clients negotiating a focus. *Counselling Psychology Review*, 24(3 & 4): 24–37.

Sutherland, G. (1987) *Breakdown: A Personal Crisis and a Medical Dilemma* (rev. edn). London: Weidenfeld and Nicolson.

Wolpert, M. (2014) Outcome measurement and the therapeutic relationship: help or hindrance? *BACP Research Conference Keynote*, London, 17 May.

RECOMMENDED READING

1. https://disequilibrium1.wordpress.com/

Disequilibrium1's Blog is a US-based website that invites clients and ex-clients of therapy to articulate their (largely unsatisfactory) experiences of therapy and therapists. Many are well informed and proffer views that are critical of the institution of therapy as well as bad individual experiences.

2. Howe, D. (1993) *On Being a Client: Understanding the Process of Counselling and Psychotherapy*. London: Sage.

A classic in the genre of learning from clients who are grappling with the process of help-seeking.

3. Yalom, I.D. and Elkin, G. (2008) *Every Day Gets a Little Closer: A Twice-told Therapy*. New York: Basic Books.

In a very unusual exercise, both Yalom and his client write up their own impressions of the two-year therapy, showing interestingly different perspectives. This book remains contentious but fascinating.

4.9 THERAPY AND THE LAW

PETER JENKINS

OVERVIEW AND KEY POINTS

Therapists are discovering that they increasingly need to have at least a basic working knowledge of the law, whatever their reservations about the legal system or the law itself. This chapter sets out some of the main parameters of the interface of counselling and psychotherapy and the law in the United Kingdom (UK). The main points of reference relate to the civil law in England and Wales, with the law in Scotland and Northern Ireland operating in distinct, but still broadly parallel, ways. The emphasis will be on describing the key trends and professional issues to be considered by practitioners, rather than setting out the precise detail, which can be followed up in the references and resources supplied. The chapter briefly sets out:

- how legal principles applying to counselling and psychotherapy are mediated by the practitioner's context for practice, employment status and client group

- legal aspects of managing professional relationships with clients
- legal obligations and options in handling risk
- legal principles applying to the management of sensitive information
- developments regarding the statutory regulation of therapists.

MAKING LINKS BETWEEN PSYCHOTHERAPEUTIC PRACTICE AND THE LAW

Therapists often look for general principles, and even for absolute certainty, when encountering the law. While, as practitioners, we try to encourage our clients and colleagues to contain, stay with and *work through* ambiguity and uncertainty, our own strong preference is very often to have clear and very definite answers to the professional dilemmas which we face. The following example might illustrate this process at work.

Paul did some unpaid weekly counselling sessions for a small voluntary agency. He became concerned about his client, Sarah, who seemed to be increasingly depressed and self-absorbed, to the extent that her pre-teenage sons, who were involved in illicit drugs and joy-riding, seemed to her to be 'running wild' and almost beyond her control as a single parent. The senior counsellor at the agency was unable to provide any clear guidance on how he should respond to the risks he perceived for the sons, given that there was no specific evidence of child abuse. Any attempt to explore her problematic relationship with her sons, or to express his own anxiety about this situation as a counsellor, seemed to produce little response from her, possibly due to her somewhat depressed emotional state. However, Paul's supervisor was increasingly concerned about the client and the risk to the sons' welfare. His supervisor felt strongly that Paul should make contact with social services to report this as a safeguarding issue, given the apparent reluctance or inability of the client to take any action herself.

From a professional and ethical point of view, a therapist's first point of reference should be with regard to their code of ethics, such as the British Association for Counselling and Psychotherapy's *Ethical Framework for the Counselling Professions* (BACP, 2016). This case contains a classic dilemma, namely of promoting client autonomy versus protecting the welfare of the client and also of third parties. From a legal point of view, the practitioner's responses will be framed by a number of key factors, which are highly specific and will vary according to:

- the *context* in which the therapist practises
- the therapist's *employment* status
- the nature of the *client group*.

The interaction of these key factors provides a clue to the complexity of the law as it relates to counselling and psychotherapy. Exploring the possible options and responses to particular legal dilemmas is often highly specific, as general principles have to be applied carefully to this particular counsellor, working in this setting, on this employment basis, with the client group. Thus, there may well be significant differences between the safeguarding requirements faced by therapists working in a statutory setting and those for a counsellor, such as Paul, who is counselling in a voluntary agency. Alternatively, a counsellor such as Paul, who is either directly employed, or who is seen by the law to approximate to 'employed' status, may have little real discretion in deciding how to respond to issues of client or third-party risk, due to agency policy. A therapist in private practice, on the other hand, generally has substantially greater freedom of action in deciding how best to work with these issues. Therapists working with children, or with adults experiencing mental health problems, may similarly face certain pressures to act, which are *not* obligatory when working with other client groups, who are deemed to be less vulnerable.

The resulting combination of legal pressures means that therapists often encounter a wider and more varied range of legal issues than do other comparable professionals, such as social workers or mental health practitioners. Therapists need, therefore, to consider carefully how well they are prepared for recognizing and responding to such professional dilemmas, which necessarily carry a *legal* element as well as an ethical or a professional set of choices (Bond, 2015).

LEGAL ASPECTS OF MANAGING PROFESSIONAL RELATIONSHIPS WITH CLIENTS

The discussion above has emphasized the *variability* of the law as applied to different psychotherapeutic situations. The following sections now provide a brief outline of more general legal principles, which will need to be adapted to a range of specific situations. The core of counselling and psychotherapy work consists of the therapeutic relationship and its essential boundaries. These mark it as being distinct from other professional stances, such as teaching or social work, or other helping relationships, such as friendship or mentoring. From a legal perspective, the key factors relating to the therapist's therapeutic relationship with clients are framed by the concepts of:

- contract
- duty of care
- liability.

DEFINING A CONTRACT

Counsellors and therapists often use the term 'contract' in a rather loose way, referring to a set of arrangements guiding contact with the client, the purpose of the counselling and psychotherapy, and arrangements for supervision and recording. While the use of formal written agreements with clients may be considered a hallmark of good practice, these documents may not be considered to constitute a contract in a proper legal sense. A legal contract requires the fulfilment of a precise set of conditions (Jenkins, 2007a: 27):

- *capacity* for the parties involved, i.e., not mentally disordered or under 18 years of age
- a firm *offer* and unequivocal *acceptance*
- a clear *intention* of both parties to create a legally binding agreement
- a contract that is supported by *consideration*, i.e., an exchange of goods or services for payment.

Many therapeutic contracts would *not* meet all these conditions, particularly regarding payment, as much counselling or therapy is provided *without* charge to the client, for example in schools, in the National Health Service (NHS), or by voluntary agencies. In private therapy or supervision practice, however, the agreement would, in all likelihood, constitute a legal contract. As a result, a therapist, supervisor, supervisee or client could take legal action for breach of a contract in the small claims section of the county court should there be an alleged breach of the contract.

Rather than applying a legal contract as such, therapists may be using a document which is actually better termed a consent form, or a working agreement. This can be useful and necessary for setting out the limits to confidentiality, for example. In this way, a client may give their advance consent to their general practitioner being contacted if they become suicidal. The counsellor then has substantial protection in law against any later charge of breach of confidence from an aggrieved client. Consent forms, or working agreements, are also important in documenting the client's *informed consent* to therapy.

DUTY OF CARE

Not all counsellors or psychotherapists will be covered by the law of contract. However, therapists will be subject to a duty of care towards their *client*, and supervisors will be similarly bound to their *supervisees*. The following fictitious vignette illustrates some features of this crucial part of the law relating to psychotherapeutic practice.

Niki was a newly qualified psychotherapist working in the NHS with clients who had been subjected to extensive domestic violence, and who often had previous histories of experiencing serious childhood sexual abuse. Interested in trauma work, Niki began experimenting by using some radical hypnotic techniques with a client after attending a week-long workshop in the USA. Unfortunately, the client's mental condition began to deteriorate rapidly soon afterwards and she was admitted for psychiatric treatment. Following this, she then brought a civil case against Niki as her former psychotherapist for breach of duty of care, alleging that the psychotherapeutic techniques had caused her lasting psychological damage and resultant substantial loss of earnings.

Action of this kind is brought under tort law, for the infliction of non-intentional harm, and requires the fulfilment of the following conditions:

- the existence of a duty of care between practitioner and client
- breach of that duty
- resultant foreseeable harm to the client as a direct result of the breach.

For counselling and psychotherapy clients, the alleged harm will normally be *psychological* rather than physical in nature. However, the law sets a very high threshold for such damage. It requires that the alleged harm meets the diagnostic criteria for a psychiatric illness, such as clinical depression, generalized anxiety disorder, or post-traumatic stress disorder, rather than simply taking the form of the more everyday human emotions of anger, distress or disappointment.

CASE LAW CONCERNING THERAPISTS

Many therapists are somewhat apprehensive of being sued by their clients, particularly when the latter are very aggrieved about some aspect of the therapy provided. However, the relative lack of reported cases in the UK suggests that the law actually presents very formidable barriers to clients successfully winning this type of case. Derived from medical case law, therapists subject to this type of action will be judged according to the *Bolam test*, namely whether their actions were consistent with the 'practice of competent respected professional opinion'. Relying on the evidence of expert witnesses, the judge needs to decide whether the therapist was working *within* the parameters of their chosen approach, such as psychodynamic, person-centred or other method. In practice, it is very difficult for clients to prove that the therapist's actions directly *caused* their psychological damage. In the case of Niki above, the client's *prior* history of abuse and possible evidence of psychiatric treatment *in the past* may well be used in court to invalidate her claim or, at the very least, reduce any damages eventually awarded to her. For more detailed discussion of relevant case law on therapist professional negligence, see Jenkins (2014).

LIABILITY

Therapists are often keen to assume a professional duty of care towards their clients, as this is consistent with their overall professional stance and their obligations under a code of ethics. From a legal point of view, liability is defined in rather narrower terms and takes specific forms, which are determined by the therapist's *employment* status rather than simply by the existence of a therapeutic relationship with the client. Liability can take the form of:

- *personal* liability, where a therapist doing paid private work holds *direct* responsibility for any non-intentional harm caused to the client
- *vicarious* liability, where an *employer* holds liability for the work of employees and volunteers.

Returning to the points made earlier, Niki's liability would be primarily determined by her status as an employee of the NHS trust. The client would need to sue her *and* the NHS trust together. To that extent, a psychotherapist in Niki's position would be 'protected' by their employer, which may have its own legal department and extensive experience in responding to claims and litigation. There remains a strong case, nevertheless, for therapists to keep their own professional indemnity insurance, rather than rely totally on the goodwill of their employer. Holding such insurance gives the therapist access to independent legal advice and, if necessary, separate legal representation in court, should this be necessary.

The barriers against clients succeeding in this case remain substantial. It needs to be remembered that clients also have access to a non-legal route of redress, namely by bringing a *complaint* against the therapist, either to the therapist's employer, or to their professional association, such as BACP or United Kingdom Council for Psychotherapy (UKCP). Given the shift towards establishing accessible and user-friendly complaints procedures by therapists' organizations, it is probably much more likely that counsellors and psychotherapists will face at least one serious professional or organizational complaint during their working career, rather than undergo actual litigation in court.

LEGAL OBLIGATIONS IN HANDLING RISK

Therapists often express real concern about the ethical tension and conflict existing between their obligations towards the client and those towards other members of society, who may be put at risk by the client's actions. In fact, the concept of risk can take a number of forms:

- risk to *client*, via deliberate self-harm, actual or attempted suicide
- risk to a *third party*, such as child abuse, domestic violence, serious crime or terrorism
- risk to *therapist*, via assault or stalking.

Therapists subscribe to an ethical commitment to promote the client's autonomy and to protect their wellbeing. This may come into conflict with real or imagined *legal* obligations, particularly when counterbalanced against an expectation that therapists should avoid harm to the client or others, by breaking client confidentiality if necessary. This might be in order to take preventive action by alerting the authorities concerned, for example, in the case of suspected child abuse.

As discussed below, therapists have a duty of trust and confidence towards clients. There are few overriding, absolute legal requirements to break confidentiality, and these concern instances of terrorism and drug money laundering. Reporting child abuse may well become a legal requirement for therapists in the near future, depending on the outcome of a policy review by the Goddard Inquiry in this area (www.iicsa.org.uk). Therapists may be required by their contract of employment or agency policy to report suspected child abuse, or threatened client self-harm or suicide, when working for statutory agencies such as health, education and social services. However, even these requirements need to be carefully balanced against the therapist's duty of trust and confidentiality towards the client.

In fact, in situations involving non-terrorist crime, therapists (outside Northern Ireland) have the *right*, but not necessarily a *duty*, to break confidentiality in the wider public interest. A therapist *could*, therefore, contact the police to report criminal activity by a client, such as an undetected murder, or a credible threat of revenge towards a former partner, or to report a client who was stalking the therapist herself. From an ethical, professional and therapeutic point of view, any such decision to report clearly needs to be prefaced wherever possible by discussion with the client, and consultation with a supervisor and experienced colleagues. However, the law will generally support such action if taken in a measured, responsible and accountable manner, as evidenced by the statutory provision for 'whistleblowing' facilities in the workplace.

LEGAL PRINCIPLES APPLYING TO THE MANAGEMENT OF SENSITIVE INFORMATION

Therapists learn a great deal of highly sensitive information about clients during the course of their work. In terms of the law, therapists owe a duty of confidence to clients, where this would be a reasonable expectation. This duty can also be assumed to apply in the case of a contract for the psychotherapeutic work (see earlier). The legal protection for client confidentiality has been further strengthened by statute, such as the client's right to *respect* for privacy under human rights legislation, and, more emphatically, by the provisions of data protection law. This requires therapists to adopt transparent forms of record keeping which are consistent with the fundamental rights of citizens to know and, wherever appropriate, to have substantial access to such records. Data protection law covers manual records kept in systematic form, as well as computerized records, together with audio- and video-tapes.

ACCESS BY THIRD PARTIES TO CLIENT RECORDS

Part of the therapist's role in managing sensitive client data has been to limit unauthorized access by other interested parties, such as the partner of a client undergoing therapy. There has been a rising interest by external agencies in requiring access to client records, for use in legal proceedings. These agencies include:

- *solicitors* representing clients in legal proceedings, such as litigation for workplace stress
- *police officers* seeking evidence for a prosecution in the case of alleged child abuse
- *courts* requiring the surrender of counselling and psychotherapy records, including personal and supervision notes, to assist the court in its deliberations.

Counsellors and psychotherapists do not possess legal privilege, unlike solicitors, and cannot simply refuse to comply with court-ordered demands for notes, except at the risk of being held in contempt of court. Practitioners faced with court-authorized demands for release of client records need to take legal advice, but are faced with the reality that client confidentiality is outweighed by the wider public interest. Therapists, trainers and professional associations need to take fuller account of this issue, where client and therapist confidentiality is ultimately provided with limited protection by the law, that is

when the law itself declares an interest in accessing client secrets confided within the therapy session (see Mitchels – Chapter 4.5, this volume).

STATUTORY REGULATION OF THERAPISTS

Therapists' organizations have been heavily engaged in lobbying for the statutory regulation of counselling and psychotherapy over the past few decades. These moves were ultimately unsuccessful, as signalled by a clear government decision *not* to implement statutory regulation for counselling and psychotherapy (Department of Health, 2011). Professional standards are managed by a combination of voluntary and statutory registers relying on professional self-regulation, overseen by the Professional Standards Authority for Health and Social Care. There is a certain degree of statutory regulation of the talking therapies, but it is partial and resembles a 'patchwork quilt', rather than anything more systematic and comprehensive in design or effect. There is limited and highly selective legal protection of Title, but only for some practitioners, such as Counselling, Clinical and Educational Psychologists, and Arts, Play and Music Therapists, who are all regulated by the Health and Care Professions Council (HCPC). In terms of Practice, adoption counselling is regulated by the Adoption and Children Act 2002 and infertility counselling by the Human Fertilization and Embryology Act 1990. The result is probably a deeply unsatisfactory compromise for the main therapists' organizations, for whom statutory regulation has been a major policy priority, almost from their very inception.

SUMMARY

Therapists need to be familiar with the broad outline of the civil law and the specific ways in which it impacts on their practice. In reality, the relationship of the law to counselling and psychotherapy is mediated by a number of factors, such as the therapist's context for practice, employment status and client group. In terms of managing professional relationships with clients, therapists need to be aware of the principles underlying contracts, if in private practice or undertaking client work for a fee, and to work within the parameters of accepted professional norms in discharging their duty of care to clients. The process of managing risk presents a number of challenges to therapists, where there are relatively few absolute requirements to break client confidentiality.

Psychologists Protection Society Seminar in June 2014 on 'Records as Evidence':

www.theprofessionalpractitioner.net/index.php/cpd-activities/14-cpd-activity-records-as-evidence

Counselling Mind-Ed (free online training material, on legal and ethical aspects of working with children and young people, such as applying the law, record keeping and safeguarding): www.minded.org.uk

British Association for Counselling and Psychotherapy legal resources (linked to the *Ethical Framework* (BACP, 2015): www.bacp.co.uk/ethics/newGPG.php

Figure 4.9.1 Therapy and the law web resources

Data protection law has eroded previous therapist latitude regarding record keeping, and subjected it to wider principles of public transparency, access and accountability. While the law is generally supportive of client confidentiality, therapists do not possess the legal protection of privilege, and must normally comply with court-authorized demands for access to client records in the public interest. A second wave of progress towards the goal of achieving statutory regulation of counsellors and psychotherapists has been halted by a change of government policy, which favours reliance on a complex combination of voluntary and statutory registers and professional self-regulation.

REFERENCES

BACP (2016) *Ethical Framework for the Counselling Professions*. Lutterworth: British Association for Counselling and Psychotherapy.

Bond, T. (2015) *Standards and Ethics for Counselling in Action* (4th ed.). London: Sage.

Department of Health (2011) *Enabling Excellence: Autonomy and Accountability for Healthcare Workers, Social Workers and Social Care Workers*. Cm 8008. London: Stationery Office.

Jenkins, P. (2007a) *Counselling, Psychotherapy and the Law* (2nd ed.). London: Sage.

Jenkins, P. (2014) *Therapists and Professional Negligence: A Duty of Care?* DVD: Counselling DVDs.

RECOMMENDED READING

1.   Daniels, D. and Jenkins, P. (2010) *Therapy with Children: Children's Rights, Confidentiality and the Law* (2nd ed.). London: Sage.

Detailed discussion of the rights of children and young people, based on case studies drawn from school-based counselling.

2.   Jenkins, P. (2007b) Supervision in the dock? In K. Tudor and M. Worrall (eds.), *Freedom to Practise*. Volume 2: *Developing Person-centred Approaches to Supervision* (pp. 176–194). Ross-on-Wye: PCCS Books.

Suggested framework for distinguishing ethical and legal aspects of supervisor's 'duty of care' to supervisees and clients.

3.   Jenkins, P. (in press) *Professional Practice in Counselling and Psychotherapy, Ethics and the Law*. London: Sage.

Student textbook analysing the key components of professional practice, based on the BACP *Ethical Framework for the Counselling Professions* (2016).

4.10 MENTAL HEALTH LAW

SOBHI GIRGIS

OVERVIEW AND KEY POINTS

The care of people with mental disorders is regulated by a host of legal provisions, not restricted to a specific mental health law. Detention in hospital could be effected by part 2 'civil' or part 3 'criminal' of the Mental Health Act (MHA) 1983, the Mental Capacity Act (MCA) 2005 or the Children Act (1989), among other legislations. Deprivation of liberty and enforcing treatment undoubtedly constitute serious encroachments on personal autonomy. Thus, the legal framework includes clear safeguards against the misuse of such powers. In 2007, significant changes were made to the MHA 1983, including the introduction of Community Treatment Orders (CTO). The Code of Practice of the MHA was revised in 2015 to provide stronger protection of people who come under compulsory powers. It puts emphasis on the compliance with the Human Rights Act (HRA) 1998, the Equality Act 2010 and the Care Act 2014.

- Most countries have their own specific mental health law, including devolved nations within the United Kingdom (UK).
- Detention in hospital for treatment of mental disorder could be effected by a number of legal provisions, and not restricted to MHA 1983.
- There are several safeguards to ensure lawful and fair treatment of people with mental disorders.
- Legal frameworks and clinical practice need to comply with HRA 1998 and the Equality Act 2010.

The care of people with mental disorder is regulated by a host of legal provisions arising from, among other sources, Acts of Parliament, secondary legislation, Case Law, the European Convention on Human Rights (ECHR), the HRA 1998 and judgments made by the European Court of Human Rights (ECtHR).

Detention in hospital is a significant encroachment on personal liberty. Most countries have a specific mental health law to regulate the use of such powers and stipulate sufficient safeguards against their misuse. Devolved UK administrations have slightly different mental health laws.

Provisions for detention in hospital are also available through other legislation, for example, the MCA 2005, the Children Act 1989, the Criminal Procedure (Insanity) Act 1964 as amended by the Criminal Procedure (Insanity and Unfitness to Plead) Act 1991, and the Homicide Act 1957. The Criminal Justice Act 2003 enables the courts to add treatment requirements to a community sentence, for example, mental health, drug or alcohol treatment requirements.

Legal provisions dealing with issues of capacity have developed over the years through common law. These were eventually codified by the MCA 2005. The latter was amended to include clear procedures and safeguards regarding deprivation of liberty. A clearer test for deprivation of liberty has been introduced through a recent Supreme Court judgment – the 'Cheshire West' case.

MENTAL HEALTH ACT 1983 (AS AMENDED BY MHA 2007)

The Act deals with care and treatment of people with mental disorders. The 2007 amendment widened the definition of mental disorder and abolished the previous four categories (mental illness, mental impairment, severe mental impairment and psychopathic disorder). Mental disorder is defined in the Act as 'any disorder or disability of the mind'. Learning disability is considered to be a mental disorder for the purpose of detention for treatment, only if it is associated with abnormally aggressive or seriously irresponsible behaviour. Dependence on alcohol or drugs *per se* is not considered a mental disorder and patients cannot be detained solely because of their dependence. However, psychiatric disorders arising from alcohol or drug misuse constitute mental disorders, for example, intoxication, withdrawal or alcoholic psychotic disorder. The 2007 amendment abolished the 'treatability' criteria for some mental disorders. Instead, it created an 'appropriate medical treatment' test which applies to all mental disorders. No longer can Electro-Convulsive Therapy (ECT) be given to a capacious adult without their consent unless it is a lifesaving treatment.

Patients can be detained in hospital under 'civil' sections (Part II of the Act) or 'criminal sections' which are issued by a Court or Ministry of Justice (Part III of the Act). Part IV regulates consent to treatment while Part V deals with appealing against detention and CTO.

Clinicians have been given new powers to impose certain conditions on patients on their release from detention and the ability to recall patients back to hospital.

The Act opened the door for professionals other than doctors, including psychologists, to become 'Approved Clinicians (ACs)' or 'Approved Mental Health Professionals (AMHPs)'. The 'Responsible Clinician (RC)' is the AC with overall responsibility for the care of patients coming under compulsion. AMHPs carry out the functions that used to be the preserve of the 'Approved Social Worker (ASW)'.

MEDICAL TREATMENT UNDER MHA

Medical treatment of mental disorders includes nursing care, psychological intervention, and specialist mental health habilitation, rehabilitation and care. The 2007 amendment explicitly included psychological intervention within the definition.

The Act defines medical treatment for mental disorder as 'medical treatment which is for the purpose of alleviating or preventing a worsening of a mental disorder or one or more of its symptoms or manifestations' (section 145(4) of the Mental Health Act). This can include treatment of physical health problems only if such treatment is part of, or ancillary to, treatment for mental disorder (e.g., treating wounds self-inflicted as a result of mental disorder). Sections 57, 58 and 58A set out types of medical treatment to which special rules apply, including, in many cases, the need for a certificate from a 'Second Opinion Appointed Doctor (SOAD)' approving the treatment. Under section 63, detained patients may be given medical treatment for any kind of mental disorder, if they consent to it, or if they have not consented to it, but the treatment is given by or under the direction of the AC in charge of such treatment (unless sections 57, 58 or 58A apply). Psychological therapies and other forms of medical treatments which, to be effective, require the patient's cooperation are not automatically inappropriate simply because a patient does not wish to engage with them. Such treatments would remain appropriate and available as long as they continue to be clinically appropriate and would be provided if the patient agrees to engage.

PART II OF THE MHA 1983

This part deals with 'civil detentions', that is, not through the criminal justice system. Section 2, lasting for up to 28 days, is for assessment or assessment followed by treatment. Section 3, lasting for up to six months, is for treatment. It can be renewed at regular intervals, initially for six months, then annually. Admission under sections 2 or 3 requires two medical recommendations and an application by an AMHP. Section 4 allows urgent detention for up to 72 hours, when only one medical recommendation could be secured. Section 5 deals with application for a 'holding' power order that allows a nurse or a doctor to keep a patient already in hospital to facilitate assessment for detention under sections 2 or 3. Section 7 concerns application for a guardianship order. Section 17 regulates granting leaves of absence. Section 20 deals with renewal of detention while section 23 regulates discharge from detention.

PART III OF THE MHA 1983

These are orders made by a criminal court in relation to offenders or by the Ministry of Justice in relation to prisoners who are in need of psychiatric treatment in hospitals. Section 37 is a Hospital Order imposed by the Magistrates or Crown Court. It operates in the same way as its civil counterpart s. 3. A Restriction Order under s. 41 can be attached to s. 37 only by the Crown Court. Section 41 aims at protecting the public from serious harm. Under s. 41, leave of absence and transfer between hospitals will require Ministry of Justice permission. Discharge can only be ordered by a Mental Health Tribunal or the Ministry of Justice. Section 38 Interim Hospital Order allows the court to remand offenders to hospital for a trial of treatment before deciding to sentence them to a Hospital Order. The courts also have other powers to remand offenders to hospital for preparation of reports (s. 35) or treatment (s. 36). Section 47 is used by the Ministry of Justice to transfer a serving prisoner to hospital. A Restriction Order s. 49 (similar to s. 41) is usually attached to s. 47. Remanded prisoners in urgent need for treatment can be transferred to hospital under ss. 48/49.

PART IV OF THE MHA 1983

This regulates medical treatment of mental disorder and issues of consent. Treatment with medication, after the first three months of their first administration (s. 58), requires the patient's consent *or* the agreement of a SOAD. In urgent cases, the RC can authorise treatment pending compliance with certification by an SOAD (s. 62). New safeguards have been introduced for ECT (s. 58A). Capacious patients cannot be given ECT without their consent unless it is lifesaving.

SAFEGUARDS FOR DETAINED PATIENTS

Patients must be given information on their detention and any safeguards. All detained patients and patients under CTOs have a new right of access to an Independent Mental Health Advocate (IMHA). Patients can appeal against detention or CTO to the Mental Health Tribunal or the Hospital Managers. The MHA gives significant powers to the nearest relative (NR), including objecting to detention in hospital for treatment (s. 3), ordering discharge of the patient, and applying for review of the patient's detention by a tribunal.

COMMUNITY TREATMENT ORDER

The 2007 amendment introduced CTO – a new regime to apply compulsory powers in the community. The RC can impose certain conditions on patients on their release from detention and recall patients back to hospital if treatment in hospital is required. An RC can recall the patient to hospital for up to 72 hours, where treatment can be given. If a longer period of care is needed, the CTO can be revoked, initiating a new six-month period of detention in hospital. In general, treatment cannot be enforced in the community, except when physical force is required to administer emergency treatment to people lacking capacity.

GUARDIANSHIP ORDERS

If there are concerns about the welfare of people with mental disorder, they can be placed under guardianship in the community rather than detained in hospital. The Local Authority most often takes the role of the guardian.

POWERS OF ENTRY AND POLICE POWERS (S. 135 AND S. 136)

Section 135 allows an AMHP to apply to a magistrate for a warrant authorising a police officer to enter specific premises, by force if necessary, if there is reasonable cause to suspect that someone with a mental disorder:

- has been or is being ill-treated, neglected or kept otherwise than under proper control on the premises; or
- is living there alone and unable to care for themselves.

The police also have powers under s. 136 in relation to people they find in a public place who appear to be suffering from mental disorder and to be in immediate need of care or control. People will then be taken to a 'place of safety' where their mental health is assessed within 24 hours.

AFTERCARE (S. 117)

Patients detained for treatment are entitled to appropriate services, according to their needs, when they leave hospital. Section 117 places an obligation on Clinical Commissioning Groups (CCGs) and Local Authorities (LAs) to provide those services free of charge. Section 117 was significantly amended by the Care Act 2014 to ensure that care plans are patient-centred.

CRIMINAL PROCEDURE (INSANITY) ACT 1964 (AS AMENDED)

People whom the court accepts to be legally insane are given the special verdict of 'not guilty by reason of insanity'. They can be admitted to hospital for treatment in a similar way to s. 37. The law was amended in 1991 to cover people who are 'unfit to plead'. Those people cannot be tried but their case will be subject to a 'trial of facts'. The jurors will decide whether the person has committed the act or the omission. The person can be admitted to hospital for treatment but can also be given guardianship, a community sentence or absolute discharge.

POLICE AND CRIMINAL EVIDENCE ACT (PACE) 1984

This legislation recognises the vulnerability of people with mental disorder when they come into contact with the police. If a police constable thinks or is told in good faith that a detained person is mentally disordered, an interview cannot be conducted in the absence of an 'appropriate adult'.

HOMICIDE ACT 1957 (AS AMENDED BY THE CORONERS AND JUSTICE ACT 2009)

This legislation introduced the partial defence of 'diminished responsibility' to a charge of murder. This defence is available to people suffering from a mental disorder which substantially impairs their mental responsibility for the killing. They receive a conviction of manslaughter rather than murder and are invariably sentenced to a hospital order with restriction. The test for diminished responsibility has been modernised by the Coroners and Justice Act 2009.

COMMUNITY CARE LAW

There has been a plethora of successive Acts covering community care. The National Assistance Act 1948, a key piece of legislation, followed the establishment of the National Health Service (NHS). It abolished the workhouses and kick-started the modern system of social benefits. Much legislation followed dealing with community care in a piecemeal manner. In the 1980s there was a shift of care from psychiatric institutions to the community, with the closure of asylums. The NHS and Community Care Act 1990 defined the responsibilities of health and LAs in providing community care services. The NHS no longer has the primary responsibility for the provision of non-hospital services for those requiring long-term care. The Act required LAs to assess the care needs of people whom they are either obliged or empowered to assist.

The Care Act 2014 is the biggest change to community care law in 60 years. It brought together a number of existing laws and introduced new duties to LAs to ensure that wellbeing, dignity and choice are at the heart of health and social care. Relevant professionals (particularly those involved in discharging or treating patients in the community) should also consider the general responsibilities of LAs under Part 1 of the Act (e.g., duty to promote wellbeing, promote integration and cooperation duties). The Act significantly amended the duties of LAs and CCGs under s. 117 of the MHA 1983.

MENTAL CAPACITY ACT 2005

This is a 'codifying' Act, as it did not create new legal principles but enshrined in statute common law principles concerning people lacking mental capacity and those who take decisions on their behalf. It replaced existing statutory schemes for enduring powers of attorney and court of protection receivers with reformed and updated provisions. The Act is underpinned by five key principles: presumption of capacity, supporting individuals to make their own decisions, not equating unwise decisions with lack of capacity, acts done on behalf of people lacking capacity must be in their best interest, and lastly, these acts should be the least restrictive of their basic rights and freedoms.

The MHA 2007 amended the MCA 2005 to introduce Deprivation of Liberty Safeguards (DoLS), a legal framework for depriving people who lack capacity of their liberty if that is in their best interests. The safeguards apply to people who are either in a hospital or in registered care homes. DoLS contain detailed requirements about when and how deprivation of liberty may be authorised. The legislation also provides detailed arrangements for renewing and challenging the authorisation of deprivation of liberty. Specifically, DoLS were introduced to prevent human rights breaches identified by the judgment of the ECtHR in the 'Bournewood' judgment.

In March 2014, the Supreme Court made a judgment in a case best known as Cheshire West. The judgment established the 'acid test' to decide whether there is deprivation of liberty. The Court asserted that people who lack capacity enjoy the same human rights enjoyed by everybody else. Patients lacking capacity to consent to admission to a psychiatric hospital where the regime amounts to deprivation of liberty, and who are objecting to being there, cannot remain 'informally'. Those patients cannot be detained under DoLS either. MHA could be a more appropriate legal framework.

HUMAN RIGHTS ACT 1998

The UK was a co-signatory of the European Convention on Human Rights (ECHR) at its inception in 1950. The HRA 1998 gives further effect in UK law to the rights contained in the ECHR. It makes available in UK courts a remedy for breach of Convention rights, without the need to go to the ECtHR. Some of the rights are absolute, some are qualified (by the needs of society), and some are limited (by other legislation). The relevant ECHR articles are listed in Table 4.10.1.

The current Conservative Government is planning to repeal the HRA 1998 and to introduce a British Bill of Rights. A consultation was due to be launched in December 2015 but, at the time of writing, this has not been conducted.

Table 4.10.1 ECHR articles

Article 2 Right to life (absolute)

Article 3 Prohibition of torture (absolute)

Article 4 Prohibition of slavery and forced labour (absolute)

Article 5 Right to liberty and security (limited)

Article 6 Right to a fair trial (limited)

Article 7 No punishment without law (absolute)

Article 8 Right to respect for private and family life (qualified)

Article 9 Freedom of thought, conscience and religion (qualified)

Article 10 Freedom of expression (qualified)

Article 11 Freedoms of assembly and association (qualified)

Article 12 Right to marry (limited)

EXAMPLES OF RELEVANCE OF THE HRA 1998

Article 5 allows the detention of people with 'unsound mind' on the basis of objective medical evidence. This principle underpins the process of detaining people with mental disorder under the MHA. Medical recommendations provide the necessary 'objective medical evidence'. Article 5 also requires speedy review by a 'court'. Following the Winterwerp case, the mental health tribunals were given the power to discharge patients to ensure compliance with article 5.

Article 6 underpins the proceedings of the tribunals and the entitlement of patients to free legal representation in connection with the review, by a tribunal, of their detention. Article 8 protects the right of detained people to privacy of their correspondence and contact with family and friends. Article 3 guards against any intervention that could be considered as 'inhumane or degrading'.

SOME LEGAL ISSUES RELEVANT TO COUNSELLORS AND PSYCHOTHERAPISTS

The current MHA made it possible for psychologists to become ACs and AMHPs. Psychological treatment has been explicitly included in the definition of 'medical treatment'. As such, appropriate medical treatment can theoretically be limited to psychological treatment, for example, in a personality disorders unit. Psychological treatment for detained patients is provided under the authority of the RC (s. 63).

It is interesting that treatment is considered as 'available' even if a detained patient refuses to engage. This poses an ethical dilemma for the therapist. If psychological treatment is the main form of treatment for a detained patient, admission to a particular unit is only possible if such intervention is available in that unit.

Following the Cheshire West case, there has been increased attention to the issues of capacity, whether the patient is objecting to admission or treatment, whether there is deprivation of liberty and best interest. Psychologists and counsellors should regularly contribute to the decision-making process around those issues.

It is unlawful for a public authority to act in a way which is incompatible with a Convention right, for example, the right to respect for private and family life. Under s. 6 of the HRA 1998, individual therapists would fall under the definition of public authority if they are working for an organisation whose functions are of a public nature, for example, an NHS hospital or a private hospital providing NHS treatment.

REFERENCES

Department of Health (2015) *Mental Health Act 1983: Revised Code of Practice*. London: Stationery Office.

STATUTES

Care Act 2014 c.23
Children Act 1989 c.41
Coroners and Justice Act 2009 c.25
Criminal Procedure (Insanity) Act 1964 c.84
Criminal Procedure (Insanity and Unfitness to Plead) Act 1991 c.25
Equality Act 2010 c.15
European Convention on Human Rights 1950: Convention for the Protection of Human Rights and Fundamental Freedoms, Rome, 4. XI.1950 available at www.echr.coe.int/Documents/Convention_ENG.pdf
Homicide Act 1957
Human Rights Act 1998
Mental Capacity Act 2005 c.9
Mental Health Act 1983 (as amended by MHA 2007) c.20
National Assistance Act 1948 c. 29 (Regnal. 11 and 12 Geo 6)
National Health Service and Community Care Act 1990 c. 19
Police and Criminal Evidence Act (PACE) 1984 c. 60

CASES

Bournewood case: HL v UK 45508/99 (2004) ECHR 471
P v Cheshire West & Chester Council; P & Q v Surrey County Council [2014] UKSC 19
Winterwerp v Netherlands 6301/73 (1979) ECHR 4

RECOMMENDED READING

1. Department of Health (2015) *Mental Health Act 1983: Revised Code of Practice*. London: Stationery Office.

The revised code is a well-written account of the principles of mental health law and their application in clinical practice. It is a statutory document for all health and social care staff in England.

2. Jones, R. (2104) *Mental Capacity Act Manual* (6th ed.) London: Sweet & Maxwell.

The book provides an up-to-date account of the legal framework of mental capacity and deprivation of liberty safeguards.

3. P v Cheshire West & Chester Council; P & Q v Surrey County Council [2014] UKSC 19.

The judgment is hugely influential in mental capacity law. It introduced a clear test for deprivation of liberty and clarifies for the first time that people with learning disability are entitled to the same degree of human rights as anybody else.

4.11 FUNDAMENTALS OF RESEARCH

JOHN MCLEOD

OVERVIEW AND KEY POINTS

At the present time there exist opposing pressures around the relevance of the scientific knowledge base that informs therapy policy and practice. On the one hand, there are demands that therapists become more tuned in to research. On the other hand, some therapists are resistant to becoming more involved in an activity that does not appear to produce advantages in respect of work with clients. This chapter explores some of the key issues and developments in relation to research in counselling and psychotherapy, and the potential value of research as a means of enhancing the quality of therapy services that are available to clients. The aims of the chapter are to:

*   provide an overview of developments in research on the process and outcomes of counselling and psychotherapy;
*   identify the key skills and knowledge required to be a research-informed practitioner;
*   discuss the critical issues and debates within this field, and their implications for the future of counselling and psychotherapy.

BACKGROUND

An awareness of research has become increasingly important for counsellors and psychotherapists in recent years. The professionalization of counselling and psychotherapy, and the emphasis placed within health care on evidence-based practice, has contributed to an expectation that therapists will be informed about research findings relevant to their work. There is a growing trend for institutions and agencies which fund therapy services, and also for consumer groups, to demand research evidence about effectiveness. The development of new therapy settings, client groups and interventions has also required research support.

It is possible to differentiate between two broad areas of focus for therapy research: outcome and process. Outcome research seeks to establish the effectiveness of different therapy interventions. Process research examines the ways in which different activities and factors contribute to outcome.

Counselling and psychotherapy process research began with the pioneering work of Carl Rogers and his colleagues in the 1940s, into the 'necessary and sufficient conditions' for therapeutic change. Since that time, a wide range of methods for studying therapy process have been developed. Some studies have used quantitative methods, such as questionnaires or rating scales completed by clients and therapists at the end of therapy sessions, or coding systems applied by independent raters to analyse processes that can be observed in video recordings of sessions. Other process research makes use of qualitative methods, such as interviews with clients and therapists, and analysis of patterns of narrative and discourse in transcripts of therapy sessions.

The largest single body of research into the process of therapy has centred on the question of the characteristics of facilitative client–therapist relationships, for example using the Working Alliance Inventory to invite clients and therapists to record their perceptions of the strength of *bond*, *task* and *goal* dimensions of the relationship. This research has produced convincing evidence that the strength of the working alliance early in therapy and successful resolution of ruptures in the alliance are significant predictors of eventual good outcome in therapy (Cooper, 2008). Other research has used qualitative methods to examine the client's experience of the therapy process, and the ways that therapists use language to maintain control of therapy interactions. There is also extensive research into the nature of psychoanalytic processes in therapy, such as the role of transference and the impact in interpretations.

Outcome research (also described as 'efficacy', 'effectiveness' or 'evaluation' research) has the primary aim of finding out how much a particular counselling or therapy intervention has helped or benefited the client. The earliest systematic research into counselling and therapy concentrated entirely on this issue. In the 1930s and 1940s, several studies were carried out into the effects of psychoanalysis. The results of these investigations suggested that, overall, around two-thirds of the psychoanalytic patients followed up improved, with one-third remaining the same or deteriorating after treatment. These early studies consisted of follow-up interviews with clients. The limitations of this kind of research design are readily apparent: it is possible that all, or some, of the clients who improved might have done so even if they had not received therapy. In response to this methodological critique, a later generation of outcome research employed the strategy of the randomized controlled trial (RCT), in which clients are assessed prior to receiving therapy and are randomly allocated to different treatment conditions. Within the design, any differences in outcome between the treatment groups at the end of therapy can be attributed to the effects of therapy, because all other factors have been held constant. From the 1970s, many hundreds of RCTs have been carried out into the impact of different therapy approaches on different client populations. Once a number of RCTs have been conducted, it is possible to look at whether a consistent pattern emerges regarding the relative effectiveness of competing therapy models with particular client groups. This procedure involves the use of a technique for systematic review of outcome literature, known as meta-analysis. Meta-analysis involves calculating the average amount of client change reported for each approach in each separate study, then combining these change scores to give an overall estimate of how much benefit a particular approach (such as psychoanalysis, client-centred therapy or behaviour therapy) yields over a set of studies comprising a large number of clients. The first comprehensive and systematic meta-analysis of therapy outcome was published by Smith, Glass and Miller (1980), and since that time many further meta-analyses have been conducted. Taken as a whole, these meta-analyses suggest that counselling and psychotherapy in general are highly effective, with clients who have received treatment reporting much more benefit than those on waiting lists or in other control conditions. The pattern of outcome in relation to specific disorders or problem areas is more mixed. There is strong evidence for the efficacy of cognitive-behavioural therapy (CBT) for most psychological problems, but this finding may reflect the fact that more outcome studies have been carried out on CBT interventions than on other approaches. Where relevant outcome studies have been conducted, there also tends to be good evidence for the efficacy of psychodynamic, person-centred/experiential and other approaches to therapy.

Although there is no doubt that RCTs represent a powerful tool for examining the effectiveness of counselling and psychotherapy, it is also clear that there are many challenging methodological issues associated with the use of this approach within the domain of research in counselling and psychotherapy. In essence, the critical factor is that the technical requirements of a good randomized trial mean that the clients who are recruited to the study, and the therapy that is provided for them, may be rather different from therapy that occurs in routine practice. As a result, the relevance of RCT findings for everyday practice can be called into question. Practice-based or naturalistic outcome studies represent a means of collecting information on the outcomes of therapy that is more faithful to the conditions of everyday therapy. In practice-based research, all clients receiving therapy from an agency or a clinic are invited to complete questionnaires at the start and end of their therapy. The development of outcome monitoring systems, in the form of brief symptom scales that clients can complete at each session, has made it possible for many practitioners and therapy service providers to engage in practice-based audit and research (Barkham et al., 2010; Overington and Ionita, 2012).

An important consequence of ready access to outcome monitoring systems has been the increasing use by practitioners of therapy outcome measures to provide real-time feedback on client progress (Boswell et al., 2015). Essentially, these initiatives involve inviting the client to complete a brief outcome measure before each session. The pattern of improvement or deterioration that is then visible can be used by the therapist, or collaboratively by therapist and client together, to inform the work they are doing. This kind of information has proved to be particularly valuable in relation to managing 'off-track' clients who are getting worse, and decisions around when to end therapy. The primary reason for the value of these sources of information is that studies have shown that therapists are not good at knowing when their clients are getting worse, or when they are well enough to terminate. Therapists can be provided with checklists of potential strategies (clinical support tools) for dealing with clients who are displaying negative outcomes (Harmon et al., 2007).

The field of counselling and psychotherapy outcome research is dominated by studies that assess outcome in terms of changes in client scores on self-report measures of symptoms of anxiety, depression and other types of distress. Some researchers have sought to broaden the range of outcome research by carrying out studies that have collected data on the economic costs and benefits of therapy (Miller and Magruder, 1999) and on the way that clients and service users define and make sense of outcome in terms of their own criteria (McLeod, 2011).

Although a vast amount of therapy research has been carried out over the past 50 years, it is not clear that this knowledge has had a consistent or significant impact on practice: the existence of a research–practice 'gap' is widely acknowledged. Few therapists read research articles or regard them as being useful sources of information in relation to practice. Practitioners complain that research depends too much on statistical generalizations and does not ask the appropriate questions (Morrow-Bradley and Elliott, 1986; Stewart, Stirman and Chambless, 2012).

ESSENTIAL RESEARCH KNOWLEDGE AND SKILLS

The topic of research methodology covers an extremely wide range of issues and methodological approaches. Even among full-time researchers, there are few, if any, individuals who can claim competence across the entire field. For practising counsellors and psychotherapists, and

those in training, the main investment of time and energy is inevitably focused on being able to offer the best possible service for clients, rather than on learning about research or conducting research studies. However, in order to be adequately research-informed, therapists need to possess knowledge in a set of key domains:

- critically analysing research articles;
- making sense of systematic reviews of research findings;
- qualitative, interview-based research;
- quantitative outcome research;
- systematic case study research;
- personal experience research.

A brief overview of each of these domains is provided below. These areas also have implications for training and continuing professional development, in relation to topics that need to be addressed to support research-informed practice.

CRITICALLY ANALYSING RESEARCH ARTICLES

A key skill for any research-informed therapy practitioner is to be able to access and read research articles. The research literature represents an immense resource for therapists. It includes articles on many different kinds of therapy applied to the problems of a diversity of client groups. It is now possible to access much of this literature through online search engines and databases. A good place to start when trying to learn about the kind of research that has been carried out is *Bergin and Garfield's Handbook of Psychotherapy and Behavior Change*, edited by Lambert (2013) and now in its sixth edition. Therapy research articles are published in a wide range of journals, including specialist research journals such as: *Counselling and Psychotherapy Research*, *Psychology and Psychotherapy*, *Journal of Consulting and Clinical Psychology*, *Journal of Counseling Psychology* and *Psychotherapy Research*. To extract information from research articles, it is necessary to develop an appreciation of how they are written. All research papers begin with an abstract which summarizes the main features and conclusions of the study. Readers can use the abstract to decide whether or not to look at the article in more detail. Although an increasing number of research studies employ qualitative methods, it is still the case that the majority rely on statistical forms of data analysis. To make sense of these papers, it is therefore necessary to have some familiarity with statistical concepts. When reading research papers it is important to adopt a critical, questioning perspective, particularly in relation to the implications of the study for practice. In research studies, the definition and measurement of key variables, the selection of participants, or the therapeutic interventions that are used may not mirror what happens in everyday therapeutic practice.

MAKING SENSE OF SYSTEMATIC REVIEWS OF RESEARCH FINDINGS

Typically, at any one time, a practitioner may have a special interest in two lines of research, and try to keep up to date with the development of knowledge in these areas. An appreciation of research findings in other areas can be gained from reading review articles that systematically summarize and evaluate findings that have accumulated around a particular theme or question. There are different types of review methodology. For example, scoping reviews aim to map out the overall landscape of research in a particular area, while narrative reviews aim to tell the story of how knowledge has been built up within a topic. Meta-analysis is a form of review methodology that looks at overall conclusions that can be drawn in relation to quantitative studies, for example, studies that have measured the effectiveness of a particular approach to therapy with a specific client population. Meta-synthesis is an approach to systematic reviewing that identifies common themes in a set of qualitative studies, for example, interview studies where clients have been invited to talk about what was helpful or hindering in the therapy they have received. In order to be an informed consumer of review articles, it is necessary to possess an appreciation of good practice in different types of review, and an understanding of what they are trying to achieve.

QUALITATIVE, INTERVIEW-BASED RESEARCH

Qualitative research seeks to explore the ways in which meaning and action are constructed. The most widely-used qualitative methodology is the research interview, although qualitative data can also be collected through diaries and other written documents, open-ended questionnaires, projective techniques, recordings of therapy sessions and direct observation. Qualitative research tends to be discovery-oriented rather than oriented at testing or conforming hypotheses, and is particularly appropriate in relation to research questions that are concerned with understanding the experiences of clients and therapists. Examples of influential and practically useful qualitative research include studies of client experience of metaphor (Angus and Rennie, 1989), and what counsellors who work with young people have learned about what is effective with this client group (Westergaard, 2013). Such

studies do not yield definitive guidelines for practice, but instead offer descriptive accounts and ways of making sense, which can help practitioners to reflect on their work. Qualitative inquiry requires imagination, sensitivity and ethical awareness, and both readers and researchers need to be familiar with criteria for evaluating the validity of this form of investigation (Elliott, Fischer and Rennie, 1999).

QUANTITATIVE OUTCOME RESEARCH

The issue of the effectiveness of therapy (how much does it help?) represents the single most important research question in the eyes of most clients, therapists, service managers and policy-makers. Although it is possible to evaluate outcomes through qualitative interviews (McLeod, 2011), the majority of outcome studies are based on analysis of data from standardized quantitative self-report measures of symptom and functioning that are administered at the start and end of therapy and at follow-up. There are two main types of quantitative outcome study. Naturalistic or practice-based studies examine the *effectiveness* of therapy as it occurs in routine practice. Randomized controlled (or clinical) trials (RCTs) examine the *efficacy* of therapy in ideal, controlled situations, for example with groups of clients with well-defined problems. By comparing outcomes across different interventions, such as CBT versus psychodynamic, or person-centred versus treatment as usual, an RCT design is able to offer robust conclusions around causal efficacy (for example, the change that was recorded can be attributed to the effect of therapy). By contrast, naturalistic studies of routine practice may be able to demonstrate that change has occurred, but are not able to determine whether that change resulted from therapy or some other factor (for instance, that a client might have improved in the absence of therapy, as a consequence of a natural healing or recovery process). As well as analysing statistical differences in scores before and after therapy, most quantitative outcome studies also calculate rates of *reliable change* (whether the client has improved sufficiently to make a tangible difference to their wellbeing) and *clinical change* (whether, by the end of therapy, the client is symptom-free or fully recovered). An overall *Effect Size* (ES) calculation is used as a means of comparing levels of change reported in different studies. For example, an ES of .2 would reflect a minimal level of change, whereas an ES of 1.0 would indicate that therapy had been successful for most clients in the sample. Because many outcome studies have been published, it is possible to develop benchmarks for success with different client groups. This allows the effectiveness of individual therapists, or counsellors in a particular agency, to be compared with results achieved by colleagues elsewhere. An important practical dimension of quantitative outcome research has consisted of studies of the proportion of clients with unplanned endings or irregular attendance. Finally, outcome research can include information about the process of therapy (process-outcome research), leading to a capacity to identify key therapy processes that contribute to change. The most influential area of focus in this type of research has consisted of a large number of studies that have shown that a healthy client–therapist working alliance is a strong predictor of eventual good outcome.

SYSTEMATIC CASE STUDY RESEARCH

The original founding figures of psychotherapy, such as Sigmund Freud and Joseph Wolpe, used case studies of their clinical practice to document and disseminate their new approaches and to explore the processes that seemed to be contributing to therapeutic change. Clinical case studies have continued to be used as a means of communicating new ideas about practice within the professional community. However, there has been a substantial amount of scepticism about the status of clinical case studies as a source of research evidence, on account of the methodological weaknesses associated with this mode of inquiry. Clinical case reports that are based solely on post-session notes made by the therapist in the case, which are then analysed and written up by that therapist, lack the kind of transparency and external scrutiny and verification that have come to be taken for granted in other spheres of counselling and psychotherapy research. As a result, there has been a decline in the number of case studies that have been published. This is regrettable, because, in principle, case studies provide a unique perspective on what happens in therapy. Compared to other types of research, case studies are better able to reflect the complexity of therapy process and outcome, and to track the ways in which key change processes unfold over time. Case studies are also particularly effective at exploring the ways in which contextual factors influence the therapy process. In recent years there has been a resurgence of case study research, based on the adoption of a set of principles for systematic case inquiry (McLeod, 2010). These principles reflect two key methodological strategies: (1) the construction of a rich dataset on the case, drawn from a range of different sources of information; and (2) the analysis of case data by a group or team of researchers (usually including the therapist, and sometimes also including the client). The implementation of these principles, and the establishment of case study

journals such as *Clinical Case Studies* and *Pragmatic Case Studies in Psychotherapy*, alongside the increasing willingness of other journals to publish systematic case studies, have meant that the case study method is now beginning to make a meaningful contribution to the evidence base for counselling and psychotherapy. This development is particularly welcome because it carries with it the potential to bridge the research–practice 'gap': practitioners are in a good position to collect and write up case study data, and practitioners enjoy reading case studies.

PERSONAL EXPERIENCE RESEARCH

An emergent area of research in counselling and psychotherapy comprises studies in which people write in detail about their own personal experience of some aspect of therapy, or about painful life experiences that have led to a need for therapy (McLeod, 2011). This type of research is often described as *autoethnography*, to indicate a fusion of *auto*biography and *ethnography* (observing everyday experience). An example of an autoethnographic study is an account by Mckenzie (2015) into her experience of the difficulty in finding appropriate therapy following loss through homicide. This study illustrates the unique descriptive intensity that can be achieved through this methodological approach, as well as the potential of this type of research as a resource for therapists faced with clients who have unusual or severe problems.

CRITICAL ISSUES AND CHALLENGES IN RESEARCH ON COUNSELING AND PSYCHOTHERAPY

It is essential to acknowledge the limitations of research into counselling and psychotherapy. Compared to a field such as biomedical science, or even a single sector of that field, such as cancer care, the number of active psychotherapy researchers is significantly smaller. This difficulty is exacerbated by the fact that the psychotherapy research community is fragmented into sub-groups associated with schools of therapy, such as CBT and psychodynamic, who pursue research questions that are not readily generalizable across the field as a whole.

The existence of schools of therapy, each with its own theoretical perspective, presents further difficulties for the psychotherapy research community in respect of researcher allegiance effects and overall research strategy. Researcher allegiance refers to the tendency for researchers conducting supposedly rigorous and well-controlled scientific outcome studies to report results that favour the therapy approach in which they have been trained at the expense of whatever approach to which it has been compared (Luborsky et al., 1999). This cause of distortion and bias has persisted in outcome research over a 20-year period (Dragioti, Dimoliatis and Evangelou, 2015).

At a strategic level, the influence of schools of therapy has resulted in a large number of outcome studies in which the effectiveness of one approach has been compared to that of a competitor model. On the whole, this type of research ends up showing that all schools of therapy are equivalent in effectiveness for most conditions – the 'Dodo bird verdict – all have won and all should have prizes'. Any minor differences in effectiveness that are reported across therapy approaches can be attributed to allegiance effects (see above). As argued by Wampold and Imel (2015), outcome equivalence can be explained on the grounds that the similarities between approaches (i.e., common factors such as the expression of emotion, the existence of a trusting therapeutic relationship, etc.) hugely outweigh any differences in technique. Wampold and Imel (2015) point out that therapist effects account for differences in outcome much more than therapy approach effects: some therapists achieve much better results than others. The implication of this perspective is that the research priority should shift, from examining the effectiveness of therapies to investigating the effectiveness of therapists.

A final set of challenging issues for counselling and psychotherapy research concerns the translation of research findings into policy and practice. The accumulation of evidence about the effectiveness of different forms of therapy for different disorders has come to the attention of health services and governments committed to the development of policies of evidence-based practice. The concept of evidence-based practice represents an inevitable and rational response of governments and other health-care providers to the intersection of increasing costs of health services and increasing demand from patients for new and expensive treatments. Evidence-based practice consists of a broad strategy of prioritizing those treatments for which reliable evidence of efficacy is available. Within most of the United Kingdom (UK), recommendations around evidence-based practice in health care are made by the National Institute for Health and Care Excellence (NICE); Scotland is covered by a parallel body, the Scottish Intercollegiate Guidelines Network (SIGN). These organizations are independent of but funded by government, and have the task of reviewing research into the efficacy of interventions for specific disorders, and publishing recommendations in the form of clinical guidelines which determine the types of treatment that are offered within the National Health Service (NHS). Guidelines emerge from a lengthy consultation process which involves all possible stakeholders, including patient groups and individuals.

There are a number of ways in which evidence-based practice policies, and the specific approach taken by NICE, can be regarded as controversial. Any form of rigorous implementation of evidence-based practice requires that counsellors and psychotherapists should assess and diagnose their clients, and only use interventions that have been supported in research studies as being efficacious for that disorder. This framework conflicts with much of current therapy practice, at least in the UK. There are many therapists who do not work in health contexts, and who do not use an illness or medical model. Even among those who are sympathetic to a diagnosis-driven approach, there is a concern that in practice very few clients fit neatly into one diagnostic category; probably the majority of people who seek help from counsellors and psychotherapists have multiple problems ('comorbidity'). Furthermore, even if a therapist is trained in one empirically validated approach to therapy, there is a tendency for practitioners to operate from a more integrative or eclectic base as they gain more experience and assimilate additional ideas and methods into their clinical repertoire. Finally, there exist many prima facie valid approaches to therapy that have not yet been the subject of controlled outcome research, and which therefore risk being eliminated from the range of resources that are offered to clients. These are all factors that make it hard to implement strict evidence-based practice policies in the field of counselling and psychotherapy. In addition, NICE guidelines working groups have been criticized for adopting a review strategy that is too heavily dominated by RCT evidence and by issues of professional status, and which does not do justice to the contribution of a sufficiently inclusive definition of what counts as evidence (Moncrieff and Timimi, 2013).

CONCLUSION

The growing emphasis that is placed on research in counselling and psychotherapy, and the multiple possible ways in which research can inform practice, have meant that it has become increasingly important for research training to be incorporated into counsellor and psychotherapist training programmes, and for research updating to be made available through continuing professional development networks. The central or core research competency that needs to be acquired during basic training is the ability to read and critically appraise the contribution that research articles and reviews can make to practice. Beyond this, trainees need to know about the strengths and weaknesses of different methods for evaluating therapy outcomes, and to be helped to develop their own position in relation to ongoing debates around the nature of evidence-based practice and the relative effectiveness of different therapy interventions for particular disorders. Finally, it is not possible to appreciate the research process without experiencing it first-hand and actually *doing* a research study of some kind. If counselling and psychotherapy are to gain and maintain credibility in a cultural environment in which the public holds expectations that professions are accountable and can produce evidence for the effectiveness of their activities, it is necessary for counsellors and psychotherapists from all sectors of the profession to come to terms with the role and meaning of research. It is important to recognize that the complexity and ethical sensitivity of therapy research presents distinctive problems. Although counselling and psychotherapy research has made significant progress over the last 50 years, in providing a rational source of evidence to inform practice, it still faces considerable challenges.

REFERENCES

Angus, L. E. and Rennie, D. L. (1989) Envisioning the representational world: the client's experience of metaphoric expressiveness in psychotherapy. *Psychotherapy, 26,* 373–379.

Barkham, M., Hardy, G. E. and Mellor-Clark, J. (eds) (2010) *Developing and Delivering Practice-based Evidence: A Guide for the Psychological Therapies.* Chichester: Wiley-Blackwell.

Boswell, J. F., Kraus, D. R., Miller, S. D. and Lambert, M. J. (2015) Implementing routine outcome monitoring in clinical practice: benefits, challenges, and solutions. *Psychotherapy Research, 25,* 6–19.

Cooper, M. (2008) *Essential Research Findings in Counselling and Psychotherapy: The Facts are Friendly.* London: Sage.

Dragioti, E., Dimoliatis, I. and Evangelou, E. (2015) Disclosure of researcher allegiance in meta-analyses and randomised controlled trials of psychotherapy: a systematic appraisal. *BMJ Open,* 5:e007206.

Elliott, R. E., Fischer, C. T. and Rennie, D. L. (1999) Evolving guidelines for the publication of qualitative research studies in psychology and related fields. *British Journal of Clinical Psychology, 38,* 215–229.

Harmon, S. C., Lambert, M. J., Smart, D. M., Hawkins, E., Nielsen, S. L., Slade, K. and Lutz, W. (2007) Enhancing outcome for potential treatment failures: therapist–client feedback and clinical support tools. *Psychotherapy Research, 17,* 379–392.

Lambert, M. (ed.) (2013) *Bergin and Garfield's Handbook of Psychotherapy and Behavior Change* (6th edn). New York: Wiley.

Luborsky, L., Diguer, L., Seligman, D. A., Rosenthal, R., Krause, E. D., Johnson, S., et al. (1999) The researcher's own therapy allegiances: a 'wild card' in comparisons of treatment efficacy. *Clinical Psychology: Science and Practice, 6,* 95–106.

Mckenzie, E. A. (2015) An autoethnographic inquiry into the experience of grief after traumatic loss. *Illness, Crisis and Loss, 23,* 93–109.

McLeod, J. (2010) *Case Study Research in Counselling and Psychotherapy.* London: Sage.

McLeod, J. (2011) *Qualitative Research in Counselling and Psychotherapy* (2nd edn). London: Sage.

Miller, N. E. and Magruder, K. M. (eds) (1999) *Cost-Effectiveness of Psychotherapy: A Guide for Practitioners, Researchers and Policymakers.* New York: Oxford University Press.

Moncrieff, J. and Timimi, S. (2013) The social and cultural construction of psychiatric knowledge: an analysis of NICE guidelines on depression and ADHD. *Anthropology & Medicine, 20,* 59–71.

Morrow-Bradley, C. and Elliott, R. (1986) Utilization of psychotherapy research by practicing psychotherapists. *American Psychologist, 41,* 188–197.

Overington, L. and Ionita, G. (2012) Progress monitoring measures: a brief guide. *Canadian Psychology/Psychologie Canadienne, 53,* 82–92.

(Continued)

(Continued)

Smith, M., Glass, G. and Miller, T. (1980) *The Benefits of Psychotherapy*. Baltimore, MD: Johns Hopkins University Press.

Stewart, R. E., Stirman, S. W. and Chambless, D. L. (2012) A qualitative investigation of practicing psychologists' attitudes toward research-informed practice: implications for dissemination strategies. *Professional Psychology: Research and Practice*, *43*,100–109.

Wampold, B. and Imel, M. (2015) *The Great Psychotherapy Debate: The Evidence for What Makes Psychotherapy Work* (2nd edn). New York: Routledge.

Westergaard, J. (2013) Counselling young people: counsellors' perspectives on 'what works' – an exploratory study. *Counselling and Psychotherapy Research*, *13*, 98–105.

RECOMMENDED READING

1. McLeod, J. (2013) *An Introduction to Research in Counselling and Psychotherapy*. London: Sage.

An overview of the history of therapy research and the contribution of different research approaches.

2. McLeod, J. (2014) *Doing Research in Counselling and Psychotherapy* (3rd edn). London: Sage.

Detailed guidelines on how to carry out, and critically evaluate, all of the main types of counselling and psychotherapy research study.

3. McLeod, J. (2016) *Using Research in Counselling and Psychotherapy*. London: Sage.

Reviews the debate around the nature of the research–practice 'gap' and how it can be addressed, and explores practical ways in which therapists can use research to enhance the effectiveness of their work with clients.

PART V

THEORY AND APPROACHES

5.1

INTRODUCING THEORY AND APPROACHES: SINGULAR MODELS, COMBINED APPROACHES AND ALTERNATIVE PERSPECTIVES

TERRY HANLEY

OVERVIEW OF THIS SECTION

This section provides an overview of a key selection of the theories and approaches to counselling and psychotherapy. As has been well chronicled previously, there are hundreds of specific theories related to therapeutic work. In the 1980s Karasu (1986) suggested there were over 500 different types of therapy, and, in more recent times, there is little evidence to suggest that the trend of developing new ones is coming to an end. Therefore, here we do not attempt to provide an overview of each and every one of these different ways of working, instead we provide an informed introduction to what we believe to be those that individuals are most likely to encounter when engaging with the therapeutic work within the UK.

To provide a framework for the multitude of theories that are introduced here we have divided them into five major subsections. These are (1) Psychodynamic, (2) Cognitive-Behavioural, (3) Humanistic and Existential, (4) Constructivist and (5) Integrative and Eclectic. Within each of these subsections, several chapters are presented which provide an overview of approaches associated with it. For instance, the subsection on psychodynamic practice includes chapters on Alderian therapy, Jungian analytic psychology, attachment-based therapy, Lacanian therapy, psychoanalytic therapy, psychodynamic therapy and psychodynamic interpersonal therapy. As is hopefully already evident, such a position spans a huge territory and reflects work that spreads across the whole history of the approach.

Each chapter is introduced by an individual, or individuals, who is well versed in the theory, practice and research related to the approach in question. The chapters follow a common pathway, notably (i) providing a brief history, (ii) an overview of the basic assumptions, (iii) the perspective on the origin and maintenance of problems, (iv) the theory of change underpinning the work, (v) the skills and strategies used by practitioners (commonly including a composite example from practice) and (vi) an introduction to the research evidence for that particular way of working. When reading through the chapters, although the same headings have been followed throughout, you will see that each chapter has a unique and different flavour. Authors have been guided by their own understanding of the theoretical perspectives and concentrated to varying degrees on the historical, theoretical, practical or research developments in that arena. This variety, as well as making the text more vibrant, also provides a thought-provoking glimpse into the different worlds of each of the ways of working being introduced. Finally, for those wishing to take the next step and continue learning about a particular approach, the authors also recommend a number of texts or sources for readers to seek out.

To end the section, the final two chapters provide counterpoints to the earlier content that has been presented. The first of these is a critical reflection on therapeutic work itself. The second then considers how therapy might sit alongside commonplace psychopharmacological interventions. Much as we hope the wide variety of therapeutic theories and approaches encourages individuals to critically consider the work that counsellors and psychotherapists engage with, these chapters aim to purposefully provide provocations that reflect alternative perspectives to those that are commonly reflected in those that come before.

SINGULAR MODELS VERSUS COMBINED APPROACHES: THE ART AND SCIENCE OF THERAPY

Although psychotherapy and counselling have become established professions in many countries, as referred to in Chapter 1.1 (Feltham and Hanley – this volume), there is far from a consensus on what forms they should take. Throughout the history of therapy we can see differences of opinions at best and serious in-fighting and schisms at worst, between the key proponents within each major approach. Individuals have aimed to refine theories or create credible alternatives in response to their own personal experiences, therapeutic work and research. As an end result some theories have lived to see another day, while others are left behind and forgotten (or at least assimilated into other approaches). What is presented in the chapters that follow are some of the more established theories and approaches that have stood the test of time.

The messiness associated with the delineations between therapeutic approaches and theories can be viewed at almost every level of consideration. For instance, if we examine the four major subsections of this section of the *Handbook* (Psychodynamic, Cognitive-Behavioural, Humanistic and Existential and Constructivist), numerous dialogues and debates exist about where these begin and end. This might be relatively unsurprising given the overlaps between key individuals in the approaches. For instance, those involved in the initial development of humanistic and existential approaches were commonly trained and influenced by classical psychoanalysis (Charles Bugental, Rollo May, Carl Rogers, etc.) and even Albert Ellis, commonly associated with the development of cognitive-behavioural therapy, described his work as a humanistic psychotherapy (Ellis, 1973). In contemporary literature such amalgamated views can be seen more explicitly in approaches such as Psychodynamic Interpersonal Therapy, Acceptance Commitment Therapy and Solution-focused Brief Therapy. Here key theorists have explicitly brought together ideas from multiple sources to aid the development of a unique theory firmly based within its core approach. For some, such occurrences have contributed to creating a grand mess and exemplify the confusion and disunity in the work of the therapy industry (Maloney, 2013), while for others the vast range of alternatives reflects the complexity and multiple needs that humans present with on a day-to-day basis.

The wide range of theories that explicitly aim to integrate different ways of working might be viewed as adding to the messiness of the therapeutic landscape. In this section we introduce seven of the most common ways of conceptualising the melding together of therapeutic theories. Each provides a slightly different view and might be classified as *eclectic* or *integrative* therapy. Hollanders (1999: 484) defines these terms as:

Eclecticism – 'The systematic use of techniques within an organising framework, but without necessary reference to the theories that gave rise with them.'

Integrationism – 'The quest for theoretical synthesis on different levels.'

As with other terminology, these concepts are not hard and fast and the eclectic/integrative definitions might be viewed at each end of a sliding scale, with the pure forms of the two positions situated at each end. In looking at these theories, the amalgamation of approaches is clearly embedded in perspectives such as Cognitive Analytic Therapy. In contrast, other theories might be viewed as integrating at a different level of

conceptualisation, with approaches such as the Skilled Helper and Pluralistic Therapy providing overarching frameworks based upon observed common therapeutic processes and factors. With such thinking in mind, Norcross and Grencavage (1989: 11) go as far as to state that 'no technical eclectic can totally disregard theory and no theoretical integrationist can totally ignore technique'. In accounting for such complexities, here we therefore refer to all those under this umbrella as being within the integrative movement.

At the heart of many of the debates surrounding the evolution of psychotherapy and counselling theory is the question: is therapy an *art* or a *science*? Without delving too deeply into the philosophical quagmire that underpins this question, it is clear that such debates have been part of the discourse that has led to the creation of so many ways of working. In history, Sigmund Freud and behavioural psychologists such as B. F. Skinner clearly viewed themselves as scientists. Also, leading humanistic psychologists, such as Carl Rogers, began their careers as researchers trying to capture the most effective ways of working therapeutically with people (e.g., Rogers and Dymond, 1954). Although time commonly treats the efforts of such individuals as poor, naïve or unethical, we cannot ignore the great contributions of their work and how this has acted as a catalyst to a wide array of developments that have ultimately aided our sensitisation to the work that therapists undertake. Further, the juggling of these different roles has led to the development of what has become known as the *scientist-practitioner*, notably individuals who have a 'research-orientation in their practice, and a practice relevance in their research' (Belar and Perry, 1992: 72). The acknowledgement of the importance of the relationship between research and practice has grown to new heights in recent years. The power of hierarchies of evidence that prize meta-analysis and randomised controlled trials (e.g., the guidelines produced by the National Institute for Health and Care Excellence (NICE)) now means that, in some sectors, the absence of evidence means that some approaches are no longer viewed as commissionable services. Such a trend is welcomed by some, and viewed as safeguarding the potentially vulnerable clients with whom therapists work. In contrast, others are more critical and challenge the fit with the work of therapists (e.g., Rennie, 1995). As with any argument, there are also those who proactively try to navigate the two worlds, thus advocating a research-*informed* (rather than *driven* or *absent*) approach to therapy (Hanley et al., 2013). This proves a happy medium but the straddling of worlds itself proves open to great philosophical challenge.

Although the scientist-practitioner position has increasingly been advocated by professional bodies and training programmes, as indicated above, some individuals find it difficult to see their work fitting in this frame. As an alternative, or complementary frame, some find the concept of the *reflective-practitioner* more fitting for their work. Here, therapeutic work is described in more dynamic and fluid terms, with practitioners being required to reflect and analyse the impact of the therapeutic work upon them, the client(s) and the relationship. Schön (1983) describes such activities as taking place *in action*, with the therapist considering the work in the moment, and *on action*, with the therapist considering the work after the event in an activity such as clinical supervision. This perspective aligns more with the view that therapy might be better conceptualised as an *art* form rather than a *science* (e.g., Bugental, 1992; May, 1992). As with the scientist-practitioner perspective, the reflective-practitioner perspective can be seen as having a significant place in the history of therapeutic literature. Authors throughout the years have aligned reflective practice with ethical practice (see Hanley and Amos (2017) for further discusion) and draw parallels between some of the most empiricist research methods, which seek a one-size-fits all approach, and the relatively futile act of chasing rainbows.

Readers can see some of these debates coming to life in the chapters that follow. In particular, as noted above, authors have prized certain areas of the brief provided to them more than others. Additionally, the way in which individuals describe the engagement with research at the end of each chapter also provides much food for thought. Some wed themselves to particular methods and methodologies (e.g., advocating research around evidence-based practices or supporting the value of qualitative research), while others pragmatically navigate between different types of research or just reflect the limited importance for their way of working. Such presentations themselves say much about the worlds which the authors inhabit and we hope you find intrigue in such differences as you read.

Ultimately, this introductory chapter is intended to have sewn some seeds about the complexity inherent in dividing up the therapeutic world into neat and tidy slices. Thus, while we acknowledge that creating these divisions helps to guide readers through the broader narrative that is presented throughout this section, the reader is asked to heed some caution in viewing the boundaries as static fixed entities.

QUESTIONS

1. The authors in this section have all had to consider theory, practice and research in their writing. Reflect upon what *you* believe creates a convincing approach? If this seems difficult, maybe, once you have read some of the chapters that follow, ask yourself which of these approaches you would recommend to someone you care about.
2. How do psychotherapists and counsellors support the people they meet? With this question in mind, consider your own answers to the following questions before reading those set out by the authors in this book:

    - What is *your* perspective on the origin and maintenance of problems?
    - What do *you* see as the key components that might influence change in a person?

3. What do you see to be the strengths and weaknesses in therapeutic integration?

REFERENCES

Belar, C. D. and Perry, N. W. (1992) 'National Conference on Scientist-Practitioner Education and Training for the Professional Practice of Psychology', *American Psychologist*, 47(1), 71–75.

Bugental, J. F. T. (1992) *The Art of the Psychotherapist: How to Develop the Skills that Take Psychotherapy beyond Science*. New York: W.W. Norton & Co.

Ellis, A. (1973) *Humanistic Psychotherapy: The Rational Emotive Approach*. New York: McGraw-Hill.

Hanley, T. and Amos, I.. (2017) 'The Scientist-Practitioner and the Reflective-Practitioner', in Galbraith, V. (ed.) *Topics in Applied Psychology: Counselling Psychology*. London: Wiley.

Hanley, T., Cutts, L., Gordon, R. and Scott, A. (2013) 'A Research-Informed Approach to Counselling Psychology', in Davey, G. (ed.) *Applied Psychology*. London: Wiley.

Hollanders, H. (1999) 'Eclecticism and Integration in Counselling: Implications for Training', *British Journal of Guidance & Counselling*, 27(4), 483–500.

Karasu, T. B. (1986) 'The Specificity versus Nonspecificity Dilemma: Toward Identifying Therapeutic Change Agents', *American Journal of Psychiatry*, 143(6), 687–695. doi: 10.1176/ajp.143.6.687.

Maloney, P. (2013) *The Therapy Industry: The Irresistible Rise of the Talking Cure, and Why It Doesn't Work*. London: Pluto.

May, R. (1992) *The Art of Counselling*. London: Souvenir.

Norcross, J. C. and Grencavage, L. M. (1989) 'Eclecticism and Integration in Counselling and Psychotherapy: Major Themes and Obstacles', *British Journal of Guidance & Counselling*, 17(3), 227–247.

Rennie, D. (1995) 'On the Rhetorics of Social Science: Let's Not Conflate Natural Science and Human Science', *The Humanistic Psychologist*, 23(3), 321–332.

Rogers, C. and Dymond, R. (1954) *Psychotherapy and Personality Change*. Chicago, IL: The University of Chicago Press.

Schön, D. (1983) *The Reflective Practitioner: How Professional Think in Action*. London: Temple Smith.

THEORY AND APPROACHES: PSYCHODYNAMIC APPROACHES

5.2 ADLERIAN THERAPY

ANTHEA MILLAR

OVERVIEW AND KEY POINTS

Adlerian therapy has developed from the philosophy, psychology and practice of Alfred Adler. He understood people as socially embedded, holistic beings, and emphasised the purposeful, goal-directed nature of human behaviour, that is influenced by our uniquely created beliefs and perceptions (the 'lifestyle'). The focus is on what we do with our experiences, rather than being solely determined by our history. A therapeutic relationship based on equality and encouragement provides the foundation for exploring mistaken assumptions and a re-education towards more constructive goals. Key aims of therapy include:

- establishing an empathic and encouraging relationship
- supporting clients to understand the beliefs and feelings, motives and goals that underlie their lifestyle
- supporting clients to gain insight into their self-defeating beliefs and behaviours
- supporting clients to consider alternatives to problematic patterns of behaviour and make a commitment to change
- supporting clients to overcome feelings of discouragement and inferiority and to develop an increased sense of equality and social interest.

BRIEF HISTORY

Alfred Adler was a Viennese psychiatrist and contemporary of Freud and Jung. He was one of the co-founders of the Viennese Psychoanalytical Society, which he left in 1911 after a disagreement with Freud. He most particularly challenged the view of the sexual instinct as omnipotent, emphasising instead the importance of social interdependence in relationships. In 1912 Adler formed his school of Individual Psychology (expressing the indivisible nature of the human being) and continued to develop his approach, also influenced by concepts of holism and evolution. His experiences as a physician in the First World War gave further impetus to his development of the concept of community feeling and the importance of social equality, regardless of gender, culture or race. After the War, Adler returned to

Vienna and focused his attention on preventative approaches and psycho-education, setting up child guidance centres, working with teachers and pupils in open sessions. He also gave lectures at the People's Institute, believing strongly that laypeople could make use of psychological insights. Adler was Jewish, and following the closure of his centres by the Nazis, he was forced to leave Vienna, emigrating to New York in 1934. Adler's ideas influenced key figures such as Viktor Frankl, Rollo May, Abraham Maslow, Albert Ellis and Carl Rogers, and also pre-empted later neo-Freudian developments, as well as cognitive constructivist approaches. After his death, a younger Viennese psychiatrist, Rudolf Dreikurs, who had also moved to the United States, further developed Adlerian therapy training, and teacher and parent education. There are presently Adlerian Institutes throughout the world, with the Adlerian approach of establishing democratic relationships used in all forms of counselling and psychotherapy and in management training as well as teacher and parent education.

BASIC ASSUMPTIONS

- *Holistic* – Adler proposed a holistic view of the personality. The *individual* of Individual Psychology is a poor translation and actually means 'indivisible'. The client's consistent overriding pattern of behaviour, goals, thoughts and emotions must be viewed as a whole. Adlerians refer to this unity of the person as the lifestyle.
- *Socially oriented* – People develop and live in a social context, and need to find a place in the group; without this the human race cannot survive. Adler considered that everyone is born with the potential to belong and contribute as a social equal. Most of us, however, also feel some feelings of inferiority, and will strive to overcome these through feelings of superiority. *Gemeinschaftsgefühl*, commonly translated as 'Social Interest' or 'Community Feeling', describes an Adlerian concept central to mental wellbeing. Therapy aims to understand the nature of each person's way of belonging, and to identify both clients' strengths and their discouraging beliefs that block them from realising their full potential as equal human beings.

- *Purposive nature of behaviour* – In contrast to a historical-causal approach, Adlerian therapy is unique in its focus on purpose, that is mostly related to finding a way to belong, and to seek a subjective sense of safety. Clients' goals are identified and the purposes of their behaviour revealed. Prior to therapy, clients are not usually aware of their goals, or the ideas and beliefs that underpin their movement through life.
- *Creative and responsible* – We create our own personalities or lifestyles extremely early in life, very much influenced by the interactions with our siblings and family. Our behaviour is the result of our own subjective perceptions; what we have inherited or experienced is less important than what we do with it (Adler, 1929). Our beliefs, which underpin our unconscious goals, are called our private logic; the ideas make sense to us but are not necessarily common sense. We are responsible for our goals, behaviour, beliefs and feelings and therefore it is in our power to change if we should wish to do so.
- *Unique* – Adler was a subjective psychologist, not interested in the facts *per se*, but in each person's unique perception of the facts. In order to understand people, we must explore their unique and subjective view of themselves, other people, the world and the decisions they have made about their movement through life.

ORIGIN AND MAINTENANCE OF PROBLEMS

Adler believed people are born with the potential to feel they belong as equal human beings, although frequently this potential is not nurtured by their early experiences. We live in a mistake-centred society where mistakes are commented upon, disruptive behaviour is responded to, competition is encouraged and personal self-esteem is considered more important than contribution to the task in hand. When a child does not feel equal, he or she will experience inferiority feelings or, more problematically, develop an inferiority complex, which invites a compensatory superiority complex, deeply impacting on self-esteem and general health. Adler challenged the practice of corporal punishment, and stressed the importance of love and encouragement in early childhood, decrying neglect and abuse. He also identified the danger of both pampering, which can result in a child feeling incapable and fearful about making decisions, and spoiling, when the child develops the mistaken view that they must always have what they want. If spoiling continues over the years, parents may either give in to the demands so the child gains power over them, or may punish the child. Punished children are likely

to feel hurt and seek revenge. In order to hurt their parents, they may also hurt themselves, for example through such revenge-seeking behaviours as failure at school, anti-social or criminal behaviour and substance abuse.

In addition to the relationship with parents, Adler emphasised the importance of sibling influence on personality development. Each child will observe their other siblings acutely, or in the case of only children, their peers as well as significant adults. Then, as a means of ensuring some form of significance, the child will construct a unique position within the family system, even if it means behaving destructively. These role choices in the family are likely to be re-enacted in adult life.

Inferiority feelings are uncomfortable, and people compensate for these feelings by striving for superiority; their goals involve elevated self-esteem and feeling better than others, often involving putting others down. This attitude towards others creates social and relationship problems, with engagement in power plays and competition, and concern with personal status in the group rather than cooperating and contributing to it. This leads to distancing from other people and/or a lack of intimacy and spontaneity. Goals of superiority are often unattainable and that causes discomfort so the person safeguards their self-esteem by developing alibis to justify why the goal is not achieved. Adler recognised neurotic behaviour in people, such as developing illnesses or disabilities or making excuses for not achieving their over-ambitious goals.

THEORY OF CHANGE

Where possible, Adlerian practitioners work on *prevention* of future difficulties through family and community education. Therapy, however, remains an important and hopeful process for facilitating change. The initial phase of therapy involves establishing a meaningful therapeutic relationship, based on equality and aligned goals. The therapist will first work to identify the client's strengths as a resource for future change, and then support the client in uncovering the hidden purpose of symptoms and mistaken ideas (private logic) using the therapeutic functions of insight and meaning. Clients are helped to understand that they are responsible for their own behaviour and for their decisions to change or not to change. The therapist offers both support and challenge, inviting the client to risk new attitudes and behaviours and greater flexibility in ways of being in the world.

Some clients may express a 'yes…but' attitude to change and it is up to the therapist to help them understand that they are trusted with their own destiny. This democratic cooperative relationship may be the first such experience for some clients where they are afforded equal rights, equal respect and equal responsibility.

Clients gain insight and become aware of their beliefs and ideas and the goals (or purpose) of their behaviour and they develop understanding of how their presenting problems have occurred due to their view of life and habitual pattern of responding. Once the goals are revealed clients can no longer pursue them with such energy.

For reorientation, the therapist must ensure that clients want to change their personal goals and ideas, and, if they do, to what extent. It takes time for the client consciously to own ideas, beliefs and goals that have been below consciousness for many years. Insight will occur first after the behaviour has taken place, then during the behaviour and lastly before the behaviour. Carefully negotiated assignments may be set which challenge the old private logic, clients agreeing to do something they do not usually do or have never done. The therapist will now be looking towards the life tasks of occupation, social life and intimate relationships, and the client's presenting problems. Full participation as an equal member of the community, with an ability to contribute and cooperate usefully in the three life tasks was considered by Adler to be the measure of a mentally healthy person. Adlerians take a flexible attitude towards the life tasks of occupation and intimacy: it is not possible or necessary for everyone to have paid employment, and there is appreciation that healthy emotional and sexual intimacy may be expressed in many forms.

Throughout therapy the client is taught the art of encouragement. Most people are discouraged to some extent, feeling bad about mistakes and dwelling on their failings. Many people also have unrealistic goals which are a constant source of discouragement because they are never attained. Clients are taught to focus on strengths and regard mistakes as an essential opportunity for learning, rather than evidence of failure. Once clients become more encouraged, they are able to encourage others, thus creating a more optimistic yet realistic environment, which will further enhance the encouragement process. This can be especially powerful in group sessions. Realistic, attainable goals and a more flexible attitude towards life will enable clients to feel good about their achievements and worth. As their feelings of inferiority diminish and their social interest develops, they are likely to feel equal to their fellows, wishing to cooperate and make their contribution, in turn increasing a sense of mental wellbeing.

SKILLS AND STRATEGIES

- *Establishing a democratic relationship based on equality* – Adler was one of the first in therapy to use two facing chairs rather than an analytic couch. A good client/therapist relationship is based on cooperation, mutual trust and alignment of goals. This develops through the therapist's own self-awareness and authenticity as an ordinary human being. Therapists participate actively, demonstrating warmth and genuine interest, listening empathically to the client in order to understand his or her point of view. As the goal in therapy is to encourage the development of social interest, the therapist needs to model this social interest him or herself. While the therapist is free to express feelings and opinions, it is crucial to maintain a respectful, non-power-based relationship, where clients are trusted to make their own decisions.

- *Encouragement* – The encouragement process is fundamental to every stage of therapy. It is seen as the antidote to the basic problem of inferiority feelings and the resulting discouragement. Encouragement takes many forms and involves both identifying the strengths of the client as well as trusting them to face challenges and gain a sense of achievement in the face of what previously felt too risky.

- *Lifestyle assessment* – In order to understand the client, a lifestyle assessment can be carried out. Information is gathered about the client and his or her presenting concerns and how the client is participating in the three life tasks. Then the therapist will elicit the client's subjective perception of their situation as a child. This involves gaining family constellation data, establishing how clients interpret their childhood position, paying special attention to birth order and sibling relationships, and the creative choices made to become the sort of people they are. Interpretations of the client's early memories are then explored with the client, and consistent patterns or themes identified.

- *Analysing and transforming early memories and dreams* – Early memories and dreams provide projective data for understanding a person's lifestyle, identifying the client's image of self, of life, of others, of the 'self-ideal' and the key strategies used to move in the direction of the self-ideal or goal. Adler's focus on selective memory that functions in association with a person's lifestyle puts the emphasis on what is *remembered* rather than what is forgotten. Therapists need to put their own interpretations and attitudes on hold so that they can truly empathise with clients and see the world through their eyes. Each hypothesised guess will have to be checked out with the client and the therapist needs to be sensitive to the client's reactions to their guesses. Early recollections can function as metaphors for a life situation or present-day problem and creative work on transforming the early memory can enable new perspectives on a here-and-now situation.

- *Mutually agreed assignments* are set that challenge the client's private logic and support new constructive behaviours and ways of being.

A wide range of processes and techniques that support the above processes may be implemented, some also used by therapists from other orientations. Examples include psychodrama, art, music and play therapy, behavioural assignments, Socratic questioning, paradoxical intention and body work. Therapy is applied in many contexts, including child guidance centres, schools, the work place, prisons, hospitals and other institutions, and with individuals, couples, families and groups, the latter a natural fit in relation to the socially oriented view. Therapy may be short-, mid- or long term, all aiming to provide a positive psycho-educational and future-oriented approach, underpinned by an enabling client/therapist relationship.

CASE EXAMPLE: MARJORIE

Marjorie, 32, presented in considerable distress, following a seemingly irreparable row with her parents, berating herself severely for expressing her anger so overtly, which she believed was the first time this had happened.

Establishing and maintaining an empathic relationship: In the first session I listened carefully to her story, responding with sincerely expressed empathic reflections while also bringing her attention to the courage she had displayed in finding a voice to express justified emotions that had been suppressed for so long. As an ongoing process, the empathic relationship was maintained and we had regular reviews to ensure our goals were aligned in terms of her needs and wants.

Exploration of beliefs, feelings, motives and goals: Marjorie's childhood history revealed serious emotional neglect, and many years of obsessive compulsive behaviours that presently impacted detrimentally on her relationships with her two young children and partner. While her history and anxiety symptoms were important to acknowledge and understand, it was crucial to identify the mistaken convictions that were maintaining this distress. Through exploration of her family constellation, and the use of early memories analysed as a metaphor, Marjorie's perception of herself, others and the world, and the strategies she had created to find her place of belonging, were revealed. The key lifestyle themes emerging were: 'I am not good enough', 'People reject me, blame me, and ignore my needs', 'The world is bewildering and uncertain', 'Therefore I must be good and perfect, cut off from my feelings, and not expect support from others'. I also explored with her how she viewed her satisfaction with the life tasks of occupation, social relationships and intimacy, this serving as a basis for identifying her progress throughout therapy.

Gaining insight: Marjorie found new understanding regarding her mistaken convictions, also discovering how the obsessions served a compensatory purpose by her being extra vigilant, perfect and in control – a means of overcoming her mistaken belief of being no good. Throughout the exploration of her lifestyle patterns, it was important to offer my hunches and interpretations tentatively, in an open-ended way that Marjorie could refute if necessary. A further essential part of these new insights involved building her awareness and acceptance of her many strengths. Offering sincere descriptive encouragement (rather than labelling praise), in doses that were manageable for her to digest, was an important aspect of the work.

Reorientation: making new choices: Developing alternative choices and building her self-esteem was an ongoing process, supported by mutually agreed and collaboratively created assignments that were realistic and manageable. Marjorie began by noticing her old patterns, 'catching herself' without judgement, then taking increasing risks in handling fears around hygiene, developing social interactions with others with decreasing fear around rejection, expressing her feelings and views in her family, with friends and at work, and a major step, reconnecting with her parents on an equal and assertive basis. In our final sessions we reviewed her work in therapy over the last 18 months, and explored how she was meeting the life tasks. In summary, she stated 'I feel connected to the world, and can belong and contribute by simply being me'.

RESEARCH EVIDENCE

Assessing the efficacy of the broad focus of Adlerian therapy through a medical model view of therapy raises many problems when attempting to measure such complex intra-psychic issues as the therapeutic relationship, the change in clients' subjective private logic and the development of social interest (Neukrug, 2011). Similarly Shelley (2008) discusses the challenges of both quantitative and qualitative research methodologies when attempting 'to capture the depth and paradoxes that a depth psychology such as Individual Psychology proposes' (p. 420). There are, however, a good number of research studies that have identified the importance of developing a positive relationship with the client (Carlson et al., 2006), which is a central aspect of Adlerian therapy. Other studies have confirmed the effects of birth order (Watkins, 2008), and identified the value of analysing early memories as a projective technique (Carlson et al., 2006). The central importance of social connection and a sense of belonging for a person's feeling of wellbeing has been clearly acknowledged (Curlette and Kern, 2010), this being confirmed by neuroscience research (Gallese et al., 2002; Porges, 2011). Also numerous studies have been conducted on the effectiveness of encouragement (Carns and Carns, 2008; Burnett, 1988), with Wong (2015) concluding that the process of encouragement is as deserving of much greater attention by psychologists.

REFERENCES

Adler, A. (1929) *The Science of Living*. New York: Greenberg.

Burnett, P.C. (1988) Evaluation of Alderian parenting programs. *Individual Psychology,* 44(1): 63–76.

Carlson J., Watts, R.E. and Maniacci, M. (2006) *Adlerian Therapy: Theory and Practice.* Washington, DC: American Psychological Association.

Carns, M.R. and Carns, A.W. (2008) A Review of the Professional Literature Concerning the Consistency of the Definition and Application of Adlerian Encouragement. In J. Carlson and S. Slavik (Eds), *Readings in the Theory of Individual Psychology*. New York: Routledge.

Curlette, W.L. and Kern, R.M. (2010) The Importance of Meeting the Need to Belong in Lifestyle. *The Journal of Individual Psychology*, 66(1), 30.

Gallese, V., Ferrari P.F. and Umilta M.A. (2002) The Mirror Matching System: A Shared Manifold for Intersubjectivity. *Behavioural and Brain Sciences*, 25(1), 35–36.

Neukrug, E.S. (2011) *Counseling Theory and Practice*. Belmont, CA: Brooks/Cole-Cengage Learning.

Porges, S.W. (2011) *The Polyvagal Theory: Neurophysiological Foundations of Emotions, Attachment, Communication, Self-regulation*. New York: W.W. Norton.

Shelley, C. (2008) Phenomenology and the Qualitative in Individual Psychology. In J. Carlson and S. Slavik (Eds), *Readings in the Theory of Individual Psychology*. New York: Routledge.

Watkins, C.E. Jr (2008) Birth Order Research and Adler's Theory. In J. Carlson and S. Slavik (Eds), *Readings in the Theory of Individual Psychology*. New York: Routledge.

Wong (2015) The Psychology of Encoragement. *The Counseling Psychologist*, 43(2), 178–216.

RECOMMENDED READING

1.   Adler, A. (1927/2009) *Understanding Human Nature*. Trans. Colin Brett. Oxford: Oneworld Publications.

Written for the general reader in 1927, it offers an accessible overview of Adler's theory and approach.

2.   Ansbacher, H. and Ansbacher, R. (Eds) (1964) *The Individual Psychology of Alfred Adler: A Systematic Presentation in Selections from his Writings*. New York: Harper.

An essential text for any researcher, with Adler's writings organised into a coherent whole, the editors' helpful commentaries alongside.

3. Oberst, U.E. and Stewart, A.E. (2003) *Adlerian Psychotherapy: An Advanced Approach to Individual Psychology*. Hove: Brunner-Routledge.

Offers an integrationist approach, highlighting the relevance of Adlerian psychotherapy in today's world.

5.3 JUNGIAN ANALYTICAL PSYCHOLOGY

RUTH WILLIAMS

OVERVIEW AND KEY POINTS

Analytical psychology is the term coined by Carl Gustav Jung to distinguish his approach from that of Sigmund Freud, with whom he had a close working association. Their first meeting famously lasted thirteen hours. There was clearly a great excitement on the part of both men on establishing a truly deep connection with each other. Freud initially saw Jung as his natural heir in the field of psychoanalysis and encouraged him to take on leading roles in the profession.

- Clinically, the cornerstone of the work is the process of individuation.
- One of the unique features of Jung's approach was to talk about archetypes, which he saw as belonging to what he called the collective unconscious, a layer of the mind which connects us to ancient mythical images and symbols which can be analysed in the work. Of course modern man often sees or experiences these images in modern dress so that the images become relevant to their place in time. A brilliant example of this is that of the rap poet Kate Tempest in her *Brand New Ancients* (2013) (available in both written and audio form, and well worth listening to since she has a unique rhythm). She writes of myth in a totally modern idiom.
- Dreams too are central to Jungian analysis. They can be seen as individual vignettes or often come in series so that a narrative might develop over time, making it important to notice the changes.

- Terms such as synchronicity, introversion, extroversion – all in common parlance now – were introduced by Jung.

BRIEF HISTORY

Analytical psychology is also referred to as Jungian analysis or psychotherapy or sometimes Jungian psychoanalysis.

Jung was born on 26 July 1875, the son of a Swiss Pastor. His disappointment in his father, whose faith he saw as rooted in dogma rather than personal experience, was critical in forming Jung's view of what we might now think of as the need for personal authenticity. His mother came from one of the oldest patrician families in Basel and he went on to marry wealthy heiress Emma Rauschenbach on Valentine's Day in 1903.

Jung worked as a psychiatrist at the Burgholzli clinic in Zurich (1900–1909) under the well-known psychiatrist Eugene Blueler (who invented the term schizophrenia, previously known as *Dementia Praecox*). During this period Jung developed the Word Association Test, which involved a list of one hundred words being given to a subject to elicit the spontaneous association to each word. Meaning was ascribed to the association itself as well as the response time to the so-called stimulus-words. When clusters of similar responses arose, these were seen as being significant and led Jung to formulate his theory of complexes. The Word Association Test is not used in contemporary practice.

On its publication in 1900, Jung read Freud's *The Interpretation of Dreams*, which he recognised as having been produced by a kindred spirit. On meeting Freud in

1906, a deep affinity was established between the two men. Freud saw Jung as his natural heir and in Freud, Jung saw a paternal figure. The relationship broke down on Jung's publication of his *Psychology of the Unconscious* (1916) when it became clear that Jung's ideas had significantly diverged from those of his mentor. The irreconcilable differences concerned whether there could be libido that was not exclusively sexual. Jung saw libido as being more broadly defined, a notion that sometimes erroneously gives rise to the notion that Jungian analysis is not concerned with sex. The trauma of this rift with Freud presaged a period of crisis for Jung, during which he developed many of his most original and creative ideas, using nature, creative media and dreams to explore his own psyche. These explorations are now available following the long-awaited publication of *The Red Book* (2009), which gives an intimate insight into Jung's personal development in both written and artistic form. *The Red Book* presents Jung's own Active Imaginations (see definition below) giving direct access to the innermost workings of his mind in the most experimental form. Of this period Jung states:

> The years when I was pursuing my inner images were the most important of my life – in them everything essential was decided. It all began then; the later details are only supplements and clarifications of the material that burst forth from the unconscious, and at first swamped me. It was the *prima materia* for a lifetime's work. (Jung, 1995 [1963]: 199)

Some of these events are covered in abridged form in *Memories, Dreams, Reflections* (written by Jung in collaboration with Aniela Jaffe) (1995 [1963]).

In 2011 David Cronenberg released his take on the relationship between Jung and Freud in a film entitled *A Dangerous Method*, named after John Kerr's 1993 book about the relationship between Freud, Jung and Sabina Spielrein, who was a patient of both men but who is more famous for her supposed relationship with Jung than for her intellectual contribution to the field. (She became an analyst in her own right and published a number of papers, most notably one entitled 'Destruction as the Cause of Coming into Being', originally published in German in *Jahrbuch* in 1912 and finally published in English in the *Journal of Analytical Psychology* in 1994 (Vol. 39: 155–186)). The film is not entirely factual but gives an entertaining account of events.

Jung's erudition expanded the field of his psychology to include religion (Eastern and Western), and the ancient art of alchemy, which he used as a metaphorical device to illustrate his ideas by drawing on some ancient woodcut images from a medieval treatise entitled the *Rosarium Philosophorum* (or rose garden of the philosophers), which he uses to illustrate and interpret modern behaviour in a quite unique and apposite way.

His interest in the esoteric has attracted a wide gamut of seekers and has been incorporated into New Age thinking (see Tacey, 2001).

Jung's ideas have been widely applied to great effect in cultural studies, in the arts and popular culture, perhaps especially in film.

The International Association for Analytical Psychology, with member organisations throughout the world, regulates the training and professional aspects of Jungian analysis. In Britain there are five affiliated societies, with distinct features ranging from the Developmental (Society of Analytical Psychology and British Jungian Analytic Association), which incorporates Kleinian ideas in regard to early human development, to the Classical (Independent Group of Analytical Psychologists and Guild of Analytical Psychologists), which pays particular heed to myth and fairy tale and thus tends to look at the personal through the lens of the collective unconscious, to the Association of Jungian Analysts, which holds the middle position between these approaches, having respect for both ends of this spectrum. The history of the divisions between these societies and an in-depth account of the differences may be found in Kirsch (2000). See Samuels (1985: Chapter 1) for an account of the 'Schools of Analytical Psychology', where Samuels systematically delineates the features of each school which, in part, includes consideration of frequency of sessions.

There is a third strand called 'archetypal psychology', which is an important off-shoot developed by James Hillman (1978) but which has not taken root as a clinical discipline.

BASIC ASSUMPTIONS

Individuation is the term used to describe the process of becoming oneself, which is the goal of analysis. It is quite distinct from individualism, which is about being overly self-reliant or self-centred in a somewhat narrow way, as opposed to individuation, which implies a striving towards greater wholeness. Individuation is the process by which a person becomes a separate psychological individual, distinct from all others.

Jung's schema consists of a *personal* and *collective unconscious*, the former being made up of the personal complexes, the latter of *archetypes*.

Archetypes may be seen as potentials. They are often referred to in the form of characters (Trickster, Hero, Mother/Father, Puer or Puella (eternal child), or Witch, for instance). These are all facets of personality to which we each have access and which vary in accordance with individual and cultural context. Archetypes are seen as deriving from radically differing origins by Jungian writers, ranging from the biological/evolutionary (Stevens, 1982, 2003), poetic (Hillman, 1983, 1994), developmental/neuroscientific (Knox, 2001, 2003) and most recently via emergence (Hogenson, 2004) (see below), to name but a few.

Psychological types – The terms *introvert* and *extrovert* both originated with Jung and are now in common usage to describe people whose principal mode of being tends to be more internally or externally focused. Jung formulated a system whereby he saw people as falling predominantly into one of four types: feeling, thinking, intuition, sensation. Although it sounds quite restrictive and over-determined, in fact this system can be used in quite a subtle fashion to enhance understanding. A person may need to give precedence to another facet of their personality to compensate (a Jungian term) for one-sidedness and this model might help gain insight into where a person needs to develop. It is also helpful in understanding interpersonal conflicts and where people(s) clash along the axis of different psychological types. This system gave rise to personality tests that are still used in commercial settings and more rarely in a clinical context.

Jung saw life as a 'continual balancing of Opposites' (1949: par. 1417). If a person is too 'nice', it is probable something less nice is being held at bay and needs to be balanced out in order for that person to become more rounded or authentic. The *Shadow* is often referred to in this context in that it contains all the elements one does not wish to identify with or admit as part of oneself. This usually means those qualities or thoughts will burst through, like the return of the repressed.

Anima (meaning soul) and *Animus* (the feminine form) are the Latin names Jung used to describe the part of ourselves which represents the internalised aspects of the opposite sex to the gender of the individual (cf. below regarding gender). These images are sometimes seen or imagined as idealised images of the beloved or desired object in dreams or waking life and can be experienced as the external person being one's 'soul mate'.

Persona is sometimes seen as a mask. It is the face one presents to the world and is not necessarily 'false'.

Self is sometimes spelt with a capital 's' in Jung's writings to emphasise the distinction from the ordinary usage of the word self. It is seen as the centre of being, sometimes with spiritual connotations. Coming more into the 'Self' is seen as an achievement in terms of *individuation*, Self being seen as the sum of all the parts

ORIGIN AND MAINTENANCE OF PROBLEMS

One factor which might account for analytical psychology being sometimes seen as less mainstream than psychoanalysis is that Jung has been accused of being anti-semitic. It is true that he wrote some things (regarding race, for instance) which were unwise and ill-considered, especially in the context of his time. These matters have been taken seriously by later generations of Jungians, who have re-evaluated Jung's work from this perspective both as historical corrective but also as necessary reparation (see Samuels, 1993: 287–316).

There have likewise had to be revisions to Jung's writing in regard to gender. Jung's wife, Emma (who was also a practising analyst), wrote *Two Essays* on *Animus and Anima* (1931) which show a more nuanced perspective than Jung's own writing in this area. See also Wehr (1987), Samuels (1989: Chapter 6) and Young-Eisendrath (2004), for instance.

There are also two new areas of study that have arisen in recent years and which contribute to the field of analytical psychology enormously. One is emergence theory and the other is the cultural complex.

The cultural complex has been developed by Singer and Kimbles as an idea only since 2000. They are building on Jung's own theory of complexes (which relates to the personal level) and extrapolating those ideas on to the individual, societal and the archetypal realm. They identify cultural complexes to be at the heart of conflicts between many groups in terms of politics, economics, sociology, etc. (Singer, 2004: 20) as well as being deeply embedded in 'tribal memories, patterned behaviours in the form of rituals and strong beliefs' (Singer, 2010: 234).

Emergence theory is based on the idea that phenomena can arise without any precursor. As such, it is at the cutting edge of attempts to explore the origin of archetypes (Hogenson, 2004).

THEORY OF CHANGE

The process of change and transformation in any psychotherapy is usually a slow one. Grappling with entrenched psychological trauma or patterns of being requires investment of time (and money if formally undertaken with an analyst or therapist), as well as deep personal application. Some see the process of *individuation* as a working through of karmic tasks. The psyche (as defined in Jungian terms as encompassing the whole person) may transform through dreams or by using creative media such as art, sand tray or dance/bodywork, etc. (see Schaverien, 1991, 1995). Talking is usually the main tool in analysis. A relationship is formed with the therapist/analyst which becomes the vessel in which the issues arise and can be worked through. It was in this context that Jung used the alchemical metaphor mentioned above to elucidate the process of analysis. The alchemists were striving to turn one substance into another, which entailed various stages of transformation. This can be seen to mirror the psychic stages of transformation undergone during the course of an analysis or psychotherapeutic journey. In psychoanalytic terms this refers to the transference, which is the framework within which matters arise and which provides the arena for working through and thus change. This is an arduous process in which one is gripped by 'real' feelings, being in a 'real' relationship. This involves coping with the vicissitudes of need and dependency. By 'working through' is meant coping with the emergence of unconscious material with a view to integrating it and gaining ways of going forward, incorporating hitherto unwanted parts of oneself. This expansion is usually felt as an enhancement of the personality and an ability to cope with and enjoy life.

SKILLS AND STRATEGIES

Dreams are central to Jungian analysis and psychotherapy. Their symbolic contents encapsulate a situation in a way words alone cannot.

The numinous is a concept unique to Jungian analysis. It refers to the mysterious, gripping, some would say spiritual, elements we all touch on in life at times and which may be encountered in dreams and synchronicities, for instance. Jung wrote 'the approach to the numinous is the real therapy and inasmuch as you attain to the numinous experiences you are released from the curse of pathology' (1945: 377).

Active Imagination was a method Jung developed during his personal crisis. In this he used creativity to identify and work problems through. This is sometimes used in contemporary practice where a flexible and open mind can facilitate exploration.

Synchronicity is the term Jung introduced to describe the co-incidence of two events which he saw as having an a-causal link. In other words, that it is not just coincidence that something happens, but that something else happens which connects the two in an inexplicable but meaningful way. The term has of course entered common parlance. Genuine synchronicities – somewhat rare as they are – can

contribute to our understanding in a clinical setting as well as outside. A dramatic example taken from Main (2007: 1–2) is as follows:

> An analyst on vacation suddenly had a strong visual impression of one of her patients she knew to be suicidal. Unable to account for the impression as having arisen by any normal chain of mental associations, she immediately sent a telegram telling the patient not to do anything foolish. Two days later she learned that, just before the telegram arrived, the patient had gone into the kitchen and turned on the gas valve with the intention of killing herself. Startled by the postman ringing the doorbell, she turned the valve off; and even more struck by the content of the telegram he delivered, she did not resume her attempt.

RESEARCH EVIDENCE

The very issue of providing research in the field of psychotherapy is somewhat contentious inasmuch as the work is not easily quantifiable. It is a highly subjective experience. Under pressure to conform to standards set by executive bodies, much effort is being put into finding ways of conducting research that does justice to the work. This has become increasingly important at a time when there has been governmental pressure to statutorily regulate the profession, and in a climate where economics has been the guiding principle in the Improving Access to Psychological Therapies (IAPT) initiative. With the IAPT programme there has been a risk of losing the essential meaning of 'therapy', shifting the focus from the 'care of souls' to a manualised practice that can be evaluated in numerical form.

Jung himself regarded his life's work to be indivisible from his life and research (Stevens, 1990).

The first Chair in Analytical Psychology was endowed in Dallas, United States of America, at the Texas A&M University in 1985. In Britain, the first Chair in Analytical Psychology was created in 1995 at the University of Essex. This is now a thriving department with pioneering research programmes in analytical psychology at BA, Masters and Doctoral level, attracting students from around the world.

REFERENCES

Freud, S. (1900) 'The Interpretation of Dreams', in *The Standard Edition of the Complete Psychological Works of Sigmund Freud*. London: Hogarth Press.
Hillman, J. (1978) *The Myth of Analysis: Three Essays in Archetypal Psychology*. New York: Harper Torch.
Hillman, J. (1983) *Archetypal Psychology: A Brief Account*. Woodstock, CT: Spring Publications.
Hillman, J. (1994) *Healing Fictions*. Woodstock, CT: Spring Publications.

Hogenson, G.B. (2004) 'Archetypes: Emergence and the Psyche's Deep Structure', in J. Cambray and L. Carter (eds), *Analytical Psychology: Contemporary Perspectives in Jungian Analysis*. Hove and New York: Brunner-Routledge.

Jung, C.G. (1916) *Psychology of the Unconscious*. London: Kegal, Paul, Trench, Trubner & Co.

Jung, C.G. (1945) 'Letter to P.W. Martin', dated 20 August 1945, in *C.G. Jung Letters* (Vol. 1). London: Routledge & Kegan Paul.

Jung, C.G. (1949) 'Foreword to Neumann: Depth Psychology and a New Ethic', in *The Symbolic Life* (Collected Works, Vol. 18). London: Routledge.

Jung, C.G. (with Jaffe, A.) (1995 [1963]) *Memories, Dreams, Reflections*. London: Fontana Press.

Jung, C.G. (2009) *The Red Book*. London and New York: W.W. Norton.

Jung, E. (1931) *Animus and Anima: Two Essays*. Woodstock, CT: Spring Publications.

Kerr, J. (1993) *A Most Dangerous Method: The Story of Jung, Freud and Sabina Spielrein*. New York: Alfred A. Knopf.

Kirsch, T. (2000) *The Jungians: A Comparative and Historical Perspective*. London and Philadelphia, PA: Routledge.

Knox, J. (2001) 'Memories, Fantasies, Archetypes: An Exploration of Some Connections between Cognitive Science and Analytical Psychology', *The Journal of Analytical Psychology*, 46(4), 613–635.

Knox, J. (2003) *Archetype, Attachment, Analysis: Jungian Psychology and the Emergent Mind*. Hove: Brunner-Routledge.

Main, R. (2007) *Revelations of Chance: Synchronicity as Spiritual Experience*. New York: SUNY Press.

Samuels, A. (1985) *Jung and the Post-Jungians*. London and New York: Routledge.

Samuels, A. (1989) *The Plural Psyche: Personality, Morality and the Father*. London and New York: Tavistock/Routledge.

Samuels, A. (1993) *The Political Psyche*. London and New York: Routledge.

Schaverien, J. (1991) *The Revealing Image: Analytical Art Psychotherapy in Theory and Practice*. London and New York: Tavistock/Routledge.

Schaverien, J. (1995) *Desire and the Female Therapist: Engendered Gaze in Psychotherapy and Art Therapy*. London and New York: Routledge.

Singer, T. (2004) 'Archetypal defences of the group spirit', in T. Singer and S.L. Kimbles (eds), *The Cultural Complex: Contemporary Jungian Perspectives on Psyche and Society*. Hove: Routledge.

Singer, T. (2010) 'The Transcendent Function and Cultural Complexes: A Working Hypothesis', *Journal of Analytical Psychology*, 55(2), 234–241.

Spielrein, S. (1994 [1912]) 'Destruction as the Cause of Coming into Being', *Journal of Analytical Psychology*, 39: 155–186.

Stevens, A. (1982) *Archetypes: A Natural History of the Self*. New York: William Morrow & Co.

Stevens, A. (1990) *On Jung*. London and New York: Routledge.

Stevens, A. (2003) *Archetype Revisited: An Updated Natural History of the Self*. Toronto: Inner City Books.

Tacey, D. (2001) *Jung and the New Age*. Hove: Brunner-Routledge.

Tempest, K. (2013) *Brand New Ancients*. London: Picador.

Wehr, D. (1987) *Jung and Feminism: Liberating Archetypes*. Boston, MA: Beacon Press.

Young-Eisendrath, P. (2004) *Subject to Change: Jung, Gender and Subjectivity in Psychoanalysis*. Hove: Routledge.

RECOMMENDED READING

1. Bair, D. (2003) *Jung: A Biography*. London: Little Brown & Co.

An exhaustive and lengthy biography of Jung, the man.

2. Samuels, A. (1985) *Jung and the Post-Jungians*. London and New York: Routledge.

A brilliant overview of the field, including contemporary developments, from a leading clinician.

3. Goss, P. (2015) *Jung: A Complete Introduction*. London: John Murray Learning.

A simple introduction to Jungian analysis.

ATTACHMENT-BASED PSYCHOANALYTIC PSYCHOTHERAPY

MARK LININGTON AND VICTORIA SETTLE

OVERVIEW AND KEY POINTS

Attachment-based psychoanalytic psychotherapy is a form of psychotherapy provided to individuals, couples, families and groups which uses both attachment theory and psychoanalytic theory as a way of understanding people, their relationships and their difficulties. It makes use of those aspects of psychoanalytic theory which elucidate the nature of the internal world but it locates attachment, rather than sexual or aggressive drives, at the heart of development.

The psychiatrist and psychoanalyst Dr John Bowlby began the development of attachment theory in the 1940s, although there have been many others significantly involved in collaboratively developing it since that time. It is an empirically based scientific theory of human relationships built on Bowlby's recognition that attachment to a primary caregiver is a biological imperative in order for the infant to survive both physically and emotionally.

The central premise of attachment-based psychoanalytic psychotherapy is that in order to explore safely, we all need to feel securely attached. This means that our clients, as *care seekers*, cannot begin to explore their internal and external worlds until they feel safe in their relationship with us as their psychotherapist or *caregiver*. This is arguably the most important contribution that attachment has made to the practice of psychoanalytic psychotherapy. This premise can be understood by applying the Circle of Security™ (Powell et al., 2014) model to attachment-based psychoanalytic psychotherapy with adults (see Figure 5.4.1).

Attachment-based psychoanalytic psychotherapy is attentive to the type of caregiving needed (McCluskey, 2005). If the client is approaching the psychotherapist in a state of fear and/or distress, the client needs type 1 caregiving. Type 1 caregiving (the provision of a 'safe haven') is characterised by soothing, comforting and the attuned regulation of feelings. When the client has become soothed they will return to their natural human state of exploratory behaviour. In this state, the client needs the support of type 2 caregiving, which recognises, validates and encourages the competency of the client in their exploration of their internal and external worlds.

Key points include:

- Difficulties in our current relationships stem from our patterns of attachment which have been shaped by our earliest relationships to our primary caregivers. Our preverbal experience makes up the core of our developing self.
- These patterns of attachment are not necessarily fixed and later relationships can offer us the opportunity to transform our sense of self.

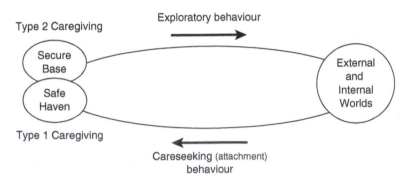

Figure 5.4.1   The Circle of Security™

Adapted from Powell, B., Cooper, G., Hoffman, K. and Marvin, B. (2014). The Circle of Security Intervention: Enhancing Attachment in Early Parent-Child Relationships. New York: The Guilford Press

- Our sense of attachment security is influenced by how we think about and reflect upon our relational experiences as well as the experiences themselves.
- The client's relationship to their psychotherapist is primary and it supplies both a secure base from which to explore and a safe haven in which to find solace.
- A sense of felt security, generated through sensitive attunement on the part of the psychotherapist, enables us to access disavowed or dissociated experiences.
- Accessing and reflecting upon these previously un-verbalised feelings and thoughts gives us a stronger and more integrated self-narrative.

BRIEF HISTORY

The early thinking of the object relations school of psychoanalysis influenced John Bowlby but he profoundly disagreed with the dominant psychoanalytic belief that infants' responses relate to their internal fantasy rather than to real-life events. He set out to develop a theory of motivation and behaviour control built on science rather than Freud's Psychic Energy model, and for this he was effectively ostracised from the psychoanalytic community.

When the Second World War broke out and children were evacuated in large numbers, Bowlby, in his outrage at the suffering of homeless and separated children, set out to produce a theory to explain why the mother was so important to the child. All the studies that he carried out had shown that children experienced intense distress when separated from their parents, even if they were fed and cared for by others. It became clear that, for the infant to thrive, the mother's constant proximity and attention were vital. Attachment theory grew out of his subsequent work on the issues raised.

In 1951 Bowlby put forward the hypothesis that 'the infant and young child should experience a warm, intimate, and continuous relationship with his mother (or permanent mother substitute) in which both find satisfaction and enjoyment' (Bowlby, 1951: xi) – the lack of which may have significant and irreversible mental health consequences.

Bowlby collaborated with social worker and psychoanalyst James Robertson in making the 1952 documentary film *A Two-Year-Old Goes to the Hospital*, which filmed the effects of separation on children in hospital and was instrumental in a campaign to alter hospital restrictions on visits by parents. Bowlby's work, coupled with Robertson's films, caused a virtual revolution in hospital visiting by parents, hospital provision for children's play, educational and social needs and the use of residential nurseries.

Bowlby's attachment theory was finally written in three volumes (Bowlby, 1969, 1972, 1980).

In the 1970s, in collaboration with Bowlby, Mary Ainsworth developed a research tool called the *Strange Situation*, which enabled observers to classify young toddlers as either *securely* or *insecurely* attached to their primary attachment figure (Ainsworth and Bell, 1970). She observed that there were differences in the attachment behaviour of the toddlers which depended upon the patterns of communication between the caregiver and the toddler. The insecurely attached toddlers were then divided into two groups, whose main patterns of attachment were either avoidant (I don't expect you to meet my needs so I won't seek you out) or ambivalent (if I push I may get my needs met so I will seek you out persistently, but I don't trust that you are there so I will push you away too).

In the 1980s the theory of attachment was developed further by Mary Main, who made two major contributions to the thinking on attachment. First, she discovered a third category of insecure attachment, which she described as *disorganised* and which she linked to high levels of stress and disturbance in both the children and their caregivers (Main and Solomon, 1990). Second, she devised the *Adult Attachment Interview* (AAI), which enabled observers to classify the adults' verbal descriptions of their childhood experiences of attachment (Main et al., 1985). The key aspect of this development was that the attachment behaviour observed directly and described by Bowlby and Ainsworth could now be studied at a representational level.

In the 1990s studies were conducted by Peter Fonagy and Miriam and Howard Steele in London. Their key contribution was their 'Reflective-Functioning' subscale, which essentially was used to measure parents' capacity to think about their own thinking – with correlations between this capacity and attachment outcomes in the Strange Situation (Fonagy et al., 1991). They observed that the more parents were able to reflect on their own and their infants' mental states, the more likely the infants were to be securely attached to them.

More recently, Fonagy and others (2005) came to understand that the capacity to mentalise was absolutely central to attachment. Fonagy put forward the idea that the *mentalising system* offers enormous survival advantages because it enables us to interpret and predict the behaviours of others. As such it is a 'cornerstone of social intelligence' and critical to work, play and all sorts of collaborations (Allen and Fonagy, 2006).

In the last decade or so, exciting new connections have been made between psychoanalysis, attachment theory and neuroscience, and there is a burgeoning of literature exploring how we might apply all of this to clinical practice. This is now the cutting-edge of attachment-based psychoanalytic psychotherapy.

Professionals in the field are revisiting how we might understand and work with dissociation in all its forms and how an attachment-based approach could work effectively with clients who have suffered severe trauma, including complex post-traumatic stress and dissociative identity disorder. The focus on the links between our real external experiences and the formation of our attachment patterns has lead clinicians to consider, in much more careful detail, the impact of racism, sexism, homophobia and other discriminatory behaviours on our sense of being securely or insecurely attached.

BASIC ASSUMPTIONS

- There is an inner world, conscious and unconscious, developed in relationship to the other.
- We essentially seek relationship from infancy through childhood and adulthood and into old age.
- Our sense of self is continuously shaped by intersubjective experience.
- What happens in reality, in the external world, profoundly impacts upon our sense of attachment security.
- The self develops in relationship to differing cultural, social and political contexts and is impacted on by the inequality of power relations.
- Trauma disrupts attachment relationships and emotional development.
- We continuously re-enact our working models of relationship and re-engage these internal working models throughout life.
- Understanding is co-created within the therapy relationship, making what was previously unconscious available to consciousness.
- Change comes from mourning, the rediscovery of meaning and the liberation of desire and creativity within the self.
- Attachment-based psychoanalytic psychotherapy should be available to everyone.

ORIGIN AND MAINTENANCE OF PROBLEMS

Attachment-based psychoanalytic psychotherapy understands the majority of our emotional and relational problems as originating in experiences of chronically insecure relationships with caregivers. These experiences can occur with detrimental consequences at different periods across the life cycle from pre-birth through to early adulthood (although chronically insecure experiences at a younger age are likely to be more negatively significant for later life). These insecure aspects of caregiving, which

are sometimes present across the generations in families, are transmitted physically, non-verbally and verbally to the infant, child and adolescent. The characteristics of these three main insecure forms of caregiving – preoccupied, dismissive, frightened/frightening (Cassidy and Shaver, 1999; Karen, 1994) – are expressed in forms of intrusiveness, high emotionality, neglect, emotional unresponsiveness and abuse. These different forms of insecure caregiving lead to the adaption of three broad complementary categories of attachment patterns: ambivalent, avoidant or disorganised (Cassidy and Shaver, 1999; Karen, 1994). The purpose of these attachment patterns (which are forms of careseeking) is to maximise the responsiveness and availability of the caregiver, given the way they relate.

These repeated experiences in caregiving relationships become working models of relationships internalised in our body and mind. These (insecure) working models of relationships, which are usually mostly outside our conscious awareness, operate as templates for expectations and ways of relating in our later relationships with peers and adult caregivers. We repeat these patterns of relating unless we have an opportunity to experience other more secure ways of relating.

Features of these patterns of relating include:

- How effectively we seek help from caregivers, including as adults with peers. When we have had insecure caregiving-careseeking experiences we are likely to have difficulties in obtaining and receiving help from caregivers in a way that effectively meets our needs.
- The way we experience our feelings in ourselves, how we communicate our feelings to others and our ability to regulate these feelings in ourselves and with others. The regulation of feelings means the ability to bring feelings into a tolerable range (see the Window of Tolerance model in Seigel, 1999).
- Our internal sense of our self as a person, including how we judge ourselves, our knowledge of our competencies and our relationship with our body.
- How we interact in peer relationships, including our ability to play easily and creatively with others, and develop and share common interests (Heard and Lake, 1997) and be romantically, physically and sexually intimate.

Such patterns of relating, originating in a person's past childhood relational experiences, are understood to emerge in the psychotherapeutic relationship (transference). The psychotherapist will utilise her or his internal responses (countertransference) to such, often unconscious, material to understand more about the nature of the person's attachment patterns.

THEORY OF CHANGE

Put briefly, the theory of change is that if our clients can feel secure in their attachment to us as psychotherapists and we can, in turn, offer attuned responses, we can enable our clients to develop a greater capacity to think about themselves, both in and out of a relationship.

It is important that, within the therapeutic relationship, the psychotherapist is able to be contingent – he or she needs to respond well to the client's spontaneous gestures or initiatives. If the psychotherapist can attune to the emotional world of the client, then feelings that would in the past have threatened to overwhelm the state of the client can be contained safely and digested by the client with the aim of being integrated into the self. Once the psychotherapist has regulated the anxiety, fear or anger expressed by the client, then exploration can safely be started, attachment wounds can be grieved and enlivenment and companionable interest sharing can follow.

Through free association, dreams, transference reenactments, sharing of countertransference and patterns in our client's developmental history, together we can begin to make sense of our client's experiences and the primary task of meaning making can begin. This process of formulating how our client thinks and feels enables him or her to understand how their inner world impacts on their everyday life. This leads to a greater clarity around their own and others' mental states which enables our clients to project less and to relate more realistically and authentically. This in turn leads to more satisfying relationships and a better quality of attachment to significant others.

Validation alone is not sufficient to bring about change. Specific moments of change are often brought about by a gentle but solid holding of one's own position, which puts the client into a kind of 'benign bind' (Holmes, 2010) that helps him or her to reintegrate repressed, disowned, projected or dissociated affects or parts of the self. This usually results in a greater sense of vitality and 'wholeness', which enhances emotional expression and allows our clients to be more flexible, more creative and less transference-driven.

SKILLS AND STRATEGIES

Attachment-based psychoanalytic psychotherapy views the psychotherapeutic session as a unique intersubjective encounter occurring moment by moment in a form that is asymmetrically co-created by the two (or more) participants ('Asymmetry' is used here to indicate the difference in the balance of power and influence operating in the interactions

in psychotherapy; see Aron, 1996). In this regard, attachment-based psychoanalytic psychotherapy has something in common with other relational forms of psychotherapy.

The key strategy of this form of psychotherapy is to provide the appropriate form of secure caregiving that will, first, enable the regulation of fear and distress and, second, facilitate reflective and narrational exploration. Secure caregiving is understood to have two broad forms (Heard et al., 2009). In order to fulfil this strategy, the attachment-based psychoanalytic psychotherapist employs a number of integrated skills:

1. **The skill of empathic attunement** (McCluskey, 2005; Stern, 1985, 1995). This skill is used predominantly non-verbally and to a large extent is outside verbal conscious awareness, but occurs in the domain of implicit relational knowledge (Stern, 2004). The understanding and development of this skill in psychotherapy has emerged from research studies into infant development in their relationships with caregivers.

2. **Attentiveness and responsiveness to fear**, with its range of responses of fight, flight, freeze and collapse. Fear (which includes its range of associated feelings, such as nervousness, anxiety, panic and distress) is understood as arising from an accurate appraisal of the *current* environment. For example, meeting a psychotherapist for the first time is realistically likely to arouse anxiety. It is also understood as arising from *past trauma* (most especially attachment trauma) from which the person has not yet recovered. Attachment-based psychoanalytic psychotherapists make use of non-verbal and verbal ways of regulating fear, including centring/grounding techniques and naming the emotion that is being experienced.

3. **The provision of secure caregiving** to increase the experience of safety and security in the relationship, with the intention of achieving the outcome of relief from distress and the increase of the natural instinct to exploration both internally and externally. Throughout this work the psychotherapist must be attentive to both the real here-and-now relationship and the links with past experiences of relating (both their own and the client's).

4. **The use of countertransference and understanding of trauma-based enactments**. Attachment-based psychoanalytic psychotherapists learn to attune to their own physiological and emotional responses when working with a client. These responses often have a connection to the unconscious emotional and relational experiences of clients. Sometimes such material is enacted in some form by the therapist and client (for example, starting a psychotherapy

session late), which then requires careful exploration between the psychotherapist and the client.

5. **The facilitation of mourning**. Mourning, while culturally influenced and structured, is also an evolved process that supports the recovery from loss and trauma. It includes the experience and expression of feelings (for example, numbness, sadness, anger, despair) and the enactment of relational behaviours (clinging, searching, withdrawing). The individual's attachment experience will significantly influence the form and path of their mourning. An attachment-based psychoanalytic psychotherapist helps the client mourn by recognising and validating the client's experiences of loss and/or trauma. The therapist pays particular attention to the emotional and relational aspects of these real-life events and helps the client over time to construct a reflective, more conscious, narrative of these distressing experiences.

RESEARCH EVIDENCE

Attachment theory is one of the most researched psychological and relational theories. Its origins are firmly rooted in several empirical longitudinal studies of attachment relationships (Grossman et al., 2005; Main et al., 2005; Sroufe et al., 2005; Steele and Steele, 2005) as well as many other smaller-scale study projects. There are important overlaps with research in three interrelated disciplines: neuroscience (Schore, 1999), infant and child development (Beebe and Lachmann, 2002; Stern, 1985, 1995) and trauma (Herman, 1992; van der Hart, 2006; van der Kolk, 2014). All of these different aspects of scientific human social research significantly influence the practice of attachment-based psychoanalytic psychotherapy. Furthermore, there is a growing development of research on psychotherapy generally, predominantly utilising outcome measures, but also looking to include explorations of the significance of the quality of the relationship on the psychotherapy (for example, at the United Kingdom Council for Psychotherapy (UKCP) Research Council; Rowland and Goss, 2000). Finally, there is a growing edge of research regarding the clinical application of attachment theory in psychotherapy (McCluskey, personal communication; The Bowlby Centre, 2012).

REFERENCES

Ainsworth, M. D. S. and Bell, S. M. (1970). Attachment, exploration, and separation: Illustrated by the behavior of one-year-olds in a strange situation. *Child Development*, *41*, 49–67.

Allen, J. G. and Fonagy, P. (2006). *Handbook of Mentalization-based Treatment*. Chichester: John Wiley.

Aron, L. (1996). *Meeting of Minds: Mutuality in Psychoanalysis*. New York: The Analytic Press.

Beebe, B. and Lachmann, F. (2002). *Infant Research and Adult Treatment: Co-constructing Interactions*. New York: The Analytic Press.

Bowlby, J. (1951). *Child Care and the Growth of Love; based by permission of the World Health Organization on the report 'Maternal Care and Mental Health'*. Harmondsworth: Penguin.

Bowlby, J. (1969). *Attachment and Loss*. Vol. 1: *Attachment*. Harmondsworth: Penguin.

Bowlby, J. (1972). *Attachment and Loss*. Vol. 2: *Separation: Anxiety and Anger*. Harmondsworth: Penguin.

Bowlby, J. (1980) *Attachment and Loss*. Vol. 3: *Loss: Sadness and Depression*. Harmondsworth: Penguin.

Cassidy, J. and Shaver P. R. (Eds.) (1999). *Handbook of Attachment: Theory, Research, and Clinical Applications*. New York: Guilford Press.

Fonagy, P., Gergely, G., Jurist, E., and Target, M. (2005). *Affect Regulation, Mentalization, and the Development of the Self*. New York: Other Press.

Fonagy, P., Steele, H. and Steele, M. (1991). Maternal representation of attachment during pregnancy predicts the organisation of infant-mother attachment at one year of age. *Child Development*, *62*, 891–905.

Grossmann, K., Grossmann, K. E. and Kindler, H. (2005). Early care and the roots of attachment and partnership representation: The Bielfield and Regensburg Longitudinal Studies. In K. E. Grossman, K. Grossman and E. Waters (Eds.), *Attachment from Infancy to Adulthood: The Major Longitudinal Studies*. New York: Guilford Press, pp. 98–136.

Heard, D. and Lake, B. (1997). *The Challenge of Attachment for Caregiving*. London: Karnac.

Heard, D., Lake, B. and McCluskey, U. (2009). *Attachment Therapy with Adolescents and Adults: Theory and Practice Post Bowlby*. London: Karnac.

Herman, J. L. (1992). *Trauma and Recovery: From Domestic Abuse to Political Terror*. New York: Basic Books.

Holmes, J. (2010). *Exploring in Security: Towards an Attachment-informed Psychoanalytic Psychotherapy*. London and New York: Routledge.

Karen, R. (1994). *Becoming Attached: First Relationships and How They Shape Our Capacity to Love*. Oxford: Oxford University Press.

Main, M., Hesse, E. and Kaplan, N. (2005). Predictability of attachment behavior and representational processes at 1, 6, and 19 years of age: The Berkeley Longitudinal Study. In K. E. Grossmann, K. Grossmann and E. Waters (Eds.), *Attachment from Infancy to Adulthood: The Major Longitudinal Studies*. New York: Guilford Press, pp. 245–304.

Main, M., Kaplan, N. and Cassidy, J. (1985). Security in infancy, childhood, and adulthood: a move to the level of representation. In I. Bretherton & E. Waters (Eds.), Growing points of attachment theory and research. *Monographs of the Society for Research in Child Development, 50 (1-2 Serial No 209)*, 66–104.

Main, M. and Solomon, J. (1990). Procedures for identifying infants as disorganized/disoriented during the Ainsworth Strange Situation. In M. T. Greenberg, D. Cicchetti and E. M. Cummings (Eds.), *Attachment in the Preschool Years: Theory, Research, and Intervention* (pp. 121–160). Chicago, IL: University of Chicago Press.

McCluskey, U. (2005). *To Be Met as a Person: The Dynamics of Attachment in Professional Encounters*. London: Karnac.

Powell, B., Cooper, G., Hoffman, K. and Marvin, B. (2014). *The Circle of Security Intervention: Enhancing Attachment in Early Parent–Child Relationships*. New York: Guilford Press.

Rowland, N. and Goss, S. (2000). *Evidence-based Counselling and Psychological Therapies: Research and Applications*. London: Routledge.

Schore, A. N. (1999). *Affect Regulations and the Origin of the Self: The Neurobiology of Emotional Development*. Hillsdale, NJ: Lawrence Erlbaum Associates.

Siegel, D. (1999). *The Developing Mind: How Relationships and the Brain Interact to Shape Who We Are*. New York: Guilford Press.

Sroufe, A. L., Egeland, B., Carlson, E. A. and Collins, W. A. (2005). *The Development of the Person: The Minnesota Study of Risk and Adaptation from Birth to Adulthood*. New York: Guilford Press.

Steele, M. and Steele, H. (2005). Understanding and resolving emotional conflict: The London Parent–Child Project. In K. E. Grossmann, K. Grossmann and E. Waters (Eds.), *Attachment from Infancy to Adulthood: The Major Longitudinal Studies*. New York: Guilford Press, pp. 137–164.

Stern, D. N. (1985). *The Interpersonal World of the Infant: A View from Psychoanalysis and Developmental Psychology*. New York: Basic Books.

Stern, D. N. (1995). *The Motherhood Constellation: A Unified View of Parent–Infant Psychotherapy*. New York: Basic Books.

Stern, D. N. (2004). *The Present Moment in Psychotherapy and Everyday Life*. New York: W. W. Norton.

The Bowlby Centre (2012). *The Spine of the Relational World*. London: The Bowlby Centre.

Van der Hart, O. (2006). *The Haunted Self: Structural Dissociation and the Treatment of Chronic Traumatization*. New York: W. W. Norton.

Van der Kolk, B. (2014). *The Body Keeps the Score: Mind, Brain and Body in the Transformation of Trauma*. Harmondsworth: Penguin.

RECOMMENDED READING

1. Bowlby, J. (1988). *A Secure Base: Clinical Applications of Attachment Theory*. London: Routledge.

Presents the most fundamental aspects of attachment theory and helps to bridge the gap between theory and practice.

2. Cozolino, L. (2016). *Why Therapy Works: Using Our Minds to Change Our Brains*. New York: W.W. Norton & Company.

Offers an accessible bridge between the neurobiology of attachment and psychotherapy.

(Continued)

(Continued)

3. Heard, D., Lake, B. and McCluskey, U. (2009). *Attachment Therapy with Adolescents and Adults.* London: Karnac.

Explores how extended attachment theory is relevant to and can be applied in the attachment-based psychotherapeutic relationship.

4. Holmes, J. (2010). *Exploring in Security: Towards an Attachment-informed Psychoanalytic Psychotherapy.* London and New York: Routledge.

Very accessible and current, this book develops thinking on the ideas about attachment that Bowlby founded.

5. Wallin, D. (2009). *Attachment in Psychotherapy.* New York: Guilford Press.

Explores the ways in which we can use attachment-based research for clinical application.

5.5 LACANIAN THERAPY

LIONEL BAILLY

OVERVIEW AND KEY POINTS

Lacanian Therapy is a psychoanalytically informed treatment aimed at individuals with disabling anxiety, failing coping strategies and problematic personality traits.

-   Lacanian Therapy is a psychological therapy nested in a theoretical model in which humans are 'speaking beings', the unconscious is structured as a language and symptoms can be seen as having a metaphoric value.
-   The overarching goal in Lacanian Therapy is to move away from the ego, understood as a fiction, to discover more of the subject and the truth of one's desire.
-   Desire results from the impossibility of a subject to properly articulate what it needs. The therapy helps a patient identify what their objects, around which desire is organised, are. These imaginary objects, called 'the object cause of desire', are closely linked with anxiety.
-   Therapists don't provide advice or guidance as they are sure to be mistaken, but are empty mirrors in which the patients can start to see themselves for what they are.

BRIEF HISTORY

In the middle decades of the twentieth century, Jacques Lacan created a model of psychoanalysis by revisiting the works of Freud in the light of developments in fields of study such as linguistics, philosophy, anthropology and mathematics.

Jacques Lacan was born in Paris on 13 April 1901. He studied medicine and psychiatry and was trained in psychiatric asylums where he acquired a wide clinical experience, including of severe psychosis. After having worked with some of the most brilliant proponents of organic psychiatry, he found in psychoanalysis the most helpful theoretical model for understanding and treating the complex patients he was dealing with. In 1938, he became a psychoanalyst of the Société Psychanalytique de Paris. Lacan believed that Freudian theory was not a perfect edifice but a work in progress, and wanted to contribute towards what he saw as a developing model. His attitude towards the development of theory was modern in that he was willing to examine any body of science that could clarify or shed new light on the phenomena he was trying to explain, and consequently he drew inspiration from biological psychiatry, genetic psychology, philosophy, structural linguistics, anthropology and even mathematics. The richness of the result has attracted students in fields far from psychoanalysis or psychiatry. His use of variations on the standard psychoanalytic treatment was sufficiently controversial for Lacan to be banned from the International Psychoanalytic Association in 1962. In 1963, he created his own school of psychoanalysis. The new organisation proved a success, and the influence and membership of Lacanian analytic institutions has continued to grow to the present day. Jacques Lacan died in Paris on 9 September 1981.

BASIC ASSUMPTIONS

Lacan's view is that the characteristic that sets human beings apart from other animals is language: we are speaking beings. If speech is what makes us human, then the fundamentals of the human psyche should be found in the particularities and structure of spoken language. Lacan made the hypothesis of a structural mirroring between what we say, the way we think and what we are – and this also applies to the unconscious, which is structured like a language. Slips of the tongue, bungled actions and also symptoms encountered in psychopathology follow this linguistic structure and can be seen as having a metaphoric value.

The ego is a fiction, 'an imaginary narrative' that the infant starts to construct as soon as he/she is able to recognise itself in the mirror, and the building blocks of the edifice are signifiers (the spoken word). The ego is not based on a perception–consciousness system or organised by the reality principle, but exists instead by dint of *méconnaissance* (obliviousness) – the obliviousness or blindness of the subject to itself.

Drawing upon Freud's idea that thought and meaning are coded in ideational representatives, Lacan pinpointed these by means of Saussurian linguistics as being signifiers – the acoustic image of words. Lacan emphasised the detachable quality of signifiers from what they signify, and that it is the signifier attached to an anxiogenic thought that becomes repressed into the unconscious, so that the anxious affect becomes displaced onto other, less terrifying signifiers (which might thereby acquire an irrationally worrying nature). The unconscious for Lacan is therefore a world of repressed signifiers, and the task of analysis is to retrieve these and restore them to consciousness in the authentic signifying chain. The patient is the only person in possession of the unconscious knowledge, and it is by paying careful attention to the patient's discourse – especially to slips of the tongue, dreams, repetitive speech, irrational narrative or neurotic preoccupations – that the analyst is able to hear the manifestations of the unconscious. The patient has no feeling of responsibility for these manifestations, which seem to him to come from somewhere else, which Lacan calls the Other (*le grand autre*). The place occupied by this Other is that from which language and laws derive.

The unconscious discourse of the patient is directed by 'master signifiers' – the foundation stones of the individual's psychological structure. These signifiers 'orient' or give direction to the patient's preoccupations and unconscious narratives. One of the main tasks of analysis is to bring into consciousness these master signifiers, so that the patient becomes aware of how they influence his/her emotions and thoughts.

Lacan builds upon Freud's Oedipus complex to arrive at the subtler formulation known as the paternal metaphor to explain how a child separates psychically from its mother and accepts its status as a less-than-perfect being. In order to explain its mother's absences and preoccupations, the child must postulate an object s/he desires more than him/herself. This imaginary object is called the phallus. Castration is not a real physical threat, but the child's reluctant acceptance that s/he does not have what it takes to keep mother's perfect attention, and the consequent hypothesis that this most desirable object must exist 'somewhere out there' in the real world. The name-of-the-father is the first signifier that the child can accept as a representative of what mother finds more interesting than him/herself; it is a metaphor and the child's acceptance of it involves an important intellectual act. For Lacan, the child's submission to this formulation initiates him/her into the ability to think metaphorically, with the flexibility of signifier substitutions that this allows, and is a keystone in the construction of the psyche.

Lacan saw desire as a condition that plays a structuring role in the subject. Desire results from the impossibility that a subject can properly articulate what it needs – the 'gap between demand and need'. The articulation of need must pass through the gates of language, and what cannot squeeze through and is left behind constitutes desire. The objects, around which desire is organised, are imaginary objects called 'the object cause of desire', and this has a genetic link with the original imagined perfect object, the phallus. The object cause of desire, or object 'a', is closely linked with anxiety, in that it appears in the place of a primordial experience of loss.

For Lacan, it is not the biological reality of sex that determines our gender identity; he saw gender as the result of a process of identification, and of a process he calls 'sexuation'. This has to do with how a subject situates itself in relation to the phallus and symbolic castration, and also to his/her identification with the mother.

ORIGINS AND MAINTENANCE OF PROBLEMS

Like Sigmund and Anna Freud, Lacanians think that 'human behaviour and its aberrations [are] being determined not by overt factors but by the pressure of instinctual forces emanating from the unconscious mind' (Freud, n.d.). Besides the classical analytical views on the origin of psychopathology, the Lacanian model suggests some specific types of difficulties.

The mirror stage represents a moment at which the baby perceives itself as a unit, and also the first time the child thinks of itself as 'I' in relation to an image that he understands as representing himself. The failure to perceive oneself in this way is seen in autistic pathologies in children. In addition, the intellectual perception of oneself is an alienating experience as the image is never as perfect as the imagined self, and splits the psyche into the part that identifies with the image and the part that becomes the active agent in building a narrative about the imaginary (from image) self. The discourse that is built upon the image is the ego, which Lacan sees as a fiction maintained and nurtured throughout one's life with the help of denegation and obliviousness (*méconnaissance*). This fictional ego can be the source of the patient's discontent and request for therapeutic help.

The ego and the subject both develop in the discourse of the Other – a way of saying that the discourse, attitudes and beliefs of the main figures in a child's development have a profound structuring effect upon the subject. The individual's master signifiers, which also derive from the Other, have a crucial role in the construction of the psychological structure of an individual and can be at the root of a subject's failure and sufferings.

The submission to the paternal metaphor allows the child to situate itself within the law, to move away from an enmeshed relationship with his/her mother and to drop his/her infantile omnipotence. For Lacan, the foreclosure of the paternal metaphor leads to the development of a psychotic structure, while other pathological modalities of dealing with it can lead to neurosis or perversion.

The subject's relationship with his object cause of desire defines the individual's unique way in which s/he seeks enjoyment, and both the nature of these objects and the specificity of the relationship can be the source of psychopathology.

THEORY OF CHANGE

Lacan was preoccupied with what exactly 'curing' means. Is it simply the disappearance of a symptom, or does one aim to change the underlying personality structure that produced it and in which it is inscribed? Is this at all achievable, and if it is, is it desirable? If it is neither achievable nor desirable, then where should curing stop – at what boundary line? Lacan clarified his position about patients and symptoms by saying that while it is reasonable that individuals expect their symptoms to disappear following an analytical treatment, the symptom has a defensive quality and it might not always be prudent to try to suppress the use of certain aspects of it. In this way, enjoyment and desire remain possible for the subject.

The Lacanian analyst knows that at some point during the course of the treatment, the patient will be faced with the decision to be cured of his/her symptom or not to be. This decision, if the treatment has been successful, could be an enlightened choice, made in the light of self-knowledge.

A patient looking to boost his/her self-esteem, or to be reassured that they are really all right and just need to rethink some of their 'coping strategies', should not go to a Lacanian analyst. Lacanians do not 'strengthen' or 'support' the ego but will try to help the patient dismantle it in order to come face-to-face with his/her own subject, to recognise the truth of his/her desire and the modalities of his/her enjoyment and to emerge from treatment with an altered ego that is closer to the fullness of the subject.

SKILLS AND STRATEGIES

As in most other forms of psychotherapy, free association is the first rule. The patient is asked to say anything that comes to mind, even if it appears superficial or unrelated to what has been discussed, and is encouraged to remember and talk about their dreams. The therapist pays particular attention to the discourse of the patient, the words used, the structure of the sentences, any unusual use of a word, patterns and repetitions, etc.

The place of counter-transference in Lacanian analysis is different from that in most other schools. Lacan recognised that the therapist experiences feelings towards his patient, but suggested that he must know not only not to give into them, but also how to make adequate use of them in his technique. If the analyst does not act on the basis of these feelings, it is not because his training analysis has drained away his passions, but because it has given him a desire which is even stronger than those passions: the desire to remain focused upon the treatment of the patient.

Lacanians use sessions of variable duration, including short sessions. The ending of the session is a meaningful act, too important to leave to mere form. One should not end a session just because the allotted time is up, especially if the analysand is in the middle of some interesting discourse. Conversely, it may be useful to be able to end the session just at the point that the analysand says something important – so that it can 'hang in the air' for further reflection until the next time; more words will often obfuscate the realisation that was emerging. In many ways, the end of the session emphasises some particularly important aspect and works almost as an interpretation.

BRIEF CASE EXAMPLE

A 30-year-old woman comes to see a therapist, explaining that she is gay and wants to have a baby. She has been in homosexual relationships since she was a teenager and is satisfied with her sexuality. Her family and colleagues at work know of her sexual orientation and it has never been a problem. Now that she wants a baby, people have suggested she should find a sperm donor but she does not want to become pregnant that way. She says: 'I want my children to be conceived like I have been conceived. I want them to grow up like I grew up, with a father and a mother. I want to be a real mother'. She is perfectly aware that this wish clashes with what her life has been, her sexual orientation and choice of love objects. The therapy focused on the object of her desire, the place the signifiers 'real mother' meant in her psyche and the exploration of the construction of her gender and sexual identity.

RESEARCH EVIDENCE

There has been no quantitative research on the outcome of psychotherapy in a Lacanian theoretical framework. In addition, a Lacanian approach would lead to questioning the ability of quantitative research to assess and measure the 'improvement' of a patient, as this can't be equated with a mere reduction in symptomatology. It is not that research is impossible, but that the impact of therapy on the individual's psyche is of a complexity far beyond the reach of symptom rating scales.

REFERENCE

Freud, A. (n.d.) (www.freud.org.uk/education/topic/40053/annafreud).

RECOMMENDED READING

1. Bailly, L. (2009) *Lacan: A Beginner's Guide*. Oxford: One World.

This book is an introduction to Lacanian theory that allows beginners to understand some of the key concepts without being overwhelmed by the complexity of Lacan's thinking and his rather difficult style.

2. Lacan, J. (1982) Guiding remarks for a congress on feminine sexuality. From *Écrits* (trans. J. Rose). In J. Mitchell and J. Rose (eds), *Feminine Sexuality*. New York: W.W. Norton.

This article introduces readers to Lacan's original and modern take on gender and sexuality.

3. Lacan, J. (2006) *Écrits* (trans. Bruce Fink). New York: W.W. Norton.

Écrits is Lacan's first published book, written to provide the founding texts of his new psychoanalytic thinking. For anybody who wants to start a serious reading of Lacan.

5.6 PSYCHOANALYTIC THERAPY

JESSICA YAKELEY

OVERVIEW AND KEY POINTS

Psychoanalytic therapy is an exploratory psychological treatment based on psychoanalytic principles and ideas that were established by Sigmund Freud at the beginning of the twentieth century and subsequently expanded and elaborated by numerous psychoanalytic thinkers and practitioners since then. Influential psychoanalysts who have shaped psychoanalytic practice and discourse include Anna Freud, Melanie Klein, Donald Winnicott and Wilfred Bion in Britain, and Heinz Hartmann, Heinz Kohut and Otto Kernberg in the United States. There are now many different 'schools' of psychoanalysis, each advocating variations in psychoanalytic theory and technique. However, many of Freud's basic psychoanalytic concepts continue to unite these different approaches, including the existence of a dynamic unconscious, resistance, transference, countertransference, defence mechanisms, free association and the repetition compulsion. This chapter focuses on Freud's original ideas and their influence on contemporary psychoanalytic thinking and practice.

The key points of psychoanalytic therapy are:

- It focuses on the patient's 'internal world' of unconscious fantasies, wishes, motivations, conflicts and defences
- It embraces a developmental perspective in which the adult personality is shaped by significant relationships and events in childhood
- It aims to effect longstanding personality change by addressing the psychological mechanisms underlying the patient's more overt symptoms and behaviours
- It is usually less structured, more intensive and longer term than other psychotherapy modalities, such as cognitive-behavioural treatment
- It was originally developed by Freud for the treatment of neuroses, but has widened its scope to treat people with a range of psychological conditions, personality difficulties and relationship problems.

BRIEF HISTORY

Sigmund Freud is one of a handful of remarkable thinkers whose ideas helped shape the twentieth century and which continue to be influential today. Originally a neurologist in Vienna working with patients suffering from hysteria, Freud experimented with hypnosis, abreaction and catharsis before discovering the 'talking cure'. Freud initially believed that neurotic symptoms were the result of the 'damming up' of affect resulting from painful childhood experiences, and if patients could be encouraged to talk about them, they would be cured. Freud particularly focused on his patients' dreams, proposing that the dream represented an attempt by the dreamer to fulfil a wish, which was usually an erotic wish. Like dreams, Freud saw neurotic symptoms as meaningful, representing compromise formations between repressed sexual impulses and the censoring agents of the mind. As he developed his thinking further, he began to see neurosis not just as the result of real trauma or childhood seduction, but due to conflict over unconscious fantasies of infantile sexual gratification stemming from early childhood.

Freud's ideas were ahead of his time, and his theory of infantile sexuality shocked his colleagues and the wider society of early twentieth-century Europe in which he lived. However, through extensive treatment of patients, as well as his own self-analysis, he continued to develop a methodology of treatment in which to test his theories of the mind, attracting a growing body of followers. Despite influential critics and controversies, Freud's ideas have endured for over a century, permeating diverse fields of thought, including education, the social sciences, literary theory, philosophy and the media. Psychoanalysis, as invented by Freud, continues today as a therapeutic treatment, a body of theoretical knowledge and as a method of investigation of the human mind.

BASIC ASSUMPTIONS

Although psychoanalysis has evolved considerably since Freud, many of his basic tenets remain central to contemporary theory and practice. Key notions include unconscious mental activity, psychic determinism and the idea that childhood experiences are critical in shaping the adult personality.

THE UNCONSCIOUS AND MODELS OF THE MIND

Part of our mind is unconscious and can never be fully known to us, but is revealed through the analysis of dreams, slips of the tongue (which Freud called *parapraxes*) and patterns of speech, which provide a window into the underlying unconscious feelings, fantasies and desires that motivate our conscious thoughts and manifest behaviour. In Freud's first *topographical model*, the mind was divided into three systems: the conscious, the preconscious and the unconscious. In the *preconscious*, mental contents can easily be brought to conscious awareness by shifting awareness, whereas the mental contents of the *unconscious* are unacceptable to the conscious mind and are therefore kept from conscious awareness by the forces of *repression* but emerge in the guise of symptoms.

In Freud's second model of the mind, the *structural model*, the psychical apparatus is divided into three parts: id, ego and superego. The *id* is a reservoir of unconscious, unorganised, instinctual sexual and aggressive drives, which are unacceptable to the social, moral and ethical values of conscious civilised thought, and must therefore be kept at bay. The id is governed by primary process thinking under the domination of the pleasure principle – the inborn tendency of the organism to avoid pain and seek pleasure via the release of tension. In the lawless world of the id, opposites co-exist, wishes are fulfilled, negatives do not exist and there is no concept of time. The *ego* mediates between the conflicting demands of id, superego and reality. It is the executive organ of the psyche, controlling motility, perception, contact with reality and, via the defence mechanisms, which are located in the unconscious part, the ego modulates the drives coming from the id. The *superego* evolves from part of the ego as the heir to the Oedipus complex, with the internalisation by the child of parental standards and goals to establish the individual's moral conscience.

PSYCHIC DETERMINISM

Freud believed that although we may think we have control over our lives and operate through free choice, our conscious thoughts and actions are actually shaped and controlled by unconscious forces. For example, our chosen vocation, choice of partner or even hobbies are not randomly selected, but are unconsciously determined by our childhood experiences. Moreover, Freud proposed that a single symptom or behaviour was multi-determined, in that it could contain multiple complex meanings and serve several functions in responding to the demands of both reality and the unconscious needs of the internal world.

DRIVE THEORY AND LIBIDO

An instinct is a hereditary pattern of behaviour, specific to a species, that unfolds in a predetermined fashion during development and is resistant to change. Freud took this biological concept to embed his psychological theory of the mind in biology with his theory of the drives. For Freud, all instincts had a *source* in a part of the body or bodily stimulus; an *aim*, to eliminate the state of tension deriving from the source; and an *object* (often another person), which was the target of the aim. Freud described libido as 'the force by which the sexual instinct is represented in the mind' (Freud, 1917a: 136). The association with sexuality is misleading, as Freud considered libido to include the notion of pleasure as a whole. In Freud's final theory of the instincts, he proposed two opposing instincts – the life instinct (Eros) and the death instinct (Thanatos). Initially aimed at self-destruction, the death instinct is later turned against the outside world and underlies aggression.

DEVELOPMENTAL STAGES

Freud believed that children were influenced by sexual drives and proposed a developmental trajectory in which the early manifestations of infantile sexuality were associated with bodily functions such as feeding and bowel control. Psychosexual development consists of libidinal energy shifting from oral to anal to phallic to genital erotogenic zones respectively, where each corresponding stage of development is characterised by particular functions and objectives, but builds upon and subsumes the accomplishments of the preceding stage. Failure to negotiate the emotional demands of each stage is linked to complex character traits in adult life. For example, excessive oral gratifications or deprivations can result in pathological narcissism and dependence on others, whereas developmental arrest at the anal stage can lead to miserliness or sadism.

THE OEDIPUS COMPLEX

Freud named the Oedipus complex after the Greek tragedy in which Oedipus unknowingly killed his father and married his mother. Freud proposed that the Oedipus complex was a normal stage of development occurring between the ages of 3 and 5 years, where the boy is attracted to his mother and develops feelings of rivalry and jealousy for his father. The equivalent constellation in the little girl is called the *Electra complex*. Castration anxiety refers to the boy's fear that his father will castrate him for his desire for the mother. Resolution of the Oedipus complex results in the formation of the superego. Freud proposed that failure to negotiate the Oedipus complex lies at the heart of neurotic illness and results in deficits in the capacity to enjoy healthy loving and sexual relations.

ORIGINS AND MAINTENANCE OF PROBLEMS

CONFLICT

Freud believed that neurotic illness was the result of *conflict* between the instinctual drives and the external world, or between different parts of the mind. This conflict between the ego and id can result in neurotic symptoms as unacceptable sexual and aggressive thoughts and feelings break through the ego's censorship barrier and are converted into substitute compromise formations to prevent them from fully entering consciousness. Conflict between the ego and superego can give rise to feelings of low self-esteem, shame and guilt due to the ego's failure to live up to the high moral standards imposed by the superego.

ANXIETY AND DEFENCE MECHANISMS

The notion of anxiety is also central to Freud's formulations regarding the origin of neurosis. In Freud's earlier model, anxiety is a direct expression of undischarged sexual energy or libido. He later revised his theory of anxiety to see anxiety as an affect experienced by the ego as a signal when faced with danger. This led Freud to the concept of defence mechanisms, manoeuvres of the ego that protect it from both internal sources of danger, anxiety and unpleasure (such as the sexual and aggressive drives) and external threats, especially those related to experiences of loss.

Freud proposed that different mental states result from different constellations of anxiety and defence mechanisms. In *neurosis*, the primary defence mechanism is repression, the pushing out of consciousness of thoughts and wishes that do not fit in with one's view of one's self. In *perversion*, the ego is split via the defence mechanism of disavowal, which allows contradictory beliefs to be held simultaneously so that the perverse person may hold a circumscribed delusional belief (such as the paedophile who believes children enjoy sexual intercourse) but the rest of the personality appears intact and functioning normally. In *psychosis*, repression fails completely and the person is overwhelmed by unconscious or id contents, and creates a delusional world via primitive defence mechanisms such as projection and omnipotence to make sense of such chaos.

TRAUMA

Massive trauma can also overwhelm the ego, breaking through its defences and rendering it helpless and unable to function. Freud coined the term *repetition compulsion* to describe a person's unconscious tendency in adult life to repeat past traumatic behaviour, in an attempt to resolve feelings of helplessness and conflict. Freud later explained this as a manifestation of the death instinct.

RESISTANCE

Freud described the antagonism of the patient to the therapist's attempt, which is frequently encountered, despite their distress and disability, to achieve insight and change as *resistance*, which represented a compromise between the forces that were striving towards recovery and the opposing ones. Resistances to treatment can take overt and covert forms, such as missing appointments, being late to sessions, being silent or not hearing interpretations. Resistance can be seen as a defence mechanism that arises during treatment to avoid experiencing the psychic pain associated with previously repressed unpleasant impulses and affects that the therapy is attempting to uncover and explore.

THEORY OF CHANGE

CONSCIOUSNESS

Freud's changing views of therapeutic action reflected his evolving conceptualisation of his models of the mind. His initial simple model of catharsis, in which therapy worked by releasing damned-up affects, reflected a model of the mind in which traumas had aroused unacceptable feelings and thoughts that had to be pushed from consciousness to maintain psychic stability. Freud's mechanism of change at this time was to 'transform what is unconscious into what is conscious' (Freud, 1917b: 293).

STRENGTHENING OF THE EGO

Freud's development of his topographical model of the mind led to his emphasis on the interpretation of defence and resistance as techniques to allow the unconscious mental contents into consciousness. When his structural model took priority over the topographical, his positioning of the Oedipal complex as the developmental crisis at the centre of all neuroses, and the increasing attention to ego defences, therapeutic effect now depended on the alteration and redistribution of energy between the three mental agencies of ego, id and superego, and in particular the strengthening of the ego.

TRANSFERENCE

Freud himself recognised the central role of the transference in effecting therapeutic change, in providing a window into the patient's unconscious fantasy life. Transference is the displacement by the patient of early wishes and feelings towards people from the past, particularly the patient's parents, onto the figure of the therapist. The safety of the analytic situation allows the patient to experience those unconscious wishes and fears as they arise in relation to the analyst, to appreciate their irrationality and origins from the past and to provide the opportunity of working through. Since Freud, increasing emphasis has been placed on the role of the transference and its interpretation in effecting therapeutic change, which includes superego modification with the introduction of a more benign superego.

RELATIONAL EXPERIENCE

While verbal interpretations of the meaning of the transferential experience are important, there has also been a shift to believing that the relational affective experience in itself is a mutative factor. This involves the internalisation of a new relationship with the therapist, who is reliable and not retaliatory, which may be very different from the relationships the patient has previously experienced.

SKILLS AND STRATEGIES

THE ANALYTIC SETTING

In psychoanalytic treatment, patients are encouraged to lie on the couch, with the analyst sitting behind them. The relative sensory deprivation and inability to see the analyst's facial expressions facilitates the patient in being able to focus on his inner thoughts and feelings, which he is encouraged to express in free association. The reclining position is also helpful in inducing a certain degree of regression and dependency that is necessary in order to establish and work through the patient's neurotic difficulties. The boundaries of the setting or parameters of treatment are important in creating a safe environment in which therapy can occur. These boundaries include consistency of the physical environment in which the therapy takes place, the reliability of regular 50-minute sessions that begin and end on time, and clearly defined interpersonal boundaries between patient and therapist, in which the therapist minimises self-disclosure and maintains confidentiality.

FREE ASSOCIATION

Free association is the cornerstone of classical Freudian psychoanalytic technique. The patient is encouraged to say whatever is in his mind, without censoring his thoughts, however embarrassing, disturbing or seemingly trivial these may be. The psychoanalyst's task, through a corresponding type of evenly suspended listening that Freud called *free-floating attention*, is to discover the unconscious themes that underlie the patient's discourse via the patient's slips of the tongue, associative links and resistances to speaking about certain topics that the patient himself is unaware of.

SPECTRUM OF INTERVENTIONS

The analyst intervenes in the form of verbal communications, which can be categorised along a spectrum that moves from the supportive to interpretative as the therapy progresses. Thus the analyst may initially make *empathic comments*; moving to *clarifications* – questioning or rephrasing to elucidate what the patient means; via *confrontations*, where the analyst will point out inconsistencies in the patient's account or draw his attention to subjects he may be avoiding; to *interpretations*.

INTERPRETATIONS

An interpretation offers a new formulation of unconscious meaning and motivation for the patient. Many contemporary psychoanalysts view transference interpretations in the 'here-and-now' or affective interchange of the analytic session as the most mutative intervention. However, more classical Freudian analysts may wait longer before interpreting the transference, holding back until the patient himself is aware of the feelings he has towards the analyst. The Freudian analyst also focuses attentively on details of the patient's past life to make reconstructive interpretations that can help the patient understand how his current difficulties have been influenced by his history. Exploration and interpretation about the patient's current external life (extra-transference interpretations) may also be helpful without minimising the importance of his internal world and unconscious fantasies.

COUNTERTRANSFERENCE

Countertransference describes the unconscious emotional reactions that the therapist has towards the patient, and is a result of both unresolved conflicts in the therapist as well as contributions or projections from the patient. Freud originally saw countertransference as a resistance to treatment, but contemporary analysts see it as a source of useful information about the patient and his internal object relations, which determine the patient's pattern of relating to others.

INTENSITY AND DURATION OF TREATMENT

Psychoanalytic therapy aims to effect long-lasting characterological change, not just alleviation of the patient's symptoms, and therefore tends to be long term, lasting years rather than months. This allows sufficient time for the *working-through* of difficulties – the integration of cognitive and affective understanding and the consolidation of new ways of functioning and relating to others. Psychoanalysis is also an intensive treatment, with the patient being seen four to five times per week, whereas in psychoanalytic psychotherapy the patient is seen once to three times a week, often face-to-face, rather than lying on the couch.

CASE EXAMPLE

Ben was a 30-year-old man presenting with depression and anxiety following his girlfriend ending their relationship because of Ben's refusal to move out of the house where he lived with his mother. He was referred by his General Practitioner (GP) to his local mental health service and, following assessment, was offered weekly psychoanalytic psychotherapy with a female therapist. Significant events in Ben's history were his father leaving the family home when he was 5 years old, and his mother becoming severely depressed and hospitalised for several months, during which Ben and his siblings were looked after by their grandparents.

At the start of the therapy, Ben appeared anxious and found silences difficult so the therapist initially limited her interventions to empathic comments and clarifications of what his current difficulties entailed. As Ben became more engaged and able to talk more spontaneously about what was on his mind, the therapist began to explore with him how his childhood experiences of loss had impacted on his adult relationships. However, she began to feel irritated with Ben's passivity and compliant attitude towards her, which she suspected concealed more aggressive feelings that he could not admit into conscious awareness. Having reflected on the possible meaning of her countertransferential feelings, and following Ben missing the session after she had unexpectedly cancelled a session due to illness, she suggested that Ben's absence might be connected to feelings of resentment that she had not been there the previous week (transference interpretation). Ben initially denied this, saying that he had felt too depressed to come, which had nothing to do with her. However, when Ben missed another session after the therapist returned from her planned leave, he admitted that he felt a bit annoyed and upset that his therapist had better things to do than see him. Over time, Ben was able to understand that his experience (in the transference) of his therapist as a rejecting, unavailable object was based on an unconscious identification with his mother as a depressed and abandoned victim of his father. As Ben worked through these difficult feelings in relation to his therapist, he was able to access previously unconscious feelings of anger towards his mother for being emotionally unavailable to him after his father left. By the end of therapy he felt he had a more balanced understanding of his parents' difficulties and their influence on his development, was able to move out of his mother's house and establish a relationship with his father that was less dominated by anger and resentment.

RESEARCH EVIDENCE

Although it is difficult to conduct outcome research on intensive psychoanalytic treatments, there is an accumulating body of empirical evidence supporting the efficacy of psychoanalytic psychotherapy. Recent meta-analyses, which pool the results of many different independent studies, including randomised controlled trials of long-term psychoanalytic psychotherapy (Leichsenring and Rabung, 2008), show that the effect sizes for psychoanalytic therapy are as large as those reported for other evidence-based therapies, such as cognitive-behavioural therapy, and that psychoanalytic psychotherapy is efficacious in common mental disorders, including depression, anxiety, personality disorders, eating disorders and post-traumatic stress disorder (Leichsenring and Klein, 2014). Moreover, patients who receive psychoanalytic therapy maintain therapeutic gains and continue to improve after cessation of treatment. The widespread scepticism regarding the scientific nature of psychoanalytic therapy is not justified, and may reflect biases in the dissemination of research findings (Shedler, 2010).

REFERENCES

Freud, S. (1917a) A Difficulty in the Path of Psycho-Analysis. In *The Standard Edition of the Complete Psychological Works of Sigmund Freud, Volume XVII.* London: Hogarth Press.

Freud, S. (1917b). Introductory Lectures on Psycho-Analysis. In *The Standard Edition of the Complete Psychological Works of Sigmund Freud, Volume XVI.* London: Hogarth Press.

Leichsenring, F. and Rabung, S. (2008) Effectiveness of long-term psychodynamic psychotherapy. *Journal of the American Medical Association*, 300: 1551–1565.

Leichsenring, F. and Klein, S. (2014) Evidence for psychodynamic psychotherapy in specific mental disorders: a systematic review. *Psychoanalytic Psychotherapy*, 28: 4–32.

Shedler, J. (2010) The efficacy of psychodynamic psychotherapy. *American Psychologist*, 65: 98–109.

RECOMMENDED READING

1. Bateman, A. and Holmes, J. (1995) *Introduction to Psychoanalysis*. London: Routledge.

A concise, introductory guide to the main principles and practice of psychoanalysis and psychoanalytic psychotherapy.

2. Gay, P. (1988) *Freud: A Life for Our Time*. London: J.M. Dent.

Biography of Sigmund Freud, incorporating new material discovered since the publication of that of Ernest Jones in 1953 (Jones, E. (1953) *The Life and Work of Sigmund Freud*. London: Penguin Books).

3. Greenson, R. (1967) *The Technique and Practice of Psychoanalysis*. New York: International Universities Press.

Clear, readable and comprehensive textbook that remains relevant to psychoanalytic practice today.

5.7 PSYCHODYNAMIC PSYCHOTHERAPY

JULIA SEGAL

OVERVIEW AND KEY POINTS

Psychodynamic psychotherapy is based on the observations and work of psychoanalysts, both past and present. The basic premise is that understanding, in the context of a one-to-one relationship with a reliable, concerned other, allows a freeing-up of the mind and makes available aspects of the self which previously were cut off. Anxieties are based on unconscious phantasies about the world, and these can be changed (and the accompanying anxieties reduced) in a relationship with a therapist who pays close attention to the emotional to-and-fro in the room.

Psychodynamic psychotherapy:

*   requires close attention to understanding emotional states and non-verbal communication as well as speech;
*   uses the fact that the therapist's understanding 'holds' the client, allowing them to feel safe enough to experience

thoughts and feelings which have been kept at bay while covertly influencing behaviour;

- uses the fact that problems in relationships in the outside world are evoked in a relationship with a therapist, where they can be understood and modified. This then changes the outside-world relationships;
- may link past losses and past experiences with aspects of the self which are cut off in the present, and which can be brought back into use through the relationship with the therapist;
- has been shown to have more long-term benefits for the client as compared with other forms of therapy.

BRIEF HISTORY

Psychoanalysis provides the basic understanding underlying insight-based counselling and psychotherapy. The techniques of free association, exploration and interpretation of unconscious motivations, emotions and drives, and the use of the relationship with the therapist as a tool for understanding patients' problems, were all discovered by Sigmund Freud in the early twentieth century and developed by him and many others, such as Melanie Klein in the United Kingdom (UK) (Klein, 1975).

Freud and his colleagues were interested in understanding the way the mind worked as well as in relieving distress by providing therapy. They developed a new language with which to talk about ways we think, feel and behave, and about the ideas, assumptions and beliefs people hold about themselves and others. The discovery, for example, that babies and infants are active participants in relationships with their mothers and others around them, having both feelings and awareness, was contrary to opinion at the time. Many psychoanalytical ideas, controversial at first, brought new possibilities for understanding and have become accepted over time.

From the mid-twentieth century there have been attempts to develop briefer, cheaper forms of therapy based on the understanding of psychoanalysts. Psychodynamic therapists and counsellors recognise and use the insights of psychoanalysts while modifying their techniques to fit the different requirements of their particular settings. Where psychoanalysts for many years insisted on seeing patients five times a week, psychodynamic psychotherapists usually work once, twice or three times a week with clients. In mainland Europe and the United States of America (USA) this distinction is not always maintained.

Historically, psychoanalytical therapists considered their work with patients was a form of research, and they communicated with each other through detailed observations of material from the consulting room. It is only relatively recently that psychodynamic psychotherapists have accepted that there are other valid ways of conducting research on their work. In the last ten years, under pressure for 'evidence-based' practice, many research projects have demonstrated that psychodynamic psychotherapy can be effective for a wide range of mental health problems, and that longer-term follow-ups demonstrate longer-term benefits.

BASIC ASSUMPTIONS

Emotional understanding is a powerful tool. An understanding relationship can allow an individual to develop their capacities to feel, to think, to understand themselves and others better.

Facing feared reality, working through the associated feelings and fantasies and grieving for real losses brings long-term reduction in anxiety. Any kind of illusion or defence is maintained by and maintains anxiety.

People often hide their own emotions from themselves. For example, someone may light up a cigarette to prevent themselves feeling angry. Exploring emotions which are kept out of conscious awareness brings new understanding of the self in relation to others.

Difficulties in relationships with caregivers (involving accepting food and other necessities, taking in and learning, for example) underlie many problems both in the past and in the present. They manifest themselves not only in relationship difficulties, but also in disturbances in the individual's relationship with themselves. The understanding of the counsellor or therapist includes the capacity to face unpleasant, destructive, shameful feelings as well as deeply loving ones, in themselves as well as in the client. Their training should ensure that they have experienced the pains as well as the pleasures of a relationship with a therapist and that they have no sense of superiority towards their clients.

However, no relationship with a therapist or counsellor is truly one of equals. The therapist offers something which the client supposedly wants. This relationship therefore has the potential to arouse emotions such as hope, longing, desire, rivalry, envy, fear of loss, anger and aggressiveness; in therapy, some of these can be understood and the associated behaviour, fears, attitudes and beliefs explored. The client's relationship with the therapist provides an opportunity to reassess the client's feelings and behaviour in connection with being cared for in the past. This can improve relations with others and with the self in the present.

The therapist's help in thinking directly about relationships with others and the self, both currently and in the past, may also bring considerable relief.

ORIGIN AND MAINTENANCE OF PROBLEMS

Our understanding of the world around us, and of ourselves in relation to it, grows with us. What Melanie Klein called 'phantasies' (H. Segal, 1981; J.C. Segal, 1985) are formed. To understand this concept, think of the way babies gradually begin to recognise people. Some kind of picture or model or 'phantasy' is formed. These phantasies are dynamic; they change and develop as the people around come and go and interact with each other. When the baby is happy, their phantasies of their world, including the people in it, are happy, loving ones; when the baby is feeling bad in some way, the phantasies may be frightening, disturbing ones.

Phantasies are unconscious constructions: we are not aware of our own contribution to our perceptions; we just see things that way. As a small child we may just *know* our father can do everything; as a teenager we may simply see him as the greatest fool in the world. One adult just knows the world is a friendly place; another lives in constant fear of attack.

As we grow up, we generally begin to see those around us more realistically. Phantasies we have of other people include characteristics derived from our knowledge and experience of ourselves: so a child who is missing a parent may believe that the absent parent is sad, for example; if the child is angry with the parent for being away, they may believe the parent is angry with them. A teenager afraid of embarrassing themselves may see a parent as embarrassing.

Problems can arise if very infantile phantasies do not get modified through play and through age-appropriate relationships with real people. Problems with our parents affect our phantasies about the world. We have phantasy relationships with our parents even when they are not there, so someone whose father disappeared when they were two may expect all men to disappear from their lives after about two years, and may behave in such a way as to make it happen. Their phantasies about sexual partners and fathers may remain on a level more appropriate to the knowledge and beliefs of a two year old. Later experiences may lead to modifications to such beliefs, but phantasies created very early on under painful conditions (such as loss) are hard to change since recurrence of the pain is feared.

Problems arise too because of the ways we manipulate phantasies and emotions in response to conflicts. For example, bad feelings can seem so frightening that they have to be separated from good ones. In order not to feel jealous, envious, angry and left out, for example,

we may see ourselves as having and being everything desirable and our mothers as poor, weak, foolish creatures with no understanding. Unfortunately, such phantasies may leave us not only vulnerable to collapse when we discover we do not live up to our own expectations, but also unable to then turn to her (in reality or in imagination) for comfort.

Reality often brings emotional pain. Perception of the world and the self can be 'split' to avoid such pain. However, the splitting itself is not only insecure but also deeply damaging. Denial, idealisation and denigration (forms of splitting used in the Madonna and Whore images, for example) may temporarily get rid of the jealous envy attached to knowing that women in general, and our mothers in particular, can have sex as well as have children, but in order to allow ourselves and others to be more rounded women (or men), we have to learn to tolerate our differences without idealising or denying, denigrating or dismissing them.

Phantasies that we can get rid of unbearable, uncontainable feelings into other people are common. We call this *projective identification*. This may be involved, for example, when a father of a small child finds a new lover. Instead of feeling left out of the relationship between his wife and the child, he feels that *they* are left out of his exciting new relationship. He may be trying to get rid of re-awoken feelings of being cruelly left out when he was a child. He does not think to himself 'I will leave my child then he or she will feel the pain instead of me'; he simply feels an overwhelming urge to be cared for and loved exclusively; the excitement helps him to split off awareness of his own cruelty. The hope must be to find a new, better solution this time. The risk is that the 'solution' will be equally or more damaging – to the father himself as well as to his family.

Both external and internal conditions can cause problems in development. A baby or child subjected to ill-treatment may respond in many ways which affect his or her long-term development. However, some babies and children seem to respond badly to even normal good and loving care, and, contrariwise, some can make use of even the smallest opportunity for love in an otherwise problematic environment. People have different capacities to use the good things and relationships they are offered and to withstand adversity. Some babies seem to enjoy life more from the beginning; others find it difficult and unpleasant, or even unbearable. Mothers who have to cope with difficult babies often blame themselves, but psychodynamic psychotherapists have a greater awareness of the contribution of the child's own physical and emotional makeup.

THEORY OF CHANGE

Change depends on modifying the underlying phantasies we have about the world and that we use to orient ourselves. We can be changed by any new learning which involves an emotional element – relationships, giving birth, work and any form of creativity. All of these have the power to evoke emotions while challenging our beliefs, assumptions and awareness of ourselves and others. However, emotions can be painful and change can be feared and avoided.

Psychodynamic practitioners emphasise the importance of bringing to consciousness significant aspects of the relationship with the therapist, in the room, particularly those associated with painful emotions. 'Transference interpretations', in which this relationship becomes the focus of work, enable a client to become aware of their experience of the relationship, while being accompanied and supported by the therapist. Endings, lateness or missed sessions all have meaning to the client which may need to be examined, uncovered and addressed, even when the client does not see (at first) that they pose any problem.

In psychodynamic therapy or counselling, the client has the opportunity to experience a relationship in which her or his emotional states can be felt, understood, tolerated and recognised in a new way.

The aim of psychodynamic counselling is to increase the client's capacity to use and accept more aspects of themselves, to free their processes of thought and feeling and to remove damaging restrictions on them. New, better possibilities for dealing with internal and external conflicts remain after counselling ends.

Grieving can initiate powerful processes of change. Grief handled alone sometimes results in attempts to get rid of the pain by cutting off parts of the self, such as the ability to think or to feel or to see in certain areas. It can also result in attempts to get rid of unbearable pain into someone else, making them feel the pain 'instead', perhaps by hitting out at them verbally, or in some more subtle way evoking a version of the same pain in them (projective identification). Grief worked through with someone (such as a psychodynamic therapist) who can help a client to tolerate painful, often humiliating, thoughts and feelings may gradually bring new awareness and new strengths.

SKILLS AND STRATEGIES

A psychodynamic practitioner is expected to have an ability to recognise and tolerate their own true state of mind in the presence of a client.

Since offering anything to a client has important implications for the relationship, skill is involved in knowing when and how to share an idea or to suggest a thought for the client to consider, and in picking up the consequences.

Skill is involved in deciding when to discuss an issue raised by the client in terms of the overt meaning, and when to pick up a more covert meaning. For example, a client complaining about their sister may need help in thinking about her – but they may also need help in thinking about ways in which the sister at this moment is being used to talk about some aspect of themselves or the counsellor. Negative feelings towards the therapist or therapy are often raised in such ways, providing an opportunity to draw attention to, discuss and modify processes of splitting.

Skill is also needed to interpret what clients bring to the counsellor, both verbally and non-verbally. Since feelings, both negative and positive, can often be hidden by the client from their own awareness, the therapist has to be aware of signals conveying them. As they were hidden in the first place for very powerful reasons, bringing them to the attention of the client raises many issues about the relationship with the counsellor as well as about the client's state of mind and, when it is done, has to be done skilfully.

Psychodynamic psychotherapists do not use self-disclosure and they maintain their privacy as far as possible in order to help clients recognise that their fantasies about other people (such as the therapist) *are* fantasies, arising from the client's mind. (Interestingly, research by an insurance broker into litigation brought by clients against therapists confirmed the wisdom of this stance. Not only any form of touch other than a formal handshake, but also personal pictures or any mention of personal matters, of holidays or family; any change in or carelessness about the therapists' clothing or appearance or arrangement of the room; any statement or behaviour which could be classed as outside the professional frame; even changes of time or place, *have been* cited by more than one client as constituting a provocative invitation to a personal, often sexual, relationship.)

RESEARCH EVIDENCE

For many years psychoanalysts and psychodynamic psychotherapists were reluctant to subject themselves and their clients to outcome studies. The 'tick-box' questionnaires demanded by large-scale studies of outcomes seemed to bear little relation to the actual problems and work of clients and therapists. Serious methodological criticisms (e.g., the unreliability of diagnostic categories) combined with practical ones (e.g., the fact that there were no accepted, agreed manuals for psychodynamic or psychoanalytic psychotherapy) meant that practitioners were reluctant to engage with research which would be acceptable to the mainstream scientific community.

With the increasing emphasis on 'evidence-based practice' and, eventually, the advent of the *Improving Access to Psychological Therapies* (IAPT) programme in the UK, the situation changed. Mental health services found their funding dependent upon the judgements of managers rather than clinicians, and these demanded a kind of evidence which Cognitive-Behavioural Therapy (CBT) therapists had been producing for many years. Faced with the threat of decimation of the profession, psychodynamic therapists have found ways of producing the evidence they needed.

The change has taken place in two ways. One is by the manualisation of psychodynamic therapy, a first step towards enabling randomised controlled trials. In *What works for Whom?* (2004), Anthony Roth and Peter Fonagy looked at the evidence for effective psychodynamic interventions for different conditions. Together with Alessandra Lemma and Mary Target, specific manualised therapies for specific diagnoses were developed, using those psychoanalytic/dynamic approaches with the strongest empirical evidence for efficacy based on the outcome of controlled trials. Mentalisation-based Therapy (MBT) emerged for people with borderline personality disorder, and Dynamic Interpersonal Therapy (DIT) for depression, anxiety and mood disorders.

At the same time, psychodynamic therapists have begun to participate in trials and to gather evidence of effectiveness. In 2002, for example, Phil Richardson at the Tavistock Clinic, London, UK, started a rigorous long-term, large-scale randomised controlled trial of long-term psychodynamic psychotherapy. The study was restricted to people suffering from major depressive disorder for more than two years who had had at least two failed treatment attempts. One hundred and twenty-nine patients were randomised to 18 months of weekly psychodynamic psychotherapy with therapists registered with the British Psychoanalytic Council or *Treatment as Usual*. Richardson died in 2007 but the study was completed by Fonagy and others, and in 2015 the results were published.

There is now a considerable body of evidence that long-term (i.e., more than one year) psychodynamic therapies produce significantly more improvements, when measured over the longer term (two to three years), than other kinds of therapy and 'treatment as usual'. There is also evidence that other therapists (such as CBT practitioners) who use psychodynamic methods do better than those who keep most strictly to their own manualised techniques. Jonathon Shedler's (2010) paper is one of the most encouraging (as well as readable) pieces of research for psychodynamic therapists in general. Looking at a large number of meta-studies, he concluded that:

> Empirical evidence supports the efficacy of psychodynamic therapy. Effect sizes for psychodynamic therapy are as large as those reported for other therapies that have been actively promoted as 'empirically supported' and 'evidence based.' In addition, patients who receive psychodynamic therapy maintain therapeutic gains and appear to continue to improve after treatment ends. Finally, non-psychodynamic therapies may be effective in part because the more skilled practitioners utilize techniques that have long been central to psychodynamic theory and practice. The perception that psychodynamic approaches lack empirical support does not accord with available scientific evidence and may reflect selective dissemination of research. (Shedler, 2010: 107)

Since he wrote this, more research, including in the UK, has appeared to confirm his observation: psychodynamic psychotherapy is now backed up by evidence which satisfies mainstream 'scientific' criteria.

Neuroscience has been another source of research evidence which supports many psychoanalytical ideas, including the idea that emotions are important in change; that attachment to caregivers and early relationships are highly significant for later life; that babies actively relate to their environment and are aware of and care about the people around them. Ideas about unconscious phantasy fit well with neuroscientists' discoveries about the ways we learn and experience the world (Gerhardt, 2004; Ledoux, 1998).

Important as these studies are for the survival of psychodynamic or psychoanalytic therapies, the reader may find the older, psychoanalytical case study form of research both enlightening and interesting. A case study is most useful for those who have the capacity to use others' insights to enhance their own. Not a manual or book of rules, it requires a therapist to use sensitivity, thought and care when applying observations from one situation to another. The earliest are Freud's *Studies on Hysteria* (1975 [1893–95]), and there is an interesting collection entitled *The Contemporary Kleinians of London*, edited by Roy Schafer in 1997. Waddell's *Inside Lives: Psychoanalysis and the Growth of Personality* (1998) and J.C. Segal's *Phantasy in Everyday Life* (1985), both written for a less intellectual readership, include many thought-provoking cases and vignettes.

REFERENCES

Fonagy, P., Rost, F., Carlyle, J., McPherson, S., Thomas, R., Fearon, R.M.P., Goldberg, D. and Taylor, D. (2015) Pragmatic randomized controlled trial of long-term psychoanalytic psychotherapy for treatment-resistant depression: the Tavistock Adult Depression Study (TADS). *World Psychiatry*, 14, 312–321.

Freud, S. (1975 [1893–95]) *Studies on Hysteria*. Vol. 2. *The Standard Edition of the Complete Psychological Works of Sigmund Freud*. Trans James Strachey. London: Hogarth Press and the Institute of Psychoanalysis.

Gerhardt, S. (2004) *Why Love Matters: How Affection Shapes a Baby's Brain*. London: Routledge.

Klein, M. (1975 [1957]) *The Writings of Melanie Klein*, Vols I, II and III. London: Hogarth Press and Institute of Psychoanalysis.

Ledoux, J. (1998) *The Emotional Brain: The Mysterious Underpinnings of Emotional Life*. London: Orion.

Roth, A. and Fonagy, P. (2004) *What Works for Whom?* (2nd ed.). New York: Guilford Press.

Segal, H. (1981) *The Work of Hanna Segal: A Kleinian Approach to Clinical Practice*. New York: Jason Aronson (republished London: Free Associations).

Segal, J.C. (1985) *Phantasy in Everyday Life*. London: Pelican Books (reprinted London: Karnac, 1995).

Shafer, R. (ed.) (1997) *The Contemporary Kleinians of London*. New York: International Universities Press.

Shedler, J. (2010) The efficacy of psychodynamic psychotherapy. *American Psychologist*, 65(2):98-109.

Waddell, M. (1998) *Inside Lives: Psychoanalysis and the Growth of Personality*. London: Duckworth.

RECOMMENDED READING

1. Waddell, M. (1998) *Inside Lives: Psychoanalysis and the Growth of Personality*. London: Duckworth.

A very readable book. Written for a non-professional readership, it includes many thought-provoking cases and vignettes.

2. Segal, J.C. (1985) *Phantasy in Everyday Life*. London: Pelican Books.

This is a very readable and accessible text that includes many vignettes.

3. British Psychoanalytic Council: www.bpc.org.uk/about-psychotherapy/evidence.

This website addresses the question of evidence for psychoanalytic psychotherapy.

5.8 PSYCHODYNAMIC INTERPERSONAL THERAPY

RICHARD J. BROWN, SARA BARDSLEY AND VANESSA HERBERT

OVERVIEW AND KEY POINTS

Psychodynamic interpersonal therapy (PIT) is a brief, largely jargon-free type of relational therapy that is easy to learn and does not require extensive knowledge of psychodynamic theory. It has theoretical roots in person-centred counselling and a number of psychodynamic traditions but is a distinct form of therapy in its own right. Key points include the following:

- PIT takes the form of an in-depth, two-way conversation focusing on the client's feelings as they emerge in the session, with a view to helping them understand and resolve interpersonal problems in their lives.

- PIT has a good evidence base, with randomised controlled trials suggesting it is efficacious as a treatment for depression, deliberate self-harm, personality disturbance and functional ('medically unexplained') symptoms.
- PIT is recognised as an efficacious treatment within the CORE competence frameworks for psychoanalytic/psychodynamic therapy and for persistent physical health problems.

BRIEF HISTORY

The conversational model (as PIT was originally known) was developed in the 1970s and 1980s by British psychiatrist and psychotherapist Robert Hobson and his Australian collaborator Russell Meares. The term PIT was adopted later when the model was manualised and evaluated as a brief intervention in United Kingdom (UK) clinical trials; Meares still uses the original name to refer to his variant of the approach, which is mainly used in Australia as a long-term treatment for borderline personality disorder (Meares, 2012).

Hobson and Meares were influenced by a range of clinical and theoretical perspectives, such as attachment theory, interpersonal psychology, psychoanalysis, person-centred counselling and existential psychotherapy, as well as non-clinical traditions, including theology, the philosophy of Ludwig Wittgenstein, and romantic poets such as Wordsworth, Blake and Coleridge. His combination and application of these influences constitutes a unique approach to psychotherapy, a comprehensive account of which is documented in Hobson's influential book, *Forms of Feeling* (Hobson, 1985).

BASIC ASSUMPTIONS

Traditional psychodynamic concepts like the avoidance of painful feelings arising from emotional conflict and the re-enactment of problematic patterns of relating are central to PIT, although Hobson's description of these concepts in *Forms of Feeling* relies very little on formal psychodynamic theory and terms, making it particularly accessible. PIT also assumes that the 'how' of therapy is often more important than the 'what', and that slavish adherence to theoretical models can often undermine the central therapeutic task, which is to develop an emotional connection with the client in order to help them solve their personal problems.

PIT assumes that thought and action are motivated by intrinsic needs that serve to maintain physical and emotional homeostasis, and that stress and anxiety arise when those needs are not met. Two needs that are afforded particular importance in this respect are the need to maintain relationships with other people and the need to maintain autonomy and a positive, coherent sense of self. How we manage the conflict that often arises between these needs has an important bearing on our wellbeing. According to Hobson, negotiating a successful balance between these needs (so-called *aloneness-togetherness*) requires us to relate to and value ourselves and others as unique, experiencing, feeling beings, that is, as 'persons' rather than 'objects' ('I–thou' and 'I–it' forms of relating respectively; Buber, 1937). When we are unable to do this, often because of difficulties in our early relationships, emotional disturbance can arise. PIT assumes that this can be addressed by understanding and optimising the balance between aloneness and togetherness during the therapy, which often involves focusing on and 'staying with' avoided feelings as they arise in the moment.

PIT assumes that helping the client to relate more as a person requires the therapist to be able to do so themselves, which means being genuine (i.e., 'yourself'), humble, emotionally present and responsive to the other person's feelings, without disregarding one's own. The model also assumes that it is easy for even well-meaning therapists to relate to their clients in ways that are counter-therapeutic, including responding in a subtly intrusive, derogatory, invalidating or opaque manner (Meares and Hobson, 1977). Being alert to this possibility is regarded as a crucial task, as is repairing ruptures in the therapuetic relationship when such instances inevitably arise.

ORIGIN AND MAINTENANCE OF PROBLEMS

According to this approach, unhelpful experiences in early attachment relationships may give rise to problems in relationships with the self and/or others, including (1) a tendency to perceive threats to attachments; (2) a tendency to see attachments as a threat to oneself; (3) problems regulating affect and engaging in reflective processing; and (4) problems representing the mental states of self and/or others. These experiences undermine the individual's ability to relate (both to themselves and other people) in adaptive ways, rendering them vulnerable to painful and conflicting feelings in relationships, particularly when there is a threat to their self-worth/autonomy and/or their relatedness with others. Psychopathology is said to arise when the individual manages the anxiety generated by these feelings in a maladaptive way, typically by disowning the feelings or engaging in other avoidance activities (defences in traditional psychodynamic theory) that keep them from awareness. These avoidance activities typically include unhelpful patterns of relating that reflect how the individual learnt to cope with their early relationships, but which are no longer optimal. These avoidance activities maintain symptoms in various ways, such as by preventing the underlying issues from being recognised and dealt with, by preventing the individual's needs from being met and by exposing the individual to unhealthy relationships.

This model provides a basis for formulation in PIT, and a key goal of the assessment is to arrive at a basic, shared formulation that incorporates some or all of these elements. As an exploratory therapy, however, the process of formulation is seen an intrinsic aspect of PIT that continues throughout the work, with a deeper, more nuanced understanding of the client's problems (and therefore possible solutions to them) emerging over time.

THEORY OF CHANGE

The aim of PIT is to create a sense of safety so that the individual's anxieties can be tolerated, allowing them to hold the hidden material (and the relational context to which it pertains) in awareness and talk about it as it arises in the moment. This fosters a process of 'symbolical transformation' (akin to the concept of emotional processing in other traditions), whereby the nature, meaning and origins of the hidden material are understood, accepted and mastered. In so doing, new 'forms' (or mental representations) of feeling are developed

that reduce the need for further avoidance activities. This renders the client more able to relate to themselves and others as persons and to test this out in the therapy and elsewhere, thereby improving their self-esteem and interpersonal relationships. Subsequent theoretical writings by Meares (2000, 2005) have focused on the development of the self through this process, although these ideas are not fundamental to how the model is understood and practised in the UK.

SKILLS AND STRATEGIES

Arguably, the personal qualities and interpersonal skills of the therapist are more important than detailed knowledge of theoretical concepts in PIT, as long as the therapist has a good understanding of the basic model and the purpose of the therapeutic conversation. There is also a specific set of core skills that are central to appropriate practice of the model. One of the strengths of PIT is that the basic interventions that characterise this approach are clearly defined, easy to learn and comparatively simple to apply (see, for example, Guthrie et al., 2004; Shaw et al., 2001). In this section, we describe some of the main interventions, using examples that might apply in the hypothetical case, *Jean*.

CASE EXAMPLE: JEAN

Jean is 46 and is coming for help with depression, which started when her youngest son left home two years ago. Jean's husband, David, is 10 years older than her and they got married the year after she left school at 16, having the first of their three children not long after that. Jean has dedicated her life since then to looking after them. Jean says she has 'the perfect marriage', describing David as 'wonderful, the ideal man … he's always provided for me and the kids'. She explains how proud she is of his successful company and how he is 'always going abroad to do some deal or another'. There are tears in Jean's eyes when the therapist wonders what it is like for her when he's out of the country; after a long pause, she says (in a far from convincing voice) 'it's good, it really allows me to concentrate on the children'.

Jean was the oldest of seven children and spent a lot of time looking after her siblings when she was growing up, particularly after her father, whom she 'adored', died when she was 12. When the therapist asks how she reacted to his death, she says 'I never really cried when he died … Mum was in such a state and the kids needed looking after … I guess I just had to put a lid on it'. Jean quickly changes the subject. Jean says she has 'a lot to be thankful for' and can't understand why she is depressed. She describes getting angry at herself for 'being selfish' and 'burdening people'.

Later in the therapy, the therapist has to cancel two sessions due to illness. When they finally meet again, the therapist wonders what it was like for her while they were away. Jean wells up and replies 'It must take its toll hearing about everyone's problems all the time…'. She seems subdued and upset and the therapist feels that it is difficult to connect with her.

The overarching strategies in PIT are to develop a personal connection and emotionally vivid 'mutual feeling language' with the client regarding their problems, with an appropriate balance of aloneness-togetherness. Feelings are focused on 'here and now' as they arise and are felt in the therapy (rather than in an abstract sense). To that end, the therapist is alert to cues pointing to the client's emotional experience during the therapy session, including what is explicit and implicit in the language, expression and behaviour of both participants. Hobson refers to this as a focus on the 'minute particulars' of therapy. The tears in Jean's eyes, the long pause and the unconvincing tone of her voice point to more mixed feelings about her husband's absence than the verbal content of her narrative alone, for example.

Where appropriate, the therapist will seek to amplify the feelings in question by noticing the cues and 'wondering about' what the client is experiencing, with a view to bringing any feelings on the edge of awareness into focus. They may also offer an informed guess or *understanding hypothesis* about what is happening for them in that moment, based on the available cues and their knowledge of the client (e.g., 'When you were talking about David then I noticed there were tears in your eyes and you paused ... I wonder if part of you feels a bit upset about him going away sometimes'). The client is encouraged to 'stay with' and talk about any feelings that have emerged (e.g., 'that sounds important ... maybe we could just stay with that upset feeling'), in a two-way, mutual conversation that evolves over time into a shared understanding of the client's emotional experience in relationships. First-person pronouns ('I', 'we' and 'you') are used to foster an explicit discussion of the relationship between client and therapist in particular.

In PIT, the style of the therapist's conversation is tentative and invites negotiation (e.g., 'This might not be quite right but I wonder if...'), communicating a wish to understand the client's difficulties and to be corrected if misunderstandings occur. A distinctive component of PIT is the use of statements (e.g., 'I wonder what's going on inside right now'), which are considered to be less anxiety-provoking and probing than questions (e.g., 'How do you feel about that?'). Statements aim to create a starting point for exploration of the person's difficulties, while providing a space for correction. Wherever possible, the client's specific words and phrases are used; in particular, their metaphors and other figurative language are picked up and used to amplify and explore feelings, with a view to broadening the client's understanding of them (e.g., 'put a lid on it ... like a pressure cooker maybe...'). Detailed questioning, jargon and expert pronouncements are explicitly proscribed: the emphasis is on a shared experience within therapy, and client and therapist perspectives being of equal value.

Over time, the therapist begins to make statements that suggest parallels between what is happening in that moment and feelings in other relationships in the client's life, both currently and in the past. These are *linking hypotheses* (e.g., 'I don't know ... you seem a bit upset ... I wonder if it felt quite difficult me being away ... a bit like when David goes away'). In so doing, previously unrelated aspects of experience can be joined up and patterns discerned. Eventually, therapist and client may begin to develop *explanatory hypotheses*, that describe possible reasons for difficulties in relationships both within and outside the therapy (e.g., 'I guess it feels really hard to say you're upset and cross with me ... like it might hurt me or what we're doing in some way ... just like you had to put your upset and grief to one side when your Dad died ... maybe you felt you had to protect your Mum ... in case you lost her too'). This provides an opportunity for conflicts, hidden feelings and avoidance activities to be acknowledged, owned and explored. Such hypotheses bear some resemblance to the transference interpretations seen in other psychodynamic therapies, but are used more sparingly and collaboratively in PIT.

In PIT, the therapist's intuitive sense of how 'connected' they are with their client is seen as a potentially useful indicator of what is happening in the therapy, and as a possible starting point for exploration. The PIT therapist may notice a possible disconnection from Jean following the unplanned break in therapy, for example, and offer an understanding hypothesis about it (e.g., 'I'm not sure, it feels like there's a bit of a distance between us today'). The therapist is also alert to the client's anxiety levels throughout, with a view to promoting meaningful exploration (which is inevitably anxiety-provoking) while ensuring that the process is tolerable for the client. This requires the therapist to use their understanding of the client, the model and their general clinical skills to determine what is safe and appropriate for that individual.

RESEARCH EVIDENCE

There is good evidence from randomised controlled trials that PIT is an effective treatment for depression (Barkham et al., 1996; Guthrie et al., 1999; Shapiro et al., 1995), functional ('medically unexplained') symptoms (Creed et al., 2003; Creed et al., 2005a, 2005b, 2005c; Creed et al., 2008; Guthrie et al., 1991; Hamilton et al., 2000; Hyphantis et al., 2009; Mayor et al., 2010; Sattel et al., 2012), deliberate self-harm (Guthrie et al., 2001; Guthrie et al., 2003) and borderline personality disorder

(Korner et al., 2006; Stevenson and Meares, 1992; Stevenson et al., 2005). PIT has not been evaluated as a treatment for other mental health problems and is therefore not normally offered as a 'frontline' therapy in these cases. However, PIT may be offered where other treatments (such as Cognitive-Behaviour Therapy) have not worked or are not suitable, where the presenting problems seem particularly amenable to an exploratory interpersonal approach, or where the client expresses a particular preference for PIT.

Process studies have shown that the focus on interpersonal difficulties in PIT is associated with improvements in self-esteem and social adjustment (Kerr et al., 1992). There is also evidence that staying with feelings helps clients to vividly experience and express emotions that are usually suppressed (Mackay et al., 1998). The quality of the therapeutic alliance in PIT is associated with improvements on a variety of therapy outcome measures, including symptoms of depression, general symptoms and interpersonal difficulties (Stiles et al., 1998).

REFERENCES

Barkham, M., Rees, A., Shapiro, D. A., Stiles, W. B. et al. (1996). Outcome of time-limited psychotherapy in applied settings: replicating the Second Sheffield Psychotherapy Project. *Journal of Consulting and Clinical Psychology*, 64, 1079–1085.

Buber, M. (1937). *I and Thou.* Edinburgh: T. and T. Clark.

Creed, F., Fernandes, L., Guthrie, E., Palmer, S., Ratcliffe, J., Read, N., Rigby, C., Thompson, D., Tomenson B. and North of England IBS Research Group (2003). The cost-effectiveness of psychotherapy and paroxetine for severe irritable bowel syndrome. *Gastroenterology*, 124(2), 303–317.

Creed, F., Guthrie, E., Ratcliffe, J., Fernandes, L., Rigby, C., Tomenson, B., Read, N. and Thompson, D. G. (2005a). Reported sexual abuse predicts impaired functioning but a good response to psychological treatments in patients with severe irritable bowel syndrome. *Psychosomatic Medicine*, 67, 490–499.

Creed, F., Guthrie, E., Ratcliffe, J., Fernandes, L., Rigby, C., Tomenson, B., Read, N. and Thompson, D. G. (2005b). Does psychological treatment help only those patients with severe irritable bowel syndrome who also have concurrent psychiatric disorder? *Australian and New Zealand Journal of Psychiatry*, 39, 807–815.

Creed, F., Ratcliffe, J., Fernandes, L., Palmer, S., Rigby, C., Tomenson, B., Guthrie, E., Read, N. and Thompson, D. G. (2005c). Outcome in severe irritable bowel syndrome with and without accompanying depressive, panic and neurasthenic disorders. *British Journal of Psychiatry*, 186, 507–515.

Creed, F., Tomenson, B., Guthrie, E., Ratcliffe, J., Fernandes, L., Read, N., Palmer, S. and Thompson, D. G. (2008). The relationship between somatisation and outcome in patients with severe irritable bowel syndrome. *Journal of Psychosomatic Research*, 64(6), 613–620.

Guthrie, E., Creed, F., Dawson, D. and Tomenson, B. (1991). A controlled trial of psychological treatment for the irritable bowel syndrome. *Gastroenterology*, 100, 450–457.

Guthrie, E., Kapur, N., Mackway-Jones, K., Chew-Graham, C., Moorey, J., Mendel, E., Marino-Francis, F., Sanderson, S., Turpin, C., Boddy, G. and Tomenson, B. (2001). Randomised controlled trial of brief psychological intervention after deliberate self-poisoning. *British Medical Journal*, 323, 135–138.

Guthrie, E., Kapur, N., Mackway-Jones, K., Chew-Graham, C., Moorey, J., Mendel, E., Marino-Francis, F., Sanderson, S., Turpin, C. and Boddy, G. (2003). Predictors of outcome following brief psychodynamic-interpersonal therapy for deliberate self-poisoning. *Australian and New Zealand Journal of Psychiatry*, 37, 532–536.

Guthrie, E., Margison, F., Mackay, H., Chew-Graham, C., Moorey, J. and Sibbald, B. (2004). Effectiveness of psychodynamic interpersonal therapy training for primary care counsellors. *Psychotherapy Research*, 14(2), 161–175.

Guthrie, E., Moorey, J., Margison, F., Barker, H., Palmer, S., McGrath, G., Tomenson, B. and Creed, F. (1999). Cost-effectiveness of brief psychodynamic-interpersonal therapy in high utilizers of psychiatric services. *Archives of General Psychiatry*, 56, 519–526.

Hamilton, J., Guthrie, E., Creed, F., Thompson, D., Tomenson, B., Bennett, R., Moriarty, K., Stephens, W. and Liston, R. (2000). A randomised controlled trial of psychotherapy in patients with chronic functional dyspepsia. *Gastroenterology*, 119, 661–669.

Hobson, R. F. (1985). *Forms of Feeling: The Heart of Psychotherapy*. London: Routledge.

Hyphantis, T., Guthrie, E., Tomenson, B. and Creed, F. (2009). Psychodynamic interpersonal therapy and improvement in interpersonal difficulties in people with severe irritable bowel syndrome. *Pain*, 145, 196–203.

Kerr, S., Goldfried, M., Hayes, A., Castonguay, L. and Goldsamt, L. (1992). Interpersonal and intrapersonal focus in cognitive–behavioral and psychodynamic–interpersonal therapies: a preliminary analysis of the Sheffield Project. *Psychotherapy Research*, 2(4), 266–276.

Korner, A., Gerull, F., Meares, R. and Stevenson, J. (2006). Borderline personality disorder treated with the conversational model: a replication study. *Comprehensive Psychiatry*, 47, 406–411.

Mackay, H. C., Barkham, M. and Stiles, W. B. (1998). Staying with the feeling: An anger event in psychodynamic-interpersonal therapy. *Journal of Counseling Psychology*, 45, 279–289.

Mayor, R., Howlett, S., Grunewald, R. and Reuber, M. (2010). Long-term outcome of brief augmented psychodynamic interpersonal therapy for psychogenic non-epileptic seizures: seizure control and healthcare utilization. *Epilepsia*, 51, 1169–1176.

Meares, R. (2000). *Intimacy and Alienation: Memory, Trauma and Personal Being*. London: Brunner-Routledge.

Meares, R. (2005). *The Metaphor of Play*. London: Brunner-Routledge.

Meares, R. (2012). *Borderline Personality Disorder and the Conversational Model*. New York: W.W. Norton.

Meares, R. and Hobson, R. F. (1977). The persecutory therapist. *British Journal of Medical Psychology*, 50, 349–359.

Sattel, H., Lahmann, C., Gündel, H., Guthrie, E., Kruse, J., Noll-Hussong, M., Ohmann, C., Ronel, J., Sack, M., Sauer, N., Schneider, G. and Henningsen, P. (2012). Brief psychodynamic interpersonal psychotherapy for patients with multisomatoform disorder: randomised controlled trial. *British Journal of Psychiatry*, 100, 60–67.

Shapiro, D., Rees, A., Barkham, M. and Hardy, G. (1995). Effects of treatment duration and severity of depression on the maintenance of gains after cognitive-behavioural and psychodynamic-interpersonal psychotherapy. *Journal of Consulting and Clinical Psychology*, 63(3), 378–387.

Shaw, C. M., Margison, F. R., Guthrie, E. A. and Tomenson, B. (2001). Psychodynamic interpersonal therapy by inexperienced therapists in a naturalistic setting: a pilot study. *European Journal of Psychotherapy, Counselling and Health*, 4(1), 87–101.

Stevenson, J. and Meares, R. (1992). An outcome study of psychotherapy for patients with borderline personality disorder. *American Journal of Psychiatry*, 149, 358–362.

Stevenson, J., Meares, R. and D'Angelo, R. (2005). Five year outcome of outpatient psychotherapy with borderline patients. *Psychological Medicine*, 35, 79–87.

Stiles, W.B., Agnew-Davies, R., Hardy, G.E., Barkham, M. and Shapiro, D.A. (1998). Relations of the alliance with psychotherapy outcome: Findings in the Second Sheffield Psychotherapy Project. *Journal of Consulting and Clinical Psychology*, 66, 791–802.

RECOMMENDED READING

1. Barkham, M., Guthrie, E., Hardy, G. and Margison, F. (2016). *Psychodynamic Interpersonal Therapy: A Conversational Model*. London: Sage.

A detailed manual and comprehensive overview of PIT research, teaching and practice.

2. Hobson, R. F. (1985). *Forms of Feeling: The Heart of Psychotherapy*. London: Routledge.

Classic presentation of the theoretical and practical aspects of the model from its founder. Core reading for all PIT therapists, novices and experts alike.

3. Meares, R. and Hobson, R. F. (1977). The persecutory therapist. *British Journal of Medical Psychology*, 50, 349–359.

In this paper, Hobson and Meares argue that a core task for all therapists is to be alert to, and minimise, the various subtle ways that we can unwittingly damage our clients.

THEORY AND APPROACHES: COGNITIVE-BEHAVIOURAL APPROACHES

ACCEPTANCE AND COMMITMENT THERAPY

JOHN BOORMAN, ERIC MORRIS AND JOE OLIVER

OVERVIEW AND KEY POINTS

Acceptance and commitment therapy (ACT) is a contextual cognitive-behaviour treatment that aims to strengthen clients' flexible responding to their internal experiences (feelings, thoughts, urges) in order to help them engage in actions and choices guided by personal values.

- The main aim is to help clients live a rich and meaningful life in accordance with their values.
- This is achieved by strengthening clients' skills in mindfully discriminating thoughts and feelings, in order to reduce unhelpful responding and foster psychological acceptance of this internal content.
- ACT also seeks to reduce clients' entanglement with what it terms the 'conceptualised self' (for example, self stories) in order to increase flexible perspective-taking on psychological distress.
- Therapy seeks to help clients engage in specific patterns of committed behavioural action, which are directly linked to what they consider are important.
- ACT has been found to be as effective as other cognitive-behaviour therapies at treating anxiety, depression, addiction and somatic health problems.

BRIEF HISTORY

Acceptance and commitment therapy (ACT, pronounced as a single word 'act') is part of an evolution of behavioural and cognitive psychotherapies that emphasise mindfulness and acceptance. These mindfulness-based interventions include, among others, dialectical behaviour therapy (DBT: Linehan, 1993) and mindfulness-based cognitive therapy (Segal, Williams and Teasdale, 2002). ACT sits within the wider science of human understanding known as Contextual Behavioural Science (Hayes, Barnes-Holmes and Wilson, 2012). One of the aims is to foster treatment development through a proposed reticulated model (Hayes et al., 2013), which describes how clinical practitioners and basic science researchers can engage in a mutually beneficial relationship in order to build a more progressive, unified psychology.

ACT is based upon the scientific philosophy of functional contextualism. Functional contextualism defines the goal of science to be the prediction and influence of behaviour, with precision, scope and depth, using empirically based concepts and methods. Behaviour is understood and influenced on the basis of function rather than form, and all actions are considered to occur within a specific context (for example, historical, situational, environmental, social, cultural and verbal influences). What is considered 'true' in this pragmatic philosophy are ways of speaking that allow for 'successful working'. Concepts or rules that do not point to what to *do* (as a therapist or scientist) are discarded. ACT incorporates elements of both the first (behaviour therapy) and second (cognitive therapy) 'waves' of Cognitive-Behaviour Therapy (CBT), while introducing new elements such as mindfulness, acceptance and defusion from thoughts.

ACT was originally developed by the American psychologist Steven Hayes, who, along with other colleagues, looked to expand upon the behaviour analytic principles first put forward by B.F. Skinner regarding verbal behaviour. At its inception in the late 1970s and early 1980s, ACT was originally called 'comprehensive distancing', a concept first suggested by Beck, where the therapy goal was to assist clients to develop healthy distancing from problematic thoughts and mental processes. Then followed a period spanning over 15 years when attention was centred upon empirical development of a therapeutic model. Central to the model was the concurrent development of a behavioural account of human language and cognition, known as relational frame theory (RFT: Hayes, Barnes-Holmes and Roche, 2001). Finally, the therapy model and procedures were comprehensively explicated in the first ACT manual in 1999 (Hayes, Strosahl and Wilson, 1999), and updated in a new edition (Hayes, Strosahl and Wilson, 2012).

BASIC ASSUMPTIONS

ACT takes the view that psychological pain is both universal and normal and is part of what makes us human. ACT therefore challenges the assumption put forward in many mainstream models of psychopathology, and perhaps by society in general, that psychological health is equated with the absence of pain, or conversely that the presence of pain is indicative of faulty or abnormal processes (biological or psychological).

Drawing upon literature into thought/emotion suppression and how humans cope with pain, ACT argues that attempts to control, avoid and/or escape from distressing thoughts and feelings can result in life restrictions and diminished functioning. A core assumption of ACT is that psychological problems are maintained by excessive avoidance of painful experiences (thoughts, feelings, memories, etc.).

Based upon the research into RFT, ACT demonstrates how everyday language processes have the ability to amplify normal psychological pain. The ACT model of psychopathology assumes that psychological suffering can occur when private experiences become the dominant source of behavioural regulation and contact with other environmental contingencies are diminished. The emphasis in ACT is therefore not to alter the frequency or form of distressing internal experiences (although naturally this will occur over the course of an ACT intervention), but rather to change the relationship (function) the client has with these experiences. This is perhaps where ACT differs most from other behavioural and cognitive approaches, which primarily look to change the form or frequency of thoughts and feelings.

The emphasis on changing the function of internal experiences (rather than their frequency or form) is always in the service of assisting clients to take actions consistent with valued life directions. Values differ from goals, which are concrete and time limited, in that they are seen as life directions that don't have an end point. Examples of valued areas that clients might find important could include relationships, family, work/education, spirituality and health. A basic assumption in ACT is to take a pragmatic view to clients solving their problems, focusing on what works to help them move towards their values, as opposed to what is right or true. This stance, also known as the *pragmatic truth criterion*, is taken from the philosophy of functional contextualism.

ORIGINS AND MAINTENANCE OF PROBLEMS

Relational frame theory (RFT) describes how psychological distress is maintained through normal language processes. RFT views the core of human language and cognition as the learned ability to relate anything to anything (or arbitrarily), mutually and in combination. In this way, potentially any internal or environmental stimulus (e.g., sights, sounds, smells, memories) has the capacity to induce painful thoughts and emotions. Research into RFT has shown that relational responding is a basic and learned aspect of language that serves important functions in the outside world, for example problem solving or prediction, but can be problematic when this method of learning is

over-applied to private experiences (Hayes et al., 2001). Importantly, relational responding has the capacity to transform the functions of any property (physical or mental) and modifies other behavioural processes, such as classical and operant conditioning. Smoking may be taken as an example to explain this process. If a smoker is asked to imagine a cigarette, they may note its formal physical properties, such as its colour (e.g., white), its shape (e.g., cylinder) and its contents (e.g., contains tobacco). In addition to the physical properties, however, a cigarette can also acquire informal or arbitrary properties through the human ability to relate anything to anything (relational responding). For example, a cigarette can also be viewed as something that is 'dependable', or like a 'good friend' who is always there in times of crisis. From an RFT perspective, as 'cigarette' and 'best friend' are brought into a relational frame of co-ordination, some of the functions of the cigarette are transformed and share the functions noted in a best friend. Importantly, these functions have the potential to dominate over other sources of behavioural regulation, such as health warnings.

Based upon RFT, ACT essentially sees human psychological problems in terms of a lack of psychological flexibility, which is fostered by two core processes, termed experiential avoidance and cognitive fusion.

Experiential avoidance occurs when an individual is unwilling to stay in contact with certain thoughts, feelings and physical sensations, and also tries to alter the content of these internal experiences even when this causes behavioural or emotional harm. While engaging in such acts of avoidance can often serve to ameliorate problems in the short term, it has the potential to lead to long-term suffering. ACT views experiential avoidance as a central process in the origin and maintenance of psychological problems, the use of which is supported by folk psychology and mainstream culture (e.g., advice to 'just get over it', 'move on', etc.). ACT highlights how significant energy can be expended in attempts to escape, avoid or otherwise control these events, and proposes psychological acceptance as the healthy and adaptive alternative.

Cognitive fusion occurs when individuals fail to notice a distinction between the contents of their thoughts and themselves as the *thinker*, and become *fused* with their thoughts. According to RFT, cognitive fusion becomes a source and maintenance process of psychological problems when people are unhelpfully guided more by the literal content of their thoughts than by what they directly experience in their environment. Clients are often asked to notice and observe the ebb and flow of their private experiences, in an attempt to create a helpful distance and space from their minds (*defusion*) to respond differently. ACT also focuses on helping clients to be in more direct contact with their actual experiences, rather than with what their thoughts are telling them is happening.

Hayes' (1989) research on verbal behaviour suggests that inflexible or unhelpful actions are frequently maintained by rigid verbal rules or beliefs, such as attempts to seek social recognition (e.g., reassurance seeking) and/or inaccurate descriptions of how thoughts and feelings work (e.g., beliefs about thought suppression, 'just get over it', etc.). Furthermore, the presence of these verbal rules can dominate to such an extent that people do not learn from their experience, especially if it does not fit with their own verbal rules. This research suggests that therapists may be more effective adopting an experiential learning approach, using metaphors and exercises that help the client to notice their own experience, rather than providing more or different verbal rules that could carry the risk of maintaining inflexibility.

While ACT does not ignore or neglect biological and social factors that can cause, influence and maintain psychological distress, it places greater emphasis on the person and how they interact with their physical and internal environments (or contexts). The ACT therapist is part of the context of the client and vice versa; the focus for the ACT therapist is on creating a therapeutic context that helps the client pragmatically change their behaviour, in the service of their chosen values.

THEORY OF CHANGE

The main therapeutic goal of ACT is to increase an individual's psychological flexibility. ACT attempts to increase a person's psychological flexibility by:

- using acceptance and mindfulness processes to develop more flexible patterns of responding to their own psychological struggles
- reducing the impact of thoughts and self-conceptualisations (self stories) on behaviour
- helping the client to be in contact with their own (actual) experiences
- increasing the frequency and variety of values-based behaviours.

ACT endeavours to help clarify what areas are important or of value in a client's life (e.g., family, relationships, work/education, etc.) and to notice what barriers (e.g., unhelpful responses to negative thoughts, avoidance patterns) are preventing them from consistently moving towards these values. The focus therefore is not on controlling or reducing painful thoughts or feelings, but

rather on directing behaviour change according to what is important to the individual.

Through acceptance and mindfulness techniques, clients are taught to become more aware and notice their internal mental, physical and emotional processes. This is in the service of allowing clients the opportunity to directly observe such processes without attempting to judge or change them. Once clients become more aware of their own private experiences, they then have the opportunity to make more informed choices on whether to be guided by such thoughts or feelings. Through developing the skills of acceptance, mindfulness and a flexible perspective-taking, an alternative choice is available: to be able to engage in behaviours that are consistent with their deepest values, while 'making room for' experiences.

SKILLS AND STRATEGIES

ACT therapists often adopt an experiential approach to therapeutic change through the use of metaphors and exercises carried out in the session. The aim is to help clients come into direct contact with their learning histories, as opposed to the verbal descriptions of these experiences. By noticing how their minds work and exploring the results of sensible but unworkable strategies, clients are encouraged to consider whether an alternative stance of being more in the present, while holding thoughts and feelings lightly and being in touch with personal values, may produce greater life vitality. The ACT therapist does not try to convince the client of this; the arbiter is the client's own lived experience of the workability of such an approach.

Within ACT there are six core processes; these are viewed as positive psychological skills as opposed to techniques or methods for avoiding and controlling psychological pain (see Figure 5.9.1). None of these six processes is an end in itself; rather, ACT views them as methods and strategies for increasing psychological flexibility and allowing values-based actions. The six core therapeutic processes of ACT are:

- *Acceptance*. The aim is to actively accept what is there, without defence or judgement. The focus is on approaching whatever painful thought or feeling shows up as opposed to avoiding, distracting or controlling these. Experiential acceptance can be thought of as an alternative to experiential avoidance.
- *Defusion*. The aim is to help clients notice the processes of thinking in order to see the functional impact this can have on their behaviour. Clients are invited to

step back and create distance from their thoughts to allow information from the environment to help shape and guide their behaviour.

- *Contacting the present moment.* This is achieved through the use of a variety of approaches, including mindfulness, whereby the therapist helps the client make contact with the here-and-now. Fundamentally, the aim is to assist the client to notice their internal private content (thoughts, feelings, bodily sensations) with a non-judgemental stance without judging, evaluating or critiquing them.
- *Self as context or flexible perspective-taking.* Helping the client to become aware that they have a place or self with which they can observe difficult thoughts and feelings without being caught up with them. Clients learn for themselves how this sense of their self remains constant, and has been with them throughout all of their life experiences.

The final two core ACT processes are known as the approach or activation strategies:

- *Values.* Clarifying with the client what areas are really important in their life. Once the client has identified particular values as important, the ACT practitioner asks the client to evaluate whether their behaviour is in accordance with these.
- *Committed action.* Clients are invited to engage in any behaviour change strategies that enable them to flexibly persist in taking values-based actions.

ACT also draws heavily upon traditional behaviour analysis in using functional analysis and therapeutic techniques derived from learning theory. ACT is not simply a collection of techniques; rather, it is a therapeutic model: practitioners flexibly introduce a variety of strategies in a formulation-based way to the areas/domains most in need of attention.

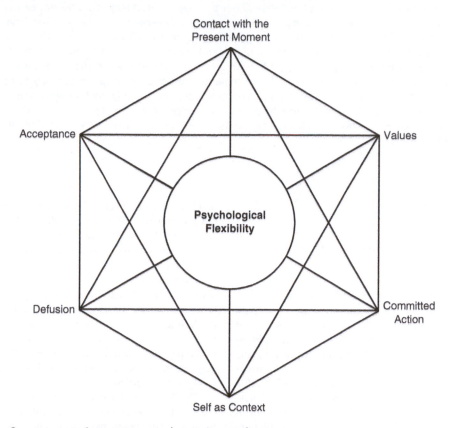

Figure 5.9.1   Core processes in acceptance and commitment therapy

Copyright Steven C. Hayes, used with permission

CASE EXAMPLE

A case example is provided to help illustrate some of ACT's core therapeutic processes. Jill is a 25-year-old woman who presented with anxiety, relationship and work-related difficulties. She reported these problems had been ongoing for the past four years and led to her experiencing a significant amount of distress. Jill was plagued by thoughts of being worthless and a failure. She avoided going into work as she was fearful of being scrutinised by her colleagues, who would realise she was incompetent. This left her with debilitating symptoms of anxiety, including palpitations and difficulty in concentrating. She also struggled to maintain personal relationships outside work, reporting her inability to trust others led to the breakdown of several intimate relationships. After completing an assessment, her therapist suggested that certain behavioural avoidance patterns (not going into work, distracting herself by isolating herself from her friends and drinking excessive amounts of alcohol) were strategies employed to cope with the verbal rules about herself in comparison to others. However, these behaviour patterns led to her feeling low, worthless and resulted in prolonged periods of struggle.

Jill was helped to identify alternative ways of responding to her distress, which included noticing how thoughts (verbal rules) about herself and others led to avoiding people. A central metaphor was introduced, the *quick sand metaphor* (Hayes et al., 1999), which describes how a client's struggle, while understandable, often can have the paradoxical effect of worsening distress. This metaphor also helped Jill make sense of her difficulties and understand her behavioural patterns in a different context, which included the short-term relief gained from avoiding people also served to move her away from sources of comfort. Jill was invited to let go of this struggle through learning to sit with this discomfort in sessions. She gradually started to accept these thoughts and feelings as being a normal, yet painful part of her experiences. After working to strengthen these processes, Jill realised relationships and work were vitally important and did not want to let the struggle her verbal content get in the way of being with others. She chose to make several behavioural commitments, including going into work and socialising more with her friends, while continuing to notice and let go of her struggle when painful thoughts and feelings showed up. This created a greater sense of joy for Jill as she was living a life which was important to her.

RESEARCH EVIDENCE

The empirical development of ACT has pursued a somewhat different path from some other behavioural and cognitive psychotherapy research. Initially, a significant amount of time was spent gaining empirical support for the basic theory behind ACT (RFT), before the focus shifted on to conducting outcome research on the therapeutic model. Research into RFT has yielded over 400 studies over a 30-year period. In addition to both the basic (RFT) and outcome (evaluating the effectiveness of ACT) research, a great deal of attention has also focused on examining the specific ACT process (e.g., acceptance, experiential avoidance, cognitive defusion, values) and how these may influence outcomes such as life satisfaction and wellbeing. Studies investigating these processes have identified that changes in levels of experiential avoidance can have an indirect effect on an individual's level of psychological distress (A-Tjak et al., 2015).

The outcome research into the efficacy of ACT has developed significantly. To date, ACT has over 200 randomised controlled trials (RCTs) conducted with a diverse range of conditions, including psychosis, anxiety, depression, substance misuse, smoking cessation, borderline personality disorder, epilepsy and weight loss. ACT has been shown to be as effective as established psychological treatments (e.g., CBT) for anxiety, depression, substance misuse and somatic problems (A-Tjak et al., 2015).

The American Psychological Association has listed ACT to be an evidenced-based treatment for the treatment of chronic pain, psychosis, addictions and anxiety and depression.

REFERENCES

A-Tjak, J.G.L., Davis, M.L., Norina, N., Powers, M.B., Smits, J.A.J. and Emmelkamp, P.M.G. (2015) A Meta-analysis of the Efficacy of Acceptance and Commitment Therapy for Clinical Relevant Mental and Physical Health Problems. *Psychotherapy and Psychomatics*, 84, 30–36.

Hayes, S.C. (ed.) (1989) *Rule-governed Behavior: Cognition, Contingencies, and Instructional Control*. New York: Plenum.

Hayes, S.C., Barnes-Holmes, D. and Roche, B. (2001) *Relational Frame Theory: A Post-Skinnerian Account of Human Language and Cognition*. New York: Kluwer.

Hayes, S.C., Barnes-Holmes, D. and Wilson, K.G. (2012) Contextual Behavioral Science: Creating a Science More Adequate to Challenge the Human Condition. *Journal of Contextual Behavioral Science*, 1, 1–16.

Hayes, S.C., Long, D.M., Levein, M.E. and Follette, W.C. (2013) Treatment Development: Can We Find a Better Way? *Clinical Psychology Review*, 33, 870–882.

Hayes, S.C., Strosahl, K. and Wilson, K.G. (1999) *Acceptance and Commitment Therapy: An Experiential Approach to Behavior Change*. New York: Guilford Press.

Hayes, S.C., Strosahl, K. and Wilson, K.G. (2012) *Acceptance and Commitment Therapy: The Process and Practice of Mindful Change*. New York: Guilford Press.

Linehan, M.M. (1993) *Cognitive-Behavioral Treatment of Borderline Personality Disorder*. New York: Guilford Press.

Segal, S.V., Williams, M.G. and Teasdale, J.D. (2002) *Mindfulness-based Cognitive Therapy for Depression*. New York: Guilford Press.

RECOMMENDED READING

1. Harris, R. (2009) *ACT Made Simple: An Easy-to-read Primer on Acceptance and Commitment Therapy*. Oakland, CA: New Harbinger.

This easy-to-read introduction into the ACT model offers the interested reader a step-by-step guide on how to use ACT clinically.

2. Oliver, J., Hill, J. and Morris, E. (2015) *ACTivate Your Life: Using Acceptance and Mindfulness to Build a Rich, Meaningful and Fun Life*. London: Robinson.

An accessible, highly practical self-help book, which introduces the reader to the ACT processes and how they can be applied to problems of depression, anxiety, anger and self-esteem.

3. Luoma, J.B., Hayes., S.C. and Walser, R.D. (2007) *Learning ACT: An Acceptance and Commitment Therapy Skills-training Manual for Therapists*. Oakland, CA: New Harbinger.

An excellent book which, complete with videos, helps the budding ACT practitioner develop their existing learning and practical understanding of how to implement ACT.

5.10

COGNITIVE THERAPY

JILL MYTTON AND HEATHER SEQUEIRA

OVERVIEW AND KEY POINTS

Cognitive therapy (CT) is an evidence-based, relatively short-term therapy for a wide range of emotional, psychological, psychosocial and medical issues. It is a collaborative approach between client and therapist that encourages individuals to reflect on and question the meaning attributed to life experiences and to re-evaluate those meanings. The invitation of CT is to experiment with alternative perspectives, strategies and actions that could be a more useful way of responding to life's challenging situations. The aim is to empower people to find effective ways of managing human problems for themselves in the long term.

- Cognitive therapy is practical, action-oriented, rational and aims to help the client gain independence and effectiveness in dealing with real-life issues.
- Cognitive therapy is the most researched and scientifically validated of any of the 'talking therapy' approaches.
- Within the therapeutic relationship is a strong emphasis on collaborative working, self-empowerment and equality.
- The main focus of therapy is on thinking, behaving, feeling and communicating in the here-and-now with an emphasis on promoting 'realistic' and 'helpful' thinking.
- Cognitive therapy helps people learn effective self-helping skills that can stay with them for life.

BRIEF HISTORY

Around the middle of the last century, two eminent American psychologists, Albert Ellis and Aaron Beck, became separately dissatisfied with the psychoanalytic approach in which they were trained. Ellis went on to develop rational emotive behaviour therapy and Beck to develop what has become the most-used cognitive approach to therapy today. Both these therapeutic approaches echo the ideas of the Greek, Roman and Eastern philosophers who argued that the way we think about our world and ourselves plays an important role in our emotions and behaviours. Gautama Buddha once observed, 'We are what we think. All that we are arises with our thoughts, with our thoughts we make the world'

and Stoic philosopher Epictetus noted, 'What disturbs people's minds is not events but their judgments on events'.

Aaron Beck had noticed that the dreams and thoughts of his depressed clients were focused on unrealistic negative ideas, and in 1963 and 1964 he published two seminal papers on the relationship between thinking and depression (Beck, 1963; Beck et al., 1964). In his pioneering studies he analysed the dreams and psychotherapeutic sessions with 50 of his patients and found evidence of 'negative bias' in their thinking. Specifically, Beck identified that people struggling with depression presented with what he termed the Negative Cognitive Triad: a negative view of (1) themselves, (2) the world and (3) the future. Beck hypothesised that depression was a form of 'thought disorder' and concluded that psychoanalytic theory was inadequate to account for his findings. Within psychotherapy this observation represented a ground-breaking shift from traditional psychoanalytic and behavioural ideas by positing the centrality of thinking in our understanding of psychological distress.

Over the next decade, Beck extended his ideas to other psychological disorders, in particular anxiety. In 1976 he published *Cognitive Therapy and the Emotional Disorders* (Beck, 1976), in which he described his model of cognitive processing and the first concepts of cognitive therapy that focused on teaching his clients to identify and alter unhelpful thought patterns. Unlike some therapeutic models that are dominated by a single theoretician, CT has been researched, extended and adapted by other influential clinicians and has differentiated into many empirically based strategies. Although Beck's CT is arguably the most influential approach, other cognitive approaches described in other chapters in this book are also widely used and researched, for example, REBT (Ellis, 2011), meta-cognitive therapy (Wells, 2013), schema therapy (Jacob and Arntz, 2013; Young, Klosko and Weishaar, 2003) and 'Third Wave' cognitive approaches (Kahl, Winter and Schweiger, 2012).

For more than 50 years, CT has delivered an evidence-based way to understand and treat psychological difficulties and has grown into what is arguably one of the most influential and widely validated psychotherapeutic models in the world. It has been extended and adapted to the treatment of many forms of psychological (and body-based) problems. Based on a solid foundation of neurological and behavioural research, there is a large body of clinical evidence supporting its efficacy, with issues including (but not limited to) depression, generalised anxiety disorder, anorexia, obsessive compulsive disorder (OCD), post-traumatic stress disorder (PTSD), phobias, personality disorders, schizophrenia and psychosis (Epp and Dobson, 2010; Naeem et al., 2016; Wykes, 2014). In addition, there is evidence that CT can aid the impact management of physical diseases such as multiple sclerosis, chronic fatigue syndrome, cancer and chronic pain (van Beugen et al., 2014; White, 2001). CT has an established evidence base for use in individual face-to-face therapy, online therapy, group therapy and family therapy.

BASIC ASSUMPTIONS

Human beings have cognitions. We process information coming through our five senses and make interpretations and evaluations about that information. In this way we interact with our life experiences and develop our own individualised meanings about our perceptions and experiences. The central role of cognition in our psychosocial and emotional health is the most basic assumption of CT (Bennett-Levy et al., 2004).

In this way, our emotional and behavioural responses to events in our lives (e.g., a traumatic life event or loss of a relationship) depend not on the event alone, but on the personal interpretation that we give to that event. This explains why people can undergo exactly the same event but experience vastly different emotional responses to the same situation.

Take an example: two people are turned down at the same job interview with similar feedback. Person One attaches the following meaning to this event:

'It's disappointing that I did not get the job, but the feedback indicates that I did not sell my skills sufficiently to prove my worth in the job. I will practise this for future interviews and this will improve my chances of getting a similar position next time.'

In contrast, Person Two attaches a different meaning to the event:

'Being rejected is further evidence that I am a useless and worthless individual. Everyone can see that I am worthless. This means I am likely to fail at future interviews and so it is not even worth trying again.'

In this fictional example, the two people place very different personal meaning on the same event. The different meanings cause (1) different emotional responses and (2) different behavioural actions. It is important to note that the meanings or appraisals that people place on life experiences can be positive or negative, helpful or unhelpful and accurate or distorted. The model CT suggests that mental health issues, such as depression or generalised anxiety, are maintained or made worse by negatively biased and distorted ways of thinking. It is held that the meanings ascribed to experiences depend to a large extent on a person's prior life experiences (particularly early childhood experiences).

Within CT, cognitions are seen to be to be interrelated with feelings, behaviour, physiology and broader life experiences (environment). This is termed 'Reciprocal Interaction'. Thus if a situation is perceived as threatening, a person is likely to experience a physiological reaction (adrenalin released, increasing the heart and breathing rate). Along with these cognitive and physiological responses the person may feel fear (emotion) and could potentially react in terms of their behaviour ('flight or fight'-type behaviour).

ORIGIN AND MAINTENANCE OF PROBLEMS

Beck's cognitive model proposes that distorted and negatively biased thinking underlies psychological disturbance because this style of thinking hinders the individual to cope in the most resilient way to aversive life events or stressful experiences.

Beck identified a number of 'logical errors' that characterise such negative automatic thoughts (NATS):

- *Arbitrary inference*: people sometimes draw conclusions about events without any supporting evidence.
- *Dichotomous or black-and-white thinking*: thinking in extreme terms. For example, using the words 'never' and 'always' rather than 'sometimes' (e.g., I never look attractive; my friend Helen always looks fantastic), or placing experiences in one of two opposite categories, such as beautiful and ugly.
- *Maximisation and minimization*: events are evaluated as much more or much less important than they really are. A normally calm mother losing her temper one day with her child may exaggerate the event (maximisation) and conclude that she is a very bad mother with poor childcare skills (minimisation).
- *Catastrophising*: assuming a negative outcome and jumping to the conclusion that this would lead to a chain of worst possible outcomes. For example, 'If I get nervous during my sales presentation I will forget what I am saying. This means that I will not make the sale, I will get fired and never get another job like this one. I won't be able to pay the mortgage so lose the house, and my young family will be homeless'.
- *Emotional reasoning*: we assume that our emotions reflect the way things actually are. For example, If we feel ignored by a friend, then we assume that we were actually ignored rather than looking for alternative

explanations (e.g., she did not see me)'. 'I feel it, therefore it is true.'

- *Mind reading*: assuming what is going on for others without checking it out. For example, 'My boss did not acknowledge my report so she obviously thinks it's not up to scratch'.
- *Fortune telling*: assuming that things will turn out badly without trying it out. For example, 'It's not worth me asking Alisha for a date as she is bound to turn me down'.

Beck describes the origin of early schemas. Schemas are the unspoken rules or underlying core beliefs often learned through early/childhood experiences, which the individual holds about the self, others and the world. They include enduring patterns of memories, bodily sensations and emotions which act as templates to filter incoming information. When an event occurs, schemas filter out unwanted information, enabling the person to attend to information that is considered important – and is often consistent with the person's earlier experiences.

Schemas can be adaptive and healthy or maladaptive (unhelpful) and unhealthy. Maladaptive schemas tend to be negative, rigid and absolute. When unhealthy schemas are activated, they affect all the stages of information processing. Thus a person with the schema 'I am worthless' will tend to distort incoming information to match this belief. Positive information that could discount this belief may be ignored or distorted: 'The teacher only gave me a good mark because she wants something from me'.

When unhealthy schemas are activated, the individual tends to be prone to negative automatic thoughts. For example, an anxious person may automatically and repeatedly think 'I can't cope with this', and a depressed person may think 'I'm useless, I'll never be able to do this, I give up'. Although people with positive mental health can also experience such automatic thoughts, they are more frequent and disruptive in people with emotional problems.

Aaron Beck and colleagues have produced extensive updates to Beck's original work incorporating perspectives from clinical, cognitive, biological and evolutionary perspectives (Beck and Bredemeier, 2016; Beck and Haigh, 2014). For example, in the Unified Model of Depression (Beck and Bredemeier, 2016), genetic predispositions and early experiences and/or trauma both contribute to the development of information-processing biases (e.g., attentional and memory biases) and biological reactivity to stress (e.g., amygdala, hypothalamic-pituitary-adrenal (HPA) axis, cortisol). The authors indicate how the combination of early experiences, cognitive biases and stress reactivity can gradually lead to the development of the 'Negative Cognitive Triad' (i.e., depressogenic beliefs about the self, world and future). In turn these beliefs heighten the impact of stressful or negative life events (such as physical disease, relationship loss, etc.) by influencing the meaning placed on the experience by the individual. As Beck and Bredemeier go on to describe, once the 'depression programme' is activated, negative thoughts tend to trigger corresponding emotions (e.g., sadness) and behavioural responses (e.g., withdrawal). Furthermore, they highlight that interventions that target predisposing, precipitating or resilience factors can reduce risk and alleviate symptoms.

THEORY OF CHANGE

Change in CT usually means alleviation or reduction of the emotional problems through the intentional adjustment of how we think and respond to our environment. Cognitions are the primary target for change, although the emotional, physiological and behavioural aspects are also clearly acknowledged (Hofmann et al., 2012). It is important to note that another key active ingredient in therapy is a sound therapeutic alliance and in recent years there has been an increased focus on the role of collaboration between the client and the therapist in bringing about change.

Psychoeducation: The process of change begins with psychoeducation about the cognitive model (i.e., that the client's inner cognitive world causally affects emotions and behaviours). The emphasis is on individually conceptualising the client's problems in relation to the cognitive model and providing some early symptom relief. The process continues with the therapist helping the client to set goals, identify and challenge cognitive errors, automatic thoughts and schema and strategies for behavioural change. Ultimately the client is helped to become 'their own therapist' and relapse management is emphasised.

Formulation and case conceptualisation: This is a shared understanding of the client's problems built collaboratively by client and therapist and used to conceptualise the client's problems. A formulation is a tentative hypothesis about the origins and maintenance of the client's difficulties and is conceptualised in terms of:

- The client's current thinking patterns by assessment of their information processing, automatic thoughts and schema.
- Precipitating factors – a consideration of current stressors will help understanding of what has precipitated the present difficulties. These might be related to home, work, family or friends, and examples would include loss, illness, traumatic events or life changes.
- Predisposing factors can include past traumatic events, childhood experiences, genetic vulnerability and personality factors.

The formulation leads to identification of personalised strategies and practical and psychological skills that will empower the client to make the desired changes (Kuyken, Padesky and Dudley, 2008). This collaborative understanding of the client's issues is developed and refined on an ongoing basis as more information and understanding is acquired through the therapeutic process.

SKILLS AND STRATEGIES

Beck maintained from the early days of the development of cognitive behaviour therapy that the context of a sound therapeutic relationship was very necessary, although not sufficient, to bring about change (Beck et al., 1979). The core conditions described by Rogers (1957) of empathy, unconditional positive regard and congruence have to be in place to facilitate the effective use of CT techniques. There is now strong empirical support that CT techniques need the context of a sound therapeutic alliance to be most effective (Beck and Dozois, 2011; Leahy, 2008; Wills and Saunders, 1997). Therapists and clients need to be able to work in a collaborative way with their clients, 'joining forces' against the problem, enabling clients to become their 'own therapist'. This stance, known as Collaborative Empiricism, empowers clients by giving them a say in their own therapeutic process and it fosters self-efficacy.

Cognitive counselling or psychotherapy uses a variety of skills and strategies to bring about change. Techniques are chosen on the basis of the case formulation and in collaboration with the client. Cognitive strategies are central to this approach and are used to help the client identify, examine, reality test and modify automatic thoughts, errors in information processing and schema. They include:

- Socratic questioning: a form of challenging dialogue using systematic questioning and inductive reasoning.
- Cost–benefit analysis: looking at the advantages and disadvantages of holding a particular belief.
- Alternative perspectives: for example, viewing their problem from the perspective of a close relative.
- The use of automatic thought diaries to help clients identify and understand how thoughts influence their emotions and behaviour.
- Emotional regulation strategies, such as distraction, reappraisal and labelling.
- Reality testing: looking at evidence 'for' and 'against' the dysfunctional and distorted thoughts.
- Cognitive rehearsal: practising coping with difficult situations either in role play with the therapist, in imagination, or in real life.

CT advocates homework assignments to encourage clients to practise their newly learned skills in the 'real world' and thus to enhance the therapeutic process. Beck and Dozois (2011) suggest that completion of homework increases the sense of mastery of new strategies and offers the client an increased sense of control over life challenges. These practised skills can equip the client against relapse.

RESEARCH EVIDENCE

CT approaches have undergone the most extensive scientific scrutiny and empirical validation of any of the psychotherapeutic approaches. Thousands of well-controlled studies on the effectiveness of CT have been conducted across a wide range of client problems so we have good understanding of its average overall effects. For example, Hofmann et al. (2012) conducted a review of 106 meta-analyses (studies that combine and analyse the results from multiple similar studies to obtain a superior understanding of how well a treatment works). Hofmann et al. found that CT has the most extensive support for anxiety disorders, hypochondriasis, body dysmorphic disorder, bulimia, anger control problems and general stress. Likewise, Tolin (2010) finds cognitive therapies to be superior over alternative therapies for clients with anxiety and depressive disorders, and argues against claims of treatment equivalence with other psychotherapeutic models. Evidence of effectiveness is also well established for substance use disorder, personality disorders, bipolar disorder and psychosis (Hofmann and Asmundson, 2011; Windgassen et al., 2016).

There is also an increasing body of neuroscientific research indicating a successful CT is correlated with changes in the activity of relevant brain regions (such as those associated with emotional regulation) and is associated with the way that the brain processes and reacts to emotional stimuli (Beevers et al., 2015; Hofmann and Asmundson, 2011). Although it is not yet clear whether these neurobiological changes are a cause or a consequence of recovery with CT, these neuroscientific studies are furthering our level of understanding regarding the possible mechanisms of how CT can bring about changes in mental health.

Contemporary CT is a huge family of interventions with proven efficacy for treating a wide range of mental health conditions. These range from mild everyday issues to the most challenging and serious of mental health problems. CT integrates clinical, emotional, cognitive, biological and evolutionary perspectives into our understanding of mental health. Above all, it is the empathic therapeutic relationship coupled with methods of scientifically proven efficacy that make it among the most useful and far-reaching methods of psychological intervention.

REFERENCES

Beck, A.T. (1963). Thinking and depression. 1. Idiosyncratic content and cognitive distortions. *Archives of General Psychiatry*, 9, 324–333.

Beck, A.T. (1976). *Cognitive Therapy and the Emotional Disorders*. New York: International Universities Press.

Beck, A.T., Allport, F.H., Beck, A.T., Bruner, J.S., English, H.B. and E.A.C., Festinger, L. and Sarbin, T.R. (1964). Thinking and depression. *Archives of General Psychiatry*, 10(6), 561–571.

Beck, A.T. and Bredemeier, K. (2016). A unified model of depression: integrating clinical, cognitive, biological, and evolutionary perspectives. *Clinical Psychological Science*, 4(4), 596–619.

Beck, A.T. and Dozois, D.J.A. (2011). Cognitive therapy: current status and future directions. *Annual Review of Medicine*, 62, 397–409.

Beck, A.T. and Haigh, E.A.P. (2014). Advances in cognitive theory and therapy: the generic cognitive model*. *Annual Review of Clinical Psychology*, 10(1), 1–24.

Beck, A. T., Rush, A., Shaw, B. and Emery, G. (1979). *Cognitive therapy of depression*. New York, NY: Guilford

Beevers, C.G., Clasen, P.C., Enock, P.M. and Schnyer, D.M. (2015). Attention bias modification for major depressive disorder: effects on attention bias, resting state connectivity, and symptom change. *Journal of Abnormal Psychology*, 124(3), 463–475.

Bennett-Levy, J., Butler, G., Fennell, M., Hackman, A., Meuller, M. and Westbrook, D. (Eds) (2004). *Oxford Guide to Behavioural Experiments in Cognitive Therapy*. Oxford: Oxford University Press.

Ellis, A. (2011). *Rational Emotive Behavior Therapy*. Washington, DC: American Psychological Association.

Epp, A. and Dobson, K. (2010). *The Evidence Base for Cognitive Behavioural Therapy*. New York: Guilford Press.

Hofmann, S.G. and Asmundson, G.J.G. (2011). The science of cognitive behavioral therapy. *Behavior Therapy*, 44, 199–212.

Hofmann, S.G., Asnaani, A., Vonk, I.J.J., Sawyer, A.T. and Fang, A. (2012). The efficacy of cognitive behavioral therapy: a review of meta-analyses. *Cognitive Therapy and Research*, 36(5), 427–440.

Jacob, G.A. and Arntz, A. (2013). Schema therapy for personality disorders: a review. *International Journal of Cognitive Therapy*, 6(2), 171–185.

Kahl, K.G., Winter, L. and Schweiger, U. (2012). The third wave of cognitive behavioural therapies. *Current Opinion in Psychiatry*, 25(6), 522–528.

Kuyken, W., Padesky, C.A. and Dudley, R. (2008). The science and practice of case conceptualization. *Behavioural and Cognitive Psychotherapy*, 36(6), 757.

Leahy, R.L. (2008). The therapeutic relationship in cognitive-behavioral therapy. *Behavioural and Cognitive Psychotherapy*, 36(6), 769.

Naeem, F., Khoury, B., Munshi, T., Ayub, M., Lecomte, T., Kingdon, D. and Farooq, S. (2016). Brief Cognitive Behavioral Therapy for Psychosis (CBTp) for schizophrenia: literature review and meta-analysis. *International Journal of Cognitive Therapy*, 9(1), 73–86.

Rogers, C.R. (1957). The necessary and sufficient conditions of therapeutic personality change. *Journal of Consulting Psychology*, 21(2), 95–103.

Tolin, D.F. (2010). Is cognitive-behavioral therapy more effective than other therapies? A meta-analytic review. *Clinical Psychology Review*, 30(6), 710–720.

van Beugen, S., Ferwerda, M., Hoeve, D., Rovers, M.M., Spillekom-van Koulil, S., van Middendorp, H. and Evers, A.W.M. (2014). Internet-based cognitive behavioral therapy for patients with chronic somatic conditions: a meta-analytic review. *Journal of Medical Internet Research*, 16(3), e88.

Wells, A. (2013). Advances in metacognitive therapy. *International Journal of Cognitive Therapy*, 6(2), 186–201.

White, C.A. (2001). Cognitive behavioral principles in managing chronic disease. *Western Journal of Medicine*, 175(5), 338–342.

Windgassen, S., Goldsmith, K., Moss-Morris, R. and Chalder, T. (2016). Establishing how psychological therapies work: the importance of mediation analysis. *Journal of Mental Health*, 25(2), 93–99.

Wills, F. and Saunders, D. (1997). *Cognitive Therapy: Transforming the image*. London: Sage

Wykes, T. (2014). Cognitive-behaviour therapy and schizophrenia. *Evidence-based Mental Health*, 17(3), 67–68.

Young, J., Klosko, J. and Weishaar, M. (2003). *Schema Therapy: A Practitioner's Guide*. New York. Guilford Press.

5.11   COMPASSION FOCUSED THERAPY

SUNIL LAD AND CHRIS IRONS

OVERVIEW AND KEY POINTS

Compassion focused therapy (CFT) was originally developed for people with chronic and complex mental health problems, often associated with high levels of shame and self-criticism. Many people with these problems have experienced difficult early relationships, often characterised by abuse, neglect and a lack of emotional warmth, care and affection. Moreover, they can often find it difficult to experience care, warmth and soothing from others, or themselves. CFT is an integrated therapy designed to address these difficulties, and draws upon a variety of sciences, including evolutionary psychology, neuroscience, developmental and social psychology, and attachment theory. It is a multi-modal therapy and utilises a range of interventions used in Cognitive-Behavioural Therapy (CBT) and other approaches.

BRIEF HISTORY

CFT was developed by Paul Gilbert after observing the difficulties many of his clients had in feeling reassured and less distressed following standard therapy interventions. While able to shift from an overly self-critical and self-blaming perspective, some clients would reflect: 'I now know that I'm not to blame for being abused as a child, but I still *feel* like I'm to blame, that there's something bad or toxic about me'. This phenomenon, sometimes referred to as 'rational-emotional dissociation' (Stott, 2007), appears to be common in therapy, and may block the effectiveness of interventions. Upon further inquiry, many clients describing this experience emphasised that the inner voice tone that was present when trying to bring alternative cognitive perspectives was frequently laden with contempt, hostility and disappointment.

So, CFT interventions began simply by helping clients to practise cultivating supportive and warm emotional tones alongside coping strategies and alternative thoughts. When encouraged to practise a more warm, caring voice tone, many struggled, finding this type of positive effect blocked, alien or even anxiety-provoking. Research has found that many people find that kindness and care can feel uncomfortable and be easily dismissed (Gilbert et al., 2014; Pauley and McPherson, 2010), so CFT involves understanding the blocks, fears and resistances to both compassionate motivation and affiliative feelings in the change process.

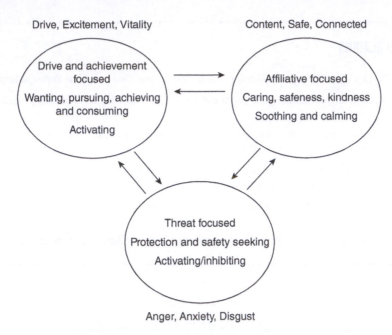

Drive, Excitement, Vitality

Content, Safe, Connected

Drive and achievement focused

Wanting, pursuing, achieving and consuming

Activating

Affiliative focused

Caring, safeness, kindness

Soothing and calming

Threat focused

Protection and safety seeking

Activating/inhibiting

Anger, Anxiety, Disgust

Figure 5.11.1   Three system model (Gilbert, 2009)

BASIC ASSUMPTIONS

CFT is grounded by insights from evolutionary psychology that stress the importance of understanding our brains and emotions in the context of how they have been shaped over millions of years (Gilbert, 2014). From this perspective, we can see that we have very old (in evolutionary terms) parts of our brains – referred to as our 'old brain' – that we share with other animals. Our old brains include basic *motives* to pursue food and reproductive opportunities, to care for our offspring and be oriented by status, basic *emotions* (e.g., anxiety, anger, disgust) and *behaviours* (e.g., fight, flight, submission). However, during the last million years or so, our ancestors evolved along a line that led to a rapid expansion of complex cognitive abilities, including the capacity to imagine, plan, ruminate, mentalise and self-monitor. These new psychologies brought wonderful things in to the world: art, literature, medicines, technology and a capacity to work on complex problems facing our species. However, these same abilities (known as 'new brain' abilities) can also, in certain circumstances, create problems for us. For example, if a zebra is chased but then escapes from a lion, it will begin to calm down and return to what it was doing prior to being chased (e.g., eating grass). However, if we escape a lion that is chasing us, it's unlikely we'd calm down quickly and return to eating our lunch; rather, under conditions of high, old-brain emotion (e.g., anxiety), our

new brains are shaped and influenced. It's likely that we would start to ruminate about what might have happened if the lion had caught us, or worry about whether it will still be there later. In turn, these new-brain patterns of thinking and imagining send signals to our old brain, keeping the threat going. As a result, through no fault of our own, we can easily get caught up in 'loops in the mind' that can drive much of our distress.

Second, building upon the work of a variety of other researchers (e.g., Depue and Morrone-Strupinsky, 2005; Panksepp, 1998), CFT suggests that we have three broad types of affect regulation systems. These are represented in Figure 5.11.1 and include:

- The threat, self-protection system – this system evolved to detect and help us respond to threats in the world. It is associated with certain protective behaviours (e.g., flight, fight, freeze and submit responses) and emotions (such as anger, anxiety and disgust). This system can often be dominant and directs attention to the nature of the threat, and creates 'better to be safe than sorry' styles of thinking (e.g., overgeneralising, catastrophising) which facilitate quick responses.
- The drive system evolved to direct an animal's attention and energy towards attaining resources that would be beneficial for them (e.g., food, shelter, sexual opportunities) and motivate and energise

them into pursuing these. When these resources are attained, this system can leave us experiencing positive emotions and feelings, such as excitement, joy and elation, which may make it more likely that we engage in similar behaviours in the future.

- The soothing-affiliative system – like the drive system, this is also related to positive emotion, but rather than being linked to attaining/achieving something, it allows animals to experience periods of calm and peacefulness when we are not seeking things, and when we are not threatened. It is sometimes referred to as the 'rest and digest' system, and is linked to a number of physiological responses (e.g., part of the parasympathetic system) which are associated with calming and slowing the body down. It is hypothesised that, over time, this system was adapted with the mammals to be linked to the experience of attachment and caring, and may therefore be linked with a 'tend and befriend' motivation.

Here, CFT overlaps with well-established literatures (e.g., Attachment Theory; Bowlby, 1969), modern neuroscience and physiological research, highlighting the powerful role that caring has upon how the brain matures and gene expression (e.g., Belsky and Pluess, 2009; Cozolino, 2007). As infants and children, turning towards caring and support from others when distressed can have a powerful impact on reducing our distress and helping us to feel safe; similarly, as adults, turning towards friends colleagues and loved ones can have similar calming effects. So working with the systems that are involved in the affiliative regulation of emotion is essential in therapy (Gilbert, 2014), and helping people to find ways to access this externally (i.e., with other people) and internally (e.g., through self-soothing, reassurance and compassion) can be an important therapeutic task.

ORIGINS AND MAINTENANCE OF PROBLEMS

CFT takes a biopsychosocial approach to understanding the origin and maintenance of problems. For example, one source of suffering emerges from an understanding that we are a biological organism, and that all organisms age, develop illnesses and diseases, and, ultimately, die. Moreover, some of us will inherit a set of genes that may leave us vulnerable to the development of certain physical and mental health difficulties. So suffering is part of the flow of life.

Within our own lives, we suggest that problems might emerge through multiple sources. Given that our emotion-motivation systems (Figure 5.11.1) are highly sensitive to social context, learning and conditioning, our social contexts can have powerful roles in the origin and maintenance of problems. There is a lot of evidence now that certain

types of relational experiences (e.g., experiencing abuse, bullying) and social/cultural experiences (e.g., deprivation, discrimination, stigma) can influence the development of our affect regulation systems and are associated with future distress. CFT therefore emphasises the importance of *social shaping* – that our experiences in life shape our biology and, consequentially, our psychology. From this perspective, the 'version' of us in the world today is just one of thousands of different versions that could have emerged, if we'd had a different set of experiences. To this end, we often ask our clients (and when training our therapists) to consider how they might be different today if they had been raised by their neighbours rather than in their house or by their family. This is an important tenet of CFT as it helps us to understand that the ways we have learnt to cope and the ways problems have developed are 'not our fault'. This may help the process of clients deshaming aspects of themselves that they had little control over, but help them to learn to take responsibility for how they would like to manage these in the future.

From this perspective, psychological problems can be maintained through a variety of processes, many of which link to various 'loops in the mind' and understandable safety strategies developed to manage fears in the external (i.e., other people) and internal (i.e., arising inside of us) world. For example, to manage concerns that others might reject, criticise or harm us (e.g., physically), we may develop strategies linked to hypervigilance, avoidance or aggression to manage these. To manage internal fears linked to feeling our emotions/memories are overwhelming, or to concerns that we are inferior or a failure, we may develop protective strategies linked to experiential avoidance, repression and/or self-criticism and rumination to manage these. Unfortunately, while all of these strategies can be helpful in the short term, they tend to link to a variety of unintended consequences over time, including keeping the threat going (and, therefore, the initial 'problem').

THEORY OF CHANGE

CFT seeks to facilitate change via the development of a compassionate mind and in building compassionate capacity to engage with one's difficulties. CFT uses a standard definition of compassion as 'a sensitivity to the suffering of self and others, with a commitment to try to alleviate or prevent it'. There are *two key psychologies* that underpin this definition. The first involves developing the ability to notice and turn *towards* and engage *with* suffering (as opposed to avoiding or dissociating from it). Given that engaging with distress and suffering is often difficult, the first psychology of compassion often involves a form of strength and courage to do this. As you will see in Figure 5.11.2 below, the inner circle contains a number of attributes that CFT suggests give

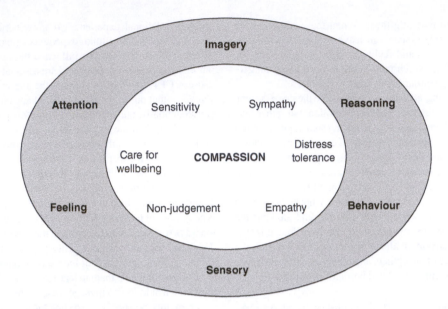

Figure 5.11.2 Compassion circles: the key attributes of compassion (inner circle) and the skills used to develop them (outer circle) (Gilbert, 2009)

rise to this first psychology of compassion: a motivation for wellbeing, sensitivity to suffering, sympathy, distress tolerance, empathy and non-judgement (see Gilbert, 2014).

The second psychology of compassion involves developing wisdom and dedication to find ways to alleviate and prevent suffering. This requires practice in developing skills and techniques that will aid our ability to manage suffering and advance our wellbeing. As a multi-modal therapy, CFT pulls upon a variety of skills training – as represented with the outer circle in Figure 5.11.2 (e.g., attention training, imagery, cognitive and behavioural work, working with cultivating positive affect). The CFT therapist will attempt to help their clients cultivate a 'compassionate mind' by using skills training in the outer circle to help stimulate various attributes of the first psychology of compassion (inner circle).

CFT views the therapeutic relationship as a key mechanism for change, and would share much here with other therapeutic approaches. CF therapists would attempt to embody in themselves the inner qualities of compassion outlined in the inner circle of Figure 5.11.2, along with other core therapeutic skills (e.g., empathy, genuineness, positive regard), as well as being skilled in key therapeutic interventions (e.g., Socratic dialoguing, guided discovery, inference chaining, exposure, behavioural experiments, the use of imagery, chair work and breathing techniques) evident in the outer circle of Figure 5.11.2.

SKILLS AND STRATEGIES

CFT has a number of key steps to help clients to become more sensitive to distress and suffering, and to develop skills to help manage and alleviate this. These include:

- Developing an empathetic and compassionate understanding of how our brains develop and function, and how, for the individual, their affect regulation systems have been sensitised by various experiences in life, and that, out of this, various protective strategies have emerged and how these are likely to have led to a number of unintended consequences. Together, this may be the foundation for an appreciation that 'this is not my fault'.

- Developing a greater awareness of, and ability to engage in and manage, unhelpful threat and drive-system processes.

- Developing capacity to experience positive affect and an inner physiology linked to the soothing-affiliative system that can help in the regulation of the threat system.

- Building the desire and commitment (motivation) to engage with and acquire the skills to alleviate distress by using a variety of trans-therapeutic, multi-modal interventions (see outer circle of Figure 5.11.2).

'James' sought therapy for help with persistently high levels of anxiety. He described concerns related to having Irritable Bowel Syndrome (IBS) and, in particular, a fear that he would not be able to get to a toilet in time when in a social situation. He also described more generalised anxiety symptoms (e.g., others would not like him or would want to harm him), and these all led to him avoiding social situations, feeling isolated and being low in mood. To help manage these feelings (temporarily at least), he described self-medicating by using a variety of substances (e.g., alcohol and cannabis).

James reported that he had experienced physical violence at the hands of his stepfather in his childhood; his mother suffered from mental health problems and regularly drank alcohol to help her cope, and James had few memories of her caring for him or showing any affection. As the eldest child, he also wanted to protect his younger siblings and would take any punishments his stepfather doled out to them. At school he was bullied by other children, but as a teenager he learnt that when he was aggressive people kept away. Unfortunately, after frequently getting into trouble for fighting, he was expelled and left school without any qualifications.

As an adult, for most situations he had learnt to escape and run away as he didn't want to hurt anyone. We formulated his difficulties through the lens of the three system model, as well as longitudinally through a threat-based formulation (see Dale-Hewitt and Irons, 2015). This helps clients to link how early experiences have led to the development of key fears and threats in the 'here-and-now', and how they have learnt to use certain key safety and protective strategies to manage these. The formulation ends with an appreciation of how, unfortunately, these safety strategies sometimes lead to unintended consequences that drive self-criticism, shame and distress. James found this helpful, as it provided an initial opportunity to understand that many of his struggles were understandable in the context of his life experiences, and were (well-intended) attempts to manage threats in the world.

As therapy progressed we formulated his 'loops in the mind' (e.g., worrying about others harming him led to IBS symptoms and then isolating himself from others), and how his three systems were being activated. We then moved into developing through a variety of compassionate mind-training skills, including: attention training and mindfulnesss, soothing rhythm breathing and imagery.

ATTENTION TRAINING AND MINDFULNESS

We explored with James how attention can be thought about like a spotlight – where it focuses, it 'lights up'. He was able to recognise that, like a rusted spotlight, his attention was often stuck 'shining' in one direction – to threat-based concerns (e.g., memories, worries, images). We practised

attention training and mindfulness exercises, and over time he described feeling more able to be aware of when his attention was caught up by his threat system, and to find ways to redirect this in helpful ways.

He learnt that specific thoughts were related to him worrying that others would be disgusted about him if his symptoms flared up, leading to him being ridiculed. As time progressed and he learnt that this threat system was easily triggered, and led to his IBS symptoms flaring up, we started to recognise what activated his threat system and possible reasons why his body was reacting in this way. We started to recognise that as a child he picked up on cues that would lead to him experiencing violence at the hands of his stepfather, and that similar cues could trigger his threat system now.

SOOTHING RHYTHM BREATHING

Like other approaches, CFT uses the emerging 'science of breathing', which suggests that certain types of breathing rhythm (e.g., slower, smoother, deeper) are associated with a variety of helpful benefits in therapy, partly through giving rise to physiological changes (e.g., increased heart rate variability) that may help to regulate threat processing. Using these insights, James learnt how to practise a 'soothing breathing rhythm', and how to utilise this to help regulate occasions in which he began to spiral into highly anxious, threat-based states. This was particularly helpful when engaging in social interactions where he could feel himself getting anxious and panicky.

IMAGERY

Within CFT, compassion can be experienced in three directions or flows. Through the use of imagery, this was generated and cultivated with James in the following ways:

- Self to others (e.g., developing his ideal compassionate self, and using this to direct compassion to others close to him).
- Other to self (e.g., developing an ideal compassionate figure who can give him warmth, care, emanating wisdom and strength at times of difficulty).
- Self to self (e.g., exploring his memories of victimisation and harm and developing a compassionate understanding of the distress, which led to him reducing blame and self-criticism and, consequently, distress).

James initially struggled when thinking about a warm and caring other who could give him compassion, as he felt that if people were nice to him, then they would harm him. As therapy progressed he saw how this was understandable, and was linked to the unpredictable nature in which he had learnt about relationships (e.g., although mostly violent, his stepfather could also be very loving and kind at times). Over time, he was able to develop his compassionate mind through practising 'compassionate letter writing' to help him express understanding, care and support regarding his current and past distress. We also used his compassionate image to help restructure trauma-like memories of his stepfather. Finally, we also used a variety of the skills to help him tolerate some of his 'here-and-now' anxiety, and, crucially, develop the courage to step back from some of his safety strategies and facilitate exposure.

RESEARCH EVIDENCE

As a relatively 'young' psychotherapeutic approach, research into CFT is reflective of this, but findings so far have been promising. For example, a recent systematic review of published CFT studies found positive results for those with mood disorders and high criticism (Leaviss and Uttley, 2015), although suggested the need for further, high-quality studies. In a randomised controlled trial on recovery from psychosis, Braehler et al. (2013) found that, compared to 'treatment as usual', CFT increased compassion and was significantly associated with reductions in depression and perceived social marginalisation, and showed low attrition rates. Additionally, positive results have been found with groups suffering with personality disorder (Lucre and Corten, 2012) and eating disorders (Gale et al., 2014), and those presenting with complex and chronic mental health problems in a day hospital (Gilbert and Procter, 2006).

REFERENCES

Belsky, J. and Pluess, M. (2009). Beyond Diathesis-Stress: Differential Susceptibility to Environmental Influences. *Psychological Bulletin*, 135(6), 885–908.

Bowlby, J. (1969). *Attachment and Loss. Vol.1: Attachment.* London: Hogarth.

Braehler, C., Gumley, A., Harper, J., Wallace, S., Norrie, J. and Gilbert, P. (2013). Exploring change processes in compassion focused therapy in psychosis: Results of a feasibility randomized controlled trial. *British Journal of Clinical Psychology*, 52, 199–214.

Cozolino, L. (2007). The neuroscience of human relationships: Attachment and the developing brain. New York: Norton.

Dale-Hewitt, V. and Irons, C. (2015). Compassion focused therapy. In D. Dawson and N. Moghaddam (eds), *Formulation in Action: Applying Psychological Theory to Clinical Practice* (pp. 161–183). Berlin: De Gruyter Open Ltd.

Depue, R.A. and Morrone-Strupinsky, J.V. (2005). A neurobehavioural model of affiliative bonding. *Behavioural and Brain Sciences*, 28, 313–395.

Gale, C., Gilbert, P., Read, N. and Goss, K. (2014). An evaluation of the impact of introducing compassion focused therapy to a standard treatment programme for people with eating disorders. *Clinical Psychology and Psychotherapy*, 21(1), 1–12.

Gilbert, P. (2009). *The Compassionate Mind*. London: Constable & Robinson.

Gilbert, P. (2014). The origins and nature of compassion focused therapy. *British Journal of Clinical Psychology*, 53(1), 6–41.

Gilbert, P., McEwan, K., Catarino, F., Baião, R. and Palmeira, L. (2014). Fears of happiness and compassion in relationship with depression, alexithymia, and attachment security in a depressed sample. *British Journal of Clinical Psychology*, 53(2), 228–244.

Gilbert, P. and Procter, S. (2006). Compassionate mind training for people with high shame and self-criticism: A pilot study of a group therapy approach. *Clinical Psychology and Psychotherapy*, 13, 353–379.

Leaviss, J. and Uttley, L. (2015). Psychotherapeutic benefits of compassion-focused therapy: an early systematic review. *Psychological Medicine*, 45(5): 927–945.

Lucre, K. and Corten, N. (2012). An exploration of group compassion-focused therapy for personality disorder. *Psychology and Psychotherapy: Theory, Research and Practice*, 86(4), 387–400.

Panksepp, J. (1998). *Affective Neuroscience*. Oxford and New York: Oxford University Press.

Pauley, G. and McPherson, S. (2010). The experience and meaning of compassion and self-compassion for individuals with depression or anxiety. *Psychology and Psychotherapy: Theory, Research and Practice*, 83, 129–143.

Stott, R. (2007). When the head and heart do no agree: A theoretical and clinical analysis of rational-emotional dissociation (RED) in cognitive therapy. *Journal of Cognitive Psychotherapy: An International Quarterly*, 21, 37–50.

RECOMMENDED READING

1. Gilbert, P. (2009). *The Compassionate Mind*. London: Constable & Robinson.

A comprehensive text on the nature of the human mind, distress and suffering, and how compassion may help. It includes various exercises to practise and try out.

2. Gilbert, P. (2010). *Compassion Focused Therapy: The CBT Distinctive Features Series*. Hove: Routledge.

A small but useful guide for therapists interested in using CFT. It takes the reader through the key steps of the therapeutic process, including assessment, formulation and key CFT interventions.

3. Kolts, R. (2016). *CFT Made Simple. A Clinician's Guide to Practicing Compassion Focused Therapy*. Oakland, CA: New Harbinger.

This is a helpful book for therapists wanting to learn about using CFT. It is full of useful examples and case dialogues.

5.12   DIALECTICAL BEHAVIOUR THERAPY

MICHAELA SWALES AND CHRISTINE DUNKLEY

OVERVIEW AND KEY POINTS

Dialectical behaviour therapy (DBT) is a behavioural treatment developed originally to reduce suicidal and self-harm behaviours for clients with a diagnosis of borderline personality disorder. Therapists work in teams and model a dialectical approach to problem solving, combining traditional cognitive-behavioural therapy (CBT) change strategies with mindfulness and Zen-inspired acceptance practices. There are five modalities to the programme of treatment, aimed at redressing clients' skills and motivational deficits:

*   DBT is a psychological therapy nested in a comprehensive programme of care delivered by a team of therapists working in a consultation team.
*   The overarching goal in DBT is 'a life worth living'.
*   Therapists rank problem behaviours by order of severity.
*   Therapy addresses skills deficits by teaching skills.
*   Therapy takes a dialectical approach to problem solving, balancing mindfulness and acceptance with behavioural change strategies.

BRIEF HISTORY

Dialectical behaviour therapy (DBT), developed by Marsha Linehan, evolved from the application of behaviour therapy to the treatment of suicidal behaviours. Linehan began working with suicidal women and subsequently identified that a diagnosis of borderline personality disorder (BPD) occurred frequently in this group. The first trial of DBT (Linehan et al., 1991) was also the first randomised controlled trial demonstrating efficacy for any treatment for clients with a BPD diagnosis. This marked the beginning of an increasing therapeutic optimism about the treatment of BPD, where previously clinicians had been hopeless about the possibility of recovery. The treatment manuals were published in 1993 (Linehan, 1993a, 1993b) and a training programme began the same year. Since then there have been an increasing number of research trials, and clinical programmes have sprung up around the world. DBT is a principle-driven treatment (Swales and Heard, 2017: Chapter 1) that focuses on the treatment of specific behaviours, most commonly suicidal behaviours, in the context of a specific diagnostic group.

BASIC ASSUMPTIONS

DBT principles are derived from three core philosophical perspectives: behaviourism, Zen and dialectics. DBT adopts a radical behaviourist stance. Thus, DBT therapists conceptualise the diagnostic criteria for BPD as a series of behaviours, both covert and overt, that can be operationalised and changed using the principles of learning theory. If clients no longer experience and report the internal behaviours of the diagnosis (e.g., sense of emptiness) and do not engage in the readily observable behaviours (e.g., suicide attempts), then the diagnosis no longer applies. A behavioural conceptualisation of diagnosis therefore provides hope that recovery from BPD is possible.

While DBT was initially developed for the treatment of individuals with a BPD diagnosis, consistent with its radical behaviourist stance, Linehan translated the problems described by the diagnosis into five separate systems of dysregulation, each of which is targeted for change within the treatment:

- Emotional dysregulation (affective lability and problems with anger)
- Interpersonal dysregulation (chaotic relationships and fears of abandonment)
- Self-dysregulation (identity disturbance and sense of emptiness)
- Behaviour dysregulation (suicidal and impulsive behaviours)
- Cognitive dysregulation (paranoid ideation and transient dissociated states)

DBT conceptualises clients' inability to regulate their emotions as driving disturbances in each of the other domains of functioning. In turn, disruption in each domain impacts on the others, which has the potential to further intensify any emotion dysregulation. Suicidal, self-harm and impulsive behaviours are seen either as natural consequences of extreme levels of dysregulation or as attempts to reregulate affect. The *Diagnostic and Statistical Manual of Mental Disorders* (5th Edition: DSM-5; American Psychiatric Association, 2013) gave extensive consideration to changing the categorical system for diagnosing personality disorder into a continuous trait-based system. The proposed revisions to the *International Classification of Diseases* (10th revision: ICD-10; World Health Organisation, 2016) are considering moving from a categorical system to one based initially on severity and then on personality traits. By translating the diagnostic 'symptoms' into these systems of dysregulation and identifying behaviours within each system, DBT remains resilient to these proposed changes within the diagnostic classification system.

In her early work, Linehan encountered several problems in applying behaviour therapy to this client group. Often clients did not complete homework tasks or implement solutions developed in therapy. They presented each week with a different problem to solve, driving numerous changes in treatment direction. Sometimes they failed to return to sessions at all. In resolving these problems, Linehan hypothesised that clients struggle to engage with the therapy because the relentless focus on change invalidates their experience of themselves and their capabilities. She proposed that when faced with multiple life problems combined with beliefs that change is impossible or undeserved, participating in a change-focused therapy presents major challenges. Tensions build as the therapist pushes harder for change but the client increasingly finds change intolerable. To mitigate the impact of a persistent change-focused agenda Linehan actively sought an acceptance-based counter-point. If the learning theorists were experts in the science of change, who were the experts in the art of acceptance? She turned to the ancient philosophy of Zen and the practice of mindfulness. This thread of acceptance weaves throughout the therapy, informing the attitudes, strategies and skills that comprise the elements of the treatment.

How can such contrasting strategies of change and acceptance form a cohesive therapy? Linehan's answer is to house them within an overarching dialectical philosophy. Dialectics emphasises the interconnectedness and wholeness of reality such that multiple perspectives on reality are not only possible, but encompass truth. Using the principles of dialectics, DBT therapists work to find the value in contrasting and opposing views on problems and solutions, to find solutions that respect the wisdom in each perspective. Embracing dialectics in this way assists to defuse the tension that often develops in a therapeutic context where the client experiences intense emotional pain and change is difficult and slow.

ORIGIN AND MAINTENANCE OF PROBLEMS

Linehan's biosocial theory of the development of BPD suggests that the disorder occurs as a result of an ongoing transactional process between emotional vulnerability in the individual and an invalidating environment. Features of emotional vulnerability include a highly sensitive nervous system with low threshold for emotional reactions. Once activated by emotional stimuli, responses are fast, extreme and slow to return to a baseline position. This pervasive emotional dysregulation adversely affects a number of different systems within the individual: cognition, interpersonal responses, identity formation and behaviour. Linehan likens the effect to a burn victim, missing a layer of 'emotional skin', so every interaction is painful. Invalidating

Table 5.12.1 Five functions of dialectical behaviour therapy

Function	Modes in standard outpatient DBT
Enhance client capabilities	Skills training group
Improve motivational factors	Individual one-to-one therapy
Assure generalisation to the natural environment	Telephone coaching
Enhance therapist capabilities	Weekly therapist consultation meeting
Structuring the environment	Case management, family/marital/community interventions

environments compound the problem, so a chain reaction occurs, intensifying the effects on both the environment and the individual until full BPD is evident.

An 'invalidating environment' is one which negates or dismisses the individual's internal experiences and behavioural responses regardless of their actual validity. Emotions are dismissed, as in 'what are you scared of? Just do it', or criticised, such as 'you're over-reacting', or simply ignored. The individual learns to ignore her own internal responses, instead searching the environment for cues on how to respond. For example, a child of alcoholic parents stops attending to internal cues of hunger, as food only arrives when her parents are sober. Instead she searches for signals in her parents that they might offer food, and her 'hunger' feelings become redundant. When ignored over time, emotions become bewildering and unmanageable. The environment struggles to provide an effective response to emotional volatility and may inadvertently reinforce dysfunctional behaviour. For example, an individual may repeatedly say, 'I can't bear it' when a demand is made on her, and is told, 'just get on with it'. Then she self-harms and the demand is removed. Even the most caring environment may become invalidating in an attempt to suppress dysfunctional behaviour. Linehan provides a no-blame model, looking at the incremental, transactional development of problems rather than ascribing a single cause.

The result of this transactional process is a skills deficit within the individual: clients cannot up-regulate physiological arousal when required, and when emotionally aroused cannot turn attention away from the stimulus. Information processing is impaired, preventing the organisation of behaviour in the service of her short- or long-term goals. Consequently, clients engage in mood-driven behaviour, which may be impulsive or destructive, and at times shut down or freeze. Self-harming or suicidal thoughts and behaviours may function to regulate affect in the short term by providing an escape from the cycle or to change an emotional state. Consequences in the environment (e.g., caregiving or rejection by others) can act to increase or reduce the likelihood of further repetitions of the behaviour in a constantly evolving set of actions and reactions. In summary, DBT conceptualises clients' problems as arising from both capability and motivational deficits that are addressed in the five modalities of a comprehensive DBT programme (see Table 5.12.1).

THEORY OF CHANGE

DBT therapists are working towards helping their clients achieve a 'life worth living' by reducing behaviours that interfere with the accomplishment of this goal and at the same time increasing and strengthening skills. The change process begins with the client entering a phase of pre-treatment, in which goals are identified and commitment is obtained, before entering the full programme. Table 5.12.1 shows the five functions of DBT and the modes through which they are delivered in a standard outpatient programme.

DBT is a team treatment where a community of therapists treats a community of clients. A client in DBT will have one primary therapist, who provides their individual therapy, and will also be expected to attend a separate skills training component of the programme. The primary therapist will also provide out-of-session help to generalise skills – usually via telephone coaching. The individual therapists and skills trainers all attend a weekly therapists' consultation meeting where they get support to adhere to the principles of the treatment and share multiple perspectives on solving clients' problems.

Each modality of therapy has its own target hierarchy. Within individual therapy, behaviours are addressed in the following order:

- Life-threatening behaviour, for example, suicidal or homicidal actions, non-suicidal self-injury, and urges to harm self or others.
- Therapy-interfering behaviour, including behaviours that prevent the therapist from delivering therapy or the patient from receiving it. For example, missing sessions, repeatedly saying 'I don't know'.

- Quality of life-interfering behaviour, including severe destabilising conditions. For example, behaviours leading to homelessness or unemployment. Also, behaviours that are part of other comorbid conditions, such as major depressive disorder or bulimia nervosa.

At the start of therapy a unique 'target hierarchy' is drawn up for each client, with specific behaviours to be changed. This may be modified during the course of treatment.

The predominant mechanism of change in DBT is behavioural rehearsal. Clients in DBT track the target behaviours on a diary card and in each individual session a behavioural chain and solution analysis is conducted on the most severe target behaviour on the card. Events preceding and following the target behaviour are analysed to identify controlling variables of that specific incident. New, more skilful, behaviours are rehearsed in session (Heard and Swales, 2015).

SKILLS AND STRATEGIES

The primary skill of the DBT therapist is to maintain a dialectical approach, welcoming tensions that arise as an opportunity to seek out the validity in both sides of the argument, and move towards synthesis. The therapist models how to move away from the characteristic black-and-white thinking by looking for new perspectives and finding a 'both/and' position. Therapists validate the functional and logical components of clients' behaviours before highlighting dysfunctional aspects. For example, if the client says, 'I know people are repulsed by my scarring, so I hide at home', the therapist will validate, 'It is reasonable to think that some people are repulsed by scarring, and staying home makes sense when you want to avoid meeting that response. Are there any other, less isolating ways to solve this?' Each problem situation is viewed as a practice opportunity for new skills, and in particular those learned in the skills training sessions (see above). The therapist favours consulting with the client on how to manage problems in her environment, rather than instructing the environment on how to manage the client.

A range of dialectical strategies is used, the main one being the balance between acceptance and change that the therapist weaves seamlessly into the solution analyses of the clients' targeted behaviours. The therapist also highlights patterns of behaviour common to BPD which Linehan (1993a) referred to as secondary targets or dialectical dilemmas:

- Active passivity versus apparent competence.
- Unrelenting crises versus inhibited grieving.
- Emotional vulnerability versus self-invalidation.

The therapist moves back and forth between a reciprocal style of communication and an irreverent off-beat manner, keeping an eye on the flow of the session and altering styles strategically to maintain therapeutic momentum.

The weekly consultation meeting is where therapists apply the principles of the therapy to themselves. Beginning with a mindfulness practice, the emphasis is then on 'therapy for the therapist' – being alert to signs of burnout, seeking out the validity in opposing opinions to ensure nothing is being missed and working towards comprehensive, dialectical solutions to any problems presented. An observer ensures the team adheres to the model.

The four skills training modules in DBT are mindfulness, emotion regulation, interpersonal effectiveness and distress tolerance (Linehan, 1993b, 2015). Mindfulness is considered a core skill. Therapists teach clients to turn the spotlight of their attention away from distressing stimuli, to identify what would be effective and to take action when needed. Together they acknowledge that change is inevitable, and that each situation that cannot be changed must be tolerated until natural change occurs. The therapist and client are encouraged to use skilful means and evaluate the outcome without judgement, slowly shaping more effective behaviour (Dunkley and Stanton, 2013). In emotion regulation, they are taught to identify emotions and their function, and how to act opposite to an unjustified emotion. In interpersonal effectiveness, they learn to assess their priorities in a given situation, to make skilful requests or decline unwanted invitations. In distress tolerance, they learn to get through a crisis without making it worse, and accept distressing situations that cannot be changed immediately or in the longer term.

CASE EXAMPLE

Sara is a 23-year-old client of the community mental health team. She lives alone and has taken three serious overdoses in 12 months. She cuts her arms and binge drinks. She started in DBT two months ago, having had four sessions of pre-treatment with her therapist, Zac. Together she and Zac identified her goal to go to college to study Art.

In pre-treatment Zac explained how Sara's behaviours are often a way to manage uncomfortable emotions. He described how developing new skills could reduce the behaviours that are preventing her from getting to college. Sara and Zac meet every Tuesday for her individual DBT therapy session.

Each day Sara fills in her diary card, keeping track of the behaviours that she and Zac placed on her target hierarchy. Also on her diary card is a list of all the skills she is learning in the skills training group. Each time she practises a skill she circles it on her card.

Sara attends the skills training group every Thursday with nine other patients. She has completed two sessions of mindfulness and a six-week module of interpersonal effectiveness. Skills trainers Jo and Gwen teach a new skill and set homework one week, then take feedback the following week to assess their clients' learning. The three modules – interpersonal effectiveness, emotion regulation and distress tolerance – are taught on a rolling programme with two sessions of mindfulness between modules.

During weekly individual therapy with Zac, Sara knows they will focus on the highest priority incident from her diary card that week. If Sara has recorded an incident of cutting her arm, then together she and Zac analyse the steps leading up to and following the cutting and actively rehearse more skilful solutions. If Sara tries a solution and it doesn't work, Zac helps analyse what went wrong; sometimes she has misapplied a skill or needs to combine two or three skills together. Last week she had urges to cut herself following a row with a neighbour, so Zac role-played the scenario with her, so that she could practise her interpersonal effectiveness skills. Afterwards he reminded her that if she was struggling to use the skill she could call him (using telephone consultation) to get some additional skills coaching.

RESEARCH EVIDENCE

Since the first research trial (Linehan et al., 1991), most studies have been conducted on the original client population: women with a diagnosis of BPD presenting with recurrent suicidal behaviour. Five further randomised controlled trials on chronically suicidal women with a BPD diagnosis have now been published (Clarkin et al., 2007; Koons et al., 2001; Linehan et al., 2006; McMain et al., 2009; Verheul et al., 2003). In summary, these trials demonstrate that DBT is efficacious in reducing suicidal behaviours (including non-suicidal self-injury and suicide ideation) and their severity, decreasing hospital stays and improving treatment retention (Koons et al., 2001; Linehan et al., 1991, 2006; Verheul et al., 2003). In later trials that have compared DBT either to a very rigorous control condition (Linehan et al., 2006; McMain et al., 2009) or to other active treatments (Clarkin et al., 2007), benefits remain but are less marked in contrast.

DBT has also been tested for efficacy with other client groups. Two trials of DBT for women with both BPD and substance dependence demonstrated benefits in decreasing substance misuse (Linehan et al., 1999, 2002). There is also an emerging evidence base for the use of DBT with adults with a diagnosis of binge-eating disorder (Telch et al., 2001) and in older adults with comorbid depression and personality disorder (Lynch et al., 2003, 2007). Studies in inpatient settings, although not randomised, have also demonstrated the usefulness of DBT in managing behavioural disturbance (Bohus et al., 2004).

REFERENCES

American Psychiatric Association (2013) *Diagnostic and Statistical Manual of Mental Disorders* (5th ed.). Washington, DC: APA.

Bohus, M., Haaf, B., Simms, T.M.F.L., Schmahl, C., Unckel, C., Lieb, K. and Linehan, M.M. (2004) Effectiveness of inpatient dialectical behavioral therapy for borderline personality disorder: a controlled trial. *Behaviour Research and Therapy*, 42: 487–499.

Clarkin, J.F., Levy, K.N., Lenzenweger, M.F. and Kernberg, O.F. (2007) Evaluating three treatments for borderline personality disorder: a multiwave study. *American Journal of Psychiatry*, 164: 922–928.

(Continued)

(Continued)

Dunkley, C. and Stanton, M. (2013) *Teaching Clients to Use Mindfulness Skills: A Practical Guide*. London: Routledge.

Heard, H.L. and Swales, M.A. (2015) *Changing Behavior in DBT®: Problem Solving in Action*. New York: Guilford Press.

Koons, C.R., Robins, C.J., Tweed, J.L., Lynch, T.R., Gonzalez, A.M., Morse, J.Q., Bishop, G.K., Butterfield, M. and Bastian, L.A. (2001) Efficacy of dialectical behavior therapy in women veterans with borderline personality disorder. *Behavior Therapy*, 32: 371–390.

Linehan, M.M. (1993a) *Cognitive Behavioral Treatment of Borderline Personality Disorder*. New York: Guilford Press.

Linehan, M.M. (1993b) *Skills Training Manual for Borderline Personality Disorder*. New York: Guilford Press.

Linehan, M.M. (2015) *DBT® Skills Training Manual*. New York: Guilford Press.

Linehan, M.M., Armstrong, H.E., Suarez, A., Allman, D. and Heard, H. (1991) Cognitive behavioral treatment of chronically suicidal borderline patients. *Archives of General Psychiatry*, 48: 1060–1064.

Linehan, M.M., Comtois, K.A., Murray, A.M., Brown, M.Z., Gallop, R.J., Heard, H.H., Korslund, K.E., Tutek, D.A., Rynolds, S.K. and Lindenboim, N. (2006) Two-year randomized controlled trial and follow-up of dialectical behavior therapy vs therapy by experts for suicidal behaviors and borderline personality disorder. *Archives of General Psychiatry*, 63: 757–766.

Linehan, M.M., Dimeff, L.A., Rynolds, S.K., Comtois, K.A., Shaw-Welch, S., Heagerty, P. and Kivlahan, D.R. (2002) Dialectical behavior therapy versus comprehensive validation plus 12-step for the treatment of opioid dependent women meeting criteria for borderline personality disorder. *Drug and Alcohol Dependence*, 67: 13–26.

Linehan, M.M., Schmidt, H., Dimeff, L.A., Craft, J.C., Kanter, J. and Comtois, K.A. (1999) Dialectical behavior therapy for patients with borderline personality disorder and drug-dependence. *The American Journal on Addictions*, 8(4): 279–292.

Lynch, T.R., Cheavens, J.S., Cukrowicz, K.C., Thorp, S., Bronner, L. and Beyer, J. (2007) Treatment of older adults with co-morbid personality disorder and depression: a dialectical behavior therapy approach. *International Journal of Geriatric Psychiatry*, 22: 131–143.

Lynch, T.R., Morse, J.O., Mendelson, T. and Robins, C.J. (2003) Dialectical behavior therapy for depressed older adults: a randomized pilot study. *American Journal of Geriatric Psychiatry*, 11(1): 33–45.

McMain, S.F., Links, P.S., Gnam, W.H., Guimond, T., Cardish, R.J., Korman, L. and Steiner, D.L. (2009) A randomized trial of dialectical behavior therapy versus general psychiatric management for borderline personality disorder. *American Journal of Psychiatry*, 166(12): 1365–1374.

Swales, M.A. and Heard, H.L. (2017). *Dialectical Behaviour Therapy: Distinctive Features*. Second edition. London: Routledge.

Telch, C.F., Agras, W.S. and Linehan, M.M. (2001) Dialectical behavior therapy for binge eating disorder. *Journal of Consulting and Clinical Psychology*, 69(6): 1061–1065.

Verheul, R., van den Bosch, L.M.C., Koeter, M.W.J., De Ridder, M.A.J., Stijnen, T. and van den Brink, W. (2003) Dialectical behaviour therapy for women with borderline personality disorder: 12-month, randomised clinical trial in The Netherlands. *British Journal of Psychiatry*, 182(2): 135–140.

World Health Organisation (2016) *International Classification of Diseases* (10th ed.) ICD-10. Geneva: WHO.

RECOMMENDED READING

1. Linehan, M.M. (2015) *DBT® Skills Training Manual*. New York: Guilford Press.

Contains instructions, clinical examples and teaching points for the delivery of the full skills training programme, and includes a link to download all the handouts in electronic format.

2. Linehan, M.M. (1993) *Cognitive Behavioral Treatment of Borderline Personality Disorder*. New York: Guilford Press.

The original text explaining Linehan's underpinning theory of DBT and the core components of treatment.

3. Heard, H.L. and Swales, M.A. (2015) *Changing Behavior in DBT®: Problem Solving in Action*. New York: Guilford Press.

Further exploration of the problem-solving strategies used in DBT, including common pitfalls in treatment delivery and how to avoid them.

5.13

EYE MOVEMENT DESENSITISATION AND REPROCESSING (EMDR)

CATHERINE KERR AND LIZ ROYLE

OVERVIEW AND KEY POINTS

Eye Movement Desensitisation and Reprocessing (EMDR) is a comprehensive psychotherapeutic approach recognised by the National Institute for Health and Care Excellence (NICE, 2005) for the effective treatment of post-traumatic stress disorder (PTSD). In her core text, Shapiro (2001) describes EMDR as an integrative psychotherapy, sharing key elements of traditional approaches. A unique aspect of EMDR is its use of Bilateral Stimulation (BLS), in the form of eye movements, tapping or tones, to process disturbing memories.

- The theoretical underpinning of EMDR is the Adaptive Information Processing model.
- This posits that the brain has an innate healing process that can be stimulated by BLS.
- It is believed that present dysfunction is caused by maladaptively stored memories of distressing events.
- EMDR unhooks the negative emotions from a memory, enabling recall without distress, and facilitates links to adaptive memory networks.
- EMDR consists of a structured eight-phase protocol.

BRIEF HISTORY

EMDR was developed by American psychologist Francine Shapiro in 1987 in something of a chance breakthrough. While out walking and experiencing some disturbing thoughts, she realised that her thought patterns were somehow improving. She started to pay attention to this process and noticed that, when she was affected by negative reflections, her eyes spontaneously moved from side to side. At the same time, her disturbing thoughts lost their negative emotional charge. She hypothesised that there was a link between these two events. Fascinated by this, she tested her theory on colleagues before embarking on rigorous research. Her first clinical study concentrated on the treatment of veterans of the Vietnam War and survivors of sexual assault (Shapiro, 1989). Clinical input was gathered from trained practitioners around the world leading to a refinement of the model. Originally called Eye Movement Desensitisation (EMD), in 1990 the approach was renamed EMDR to incorporate the cognitive and emotional restructuring elements. Subsequent extensive research further developed the principles, protocols and procedures of the psychotherapeutic approach of EMDR as we know it today.

BASIC ASSUMPTIONS

EMDR is underpinned by the belief that the brain has the same self-healing capacity as the body. Just as the body fights infection and strives for physical balance, so the brain strives to move on from traumatic events and regain psychological balance. *It is posited that the BLS used within EMDR triggers this innate healing process.*

Many psychotherapeutic approaches hold that the majority of our adult belief systems are rooted in childhood experiences. The Adaptive Information Processing (AIP) model of EMDR (Shapiro, 2001, 2007) similarly suggests that most psychopathology has its roots in distressing past experiences that have been maladaptively stored. This prevents the associated thoughts, images, emotions and physical sensations being correctly processed, thus remaining intrusive, easily triggered and leading to current dysfunctions. Such maladaptively stored memories are not able to link to more adaptive memory networks. An example of this is someone who, as a child, was humiliated in a classroom situation. The associated shame, beliefs of defectiveness and physical feelings, such as blushing and anxiety, are kept alive and easily triggered even as an adult. This may lead to social anxiety or general feelings of low self-esteem. There is no emotional link with adaptive information, such as 'I was a child – the teacher was the one who was defective for allowing this'. EMDR seeks to link the old negative belief to a more positive one that can be believed both intellectually and emotionally. This is then 'installed' with the desensitised memory. AIP theory suggests that the mind will not accept a positive cognition that is not ecologically valid. Therefore it would not be possible to install 'It's not my fault' when processing a road traffic accident where the client was drink-driving and entirely to blame. Another example of an invalid positive cognition would be 'I'm safe' where the client faces ongoing danger. In such cases, a more adaptive positive cognition may be 'I can learn from this', 'It's over' or 'I can make changes'.

ORIGIN AND MAINTENANCE OF PROBLEMS

EMDR case conceptualisation takes a three-pronged approach. It aims to locate the *past events* that underpin the current dysfunction. These may be obvious or very subtle and can even include pre-verbal events. In cases of multiple traumatic events, the clinician will aim to cluster memories that share a common aspect. An example could be a common belief, such as 'I am worthless', or a theme, such as multiple incidents of sexual abuse. Where possible, they will be aiming for a generalisation effect, whereby targeting one memory in a cluster processes many others simultaneously.

The clinician will next process *current situations* that exacerbate the problem. Finally, they will target *future events* where a different response is desired. Often once the past events have been processed, the present triggering events and the anticipation of future dysfunction have largely resolved, although some clients may need help in learning new skills, such as assertiveness. Having changed beliefs that they may have held for a lifetime can mean they need support in creating their new life.

A useful analogy here is that of a weed. The client can be helped to remove the head of the weed, effectively managing symptoms and making state changes or EMDR can be used to target the 'touchstone' memory, the earliest occurrence of a negative belief. By processing this, the root of the weed is removed, thus making trait changes.

THEORY OF CHANGE

As with other psychotherapies, there is not a definitive answer to how EMDR works. BLS (particularly via eye movements) is viewed as the mechanism of change in EMDR. Questions have been raised about the necessity of this aspect of EMDR, but research has shown a moderate and significant enhancing effect of eye movements (Lee and Cuijpers, 2013). Varied theories have emerged relating to how BLS effects change.

Eye movements are theorised to reduce the vividness of emotional images by interfering with working memory processes (van den Hout et al., 2014). Put simply, desensitisation occurs due to the inherent limitations of viseo-spatial and central executive working memory resources.

Many studies have investigated the neurobiological mechanisms of BLS. Neuro-imagery studies of EMDR consistently show that BLS has the ability to facilitate the activation of areas of the frontal lobes (Bergmann, 2010).

Increased interhemispheric communication potentially enhances the retrieval of episodic memories which, once processed, can be properly consolidated and stored (Propper and Christman, 2008).

Another theory is that BLS links into the same processes that occur during Rapid Eye Movement (REM) sleep (Stickgold, 2002) when the brain is most active in sifting through the day's events and laying down new memories. In the authors' opinion, this would better explain the forging of adaptive links that occur as the brain naturally seeks to extract learning and gain insight from each new experience.

During processing, the images, sounds and thoughts related to the target can change. Clients may remember further details or associate to other related instances as memory networks are activated. There may be changes in emotions and somatic sensations, with these rising, peaking then falling away or changing. The overall effect will be to reduce the disturbance and for the client to spontaneously and naturally begin to have more adaptive thoughts and emotions about the event.

SKILLS AND STRATEGIES

EMDR is a structured protocol consisting of eight phases, including history-taking and treatment planning, preparation, assessment, desensitisation, installation, body scan, closure and re-evaluation (Shapiro, 2001).

PHASE 1: HISTORY-TAKING

In phase 1, the clinician takes a full client history and explores current symptoms, goals and preferences for therapy. The clinician conceptualises the case in accordance with AIP theory and, from this, determines which memories to target and in what order. Safety factors and the client's current level of functioning are explored and it is particularly important to screen for dissociative disorders and poor ego strength as the standard EMDR protocol is not appropriate for these presentations.

PHASE 2: PREPARATION

Although it is important to maintain fidelity within the standard protocol, this is not at the expense of building a solid therapeutic alliance and ensuring the client has a safe space to make sense of their distress. In phase 2, the therapeutic relationship is being strengthened and a clear explanation of EMDR processing given. It is important that the client understands the process and that any fears or expectations are addressed. As part of this, eye movements or other forms of BLS are tested and the clinician checks that the client can maintain dual awareness between past distress and their present safety. This balance of 'a foot in the past and a foot in the present' provides the optimal state for processing.

The clinician teaches self-soothing, affect management and stabilisation techniques so that they and their client are confident that any disturbance can be tolerated. BLS can be used to stimulate positive memory networks and are often introduced in this phase. The clinician can enhance the client's inner resources, such as states of calm, self-compassion and strength, with BLS.

In reality, phases 1 and 2 may run concurrently and may take several weeks, particularly for complex trauma.

PHASE 3: ASSESSMENT

In the assessment phase the client is helped to identify the components of the target memory in a structured way. This includes:

- A target image representing the worst aspect of the memory.
- An associated negative belief about the self (the negative cognition) that is a currently held, irrational and negative thoughts, e.g., I am in danger, I am helpless.
- The emotions and body sensations that arise when the memory is accessed.
- A positive cognition that the client would prefer to believe about themselves both now and in respect to the target memory. This helps activate any adaptively stored material.

The clinician establishes baseline measures so that subsequent progress can be checked. The Subjective Units of Disturbance (SUD) scale is used to measure the total disturbance and the Validity of Cognition (VOC) scale measures how much the client believes the positive cognition at an emotional, not an intellectual, level.

Drawing out the components in this way activates the memory ready for processing.

PHASE 4: DESENSITISATION

In phase 4, the clinician provides BLS while the client processes the memory.

As AIP posits that the BLS stimulates the brain's innate healing process, the clinician needs to intervene minimally. Their role now is to reassure the client and maintain optimal levels of arousal for effective processing. Clients are asked to just notice whatever comes up during processing and the clinician will take very brief feedback between sets of BLS so as to be able to oversee the process. Occasionally processing gets stuck and the clinician will have a range of interventions to facilitate the return to processing.

At the end of phase 4, the SUD for the target will be reduced to 0 or 1 out of 10.

PHASE 5: INSTALLATION

The clinician helps the client to re-evaluate the suitability of the positive cognition, then, using BLS, integrates this with the targeted memory, thereby strengthening and enhancing associations to positive memory networks. The VOC scale is used to evaluate the effectiveness of the positive cognition.

PHASE 6: BODY SCAN

The clinician moves on to check for any residual somatic disturbance that may be raised when the client holds the original memory in mind while considering the positive cognition. They help the client to scan for any tension, discomfort or unusual sensations that need to be processed with BLS.

PHASE 7: CLOSURE

Not every target is fully processed in a single session, so the clinician needs to be able to contain the remaining disturbance and stabilise the client before they leave the session.

Whereas in phase 4, discussion was deliberately avoided so as not to interfere with processing, now there is an opportunity for debriefing and exploration of insights gained. The clinician may close with a relaxation exercise and will help the client to identify helpful self-care strategies for the week ahead. Processing will continue for some time after the session so clients are asked to keep a log to note any new thoughts, feelings, behaviours, dreams or memories that arise in between sessions. This information is crucial for the next phase of the protocol.

PHASE 8: RE-EVALUATION

Re-evaluation is done at the beginning of every session following a desensitisation session. The clinician reviews the client's experiences in the week and reassesses the targets that were processed. All this is fed into the consideration of subsequent targets and the overall treatment plan. As therapy progresses, the clinician and client will review whether all the necessary targets have been processed in relation to the past, present and future approach.

CASE EXAMPLE

The following composite case study illustrates a typical EMDR processing session for a single adult trauma.

Adam was referred for treatment after a road traffic collision (RTC). He had been diagnosed with post-traumatic stress disorder (PTSD) as defined in the *Diagnostic and Statistical Manual of Mental Disorders* (5th edition; American Psychiatric Association, 2013) (DSM-5). Following a diagnostic assessment carried out by a clinical psychologist, 12 sessions of EMDR were recommended.

Thorough history-taking revealed no earlier associated trauma, the therapist then taught Adam several self-soothing and grounding techniques to help him manage his levels of arousal. It was important that this, and a good therapeutic relationship, were in place prior to addressing the traumatic material.

The processing session began with phase 3 – the assessment of the target memory. This drew out:

- The image representing the worst aspect of the memory – coming around a blind bend into a queue of stationery traffic.
- The negative belief – 'I'm in danger' – in keeping with the currently held, irrational fear that was blighting his life.
- The emotions and body sensations of fear, a tight chest and clenching stomach. Adam rated these as 8/10 on the SUD scale.

He wanted to believe that he was safe and it was over, but this only rated a 2/7 on the VOC scale.

Adam was asked to hold these components of the memory in mind and the clinician began phase 4 with BLS. In between each set of eye movements, Adam was asked for short feedback. What he reported is summarised below:

- His anxiety initially rose as he remembered more details of the moment of impact.
- He felt tension throughout his body as though he were bracing for impact.
- He remembered hearing the screams from an injured driver.
- He recalled feeling trapped in his vehicle and seeing broken glass glinting in the sunlight.
- He reported being aware of the fact that another car could come around the corner and plough into him and his anxiety peaked at that point.
- He remembered sirens as the emergency services arrived.
- He remembered someone coming to help him and telling him he was going to be okay.
- He reported feeling a relief and a sense of being protected by their presence behind his vehicle.
- He recalled people being out of their cars and standing at the side of the road – at this point he spontaneously said aloud 'it had already happened – it wasn't my fault'. It was only then that he realised he had felt some level of responsibility for the accident. This was a massive insight for him and he experienced a surge of relief.
- He had a thought about how his choice of car had been a factor in his lack of physical injuries and this led to him feeling protected.
- He continued to realise how many different elements generally contributed to his safety on the road – then and now – for example, his driving experience, choice of vehicle and road awareness. This gave him a sense of some control and he began to feel calmer.
- His calmness increased as BLS continued.

Once his SUD had reduced to 0, Adam was asked what words best went with that memory now. It was very natural and easy for him to say 'I'm safe now', and the clinician installed this positive cognition with BLS and checked there was no residual somatic disturbance. The session was closed with a debriefing of his experience of the processing and a relaxation exercise.

When Adam returned, the next session began with the re-evaluation and consideration of next steps.

EMDR is sometimes wrongly viewed as rigid and formulaic. The eight phases can be viewed as a cradle holding a wide range of therapeutic skills. How individual clinicians take a history and stabilise a client will vary, depending on their therapeutic background and experiences. The clinician must be able to build understanding and control by teaching containment, emotional tolerance, grounding strategies and providing psycho-education. Only then should they consider addressing the desensitisation of the traumatic memories. Consequently, EMDR is more fluid than would first appear and is not a linear process. As well as the strong relational aspect, clinicians should be culturally competent and informed about innovative strategies and working with special populations (Nickerson, 2016).

RESEARCH EVIDENCE

EMDR is recommended as one of the therapeutic approaches for the effective treatment of PTSD and much research has been focused in this area (NICE, 2005). However, published non-randomised studies have suggested the effectiveness of EMDR for other presentations, such as borderline personality disorder (Brown and Shapiro, 2006), generalised anxiety disorder (Gauvreau and Bouchard, 2008), bulimia nervosa (Kowal, 2005), phobia (De Jongh et al., 1999) and pain management (Ray and Zbik, 2001). Shapiro (2001) refers to trauma in terms of large 'T', the major, obvious traumatic incidents, and small 't' traumas. The latter are 'those experiences that give one a lesser sense of self-confidence and assault one's sense of self-efficacy' (Parnell, 2007: 4). Where small 't' trauma is posited to be at the root of dysfunction, EMDR may also be beneficial. Examples include social anxiety and low self-esteem.

Fidelity to the protocol is important and training and supervision are vital in this. Further details of recognised training providers can be found at EMDR Association UK and Ireland (www.emdrassociation.org.uk), EMDR Europe (www.emdr-europe.org) and EMDR International Association (www.emdria.org).

REFERENCES

American Psychiatric Association (2013). *Diagnostic and Statistical Manual of Mental Disorders* (5th ed.). Washington, DC: APA.

Bergmann, U. (2010). EMDR's neurobiological mechanisms of action. *Journal of EMDR Practice and Research*, 4(1), 9–24.

Brown, S. and Shapiro, F. (2006). EMDR in the treatment of borderline personality disorder. *Clinical Case Studies*, 5, 403–420.

De Jongh, A., ten Broeke, E. and Renssen, M. (1999). Treatment of specific phobias with EMDR. *Journal of Anxiety Disorders*, 13, 69–85.

Gauvreau, P. and Bouchard, S. (2008). Preliminary evidence for the efficacy of EMDR in treating generalized anxiety disorder. *Journal of EMDR Practice and Research*, 2, 26–40.

Kowal, J.A. (2005). QEEG analysis of treating PTSD and bulimia nervosa using EMDR. *Journal of Neurotherapy*, 9, 114–115.

Lee, C.W. and Cuijpers, P. (2013). A meta-analysis of the contribution of eye movements in processing emotional memories. *Journal of Behavior Therapy and Experimental Psychiatry*, 44, 231–239.

National Institute of Clinical Excellence (2005). *Post Traumatic Stress Disorder (PTSD): The Management of PTSD in Adults and Children in Primary and Secondary Care* (Clinical Guideline 26). London: NICE.

Nickerson, M. (2016). *Cultural Competence and Healing Culturally-based Trauma with EMDR Therapy: Innovative Strategies and Protocols*. New York: Springer.

Parnell, L. (2007). *A Clinician's Guide to EMDR: Tools and Techniques for Successful Treatment*. New York: W.W. Norton.

Propper, R. and Christman, S. (2008). Interhemispheric interaction and saccadic horizontal eye movements: implications for episodic memory, EMDR, and PTSD. *Journal of EMDR Practice and Research*, 4, 269–281.

Ray, A. and Zbik, A. (2001). Cognitive behavioral therapies and beyond. In C. Tollison, J. Satterhwaite and J. Tollison (Eds.), *Practical Pain Management* (3rd ed., pp. 189–208). Philadelphia, PA: Lippincott.

Shapiro, F. (1989). Efficacy of the eye movement desensitization procedure in the treatment of traumatic memories. *Journal of Traumatic Stress Studies*, 2, 199–223.

Shapiro, F. (2001). *Eye Movement Desensitization and Reprocessing: Basic Principles, Protocols and Procedures* (2nd ed.). New York: Guilford Press.

Shapiro, F. (2007). EMDR, adaptive information processing, and case conceptualization. *Journal of EMDR Practice and Research*, 1, 68–87.

Stickgold, R. (2002). EMDR: a putative neurobiological mechanism of action. *Journal of Clinical Psychology*, 58, 61–75.

van den Hout, M.A., Eidhof, M.B., Verboom, J., Littel, M. and Engelhard, I.M. (2014). Blurring of emotional and non-emotional memories by taxing working memory during recall. *Cognition and Emotion*, 28(4), 717–727.

RECOMMENDED READING

1. Royle, E. and Kerr, C. (2010). *Integrating EMDR into your Practice*. New York: Springer.

This book helps novice practitioners integrate EMDR into their current practice whatever their theoretical orientation.
   These next two books are authored by the creator of EMDR and detail the history, development and basic principles, protocols and procedures of this therapeutic approach.

2. Shapiro, F. and Forrest, M.S. (1997). *EMDR the Breakthrough 'Eye Movement' Therapy for Overcoming Anxiety, Stress, and Trauma*. New York: Brunner-Routledge.

3. Shapiro, F. (2001). *Eye Movement Desensitization and Reprocessing: Basic Principles, Protocols and Procedures* (2nd ed.). New York: Guilford Press.

5.14   MINDFULNESS BASED COGNITIVE THERAPY

ADAM J. SCOTT AND KATE ADAM

OVERVIEW AND KEY POINTS

This chapter will explore Mindfulness Based Cognitive Therapy (MBCT), an evidence-based and integrative form of Cognitive-Behavioural Therapy (CBT) used to treat a range of psychological issues. As MBCT was originally developed to work with clients experiencing recurrent episodes of major depression, the chapter will focus on this psychological presentation. The key points of the chapter are as follows:

*   MBCT is part of the third wave of CBT.
*   MBCT argues that *rumination* and *experimental avoidance* are two thought processes which make clients vulnerable to recurrent depressive episodes.
*   MBCT makes use of cognitive therapy and mindfulness techniques to enable clients to become self-aware, so they can learn to de-centre from distressing thoughts, feelings, bodily sensations and behaviours.
*   MBCT has a growing evidence base and is recommended by the National Institute for Health and Care Excellence (NICE) (2009) as a treatment for major recurrent depression.

BRIEF HISTORY

MBCT is informed by mindfulness meditation practices and cognitive therapy theory (Segal, Williams and Teasdale, 2012). Mindfulness is a form of meditation found in most world faiths, although mindfulness practices used within counselling and psychotherapy tend to be Buddhist in nature. It is important to remember that mindfulness within religious practice differs from that within counselling and psychotherapy, the former focusing on enlightenment, devotion and worship and the latter on psychological wellbeing (Rohr, 2003).

Mindfulness is used in three main ways in the field of counselling and psychotherapy: (1) as a self-help tool (Williams and Penman, 2011), (2) as a technique within an eclectic approach to therapy or (3) as an integrative form of CBT, such as MBCT and Compassion Focused Therapy and Dialectical Behaviour Therapy (Mansell and Taylor, 2012). MBCT is an integrative approach based on John Kabat-Zinn's (1990) Mindfulness Based Stress Reduction (MBSR). MBSR was developed for clients experiencing chronic pain, mental health issues and other life-limiting illnesses. Using Buddhist meditative practices (mindfulness), this approach encourages clients to accept the discomfort they experience rather than resisting it. Interestingly, through acceptance comes an alleviation of their psychological and physical distress. Segal, Williams and Teasdale (2012) further developed MBSR into MBCT by integrating it with aspects of cognitive therapy in order to effectively help those experiencing recurrent depressive episodes.

BASIC ASSUMPTIONS

MBCT is part of the third wave of CBT, a group of integrative variants of CBT (Mansell and Taylor, 2012). Therefore, the assumptions that underpin MBCT are those of CBT more broadly. Sanders (2010) provides a clear summary of the key assumptions of CBT which have been applied to MBCT below:

- Collaboration – it is essential clients feel they are playing an active role in therapy, whether MBCT is used within a group or individual setting. Collaboration is facilitated through group discussion and tasks to complete at home.

- Formulation – MBCT does not necessitate the creation of a written formulation, but it does require the client to learn to formulate their presenting problem with MBCT theory in mind.
- Structured, psychoeducational and focused – MBCT is a psychoeducation group or one-to-one therapy programme designed to treat specific mental health issues (i.e., depression, anxiety, psychosis, etc.).
- Time-limited – MBCT groups are designed to last for eight weeks, although if used in individual therapy may last longer.
- Cognitive and behavioural – MBCT is integrative in nature and draws from a number of therapeutic sources, namely mindfulness meditation, but is firmly grounded in cognitive therapy theory and practice.
- Homework – MBCT requires all clients to carry out tasks at home and reflect on these in the therapy sessions. This homework is a central part of the therapeutic process.

ORIGIN AND MAINTENANCE OF PROBLEMS: INTRODUCING JEREMY

Jeremy is a 45-year-old man who has come to therapy because he is experiencing recurrent episodes of depression. He first had a depressive episode when he was 27 after a particularly stressful time at work and a relationship breakdown. He currently experiences between two to three episodes of depression a year. These are moderate in nature and generally last from two and six weeks. While he can work when feeling depressed, he finds it difficult due to the symptoms he experiences – lack of concentration, waking in the night worrying, tiredness and low motivation. Jeremy takes antidepressants and has had person-centred therapy in the past, which he found helpful. Jeremy has been referred for MBCT because his GP told him it may help to better manage his depression.

Thought patterns are central to MBCT's understanding of why people are vulnerable to mental health concerns such as recurrent depression (Piet and Hougaard, 2011). The approach argues there are two ways of thinking which can trigger and maintain depressive episodes. The first is called *rumination* and the second *experimental avoidance* (Crane, 2009). While the term *rumination* may be unfamiliar, the experience of a negative ruminative is a common one. Most people have experienced waking up in the middle of the night worrying about something, and once they begin to worry about one thing, another worry is triggered, and so on, which culminates in a cycle of worry which is difficult to escape from (Williams and Penman, 2011). Therefore, *rumination* can be experienced as a spiral of distressing emotions, thoughts and sensations in our

bodies and behaviours. This common experience can lead to a poor night's sleep, although, for people like Jeremy, with previous experience of a pathological depression, *rumination* may trigger a further episode of depression.

Depressive rumination is distressing and when Jeremy experiences it he seeks to escape his uncomfortable thoughts, feelings, bodily sensations and behaviours. MBCT defines this as *experiential avoidance* (Crane, 2009). When awoken in the night with worry, Jeremy tries to avoid his worries by forcing himself to stop thinking about the issue he is worrying about, or by engaging in an internal dialogue which seeks to resolve his concerns through problem-solving. Unfortunately, these actions usually lead to frustration, further distress and even strengthen the ruminative pattern. During the day Jeremy tries to use coping strategies to distract himself from his distressing experiences – he tends to spend longer at work when he begins to feel down so that he is distracted from his *ruminations*, a behaviour which can work in the short term but soon exacerbates his problems. MBCT theory suggests Jeremy can learn to manage *depressive rumination* by (a) becoming aware of what triggers *rumination*, (b) recognising when he is ruminating and (c) *de-centre* or detach from the negative thoughts feelings, bodily sensations and behaviours by learning to observe and accept them rather than avoid or fight them (Piet and Hougaard, 2011).

PROCESS OF CHANGE

MBCT suggests that in order to learn to *de-centre*, clients need to be able to recognise the two *modes of mind* – the *being mode* and the *doing mode* (Crane, 2009). The *doing mode of mind* is most useful for problem-solving, analysing and comparing current problems with things that happened in the past or predicting what might happen in the future (Williams and Penman, 2011). However, it becomes less useful when allied with *depressive rumination*. For example, Jeremy works in a busy marketing agency and when a large contract is near completion he often has to work extra hours. This can lead to him being overwhelmed (feeling), to think that he does not have the ability to do his work (thought), to have stress-related headaches (bodily sensations) and to begin to isolate himself from others so he has more time to work (behaviours). He can use the *doing mode* to problem-solve this situation by thinking 'I know I am feeling overwhelmed but this contract will be finished soon and if I just put in another couple of day's work everything will be fine'. However, there are times when this type of problem-solving does not help and Jeremy feels he cannot 'switch off' and he begins to get caught in the *doing mode* which promotes *depressive rumination* (Papageorgiou and Wells, 2004). During these stressful times at work, Jeremy can wake up at night and begin to worry, thinking about times in the past when he felt he could not cope with stress at work and being fearful that he may be getting depressed. As we have already said, the fact that Jeremy tries to problem-solve these thoughts can lead him into a spiral of worry that he finds difficult to get out of. The problem with these ruminative patterns is they can become automatic, which means Jeremy may not be aware he is engaging in them. MBCT calls this lack of awareness the *automatic pilot* (Segal, Williams and Teasdale, 2012).

We all have an *automatic pilot* which governs thinking, feeling or behaviour processes that have become routine. For example, leaving the house and walking to the bus and then thinking 'did I lock the front door?' The reason

we cannot remember locking the door is because we do it automatically and without self-awareness. It is important to note the *automatic pilot* is not a problem which we need to eradicate as it has a positive function in our lives, such as helping us with complex activities like driving a car (Williams and Penman, 2011). However, MBCT encourages people to be aware of our *automatic pilot* because by becoming aware of it clients can recognise when they are caught in negative patterns of thoughts which can leave them vulnerable to further episodes of depression.

In MBCT theory, the *being mode* of mind stands alongside the *doing mode*. In the *being mode* of mind, we experience a sense of homeostasis, for example, sitting on a park bench on a spring morning, the sweet smell of new flowers, the warm sunshine on your skin, the sound of birds singing and the experience of being at peace. Mindfulness is an aspect of the *being mode* and can be defined as 'paying attention ... on purpose in the present moment with curiosity and kindness ... to things as they are' (Kabat-Zinn, 1994: 4). Most importantly, by becoming mindful we can shift from the *doing* to the *being* mode of mind. Similarly, Jeremy can shift from the doing to the being mode by using mindfulness when he is overwhelmed by work stress, by observing and de-centring from the distressing thoughts, emotions, bodily sensations and behaviours he is experiencing.

In summary, by bringing together cognitive therapy with mindfulness mediation, MBCT teaches clients to learn to increase their self-awareness in order to recognise potential triggers to depressive rumination and experiential avoidance. Through this self-awareness and with training in mindfulness, the client has the opportunity to respond differently to their automatic thought processes and learn to *de-centre* before they spiral into psychological distress (Chiesa and Serretti, 2010).

SKILLS AND STRATEGIES

This section will provide a brief overview of the eight sessions of the MBCT group intervention from Jeremy's perspective. It is based on the sessions outlined by Segal, Williams and Teasdale (2012) and Williams and Penman (2011). Each session has a clear structure and a number of elements, which include an *in vivo* mindfulness practice, discussion on a set topic and homework being set and reflected upon.

SESSION 1

In the first session Jeremy is introduced to the group in order to build rapport. He is taught about the automatic pilot and its impact on his wellbeing. The therapist introduced mindfulness by inviting the group to take a raisin and mindfully explore its appearance, texture, smell and taste as though they had never seen one before. The group also completed their first body scan, a similar exercise to the raisin meditation but this time they focused on the sensations in different parts of their bodies. Jeremy found both these exercises helpful as introductions to mindfulness, particularly in becoming aware of how distracted his mind could be when trying to focus. The group was asked to practise these exercises each day before the next session.

SESSION 2

The group discussed their homework from last week and Jeremy spoke about his growing awareness of the *chatter* in his mind when trying to meditate. The group explored the impact this *chatter* could have on their thoughts, feelings, bodily sensations and behaviours, and were introduced to the concept of *de-centring* by noticing and letting go. The therapist practised another mediation with them called the *sitting meditation*. This was added to their homework, as was a task which required the group to keep a diary of pleasant experiences.

SESSION 3

The group reviewed their homework and discussed relevant issues. Jeremy was enjoying the meditation homework even though it was challenging at times. The therapist introduced a new exercise called mindful movement. This involved using mindfulness alongside basic yoga, stretching and walking. As he had reported struggling with some of these, he found the technique of being aware of his breath, as an anchor in the present, very helpful. This exercise was added to the group's homework for the week.

SESSION 4

In this session the group focused on staying present when their minds are caught by some thoughts while avoiding others. They learned that mindfulness facilitates taking a broader perspective and relating differently to our emotions, body sensations, thoughts and behaviours. The group explored depression and Jeremy formulated an understanding around what may have contributed to the development of his difficulties. He recognised that his relationship breakdown and stress at work had impacted on the development of his depression, although the real issue was how his thoughts were subsequently interpreting interactions and experiences in the present. The homework for next week involved practising mediations and breathing spaces.

SESSION 5

In this session the group learned to allow experiences to be as they are, without judgement, by using skills like acceptance, holding, allowing and letting be. This attitude towards experiences facilitated Jeremy to see more clearly and evaluate how he best cared for himself. He recognised that a situation at work where he had an increased workload due to a contract coming to an end was causing him significant anxiety. He realised that the anxiety he was experiencing could be a 'normal' response for people in this situation, which did not mean he was necessarily getting depressed. He decided to focus on how best to look after himself during this time instead of getting caught up in negative ruminative patterns. The session also included sitting meditation and an expanded breathing space, which formed part of Jeremy's homework.

SESSION 6

This session focused on the idea that *thoughts are not facts* and explored how depressive thoughts can affect our ability to relate to our experiences – acknowledging thought patterns empowered the group members to decide whether or not they wished to engage with particular thoughts. The therapist encouraged the group to be aware that the end of therapy was approaching and to integrate mindfulness practice into their daily life. Jeremy discussed with the group his feeling that he has more control of his depression rather than being an inactive passenger of it, although he also said he was struggling to take the time needed to complete his meditative exercises. The group discussed some ways he could address this.

SESSION 7

The group learned the importance of being proactive in managing their depression and reflected on self-care skills. They discussed the impact of activity on mood and the importance of planning mindfulness and positive activities into their lives. Jeremy recognised going for a pint with friends or walking his dog, rather than just watching TV after work, led him to feel more positive. The therapist facilitated a discussion on recognising signs of relapse and depressive symptoms. Jeremy identified thoughts where he believed others criticising him could lead to getting caught in depressive emotions and behaviours. Using the breathing space, he was able to explore these further and continued to consolidate his progress though his homework.

SESSION 8

The final session focused on *using what has been learned to deal with future moods*. It reviewed the journey the group and the individuals in it had made. The group discussed how to continue the mindfulness practices and maintain their learning. Jeremy shared that he and others were looking to attend yoga classes and perhaps set up a weekly space for mindfulness meditations. The group made practical plans for the future, during which Jeremy wrote a list to remind himself why it was important to sustain his mindfulness practice. He also recognised that since starting the group he enjoyed life more and that acceptance was something he wanted to continue to work on. He recorded he was most motivated to stay healthy by wanting to have a good relationship with his partner and being around friends and family. The session closed with a meditation.

RESEARCH EVIDENCE

The effectiveness of MBCT has been extensively explored in the research literature as an evidence-based treatment of recurrent major depression and is recommended by the National Institute for Health and Care Excellence (NICE, 2009). Studies on its longitudinal effects on this presentation are also proving promising (Mathew, Whitford, Kenny and Denson, 2010). In this chapter we have focused on MBCT for depression, although there is a growing evidence base for the use of MBCT with other disorders, such as bipolar disorder, generalised anxiety disorder, panic disorder and psychosis (Abba, Chadwick and Stevenson, 2008; Chiesa and Serretti, 2010). Interestingly, there are also studies which suggest mindfulness interventions such as MBCT and MBSR are effective for the development of resilience and wellbeing in therapists and trainee therapists (Hopkins and Proeve, 2013).

REFERENCES

Abba, N., Chadwick, P. and Stevenson, C. (2008). Responding mindfully to distressing psychosis. *Psychotherapy Research*, 18(1), 77–87.

Chiesa, A. and Serretti, A. (2010). Mindfulness-based cognitive therapy for psychiatric disorders: A systematic review and meta-analysis. *Psychiatry Research*, 178(3), 441–453 (www.elsevier.com/locate/psychres).

Crane, R. (2009). *Mindfulness-based cognitive therapy*. London: Routledge.

Hopkins, A. and Proeve, M. (2013). Teaching mindfulness-based cognitive therapy to trainee psychologists: Qualitative and quantitative effects. *Counselling Psychology Quarterly*, 26(2), 115–130.

Kabat-Zinn, J. (1990). *Full catastrophe living*. New York: Delacorte.

Kabat-Zinn, J. (1994). *Wherever you go, there you are*. London: Piatkus.

Mansell, W. and Taylor, J. L. (2012). What is CBT and what isn't CBT? In W. Dryden and R. Branch (Eds.), *The CBT handbook* (pp. 5–74). London: Sage.

Mathew, K. L., Whitford, H. S., Kenny, M. A. and Denson, L. A. (2010). The long-term effects of mindfulness-based cognitive therapy as a relapse prevention treatment for major depressive disorder. *Behavioural and Cognitive Psychotherapy*, 38(5), 561–576.

NICE (2009). *Depression: The treatment and management of depression in adults*. London: National Institute for Health and Care Excellence (www.nice.org.uk/nicemedia/pdf/CG90NICEguideline.pdf).

Papageorgiou, C. and Wells, A. (2004). Nature, function and beliefs about depressive rumination. In C. Papageorgiou and A. Wells (Eds.), *Depressive rumination: Nature, theory and treatment* (pp. 3–20). Chichester: Wiley.

Piet, J. and Hougaard, E. (2011). The effect of mindfulness-based cognitive therapy for prevention of relapse in recurrent major depressive disorder: A systematic review and metaanalysis. *Clinical Psychology Review*, 31, 1032–1040.

Rohr, R. (2003). *Simplicity: The freedom of letting go*. New York: Crossroad Publishing.

Sanders, S. (2010). Cognitive behavioural approaches. In R. Woofle, S. Strawbridge, B. Douglas and W. Dryden (Eds.), *Handbook of counselling psychology* (3rd ed., pp. 105–129). London: Sage.

Segal, Z. V., Williams, J. M. G. and Teasdale, J. D. (2012). *Mindfulness-based cognitive therapy for depression: A new approach to preventing relapse (2nd ed.)*. New York: Guilford Press.

Williams, M. and Penman, D. (2011). *Mindfulness: Finding peace in a frantic world*. London: Piatkus.

RECOMMENDED READING

1. Segal, Z. V., Williams, J. M. G. and Teasdale, J. D. (2012). *Mindfulness-based cognitive therapy for depression: A new approach to preventing relapse*. New York: Guilford Press.

This core text is accessible to students and clinicians. It introduces the reader to MBCT's development, current theory, practice and relevant research. Its exploration of MBCT theory and research is engaging and provides an excellent grounding for practitioners. It is also practical in nature and provides a step-by-step overview of how to conduct the eight sessions of the MBCT group programme. The fact that it provides handouts for each session and an audio CD of mindfulness meditations makes it a must-have for those considering running an MBCT group.

2. Crane, R. (2009). *Mindfulness-based cognitive therapy*. London: Routledge.

This is an excellent reference text in the 'CBT Distinctive Features Series'. It provides a brief overview of the theory and structure of the approach. It is suitable for those exploring MBCT for the first time and for more experienced practitioners who want a text for quick reference.

3. Williams, M. and Penman, D. (2011). *Mindfulness: Finding peace in a frantic world*. London: Piatkus.

This self-help book is structured around the eight-week MBCT programme but applies it to an individual setting. It is written in a clear and understandable way, which makes it suitable to recommend to clients. The book comes with a CD of mindfulness meditations to guide clients in mindfulness practices and has a supporting website (www.franticworld. com) where clients can access free online meditations. It is an excellent resource for counsellors and psychotherapists wanting to structure one-to-one therapy around MBCT.

5.15 RATIONAL EMOTIVE BEHAVIOUR THERAPY

WINDY DRYDEN

OVERVIEW AND KEY POINTS

Rational emotive behaviour therapy (REBT) is a distinctive approach within the cognitive-behavioural tradition of psychotherapy that was developed by Albert Ellis (1913–2007). It is generally regarded to be the first cognitive-behavioural approach and has recently celebrated its 60th birthday.

- REBT emphasises the interdependence of cognition, emotion and behaviour.
- It argues that rigid and extreme beliefs are at the core of psychologically disturbed responses to adversity and flexible and non-extreme beliefs are at the core of psychologically healthy responses to the same adversity.

- It follows that a central task of REBT therapists is to encourage clients to develop flexible and non-extreme beliefs about adversity.
- In carrying out this central task, effective REBT therapists need to be good therapists, good psychological educators and tend to practise in their own lives what they 'preach' in the consulting room.
- Meaningful psychological change is deemed to be difficult and clients need to commit themselves to an ongoing routine of thinking flexibly and in non-extreme ways in the face of adversity and of taking action that supports and reinforces such thinking. Therapists need to help clients to make this commitment in the first place and to renew this commitment during the therapeutic process and beyond.

BRIEF HISTORY

Rational emotive behaviour therapy (REBT) was founded in 1955 by Albert Ellis, an American clinical psychologist who had become increasingly disaffected with psychoanalysis, in which he trained in the late 1940s. Originally, the approach was called rational therapy (RT) because Ellis wanted to emphasise its rational and cognitive features. In doing so, Ellis demonstrated the philosophical influences (largely Stoic) on his thinking. In 1961 he changed its name to rational-emotive therapy to show critics that it did not neglect emotions, and over 30 years later (in 1993) Ellis renamed the approach yet again, calling it rational emotive behaviour therapy to show critics that it did not neglect behaviour.

In 1962, Ellis published *Reason and Emotion in Psychotherapy*, a collection largely of previously published papers or previously delivered lectures, but which became a seminal work in the history of psychotherapy and which was revised 32 years later (Ellis, 1994 [1962]). Most of REBT's major present-day features are described in this book: the pivotal role of cognition in psychological disturbance; the principle of psychological interactionism where cognition, emotion and behaviour are seen as interacting, not separate, systems; the advantages of self-acceptance over self-esteem in helping clients with their disturbed views of their selves; and the importance of an active-directive therapeutic style, to name but a few.

Albert Ellis died in 2007 after an unfortunate period during which he was in dispute on a number of issues with the institute that continues to bear his name. Despite this, the legacy that Ellis left REBT and the wider field of psychotherapy is untarnished and unquestioned.

REBT is practised all over the world and has many different therapeutic, occupational and educational applications. However, it tends to live in the shadow of Beck's cognitive therapy, an approach to cognitive-behaviour therapy which has attracted a greater number of practitioners and is more academically respectable.

BASIC ASSUMPTIONS

Rationality is a concept that is normally applied to a person's beliefs. Rational beliefs, which are deemed to be at the core of psychological health, are flexible or non-extreme, consistent with reality, logical, and both self and relationship enhancing. Irrational beliefs, which are deemed to be at the core of psychological disturbance, are rigid or extreme, inconsistent with reality, illogical, and both self and relationship defeating.

There are four types of rational belief: flexible beliefs ('I want to be approved of, but I don't have to be'); non-awfulising beliefs ('It's bad to be disapproved of, but it isn't the end of the world'); discomfort tolerance beliefs ('It is difficult to face being disapproved of, but I can tolerate it and it is worth it to me to do so'); and acceptance beliefs (e.g., self-acceptance, 'I can accept myself if I am disapproved of'; other acceptance, 'You are not horrible if you disapprove of me'; and life acceptance, 'Even though this tragedy happened, life is not all bad and comprises good, bad and neutral events').

Similarly, there are four types of irrational belief: rigid beliefs ('I must be approved of'); awfulising beliefs ('If I'm disapproved of, it's the end of the world'); discomfort intolerance beliefs ('I can't tolerate being disapproved of'); and depreciation beliefs (e.g., self-depreciation, 'I am worthless if I am disapproved of'; other depreciation, 'You are horrible if you disapprove of me'; and life depreciation, 'Life is all bad because this tragedy happened').

REBT advocates a situational 'ABC' model of psychological disturbance and health. 'A' stands for adversity, which occurs within a situation and can be actual or inferred. 'A' represents the aspect of the situation that the person focuses on and evaluates. 'B' stands for belief (rational or irrational). 'C' stands for the consequences of holding a belief about 'A' and can be emotional, behavioural and cognitive. Thus, 'As' do not cause 'Cs' but contribute to them. 'Bs' are seen as the prime but not the only determiners of 'Cs'.

Holding a rational belief about an 'A' leads to healthy emotions, functional behaviour and realistic and balanced subsequent thinking. Holding an irrational belief about the same 'A' leads to unhealthy emotions, dysfunctional behaviour and unrealistic subsequent thinking that is highly skewed to the negative.

REBT's view of human nature is realistic. Humans are seen as having the potential for both rational and irrational thinking. The ease with which we transform our strong desires into rigid demands suggests that the tendency towards irrational thinking is biologically based, but can be buffered or encouraged by environmental contexts.

Clients often have the unfortunate experience of inheriting tendencies towards disturbance and being exposed to their parents' disturbed behaviour. REBT is optimistic and realistic here. It argues that if such clients work persistently and forcefully to counter their irrational beliefs and act in ways that are consistent with their rational beliefs, then they can help themselves significantly. However, REBT also acknowledges that most clients will not put in this degree of effort over a long period of time and will therefore fall far short of achieving their potential for psychological health.

ORIGIN AND MAINTENANCE OF PROBLEMS

People are disturbed not by events but by the rigid and extreme views that they take of them. This means that while negative events contribute to the development of disturbance, particularly when these events are highly aversive, disturbance occurs when people bring their tendencies to think irrationally to these events.

REBT does not have an elaborate view of the origin of disturbance. Having said this, it does acknowledge that it is very easy for humans when they are young to disturb themselves about highly aversive events. However, it argues that even under these conditions people react differently to the same event and thus we need to understand what a person brings to and takes from a negative activating event. People learn their standards and goals from their culture, but disturbance occurs when they bring their irrational beliefs to circumstances where their standards are not met and their pursuit of their goals is blocked.

REBT has a more elaborate view of how disturbance is maintained. It argues that people perpetuate their disturbance for a number of reasons, including the following:

- They lack the insight that their disturbance is underpinned by their irrational beliefs and think instead that it is caused by events.
- They wrongly think that once they understand that their problems are underpinned by irrational beliefs, this understanding alone will lead to change.
- They do not work persistently to change their irrational beliefs and to integrate the rational alternatives to these beliefs into their belief system.
- They continue to act in ways that are consistent with their irrational beliefs.
- They lack or are deficient in important social skills, communication skills, problem-solving skills and other life skills.
- They think that their disturbance has payoffs that outweigh the advantages of the healthy alternatives to their disturbed feelings and/or behaviour.
- They live in environments which support the irrational beliefs that underpin their problems and they think that as this is the case they cannot do anything to help themselves.

THEORY OF CHANGE

REBT therapists consider that the core facilitative conditions of empathy, unconditional acceptance and genuineness are often desirable, but neither necessary nor sufficient for constructive therapeutic change. For such change to take place, REBT therapists need to help their clients to do the following:

- realise that they largely create their own psychological problems and that while situations contribute to these problems, they are in general of lesser importance in the change process
- fully recognise that they are able to address and overcome these problems
- understand that their problems stem largely from irrational beliefs
- detect their irrational beliefs and discriminate between them and their rational beliefs
- question their irrational beliefs and their rational beliefs until they see clearly that their irrational beliefs are false, illogical and unconstructive while their rational beliefs are true, sensible and constructive
- work towards the internalisation of their new rational beliefs by using a variety of cognitive (including imaginal), emotive and behavioural change methods
- refrain from acting in ways that are consistent with their old irrational beliefs
- extend this process of challenging beliefs and using multimodal methods of change into other areas of their lives and to commit to doing so for as long as necessary.

All this is best done when effective REBT therapists develop, maintain and suitably end a good working alliance with clients (Dryden, 2009). This involves:

- therapists and clients having a good working bond
- therapists and clients sharing a common view of the determinants of the latter's problems and how these can best be addressed
- therapists and clients working towards agreed goals
- therapists and clients executing agreed tasks designed to facilitate goal achievement.

SKILLS AND STRATEGIES

REBT therapists see themselves as good psychological educators and therefore seek to teach their clients the ABC model of understanding and dealing with their psychological problems. They stress that there are alternative ways of addressing these problems and strive to elicit from their clients informed consent at the outset and throughout the counselling process. If they think that a client is better suited to a different approach to therapy, they do not hesitate to effect a suitable referral.

REBT therapists frequently employ an active-directive counselling style and use both Socratic and didactic teaching methods. However, they vary their style from client to client. They begin by working with specific examples of identified client problems and help their clients to set healthy goals. They employ a sequence of steps in working on these examples which involves using the situationally based ABC framework, challenging beliefs and negotiating suitable homework assignments with their clients.

Helping clients to generalise their learning from situation to situation is explicitly built into the counselling process. So, too, is helping clients to identify, challenge and change core irrational beliefs which are seen as accounting for disturbance across a broad range of relevant situations.

A major therapeutic strategy involves helping clients to become their own therapists. In doing this, REBT therapists teach their clients how to use a particular skill, such as challenging irrational beliefs, model the use of this skill and sometimes give the clients written instructions on how to use the skill on their own. Constructive feedback is given to encourage the refinement of the skill. As clients learn how to use the skills of REBT for themselves, their therapists adopt a less active-directive, more prompting therapeutic style in order to encourage them to take increasing responsibility for their own therapeutic change.

REBT may be seen as an example of theoretically consistent eclecticism in that its practitioners draw upon procedures that originate from other counselling approaches, but do so for purposes that are consistent with REBT theory. REBT therapists are judiciously selective in their eclecticism and avoid the use of methods that are inefficient, or mystical, or of dubious validity.

REBT therapists have their preferred therapeutic goals for their clients, namely to help them to change their core irrational beliefs and to develop and internalise a set of core rational beliefs. However, they are ready to make compromises with their clients on these objectives when it becomes clear that their clients are unable or unwilling to change their core irrational beliefs. In such cases, REBT therapists help their clients by encouraging them to change their distorted inferences, to effect behavioural changes without necessarily changing their irrational beliefs or to remove themselves from negative activating events.

CASE EXAMPLE

Once Marie had made progress in developing her self-accepting belief, I helped her to stand back and question her inference that others would invariably judge her negatively if her mind did go blank when giving a public presentation and for other public displays of what she judged as a weakness. Marie concluded that not everybody would judge her negatively: some would do so, others would not notice and yet others would empathise with her. Also, Marie questioned that such displays were signs of weakness. Rather, she concluded they were signs of fallibility.

RESEARCH EVIDENCE

There is quite a lot of research indicating that psychological disturbance is correlated with irrational beliefs. For example, awfulising is involved in both anxiety and pain, and self-depreciation is a fundamental component of depressed mood (see Dryden, David and Ellis, 2010).

Two rigorous meta-analyses have shown REBT's effectiveness with a range of clinical and non-clinical problems (Engels, Garnefsky and Diekstra, 1993; Lyons and Woods, 1991), although the quality of much of this research could have been improved. Well-controlled trials of REBT need to be done with clinical populations, employing well-trained REBT therapists who can be shown to adhere to a properly designed REBT competency scale (Dryden, Beal, Jones and Trower, 2010). Finally, Dan David's (2015) research consistently shows that REBT does as well as other cognitive-behioural approaches in comparative outcome studies.

REFERENCES

David, D. (2015). Rational emotive behavior therapy. In R.L. Cautin and S.O. Lilienfeld (Eds.), *Encyclopedia of Clinical Psychology*. Hoboken, NJ: Wiley-Blackwell, pp. 1–8.

Dryden, W. (2009). *Skills in Rational Emotive Behaviour Counselling and Psychotherapy*. London: Sage.

Dryden, W., Beal, D., Jones, J. and Trower, P. (2010). The REBT competency scale for clinical and research applications. *Journal of Rational-Emotive and Cognitive-Behavior Therapy*, 28(4), 165–216.

Dryden, W., David, D. and Ellis, A. (2010). Rational emotive behavior therapy. In K.S. Dobson (Ed.), *Handbook of Cognitive-Behavioral Therapies* (3rd ed., pp. 226–276). New York: Guilford Press.

Ellis, A. (1994 [1962]). *Reason and Emotion in Psychotherapy* (rev. ed.). New York: Birch Lane.

Engels, G.I., Garnefsky, N. and Diekstra, F.W. (1993). Efficacy of rational-emotive therapy: A quantitative analysis. *Journal of Consulting and Clinical Psychology*, 61, 1083–1090.

Lyons, L.C. and Woods, P.J. (1991). The efficacy of rational-emotive therapy: A quantitative review of the outcome research. *Clinical Psychology Review*, 11, 357–369.

RECOMMENDED READING

1. DiGiuseppe, R.A., Doyle, K., Dryden, W. and Backx, W. (2014). *A Practitioner's Guide to Rational Emotive Behavior Therapy* (3rd ed.). New York: Oxford University Press.

This book is the most comprehensive presentation of the philosophy, theory and clinical practice of rational emotive behaviour therapy.

2. Dryden, W. (2001). *Reason to Change: A Rational Emotive Behaviour Therapy (REBT) Workbook.* Hove: Brunner-Routledge.

This is a comprehensive client workbook which takes clients through the process of REBT, teaching them the necessary skills which will help them get the most from this process.

3. Ellis, A. (2002). *Overcoming Resistance: A Rational Emotive Behavior Therapy Integrated Approach* (2nd ed.). New York: Springer.

This is perhaps Ellis's best book on REBT, devoted to helping therapists address their clients' many resistances to initiating and maintaining therapeutic change.

THEORY AND APPROACHES: HUMANISTIC-EXISTENTIAL APPROACHES

5.16 ECOTHERAPY

NICK TOTTON

OVERVIEW AND KEY POINTS

Ecotherapy (also ecopsychology, nature therapy, nature-assisted therapy, outdoor therapy) is an umbrella term for several approaches which combine psychological therapy with green environments. It believes that spending time outdoors around growing things and living creatures is inherently good for us, and works to amplify this effect through various exercises and techniques, and through a therapeutic relationship in the outdoors. Most ecotherapists also believe that our civilisation suffers from a 'nature deficit', an alienation from the rest of life which is at the root of many of our cultural ills, including climate change and other environmental emergencies, so ecotherapy hopes to heal the culture as well as the individual. Ecotherapy:

- takes an ecosystemic view of human problems
- largely happens outside the therapy room in green surroundings
- avoids the approach of 'using' the other-than-human, which is normal to our culture, encouraging clients to find their own way into relationships with other-than-human beings
- often has a spiritual attitude of reverence for living systems
- at times directly engages with environmental politics.

BRIEF HISTORY

Although many people have independently contributed to the development of ecotherapy and ecopsychology, if there is a founding figure it is the American psychologist Theodore Roszak, through his book, *The Voice of the Earth* (Roszak, 2002 [1993]), and the collection which he co-edited, *Ecopsychology: Restoring the Earth, Healing the Mind* (Roszak, Gomes and Kanner, 1995). A number of others, mostly in the USA, have since taken the work in a variety of directions (there is no central organisation or authority). The best known of these include Joanna Macy, John Seed, David Abram, Andy Fisher and Bill Plotkin. It is indicative of the unusual origins of ecotherapy/ecopsychology that many of these are not actually psychotherapists or counsellors. In the United Kingdom (UK), significant figures include Mary-Jayne Rust, Hilary Prentice, David Key, Martin Jordan and Nick Totton.

True to its philosophy, ecotherapy has grown like a forest rather than a plantation, with few rules, organisations and institutions. To switch metaphors, it resembles a complex river delta, with many water courses flowing side by side, branching and braiding until it is impossible to identify which is which. Although Roszak's ecopsychology is a crucial component, many ecotherapists have come through other routes: adventure and outdoor therapy and bushcraft, art and art therapy, spirituality, horticulture, permaculture, ecology, environmental activism and of course, counselling and psychotherapy, have all led people to the practice of ecotherapy.

Also important is the large and growing field of animal-assisted therapy (AAT), closely associated and in some ways overlapping with ecotherapy. AAT (also known as animal-facilitated therapy) originally based itself on the perceived benefits for sick or disturbed children from being around animals (see the discussion below of biophilia). However, it has become apparent that many animals, especially perhaps dogs and horses, are highly sensitive to human emotional fields, and in fact actively seek to take part in the therapeutic process. Equine therapy in particular, with both children and adults, has become very popular in recent years (Karol, 2007; Kohanov, 2001).

It should be noted that references to 'ecotherapy', both in the popular media and in research papers, quite frequently concern only the beneficial effects of being in green spaces, and lack any psychotherapeutic element. This should be distinguished from the ecotherapy being discussed here.

BASIC ASSUMPTIONS

A striking aspect of ecotherapy is its heterogeneity, mirroring the diversity of the ecosystems which are central to its practice. It is therefore difficult to make realistic generalisations about the whole field, but here are some positions which probably all ecotherapists share to varying degrees.

Ecotherapy's philosophical foundations are in ecology, deep ecology (Sessions, 1995) and ecosystemic thinking (Bateson, 1980). It situates human beings within, rather than above or beyond, the whole web of life forms on this planet, and identifies our sense of separateness from the rest of life as the source of many of our problems. Hence, a powerful source of healing is immersion in the 'wild', in the other-than-human (Totton, 2011), and ecotherapy seeks to offer opportunities for this, trying to balance familiarity and adventure, safety and risk, at the level which works best for each individual or client group (Totton, 2014).

Important to many ecotherapists is Edward O. Wilson's concept of biophilia (Wilson, 1990): the hypothesis that humans have an innate attraction towards other life forms, which, given the opportunity, expresses itself as love and nurturing. We often see this clearly in small children's love and awe of other animals, but of course we also often see cruelty and destructiveness as well. These two strands continue into adulthood, with the love and awe perhaps often increasingly masked. Ecotherapy practitioners are accustomed to noticing and nurturing the small signs of biophilia in many of their clients who have hardened against other life forms until eventually a breakthrough may reconnect them with their childhood love for the other-than-human, and their grief about its loss.

Ecotherapists have employed many mainstream therapy concepts to help make sense of our difficult relationship with the rest of the living world. These include attachment theory (Jordan, 2009), addiction (Glendinning, 1995; Maiteny, 2012), eating disorder (Rust, 2005) and autism (Chatalos, 2012). However, these connections sometimes function as much as productive analogies as direct theoretical links. A more central concept is ecosystemic thinking (Bateson, 1980; Keeney, 1979; Totton, 2011).

To think ecosystemically about a person is to see them not as an isolated individual, but as an open system nested within other open systems, and with yet other open systems nested within us. This complex field of being is always present in the therapy room: when therapist and client meet, a new field is created from their relationship. And at any moment the creative spark of growth can come from anywhere in the field. This way of experiencing the therapeutic nexus is at the heart of ecotherapy, and a key way that working outdoors can influence working in the therapy room.

ORIGIN AND MAINTENANCE OF PROBLEMS

It follows from the biophilia hypothesis that many psychological problems either originate in, or are exacerbated by, alienation from the other-than-human. Among the many conditions where this link can convincingly be argued are anomie and the experience of meaninglessness (Hay, 2005), depression (Kidner, 2007; Macy, 1995), addiction (Seifert, 2014; Wilshire, 1999) and compulsive consumption (Kanner and Gomes, 1995; Rust, 2008a).

Most ecotherapists also agree that there are specific psychological consequences from the conscious or semi-conscious awareness of environmental catastrophe (Bodnar, 2008; Rust, 2008b). These can range between frantic anxiety, despair, numbness and 'manic defences' like drinking, drugging, compulsive consumption and promiscuity. Sometimes, as an ecotherapy client reconnects with their love for other-than-human life, the destruction of global ecosystems hits them like a hurricane, and they need deep support in assimilating this reality and moving towards some sort of reparative action.

THEORY OF CHANGE

Ecotherapy's basic theory of change is that immersion in and engagement with the other-than-human world, the world of 'nature' and 'wildness', has an inherently transformative tendency. A part of the reason for this is that spending task-free time outdoors tends to stimulate relaxation and spaciousness, through what has been termed 'soft fascination' (Kaplan and Kaplan, 1989; Kaplan, 1995): phenomena like clouds, leaves and running water capture our involuntary attention with a complexity which gives pleasure without demanding cognitive processing, enabling a meditative state. A quite different sort of ecotherapy emphasises task, quest and achievement – for example, climbing and trekking – as a way towards empowerment and individuation (Gillis and Ringer, 1999).

There is also a relational approach to ecotherapy. In many ways, the therapist's role changes from dyadic partner to witness and accompanier of the client's journey into relationship with the other-than-human. It can be striking how, so to speak, the burden of transference lifts, and a more equal, adult-to-adult relationship becomes possible between therapist and client (Berger, 2007): the transferential focus shifts to tree, or animal, or plant, or river (Totton, 2014). Very often, the client experiences a unique degree of non-judgemental acceptance from the other-than-human – what in person-centred work would be termed 'unconditional positive regard'. We can treat this as a projection of the client's own healthy core, or, from a more spiritual viewpoint, accept that the experience is meaningful in its own terms and that we can receive love and acceptance from the other-than-human. Either way, it can be transformative; it can also teach practitioners who experience it how to offer their clients a deeper level of acceptance.

SKILLS AND STRATEGIES

A number of practices have been developed towards ecotherapy's goal of reconnecting clients with the living world around them. Here are a few examples.

THERAPEUTIC GARDENING

The therapeutic content here can range from an opportunity for exercise and to experience the calming and grounding effects of working in a garden, perhaps with individual or group therapy happening alongside this, to much more radical fusions of the two. The Natural Growth Project, a trailblazing scheme set up by the Medical Foundation for the Victims of Torture, was established on 30 allotments and in a large garden (for those too disabled by torture to manage an allotment). Those on the allotments are visited weekly by a psychotherapist and a gardener.

> The therapist's role is not to co-ordinate activities but rather to reflect on the experience of the client through the contact with nature. Using nature as a metaphor, it is possible very quickly to access deeply traumatic events and to work on the most difficult feelings, and the life cycle embodied in nature carries the promise of healing. (Linden and Grut, 2002: 12)

SOLO/VISION QUEST

A core element of wilderness and adventure therapy is the 'solo': a period of time spent in the wild outdoors on one's own. An irreducible aspect of this is *survival*, physical and psychological – testing oneself against the wild. For ecotherapy, there is also an aspect of *encounter*, opening oneself to being touched and changed by the wild.

The 'solo' structure is also central to spiritual practices of the wild, like the Native American Vision Quest, and there has been a fruitful interplay between these approaches and ecotherapy. The original vision quest involved going naked and fasting into the wild for four days, taking only a blanket and sacred pipe; contemporary Western versions are often more moderate, perhaps only a day or less, but still serious undertakings.

Some stay close to the original. Caswell (2007) describes a vision quest in Death Valley consisting of four days of preparation ('severance'), four days of fasting alone in a wild landscape (the 'threshold') and four days of group work to interpret and understand the threshold experience ('incorporation'). In the altered state induced by fasting, solitude and 'severance', every event takes on meaning, as the other-than-human is set free to speak to us and we are set free to listen. 'The exterior landscape and its creatures are an inseparable part of the interior landscape, the landscape of the spirit and the heart' (Caswell, 2007: 609).

MEDICINE WALK

A variation on the vision quest is the medicine walk (Foster and Little, 1988). Rather than sitting on one spot, one moves through a landscape holding a question about one's life and attending to what one encounters as a message about one's question. A full-scale medicine walk lasts at least from dawn to sunset, alternating walking and resting. Participants are encouraged to fast. The medicine walk can be used as part of the preparation for a vision quest or some other rite of passage. It can also be used in a smaller-scale way in an individual therapy session or as part of an ecotherapy workshop, often with a walker and a witness/accompanier.

MAKING CONTACT

A key technique for the more relational forms of ecotherapy is to let oneself be drawn towards a particular being or landscape element – an animal, bird, plant, tree, rock, water or cave, for example – and find a way to enter into contactful relationship with it. This might involve sitting with it, observing it, touching it, smelling it, climbing on or into it, vocalising to or with it or having a silent conversation with it, dancing with it, sleeping and dreaming by it – the options are enormous, once one has taken the key step of allowing the possibility of relating.

This is clearly a form of play, offering an opportunity to re-enter the world of childhood, where the whole environment is alive and intelligent. Many people who adventure in this way find themselves returning with gifts and messages from the other-than-human, which can then be worked with and understood over time.

NATURE ART

A further way of developing contact with the other-than-human is to make art (Siddons Heginworth, 2011): to draw or paint or sculpt, to make structures and patterns in particular locations out of what one finds there (Berger, 2007), to create masks to represent one's connection with magical beings.

RESEARCH EVIDENCE

There is considerable evidence, both quantitative and qualitative, for the positive effect that spending time outdoors in green environments has on psychological and physical wellbeing. As well as research on the general benefits (MIND, 2013), this includes work focused on:

- recovery from illness and surgery (Ulrich, 1984)
- children and young people (Louv, 2010)
- the elderly (Gigliotti, Jarrott and Yorgason, 2004; Watts and Hsieh, 2010)
- mental patients (Wilson, Ross, Lafferty and Jones, 2008)

- addiction (Black, 2015; Cornille, Rohrer, Phillips and Mosier, 1987)
- depression (Gonzalez et al., 2010)
- asylum seekers (Linden and Grut, 2002)

Some of this work (notably Linden and Grut, 2002) is focused specifically on ecotherapy proper, while some of it simply reports on the beneficial effects of being in or able to see green spaces.

Perhaps the best meta-study so far of ecotherapy is Annerstedt and Wahrborg (2011), which analysed three meta-analyses, six pieces of research classified as high evidence grade, and 29 classified as low to moderate evidence grade. The study concluded that 'a rather small but reliable evidence base supports the effectiveness and appropriateness of Nature-Assisted Therapy (NAT) as a relevant resource for public health. Significant improvements were found for varied outcomes in diverse diagnoses, spanning from obesity to schizophrenia' (2011: 371). Another valuable, if more discursive, research survey is Chalquist (2009), which argues for ecotherapy rather than taking a neutral position. Finally, David Key and Margaret Kerr have provided several papers of qualitative research around their training model, the Natural Change Project (Key and Kerr, 2012; Key, 2015), and also a critique of quantitative research which advocates a new research model specifically for ecotherapy and ecopsychology (Kerr and Key, 2011; Key and Kerr, 2011).

REFERENCES

Annerstedt, M. and and Wahrborg, P. (2011) Nature-assisted therapy: Systematic review of controlled and observational studies. *Scandinavian Journal of Public Health*, 39(4), 371–388.

Bateson, G. (1980) *Mind and Nature: A Necessary Unity*. London: Fontana/Collins.

Berger, R. (2007) Nature Therapy: Developing a Framework for Practice. PhD thesis, University of Abertay, Dundee.

Black, M. (2015) 'The Trees Were Our Cathedral': A Narrative Enquiry into Healing from Addiction through a Relationship with Nature. Dissertation submitted to the faculty of the California Institute of Integral Studies. (http://pqdtopen.proquest.com/doc/1757513031.html?FMT=ABS)

Bodnar, S. (2008) Wasted and bombed: Clinical enactments of a changing relationship to the earth. *Psychoanalytic Dialogues*, 18(4), 484–512.

Caswell, K. (2007) Hunger on the mountain. *Janus Head*, 9(2), 605–624.

Chalquist, C. (2009) A look at the ecotherapy research evidence. *Ecopsychology*, 1(2), 64–74.

Chatalos, P. (2012) Gaia living with AIDS: Towards reconnecting humanity with ecosystem autopoiesis through using metaphors of the immune system. In M.-J. Rust and N. Totton (eds), *Vital Signs: Psychological Responses to Ecological Crisis* (pp. 33–45). London: Karnac.

Cornille, T., Rohrer, G., Phillips, S. and Mosier, J. (1987) Horticultural therapy in substance abuse treatment. *Journal of Therapeutic Horticulture*, 2(1), 3–8.

Foster, S. and Little, M. (1988) *The Book of the Vision Quest*. New York: Prentice-Hall.

Gigliotti, C., Jarrott, S. and Yorgason, J. (2004) Harvesting health: Effects of three types of horticultural therapy activities for persons with dementia. *Dementia*, 3(2), 161–180.

Gillis, H.L. and Ringer, M. (1999) Adventure as therapy. In J.C. Miles and S. Priest (eds), *Adventure Programming* (pp. 29–37). State College, PA: Venture Publishing.

Glendinning, C. (1995) Technology, trauma, and the wild. In T. Roszak, M.E. Gomes and A.D. Kanner (eds), *Ecopsychology: Restoring the Earth, Healing the Mind* (pp. 41–54). San Francisco: Sierra Club Books.

Gonzalez, M.T., Hartig, T., Patil, G.G., Martinsen E.W. and Kirkevold, M. (2010) Therapeutic horticulture in clinical depression: A prospective study of active components. *Journal of Advanced Nursing*, 66(9), 2002–2013.

Hay, R. (2005) Becoming ecosynchronous, part 1: The root causes of our unsustainable way of life. *Sustainable Development*, 13, 311–325.

Jordan, M. (2009) Nature and self: An ambivalent attachment? *Ecopsychology*, 1(1), 26–31.

Kanner, A.D. and Gomes, M.E. (1995) The all-consuming self. In T. Roszak, M.E. Gomes and A.D. Kanner (eds), *Ecopsychology: Restoring the Earth, Healing the Mind* (pp. 77–91). San Francisco, CA: Sierra Club Books.

(Continued)

(Continued)

Kaplan, R. and Kaplan, S. (1989) *Experience of Nature*. Cambridge and New York: Cambridge University Press.

Kaplan, S. (1995) The restorative benefits of nature: Towards an integrative framework. *Journal of Environmental Psychology*, 16, 169–182.

Karol, J. (2007) Applying a traditional individual psychotherapy model to equine-facilitated psychotherapy (EFP): Theory and method. *Clinical Child Psychology and Psychiatry*, 12, 77–91.

Keeney, B.P. (1979) Ecosystemic epistemology: An alternative paradigm for diagnosis. *Family Process*, 18, 117–129.

Kerr, M.H. and Key, D.H. (2011) The Ouroboros (Part 1): Towards an ontology of connectedness in ecopsychology research. *European Journal of Ecopsychology*, 2, 48–60.

Key, D.H. (2015) Transpersonal patterns in the Natural Change Project. *Self and Society*, Summer, 43(2), 106–119.

Key, D.H. and Kerr, M.H. (2011) The Ouroboros (Part 2): Towards an intersubjective-heuristic method for ecopsychology research. *European Journal of Ecopsychology*, 2, 61–75.

Key, D.H. and Kerr, M.H. (2012) The Natural Change Project. In M.-J. Rust and N. Totton (eds), *Vital Signs: Psychological Responses to Ecological Crisis* (pp. 239–250). London: Karnac.

Kidner, D.W. (2007) Depression and the natural world: Towards a critical ecology of psychological distress. *International Journal of Critical Psychology*, 19(Spring), 123–143.

Kohanov, L. (2001) *The Tao of Equus*. Novato, CA: New World Library.

Linden, S. and Grut, J. (2002) *Healing Fields: Working with Psychotherapy and Nature to Rebuild Shattered Lives*. London: Frances Lincoln.

Louv, R. (2010) *Last Child in the Woods: Saving Our Children from Nature-deficit Disorder*. Chapel Hill, NC: Algonquin Books.

Macy, J. (1995) Working through environmental despair. In T. Roszak, M.E. Gomes and A.D. Kanner (eds), *Ecopsychology: Restoring the Earth, Healing the Mind* (pp. 240–259). San Francisco, CA: Sierra Club Books.

Maitney, P. (2012) Longing to be human: Evolving ourselves in healing the earth. In M-J. Rust and N. Totton (eds), Vital Signs: Psychological Responses to Ecological Crisis (pp. 47–60). London: Karnac.

MIND (2013) *Feel Better Outside, Feel Better Inside: Ecotherapy for Mental Wellbeing, Resilience and Recovery*. London: MIND.

Roszak, T. (2002 [1993]) *The Voice of the Earth: An Exploration of Ecopsychology*. Grand Rapids, MI: Phanes Press.

Roszak, T., Gomes, M.E. and Kanner, A.D. (eds) (1995) *Ecopsychology: Restoring the Earth, Healing the Mind*. San Francisco, CA: Sierra Club Books.

Rust, M.-J. (2005) Ecolimia nervosa? *Therapy Today*, 16(10), 11–15.

Rust, M.-J. (2008a) Consuming the Earth: Unconscious Processes in Relation to Our Environmental Crisis. Keynote Lecture for Climate of Change conference, Bristol. 2008. (www.mjrust.net/downloads/Consuming%20the%20Earth.pdf).

Rust, M.-J. (2008b) Climate on the couch: Unconscious processes in relation to our environmental crisis. *Psychotherapy and Politics International*, 6(3), 157–170.

Seifert, A.-R. (2014) Cultivating new lives: An ethnographic pilot study of eco-therapy provision for people with alcohol-related problems in Northern Ireland. *Anthropology in Action*, 21(1), 4–12.

Sessions, G. (ed.) (1995) *Deep Ecology for the 21st Century: Readings on the Philosophy and Practice of the New Environmentalism*. Boston, MA: Shambhala.

Siddons Heginworth, I. (2011) *Environmental Arts Therapy and the Tree of Life*. Exeter: Spirit's Rest Books.

Totton, N. (2011) *Wild Therapy: Undomesticating Inner and Outer Worlds*. Ross-on-Wye: PCCS Books.

Totton, N. (2014) The practice of Wild Therapy. *Therapy Today*, 25(5), 14–17.

Ulrich, R. (1984) View through a window may influence recovery from surgery. *Science*, 224(4647), 420–421.

Watts, C. and Hsieh, P.-C. (2010) The use of horticulture-based programs to promote engagement for older adults with dementia. *Therapeutic Recreation Journal*, 49(3), 257.

Wilshire, B. (1999) *Wild Hunger: The Primal Roots of Modern Addiction*. Lanham, MD: Rowman and Littlefield.

Wilson, E.O. (1990) *Biophilia*. Cambridge, MA: Harvard University Press.

Wilson, N., Ross, M., Lafferty, K. and Jones, R. (2008) A review of ecotherapy as an adjunct form of treatment for those who use mental health services. *Journal of Public Mental Health*, 7(3), 23–35.

RECOMMENDED READING

1. Roszak, T., Gomes, M.E. and Kanner, A.D. (eds) (1995) *Ecopsychology: Restoring the Earth, Healing the Mind.* San Francisco, CA: Sierra Club Books.

The classic text of ecotherapy and ecopsychology. It is an anthology of substantial and often theoretical writings which did a great deal to establish the field. US focused.

2. Rust, M.-J. and Totton, N. (2012) *Vital Signs: Psychological Responses to Ecological Crisis.* London: Karnac.

A more recent collection showcasing the varied approaches to theory and practice. Largely, though not entirely, focused towards practitioners in the United Kingdom.

3. Buzzell, L. and Chalquist, C. (2009) *Ecotherapy: Healing with Nature in Mind.* San Francisco, CA: Sierra Club Books.

An anthology of short pieces from a wide variety of sources, addressing different aspects and practices. Focused on practitioners in the USA.

5.17 EMOTION-FOCUSED THERAPY

LADISLAV TIMULAK

OVERVIEW AND KEY POINTS

Emotion-focused therapy (EFT) is a humanistic-experiential treatment building on the traditions of person-centred and Gestalt therapy, integrating research-informed developments in this and other forms of therapy. The basic premise of EFT is that the core chronic painful maladaptive emotion schemes which influence a client's emotional processing need to be accessed and transformed in therapy, in order that adaptive emotion schemes can be established. Thus, EFT is:

- a form of research-informed humanistic-experiential therapy;
- a therapy that focuses on the transformation of chronic painful emotion by accessing underlying emotion schemes and transforming them with adaptive emotions;
- a therapy that values the therapeutic relationship, which it views as pivotal in bringing about lasting therapeutic change in clients; and

- a therapy that is highly developed as a treatment for depression, complex trauma and couple distress, with new developments in the areas of eating disorders, anxiety disorders and family distress.

BRIEF HISTORY

Emotion-focused therapy (EFT) is primarily associated with the work of Leslie (Les) Greenberg (2011, 2015). It has strong roots in the research tradition of client-centred therapy. Greenberg's mentor, Laura Rice, was a student of Carl Rogers, and Rice's work on the evocative functions of empathy in client-centred therapy significantly informed the early development of emotion-focused therapy. Greenberg also trained in Gestalt therapy and his couples work was further influenced by systemic training. Greenberg's early interest in the subject of emotion in psychotherapy (e.g., Greenberg and Safran, 1987) resulted in a research programme that led first to the development of a model for couples therapy (initially named *emotionally focused couple therapy*, in collaboration with his student Sue Johnson (Greenberg and Johnson, 1988)) and later, to the development of an individual therapy modality (initially named *process-experiential therapy* (Greenberg, Rice and Elliott, 1993) and subsequently renamed *emotion-focused therapy* (Greenberg, 2015; Greenberg and Paivio, 1997)). The tradition of research in EFT is such that EFT as an individual therapy has arguably more process studies than any other therapy; in EFT virtually all therapist interventions are informed by research-based observations. This research programme has also produced a number of randomized clinical trials (RCTs), most notably RCTs of EFT as a treatment for depression (see Elliott, Greenberg, Watson, Timulak and Freire (2013) for an overview of process and outcome research in EFT). Development in the area of couples work was mainly furthered by Sue Johnson (2004) and her collaborators, although Greenberg has also, in collaboration with Rhonda Goldman, made a return to research and writing in this area (Greenberg and Goldman, 2008). Current practice of EFT is well summarized in the American Psychological Association's bestseller, *Learning emotion-focused therapy* (Elliott, Watson, Goldman and Greenberg, 2004) and in several other books describing EFT work with depression (Greenberg and Watson, 2006), complex trauma (Paivio and Pascual-Leone, 2010) and emotional distress more generally (Greenberg, 2015; Timulak, 2015).

BASIC ASSUMPTIONS

Emotion-focused therapy (EFT) is a neo-humanistic treatment that relies on a constructivist epistemology (Greenberg, 2011). According to Greenberg (2011: 32) 'people are seen as constantly synthesizing conscious experience out of many levels of processing'. These levels of processing include sensorimotor, emotion schematic and conceptual processing. In EFT, Rogers' concept of congruence between experience and symbolized awareness is replaced by a concept of coherence between various levels of processing (Greenberg, 2011). As within Rogers' theory, people are seen as striving for adaptive functioning in the context of interaction with their environment. According to Greenberg (2011: 35), 'people are dynamic self-organizing systems in constant interaction with the environment … [while] … affect regulation is seen as a core aspect of motivation'. Indeed, in EFT (Elliott et al., 2004; Greenberg, 2011, 2015) emotions are seen as important sources of information that tell us whether our interaction with the environment is adaptive, promoting survival and growth. Emotions inform us about the extent to which our needs are met (Greenberg, 2011, 2015; Timulak, 2015).

EFT differentiates between various aspects of emotional experience. For instance, it differentiates between primary, secondary and instrumental emotions (Greenberg and Safran, 1987). Within this framework, primary emotions are the very first reactions we feel in response to a situation (e.g., fear when we are threatened). Secondary emotions are usually emotional responses to primary emotions or accompanying thoughts (e.g., I do not like my fear, so I become angry). Instrumental emotions are emotions deliberately expressed in order to influence others (e.g., crocodile tears engaged in to elicit comfort from others). EFT theory recognizes also a distinction between adaptive and maladaptive emotions (assessed on the basis of whether they inform or do not inform adaptive action; see Greenberg, 2015) and focuses as an intervention on accessing chronic primary maladaptive emotions in order that they can be transformed in therapy though the accessing of primary adaptive emotions. EFT theory also recognizes different levels of emotional arousal (Warwar and Greenberg, 1999) and there is a focus in therapy on attaining an optimal level of emotional arousal in order that emotions are not only talked about, but are actually accessed, experienced and expressed within the therapy session. It is also understood that maladaptive emotions can only be transformed in therapy when those emotions are activated within the session. EFT theory also distinguishes between productive and unproductive in-session emotional experiencing; while primary, adaptive emotions are perceived as being productive, the experiencing of maladaptive primary emotions is regarded as productive only if such emotion is experienced in a way that is not overwhelming, is owned and is well differentiated (Greenberg, Auszra and Herrmann, 2007).

ORIGIN AND MAINTENANCE OF PROBLEMS

An important part of our processing of interactions with the environment occurs through schematic processes. In EFT, these 'internal memory structures that synthesize affective, motivational, cognitive, and behavioural elements into internal organizations [which] are activated rapidly, out of awareness, by relevant cues' (Greenberg, 2011: 38) are called emotion schemes. Psychopathology occurs either when information contained in these emotion schemes is not symbolized in the individual's awareness, or when emotion schemes are maladaptive (Greenberg et al., 1993; Greenberg and Watson, 2006). Psychopathology thus develops (1) out of non-optimal (maladaptive) use of emotional processing, that is, our more conceptual processing (meaning-making) does not utilize the full potential of the information involved in faster emotional processing, or (2) out of problematic emotional processing based in maladaptive emotion schemes which results in chronic painful feelings that do not inform adaptive action. The origins of these types of problematic processing typically lie in early development; for example, when the emotional support provided to the individual was suboptimal, or when emotional experiences were so difficult (traumatic) that they disrupted the formation of healthy ways of interacting with the individual's environment. Even later in a person's development, significant traumatic experiences may impact on the quality of emotional/conceptual processing of interactions with the interpersonal and social environment, and may lead to non-optimal or limited use of own capacities. Similarly, biological vulnerabilities and their interplay with the (social) environment may be responsible for the formation of problematic emotion schemes.

THEORY OF CHANGE

Therapeutic change in EFT is based on (1) increasing the client's awareness of the richness of information contained in emotional schematic processing, thus facilitating the client to optimally use this information at a conceptual (meaning-making) level of processing, and (2) on the reworking of problematic emotional schemes, particularly through the use of adaptive emotional experiences to counteract maladaptive ones. Therapy thus focuses on bringing an optimal level of emotional arousal (e.g., overcoming emotional avoidance), on broadening awareness of emotional experiences, on regulating dysregulated emotions, on transforming chronic maladaptive emotions (schemes) through the experiencing of adaptive emotions in the context of maladaptive emotions, and finally on meaning-making that takes into account the wealth of information contained in the emotional experience (Greenberg, 2011, 2015).

The process of change can also be understood in terms of a productive sequence of emotional experiencing (Pascual-Leone and Greenberg, 2007; Timulak, 2015) that starts with (1) problematic, secondary, global undifferentiated distress (e.g., I feel hopeless, helpless, down, etc.) and emotional/behavioural avoidance (e.g., I do not want to feel the pain, I am afraid of situations that may bring it); followed by (2) the accessing of core painful (maladaptive) feelings (e.g., I feel worthless, unlovable) which are sparked by the client's interaction with the environment (e.g., they do not love me) and problematic self-treatment (e.g., it is all my fault); (3) the identification of unmet needs (e.g., I want to feel loved and accepted); and responded to by (4) experiences of adaptive emotions such as compassion (e.g., I feel loved) and healthy protective anger (e.g., I deserve to be loved), in turn gradually leading to grieving (e.g., it is sad what I had to go through, but I can

let go of it now) and a sense of empowerment (e.g., I feel stronger inside now). This particular emotional sequence was initially discovered and conceptualized by Pascual-Leone and Greenberg (2007; Pascual-Leone, 2009) and eventually studied by others (e.g., Timulak, 2015).

SKILLS AND STRATEGIES

Therapeutic work in EFT is embedded in the therapist's provision of a Rogerian authentic, caring and unconditional relationship. The default position of the therapist is one of empathic attunement to the client's affective experience, a position very similar to that found in person-centred therapy. The therapist facilitates the client's exploration by empathic exploration and empathic understanding-focused interventions. The therapist's empathy is, however, more active than would be the case in person-centred therapy, with the therapist using empathic responses to evoke emotional experience, refocus the client on emotional processes, or empathically conjecture as to the nature of the client's emotional experience (Elliott et al., 2004). All of these strategies are employed with the goal of promoting access to the client's emotional experience.

The EFT therapist's work is also influenced by case formulation. EFT case formulation (Goldman and Greenberg, 2015) considers the client's presenting issue, focuses on the underlying painful emotions, considers the client's emotional processing style and assesses whether painful emotions are linked to identity or attachment issues. It then focuses on identifying the primary maladaptive emotion schemes that need to be accessed and transformed through the use of experiential tasks (see below). Timulak and Pascual-Leone (2015) also offer a framework that can inform EFT therapist strategy; conceptualization within this framework focuses on identifying painful triggering situations; the client's self-treatment in the context of these situations; the client's typical secondary emotions in those situations (global distress); the client's apprehension and avoidance of the situations that bring painful feelings; the client's core painful maladaptive feelings (i.e., loneliness, shame and fear) in those triggering situations; and the unmet needs embedded or contained in core painful, primary maladaptive feelings. The therapy then focuses on accessing these painful primary feelings and facilitating the articulation of unmet needs (e.g., to be loved, accepted and/ or safe); the articulation of which typically invites adaptive experiential responses from the client (typically compassion and protective anger) that lead to emotional transformation.

EFT is also a 'marker'-driven therapy, which means that when certain markers present themselves in the session (e.g., self-criticism) the therapist introduces experiential tasks, during which the therapist actively guides the client to access their emotional experience, own it, regulate it if needed and transform it if needed. Experiential tasks (see Elliott et al., 2004) include for instance: *systematic evocative unfolding* (in which the client is guided to recall in a slow-process situations that troubled him or her in order to get a sense of what it was within that situation that sparked an unexpected or problematic reaction); *clearing a space* (an emotional regulation-promoting task); *experiential focusing* (a task that allows the client to access emotional experience and symbolize them in awareness); *two chair dialogue for self-criticism* (in which the client enacts problematic self-treatments such as self-criticism in order to transform the maladaptive schemes); *two chair dialogue for self-interruption* (an imaginary dialogue in which the client accesses previously avoided emotional experience); and *empty chair dialogue* (in which the client engages in an imaginary dialogue with a significant other in order to identify emotional injuries in relation to that significant other and in order to transform the underlying maladaptive emotion schemes rooted in such injuries). In short-term therapies, approximately 50% of the time is spent in various experiential tasks, predominantly self–self or self–other chair dialogues.

CASE EXAMPLE

To illustrate the nature of therapeutic work in EFT, I will use a case presented by McNally, Timulak and Greenberg (2014; also McNally, 2012). The client, Jane (pseudonym), sought out therapy for depression. She presented with many somatic symptoms related to emotional distress, and she reported feeling down, irritable and profoundly hopeless. As therapy proceeded, it emerged that Jane felt ostracized from, and judged by, her family of origin (in particular, she felt judged by her mother). She also married at a young age, and her husband had been abusive. She felt very guilty for not having being able to protect her children from her abusive husband. Although she was now remarried, she also felt let down by her current husband. She was very self-critical of herself (e.g., *There is something wrong with me; Nobody loves me; I let down my children; I am a bad mother; I am a bad daughter*); felt shamed and alone and still felt traumatized by the abusive attacks of her ex-husband. She was very avoidant of her core painful feelings, and despite her presenting irritability was not able to stand up for herself without feeling tremendous guilt.

In therapy Jane was able to access her pain in the context of soothing responses from her therapist. For instance, in session 12 she touched on the pain of missing her children when she had to withdraw from an abusive situation. In a two chair dialogue, with the judging/critical part of herself in the Critic chair (e.g., voicing judgement and criticism about how she failed to protect her children) and the impacted, ashamed part of herself in the Experiencer chair, Jane describes her pain thus:

Jane [speaking from the Experiencer chair to the Critic chair]:
    I used to come home every night from work and go into their (Jane's children) empty rooms (sniffs) and walk around as though I was lost (sighs). I used to have this ache in my heart all the time, that I wanted them there with me (crying) and I couldn't have them (sniffs)

Therapist: What was that ache like? Seems like you're feeling...

Jane: (sniffs) It just...

Therapist: Right now...

Jane: (sniffs) It was like a – a physical hurt, ah (sniffs) and it hurt so much and I used to – without thinking about it – set the table and call them (Jane's children) for dinner – and I'd realize that they were not there (sniffs)...

...

Therapist: Mm-hm it really tore you apart.

One session prior to this exchange, she touched on the vulnerability she felt in the presence of her husband, a sense of not feeling loved. In an empty chair dialogue with her imagined husband in the other chair, she articulated what she needed from her husband when feeling unloved, overlooked and uncared for (Unmet Need):

Jane: I still need you (client's husband) there – to protect me (crying) – even though I might – come across that I don't need it all the time, I still need you there to protect me – I want – you once – to put me ahead of everybody else (sniffs)...

Therapist: So I want to be ahead – (C. sigh) – of (C. sniff) everyone – else.

Jane: I want to be number one in your life – ah – not after everybody else – (sniff)...

When enacting her husband's response to this unmet need (Jane was asked to sit in the other chair and witness the expressed pain and unmet need), Jane unexpectedly communicated a very caring and loving response, which she (sitting back in 'her' chair and asked to feel how it was like to get this response) in turn experienced as very soothing.

In session 12 she was also able to stand up to the judgement she had always felt from her mother (e.g., for failing as a daughter, as a wife and a mother of her own children). In the empty chair dialogue with her imagined mother, she stood up for herself (Protective Anger):

Jane: I have to live up to these expectations (her mother's expectations) (sniffs)... I don't want to do it anymore, it's too hard (sniffs). I want to get off of it, I don't want to do it anymore, it's hard (sniffs) I feel hurt... I don't deserve it.

....

Jane: Ah, I'd like you (client's mother) just to accept me for myself, even if I'm not that good all the time (sniffs)...

Therapist: Mm-hm, so you want to be accepted.

Jane: I want to be accepted for myself (sniffs).

This expression left Jane feeling calm and empowered, and the session appeared to be quite pivotal in the overall case.

RESEARCH EVIDENCE

Emotion-focused therapy is particularly well researched as a treatment for depression, with research indicating that it was somewhat more effective than classical person-centred therapy and comparably effective to cognitive-behavioural therapy (a summary of these studies can be found in Elliott et al., 2013). Sandra Paivio and her colleagues have also assessed the efficacy of EFT in the treatment of complex trauma stemming from child abuse (a summary of that work can be found in Paivio and Pascual-Leone, 2010). Emotion-focused therapy is heavily influenced by psychotherapy process research and has in turn contributed to that research field. The latest summary of this research is captured in two excellent research reviews by Elliott et al. (2013) and Angus, Watson, Elliott, Schneider and Timulak (2015). The couples' version of EFT (Greenberg and Goldman, 2008; Greenberg and Johnson, 1988; Johnson, 2004) is also one of the most researched couples therapies in the world.

REFERENCES

Angus, L., Watson, J. C., Elliott, R., Schneider, K. and Timulak, L. (2015). Humanistic psychotherapy research 1990–2015: From methodological innovation to evidence-supported treatment outcomes and beyond. *Psychotherapy Research*, *25*, 330–347.

Elliott, R., Greenberg, L. S., Watson, J., Timulak, L. and Freire, E. (2013). Research on humanistic-experiential psychotherapies. In M. J. Lambert (Ed.), *Bergin & Garfield's handbook of psychotherapy and behavior change* (pp. 495–538). New York: John Wiley.

Elliott, R., Watson, J. C., Goldman, R. N. and Greenberg, L. S. (2004). *Learning emotion-focused therapy: The process-experiential approach to change*. Washington, DC: American Psychological Association.

Goldman, R. N. and Greenberg, L. S. (2015). *Case formulation in emotion-focused therapy*. Washington, DC: American Psychological Association.

Greenberg, L. S. (2011). *Emotion-focused therapy*. Washington, DC: American Psychological Association.

Greenberg, L. S. (2015). *Emotion-focused therapy: Coaching clients to work through their feelings* (2nd ed.). Washington, DC: American Psychological Association. (The first edition published in 2002.)

Greenberg, L. S., Auszra, L. and Herrmann, I. R. (2007). The relationship among emotional productivity, emotional arousal and outcome in experiential therapy of depression. *Psychotherapy Research*, *17*, 482–493.

Greenberg, L. S. and Goldman, R. N. (2008). *Emotion-focused couples therapy: The dynamics of emotion, love, and power*. Washington, DC: American Psychological Association.

Greenberg, L. S. and Johnson, S. M. (1988). *Emotionally focused therapy for couples*. New York: Guilford Press.

Greenberg, L. S. and Paivio, S. C. (1997). *Working with emotions in psychotherapy*. New York: Guilford Press.

Greenberg, L. S., Rice, L. N. and Elliott, R. (1993). *Facilitating emotional change: The moment by moment process*. New York: Guilford Press.

Greenberg, L. S. and Safran, J. D. (1987). *Emotion in psychotherapy: Affect, cognition, and the process of change*. New York: Guilford Press.

Greenberg, L. S. and Watson, J. (2006). *Emotion-focused therapy for depression*. Washington, DC: American Psychological Association.

Johnson, S. M. (2004). *The practice of emotionally focused couples therapy: Creating connections* (2nd ed.). New York/London: Brunner-Routledge.

McNally, S. (2012). *Transforming emotion schemes in emotion focused therapy*. Unpublished dissertation. Trinity College Dublin.

McNally, S., Timulak, L. and Greenberg, L. S. (2014). Transforming emotion schemes in emotion focused therapy: A case study investigation. *Person-Centered & Experiential Psychotherapies*, *13*, 128–149.

Paivio, S. C. and Pascual-Leone, A. (2010). *Emotion-focused therapy for complex trauma: An integrative approach*. Washington, DC: American Psychological Association.

Pascual-Leone, A. (2009). Emotional processing cycles in experiential therapy: 'Two steps forward, one step backward'. *Journal of Consulting and Clinical Psychology*, *77*, 113–126.

Pascual-Leone, A. and Greenberg, L. S. (2007). Emotional processing in experiential therapy: Why 'the only way out is through'. *Journal of Consulting and Clinical Psychology*, *75*, 875–887. doi: 10.1037/0022-006X.75.6.875.

Timulak, L. (2015). *Transforming emotional pain in psychotherapy: An emotion-focused approach*. London: Routledge.

Timulak, L. and Pascual-Leone, A. (2015). New developments for case conceptualization in emotion-focused therapy. *Clinical Psychology & Psychotherapy*, *22*, 619–636.

Warwar, S. and Greenberg, L. S. (1999). Client emotional arousal scale–III. Unpublished manuscript, York University, Toronto, Ontario, Canada.

RECOMMENDED READING

1. Elliott, R., Watson, J. C., Goldman, R. N. and Greenberg, L. S. (2004). *Learning emotion-focused therapy: The process-experiential approach to change*. Washington, DC: American Psychological Association.

This is an excellent introduction to EFT for students. It provides a thorough description of the experiential tasks used in EFT. Written in a student-friendly manner.

2. Greenberg, L. S. (2015). *Emotion-focused therapy: Coaching clients to work through their feelings* (2nd ed.). Washington, DC: American Psychological Association.

This is the latest book from the primary EFT developer Les Greenberg. It is a summary of his latest thinking, written for professionals of all theoretical orientations. It contains examples of exercises that can be used as standalone pieces and which can be incorporated into one's practice.

3. Timulak, L. (2015). *Transforming emotional pain in psychotherapy: An emotion-focused approach.* London: Routledge.

This is a relatively short presentation of EFT through the lens of emotion transformation embedded in the theoretical framework presented in this chapter. The book uses plenty of clinical examples.

5.18 EXISTENTIAL THERAPY

EMMY VAN DEURZEN

OVERVIEW AND KEY POINTS

Existential therapy is a philosophical form of counselling and psychotherapy, with long roots into philosophy and a century of development. There are many forms of existential therapy, including an analytical version, Daseinsanalysis (Binswanger, Boss), a meaning-based approach, called Logotherapy (Frankl, Längle), an existential/humanistic or existential/integrative approach (Yalom, Schneider) and an existential-phenomenological approach (Deurzen, Spinelli). All these varied forms of existential therapy search for a direct engagement with people's problems in living, without pathologizing these. Existential therapists consider human existence to be intrinsically difficult. They aim to enable people to get better at tackling their problems in living, by gaining greater understanding. Existential therapy:

*   engages with the big questions
*   emphasizes paradoxical concepts like freedom and responsibility
*   focuses on the way in which purpose, values and beliefs shape our lives
*   reminds people of the limits of the human condition
*   enables people to regain their passion for life.

BRIEF HISTORY

Existential therapy finds its origin in applied philosophy. The original idea of philosophy, literally the love of wisdom, was to actively search for the secret of a well-lived life. Hellenistic philosophers used the Socratic method of dialectical discussion to reveal and unravel the truth about personal and universal issues and dilemmas. This practice fell into desuetude but was revitalized at the beginning of the twentieth century when a number of psychiatrists began applying the thinking of existential philosophers such as Kierkegaard, Nietzsche and Heidegger to their clinical work (Deurzen, 2010). Karl Jaspers, Ludwig Binswanger and Medard Boss were the first to formulate some principles for existential psychotherapy (May et al., 1958). Their work, based mainly in Germany and Switzerland, was known as *Daseinsanalysis* or existential analysis.

Authors such as Paul Tillich (1952) and Rollo May (1969) then spread the approach far more widely in the United States. Their influence on the human potential movement and on humanistic psychotherapy and counselling was extensive. There are obvious existential elements in approaches such as person-centred therapy and Gestalt psychotherapy, while Irvin Yalom (1980), James Bugental (1981) and Alvin Mahrer (1996) have made direct contributions to the development of existential/humanistic forms of psychotherapy in North America. More recently, Kirk Schneider has taken existential therapy into a more spiritual direction (Schneider and Krug, 2009).

In Europe existential psychotherapy was further developed by Victor Frankl's (1964 [1946]) Logotherapy, which is a largely meaning-driven approach, now spread more widely around the world. More recently, Alfried Längle has added further layers of practice to Logotherapy, calling it existential analysis (Längle, 1990). In the United Kingdom (UK) the work of R.D. Laing (1960) was much inspired by the existentialist writing of Jean-Paul Sartre (1956 [1943]). It facilitated the flourishing of existential psychotherapy in the UK, which was firmly established from 1988 with the founding of the Society for Existential Analysis, together with its journal *Existential Analysis*. A number of training courses at the Philadelphia Association, Regent's University, Surrey University and the New School of Psychotherapy and Counselling, at the Existential Academy, were developed and the existential-phenomenological approach characteristic of the UK is now widespread. A number of noteworthy publications made the existential approach better known (see Cohn, 1997; Deurzen, 2010, 2012, 2015; Spinelli, 2014). Existential-phenomenological therapy has been adopted by many psychotherapists across the world, as became evident at the first World Congress for Existential Therapy in London, in 2015.

BASIC ASSUMPTIONS

Existential therapy helps people in coming to terms with their lives in all its complexity rather than just addressing psychological or relationship problems.

Many problems are the natural and inevitable consequence of the challenges and limitations of the human condition, such as death, loneliness, failure, weakness, guilt, anxiety, poverty, illness and futility.

The objective is not to cure people of pathology, which is an unhelpful and misleading concept borrowed from the medical model, but rather to assist them in coming to terms with the contradictions, dilemmas and paradoxes of their everyday existence. Several concepts are distinctive for existential therapy.

Anxiety is a valuable instrument in helping us become more aware of the demands of reality. It is a form of life energy and when embraced can help live life to the full.

Human beings often feel alone, but are never in isolation. They are always in a given world, with other people and in a situation, which affects their experience. Problems need to be seen in their cultural, social and political context.

We all tend to hide away and deceive ourselves about life and our own position in it. Facing the truth and aiming for a more authentic way of being are important goals.

The concept of 'self' is a relative one. It is only as I act in the world and connect to objects, people and ideas in the world, that I create a sense of self. There is no such thing as a solid, immutable self. We are in constant transformation and flux and can change and redefine ourselves.

Existential therapists work with what is unknown and hidden. They do not accept the idea that there is an inner place called 'the unconscious'. Nor is there such a thing as absolute truth. They explore multiple interpretations of reality at different levels of existence.

People need purpose and meaning in life. Tuning into personal yearnings and longings helps finding a life project, in line with beliefs and values.

Vitality comes from accepting both positives and negatives in life. There can be no life without death and no health without illness, no happiness without unhappiness (Deurzen, 2009).

We live in time. We recollect ourselves from the past. We present ourselves in the now and project ourselves into the future. All these dimensions of time are equally important. Temporality is a core aspect of existential work.

We live in space, on a number of different dimensions. We are embodied in a physical world where we interact with material objects. We are with other people in a social world. We relate to ourselves in a personal, inner world. We form theories and ideas that give meaning to life at a spiritual or ideological level.

ORIGIN AND MAINTENANCE OF PROBLEMS

Life is intrinsically problematic as tensions are created at all levels. Every day we encounter problems of all sorts. We need to build confidence in our ability to tackle and solve these problems and improve our competence in dealing with increasingly tougher situations. We find pleasure in the vitality that comes with a resolute and courageous attitude to living.

Sometimes we might try to make things easier for ourselves by escaping from reality and living with illusions. One of the ways in which we deceive ourselves is by imagining that we can't change. We can learn to embrace our freedom and responsibility and make our own choices and changes in life.

Sometimes people feel so overwhelmed that they withdraw from the world completely, in isolation or chaos, losing their foothold on reality and giving up their remaining strength and vitality.

One of our constant causes for concern is the presence of others. We might see our fellow human beings as potential threats and as untrustworthy. Our destructive interactions or avoidance of interaction with others can become a self-fulfilling prophecy of doom.

We often live with regret over what happened yesterday, in fear of what may be demanded of us tomorrow and in guilt over what we have not yet accomplished today. We are quite capable of emotionally paralysing ourselves in this manner. Working with moods and feelings is central to existential therapy and is done by tracing the values that are at the root of feelings.

Some people are in situations that significantly restrict or constrict their outlook and their freedom of action. Genetic, developmental, accidental, class, cultural or gender factors can all generate apparently insurmountable obstacles. Everyone's life presents numerous difficulties that have to be accommodated or overcome. Some people manage to surmount substantial initial disadvantages or adversity, whereas others squander their advantage or flounder in the face of minor misfortunes.

Every problem has several solutions. Facing the situation and putting it in perspective is always possible, given some time and with some assistance, and this will lead to finding new ways of viewing the problem.

Existential therapy encourages resolute living, which is based in the capacity to meet whatever may come with steadfastness and in a spirit of adventure.

THEORY OF CHANGE

Change takes place continuously in life. We spend much energy trying to keep things the same. When aiming for stability and safety we may find it difficult to allow changes to happen, even when this could be beneficial. We may fear the process of transformation that everything in this world is subject to and fend it off.

When clients come to therapy they do so because they want to find the strength and confidence to allow changes for the better to happen in their lives. They need the therapist to help them to be steady when confronting their fears and doubts, so as to find a way through.

The objective of existential work is to enable clients to become more open to their own experience in all its paradoxical reality. They will become more tolerant of their anxiety and more understanding of themselves by self-reflection. They gain awareness of their worldview and interpretation of reality, reshaping their story and thus their future as well.

Becoming aware of strengths, talents and abilities is as important as to explore the darker side of experience. Hidden passions and yearnings bring new energy for change.

For those who are in a situation of crisis, which is a moment of danger and loss, the challenge is to find new opportunities instead of being thrown into a state of confusion. Existential therapy explores new paths and new directions, ensuring that the crisis is a point of breakthrough rather than breakdown.

Even when circumstances are dire or unfair, it is still possible to find courage and create new ways of improving your fate, perhaps by finding new meaning in it.

SKILLS AND STRATEGIES

The existential approach is in principle against techniques, as these hamper human interaction at a deep, direct and real level. The therapeutic encounter consists of an authentic human exchange, in dialogue. Skills are drawn largely from the method of phenomenology, the scientific study of human consciousness. But we might also other philosophical methods, such as logic, dialectics, hermeneutics and maieutics. These will be described and illustrated by the example of a fictitious existential therapy client called Millie. Millie is a young woman in her early twenties who seeks therapy when she feels frozen and incapacitated by constant fear and anxiety, which is stopping her living a normal life.

When Millie arrives for therapy she finds herself in a welcoming conversation with her existential therapist, who freely asks questions as well as answering them. The therapist may think of this conversational strategy as a Socratic dialogue, where the client is helped to pinpoint inner knowledge she was not aware of. Millie will be encouraged to trace a deep personal sense of her predicament and articulate this. Millie's therapist will help her discover paradoxical realities that have confused her in her life. Millie will find her therapist very real in the dialogue. The relationship between them will be up for constant scrutiny. The dynamic between them is up for an honest appraisal. This will help Millie to become more reflective about the way in which she responds and relates to the outside world and its challenges. Her way of being will never be pathologized. She will soon begin to feel freer in her descriptions of what matters to her, as her therapist becomes an ally. Together they will ponder how Millie makes sense of her world and how she can look at things from new angles. In this way she will soon start to see the conflicts and troubles she is dealing with as something temporary and situational rather than permanent. She sees it is possible to understand and confront reality.

Existential therapists encourage an attitude of openness and directness. Millie and her therapist speak in everyday language. She is not mollycoddled either, but will be treated with utmost respect and care. Millie will start focusing on strengths she had already developed and can learn to master further. She will soon get used to becoming tougher on herself than she has been in the past. Millie will then be more curious about her difficulties and where they come from, tracking the circumstances that created them. As the situation is elucidated Millie will gain strength and take courage in being able to understand things better. She can begin to take charge of the process and be in the world in a much more determined way. She will get continuous feedback from her therapist when she forgets to notice her own progress. She will get bolder at experimenting. She will recognize what gives her safety and comfort in unfamiliar situations and build confidence that she can follow her own purpose and direction. She will learn to move forward, as if she is learning to ride a bike by keeping her eyes on where she is going, to stay in tune with the forces of gravity.

In line with phenomenological principles, Millie's therapist will help her to make explicit her assumptions about the world. She will get to know her values and beliefs, until a clear worldview emerges. Sometimes the therapist will help her confront contradictions. At other times the therapist might point to consequences or implications of her beliefs or ideas. In this way Millie may discover that she is much more judgemental of other people and herself than she realized. She will find that it is this tendency to dismiss herself and others that gets her into trouble and confusion. Initially the therapist will just stay with Millie's usual mode of being, but soon will challenge it and invite Millie to experiment with new ways of being. They will speak about her past, her present and her future. They will explore her relationship to herself in her inner world. They will examine how she is with others, and how she is when alone. In this process she will come to know herself from many different angles. She will remember more and more about the talents and abilities she has hidden away and that she was afraid of developing.

Her existential therapist will not tell her how to be, but will draw her out of hiding. Her therapist will help her look at problems in a brave and creative manner. Millie will start to unfold and care for herself better. She will discover ways in which she has constricted her world or outreached herself. She will reclaim her freedom. She will gain trust in the world around her as she becomes more confident. She will see new opportunities. Her therapist will facilitate this journey of discovery until Millie takes the lead.

The existential therapist keeps track of Millie's state of mind, following her moods and attitudes, feelings and intuitions to their source, till a deeply felt sense of what truly matters emerges.

The therapist is personal, direct, gentle and respectful, though sometimes also quite challenging. They will face fears and terrors and they will laugh together. The therapy is a collaborative process, where Millie learns to be alive in a more open, confident and aware manner. Her vitality is encouraged and stimulated. Millie becomes inspired by the idea of finding new purpose in her life.

Millie learns that her troubles and doubts do not define her but are part of life. She becomes more resilient and more resolute in facing up to dangers and changes. She accepts the limits of life and does not expect herself to become perfect. She now feels able to face new difficulties in her life as her mother's decline requires her to look after mom. This time when she feels anxious about this, she welcomes the feeling as proof that she is readying herself for a new challenge.

RESEARCH EVIDENCE

There is little outcome research in existential therapy because such research is generally based on the medical model, which seeks symptom relief. There is, however, a growing body of qualitative research which is done by the many doctoral counselling psychology students and their tutors, who use phenomenological methods to investigate various human issues (Edwards and Milton, 2014). There is also research that deals with existential concerns, showing these to be at the core of the therapeutic change process:

- Yalom (1970) in his work with groups found existential factors to be vital to client change.
- Much of the research on person-centred therapy is relevant to existential therapy, especially where it demonstrates the importance of genuineness or authenticity on the part of the therapist (Carkhuff and Truax, 1965).
- Bergin and Garfield (1994) recognized a number of existential factors as determining positive outcome in psychotherapy.
- Rennie's (1992) qualitative research shows the importance of a number of existential factors.
- There is much research evidence for the importance of meaning creation in the successful processing of traumatic events (Clarke, 1989).
- Recent research in positive psychology demonstrates the importance of such existential factors as authenticity (Seligman, 2002) and meaning (Baumeister, 1991).

- Some research on outcome has now been done in existential therapy and is looking promising in terms of its effectiveness and relevance (Rayner and Vitali, 2014; Vos et al., 2015).

- Evidence on the importance of phenomenological methods of research can be found in the work of several researchers (Deurzen, 2014; Deurzen-Smith, 1990; Milton, 2010; Willig, 2001).

REFERENCES

Baumeister, R.F. (1991) *Meanings of Life*. New York: Guilford Press.

Bergin, A. and Garfield, S. (eds) (1994) *Handbook of Psychotherapy and Behavior Change* (4th ed.). New York: Wiley.

Bugental, J.F.T. (1981) *The Search for Authenticity*. New York: Irvington.

Carkhuff, R. and Truax, C. (1965) Training in counseling and therapy: an evaluation of an integrated didactic and experiential approach. *Journal of Consulting Psychology*, 29: 333–336.

Clarke, K.M. (1989) Creation of meaning: an emotional processing task in psychotherapy. *Psychotherapy*, 26: 139–148.

Cohn, H. (1997) *Existential Thought and Therapeutic Practice*. London: Sage.

Deurzen, E. van (2009) *Psychotherapy and the Quest for Happiness*. London: Sage.

Deurzen, E. van (2010) *Everyday Mysteries: Handbook of Existential Psychotherapy* (2nd ed.). London: Routledge.

Deurzen, E. van (2012) *Existential Counselling and Psychotherapy in Practice* (3rd ed.). London: Sage.

Deurzen E. van (2014) Structural Existential Analysis (SEA): a phenomenological research method for counselling psychology. *Counselling Psychology Review*, 29(2): 70–83.

Deurzen, E. van (2015) *Paradox and Passion in Psychotherapy* (2nd ed.). Chichester: Wiley.

Deurzen-Smith, E. van (1990) Philosophical underpinnings of counselling psychology. *Counselling Psychology Review*, 5: 8–12.

Edwards, W. and Milton, M. (2014) Retirement therapy? Older people's experiences of existential therapy in their transition to retirement, *Counselling Psychology Review*, 29(2): 43–53.

Frankl, V.E. (1964 [1946]) *Man's Search for Meaning*. London: Hodder and Stoughton.

Laing, R.D. (1960) *The Divided Self*. London: Tavistock.

Längle, A. (1990) Existential Analysis psychotherapy. *International Forum of Logotherapy* (Vienna), 13: 17–19.

Mahrer, A.R. (1996) *The Complete Guide to Experiential Psychotherapy*. New York: Wiley.

May, R. (1969) *Love and Will*. New York: W.W. Norton.

May, R., Angel, E. and Ellenberger, H.F. (1958) *Existence*. New York: Basic Books.

Milton, M. (2010) *Therapy and Beyond: Counselling Psychology Contributions to Therapeutic and Social Issues*. Chichester: Wiley-Blackwell.

Rayner, M. and Vitali, D. (2014) 'CORE blimey! Existential therapy scores GOALS!' *Existential Analysis*, 25: 296–313.

Rennie, D.L. (1992) Qualitative analysis of the client's experience of psychotherapy: the unfolding of reflexivity. In S. Toukmanian and D.L. Rennie (eds), *Psychotherapy Process Research: Paradigmatic and Narrative Approaches*. Newbury Park, CA: Sage.

Sartre, J.-P. (1956 [1943]) *Being and Nothingness: An Essay on Phenomenological Ontology*. Trans. H. Barnes. New York: Philosophical Library.

Schneider, K.J. and Krug, O.T. (2009) *Existential-Humanistic Therapy*. Washington, DC: American Psychological Association.

Seligman, M.E.P. (2002) *Authentic Happiness*. New York: Free.

Spinelli, E. (2014) *Practising Existential Psychotherapy: The Relational World* (2nd ed.). London: Sage.

Tillich, P. (1952) *The Courage To Be*. New Haven, CT: Yale University Press.

Vos, J., Craig, M. and Cooper, M. (2015) Existential therapies: a meta-analysis of their effects on psychological outcomes. *Journal of Consulting and Clinical Psychology*, 83(1): 115–128.

Willig, C. (2001) *Introducing Qualitative Research in Psychology: Adventures in Theory and Method*. Buckingham: Open University Press.

Yalom, I.D. (1970) *The Theory and Practice of Group Psychotherapy*. New York: Basic Books.

Yalom, I.D. (1980) *Existential Psychotherapy*. New York: Basic Books.

RECOMMENDED READING

1. Deurzen, E. van and Adams, M. (2016) *Skills in Existential Counselling and Psychotherapy* (2nd ed.). London: Sage.

One of the most comprehensive, easy-to-follow manuals for existential-phenomenological therapy, which is practice-based and yet firmly rooted in philosophy.

2. Cooper, M. (2016) *Existential Therapies* (2nd ed.). London: Sage.

This book provides an overview of all the different forms of existential therapy and gives a good sense of how existential therapy is different from any other form of psychotherapy.

3. Yalom, I.D. (1980) *Existential Psychotherapy*. New York: Basic Books.

This is one of the best-known books on existential psychotherapy and is regarded as a classic on existential/humanistic psychotherapy.

5.19 GESTALT THERAPY

MICHAEL ELLIS AND JONATHAN SMITH

OVERVIEW AND KEY POINTS

Gestalt therapy is an approach to psychotherapy which emphasises the central role of here-and-now awareness, including awareness of all aspects of the person, including one's body, feelings, thoughts and beliefs, and one's surrounding environment and history (the 'field'). Gestalt emphasises the importance of responsibility and choice and seeks to enhance clients' awareness of their ownership of their lives. The relationship between therapist and client is central to the work, and how they experience each other will be explored through dialogue and experiment. Gestalt therapy:

-   focuses on the here-and-now
-   pays attention to the body and how people 'embody' themselves
-   explores how clients make contact with others in their world, including the therapist
-   uses active experiments such as movement and role-playing to broaden and deepen clients' awareness of themselves and their relationships.

BRIEF HISTORY

Gestalt theory and practice were first developed by Frederick (Fritz) Perls and Laura Perls along with Paul Goodman and others in New York in the 1950s. *Gestalt Therapy: Excitement and Growth in the Human Personality* was published in 1951 (Perls et al., 1951). This has been for many years the definitive text on gestalt theory. Prior to this, while in South Africa, Fritz Perls published *Ego, Hunger and Aggression* (1947), in which he laid the foundations for this approach to therapy.

Perls was born in Berlin and educated at the University of Freiburg and Frederick Wilhelm University in Berlin. He received his MD in 1921. Before this he had served as a Medical Officer in the German army. He then trained in psychoanalysis in Berlin, Frankfurt and Vienna. Thus Perls brought a strong foundation in psychoanalysis, particularly influenced by Wilhelm Reich and Karen Homey. His wife Laura Perls studied gestalt psychology with Kurt Goldstein (from which the approach takes its name), worked with Paul Tillich and was greatly influenced by Martin Buber. Paul Goodman, a philosopher, libertarian and anarchist, contributed a social and political dimension to their thinking.

GESTALT PSYCHOLOGY

The word *Gestalt* does not have a direct translation into English; definitions include pattern, configuration, form and whole. The work of the gestalt psychologists in the early part of the twentieth century focused primarily on perception and learning. Wertheimer and Ehrenfels proposed that we perceive our environment in terms of 'wholes'. As best as we are able, we make meaning, we create a form or gestalt, from what we experience. The gestalt includes what is 'figure' for us in relation to what is in the background. Hence the importance in gestalt work of figure and ground. An additional contribution of the gestalt psychologists was the concept of 'closure'. In its original sense, it refers to the tendency of the perceptual system to 'close' or round off any incomplete shape or form. Perls expanded the notion of closure to include the push to bring any kind of experience or impulse to its natural conclusion – to complete 'unfinished business'.

The work of the above psychologists and others, including Koffka and Köhler, was extended into the realms of personality by Kurt Goldstein and Kurt Lewin. The work of these men was key for the development of gestalt theory and practice, although Lewin's influence has only recently been acknowledged. Goldstein developed his 'organismic theory' from gestalt principles, and particularly the centrality of 'self-actualisation' for the unfolding of the individual's potential. Lewin, also an associate of Wertheimer and Köhler, developed the concept of the individual as part of a dynamic field. He emphasised the importance of the person in relation to their environment and the significance of the present forces or vectors acting on the individual from the surrounding dynamic field.

EXISTENTIALISM

Gestalt theory has been influenced by a number of existentialist thinkers, such as Paul Tillich, Martin Buber and Jean-Paul Sartre. It is an existential phenomenological approach and explores the individual's existence as experienced by them. There is considerable emphasis on the individual being responsible for their own existence, on the importance of the here-and-now (experience in the present) and on the meeting of therapist and client in an authentic 'I–Thou' relationship.

EASTERN RELIGION

The influence of Eastern religions, particularly Taoism and Zen (Fritz Perls spent almost a year in Japan studying Zen), are evident in the importance of awareness of the present moment as a goal and a method in gestalt work,

which may lead to a 'satori'-like insight, a sudden realisation which results in a reconfiguration of the phenomenal field, a new gestalt, or a reorganisation of the person's experience. Also significant is the focus on 'organismic functioning' rather than an over-emphasis on thinking, and on the use of paradox and the ideas and practice of non-doing, of standing out of the way and allowing one's experiences to emerge and evolve of their own accord.

DRAMA AND MOVEMENT

Fritz Perls was very interested in the nature of theatre and drama and incorporated some of Jacob Moreno's psychodrama techniques. Laura Perls also studied dance for many years. These influences have given gestalt methodology a strong expressive/creative bias.

BASIC ASSUMPTIONS

- *Holism.* That nature is a coherent whole; different elements are in relation with each other in a continually evolving process. Holistically, we cannot understand ourselves by analysing aspects in isolation because 'the whole is more than the sum of the parts'.
- *Field theory.* Originally formulated by Kurt Lewin, field theory maintains that the person is never separated from their environment, both their internal physical and psychological environment and their external social and cultural context. The meaning we give to any figure, or stimulus, will then be dependent on its context or field. The Belgian gestaltist George Wollants has offered a re-formulation of field theory in his book *Gestalt Therapy: Therapy of the Situation* (Wollants, 2012), where he argues that the whole focus of therapeutic work needs to be directed towards the person-in-the-situation rather than the person in themselves.
- *Growth.* The process of organismic self-regulation occurs through contact with our environment, of which we are a part. In health we do this by a process of forming figures against a background based on our current most important need. At a given moment a need will emerge, become 'figural', be met and then recede into the background as another need emerges from the 'ground'. For example, I become aware of a dry mouth, decide I need a drink, take action to get a drink and then focus on the paper I was about to read.
- *Self-actualisation.* We have an innate tendency to realise our potential, to become who we can be. Perls wrote: 'Every individual, every plant, every animal

has only one inborn goal – to actualize itself as it is' (1969: 31).

- *Awareness*. Increasing awareness is at the core of gestalt practice. Through the development of 'organismic' experienced awareness (rather than just intellectual understanding) we are able to be responsible and proactive and allow the healthy flow of self-regulation for the whole organism.

- *Contact and dialogue*. Contact refers to the way we meet, interact and exchange with the environment, including other people. Gestalt work always aims for lively contact which can be enhanced through the use of dialogue. Dialogue means meeting in the here-and-now and recognising one another 'in our uniqueness, our fullness and our vulnerability' (Hycner and Jacobs, 1995: 9). Healing occurs through meeting another as a person. Each individual, acknowledged as separate, is capable of risking meeting the other in an I–Thou relationship, as defined by Martin Buber. Buber described two contrasting attitudes that an individual can take towards others: the *I–It* way of relating and the *I–Thou* way of relating. Both are needed for living. The I–It attitude is more present when there is a purpose in the meeting, when one or other or both have a goal of some sort. The I–Thou attitude is one of being as open and present as possible with another, without consideration of any purpose or goal and with an appreciation of the uniqueness of the other as a person.

ORIGIN AND MAINTENANCE OF PROBLEMS

A healthy person in gestalt theory allows himself or herself a fluent exchange and adjustment in relation with the environment (organismic self-regulation). This healthy process of forming figures against the background based on our needs is known as the gestalt formation and destruction cycle and is also called the contact/withdrawal cycle.

Problems are seen as disturbances of this natural healthy functioning. Significant early relationships are important in the initial disturbance of the contact/withdrawal cycle. These disturbances may develop as a creative way of surviving in the face of danger, lack of love, care and attention. However, they become embedded in the personality and in adulthood limit any further creative adjustment with the current environment, so functioning becomes rigid, habitual and over-controlled.

Perls defined four 'neurotic mechanisms' or contact boundary disturbances which can restrict and limit individuals' healthy exchange with their environment, whether physical, emotional or intellectual. All these processes have a healthy, functional aspect; it is when they are habitual and chronic that healthy functioning is limited. The mechanisms are:

- *Introjection*. In this, something is taken in whole, 'swallowed down' without assimilation or reflection. This may be an attitude, a belief, an idea or a behaviour.
- *Projection*. Here traits, attitudes, behaviours, beliefs, etc. are attributed to others or to objects in the environment.
- *Retroflection*. This involves turning energy 'back in' against oneself which in healthy functioning would be allowed to go out to contact the environment. For example, somebody who has learnt that expressing their irritation or anger is risky may come to withhold aggressive energy, possibly causing headaches, muscle tension or other physiological distress, thus turning energy against themselves.
- *Confluence*. This is a state of being in which the individual is unclear about boundaries, with others, with the environment. There is a merging of ideas, beliefs, feelings, etc. and no clear sense of separateness.

Since Perls, more recent theorists have described another mechanism:

- *Deflection*. Here the individual turns away from healthy contact with the environment and the contact is experienced as unclear, weak, vague (a weak gestalt). Sometimes the impulse is redirected (deflected) towards an undeserving but convenient substitute.

These are processes by which problems are maintained and result in 'unfinished business' (incomplete gestalten) which inhibits energy and healthy functioning. If extremely chronic, this can result in severe disturbance in functioning for the individual.

THEORY OF CHANGE

Therapeutic change occurs with the rediscovery of the gestalt process of *organismic self-regulation*. This involves close attention to how the client does what she or he does, how they function in the world and in the relationship with the therapist.

Awareness is the key in this work: to become more aware of the sorts of disturbances described in the previous section brings a recovery of contactfulness with aspects of self and others. The sort of awareness sought is not just intellectual but is holistic in that it is an experience involving intellect, emotions and physical sensations.

As part of the therapy the client works to complete unfinished business through closure and resolution of issues from the past which still affect the client's current functioning.

Another aspect of change is that of exploring/experimenting with new sorts of behaviour as the energy bound up in old patterns is released. Such experimentation develops from an underlying willingness by the client to discover more of who they are.

Change in gestalt therapy comes from becoming more fully ourselves: this is known as the 'paradoxical theory of change', first formulated by Beisser in 1970: 'Change occurs when one becomes what he is, not when he tries to become what he is not' (Beisser, 1970: 88). This can only happen through awareness, now, of what we are actually doing and how we are functioning.

Yontef (2005) emphasises the central role of the relationship with the therapist in the work of change. The gestalt therapist works with dialogic contact to enliven and enhance awareness. Dialogic contact requires four elements: *inclusion* (a deep entering into the world of the client); *confirmation* (the full acceptance and validation of the client's existence and experience); *presence* (the therapist bringing themselves fully and authentically to the encounter); and a surrender to the *between* (trusting the outcome of the meeting will emerge unpredictably as it unfolds).

SKILLS AND STRATEGIES

The gestalt therapist's approach is phenomenological: to facilitate clients deepening their awareness of themselves and their relationship with others through attending, engaging with the clients, exploring their experience, describing what is.

The authenticity of the therapist, their genuineness, their wholeness and presence are central. The therapist engages and participates in the relationship and also observes. The therapist interacts with the client with an I–Thou attitude where possible, a willingness to relate authentically and meet the client as a person. What sort of contact is made and how that is 'interrupted' is the focus of the work.

Therapists must therefore use their creativity, working from a clear understanding of gestalt theory: the centrality of gestalt formation and destruction, awareness of present experience and the theory of change.

Gestalt sessions can be quite active, with the therapist suggesting behavioural or experiential experiments for the client to try out, with a view to enhancing their awareness of their feelings, aspects of their relationships with others, or subliminal thoughts or assumptions they may be carrying around with them.

Examples of such experiments might be:

- focusing' on body awareness, e.g. encouraging the client to become more aware of felt sensations within the body
- exaggerating movements or phrases, repeating them and allowing them to grow or lead to some deeper awareness
- attention to language, e.g. noticing how the client constructs sentences, one aspect being whether the client uses impersonal pronouns (it, they, one) to distance themselves from their experience
- psychodramatic work, e.g. 'empty chair' work in which a client explores their relationship with others, or aspects of themselves, by imagining others to be present and engaging in dialogue with them
- exploring the contact with the therapist, e.g. by experimenting with sitting at different distances from each other.

Joyce and Sills (2014) and Mann (2010) discuss a variety of skills and strategies which can be used in gestalt counselling settings, although it should be remembered that the use of such interventions will arise out of the ongoing dialogue and exploration between client and therapist rather than being used merely as techniques. The aim is always to enhance the awareness of clients, to facilitate their recovery of their organismic self-regulation.

Since the turn of the century, an increasing range of applications of gestalt have been explored. Houston (2003) has shown how the gestalt approach can be tailored for use in short-term, brief therapy settings. Woldt and Toman (2005) have included a number of chapters in their edited book discussing gestalt applications to a range of populations and settings, including children and adolescents, families and couples, groups and organisations, community mental health, substance abuse and in education. O'Leary et al. (2003) have explored the use of gestalt group approaches in working with older adults.

CASE EXAMPLE

Rob presented as a 34-year-old man with a history of unsatisfactory relationships with women and thinking himself to be depressed. His body was hunched and self-protective and his eye contact minimal, rarely looking at me. I asked him to feel the way he was sitting and holding himself. I said 'What is your body saying?' For a while he sat silently, eventually saying 'Stay away from me'. I asked him to repeat those words: 'stay away from me; stay away from me'. 'Who are you speaking to?' I asked. He paused before offering 'The world' then 'my mother'. 'What else do you have to say to your mother?' He began then to recall a number of recriminations and hurts he was holding towards his mother and as he voiced these, his energy slowly changed, becoming more feelingful, eventually bursting into a mix of sobs and rage. From this beginning, a painful story of neglect and humiliation unfolded. Later in the therapy his angry and resentful feelings turned towards me, his therapist, and we explored how I had let him down, in his mind. I wanted to allow him to use me as a transferential object, to allow the pent-up feelings' full scope to emerge and be expressed, while at the same time bringing my own real self into the room, sharing back to him some of my own sense of sorrow and hurt at being so accused; thus working to give him an alternative experience of authentic contact with another in his real, present world.

RESEARCH EVIDENCE

Until the 1980s gestalt therapy had a limited research literature. During that decade Greenberg began to publish a series of papers exploring the benefits of two-chair work. That work was summarised by Eleanor O'Leary (1992) in her review of the research literature, and since then an increasing number of research papers have been published. In the latest edition of *Bergin and Garfield's Handbook of Psychotherapy and Behavior Change* (Lambert, 2004), gestalt therapy is identified as one of the three 'major subapproaches' to experiential/humanistic therapy, alongside person-centred and existential approaches (Elliott et al., 2004). Another large-scale review article was published by Strumpfel (2004), which summarised 60 studies providing some good evidence for the effectiveness of gestalt methods.

Many of the studies are concerned with the effectiveness of the two chair technique. For example, Paivio et al. (2001) found that the degree of engagement in imagined confrontations with abusive carers in empty chair work predicted resolution of child abuse issues. Johnson and Smith (1997) compared systematic desensitisation and gestalt empty chair procedures with a no-therapy control group in the treatment of phobia sufferers, and found that, following treatment, both treatment groups were significantly less phobic than the no-therapy group.

In the UK, Stevens et al. (2011) have shown how the CORE outcome measure (a generic questionnaire used widely in a range of settings to monitor the effectiveness of counselling) can be used to demonstrate levels of improvement from pre- to post-therapy in samples of gestalt clients, which are equivalent to the improvements shown in other large-scale studies comparing cognitive-behavioural, person-centred and psychodynamic samples.

The gestalt approach is beginning to be recognised and practised in non-European settings: Saadati and Lashani (2013) showed how the use of gestalt methods with a group of Iranian divorced women produced significantly higher scores on a measure of self-efficacy as compared with a non-treated control group.

In the last 10 to 15 years gestalt therapy research has benefited from the upsurge of interest in qualitative methods. Phenomenological research methods have been a recognised approach to social science methodology generally since the 1960s (Moustakas, 1994), but their affinity with gestalt theory has only recently been highlighted. Paul Barber, in particular, has offered a specifically gestalt account of qualitative research (Barber, 2006; Barber and Brownell, 2008; Finlay and Evans, 2009). Joanna Hewitt Taylor (2002) provides an example of this kind of gestalt-informed phenomenological enquiry into the ways a group of abused black women in Britain make meaning out of their experiences, and how their accounts can be interpreted from a gestalt perspective.

REFERENCES

Barber, P. (2006) *Becoming a Practitioner-Researcher: A Gestalt Approach to Holistic Enquiry*. London: Middlesex University Press.

Barber, P. and Brownell, P. (2008) Qualitative research. In P. Brownell (ed.), *Handbook for Theory, Research and Practice in Gestalt Therapy* (pp. 37–63). Newcastle: Cambridge Scholars.

Beisser, A.R. (1970) The paradoxical theory of change. In J. Fagan and I.L. Shepherd (eds), *Gestalt Therapy Now*. Harmondsworth: Penguin.

Elliot, R.L., Greenberg, L.S. and Lietaer, G. (2004) Research on experiential psychotherapies. In M.J. Lambert (ed.), *Bergin and Garfield's Handbook of Psychotherapy and Behavior Change* (5th ed.). New York: Wiley.

Finlay, L. and Evans, K. (2009) *Relational-centred Research for Psychotherapists*. Chichester: Wiley-Blackwell.

Houston, G. (2003) *Brief Gestalt Therapy*. London: Sage.

Hycner, R.A. and Jacobs, L. (1995) *The Healing Relationship in Gestalt Therapy*. Highland, NY: Gestalt Journal Press.

Johnson, W.R. and Smith, E.W.L. (1997) Gestalt empty-chair dialogue vs systematic desensitisation in the treatment of a phobia. *Gestalt Review*, 1: 150–162.

Joyce, P. and Sills, C. (2014) *Skills in Gestalt Counselling and Psychotherapy* (3rd ed.). London: Sage.

Lambert, M.J. (ed.) (2004) *Bergin and Garfield's Handbook of Psychotherapy and Behavior Change* (5th ed.). New York: Wiley.

Mann, D. (2010) *Gestalt Therapy: 100 key points and techniques*. London: Routledge.

Moustakas, C. (1994) *Phenomenological Research Methods*. London: Sage.

O'Leary, E. (1992) *Gestalt Therapy: Theory, Practice and Research*. London: Chapman and Hall.

O'Leary, E., Sheedy, G., O'Sullivan, K. and Thoreson, C. (2003) Cork Older Adult Intervention Project: outcomes of a gestalt therapy group with older adults. *Counselling Psychology Quarterly*, 16(2): 131–143.

Paivio, S.C., Hall, I.E., Holowaty, K.A.M., Jellis, J.B. and Tran, N. (2001) Imaginal confrontation for resolving child abuse issues. *Psychotherapy Research*, 11: 433–453.

Perls, F. (1947) *Ego, Hunger and Aggression: A Revision of Freud's Theory and Method*. London: Allen and Unwin.

Perls, F. (1969) *Gestalt Therapy Verbatim*. Moab, UT: Real People.

Perls, F., Hefferline, R. and Goodman, P. (1951) *Gestalt Therapy: Excitement and Growth in the Human Personality*. New York: Julian.

Saadati, H. and Lashani, L. (2013) Effectiveness of gestalt therapy on self-efficacy of divorced women. *Procedia – Social & Behavioural Sciences*, 84: 1171–1174.

Stevens, C., Stringfellow, J., Wakelin, K. and Waring, J. (2011) The UK Gestalt Psychotherapy CORE Research Project: the findings. *The British Gestalt Journal*, 20(2): 22–27.

Strumpfel, U. (2004) Research on gestalt therapy. *International Gestalt Journal*, 12(1): 9–24.

Taylor, J.H. (2002) Childhood abuse as experienced by black women living in Britain – a phenomenological exploration. *British Gestalt Journal*, 11(2): 91–98.

Woldt, A.L. and Toman, S.M. (2005) *Gestalt Therapy: History, Theory and Practice*. London: Sage.

Wollants, G. (2012) *Gestalt Therapy: Therapy of the Situation*. London: Sage.

Yontef, G.M. (2005) Gestalt therapy theory of change. In A.L. Woldt and S.M. Toman (eds), *Gestalt Therapy: History, Theory and Practice*. London: Sage.

RECOMMENDED READING

1.   Joyce, P. and Sills, C. (2014) *Skills in Gestalt Counselling and Psychotherapy* (3rd ed.). London: Sage.

A straightforward account of the theory and practice of gestalt therapy. This new edition includes chapters on working with trauma, depression and anxiety.

2.   Mann, D. (2010) *Gestalt Therapy: 100 Key Points and Techniques*. Hove: Routledge.

A clear outline of basic concepts and techniques used by contemporary gestaltists, with 100 short chapters, each describing either a theoretical point or an aspect of practice.

3.   Houston, G. (2013) *Gestalt Counselling in a Nutshell*. London: Sage.

A succinct account of the gestalt approach with some helpful vignettes showing therapeutic interactions.

5.20 PERSON-CENTRED THERAPY

KEITH TUDOR

OVERVIEW AND KEY POINTS

Person-centred therapy (PCT) is the therapeutic manifestation and application of the broader person-centred approach to life. Initially developed by Carl Rogers, PCT:

- is a form of therapy that centres on the whole person and being of the client;
- emphasises the view that therapy *is* the relationship between therapist and client, and has contributed to thinking about the nature of the therapeutic relationship;
- is informed by practice-based research; and
- is influenced the development of humanistic psychology.

BRIEF HISTORY

'Person-centred therapy' (PCT) or 'client-centred therapy' (CCT) was originally developed by Carl Rogers and his colleagues in the USA from the late 1930s onwards. For a short while the approach now known as PCT was referred to as 'non-directive therapy', a term that fell into disuse, although 'non-directivity' as a concept and a principled attitude has remained at the centre of PCT and has been the subject of some recent revival (see Levitt, 2005). A key date in the history of PCT is 10 December 1940, when Rogers spoke at the University of Minnesota on 'Some newer concepts of psychotherapy'. CCT was further expanded by Rogers and his colleagues at the University of Chicago and included the development of a theory of personality and behaviour, as well as a more detailed description of the characteristics of person-centred therapy (see Rogers, 1951).

Between 1953 and 1954, and based on his research, Rogers formulated his now famous hypothesis of certain necessary and sufficient conditions of therapeutic personality change (published in 1957 and 1959). These papers established Rogers and his colleagues as innovators in the field of therapy, and stimulated a great deal of debate and research, for a summary of which see Patterson (2000 [1984]) and Tudor and Merry (2002) – research which finds expression in more recent research into 'common factors' across therapeutic modalities. Rogers himself identified more with an emerging 'third force' of psychology, i.e., humanistic psychology, and is widely recognised as one of its founders; and PCT became established as one of the most influential of the humanistic approaches to therapy. Mearns and Thorne (2000: 27), however, have suggested that, in 'its forsaking of mystique and other "powerful" behaviours of therapists', PCT is as different from many humanistic therapies as it is from other traditions, such as behaviourism and psychoanalysis. In the later years of his life Rogers became interested in the wider application of the principles of person-centred psychology (PCP) to education and learning; groups, group facilitation and conflict resolution; and politics. He also become more open to and interested in mystical experiences, which led Rogers to speculate about the importance of 'presence', and others to consider the interface between PCT and spirituality, notably Thorne (2000 [1991], 2002, 2008, 2012). Person-centred *therapy* is now viewed as one application of what has become more broadly referred to as the 'person-centred *approach*' (PCA), for an outline and development of which see Embleton Tudor et al. (2004).

Although its influence in the USA has diminished in recent decades, currently PCT is widely practised and studied in Europe, Japan and South America, and there is a thriving World Association of Person-Centered and Experiential Psychotherapy and Counseling (www.pce-world.org), which has individual and organisational members in over 30 countries, holds a biennial international conference and publishes a quarterly journal, *Person-Centred and Experiential Psychotherapies*. English-language publications have been fostered by the presence of PCCS Books (www.pccs-books.co.uk), which, in a period of 23 years, has published over 60 books on person-centred psychology and its various manifestations, including PCT. There is also a considerable and growing international literature, including publications and journals in Dutch, French, German, Italian, Japanese, Portuguese and Spanish.

BASIC ASSUMPTIONS

There are a number of basic assumptions which underlie PCT. Here they are clustered under three core principles (see Sanders, 2000; Tudor and Worrall, 2006).

1 THAT THE HUMAN ORGANISM TENDS TO ACTUALISE

The view that the human organism, as other organisms, tends to actualise – i.e., to maintain, enhance and reproduce the experiencing organism – represents the sole motivational construct in PCP. The theory of actualisation is a natural science theory, not a moral theory. While no specific moral values are implied by the theory, two values implicit in the person-centred approach to the person are fluidity (as distinct from fixity or rigidity) and creativity.

One function of the fact that we tend to actualise is that we differentiate a portion of our experience into an awareness of self and the organisation of a self-concept. The self-concept or self-structure is a fluid but consistent pattern of perceptions of the 'I', 'me' – and 'we' – in relation to the environment, personal and social values, goals and ideals. One aspect of organismic actualising, self-actualising, appears after the development of the self-concept and acts to maintain that concept. Self-actualising – or, more commonly, 'self-actualisation' – does not always result in optimal functioning because each person, whether psychologically healthy or unhealthy, is self-actualising to the extent that each has a self-structure to maintain and enhance. Thus, if an aspect of someone's self-concept is to be pleasing, then s/he may act socially to support that, at the expense of her/his organismic direction.

Awareness of self is termed 'self-experience'. When any self-experience is evaluated by others as being more or less worthy of positive regard, a person's self-regard becomes vulnerable to these external judgements. When self-experiences become sought after or avoided because they are more or less deserving of self-regard, the individual is said to have acquired conditions of worth, which are the basis of person-centred theories of psychopathology (see Bozarth, 1996; Joseph and Worsley, 2005; Tudor and Worrall, 2006).

2 IN ORDER TO SUPPORT GROWTH AND CHANGE, THE THERAPIST/FACILITATOR NEEDS TO EMBRACE AND EMBODY A NON-DIRECTIVE APPROACH AND ATTITUDE

This follows from the first assumption. If you think that the fact that the organism tends to actualise is an expression of an inherent and trustworthy directionality, then, as a therapist or facilitator, you would tend to support the client's direction.

The view of human nature underlying this approach is positive, constructive and co-creative. It does not, however, deny the capacity for harmful, destructive and anti-social behaviour. It focuses, rather, on the potential for positive, personal and social change to occur throughout life; and takes the view that environmental influences, particularly those concerning relationships with others, including therapeutic and facilitative relationships, are critical factors in determining either positive or negative self-concepts and, hence, healthy or unhealthy functioning. PCP recognises that the outward and, indeed, inward manifestations of harmful behaviour can have serious and extreme consequences. In response, the practice of PCT understands or attempts to understand, and helps the client to understand, the motivation and needs which underlie her/his behaviour – and, generally, views behaviour as a needs-driven expression of a unitary theory of motivation (see Rogers, 1951).

3 THAT, TOGETHER, THERAPIST AND CLIENT CO-CREATE CERTAIN FACILITATIVE CONDITIONS WHICH PROMOTE GROWTH, CHALLENGE AND CHANGE

In PCP, people are regarded as trustworthy, creative, social, contactful, congruent or integrated in themselves, and in relationships, loving, understanding, receptive and resourceful. Given the right conditions, we are able to admit all experiencing into awareness without distortion or denial, which are the two defence mechanisms postulated in PCP. Everyone has the capacity to rediscover their organismic valuing process and direction in a relationship in which power and control are shared between therapist and client, and this capacity can be nurtured in a climate of facilitative psychological attitudes or conditions (described below). This climate can exist within a therapeutic setting or elsewhere, for example, in groups, families, tribes, communities, schools and workplaces.

ORIGIN AND MAINTENANCE OF PROBLEMS

Disturbance exists whenever there is antagonism between a person's tendency to actualise in one direction and her or his self-actualisation, which may lie in another direction. Incongruence exists to the extent that these two tendencies diverge.

At the beginning of life, a person is fully congruent, that is, able to allow all experiencing into awareness without distortion or denial. Later – and developmental studies show that this can take place *in utero* – the person encounters threat, disruption, disapproval, rejection and, as a result, becomes anxious in the face of the continuing need for positive regard from significant others. The formation of the person's self-concept becomes conditioned by these negative experiences, conditions of worth become internalised and the person seeks protection from further negative experiences. The conditioned self-concept can become so reinforced that the person becomes completely alienated from any sense of themselves and their organismic direction – which is why 'psychopathology' is best understood in terms of alienation (see Tudor and Worrall, 2006). The dichotomy between the self-concept and experiencing leads to increasingly distorted perception. A condition of incongruence now exists, and the person's psychological functioning is disturbed.

Disturbance is maintained through the continuation of a high degree of reliance on the evaluations of others for a sense of self-worth or self-esteem. Anxiety, threat and confusion are created whenever incongruence is experienced between the self-concept, with its internalised conditions of worth, and actual experience. Whenever such anxiety arises, or is threatened, the person will continue to default to defences of distortion or denial of experiencing. If experiences are extremely incongruent with the self-concept, a person's defence system may be unable to prevent such experiences from overwhelming the self-concept. Resulting behaviour may be destructive, disorganised and chaotic.

THEORY OF CHANGE

Effective therapy occurs in a relationship in which the therapist holds certain attitudes or conditions and the client receives/perceives or, more precisely, engages with how s/he receives/perceives these – or not. In addition, Rogers identified certain client conditions which prefigure more recent concerns about the relational, dialogic and co-creative nature of therapy. Indeed, Rogers first referred to his work as 'relationship therapy'.

The therapist's conditions (from Rogers, 1959: 213) are:

1. 'That two persons are in contact', a condition which requires both therapist and client to be actively present, both in a social sense of meeting and agreeing to work together (or not) and in a more psychological sense. Clearly some more disturbed clients are less contactful or contactable and, with advances in the theory and practice of 'pre-therapy' (Prouty, 1994), this condition is currently receiving more attention in PCT.
2. The therapist is congruent within the relationship, that is, is authentic, genuine or real, putting up no professional façade. This includes the therapist admitting into awareness all experience of the relationship so that such experiencing is available for direct communication to the client, when appropriate. This condition is more about experiencing than self-disclosing. It is not necessary for the therapist directly to communicate any particular experience of the relationship, except when the failure to do so impedes the practitioner's ability to experience

unconditional positive regard and to understand the client empathically, in which circumstances it may become necessary for the therapist to communicate their experiencing.
3. The therapist experiences unconditional positive regard for the client, that is, s/he maintains a positive, non-judgemental and accepting attitude.
4. The therapist experiences an empathic understanding of the internal, subjective frame of reference of the client.

There is a difference between Rogers' two formulations of these hypotheses (published in 1957 and in 1959) about the extent to which the therapist should communicate these last two conditions.

The requirements of a client, which we may refer to as the 'client's conditions' (see Tudor, 2000, 2011) are:

1. 'That two persons are in contact' (as above).
2. That, by virtue of being vulnerable or anxious, s/he is in some way incongruent or (as discussed above) experiencing a discrepancy between organismic and self-actualising tendencies.
3. That s/he perceives the therapist's unconditional positive regard and empathic understanding 'at least to a minimal degree' (whether the therapist directly or explicitly communicates this or not). In one paper, Rogers (1967 [1958]) refers to this as the 'assumed condition', by which, in effect, all therapy is evaluated or assessed.

As discussed (above), a major characteristic of PCT is that it is non-directive. In other words, the therapist has no specific goals for the client and, classically, does not suggest that the client attend to any particular form of experiencing. The therapist refrains from interpreting the client's experience, but, rather, focuses on non-judgemental acceptance and understanding of the client's experience.

Change in the present is encapsulated in moments of therapeutic movement which consist of experiences of profound self-acceptance and integration. Typically, such moments have the following characteristics: they are immediate and consist of total experiences, not thoughts or intellectual understandings, although these may follow or accompany the experience; they are new in that, while they may have been experienced before, at least, in part, they have never been experienced completely or with awareness combined with appropriate physiological reactions; they are self-accepting in that they are owned as a part of the self; and they are integrated into the self-structure without distortion.

SKILLS AND STRATEGIES

In person-centred theory and practice, being in contact, congruent, acceptant and understanding are conceptualised more as qualities of the therapist – and of the relationship – than as skills, strategies or techniques. It is, moreover, unhelpful to conceptualise PCT in terms of behavioural strategies, since the therapist's only intention is to maintain and enhance a way of relating with the client, based on the conditions described above, and 'strategies' suggest a certain direction based on the therapist's frame of reference. A skilled therapist is one who can communicate her/his contactfulness, authenticity, positive regard and empathic understanding in ways that the client experiences as non-threatening, as experiencing these conditions without threat enables the client to become increasingly free of the need to deny her/his experience and/or distort her/his perceptions.

Although opinions among person-centred and especially experiential therapists vary, many would agree that it is possible, even within the strictest theoretical understanding of PCT, to utilise techniques associated with other forms of counselling and psychotherapy *providing* that such techniques, as Rogers (1957: 102) put it, 'serve as channels for fulfilling one of the conditions'. Clearly such techniques would not be imposed by the therapist; would be used only when requested by the client to further a particular purpose; and the client should retain control over the extent of their use. The use of such techniques by person-centred practitioners, however, is minimal.

CASE EXAMPLE

In the last session of what had been two years of regular, more or less weekly therapy, Kay summarised her experience. She told her therapist how important his consistency, calmness and caring had been. She went on to describe a number of other qualities that she had valued: his kindness, warmth, gentleness, experience, realness (in showing her, at times, what he was feeling and thinking) and mindfulness (in holding her in mind between sessions), as well as a certain protectiveness. While her description was about and true of the therapist, clearly it was also naming qualities that she valued and found important. Some people regard all feedback as projection (and use that to reject the feedback). I consider and suggest that all feedback is, rather, reflective of a co-created relationship and the client's experience of that relationship. Thus, the projective nature and quality of feedback do not make it any the less true or useful. In this sense, from a person-centred perspective, and especially with reference to the importance of the sixth, assumed condition, Kay was describing those aspects of the therapist's unconditional positive regard and empathic understanding – and, behind that, his authenticity and contactfulness – that she had experienced and found important. That the evaluation and assessment of PCT is – or should also be – person-centred places the client at the centre of such evaluation, a process which also means that acceptance and empathy are more particularly and usefully described and specified – by the client.

RESEARCH EVIDENCE

Rogers himself was one of the leading pioneers of research into counselling and psychotherapy (see Rogers and Dymond, 1954), conducting a major research study of psychotherapy with schizophrenics (Rogers et al., 1967). Partly because of its longevity, PCT itself has both been the subject of and generated more research than many other approaches. In the 1950s, using the Q-sort technique, Rogers and Dymond (1954) showed that person-centred therapy results in changes to the self-concept, whereby the perceived self becomes closer to the ideal self, and the self as perceived becomes more comfortable and adjusted.

Research evidence that the therapeutic conditions are both necessary and sufficient is not unequivocal, though much of it suffers from inadequate methodology and the possibility of poorly reported and discussed results. For a useful summary of four decades of research evidence, see Bozarth (1993). Most research strongly supports the hypothesis that the conditions are necessary for effective counselling, whether this is person-centred or not; research which forms the basis of the mainstream view in therapy that the therapeutic relationship is the key factor in successful outcome, and that Rogers' conditions describe significant 'common factors' across theoretical orientations.

Two independent studies, based on randomised, controlled assessments (Friedli et al., 1997; King et al., 2000), have concluded that person-centred, non-directive psychotherapy/counselling more than holds its own in comparison with other forms of therapy and helping. The book *Person-centered and experiential therapies work* (Cooper, Watson and Hölldampf, 2010) offers a useful review of research on person-centred counselling, psychotherapy and related practice; *Person-centered and Experiential Psychotherapies* (PCEP) publishes peer-reviewed articles on research; and, for a number of years, high-quality research into person-centred, experiential and humanistic-existential approaches to therapy has been conducted in the Counselling Unit at the University of Strathclyde.

REFERENCES

Bozarth, J. D. (1993). Not necessarily necessary, but always sufficient. In D. Brazier (Ed.), *Beyond Carl Rogers* (pp. 92–105). London: Constable.

Bozarth, J. D. (1996). A theoretical reconceptualization of the necessary and sufficient conditions for therapeutic personality change. *The Person-Centered Journal, 3*(1), 44–51.

Cooper, M., Watson, J. C. and Hölldampf, D. (Eds.) (2010). *Person-centered and experiential therapies work: A review of the research on counseling, psychotherapy and related practices.* Ross-on-Wye: PCCS Books.

Embleton Tudor, L., Keemar, K., Tudor, K., Valentine, J. and Worrall, M. (2004). *The person-centred approach: A contemporary introduction.* Basingstoke: Palgrave.

Friedli, K., King, M., Lloyd, M. and Horder, J. (1997). Randomised controlled assessment of non-directive psychotherapy versus routine general practitioner care. *Lancet, 350,* 1662–1665.

Joseph, S. and Worsley, R. (2005). Psychopathology and the person-centred approach: Building bridges between disciples. In S. Joseph and R. Worsley (Eds.), *Person-centred psychopathology: A positive psychology of mental health* (pp. 1–8). Ross-on-Wye: PCCS Books.

King, M., Lloyd, M., Sibbald, B., Gabbay, M., Ward, E., Byford, S. and Bower, P. (2000). Randomised controlled trial of non-directive counselling, cognitive behaviour therapy and usual general practitioner care in the management of depression as well as mixed anxiety and depression in primary care. *Health Technology Assessment, 4*(19)

Levitt, B. E. (Ed.) (2005). *Embracing non-directivity: Reassessing person-centered theory and practice in the 21st century* (pp. i–iii). Ross-on-Wye: PCCS Books.

Mearns, D. and Thorne, B. (2000). *Person-centred therapy today: New Frontiers in theory and practice.* London: Sage.

Patterson, C. H. (2000 [1984]). Empathy, warm and genuineness in psychotherapy: A review of reviews. In C. H. Patterson, *Understanding psychotherapy: Fifty years of client-centred theory and practice* (pp. 161–173). Ross-on-Wye: PCCS Books.

Prouty, G. (1994) *Theoretical Evolutions in Person-Centered/Experiential Therapy: applications to schizophrenic and retarded psychoses.* Westport, CN: Praeger.

Rogers, C. R. (1951). *Client-centered therapy.* London: Constable.

Rogers, C. R. (1957). The necessary and sufficient conditions of therapeutic personality change. *Journal of Consulting Psychology, 21,* 95–103.

Rogers, C. R. (1959). A theory of therapy, personality and interpersonal relationships, as developed in the client-centered framework. In S. Koch (Ed.), *Psychology: A study of science.* Vol. 3: *Formulation of the person and the social context* (pp. 184–256). New York: McGraw-Hill.

Rogers, C. R. (1967 [1958]). A process conception of psychotherapy. In C. R. Rogers, *On becoming a person* (pp. 125–159). London: Constable.

Rogers, C. R. and Dymond, R. F. (Eds.) (1954). *Psychotherapy and personality change.* Chicago, IL: University of Chicago Press.

Rogers, C. R., Gendlin, E. T., Kiesler, D. J. and Truax, C. B. (Eds.) (1967). *The therapeutic relationship and its impact: A study of psychotherapy with schizophrenics.* Madison, WI: University of Wisconsin Press.

Sanders, P. (2000). Mapping the person-centred approaches to counselling and psychoterhapy. *Person-Centred Practice, 8*(2), 62–74.

Thorne, B. (2000 [1991]). *Person-centred counselling: Therapeutic and spiritual dimensions.* London: Whurr.

Thorne, B. (2002). *The mystical power of person-centred therapy.* London: Whurr.

Thorne, B. (2008). *Person-centred counselling and Christian spirituality: The secular and the holy.* London: Whurr.

Thorne, B. (2012). *Counselling and spiritual accompaniment: Bridging faith and person-centred therapy*. London: Wiley-Blackwell.

Tudor, K. (2000). The case of the lost conditions. *Counselling, 11*(1), 33–37.

Tudor, K. (2011). Rogers' therapeutic conditions: A relational reconceptualisation. *Person-Centered & Experiential Psychotherapies, 10*(3), 165–180.

Tudor, K. and Merry, T. (2002). *Dictionary of person-centred psychology*. London: Whurr.

Tudor, K. and Worrall, M. (2006). *Person-centred therapy: A clinical philosophy*. London: Routledge.

RECOMMENDED READING

1. The journal *Person-Centered and Experiential Psychotherapies* (2002–present).

This peer-reviewed journal 'seeks to create a dialogue among different parts of the person-centered and experiential tradition, to support, inform, and challenge each other and to stimulate their creativity and impact in a broader professional, scientific and political context' (www.pce-world.org/pcep-journal.html). The journal has established and maintained a consistently high quality of articles which advance this tradition.

2. Tudor, K. and Worrall, M. (2006). *Person-centred therapy: A clinical philosophy*. London: Routledge.

Part of a series of books on 'Advancing Theory in Therapy', this book examines the roots of person-centred thinking, especially with regard to existential, phenomenological and organismic philosophy and psychology. It demonstrates how recent research in areas such as neuroscience supports the philosophical premises of PCT and updates Rogers' original vision of a therapy based on relationship.

3. Lago, C. and Charura, D. (Eds.) (2016). *Person-centred counselling and psychotherapy: Origins, developments and contemporary applications*. Buckingham: Open University/McGraw Hill.

At the time of going to press, this is the most recently published book on PCT and is certainly one of the most comprehensive. Bringing together 34 authors from a number of different countries, the book covers the history and development of the person-centred approach, contributions to its theory and practice, including new theoretical paradigms and practice, research, as well as differences, diversity, its position, and the future.

5.21   PSYCHODRAMA

CLARK BAIM

OVERVIEW AND KEY POINTS

Psychodrama is a holistic method of psychotherapy in which people are helped to explore their psychosocial and emotional difficulties using sensitively guided enactment. Psychodrama uses a wide range of action-based techniques to help people examine troubling episodes from their life, their current or past relationships, unresolved situations, desired roles or inner thoughts, feelings and conflicts. Psychodrama is notably different from talk-based therapy because in psychodrama all aspects of life are not only discussed but are re-created, worked through in action and integrated in the 'here and now' of the therapy session. This active involvement can deepen learning, recovery and growth. The aims are:

- to promote insight, emotional release, resolution of trauma and loss and integration;
- to help the person to understand and transform the impact of their experiences and relationships; and
- to develop new responses.

BRIEF HISTORY

Psychodrama was first devised in the 1920s and 1930s by the psychiatrist Dr Jacob Levy Moreno, and further elaborated over several decades in collaboration with his wife Zerka Toeman Moreno. Among Moreno's extensive writing, his essential texts include *Who Shall Survive* (1934) and *Psychodrama* (1946–1969, three volumes; Volumes 2 and 3 co-authored with Zerka Moreno).

Psychodrama was the first recognised method of group psychotherapy. It has gained wide acceptance as an effective approach to psychological and emotional healing, and is practised in more than 100 countries by more than 10,000 professionals. It has an extensive literature of more than 7,300 publications, with many national and regional journals, associations and training organisations around the world. A comprehensive bibliography of world psychodrama can be found at www.pdbib.org.

Moreno was born in Romania and spent his formative years as a young doctor in Vienna during its renowned period of cultural ferment. During the First World War he was a medical superintendent at a resettlement camp. After emigrating to the USA in 1925, Moreno lived the rest of his life in New York City and in upstate New York, where he founded a private sanatorium in Beacon, which also served as a training centre for the early generations of psychodramatists. Three very different and inspiring accounts of his life and ideas can be found in Marineau (1989), J. D. Moreno (2014) and Nolte (2014).

In addition to being a medical doctor and psychiatrist, Moreno was also a philosopher and visionary. He was a highly ebullient and charismatic figure, with an inspirational vision that human beings have the potential to be – in his terms – co-creators of the cosmos, with vast reserves of untapped creative power to change the world for the better. His far-reaching vision was that therapy should be for all humankind just as much as it is for individual human beings. He coined the term *sociatry* – the healing of society – as a counterpart to the term *psychiatry* – the healing of the individual mind. His development of methods such as sociodrama and sociometry were important contributions to his broader aim of sociatry for all of humanity.

BASIC ASSUMPTIONS

SPONTANEITY AND CREATIVITY

In his young adulthood, Moreno first became interested in the healing potential of spontaneity and creativity when watching children play in the parks of Vienna and joining them as a storyteller. He observed that children often appeared able to solve their conflicts with play and without adult intervention. He also noted that children who repeatedly took the same roles in their play had more difficulty in showing creativity and making friends. With encouragement to try new roles, the children became more spontaneous and vital in their interactions and better integrated with the group.

These observations led Moreno to the underlying premise of psychodrama, which is that all human beings are born with an innate will to survive, which includes the drives of spontaneity and creativity. Spontaneity is the capacity to find adequate responses to new situations or new responses to old situations in order to best meet the challenges and opportunities that life presents.

Moreno often wrote about the many forces within families and society that constrain spontaneity and creativity from infancy onwards, resulting in robot-like thinking, feeling and behaviour. One way to encapsulate the purpose of psychodrama is that it is a process of rediscovering and unblocking our innate spontaneity in order to 'heal ourselves' and free ourselves from the tendency towards becoming automatons. To further develop this point, we see that in the terminology of psychodrama, the client is called the 'protagonist', a term borrowed from the ancient Greek theatre meaning 'the first actor'. Psychodrama is intended to help each person find the courage to act with authenticity and to take centre stage as the primary actor in their own life story.

ENCOUNTER

An important aspect of psychodrama is that the client is part of the action. As part of the action, they are encouraged to encounter the other people in the group. (Psychodrama is normally a group process, although it also used effectively in one-to-one sessions.) The challenge and energy of encounter are among the prime healing forces in psychodrama; it is through authentic here-and-now encounters with other people that we are best able to gain an understanding of how our behaviour affects other people, to get feedback from others about how they perceive us and hence to know if we are 'getting better'.

CATHARSIS AND INTEGRATION

Catharsis is a term first used by the Greek philosopher Aristotle to describe how drama can lead to emotional purging among audience members and in the characters in the drama. In psychodrama, it is common for group members to experience *catharsis of emotion*, particularly a release of deeply held emotions, such as sadness, fear or anger. It should also be noted that, for some people, particularly those who are typically overwhelmed by emotion, psychodrama can be used just as effectively to help them contain rather than express emotion, or to help them express the 'forbidden' emotion that they are not able to express (such as the anger behind sadness, or the fear beneath a defiant exterior).

There is another important form of catharsis, which is the *catharsis of integration*. Emotional release may have limited value if it is not then integrated into the person's psychosocial functioning. The catharsis of integration usually takes place towards the end of a psychodrama, when the protagonist is helped to put into practice their new learning and apply it to daily living.

ORIGIN AND MAINTENANCE OF PROBLEMS

Psychodrama is deeply rooted in role theory (Moreno, 1946). One of the principles of role theory is that, in the course of our lives, we carry out many roles. When we know how to perform a given role, it can be said to be in our *role repertoire*. In general, the greater the number of integrated roles we have in our repertoire, the better able we are to meet our needs and function successfully because we have a wide variety of strategies from which to choose. This flexibility of roles is essential if we are to meet the demands of the moment, because our behaviour may need to alter radically when we move from one context to another.

SOMATIC ROLES

Role theory also provides a way of understanding the origin and maintenance of emotional and psychosocial problems. For example, Moreno observed that, in order to survive, a baby must carry out somatic roles (*somatic* meaning 'of the body'), such as the role of breather, drinker, eater, crier or signaller of distress. These roles may develop smoothly and instinctively, or they may be full of conflict and distress, depending on a wide range of variables influencing the baby, the parents and their environment. If there are significant disturbances in the development of somatic roles, this may lead to illness or vulnerability related to breathing, eating, intestinal function, mobility, bodily shape and posture, sensory processing, emotional self-regulation and expression and other somatic processes. The body remembers even if the mind forgets (van der Kolk, 2014). This is where psychodrama comes into its own as an action method, because many of the problems people face are literally 'beyond words'. For this reason,

psychodrama focuses on emotion and action just as much as the higher functions of thinking, speaking and reflection.

SOCIAL/CULTURAL ROLES

The next category of roles includes the social/cultural roles, such as son, daughter, mother, father, shopper, commuter, partner, lover, teacher, etc. Each role consists of a constellation of behaviours that are associated with that role in a given cultural context. Most of these roles are subject to social learning, and are heavily influenced by role models within the family and within the broader culture. Given a sufficiently stable and conducive environment, a person can develop appropriate and effective social roles that help them survive and that best suit them, their abilities and their goals. Problems may develop, however, if the person is allowed only to learn and carry out a very restricted range of roles, or if one role is over-developed to the detriment of other roles. Another type of problem arises when roles are in conflict and the person is faced with a dilemma.

FANTASY/PSYCHODRAMATIC ROLES

The next category of roles is the fantasy/psychodramatic roles. These are the roles that develop through imagination and through myths, stories and dreams. When used in an integrated way, the psychodramatic roles can strengthen and inspire us. (Think of the strength one may find in stories, music, art, poetry, film and drama.) However, these roles can also become over-developed; if we are too identified with our psychodramatic roles, we may lose touch with reality.

ROLES AND THE EMERGENCE OF THE SELF

Summarising the relationship between roles and the development of our sense of self, Moreno (1946) observed that *roles do not emerge from the self, but the self may emerge from roles*. In other words, the person that we are – our deepest sense of what constitutes our self – develops out of all the roles we are encouraged and permitted to carry out. This description of the formation of self-identity has disturbing implications when we consider what sort of self emerges from conflicted roles, from over-rigid roles, or from self-doubting, antisocial or victim roles.

THEORY OF CHANGE

Psychodrama offers a medium for 'rewriting the script' of our lives and rehearsing new behaviours and roles. Where the issue is unresolved trauma and loss, it is necessary that the person should have his or her suffering acknowledged and believed. Resolution is often achieved by revisiting the scene of the hurt in a structured way and providing an opportunity for emotional release and also a comforting and empowering new experience.

In its so-called 'classical' form, a psychodrama often begins with a current problem or difficulty and traces it back to earlier life situations. Here, the participant (the protagonist) may have the chance to experience what was missing but needed at that time. The enactment then returns to the present, where new learning can be integrated and put into practice. At the end of the drama, the group members share how they relate to the participant's issues and problems. The sharing portion of the session is very important, as it offers the group members an opportunity to speak about their own emotional burdens. It also lets the protagonist know that they are not alone in their suffering.

SKILLS AND STRATEGIES

Five elements are present in a psychodrama session:

- *The protagonist.* The person whose story or issue is the primary focus of the session.
- *The auxiliary egos.* Group members or trained members of staff who assume the roles of significant others in the drama. This may include significant people, objects or even aspects of the self or a person's internal world, e.g., 'my optimistic self' or 'my negative thoughts'.
- *The audience/group.* Group members who witness the drama and who may become involved as auxiliary roles. The emphasis is on creating a safe and supportive environment where each person is a potential therapeutic agent for the others.
- *The stage.* The physical space in which the drama is conducted. It may be an actual stage or simply a designated space.
- *The director.* The trained therapist who guides participants through each phase of the session.

Psychodrama uses a very wide array of active techniques, and many of these have been incorporated into other therapies (Moreno, 1959; Blatner, 1996). Key psychodrama techniques include:

- *Role reversal.* In this technique, one person reverses roles (changes places) with another person and speaks from their point of view. It is a fundamental technique for encouraging empathy and insight into the mind of other people.
- *Doubling.* In this technique, we try to become the 'double' of another person by speaking what we imagine to be their inner thoughts, feelings and beliefs. Doubling can be helpful when people struggle to voice their authentic thoughts and feelings.
- *Parts of self or internal roles.* In this technique, the client is encouraged to speak from the various 'parts' of himself, such as 'the part of me that hates myself and doesn't care about having a decent life' and 'the part of me that likes myself and wants to live a better life'.
- *Role training and role play.* This is perhaps the most widely adopted of the techniques derived from psychodrama. As the name implies, in role training the client is encouraged to learn and practise virtually any human skill.
- *Empty chair.* The client speaks directly to a person or concept being represented by an empty chair. This technique can be used to address unfinished business from the past or to have a 'conversation with myself', to offer just two of the myriad applications of this technique. A chair is often useful when it is too difficult to speak directly to a person.
- *Concretisation.* In psychodrama, it is common to find ways of putting the 'inner world outside' by making the intangible real or 'concrete'. So, objects, symbols, drawings, chairs or other group members may be used to represent internal processes.

EXAMPLES OF PSYCHODRAMAS (ANONYMISED)

Gerry has suffered a string of relationship breakdowns. During his psychodrama, he traces his difficulties back to his early relationship with his mother, whom he experienced as cold and distant. Speaking to a group member who is in the role of his mother, Gerry angrily expresses his unmet need for love and care from her. Within the drama, Gerry then experiences an emotionally attuned mother. He allows himself to be held, and he weeps. He speaks about all the times he has run away from intimacy, or treated women badly because he could not bear to be vulnerable and then rejected by them. His more attuned, psychodramatic mother encourages him to form intimate relationships and to allow himself to love and be loved, without fear. Following this, Gerry is given time to practise a new way of being in intimate relationships, drawing from this experience of attuned mothering.

Meredith chooses a group member to represent the child she never had. In the drama, she holds the child she always wanted, but could not have for medical reasons. She expresses her grief and longing, while gently stroking the child's hair and face. After a long and sensitive encounter with this much-wanted child, she is helped to explore ways in which she can still carry out her desired role of 'loving mother' with her nieces and nephews and in her community. She finds hope for her future, beyond her despair, as she interacts with an immigrant family of two children and their struggling mother (played by group members) who live in her street. She reflects that there are creative and valuable ways to carry out her mothering role that don't involve being a biological mother.

As a child, Tom was sexually assaulted by a neighbour who had 'befriended' him. Twenty years later, he is still terrified by the memory of this event. In the psychodrama, Tom expresses his fear and grief, and summons up his rage about the abuse. Tom takes back his ability to say 'No!' as he accuses his abuser and sees him brought to justice in a psychodramatic 'courtroom'. Tom receives supportive hugs from the group members and tells them it is a relief to be believed and understood. He feels relieved of the pressure to keep secrets and the burden of guilt and shame that he has held onto for so long.

RESEARCH EVIDENCE

In recent years, there has been an increasing number of systematic quantitative and qualitative analyses of psychodrama's effectiveness in the treatment of addictions, offending behaviour, unresolved trauma and loss, and a wide range of mental health disorders (Stadler et al., 2016). These studies have shown that psychodrama can be an effective therapeutic method, although there is significant variation in the types of instrument and the criteria used to measure effectiveness. A summary of studies into psychodrama's effectiveness can be found in Weiser (2007). A meta-analysis of psychodrama research conducted by Kipper and Ritchie (2003) documented an improvement effect similar to or better than that commonly reported for group psychotherapy. The techniques of role reversal and doubling emerged as the most effective interventions. Hudgins and Toscani (2013) have found increasing consensus among therapists focusing on post-traumatic stress disorder (PTSD) that active methods, including psychodrama, are not only effective in working with unresolved trauma, but are indeed the treatment of choice for people suffering with unresolved trauma.

One important finding from the research is that psychodrama needs adaptation to meet the needs of different groups and people with different diagnoses. Given the very wide range of techniques available in psychodrama, it is a method that is particularly amenable to such flexible application. It is always possible for a skilled practitioner to find the 'shoe that fits' a particular person and group.

Psychodrama has been applied in every type of therapeutic and mental health setting, and is also used in personal development, relationship and marital counselling, community building, professional training and business and industry. While there is still much room for additional evidence of psychodrama's effectiveness in these areas and in the clinical domain, it is fair to say that much of the research into the effectiveness of all group therapy is likely to apply to psychodrama as well.

REFERENCES

Blatner, A. (1996). *Acting-In: Practical Applications of Psychodramatic Methods* (3rd ed.). London: Free Association.
Hudgins, K. and Toscani, F. (Eds.) (2013). *Healing World Trauma with the Therapeutic Spiral Model: Psychodramatic Stories from the Front Lines*. London: Jessica Kingsley.

(Continued)

(Continued)

Kipper, D. A. and Ritchie, T. D. (2003). The effectiveness of psychodramatic techniques: a meta-analysis. *Group Dynamics: Theory Research and Practice*, 7(1): 13–25.

Marineau, R. (1989). *Jacob Levy Moreno: Father of Psychodrama, Sociometry and Group Psychotherapy*. London: Tavistock/Routledge.

Moreno, J. D. (2014). *Impromptu Man: J.L. Moreno and the Origins of Psychodrama, Encounter Culture, and the Social Network*. New York: Belleview Literary Press.

Moreno, J. L. (1934). *Who Shall Survive? A New Approach to the Problem of Human Interrelations*. Washington, DC: Nervous and Mental Disease Publishing.

Moreno, J. L. (1946). *Psychodrama* (Vol. 1). New York: Beacon.

Moreno, J. L. (1946–1969). *Psychodrama* (Vols 1–3; Vols 2 and 3 with Z. T. Moreno). New York: Beacon.

Moreno, Z. T. (1959). A survey of psychodramatic techniques. *Group Psychotherapy*, 12: 5–14.

Nolte, J. (2014). *The Philosophy, Theory and Methods of J.L. Moreno: The Man Who Tried to Become God*. London: Routledge.

Stadler, C., Wieser, M. and Kirk, K. (Eds.) (2016). *Psychodrama: Empirical Research and Science 2*. Heidelberg: Springer.

van der Kolk, B. (2014). *The Body Keeps the Score: Brain, Mind, and Body in the Healing of Trauma*. New York: Viking.

Weiser, M. (2007). Studies on treatment effects of psychodrama psychotherapy. In C. Baim, J. Burmeister and M. Maciel (Eds.), *Psychodrama: Advances in Theory and Practice*. London: Routledge.

RECOMMENDED READING

1. Blatner, A. (1996). *Acting-In: Practical Applications of Psychodramatic Methods* (3rd ed.). London: Free Association.

This is a very good introductory text about psychodrama. It is written in a highly accessible style and has for many years been a key text for students of the method.

2. Dayton, T. (2005). *The Living Stage: A Step-by-step Guide to Psychodrama, Sociometry and Experiential Group Therapy*. Deerfield Beach, FL: Health Communications.

This is a superb overview of psychodrama, sociometry and group therapy. It is written in an accessible style and offers comprehensive coverage of theory and practice. The book has many useful checklists and practical tips for therapists and group leaders.

3. Moreno, J. D. (2014). *Impromptu Man: J.L. Moreno and the Origins of Psychodrama, Encounter Culture, and the Social Network*. New York: Belleview Literary Press.

This is a biography of J. L. Moreno written by his son, Jonathan Moreno. It is an excellent book and offers not only an account of Moreno's life, but also a detailed and insightful overview of his impact on society, including his impact on the encounter culture, many forms of psychotherapy, social networking and the theatre.

5.22

PSYCHOSYNTHESIS THERAPY

HELEN SIERODA

OVERVIEW AND KEY POINTS

Psychosynthesis is rooted in both Western and Eastern philosophical and mystical thinking as well psychoanalysis. It is part of a wider movement of psychospiritual development sometimes called 'transpersonal'. It is an open system, not identified with any specific technique or practice. This inclusiveness allows it to draw upon a wide range of approaches and develop many techniques and methods. However, it would be a mistake to assume this has led to an eclectic mishmash; psychosynthesis possesses its own original and central essence, outlined under 'Basic Assumptions'. In short, psychosynthesis is:

- a synthetic approach, drawing upon diverse methodologies in the service of addressing human suffering and human potential
- inclusive, integrating and embracing individuality and universality, human suffering, psychopathology, spiritual experience and deeper questions of meaning and purpose
- broad in scope, engaging with the realisation of potential in individuals, organisations and society.

BRIEF HISTORY

Roberto Assagioli (1888–1974), the founder of psychosynthesis, was a student of Freud and Bleuler, a contemporary of Jung, and a pioneer of psychoanalysis in Italy. He was actively involved in the birth of depth psychology, writing articles and participating in the Zurich Freud Society, but his participation in the psychoanalytic movement between 1909 and 1912 was brief. Assagioli's conception of the person was radically different from Freud's and as early as 1910, in his doctoral thesis, he was beginning to develop psychosynthesis. He argued that Freud's vision of the person was incomplete because it did not include the healthy or spiritual aspects of being human. He envisioned a holistic psychology which could integrate psychoanalysis with psychosynthesis and 'depth psychology' with 'height psychology'. Psychosynthesis builds upon Freud's theory of the unconscious; it addresses psychological distress, and

intra-psychic and interpersonal conflict, *as well as* actualisation of human potential, the capacity for wholeness and the search for deeper meaning and purpose.

Assagioli drew inspiration for his approach to human development from diverse sources (a full account of these can be found in Hardy, 1987). He was influenced by Western philosophical and mystical thinking and had a serious interest in Eastern traditions. In order to gain a deeper understanding of the development of psychosynthesis it is necessary to appreciate the broader currents of European culture at the end of the nineteenth century. This was a period characterised by anticipation of radical change. Assagioli's vision of personal transformation and cultural revitalisation and his attempt to marry the emerging science of psychology with mysticism reflect both the spiritual and scientific quests of the *fin de siècle*. The creative tensions and contradictions of this period seem fundamental to the birth and later development of the synthetic, integrative vision of psychosynthesis.

The Istituto di Psicosintesi was founded in Rome in 1926. Following this, a number of other centres were established in Europe and in 1957 the Psychosynthesis Research Foundation was founded in the United States. Although Assagioli did not enjoy wide recognition until the late 1950s, he developed and practised his ideas 50 years before 1960s counterculture and the birth of humanistic and transpersonal psychology. He played a part in the development of both of these movements, serving on the board of editors for the *Journal of Humanistic Psychology* and the *Journal of Transpersonal Psychology*.

Assagioli envisaged psychosynthesis as an approach (rather than a school) with no central, formal authority, structure or institute. Shortly before his death he issued a statement indicating that the relationship of centres 'should be not that of a "solar system" but that of a "constellation"' (Assagioli, 1974). Whereas this undoubtedly created a context where immense richness, diversity and creative freedom could flourish, it does make keeping track of the international development and impact of psychosynthesis a challenge.

Psychosynthesis has moved on in the decades since Assagioli's death and is flourishing in numerous centres worldwide. There are well-established training centres throughout Europe and in the UK.

BASIC ASSUMPTIONS

Assagioli outlined seven core principles underpinning the psychosynthesis approach, which together convey its essence. Although by no means limited to these, their inclusion is central to any full account of psychosynthesis. These are:

- transpersonal self or 'Self' often written with a capital 'S'
- superconscious
- dis-identification
- personal self or 'I'
- the will
- ideal model
- synthesis.

Central to psychosynthesis is a celebration of the vast potential of the human spirit. In this respect it could be seen as a forerunner of positive psychology. Both human suffering and potential are held in a broad psychospiritual context, based on the understanding that a deeper connection with our spiritual source or transpersonal self (often referred to simply as 'self') is at the heart of the human condition and is the foundation of psychological health. Transpersonal self is not psychologised, understood as a God concept, archetype or symbol; Assagioli maintained that self is a spiritual, metaphysical reality. Psychosynthesis holds that each of us essentially *is* a self and has the potential to develop a relationship with this source, not only at times of mystical or 'peak' experiences at the higher levels of the superconscious, but also in the midst of our everyday lives.

One fundamental proposition is that the transpersonal infuses all levels of the personality and all levels of consciousness through every stage of life. Just as we have a lower unconscious containing sexual and aggressive drives, instincts, complexes and pathological symptoms, we also have a higher unconscious or superconscious which is the source of creative imagination, inspiration, intuition, ethical imperatives and the pull towards spiritual maturity. The latter is as basic to human nature as the former. Spiritual development is not conceived of as a linear journey from here outward to some lofty and distant destination. It is described as an unfolding process which includes all of life participating in a spiritually evolving cosmos. The goal is a regenerated personality aligned with this wider context, and the process combines attending to the lower unconscious with utilising superconscious energies and the imagination to create a realistic and attainable ideal (as opposed to idealised) model of what we can become.

Though psychosynthesis has an optimistic view of the person, it actively addresses the destructive potential in human nature, while holding the possibility for positive change. Much of the work of psychosynthesis involves increasing awareness or uncovering the 'split-off' or disowned parts of ourselves and facilitating the integration of contradictions and multiplicity within the personality. This includes the psychological functions: desires, sensation, feeling, thinking, imagination and intuition. It is an approach which sees the person as carrying within themselves the resources to become whole.

Assagioli frequently stressed that superconscious or mystical experiences are not to be seen as an end in themselves. Rather, these experiences should be a source of inspiration for engaging with the world in pragmatic ways, in a spirit of service similar to the bodhisattvic endeavour of Buddhism. He conceived of society as a reflection of human consciousness, with psychosynthesis playing a part in social and political transformation. This orientation has facilitated the emergence of social or applied psychosynthesis which offers a pragmatic response to the psychological reductionism and socio-political disconnection of which counselling and psychotherapy in general are often accused.

Psychosynthesis embraces a transpersonal context for our life journey and is often linked with the transpersonal movement. Like transpersonal psychology, it has developed a variety of techniques for working with the symbolic, with images, dreams and the realm of the superconscious. Like transpersonal psychology, it addresses the 'dark night of the soul', spiritual emergence and emergency. However, the transpersonal movement and some New Age offshoots are often associated with an exclusive focus on the attainment of spiritual experiences and the cultivation of superconscious energies. This emphasis can make an association with the transpersonal movement problematic. This movement does not accurately reflect the work of the majority of psychosynthesis practitioners when there is a valuing of transcendence or higher states of consciousness *to the exclusion of other perspectives*, or where repression of our earthly lives is confused with transpersonal development. An overemphasis on height creates a problem of duality and an uneasy polarisation of higher and lower, personal and transpersonal, psyche and spirit, self and world. For this reason, many practitioners adopt the term 'psychospiritual'. Nevertheless, psychosynthesis has historically made an important contribution to the development of the transpersonal movement and is also enriched by transpersonal thinkers. Wilber's (2000) quadrant model is routinely found on the curriculum of psychosynthesis training. Jorge Ferrer's (2002) participative view of the transpersonal, A.H. Almaas's (2001) approach to fundamental narcissism, and the work of other transpersonal theorists are all recognised within psychosynthesis.

ORIGIN AND MAINTENANCE OF PROBLEMS

From a psychosynthesis perspective, psychological disturbances are not merely disturbances to self-concept but, crucially, are a disconnection from self. Assagioli asserted that much psychological dysfunction stems from a case of mistaken identity, an estrangement from our essential nature which leads to a lack of meaning and purpose in our lives. He proposed that the purpose of psychosynthesis was to recognise a deeper pull to meaning in our lives and to connect with this deeper source of identity. The personal self or I is the point of connection with self at the level of the personality and makes possible the integration and synthesis of the various (often competing) pulls within the personality.

From a developmental perspective, early environment frequently contributes to a failure to develop into all that we might be in later life. This happens where parents or caregivers require us to become radically different from who we truly are. For example, we may grow up in a repressive environment where our emotions, drives and impulses are not accepted and are driven underground, or when our unique individuality, qualities and gifts are not recognised, encouraged and sustained. We could say that under circumstances like these, the seed of self lacks vital conditions to support its emergence and development. Under these conditions our growth is stunted; as children we adapt to our surroundings in order to survive. As time goes on, most of us habitually settle for living far short of all that we can be, making choices based on what others want or expect, or what causes least discomfort or disruption. To the extent that we are not being true to ourselves, this creates a rupture in the relationship between soul and self. The work of personal development and transpersonal development are not seen as separate processes; the task is to work with blocks and obstacles that prevent the emergence of self wherever they occur.

Every human life is confronted with tragedies, loss, change and uncertainty. Sometimes our usual defences and coping mechanisms don't work, leading to a sense of powerlessness, trepidation or alarm as our lives seem to be unravelling. In psychosynthesis, this psychological distress is understood in the context of a larger mystery which unfolds over time. The lifelong journey of navigating pain, crisis and failure presents an opportunity for awakening to the deeper psychospiritual context of our lives.

THEORY OF CHANGE

Life is uncertain; it confronts us all with the challenge of change. Often we attempt to maintain the illusion of permanence in the face of a dynamic and changing world, experiencing enormous resistance and anxiety at the prospect of change. Psychosynthesis recognises two different orientations towards change. The first is *regressive* – trying to hold on to a situation, behaviour or worldview which we have outgrown or is no longer serving us. This orientation generates more pain. The second is *progressive* – taking responsibility for our lives, choosing to let go of (or dis-identify from) a pattern of thinking, behaviour or state of affairs, or conversely choosing to engage with a tough, challenging situation which we might prefer to avoid. This orientation can also be challenging and disruptive, with painful awakenings, but it leads to inner freedom, for it involves the perspective of the I, the essential spark or seed of the self which is available to us all at the core of our personality. Access to this centre opens the possibility to transform, through the engagement of awareness and will (basic functions of the I), both ourselves and the situation. Even in conditions like sickness, ageing and death, where we have no power over external circumstances, we can choose how we respond to the inevitable (Assagioli, 1974).

SKILLS AND STRATEGIES

Psychosynthesis practitioners respond to the client's own understanding of their experience, adapting strategies, techniques and the application of core principles contextually.

The empathic support provided within the therapeutic relationship is fundamental to the work of helping the client to experience and understand how they have been betrayed by their early environment and/or turned from their true nature or self in order to survive. A vital component within this process is the ability of the therapist to hold what is sometimes called a 'bifocal' perspective: seeing the client as more than their problems, as *both* a spiritually whole self *and* at the same time a personality with pain, problems and pathology.

Psychosynthesis is often associated with subpersonalities. Subpersonalities are a way of making sense of the sometimes bewildering complexity of the human condition and the stormy juxtaposition between different parts of ourselves. Working with subpersonalities creates an awareness of the multiplicity of our inner world, making our inner conversations explicit. It provides a powerful and effective tool for working with intra-psychic conflict while simultaneously addressing the pushes and pulls from the wider world in which we live. Central to this is the development of non-judgemental awareness and the technique of dis-identification which facilitates integration or synthesis within the personality. This brings depth and power to a psychosynthesis approach to subpersonalities. Psychosynthesis has made a great contribution to developing and refining a dialogical approach to working with subpersonalities. However, subpersonalities *per se* are not essential to the practice of psychosynthesis.

A goal of psychosynthesis is to cultivate the ability to purposefully direct psychological energies through the I in line with our highest values, deepest aspirations and a sense of meaning. This includes subpersonalities as well as other psychological functions: desire, sensation, feeling, thinking, imagination, intuition. Working with meaning and purpose might take the form of asking what legacy we wish to leave, what difference we choose to make in the lives of those we touch, or what deeply matters to us, 'what makes our heart sing'. This is an area for challenging clients to engage their vision, gifts and talents. The goal is to develop the courage, insight and vision to grow through both the successes and the difficulties of life.

To sum up, in psychosynthesis the development and refinement of the personality or 'personal psychosynthesis' involve gaining a wide-ranging knowledge of one's personality, learning to direct and coordinate its diverse constituents. This work involves the discovery of the unifying centre or I and the integration of the personality around this centre. The transpersonal aspect of this process involves strengthening the relationship between I and self in the midst of life and engaging with the energies of the superconscious. These are not separate stages that happen in a particular order, but rather interweaving elements in a complex emergent process.

CASE EXAMPLES

Arielle was a beautiful 30-year-old woman, who appeared young and fragile. During the initial interview, her laugh seemed brittle. As part of the initial assessment, her therapist asked her to work on a timeline of significant points in her life. A crisis had occurred as a teenager. Following an idyllic holiday to Africa, she had returned with a chronic virus and spent time in hospital. The trauma of that illness kept her locked in a regressive place of feeling vulnerable and reliant on others, she developed a strong 'pleaser-victim' subpersonality. Her timeline thereafter was littered with skin allergies and more recently alopecia (patches of hair loss).

Arielle felt unattractive, insecure and unsure of how to leave the service/hospitality industry where she felt under-appreciated and subservient. She spent her energy pleasing others, any potential conflict felt oppressive; she described a churning stress, where she 'wound' herself up. The therapeutic work centred on increasing awareness of patterns and subpersonalities; developing a unifying centre (I); engaging will, which enabled her to make new choices to support the development of her strengths and qualities and integrating the energy of the superconscious by reconnecting to her vitality and purpose in life. The lowest point came when Arielle spoke about failure and returning to her parental home, as making a living in London wasn't working. Meeting her in this place, the therapist asked when she would make this change. The intervention melted her resistance and re-ignited her determination to succeed. Over the next weeks, she set realistic goals; her 'ideal model' became realisable and attainable. The therapist's 'bifocal vision' and belief in Arielle's ability to make her own choices supported her to take charge of her life, put herself first and step into her future. As she learned to let go of her anxieties and pursue her own purpose, she found an intense inner will. Letting go of her outmoded identification as a fragile woman allowed her to 'let go' of the opposing contradictory pull to save others. She started to speak with confidence of her hopes and desires, telling her family that though they might not agree with her decisions and she might make mistakes, this was simply the process of living her life.

Another client, Andy, was faced with depression. Developing creativity and intuition through imaginative exercises helped to re-establish his connection with a unifying centre (I) and superconscious qualities. His father left when he was four years old. Four decades later, he realised that much of his life was spent trying to make his absent father proud of him. Recognising his father's unavailability was immensely painful. As his acceptance and understanding grew, Andy began to integrate life-giving superconscious energy that had previously been abandoned and ignored; he started to feel his potency and to reconnect to his own sense of purpose. A series of sessions working with guided imagery, mapping his inner world, furnishing the rooms of his inner house, from the basement to the attic, helped Andy reclaim and integrate exiled subpersonalities, develop his sense of purpose and inner freedom, bringing the strength to face and acknowledge the bewildering and unescapable truth; he could not make his father love him.

RESEARCH EVIDENCE

Like many humanistic-existential and integrative approaches, published research in psychosynthesis is sparse. This is despite partnerships with universities offering masters-level psychosynthesis qualifications. Research-oriented conferences are held, but little finds its way into peer-reviewed journals.

Perhaps research is abandoned once training is completed and private practice established. A more likely explanation is a historic ambivalence towards traditional research methods. These methods, relying on statistical data analysis, can be seen as hyper-rational and reductionist. From the perspective of the quantitative research, a subjective, contextual approach lacks rigour; from a psychosynthesis viewpoint, therapy is a creative, emergent process – more improvisation than set-piece. The mystery of life cannot easily be squeezed into predetermined models or step-by-step, tick-box recipes. Arguably, the research dilemma goes beyond epistemological, theoretical and methodological issues to encompass competing philosophical paradigms. Nevertheless, the importance of research to demonstrate a credible epistemological basis for psychosynthesis is increasingly being recognised.

A significant example of qualitative and quantitative research is found in the work of 'Teens and Toddlers', a charity supporting disengaged teenagers from disadvantaged areas to build the life skills and self-belief they need to succeed at school, in work and in the community (see www.teensandtoddlers.org). 'Disadvantage' is identified through poverty/free school meals, disengagement/exclusion from education and likelihood of risky behaviour.

Although not explicitly presented as such, the approach is grounded in psychosynthesis. The programme (developed by Diana Whitmore, founder and co-chair of the Psychosynthesis Trust) provides a holistic, evidence-based approach effective in engaging young people who are notoriously difficult to reach.

Their research delivers solid, methodical evaluation, surveying the effectiveness of short- and long-term impacts, evaluated against standard measures for self-esteem, self-efficacy and behaviour. Programmes have been evaluated since 2001, and as of 2015 more than 14,000 young people have participated. Their impact report scored maximum points when assessed and peer-reviewed by the Centre for Analysis of Youth Transitions (CAYT), a Department for Education-sponsored research centre that brings together leading educationalists and social scientists from the Institute for Fiscal Studies, Institute of Education and National Centre for Social Research.

REFERENCES

Almaas, A.H. (2001) *The Point of Existence*. Boston, MA: Shambhala.
Assagioli, R. (1974) Training. Unpublished paper.
Ferrer, J.N. (2002) *Revisioning Transpersonal Theory*. New York: SUNY Press.
Hardy, J. (1987) *A Psychology with a Soul: Psychosynthesis in Evolutionary Context*. London: Routledge and Kegan Paul.
Wilber, K. (2000) *Integral Psychology*. Boston, MA: Shambhala.
With thanks to Kim Schiller for providing case study examples.

RECOMMENDED READING

1. Assagioli, R. (1965) *Psychosynthesis: A Collection of Basic Writings*. Wellingborough: Turnstone.

Containing many early writings, this is a key work for understanding the principles, techniques and application of psychosynthesis.

2. Firman, J. and Gila, A. (2002) *Psychosynthesis: A Psychology of the Spirit*. New York: SUNY Press.

A comprehensive account of psychosynthesis, providing a transpersonal integration of developmental, personality and clinical theory.

3. Whitmore, D. (1991) *Psychosynthesis Counselling in Action*. London: Sage.

A definitive introduction to the principles and techniques of psychosynthesis. A guide to the four main stages of the counselling journey, explaining how a wide range of practical methods can be tailored to different client needs.

THEORY AND APPROACHES: CONSTRUCTIVIST APPROACHES

5.23 NARRATIVE THERAPY

JOHN MCLEOD

OVERVIEW AND KEY POINTS

Narrative therapy is primarily associated with the work of Michael White and David Epston. This chapter offers an introduction to the key assumptions and skills of the narrative therapy tradition that grew from the publication of *Narrative Means to Therapeutic Ends* (White and Epston, 1990), and which is now applied in therapy with individuals and couples, and in various community interventions, as well as in work with families. The aims of the chapter are to:

- offer an introduction to the main ideas and methods used in narrative therapy;
- provide an account of the distinctive features of the narrative therapy approach, arising from its adoption of philosophical stance that is more socially oriented than mainstream models of therapy;
- explain how narrative therapy works in practice;
- evaluate the research evidence for this approach.

BRIEF HISTORY

The founders of narrative therapy, David Epston and Michael White, originally trained in family therapy in the 1980s. At that time, in the field of psychology and psychotherapy as a whole, there was a growing interest in narrative perspectives, centred on the idea that storytelling represented a fundamental human means of communication and sense-making (McLeod, 1997). Although the 'narrative turn' within psychology, philosophy and the social sciences had a significant impact on many approaches to therapy, narrative therapy represents its most tangible legacy. Narrative therapy training is now available in most countries, and there is a thriving network of events and conferences that support the ongoing development of the approach. Because of its distinctive philosophical and politically aware roots, narrative therapy represents a way of working that is not readily integrated with other therapy approaches. However, there have been initiatives to integrate narrative therapy with experiential, emotion-focused ways of working (Angus and Greenberg, 2011; Seo, Kang, Lee and Chae, 2015) and with Cognitive-Behavioural Therapy (CBT) (Ikonomopoulos,

Smith and Schmidt, 2015). Within the broad systemic tradition, there are also other narrative-informed models of therapy (Sundet and McLeod, 2016).

BASIC ASSUMPTIONS

Narrative therapy has been influenced by the ideas of the French poststructuralist philosopher Michel Foucault and other postmodern writers, who are critical of the assumption that is made within contemporary psychology that cognitive, biological and emotional structures within the individual person are the source of human action and decision-making. These writers propose an alternative way of making sense of people, in terms of relationships and connections between individuals and participation in a shared language which incorporates and conveys layers of historical meaning. Within this perspective, stories play a crucial role in mediating between the person and the culture within which he or she lives their life. As a result, narrative counselling and psychotherapy are based on a complex set of ideas or assumptions about the role of narrative in human communication, identity and meaning-making. These ideas are as follows.

Stories are the basic way in which people make sense of their experience. Relating a story about an event conveys the intentionality and purpose of the teller and their understanding of relationships and the social world, expresses feelings and communicates a moral evaluation of what has happened.

We tell our own personal tales, but do so by drawing on a cultural stock of narrative forms. We are born into the story of our family and community, and the story of who we are (e.g., our birth story, the story behind our name). As we grow up we adopt narrative templates provided by myths, films, novels and other cultural resources to give shape and meaning to our individual life narrative.

People are social beings, and have a basic need to tell their story. Holding back on telling the story involves a process of physiological inhibition that can have negative effects on health. Telling one's story promotes a sense of knowing and being known, and leads to social inclusion.

Personal experience and reality are constructed through the process of telling stories. The stories that we tell are always co-constructed, and are told in the presence of a real or implied audience. There is a dialogic aspect to stories. Constructing a story is a situated performance, a version of events created at a particular time and place to have a specific effect. A story is something that is created *between* people rather than existing in one person's mind. The narrativization of experience is an open-ended process. There are always other stories that can be told about the same events or experiences.

The concept of *voice* refers to the way in which a story is told. The life narrative represents a weaving together of multiple voices. For example, the story of someone's life, or episodes in that life, can be narrated through an official, psychiatric/medical voice, a personal and vulnerable voice or the harsh critical voice of an angry parent. One of the tasks of therapy is to distentangle these voices. The concept of voice also conveys something of the embodied nature of storytelling, by drawing attention to the physical qualities of *how* the story is told, in terms of volume, tone, rhythm and the use of speech forms such as metaphor, repetition and contrast.

It is useful to distinguish between oral and literary (written) forms of narration. Writing down a story tends to produce a more logically structured version, which can function as a permanent record. People attribute authority and legitimacy to written stories. Oral versions of stories, by contrast, are generally more relational, improvised, emotionally involving and transient.

ORIGIN AND MAINTENANCE OF PROBLEMS

These underlying assumptions suggest a distinctive narrative perspective on the origins and maintenance of the problems that can lead people to seek therapy. The elements of this perspective are as follows.

The experience of being *silenced* is emotionally painful and problematic for most people. Silencing can be a consequence of the social isolation that can result in many situations, such as bereavement, emigration/exile, illness and disability. Silencing can also be produced through purposeful oppression of persons, for example those who may have been sexually, physically or emotionally abused by family members or those who are members of political, ethnic, religious or sexual orientation minority categories.

A life story that is silenced or that is habitual minimizes the possibility of dialogical engagement with other persons. 'Problems' can be understood as being those areas of personal experience around which the person is not able, or willing, to engage in conversation.

The life narrative templates available within a culture, community or family may be difficult or impossible to reconcile with the circumstances of actual lived experience. For example, the *dominant narratives* within a culture may prescribe gender, age or social class 'scripts' which deny many or most of the possibilities for creative human encounter.

The trajectory of some lives may contribute to the production of narratives which are *incomplete* or *incoherent*. For example, when a person has experienced trauma, he or she may end up with a 'fractured' life narrative in which crucial elements of the trauma event are too hard to disclose, and as a result are not included in the stories that the person tells about their life.

Some people can develop a style of telling personal stories that is almost wholly *problem saturated*. This tendency can be exacerbated by over-involvement with mental health ideologies.

THEORY OF CHANGE

The change process in narrative therapy involves the construction of opportunities for stories to be told, leading to a phase of reflection and then finally the possibility that the story might be modified or changed. White and Epson (1990) use the term *reauthoring* to characterize this change process.

People find it helpful to have an opportunity to tell their story in a setting in which what they have to say is accepted and valued by others. The basic experience of another person becoming a witness to one's account of troubles is meaningful and worthwhile.

It can be useful to be given the opportunity to generate different versions of a story concerning life issues. Usually, the telling and retelling of the story produces narratives of strength, resourcefulness and courage, which eventually may replace the more habitual, problem-saturated accounts of troubles that the person has brought into therapy.

The ritual of therapy makes it possible for the person to articulate their life narrative with support and without interruption or competition. This gives the person a chance to reflect upon their story, and to consider whether there are any parts of it that perhaps they might seek to articulate in different ways. Unfolding the story in its entirety is a means of retrieving and preserving the meaning of that life narrative, and in itself leads to a more meaningful life.

The notion of *externalizing* the story conveys the idea that the person creates the stories he or she tells (and therefore can tell different stories). The person is not identified with their story but has a relationship with it.

Narrative therapy methods involve the construction of a more satisfying or coherent life narrative through a process of broadening the narrative horizon. The person may find that stories of current troubles may make sense when understood in the light of earlier 'chapters' in the life story.

People who are seeking to change aspects of their life story may engage in a search for examples of more convivial or suitable narrative forms they can live within. This search may involve exploring literary sources, meeting new people or learning from fellow members of a therapy or self-help group.

The act of narrating a life in a changed way may necessitate disrupting or deconstructing habitual narratives. This process can be facilitated by the use of figurative and concrete language and different modes of telling (e.g., writing). Therapists encourage the telling of vivid, meaningful and emotionally resonant personal stories rather than bland, abstract reports.

Telling a different story about oneself can require recruiting new audiences, and challenging the ways in which pre-existing audiences and communities promote problem-saturated narratives.

SKILLS AND STRATEGIES

The skills and strategies employed in narrative therapy can be understood as comprising two broad dimensions: a poststructuralist worldview from which the client is regarded as a person with strengths and resources, and the use of specific narrative interventions. Narrative therapy practice requires sensitivity and awareness in relation to language use and narrative forms, and genuine curiosity about the stories through which people create and maintain their identities and relationships. In narrative therapy, the role of the counsellor or psychotherapist includes being both witness to, and co-editor of, the stories told by the person seeking help. The client–therapist relationship is not regarded as being at the centre of the therapy process (as it would be in psychodynamic or person-centred therapy). Instead, the aim is to 'decentre' the therapy relationship in ways that invite the client to become aware of how they relate to other people in their real everyday life. The narrative therapy worldview is critical of oppression and inequality in society. Narrative therapists seek to minimize the danger that the therapeutic experience will function as a means of reinforcing dominant cultural narratives. One of the ways in which they do this is by adopting a *not-knowing* stance, which involves honouring the teller as the expert on their own story. Users of therapy are seen as consultants to the therapeutic process, and are asked for advice on what is helpful.

The second dimension of narrative practice concerns the specific interventions or procedures that have been developed within the narrative therapy tradition. Some narrative-informed therapists use techniques based on writing, such as a letter written to clients or documents written by clients, rather than relying solely on spoken dialogue. The purpose of writing is to exploit the value of a communication format that is permanent, and allows reauthored stories to be recorded and reread. Most narrative therapists make use of the technique of *externalizing* the problem, based on inviting the client to find a way of talking about their problem as something separate from. This strategy opens up a space for exploring the influence of the person on the problem, and the problem on the person. It also enables the therapist to invite the client to consider times when they were problem-free (unique exceptions) and to build an alternative narrative around these hitherto silenced or disregarded 'glittering moments'. An important aspect of narrative therapy involves the recruitment of new audiences for the reauthored story that is emerging from therapy; the aim is not to be able to tell this story in the therapy room, but to make it part of everyday life. Some narrative therapists will invite family or community members into therapy sessions to act as *witnesses* to the client's new story, or will encourage the client to seek opportunities within their life to recruit friends, family and work colleagues as witnesses. In some situations, where the social pressure and control of the dominant narrative is particularly strong, the therapist may facilitate the creation of support groups of people who are engaged in similar reauthoring 'projects'. An example of this kind of social action approach can be found in the 'anti-anorexia league' (Maisel, Epston and Borden, 2004), a support network and political action group for people fighting to free themselves from a 'voice of anorexia' that is powerfully reinforced through media images. Further information on recent developments in narrative therapy skills and strategies can be found in White (2011).

An example of how narrative therapy can operate in practice is the case of Jane, who sought help from a counsellor because of panic attacks and general anxiety. In their first meeting, the counsellor asked questions that have the effect of inviting Jane to experiment with a different way of talking about her difficulties: 'I allowed the *fog of panic* to take over my life', rather than 'I panicked'. This way of talking opened up further conversations around the characteristics of the 'fog' and whether there might have been some occasions when Jane had been able to resist or outwit the 'fog'. The counsellor showed great curiosity around these moments of success, and what had made them possible. She then invited Jane to identify other people in her life who would not have been surprised about these accomplishments. Jane thought about this, and mentioned a close friend who 'is always on my side'. These steps allowed, over the next few sessions, a process to unfold where Jane became able to become more aware of her own resources in relation to the 'fog' and to use counselling to celebrate and reflect on her successes around 'just letting it pass me by'. After each session, her counsellor sent Jane an email that documented and reinforced the new story she was beginning to construct about who she was and what she stood for, and encouraged her to find audiences for this story within her circle of family, friends and work colleagues.

RESEARCH EVIDENCE

Narrative therapy theory and practice is informed by a critical philosophical, ethical and sociological perspective that is not consistent with the assumptions of mainstream research in counselling and psychotherapy. For example, studies that rely on psychiatric diagnostic categories may have the effect of disseminating and supporting a 'language of deficit' that labels and excludes individuals. As a result, the narrative therapy community has been cautious in its engagement with the need for research evidence to support the development of the approach.

In recent years, a broad-based narrative therapy research literature has begun to emerge. There have been a number of participatory action research studies that document the efforts of particular groups of people to overcome specific problems (see, for example, Denborough, 2008) and to communicate what they have learned to others who are engaged in similar struggles. Qualitative research interviews have been used to explore client and therapist experience of various aspects of narrative therapy in practice (Keeling and Nielson, 2005; O'Connor et al., 2004; Young and Cooper, 2008). Process analysis of narrative practice has been conducted using coding of therapy session transcripts (Ramey, Young and Tarulli, 2010; Santos, Gonçalves and Matos, 2011). Systematic case studies of narrative therapy have been published by Ikonomopoulos, Smith, and Schmidt (2015) and Palgi and Ben-Ezra (2010). Quantitative studies of the effectiveness of narrative therapy for depression, using standard outcome measures, have levels of improvement similar to CBT (Lopes et al., 2014; Vromans and Schweitzer, 2011). Taken together, these studies provide credible support for the therapeutic processes included in narrative therapy, and for the effectiveness of the approach as a whole.

REFERENCES

Angus, L.E. and Greenberg, L.S. (2011) *Working with Narrative in Emotion-focused Therapy: Changing Stories, Healing Lives*. Washington, DC: American Psychological Association.

Denborough, D. (2008) *Collective Narrative Practice: Responding to Individuals, Groups, and Communities Who Have Experienced Trauma*. Adelaide: Dulwich Centre.

Ikonomopoulos, J., Smith, R.L. and Schmidt, C. (2015) Integrating narrative therapy within rehabilitative programming for incarcerated adolescents. *Journal of Counseling and Development, 93*, 460–470.

Keeling, M.L. and Nielson, L.R. (2005) Indian women's experience of a narrative intervention using art and writing. *Contemporary Family Therapy, 27*, 435–455.

Lopes, R.T., Gonçalves, M.M., Fassnacht, D.B., Machado, P.P.P. and Sousa, I. (2014) Long-term effects of psychotherapy on moderate depression: a comparative study of narrative therapy and cognitive-behavioral therapy. *Journal of Affective Disorders, 167*, 64–73.

Maisel, R., Epston, D. and Borden, A. (2004) *Biting the Hand that Starves You: Inspiring Resistance to Anorexia/Bulimia*. New York: W.W. Norton.

McLeod, J. (1997) *Narrative and Psychotherapy*. London: Sage.

O'Connor, T.S., Davis, A., Meakes, E., Pickering, R. and Schuman, M. (2004) Narrative therapy using a reflecting team: an ethnographic study of therapists' experiences. *Contemporary Family Therapy, 26*, 23–39.

Palgi, Y. and Ben-Ezra, M. (2010) "Back to the Future": Narrative Treatment for Post-Traumatic, Acute Stress Disorder in the Case of Paramedic Mr. G. *Pragmatic Case Studies in Psychotherapy, 6*(1), 1–26.

Ramey, H.L., Young, K. and Tarulli, D. (2010) Scaffolding and concept formation in narrative therapy: a qualitative research report. *Journal of Systemic Therapies, 29*, 74–91.

Santos, A., Gonçalves, M.M. and Matos, M. (2011) Innovative moments and poor outcome in narrative therapy. *Counselling and Psychotherapy Research, 11*, 129–139.

(Continued)

(Continued)

Seo, M., Kang, H.S., Lee, Y.J. and Chae, S.M. (2015) Narrative therapy with an emotional approach for people with depression: improved symptom and cognitive-emotional outcomes. *Journal of Psychiatric and Mental Health Nursing, 22,* 379–389.

Sundet, R. and McLeod, J. (2016) Narrative approaches and pluralism. In M. Cooper and W. Dryden (eds), *Handbook of Pluralistic Counselling and Psychotherapy.* London: Sage.

Vromans, L.P. and Schweitzer, R. (2011) Narrative therapy for adults with major depressive disorder: improved symptom and interpersonal outcomes. *Psychotherapy Research, 21,* 4–15.

White, M. (2011) *Narrative Practice: Continuing the Conversations.* New York: W.W. Norton.

White, M. and Epston, D. (1990) *Narrative Means to Therapeutic Ends.* New York: W.W. Norton.

Young, K. and Cooper, S. (2008) Toward co-composing an evidence base: the narrative therapy re-visiting project. *Journal of Systemic Therapies, 27,* 67–83.

RECOMMENDED READING

1.   Combs, G. and Freedman, J. (2012) Narrative, poststructuralism, and social justice: current practices in narrative therapy. *Counseling Psychologist, 40,* 1033–1060.

An overview of theory and practice in narrative therapy from two of the leading figures in this approach.

2.   Denborough, D. (2014) *Retelling the Sories of Our Lives: Everyday Narrative Therapy to Draw Inspiration and Transform Experience.* New York: W.W. Norton.

Recent developments in narrative therapy and community practice, with an emphasis on the political and community dimensions of the approach.

3.   Morgan, A. (2000) *What is Narrative Therapy? An Easy-to-read Introduction.* Adelaide, South Australia: Dulwich Centre.

Accessible starting point for anyone wishing to learn about narrative therapy. The Dulwich Centre website provides a wealth of information and resources on the approach (http://dulwichcentre.com.au).

5.24   NEURO-LINGUISTIC PROGRAMMING

JO COOPER

OVERVIEW AND KEY POINTS

Neuro-linguistic programming (NLP) offers a model – and a modelling process – of how humans function, as well as ways of applying the models to facilitate change. The basic model of NLP is that humans take in information through their senses – they see, hear, feel, smell and taste. They use the same senses to process that information internally, building an individual and unique model of the world that is constantly updated. It is this model that informs behaviour. While NLP is not in itself a therapy, it can be remarkably effective when used therapeutically to help a client adjust their model of the world in order to function more effectively.

- NLP can be thought of as 'the study of the structure of subjective experience'.
- It is a systemic model perceiving the mind–body as one system and involves the whole system in change.
- It focuses on process and pattern rather than content.
- NLP helps the client to recognize the resources already available to them, to add choice and to help them to move forward effectively towards and beyond their present goals.

BRIEF HISTORY

NLP was founded in the early 1970s by Richard Bandler, a mathematician and information scientist, and John Grinder, an associate professor of linguistics at the University of California at Santa Cruz. They were interested in what made the difference between people whose work was generally perceived as brilliant and others whose work was competent but less remarkable. They were curious as to how the structure of subjective experience informs behaviour. Their form of study was to 'model' people who were experts in their fields, then to design 'models' that they could use themselves and that they could teach to others.

Bandler and Grinder's best-known modelling was of the work of three major therapists: gestalt therapist Fritz Perls, family therapist Virginia Satir and Milton H. Erickson, doctor and founder of the American Society of Clinical Hypnosis. Bandler (2010: 22) explains:

> We watched them at work, and instead of getting caught up in the content of what they were doing, we looked at the syntax of what they were saying and doing. As soon as we looked at it in that way, the patterns popped out everywhere – in the questions they asked, the words they used, the gestures they made, the tonality and rate with which they spoke.

Bandler and Grinder's first books, *Structure of Magic I* (Bandler and Grinder, 1975a) and *Structure of Magic II* (Grinder and Bandler, 1976) were the result of their modelling of Perls, Satir and others, and were initially directed towards therapists. Their model of the work of Milton Erickson was set out in *Patterns of the Hypnotic Techniques of Milton H. Erickson, MD*, Volumes 1 and 2 (Bandler and Grinder, 1975b; Grinder et al., 1977) and again more recently by Bandler (2010).

BASIC ASSUMPTIONS

The name that Bandler and Grinder chose for their work can be thought of as descriptive:

- *Neuro* refers to neuro-physiology, the functioning of the nervous system within the physiological structure of the human body, thought of as 'one system'.
- *Linguistic* refers to the use of language to communicate – both verbal and non-verbal.
- *Programming* refers to the patterns and sequences evident in neurological processing, demonstrated in behaviour, which can be thought of as representing personal 'programmes'.

At its simplest, NLP assumes that human beings use their senses (seeing, hearing, feeling, smelling and tasting – or, as usually referred to in NLP, visual, auditory, kinaesthetic, olfactory and gustatory) to perceive and process information – their subjective experience. As they continuously process their experience, individuals develop their own unique models of their world.

For practical purposes, human modelling (the individual's creating and updating of their model of the world) can be thought of as the systemic interrelationship of neuro-linguistic patterning and behaviour. A key assumption in NLP is that experience has structure – it is never random – and that all behaviour is informed by the individual's model of the world, however bizarre or extreme it may seem to others. Bandler and Grinder (1975a) said that identifying the assumptions in a client's modelling is the equivalent of understanding how the client's behaviour 'makes sense'.

Similarly, NLP itself 'makes sense' when its basic assumptions are understood. These were initially identified by its originators and have become known as the *NLP presuppositions*.

Perhaps the best known of the NLP presuppositions is 'the map is not the territory': the individual's *model of the world* is not the world. Many problems and misunderstandings occur when people confuse their model of the world with the world itself, believing that their model is 'true' and shared by others.

NLP is a systemic model. This is difficult to describe in 'linear' language; at best we can say that the 'body–mind' (or 'mind–body') is one system and that life and mind are *systemic processes*. Two other NLP presuppositions follow from this. The first is that any change in one element of a system will, in some way, be *detectable throughout the system*, and secondly, that the element of the system with the greatest *flexibility of behaviour* has the most influence in the system.

Cybernetic models were central in the development of NLP. A key conceptual model adopted by the originators was the test–operate–test–exit (TOTE) model, developed by Miller et al. (1960). The TOTE model maintains that all behaviour is goal-oriented, and feedback is provided by testing the goal against the evidence criteria for its achievement. This is encapsulated in the NLP presuppositions that all behaviour has a *positive intention* (in which 'positive' refers to purposeful, not to a value judgement as to its worth) and that in communication there is no failure, only *feedback*, the constant evaluating of the goal and evidence.

The NLP presuppositions, taken together, generate the possibility of choice, in that a particular behaviour is chosen to accomplish a purpose. NLP presupposes that individuals will make the *best choice* they can, given their model of the world and the resources they perceive to be available to them. Implicitly, individuals can be limited as much, if not more, by their models of the world and the choices they make as by the world itself.

Internal resources are a function of the development and sequencing of representational systems in internal processing. So provided that they have the necessary neurophysiology, everyone either has, or has the potential to develop, *all the resources they need to act effectively*.

ORIGIN AND MAINTENANCE OF PROBLEMS

The domain of NLP is subjective experience – how human beings model and structure their experience. Bandler and Grinder proposed three sets of 'filters' that affect this modelling process:

1. Neurological constraints, the limits imposed by the human nervous system.
2. Social genetic factors, which are shared by members of the same socio-linguistic community.
3. Individual constraints, which provide the basis for the most far-reaching differences between individuals.

It is the combination of these filters that ensures that the experience of each individual is unique and that each individual generates their own unique model of the world. Bandler and Grinder (1975a: 12) said that 'these uncommon ways [in which] each of us represents the world will constitute a set of interests, habits, likes, dislikes and rules for behaviour which are distinctly our own'.

In NLP a 'problem' occurs when an individual is aware of a difference between their present state and desired state but perceives that they have little or no choice. The NLP practitioner's intention is to help their client to enrich their model of the world and to restructure their experience in such a way as to enhance choice.

THEORY OF CHANGE

Over the years NLP modelling has become more detailed and precise as finer distinctions have been made. In the early days, for example, it was recognized that human beings process their experience in sensory modalities, see images in their mind's eye, hear internal sounds and voices (including their own voice) and have feelings that are internally generated.

The significance of changes in 'submodalities' was explored later. Submodalities are the finer distinctions within each representational system, for example the colour, brightness, shape and location of an image; the tone, pitch, volume and tempo of a sound; and the location and intensity of a feeling.

Deliberate and systematic NLP modelling can enable the practitioner to identify specific neuro-linguistic patterns and sequences in order to make sense of, and re-create, aspects of the behaviour of their 'subject'. In the therapeutic context, this process is used to elicit how the client maintains their 'problem' and to design ways of facilitating change.

Bandler and Grinder (1975a) claimed that all successful therapy, whatever its emphasis or method of treatment, characteristically involves a change in the client's representation or model of the world.

Individuals process vast amounts of sensory information. Some of this is in conscious awareness but most is processed unconsciously (in NLP 'unconscious' simply refers to processing that is outside conscious attention).

Sensory experience is transformed by what Bandler and Grinder referred to as the three universal modelling processes: deletion, generalization and distortion. Deletion occurs when information is left out, generalization when information is expanded so as to exclude counterexamples and distortion when there is an assumption of causal connections and equivalencies. These are natural processes that are essential for the processing and coding of information and can be both limiting and empowering.

In *Structure of Magic I* Bandler and Grinder (1975a) showed how the universal modelling processes can be identified in an individual's language patterns. The words and phrases that people use can be regarded as 'surface structure', which is derived from 'deep structure' (full linguistic representation), which in turn is derived from the sensory representation of the individual's model of the world.

By observing the client's behaviour and listening to their language patterns, an NLP practitioner can identify deletion, generalization and distortion in the client's modelling. By using language and behaviour in specific and precise ways, the NLP practitioner can help the client enrich their model and expand its boundaries.

When an NLP practitioner and client work together, it is always with the active, creative participation of the client. The practitioner uses sensory acuity, an understanding of modelling processes and behavioural flexibility to influence the system and to create a context in which the client is able to access new choices.

SKILLS AND STRATEGIES

The skills needed by the NLP practitioner can be thought of from three perspectives: conceptual, analytical and behavioural. Conceptual skills include the understanding and application of NLP models. Analytical skills include the ability to analyse the system (including the practitioner's and the client's behaviour). Behavioural skills include the practitioner's ability to vary their own behaviour to influence the system and to facilitate the client's ability to change.

NLP is a systemic model and the TOTE model described earlier is a key concept. Other conceptual models in NLP are language models, representation systems (the way in which experience is processed in different sensory systems), accessing cues (signalling how individuals access information internally), anchors (the patterns of association between external cues and internal experience) and rapport (pacing and leading).

Analytical skills can be thought of as the ability to analyse the 'system'. Practitioners make use of the TOTE when they model the client's behaviour and as a structure for their own participation in the system (Dilts, 1998; Dilts and DeLozier, 2000). They need to be able to chunk information at different levels, to identify patterns and sequences of behaviour, language patterns and naturally occurring anchors.

Behavioural skills include the use of sensory acuity to be aware of what is happening in the system as it occurs. There is always external evidence of internal processing, including posture, gesture, breathing rate and location, eye movements, language patterns, voice tone, tempo and pitch, and much more in every sensory system. The more highly developed the acuity of the practitioner and the better the feedback in the system, the more the practitioner will be able to vary their behaviour to influence the system. Behavioural skills also include the ability to match the client and to lead the client to change their behaviour, to anchor specific states and to use language precisely to achieve specific outcomes.

In the early days of NLP, Bandler and Grinder summed up the necessary components of NLP as to gather information, to evolve the system and to solidify change. Over the years there has been a tendency for the application of recipe-like 'techniques' to be confused with NLP. Bandler is often quoted as saying that NLP is an attitude (of curiosity) and a methodology (of modelling), which leave behind a trail of techniques.

In practice NLP can be remarkably simple. For example, Mr A, a manager in a large engineering company, was worried that he could no longer communicate with his team. He was so anxious that he felt unable to walk into the workshop where his team was based. The first step was to ask him about the situation and to assess the 'present state'. While explaining that he wanted his team to do well and to achieve their goals, he made no reference to what they had already achieved. In fact, his eye movements only followed the pattern that would be expected of someone accessing present and future information. When he was asked what had already been achieved he was dismissive and talked again of what was yet to be done.

The practitioner then asked him if he had any personal projects that he was working on outside work. He said that he was building a conservatory and again explained his goal and everything that he had not yet achieved, with no reference to what he had already done.

The practitioner used the language patterns of NLP to direct the manager's attention to what he had already achieved and to observe changes in his behaviour, including changes in his eye-accessing cues.

The practitioner then used the manager's personal experience as a metaphor for the issues with his team, and directed his attention to their achievements. The manager recognized that he could show appreciation of his team's efforts as well as planning the next steps to reach their goals. He then practised what he would do in his next meeting with his team.

A few weeks later the practitioner met Mr A and asked how he was getting on with his team. He looked slightly puzzled and said they were 'a great bunch of lads'. When asked if he'd resolved the issues from a few weeks earlier, he didn't recall having any issues and just repeated that everything was going well!

This example includes gathering evidence about the present state, establishing a goal, looking for behavioural cues as to how the client is structuring his internal experience, finding an example of a similar situation that demonstrated the same pattern with more personal relevance and then applying that to his work situation. The final step was to mentally rehearse the actions he planned to take so that they became familiar to him.

RESEARCH EVIDENCE

There have been numerous efforts to research NLP, and many of them are listed in a database that is published on the NLP Research Data Base (www.nlp.de/research/ – compiled and edited by Dr Daniele Kammer and published by Dr Franz-Josef Hücker).

NLP research can be thought of in two categories: first, research into the conceptual models formulated by Bandler and Grinder; and second, research into the efficacy of the application of NLP.

The conceptual models present a difficulty for researchers in that Bandler and Grinder used the word *model* advisedly. They said in *Frogs into Princes*:

> We call ourselves *modelers* … We are not psychologists, and we're also not theologians or theoreticians. We have *no* idea about the 'real' nature of things, and we're not particularly interested in what's 'true'. The function of modelling is to arrive at descriptions which are *useful*. So, if we happen to mention something that you know from a scientific study, or from statistics, is inaccurate, realize that a different level of experience is being offered you here. We're not offering you something that's *true*, just things that are *useful*. (Bandler and Grinder, 1979: 7)

Research into the application of NLP, and especially into NLP 'techniques', is difficult to design. Skilled NLP practitioners who have integrated NLP into their own models of the world are aware of sensory feedback within the system and vary their behaviour accordingly. Their choice of behaviour is made in relation to the way the client is structuring their experience, rather than the application of a standardized format. Traditional research, however, has typically required the construction of a boundary around an aspect of behaviour in the belief that it is possible to measure the effectiveness of one element of behaviour in isolation. When NLP practitioners work with their clients the NLP is in the intentional and purposeful application of the model, rather than in any specific behaviour.

In his introduction to a book introducing NLP to health professionals, Bandler (2008: ix) wrote: 'I have for years been very good at modelling successful healers, but have fallen short on providing the science. … It seems obvious to me that the more we know about the brain and how it works well, the better off we will be'.

Many of the key presuppositions of NLP are gaining support from neuroscience. The ideas that individuals operate from their unique, individual model of the world, and that behaviour is intentional rather than reactive, were radical in the early 1970s, but now neuroscientists are reporting similar conclusions.

In their book about the emerging science of body maps, Blakeslee and Blakeslee (2008: 62) write: 'Perception and action are inherently predictive. Your brain creates mental models of your body and the world, and is constantly updating those models with newly arrived information from the senses and constantly extrapolating predictions from them'.

Discoveries in neuroscience are bringing further credibility to key concepts and methods of NLP. There has for many years been talk in NLP of 'building new synapses' and recent research and understanding of neuroplasticity demonstrate this happening. In his book *The Brain's Way of Healing*, Norman Doidge (2015: xiii) describes neuroplasticity as 'the property of the brain that enables it to change its own structure and functioning in response to activity and mental experience'. He goes on to say that the ways of healing described in his book:

> frequently use the body and the senses as primary avenues to pass energy and information into the brain … these are the avenues the brain uses to connect with the world, and so they provide the most natural and least invasive way to engage it. (Doidge, 2015: xvii)

The key methodology of NLP – the modelling process – has been supported by the 1990s development of the concept of mirror neurons. NLP practitioners are encouraged to be 'in rapport' with their clients to assist in the process of modelling how the client is structuring their subjective experience. The concept of mirror neurons offers a possibility of how this can facilitate the modelling process. Ramachandran (2011: 23) writes that within the brain:

> there is a special class of nerve cells called mirror neurons. These neurons fire not only when you perform an action, but also when you watch someone else perform the same action. This sounds so simple that its huge implications are easy to miss. What these cells do is effectively allow you to empathise with the other person and 'read' her intentions – figure out what she is really up to.

At a time of rapid developments in the field of neuroscience, practitioners wanting to take their practice forward, and to develop new ways of applying NLP, can benefit from directing their curiosity not only to the study of NLP and its continuing development, but also to current research in neuroscience and especially to neuroplasticity, which is giving increasing validity to the basic tenets of NLP.

REFERENCES

Bandler, R. (2008) Introduction. In G. Thomson and K. Khan (eds), *Magic in Practice: Introducing Medical NLP: The Art and Science of Language in Healing and Health*. London: Hammersmith Books.

Bandler, R. (2010) *Richard Bandler's Guide to Trance-Formation*. London: Harper Element.

Bandler, R. and Grinder, J. (1975a) *Structure of Magic I*. Palo Alto, CA: Science and Behavior.

Bandler, R. and Grinder, J. (1975b) *Patterns of the Hypnotic Techniques of Milton H. Erickson, MD* (Vol. 1). Cupertino, CA: Meta Publications.

Bandler, R. and Grinder, J. (1979) *Frogs into Princes*. Moab, UT: Real People.

Blakeslee, S. and Blakeslee, M. (2008) *The Body Has a Mind of Its Own*. New York: Random House.

Dilts, R. (1998) *Modeling with NLP*. Capitola, CA: Meta Publications.

Dilts, R. and DeLozier, J. (2000) *Encyclopedia of Systemic NLP and NLP New Coding*. Santa Cruz, CA: NLP University Press.

Doidge, N. (2015) *The Brain's Way of Healing*. New York: Penguin Random House.

Grinder, J. and Bandler, R. (1976) *Structure of Magic II*. Palo Alto, CA: Science and Behavior.

Grinder, J., Delozier, J. and Bandler, R. (1977) *Patterns of the Hypnotic Techniques of Milton H. Erickson, MD* (Vol. 2). Capitola, CA: Meta Publications.

Miller, G.A., Galanter, E. and Pribram, K.H. (1960) *Plans and the Structure of Behavior*. New York: Holt, Rinehart and Winston.

Ramachandran, V.S. (2011) *The Tell-Tale Brain*. London: Heinemann.

RECOMMENDED READING

1. Bandler, R. (2010) *Richard Bandler's Guide to Trance-Formation*. London: Harper Element.

In this book Richard Bandler revisits some of the patterns described in the earliest books that he wrote or co-wrote in the 1970s and 1980s, some of them written before NLP was named, and looks at them from the perspective of using and developing them over 30–40 years. It includes exercises, resource pages that give a brief introduction to the major patterns of NLP and transcripts of Bandler working with clients. It includes a description of the connections between NLP and hypnosis, and the ways in which trance is universal. This is a book that is easy to read and deceptively complex, offering new ideas and perspectives with every reading.

2. Thomson, G. and Khan, K. (2015) *Magic in Practice: The Art and Science of Language in Healing and Health* (2nd ed.). London: Hammersmith Health Books.

Written for health professionals, this book is equally relevant to counsellors, psychotherapists and coaches who want to understand and improve the effects of how and what they communicate to their patients and clients, consciously and unconsciously. Language, verbal and non-verbal, is a powerful catalyst for change. This book demonstrates the ways in which practitioners can communicate in ways that are helpful and empowering and can facilitate, rather than obstruct, the process of healing and change.

3. Dilts, R. and DeLozier, J. (2000) *Encyclopedia of Systemic NLP and NLP New Coding*. Santa Cruz, CA: NLP University Press. (http://nlpuniversitypress.com/)

(Continued)

5.25 PERSONAL CONSTRUCT COUNSELLING AND PSYCHOTHERAPY

DAVID WINTER AND FAY FRANSELLA

OVERVIEW AND KEY POINTS

Personal construct theory was developed in the clinical sphere by George Kelly, and while its applicability is by no means limited to this field, it has provided a basis for a particular form of constructivist counselling and psychotherapy. The theory considers that each of us constructs our world but that people who present psychological problems have become stuck in constructions that are not revised despite being invalidated. The aim of personal construct counselling and psychotherapy is therefore to help them to engage in a process of reconstruction. This generally involves the exploration of the client's construing, perhaps using personal construct assessment techniques such as the self-characterization or the repertory grid, and the facilitation of experimentation with construing. The flexibility of the approach makes it applicable to various client groups across the life span, and it has a good evidence base. Key points include:

- Personal construct counselling and psychotherapy are derived from George Kelly's personal construct theory.
- It was the first example in a psychological theory of what has come to be termed a constructivist approach.
- The theory asserts that people construct their worlds and, when their constructions are invalidated, reconstruct them, but that this process becomes blocked in people with psychological problems.

- Personal construct counselling and psychotherapy use a range of techniques to facilitate the process of reconstruction.
- This approach to counselling and psychotherapy has a good evidence base.

BRIEF HISTORY

Personal construct counselling and psychotherapy are based directly on George Kelly's *The Psychology of Personal Constructs* (1991), set out in two volumes published in 1955. His first degrees were in physics and mathematics, followed by postgraduate degrees in sociology, education and, eventually, psychology. He spent much of his academic life at Ohio State University and overlapped there with Carl Rogers for a short time. In his theory of personal constructs, George Kelly aimed to encompass the person's experiencing of the world in its entirety. Feeling involves thinking and behaving just as behaviour involves feelings and thoughts. The theory had a mixed reception on its publication as it was explicitly against the current climate in the psychology of behaviourism, on the one hand, and psychoanalytic theories on the other. Its influence, both as a theory of personality and as an approach to counselling and psychotherapy, was felt first in Great Britain and spread into Europe before being taken up in any substantial way in its birthplace, the United States of America. (See Fransella (1995) for more details of the man and his theory, and Walker and Winter (2007) and Winter and Reed (2016) for details of how personal construct psychology has been developed and applied since Kelly introduced it.)

Early critics of the theory insisted that it explained 'cognitions' very well but did not deal adequately with emotions. In spite of arguments to the contrary, in 1980 Walter Mischel called George Kelly the first cognitive psychologist. He said: 'There is reason to hope that the current moves towards a hyphenated cognitive-behavioral approach will help fill in the grand outlines that Kelly sketched years before anyone else even realized the need' (Mischel, 1980: 86). The argument about this issue continues today, but suffice it to say that many personal construct psychologists would not be happy with the not uncommon classification of personal construct theory in textbooks as cognitive-behavioural, instead considering that it has more in common with humanistic, integrative or narrative approaches.

Of great influence has been George Kelly's philosophy of *constructive alternativisim*, which underpins the theory throughout. That philosophy is seen as one of the main precursors of the movement of *constructivism*, which has swept through psychology as well as psychotherapy and counselling (Chiari and Nuzzo, 2010; Neimeyer, 2009) during the last few years. The philosophy sees reality as residing within the individual. While 'true' reality may indeed be 'out there', we, as individuals, are only able to place our own personal interpretations on that external reality.

Personal construct counselling and psychotherapy are practised around the world, but are not as popular as some other approaches. The main reason, no doubt, is the fact that the personal construct approach is based on a very complex theory about how all individuals experience their worlds. Personal construct therapy is one application of that theory designed to help those who are experiencing problems in dealing with their world.

BASIC ASSUMPTIONS

Constructive alternativism states that there are always alternative ways of looking at events. That means that no one needs to be the victim of their past since that past is always capable of being seen in a different way – it can be *reconstrued*. However, we can trap ourselves by our past if we construe it as fixed.

The philosophy gives a positive and optimistic view of life since there is always the possibility of change – no matter how difficult that change may be. We have created the person we now are, and so can re-create ourselves.

Personal constructs are essentially discriminations. We see some events, or people, or behaviours as being alike and, thereby, different from other events. These dichotomous personal constructs are formed into a system and it is through that system of personal constructs that we peer at the world of events milling around us.

We place an interpretation on an event by applying certain of our repertoire of personal constructs to it and, thereby, predict an outcome. You see someone smiling at you across the street and predict, perhaps, that he is about to cross the road to say hello. You act accordingly.

Behaviour is the experiment we conduct to test out our current prediction of a situation. The man does cross the street and you put out your hand to shake his only to find he is smiling at someone behind you. In the language of personal construct theory, you have been invalidated.

The theory is couched in the language of science. Kelly suggested we might look at each person 'as if' we were all scientists. We have theories (personal construing), make predictions from those theories and then test them out by behaving.

The person is a form of motion. No sooner have we conducted one behavioural experiment than the answer leads us into another situation and another cycle of construing.

'Negative' feelings are experienced when we become aware that our current ways of construing events are not serving us well. We become aware that the current situation means we are going to have to change how we see our 'self' – we are threatened; or we become aware that we cannot make sense of what is happening and, until we do, we experience anxiety; or we become aware that we have behaved in a way which is 'not me' – and feel guilty. Sometimes, when our constructions are invalidated, we attempt to change the world to make it fit with them, rather than vice versa, and show 'hostility' in Kelly's sense of this term.

Personal construct therapists use various ways of helping the client to find alternative possibilities of construing events and life that will enable them to conduct more productive behavioural experiments, but the client is the expert and the client has the answers. However, those answers may well not be available to conscious awareness.

Construing takes place at different levels of cognitive awareness. The lowest level of cognitive awareness is what is termed *pre-verbal*, that is, discriminations that have been made before the acquisition of language.

An essential feature of personal construct theory is its reflexivity. It accounts for the construing of the counsellor and therapist as well as that of the client.

ORIGIN AND MAINTENANCE OF PROBLEMS

There is no list for the personal construct therapist of ways in which problems start. The answer lies with the client who is presenting that problem.

A person decides they have a psychological problem when their present way of construing and predicting events is not working well. Predictions and behavioural experiments are being invalidated but the person is not able to modify those predictions and behaviours in the light of experience.

THEORY OF CHANGE

Since each person is a form of motion, change is the norm. The person with a psychological problem is seen as being 'stuck'. The goal of therapy and counselling is to help the person 'get on the move again'. At the most superficial level, this might involve the client changing the use of their existing constructs, but more fundamental changes include modification of these constructs or their replacement by new constructs (see Fransella and Dalton (2000) for more detail of the change process).

A collaborative therapist–client relationship, which Kelly saw as analogous to that between a research supervisor and their student, is necessary to facilitate change. As part of this, the therapist uses the 'credulous approach'. He or she takes at face value everything the client relates – even if it is known to be a lie. Credulous listening helps the therapist get a glimpse into the client's world. A therapeutic plan cannot be drawn up, and certainly not put into action, until the practitioner has some idea of what certain changes may mean to the client. The therapist essentially provides a climate of sufficient validation to enable the client to risk experimentation with, and the possibility of some invalidation of, their construing.

Somewhere in the client's construing system are the reasons why he or she cannot get on with the business of living. The therapist uses the theory of personal constructs to make a temporary *diagnosis* or formulation (Winter and Procter, 2013) of why the client has the problem.

That theoretical diagnosis leads to the therapeutic plan of action. It may, for instance, focus on the *looseness* of the client's construing process. The client cannot make enough sense of events to conduct meaningful behavioural experiments; or the client may be thought to be resisting any change because that change has some unacceptable implications. For instance, being *anxious all the time* may be seen as indicating that one is a *sensitive*, *thoughtful* and *caring* person whereas being *anxiety-free* means one is the opposite.

The focus of the process of change is mostly in the here and now. It is how the client construes things now that is important. Sometimes, the client links the present with a past event. In that case, the counsellor explores, with the client, that past event. But there is nothing in the theory that makes it mandatory to explore the past with the client.

SKILLS AND STRATEGIES

Personal construct counselling and psychotherapy are largely value-free. There is little in personal construct theory that dictates how a person should be. Therefore, the therapist or counsellor needs to be able to suspend his or her own personal construct system of values. Without that ability, it is not possible to step into the client's shoes and look at the world through the client's eyes, because the therapist's personal values get in the way. In the place of a personal system of constructs, the therapist peers through the system of professional constructs provided by personal construct theory. That means the therapist needs to be well versed in the use of theoretical constructs.

Kelly (1991 [1955]) suggests the personal construct practitioner needs several other skills, including creativity and good verbal ability. The need for creativity stems from the fact that the theory is eclectic in terms of tools available to the counsellor or therapist. The aim is to help the client find alternative ways of dealing with personal events and any means may be used to attain that goal. Kelly (1991 [1955]: 600–601) put it like this:

> Creation is therefore an act of daring, an act of daring through which the creator abandons those literal defenses behind which he might hide if his act is questioned or its results proven invalid. The … [therapist] who dares not try anything he cannot verbally defend is likely to be sterile in a [counselling/ psychotherapy] relationship.

Kelly described two specific tools that allow the exploration of the client's construing:

- *Self-characterization* – stems from Kelly's first principle: 'If you want to know what is wrong with a person, ask him, he may tell you'. It consists of a statement written by the client, in the third person, describing him/herself in a sympathetic way. The client is free to say whatever he or she likes.
- *Repertory grid technique* – is a method which can assess both the content and the structure of the client's personal construct system, by such means as indicating the strength of mathematical relationships between personal constructs, between the elements to which they may be applied and between constructs and elements. It was a way Kelly suggested psychologists could 'get beyond the words'. This technique has been widely used in counselling and psychotherapy, for example, as a means of identifying the client's dilemmas, which may then be the focus of therapy (Feixas and Saúl, 2005). However, as with all else, its use is by

no means a requirement (see Fransella et al. (2004) for details on how to use this technique, and Caputi et al. (2011) and Bell (2016) for developments of this and other personal construct assessment methods).

A specific therapeutic technique developed by Kelly for use with some, but by no means all, clients is *fixed-role therapy*. It involves the therapist or counsellor writing a sketch of a new character whom the client is invited to become for a week or more. This character is not the opposite of the client, but rather will involve the elaboration of some new theme which might be valuable for the client to explore. The client must agree that the character portrayed is understandable and acceptable. The new role that the client plays shows him or her that making changes to oneself also produces changes in how others respond to us, how we feel, and so forth. Most importantly, it shows we can re-create ourselves (see Epting et al., 2005). Fixed-role therapy is but one of many ways by which the personal construct counsellor or psychotherapist may facilitate the client's experimentation. Since personal construct counselling and psychotherapy are technically eclectic, several of these may be borrowed from other therapeutic models but the reasons for their selection and mode of action will be conceptualized in personal construct theory terms.

Fixed-role therapy was one of the techniques used with a client, Tom, who presented with difficulties in interpersonal relationships, including in being assertive (Winter, 1987). Repertory grid technique and other personal construct assessment methods revealed the dilemmas underlying these difficulties, not least that he contrasted being *assertive* with being *reasonable*, and associated extraversion and assertiveness with various characteristics that, for him, were undesirable, such as being *demanding*, *aggressive* and *selfish*. Exploration of the origins of this pattern of construing led him to consider his childhood relationship with his mother, who was generally very silent but at times when she expressed her opinions became verbally and physically abusive towards him and his father. It was suggested to Tom that his way of construing assertiveness was perfectly understandable as a way of anticipating his mother's behaviour when he was a child, but that it perhaps could be limited to his construing of her at that time, giving him freedom to experiment with ways of being more assertive and extraverted without the possible negative implications that were previously associated with these ways of behaving. Part of this experimentation involved fixed-role therapy using a sketch of a character which elaborated themes of showing a lively curiosity in other people, and a commitment to everything that he does. Since his self-characterization had indicated that his construing and behaviour were dominated by a relentless and unproductive focus on finding a girlfriend, the fixed-role sketch deliberately avoided any mention of this particular concern. Post-treatment assessment revealed not only clinically significant changes on measures of symptoms and social difficulties, but also changes on grid measures indicative of more favourable self-construing and resolution of his dilemmas concerning extraversion and assertiveness.

Over the years, personal construct counselling and psychotherapy have been employed with a wide range of client groups throughout the age range, and in individual, couple, family and group settings (Winter, 1992; Winter and Viney, 2005).

RESEARCH EVIDENCE

The evidence base for personal construct counselling and psychotherapy includes research, mostly using the repertory grid, into changes in construing resulting from personal construct interventions, and evidence that the outcome of this form of counselling and psychotherapy is comparable to that of other major therapeutic approaches (Metcalfe et al., 2007; Winter, 2005).

REFERENCES

Bell, R.C. (2016). Methodologies of assessment in personal construct psychology. In D.A. Winter and N. Reed (Eds.), *Wiley Handbook of Personal Construct Psychology*. Chichester: Wiley-Blackwell.

Caputi, P., Viney, L.L., Walker, B.M. and Crittenden, N. (Eds.) (2011). *Personal Construct Methodology*. Chichester: Wiley-Blackwell.

Chiari, G. and Nuzzo, M.L. (2010). *Constructivist Psychotherapy: A Narrative Hermeneutic Approach*. London: Routledge.

(Continued)

(Continued)

Epting, F., Germignani, M. and Cross, M.C. (2005). An audacious adventure: personal construct counselling and psychotherapy. In F. Fransella (Ed.), *The Essential Practitioners' Handbook of Personal Construct Psychology*. Chichester: Wiley.

Feixas, G. and Saúl, L.A. (2005). Resolution of dilemmas by personal construct psychotherapy. In D.A. Winter and L.L. Viney (Eds.), *Personal Construct Psychotherapy: Advances in Theory, Practice and Research*. London: Whurr.

Fransella, F. (1995). *George Kelly*. London: Sage.

Fransella, F., Bell, R. and Bannister, D. (2004). *A Manual for Repertory Grid Technique* (2nd ed.). Chichester: John Wiley & Sons.

Fransella, F. and Dalton, P. (2000). *Personal Construct Counselling in Action* (2nd ed.). London: Sage.

Kelly, G.A. (1991 [1955]). *The Psychology of Personal Constructs* (Volumes I and II). New York: Routledge. (Originally published by W.W. Norton in 1955.)

Metcalfe, C., Winter, D. and Viney, L. (2007). The effectiveness of personal construct psychotherapy in clinical practice: a systematic review and meta-analysis. *Psychotherapy Research*, 17: 431–342.

Mischel, W. (1980). George Kelly's appreciation of psychology: a personal tribute. In M.J. Mahoney (Ed.), *Psychotherapy Process: Current Issues and Future Directions*. New York: Plenum Press.

Neimeyer, R.A. (2009). *Constructivist Psychotherapy*. London: Routledge.

Walker, B.M. and Winter, D.A. (2007). The elaboration of personal construct psychology. *Annual Review of Psychology*, 58: 453–477.

Winter, D.A. (1987). Personal construct psychotherapy as a radical alternative to social skills training. In R.A. Neimeyer and G.J. Neimeyer (Eds.), *Personal Construct Therapy Casebook*. New York: Springer.

Winter, D.A. (1992). *Personal Construct Psychology in Clinical Practice: Theory, Research and Applications*. London: Routledge.

Winter, D.A. (2005). The evidence base for personal construct psychotherapy. In F. Fransella (Ed.), *The Essential Practitioners' Handbook of Personal Construct Psychology*. Chichester: John Wiley & Sons.

Winter, D.A. and Procter, H.G. (2013). Formulation in personal and relational construct psychotherapy. In L. Johnstone and R. Dallos (Eds.), *Formulation in Psychology and Psychotherapy*. London: Routledge.

Winter, D.A. and Reed, N. (Eds.) (2016). *Wiley Handbook of Personal Construct Psychology*. Chichester: Wiley-Blackwell.

Winter, D.A. and Viney, L.L. (Eds.) (2005). *Personal Construct Psychotherapy: Advances in Theory, Practice and Research*. London: Whurr.

RECOMMENDED READINGS

1. Caputi, P., Viney, L.L., Walker, B.M. and Crittenden, N. (Eds.) (2011). *Personal Construct Methodology*. Chichester: Wiley-Blackwell.

Describes personal construct assessment methods, including those originally devised by Kelly and subsequent developments.

2. Fransella, F. and Dalton, P. (2000). *Personal Construct Counselling in Action* (2nd ed.). London: Sage.

A clear introduction to personal construct counselling and psychotherapy.

3. Winter, D.A. and Viney, L.L. (Eds.) (2005). *Personal Construct Psychotherapy: Advances in Theory, Practice and Research*. London: Whurr.

Contains examples of developments in personal construct psychotherapy and their theoretical and research base, together with several examples of applications in clinical practice.

5.26 SOLUTION-FOCUSED BRIEF THERAPY

GUY SHENNAN

OVERVIEW AND KEY POINTS

Solution-focused brief therapy (SFBT) was first developed in the early 1980s by a group of therapists in the United States of America (de Shazer et al., 1986). Its subsequent development has led to a number of versions emerging, with the one described here being that predominantly used today in the United Kingdom (UK) (Ratner, George and Iveson, 2012; Shennan, 2014). Its starting point is to develop a forward-facing orientation for the work based on what the client wants from it. The major therapeutic activity from that point on consists of helping the client to describe in detail how they and their lives would be if what they wanted from the work was realised, to describe in detail the progress they are already making towards this 'preferred future', and to consider how they are making that progress. In short, a solution-focused brief therapist:

- focuses on what is wanted rather than on what is not wanted
- assumes that people are already on the way to realising what they want
- does not try to solve problems or find solutions, but rather elicits descriptions of preferred futures and progress being made towards them
- is not gathering or analysing information or trying to understand the client
- tries to find questions to ask that connect with the client's answers and help the client to continue to think and talk in ways that become useful to them.

BRIEF HISTORY

The original SFBT blueprint was developed at the Brief Family Therapy Center in Milwaukee in the early 1980s, by therapists mainly from the brief/strategic and family therapy traditions. Like most therapists, their (pre-solution-focused) starting point is to focus on the client's problems, which they viewed interactionally rather than as situated within the client's individual psyche, and which they believed to be maintained by actions the client was taking in unsuccessful attempts to resolve them. In this view of problem causation or maintenance they were

following the brief therapists of the Mental Research Institute (MRI) in Palo Alto (Watzlawick, Weakland and Fisch, 1974), by, in short, focusing on what the client was doing that was not working. The therapists often worked as a team, with one therapist conducting the session with the client(s) and the others observing via a one-way screen or monitor. The conductor's role was to elicit information from the client, in particular about what was not working, so that the observing team could develop an appropriate task for the client that would encourage them to do something different, which would work.

The shift from this problem focus to what became seen as a solution focus was a gradual one, though one incident was pivotal (Lipchik et al., 2011). The team sometimes gave the client the task of writing down all the things they wanted to change. During one session a team member suggested they ask the family to list instead all the things they observed happening between sessions which they did not want to change. At the next session the family reported, in concrete terms, the positive changes that had taken place, and the team was encouraged to give other clients a similar task, frequently with the same results.

This contributed to a realisation that, whatever problems a client had come with, there was always something that was working, and that focusing on this appeared to lead to positive changes taking place. So, as well as giving what they had labelled the Formula First Session Task, the team began to ask clients to talk about these 'exception' times. In these ways they shifted their attention from what was not working to what was working and engaged clients in 'change talk' rather than 'problem talk' ever earlier in the work (Gingerich, de Shazer and Weiner-Davis, 1988). The other major focus of the approach developed from the goal orientation of brief therapy, based on the idea that if it was not known what needed to happen for therapy to end, it could in theory continue forever. One technique devised to establish the endpoint of the work was the 'miracle question' (de Shazer, 1988). As this question was increasingly used and became a series of questions, it was clear that it had more useful effects than just setting end goals, and so a focus on 'preferred futures' came to join the focus on what was working as the main pillars of the approach.

BASIC ASSUMPTIONS

The most basic assumption of SFBT is that if someone has made the decision to talk to a person in a helping role, then they must want something to come from this. The assumption is one of motivation. Every client must be motivated for something, or else they would not be talking to someone, though it will often not be clear to the client at the outset what this is. As the brief therapist John Weakland once said, therapy is 'two people talking together, trying to figure out what the hell one of them wants' (de Shazer, 1999, p35). So, establishing what the client wants is a co-constructive process, which the solution-focused therapist begins with their first question to the client: What are your best hopes from our work together?

Another assumption of SFBT is that change, and so therapy, can occur rapidly, which is supported by research, as we will see below (Gingerich and Peterson, 2013). In fact, in SFBT it is assumed that change is not only possible, but inevitable (de Shazer, 1985), and that it is happening all the time. Furthermore, it is assumed that there will be some positive change happening, that there are always exceptions to problems and that the client is an active agent of change. The task of the solution-focused therapist, then, is to help to highlight and amplify positive change that is already underway.

It is also assumed that the particular activities a solution-focused therapist engages in are helpful. However, it is not the therapist's questions that are seen to lead to change happening, but the thinking and talking by the client that the questions generate. In other words, it is assumed that talking about preferred futures and the progress being made towards them are helpful things for a client to do.

ORIGIN AND MAINTENANCE OF PROBLEMS

A distinctive aspect of SFBT is that it is not based on a theory about the aetiology of problems. Before developing the approach, the Milwaukee team were influenced by the MRI idea that problems arise and are maintained by the mishandling of ordinary life difficulties. This tends to normalise problems and to minimise the pathologising and blame that can be associated with locating their cause. As the team moved from a problem to a solution focus, they took this normalising and depathologising a step further, seeing problems as just 'damned bad luck' (de Shazer, 1985: 18).

In the early stages of the approach, its movement was away from the problems that brought the client to therapy, by the focus on exceptions to these problems.

Then as the future focus increased in importance, the movement turned towards what is wanted. This has been accompanied by a focus on instances of where this is already happening, rather than on exceptions to problems, so any focus by the therapist on problems has become less necessary. Of course, clients will frequently feel the need to talk of their problems, and then the therapist must listen and show they have heard how difficult those problems are. However, what they will be curious about at these moments is not how the client got into the problems, but how they are getting through them and what they want to be happening instead.

When a client states a wish to understand the causes of the problems they are having, a solution-focused therapist will ask what they hope such an understanding will lead to, which usually paves the way for a focus on a preferred future and progress being made towards it.

THEORY OF CHANGE

The founders of SFBT stressed the pragmatic nature of its development, claiming it was not based on theory, or at least on any 'grand theory', but on many hours of 'disciplined observation' of what works in therapy. However, to talk of observing what works invites the question of what is meant by 'working' and what the criterion of this is. It cannot relate to an eventual positive outcome of the therapy, as this cannot be observed while the therapy is taking place. When the developers of SFBT talked of something working, the initial criterion they appeared to be using is that the client is able to report recent positive changes in concrete ways. For example, this is how they judged that the First Session Formula Task 'worked'. Their theory of change then became evident as they chose to focus on recent positive changes, by asking questions that encouraged the client to talk about them. Then what 'worked' within a session was whatever the therapist did that facilitated 'change talk' rather than 'problem talk' (Gingerich, de Shazer and Weiner-Davis, 1988). So, SFBT has a language-based theory of change based on the simple idea that what we talk about concerning ourselves influences how we think of ourselves and who we can become.

Additionally, talking about future preferences is seen to engender hope. Once a client is able to articulate a wish and to describe a desired future in detail, their sense that this is possible grows, which in turn leads to increased hope. When the client is encouraged to recall and talk about times when they have already achieved at least some of this, then hope can be transformed into expectation, having the effect of a self-fulfilling prophecy.

SKILLS AND STRATEGIES

In a general sense the solution-focused brief therapist engages in three activities with the client:

- Asking questions
- Listening – with a constructive ear
- Responding – echoing and summarising.

Questions serve different purposes, and are often used to seek information. This is how they are used in many therapeutic approaches, with the information gathered guiding, for example, the therapist's formulations or interpretations or the setting of between-session tasks. The solution-focused brief therapist, however, does not ask questions to gather information but simply to help the client talk in ways that become useful for them. Each question is constructed so that it fits overall within the solution-focused process and connects with the client's previous answer, thus helping the client to incrementally build their descriptions of a preferred future and progress towards this.

Listening closely to the client is essential in ensuring that the next question connects with the previous answer, and 'listening with a constructive ear' (Lipchik, 1988) ensures that the question fits the solution-focused process. What a therapist listens for is determined by their therapeutic orientation, and the constructive ear of the solution-focused therapist is alert for what the client is wanting, the signs of that emerging and anything they are doing that fits with the possibility of achieving this.

This process of asking a question, listening to the answer, constructing a question that connects with that answer, listening to the next answer and so on, elicits descriptions of preferred futures and progress that are built from the client's words, which are centred in the process. When the therapist engages in the third activity listed above, responding, it is therefore important that they do so in the main by simply echoing or summarising the client's words.

Excerpts from the first session with Sonia, an 18-year-old woman referred for therapy by a worker in a young people's advice service, will illustrate this and the three parts of the solution-focused process.

1 SETTING A DIRECTION TOWARDS A DESIRED OUTCOME

After some introductions the therapist's first questions aimed to develop a forward-looking orientation for the work:

Therapist:	What are your best hopes from this?
Sonia:	Well, I've got a few problems with anxiety. And since I got pregnant I've had really bad depression…

As Sonia continued to list her difficulties, the therapist listened, before acknowledging the difficult time Sonia was going through, and asking:

Therapist:	And how would you know that coming here had been useful to you?
Sonia:	I'm stressed a lot, and I like having someone to talk to when I'm low and when I'm depressed, so that someone can help me. I just want help.
Therapist:	So if this does prove to be helpful, what will it tell you, what will you notice about yourself that will tell you this has proved to be helpful?
Sonia:	I wish that I didn't feel so anxious. I hope that I can get help with feeling anxious all the time…

A movement for the work had been established, away from anxiety. Moving towards something actively desired rather than away from a problem can provide a more positive and energising context for the work:

Therapist:	What would you like to be feeling instead?
Sonia:	I just want to feel happy.

The therapist was not concerned by the generality of a desire to be happy. What had happened through this opening exchange was a shift in orientation, so that the work could now proceed with client and therapist looking towards something wanted rather than looking down and back at the problems Sonia has come with.

2 DESCRIBING A PREFERRED FUTURE

Therapist:	Suppose when you wake up tomorrow, you find anxiety isn't a problem for you and you're able to feel happy as you'd like to – what's the first thing you'd notice about yourself?

Sonia: I'd have a clear head. I wouldn't be thinking so much about my problems. Because problems make you anxious. When you don't think you're not anxious, are you?

Therapist: So what might you be thinking about tomorrow instead, if you woke up feeling how you'd like to?

Sonia: I'd be more into taking more care of my little girl, more into taking care of myself and getting into my hobbies and interests as well, and not letting my relationship get the best of me really.

The therapist proceeded to help Sonia to describe in detail the differences she might notice in these areas of her life, which would both accompany and show the realisation of her hopes from the therapy. Situating these descriptions in the immediate future of tomorrow helped to ensure they were connected to the actual situation in which Sonia was living. The therapist's questions were then designed to help Sonia both 'zoom in' to the smallest details she would notice in herself – What's the first thing you would do tomorrow if you were taking care of yourself more? – and to 'widen her lens' – Where else tomorrow would you notice these differences?

Making descriptions interactional, so that clients consider themselves from others' perspectives and their effects on those others, enhances their emotional content:

Therapist: What would your little girl notice about you?

Sonia: That I'd be playing with her more. And I'd be much more patient if she starts crying and I don't know what the reason is. I'd have more energy to be patient with the baby.

Therapist: Playing more, and patient, right. What sorts of things would you play?

Sonia: Oh, I'd sing to her, I'd read books to her, I'd make her stand up, I already do, but I feel I would do more than I do right now. I'd play with her, I'd make her feel she's walking around everywhere.

Therapist: Would she enjoy you doing those things with her?

Sonia: I'm sure she would!

Therapist: How would you know?

Sonia: She'd look up at me when I walked her around, and be smiling.

3 DESCRIBING PROGRESS TOWARDS AND INSTANCES OF THE PREFERRED FUTURE

A shift from preferred futures to times when they are already happening ('instances') can be facilitated simply by listening out for mentions of the latter. While Sonia was describing her future self being more assertive with her partner, by asking him not to phone her while he was working a night shift, she added: 'Because when I had depression I couldn't sleep all night, and it's only recently I've started to sleep well, and I'd like to continue sleeping well'.

The therapist's curiosity about Sonia's having started to sleep well showed itself in the following questions, which are typically asked in such circumstances:

How did you do that? How have you managed to start sleeping well? What differences has it made?

A common way to elicit instances and details of progress being made is to use scaling questions. The therapist introduced a scale to Sonia in the following manner:

Think of a scale from 0 to 10, where 10 is that things are just like you've described tomorrow, able to be happy, anxiety not a problem, so with all that stuff happening for you, and 0 is the furthest you have been from that…

Sonia stated she was at 4. The solution-focused therapist observes at this point that 4 is higher than 0, which opens up a range of questions, beginning with those that elicit descriptions of the progress made:

What tells you it's 4 and not 0? What's different? What are you doing now that you weren't doing at 0? Who else has noticed differences and what have they noticed?

These can be augmented by questions similar to those asked of Sonia about sleeping well, that is, questions about Sonia's agency in bringing about the changes signified by being at 4. These have been usefully divided into 'strategy' questions – How did you do that? – and 'identity' questions – What qualities do you have that enabled you to make that change? (Ratner, George and Iveson, 2012).

The scale can also be used to make achieving progress seem more possible, by asking about a 'good enough' point, and by helping the client to 'think small' by asking about moving one point up the scale.

FIRST AND FOLLOW-UP SESSIONS

The structure of a first session can be discerned in the excerpts of the session with Sonia: a focus on the desired future first, and then on progress being made towards it. Follow-up sessions typically reverse the order, so that progress between sessions is asked about first: What's better, since we met? This is detailed as described above, before a return to the future, often punctuated by the use of the scale: Thinking of the scale we used last time, with 10 being you've got what you want from this, and 0 the opposite, where are you now? How would you know you were moving further up the scale?

'IT'S WORSE'

If a client says that they are at 0 on the scale, or that nothing is better since last time, the solution-focused therapist will acknowledge the extent of the client's difficulties while at the same time holding open the possibility of change. Ways to do this include asking coping questions – How are you managing to keep going? – listening for exceptions to the problems and asking how the client has prevented things from becoming even worse. Future-focused questions can then be returned to cautiously: Suppose you started to get back on track, what's the first, tiny signs you might notice?

RESEARCH EVIDENCE

The three most useful sources of evidence currently are:

- The evaluation list maintained by Alasdair Macdonald, the former research co-ordinator of the European Brief Therapy Association. His latest update (2017) refers to 308 relevant outcome studies, including 134 randomised controlled trials showing benefit from solution-focused approaches with 87 showing benefit over existing treatments, and 94 comparison studies, of which 66 favour solution-focused therapy.
- A major text reviewing the current state of the research, which provides an overview of the effectiveness of solution-focused therapy in a wide range of contexts (Franklin et al., 2011).
- A systematic review of 43 controlled studies, where the outcomes were indicated by observed changes in the client, which concludes that: 'SFBT is an effective treatment for a wide variety of behavioral and psychological outcomes and, in addition, it appears to be briefer and less costly than alternative approaches' (Gingerich and Peterson, 2013: 281).

REFERENCES

de Shazer, S. (1985). *Keys to Solution in Brief Therapy*. New York: W.W. Norton.

de Shazer, S. (1988). *Clues: Investigating Solutions in Brief Therapy*. New York: W.W. Norton.

de Shazer, S. (1999). John Weakland: master of the fine art of "doing nothing". In W. Ray and S. de Shazer (Eds.), *Evolving Brief Therapies: In Honor of John Weakland* (pp.30–43). Galena, IL: Geist & Russell Companies.

de Shazer, S., Berg, I. K., Lipchik, E., Nunnally, E., Molnar, A., Gingerich, W. and Weiner-Davis, M. (1986). Brief therapy: focused solution development. *Family Process*, 25(2), 207–221.

Franklin, C., Trepper, T., Gingerich, W. and McCollum, E. (Eds.) (2011). *Solution-focused Brief Therapy: A Handbook of Evidence-based Practice*. New York: Oxford University Press.

Gingerich, W., de Shazer, S. and Weiner-Davis, M. (1988). Constructing change: a research view of interviewing. In E. Lipchik (Ed.), *Interviewing* (pp. 21–32). Rockville, MD: Aspen.

Gingerich, W. and Peterson, L. (2013). Effectiveness of solution-focused brief therapy: a systematic qualitative review of controlled outcome studies. *Research on Social Work Practice*, 23(3), 266–283.

Lipchik, E. (1988). Interviewing with a constructive ear. *Dulwich Centre Newsletter*, Winter, 3–7.

(Continued)

(Continued)

Lipchik, E., Derks, J., Lacourt, M. and Nunnally, E. (2011). The evolution of solution-focused brief therapy. In C. Franklin, T. Trepper, W. Gingerich and E. McCollum (Eds.), *Solution-focused Brief Therapy: A Handbook of Evidence-based Practice*. New York: Oxford University Press.

Macdonald, A. (2017). Solution-focused brief therapy evaluation list. www.solutionsdoc.co.uk/sft.html (accessed 12 July 2017).

Ratner, H., George, E. and Iveson, C. (2012). *Solution Focused Brief Therapy: 100 Key Points and Techniques*. Hove: Routledge.

Shennan, G. (2014). *Solution-Focused Practice: Effective Communication to Facilitate Change*. Basingstoke: Palgrave Macmillan.

Watzlawick, P., Weakland, J. and Fisch, R. (1974). *Change: Principles of Problem Formation and Problem Resolution*. New York: W.W. Norton.

RECOMMENDED READING

1. de Shazer, S. (1988). *Clues: Investigating Solutions in Brief Therapy*. New York: W.W. Norton.

The development of the approach can be traced in the books written by Steve de Shazer between 1985 and 1994. By the time he wrote *Clues* in 1988, the approach could be seen clearly emerging from the brief therapy that preceded it, and the reader is drawn into the excitement of discovery that permeated the original Milwaukee team.

2. Ratner, H., George, E. and Iveson, C. (2012). *Solution Focused Brief Therapy: 100 Key Points and Techniques*. Hove: Routledge.

Harvey Ratner, Evan George and Chris Iveson introduced the approach to many of us in the UK, and this accessible book contains many useful pointers for its successful use.

3. Shennan, G. (2014). *Solution-Focused Practice: Effective Communication to Facilitate Change*. Basingstoke: Palgrave Macmillan.

In my book I provide a systematic account of how to use the approach, following the version designed by Ratner and his colleagues. It includes many real-life case examples.

THEORY AND APPROACHES: INTEGRATIVE AND ECLECTIC APPROACHES

5.27 COGNITIVE ANALYTIC THERAPY

CLAIRE POLLITT

OVERVIEW AND KEY POINTS

Cognitive analytic therapy (CAT) was proposed as a formal psychotherapy model in the 1980s by Anthony Ryle, who viewed conceptual integration as key to the development of a comprehensive psychological theory. CAT integrated both cognitive and analytic ideas within its early framework, particularly drawing on personal construct theory (Ryle, 1982) and object relations theory (Ryle, 1985). In later years, it also incorporated concepts from Vygotsky and Bahktin (Leiman, 1992). These significant and influential ideas were revised and harmonised to form a coherent model of psychological functioning, which has explanatory power in relation to psychopathology, and creates a sound framework for therapeutic intervention.

CAT proposes that through early social experiences, we develop a repertoire of reciprocal roles (RRs), which become internalised as working models for conducting relationships. They are reciprocal in that any role we occupy can only be understood in relation to the complementary role of another. During interaction both social parts are learnt, and we can enact these both towards ourselves and others, while creating expectancy that the other person will occupy the alternate position. When these RRs are activated, they manifest as repeating patterns (reciprocal role procedures), which are observable in how we relate to others, and form the basis of self-management and self-regulation.

The key points of CAT are as follows:

- CAT aims to develop client self-reflective capacity and recognition of problematic roles and procedures, in order to revise them.
- CAT is transdiagnostic, and has been applied to a wide array of clinical difficulties (Calvert and Kellett, 2014).
- CAT is commonly used within a 16-session individual therapy format, or 24 sessions for more complex presentations.

BRIEF HISTORY

The evolution of CAT theory can be traced by the emergence of three psychological models, outlined below.

The procedural sequence model (PSM; Ryle, 1982) was informed by Kelly's view of cognitive processes (Kelly, 1955). Kelly proposed that people develop models of reality based on 'constructs', which are understood in polarity to each other (e.g., 'hot' in relation to 'cold'), and shape our expectations and behaviours. Kelly thought that, like scientists, people develop constructs based on observation and experimentation, and that we make amendments according to our findings. Ryle developed this idea by introducing the concept of 'procedures', which combine cognition, affect and behaviour in a sequential pattern. Procedures consist of an appraisal and action, followed by an evaluation of consequences and either confirmation or revision. Ryle suggested that psychological distress can be accounted for by a restricted range of procedures that were dysfunctional and/or resistant to revision.

With the introduction of the concept of RRs, the procedural sequence object relations model (PSORM; Ryle, 1985) incorporated the psychoanalytic premise of an internal world. However, this was not based upon instincts, 'phantasy' and reified internal objects, as in the work of Klein (1946). Ryle shared Fairburn's (1986) perspective on the importance of external relationships in shaping an individual's inner world, with reciprocal roles deriving from internalised interactions with key carers. The influence of wider culture was later emphasised with Lieman's (1992) reflections on the work of philosopher Bakhtin (1986), who proposed that thought itself is dialogical, mirroring the person's conversation with key carers and society. The stability of the reciprocal role is maintained by the individual seeking and eliciting the complementary response in others. This notion incorporates the psychoanalytic concepts of transference, counter-transference and projective identification. However, CAT demystifies these processes, making them observable and applicable outside the confines of the therapeutic relationship.

Seeking to account for the difficulties observed within borderline personality disorder (BPD), the multiple self states model (MSSM; Ryle, 1997) extended CAT theory by introducing the concept of three interdependent levels of psychological functioning. Ryle proposed that within BPD there is damage to all levels. Level one relates to the degree to which the individual has a multiplicity of healthy reciprocal roles. Level two relates to how higher-order procedures, which are meta-cognitive in nature, continuously select and integrate within the repertoire of RRs, according to the context and the individual's aims and values. Level three relates to conscious self-awareness and self-reflective capacity, which is itself seen as a procedure originating from internalised interactions with attentive caregivers.

BASIC ASSUMPTIONS

- CAT is collaborative, emphasising the importance of joint activity and conceptual tools (e.g., diagrams and therapeutic letters) in supporting the client to develop a self-reflective capacity.
- CAT involves the therapist's active use of self (including emotional responses), in order to build a shared understanding of the client's roles and procedures, and to avoid enacting these unhelpfully within the therapeutic relationship.
- The client is an active participant in change, engaging in self-monitoring and testing out what has been learnt within therapy within their 'everyday' lives.
- Therapy is time-limited, and uses this constraint to mobilise and focus the therapy.

ORIGIN AND MAINTENANCE OF PROBLEMS

DYSFUNCTIONAL RECIPROCAL ROLES AND PROCEDURES

The internalisation of destructive or limited RRs is seen as a primary source of distress, interpersonal problems and self-management difficulties. For example, if an individual has received parenting that is harsh and critical they may internalise the following reciprocal role (see Figure 5.27.1).

The top 'pole' signifies the parental position, while the bottom reflects the lived experience of the individual. Both parts are internalised, and may be enacted in three keys ways:

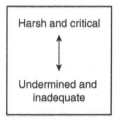

Figure 5.27.1 An example of dysfunctional reciprocal roles and procedures

- Self to self – Sets perfectionist standards and become self-critical if these aren't met.
- Self to other – Sets unrealistic standards of others and becomes critical if these aren't met.
- Other to self – 'Invites' others to be critical towards them through their rigidity and negative judgement. Demonstrates a cognitive bias towards perceiving others as attacking.

The more limited the individual's repertoire of roles, the stronger the 'pull' of reciprocation is likely to be. Outlined below are further examples of problematic RRs:

- mocking to humiliated;
- smothering to stifled;
- controlling to dominated;
- rejecting to 'thrown away' and defective;
- withholding to deprived; and
- abandoning to vulnerable and alone.

Problematic procedures are those that are self-limiting, have negative consequences or fail to reduce distress/meet the individual's emotional needs. They may have originated as adaptive responses to early life experiences, which have since become outdated and unhelpful. For example, an individual who has been mistreated by a parent could understandably develop a placatory procedure. However, as an adult, such behaviour may leave them vulnerable to further mistreatment. Problematic procedures are resistant to revision either because of their circularity (traps), because of false polarised choices (dilemmas), or because of the abandonment of appropriate goals due to maladaptive beliefs (snags).

An illustration of each is given in relation to the case example:

- Dilemma – Either I am anxiously striving for perfection or I feel guilty and become self-critical.
- Trap – To avoid feeling like a failure, and being criticised by myself and others, I avoid situations and activities where I feel unsure of myself. This avoidance undermines my development and my confidence, leaving me feeling more like a failure and self-critical.
- Snag – Feeling inadequate, I sabotage good things in my life as if I do not deserve them.

DIMINISHED RR INTEGRATION AND SELF-REFLECTIVE CAPACITY IN BPD

CAT proposes that in BPD presentation, at level one, there is a very limited repertoire of RRs, formed through extreme experiences of abuse and neglect. At level two, higher-order procedures concerned with integration and selection within the reciprocal role repertoire are incomplete or disrupted. This is thought to occur due to trauma-induced dissociation and/or exposure to incoherent, neglectful or contradictory experiences. Dissociation initially occurs as a response to unmanageable external threat, but is re-triggered with memories or perceived repetitions of the threat. This process can lead to RRs and their procedures becoming partially dissociated, so that when in one particular role the person has limited awareness of or access to alternates. These partially dissociated RRs, known as self-states, are thought to account for the rapid changes in being that can be seen within BPD, with the noted lack of sequential awareness of what has led to the sudden shift. This dysfunction results in further impairment at level three, which relates to self-awareness and capacity for self-reflection.

THEORY OF CHANGE

The CAT process involves building a reformulation of the client's difficulties, with the subsequent recognition and revision of problematic RRs and procedures.

The therapist and client agree a list of target problems. The procedures which are seen as maintaining these are named as target problem procedures, and these become the focus for change.

The CAT theory of change is influenced by Vygotsky's (1978) work on sign mediation and the zone of proximal development (ZPD).

Vygotsky suggested that meaning is formed through shared activity, whereby joint signs (such as those found within language) are created through repeated parental responses to the child's gestures and verbal expressions. Once internalised, these signs enable the development of psychological tools, which in turn shape the mind's capacities. A memory mnemonic is an example of such a tool. CAT therefore emphasises the co-creation of psychological tools in the form of a therapeutic letter and a sequential diagram of the reciprocal role repertoire. Once internalised, these tools can represent the client's inner world, thereby facilitating self-reflection and subsequent change.

Vygotsky described the ZPD as the distance between the individual's actual developmental level and the level of current potential development (determined through problem-solving ability with more-capable others). Growth occurs when the individual is working within their ZPD, where the task is experienced as challenging, but not so novel or demanding that it cannot be accomplished by the individual themselves with appropriate support. Through repetition, the aided task becomes one that the individual can perform independently. Within CAT this concept helps the therapist identify the optimal conditions for effective

therapeutic intervention by informing the appropriate pace of therapy, the required level of therapist guidance and likely achievable 'exits' to problematic procedures.

SKILLS AND STRATEGIES

REFORMULATION

Reformulation involves building a joint understanding with the client of their difficulties and how these are being maintained by problematic RRs and procedures. This process involves the creation of a sequential diagrammatic reformulation (SDR) and a prose reformulation letter.

From assessment, the therapist begins mapping the client's reciprocal roles and procedures with them to form the SDR. This is amended and elaborated upon as the client develops new understandings about themselves. Such joint activity, characterised by curiosity, care and persistence in understanding the client's inner world, can subsequently be internalised to form the basis of a healthy self-management procedure. The SDR is based upon descriptions of the client's relationship history, functional analysis of current behaviours and observations of interactions within the therapeutic relationship. It is designed to provide the client with perspective on their difficulties, to help generate 'exits'. Figure 5.27.2 describes a partial SDR for the aforementioned case example.

An initial reformulation letter is typically read aloud to the client around session four. The letter outlines target problems and procedures, but it has the added value of placing these within a historical context, framing them as survival modes that once had appropriate and protective functions. It aims to connect past neglect, abuse and trauma with the current RRs and procedures of the client, in a manner which conveys warmth and understanding for the person's struggle. This can provide a powerful means of validation and normalisation, which strengthens the therapeutic relationship early in the alliance.

RECOGNITION

Having built an understanding of their RRs and procedures, the client is encouraged to recognise them as they occur, as a prerequisite to revision. The therapist may introduce personalised self-monitoring diaries or mindfulness practice to facilitate this skill development between sessions. In each session, the client rates their target problem in terms of how rapidly they noticed the associated problematic procedure, and later how effectively it was addressed. The SDR tool is used in every session to assist the client to recognise RRs and procedures as they occur, both in the narratives of their life which they bring to therapy and within the therapeutic relationship.

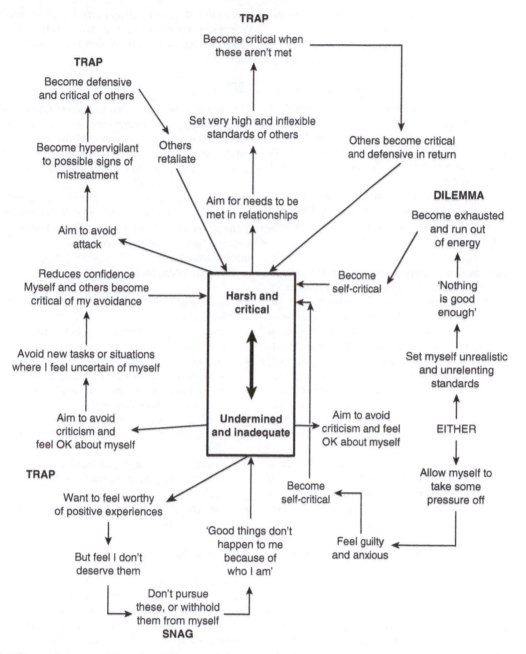

TRAP

Become critical when these aren't met

TRAP

Become defensive and critical of others

Become hypervigilant to possible signs of mistreatment

Set very high and inflexible standards of others

Others retaliate

Others become critical and defensive in return

DILEMMA

Become exhausted and run out of energy

Aim for needs to be met in relationships

Aim to avoid attack

Reduces confidence Myself and others become critical of my avoidance

Become self-critical

'Nothing is good enough'

Harsh and critical

Set myself unrealistic and unrelenting standards

Avoid new tasks or situations where I feel uncertain of myself

Aim to avoid criticism and feel OK about myself

Undermined and inadequate

Aim to avoid criticism and feel OK about myself

EITHER

Allow myself to take some pressure off

TRAP

Want to feel worthy of positive experiences

Become self-critical

Feel guilty and anxious

But feel I don't deserve them

'Good things don't happen to me because of who I am'

Don't pursue these, or withhold them from myself

SNAG

Figure 5.27.2 Example of a partial SDR

REVISION

Revision involves the client amending problematic RRs and procedures by finding 'exits' to replace them with healthier patterns of relating to themselves and others.

Various change methods from other therapies may be utilised, generating therapeutic richness and flexibility. However, methods must be carefully selected and applied to ensure that they are theoretically consistent with CAT and are reformulation-driven.

Outlined below are several change methods and examples of their possible application within CAT:

- Assertiveness skills – Addressing dilemma related to either 'I am a bully or a victim'.
- Self-soothing skills – Addressing a self-harm procedure in which the function of the behaviour is to manage feelings of distress.
- Use of empty chair technique or non-send letters – To process past losses related to dilemma of 'I get involved with others and get hurt, or I am in control but totally alone'.
- Psychoeducation and cognitive restructuring – Reducing shame in sexual abuse victims who have a self-sabotage snag, based upon feeling non-deserving.

In the case example, change methods could include a behavioural experiment, to test out the impact of positive self-encouragement versus self-criticism on motivation levels. Thought-challenging diaries and psychoeducation around thought biases can be employed to address the tendency to perceive others as critical, while assertiveness practice may include saying 'no' to excessive work demands. The intervention may also include helping the client to extend their social and recreational interests, in order to establish activities outside those based upon 'self-improvement', and to address avoidance of situations where they feel unconfident or 'non-deserving'.

Irrespective of other methods employed, within CAT the therapeutic relationship is the major vehicle of change. The therapist's key role is to resist the pull to adopt the expected reciprocal role. Regular CAT supervision is important, and therapists must be aware of how their own RRs and procedures may collude with those of the client. Through direct experience of acknowledging and exploring RRs through the therapeutic relationship, the client is able to negotiate new ways of being. These new behavioural styles, and a positive experience of the therapist, can form the basis of healthier RRs and procedures to be practised outside the therapeutic relationship. Research indicates that good therapy outcomes are associated with therapists who recognise problematic enactments within the therapy relationship and collaboratively work with the client to resolve them (Bennett et al., 2006; Daly et al., 2010).

In the case example, possible enactments could include the client avoiding homework tasks when they feel unable to perform them perfectly, experiencing the therapist as critical and acting defensively or becoming attacking due to perceiving that not enough has been achieved.

ENDING

The ending is explicitly used to address unresolved grief issues, unhelpful procedures related to managing loss and RRs characterised by rejection or abandonment. To facilitate the transition, the client is either offered a follow-up at one month (16-session CAT) or four follow-ups over six months (24-session CAT).

Both the therapist and client exchange 'goodbye letters'. Their key function is to facilitate the expression of feelings regarding therapy ending, and to keep the experience and learnt 'exits' active in the client's mind following therapy completion.

Both letters can include:

- naming of 'exits' with specific examples applied during therapy;
- acknowledgement of challenges that the client found particularly difficult;
- significant moments within the therapeutic relationship, such as resolving reciprocal role enactments;
- naming possible feelings of disappointment in relation to initial hopes for change;
- naming of thoughts and feelings in relation to ending, and its meaning within the context of the client's history;
- naming of possible problematic RRs and procedures that may be triggered by ending, with possible 'exits'; and
- indications for future work, particularly during the follow-up period.

RESEARCH EVIDENCE

In a review of the outcome evidence base for CAT, Calvert and Kellet (2014) examined 25 studies published between 1960 and 2013, which met the criteria of having adequate outcome measures and pre- and post-outcome scores. Of the 25 studies reviewed, five were case studies, four were single case experimental designs, five were randomised controlled trials (RCTs) and 11 were effectiveness studies. Overall, 52% (13/25) of the studies met criteria for high-quality outcome data, with the case studies being assessed as poorest in methodological quality.

The authors outlined that due to methodological limitations and the small number of studies, there was insufficient current evidence for the efficacy of CAT for dissociative disorders, morbid jealousy and childhood sexual abuse survivors experiencing a range of difficulties. Likewise, they stated that it was difficult to draw any strong conclusions regarding CAT effectiveness for physical health conditions, because of differences in outcome methodologies and the populations studied. In relation to the treatment of anxiety and depression, only two out of the six studies in this area were deemed high in quality, with a notable lack of research in this area.

The review indicated that more research has been directed at populations with personality disorders, with 11 of the 25 studies being focused upon this client group. The authors concluded that these studies (eight assessed as high quality, with two being randomised controlled trials (RCTs)) suggest that CAT can produce positive outcomes for clients with PD, both in routine clinical practice and under trial conditions. Encouraging results were also indicated for anorexia nervosa, with two high-quality RCT studies producing positive outcomes.

Overall, the research suggests growing evidence for the effective use of CAT, especially with clients with personality pathology. Within this context, CAT has been included as a potential treatment within the National Institute for Health and Care Excellence (NICE) guidelines for both *Eating Disorders* (NICE, 2004) and *Borderline Peronality Disorder* (NICE, 2009). However, a co-ordinated research strategy is needed to extend both the breadth and depth of the CAT evidence base, particularly in relation to common mental health problems (Calvert and Kellet, 2014).

REFERENCES

Bakhtin, M.M. (1986) *Speech Genres and Other Late Essays.* Austin, TX: University of Texas Press.

Bennett, D., Parry, G. and Ryle, A. (2006) Resolving threats to the therapeutic alliance in cognitive analytic therapy of borderline personality disorder: a task analysis. *Psychology and Psychotherapy: Theory, Research and Practice*, 79: 395–418.

Calvert, R. and Kellett, S. (2014) Cognitive analytic therapy: a review of the outcome evidence base for treatment. *Psychology and Psychotherapy: Theory, Research and Practice*, 87: 253–277.

Daly, A.M., Llewelyn, S., McDougall, E. and Chanen, A.M. (2010) Rupture resolution in cognitive analytic therapy for adolescents with borderline personality disorder. *Psychology and Psychotherapy: Theory, Research and Practice*, 83: 273–288.

Fairburn, F.W. (1986) *Psychoanalytic Studies of the Personality*. London: Tavistock.

Kelly, G.A. (1955) *The Psychology of Personal Constructs*. New York: W.W. Norton.

Klein, M. (1946) Notes on some schizoid mechanisms. In M. Klein, P. Heiman, S. Isaacs and J. Riviere (eds), *Developments in Psychoanalysis*. London: Hogarth.

Leiman, M. (1992) The concept of sign in the work of Vygotsky, Winnicot and Bakhtin: further integration of object relations theory and activity theory. *British Journal of Medical Psychology*, 67: 97–106.

NICE (2004) *Eating Disorders: Core Interventions in the Treatment and Management of Anorexia Nervosa, Bulimia Nervosa and Related Eating Disorders*. Clinical Guideline 9. London: National Institute for Health and Clinical Excellence.

NICE (2009) *Borderline Personality Disorder: Treatment and Management*. Clinical Guideline 78. London: National Institute for Health and Clinical Excellence.

Ryle, A. (1982) *Psychotherapy: A Cognitive Integration of Theory and Practice*. London: Academic Press.

Ryle, A. (1985) Cognitive theory, object relations and the self. *British Journal of Medical Psychology*, 58: 1–7.

Ryle, A. (1997) *Cognitive Analytic Therapy and Borderline Personality Disorder: The Model and the Method*. Chichester: John Wiley.

Vygotsky, L.S. (1978) *Mind and Society: The Development of Higher Psychological Processes*. Cambridge, MA: Harvard University Press.

RECOMMENDED READING

1. Hepple, J. and Sutton, L. (eds) (2004) *Cognitive Analytic Therapy and Later Life*. Hove: Bruner-Routledge.

A good introductory text, which is helpful in providing examples of prose reformulations.

2. Ryle, A. and Kerr, I. (2002) *Introducing Cognitive-Analytic Therapy: Principles and Practice*. Chichester: John Wiley.

This text provides a comprehensive overview of CAT theory.

3. Wilde McCormick, E. (2012) *Change for the Better: Self-help through Practical Psychotherapy* (4th ed.). London: Sage.

Being a self-help book, this text provides plenty of case material.

5.28   INTERPERSONAL PSYCHOTHERAPY

ELIZABETH ROBINSON AND GRAHAM DYSON

OVERVIEW AND KEY POINTS

Interpersonal psychotherapy (IPT) is a brief, time-limited therapy initially developed for the treatment of depression but has been adapted to treat other disorders. Interpersonal therapists link the client's experience of depression to the interpersonal context. Therapy focuses on different interpersonal problem areas with two related aims: to improve the interpersonal functioning in a given area and to reduce depressive symptoms.

*   A here-and-now focus targets depression in the interpersonal context.
*   Goals and strategies are used to deal with interpersonal problem areas.
*   The optimistic stance of the therapist helps the client celebrate their achievements and deal with their depression.
*   The client is encouraged to make the most of their own social network to ease symptoms and improve interpersonal functioning.

BRIEF HISTORY

Interpersonal psychotherapy was developed as a treatment for depression. Researchers from the Boston New Haven Collaborative Project drew from interpersonal theories of depression (Meyer, 1957; Sullivan, 1953) and attachment theories (Bowlby, 1969) when they developed and manualised (Klerman et al., 1984) interpersonal psychotherapy (IPT), which was compared to antidepressant medication in clinical trials in the 1970s. The researchers found that both treatments were effective, although IPT took longer to take an effect (Klerman et al., 1974; Weissman et al., 1979). Research and development in IPT for depression continued in adolescent and old age groups: both were considered to be effective interventions (Mufson et al., 2004; Reynold et al., 1996). IPT is currently recommended by the National Institute for Health and Care Excellence (NICE) as a treatment for moderate and severe depression based on the research evidence. IPT has also been adapted for use in other mental health problems, including eating disorders (Fairburn et al., 1996), social anxiety disorder (Lipstiz, 2012) and post-traumatic stress disorder (Markowitz et al., 2015). IPT can be delivered as an individual therapy, by telephone (Miller and Weissman, 2002) or in groups (Wilfey et al., 2000).

BASIC ASSUMPTIONS

Interpersonal psychotherapy (IPT) is a manualised (Klerman et al., 1984), time-limited, supportive and structured therapy which is used primarily for the treatment of depression. IPT has a dual focus, to reduce depressive symptoms by dealing with the associated interpersonal problems. Depression is framed by the therapist as a medical illness which is not the client's fault and is treatable. 'Sick role work' in IPT helps the therapist work with the client to look at ways they can make changes to help with their recovery. This may include increasing, varying or moderating activity and optimising support from others. It may be appropriate in some circumstances to assist the client in temporarily relinquishing work activities (Wilfey et al., 2000). The IPT therapist helps the client explore and understand the interpersonal context of their current depression. This may be due to disharmony or dissatisfaction in one or a number of relationships, social isolation, bereavement or a loss or change in a role. Once a link is made between the interpersonal context (problem area) and the depression there are specific techniques (Klerman et al., 1984) to help the client work towards interpersonal changes in order to move forward and ease their depression. The therapist helps the client optimise their current support network throughout this process.

ORIGIN AND MAINTENANCE OF PROBLEMS

IPT is delivered over 16 weekly sessions and involves three phases: an initial, middle and end. The *initial phase* (sessions 1 to 4) explores the origin and maintenance of problems by identifying details of the client's depression and relating it to the interpersonal context. The therapist explores with the client links between interpersonal events and their mood. An overview of the therapy is provided at the start of the process, setting a framework for treatment. The therapist initially confirms a diagnosis of depression using diagnostic criteria (American Psychiatric Association, 2013), and reinforces that depression is a condition that is treatable. Measurements of the severity of depression are taken at the start of the process using either clinician-rated scales, such as the Hamilton depression scale (Hamilton, 1960), which was recommended in the IPT manual (Klerman et al., 1984), or, in many clinical services in the UK, a self-rated measure, the Patient Health Questionnaire (PHQ9) (Kroenke and Spitzer, 2002), is widely used. At this stage, the therapist will work together with the client to consider what steps they can take to actively help with their recovery. They may need to alter some expectations of themselves in the short term (reduce workload at home/work if appropriate), add in other activities (such as pursuing a pleasurable activity as an antidepressant) and look to see how they can access help/support that facilitate their recovery. This is known

as a 'sick role work' (Klerman et al., 1984). A history of current and previous episodes of depression is gathered, considering the interpersonal context at the time.

An interpersonal inventory then gives valuable insight into the client's interpersonal world. The inventory is used to identify helpful relationships, which may provide a positive resource to build on, as well as negative relationships, which may serve as an emotional drain and contribute to the current depression. Detailed information gained about each relationship might include: frequency of contact, level of satisfaction, expectations, disagreements or disharmony and what the client may like to change. It may draw attention to any specific interpersonal issue, such as relationship struggles or changes (i.e., separation), or grief, which gives further context to the client's experiences of their current depression.

At the end of the initial phase the therapist offers an interpersonal formulation (Markowitz and Swartz, 2007). Drawing upon the information obtained from the history, time line and interpersonal inventory, a link is made between the onset and maintenance of the current depressive episode and the client's social and interpersonal situation. This is a collaborative approach whereby the therapist seeks to reach agreement with the client regarding the possible focal area. The four potential focal areas in IPT are: role transition, role dispute, interpersonal sensitivities and complicated bereavement. Having identified one or a maximum of two linked focal areas with the client, achievable goals, linked to the focal area, are agreed and a treatment contract is set between the therapist and client.

THEORY OF CHANGE

The *middle phase* of IPT (sessions 5 to 12) forms the main focus of treatment, targeting an interpersonal problem area that is fuelling the client's depression. Having identified one or two focal areas with the client during formulation at the end of the initial phase, specific treatment approaches for the particular focal area are implemented. The IPT manual clearly defines strategies for each focal area (Klerman et al., 1984). The aim for the therapist is to work with the client to increase their interpersonal functioning and help them address the interpersonal problem area, which in turn reduces depressive symptoms.

The four problem areas used in IPT are outlined below.

ROLE DISPUTE

Interpersonal disputes are common and may manifest in various ways. The client may be in open dispute or disagreement with an individual or group of individuals, which could include friends, family or work colleagues.

Non-reciprocal role expectations may contribute to the role dispute and associated depression.

ROLE TRANSITION

This is a broad area and can involve any changes in role, such as promotion, demotion, retirement or redundancy, separation, divorce, moving house, getting married, having a baby or receiving a diagnosis of a medical illness. It is important to identify the existing role that is a struggle to the client and how adapting to that particular role leads to or maintains the current depressive episode.

COMPLICATED BEREAVEMENT

The client has experienced a death of a loved one and for whatever reason has not been able to grieve for this loss. Typically, the therapist will identify with the client how they may not have effectively worked through the mourning process and how this has led to ongoing symptoms of depression.

INTERPERSONAL DEFICIT/SENSITIVITIES

There are some individuals who have limited or no satisfying or rewarding interpersonal relationships, which leads to social isolation and depression. Alternatively, any client who has relationships that are transient, superficial or disruptive can also result in social isolation and depression.

Once the IPT therapist has collaboratively identified and agreed the problem area, they will work through the strategies highlighted in the IPT manual, with the aim of reducing depressive symptoms and increasing interpersonal functioning. Specific goals linked to the focal area will be worked towards during this process.

SKILLS AND STRATEGIES

ROLE DISPUTE

The client may have a disputed relationship with their partner that is fuelling the depression. The therapist will explore with the client the differences in expectations that both parties hold, how the communication works, what works well and where things may go off track. Specific techniques, such as communication analysis, provide an opportunity to review the quality and nature of the interaction, and inform the client what role they play in the disputed relationship. Work may then focus on helping the client review their expectations in the relationship and look at alternative ways of communicating in order to address the dispute.

ROLE TRANSITION

The client may be struggling in adjusting to a role change, such as a relationship split, which is maintaining their depressive symptoms. The therapist helps the client mourn this relationship by starting with an exploration of what they liked/disliked about the lost relationship, in so doing obtaining lots of detail about this part of the client's experience. The therapist encourages a realistic evaluation of this relationship, facilitating a processing of emotions. Further work is undertaken to explore how the split took place, such as: was this unexpected? How much choice did the client have? How quickly did this happen? Again, work targeting the expression and facilitation of emotional processing gives way to allow the client to move on. Finally, opportunities in their current situation are explored, namely, how can they make the most of this current situation?

COMPLICATED BEREAVEMENT

The client may have lost a significant relationship, such as the death of a parent, which led to the ongoing depression. The aim of the work is to help the client start to mourn this loss in order to ease their depression. Exploration of the relationship covers a broad range of aspects of the relationship, including things they missed, enjoyed, treasured – the happy moments as well as the things they may not miss, or were perhaps frustrated with. There is a need to ensure this is a balanced review so that the client is not led to idealise their loved one as a 'saint', which would keep them stuck in the mourning process. Events leading up to and surrounding the death are also sensitively explored. Much of the work is geared towards facilitating affect release and encouraging the mourning process. This is done both inside and outside sessions where the client is encouraged to use social support to help them manage their loss.

INTERPERSONAL DEFICIT/SENSITIVITIES

The client may struggle in a number of relationships and a lack of sufficient quality relationships may be isolating and maintain their depression. The therapist reviews the client's current and past relationships to identify positive ones (that can be used as an example) and relationship struggles. Areas of difficultly and repeating patterns are identified and alternative options for getting relationships started or keeping them going are explored. The development of new social and communication skills is important, and opportunities to practise these skills both within and outside the session are provided. Encouragement and support also play a large part in allowing the client to increase interpersonal interaction.

Throughout all of the problem areas in IPT, the therapist engages the client to consider how they can source help and support from others outside the sessions to help deal with the interpersonal problem area, and, as a consequence, their depression.

The *end phase* of IPT (sessions 13 to 16) continues alongside the middle-phase strategies. Preparing for the end of therapy is a key task, exploring how the client feels (modelling healthy endings), evaluating the course of therapy and identifying as well as celebrating their achievements. Given that depression is a recurrent condition (Kupfer et al., 1992), IPT proactively manages future risk, with the therapist helping the client look forward to consider what they need to do to maintain improvements once therapy has ended. This may run concurrently with advice on the need for prophylactic antidepressant medication, depending on the assessed level of risk. The IPT therapist provides advice on how to deal with a potential subsequent episode, ensuring the client is confident about how to access health services. Identification of the client's symptom signature at the start the initial phase of treatment provides information to recognise early warning signs of a further episode.

RESEARCH EVIDENCE

IPT has been found to be effective in treating depression across all age groups: adults, old age and adolescents (Mufson et al., 2004; Reynolds et al., 1996; Weissman et al., 1979). The National Institute of Health and Care Excellence (NICE) recommend IPT as a treatment for moderate or severe depression in adults and adolescents (NICE, 2010, 2015). IPT alone has been found to minimise the risk of a recurrent episode, although combining IPT and medication is superior in highly recurrent depression in both adults (Frank et al., 2000) and older-age adults. However, it is notable that the latter group tends to demonstrate a slower response to treatment and earlier relapse (Reynolds et al., 1999). Additionally, IPT has helped improve compliance with medication (Miller et al., 2001), and has been combined with medication therapy for chronic treatment-resistant depression (Murray et al., 2010; Schramm et al., 2007).

IPT has demonstrated efficacy in postpartum depression (Spinelli and Endicott, 2003), with improvements in social adjustment and mother–infant bonding reported (O'Hara et al., 2000).

IPT can be delivered by telephone (Miller and Weissman, 2002) and in groups, in a range of cultures (Verdeli et al., 2003; Zlotnick et al., 2001). It is also manualised to be delivered in groups for adults (Wilfey et al., 2000) and for adolescents as a preventative programme for depression (Young et al., 2016).

IPT has been used in eating disorders (Fairburn et al., 1996), social phobia, social anxiety disorder and panic disorder (Lipsitz, 2012), and has been manualised as a non-exposure-based alternative to treating post-traumatic stress disorder (Markowitz, 2016).

REFERENCES

American Psychiatric Association (2013). *Diagnostic and Statistical Manual of Mental Disorders* (5th ed.). Washington, DC: American Psychiatric Association.

Bowlby, J. (1969). *Attachment and Loss. Volume 1: Attachment*. London: Hogarth Press.

Fairburn, C.G., Norman, P.A., Welch, S.L., O'Connor, M.E., Doll, H.A. and Peveler, P.C. (1996). A prospective study of outcome in bulimia nervosa and the long term effects of three psychological treatments. *Archives of General Psychiatry*, 52: 304–312.

Frank, E., Grochocinski, V.J., Spanier, C.A., Buysse, D.J., Cherry, C.R., Houck, P.R., Stapf, D.M. and Kupfer, D.J. (2000). Interpersonal psychotherapy and antidepressant medication: evaluation of a sequential treatment strategy in women with recurrent major depression. *Journal of Clinical Psychiatry*, 61(1): 51–57.

Hamilton, M. (1960). A rating scale of depression. *Journal of Neurology, Neurosurgery and Psychiatry*, 23: 56–62.

Klerman G.L., Dimascio, A., Weissman, M., Prusoff, B. and Paykel, E.S. (1974). Treatment of depression by drugs and psychotherapy. *American Journal of Psychiatry*, 131(2): 186–191.

Klerman, G.L., Weissman, M.M., Rounsaville, B.J. and Chevron, E. (1984). *Interpersonal Psychotherapy for Depression*. New York: Basic Books.

Kroenke K. and Spitzer, R.L. (2002). The PHQ-9: a new depression diagnostic and severity measure. *Psychiatric Annals*, 32(9): 509–515.

Kupfer, D.J., Frank, E., Perel, J.M., Cornes, C., Mallinger, A.G., Thase, M.E., McEachran, A.B. and Grochocinski, V.J. (1992). Five-year outcome for maintenance therapies in recurrent depression. *Archives of General Psychiatry*, 49: 769–773.

(Continued)

(Continued)

Lipstiz, J.L. (2012). Interpersonal psychotherapy for social anxiety disorder. In J.C. Markowitz and M.M. Markowitz (Eds) (2016). *Interpersonal Psychotherapy for Posttraumatic Stress Disorder*. Oxford: Oxford University Press.

Markowitz, J.C. (2016). *Interpersonal Psychotherapy for Posttraumatic Stress Disorder*. Oxford: Oxford University Press.

Markowitz, J.C., Petkova, E., Neria, Y., Ven Meter, P.E., Zhao, Y., Hembree, E., Lovell, K., Biyanova, T. and Marshall, R.D. (2015). Is exposure necessary? A randomised clinical trial of interpersonal psychotherapy for PTSD. *American Journal of Psychiatry*, 172: 1–11.

Markowitz, J.C. and Schwartz, H.A. (2007). Case formulation in interpersonal psychotherapy of depression. In T.D. Eells (Ed.), *Handbook of Psychotherapy Case Formulation* (2nd ed., pp. 221–250). New York: Guilford Press.

Meyer, A. (1957). *Psychobiology: A Science of Man*. Springfield, IL: Charles C. Thomas.

Miller, L. and Weissman, M. (2002). Interpersonal psychotherapy delivered over the telephone to recurrent depressives: a pilot study. *Depression and Anxiety*, 16: 114–117.

Miller, M.D., Cornes, C., Frank, E., Ehrenpreis, L., Silberman, R., Schilernitzauer, M.A., Tracey, B., Richards, V., Wolfson, L., Zaltman, J., Bensasi, S. and Reynolds, C.F. (2001). Interpersonal psychotherapy for late-life depression past, present and future. *Journal of Psychotherapy Practice and Research*, 10: 231–238.

Mufson, L., Pollack Dorta, K., Wickranaratne, P., Nomura, Y., Olfson, M. and Weissman, M.M. (2004). A randomised effectiveness trial of interpersonal psychotherapy for depressed adolescents. *Archives of General Psychiatry*, 61: 577–584.

Murray, G., Michalak, E.E., Axler, A., Yaxley, D., Hayashi, B., Westrin, A., Ogrodniczuk, J.S., Tam, E.M., Yatham, L.N. and Lam, R.W. (2010). Relief of chronic or resistant depression (Re-ChORD): a pragmatic, randomized, open-treatment trial of an integrative program intervention for chronic depression. *Journal of Affective Disorders*, 123(1–3): 243–248.

National Institute for Health and Care Excellence (NICE) (2010). *The Treatment and Management of Depression in Adults* (Updated Edition). National Clinical Practice Guideline 90. National Collaborating Centre for Mental Health. Commissioned by the National Institute of Health and Clinical Excellence. London: The British Psychological Society and The Royal College of Psychiatrists.

National Institute for Health and Care Excellence (NICE) (2015). *Depression in Children and Young People: Identification and Management*. London: NICE.

O'Hara, M.W., Stuart, S., Gorman, L.L. and Wenzel, A. (2000). Efficacy of interpersonal psychotherapy for postpartum depression, *Archives of General Psychiatry*, 57: 1039–1045.

Parsons, T. (1951). Illness and the role of the physician: a sociological perspective. *American Journal of Orthopsychiatry*, 21: 452–460.

Reynolds, C.F., Frank, E., Dew, M.A., Houck, P.R., Miller, M., Mazumdar, S., Perel, J.M. and Kupfer, D.J. (1999). Treatment of 70+ year-olds with recurrent major depression. *American Journal of Geriatric Psychiatry*, 7(1): 64–69.

Reynolds, C.F., Frank, E., Perel, J.M., Mazumdar, S., Dew, M.A., Begley, A., Houck, P.R., Hall, M., Mulsant, B., Shear, M.K., Miller, M.D., Cornes, C. and Kupfer, D.J. (1996). High relapse rates after discontinuation of adjunctive medication in elderly persons with recurrent major depression. *American Journal of Psychiatry*, 152: 1418–1422.

Schramm, E., Van Calker, D., Dykierek, P., Lieb, K., Kech, S., Zobel, I., Leonhart, R. and Berger, M. (2007). An intensive treatment programme of interpersonal psychotherapy plus pharmacotherapy for depressed inpatients: acute versus long term results. *American Journal of Psychiatry*, 164: 768–777.

Spinelli, M.G. and Endicott, J. (2003). Controlled clinical trial of interpersonal psychotherapy versus parenting education program for depressed pregnant women. *American Journal of Psychiatry*, 160(3): 555–562.

Sullivan, H.N. (1953). *The Interpersonal Theory of Psychiatry*. New York: W.W. Norton.

Verdeli, H., Clougherty, C., Bolton, P., Speelman, E., Ndogoni, L., Bass, J., Neugebauer, R. and Weissman, M. (2003). Adapting group IPT for a developing country: an experience in rural Uganda. *World Psychiatry*, 2(2): 112–120.

Weissman, M.M., Prusoff, B.A., Dimasccio, A., Neu, C., Goklaney, M. and Klerman, G.L. (1979). The efficacy of drugs and psychotherapy in the treatment of acute depressive episodes. *American Journal of Psychiatry*, 136(4B): 555–558.

Wilfey, D.E., Mackenzie, K.R., Welch, R.R., Ayres, V.E. and Weismann, M.M. (2000). *Interpersonal Psychotherapy for Groups*. New York: Basic Books.

Young, J.F., Mufson, L. and Schueler, C.M. (2016). *Preventing Adolescent Depression: Interpersonal Psychotherapy – Adolescent Skills Training*. Oxford: Oxford University Press.

Zlotnick, C., Johnson, S.L., Miller, I.W., Pearlstein, T. and Howard, M. (2001). Postpartum depression in women receiving public assistance: pilot study of an interpersonal therapy oriented group intervention. *American Journal of Psychiatry*, 158(4): 638–640.

5.29   MULTIMODAL THERAPY

STEPHEN PALMER

OVERVIEW AND KEY POINTS

Multimodal therapy is a technically eclectic therapeutic approach as it uses techniques taken from many different psychological theories and systems. The techniques and strategies are applied systematically, based on data from client qualities, specific techniques and the therapist's clinical skills (Palmer, 2015).

Multimodal therapy is a technically eclectic and systematic therapeutic approach.

- Human problems are multilevelled and multilayered. Few problems have a single cause or simple solution.
- The dimensions of personality are Behaviour, Affect, Sensations, Images, Cognitions, Interpersonal and Drugs/biology, known by the acronym, BASIC ID.
- The multimodal approach postulates that unless the seven BASIC ID modalities are assessed, therapy is likely to overlook significant concerns.

BRIEF HISTORY

During the 1950s Arnold Lazarus undertook his formal clinical training in South Africa. The main focus of his training was underpinned by Rogerian, Freudian and Sullivanian theories and methods. He attended seminars by Joseph Wolpe about conditioning therapies and reciprocal inhibition and in London he learned about the Adlerian orientation. He believed that no one system of therapy could provide a complete understanding of either human development or the human condition. In 1958 he became the first psychologist to use the terms 'behavior therapist' and 'behavior therapy' in an academic article.

Lazarus conducted follow-up inquiries into clients who had received behaviour therapy and found that many had relapsed. However, when clients had used both behaviour and cognitive techniques, more durable results were obtained. In the early 1970s he started advocating a broad but systematic range of cognitive-behavioural techniques, and his follow-up inquiries indicated the importance of breadth if therapeutic gains were to be maintained. This led to the development of multimodal therapy, which places emphasis on seven discrete but interactive dimensions or modalities which encompass all aspects of human personality.

BASIC ASSUMPTIONS

Individuals are essentially biological organisms (neuro-physiological and biochemical entities) who behave (act and react), emote (experience affective responses), sense (respond to olfactory, tactile, gustatory, visual and auditory stimuli), imagine (conjure up sights, sounds and other events in the mind's eye), think (hold beliefs, opinions, attitudes and values) and interact with one another (tolerate, enjoy or suffer in various interpersonal relationships). These dimensions of personality are usually known by the acronym BASIC ID, derived from the first letters of each modality, namely Behaviour, Affect, Sensations, Images, Cognitions, Interpersonal and Drugs/biology.

Modalities may interact with each other: for example, a negative image or cognition may trigger a negative emotion. Modalities may exist in a state of reciprocal transaction and flux, connected by complex chains of behaviour and other psycho-physiological processes.

The multimodal approach rests on the assumption that unless the seven modalities are assessed, therapy is likely to overlook significant concerns. Clients are usually troubled by a multitude of specific problems which should be dealt with by a similar multitude of specific interventions or techniques.

Individuals have different thresholds for stress tolerance, frustration, pain, and external and internal stimuli in the form of sound, light, touch, smell and taste. Psychological interventions can be used to modify these thresholds but often the genetic predisposition has an overriding influence in the final analysis.

Individuals tend to prefer some of the BASIC ID modalities to others. They are referred to as 'cognitive reactors' or 'imagery reactors' or 'sensory reactors', depending upon which modality they favour.

Human personalities stem from interplay among social learning and conditioning, physical environment and genetic endowment. Therefore, each client is unique and may need a personalized therapy.

Individuals usually benefit from a psycho-educational approach to help them deal with or manage their problems.

Although the therapist and client are equal in their humanity (the principle of parity), the therapist may be more skilled in certain areas in which the client has particular skills deficits. It is not automatically assumed that clients know how to deal with their problems or have the requisite skills, and the therapist may need to model or teach the client various skills and strategies.

No one theory has all the answers when helping clients. Multimodal therapy is underpinned by a broad social and cognitive learning theory, while drawing on group and communications theory and general systems theory. However, multimodal therapists can choose not to apply these theories obsessively to each client.

Technically speaking, 'multimodal therapy' *per se* does not exist; multimodal counsellors and psychotherapists, as technical eclectics, draw from as many other approaches or systems as necessary. To be accurate, there is a multimodal assessment format and a multimodal framework or orientation.

ORIGIN AND MAINTENANCE OF PROBLEMS

Human problems are multilevelled and multilayered. Few problems have a single cause or simple solution.

According to Lazarus, psychological disturbances are the product of one or more of the following:

- conflicting or ambivalent feelings or reactions
- misinformation
- missing information which includes ignorance, *naïveté* and skills deficits
- maladaptive habits, including conditioned emotional reactions
- issues pertaining to low self-esteem and lack of self-acceptance
- inflexible and rigid thinking styles and attitudes
- unhelpful core schemas
- tendency to cognitively or imaginally 'awfulize' events and situations
- unhelpful beliefs maintaining a low frustration tolerance (e.g., 'I can't stand it-itis')
- information-processing errors (cognitive distortions)
- interpersonal inquietude, such as misplaced affection, undue dependency or excessive antipathy
- biological dysfunctions.

Individuals avoid or defend against discomfort, pain or negative emotions, such as shame, guilt, depression and anxiety. This is known as 'defensive reactions' and should not be confused with psychodynamic concepts.

The principal learning factors which are responsible for behavioural problems and disorders are conditioned associations (operant and respondent); modelling, identification and other vicarious processes; and idiosyncratic perceptions.

Non-conscious processes are often involved in learning. Stimuli that can influence feelings, conscious thoughts/images and behaviours may go unrecognized by the person concerned.

Interactions between two or more people involve communications and meta-communications (i.e., communication about their communication). Communication can disintegrate when individuals are unable to stand back from the transaction, thereby failing to examine the content and process of ongoing relationships.

Individuals may have a genetic predisposition or vulnerability to certain disorders or distress.

THEORY OF CHANGE

A good therapeutic relationship, a constructive working alliance and adequate rapport are usually necessary but often insufficient for effective therapy. The therapist–client relationship is considered as the soil that enables the strategies and techniques to take root. The experienced multimodal therapist hopes to offer a lot more by assessing and treating the client's BASIC ID, endeavouring to 'leave no stone (or modality) unturned'.

Usually an active-directive approach to therapy is taken. However, this depends upon the issues being discussed and upon the client concerned.

The process of change commences with the counsellor explaining the client's problems in terms of the seven modalities, that is the BASIC ID, and then negotiating a counselling programme which uses specific techniques or interventions for each particular problem. This is usually undertaken in the first or second session and the completed modality profile is developed (see Table 5.29.1).

Multimodal therapists take Paul's mandate very seriously: '*What* treatment, by *whom*, is most effective for *this* individual with *that* specific problem and under *which* set of circumstances?' (1967: 111). In addition *relationships of choice* are also considered.

Positive, neutral or negative change in any one modality is likely to affect functioning in other modalities.

The approach is psycho-educational and the therapist ensures that the client understands why each technique or intervention is being used. Bibliotherapy is frequently used to help the client understand the methods applied and also to correct misinformation and supply missing information. A self-help coaching book provides details regarding the majority of multimodal techniques and how to develop a modality profile (Palmer et al., 2003).

The approach is technically eclectic as it uses techniques and methods taken from many different psychological theories and systems, without necessarily being concerned with the validity of their theoretical principles.

Multimodal therapists often see themselves in a coach/trainer–trainee or teacher–student relationship as opposed to a doctor–patient relationship, thereby encouraging self-change rather than dependency.

Flexible interpersonal styles of the therapist which match client needs can reduce dropout rates and help the therapeutic relationship. This approach is known as being an 'authentic chameleon'. The term 'bespoke therapy' has been used to describe the custom-made emphasis of the approach.

Lazarus summed up briefly the main hypothesized ingredients of change when using the multimodal approach:

- *Behaviour*: positive reinforcement; negative reinforcement; punishment; counter-conditioning; extinction
- *Affect*: admitting and accepting feelings; abreaction
- *Sensation*: tension release; sensory pleasuring
- *Imagery*: coping images; changes in self-image
- *Cognition*: greater awareness; cognitive restructuring; modification of unhelpful core schema and information-processing errors
- *Interpersonal*: non-judgemental acceptance; modelling; dispersing unhealthy collusions
- *Drugs/biology*: better nutrition and exercise; substance abuse cessation; psychotropic medication when indicated.

SKILLS AND STRATEGIES

Therapists should practise humility; Lazarus stresses that therapists should know their limitations and other therapists' strengths. The therapist tries to ascertain whether a judicious referral to another therapist may be necessary to ensure that the client's needs are met. In addition, a referral to other health practitioners, such as medical doctors or psychiatrists, may be necessary if the client presents problems of an organic or a psychiatric nature.

Therapists take a flexible interpersonal approach with each client to maximize therapeutic outcome and reduce dropout rates.

Techniques and interventions are applied systematically, based on client qualities, therapist qualities, therapist skills, therapeutic alliance and technique specificity

Table 5.29.1 John's full modality profile (or BASIC ID chart)

Modality	Problem	Proposed programme/treatment
Behaviour	Eats/walks fast, always in a rush, hostile, competitive; indicative of type A behaviour	Discuss advantages of slowing down; disadvantages of rushing and being hostile; teach relaxation exercise; dispute self-defeating beliefs
	Avoidance of giving presentations	Exposure programme; teach necessary skills; dispute self-defeating beliefs
	Accident proneness	Discuss advantages of slowing down
Affect	Anxious when giving presentations; guilt when work targets not achieved	Anxiety management; dispute self-defeating thinking
	Frequent angry outbursts at work	Anger management; dispute irrational beliefs
Sensation	Tension in shoulders	Self-message; muscle relaxation exercise
	Palpitations	Anxiety management, e.g., breathing relaxation technique, dispute catastrophic thinking
	Frequent headaches	Relaxation exercise and bio-feedback
	Sleeping difficulties	Relaxation or self-hypnosis tape for bedtime use; behavioural retraining; possibly reduce caffeine intake
Imagery	Negative images of not performing well	Coping imagery focusing on giving adequate presentations
	Images of losing control	Coping imagery of dealing with difficult work situations and with presentations; 'step-up' imagery (Palmer and Dryden, 1995)
	Poor self-image	Positive imagery
Cognition	I must perform well otherwise it will be awful and I couldn't stand it	Dispute self-defeating and irrational beliefs; coping statements; cognitive restructuring; ABCDE paradigm
	I must be in control	
	Significant others should recognize my work	(REBT) bibliotherapy
	If I fail, then I am a total failure	Coping imagery (Palmer and Dryden, 1995)
Interpersonal	Passive/aggressive in relationships; manipulative tendencies at work; always puts self first; few supportive friends	Assertiveness training
		Discuss pros and cons of behaviour
		Friendship training (Palmer and Dryden, 1995)
		Improve sleeping and reassess; refer to GP
Drugs/biology	Feeling inexplicably tired	Refer to GP; relaxation exercises
	Taking aspirins for headaches	
	Consumes 10 cups of coffee a day	Discuss benefits of reducing caffeine intake
	Poor nutrition and little exercise	Nutrition and exercise programme

Source: Palmer (1997: 159–60)

(Palmer, 2015). For example, research data will suggest various techniques that could be applied for a specific problem, although the therapist may only be proficient in using a number of them, while the client may only be able to tolerate one or two of the suggested interventions due to having a low tolerance to pain or frustration. Finally,

a poor therapeutic alliance may increase the chances of attrition (dropout) occurring if a high-anxiety-provoking technique is applied.

A wide range of cognitive and behavioural techniques is used in multimodal therapy. In addition, techniques are taken from other therapies, such as gestalt therapy

Table 5.29.2 Frequently used techniques in multimodal therapy and training

Modality	Techniques and interventions	Modality	Techniques and interventions
Behaviour	Behaviour rehearsal		Correcting misconceptions
	Empty chair		Disputing irrational beliefs
	Exposure programme		Focusing
	Fixed role therapy		Positive self-statements
	Modelling		Problem-solving training
	Paradoxical intention		Rational proselytizing
	Psychodrama		Self-acceptance training
	Reinforcement programmes		Thought stopping
	Response prevention/cost	Interpersonal	Assertion training
	Risk-taking exercises		Communication training
	Self-monitoring and recording		Contracting
	Stimulus control		Fixed role therapy
	Shame attacking		Friendship/intimacy training
Affect	Anger expression/management		Graded sexual approaches
	Anxiety management		Paradoxical intentions
	Feeling identification		Role-play
Sensation	Bio-feedback		Social skills training
	Hypnosis	Drugs/biology	Alcohol reduction programme
	Meditation		Blood pressure reduction programme
	Relaxation training		Cholesterol lowering programme
	Sensate focus training		Lifestyle changes, e.g., exercise, nutrition
	Threshold training		Referral to physicians or other specialists
Imagery	Anti-future shock imagery		Stop smoking programme
	Associated imagery		Weight reduction and maintenance programme
	Aversive imagery		
	Compassion-focused imagery		
	Coping imagery		
	Goal-focused imagery		
	Implosion and imaginal exposure		
	Motivation imagery		
	Positive imagery		
	Rational emotive imagery		
	Time projection imagery		
	Trauma-focused imagery		
Cognition	Bibliotherapy		
	Challenging faulty inferences		
	Cognitive rehearsal		
	Coping statements		

Source: adapted from Palmer (1996: 55–56)

(e.g., the empty chair). Table 5.29.2 illustrates the main techniques used in therapy.

A 15-page Multimodal Life History Inventory (MLHI) (Lazarus and Lazarus, 1991) is often but not invariably used to elicit information about each of the client's modalities, general historical information and expectations about therapy and the therapist. The client usually completes the MLHI at home between sessions 1 and 2. If the client is not up to undertaking the task due to inadequate skills or severe depression, the therapist can use the MLHI questions as a guide in the session (Palmer and Dryden, 1995).

Second-order BASIC ID is a modality profile which focuses solely on the different aspects of a resistant problem. It is undertaken when the interventions or techniques applied to help a specific problem do not appear to have resolved it.

To obtain more clinical information and also general goals for therapy, a structural profile is drawn up (Lazarus,

1989). This can be derived from the MLHI or by asking clients to rate subjectively, on a scale of 1 to 7, how they perceive themselves in relation to the seven modalities. The counsellor can ask a number of different questions that focus on the seven modalities:

- *Behaviour*: How much of a 'doer' are you?
- *Affect*: How emotional are you?
- *Sensation*: How 'tuned in' are you to your bodily sensations?
- *Imagery*: How imaginative are you?
- *Cognition*: How much of a 'thinker' are you?
- *Interpersonal*: How much of a 'social being' are you?
- *Drugs/biology*: To what extent are you health conscious?

Then, in the session, the therapist can illustrate these scores graphically by representing them in the form of a bar chart on paper (see Figure 5.29.1). Then clients are asked in what way they would like to change their profiles during the course of therapy. Once again, the client is asked to rate subjectively each modality on a score from 1 to 7 (see Figure 5.29.2).

Tracking is another procedure regularly used in multimodal therapy. Here the 'firing order' of the different modalities is noted for a specific problem. Therapy interventions are linked to the sequence of the firing order of the modalities. This is particularly useful for dealing with panic attacks.

Multimodal therapists deliberately use a 'bridging' procedure to initially 'key into' a client's preferred modality, before gently exploring a modality (e.g., affect/emotion) that the client may be intentionally or unintentionally avoiding (Lazarus, 1997; Palmer, 2015).

RESEARCH EVIDENCE

The majority of techniques used are taken from behaviour and cognitive therapy. These approaches, and, more recently, the techniques that are applied to specific problems and disorders, have been shown to be more effective than other forms of therapy. Specific research is still being undertaken in multimodal therapy (e.g., Mikaeili et al., 2015).

Controlled outcome studies have supported the benefits of multimodal assessment and counselling programmes. In addition, Kwee's (1984) outcome study on 84 hospitalized clients suffering from phobias or obsessive compulsive disorders resulted in substantial recoveries and durable follow-ups. The MLHI was also evaluated and results indicated that participants consistently evaluated it as more helpful, comprehensive and efficient compared to the Integral Intake, which is another initial assessment inventory (see Marquis, 2002).

The application of the multimodal approach to coaching is a developing area for research (Palmer, 2008; Palmer and Gyllensten, 2008), including multimodal health coaching (Rose et al., 2010).

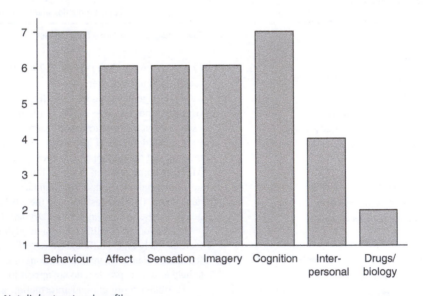

Figure 5.29.1 Natalie's structural profile

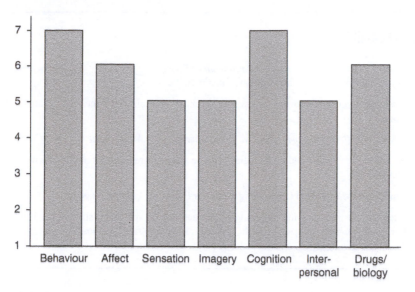

Figure 5.29.2 Natalie's desired structural profile

REFERENCES

Kwee, M.G.T. (1984) *Klinische Multimodale Gegragtstherapie*. Lisse: Swets and Zeitlinger.

Lazarus, A.A. (1989) *The Practice of Multimodal Therapy: Systematic, Comprehensive and Effective Psychotherapy*. Baltimore, MD: Johns Hopkins University Press.

Lazarus, A.A. (1997) *Brief but Comprehensive Psychotherapy: The Multimodal Way*. New York: Springer.

Lazarus, A.A. and Lazarus, C.N. (1991) *Multimodal Life History Inventory*. Champaign, IL: Research Press.

Marquis, A. (2002) Mental health professionals' comparative evaluations of the Integral intake, the life-style introductory interview, and the multimodal life history inventory. Unpublished PhD Dissertation, University of North Texas.

Mikaeili, N., Hajloo, N., Narimani, M. and Pournikdast, S. (2015) Effectiveness of multi-modal Lazarus and multi-modal spiritual – religious, of physical symptoms and quality life in patients with functional dyspepsia. *Journal of Asian Scientific Research*, 5(12): 534–544.

Palmer, S. (1996) The multimodal approach: theory, assessment, techniques and interventions. In S. Palmer and W. Dryden (eds), *Stress Management and Counselling: Theory, Practice, Research and Methodology*. London: Cassell.

Palmer, S. (1997) Modality assessment. In S. Palmer and G. McMahon (eds), *Client Assessment*. London: Sage.

Palmer, S. (2008) Multimodal coaching and its application to workplace, life and health coaching. *The Coaching Psychologist*, 4(1): 21–29.

Palmer, S. (2015) Multimodal therapy. In S. Palmer (ed.), *The Beginner's Guide to Counselling and Psychotherapy*. London: Sage.

Palmer, S., Cooper, C. and Thomas, K. (2003) *Creating a Balance: Managing Stress*. London: British Library.

Palmer, S. and Dryden, W. (1995) *Counselling for Stress Problems*. London: Sage.

Palmer, S. and Gyllensten, K. (2008) How cognitive behavioural, rational emotive behavioural or multimodal coaching could prevent mental health problems, enhance performance and reduce work related stress. *The Journal of Rational Emotive and Cognitive Behavioural Therapy*, 26(1): 38–52.

Paul, G.L. (1967) Strategy of outcome research in psychotherapy. *Journal of Consulting Psychology*, 331: 109–118.

Rose, S., Palmer, S. and O'Riordan, S. (2010) A HEALTHY development from the multimodal approach to coaching. *The Coaching Psychologist*, 6(2): 88–96.

RECOMMENDED READING

1.   Lazarus, A.A. (1989) *The Practice of Multimodal Therapy: Systematic, Comprehensive and Effective Psychotherapy*. Baltimore, MD: Johns Hopkins University Press.

This edition of the book by Lazarus provides an excellent overview to multimodal therapy. Lazarus's approach comes alive in each chapter.

2.   Lazarus, A.A. (1997) *Brief but Comprehensive Psychotherapy: The Multimodal Way*. New York: Springer.

In this book Lazarus describes how multimodal therapy can be a brief therapeutic intervention without losing the thoroughness of the approach.

3.   Palmer, S. and Dryden, W. (1995) *Counselling for Stress Problems*. London: Sage.

Palmer and Dryden demonstrate how the multimodal approach can be applied to stress-related problems. For each modality it includes a range of techniques, with the indications and contraindications for their use. It contains many real case studies.

5.30   PLURALISTIC THERAPY

JOHN MCLEOD AND MICK COOPER

OVERVIEW AND KEY POINTS

Pluralistic counselling and psychotherapy is an integrative approach that draws on concepts and interventions in ways that are tailored to the specific needs of each client. The client is regarded as a person who has strengths, resources, and knowledge that are relevant to the resolution of the problems in living that have led them to seek therapy. A pluralistic approach places a strong emphasis on the importance of the client and therapist working collaboratively to decide on the goals and tasks of therapy, and find methods through which these outcomes can be achieved.

The aims of the chapter are to:

*   introduce the main ideas and methods used in pluralistic therapy;
*   provide an account of the distinctive features of the pluralistic therapy approach;
*   explain how pluralistic therapy works in practice;
*   evaluate the research evidence for this approach.

BRIEF HISTORY

The emergence of counselling and psychotherapy in the middle of the twentieth century was associated with a proliferation of different and competing therapeutic approaches. Such diversity did much to foster creativity and growth within the field. However, the development of 'schools' has also tended to lead to an unproductive 'schoolism'. Here, adherents of particular approaches have become entrenched in the 'rightness' of their model, and blind to ways of working that might be more helpful for particular clients.

As a response to this, some therapists from the 1930s onwards have attempted to develop more integrative and eclectic practices. Yet these, too, can end up as relatively discrete and fixed models of therapy (e.g., Cognitive Analytic Therapy or Egan's skilled helper model). Moreover, in most of these approaches, the decision as to which methods or understandings to use tends to remain primarily with the therapist.

Pluralistic therapy, as developed by Cooper and McLeod (2007, 2011) – and further articulated in McLeod et al. (2013), McLeod (2017), and Cooper and Dryden (2016) – comprises a framework for therapy that is intended to overcome some of these limitations, while drawing on the most valuable features of these previous models. It is not one specific therapeutic practice, but a set of principles and meta-strategies that can be adopted by therapists from a wide range of backgrounds.

Pluralistic counselling and psychotherapy was developed at the beginning of the twenty-first century, and reflect some of the key cultural developments in this era. Pluralistic therapy reflects a postmodern suspicion of 'grand narratives', such as all-encompassing psychological theories, and a preference instead for 'local' solutions. It builds on the increasing tendency for people to be informed consumers of health care, whose use of the internet and other media enables them to develop their own ideas about what ails them and how they might be helped. Also relevant is a high level of global, or multicultural, sensitivity, which takes the form of acknowledgement of the potential value of healing practices from other cultures. Pluralistic therapy also recognises the value of non-hierarchical social networking and knowledge-building structures, such as the various wiki systems. The historical context of the development of pluralistic therapy has meant that the approach emerged at a time when a massive amount of research evidence was available around what works in therapy (see Cooper, 2008; Lambert, 2013). The pluralistic framework for practice has therefore been able to draw on this body of knowledge in designing research-informed procedures through which pluralistic principles can be applied.

BASIC ASSUMPTIONS

Pluralism is a term that is widely used in politics, theology, and philosophy, and refers to the idea that, in the arena of social life, any substantial problem admits to a multiplicity of reasonable and plausible answers. A pluralistic stance implies that a person is willing to accept the validity of other answers to a question, even while adopting a specific position (e.g., atheist, Christian or Islamic). Pluralism is associated with a strong ethical commitment to the intrinsic value of connection and dialogue between people – active curiosity and interest rather than disengaged tolerance. In relation to models of therapy integration, the concept of pluralism represents a form of theoretical integration that is not constructed around any specific set of psychological concepts, but instead is held together by a philosophical and ethical valuing of diversity. Theoretical integration on the basis of any psychological concept always has the

effect of privileging that idea while downplaying other psychological ideas. By contrast, the concept of pluralism opens a conceptual space in which all psychological theories (and other ideas, from sociology, human ecology, and other disciplines) can coexist.

Within the domain of counselling and psychotherapy, the application of pluralism takes the form of an acceptance that there are many factors that can contribute to the problems for which people seek help, and many mechanisms of change through which therapeutic help can be delivered. Moreover, it holds the view that a plurality of perspectives – the client's as well as the therapist's – should inform the direction of the therapeutic work. If a client comes to see a therapist with questions such as 'What is wrong with me?' or 'How can I get better?', it is likely that *both* of them will have some ideas about how to answer these questions. In addition, there are other potential answers available within the wider culture that may be valuable to this client and therapist but which they have not yet discovered. Pluralistic counselling and psychotherapy involve the therapist finding ways to enable his or her client to select from all of these possibilities, in order to address their specific problem.

Pluralistic counselling and psychotherapy are based on further assumptions about the characteristics of clients and therapists. Clients are viewed as active agents, with important personal strengths, who are engaged in using whatever tools and resources are available to them in order to construct a more satisfying life (Bohart and Tallman, 1999). In responding to the needs of their clients, pluralistic therapists are required to possess a solid foundation of counselling skills and self-awareness, an overview and critical appreciation of a range of therapy approaches, and in-depth practical knowledge of at least one approach (e.g., person-centred, psychodynamic, cognitive-behaviour therapy (CBT)). Pluralistic therapists are not expected to be omni-competent, but to be open-minded and curious about a range of therapy ideas and methods, and to be committed to a process of ongoing lifelong learning in which they continue to incorporate ideas and methods from different therapy approaches into their practice.

ORIGIN AND MAINTENANCE OF PROBLEMS

Within the counselling and psychotherapy literature, and the wider stock of cultural knowledge, there exists a multiplicity of ideas and theories around the origins of personal, emotional, and behavioural problems. A pluralistic stance implies that any of these accounts, or a combination of them, may be valid in any particular case. For example, if a person seeks counselling because of fearfulness around meeting other people, it may be that this pattern is due to previous trauma (being humiliated in front of peers at school), lack of social skills (growing up in a reclusive family), biological factors (being too tall or too fat to be accepted by others), and so on. A therapist who works pluralistically seeks to keep an open mind about the possible origins of their clients' problems. As a means of keeping the options open, in respect of the nature of a client's problems, some pluralistic therapists use the very general term 'problems in living' as their starting point. The process of pluralistic therapy involves the therapist and client being willing to share their ideas about the origins of the client's problems, and to work together to evaluate and test out which explanations seem most relevant.

Just as there exists a multiplicity of possible origins for the problems presented by clients, so a pluralistic approach holds that there may be a multiplicity of factors contributing to the maintenance of these problems. The role of the client in maintaining problems is of particular relevance because it is assumed that he or she would have done all they could to resolve their problems in advance of seeking help from a therapist. It may be that the coping strategies that the client has adopted have been ineffective, have not been pursued vigorously enough, or require to be modified. It may be that the client has an absence of appropriate strategies, or that there are strengths and resources that are potentially available to them but are being disregarded for some reason. By inviting discussion with the client around the issue of how their problems are being maintained, and their sense of what might help, a pluralistic therapist seeks to identify ways of making a difference that are grounded in the client's world-view and life experience, rather than externally imposed.

THEORY OF CHANGE

From a pluralistic perspective, there are many processes of change that may be relevant within therapy and may be activated through the work that the client and therapist do together. The counselling and psychotherapy theoretical literature includes descriptions of a wide range of different change processes: insight, altering patterns of behaviour through reinforcement, acquiring new social or cognitive skills, developing new relationships, working through the impact of trauma and loss, and so on. There are further change processes that may be meaningful to some clients, such as beginning or ending medication, participation in exercise or spiritual activity, and making changes to life situations (e.g., leaving home, starting a new job). It is likely that several of these change processes will occur at the same time, no matter which therapy intervention is used. For example, a standard CBT intervention such as training the client in relaxation skills as a means of counteracting anxiety may also be inter-

preted by the client in terms of greater connectedness in – and trust of – a therapist who cares about them, and/or as a shift in self-definition ('Yes, I can take responsibility for doing something different in my life'). Ultimately, the aim of pluralistic therapy is to facilitate the client in engaging with the change processes or mechanisms that make a difference for them, in terms of allowing them to move on in their life. Pluralistic therapists therefore need to discipline themselves to retain an open mind about the pathways of change that may be right for an individual client, and also the pace, location, and extent of change. Some clients can get what they need in one session, while others require a lot of time. Some clients can be observed undergoing moments of insight or catharsis in the therapy room, while for others the change happens in everyday life and the therapist is someone who is used as a source of support and an aid to reflection.

SKILLS AND STRATEGIES

The core therapeutic skills and strategies that are used by pluralistic practitioners are drawn from established theories of counselling/psychotherapy and models of counselling skills (Cooper and Dryden, 2016; McLeod and McLeod, 2011). For example, the skill of empathic reflection is well defined within person-centred counselling, and the strategy of using a case formulation to structure planned cognitive and behavioural change is similarly well defined within the CBT literature. However, working pluralistically requires the development of a number of meta-strategies that are necessary in order to facilitate the effective combination of ideas and methods from different therapy approaches. These are as follows.

CAPACITY TO DECONSTRUCT EXISTING THERAPY APPROACHES

To function as a pluralistic therapist it is essential to appreciate that existing therapy approaches consist of assemblages of ideas and practices that reflect the personal interests of the founders of the approach and the socio-historical context in which the approach was first developed. Often, there is no fundamental or necessary logical coherence to any of the mainstream therapy approaches; they each comprise bundles of ideas and practices that can be dismantled and used separately. For example, empathic reflection is a core skill within person-centred counselling but can be used by any therapist without necessarily buying into other person-centred ideas, such as the notion of an actualising tendency. This kind of conceptual flexibility is essential if pluralistic therapy is to be tailored to the specific preferences of particular clients.

ENABLING CLIENTS TO PARTICIPATE ACTIVELY IN THERAPY

It is unrealistic to expect that all clients will enter therapy with clearly formed ideas about what will help them, and how they want to work. Nevertheless, from a pluralistic perspective it is assumed that the client will have spent a lifetime being a 'self-therapist', and will have various ideas and preferences around what has been useful (or otherwise) for them. In addition, when presented with different options, most clients are drawn to some possibilities and intuitively know that other possibilities are not appropriate for them. A key skill in pluralistic therapy involves being able to assist the client to be more aware of their own preferences, and the broader 'therapy menu' that is potentially available to them. Strategies for achieving this outcome include:

- providing the client with information about how they can be involved in the therapy process, during intake or assessment, and through written materials, and reinforcing these inputs by regularly checking out with the client that they have read and understood the material;
- taking opportunities within therapy to engage in conversations with clients around key choice points in the therapy process, such as their goals, the immediate tasks that need to be accomplished in order to achieve these goals, and the methods or activities that might help them in making progress.

ROUTINE MONITORING OF WHAT WORKS

If therapy is to be constructed around what works for each particular client, it is important to know about whether the way that the therapist and client are working together is producing satisfactory results. This can be carried out through inviting the client on a weekly basis to complete an outcome scale such as one of the Clinical Outcomes in Routine Evaluation (CORE) questionnaires, or a goal rating scale in which they evaluate the extent to which they have progressed towards their own goals. Other instruments that can be used to monitor whether the client is getting what they want from therapy include the Helpful Aspects of Therapy scale, which measures the client's perception of therapeutic alliance, or the Inventory of Client Preferences (Cooper and Norcross, 2015). Further information on these techniques can be found in Cooper and McLeod (2011). The aim is to use such instruments as 'conversational tools' that supplement and extend what emerges from review sessions and the ongoing feedback

that clients offer to their therapists. An assumption that informs the use of these tools is that some clients may lack a language for conveying their experience of therapy, or may feel inhibited in passing comment by the professional status of their counsellor. These instruments therefore give clients a voice, and serve to externalise their evaluations of the therapy in a form in which client and therapist can reflect together on what it implies (Sundet, 2012).

SHARED DECISION-MAKING AS A PROCESS

The pluralistic commitment to collaboration and dialogue, as a means of weaving together the knowledge and experience of the therapist with that of the client, is no easy matter. It takes time for clients to articulate what they want and their sense of the types of activity that might facilitate these goals. The focus of therapy may change over time, as that client uncovers new aspects of an issue, or re-prioritises across multiple presenting issues. The dynamics of collaboration can be subtle, with exploration of moments of disagreement and resistance playing an equally important role as areas of consensus. It is therefore essential to regard shared decision-making as a process, rather than a single even that takes place at the start of therapy. Aspects of this process take the form of moment-by-moment meta-communication of intentions and responses, and conversations facilitated by completion of feedback measures. For many pluralistic therapists, a key stage in shared decision-making involves a session, or most of a session, devoted to a collaborative case formulation exercise in which the client and therapist may work together to map out, on a large sheet of paper, their ideas about the nature of the client's problem and goals for therapy, how the problem has developed, relevant strengths and resources, and possible ways forward.

ACTIVATING CLIENT STRENGTHS AND CULTURAL RESOURCES

Pluralistic therapy takes account of the substantial evidence that is available around the value to mental health and wellbeing of cultural resources such as art-making, reading, outdoor activities and sport, spiritual practice, voluntary work, and many other activities. In pluralistic therapy, it is assumed that the client has previous experience in their life of making use of such resources to promote connection with others, meaning in life, and self-esteem. Part of the process of therapy therefore involves reviewing the relevance of resources that may be applicable in the resolution of current problems in living, and devising strategies for activating these resources.

CASE EXAMPLE

Silvia was a single woman of 70 who had retired following a successful professional career. As an unexpected consequence of a minor surgical procedure, she suddenly lost her sight and became blind. Although she was provided with a live-in carer and appropriate technological adjustments to her living environment, Silvia became increasingly depressed and socially isolated. Six sessions of pluralistic counselling had a significant impact on her sense of wellbeing, acceptance of her condition, and hope for the future. During therapy, her counsellor regularly sought Silvia's views on what would be helpful, and whether the activities they were pursuing in therapy sessions were making a difference for her. Overall progress across therapy was monitored using a verbally administered version of the CORE outcome questionnaire. A range of therapeutic tasks were explored: (1) feeling that someone else understood what she was going through; (2) being able to express emotions around the loss of sight; (3) finding a new identity; (4) finding ways to cope with fear, loss, dependency, and other people's perceptions; (5) exploring the possibility of a positive future without sight; (6) making sense of things; and (7) finding ways to become more socially connected. Some sessions involved intensive exploratory listening and meaning-making, whereas other phases of therapy involved planning for behaviour change. Important change events within therapy included a decision to find ways to re-engage in hill-walking, and an appreciation of how she could make better use of the presence and support of her live-in carer. This case demonstrates how careful and deliberate alignment of therapy with the needs, interests and resources of the client, following pluralistic principles, can lead to meaningful and significant change within a limited number of sessions. A more detailed account of this case can be found in Thurston, McLeod and Thurston (2013).

RESEARCH EVIDENCE

The pluralistic approach to therapy was specifically developed as a framework that could incorporate the widest possible range of findings on what clients might find helpful in therapy. Furthermore, a growing body of evidence indicates that attuning therapeutic interventions to clients' individual wants *does* lead to improved outcomes. For instance, in a study by Berg, Sandahl and Clinton (2008), client preferences for particular types of change process were assessed before they entered therapy. At the end of treatment, those who reported that they had received the kinds of therapeutic experiences that they preferred were found to have benefited more from therapy than those whose preferences had not been fulfilled. In two independent meta-analyses of the relevant research literature, both Swift, Callahan, and Vollmer (2011) and Lindheim et al. (2014) found that clients whose preferences were reflected in the therapy they received had better outcomes, and were much less likely to drop out of therapy. Carey, Tai, and Stiles (2013) found that allowing clients to express preferences around session scheduling reduces rates of client non-attendance and unplanned endings. The process and outcomes of pluralistic therapy have been investigated through single-case research (Miller and Willig, 2012). There has also been a multisite evaluation of pluralistic therapy for depression (Cooper et al., 2015), which found acceptable levels of clinical outcomes and low levels of drop out across the 42 participants.

REFERENCES

Berg, A.L., Sandahl, C. and Clinton, D. (2008). The relationship of treatment preferences and experiences to outcome in generalized anxiety disorder (GAD). *Psychology and Psychotherapy: Theory, Research and Practice, 81*, 247–259.

Bohart, A.C. and Tallman, K. (1999). *How Clients Make Therapy Work: The Process of Active Self-Healing*. Washington, DC: American Psychological Association.

Carey, T.A., Tai, S.J. and Stiles, W.B. (2013). Effective and efficient: using patient-led appointment scheduling in routine mental health practice in remote Australia. *Professional Psychology: Research and Practice*, *44*, 405–414.

Cooper, M. (2008). *Essential Research Findings in Counselling and Psychotherapy: The Facts are Friendly*. London: Sage.

Cooper, M. and Dryden, W. (Eds.) (2016). *Handbook of Pluralistic Counselling and Psychotherapy*. London: Sage.

Cooper, M. and McLeod, J. (2007). A pluralistic framework for counselling and psychotherapy: implications for research. *Counselling and Psychotherapy Research*, *7*, 135–143.

Cooper, M. and McLeod, J. (2011). *Pluralistic Counselling and Psychotherapy*. London: Sage.

Cooper, M. and Norcross, J.C. (2015). A brief, multidimensional measure of clients' therapy preferences: the Cooper-Norcross Inventory of Preferences (C-NIP). *International Journal of Clinical and Health Psychology*, *16*, 87–98.

Cooper, M., Wild, C., van Rijn, B., Ward, T., McLeod, J., Cassar, S., Antoniou, P., Michael, C., Michalitsi, M. and Sreenath, S. (2015). Pluralistic therapy for depression: acceptability, outcomes and helpful aspects in a multisite study. *Counselling Psychology Review*, *30*, 6–20.

Lambert, M.J. (Ed.) (2013). *Bergin and Garfield's Handbook of Psychotherapy and Behavior Change* (6th ed.). Hoboken, NJ: John Wiley & Sons.

Lindheim, O., Bennett, C.B., Trentacosta, C.J. and McLear, C. (2014). Client preferences affect treatment satisfaction, completion, and clinical outcome: a meta-analysis. *Clinical Psychology Review*, *34*(6), 506–517.

McLeod, J. (2017). *Distinctive Features of Pluralistic Therapy*. London: Routledge.

McLeod, J. and McLeod, Julia (2011). *Counselling Skills* (2nd ed.). Maidenhead: Open University Press.

McLeod, J., McLeod, Julia, Cooper, M. and Dryden, W. (Eds.) (2013). Pluralistic therapy. In W. Dryden and A. Reeves (Eds.), *Handbook of Individual Therapy* (6th ed.). London: Sage.

Miller, E. and Willig, C. (2012). Pluralistic counselling and HIV-positive clients: the importance of shared understanding. *European Journal of Psychotherapy and Counselling*, *14*, 33–45.

Sundet, R. (2012). Therapist perspectives on the use of feedback on process and outcome: patient-focused research in practice. *Canadian Psychology*, *53*, 122–130.

Swift, J.K., Callahan, J.L. and Vollmer, B.M. (2011). Preferences. *Journal of Clinical Psychology*, *67*(2), 155–165.

Thurston, M., McLeod J. and Thurston, A. (2013). Counselling for sight loss: using systematic case study research to build a client informed practice model. *British Journal of Visual Impairment*, *31*, 102–122.

RECOMMENDED READING

1. Cooper, M. and Dryden, W. (Eds.) (2016). *Handbook of Pluralistic Counselling and Psychotherapy*. London: Sage.

A comprehensive account of recent developments in pluralistic therapy.

2. Levine, B.E. (2007). *Surviving America's Depression Epidemic: How to Find Morale, Energy, and Community in a World Gone Crazy*. White River Junction, VT: Chelsea Green Publishing.

An uplifting and informative book that discusses multiple causes and cures for depression.

3. McLeod, Julia (2013). Process and outcome in pluralistic Transactional Analysis counselling for long-term health conditions: a case series. *Counselling and Psychotherapy Research*, *13*, 32–43.

Uses a case study approach to explore how therapeutic tasks can change over the course of therapy, and how clients and therapists work together to devise strategies to address them.

5.31 SCHEMA THERAPY

KONSTANTINA KOLONIA AND HELEN KYRITSI

OVERVIEW AND KEY POINTS

Schema therapy is an integrative and unifying approach to treatment that combines elements of cognitive-behavioural therapy with psychodynamic, gestalt and interpersonal therapies, to create a sound theoretical and therapy model. It is designed specifically for people whose psychological difficulties are stemming from early childhood experiences and which are chronic and 'difficult to treat'.

- It focuses on unmet core emotional needs in childhood and the development of self-defeating, self-perpetuating and resistant-to-change emotional and cognitive patterns (early maladaptive schemas).
- The goal is to help individuals challenge and modify these negative patterns of thinking, feeling and behaving and build up the individual's healthy side so those unmet needs can be met in adulthood in an adaptive manner.
- Schema therapy goes beyond an intellectual understanding of clients' problems to actually achieving in-depth emotional change.
- The therapist–client relationship is vital for schema healing.
- Limited re-parenting and empathic confrontations are key relational tools.

BRIEF HISTORY

TRANSITION FROM CBT TO SCHEMA THERAPY

Schema therapy (ST) is an innovative and evidence-based psychotherapy that was developed by Jeffrey Young (1999 [1990]) and is specifically designed to address the issues that face cognitive-behavioural therapy (CBT) when working with challenging and complex patients, who often present with vague yet pervasive and chronic problems, difficulties in establishing and maintaining relationships and highly avoidant and rigid patterns of coping.

It places greater emphasis on the therapeutic relationship; aims to help patients gain access to and connect with their feelings, thoughts and memories, which can otherwise be inaccessible; addresses both current issues as well

as childhood origins; and focuses on coping styles and core themes (Rafaeli et al., 2011). ST is broader than CBT and psychodynamic models with regards to a conceptual model as well as a range of treatment strategies and has been proven successful in treating Cluster B and Cluster C personality disorders, as well as eating disorders and substance misuse, and can be used with individuals, couples and groups.

BASIC ASSUMPTIONS

One of the basic assumptions of schema therapy is that all human beings have *core emotional needs* that are present from childhood. Young et al. (2003) hypothesized that these include:

- Secure attachment to others (e.g., need for safety, nurturance, stability and acceptance)
- Freedom to express one's valid emotions and needs
- Autonomy, competence and a sense of identity
- Spontaneity and play
- Realistic limits where the emergence of self-control is nurtured.

The schema therapy model works on the premise that getting a child's emotional needs met early on in his/her life is of paramount importance for the development of a psychologically healthy individual with the ability to meet those core emotional needs in adaptive ways in adulthood (Rafaeli et al., 2011).

ORIGINS AND MAINTENANCE OF PROBLEMS

EARLY MALADAPTIVE SCHEMAS

According to Young (1999 [1990]), early maladaptive schemas (EMS) refer to dysfunctional, extremely rigid and enduring themes or patterns that develop usually within the first seven years of a child's life, and which are then elaborated further throughout adulthood. They are themes or patterns that provide a template for how one perceives themselves and others, and they consist of feelings, thoughts, memories and bodily sensations.

SCHEMA ACQUISITION

Young et al. (2003) postulate that EMS develop when children's core emotional needs are not met in a profound and consistent manner. They propose four types of *early childhood experiences* which can lead to the development of maladaptive schemas:

1. *Toxic frustration of needs* refers to experiences where there is a total absence of healthy experiences or too little of it, if any.
2. *Traumatization or victimization* reflects experiences of abuse and trauma.
3. *Too much of a good thing* occurs when there is parental failure to set realistic limits, overprotection or over-involvement.
4. *Selective internalization or identification with significant others* – the child selectively identifies with and internalizes some aspects (e.g., thoughts, feelings and/or behaviours) of significant others.

They also argue that two other important factors that are considered to contributing in maladaptive schema acquisition are the child's *emotional temperament* and the child and family's *cultural influences* (Young et al., 2003).

SCHEMA PERPETUATION

Because schemas are held as unconditional beliefs about oneself, they are by their nature self-perpetuating. 'Schema perpetuation' is the term that is given to the process by which an individual acts in ways that maintain and even strengthen his/her schemas. Schema perpetuation occurs through three main mechanisms (Young, 1999 [1990]):

COGNITIVE DISTORTIONS. Cognitive distortions are the mechanism by which the patient tends to make sense of life experiences by attending to information that confirms the schemas and avoids or discards information that is contrary to the schemas.

SELF-DEFEATING PATTERNS. Self-defeating patterns, like 'self-fulfilling prophecies', can occur on a behavioural, affective and interpersonal level. Patients might detach from painful emotions, thus preventing them from being able to make conscious changes. Their actions and behaviours might be such that reinforce them to remain in unhealthy situations or relationships that trigger and perpetuate their schemas.

COPING STYLES. In order to cope with the threat of the schemas, the unmet emotional needs and the corresponding painful emotions, patients develop certain coping styles early in childhood. These coping styles start off as adaptive and healthy ways of survival for the child, but become maladaptive in adulthood, resulting in schema perpetuation, even when the life circumstances have changed. In schema therapy, behaviours are not part of the schemas but part of the coping responses, which are driven by the schemas. Coping mechanisms, although primarily behavioural, can also include emotional and cognitive strategies.

There are three maladaptive coping styles: schema surrender, schema avoidance and schema overcompensation (Young et al., 2003). Patients may use different coping styles to manage different schemas or they might switch between coping styles to manage the same schemas at different times.

1. *Schema surrender* refers to the process of passively accepting that the schemas are true and therefore giving in to the messages that they provide. Patients will behave in such a way that will confirm the schemas.
2. *Schema avoidance* is the attempt to avoid any situation that might trigger the schemas. At an extreme level, avoidance will also include thoughts and feelings, resulting in the patient becoming at times emotionally disconnected and detached.
3. *Schema overcompensation* can be perceived as the healthiest of the three coping styles, as patients attempt to fight their schemas in order to meet their core emotional needs. Unfortunately, patients tend to display 'over-the-top' behaviours that go to the opposite extreme and result in chasing unobtainable standards or driving others away, ultimately maintaining and reinforcing the schemas (Young et al., 2003).

SCHEMA HEALING

The goal of schema therapy is *schema healing*, where therapist and patient work together as allies to fight the schemas, using cognitive, behavioural, experiential and interpersonal strategies. This will result in reducing the intensity of the painful emotions associated with childhood memories, diminishing the conviction with which schemas are held, and replacing the maladaptive coping styles with healthier behaviours that will enable patients to finally meet their core emotional needs and build healthier interpersonal relationships (Young et al., 2003).

SCHEMA MODES

Clients with personality disorders often present with rapid changes to their mood, behaviour and choice of coping style, while a number of different schemas might be triggered all at once. This poses a particular challenge in the traditional schema therapy approach, as it is impractical to attempt to trace the moment-to-moment changes as they are happening both within the therapy session and outside. To overcome this difficulty, the concept of schema modes was developed (Young et al., 2003) to represent the temporary manifestation of emotional and coping responses that the client finds themselves in, in response to a number of schemas being triggered.

In schema mode therapy, the client is supported to identify their predominant schema modes, make links with their childhood origins and develop a plan for dealing with each schema mode accordingly. Young et al. (2003) have developed specific mode models for borderline and narcissistic personality disorders, whereas other models (e.g., for forensic populations) are under development.

SKILLS AND STRATEGIES

Schema therapy is divided in two phases where different skills and strategies are employed: the assessment and education phase and the schema change phase.

ASSESSMENT AND EDUCATION

The first phase of schema therapy is the assessment and education.

Schema therapists' initial evaluation briefly assesses the patient's presenting symptoms and difficulties, goals for therapy as well as suitability for schema therapy. Patients presenting with psychotic experiences, an acute and severe Axis I disorder, current drug or alcohol abuse severe enough to be therapy-interfering or a major crisis are not considered suitable while those problems are still ongoing and need to be addressed first by other evidence-based approaches.

Once suitability for schema therapy has been established, then the assessment phase takes place over a number of sessions aiming to collect information on the patient's dysfunctional life patterns by using various assessment methods. The focus of this process is on understanding the patient's early maladaptive schemas, ways of coping and predominant modes as well as the developmental origins of those (Young et al., 2003).

The main assessment methods used in the schema assessment phase are the following:

- *Focused life history.* Attention is paid on gaining an intellectual understanding of the patient's symptoms, onset and triggers (historical and current) of psychological difficulties as well as of their EMS and coping styles.
- *Schema inventories.* There are four self-report inventories that are widely used and can be administered early on to further inform the assessment phase.
- *Self-monitoring.* The self-monitoring tools that are used are similar to the ones employed in other evidence-based approaches (e.g., CBT) and they aim to gather information on the patient's thoughts, feelings and behaviours that arise in response to everyday events.
- *Imagery assessment.* It is used to help the patient to express strong emotions that are often associated with their schemas and heavily informs schema therapy interventions in the change phase.
- *Therapy relationship.* The therapy relationship is used as a vehicle to initially understand those dysfunctional patterns that are also played out in the patient's everyday life and later 're-parent' and teach healthier ways of relating to self and others (Rafaeli et al., 2011).

Psycho-education is a parallel and integral part of the assessment phase. The therapist's role is to educate the patient about the schema therapy model by making them aware of their core emotional needs, their schemas and modes, the developmental origins of those and their coping styles.

All the information gathered from the assessment and education phase conclude in *a written case conceptualization* which is shared with the patient and it is updated and informed throughout therapy as needed.

THEORY OF CHANGE

The skills and interventions acquired in the change phase have a mixture of cognitive, experiential and behavioural strategies.

COGNITIVE TECHNIQUES

Cognitive strategies are often the first step in schema therapy as the patients need to challenge cognitive distortions and the validity of the schemas on a cognitive level. The therapist guides the client to develop a healthier understanding of their difficulties and discover that the origin of their schemas lies in emotional deprivation and unmet emotional needs early in childhood, within the context of which the schemas were taught (Young et al., 2003).

EXPERIENTIAL TECHNIQUES

Emotion-focused techniques are considered to be one of the pivotal elements for the efficacy of schema therapy as they are thought to produce change at the deepest level possible (Kellogg and Young, 2006). The rationale of using those techniques is to evoke the strong feelings that are often associated with the early maladaptive schemas of the patient and challenge and heal those on an emotional level. The schema therapist aims to create new and healing experiences through limited re-parenting and modelling of new adaptive ways to meet unmet childhood needs associated with his/her patient's schemas (Rafaeli et al., 2011). The three central experiential techniques used are: (i) imagery; (ii) role plays/chair work; and (iii) letter writing.

(I) IMAGERY. Guided imagery is a powerful tool that is used to help the patient actually 'feel' their schemas and connect with those childhood memories that have led to their development. The focus is to help the patient understand that although changing adverse past experiences is not possible, imagery can help in altering the meaning attached to such experiences both on a cognitive and an affective level.

In a typical imagery exercise the therapist invites the patient to revisit a negative childhood memory and play it out in his/her mind as if it was happening in the here and now. The patient's interactions with others are explored and his/her thoughts and feelings are experienced and expressed. Imagery re-scripting then follows to challenge schemas affectively and meet the child's needs. Initially the re-scripting is taking place by the therapist modelling a healthy adult, but at a later stage in therapy the patient's healthy adult part is invited to meet the child's needs (Arntz and Van Genderen, 2009).

(II) ROLE PLAYS/CHAIR WORK. Another widely used experiential technique is role play. It can be focused on past or present experiences from the patient's life and interactions with others. The therapist guides the patient to play various roles and to carry out dialogues between them. The aim is to develop and strengthen the patient's healthy adult part and consequently weaken his/her early maladaptive schemas. The gestalt chair work technique is often used in schema therapy to conduct dialogues among the different modes of the patient (Kellogg, 2015).

(III) LETTER WRITING. Patients are also encouraged to write letters describing how they were wronged by significant others (in most cases the parent/s) and expressing their memories, thoughts and feelings. They are supported by the therapist to express what they needed from them that they did not get, both in the past and in the here and now, and to assert their rights. The letters are usually read out to the therapist and are not sent to whomever they are addressed. The rationale of why the letter is not to be sent is discussed, especially at times when the patient feels otherwise, and potential ramifications are considered (Ohanian and Rashed, 2012).

BEHAVIOURAL PATTERN-BREAKING TECHNIQUES

Behavioural pattern-breaking techniques are the final and more crucial component of the change phase in schema therapy as they are focused on replacing the existing schema-driven patterns of behaviour with healthier, more adaptive ways of coping. Depending on the need, the schema therapist can use either traditional behavioural techniques (e.g., relaxation, social skills training, etc.) and/or incorporate the other schema strategies, such as imagery and dialogues, to get the patient to alter his/her unhealthy coping styles (Rafaeli et al., 2011).

THERAPEUTIC RELATIONSHIP

The therapeutic relationship is considered to be one of the most key ingredients for any successful psychological intervention. However, in schema therapy, the therapeutic relationship has an even more important role as it provides an 'antidote' to the patient's schemas and it serves to begin to meet their core emotional needs. As such, the therapist plays a much more active role in the therapy, becoming a 'role model' of the 'healthy adult' or 'good parent', which in turn gets internalised by the patient to help fight against the schemas.

There are two important elements of the therapeutic relationship that stand out in schema therapy: (i) limited re-parenting; and (ii) empathic confrontation.

(I) LIMITED RE-PARENTING. Limited re-parenting is an interpersonal technique which aims to provide patients with the appropriate core emotional needs that were not met in childhood by their parents, within the limits of the therapeutic relationship (Young et al., 2003). As such, the therapist is encouraged to express care, warmth, acceptance, encouragement, which is genuinely felt towards the patients, and to create a space that provides safety and stability.

(II) EMPATHIC CONFRONTATION. Empathic confrontation (Young et al., 2003) aims to tackle the schemas and maladaptive coping styles as they get re-enacted within the therapeutic relationship, as well as outside the therapy room. The therapist shows empathy and understanding of the patient's difficulties but gently confronts the dysfunctional behaviours and coping styles in order for them to change.

RESEARCH EVIDENCE

The popularity that schema therapy gained over the last years was followed by the need for rigorous research on both the Young's schema and mode model and therapy.

The psychometric properties of the Young Schema Questionnaire have been investigated in several studies with satisfactory outcomes (e.g., Schmidt et al., 1995). Also, a shortened version of the original Schema Mode Inventory (Young et al., 2007) has been found to be reliable in the assessment of modes (Lobbestael, 2012a).

Experimental research on the ST theoretical model as well as the schema modes is still in the early stages and more research is needed in the future. However, a significant number of experimental studies have been conducted on both the schemas and the schema modes (e.g., Lobbestael, 2012b; Sieswerda, 2012).

The effectiveness of schema therapy has been explored and its efficacy is documented in the scientific literature (Bamelis et al., 2012), although due to the small number of studies available at present the results should be interpreted with some caution. The main body of research, so far, has primarily explored the effectiveness of the schema mode model in borderline personality disorder. Studies focusing on the clinical and cost-effectiveness of the model with other personality disorders (e.g., avoidant, histrionic, etc.) and with forensic patients are under way (Bamelis et al., 2012).

REFERENCES

Arntz, A. and Van Genderen, H. (2009) *Schema Therapy for Borderline Personality Disorder*. Chichester: Wiley.

Bamelis, L., Bloo, J., Bernstein, D. and Arntz, A. (2012) Effectiveness studies. In M. Van Vreeswijk, J. Broersen and N. Nadort (eds), *The Wiley Blackwell Handbook of Schema Therapy Theory, Research, and Practise*. Chichester: Wiley.

Kellogg, S.H. (2015) *Transformational Chair Work: Using Psychotherapeutic Dialogues in Clinical Practise*. Lanham, MD: Rowman & Littlefield.

Kellogg, S.H. and Young, J.E. (2006) Schema therapy for borderline personality disorder. *Journal of Clinical Psychology*, 62, 445–458.

Lobbestael, G. (2012a) Validation of the Schema Mode Inventory. In M. Van Vreeswijk, J. Broersen and N. Nadort (eds), *The Wiley Blackwell Handbook of Schema Therapy Theory, Research, and Practice*. Chichester: Wiley.

Lobbestael, G. (2012b) Experimental studies of schema modes. In M. Van Vreeswijk, J. Broersen and N. Nadort (eds), *The Wiley Blackwell Handbook of Schema Therapy Theory, Research, and Practice*. Chichester: Wiley.

Ohanian, V. and Rashed, R. (2012) Schema therapy. In W. Dryden (ed.), *Cognitive Behavioural Therapies*. London: Sage.

Rafaeli, E., Bernstein, D. and Young, J. (2011) *Schema Therapy: The CBT Distinctive Features Series*. London: Routledge.

Schmidt, N.B., Joiner, T.E., Young, J.E and Talch, M.J. (1995) The schema questionnaire: investigation of psychometric properties as to the hierarchical structure of a measure of maladaptive schemas. *Cognitive Therapy and Research*, 19(3), 295–321.

Sieswerda, S. (2012) Experimental studies for schemas. In M. Van Vreeswijk, J. Broersen and N. Nadort (eds), *The Wiley Blackwell Handbook of Schema Therapy Theory, Research, and Practice*. Chichester: Wiley.

Young, J. (1999 [1990]) *Cognitive Therapy for Personality Disorders: A Schema-focused Approach*. Sarasota, FL: Professional Resources Press.

Young, J. E., Arntz, A., Atkinson, T., Lobbestael, J., Weishaar, M. E., van Vreeswijk, M. F., et al. (2007) The Schema Mode Inventory. New York: Schema Therapy Institute.

Young, J., Klosko, J. and Weishaar, M. (2003) *Schema Therapy: A Practitioner's Guide*. New York: Guilford Press.

5.32   THE SKILLED HELPER MODEL

VAL WOSKET AND PETER JENKINS

OVERVIEW AND KEY POINTS

Since it first emerged on the counselling scene in the mid-1970s, the skilled helper model developed by Professor Gerard Egan of Loyola University, Chicago, has been continuously revised and expanded. The model has evolved from Egan's early writings on interpersonal skills in group and individual contexts and has moved through presenting a sequential process model of individual counselling to the development of change agent models and skills within the broader field of organisational change. In this chapter we will consider the model as it applies to the field of one-to-one counselling. Key elements of the approach include:

- a three-stage model for helping clients to change;
- an evolving evidence base, which underpins the model;
- use of client goals to effect change;
- a 'deficit', rather than a 'pathology', model of client difficulties.

BRIEF HISTORY

Early and enduring influences on the skilled helper model include the work of Rogers and Carkhuff, which provide its person-centred values and principles. The model's cognitive-behavioural elements are closely informed by figures such as Bandura, Beck, Ellis, Seligman and Strong. While a three-stage map of the helping process has remained a constant during the various editions of the model, there have been a number of significant adjustments that take account of emerging research and developments in integrative practice. For instance, the third edition of Egan's *The Skilled Helper*, published in 1986, evidenced a shift from problem management to opportunity development; and in 1990, the fourth edition carried an increased emphasis on challenge and action running through all stages of the counselling process. In 1994, the fifth edition engaged more forcefully with debates about eclecticism and integrationism. In this text, the fundamentally flexible, non-linear characteristics of the model and the importance of addressing shadow-side elements of the helping process were highlighted.

In the book's seventh edition, Egan incorporated positive psychology. In the eighth edition there was an evident shift in focus, from the problem management process to a greater emphasis on relationship, dialogue difference and diversity. The model is now in its tenth edition (Egan, 2014) and continues to build on a positive psychology, solution-focused theme, including discussion of evidence-based practice.

The skilled helper model has been expanded and updated for counsellors working in the United Kingdom (UK) by Wosket (2006), in consultation with Gerard Egan. Wosket's approach illustrates how the model can be applied in a variety of clinical settings and emphasises how it can be used as an integrative framework for developing a personally authentic style of counselling. The model is 'dejargoned' and translated from the American idiom into terminology more commonly used by therapists (and their clients) in the UK. How the model can be applied to supervision and training is discussed and a number of guidelines and exercises which can be used in training are included. This version of the skilled helper model also endeavours to address some of the perceived omissions in the conceptualisation and development of the model, through a consideration of how it can evolve and adapt to fit a range of client issues and counselling contexts. These include working in the long term with complex issues, such as trauma and abuse; adopting a more relational approach that takes account of the client's past inter- and intrapersonal history; and working with unconscious and dissociated processes.

Stated in simple terms, the three stages of the skilled helper model are concerned with:

1. Problem definition.
2. Goal setting.
3. Action planning.

Egan has used different terminology in the various editions of *The Skilled Helper* to describe the three stages. In the current tenth edition (2014: 23), these are as follows:

- Stage 1: 'What's going on?'
- Stage 2: 'What do I need or want?'
- Stage 3: 'How do I get what I need or want?'

Underpinning the three stages of the model is an emphasis on *action*: 'How do I make it all happen?'

It is sometimes debated whether the model, as currently practised, is integrative or eclectic, as such divisions are not always clear-cut (Wosket, 2006). The model can be thought of as integrative in that it provides an overarching framework for the helping process, yet it does not have an over-reliance on theory. It is derivative in that it draws on person-centred values and principles, and cognitive-behavioural approaches. Egan himself has described the model as atheoretical – meaning it moves beyond theory, in searching for a framework or map, which is built on pragmatism (what has been shown to work), rather than on theoretical constructions.

The model is designed to provide a versatile and adaptable framework for developing a personal style of working that takes proper account of different client populations, issues and contexts (Wosket, 2006). At its best, it is a shared map that helps clients participate more fully in the helping process. The stages and steps of the model become orientation devices that keep the helping process on course and prevent it deteriorating into a random set of events.

BASIC ASSUMPTIONS

As noted above, Egan has explicitly adopted a positive psychology approach to helping, in more recent editions of *The Skilled Helper*. This involves taking the view that managing problems is more a proactive, than a reactive, process. As such, problem management is considered to provide opportunities for clients to learn effective, life-enhancing skills.

Two core functions of the skilled helper model are: (1) providing a 'geographical' map for the terrain of helping and (2) outlining the tasks of helping and how these tasks interrelate. Egan describes the three principal goals of helping encompassed by the model as follows:

- GOAL 1: Life-enhancing Outcomes. Help clients manage their problems in living more effectively and developing unused or underused resources and opportunities more fully.
- GOAL 2: Learning Self-help. Helps clients become better at helping themselves in their everyday lives.
- GOAL 3: Developing a Prevention Mentality. Helps clients develop an action-oriented prevention mentality in their lives. (Egan, 2014: 9–12)

In the service of these three goals for the helping process, counsellors need to be both skill learners and skill trainers.

The key values that underpin the culture of helping, as understood by Egan, are client empowerment and the Rogerian core qualities of respect, genuineness and empathy. These core values suffuse the communication skills that drive the model. While Rogers considered empathy to be a facilitative condition and one of the core qualities of the helping relationship, Egan views empathy both as 'a basic value that informs and drives all helping behavior' and as an interpersonal communication skill (2014: 48). As a value, empathy places a requirement on the counsellor to understand clients as fully as possible in three particular ways:

1. Understanding the client from his or her point of view.
2. Understanding the client in and through the context (the social setting) of her or his life.
3. Understanding the dissonance, wherever it appears to exist, between the client's point of view and current reality.

Client empowerment is linked to the three goals of helping outlined above. According to Egan, helpers do not *empower* clients, 'rather they help clients discover, acquire, develop, and use the power they have at the service of constructive life change' (2014: 58). It is recognised that counsellors are, by virtue of their role and status, in a more powerful position than those who seek their help. On the negative side, helpers can misuse their power, wherever they encourage deference, or dependency, and when they oppress others. More positively, helpers can use the power inherent in their position, within a social-influence process, that can enable clients to become more effective at managing their own problems. A positive psychology approach encourages helpers *not* to see their clients as victims, even 'if victimising circumstances have diminished a client's degree of freedom', but instead to 'work with the freedom that is left' (Egan, 2014: 60). Egan therefore suggests that helpers who use the model think of themselves as consultants and facilitators, who provide as much, or as little, assistance as the client needs in order to better manage the problem situations in their lives. Minimum intervention is considered to be the optimum way of working.

ORIGIN AND MAINTENANCE OF PROBLEMS

Egan's view of the person comprises a 'deficit' rather than a pathology model. The problems that clients bring to counselling arise, in most part, from their difficulties in harnessing energy and resources (both internal and external) to realise their best potential. Egan considers that unused human potential constitutes a more serious social problem than psychological or emotional disorders, because it is more widespread.

Egan identifies the healthy and functional personality as someone who has the necessary knowledge, skills and resources to successfully complete developmental tasks and to handle upsets and crises when they occur. The individual's ability to accomplish life's challenges will be affected by external factors in the environment and may be reduced by these. Such limiting factors might include economic and social constraints, racism and oppression of minority populations and dysfunctional family environments.

Psychological disturbance is mainly attributed to:

- being out of community, i.e., isolated or alienated from key social systems;
- the inability to successfully negotiate developmental tasks;
- being out of touch with developmental resources (intrapersonal, interpersonal and environmental).

The helper is dealing with unique human beings at particular points in their lives. Pathologising clients, through general diagnostic labels, is seen as unhelpful and perpetuates a remedial, rather than a positive psychology, approach to helping. Psychiatry and psychoanalysis have been too much focused on the individual at the expense of the social and cultural context in which the individual exists. Egan argues that the horizons of the helper need to be expanded to include these systems and settings.

People become estranged from their capacity to realise their full potential through factors such as passivity, learned helplessness and their experience of undermining social systems and environmental conditions. Abnormal behaviour and emotional disturbance are seen as ineffective behaviour and its consequences, which arise from a lack of knowledge or skills. Skills and knowledge have to be acquired at each stage of development in order for the individual to accomplish increasingly complex tasks and fulfil new roles. Helpers need to be accomplished skill trainers, or act as points of referral to external sources of information and skills that clients may need to make progress through developmental impasses. For instance, the counsellor might spend time helping the client to develop and practise the interpersonal skills of conflict management to help them move out of established patterns of passivity or deference to others.

THEORY OF CHANGE

Changes in self-concept come about through empowerment as clients learn to be more effective at problem management and opportunity development. Therapy can help to overcome early developmental deficits by enabling the client to acquire skills in living, in particular interpersonal and problem management skills.

Counselling is seen as a social-influence process. People are capable of realising their potential and rising above 'the psychopathology of the average' when they are given optimum amounts of supportive challenge within a strong therapeutic relationship. Helpers aim to be directive of the *process*, but not the *content*, of therapy. The model is collaborative and designed to be 'given away' to clients so that the process is shared with them and owned by them. The client is considered to be the expert on himself or herself and the counsellor acts as consultant to, and facilitator of, the client's process. The quality of the therapeutic relationship importantly mediates the effectiveness of the change process, but is not an end in itself. Reluctance and resistance are seen as natural aspects of the change process.

Egan asserts that it is a mistake to over-identify the helping process with the communication skills that are merely the tools that serve it. Communication skills do not, in themselves, constitute the problem management process, and 'being good at communication skills is not the same as being good at helping' (Egan, 2007: 136). Communication skills are principally helpful in establishing a good working relationship with the client. The working alliance provides a solid foundation for intentional counselling, which Egan views, first and foremost, as a systematic process of 'social-emotional reeducation' (2007: 136).

Change comes about through *action*. However, action is not limited to behavioural change outside counselling sessions. Action can be understood as both *internal* (an inner shift or change in thinking or feeling) and *external* (observable action in behavioural terms) and as happening both within and between sessions.

SKILLS AND STRATEGIES

The first stage of the counselling process is about helping clients to construct a coherent personal narrative or story. Stories may consist of both problems and missed opportunities. The counsellor enables the client to tell their story through the active listening skills of attending (verbal and non-verbal), listening, reflecting back (content, thoughts and feelings), summarising and clarifying. These communication skills help to convey the key quality of empathy, through which the counsellor demonstrates their understanding and acceptance of the client.

In order to elicit as clear a story as possible, the counsellor encourages the client to give concrete examples of behaviours, experiences and feelings. Empathic challenges are introduced to invite the client to begin to explore possible blind spots and to develop new perspectives on their situation. In the eighth edition of *The Skilled Helper*, the term 'new perspectives' was introduced in preference to 'blind spots', which is in line with the shift to positive psychology. Here, the emphasis is more on the 'task' of helping clients reframe their stories and develop new perspectives than on the notion of the helper challenging the client's lack of awareness. Through a balance of support and challenge, the counsellor helps the client search for what is termed 'value' in the ninth edition and was called 'leverage' in previous editions. The task described is to 'help clients work on issues that will add value to their lives' (Egan, 2014: 270) and the helper does this through using the skills of advanced empathy, immediacy, probing, questioning, summarising and clarifying.

The second stage of the counselling process is about helping the client gain a clearer view of what they need and want. Where people have difficulty managing problems, this is frequently down to a tendency to link problems to actions, as in 'What do I *do* about this?', rather than to link action to outcomes, as in 'What do I *need to do* to get what I want?' An axiom that Egan continuously emphasises is that *goals*, not problems or strategies, should drive action.

The second stage involves helpers assisting their clients first to see options for a better future and then to turn these into workable objectives that can drive action. The additional skills needed by the helper here are those related to goal setting, including future-oriented questioning, goal shaping and working with reluctance and resistance, to generate hope and commitment. In the eighth edition, the term 'preferred picture' was introduced, in preference to the 'preferred scenario' used in previous editions, as this phrase is considered to be clearer and more understandable for clients and helpers.

The third stage of the helping process is concerned with enabling the client to identify and implement strategies for action that will result in positive and sustainable outcomes. Here, the helper assists the client in achieving their identified goals, using the skills of creative and divergent thinking, force field analysis and sequential action planning.

Jenkins (2000) provides an example of how the skill of challenging the client's basic assumptions can help to trigger a rapid process of client-led change. The anonymised composite case example is of work with a young man aged 21, who was experiencing a number of interrelated problems affecting his work, career choices, relationships, coping with losses and, more generally, making decisions about where to go with his life. He was owed money by

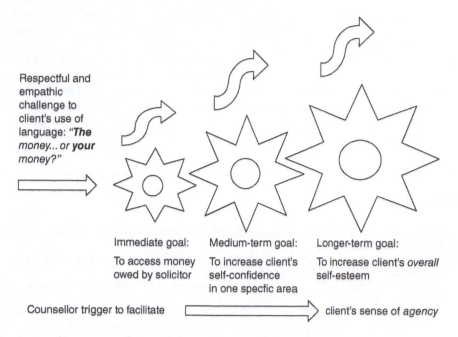

Respectful and empathic challenge to client's use of language: *"The money... or your money?"*

Immediate goal:

To access money owed by solicitor

Medium-term goal:

To increase client's self-confidence in one specfic area

Longer-term goal:

To increase client's *overall* self-esteem

Counsellor trigger to facilitate

client's sense of *agency*

Figure 5.32.1 Potential interaction of counsellor challenge and client realisation of immediate, short-term and longer-term therapeutic goals within the skilled helper model

his solicitor but felt unable to ask for it to be handed over, consistently referring to it simply as '*the* money'. 'I challenged him, fairly gently, and suggested that he look at it as "*his* money", which the solicitor, rightly or wrongly, was keeping back from him. The effect of this reframing was very powerful. He set himself a goal of phoning the solicitor during the next week. Within a matter of weeks, he had received the full amount owing to him, to our shared amazement' (Jenkins, 2000: 176). This challenge helped the client to set and achieve an immediate, realisable goal, which, in turn, catalysed his progress towards achieving other linked, but possibly more daunting, life changes (see Figure 5.32.1).

Although this brief summary is presented in a linear fashion, for ease of understanding, it is important to emphasise that, in skilled hands, the model is rarely applied in this fashion. The truly skilled helper learns to offer the stages of the model in a flexible and fluid manner, where steps frequently overlap and merge into one another, as counsellor and client move back and forth, in the ebb and flow of the helping process.

RESEARCH EVIDENCE

As with any integrative model that is largely mediated by the way the individual therapist adapts and applies it, the

skilled helper model is not accessible to outcome research in the way that a more singular approach might arguably be. The model is not a set of treatment techniques that exists in any useful way independently of the practitioner who uses it. As such, it is not accessible to empirical research in the way that a therapeutic approach with strictly definable techniques that can be replicated using a treatment manual might be. The skilled helper's approach to skills is clearly indebted to the crucial earlier research by Truax and Carkhuff (1967). This signalled a departure from the classical person-centred paradigm in concluding that the core conditions do not account for *all* perceived differences in counsellor effectiveness (Truax and Carkhuff, 1967: 114). Other studies have confirmed the positive impact of more generic problem-solving therapies within primary care (Mynors-Wallis et al., 2000), the crucial role of goal-setting in work with young people (Rupani et al., 2014) and the value of the skilled helper model itself in the training of social work students (Riggall, 2016).

Wosket's (2006) publication on the skilled helper model engages in-depth with the critical debate around the perceived lack of research activity relating to the model. She argues that Egan 'has developed a process for counselling that makes use of sequential patterns in problem management that have been empirically validated by researchers' (Wosket, 2006: 171) and discusses at length research elements underpinning the model. This publication includes a wealth of qualitative data on the client's experience of the model, through a range of clinical case studies that show its application to different contexts and client populations.

While empirical studies into the effectiveness of the model may be limited, the model itself is built on a firm foundation of research into the helping process. Egan is at pains to point out the bedrock of research upon which the various components of the model are founded. So, for instance, he draws extensively on research into cognitive dissonance theory, social learning, motivation and positive psychology, which inform past and current versions of the model. That the skilled helper model continues to be highly influential in the training and supervision of therapists in the UK and beyond (Page and Wosket, 2015; Wosket, 2006) attests to its enduring popularity as a pragmatic and adaptable framework, for both students and established practitioners.

REFERENCES

Egan, G. (2007) *The Skilled Helper: A Problem Management and Opportunity-Development Approach to Helping* (8th ed.). Belmont, CA: Brooks/Cole.

Egan, G. (2014) *The Skilled Helper: A Problem Management and Opportunity-Development Approach to Helping* (10th ed.). Belmont, CA: Brooks/Cole Cengage.

Jenkins, P. (2000) Gerard Egan's skilled helper model. In S. Palmer and R. Woolfe (eds). *Integrative and Eclectic Counselling and Psychotherapy* (pp. 163–180). London: Sage.

Mynors-Wallis, L., Gath, D., Day, A. and Baker, F. (2000) Randomised controlled trial of problem solving treatment, antidepressant medication, and combined treatment for major depression in primary care. *British Medical Journal*, 320(7226): 26–30.

Page, S. and Wosket, V. (2015) *Supervising the Counsellor and Psychotherapist: A Cyclical Model* (3rd ed.). London: Brunner-Routledge.

Riggall, S. (2016) The sustainability of Egan's skilled helper model in students' social work practice. *Journal of Social Work Practice*, 30(1): 81–93.

Rupani, P., Cooper, M., McArthur, C., Pybis, J., Cromarty, K., Hill, A., Levesley, R., Murdoch, J. and Turner, N. (2014) The goals of young people in school-based counselling and their achievement of these goals. *Counselling and Psychotherapy Research*, 14(4): 306–314.

Truax, C. and Carkhuff, R. (1967) *Toward Effective Counseling and Psychotherapy*. New York: Aldine.

Wosket, V. (2006) *Egan's Skilled Helper Model: Developments and Applications in Counselling*. London: Routledge.

RECOMMENDED READING

1. Egan, G. (2006) *Essentials of Skilled Helping: Managing Problems, Developing Opportunities*. Pacific Grove, CA: Brooks/Cole.

This represents Egan's succinct translation of the model for an international audience, emphasising the cross-cultural value of problem-management approaches.

2. Egan, G. (2014) *The Skilled Helper: A Problem Management and Opportunity-Development Approach to Helping* (10th ed.). Belmont, CA: Brooks/Cole Cengage.

This is the latest updating of Egan's classic three-stage model of problem management, acknowledging the key contribution of recent developments in positive psychology.

3. Wosket, V. (2006) *Egan's Skilled Helper Model: Developments and Applications in Counselling*. London: Routledge.

A balanced and incisive overview of Egan's model, making it more accessible and relevant to a UK readership.

TRANSACTIONAL ANALYSIS

CHARLOTTE SILLS AND KEITH TUDOR

OVERVIEW AND KEY POINTS

Transactional analysis (TA) proposes theories of personality, child development and psychopathology, all of which provide the basis for a theory of clinical practice, i.e., psychotherapy and counselling. It also has a theory of communication which may be applied to individuals and systems such as groups and organisations. This chapter offers a brief overview that encompasses:

- a brief history of TA;
- a summary of its basic operating assumptions;
- a brief introduction to its central theory, i.e., transactions, ego states, scripts and rackets and psychological games, as well as its theory of change;
- fundamental TA skills and strategies, illustrated with reference to a brief case study; and
- a brief comment on TA and research.

BRIEF HISTORY

TA was founded by Eric Berne, a Canadian psychiatrist who originally trained as a psychoanalyst. TA has its theoretical roots in the psychoanalytic tradition, although it is also substantially influenced by the cognitive-behavioural approach and social theory, while being philosophically rooted in a humanistic/existential tradition that promotes the power of the individual to take charge of his or her life, to make changes and to live in harmony with him or herself and others. Berne was particularly influenced by Paul Federn, who, from 1941, was his training analyst in New York. Federn's system of ego psychology was seminal in Berne's later development of the ego state theory of personality. In 1947, Berne moved to California and became an analysand of Eric Erikson, from whom he learned about sequential life stages and the importance of social influences in psycho-social development. In the early 1950s Berne was beginning to take a more critical view of psychoanalysis and its conceptualisation of the unconscious, and a break with psychoanalysis came in 1956 when his application for membership of the San Francisco Psychoanalytic Institute was rejected. He established a series of weekly meetings of mental health professionals interested in TA, under the name The San Francisco Social Psychiatry Seminar, which,

in 1960, became an incorporated educational body and, in turn, led to the foundation in 1964 of the International Transactional Analysis Association (ITAA). In 1961 Berne published *Transactional analysis in psychotherapy*, which drew together all his previous writings on TA and still represents a complete view of TA personality, psychotherapy and communication theory. The publication in 1964 of Berne's *Games People Play* marked a blossoming of interest in TA, especially in the USA, as demonstrated by the passage into common usage of TA terms such as 'OK' (as in 'I'm OK, You're OK'), psychological 'games' (mutual transferential processes) and 'strokes' (gestures of recognition).

Since the 1960s, TA has developed its theory, applications and organisation. Since Berne's death, a number of different traditions within TA have emerged (see Tudor and Hobbes, 2007), and it is possible to train for qualification and certification in education and organisational applications as well as counselling and psychotherapy. To date, there are over 10,000 members and TA organisations in over 90 countries, 45 of which have their own national organisation(s). Three international organisations – the International TA Association (ITAA), the European Association for TA (EATA) and the Australasian Federation of TA Associations (FTAA) – co-ordinate international certifying examinations which accredit both practitioners in the four different fields of application and also teachers and supervisors of TA. In Britain, TA has grown from initial seminar groups in the early 1960s through to the first national conference of the (United Kingdom) Institute of Transactional Analysis in 1974 to a flourishing community comprising over 1,000 people in four national TA organisations.

BASIC ASSUMPTIONS

Despite in many ways being relentlessly cynical about human behaviour, Berne nevertheless founded his work on deeply aspirational values:

- People are born with a basic drive for growth and health – in TA terms: 'OKness', which is encapsulated in the phrase 'I'm OK, You're OK', representing mutual respect for self and other and a conviction and faith in human nature to live harmoniously if given the right conditions. In his last book, *What do you say after you say hello* (1975 [1972]), Berne added to the two-person I–You, the third 'They', thereby acknowledging the wider social context of such life positions and pointing to a total life direction or destiny, and, beyond that, planetary OKness (for a summary and discussion of which, see Tudor, 2016).

- Similarly, Berne asserted that there is a creative force in nature which strives for growth and completion. Alongside Freud's instinctual drives – *thanatos* (death instinct) and *eros* (sexual instinct) – Berne proposed that there is a third drive, *physis*, which describes the creative life instinct. In his work and writing, Berne also referred to *vis medicatrix naturae* or the curative power of nature.
- A general goal in life for people is autonomy, a word that has a particular meaning in TA. Berne defined autonomy as the release or recovery of our capacity for awareness, spontaneity and intimacy. In this sense, autonomy is not a selfish, individual goal; it is an outcome that requires relationships with others and, indeed, one that may be viewed as a social goal not only for individuals but also for groups, organisations, communities and societies.
- Everyone has the capacity to think – and, therefore, to take responsibility for their actions.
- People decide their own destiny and, therefore, these decisions can be changed. These decisions may be cognitive and conscious in the ordinary sense of the word; they can also be unconscious, preverbal, bodily or visceral 'decisions'. This assumption is the basis of redecision work in TA.

ORIGIN AND MAINTENANCE OF PROBLEMS

In common with most approaches to psychological therapy, TA recognises that the past influences the present. In TA this process is called *script* or 'life plan', which starts with the interplay between psychobiological hungers (Berne, 1963, 1966) – the needs and desires with which the infant comes into the world – and the experiences of early life. From the first moment, we are shaped by what happens to us, by the experiences and events, and, importantly, the relationships that we see around us and in which we are involved. We internalise these early relationships as *ego states* and we form conclusions (*script decisions*) about ourselves, others and the world. Thus our personality is formed, and becomes the frame of reference or filter through which we interpret our experiences later in our lives. In the present, as we engage with people and events, we respond with internal experience (thoughts, feelings, embodied adaptations, relational expectations, and so on) and then behaviour (*transactions*, *games*), all of which arise from our frame of reference and also reinforce it by

bringing about repeating outcomes and patterns of relating. Some of these learned ways of being can be fluid, adaptable and effective, simply providing containment and sufficient structure as we engage responsively with our environment. Some, however, are fixed and limiting. Whether as a result of trauma or lack of environmental support, script beliefs and adaptations become the only way we know of getting our needs met enough to survive; early relational patterns, the only way we know of being in relationship.

TA has a wealth of concepts to help people understand the process by which all this happens and how they have become who they are. Here, we introduce just a few of them.

THE STRUCTURE OF THE PERSONALITY

An ego state is 'the subjectively experienced reality of a person's mental and bodily ego with the original contents of the time period it represents' (Clarkson, Gilbert and Tudor, 1996: 222). Drawing on the work of Federn, Weiss and Glover, Berne identified three types of ego state: Parent, Adult and Child (see Figure 5.33.1).

The Parent and Child ego states are archaic in that they represent past influences:

> the Parent ego state is a set of feelings, attitudes, and behavior patterns which resemble those of a parental figure. … The Child ego state is a set of feelings, attitudes and behavior patterns which are relics of the individual's own childhood. (Berne, 1975 [1961]: 75–77)

By contrast, the Adult ego state is characterised by autonomous, here-and-now feelings, attitudes and behaviours. There have been and are lively debates within TA about the nature of ego states, for further discussions of which, see Sills and Hargaden (2003) and Tudor (2010).

Ego states are ascertained or diagnosed in four ways:

1. Behavioural – based on observable words, voice tones, gestures, expressions, etc.
2. Social – i.e., the reactions the subject elicits from other people.
3. Historical – knowing that the experience can be traced to a past which did actually occur.
4. Phenomenological – based on subjective self-experience.

All four diagnoses are necessary for a sufficient identification of an ego state, and Berne emphasised the need for *both* observable and phenomenological verification of intuitive diagnosis – thus requiring the collaboration of both therapist and client.

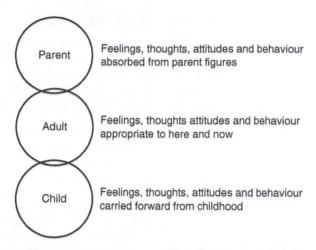

Feelings, thoughts, attitudes and behaviour
absorbed from parent figures

Feelings, thoughts attitudes and behaviour
appropriate to here and now

Feelings, thoughts, attitudes and behaviour
carried forward from childhood

Figure 5.33.1 Structural diagram of a personality

Figure from TRANSACTIONAL ANALYSIS IN PSYCHOTHERAPY by Eric Berne, MD, copyright © 1975 by Eric Berne. Used by permission of Ballantine Books, an imprint of Random House, a division of Penguin Random House LLC

PSYCHOPATHOLOGY

This involves the exclusion or 'contamination' (unaware influence) of ego states, or symbiosis i.e., when two (or more) individuals develop a co-dependent relationship based on script decisions.

HERE-AND-NOW MANIFESTATIONS OF SCRIPT

INTERNAL EXPERIENCE. TA has a number of concepts that describe the process of viewing the world through a scripted frame of reference, including '*discounting*' (ignoring or minimising) some aspects of ourselves, others or the situation, while exaggerating others, and re-experiencing familiar *racket* feelings that accompany equally familiar thoughts and conclusions about self and life.

EXTERNAL MANIFESTATIONS OF SCRIPT. Berne gave the name '*transaction*' to an interaction or relational interchange. All communication can be analysed in terms of transactions between ego states. This helps to understand how human beings engage with each other, both in achieving real contact and intimacy, but also in repeating limited patterns of relating (games). In analysing such transactions, Berne (1966) identified three 'rules' of communication:

1. When we communicate or transact from complementary ego states, i.e., between Parent and Parent, Adult and Adult, Child and Child, and Parent and Child, communication can continue indefinitely. As Berne (1966: 223) put it: 'as long as the vectors are parallel, communication can proceed indefinitely'.

2. A break in communication is described as a crossed transaction. When a transaction is crossed – in other words, the ego state that responds to a communication is not the one that was addressed – there is a break in communication and one or both individuals will need to shift ego states in order to re-establish a connection. Crossed transactions can be problematic; they can also be therapeutic, for example, when a therapist or a client 'crosses' an unhelpful, repetitive communication.

3. 'The behavioural outcome of an ulterior transaction is determined at the psychological and not at the social level' (Berne, 1966: 227). This is based on the idea that non-verbal or 'ulterior', psychological communications have more effect than social-level communications. Berne's understanding of an ulterior transaction was that it is likely to be driven by script. Novellino (2003) identified a fourth rule or type of communication by which an unconscious message is transmitted from Adult to Adult (for example, from client to therapist), not as a script enactment but in order to communicate an important but unconscious experience.

Game is the name Berne gave to describe those repeating patterns of interaction with others in which script beliefs are enacted relationally and lead to a 'pay-off' or reinforcement of the script, normally for both or all people involved. The word 'game' is not intended to imply pleasure or fun – on the contrary, games are the most painful ways we relate to others, leading to an unconscious mutual confirmation of our scripts. In classical TA, practitioners sought to avoid games with their clients, using clear contracts and constant vigilance. They challenged clients about their patterns and invited here-and-now self-responsibility. Nowadays, relational transactional analysts recognise that sometimes it is only through our games that unconscious processes are revealed (Stuthridge and Sills, 2015). They – we – therefore welcome games in the consulting room as being the source of important understanding and learning for the client.

THEORY OF CHANGE

Berne, a medical doctor, defined change in terms of 'cure', which he viewed as a progressive process involving four stages:

1. Social control – i.e., the control of dysfunctional social behaviours.
2. Symptomatic relief – the personal relief of subjectively experienced symptoms.
3. Transference cure – when the client can stay out of their script, as long as the therapist is around, either literally or 'in their head'.
4. Script cure – by which the person's own Adult ego state takes over the previous role of the therapist and the person makes autonomous decisions.

In recent years, while the understanding of change, cure and, indeed, health and learning, is generally considered in the context of cultural and social attitudes, pressures and circumstances, and much more in the context of a mutually influencing relationship, the conceptualisation of a progression from behavioural change through to characterological transformation and liberation is, nevertheless, still useful.

SKILLS AND STRATEGIES

TA originally took a unilateral, actionistic approach to change and 'treatment', focusing largely on material that was amenable to conscious cognitive awareness. Based on the contractual method and their diagnosis of the client, TA practitioners negotiated, defined and followed a mutually agreed treatment plan. The role of the therapist was to closely observe the client's here-and-now words, gestures, facial expressions as well as content, and aimed to help the client to see how their script was playing out in the present. Berne (1966) offered a precise sequence of 'operations', starting with inquiring into the situation, then raising awareness (strengthening, the Adult ego state) of script beliefs and patterns, and, finally, interpreting deeper unconscious processes.

Later developments have reflected changes in the wider field of psychotherapy. These include narrative or constructivist approaches that take account of new understandings in relation to memory and meaning-making. They also include psychoanalytic TA (Moiso and Novellino, 2000), and relational TA (Hargaden and Sills, 2002), which examines the 'deconfusion' of the Child by elaborating Berne's therapeutic 'operations' as 'empathic transactions'. In relational therapy, the relationship between therapist and client is the vehicle in which the client can express both his self-experience and patterns of relating, including sometimes deeply unconscious or unsymbolised processes, which often emerge as games (Stuthridge and Sills, 2015). Summers and Tudor (2000) describe co-creative TA, a present-centred theory of expanding Adult (see also Tudor, 2003; Tudor and Summers, 2014); and the 'relational turn' in psychotherapy in general is reflected and well articulated in TA in these and other publications (see Cornell and Hargaden, 2005; Fowlie and Sills 2011) and in the development of an International Association for Relational TA (see www.relationalta.com).

CASE EXAMPLE

In practice, James was one of those clients that therapists usually dread! As he explained on the phone, he was being 'sent' by his wife, who had told him that if he 'didn't get his act together' she would leave him. As I (Charlotte) waited for him to arrive for his first appointment, I expected to meet a good deal of ambivalence in a man who had come to therapy under threat. However, I was interested that he appeared meekly and enthusiastically committed to his development – smiling appreciatively at me, nodding his agreement and managing to curl his two-metre height so that he could still look up at/to me. I provisionally 'diagnosed' a Child ego state (some time later, he agreed to this assessment) and I took care to meet him with a blend of complementary transactions (to establish an empathic connection) and crossed ones (to establish empathic understanding) as, together, we made sense of the situation.

James's wife suffered from anxiety, which was made tolerable if she could feel fully in charge of things. James sympathised with his wife, whom he loved very much, and did his best to make their life predictable together. However, he was a man of thoughts and dreams rather than action, and he often made small mistakes – from forgetting to buy the sausages on his way home to forgetting that they had agreed to have supper with friends. These mistakes were greeted with enraged fury by his wife, who, it appeared, covered her anxiety with a rigid and punishing Parent ego state. The pair were playing a painful game by which she confirmed that the world was unsafe and she could not rely on anyone, and he confirmed that no matter how hard he tried, he could never be good enough. His most recent mistake was forgetting to do his taxes and finding unexpectedly that he had a large tax bill to pay. This had caused his precipitation into therapy.

We analysed the relational pattern and James began to experiment with having more Adult conversations with his wife, making clear agreements with her about what he would do and when. Things improved, but weren't transformed: when he reported their interaction, it sounded as if the agreements they made still represented a Child–Parent dynamic.

After a while, I began to notice that James had developed the habit of arriving five minutes late and apologising. Also he twice forgot his cheque book and couldn't pay. I felt annoyed and talked with him about the importance of boundaries – but there was an uncomfortable feeling in my stomach. It felt familiar to me, to be trying to get someone to do something (my son probably), and I also heard in my words the voice my own mother had used whenever *I* was forgetful.

I took a different tack and began to explore what might be going on between us. I wondered aloud whether I had become another demanding woman in his life, and how that felt. Gradually James began to access the deeper levels of rage, fear and guilt that had their origins in his childhood with a demanding mother who had died when he was seven. As his feelings emerged – to be received, accepted and named between us – something loosened for him in his relationship with his wife. Slowly he started to build a different sort of connection with her in which both their vulnerabilities and their Adult(s) had a place.

RESEARCH EVIDENCE

Berne (1966) argued that research and therapy must be clearly separated, to the extent that a research group should be designated as such and any therapeutic results regarded as secondary. He also discussed issues of motivation and possible psychological games involved in research, as well as the effect of the presence of the investigator. Nevertheless, Berne himself pre-figured the more recent concept of the reflective practitioner who is more aware of research. Berne's own writing, as well as that of other TA practitioners, reflects a broad concern in the TA community to observe the external manifestations of internal, phenomenological realities and to operationalise the conclusions.

It follows that most TA concepts are amenable to research: the life script through questionnaires; functional modes of ego states through the egogram; passivity and discounting through the discount matrix; the stroke economy through the stroking profile, etc. (for an explanation of these and other TA concepts, see Lapworth and Sills, 2011; Stewart and Joines, 1987). In the last 20 years, research articles have appeared in the *Transactional Analysis Journal* (*TAJ*) and the *EATA News* on, for example, self-esteem in a self-reparenting programme, the impact of TA in enhancing adjustment in college students, ego states, the effects of TA psychotherapy on self-esteem and quality of life, stress among high school students, egograms, functional fluency (using the functional modes of ego states) and the use of TA in treatment centres for addiction and others. Relational TA has been the spring-board for some qualitative action research (van Rijn et al., 2008). In 2010, EATA launched the *International Journal of Transactional Analysis Research* (*IJTAR*), an article in the first issue of which provided a reference list of TA research published in TA journals since the 1960s (Ohlsson, 2010a, 2010b). To date, *IJTAR* has published some 44 articles and this year, a special issue of the *TAJ* will be devoted to research.

REFERENCES

Berne, E. (1963*). The Structure and Dynamics of Organizations and Groups*. New York: Grove Press.
Berne, E. (1964). *Games People Play*. New York: Grove Press.
Berne, E. (1966). *Principles of group treatment*. New York: Grove Press.

(Continued)

(Continued)

Berne, E. (1975 [1961]). *Transactional analysis in psychotherapy*. London: Souvenir Press.

Berne, E. (1975 [1972]). *What do you say after you say hello?* London: Corgi.

Clarkson, P., Gilbert, M. and Tudor, K. (1996). Transactional analysis. In W. Dryden (Ed.), *Handbook of individual therapy* (pp. 219–253). London: Sage.

Cornell, B. and Hargaden, H. (Eds.) (2005). *From transactions to relations: The emergence of a relational tradition in transactional analysis*. Chadlington, UK: Haddon Press.

Fowlie, H. and Sills, C. (2011) *Relational Transactional Analysis: Principles in Practice*. London: Karnac.

Hargaden, H. and Sills, C. (2002). *Transactional analysis: A relational perspective*. London: Brunner-Routledge.

Lapworth, P. and Sills, S. (2011). *An introduction to transactional analysis* (rev. ed.) London: Sage.

Moiso, C. and Novellino, M. (2000). An overview of the psychodynamic school of transactional analysis and its epistemological foundations. *Transactional Analysis Journal, 30*(3), 182–191.

Novellino, M. (2003). On closer analysis: A psychodynamic revision of the rules of communication within the framework of transactional analysis. In C. Sills and H. Hargaden (Eds.), *Ego states* (pp. 149–168). London: Worth Publishing.

Ohlsson, T. (2010a). Scientific evidence base for transactional analysis in the year 2010 Annex 1 – The big list: References to transactional analysis research 1963–2010. *International Journal of Transactional Analysis Research, 1*(1), 12–23.

Ohlsson, T. (2010b). Scientific evidence base for transactional analysis in the year 2010 Annex 2 – The psychotherapy list: References to research on transactional analysis psychotherapy effects 1963–2010. *International Journal of Transactional Analysis Research, 1*(1), 24–29.

Sills, C. and Hargaden, H. (Eds.) (2003). *Ego states*. London: Worth Publishing.

Summers, G. and Tudor, K. (2000). Cocreative transactional analysis. *Transactional Analysis Journal, 30*(1), 23–40.

Stewart, I. and Joines, V. (1987). *TA today*. Nottingham, UK: Lifespace.

Stuthridge, J. and Sills, C. (2015). Psychological games and intersubjective processes. In R. Erskine (Ed.), *Transactional analysis in contemporary psychotherapy* (pp. 185–208). London: Karnac.

Tudor, K. (2003). The neopsyche: The integrating Adult ego state. In C. Sills and H. Hargaden (Eds.), *Ego states* (pp. 201–231). London: Worth Publishing.

Tudor, K. (2010). The state of the ego: Then and now. *Transactional Analysis Journal, 40*(3&4), 261–277.

Tudor, K. (2016). 'We are': The fundamental life position. *Transactional Analysis Journal, 46*(2), 164–176.

Tudor, K. and Hobbes, R. (2007). Transactional analysis. In W. Dryden (Ed.), *The handbook of individual therapy* (5th ed., pp. 256–286). London: Sage.

Tudor, K. and Summers, G. (2014) *Co-creative Transactional Analysis*. London: Karnac

van Rijn, B., Sills, C., Hunt, J., Shivanath, S., Gildebrand, K. and Fowlie, H. (2008). Developing clinical effectiveness in psychotherapy training: action research. *Counselling and Psychotherapy Research, 8*(4), 261–268.

RECOMMENDED READING

1. Berne, E. (1975 [1972]). *What do you say after you say hello?* London: Corgi.

Berne's last book and by far the most readable of his nine books. In it he brings together his development of TA over some 20 years, together with his interest in cross-cultural psychology, and uses independent (Martian) thinking and fairy tales to illustrate 'the psychology of human destiny' from the cradle to the grave.

2. Widdowson, M. (2009). *100 key points and techniques*. London: Routledge.

Informed by contemporary, relational thinking about psychology and psychotherapy in general, this is a very useful book on TA theory and techniques, which both informs the reader and invites them to reflect on their practice. It is written in a very direct and engaging way.

3. Lapworth, P. and Sills, S. (2011). *An introduction to transactional analysis* (rev. ed.) London: Sage.

Drawing on the best of traditional TA theory and revitalising some TA theory that is not always presented in an introductory book, this revised edition presents a contemporary and vibrant TA, with many practical and useful examples aimed at enhancing the development of relational skills and relational thinking.

THEORY AND APPROACHES: ALTERNATIVE APPROACHES TO COUNSELLING AND PSYCHOTHERAPY

PSYCHOPHARMACOLOGY

DIGBY TANTAM

OVERVIEW AND KEY POINTS

This chapter focuses upon psychopharmacology and its relationship to counselling and psychotherapy. Key points include:

- Psychopharmacology is an enormous industry as well as a major research area.
- Drugs and psychotherapy both have a substantial placebo effect.
- The use of one may interfere with the use of the other but they may also supplement each other. Therapists may therefore underestimate the value of combined drug therapy, and may even be prejudiced against it for reasons that I give in this chapter.
- Therapists should be aware both of the value of drugs and also of their side effects on those occasions when these may interfere with therapy.

MEDICATION, DRUG TREATMENT, PEPTIDES, TRANSMITTERS, OXYTOCIN, PLACEBO

Psychopharmacology is the generic term for the study and use of drugs to alter brain functioning with the aim of changing mental function. This definition includes the study and use of recreational drugs; of mind or pleasure enhancers that are supposed to improve on normal functioning; of drugs that are intended to complement other medical or psychological treatments, including drugs designed to enhance the efficacy of psychotherapy; of drugs that are intended to treat physical disorders, but have incidental or occasional effects on the mind; of drugs that are intended to restore people to normal functioning; and of drugs that counteract the effects of other drugs. I shall give at least one example from each of these classes, but will give most examples from the latter classes since these include the prescribed drugs and therefore the drugs or medication that psychotherapists will most often encounter in their clients.

I shall concentrate on the impact of drugs on the experience of being a client in therapy. However, taking medication may also affect the therapist and so questions may sometimes arise about the ethics of taking a particular drug at all or in a particular dose while performing therapy.

A considerable amount of information about drugs is available on the internet, much of it published by reputable bodies for the benefit of practitioners or patients. Careful research may provide reliable information even if no access can be gained to the carefully edited information available to professionals, for example that provided in the online version of the *British National Formulary*. I shall not therefore write in detail about any particular drug, but try to address some of the more general issues that might arise when drug use or abuse are combined with psychotherapy and to consider some of the principles that underlie prescribing decisions.

IS PSYCHOPHARMACOLOGY EVER JUSTIFIED?

Radical criticisms of the use of drugs in psychiatry have often been made, sometimes extending to complete opposition to the use of drugs at all. These views are often endorsed by the public who, in surveys, regularly prefer talking treatments to drug treatments in psychological disorders.

One kind of argument is a theological one: man is created in God's image, and is therefore already perfect in form. To believe that one can improve upon God's perfection by the use of drugs is a kind of heresy. Many people would endorse this argument when it comes to cognitive or other enhancements, for example the use of stimulants to help people to study or of amyl nitrate to increase sexual pleasure. However, although some would argue that illness is also part of God's design for the world, and should not be tampered with, it is difficult to argue that illness is a kind of perfection. In fact, most people would probably accept that wounds or diseases render a person imperfect and that treatment of them is in pursuit of God's purposes. My intuition is that most people would say that treatment of, say, a child with pneumonia with an antibiotic is also in line with God's purpose or, to put it in humanistic terms, enables the child to have their true destiny or to reach their full potential. But some people might argue that this does not apply to a condition that is 'purely' mental, such as a person who is stricken with grief.

Some psychiatric disorders do approximate to the disease model: the inexorable course of schizophrenia in some people is one example; another is the onset of self-destructive episodes of mania or of profound depression in some people with bipolar disorder. Although psychotherapists may contribute to the amelioration of these conditions, their primary treatment is usually medical. This may be considered inappropriate by a few critics of psychopharmacology, but the strongest criticism is reserved for psychopharmacology in anxiety-related disorders or unipolar depression (i.e., depression not associated with a past history of being high or 'hypomanic').

Objections to the use of medication in these conditions are made not just on the ethical or religious grounds mentioned, but on moral and practical grounds too.

DOES TAKING DRUGS PREVENT PEOPLE FROM OVERCOMING THEIR OWN PROBLEMS?

The moral objections to psychopharmacology often rest on the concept of agency or responsibility. At the height of the use of benzodiazepines by doctors during the 1980s in the UK, one of the feminist arguments against their use was that women who were distressed by adverse home circumstances – an abusive husband, for example – were sedated by their doctors and so lost the will to try to rectify the situation. Use of antidepressants or anxiolytics may be seen to be a voluntary abrogation of the responsibility to change one's life, or a denial of the power or agency to do so, because taking medication is to frame the problem as a kind of disease in oneself. Not only that, but taking tranquillizers quells or suppresses the negative emotions that might power a change.

Related to this is the perception by some psychotherapists that taking medication might be a kind of escape from the work of self-reflection and therefore from being honest about oneself and one's situation. This may be linked to the common idea that counselling and psychotherapy are undermined by combining them with psychoactive medication. I consider this later.

People who have regularly taken medication for emotional problems do seem more likely to think of medication as their first-line strategy when new problems emerge. So it seems likely that the use of psychoactive drugs does alter a person's preferred choice of coping strategy. But whether this makes them, in the long run, less resilient in the face of future adversity, as many psychotherapists might argue, cannot be assumed; I shall consider the evidence in a later section.

ARE PSYCHOACTIVE DRUGS A KIND OF PSYCHOTHERAPY?

Comparisons of the response to drugs and to psychotherapy in people with unipolar depression or anxiety disorders suggest that the outcomes are much more similar than might be expected (Tyrer et al., 1988). The most likely explanation is

that both act through a process of what Jerome Frank (1961) memorably called 'remoralization'. When medicine was more paternalistic, doctors would sometimes capitalize on this by giving their patients sugar-coated pills that were psychopharmacologically inert. To conceal this from their patients, they would term these pills 'placebos' (from the Latin placebo, 'I will please') and the pharmacist would have a stock of these inert pills to dispense. The placebo effect remains an important hidden element in psychiatry. A recent reanalysis of the effects of antidepressants that included unpublished as well as published studies demonstrated, for example, that the outcome of antidepressants and the outcome of placebo was no different in people with mild or moderate depression, even though the published studies suggested otherwise (Kirsch et al., 2008).

The passage of time might account for some of the placebo effects: sharp dips in mood or rises in anxiety may just remit given change in the circumstances that caused the dip in the first place. But in many studies, outcome is compared to being on a waiting list and the outcome of the treated group is normally better than that of the waiting list group, indicating that the placebo effect is a real treatment effect.

Frank argued that the placebo effect accounted for the therapeutic effect of psychotherapy as well as of drugs. There has been continual interest in how it is produced, and what factors increase or decrease it. It is plausibly assumed that believers in drugs benefit more from drug placebos and believers in therapy more from talking treatments: however, there is some evidence against this (Chilvers et al., 2001).

COST–BENEFIT ANALYSIS

Drugs cost money, sometimes a lot of money. New drugs cost more than old ones, often because old ones can be made in factories by companies who just make drugs rather than go to the additional expense of developing them. These generic drugs are the pharmacological equivalent of the eclectic or non-branded therapies, provided by psychotherapists who have not gone to the expense of acquiring the licence to provide an acronymic treatment like Cognitive-Behavioural Therapy (CBT). Money is not the only cost. Psychotherapy and counselling have time costs. It has been argued that they may cost more than that. Fay Weldon argued in her novel *Affliction* (1993) that they may cost relationships, too. (*Affliction* was written after Weldon broke up with her second husband Ron Weldon, who, according to Wikipedia, left her after being told by an 'astrotherapist' that their star signs were incompatible.)

These costs have to be set against benefits. Benefits, too, may be varied: there may be offset effects in a reduction of the need for other treatment, a decrease in disability leading to increased income, and, of course, a reduction of symptoms. In order to compare symptoms one with another, they are often recast as increments of quality of life.

As placebos are inert, it is sometimes assumed that they have no costs, but this is not so. There may be travel costs, time off work costs, the reduced quality of life for people who get worse with placebos (the 'nocebo' effect), the costs of delaying more active treatment, and, most importantly, the costs of reducing resilience if, indeed, treatment may do that.

SHOULD PSYCHOTHERAPISTS KNOW ABOUT DRUGS?

A little knowledge is a dangerous thing, so people say. So is it better for psychotherapists to have no knowledge at all about drugs? The answer to this partly depends on the practice of the psychotherapist or counsellor. Working in private practice will often mean working with a clientele who is rarely taking psychoactive drugs; working in a general practice, the opposite. Working in a school or college setting may often mean working with students who are using street drugs, and working in a substance misuse clinic will almost always mean this.

I would argue that any therapist or counsellor who is likely to work with people taking psychoactive drugs needs to know about them. My primary reason is that I think of counselling or therapy as a kind of primary care, and not as a specialized add-on to other health services. So a counsellor's role will include recognizing possible side effects of medication and recommending to a client that they have these investigated. It will also include evaluating if the use of a psychoactive drug is adversely affecting counselling and, more rarely but no less importantly, if a client might benefit from psychotherapy.

The justification that I have just given for knowing about drugs focuses more on knowing the costs of psychoactive drugs and less on the benefits. This is the inverse of psychopharmacology training for doctors and, rather unusually, I will therefore consider drugs according to the categories of their side effects rather than the customary classification of drugs by the expected benefits – antidepressants, anxiolytics, and so on. Fortunately this side-effect classification is actually simpler than a classification according to main effects. The reason for this is that most of the drugs currently used in psychiatry are presumed to act by either augmenting or competing with naturally occurring chemicals – transmitters – that mediate electrical transmission in brain, spinal cord, and smooth muscle.

WHEN ARE DRUGS INDICATED?

There is strong evidence that severe depression, mania, psychosis and attention deficit disorder improve with drug treatment. Panic disorder and obsessive compulsive disorder may also respond. The first three are disorders that I have previously, mentioned are most 'disease-like' in the minds of many people. Treatability is not in itself an indication that drugs should always be used in these conditions. Depression, for example, spontaneously remits in as many as 85 per cent of people. However, this eventual recovery may take years, and without treatment it is associated with an increased mortality. This is also true of schizophrenia and even attention deficit hyperactivity disorder (ADHD).

Mortality is not the only indication that doctors give for treatment. Increasing quality of life (that is, reducing dysphoria and/or reducing disability) is also often given as an indication by doctors but is one that has more opponents. One argument is that dysphoria may be the driver for personal initiatives that might lead to a resolution of the condition and not just an amelioration. One such initiative is psychotherapy or counselling. So some psychotherapists believe that psychotherapy is less likely to be successful if people are taking prescribed psychoactive drugs for this reason. Another contra-indication to medication sometimes given by psychotherapists or counsellors is that psychoactive drugs may affect thinking and feeling and so interfere with the process of therapy.

Psychotherapists do not have to prescribe drugs and are not in a position to either recommend or counsel against their use. What they do need to know, though, are the side effects of medication, particularly as these may affect the therapy or counselling itself.

BALANCING OPTIMISM AND SCEPTICISM

Most of the psychoactive drugs have been around a surprisingly long time. Brand new types of drug have proved surprisingly hard to find, and are very expensive to develop. Not surprisingly, drug companies make considerable claims when they do launch them. They want to recoup their costs. When a drug does become a hit, the rewards are enormous. So there is a temptation to make over-inflated claims that, in the end, just feed scepticism about the drug industry. Sometimes the claims are based on some preliminary science. Agomelatine was a new antidepressant that was supposed to have a novel action, targeting the receptor for melatonin, a peptide that is involved in sleep induction. The marketers cleverly made the name very like melatonin. Unfortunately, it turns out to have no different effect on sleep than other antidepressants. It is now being re-launched as a treatment for anxiety. Obtaining a licence for a drug to be used in a specific condition is another way of marketing. One drug that is promoted for, say, obsessional disorder, may be identical in its action to another drug that is promoted for depression. The drugs are not different in action, only in their chosen market.

It seems very likely that all medication, whether over the counter (the biggest market by far) or prescribed, is over-used but it would be unwise to dismiss every use as without any effect other than placebo. There is a case for us all to know the use of drugs better and to avoid using them or asking for them unless there is a clear reason to believe that they are necessary. This applies to antibiotics just as much as to antidepressants.

TYPES OF PSYCHOPHARMACOLOGICAL TREATMENTS

The types of psychopharmacological treatment are shown in Table 5.34.1. The psychopharmacology of the common psychiatric disorders and their 'normalization' is dominated by the pharmacology of a limited number of types of drugs acting on an even more limited number of transmitters (see Table 5.34.2). Many new drugs turn out to be variants of old ones (see Table 5.34.3).

Table 5.34.1 Types of psychopharmacological treatment

Enhancers	These drugs aim to increase function above normal. They include stimulants like caffeine and khat, and disinhibitors like ethanol. They also include nitric oxide sexual stimulants like Viagra and amyl nitrite (both potentiators of nitric oxide), amphetamines and cocaine (for reduced fatigue and greater focused attention), *proper name* Ecstasy for better clubbing, and anticholinesterase inhibitors for enhanced memory.
Normalizers	This class of drugs overlaps with the previous one but is justified on the basis that they do not increase function but 'correct' dysfunction. They include anticholinesterases that reduce the early effects of Alzheimer-type dementia; dopamine precursors that reduce the early symptoms of Parkinson's disease, including those of early dementia; dopamine blockers that reduce some of the symptoms of schizophrenia; drugs that increase frontal lobe function in ADHD by combining an enhancement of both dopamine and serotonin function; and drugs that reduce low mood in depression by enhancing catecholamine and serotonin function. There are also peptide drugs that may prove of value in the future, including opiates that some think may reduce the likelihood of repeated self-injury through stimulating endorphin transmission, and a possible class of future drugs for attachment disorders that will work through oxytocin or vasopressin transmission.
Treatments	Most psychological disorders are 'endogenous' *questionable*. Those that are not are most often the result of psychosocial adversity for which there is no drug treatment. The number of psychological disorders that are caused by a remediable cause are few, and many of those are the consequences of drug treatments (iatrogenic disorders) or of drug misuse rather than caused by some external, physical agent that can be counteracted by medication. Some inflammations of the brain may present as mental disorders, and so treatment of, for example, cerebral malaria presenting as psychosis constitutes a treatment of a mental disorder. Gene therapies or drugs that can directly affect neuronal growth or connectivity may provide treatments in the future.

Table 5.34.2 'Normalizers' by condition

Condition	Supposed cause	Treatment
Alzheimer's disease (the most common cause of dementia) and other dementias	Destruction of nerve cells, selectively affecting nerves that release acetylcholine (cholinergic neurons). The accumulation of a waste protein ('amyloid') may be one of the neurotoxic agents.	Drugs that block the enzymes (cholinesterases) that break down acetylcholine, and so increase acetylcholine release. Antibodies that target the waste protein.
Depression	Reduced catecholamine release (release of norepinephrine particularly) and reduced serotonin release.	Drugs that enhance norepinephrine, serotonin, or both.

(Continued)

Table 5.34.2 (Continued)

Condition	Supposed cause	Treatment
Schizophrenia	Over-production of dopamine in the cerebral cortex relative to an under-production of other transmitters such as glutamate or HDMA.	Drugs with complex effects on transmitters but commonly block dopamine and enhance acetylcholine.
Anxiety	Complex and probably depend on type of anxiety.	Drugs that enhance gamma-aminobutyric acid (GABA) transmission.
		Drugs that enhance serotonin transmission.
		Drugs that block histamine receptors, e.g., several of the antipsychotics.
		Drugs that block specific symptoms such as drugs for sleep, or drugs for tremor, by blocking the effects of epinephrine and norepinephrine.
Attention deficit hyperactivity disorder	ADHD presents with symptoms that vary from person to person and may change with age but many if not all of the primary symptoms involve impulsivity, overactivity, impersistence, working memory impairment, and dysexecutive syndrome, along with impaired interpretation of facial expression.	Like other neurodevelopmental conditions, ADHD is associated with reduced connectivity between frontal and afferent areas. One long-standing idea is that reward systems originating in the nucleus accumbens are particularly involved, and dopaminergic drugs are effective for some ADHD symptoms. There is a link with anxiety and the serotinergic system, too, and many of the effective drugs enhance both dopamine and serotonic: the paradigm of these is amphetamine.

Table 5.34.3 Transmitters, drugs affecting them, their mode of action on the transmitter, and side effects particularly relevant to participation in psychotherapy*

Transmitter	Enhance (+) or counteract (-)	Common drugs affecting this transmitter	Side effects with particular impact on therapy (NB Do not occur in everyone taking the medication or may be very mild)	Other selected side effects that may be problematic in some users and are often dose related
Dopamine (D$_2$ receptor)	+	Drugs for Parkinson's disease, e.g., L-dopa Drugs for ADHD, e.g., amphetamine, methylphenidate		Increased gambling, increased libido, addiction to the drug itself, psychosis
	-	Antipsychotics, especially high-potency antipsychotics	Lack of reward-seeking, reduced task-driven behaviour, with a reduction of thoughts and 'blunting' of feelings, inner restlessness, sedation	Stiffness, tremor, other symptoms similar to Parkinson's disease; milk production in some people 'Metabolic syndrome' esp. with olanzepine: increased appetite, weight gain, cardiovascular disease, type 2 diabetes
Serotonin (5-HT$_{2c}$ receptor)	+	Some antidepressants and anxiolytics, e.g., selective serotonin reuptake inhibitors (SSRIs), some antipsychotics	Possible impulsivity, dominant behaviour	'Toxic confusion' may lead to death in rare cases

Transmitter	Enhance (+) or counteract (-)	Common drugs affecting this transmitter	Side effects with particular impact on therapy (NB Do not occur in everyone taking the medication or may be very mild)	Other selected side effects that may be problematic in some users and are often dose related
	-	Lipid lowering drugs, e.g., statins, diet	Panic attacks in predisposed individuals with sensitivity to suffocation, low mood (Miller et al., 2000)	Cravings
Catecholamines (epinephrine and norepinephrine)	+	Serotonin and norepinephrine reuptake inhibitors (SNRIs), e.g., venlafaxine, duloxetine, sympathomimetic drugs such as some first-generation tricyclic antidepressants, e.g., amitryptiline	Sometimes conflicting effects, depending on whether alpha or beta receptors blocked more, but may be agitation, anxiety, rapid heart, irritability	Conflicting effects but blood pressure may be raised along with other physical symptoms associated with stress
	-	Some atypical antipsychotics, e.g., quetiapine, clozapine, sertindole, zotepine, some antidepressants, e.g., mianserin, mirtazepine	Sedation	Conflicting effects but may include weight gain, rapid heart rate, dizziness on standing
Acetylcholine (muscarinic receptor)	Agonist	Anticholinesterase inhibitors for dementia		Diarrhoea and vomiting
	Antagonist	A very large number of commonly prescribed drugs, including the low-potency antipsychotics (usually dose over 50 mg per day), e.g., chlorpromazine, clozapine, loxepine, quetiapine, and some tricyclics, e.g., amitriptyline	Sedation	Constipation, dry mouth, blurred vision, difficulty in passing water, eyes more sensitive to light, increase in heart problems, possible increase in cognitive decline, and possibly increased risk of Alzheimer's disease in elderly, risk of death in overdose
Glutamate (NMDA receptor)	+			Linked to cell death
	-	Drugs to alter conscious level, e.g., methadone (also an opiate), alcohol, phencyclidine, ketamine Drugs for Parkinsonism, e.g., amantadine	Disinhibition, reduced ability to store current events in memory, dissociation, psychotic symptoms	
GABA (A receptor)	Agonist	Antiepileptic drugs, benzodiazepines, barbiturates	Impaired memory of current events, sedation (Czubak et al., 2010). Dependence	

*This is not a complete list of the side effects of each medication mentioned. This can be found on guides to drugs such as the British National Formulary or on the drug packaging.

NEW DIRECTIONS

There was a hope that targeting a particular transmitter would have a specific effect. This would provide the kind of 'magic bullet' that used to be dreamt about when antibiotics were introduced against specific infective agents: getting rid of a disease agent while causing no perturbation to the organism. It remains true that dopamine D2 receptors are over-active in psychoses, and that catecholamine receptors are implicated in mood disorders. So they could be down- or upregulated, respectively, without anything else being affected. But receptors for dopamine, serotonin, and norepinephrine occur throughout the brain. Selective targeting is just not possible. Anyway, selective targeting may produce its own problems. Methylenedioxy-methamphetamine (MDMA or 'Ecstasy') is a potent agonist for dopaminergic as well as serotoninergic neurons but may in chronic and high dose use result in irreversible damage to these neurons, causing Parkinson's disease.

Peptides were hoped to be the answer. It was thought that they would be much more closely linked to specific behavioural symptoms. They have one big drawback. They are broken down in the gut. So they have to be administered as a nasal spray. One peptide, oxytocin, has caught the popular imagination. Sometimes known as the 'love hormone', it is said to increase attachment to other people and has been suggested as a possible treatment for anxiety or as an enhancer of the therapist–patient relationship (MacDonald and Feifel, 2014). As the reader will by now expect, it is much more complicated than that. It looks likely that oxytocin does increase empathy but only to people who are in one's 'in group'. It may actually increase hostility towards out-group members. So it might worsen the effects of any ethnic, gender or other mismatch between therapist and client.

REFERENCES

Chilvers, C., Dewey, M., Fielding, K., Gretton, V., Miller, P., Palmer, B., et al. (2001) Antidepressant drugs and generic counselling for treatment of major depression in primary care: randomised trial with patient preference arms. *British Medical Journal*, 322(7289): 772–775.

Czubak, A., Nowakowska, E., Burda, K., Kus, K. and Metelska, J. (2010) Cognitive effects of GABAergic antiepileptic drugs. *Arzneimittelforschung*, 60(1): 1–11.

Frank, J. (1961) *Persuasion and Healing*. Baltimore, MD: Johns Hopkins University Press.

Kirsch, I., Deacon, B.J., Huedo-Medina, T.B., Scoboria, A., Moore, T.J. and Johnson, B.T. (2008) Initial severity and antidepressant benefits: a meta-analysis of data submitted to the Food and Drug Administration. *PLoS Medicine*, 5(2): e45.

MacDonald, K. and Feifel, D. (2014) Oxytocin's role in anxiety: a critical appraisal. *Brain Research*, 1580: 22–56.

Miller, H.E.J., Deakin, J.F.W. and Anderson, I.M. (2000) Effect of acute tryptophan depletion on CO_2-induced anxiety in patients with panic disorder and normal volunteers. *The British Journal of Psychiatry*, 176(2): 182–188.

Tyrer, P., Seivewright, N., Murphy, S., Ferguson, B., Kingdon, D., Barczak, P. et al. (1988) The Nottingham study of neurotic disorder: comparison of drug and psychological treatments. *Lancet*, 2: 235–240.

Weldon, F. (1993) *Affliction*. London: HarperCollins.

RECOMMENDED READING

1. Freeth, R. (2007) *Humanising Psychiatry and Mental Health Care*. Oxford: Radcliffe Publishing.

A book that advocates a person-centred approach to working within mental health settings. It discusses ways of working and emphasises the need for humanistic values within psychiatry.

2. Eckpunkte des Bundesministeriums für Gesundheit zur Novellierung der usbildung zum Psychologischen Psychotherapeuten (www.aai.berlin/news-details/bmg-eckpunktepapier-und-rechtsgutachten-zur-novellierung-des-psychotherapeutengesetzes.html?file=files/pdfs/BMG_PsychThG_EckpunkteDirektausbildung.pdf).

The German Health Ministry has issued guidelines for the new procedure for licensing psychotherapists. Sixty hours of pharmacology training are required. This text is in German.

3. Goldacre, B. (2012) *Bad Pharma: How Medicine is Broken, and How We Can Fix It*. London: Fourth Estate.

An easy-to-read critique of the pharmaceutical industry.

5.35 CRITICAL APPROACHES TO PSYCHOTHERAPY AND COUNSELLING

COLIN FELTHAM

OVERVIEW AND KEY POINTS

Critiques of psychological therapy have existed since Freud's time, with Karl Kraus being one of the most well-known early critics. These critiques range from moderate objections to aspects of theory and practice, through partial reconstruction of traditions, to full-scale condemnation. This chapter considers these views further. Key points include:

- The very proliferation of therapeutic models and practices across the twentieth century, in a sprawling, organic and unaccountable manner more akin to the spread of religious denominations and cults, and based on an affect heuristic rather than objective evaluation, has been largely responsible for attracting critical attacks.
- Well-known critics include Eysenck, Masson, Fuller Torrey, Szasz, Epstein, Crews, Smail and Webster. Lay critiques include the charge that therapy is an unnecessary American export, a cottage industry, tea and sympathy, ritualised friendship, or psychological prostitution.
- Some dissatisfied ex-clients have offered their own critiques (Bates, 2005).

- This chapter aims to build on earlier work (Feltham, 1999a) to suggest ways in which critique, or 'critico-creative thinking', might be relevant and even constructive.

LACK OF INTELLECTUAL RIGOUR

Psychoanalysis emerged from Freud's study of neurology, experiments with hypnosis and catharsis, but Freud was informed by philosophers such as Eduard von Hartmann, whose work helped him formulate his theory of the unconscious. The broader talking therapy enterprise drew heavily from psychology from around the 1950s, both in its behavioural and humanistic forms. But philosophy and other cognate disciplines have been marginalised, in spite of the therapeutic core of many ancient Greek philosophical schools (Nussbaum, 2009), the roots of Cognitive-Behaviour Therapy (CBT) lying in Stoicism and existential therapy resting largely on the existential philosophy of the twentieth century. Much psychotherapy and counselling has developed its identity from intuitive, emotional, hope and belief-based sources, or anti-scientific, professionally anomalous, non-rational and non-sceptical bases (classic texts, such as Frank (1961) and Halmos (1978) have sympathetically indicated this long ago). Even CBT, while drawing on selective Socratic methods, has not subjected its own theories and practices to much rigorous critical reasoning.

CRITIQUE AS THE BASIS FOR CONFLICT AND CHANGE

It is self-evident that the schisms and divisions characterising the pluralistic field of therapy have resulted at least partly from the dissatisfaction expressed by Jung and Adler, and later Assagioli, Beck, Berne, Ellis, Perls, Janov, Reich and others. In other words, internal critique has changed theory and practice significantly, resulting, however, in far too many new models of therapy. The field contains no consensus on whether these schisms emanate from genuine epistemological differences, personality differences, commercial interests or other sources. Some conflicts exist between defenders of original or 'pure' models and theoretical rebels, or between those who advance considered theoretical refinements and others who reject major aspects of valued theory in favour of advancing their own agenda and new practice. However, theoretical and clinical differences also drive models of integrative, eclectic and pluralistic therapy, which are applied to conscientious reflection in practice and supervision. It is nevertheless an open secret, but one insufficiently explored, that some theorists and practitioners not merely politely disagree with each other, but sometimes condemn or wilfully ignore each other (Feltham, 1997).

CLINICAL PROFESSIONALS AT LOGGERHEADS

Many working in the mental health field under different professional titles and/or with different theoretical affiliations are critical of fellow practitioners on a number of grounds. Eysenck (1952) famously criticised psychoanalytic psychotherapy for producing no evidence of superiority to client outcome when compared with the mere passage of time without therapy (spontaneous remission), but he did this from the position of a clinical psychologist and champion of behaviour therapy. Many writers have criticised psychoanalysis, so that much more anti-psychoanalytic literature exists than that critiquing other models, but this is partly due to psychoanalysis being older than other models. For some balance, readers might see, for example, Grogan (2013) on humanistic therapy and Loewenthal and House (2010) on CBT.

The critique of some psychoanalysts of the 'diluted' forms of psychoanalytic psychotherapy and psychodynamic counselling is well known. Psychoanalytic belief in the necessity of lengthy uncovering of unconscious dynamics logically critiques humanistic therapies and CBT (Weatherill, 2004). Some clinical psychologists purport to represent the best in the field, critiquing what they regard as 'pseudoscience', often aimed at humanistic and innovative therapies (Lilienfeld et al., 2003). An implicit professional hierarchy exists, again insufficiently explored, in which mental health professions can be ranked. In terms of status and salary, psychiatrists sit atop this hierarchy, followed by clinical psychologists, counselling psychologists (with psychoanalysts sitting somewhere alongside), followed by psychotherapists, mental health nurses and counsellors. While these arguably muddled mental health traditions are disguised by outwardly seamless co-operation, anecdotally there is much concern, not least among distressed individuals trying to understand and access the confusing variety of sources of help.

We have witnessed decades of unedifying turf wars between the psy-professions, often under the guise of responsible professionalisation. On the face of it, this movement was always honourable and about protecting the public from poorly trained, unlicensed and unscrupulous practitioners. Psychiatry and clinical psychology were long ago protected as legal titles, but it took further decades and many iterations for psychotherapy, counselling and counselling psychology to approach anything like a statutory seal of approval. Here I remind readers of just one or two of the machinations involved. One historical driving factor was the anxiety to distinguish psychotherapy from scientology in the 1970s. Members of professional bodies were split between opposing statutory recognition and being appalled that anyone could oppose it. In the process, the Psychotherapists and Counsellors Professional Liaison Group, reporting to the Health and Care Professions Council (HCPC), after much deliberation found it impossible to persuade the HCPC about the alleged distinctions between counselling and psychotherapy, let alone establish meaningful distinctions between theoretical models. Even now, the push towards statutory or voluntary regulation on the one hand, and resistance to centralised control on the other, reveals a deep rift. Part of this conflict can be attributed to scepticism about the place of psychology in therapy. Do we know if extensive doctoral training in counselling psychology leads to more effective therapy? But it is also about academia and government having unwarranted oversight versus the view that clients and practitioners should be trusted to make their own decisions. The more control shifts from individuals and communities, runs this argument, the more we see the rise of powerful vested interests, questionable research projects, accreditation procedures and conservative practice. See House and Totton (2011) for some of the arguments against professionalisation and Feltham (1999b) for further views.

CRITIQUES BY PHILOSOPHERS, SOCIOLOGISTS AND SCIENTISTS

Let us briefly consider critiques put forward by certain philosophers, sociologists and scientists. Distinguished philosophers, such as Wittgenstein, Popper, Gellner, Grünbaum and Erwin, have all expressed reservations about the claims of psychotherapy. Dufresne (2006) provides one such negative philosophical analysis of psychoanalysis. It is of course natural that most therapists should regard psychology, not philosophy, as their mother discipline. A few therapists, like Eugene Gendlin, have philosophy backgrounds, and existentialist therapists from Binswanger and Laing, through to Heaton and van Deurzen, draw extensively from continental philosophy. Howard (2000) offers a rare guide to the use of philosophy by therapists. Given the many epistemological problems facing our field, we might welcome greater philosophical attention. Arguably of most relevance are the philosophies of mind, science and mental health, whereby detailed logical analysis is focused on questions like these: What is mental health? What is meant by mental disorder? Are psychiatric classifications meaningful? What do we know about the mind–body problem? How can we evaluate concepts such as the unconscious, the actualising tendency and negative automatic thoughts? Can we say that the self exists? Do we have free will? What is the nature of happiness? Some of these are addressed by Graham (2010).

Sociologists as different as Rose, Epstein and Furedi have articulated strongly negative views on psychotherapy. A common theme centres on psychological distress being wrongly understood as issuing from within individuals and being their responsibility to correct. Indeed, from a sociological or socio-economic perspective, the twentieth century is often considered by authors such as Rieff and Lasch as the birthplace of the 'therapeutic state', in which most human problems can be conceived and addressed privately, and we are encouraged to feel vulnerable and aggrieved (Furedi, 2003). From Freud's original concepts, we inherited patriarchal assumptions about mental health and illness, which feminists decried from about the 1970s onwards (McLellan, 1995). Some are now thinking in terms of 'affect studies', which highlight social causes of distress. Epstein (2006) regards therapy as a false enterprise, replacing religion and diverting attention away from needed political reforms.

As an extension of such critiques we should note that the talking therapies and their theoretical justifications are overwhelmingly spawned by middle-class, secular, Euro-American culture. It is ironic that some of the most powerful and sustained critiques we might dub 'sociological' come from clinical and counselling psychologists like David Smail, David Pilgrim and Paul Moloney. The 'therapy industry' (Moloney, 2013) continues to assert its research credentials without justification, to insist on its effectiveness against objections, to ignore problems of clinical epistemology (what Grünbaum (1992) referred to as 'epistemic ravages') and to endorse a spurious

programme of wellbeing initiatives, including the positive psychology movement. Smail, Moloney and others espouse instead a social-materialist psychology aiming to avoid false claims and raise awareness of the socio-political aetiology of distress.

The Nobel Prize winner for medicine Peter Medawar (1975) famously opined that psychoanalysis was 'the most stupendous intellectual confidence trick of the twentieth century'. Sokal and Bricmont (1998), both physicists, took to task a number of postmodern intellectuals, among whom the French psychoanalysts Jacques Lacan and Julia Kristeva ranked very highly. Like other critics of Lacan, notably Chomsky, they accused him of charlatanism, obfuscation, superficial erudition and cryptic writing style. The psychotherapy world appears to deal with scientists' criticisms by ignoring them, claiming to be misunderstood, or in some cases continuing to seek a scientific identity for psychotherapy (see Scharnberg, 2007). Some unresolved debates between neuroscientists and neurophilosophers, and psychologists and therapists, focus on the extent to which the brain and mind are identical, and on determinism versus neuroplasticity. Similar arguments are found in the field of genetics and epigenetics, concerning inherited psychological dysfunctions and our ability to avoid or modify them. Again, we can see divisions at work between therapy's different models when we read of the putative 'science of happiness' and its close links with evidence-based CBT but implicit mistrust of humanistic and psychodynamic models. Clinical psychologists also continue to espouse a scientist-practitioner model which is at odds with the 'softer' claim of 'reflexive-practitioner' identity of counselling psychologists.

FLAWED THERAPISTS

Masson's (1992) landmark critique of therapy identified a number of well-known figures, such as Freud, Ferenczi, Jung, Rosen and Perls, as fair game for exposure. Among their manifest problems could be seen examples of authoritarianism, physical and sexual abuse, pushing clients towards suicide, and otherwise breaching ethical expectations. In Masson's view, if it is so easy to find glaring faults in leading figures, we should assume that among the thousands of practitioners not in the limelight many similar abuses could be unearthed. Masson worked at the heart of the psychoanalytic establishment, and found a great deal to criticise among leading Freudians as well as in his own training analyst. Less concerned with abusive behaviour than with honestly exposing the fallible humanity of ordinary therapists, Adams' (2014) research unearthed many examples of the 'feet of clay' reality of therapists' own lives. Far from being models of positive mental health, they suffered from chronic depression and other psychological maladies and were as vulnerable to negative life events as anyone else. If we add to the myth of neurosis-free therapists the list of those who have sadly committed suicide, we have to conclude that one's own therapy does not reliably prevent such problems, and face the possibility that some therapists' behaviour confirms that unhappy people are often drawn to this profession.

Of course, many further criticisms exist, for example deterioration within therapy, poor training, insufficient and weak research, costs of private practice, and so on. See Feltham (1999b) for a selection of just 15 of such items, and Feltham (2010) for a list of 60 items.

CRITICAL THEORY, CRITICAL PSYCHOLOGY, AND CRITICAL PSYCHOTHERAPY AND COUNSELLING

Critical theory is an intellectual tradition stemming from a critique of society by early twentieth-century thinkers like Horkheimer, Adorno and Marcuse, associated with the Frankfurt School, and applied particularly to the field of psychoanalysis and therapy by Erich Fromm and others. Using selective sociological, economic and psychological theories, these writers laid the foundation for a neo-Marxist critique of culture. This was fleshed out later and applied by psychologists from many countries who were discontented with the status quo nature of the psychology profession, and who trace the origins of most psychological distress to the socio-economic conditions perpetrated by capitalism. In a wider arena, the celebrated philosopher Slavoj Žižek has drawn from Hegel, Marx, Freud and Lacan to critique social norms. Parker and others actively challenge the psychology establishment, focusing especially on the psychological neglect of individuals who are poor, working-class, disabled and oppressed for their identity as minority ethnic members, sexual minorities, of female gender or from the developing world (Parker, 2015).

FULL-SPECTRUM CRITICAL THINKING

It is necessary to address a common misunderstanding that academic criticism and critical theory concepts are the only pertinent ones for our consideration. Critical thinking itself can be traced back to both Buddhist and Socratic traditions about 2,500 years ago. Most philosophy rests on sceptical-analytical methods that carefully weigh up assumptions and assertions and logically test them for flaws and cogency. In the twentieth century a great deal of psychological research has been brought to bear on the ways in which we commonly make cognitive errors, and critical thinking has emerged as a significant

academic discipline (Davies and Barnett, 2015). Here we see concepts like cognitive dissonance, confirmatory bias, optimism bias, sunk costs, path dependency, narrative smoothing and many others. Not only clients but also therapists sometimes indulge in 'magical thinking'. Calne and O'Reilly (2013) argue that all mature scientific and professional disciplines must take on due sceptical thought.

In spite of the real contribution of critical thinking, and in its applied forms in our field, some neglected areas should be addressed. Parker (2015), for example, for all its intellectual breadth and social justice focus, contains virtually nothing on death awareness and its impact on individual distress; nor does it devote much space to the most common of mental health problems, depression. But perhaps most 'critically', texts of this kind are based on an unexamined assumption that criticality equates with a politically left-wing position. A full-spectrum version of critical thinking should surely allow for the widest possible analysis of phenomena, using independent thought, free speech and even 'exuberant scepticism'. While Foucault's writings have been amply cited in postgraduate research, his commendation of *parrhousia* or fearless honest speech (Foucault, 2011), has been interpreted in an almost exclusively left-wing manner. While legitimate enough, such critique has not usually made its partisan politics explicit.

Arguably, we have never established exactly what we mean by mental health, nor can we assume that therapy is the best method for addressing all 'mental health problems', nor should we prematurely exclude non-psychological aetiologies. However, what we frequently find in radical texts in our field are the following assumptions: capitalism is itself a source of most distress. Commercial psychopharmacology (or 'Big Pharma') causes distress, indeed it is often considered 'evil'. Biomedical psychiatry, its dehumanising use of power, labelling and classificatory systems, should be reviled. Evolutionary psychology is often mistakenly considered equivalent to sociobiology, that is, as deterministic theory to be resisted or ignored. Neurophilosophical challenges to assumptions that humans possess a self and free will are to be resisted. Certain categories of suffering or oppression are considered to be beyond critique or off limits, notably all that territory that can be designated as 'political correctness'. Finally, the very common assumption that life is good and antinatalism and suicide are bad receives almost no sceptical attention in psychotherapy publications.

CRITICAL THINKING AS AN IRRELEVANT ACADEMIC LUXURY?

For many practitioners this kind of critical exercise seems a polemical irrelevance or, worse, an unhelpful interruption of the urgent business of everyday therapeutic practice, a dispiriting diversion and evidence of professional disloyalty. Professional participation in counselling and psychotherapy frequently begins with experience as a satisfied client, followed by passionate faith as a trainee and immersion in clinical practice which overlaps heavily with livelihood. Few of us are paid to critique the field and, arguably, even most researchers in academic departments, whose remit is to conduct rigorous objective evaluation of therapy, are also practitioners or dependent on the therapy field for their own livelihood. Nevertheless, we should not hide from critiques, especially when clients are asked to be truthful, lay themselves bare and be as non-defensive as possible. As Kahneman (2011) argues, clinicians are often accurate about psychological micro-processes and interpersonal nuances but poor at understanding the longer-term macro-implications of their work. This suggests that well-meaning, skilful immersion in practice, while perhaps producing short-term feel-good outcomes, may not translate into durable client behaviours in a complex, real-world setting.

One compelling inference from all the above may be made: that if only some of these critiques are valid, and yet it is also true that a majority of clients report being positively helped, then the mechanisms by which they are helped, or believe they are helped, probably are in the main common relational or placebo factors. Purton (2014) extends this reasoning to suggest a transcendence of traditional models and a strong link with commonsense in therapeutic practice. Another related point is that if successful therapy does indeed rely on relationality and warm affect, then much clearer explanations of these are demanded. For all the research now being engaged in and published (with no real evidence that mountains of research significantly enhance therapeutic effectiveness), and even having extra criticality injected into it (Schostak and Schostak, 2013), we are still a long way from addressing most of the above critiques.

REFERENCES

Adams, M. (2014) *The Myth of the Untroubled Therapist*. London: Routledge.

Bates, Y. (ed.) (2005) *Shouldn't I Be Feeling Better by Now? Client Views of Therapy*. London: Palgrave.

Calne, R. and O'Reilly, W. (eds) (2013) *Scepticism: Hero and Villain*. New York: Norinka.

Davies, M. and Barnett, R. (eds) (2015) *The Palgrave Handbook of Critical Thinking in Higher Education*. London: Palgrave.

Dufresne, T. (2006) *Killing Freud: 20th Century Culture and the Death of Psychoanalysis*. London: Continuum.

Epstein, W.M. (2006) *Psychotherapy as Religion: The Civil Divine in America*. Reno, NV: University of Nevada Press.

Eysenck, H.J. (1952) The effects of psychotherapy: an evaluation. *Journal of Consulting Clinical Psychology*, 16, 319–324.

Feltham, C. (ed.) (1997) *Which Psychotherapy? Leading Exponents Explain Their Differences*. London: Sage.

Feltham, C. (1999a) Facing, understanding and learning from critiques of counselling. *British Journal of Guidance and Counselling*, 27(3), 301–311.

Feltham, C. (ed.) (1999b) *Controversies in Psychotherapy and Counselling*. London: Sage.

Feltham, C. (2010) *Critical Thinking in Counselling and Psychotherapy*. London: Sage.

Foucault, M. (2011) *The Courage of Truth*. New York: Palgrave.

Frank, J.D. (1961) *Persuasion and Healing: A Comparative Study of Psychotherapy*. Baltimore, MD: Johns Hopkins University Press.

Furedi, F. (2003) *Therapy Culture: Cultivating Vulnerability in an Uncertain Age*. London: Routledge.

Graham, G. (2010) *The Disordered Mind: An Introduction to Philosophy of Mind and Mental Illness*. New York: Routledge.

Grogan, J. (2013) *Encountering America: Humanistic Psychology, Sixties Culture and the Shaping of the Modern Self*. New York: Harper Perennial.

Grünbaum, A. (1992) *The Foundations of Psychoanalysis: A Philosophical Critique*. Berkeley, CA: University of California Press.

(Continued)

(Continued)

Halmos, P. (1978) *The Faith of the Counsellors* (2nd ed.). London: Constable.

House, R. and Totton, N. (eds) (2011) *Implausible Professions: Arguments for Pluralism and Autonomy in Psychotherapy and Counselling* (2nd ed.). Ross-on-Wye: PCCS Books.

Howard, A. (2000) *Philosophy for Counselling and Psychotherapy: Pythagoras to Postmodernism*. London: Palgrave.

Kahneman, D. (2011) *Thinking, Fast and Slow*. London: Penguin.

Lilienfeld, S.O., Lynn, S.J. and Lohr, J.M. (2003) *Science and Pseudoscience in Clinical Psychology*. New York: Guilford Press.

Loewenthal, D. and House, R. (2010) *Critically Engaging CBT*. Maidenhead: Open University Press.

Masson, J.M. (1992) *Against Therapy*. London: Flamingo.

McLellan, B. (1995) *Beyond Psychoppression: A Feminist Alternative Therapy*. Melbourne, Vic.: Spinifex.

Medawar, P. (1975) Victims of psychiatry. *New York Review of Books*, 23 January, p. 21.

Moloney, P. (2013) *The Therapy Industry: The Irresistible Rise of the Talking Cure, and Why It Doesn't Work*. London: Pluto.

Nussbaum, M.C. (2009) *The Therapy of Desire: Theory and Practice in Hellenistic Ethics*. Princeton, NJ: Princeton University Press.

Parker, I. (ed.) (2015) *Handbook of Critical Psychology*. London: Routledge.

Purton, C. (2014) *The Trouble with Psychotherapy: Counselling and Commonsense*. London: Palgrave.

Scharnberg, M. (2007) *Tales from the Vienna Woods: Psychoanalysts' Postulations about Scientific Verifications of their Interpretations*. (Psykiatrie-und-ethik.de/infc/en/max_scharnberg.htm).

Schostak, J. and Schostak, J. (2013) *Writing Research Critically*. London: Routledge.

Sokal, A. and Bricmont, J. (1998) *Fashionable Nonsense: Postmodern Intellectuals' Abuse of Science*. New York: Picador.

Weatherill, R. (2004) *Our Last Great Illusion: A Radical Psychoanalytical Critique of Therapy Culture*. Exeter: Imprint Academic.

RECOMMENDED READING

1. Feltham, C. (2013) *Counselling and Counselling Psychology: A Critical Examination*. Ross-on-Wye: PCCS Books.

Looks at the problems of the psychodynamic and humanistic approaches, training, supervision and research, and socio-cultural issues.

2. Masson, J.M. (1992) *Against Therapy*. London: Flamingo.

A classic exposure of the practice and personalities of many well-known (mainly American) psychotherapists, demonstrating common malpractice, and concluding with a condemnation of the profession.

3. Moloney, P. (2014) *The Therapy Industry: The Irresistible Rise of the Talking Cure, and Why It Doesn't Work*. London: Pluto.

A critique of the sprawling nature and contestable claims of the field, with an emphasis on the socio-political aetiology of mental distress.

PART VI

CLIENT PRESENTING PROBLEMS

6.1 INTRODUCING CLIENT PRESENTING PROBLEMS: A CRITICAL APPROACH TO DIAGNOSIS AND 'PSYCHOPATHOLOGY'

LAURA ANNE WINTER

OVERVIEW OF THIS SECTION

Part VI of this *Handbook* focuses on a range of client 'presenting problems' we might encounter as counsellors and psychotherapists. In this introductory chapter I provide a brief overview of the chapters which are included within this part of the book. In addition, I also aim to provide a brief reflection on some core issues which surround the topic and seem particularly pertinent to give space to. Specifically, I reflect on issues of comorbidity and present a critical perspective of diagnosis and viewing 'presenting issues' as 'disorders' or 'psychopathologies'. Finally, I leave readers to consider three questions which relate to the subject of client presenting problems in counselling and psychotherapy.

This section of the book includes 20 chapters, covering the different issues that clients might come to us with. These are wide-ranging, covering issues such as stress, self-harm, trauma, sexual abuse, low self-esteem and depression. Some of these might be classed as more 'complex' presentations and problems, for example 'psychosis' or 'personality disorders', while others might fall into the category which therapists often refer to as 'problems of living', such as bereavement or relationship problems. Clients might specifically use some of the diagnostic categories we see here, such as 'panic' or 'depression', whereas some labels or phrases might be applied by services or individual practitioners. The presenting issues have been separated and considered in turn for ease of reference and in order to give sufficient space for topics to be considered by authors with specific expertise and knowledge. However, we do not mean to suggest that these issues can be neatly boxed off into separate 'chapters' in a similar way in practice, or in clients' experiences. There are large rates of comorbidity across presenting problems and clinical diagnoses, with individuals often diagnosed with more than one 'disorder'. This should not go unrecognised, and is important for readers to bear in mind as they progress through the chapters in this section. Indeed, it is an issue which many of the authors have picked up within their specific chapters. I continue to reflect on the issue of 'comorbidity' and the multiplicity of 'presenting problems' in the section below on critical perspectives.

Each chapter within the section follows a similar structure. Authors first provide a *definition(s)* of the presenting issue they are discussing, before talking about the *aetiology* (the authors' suggested explanation for the development of the presenting issue), issues to consider within an *assessment*, how therapists might think about *formulation* and how to bring together information gained about the client and the presenting issue, possible therapeutic *intervention(s)*, and the *evaluation* of such work. As with all chapters in this *Handbook*, authors have also provided an *Overview* and some *Key Points*, as well as *References* and *Recommended Reading*. We acknowledge that this frame might be interpreted as, or critiqued for, adopting a 'medical model' approach. This is not our (the editorial team's) intention. Instead, we have encouraged authors to provide a range of contributions to this section of the book, including those which advocate a single or particular understanding or way of working with a particular problem, those which outline a variety of approaches, and those which have a more pluralistic understanding. We have also encouraged authors to consider a critical approach, as described in this introductory chapter. This frame hopefully ensures that in all of the chapters, readers get a sense of a similar range of issues in relation to the often very different subjects under question. Terms like 'aetiology' allow us to look at these issues in a variety of ways, but are not to be taken uncritically. We have also encouraged authors to be clear and transparent about the limitations of particular diagnoses or ways of viewing the world. In the next section of this introductory chapter I reflect on critical perspectives and the issue of psychiatric diagnosis in counselling and psychotherapy.

CRITICAL PERSPECTIVES AND THE ISSUE OF 'PSYCHOPATHOLOGY' AND PSYCHIATRIC DIAGNOSIS

Counselling and psychotherapy have generally been seen to take a more holistic and humanistic approach to working with individuals, rather than adopting what might be construed as a reductive 'medical model'. What is commonly referred to as the 'medical model' in these fields is a perspective which views psychological distress in the same way as a broken arm: a problem for which there is a medical or biological explanation, which can be diagnosed, and a treatment can be prescribed on the basis of that particular diagnosis. Nevertheless, as therapists, we work with a range of 'presenting problems', some of which might be potentially classed as mental health disorders or fall into categories labelled as psychiatric diagnoses. These diagnoses are typically given by professionals such as psychiatrists, but many clients may also present their own struggles in a medicalised discourse which align neatly with classification systems (Strong, Ross and Sesma-Vazquez, 2015). The two classification systems most often used internationally are the *Diagnostic and Statistical Manual of Psychiatric Disorders* (DSM), which is currently in its fifth edition (DSM-V) (American Psychiatric Association, 2013) and the *International Classification of Diseases*, tenth revision (ICD-10) (World Health Organisation, 1992). As noted above, typically, counselling and psychotherapy have adopted a more humanistic approach to human distress than that reflected in such diagnostic manuals and by the 'medical model'.

Over many years, there has been significant critique of the system of psychiatric diagnosis. Such critiques have typically focused on the

> failure to find biomarkers, which might validate categories; extensive overlap across categories and variation of symptoms within them; and the absence of treatment specificity so that, for example, neuroleptics have been recommended for schizophrenia, depression, anxiety, bipolar disorder, personality disorder, and attention deficit hyperactivity disorder. Perhaps more worryingly, although some service users experience diagnosis as a relief, a substantial number of other users testify that it conveys messages of deficit and despair. (Boyle and Johnstone, 2014: 409)

As noted earlier in this introduction, there are high rates of comorbidity across numerous of the supposedly discrete categories presented in the DSM and ICD. For example, a recent study which looked at anxiety disorders in adolescents found that only 5% of their sample was diagnosed with a single anxiety disorder (Olofsdotter, Vadlin, Sonnby, Furmark and Nilsson, 2016). As you can see in the quote above, the high rates of comorbidity have been one issue that critics of psychiatric diagnosis have cited with the current system: if the 'disorders' overlap so much, are they really discrete categories or separate 'disorders' at all? (Boyle and Johnstone, 2014). Elsewhere, authors such as Bentall (2010) present important challenges to the idea that 'mental disorders' such as schizophrenia and bipolar disorder are 'diseases of the brain', and, more recently, Moncrieff (2013: 74) argues that the hypothesis that variance in dopamine function can explain schizophrenia has acted as a 'smokescreen' which has fuelled, in her opinion, a flawed, disease-centred model of anti-psychotic drugs (and mental health problems more broadly). Furthermore, critics suggest that when viewing 'presenting problems' as discrete categories, which can be clearly diagnosed with treatment prescribed accordingly, issues of the medicalisation of normal human experience arise. For example, the recent DSM-V has amended the 'bereavement exclusion' criteria within the diagnosis of depression so that an individual may now be diagnosed with major depression after two weeks of experiencing symptoms, regardless of how recent their loss was (Bandini, 2015). Is this suggesting that an individual is 'ill' or has a 'disorder' if they experience low mood, loss of appetite and other depressive symptoms three weeks after losing their partner? Criteria for psychiatric diagnosis also typically do not take into account the wider social and political issues which might be underpinning an individual's problems: because, as noted above, the system assumes that the problem is rooted within the individual. Current systems of psychiatric diagnosis, then, are perhaps both overly medical and reductionist (Boyle and Johnstone, 2014), and overly individualistic (Rogers and Pilgrim, 2014).

In contrast to this 'psychopathology'-driven approach, critics of psychiatric diagnosis, while not ignoring the influence of biological and genetic factors in the development of distress, argue that social and relational factors play an important causal role in the development of what ends up being defined by categories of psychiatric diagnosis (Grant, 2015). This approach is consistent with the 'social justice agenda' that is seen in counselling, psychotherapy and psychology, and which is discussed in the introduction to Part II of this *Handbook* (Winter – Chapter 2.1, this volume), and has recently been advocated as a 'paradigm shift' in Clinical Psychology (British Psychological Society Division of Clinical Psychology, 2013). I would therefore encourage the reader to continue through this section of the book with a critical eye, viewing each 'presenting problem' as just that: an issue which a client might one day bring to you in your work in therapeutic practice. The chapters covered here also undoubtedly only expose readers to a fraction of the range of experiences with which your clients will come to you. Furthermore, given discussions above, it is likely to be rare that clients present with one single 'problem'.

Finally, I also urge readers to consider the broad picture when thinking about explanations or understandings of human distress, and not to forget the issues discussed in Chapter 2.1 around 'diversity and difference' and the role of social, cultural and political factors in understanding such 'presenting problems' (see also Winter, Guo, Wilk and Hanley, 2016).

QUESTIONS

1. How do you think you would feel about being given a psychiatric diagnosis if you went to your GP when feeling distressed? What factors do you think would influence this reaction?
2. Choose one of the 'presenting problems' covered in the chapters in this *Handbook*. How would you work with someone coming to therapy for this issue? Would it be similar to or different from the approach(es) described in the chapter? Why?
3. Why do you think rates of comorbidity are so high across diagnosed mental health problems?

REFERENCES

American Psychiatric Association (2013). *Diagnostic and Statistical Manual of Mental Disorders* (5th ed.). Washington, DC: American Psychiatric Publishing.

Bandini, J. (2015). The medicalization of Bereavement: (Ab)normal Grief in the DSM-5. *Death Studies*, *39*(6), 347–352.

Bentall, R. P. (2010). *Doctoring the Mind: Why Psychiatric Treatments Fail*. London: Penguin Books.

Boyle, M. and Johnstone, L. (2014). Alternatives to psychiatric diagnosis. *The Lancet*, *1*, 409–411.

British Psychological Society Division of Clinical Psychology (2013). *Classification of Behaviour and Experience in Relation to Functional Psychiatric Diagnoses: Time for a Paradigm Shift*. Division of Clinical Psychology Position Statement. Leicester: BPS.

Grant, A. (2015). Demedicalising misery: Welcoming the human paradigm in mental health nurse education. *Nurse Education Today*, *35*(8), e50–e53.

Moncrieff, J. (2013). *The Bitterest Pills: The Troubling Story of Antipsychotic Drugs*. New York: Palgrave Macmillan.

Olofsdotter, S., Vadlin, S., Sonnby, K., Furmark, T. and Nilsson, K. W. (2016). Anxiety disorders among adolescents referred to general psychiatry for multiple causes: Clinical presentation, prevalence, and comorbidity. *Scandinavian Journal of Child and Adolescent Psychiatry and Psychology*, *4*(2), 55–64.

Rogers, A. and Pilgrim, D. (2014). *A Sociology of Mental Health and Illness* (5th ed.). Maidenhead, Berkshire: Open University Press.

Strong, T., Ross, K. H. and Sesma-Vazquez, M. (2015). Counselling the (self?) diagnosed client: Generative and reflective conversations. *British Journal of Guidance and Counselling*, *43*(5), 598–610.

Winter, L. A., Guo, F., Wilk, K. and Hanley, T. (2016). Difference and diversity in pluralistic therapy. In M. Cooper and W. Dryden (eds), *The Handbook of Pluralistic Counselling and Psychotherapy*. London: Sage.

World Health Organisation (1992). *The ICD-10 Classification of Mental and Behavioural Disorders: Clinical Descriptions and Diagnostic Guidelines*. London: Churchill Livingstone.

6.2 ALCOHOL PROBLEMS

RICHARD VELLEMAN

OVERVIEW AND KEY POINTS

There is no 'one-size-fits-all' when counselling people with alcohol problems. Clients are deeply individual. To help them, we need to work with them and their families to deal with both their alcohol use and their other difficulties. In assessing a client's alcohol problems, we should examine alcohol use; the drinking behaviour; the effects of the use of alcohol; their thinking concerning the alcohol use (e.g., definition of the problem and cause); and the context (family, employment, social). Counselling clients with drinking problems requires the same skills as counselling any other problem. We need to develop trust, explore the problem, help to set goals, empower clients to take action, and help them to maintain changes. There are techniques which are especially relevant to problem drinkers: giving information and simple advice on cutting down or giving up; helping set achievable short-term goals; helping identify issues which push them towards drinking; using more active techniques to help them rethink what they can do. Clients may decide to either stop drinking, or control their drinking. This latter is a legitimate goal, although clients should be aware that controlled drinking is more difficult than abstaining. Relapse management is like the other parts of counselling: understanding the reasons for a client's behaviour; understanding the central role a client's expectations and beliefs play in determining behaviour; and enabling a client to learn new, and utilise already learnt, skills. And if clients do relapse, they need to know that we want them to return and discuss the situation with us. Relatives of problem drinkers have many problems to contend with. It is not surprising that many seek help, yet often they do not receive it. There are many ways that we can help these family members, either by offering them help in their own right, or by including them within our work with the problem drinker.

Key points relating to alcohol problems are:

- People are individuals who do things for individual reasons; problem drinkers also drink for reasons.
- Counselling helps clarify these reasons through a process of reflecting, clarifying, challenging, and exploring.

- Alcohol use lies along a continuum: there is no simple dividing line between 'alcoholic' drinkers and the rest of the population.
- Individuals learn how to behave towards alcohol, and this is open to change.

A CRITICAL PERSPECTIVE

There are many controversies related to counselling people with alcohol problems. These relate to: definitions and terminology, through assessment, to intervention methods and techniques. These controversies often relate to the very negative views which many people hold of those with alcohol problems, and about whether or not they can be helped. This chapter takes the view that most of these controversies are bound up in myth, all of which increase the negative ways in which people perceive working with clients with drinking problems.

These myths include beliefs that 'all alcoholics are liars or in denial', 'one can't work with someone unless he/she has admitted he/she is an alcoholic', 'one can't work with people unless they have reached rock-bottom', 'there's no point in trying to help alcoholics, treatment successes are a real rarity'. There is good evidence that not one of these myths is true (see Velleman, 2011).

If one adopts both compassionate and evidence-based stances towards counselling problem drinkers, it becomes very difficult to agree with any of these myths.

DEFINITION

Many people in the United Kingdom (UK) and across the world, drink at excessive levels, and cause themselves and others immense problems. On a typical UK day, some 10,000 individuals seek help for their own or someone else's drinking problem; on a typical day in the United States of America (USA), more than 700,000 people are treated for 'alcoholism'. The World Health Organisation (WHO) estimates that, worldwide, 3.3 million deaths, or 5.9% of all global deaths, were attributable to alcohol consumption (WHO, 2015). In Europe, alcohol causes nearly 10% of all ill-health and premature deaths.

Examining the huge range of statistics (see, for example, UK Government Statistical Service, 2016) reveals that:

- Almost half of British adults drink in excess of sensible limits (some alcohol-free days, no more than 2–3 units of alcohol on each drinking day, no more than 14 units per week): in 2014, 12.9 million people (45% of the UK population; 52% of men, 37% of women) drank more than 4.5 units on at least one day of the week. The rise over the last 25 years has been huge: in 2007 it was 37% (41% of men, 34% of women) who drank at this level; in 1988 it was much lower, with around a quarter of men and 10% of women drinking at more than the recommended limits.
- In England, 26% of adults aged 16–64 have an alcohol use disorder (38% of men and 16% of women). This is equivalent to approximately 8.2 million people in England. In England in 2013–14, 80,929 people started new alcohol treatment. Over 17.5 million people in the USA have alcohol-related problems. Each of these individuals will have contact with and will influence a wide range of other people.

The seriousness of some of these issues cannot be overstated:

- Deaths attributable to alcohol are around 40,000 per year in England and Wales, and 100,000 per year in the USA. This includes up to 63% of all deaths following falls, up to 61% of all deaths by fire, up to 47% of all deaths by drowning, around 40% of all deaths following assaults, and around one-third of driving fatalities.
- The following are alcohol related: about 50% of all crime, 60% of stranger violence, 46% of domestic violence, between one-third and one-half of all child abuse cases dealt with by social services, and up to 80% of weekend arrests.
- In 2012–13 there were over a million admissions to National Health Service hospitals related to alcohol consumption. Again, these figures show huge rises: in 2005–06 there were over a quarter of a million such admissions, and that number was double the number of admissions in 1997. Up to 40% of all accident and emergency attendances and ambulance costs are alcohol related; between 12 midnight and 5 am, 70% of accident and emergency attendances are alcohol related.

A SIMPLE DEFINITION

Alcohol is related to lots of different types of problem. But as counsellors, what do we mean when we say that someone has an alcohol problem? My definition is:

If someone's drinking causes problems for him or her, or for someone else, in any area of their lives, then that drinking is problematic.

This could include problems with health, finances, the law, work, friends or, relationships. Hence, drinking problems are not determined by fixed quantities of alcohol, or timings, but by whether or not they cause problems, for the drinker or anyone else.

OTHER DEFINITIONS

A very commonly used term is *alcoholism*. Alcohol problems are seen as a disease or psychiatric condition or an allergy. There are advantages and disadvantages to using this term. Some find the disease concept useful; and conceptualising it as an illness has allowed a more helpful approach to be developed within the workplace, where people with problems can be helped as opposed to being disciplined. Disadvantages include the idea of the 'disease' being a medical problem and that the solution is not the person's responsibility but that of the doctors. The term also dissuades many people from seeking help because they do not want to be labelled an 'alcoholic', or because they are nothing like their stereotype of what an alcoholic is like.

Due to some of these reasons, the WHO in 1977 (Edwards et al., 1977) suggested replacing the term 'alcoholism' with *alcohol dependence syndrome* (ADS). In many ways, this is an improvement as it suggests that a drinking problem can be described in terms of three factors – that is, the degree to which: a person's drinking behaviour is abnormal; they feel there is something wrong with their drinking; and they have an altered physiological response to alcohol (tolerance and withdrawal symptoms). However, although officially ADS has replaced 'alcoholism', it is the latter term which is commonly used by both the general public and many counsellors.

Many argue that, although the development of the ADS is an improvement, it is still a medical, disease notion of what is fundamentally a non-medical problem. However, others argue that because people do develop problems with their consumption of an addictive drug, it is reasonable to use such a medical notion.

I use 'problems' because I believe that people can change the ways that they think and feel about, and behave towards, alcohol. The term 'alcoholism' implies that a client has some irreversible disease which is not really amenable to a counselling intervention.

AETIOLOGY

There are lots of theories purporting to explain the causes of alcohol problems (Velleman, 2011). Some are based on factors within the individual, or within the social context, or on overall cultural factors.

My own view is that there is no single cause for all alcohol problems. People must be dealt with on an individual basis, not according to some pre-existing formula based on any single theory of causation. Any person's vulnerability towards developing an alcohol problem will exist on a continuum, from highly vulnerable to highly invulnerable.

ASSESSMENT

Alcohol problems are both similar to and different from other problems.

The types of emotional difficulty with which clients with alcohol problems present are similar to those of many other clients. These may include grief, depression, anger, uncertainty, bewilderment, anxiety, etc., and may also include problems with relationships, the law, jobs, health, finances, or housing.

But there are also issues which relate specifically to clients' alcohol consumption. Because alcohol is an addictive drug, it can give rise to problems of tolerance and withdrawal, dependency, craving, and a strong ambivalence about whether or not giving up or reducing use is either possible or desirable. Further, public and professional attitudes to drinking problems are so negative that clients will often find it difficult to get help when they need it.

In assessing a client's alcohol problems, we should examine the alcohol use; the drinking behaviour and effects; the client's thinking concerning the alcohol use (expectations, values, definition of the problem, understanding of its cause); and the context (family, employment, social).

FORMULATION

The most important insight into helping people with their alcohol problems is to realise that people drink for individual reasons. They may not understand what these reasons are, or else they would change without our help. Our two most important tasks as the counsellor are to help our clients understand what their reasons are for behaving in the ways that they do, and then to empower them to change, so that they no longer need to behave in these ways.

INTERVENTION

Five simple principles should underpin our counselling work (Velleman, 2011):

- People drink problematically for reasons.
- Working with alcohol-misusing clients means we need to deal simultaneously with their alcohol use and other difficulties.
- People cannot be dealt with in isolation from the rest of their lives (family, friends).
- Counselling clients with these problems is no different from working with people with other types of difficulty.
- It is not necessary to be a specialist counsellor to help clients with alcohol-related problems.

There are also four simple assumptions which are useful (Velleman, 2011):

- Alcohol use lies along a continuum: there is no simple dividing line between 'alcoholic' drinkers and the rest of the population.
- Individuals can move along this continuum, in either direction.
- Individuals learn how to behave towards alcohol, and this is open to change.
- We know from a lot of research that most people who develop alcohol problems go on to change without recourse to outside professional help. This implies that people who need our assistance will have perpetuating factors which block them from changing on their own.

These principles and assumptions can help us counsel people with alcohol problems. We help people by using the same skills that we use in counselling any person with any problem, and the same understanding of the counselling process that we use with any other kind of presenting problem.

This counselling process needs to go through a number of steps or stages as we work through our tasks in counselling. We need to:

- develop trust;
- help the client to explore the problem;
- help to set goals;
- empower clients to take action;
- help them to maintain changes; and
- agree when the time comes to end our counselling relationship.

In counselling, *we* are responsible for this process and for ensuring that these tasks are undertaken and fulfilled. The main responsibility for the content of the sessions (instead of the process) lies with the client.

As well as these processes, there are other techniques which are especially relevant to problem drinkers:

- giving clients information and simple advice as to how to cut down or give up;
- helping the client to set intermediate, short-term goals which are (and seem to the client to be) achievable;
- helping problem drinkers to become more aware of the forces within their environments which push them towards drinking; and
- using more active techniques to help them to rethink what they can do.

Other important techniques and ideas which have been developed within the alcohol field have proved very effective, including the Prochaska and DiClemente cycle of change (Prochaska and DiClemente, 1994) and motivational interviewing (Miller and Rollnick, 1991).

The *cycle of change* has two important ideas: that *change has various stages* and that *the change process is a cycle*. People usually make more than one attempt before succeeding. This clear model (see Figure 6.2.1) suggests that when clients arrive for counselling, they may be at one of a variety of stages, to each of which the authors gave a name:

- *pre-contemplation* (an individual may not be aware that his/her drinking is causing problems, or may not really think about the problematic side of their drinking);

- *contemplation* (an individual acknowledges the link between behaviour and problems; they try to work out what is going wrong; they start to think about their inappropriate use);
- *preparation* (a serious commitment to action, and to a change plan to be implemented in the short term, is made);
- *action* (the client implements the proposed action or change, and constantly practises new skills which have been learnt to enable change, so as to maintain the new habits or behaviours);
- *maintenance* (an attempt to integrate the behaviour change into their lifestyle, trying to maintain the chosen direction);
- *termination* or *lapse/relapse* (either the new behaviour has been successfully learnt, and the new coping methods are successfully incorporated into the client's repertoire, or the person succumbs to the pressures to resume problematic drinking).

Motivational interviewing is a powerful technique that accepts that ambivalence about changing behaviour is normal. We need to work with this ambivalence from the outset, as opposed to ignoring it until a client 'fails', whereupon explanations are couched in terms of 'lack of motivation'.

Effective interventions generally include working with ambivalence and working with clients at whichever stage of the cycle of change that they are at.

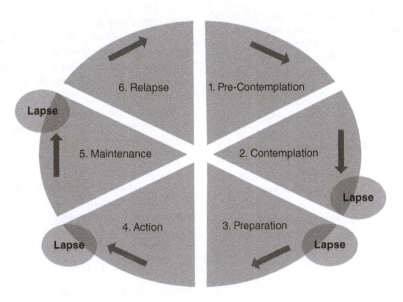

Figure 6.2.1 The cycle of change

Source: adapted from Prochaska and DiClemente (1982).

SKILLS

To help clients develop their own abilities to solve problems, it is important they acquire and practise relevant skills, as opposed to merely discussing the issues with us. Our clients must learn and practise alternative ways of coping with the triggers which normally push them into drinking. Those clients who can engage in alternative ways of behaving, and who can adopt a positive style of coping with problems, appear to do well in the long term.

Many of the techniques outlined above are based on cognitive-behavioural therapy (CBT) ideas. But it is important to remember that research which has looked at the relative efficacy of different sorts of therapy has found that *all* therapies with a good evidence base and which are well delivered seem to be equally effective. The phrases 'good evidence base' and 'well delivered' are key: I am not arguing that all therapies or all therapists are equally effective. But it seems clear that the important issues are whether the therapist or counsellor:

- has key counselling skills;
- is using interventions which they are happy and confident about;
- is using an intervention which is evidence based.

As well as the techniques mentioned above, there also will be specific issues relating to alcohol which we ought to understand. It is useful:

- to know a bit about alcohol's effects;
- to understand that alcohol is an addictive drug; but also
- to understand that people with drinking problems can control their behaviour – they are not overcome by an impossible-to-resist urge to consume alcohol.

It is also useful to know that 'controlled drinking' goals are legitimate ones for clients to aim towards (if the client wishes to), although both we and our clients should realise that controlled drinking is more difficult than abstaining. Related to that, if we think clients are aiming for the wrong goal (drinking or otherwise), we should tell them, on the one hand, that we are happy to back them up and help them, but, on the other hand, we think they have chosen incorrectly, and why we think this.

Another key area (in common with all addictive and mental health problems) is relapse: the situation where a client is making progress towards achieving their goals and then they gradually or suddenly take a number of steps backwards. Clients need to know that even if they do relapse, we want them to return and discuss the situation with us.

CASE EXAMPLE: WORKING WITH RELAPSE

When Steve first came to see me, he had tried lots of different approaches – Alcoholics Anonymous, private treatment agencies, and so on – and had relapsed frequently. We discussed this at an early stage, and made two decisions: first, that we needed to work through possible relapse-inducing situations, and second, that if a relapse occurred, it was vital that he return so we could discuss and learn from it.

Steve made many apparently irrelevant decisions which contributed to relapse. For example, one strategy to improve his social life that we decided upon was to invite friends round for a meal, and Steve did not think through what he would do when people arrived bearing a bottle of wine.

Steve became better at recognising when situations were likely to become risky, and he developed many skills at avoiding these at-risk situations. For example, he arranged with the friends who came for a meal that they would take away with them any leftover alcohol, so he would not need to keep any in the house. I got him to rehearse out loud in the sessions how well he was doing – and indeed, he remained abstinent for a longer period than he had ever done in the previous 30 years.

However, Steve did start to drink again. He came to me in distress because he had drunk two pints. We discussed the detail of what had happened. As a result of this lapse, he decided he wanted to try controlled drinking. I told him of my view that the evidence suggested this would not be a good idea; but he still wished to try, and so I supported him in this.

(Continued)

(Continued)

He then had a major relapse. He telephoned me rather than coming to an appointment, slurring his words. I pressed him to come anyway, but he refused, feeling he had let both himself and me down. I made another appointment, and he did not come. I wrote twice more and telephoned once. In all, I had three conversations with an intoxicated and terribly ashamed Steve. Finally, he returned after two months. I saw this as a great success – I had managed to convince him that we could still work together, in spite of his 'failure', as he saw it.

I worked to enable Steve to reframe the situation, to see the relapse as a tremendous learning experience. We reverted to an abstinence goal, and to continuing to work on analysing at-risk situations, developing better coping skills, and raising confidence and self-esteem. We also worked on dealing with any future lapses in such a way that they did not turn into relapses. After two months, we moved to fortnightly sessions, then to monthly, and to three-monthly follow-ups.

FAMILIES

Most counselling of problem drinkers is undertaken in individual sessions. However, there is increasing evidence (Copello et al., 2005) that the involvement of family members (spouses, parents, other close and affected people) can lead to better outcomes. Sometimes relatives of problem drinkers do not wish to get involved; they often have had very negative experiences while living with a problem drinker and may just want the drinker to 'sort themselves out'. Indeed, often these relatives need help in their own right, although frequently they do not receive it. But if we can involve interested and affected family members in our counselling of clients with alcohol problems, it is likely that help to both the drinker and the relative will be more effective.

EVALUATION

There is clear evidence that some forms of help are better than others (Miller and Wilbourne, 2002). It has become evident that, as long as one uses interventions which *do* have good evidence, then any of these 'good interventions' is as effective as any other.

Project MATCH was the largest and most rigorous trial ever undertaken – not just in the alcohol field but in any area of psychotherapy. Project MATCH compared three different evidence-based methods of helping people with serious alcohol problems: cognitive-behavioural therapy (CBT), motivational enhancement therapy (MET), and 12-step facilitation (TSF). There were no major differences in how well people did, irrespective of which form of help they received (Project MATCH Research Group, 1997). The United Kingdom Alcohol Treatment Trial (UKATT Research Team, 2005) built upon the findings of MATCH, comparing one of the therapeutic methods that had been used in that project (MET) with results from using a quite different method, based around ideas related to family and social support and social networks (Social Behaviour and Network Therapy, SBNT). Again, UKATT showed that there were no differences in how well people did, irrespective of which form of help they received.

Importantly, as well as showing that all these well-evidenced interventions seem to work as well as each other, what both Project MATCH and UKATT also showed was that *treatment works*. In both trials, substantial reductions in alcohol consumption, dependence and problems, and better mental-health-related quality of life, were reported.

REFERENCES

Copello, A., Velleman, R. and Templeton, L. (2005) Family interventions in the treatment of alcohol and drug problems. *Drug and Alcohol Review*, 24: 369–385.

Edwards, G., Gross, M. M., Keller, M., Moser, J. and Room, R. (1977) *Alcohol Related Disabilities*. WHO Offset Publication 32, Geneva.

Miller, W. and Rollnick, S. (1991) *Motivational Interviewing: Preparing People for Change* (3rd ed., 2012). New York and London: Guilford Press.

Miller, W. and Wilbourne, P. (2002) Mesa Grande: a methodological analysis of clinical trials of treatments for alcohol use disorders. *Addiction*, 97(3): 265–277.

Prochaska, J. and DiClemente, C. (1982) Transtheoretical therapy: toward a more integrative model of change. *Psychotherapy: Theory, Research and Practice*, 19(3): 276–88.

Prochaska, J. and DiClemente, C. (1994) *The Transtheoretical Approach: Crossing Traditional Boundaries of Therapy.* New York: Krieger..

Project MATCH Research Group (1997) Matching alcoholism treatments to client heterogeneity: Project MATCH post-treatment drinking outcomes. *Journal of Studies on Alcohol*, 58: 7–29.

UK Government Statistical Service (2016) Statistics on Alcohol England, 2016. (http://digital.nhs.uk/catalogue/PUB20999/alc-eng-2016-rep.pdf).

UKATT Research Team (2005) Effectiveness of treatment for alcohol problems: findings of the randomised UK Alcohol Treatment Trial (UKATT). *British Medical Journal*, 331: 541–544.

World Health Organisation (2015) Retrieved on 19 June, 2017 from http://www.who.int/mediacentre/factsheets/fs349/en/

Velleman, R. (2011) *Counselling for Alcohol Problems* (3rd ed.). London: Sage.

RECOMMENDED READING

1. Galvani, S. (2011) *Supporting People with Alcohol and Drug Problems: Making a Difference* (Social Work in Practice). London: Policy Press.

A book focusing on a social work practice approach to helping problem drinkers, anchored in relevant research.

2. Miller, W. and Rollnick, S. (1991) *Motivational Interviewing: Preparing People for Change* (3rd ed., 2012). New York and London: Guilford Press.

Motivational interviewing is the leading method of engaging with and helping those with alcohol problems, and this is the best introduction, by its originators.

3. Velleman, R. (2011) *Counselling for Alcohol Problems* (3rd ed.). London: Sage.

A highly practical guide to the steps that counsellors can take on a day-to-day basis to help those who have problems with their use of alcohol. The key book recommended by most alcohol counselling courses in the UK and a number of other countries, including the Scottish National Alcohol Counsellors Training Scheme.

6.3 ANXIETY AND PANIC

GILL DONOHOE AND TOM RICKETTS

OVERVIEW AND KEY POINTS

Problematic anxiety is a common and pervasive difficulty which manifests in many ways. Along with social anxiety disorder and post-traumatic stress disorder, generalised anxiety disorder (GAD) and panic are the most common anxiety disorders encountered in primary care services and are the focus of this chapter. Given the increasing effectiveness of cognitive-behavioural approaches to these disorders, this is the perspective which will be taken throughout.

This chapter will first outline the defining features of panic disorder and generalised anxiety disorder and guidance on assessment. Key models for understanding these difficulties will be introduced, along with case examples, to demonstrate clinical formulation and interventions based on the model. Finally, research and updates on the findings in relation to delivery options and core reading will be recommended.

DEFINING PANIC AND GENERALISED ANXIETY DISORDER

In the first, panic disorder, the main problem is recurrent panic attacks which occur unexpectedly at times when the individual does not anticipate anxiety. A panic attack is a discrete period of intense fear or discomfort that is accompanied by a range of somatic or cognitive symptoms (see Table 6.3.1). Panic attacks are often accompanied by a sense of imminent danger or impending doom and an urge to escape. They may be cued, that is triggered by specific situations, such as in phobic conditions or following trauma, or may be spontaneous. Unexpected or spontaneous panic attacks are important in the *diagnosis* of panic disorder, where more than one attack needs to have occurred unexpectedly and with at least four of the symptoms outlined in Table 6.3.1. Panic disorder and agoraphobia commonly occur together, with the fear and avoidance of a wide range of situations common in agoraphobia often being linked to a fear of the recurrence of panic attacks. In the most recent *Diagnostic and Statistical Manual of Mental Disorders* (DSM-5) (American Psychiatric Association, 2013), panic disorder and agoraphobia have been separated to recognise that panic may not be present in all cases of agoraphobia, and describing attacks as 'expected' or 'unexpected' rather than 'situationally bound' highlights that people often experience both types. Other features of panic disorder are that sufferers experience persistent concern about having additional attacks, worry about the implications of the attack or its consequences or a significant change in behaviour related to having had a panic attack.

Individuals may also experience panic attacks as a result of substance use, or as part of a medical condition such as hyperthyroidism. These possible explanations for symptoms should be explored in assessment.

In the second type of anxiety disorder, generalised anxiety disorder (GAD), the main defining feature is excessive anxiety and worry. To meet diagnostic criteria these feelings must be experienced more days than not for at least six months, must be about a range of different events or

Table 6.3.1 Criteria for a panic attack

A discrete period of intense fear or discomfort, in which four or more (at least once for full-symptom panic) of the following symptoms developed abruptly and reached a peak within minutes:

1	palpitations, pounding heart or accelerated heart rate
2	sweating
3	trembling or shaking
4	sensations of shortness of breath or smothering
5	feeling of choking
6	chest pain or discomfort
7	nausea or abdominal distress
8	feeling dizzy, unsteady, light-headed, or faint
9	derealisation or depersonalisation
10	fear of losing control or going crazy
11	fear of dying
12	paresthesias (pins and needles in extremities)
13	chills or hot flushes

Table 6.3.2 Diagnostic features of generalised anxiety disorder

Excessive anxiety and worry, occurring more days than not for at least six months, about a number of events or activities (such as work or school performance). At least three out of the following symptoms:

1	restlessness or feeling keyed up or on edge
2	being easily fatigued
3	difficulty concentrating or mind going blank
4	irritability
5	muscle tension
6	sleep disturbance

The anxiety, worry or physical symptoms must lead to significant distress or impairment in important areas of functioning

The focus of the anxiety or worry is not exclusively related to another psychiatric disorder

activities and must cause significant interference with the individual's functioning. Table 6.3.2 shows other diagnostic features for generalised anxiety disorder.

Overall, the symptoms experienced in generalised anxiety disorder are less intense than in panic disorder, onset is more gradual and the central feature is the repeated experience of excessive worry. Although less intense, GAD can be very difficult to control (which is in itself one of the defining features) and the condition tends to be under-recognised, although prevalence rates, difficulties in diagnosis and the chronic course of the untreated disorder have been recognised (McManus et al., 2009).

AETIOLOGY OF PANIC DISORDER AND GENERALISED ANXIETY DISORDER

It is useful when considering the causes of anxiety, to consider the range of both general and problem-specific factors. These can be broadly considered as an interacting set of vulnerabilities, including biological, psychological and more specific learning experiences which may influence the development of specific disorders (Barlow, 2002). Biological factors can include genetic contributions towards certain common traits, such as a neurotic or anxious predisposition. Environmental and learning experiences in each individual's history can then contribute to psychological vulnerabilities. An example of a key psychological factor relevant in the case of anxiety is a persistent sense of anticipated threat and lack of control. In the case of specific disorders, for example, panic, there may be a clear learning history which places particular emphasis on the dangerousness of somatic symptoms. In the case example described below, Jo's mother had herself experienced anxiety and panic as a parent, and had reacted to any unusual or sudden physical symptoms in herself or her children with alarm. She had regularly sought advice and reassurance from medical agencies. This could be considered as a form of vicarious learning and the development of cognitions regarding threat related to somatic experiences.

ASSESSMENT OF ANXIETY AND PANIC

Interventions for anxiety or panic should be based on a detailed assessment and analysis of the presenting difficulty along with any other associated problems. This will include taking a history of the development of the problem, identifying goals for therapy and the use of measurement tools to assist in the process and review outcomes. The assessment information is then discussed with the client within a cognitive-behavioural framework.

FORMULATION

PANIC DISORDER

In the cognitive model of panic disorder, it is proposed that panic attacks result from the misinterpretation of certain bodily sensations, with the sensations being perceived as much more dangerous than they actually are. Examples would be an individual perceiving palpitations as evidence of an impending heart attack, or perceiving a shaky feeling as evidence of loss of control and insanity.

Figure 6.3.1 illustrates the model. Triggers can be either external (e.g., a department store for a client suffering from agoraphobia, as in the case below), or internal (e.g., bodily sensations, thoughts or images), or both. If the trigger is experienced as threatening, a mild state of apprehension occurs. This is accompanied by a range of bodily sensations, which are then interpreted as catastrophic. This interpretation becomes the next perceived threat, and the vicious circle continues, culminating in a panic attack.

Once panic attacks have become established, the individual develops further responses to panic which serve to maintain the problem, namely selective attention, safety behaviours and avoidances. Selective attention relates to the way in which clients are watching out for physical symptoms constantly, and therefore notice them more, activating the panic cycle. Safety behaviours develop to prevent the feared catastrophic consequence from occurring, and include such things as holding on to walls or sitting down to prevent collapse. These behaviours give the individual an alternative explanation for why the feared event did not occur, and prevent changes in thinking during panic attacks. An example would be the individual thinking that they did not collapse because they sat down. Avoidances develop which restrict the individual's contact with anxiety-inducing situations, thereby reducing opportunities for discovering that the feared consequences do not occur.

The cognitive model proposes that panic disorder develops as a result of the triggering of pre-existing learnt assumptions about physical symptoms such as 'bodily symptoms are always an indication of something being wrong'. These assumptions are viewed as being developed through a range of routes, such as parental response to illness, perceived medical mismanagement and sudden deaths of significant others. Such assumptions are argued to be relatively stable (Beck, 1976), but to become more pertinent when triggered by events such as the individual experiencing illness themselves, or a first panic attack.

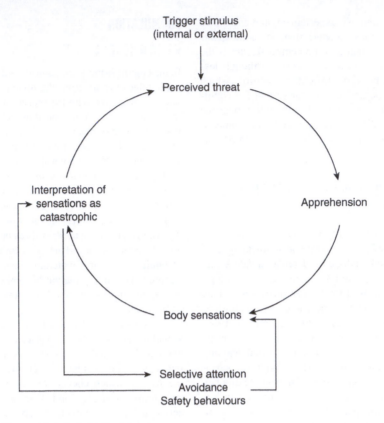

Figure 6.3.1 Cognitive model of panic disorder

Source: adapted from Clark (1986), Wells (1997)

PANIC CASE EXAMPLE

Four months previously, Jo gave birth to her first daughter and six weeks ago experienced her first panic attack. The birth of her daughter was complicated, leading to an emergency C-section, but this was well managed and despite the baby requiring initial intensive care, all was well and she returned home within a week. On the day she experienced her first panic attack Jo was feeling tired and stressed as usual, but needed to go to the local supermarket to pick up items for the baby. She started to feel unwell in the shopping aisle. She continued with her shopping but at the queue started to have difficulty with her breathing, pounding heart and experienced a strong sense of dread. This rapidly intensified to the point that she felt that she couldn't breathe and that her heart was going to explode. She felt hot and shaky and didn't know what was happening to her, but believed she was about to die. She managed somehow to pay for her items and quickly get out to the car. Once there she felt a little better and although still feeling very shaky and light-headed, managed to get home where, after a short time, she felt recovered. Jo, however, continued to experience attacks, usually when out in public places and sought advice from her General Practitioner (GP) as she was concerned about both her health and her ability to care for her family.

In the next section, reference will be made to Jo in terms of how interventions were used to help her to manage her symptoms of panic and reduce the impact on her life.

GENERALISED ANXIETY DISORDER

Models of generalised anxiety disorder (Dugas et al., 1998; Zinbarg et al., 2006) all share a focus on the central element of worry. This is consistent with developments in the understanding of the nature of the disorder, and changes from the initial diagnostic manual (*DSM*) (American Psychiatric Association, 1987). Further revisions supported the need to categorise GAD as a chronic and disabling disorder, identifiable even if coexisting

with another anxiety disorder and present for at least six months (instead of just one month).

A model outlined by Dugas and colleagues (1998) represents the considerable advancement in the understanding of GAD over the last 15–20 years, and forms the basis of a step-by-step treatment approach now recommended by the Department of Health in the United Kingdom (UK) (IAPT, 2007). Figure 6.3.2 outlines this model. Central to the Dugas model is the tendency of the individual to have a set of negative beliefs around uncertainty and its implications. An example is the belief that uncertainty is unfair or upsetting and should be avoided at all costs. This enduring tendency is described as an 'intolerance of uncertainty'

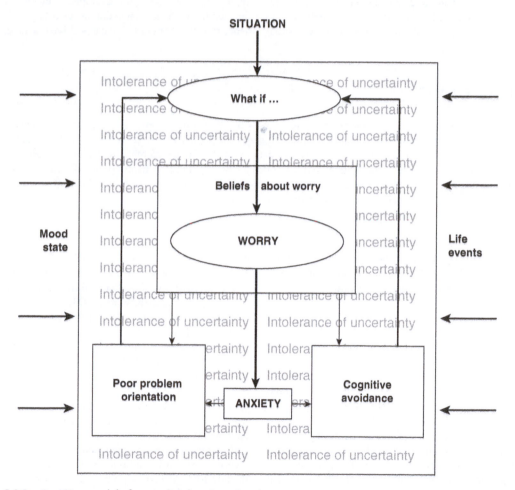

Figure 6.3.2 Cognitive model of generalised anxiety disorder

Source: Dugas et al. (1998), reprinted with permission from Elsevier

and is usually overtly manifested in the 'what if?' style of thinking which feeds the worry, and a range of possible approach or avoidance behaviours. These can include, among others, repeated checking, reassurance seeking, not being able to delegate, procrastination or avoidance of commitment. Consistent with previous models, the beliefs the individual holds about the worry itself have an important part to play in the development and maintenance of the problem. These can be either negative or positive. An example of a negative belief would be that the 'worrying will send me crazy', whereas a positive belief may be that 'worrying can prevent bad things from happening' or 'I need to worry to help me solve my problems'. Although both negative and positive beliefs may require targeting in therapy, Dugas and colleagues (1998) have helped to focus attention on the key role that positive beliefs may have in that if the act of worrying leads to a desired outcome (even if this may be coincidental), then the beliefs, and in turn the worry, will be reinforced. An example of negatively reinforced worry would be where a negative outcome is avoided.

The two other key aspects of the Dugas model are negative problem orientation and cognitive avoidance. Cognitive avoidance incorporates both emotional and cognitive features. The role of cognitive avoidance has had important implications for the treatment of GAD as it has led to the incorporation of exposure approaches where appropriate – methods traditionally associated primarily with phobic anxiety. Negative or poor problem orientation seems to be closely linked to the intolerance of uncertainty and relates to the way an individual approaches problems, for example, viewing them as threatening, with associated doubts regarding their confidence to solve them or to have a positive outcome.

GAD CASE EXAMPLE

John has always been a worrier. He cared for his younger brother from an early age as he had problems with learning difficulties and his parents separated when he was in his early teens. He managed well at school and became a teacher. His problems with worry and anxiety became more problematic when he got married and had a daughter. Along with work stress and a range of concerns regarding the health of his wife and his daughter's progress at school, he found he was struggling to sleep, to sustain work tasks and found the worry and associated symptoms to be increasingly difficult to control.

These explanations of panic disorder and generalised anxiety disorder have led to the development of specific interventions, which will be outlined below.

INTERVENTIONS

A considerable proportion of individuals with anxiety may be managed within primary care, adopting a self-help approach with more limited therapist involvement but still within the framework described in this section. The National Institute for Health and Care Excellence guidance on anxiety (NICE, 2011a) reinforces the role of a stepped-care framework to assist in the management of GAD. Low-intensity interventions following assessment and identification of anxiety can enable individuals to access help more quickly, and in less severe cases yield considerable benefits. Self-help may be non-facilitated with minimal therapist contact over approximately six weeks or guided with regular face-to-face or telephone sessions by an experienced practitioner. Psycho-education groups are further low-intensity (Step 2) options delivered over at least six weeks. Stress Control courses are a recognised and well-evaluated format delivered widely (Delgadillo et al., 2016; White, 1998).

Stepped-care interventions delivered within primary care have enabled sufferers to access help more rapidly. NICE guidance recommend that the range of options described above are all clearly available but that if these are not effective or the presentations are more severe, then intensive (Step 3) approaches are required and with a choice of psychological or pharmacological interventions.

For both anxiety and panic, cognitive-behavioural approaches have been shown to be effective, along with earlier methods based upon conditioning and learning theories (see Craske and Barlow, 2007). The first stage of therapy for any anxiety problem is to educate the client on the principles of the approach and the rationale for the treatment plan based upon their difficulties. It is therefore important to start this process from the very onset, ideally developing a formulation with the client at session one, particularly in the case of panic disorder. In cases of GAD, the formulation may be progressively developed in stages over the course of therapy in line with the interventions and model described in this chapter. In all cases, it is important to make use of recommended outcome measures designed to monitor progress on a session-by-session basis.

INTERVENTIONS FOR PANIC DISORDER

- *Education about anxiety.* Given the importance of catastrophic misinterpretations of bodily symptoms in panic disorder, education regarding the features of normal anxiety is a first stage in treatment. In the case example described, Jo was reassured by being provided with clear verbal and written details on anxiety and panic, along with the formulation to make sense of why it was understandable and natural to experience the body's normal response to perceived threat and how this would be an adaptive response to actual current danger. Experiments can also be utilised to enhance socialisation to the model, for example, the 'paired associates task' (Clark et al., 1988), where Jo was instructed to read aloud and focus on symptoms, such as (dizziness), paired with typical misinterpretations (fainting), to test whether attention alone has an impact on symptoms.
- *Dealing with misinterpretations of physical symptoms.* This part of the treatment focuses on enabling the client to identify thoughts associated with concerns about physical symptoms, and then to begin to develop alternative perspectives on those same symptoms. The previous educational and socialisation interventions regarding the nature of anxiety and panic provides the client with a starting point for identifying an alternative perspective. Once an alternative perspective has been developed, current evidence for each of the two perspectives should be considered in detail, and a behavioural experiment agreed. Within this process the therapist is directive in engaging the client in consideration of their thoughts regarding symptoms, but the alternative views need to be elicited from the client, rather than presented by the therapist. When experiencing palpitations Jo continued to automatically see herself at risk of an imminent heart attack rather than as being the result of the release of adrenalin into her bloodstream. An example of a behavioural experiment for Jo involved running up and down stairs vigorously, at first in the treatment setting in order to test her belief regarding the dangerousness of her heart racing.
- *Dealing with avoidance.* Following a reduction in the degree of belief in the dangerousness of physical

symptoms, the client should gradually resume all avoided behaviours, utilising a graded exposure approach as described within the chapter on phobias in this volume (Ricketts and Donohoe – Chapter 6.14, this volume). These can be framed as experiments to continue to challenge beliefs, for example, 'if I get hot and it is busy in the shop, then I will faint and make a fool of myself'.

- *Reduction of safety behaviours.* The use of safety behaviours by panic sufferers helps to explain how, despite the repeated failure of the feared consequence to occur during panic attacks, they continue to believe that it may occur next time. Safety behaviours will therefore prevent the cognitive approach outlined earlier from being effective. As for avoidances, safety behaviours (such as having to hold on to the trolley) should be gradually reduced as the client becomes more confident in the alternative explanations for their symptoms.
- *Relapse prevention.* Consideration of the patterns of unhelpful behaviours which the client had engaged in, together with discussion and reconsideration of any long-standing assumptions regarding the dangerousness of physical symptoms, should occur towards the end of treatment, with a view to maintenance of change.

INTERVENTIONS FOR GENERALISED ANXIETY DISORDER (GAD)

- *Education.* As with panic disorder, educating the client about the normal features of anxiety is a first component of treatment. This should include an explanation of the model, for example, as outlined above, and the central role of worry. Anxiety and worry in GAD should be explained as the extreme end of a normal and universal mental phenomenon. Dugas and colleagues (1998) suggest that the treatment model and approach should be presented to the client in a step-by-step fashion. Following and alongside psycho-education, the client is instructed to keep a 'worry diary'. This helps the client to recognise the triggers for worry and the types of worry they experience. Worries are then classified into two main types: worries about current problems and worries about future hypothetical situations. In the case example outlined above, John found it helpful to identify that although some of the worries regarding his work were current and practical, the majority of his concerns were possible future scenarios that may not arise.
- *Modifying beliefs about worry.* As with panic disorder, a process of identifying and then reconsidering beliefs about the nature of symptoms, in this case worry, is

central to treatment of generalised anxiety disorder. Other strategies seek to disconfirm beliefs, both positive and negative, about worry, specifically through behaviour change. Behavioural experiments can be used to increase tolerance of uncertainty by targeting avoidance or reducing other behaviours, such as checking or reassurance seeking. To engage the client in experiments they are first helped to identify the range of behaviours which they have been adopting in an attempt to be more certain but which in effect fuel the worry. Tolerating uncertainty experiments are planned and recorded. For example, a homework experiment may be to go to an unknown restaurant without first checking or to invite a colleague or friend out for the evening. John agreed to stop checking his work emails every evening for a one-week period in order to test whether this would increase or reduce his work problems and worry. Other more internal behaviours, such as thought control, can also be abandoned in a controlled therapeutic experiment. Challenging thoughts about the usefulness of worry (targeting positive beliefs about worry) may follow. For example, 'worry helps me to prepare and perform better at work'. Beliefs should be identified and sensitively challenged through non-judgemental questioning and discussion. See Dugas and Robichaud (2007) for a list of possible approaches. Negative beliefs can also be targeted. An example of a strategy which may be incorporated here includes the use of controlled worry periods, in which a 15-minute period each day is set aside to actively worry about issues. Throughout the rest of the day, when worry is identified, it is deferred until the planned worry period. This can be utilised to challenge perceptions of the uncontrollability of worry. Another example could be where the client is encouraged to 'lose control' of worry, or actively exaggerate their worries, so that the possible feared consequence of mental illness or complete loss of control is disconfirmed.

- *Problem-solving training.* In line with recent developments in the understanding of worry and GAD (Dugas and Robichaud, 2007), two aspects to problem-solving approaches should be considered – problem-solving orientation and problem-solving skills. Strategies to improve problem-solving orientation incorporate a number of cognitive and behavioural approaches, such as assisting the individual to view problems as opportunities rather than threats and identifying and approaching problems earlier (rather than putting off or avoiding). Actual problem-solving skills can then follow with a step-by-step method for identifying and dealing with problems and decision-making.

- *Imaginal/cognitive exposure.* The roles of avoidance, thought suppression and neutralisation are explained to clients along the lines of that which would be considered in the treatment of a phobia. The individual is then helped to identify core fears associated with worry. A scenario is then developed with the client, which can be drafted and eventually audio-recorded. This forms the material for exposure sessions and is repeatedly presented until anxiety levels reduce. It is important that the exposure scenario does not include neutralisation, for example, self-reassuring statements, and that core fears are addressed but without them being taken to a ridiculous extreme. Sessions are initially conducted in clinic but can be repeated for homework.

- *Relaxation training.* Given the tension and restlessness evident in GAD, there is a place for the teaching of progressive and applied relaxation for clients. It is important to recognise applied relaxation as a stand-alone approach which, if utilised, should adhere to a standard protocol and, like cognitive-behavioural therapy (CBT), be delivered over approximately 12–15 sessions (see NICE, 2011a; Ost, 1987). This does not mean, however, that relaxation skills may not be utilised with other approaches. Caution should be exercised that doing the relaxation 'right' does not become another source of worry for the client.

EVALUATION

Treatment outcome studies into the cognitive treatment of panic disorder have shown generally good results, despite some studies having relatively small sample sizes. Cognitive therapy has been shown to be more effective than supportive therapy (Beck et al., 1992), applied relaxation (Clark et al., 1994) and imipramine (Clark et al., 1994). Cognitive therapy targeting catastrophic misinterpretations of physical symptoms, and excluding all exposure elements, has been found to be successful in reducing panic frequency. The addition of exposure-based approaches does appear to strengthen treatment effects, however. Where research has focused on panic disorder with agoraphobia, the superiority of cognitive therapy over exposure therapy alone is less clear-cut, with Bouchard et al. (1996) finding no significant difference.

Research into the treatment of generalised anxiety disorder by cognitive therapy is more recent, but results are promising. Cognitive-behavioural therapy has been found to be more effective than behaviour therapy alone (Butler et al., 1991), having good effects on thoughts, expectations and beliefs about worry in something less than half the clients. Hunot et al. (2007) conducted a

Cochrane review into the effectiveness of psychological therapies for GAD and found that CBT was effective for short-term treatment of anxiety. For both panic disorder and generalised anxiety disorder, if medication is to be offered, an antidepressant from the selective serotonin reuptake inhibitor (SSRI) group has generally been shown to be most effective, with sertraline most highly recommended in the case of GAD. The National Institute for Health and Care Excellence (NICE, 2011b) recommends that psychological therapy (cognitive-behavioural therapy, applied relaxation) or drug treatment should be offered if a less intensive approach, for example self-help or psycho-educational group, is not effective, and this should be before a referral is made to specialist mental health services.

The expansion of the Improving Access to Psychological Therapies (IAPT) programme and increased access to clinical data (session-by-session symptom measurement) has informed recent evaluation and the importance of the variables which may influence the recovery of individuals with anxiety across the range of treatment intensities at different steps. The development of the NICE Guidance *Common Mental Health Problems: Identification and Pathways to Care* (2011b) builds on the recommendations (Kaltenhaler et al., 2004) for further research on the effectiveness of formats and types of intervention in low-intensity approaches, including computerised cognitive-behavioural therapy and other guided and non-facilitated self-help methods. For example, in the NICE Evidence Update for generalised anxiety disorder (NICE, 2012), all evidence reviewed supported the pathways and interventions for anxiety and panic but with further recommendations on comparing the methods of delivery of guided self-help. For the proportion with complex problems and increased risk of self-harm, which require a combined approach, then a collaborative care intervention including psychological and pharmacological methods should be utilised and further work is required in this endeavour.

REFERENCES

American Psychiatric Association (1987) *Diagnostic and Statistical Manual of Mental Disorders* (3rd ed.). Washington, DC: American Psychiatric Association.

American Psychiatric Association (2013) *Diagnostic and Statistical Manual of Mental Disorders* (5th ed.). Washington, DC: American Psychiatric Association.

Barlow, D.H. (2002) *Anxiety and It's Disorders. The Nature and Treatment of Anxiety and Panic* (2nd ed.). New York: The Guilford Press.

Beck, A.T. (1976) *Cognitive Therapy and the Emotional Disorders.* New York: International Universities Press.

Beck, A.T., Sokol, L., Clark, D.A., Berchick, B. and Wright, F. (1992) Focused cognitive therapy for panic disorder: a crossover design and one-year follow-up. *American Journal of Psychiatry*, 147: 778–783.

Bouchard, S., Gauthier, J., Laberge, B., French, D., Pelletier, M.H. and Godbout, C. (1996) Exposure versus cognitive restructuring in the treatment of panic disorder with agoraphobia. *Behaviour Research and Therapy*, 34: 213–224.

Butler, G., Fennell, M., Robson, P. and Gelder, M. (1991) A comparison of behavior therapy and cognitive behavior therapy in the treatment of generalized anxiety disorder. *Journal of Consulting and Clinical Psychology*, 59: 167–175.

Clark, D.M. (1986) A cognitive approach to panic disorder. *Behaviour Research and Therapy*, 24: 461–470.

Clark, D.M., Salkovskis, P.M., Gelder, M., Koehler, C., Martin, M., Anastasiades, P., Hackman, A., Middleton, H. and Jeavons, A. (1988) Tests of a cognitive theory of panic. In I. Hand and H.V. Wittchen (Eds), *Panic and Phobias.* Berlin: Springer.

Clark, D.M., Salkovskis, P.M., Hackmann, A., Middleton, H., Anastasiades, P. and Gelder, M.G. (1994) A comparison of cognitive therapy, applied relaxation and imipramine in the treatment of panic disorder. *British Journal of Psychiatry*, 164: 759–769.

Craske, M.G. and Barlow, D.H. (2007) *Mastery of Your Anxiety and Panic (Therapist Guide)* (4th ed.). Oxford: Oxford University Press.

(Continued)

(Continued)

Delgadillo, J., Kellett, S., Ali, S., MacMillan, D., Barkham, M., Saxon, D., Donohoe, G., Stonebank, H., Mullaney, S., Eschoe, P., Thwaites, R. and Lucock, M. (2016) A multi service practice research network study of large group psych-oeducational cognitive behavioural therapy. *Behaviour Research & Therapy*, 67: 155–161.

Dugas, M.J., Gagnon, F., Ladouceur, R. and Freeston, M.H. (1998) Generalized anxiety disorder: a preliminary test of a conceptual model. *Behaviour Research and Therapy*, 36: 215–226.

Dugas, M.J. and Robichaud, M. (2007) *Cognitive-Behavioural Treatment for Generalized Anxiety Disorder: From Science to Practice*. London: Routledge.

Hunot, V., Churchill, R., Silva de Lima, M., et al. (2007) Psychological therapies for generalised anxiety disorder. *Cochrane Database of Systematic Review*, CD001848.

IAPT (2007) *The Competencies Required to Deliver Effective Cognitive and Behavioural Therapy for People with Depression and with Anxiety Disorders: Improving Access to Psychological Therapies*. London: Department of Health.

Kaltenthaler, E., Parry, G. and Beverley, C. (2004) Computerized cognitive behaviour therapy: a systematic review. *Behavioural and Cognitive Psychotherapy*, 32: 31–55.

McManus, S., Meltzer, H., Brugha, T., et al. (2009) *Adult Psychiatric Morbidity in England, 2007: Results of a Household Survey*. Leeds: NHS Information Centre for Health and Social Care.

NICE (2011a) *Generalised Anxiety Disorder and Panic Disorder (with or without Agoraphobia) in Adults: Management in Primary, Secondary and Community Care*. Clinical Guideline 113. London: NICE.

NICE (2011b) *Common Mental Health Problems: Identification and Pathways to Care*. Clinical Guideline 123. London: NICE.

NICE (2012) *Generalised Anxiety Disorder in Adults: Evidence Update: A Summary of Selected New Evidence Relevant to NICE Clinical Guideline 113*. NHS Evidence Update 22. London: NICE.

Ost, L.G. (1987) Applied relaxation: description of a coping technique and review of controlled studies. *Behaviour Research and Therapy*, 25: 397.

Wells, A. (1997) *Cognitive Therapy of Anxiety Disorders: A Practice Manual and Conceptual Guide*. Chichester: Wiley.

White, J. (1998) 'Stress control' large group therapy for generalized anxiety disorder: two year follow-up. *Behavioural and Cognitive Psychotherapy*, 26: 237–245.

Zinbarg, R.G. Craske, M.G., and Barlow, D.A. (2006). *Mastery of your Anxiety and Worry*. Oxford: Oxford University Press.

RECOMMENDED READING

1.   Barlow, D.H. (2002) *Anxiety and Its Disorders: The Nature and Treatment of Anxiety and Panic* (2nd ed.). New York: Guildford Press.

This is a thorough and extensive book covering the full range of theories relevant to the understanding and management of all of the anxiety disorders and the nature of the emotion.

2.   Wells, A. (1997) *Cognitive Therapy of Anxiety Disorder: A Practice and Conceptual Guide*. Chichester: Wiley.

This book is an excellent manual for the range of anxiety disorders, with clear models, case formulations and treatment interventions, delivered in a way which clearly connects with cognitive theory and the skills required to deliver therapy.

3.   Dugas, M.J. and Robichaud, M. (2007) *Cognitive-Behavioural Treatment for Generalized Anxiety Disorder: From Science to Practice*. London: Routledge.

This book provides the step-by-step treatment manual and formulation for the treatment of generalised anxiety which emphasises the critical role of dealing with uncertainty. Research and examples are clearly provided to guide the clinician.

6.4 BEREAVEMENT

LINDA MACHIN

OVERVIEW AND KEY POINTS

A psychodynamic perspective dominated the study of grief in the twentieth century. Contemporary researchers have built on the foundational work of seminal theorists like Bowlby but challenged the bias towards predominantly emotion-focused and pathological perspectives on grief. They have countered traditional notions by embracing a wider view of grief to include behavioural and social consequences and adaptations, and recognised the prevalence of resilience in those who grieve. This chapter will use the Range of Response to Loss (RRL) model, which echoes the concepts of contemporary theory, as the framework for exploring work with bereaved people. It was developed from research and practice, and alongside it the Adult Attitude to Grief (AAG) scale, which parallels the concepts in the model, is a tool used to capture the grieving characteristics of clients presenting for bereavement support. The diverse experiences and expressions of grief encapsulated in the AAG responses provide the rationale for a pluralistic approach to therapeutic interventions. Key points in this chapter include:

- Changing perspectives in grief theory
- Identifying the diverse reactions and responses to bereavement
- A measure to profile individual grief
- A pluralistic approach to counselling the bereaved.

DEFINITION

The primary focus of this chapter is bereavement, the experience of loss through the death of someone of significance, and the therapeutic approach to working with grief, the multifaceted range of reactions and responses to loss. While the term 'grief' will be used here in relationship to bereavement, it is important to remember that grief can also be activated by any experience of loss and the suggested theoretical and therapeutic approaches applied to them.

AETIOLOGY

The study of grief as a psychosocial reaction to bereavement was dominated during the twentieth century by psychodynamic perspectives. Central to this school of thought was the seminal work of John Bowlby (1980). The work on attachment provided a concept for understanding the nature and variability of reactions to separation and loss, and was the foundation for research and practice in the field of loss and bereavement (Cassidy and Shaver, 1999; Fraley and Shaver, 1999; Mikulincer and Florian, 1998; Parkes, 1972/1986/1996, 2006; Raphael, 1984). A significant challenge to the classic theories of grief came with the development of the Dual Process Model (DPM), which provided a more holistic account of loss response (Stroebe and Schut, 1999), attending to ongoing life demands (restoration orientation) as well as focusing on the emotional consequences of loss (loss orientation). The capacity to move between these two orientations (oscillation) demonstrates adjustments to loss taking place across the emotional domain and the cognitive/behavioural/social domain. This shift in emphasis has been very influential in the practice of bereavement and palliative care (Archer, 1999; Dallos, 2006; Hindmarch, 2009; Payne et al., 1999; Quinn, 2005; Stokes, 2007; Thompson, 2002). Additionally, contemporary research is suggesting that an apparent absence of grief is not necessarily indicative of pathology, as formerly thought, and that resilience in the face of loss is more common than frequently believed (Bonanno, 2004).

Nevertheless, identifying the psychological components of complicated grief still remains a challenge both for researchers and practitioners, whose interest is concerned with those at risk in bereavement (Sanders, 1993). Foremost in this field of research have been Prigerson and Maciejewski (2006), who have produced a measure of Prolonged Grief Disorder (PGD). It is worth noting that, while other psychiatric conditions such as depression (Kroenke and Spitzer, 2002) or anxiety (Spitzer et al., 2006) have been regarded as components of complicated grief, they do not provide a complete definition of the complex spectrum of grief responses which might make a person vulnerable in their bereavement.

Alongside this contemporary shift in theory, the Range of Response to Loss model (RRL) was created (Machin, 2001, 2014) as a result of listening to the experiences of grieving people in both clinical practice and research.

The model, while reflecting the language brought to therapy by clients, parallels the concepts of both attachment theory and the Dual Process Model. The RRL is a two-dimensional model reflecting the dynamic between stressors and coping (Stroebe et al., 2006). The first dimension characterises the reflexive reaction to grief (stressor) on a feeling and functioning spectrum, expressed in the RRL model as overwhelmed to controlled, and the second dimension characterises cognitively aware coping in a range from resilience to vulnerability.

The Adult Attitude to Grief (AAG) scale was devised initially to test the validity of the proposed elements in the RRL model. The self-report statements in the scale reflect the RRL categories – overwhelmed, controlled and resilient – while an indication of vulnerability is quantitatively calculated by combining the scores of the overwhelmed and controlled reactions (scoring on a 5-point Likert scale, in a range from 4 for 'strongly agree' through to 0 for 'strongly

disagree', providing a range from 0–36) and reversing the scoring of the resilient responses (see Figure 6.4.1 and Table 6.4.1, below). Sim et al. (2013) established support for the psychometric properties of the AAG scale, for its use to determine an indication of vulnerability and for the classification of different levels of vulnerability:

Severe vulnerability	>24
High vulnerability	21–23
Low vulnerability	<20

It became clear in the research process that in addition to giving support to the concepts in the RRL model, the AAG scale provided a profile of client grief. Further testing of the AAG scale as a clinical tool (Machin, 2007; Machin and Spall, 2004), and reported use in practice, has resulted in the increased use of the scale across the bereavement care sector.

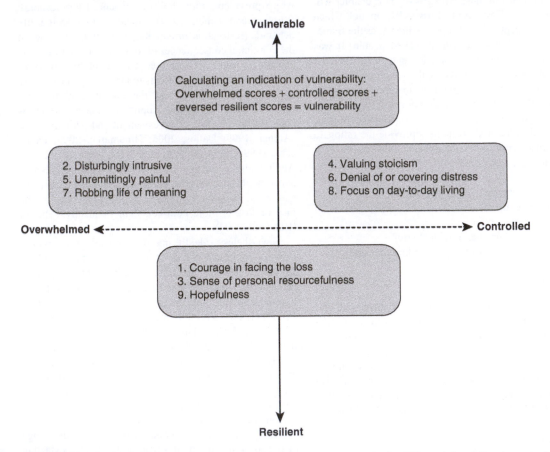

Figure 6.4.1 The interacting core grief reactions and coping responses in the RRL model and the characteristics of the model reflected in the AAG scale

ASSESSMENT

The RRL model provides a conceptual base from which to appraise the impact of bereavement loss by exploring a client's core grief reactions and their relative vulnerability/resilience in coping with the consequence of loss. The AAG scale provides more specific quantitative and qualitative profiling of client grief, as seen in the case study below. The RRL model and the AAG measure can be used throughout intervention for appraisal and measurement of change.

Not all grief requires intervention (Neimeyer, 2000, 2010; Schut, 2010), and increasingly the three-tier system describing varied levels of need is being used as guidance (see Figure 6.4.2). Services are beginning to look more rigorously at distinguishing those bereaved people with complex needs from those whose grief is normal and who require minimal professional intervention.

FORMULATION

It is clear that if the experience and expression of grief is diverse, then the approaches to working with it need to reflect that diversity. No longer will a one-size-fits-all approach based on a belief generated in the early literature

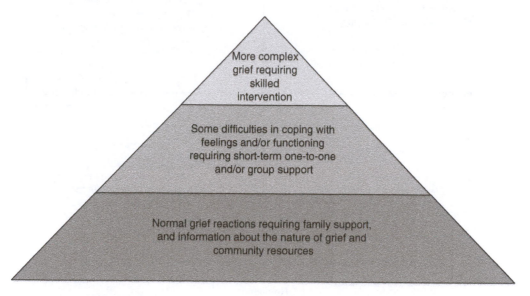

Figure 6.4.2 Levels of bereavement need associated with AAG vulnerability indicator scores and the linked intervention

about a universal linear grief process and/or training within a single school of psychotherapy meet the widely varied expressions of grief. A pluralistic counselling approach (Cooper and McLeod, 2011), therefore, is best suited conceptually and practically to working with bereaved people (Machin, 2014). This section will provide a rationale for integrating the RRL model and pluralistic counselling (based on the domains of **goals**, **tasks** and **methods**). Exploring this connection will inevitably entail some analysis and disaggregation of the helping process, which in practice will be a combined synergy of these factors.

The RRL model provides two distinct areas for therapeutic attention and potential **goal** focus. The first, associated with the overwhelmed/controlled spectrum of reactions to bereavement, aims to bring to the client an awareness of what has been expressed instinctively. The goal in achieving this will address any lack of balance between feeling and functioning. Where there is a bias towards feeling overwhelmed, the goal is to counter this by exploring strategies for more effective functioning. Conversely, where there is an instinctive bias towards control, but this is undermined by the wider impact of the loss, the goal is to explore the feelings which are inhibiting effective functioning.

The second RRL dimension of goal focus is that of coping responses on a spectrum from vulnerability to resilience. For those people needing therapy, the goal initially is to identify the nature of the vulnerability and those circumstantial factors which are adding complexity to the psychosocial aspects of grief (e.g., health problems, economic problems, caring demands, etc.). Some of these issues may need to be dealt with by other services. The longer-term therapeutic goal will be to explore the story of loss and help the client accept what cannot be changed, engage with necessary life adjustments and explore the meanings that they can draw from the experience of loss (see Figure 6.4.3).

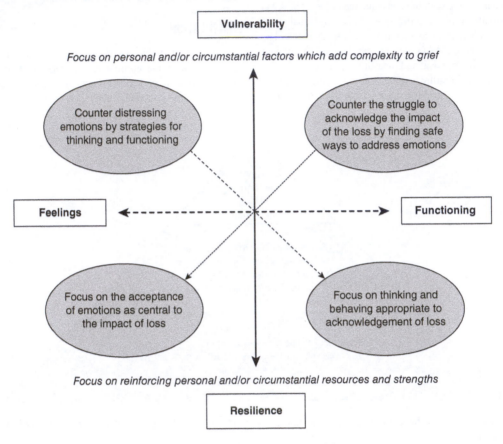

Figure 6.4.3   Therapeutic goals set within the framework of the RRL model

The **tasks**, seen as a second domain in pluralistic counselling, are well established in the field of grief counselling and link directly to the four tasks Worden (2009) identified as necessary for addressing loss:

1. To acknowledge the reality of the loss.
2. To process the pain of grief.
3. To adjust to the world without the deceased.
4. To find an enduring connection with the deceased in the midst of embarking on a new life.

The tasks provide a framework within which the individual mediating factors – relationship to the deceased, nature of the death, levels of support, etc. – can be explored with the client.

The third domain of the pluralistic approach is that of **methods** (i.e., the way in which goals and tasks are undertaken therapeutically). Underpinning all the other methods which might be appropriately used are a person-centred way of being with a bereaved person, receiving the uniqueness of their experience and expressions of grief, together with a narrative approach which holds the story of grief and its components as central to an understanding of the dynamics which make it up (Machin, 2014). Using the RRL framework and listening to the story of loss can help clarify those areas which are troubling to the client (see Table 6.4.1.)

Table 6.4.1   Applying the narrative process to the Range of Response to Loss model

(The link with the attitudinal statements in the Adult Attitude to Grief scale is indicated by the numbers.)

Narrative process (Angus and Hardke, 1994)	Range of Response to Loss (Machin, 2001)		
	Overwhelmed	Balanced/Resilient	Controlled
External narrative (what happened, when and how...)	Story told in great detail with emphasis upon the awfulness of experience.	Story told with coherence and attention given to the positive and negative aspects of experience.	Story told with minimum detail and with an emphasis upon factual aspects of experience.
Internal narrative (the impact of events upon the teller)	The engulfing nature of grief is described (2) and the teller may assume the role of victim.	The pain of loss (1) is countered by a positive sense of personal resourcefulness (3).	The desire for control (6) and bravery (4) dominates and accounts of pain are minimised.
Reflexive narrative (a process of making sense of the experience)	A lack of hopefulness about the outcome of grief (5) and difficulty in finding a sense of meaning within it (7). Personal identity may be defined in terms of the loss.	A sense of optimism in spite of the pain (9), a capacity to find meaning, and awareness of the strength which might result from an experience of loss.	A diversion from the painful elements of loss and a need to find meaning in the stoical meeting of adversity (8).

Engaging fully and empathically with a client and their grief as they are currently experiencing and expressing it is crucial. Only when they feel fully heard and accepted can the challenges to find new ways of understanding their loss and of coping with its consequences be undertaken. The following approaches are suggested to address the goals in the RRL model (see Figure 6.4.3):

- Overwhelming grief can be addressed with a cognitive approach to refocus on functioning strategies.
- Controlled grief can be addressed with a psychodynamic/attachment theory approach to re-examine relationships and emotions.

- Vulnerability can be addressed with a systems theory approach which locates the client fully in the context of their daily experience.
- Resilience can be enhanced by a meaning reconstruction approach which can enhance deep reflection on bereavement and its consequences.

INTERVENTION

The following case study illustrates the use of the RRL concepts as they were revealed in dialogue with the therapist and in the completion of the AAG scale (see Table 6.4.2).

CASE EXAMPLE

Hannah was in her late 70s and was referred for psychological help. She had suffered a stroke, which was seriously complicating the grief she felt for her deceased husband. The physical limitations resulting from the stroke defeated the 'getting on with life' approach she had previously used to adjust to the loss of her husband. The AAG scale was used to profile Hannah's grief (see Table 6.4.2). A severe level of vulnerability was evident from the VI score of 31. In looking more closely at the categories within the scale, Hannah was recording similar levels of agreement with both the overwhelmed and controlled items. This indicates considerable tension between

(Continued)

(Continued)

the automatic pull towards functioning and the overpowering feelings of grief. Alongside this tension was an absence of agreement with the resilient items. This grief picture was also evident in the qualitative comments which Hannah made in response to the AAG scale.

The **goals** of therapy, as agreed with Hannah, were to help her in the **tasks** of (1) addressing the emotional impact of her husband's death and (2) adjusting to his death in the changed circumstances of her physical limitations.

At the time of her bereavement Hannah had coped by not processing the pain of her grief. The **method** of addressing this task was by looking at her attachment history, the nature of relationships and the way in which feelings were expressed and experienced. This helped Hannah to recognise the practical strengths she had acquired during her life as a daughter, caring sibling, wife and mother, but also to see that emotional expression had been limited. The attachment narrative prompted her to consider situations when she had been confronted with difficulties but found the resourcefulness to cope well. In identifying this resourcefulness, a component of resilience, she could reflect on its application to the currently overwhelming experiences of bereavement and her seriously disabling illness. Cognitive strategies addressing practical ways of accommodating her physical limitations included ways of dealing with panic attacks and undertaking modified relaxation exercises. Hannah achieved a more balanced cognitive perspective but fuller emotional equilibrium was not reached in the face of her major life losses.

Table 6.4.2 Hannah's combined quantitative and qualitative responses to the AAG scale

AAG Practitioner Record Sheet

(**R** = Resilient items **1,3,9; C**= Controlled items **4,6,8; O** = Overwhelmed items **2,5,7**)

Adult Attitude to Grief scale (© *Linda Machin 2001*)	Strongly agree	Agree	Neither agree nor disagree	Disagree	Strongly disagree	Additional responses/comments
R	0	1	2	3	4	Difficult to face it on your own.
1. I feel able to face the pain which comes with loss.					X	
O	4	3	2	1	0	I think about him every day. On a bad day I wish he was here.
2. For me, it is difficult to switch off thoughts about the person I have lost.		X				
R	0	1	2	3	4	I'm a survivor like my mother. I've coped with a number of deaths but this is different.
3. I feel very aware of my inner strength when faced with grief.				X		
C	4	3	2	1	0	I have to be brave for the sake of my children. It's not good if I moan to my daughters.
4. I believe that I must be brave in the face of loss.		X				

Adult Attitude to Grief scale (© Linda Machin 2001)	Strongly agree	Agree	Neither agree nor disagree	Disagree	Strongly disagree	Additional responses/comments
O	4	3	2	1	0	I'm finding it very difficult to get over my husband's death. I get upset if anybody talks about him. Anything sad can trigger it off.
5. I feel that I will always carry the pain of grief with me.	X					
C	4	3	2	1	0	I can't do anything about it so why keep crying about it but I wish I could put it all to the back of my mind.
6. For me, it is important to keep my grief under control.	X					
O	4	3	2	1	0	I believe that nothing will ever be the same. It isn't living is it, sitting alone in a chair all day?
7. Life has less meaning for me after this loss.	X					
C	4	3	2	1	0	I need to get on with life because there is nothing else I can do. You've got to cope; there's no alternative but it's very hard.
8. I think it's best just to get on with life and not dwell on this loss.*		X				
R	0	1	2	3	4	I'm afraid my grief might get worse not better. I have come through, in a way, but there is deep depression and I don't think it will ever go away.
9. It may not always feel like it but I do believe that I will come through this experience of grief.				X		

© Linda Machin 2010 (* modified 2013) **Vulnerability Indicator score** = total score for the 9 items (N.B. resilient scores reversed to permit a simple addition)

EVALUATION

Recognising the human capacity for resilience, while understanding the risk associated with vulnerability, determines the likely incidence of need for counselling in the bereaved population. The Range of Response to Loss model offers a conceptual indicator for both of these factors and the Adult Attitude to Grief scale provides a measure to capture a more detailed quantitative and qualitative profile of client grief. These linked approaches can be used for initial assessment, therapeutic review and evaluation of outcome.

REFERENCES

Angus, L. and Hardke, K. (1994) Narrative processes in psychotherapy. *Canadian Psychology*, 55: 1255–1270.
Archer, J. (1999) *The Nature of Grief*. London: Routledge.
Bonanno, G.A. (2004) Loss, trauma and human resilience. *American Psychologist*, 59(1): 20–28.
Bowlby J. (1980) *Loss: Sadness and Depression*. Vol. 3: *Attachment and Loss*. London: Hogarth Press.
Cassidy, J. and Shaver, P.R. (eds) (1999) *Handbook of Attachment: Theory, Research and Clinical Application*. New York: Guilford Press.

(Continued)

(Continued)

Cooper, M. and McLeod, J. (2011) *Pluralistic Counselling and Psychotherapy*. London: Sage.

Dallos, R. (2006) *Attachment Narrative Therapy*. Maidenhead: Open University Press.

Fraley, R.C. and Shaver, P.R. (1999) Loss and bereavement: Attachment theory and recent controversies concerning grief work and the nature of detachment. In J. Cassidy and P.R. Shaver (eds), *Handbook of Attachment: Theory, Research, and Clinical Applications* (pp. 735–759). New York: Guilford Press.

Hindmarch, C. (2009) *On the Death of a Child*. Oxford: Radcliffe Publishing.

Kroenke, K. and Spitzer, R.L. (2002) The PHQ-9: A new depression and diagnostic severity measure. *Psychiatric Annals*, 32: 509–521.

Machin, L. (2001) Exploring a framework for understanding the range of response to loss: A study of clients receiving bereavement counselling. Unpublished PhD thesis, Keele University, UK.

Machin, L. (2007) The Adult Attitude to Grief Scale as a tool of practice for counsellors working with bereaved people: A study report sponsored by Age Concern, Tameside and Keele University.

Machin, L. (2014) *Working with Loss and Grief* (2nd ed.). London: Sage.

Machin, L. and Spall, R. (2004) Mapping grief: A study in practice using a quantitative and qualitative approach to exploring and addressing the range of response to loss. *Counselling and Psychotherapy Research*, 4: 9–17.

Mikulincer, M. and Florian, V. (1998) The relationship between adult attachment styles and emotional and cognitive reactions to stressful events. In J.A. Simpson and W.S. Rholes (eds), *Attachment Theory and Close Relationships* (pp. 143–165). New York: Guilford Press.

Neimeyer, R.A. (2000) Searching for the meaning of meaning: Grief therapy and the process of reconstruction. *Death Studies*, 24: 541–558.

Neimeyer, R.A. (2010) Grief counselling and therapy: The case for humility. *Bereavement Care*, 29: 4–7.

Parkes, C.M. (1972/1986/1996) *Bereavement: Studies of Grief in Adult Life*. London: Routledge.

Parkes, C.M. (2006) *Love and Loss: The Roots of Grief and its Complications*. London: Routledge.

Payne, S., Horn, S. and Relf, M. (1999) *Loss and Bereavement*. Buckingham: Open University Press.

Prigerson, H.G. and Maciejewski, P.K. (2006) A call for sound empirical testing and evaluation of criteria for complicated grief proposed by the DSM V. *Omega*, 52: 9–19.

Quinn, A. (2005) The context of loss, change and bereavement in palliative care. In P. Firth, G. Luff and D. Oliviere (eds), *Loss, Change and Bereavement in Palliative Care* (pp. 1–17). London: Open University Press.

Raphael, B. (1984) *The Anatomy of Bereavement*. London: Unwin Hyman.

Sanders, C. M. (1993) Risk factors in bereavement outcome. In M.S. Stroebe, W. Stroebe and R.O. Hansson (eds), *Handbook of Bereavement: Theory, Research and Intervention* (pp. 255–267). Cambridge: Cambridge University Press.

Schut, H. (2010) Grief counselling efficacy – have we learned enough? *Bereavement Care*, 29: 8–9.

Sim, J., Machin, L. and Bartlam, B. (2013) Identifying vulnerability in grief: Psychometric properties of the Adult Attitude to Grief scale. *Quality of Life Research*, 23(4): 1211–1220.

Spitzer, R.L., Kroenka, K. and Williams, J. (2006) A brief measure for assessing generalised anxiety disorder: The GAD-7. *Archives of Internal Medicine*, 166: 1092–1097.

Stokes, J. (2007) Resilience and bereaved children: Helping a child to develop a resilient mind-set following the death of a parent. In B. Monroe and D. Oliviere (eds), *Resilience in Palliative Care: Achievement in Adversity* (pp. 39–65). Oxford: Oxford University Press.

Stroebe, M.S., Folkman, S., Hansson, R.O. and Schut, H. (2006) The prediction of bereavement outcome: Development of an integrative risk factor framework. *Social Science and Medicine*, 63: 2440–2451.

Stroebe, M.S. and Schut, H. (1999) The Dual Process Model of coping with bereavement: Rationale and description. *Death Studies*, 23: 197–224.

Thompson, N. (ed.) (2002) *Loss and Grief*. Basingstoke: Palgrave.

Worden, W. (2009) *Grief Counselling and Grief Therapy*. London: Tavistock/Routledge.

RECOMMENDED READING

1. Machin, L. (2014) *Working with Loss and Grief*. London: Sage.

The book sets the Range of Response to Loss model and the Adult Attitude to Grief scale, as practice-based tools, in the wider context of theories of loss, grief and counselling. It uses case studies to demonstrate this approach to working with grief.

2. Worden, W. (2009) *Grief Counselling and Grief Therapy*. London: Tavistock/Routledge.

The task model which William Worden has developed has been very influential in the practice of bereavement counselling. With each new edition of his book the model has evolved to embrace new contemporary insights from research and practice, including meaning-making, resilience, complicated grief and individual differences in adjustment to bereavement.

3. Cooper, M. and Mcleod, J. (2011) *Pluralistic Counselling and Psychotherapy*. London: Sage.

This book moves away from the orientation-specific approach to counselling, offering instead a rationale and a framework for applying a range of therapeutic methods to the individual needs of clients. The pluralistic approach fits well with contemporary theories of grief and their emphasis on understanding individual difference in reacting and responding to loss.

6.5   *DEPRESSION*

DENIS O'HARA

OVERVIEW AND KEY POINTS

Depression is one of the most common and pervasive of mental health conditions with 5–12% of the world population being depressed at any given time (Kessler and Bromet, 2014). While there is evidence for the increase in the incidence of depression globally, depression has been recognised as a condition even in antiquity. Depression comes in many forms and in varying degrees of intensity. For some, depression comes and goes relatively quickly and for others it is experienced as a lifetime struggle. While the various forms of depression have symptoms or characteristics in common, there is also variety in its expression. For example, in one person low mood is accompanied by insomnia, while for another it is accompanied by hypersomnia. Another feature of depression is that it is often part of a complex of other mental health problems, resulting in different combinations of comorbidity. In this respect,

depression can be thought of as a problem in its own right but also a signal that a person is experiencing a complex of mental health problems which interrelate, making both diagnosis and treatment challenging. The key points explored in this chapter are:

*   Depression is expressed in different ways and in varying degrees of severity and is often associated with other mental health conditions.
*   It is a complex condition with various causes and associated individual personal vulnerabilities.
*   Given the fact that there are multifactorial causes for depression, counsellors and psychotherapists are required to consider a wide range of factors in any psychological assessment.
*   There are several well-researched psychotherapeutic models developed to work therapeutically with those who are depressed.

DEFINITION

Even though depressive states have been recognised for millennia, the term 'depression' is a relatively new one, only coming into common usage in the twentieth century. Historically, depression was referred to as 'melancholia' and described a state of lowered mood and life energies. The word 'depression' comes from the Latin verb *deprimere*, 'to press down' and it is this usage which gradually became the typical reference within medicine. It should be noted, however, that depression as understood in Western countries, is not necessarily a recognised concept in other countries. In many Eastern languages, for example, there is no directly equivalent word for depression. In such societies, what might be identified as depression in Western diagnostic manuals would more typically be understood as dysfunctional social and behavioural characteristics, rather than as a specified condition (American Psychiatric Association (APA), 2013; World Health Organisation (WHO), 1992).

The fifth edition of the *Diagnostic and Statistical Manual of Mental Disorders* (DSM-V) (APA, 2013) sets out a list of criteria which, when appropriately identified, constitute a diagnosis of depression. The following list, while not representing the full set of criteria, constitutes the key features of what is referred to as 'major depressive episode'. They include:

A. Five or more of the following symptoms have been present during the same two-week period, represent a change from previous functioning, and include either depressed mood or loss of interest or pleasure.

- Depressed mood
- Marked diminished interest or pleasure
- Significant weight loss or weight gain
- Insomnia or hypersomnia
- Psychomotor agitation or retardation
- Fatigue or loss of energy
- Feelings of worthlessness or excessive guilt
- Diminished ability to concentrate
- Recurrent thoughts of death or suicidal ideation

B. The symptoms cause clinically significant distress or impairment in social, occupational, or other important areas of functioning. (APA, 2013)

There are other criteria which refer to the need to assess if symptoms are due to other medical or mental health conditions. It should also be noted that in the DSM-V revision, the two-month exclusion of bereavement from the onset of the depression as a diagnostic caveat has been withdrawn.

AETIOLOGY

Depression has no single cause. Unlike pathogenic diseases, there is no blood test which will identify a pathogen for depression. Rather, there are multiple factors involved in its development. A useful way of examining different aetiological elements of depression is to consider a range of human vulnerabilities. These include:

- Genetic factors
- Early life attachment problems
- Temperament type
- Negative attributional style
- Interpersonal factors
- Stressful life events (Hankin et al., 2009).

Recently, research attention has been given to the potential influence of genes on the development of depression. While there is emerging evidence that genes do play a role in an individual's susceptibility to depression, genes are not a singular causal determinant. Rather, it is highly likely that genes play a mediating role in the complex of factors which together predispose an individual to depression (Gibb, Beevers and McGeary, 2013; Poulton, Moffitt and Silva, 2015; Sullivan, Daly and O'Donovan, 2012).

It has long been recognised that early life experiences which influence attachment and family relationships often play a part in mental health problems. Secure attachment relationships with parents and caregivers provide for the individual a sense of safety and a secure emotional base from which to explore the world. When attachment relationships are confused or disrupted it can limit an individual's capacity to feel emotionally secure and to form other healthy relationships. Studies have demonstrated that insecure attachment in children and adolescence can lead to depression well into early adulthood (Agerup et al., 2015). Importantly, adolescent depression is acknowledged as a predictor of ongoing adult mental health problems (Naicker et al., 2013). As early life relationships form the foundation for a healthy sense of self, others and the world, any disruptions in these relationships make a person more vulnerable to developing depression.

Personality temperament can also be a vulnerability factor in developing depression (Cloninger, Svrakic and Przybeck, 1993; Eysenck, 1991). Different temperament schemes have in common a trait-based view of personality, which is theorised to be developed from both genetic and environmental factors. A number of studies have demonstrated a link between certain temperament sub-types and depression (Marijnissen et al., 2002). For example, as measured by the Temperament and Character Inventory, high scores on the sub-type of Harm Avoidance and low scores on the Self-Directedness sub-type have been consistently linked with depression (Tomita et al., 2016).

A separate but related vulnerability to depression is attributional style. Attributional style refers to how people explain or attribute meaning to life events. Individual events can be explained in a number of different ways, leading to either positive or negative conclusions. As is the case with personality temperaments, individuals have a tendency to perceive the world in certain predisposing ways and, as a result, interpret their experiences through cognitive filters. Those with a positive attributional style tend to construct meaning of events in ways that maintain a positive psychological frame. Alternatively, others are more inclined to interpret life events in more customarily negative ways. Evidence suggests that those who are oriented towards a more negative attributional style are more susceptible to depression (Romens et al., 2011).

Interpersonal factors are also identified as a vulnerability factor in the development of depression. Such factors as communication skills, social relating, coping style and social supports, when well developed, act as buffers against low mood. Those individuals who rate poorly on interpersonal communication and relating and who have limited social support are much more susceptible to depression (O'Shea, Spence and Donovan, 2013). Coping style is also an important interpersonal factor as approaches to coping which orientate an individual towards social engagement as opposed to disengagement strengthen an individual's resistance to depression. Those who are able to employ positive coping strategies when confronted by life stressors have been shown to be less likely to become depressed (Adler, Conklin and Strunk, 2013).

The different vulnerabilities to depression can function as individual factors but quite often interrelate and combine to increase an individual's susceptibility to depression. One of the overarching vulnerabilities is life stress. This is because stress can act as a catalyst for responding negatively to experiences. The Diathesis Stress Model proposes that some individuals are less equipped to manage different stressors than others (Ingram and Luxton, 2005). In this respect, stress itself is the vulnerability factor. Ultimately, there is no one variable which explains how depression is initiated and developed in humans. Future studies are likely to provide a clearer understanding of the complex interplay of genes, biological, cognitive/emotional, relational and environmental factors in this challenging mental health condition.

ASSESSMENT

Diagnostic manuals provide a useful guide to the assessment of symptoms but assessment requires the gathering of further information across a range of human functions, including psychological, social and biological factors.

PSYCHOLOGICAL – COGNITIVE AND AFFECTIVE

- Mood level (including feelings about self and others)
- Self-talk and attributional style and whether it is dominantly self-blaming and focused on shame and social comparisons
- Whether cognitions are predominantly ruminative and fixed
- Any changes in ability to concentrate
- If there is a sense of being stuck or trapped
- The degree of loss of enjoyment of previously enjoyed activities
- How long the depressed state has existed
- The degree of hope for the future.

SOCIAL

- Major life events that may have contributed to triggering and perpetuating the depression
- The social environment – quality and nature of relationships
- The degree of social supports
- The quality of the work environment
- Practical life issues that may be a source of stress, such as finances and accommodation.

BIOLOGICAL

- The degree of fatigue and energy loss
- Changes in sleep patterns, e.g., difficulty getting to sleep, waking after being asleep, intermittent sleep
- Major changes in appetite and weight
- Psychomotor changes – agitation or retardation
- Existing medication that may compound depressive symptoms.

A fundamental feature of any form of depression is anhedonia and its interplay with a wider set of emotions as well as cognitive and behavioural effects. There are a range of assessment instruments for depression that are routinely used to assist in assessment and case formulation. The most important of these is the clinical interview followed by standardised tests.

FORMULATION

Formulation or case conceptualisation is the task of understanding the nature of a presenting problem based on all the available information gathered in the assessment of the case. How a case formulation is arrived at will depend on several factors, especially the theoretical orientation of the therapist, the assessment tools used and the wider context within which therapeutic help is sought. The theoretical orientation of the therapist will, to a certain degree, orientate the therapist to focus on some vulnerabilities more than others. However, counsellors and psychotherapists are trained to construct formulations on the basis of a comprehensive set of symptoms and theoretical considerations. These should include the potential influence of the different aetiological and vulnerability factors mentioned above. In any formulation for depression, it is important to assess the degree of severity of the particular case. Depression can range from mild, moderate to severe forms with associated degrees of risk. In more severe cases the risk of self-harm and suicidal ideation is greatly increased.

INTERVENTION

As is well known, there are many different approaches to psychotherapeutic change. While counsellors and psychotherapists can facilitate significant positive change in clients via a singular theoretical approach, it is more common to include a variety of approaches, adjusting therapy to clients' needs. As many counselling and psychotherapy theories are well supported by research, it is important to consider their respective contributions to the understanding of the change process. What research has also demonstrated is that all effective counselling and psychotherapy approaches have many active components in common (Laska, Gurman and Wampold, 2014).

Psychodynamic approaches pay special attention to interpersonal factors, and how attachment issues and early life experiences influence individuals' unconscious view of self, others and the world. A central focus is the identification of recurring conflictual relationship themes and the emotions related to these themes. The aim of therapy is to help the client make conscious the relational patterns and emotional states experienced and to explore how they function and the meaning they hold (Lemma, Target and Fonagy, 2013; Luborsky and Crits-Christoph, 1990; Meares, 2006).

Humanistic approaches highlight the importance of subjective and intersubjective experiences and emotional states with a focus on the here-and-now. An important feature of such approaches is the high value placed on the person's subjective and embodied experience. From this perspective, depression is first seen as an experience reflective of conflict between different parts of the self, an incongruence between the real and ideal self. When there is a discrepancy between one's ideal view of self, as possibly portrayed by primary others, and one's actual or real self, the inner dialogue between these different self-portrayals can lead to conflict, resulting in depression. When such inner conflict is sustained it can lead to a shutting down of emotions and of connection with embodied experience. Humanistic approaches seek to validate lived experience while encouraging clients to explore the discrepancies between self and experience (Elliott, 2012; Sanders and Hill, 2014).

Cognitive-behavioural approaches pay particular attention to the vulnerabilities associated with personality temperaments, cognitive attributions and the impact of stress on biological and psychological coping. The aim of therapy is to identify and realign an individual's attributional style, and strengthen coping strategies through psycho-educational means. Therapeutic strategies are also designed to respond to biological and behavioural weaknesses through behaviour management (Gilbert, 2009).

SKILLS AND STRATEGIES

Travis is a 27-year-old single male who lives in a shared flat with a male friend from his university days. He is a qualified engineer who works with a building and design firm. Until recently Travis has enjoyed work, but over the past couple of months he has found it a struggle to go to work due to feeling very flat in mood, fatigued and lacking in interest in any of his normal social pursuits. Travis has also experienced a shift in his sleeping pattern, tending to wake in the early hours of the morning and struggling to go back to sleep. Of late, his flat mate noticed a marked shift in Travis's social interactions, both at home and with friends. While he was never overly gregarious, Travis was now withdrawn often turning down invitations to social outings with friends.

One of the first priorities in working with Travis from a humanistic perspective is to privilege his experience and story and to facilitate the therapeutic relationship. Attention would be paid to felt experience both in terms of emotional states and physiological experience. Felt experiences are seen as potential points of access for both the client and the therapist to identify incongruencies between different internal dialogues and lived experience. In the case of Travis, one inner voice may berate him for not taking his career more seriously by pursuing faster advancement in his firm or at least a higher, postgraduate, qualification. The other voice may defend against this demand, taking the view that he had already worked hard to get his engineering degree and a good job and now deserved to slow down and enjoy the fruits of his labour, travelling and enjoying a social life. The task of the therapist is to assist Travis to observe the intensity of this conflict split and to explore the physical and emotional impact it is having on him. It is common in depressive states for there to be a strong self-critical voice which is often associated with shame and self-loathing. The circular nature of the inner conflict split serves to make the sufferer feel stuck with no hope of resolution. This experience is usually associated with overwhelming emotions, which also serve to disable the individual from taking action to resolve the situation.

Within humanistic theory, conflict splits are understood to arise from different aspects of the self. The *ideal self* in the above example promotes a driven sense of career advancement while the *real self* argues for a balanced life experience. The challenge for the individual is to step outside the inner struggle and to become aware of the priorities and values of the real or actual self and to live in a fashion which is genuine and congruent with it. As in the above case, the therapist's task is to help the client get in touch with his or her authentic self and associated desires and in so doing regain hope in a positive future (O'Hara, 2013; Sanders and Hill, 2014).

RESEARCH EVIDENCE

Research within mental health is based on establishing sufficient and appropriate evidence for efficacy and effectiveness of any given treatment. This approach, called evidence-based practice, is founded on the notion that best practice is based on the combination of the best available research and clinical experience. Counsellors and psychotherapists agree with this foundational principle while recognising that there is debate about what constitutes acceptable evidence. There are many different research designs, some of which favour certain aspects of practice over others. Many researchers acknowledging this dilemma have increasingly sought to establish evidence based on practice. This form of research, known as practice-based evidence, utilises the data that results from the naturalistic practice of counselling and psychotherapy.

There is now a vast array of research on depression using various study designs. While more studies have been conducted on the efficacy of cognitive-behavioural therapy, increasingly, further studies are conducted on the efficacy of psychodynamic and humanistic approaches, among other approaches. Encouragingly, the evidence continues to demonstrate that these well-established therapies are effective. As evidence emerges, national mental health guidelines increasingly recognise a range of approaches as recommended treatments (Australian Psychological Society, 2010; National Institute for Health and Clinical Excellence, 2016).

REFERENCES

Adler, A. D., Conklin, L. R. and Strunk, D. R. (2013). Quality of coping skills predicts depressive symptom reactivity over repeated stressors. *Journal of Clinical Psychology*, *69*(12), 1228–1238.

Agerup, T., Lydersen, S., Wallander, J. and Sund, A. M. (2015). Associations between parental attachment and course of depression between adolescence and young adulthood. *Child Psychiatry and Human Development*, *46*, 632–642.

American Psychiatric Association. (2013). *Diagnostic and statistical manual of mental disorders* (5th ed.). Washington, DC: American Psychiatric Publishing.

Australian Psychological Society. (2010). *Evidence-based psychological interventions in the treatment of mental disorders: A literature review*. Melbourne: Australian Psychological Society.

(Continued)

(Continued)

Cloninger, C. R., Svrakic, D. M. and Przybeck, T. R. (1993). A psychobiological model of temperament and character. *Archives of General Psychiatry, 50*, 975–990.

Elliott, R. (2012). Emotion focused therapy. In P. Sanders (ed.), *The tribes of the person-centred nation: An introduction to the schools of therapy associated with the person-centred approach.* Ross-on-Wye: PCCS Books.

Eysenck, H. J. (1991). Dimensions of personality: 16, 5 or 3. Criteria for a taxonomic paradigm. *Personality and Individual Differences, 12*, 773–790.

Gibb, B. E., Beevers, C. G. and McGeary, J. E. (2013). Toward an integration of cognitive and genetic models of risk for depression. *Cognition and Emotion, 27*(2), 193–216.

Gilbert, P. (2009) *Overcoming depression* (3rd ed.). London: Constable Robinson.

Hankin, B. L., Oppenheimer, C., Jenness, J., Barrocas, A., Shapero, B. G. and Goldband, J. (2009). Developmental origins of cognitive vulnerabilities to depression: Review of processes contributing to stability and change across time. *Journal of Clinical Psychology, 65*(12), 1327–1338.

Ingram, R. E. and Luxton, D. D. (2005). Vulnerability-stress models. In B. L. Hankin and J. R. Z. Abela (eds.), *Development of psychopathology: A vulnerability stress perspective* (pp. 32–46). Thousand Oaks, CA: Sage.

Kessler, R. C. and Bromet, E. J. (2014). The epidemiology of depression across cultures. *Annual Review of Public Health, 34*, 119–138.

Laska, K. M., Gurman, A. S. and Wampold, B. E. (2014). Expanding the lens of evidence-based practice in psychotherapy: A common factors perspective. *Psychotherapy, 51*, 467–481.

Lemma, A., Target, M. and Fonagy, P. (2013). Dynamic Interpersonal Therapy (DIT): Developing a new psychodynamic intervention for the treatment of depression. *Psychoanalytic Inquiry, 33*, 552–566.

Luborsky, L. and Crits-Christoph, P. (1990). *Understanding transference: The core conflictual relationship theme method.* New York: Basic Books.

Marijnissen, G., Tuinier, S., Sijben, A. E. S. and Verhoeven, W. M. A. (2002). The temperament and character inventory in major depression. *Journal of Affective Disorders, 70*(2), 219–223.

Meares, R. (2006). Attacks on value. *Psychotherapy in Australia, 12*(3), 62–68.

Naicker K., Galambos N. L., Zeng, Y., Senthilselvan, A. and Colman, I. (2013). Social, demographic, and health outcomes in the 10 years following adolescent depression. *Journal Adolescent Health, 52*(5), 533–538.

National Institute for Health and Clinical Excellence. (2016). *Depression in adults: Recognition and management.* London: NICE. (www.nice.org.uk/guidance/cg90/chapter/1-Guidance#treatment-choice-based-on-depression-subtypes-and-personal-characteristics).

O'Hara, D. J. (2013). *Hope in counselling and Psychotherapy.* London: Sage.

O'Shea, G., Spence, S. H. and Donovan, C. L. (2013). Interpersonal factors associated with depression in adolescents: Are these consistent with theories underpinning interpersonal psychotherapy? *Clinical Psychology and Psychotherapy, 21*, 548–558.

Poulton, R., Moffitt, T. E. and Silva, F. A. (2015). The Dunedin Multidisciplinary Health and Development Study: Overview of the first 40 years, with an eye to the future. *Social Psychiatry Psychiatric Epidemiology, 50*(5), 679–693.

Romens, S. E., MacCoon, D. G., Abramson, L. Y. and Pollak, S. D. (2011). Cognitive style moderates attention to attribution-relevant stimuli. *Cognitive Therapy and Research, 35*, 134–141.

Sanders, P. and Hill, A. (2014). *Counselling for depression.* London: Sage.

Sullivan, P. F., Daly, M. J. and O'Donovan, M. (2012). Genetic architectures of psychiatric disorders: The emerging picture and its implications. *Nature Reviews Genetics, 13*, 537–551.

Tomita, T., Yasui-Furukori, N., Kaneda, A., Ishioka, M., Sugawara, N., Nakagami, T. and Nakamura, K. (2016). An attempt to construct a 7-item short version of the temperament and character inventory to predict the treatment response of patients with depression: A validation study. *BMC Psychiatry, 16*, 290.

World Health Organisation. (1992). *The ICD-10 classification of mental and behavioural disorders: Clinical descriptions and diagnostic guidelines.* London: Churchill Livingstone.

RECOMMENDED READING

1. Busch, F. N., Rudden, M. and Shapiro, T. (2016). *Psychodynamic treatment of depression*. Washington, DC: American Psychiatric Publishing.

This book provides a comprehensive overview of depression, especially in terms of biological and psychological vulnerabilities. The authors explore key psychodynamics principles and approaches to the treatment depression.

2. Gilbert, P. (2009). *Overcoming depression* (3rd ed.). London: Constable Robinson.

Paul Gilbert provides a thorough and detailed examination of depression, with particular attention to cognitive-behavioural approaches to treatment and an emphasis on compassion-focused strategies.

3. Sanders, P. and Hill, A. (2014). *Counselling for depression: A person-centred and experiential approach to practice*. London: Sage.

This book provides a fresh review and outline of the central features of humanistic and experiential approaches to working with depression. Emphasis is placed on practitioner competencies and on the value of research evidence.

6.6   COUNSELLING FOR DRUG-RELATED PROBLEMS

ANDREW GUPPY AND SALLY WOODS

OVERVIEW AND KEY POINTS

This chapter provides an insight into the special challenges and opportunities within the field of drug misuse counselling. The next section outlines what we are referring to by the term 'drug-related problems', describing the types of substance and the expected range of problems. Following this, the types of intervention environment are then explored more deeply, focusing on the main approaches to counselling and with some background to their underlying theory. Some practical considerations of counselling substance-related problems are then presented.

Key points include:

- Around 9% of adults and 19% of young adults in the United Kingdom (UK) report taking an illicit drug sometime in the previous 12 months.
- Biological, psychological and social factors all contribute to the development of substance use disorders within individuals.

- A range of psychosocial interventions have been successful in supporting clients with Cognitive-Behavioural Therapy (CBT), Motivational Enhancement, Relapse Prevention and Contingency Management approaches all receiving support.
- Self-help recovery-based interventions such as Narcotics Anonymous are also useful in supporting clients.
- Pharmacological interventions alongside psychosocial interventions have also demonstrated success for particular substance use disorders.

DEFINITIONS

Initially, it is necessary to clarify what is meant by the concept of 'substance misuse'. In the *Diagnostic and Statistical Manual of Mental Disorders* (DSM-V) (American Psychiatric Association, 2013), substance use disorder (SUD) was defined as present if two or more of the following criteria are met:

- Taking the substance in larger amounts or for longer than the user meant to
- Wanting to cut down or stop using the substance but not managing to
- Spending a lot of time getting, using or recovering from use of the substance
- Cravings and urges to use the substance
- Not managing to do what the user should at work, home or school, because of substance use
- Continuing to use, even when it causes problems in relationships
- Giving up important social, occupational or recreational activities because of substance use
- Using substances again and again, even when it puts the user in danger
- Continuing to use, even when the user knows he/she has a physical or psychological problem that could have been caused or made worse by the substance
- Needing more of the substance to get the effect the user wants (tolerance)
- Development of withdrawal symptoms, which can be relieved by taking more of the substance.

A diagnosis of 'mild SUD' would be offered if 2–3 symptoms are present, 'moderate' if 4–5 are present and 'severe' if over five symptoms are present. In addition to clinical definitions, it may be useful for practitioners to be aware of the various substances that are commonly misused. Useful websites for such information (and much more) are described at the end of the chapter.

AETIOLOGY

Recent guidelines (National Collaborating Centre for Mental Health, 2008; National Institute for Health and Clinical Excellence, 2011) emphasise that there are a range of factors that contribute to the aetiology and maintenance of substance use problems. From a genetic perspective, studies such as Agrawal et al. (2008) have suggested that regions on chromosomes 2, 13 and especially 10 might be associated with genes that provide a biological basis for SUD. However, it is likely that the influence of genetic factors would be indirect and more likely in terms of a gene–environment interaction where for certain people under certain circumstances drug use may become more likely. The influence of family and peers as well as negative childhood experiences may all contribute to initial experiences with drugs. The rewarding nature of early experiences will then, for some people, lead to increased use and reliance on substances for release, relaxation and respite. Abrams and Niaura (1987) noted that prolonged

heavy substance use becomes reinforced and alternative coping is reduced, which leads to a 'vicious circle of negative person–environment interactions, poor models and reciprocal determinism'.

ASSESSMENT

There are a range of psychometric tools for assessing substance misuse, abuse and dependence, and it is felt that the overlap with SUD is sufficient for these to continue to be useful in assessment. There are some useful short screening tools, such as the 5-item Severity of Dependence Scale (SDS) (Gossop et al., 1995).

There are also a few much longer, structured interview methods, such as the Maudsley Addiction Profile (MAP) (Marsden et al., 1998) and the Addiction Severity Index (McLellan et al., 1985), that might also be appropriate in more formal settings.

However, it may be worth considering the Drug Use Disorder Identification Test (DUDIT) and the extended version (DUDIT-E). The DUDIT has reasonable psychometric performance, as indicated in Hildebrand's (2015) review. The DUDIT-E has additional benefits of scales measuring the positive and negative consequences of drug-taking alongside indicators of readiness to change (see also SOCRATES by Miller and Tonigan (1996)). The responses to these items might be useful to help focus the conversation with the client in the early stages.

FORMULATION

The formulation should develop hypotheses about how the client's underlying views shape their thoughts, feelings and behaviour within an appropriate theoretical structure (Persons, 2001). From a Social Learning Theory perspective, Abrams and Niaura (1987) suggested that one's initial interactions with drugs may be based on individual factors interacting with typical 'socializing agents', such as family and peers, but then the feedback from these initial experiences develops a pattern of use. Expectations and deficiencies in alternative ways of coping then combine to increase the frequency of substance use, and particularly substance use as a means of coping. Two other perspectives may help to construct further hypotheses. From the Trans-theoretical Model described by Prochaska and DiClemente (1983), a readiness to change is required for success to be more likely. This perspective emphasises the need for motivational elements to be present near the beginning of a successful intervention and these might be provided by the client (for example, by embracing early steps in Narcotics Anonymous) or by a motivational counsellor (using MI/MET approaches). Another component which seems beneficial is that of relapse risk management, where known situations or cues that might promote relapse are identified and planned for either in group or individual sessions.

INTERVENTION

HARM REDUCTION AND PRESCRIBING

Before considering psychological interventions, it is worth a brief look at the issues of harm reduction, including prescribing alternative drugs. The essence of the harm reduction approach to substance misuse is a focus of service provision on meeting and working with drug users on their terms. It is a feature of such an approach that at times these terms may be out of line with mainstream social, government or service provision policy. Critics of this approach have long argued that by being supportive, in reality giving drugs to drug users, the services may be encouraging these individuals to maintain their current patterns of use, with no compelling reason to stop (e.g., Edwards, 1969). Supporters of the harm reduction approach would argue that it is an attempt to bridge the gap between the expectations of drug users and service providers with realistic rather than moralistic methods of intervention.

Usually the first step in harm reduction involves the stabilisation of the client's illicit use, which includes provision of sterile equipment and other harm reduction resources (e.g., condoms). The next step would normally involve reduction of use, often paired with General Practitioner (GP) or specialist prescribing. Generally, counselling is offered throughout this process but is particularly encouraged during periods of change (reduction in script). Group counselling is generally available via most community Drug Action Teams, though the particular approach adopted may be varied. Clients would normally keep close contact with a key worker whose remit includes social and welfare support as well as specific drug-related matters. To some extent, problem-oriented, directive counselling occurs with this key worker. In many environments this relationship may be maintained within a 'contract' situation where support from the key worker is dependent on the client complying with the 'script regime' (e.g., cessation of illicit use). Interesting research related to this approach has come from the Drug Treatment Outcome Research Study, indicating that positive outcomes can be found even within clients referred via the criminal justice system (Jones et al., 2009).

One of the primary benefits of this approach tends to be in the realistic perspective on relapse management. As the approach does not rely on abstinence as the only acceptable alternative to harmful use, the relapse event may be more accepted within the treatment regime and the re-establishment of the treatment process is much easier. However, one possible drawback to the most commonly encountered harm reduction approach is the potential lack of detailed counselling support. To some extent, the process may focus on the management of the intake reduction and ignore underlying deficiencies in terms of self-perceptions and coping skills.

A TYPICAL PSYCHOLOGICAL APPROACH TO SUBSTANCE MISUSE COUNSELLING

A number of community-based agencies focusing on alcohol and drug misuse can provide a mixture of intervention methods added to a more traditional counselling approach. Thus one may see agencies providing certain features core to the harm reduction approach, but also advocating a move towards abstinence, while featuring a range of group and individual sessions focusing on elements central to cognitive-behavioural and rational emotive behaviour therapies.

The elements of harm reduction education and support in the provision of information and advice (as well as equipment in terms of syringes, etc.) would normally occur early on in the process. Later, the discussion of eventual outcome goals could be approached and specific input relating to unhelpful cognitions and behaviours would be the focus of later sessions. In particular, the use of group sessions focuses on the uptake of alternative behaviours in order to positively replace the effects of drug-taking.

Beyond the drug-specific information, the main difference in substance misuse counselling concerns the focus of activities (towards abstinence or 'controlled' use) rather than the actual activities themselves (e.g., role-playing within a general social skills development package). It is common for some time to be devoted to obvious substance-related issues as 'saying no'. Additionally, a lot of effort is directed towards 'relapse prevention' within the substance misuse field. Within this general package, material focusing on stress management and assertiveness training could be included, as would other exercises on self-awareness and the development of positive ways of spending leisure time (other than substance use).

Increasing attention has been focused on the benefits of Motivational Interviewing (Miller and Rollnick, 2002) methods in dealing with substance misuse problems. Motivational approaches seem to be effective at the earlier stages of engagement in promoting the perspective that change is desirable and achievable. There is an increasing evidence base for the effectiveness of this approach across a wide range of substances (Wanigaratne et al., 2005).

Jay had been using illicit drugs (speed, LSD, ecstasy and cannabis) recreationally for some years. However, alongside relationship changes and work problems, he started using crack cocaine and then heroin. For about a year he supported his habit through work, but his business collapsed and he had to find other ways of paying for drugs. At first he started dealing, but quickly smoked away the profits. He began to lie to his family and steal from shops and he was eventually arrested for shoplifting. After this he tried to give up heroin and although he found it easy to kick the habit at first, he found it impossible to stay off the drug for any length of time. Jay was arrested again and got another conviction.

Jay was put in touch with a local short-stay respite project.

'I was put on a methadone script with no pressure to reduce. In fact I was encouraged to take my time. Heroin addiction can't be cured in days or weeks, it takes months or years. I then realised what [the] Lodge was; it was what I wanted it to be. The methadone took care of the physical side of my addiction and the staff at [the] Lodge helped me with the psychological side, helping me increase my confidence and regain my self-respect. Over the next three months I gradually reduced my methadone and then went onto Subutex [buprenorphine]. I am now drug free and the first stage of my recovery is complete.'

In Jay's case, the use of prescribed methadone within a short-term therapeutic community brought a halt to the downward spiral. The input from staff and within group sessions focused on raising self-esteem and perceived control while improving coping skills. The extended outreach work by project staff meant that these improvements could be consolidated over the months after coming out of the residential phase. In addition to these core elements of a broad CBT-based approach, there would have been significant work in relation to relapse prevention. The issue of transfer of training in relapse prevention from a residential setting back into the community was assisted by the extensive outreach work of the project. This allowed new perspectives and coping skills to be developed in the real world while being regularly supported by project staff.

ELEMENTS IN DRUG COUNSELLING

MOTIVATIONAL ENHANCEMENT. In this approach the counsellor works on developing the client's motivation and commitment to change with the emphasis on the client's responsibility for doing the work. From Miller and Rollnick (1991), five key elements can be seen. The first, 'expressing empathy' means the therapist's role is a mixture of a supportive companion and knowledgeable consultant, 'listening rather than telling'. For clients early in the process, who may not be ready for change, the notion of 'developing discrepancy' is used to highlight differences between where they are and where they want to be. The element 'avoiding argumentation' is emphasised so that the client is not pushed into a defensive position, resisting change. The principle is that it is 'the client and not the therapist that voices the arguments for change' (Miller and Rollnick, 1991). When resistance occurs, another element of the approach involves 'rolling with resistance' instead of opposing it, and emphasising

that it remains up to the client what they will choose to do. Finally 'supporting self-efficacy' focuses on the specific belief that the client can change their drug-taking behaviour and that things can improve.

COPING SKILLS TRAINING. A significant element in many intervention approaches, especially CBT, involves discussing and rehearsing methods of coping. These can be in relation to specific urges to take drugs or they can be in a wider context about how to deal with life's challenges without using substances to cope. Kadden et al. (2003) suggest learning to recognise common 'urge triggers' and also the use of urge diaries, recording the circumstances and triggers and ways used to deal with them. Emphasis is often placed on distraction, discussing the craving with others, or developing positive self-talk strategies. At the more general level, the emphasis is on developing general self-efficacy perceptions so that the choice of problem-focused coping strategies becomes more natural when things can be changed. On the other hand, developing cognitive coping strategies such as devaluation ('it wasn't such a big deal after all') or accommodation ('I adjusted my expectations to meet the situation') has great benefit in helping people deal with problems that are difficult to change.

RELAPSE MANAGEMENT. This has been one of the key features of a range of substance misuse intervention approaches (for example, see Marlatt and Donovan, 2005). If substance use/misuse has become the most important and reliable method of coping behaviour within the individual over a period of years, it is quite likely that during or after assistance the client may 'return' to a pattern of substance use. The use of inverted commas around 'return' is important as the aim is for the individual to continue to progress such that they are not returning to substance use with the same set of cognitions or perspectives that they started with. Even in successful cases, relapse can occur, but the process is more likely to lead to eventual success if it is managed properly and if the individual feels able to call on support as soon as possible. One of the criticisms of the Narcotics Anonymous/ Alcoholics Anonymous (NA/AA) philosophy was that it made it difficult to maintain self-esteem following a relapse and that the distance in days from the last occasion of substance use seemed more important than how you may have developed along the way. However, this perspective is thankfully changing and one of the very useful elements of the group counselling environments found within NA/AA and elsewhere is the sharing of experience in relapse management, such as identifying high-risk situations or times and sharing ideas for alternative cognitions and behaviours.

NARCOTICS ANONYMOUS. Although this kind of 'intervention' may appear to be different from usual forms of 'counselling', NA quite clearly provides a well-known type of support for those with problems. The spread and level of activity of NA in the UK is considerably less than its sister organisation AA, although the broad philosophy of this approach can also be found in a number of residential and outpatient treatment facilities.

The principles of the NA (and AA) approach are covered in the 'Twelve Steps'. These steps principally involve six stages. First, there is an admission of powerlessness over substance use and that life has become 'unmanageable'. The second stage involves an acceptance of assistance from a 'higher power'. Stage three is about becoming aware of the 'nature of our wrongs' with the fourth stage working on removing 'defects of character' and 'shortcomings'. A penultimate stage is about promising to make amends to those who have been harmed and the final stage emphasises the maintenance of progress through prayer, meditation and a commitment to helping others in similar need. An interesting perspective on the active psychological ingredients embedded within these stages can be found in the review by Moos (2008), which helps to explain the effectiveness of Twelve-Step approaches from a social-cognitive perspective.

It has been noted that there are variations across AA (and perhaps more so NA) groups in terms of the emphasis placed on the 'higher power principle' (some are more spiritual rather than religious). The principle that does not vary within the Twelve-Steps approach concerns the goal behaviour of abstinence. This has some implications for those who are opiate abusers, where a common alternative involves methadone substitution (described below), which may be seen as incompatible with an abstinence approach by some.

EVALUATION

Success in treating drug misuse has been achieved by many different therapeutic approaches (Wanigaratne et al., 2005). However, it is clear that success needs to be carefully defined and must incorporate a number of dimensions rather than simply focusing on the volume or weight of the substance consumed. Thus modern researchers advocate a range of outcome measures to include wider aspects of psychological and social functioning as well as the more usual substance and symptom-oriented measures (Guppy and Marsden, 2002).

Where outcome evidence has been examined in the field of substance misuse, there is support for virtually all the interventions described above (Gates et al., 2016). Thus Twelve Step, harm reduction, rational emotive behaviour therapy (REBT) and CBT approaches have positive outcomes, though the prognosis tends to be less positive for those with heavier and longer patterns of misuse, perhaps particularly when misuse ranges over more than one substance. From experience, it seems that some individuals need to try a number of intervention approaches before they achieve much success. However, it remains unclear whether such success is necessarily dependent on a strength of that particular intervention or is a result of coincidental changes within the individual achieved largely outside the counselling process.

REFERENCES

Abrams, D. B., & Niaura, R. S. (1987). Social learning theory. In H. T. Blane and K. E. Leonard (Eds.), *Psychological theories of drinking and alcoholism* (pp. 131–178). New York: Guilford Press.

Agrawal, A., Hinrichs, A.L., Dunn, G., et al. (2008) Linkage scan for quantitative traits identifies new regions of interest for substance dependence in the Collaborative Study on the Genetics of Alcoholism (COGA) sample. *Drug and Alcohol Dependence*, 93, 12–20.

American Psychiatric Association (2013) *Diagnostic and Statistical Manual of Mental Disorders* (5th ed.). Washington, DC: American Psychiatric Publishing.

Edwards, G. (1969) The British approach to the treatment of heroin addiction. *The Lancet*, 7598, 768–772.

Gates, P.J., Sabioni, P., Copeland, J., Le Foll, B. and Gowing, L. (2016) Psychosocial interventions for cannabis use disorder. *Cochrane Database of Systematic Reviews*, Issue 5. Art. No.: CD005336. DOI: 10.1002/14651858.CD005336.pub4.

Gossop, M., Darke, S., Griffiths, P., Hando, J., Powis, B., Hall, W. and Strang, J. (1995) The Severity of Dependence Scale (SDS): psychometric properties of the SDS in English and Australian samples of heroin, cocaine and amphetamine users. *Addiction*, 90(5), 607–614.

Guppy, A. and Marsden, J. (2002) Alcohol and drug misuse and the organization. In M. Shabracq, J.A. Winnubst and C.L. Cooper (eds), *Handbook of Work and Health Psychology* (2nd ed.). Chichester: Wiley.

Jones, A., Donmall, M., Millar, T., Moody, A., Weston, S., Anderson, T., Gittins, M., Abeywardana, V. and D'Souza, J. (2009) *The Drug Treatment Outcomes Research Study (DTORS): Final Outcomes Report*. Home Office Research Report 24. London: Home Office.

Marlatt, G.A. and Donovan, D.M. (2005) *Relapse prevention* (2nd ed.). New York: Guilford Press.

Kadden, R., Carroll, K., Donovan, D., et al. (2003). *Cognitive-Behavioral Coping Skills Therapy Manual: A Clinical Research Guide for Therapists Treating Individuals with Alcohol Abuse and Dependence*. Rockville: National Institute on Alcohol Abuse and Alcoholism.

Marsden, J., Gossop, M., Stewart, D., Best, D., Farrell, M., Lehmann, P., Edwards, C. and Strang, J. (1998) The Maudsley Addiction Profile (MAP): A brief instrument for assessing treatment outcome. *Addiction*, 93(12), 1857–1867.

McLellan AT, Luborsky L, Cacciola J, Griffith J, Evans F, Barr HL, O'Brien CP (1985). New data from the Addiction Severity Index. Reliability and validity in three centers. *The Journal of nervous and mental disease*, 173, 412–423.

Miller, W. and Rollnick, S. (1991) *Motivational Interviewing: Preparing People for Change* (3rd ed., 2012). New York and London: Guilford Press.

Miller, W.R. and Rollnick, S. (2002) *Motivational Interviewing* (2nd ed.). New York: Guilford Press.

Miller, W.R. and Tonigan, J.S. (1996) Assessing drinkers' motivation for change: The Stages of Change Readiness and Treatment Eagerness Scale (SOCRATES). *Psychology of Addictive Behaviors*, 10, 81–89.

Moos, R.H. (2008) Active ingredients of substance use-focused self-help groups. *Addiction*, 103, 387–396.

National Collaborating Centre for Mental Health (2008) *Drug Misuse: Psychosocial Interventions*. Clinical Practice Guideline 51. London: The British Psychological Society and The Royal College of Psychiatrists.

National Institute for Health and Clinical Excellence (NICE) (2011) *Alcohol Use Disorders*. Clinical Guideline 115. London: NICE.

Prochaska, J.O. and DiClemente, C.C. (1983) Stages and processes of self-change of smoking: Toward an integrative model of change. *Journal of Consulting and Clinical Psychology*, 51, 390–395.

Wanigaratne, S., et al. (2005) *The Effectiveness of Psychological Therapies on Drug Misusing Clients*. London: NHS National Treatment Agency for Substance Misuse. (www.nta.nhs.uk/uploads/nta_effectiveness_psycho_therapies_2005_rb11.pdf).

RECOMMENDED READING

1. National Institute for Health and Clinical Excellence (NICE) (2011) *Alcohol Use Disorders*. Clinical Guideline 115. London: NICE. (www.nice.org.uk/guidance/cg51).

Provides the NICE Guidelines for working with individuals struggling with alcohol use.

2. The Australian Government's Department of Health online guidance around interventions for regular amphetamine use. (http://health.gov.au/internet/publications/publishing.nsf/Content/drugtreat-pubs-cogamph-toc~drugtreat-pubs-cogamph-3~drugtreat-pubs-cogamph-3-1~drugtreat-pubs-cogamph-3-1-4).

3. The Project MATCH monograph series. (http://pubs.niaaa.nih.gov/publications/ProjectMatch/matchIntro.htm).

Includes manuals for CBT and Motivational Enhancement.

6.7

WORKING WITH SURVIVORS OF DOMESTIC VIOLENCE

CHRISTIANE SANDERSON

OVERVIEW AND KEY POINTS

Working with survivors of domestic abuse (DA), while highly rewarding, can be extremely challenging and demanding. To fully understand the impact and long-term effects of DA, therapists need to view such abuse within the context of complex trauma in which bodily and psychological integrity is threatened and the attachment system is compromised (Sanderson, 2010, 2013). When working with survivors of DA, practitioners need to consider the principles of a trauma-informed practice (TIP) model alongside their preferred model, which titrates the therapeutic process through an approach consisting of three phases – Stabilisation, Processing and Integration – to promote post-traumatic growth (Herman, 1992a; Sanderson, 2013). In addition, clinicians need to be mindful of the impact of bearing witness to clients' experiences of DA to minimise vicarious traumatisation.

- To work with survivors of Domestic Abuse (DA) counsellors need to be aware of the spectrum of DA behaviours, and understand that these are not confined to physical abuse but include coercion and control, emotional and psychological abuse, neglect, as well as physical, sexual, financial and spiritual abuse, and that both males and females are at risk of DA.
- It is essential that counsellors contextualise DA within a trauma framework in which prolonged coercion and control give rise to a range of psycho-biological symptoms which are normal reactions to trauma rather than indices of individual pathology or personality disturbance.
- Counsellors need to validate and legitimise the DA experiences, restore reality and avoid pathologising survivors by contextualising DA within a psychobiological as well as a socio-political framework.
- Counsellors need to be mindful of the safety of the survivor and any dependents through continuous

risk assessment, and balance this with safety planning and restoring survivors' autonomy to make their own choices.
- The core therapeutic goals are best attained using a TIP model which consists of a phased approach to titrate the therapeutic process. The three phases are: 1. Stabilisation, 2. Processing and 3. Integration to promote post-traumatic growth (Herman, 1992b; Sanderson, 2013).

DEFINITION

The current definition of domestic violence and abuse is 'any incident or pattern of incidents of controlling, coercive, threatening behaviour, violence or abuse between those aged 16 or over who are, or have been, intimate partners or family members regardless of gender or sexuality. The abuse can encompass, but is not limited to: psychological, physical, sexual, financial, emotional' (Home Office, 2015: 3).

Since 2015, coercive or controlling behaviour is classified as an offence as it represents extreme psychological and emotional abuse without serious physical assault and carries a maximum of five years' imprisonment (Home Office, 2015). Controlling behaviour is defined as 'a range of acts designed to make a person subordinate and/ or dependent by isolating them from sources of support, exploiting their resources and capacities for personal gain, depriving them of the means needed for independence, resistance and escape and regulating their everyday behaviour' (Home Office, 2015: 3), in which victims are made subordinate to, or dependent on the abuser, exploiting their resources and depriving them of independence.

Coercive behaviour is defined as 'an act or a pattern of acts of assault, threats, humiliation and intimidation or other abuse that is used to harm, punish, or frighten their victim' (Home Office, 2015: 3). This commonly manifests in repeated put downs, verbal abuse, enforcing rules that degrade or dehumanise, isolating the victim from family, friends and social world, financial abuse or threat to reveal private information. Coercive and controlling behaviour as an offence applies not only to intimate partners or family members, but also former partners who still live together and acknowledges that both men and women, irrespective of sexual orientation are at risk of DA across all ages, including young people below the age of 18.

Concomitant to controlling or coercive behaviour is revenge porn, in which private sexual photographs or films are made public (Home Office, 2015). Such coercion and control is often combined with deception, denial and shaming behaviour, not only to control the survivor, but also to ensure silence and secrecy and minimise the risk of disclosure (Sanderson, 2013).

AETIOLOGY

Controlling or coercive behaviour is typically seen in the early stages of abusive relationships, which can escalate into physical violence. Sarah's abuse was initially subtle, with her partner wanting to spend as much time with her as possible yet isolating her from her friends. This masked his pathological jealousy and restricted her contact with the outside world. He started to monitor her phone and became verbally abusive in referring to her as fat and undesirable. He would often use sex as a way of controlling her either by withholding it or forcing her to perform degrading sexual acts. The aim was to force her to surrender, obliterate any sense of self-agency and engender mental defeat (Sanderson, 2013). Over time Sarah was trapped in a cycle of abuse from which she was too afraid to escape and which led to post-traumatic stress disorder (PTSD) and dissociative states.

Controlling and coercive behaviour is commonly seen in female perpetrators of DA, in which constant criticism of the partner's masculinity or femininity and their behaviour which becomes a source of shame. With Charles this manifested in repeated verbal aggression from his wife alongside micro-managing his behaviour, monitoring his phone calls, text messages and emails, as well as tracking his car satellite navigation system. This would often be accompanied by threats of suicide if he did not comply or submit to her demands.

The dynamics of DA are a subtle and gradual escalation of coercion and control, starting with loving care and attention, or 'love bombing', to entrap the partner which escalates into the increased use of threats, intimidation and violence in order to dominate and ensure total submission. These dynamics are part of the cycle of abuse (Herman,

1992b; Sanderson, 2008) in which the tension-building phase leads to an assault, followed by the conciliation or honeymoon phase. The intermittent reinforcement in this cycle ultimately leads to traumatic bonding (Dutton and Painter, 1981), dissociation and 'betrayal blindness' as the survivor tries to manage the cognitive dissonance inherent in the oscillation between love and hate, affection and brutalisation, caring and dehumanisation (Sanderson, 2008, 2013).

Although perpetrators of DA are not homogenous, there are a number of commonalities, such as the need to control and dominate through the use of coercion, control, threat and violence. Abusers also commonly display pathological jealousy, which indicates insecure attachment and fear of abandonment or rejection, underpinning the need to control and dominate (Dutton, 2007; Sanderson, 2013). Moreover, the terror of abandonment renders the victim most at risk of being murdered when they attempt to leave the relationship (British Medical Association, 2007; Sanderson, 2008). These genuine fears of violence or death when attempting to leave or report DA are what prevents many survivors from disclosing their abuse or seeking help.

ASSESSMENT

Counsellors need to be mindful of the safety of the survivor and any dependents through continuous risk assessment, and balance this with safety planning and restoring survivors' autonomy to make their own choices. Assessment of DA is often complicated, with many survivors being too scared or ashamed to disclose their abuse, making it difficult to identify. Alongside this, the distortion of reality and the belief that they are complicit in their abuse generates fears of not being believed, or being judged, or being controlled or coerced by professionals, including counsellors (Dutton, 1992).

Many survivors enter therapy not able to talk about their abuse either through sheer terror, shame or fear of re-traumatisation. It is crucial that practitioners adopt a sensitive approach to enable disclosure (British Medical Association, 2007; Sanderson, 2013) and ensure confidentiality. Some survivors may enter therapy as a result of legal proceedings or referral from children's services, but may be reluctant to engage as they do not feel entirely safe and fear potential repercussions for having reported the abuser.

While both males and females are at risk of DA, the most at-risk group is females, with on average two women a week murdered in the United Kingdom by their partner or ex-partner (Walby and Allen, 2004). DA is also the highest killer of unborn children and can lead to adverse long-term consequences for children raised in DA environments (British Medical Association, 2007). Other high-risk groups are young women, Black, Asian, Minority Ethnic (BAME) females, those with disabilities, trafficked women and refugees who fear deportation. As children in DA environments are considered to be at risk, it will be necessary to implement safeguarding procedures and conduct a risk assessment for both the survivor and any dependent children or vulnerable adults.

Many therapists get caught up in safeguarding procedures and risk assessment yet neglect to assess the impact DA has had on the survivor and their clinical needs. It is critical that counsellors assess for the degree of traumatisation and trauma symptoms, especially dissociation (Sanderson, 2013). The systematic and repeated use of DA leads to complex trauma (Herman, 1992b), including the range of symptoms seen in PTSD, especially the sub-type of PTSD with prominent dissociative symptoms. It is also frequently comorbid with depression, anxiety, self-harm or substance misuse as a way of medicating the abuse, somatisation disorder or dissociative disorder (Sanderson, 2013). It is critical to assess for these in order to create a comprehensive formulation and care plan.

FORMULATION

The systematic and repeated brutalisation characteristic of DA activates psychobiological survival mechanisms, which elicit a range of psychological and physical responses. In the presence of overwhelming and life-threatening danger, the body's alarm system is activated through the release of a cascade of neurochemicals to prepare the body for fight, flight or freeze. If the danger is inescapable, as in DA, the only option is to freeze, which prevents the neurochemicals from being discharged and thereby becoming trapped in the body. As a result, the alarm system remains on high alert and is easily tripped by external cues that resemble the original trauma, or by internal triggers such as thoughts or feelings (Sanderson, 2016), leading to a number of traumatic reactions such as hyperarousal, hypervigilance, irritability, avoidance, flashbacks, panic attacks, intrusive memories and nightmares, or hypo-arousal such as dissociation and a disconnection in normally integrated systems in the mind, body and brain (Sanderson, 2016; van der Kolk, 2014).

While some survivors of DA experience hyperarousal, many experience hypo-arousal, such as dissociation, wherein they detach from their surroundings and inner

experiencing to anaesthetise their pain. This is aided by 'betrayal blindness', in which the abuse is split off, allowing the survivor to retain a positive image of the abuser and, in turn, a negative image of the self. Such knowledge isolation (Sanderson, 2008) enables the survivor to humanise rather than demonise their partner as it seals off anger and rage, as the expression of such feelings could escalate the abuse. It also allows them to manage the paradox of *knowing* and yet *not-knowing*, to tolerate the intolerable and bear the unbearable (Sanderson, 2013).

Repeated assaults and dissociation leads to a split between what the mind cannot acknowledge or bear and what the body is forced to endure (Sanderson, 2016). As trauma is stored in the sensorimotor system, the abuse is split off from cognitive understanding and processing as the body keeps the score (van der Kolk, 2014). As survivors become increasingly numb and shut down, their behaviour becomes automatised, or robotic like, and they can present as emotionless and unfeeling.

Repeated traumatisation and dissociation prevents the survivor from processing the trauma and integrating their experiences, which further intensifies the trauma reactions and impairs affect regulation (Sanderson, 2013). Lack of processing means the trauma remains 'on line' and can lead to PTSD, Complex PTSD (C-PTSD) (Herman, 1992b) and dissociative disorders (Sanderson, 2016) in which alterations in perception of self and others predominate, leading to mental health difficulties, relational disturbances as well as compromised physical health (Sanderson, 2016; van der Kolk, 2014). In addition, to manage trauma reactions survivors may resort to self-medication to alter internal mood states through food, alcohol, drugs, gambling, sex, work, exercise or risky behaviours.

Survivors of DA also learn that to be visible is dangerous as they are more likely to be attacked, so they feel compelled to become invisible, even though this threatens their very existence. This existential conflict pervades all future relationships, in which the survivor oscillates between 'approach and avoid' behaviours. To protect themselves from further harm some survivors conceal their vulnerability and dependency needs and replace these with a façade of strength, a sense of invincibility and fierce self-reliance. This not only conceals their fear of dependency, but also has considerable impact on relational dynamics, including the therapeutic relationship (Sanderson, 2013). In addition, the fear of re-experiencing the trauma can prevent them from seeking appropriate help, which in turn leads to further isolation and withdrawal.

Repeated acts of brutalisation in which abusive behaviour alternates with loving and caretaking behaviour can lead to traumatic bonding (Dutton and Painter, 1981). Such oscillation elicits extremely strong emotional attachments, which act as a superglue to bond the relationship (Sanderson, 2008) and intensifies feelings of fear and terror, which are often misinterpreted as passion and excitement (Herman, 1992a).

In addition, many survivors of DA blame themselves for their abuse, especially when they believe they have provoked the abuser into attacking them. It is critical that practitioners understand the function of provocation as a way to gain control and predictability over when they are likely to be attacked. In provoking the abuser, the victim can have a semblance of control of the timing of the abuse, and prepare for the assault rather than remain in thrall to an anticipated attack. It is critical that these dynamics are understood within the context of an abuse or trauma framework rather than pathologising the client or colluding with the abuser in blaming them for their abuse.

INTERVENTION: WORKING WITH SURVIVORS OF DA

Therapists need to be aware of the impact of complex trauma on relational functioning to minimise the replication of abuse dynamics in the counselling process (Herman, 1992b). In this they need to establish a safe and secure base in which to develop a sensitively attuned therapeutic relationship (Pearlman and Courtois, 2005). Survivors of DA find it difficult to trust and can oscillate between hostility and extreme neediness. Practitioners need to be mindful that trust is not finite and that survivors may regularly test the commitment of the therapist, which can create ruptures in the therapeutic relationship. Therapists must understand these within the context of the survivor's experience and not personalise such ruptures or reject, shame or punish the survivor (Sanderson, 2015). Instead they must provide an authentic human relationship to counteract and undo the effects of dehumanisation and facilitate post-traumatic growth.

CORE THERAPEUTIC GOALS

- Validate and legitimise the DA.
- Provide a secure and safe space to establish a sensitively attuned therapeutic relationship in which to develop trust and restore relational worth.
- Use psycho-education to raise awareness of DA, minimise shame, self-blame and restore reality.

- Implement a phased approach to titrate the therapeutic process through a trauma-informed practice model which focuses on stabilisation, processing and integration.
- Facilitate autonomy to enable survivors to make their own choices and post-traumatic growth.

When working with survivors of DA, counsellors need to consider the fundamental principles of TIP (Herman, 1992a; Sanderson, 2013), which emphasises a phased approach alongside their own therapeutic model. The fundamental principles of a TIP model are to titrate the therapeutic process into three phases consisting of: 1. Stabilisation, 2. Processing and 3. Integration.

Stabilisation consists of psycho-education, grounding skills and affect regulation to widen the window of tolerance and increase distress tolerance (Sanderson, 2016). Psycho-education enables survivors to link physiological responses to their abuse and see these as normal reactions to trauma rather than a loss of their sanity (Sanderson, 2013). Alongside this, developing skills such as mindfulness and grounding techniques enable survivors to regain control of trauma reactions and come back into the body to live in the present without being catapulted back into the terrifying past (van der Kolk, 2014). This needs to be supported by enabling survivors to access a range of sources that can offer support, such as police, advocacy, housing and specialist support groups.

Once survivors have gained mastery over their trauma reactions, they can move into phase two to process flashbacks, intrusive memories, nightmares and traumatic experiences. In exploring the trauma and developing a more coherent narrative, the survivor can begin to gain meaning and make sense of his or her experience and restore reality (Sanderson, 2013, 2016). As survivors process their experiences and gain meaning, they can move into the final phase and begin to integrate mind, body and brain, and reconnect sensations, feelings and thoughts, and experience post-traumatic growth. While these phases are not linear, and not all survivors experience post-traumatic growth, many are able to restore control over their symptoms and regain a sense of agency and autonomy.

A fundamental goal throughout the three phases is the building and maintenance of a therapeutic relationship in which the survivor can learn and practise relational skills (Pearlman and Courtois, 2005). This is pivotal to rebuilding relational worth and to discover more authentic ways of relating, in which needs, feelings and thoughts can be expressed without fear of being punished or humiliated. It is through the therapeutic relationship that the survivor can begin to reconnect to self and others with renewed trust (Sanderson, 2013). This will enable the survivor to restore reality and challenge distorted perceptions, especially those imposed by the abuser. In addition, therapists need to restore power and control to the survivor so that they can regain autonomy and self-agency to make their own choices, including whether to leave or not. If the survivor is working towards leaving the abusive relationship, counsellors need to support this by implementing careful safety planning to minimise the risk of further violence (Sanderson, 2008; Women's Aid Federation, 2005).

While some survivors of DA enter therapy immediately after being traumatised, many survivors remain silent for many years as they are too ashamed to talk about their experiences until trust has been established. In such cases, therapists need to work on two parallel levels, one which focuses on the DA experience in the past and the other in the present to alleviate current stress and symptoms.

CASE EXAMPLE: SOPHIE

Sophie met and married her partner when they both had successful careers but wanted to start a family as soon as possible. They had three children in quick succession with Sophie taking a career break to look after the children. Sophie's husband was extremely charming, a seemingly caring and loving husband, and doting father. Shortly after the birth of the third child, a son, Sophie's husband began to express concerns about Sophie's mothering and her mental health, and started to control and intimidate her. Despite the lack of any evidence to substantiate these concerns, he escalated his coercive behaviour to the point of instigating custody proceedings.

When Sophie entered therapy she suffered from a number of PTSD symptoms, including hypervigilance, hyperarousal, flashbacks and extremely negative beliefs about her self and her relational worth. The first phase of the therapeutic process focused on providing a place of safety for Sophie to regain some control over her PTSD symptoms and her life. This necessitated a degree of psycho-education to understand her DA experiences and to validate and legitimise her experiences, restore reality and challenge the false beliefs imposed on her by her husband. Through the mastery of grounding skills she was able to re-regulate her trauma responses, develop affect regulation and increase her window of tolerance. From this she was able to process her abuse experiences and integrate these. Overtime she was able to restore trust and belief in herself, gain meaning and purpose in life, and begin her journey to post-traumatic growth. The therapeutic setting became a sanctuary or holding environment for Sophie to just 'be', rather than having to be hypervigilant or feel overpowered or controlled by someone else, and it allowed her the autonomy to make her own decisions or choices without fear of abuse.

EVALUATION

It is difficult to evaluate the outcome of the therapeutic process when working with survivors of DA as this will vary enormously. For some survivors, the goal is to leave their partner, while for others it might be acquiring the skills necessary to manage the DA. Essential for all is validating the abuse, restoring control over trauma symptoms through affect regulation and widening the window of tolerance to allow for processing and integration of the trauma and facilitate post-traumatic growth (Sanderson, 2013).

There are a number of therapeutic challenges inherent in working with survivors of DA, not least the need for flexibility and the ability to tolerate uncertainty. In addition, bearing witness to DA can impact on practitioners and lead to vicarious traumatisation and secondary traumatic stress (Sanderson, 2013). To minimise this, and avoid being overwhelmed by the enormity of DA, counsellors need to ensure that they have access to professional and personal support so that they can enable survivors to move towards living life more authentically, with greater self-agency and equality, without the fear of further abuse.

REFERENCES

British Medical Association (2007) *Domestic Abuse*. London: BMA.

Dutton, D.G. (2007) *The Abusive Personality: Violence and Control in Intimate Relationships* (2nd ed.). New York: Guilford Press.

Dutton, D.G. and Painter, S.L. (1981) Traumatic bonding: the development of emotional attachment in battered women and other relationships of intermittent abuse. *Victimology: An International Journal*, 6, 139–155.

Dutton, M.A. (1992) *Empowering and Healing Battered Women: A Model for Assessment and Intervention*. New York: Springer.

Herman, J.L. (1992a) *Trauma and Recovery*. New York: Basic Books.

Herman, J.L. (1992b) Complex PTSD: a syndrome in survivors of prolonged and repeated trauma. *Journal of Traumatic Stress*, 5, 377–392.

Home Office (2015) *Controlling or Coercive Behaviour in an Intimate or Family Relationships*. Statutory Guidance Framework 15. London: Home Office.

Pearlman, L.A. and Courtois, C.A. (2005) Clinical applications of the attachment framework: relational treatment of complex trauma. *Journal of Traumatic Stress*, 18, 449–459.

Sanderson, C. (2008) *Counselling Survivors of Domestic Abuse*. London: Jessica Kingsley Publishers.

Sanderson, C. (2010) *Introduction to Counselling Survivors of Interpersonal Trauma*. London: Jessica Kingsley Publishers.

Sanderson, C. (2013) *Counselling Skills for Working with Trauma: Healing from Child Sexual Abuse, Sexual Violence and Domestic Abuse*. London: Jessica Kingsley Publishers.

Sanderson, C. (2015) *Counselling Skills for Working with Shame*. London: Jessica Kingsley Publishers.

Sanderson, C. (2016) *The Warrior Within: A One in Four Handbook to Aid Recovery from Childhood Sexual Abuse and Sexual Violence* (3rd ed.). London: One in Four.

van der Kolk, B.A. (2014) *The Body Keeps the Score London*. London: Allen Lane.

Walby, S. and Allen, J. (2004) *Domestic Violence, Sexual Assault and Stalking: Findings from the British Crime Survey*. Home Office Research Study No. 276. London: Home Office.

Women's Aid Federation (2005) *The Survivor's Handbook*. Bristol: Women's Aid Federation.

RECOMMENDED READING

1.   British Medical Association (2007) *Domestic Abuse*. London: BMA.

An excellent resource that introduces the nature of domestic abuse (DA) and its medical, psychological and social impact on individuals. It also includes advice on how to facilitate disclosure and guidance on how access other support services.

2.   Herman, J.L. (1992) *Trauma and Recovery*. New York: Basic Books.

This is a classic text that examines the nature and dynamics of DA and how this impacts on survivors. It is an in-depth exploration of how DA affects psychobiological and psychosocial functioning.

3.   Women's Aid Federation (2005) *The Survivor's Handbook*. Bristol: Women's Aid Federation.

Although aimed at survivors, this handbook is an excellent resource for understanding DA and offers guidance on safety planning and how to access a range of support services, such as support groups, advocacy and legal advice.

6.8 EATING DISORDERS

CAROLINE VERMES

OVERVIEW AND KEY POINTS

Eating disorders are complex problems with potentially serious, and sometimes life-threatening, psychological and medical consequences. Eating disorders have an anecdotal reputation for being 'difficult to treat', yet this need not be the case when therapy is theoretically well-grounded and its practice well-conducted. The key points addressed in this chapter are:

- Eating disorders are the extreme sequelae of culturally mandated self-control of diet and body image.
- Eating disorders are caused and maintained by specific behavioural and psychological processes that can be effectively addressed with evidence-based therapy.
- The practitioner needs to pay particular care to relational warmth and empathic attunement with eating disorder clients, to protect against the risk of premature drop-out.

DEFINITION

Eating disorders are the behavioural and psychological expression of the over-evaluation of control of one's food intake, body weight and shape. This defining characteristic is present in all eating disorders. If this characteristic is absent, a diagnosis other than eating disorder may be warranted. Although some people with eating disorders deny that diet and body image are of concern to them, perceptive clinical interviewing can uncover various signs of this preoccupation. Most eating disorder cases develop in adolescent and young adult women. However, diagnostic stereotyping may cause males with eating disorders to be underrepresented in treatment services (Andersen, 2014). The fifth edition of the *Diagnostic and Statistical Manual of Mental Disorders* (DSM-V) (American Psychiatric Association, 2013) and the *International Statistical Classification of Diseases and Related Health Problems* (ICD-10) (World Health Organisation, 2010) include descriptions for anorexia, bulimia, binge eating disorder as well as other eating disorder variants. But although the eating disorders have distinguishing clinical characteristics, they also feature a common cluster of behavioural

and cognitive processes (Fairburn et al., 2003). Here we review those processes, as they are most clearly responsible for causing and maintaining eating disorders.

BEHAVIOURAL PROCESSES

The primary causal and maintaining behaviour in most eating disorders is rigid dietary restriction, or other forms of avoidance of eating a well-balanced diet. Restrictive eating may be intermittent or continual, with episodes lasting days, months or years at a time. Sustained undernourishment (sometimes compounded by compulsive exercise) can lead to **anorexia**, which is characterised by deliberate suppression of weight to a point that is below Body Mass Index (BMI) 18. Anorexia causes reproductive hormone insufficiency, which in women can disrupt or arrest the menstrual cycle (amenorrhoea) and which over time can lead to bone loss (osteoporosis). Anorexia can cause serious medical and mental health complications. While anorexia is a rare condition, occurring in approximately 0.3% of the population in Western countries (Hoek, 2006), it is estimated that up to 20% of people with anorexia die from system failure or suicide (Mitchell et al., 1997).

Another common maintaining behaviour is binge eating. Strong feelings of hunger or deprivation caused by strict dieting inevitably lead some people occasionally, or regularly, to lose control over their appetite. Binge eating episodes can be 'objective', consisting of thousands of calories eaten rapidly, or they may be 'subjective', when a person who is accustomed to eating little, eats more than they planned, but not much more than a non-eating disordered person might eat. Binges are commonly followed by feelings of regret or shame, because they breach an idealised state of self-control, and they risk weight gain. Binges are typically followed by renewed resolve to rigidly control eating. **Binge eating disorder** is the most prevalent of the eating disorders, occurring in approximately 2.5% of the population of Western countries (Hoek, 2006). It is estimated that up to 30% of people accessing treatment for obesity may experience binge eating disorder (De Zwaan, 2001).

After a binge some people may try to disrupt the digestive process by making themselves sick, or by misusing laxatives, a process called purging. These compensatory behaviours are most commonly associated with **bulimia**, but are also sometimes seen in anorexia. Bulimia occurs in approximately 1% of the population of Western countries (Hoek, 2006). Self-induced vomiting is a relatively ineffectual method of purging, as much of the food remains in the stomach to be digested (Fairburn, 2008). Habitual vomiting can cause cardiac, gastrointestinal, dental and reproductive complications (Herzog and Eddy, 2007). Laxative misuse is an entirely ineffectual method of purging, and poses serious health risks that in some cases can become life-threatening (Roerig et al., 2010). The ineffectiveness of purging in preventing absorption of energy helps explain why the weight of people with binge-purge eating patterns tends to fluctuate in the normal or higher-than-average range. People with bulimia may be naturally a higher weight than their peers, which could trigger dieting in the first place (Fairburn et al., 1997).

PSYCHOLOGICAL PROCESSES

People with eating disorders invest a disproportionate amount of their self-worth in attempts to control their eating and body image. Repeated, yet inevitable, failure to attain or sustain unrealistic weight or eating goals further injures self-esteem. Additionally, undernourishment negatively impacts the brain's ability to perform a wide range of social and cognitive functions. In underweight clients, psychological effects include constant hunger (although this may be denied), intrusive thoughts about food, cognitive rigidity, indecisiveness, impaired concentration, anxiety, irritability, obsessiveness, ritualistic habits and social withdrawal. Loss of insight into illness and denial of problems intensify at lower weights. All these effects serve to further maintain the eating disorder (Fairburn, 2008).

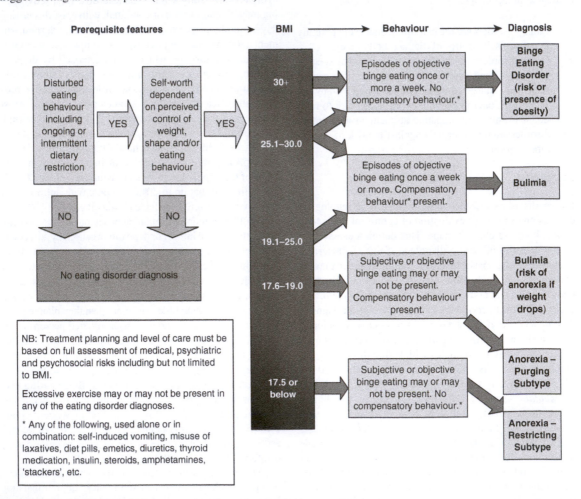

Figure 6.8.1 A simple guide to understanding eating disorder categorisation

Figure 6.8.1 provides a guide to understanding different eating disorder diagnoses. Checking for the presence of prerequisite features will initially determine if someone may have an eating disorder. Then, considering their BMI as well as the presence and absence of eating disordered behaviours are important in determining which type of eating disorder they may have.

AETIOLOGY

Now that we have summarised the behavioural and psychological factors that directly cause and maintain eating disorders, we turn to look at some background factors that predispose some people to develop eating problems. Risk factors fall into two interrelated domains: family psychobiological factors and socio-cultural factors.

FAMILY PSYCHOBIOLOGICAL RISK FACTORS

Eating disorders tend to aggregate in families. Heritable family personality and behavioural characteristics may account for this. Perfectionism (Fairburn et al., 1997, 1999) and obsessive compulsive traits (Lilenfeld et al., 1998) are risk factors in anorexia and bulimia. Research on neurotransmitter activity in people with long-term recovered anorexia has suggested an association between elevated concentrations of cerebral spinal fluid serotonin pre cursor 5-hydroxyindoleacetic acid (CSF 5-HIAA) and behavioural over-control, exactness, perfectionism and obsessionality (Kaye et al., 1991). These traits are triggered or exacerbated by malnutrition brought on by precursory dieting. Parental alcohol problems (Fairburn et al., 1997) and depression (Fairburn et al., 1998) are risk factors for bulimia and binge eating. Both are familial issues with genetic predisposition (Cloninger et al., 1981; Southwick et al., 2005).

SOCIO-CULTURAL RISK FACTORS

Western culture idealises physical attributes including slimness and fitness. Although 'appearance scrutiny' of self and others affects both males and females, it can be more pronounced for females throughout the lifespan and particularly in developmental periods, rendering adolescents vulnerable to channelling negative self-evaluation into unhealthy manipulation of eating, body size and shape in the belief this will improve personal and social acceptance. Repeated exposure to negative comments about weight and eating is a risk factor for binge eating disorder (Fairburn et al., 1998). Gender-sensitive adverse childhood experiences, including sexual abuse, are risk factors for all eating disorders (Wooley, 1994).

ASSESSMENT

It is recommended that therapists use evidence-based eating disorders assessment questionnaires to build a thorough picture of the nature, extent and effects of eating disorder symptoms. This process helps inform an accurate psychological and medical risk profile, and points to the most appropriate treatment options. The Eating Disorders Examination (EDE) 16.0D (Fairburn et al., 2008) is a semi-structured interview schedule that systematically directs clinical information gathering and incorporates a scoring system for understanding the severity of various eating disorder features. The EDE-Q 6.0 (Fairburn and Beglin, 2008) is a client self-report version of the EDE. Modifications to the EDE for use with children (for instance, using sorting tasks to assess ideas about weight and shape) is described by Bryant-Waugh et al. (1996).

In the United Kingdom, regional and national care pathways for children and adults with eating disorders provide guidance on appropriate care settings and service requirements (e.g., NHS England and NCCMH, 2015). For clients with weight below BMI 19 and/or other co-existing mental health difficulties, it is important to obtain medical and psychiatric assessment from appropriately trained consultants. Also, specialist dietitians provide helpful advice and support to eating disorder clients (e.g., Wakefield and Williams, 2009). The outpatient therapist must collaborate closely with these professionals, and promptly refer clients to more intensive services where indicated.

FORMULATION

The task of formulation in eating disorders treatment is for therapist and client to come to (a) a collaborative and evolving understanding of how specific behaviours and beliefs maintain the client's problems, and (b) an agreement about changes required to achieve the improvements the client seeks. Psycho-education helps the client understand how their weight control efforts are counterproductive to their emotional and physical wellbeing. Persistent and patient work by both therapist and client helps to dismantle deeply held beliefs about the necessity of a 'dieting' lifestyle and fears about weight gain that are characteristic of all eating disorders.

INTERVENTION

Outpatient therapy is recommended as the first step in the treatment of anorexia (National Collaborating Centre for Mental Health, 2004), while self-help approaches (e.g., Fairburn, 2013) are the recommended first step for bulimia and binge eating disorder. A helpful strategy in eating disorders treatment is to focus on behavioural change first, as improvements in eating patterns and nourishment naturally ameliorate other psychological problems commonly faced by the client, including depression and anxiety. Once behavioural improvements are underway, residual cognitive and emotional issues can be addressed. Cognitive-behaviour therapy (CBT) for eating disorders includes special modules for the minority of clients who present with severe additional problems, including clinical perfectionism, core low self-esteem and interpersonal issues (Fairburn, 2008). An effective course of therapy may take 6–12 months to complete. Here we will look at the core 'transdiagnostic' behavioural and psychological tasks that help clients towards recovery.

BEHAVIOURAL INTERVENTION

The key behavioural tasks in eating disorders treatment are restoring regular eating patterns and appropriate energy levels. This reverses emaciation and related problems in anorexia; and eliminates hunger and deprivation as primary causes of binge eating in other eating disorders. Purging typically self-resolves with the cessation of binge eating.

PSYCHOLOGICAL INTERVENTION

The key psychological task is replacing weight control as the basis of self-worth with more meaningful expressions of personal value. The most potent of these are relational in nature. Achieving this task in anorexia requires adjustment to weight restoration; and in all eating disorders, acceptance of realistic weight goals for long-term health maintenance. Developing tolerance of strong moods and difficult events without eating disturbance is another important task of recovery.

CHILDREN AND ADOLESCENTS

Family treatment is the first-line recommended treatment for children and adolescents with eating disorders (Lock, 2011; National Collaborating Centre for Mental Health, 2004). Family-based approaches have been found to produce superior results in facilitating full remission and fewer hospitalisations in adolescent anorexia when compared to individual therapy (Lock et al., 2010). The therapist provides reassuring family psycho-education about illness, recovery and treatment tasks. Where appropriate, the therapist may teach parents to actively manage their child's eating disorder, particularly at family mealtimes, and then to gradually transition control back to the child in an age-appropriate manner (Lock and Le Grange, 2012).

PHARMACOLOGY

Few psychotropic medications are recommended for use in people aged under 18. There is little scientific evidence that medications are helpful in the treatment of anorexia. On the other hand, there is some evidence that selective serotonin reuptake inhibitors (SSRIs) may be helpful in reducing binge eating (National Collaborating Centre for Mental Health, 2004).

TREATMENT RETENTION

Eating disorder clients may be at greater risk of treatment drop-out than people with more common psychological issues (Fassino et al., 2009). While there are no consistent predictors of drop-out, it might be surmised that in some cases clients find elements of treatment aversive. For these reasons, eating disorders treatment providers must pay particular care to empathic relational engagement, from first to final points of contact.

CASE EXAMPLE: CBT-E PLUS BRIEF FAMILY THERAPY

Rochelle (aged 17) was commencing her A-level year when she entered treatment. She had provisionally accepted a good university offer, having excelled in academic subjects and athletics throughout secondary school. However, in the past 18 months she had channelled her high personal and academic expectations into 'healthy eating and exercise', because, she said, most of her friends were competitively dieting. Excessive dietary restriction and exercise had quickly propelled her into anorexia. She was experiencing episodes of uncontrolled binge eating at least twice a week, which she followed with self-induced vomiting. At the start of treatment Rochelle was visibly emaciated with a BMI of 15.5. She was experiencing coldness, high anxiety and disruptive preoccupation with thoughts about food. She saw her GP monthly for check-ups and bloodwork, which remained normal. Rochelle was initially unwilling to accept that she would have to re-gain all her weight in order to recover. However, with her therapist's encouragement, she diligently followed the core CBT-E activities, including self-monitoring and regular eating. Accepting the advice of her dietitian, she improved her energy intake. The binges and vomiting quickly stopped as her hunger reduced. Her parents attended two information sessions with Rochelle and her therapist, to understand her treatment. They provided helpful support at home to ensure Rochelle stuck to her meal plans and persisted in her efforts to diversify her diet. As Rochelle's weight and energy improved she was able to tell her therapist how badly she and her father got on. She said their relationship was marked by angry standoffs, particularly when her father had been drinking alcohol. Rochelle and her therapist created a genogram which showed significant intergenerational stress impacting her father, which helped Rochelle understand him better. She decided she wanted to leave home on good terms with him. Her therapist arranged four sessions with Rochelle and her father to talk about their relationship. Her father was willing to engage in this work, and, to Rochelle's surprise, expressed admiration and love for her. He reduced his drinking. Rochelle said this work made a huge difference in her self-acceptance, and contributed to a significant improvement in relations at home. Further therapy focused on Rochelle being able to 'take a stand against dieting' with her friends, and to demonstrate her self-acceptance by eating well and focusing her energies on more important pursuits. Therapy was complete with six family sessions and 14 individual sessions. Rochelle went to university having maintained a healthy weight for eight weeks. She and her family were confident she was making the right decision.

EVALUATION

It has been estimated that after completing treatment, over a third of people with eating disorders get fully better, half may retain some elements of the disorder, and a small proportion stay markedly unwell (Bloks et al., 2004). Some people may get better by themselves after dropping out of treatment (DiPietro et al., 2002). Others get better with self-help or no treatment at all. People who decide to actively tackle their eating disorder, and seek social support while doing so, seem to have better outcomes (Bloks et al., 2004).

REFERENCES

American Psychiatric Association (APA) (2013). *Diagnostic and Statistical Manual of Mental Disorders* (5th ed.). Washington, DC: American Psychiatric Publishing.

Andersen, A.E. (2014). Diagnosis and treatment of males with eating disorders. In A. Andersen (Ed.), *Males with Eating Disorders* (pp. 133–162). London: Routledge.

Bloks, H., Furth, E.F., Callewaert, I. and Hoek, H.W. (2004). Coping strategies and recovery in patients with a severe eating disorder. *Eating Disorders*, 12(2), 157–169.

Bryant-Waugh, R.J., Cooper, P.J., Taylor, C.L. and Lask, B.D. (1996). The use of the eating disorders examination with children: a pilot study. *International Journal of Eating Disorders*, 19(4), 391–397.

Cloninger, C.R., Bohman, M. and Sigvardsson, S. (1981). Inheritance of alcohol abuse. *Archives of General Psychiatry*, 38, 861–868.

De Zwaan, M. (2001). Binge eating disorder and obesity. *International Journal of Obesity and Related Metabolic Disorders*, 25, S51.

Di Pietro, G., Valoroso, L., Fichele, M. et al. (2002). What happens to eating disorder outpatients who withdrew from therapy? *Eating and Weight Disorders*, 7, 298–303.

Fairburn, C.G. (2008). *Cognitive Behaviour Therapy and Eating Disorders*. New York and London: Guilford Press.

(Continued)

(Continued)

Fairburn, C.G. (2013). *Overcoming Binge Eating* (2nd ed.). New York and London: Guilford Press.

Fairburn, C.G. and Beglin, S. (2008). Eating Disorder Examination Questionnaire (EDE-Q 6.0). In C.G. Fairburn (Ed.), *Cognitive Behavior Therapy and Eating Disorders* (pp. 309–313). New York and London: Guilford Press.

Fairburn, C.G., Cooper, Z., Doll, H.A. and Welch, S.L. (1999). Risk factors for anorexia nervosa: three integrated case-control comparisons. *Archives of General Psychiatry*, 56(5), 468–476.

Fairburn, C.G., Cooper, Z. and O'Connor, M.E. (2008). Eating Disorder Examination (EDE 16.0D). In C.G. Fairburn (Ed.), *Cognitive Behavior Therapy and Eating Disorders* (pp. 265–308). New York and London: Guilford Press.

Fairburn, C.G., Cooper, Z. and Shafan, R. (2003). Cognitive behaviour therapy for eating disorders: A 'transdiagnostic' theory and treatment. *Behaviour Research and Therapy*, 41, 509–528.

Fairburn, C.G., Welch, S.L., Doll, H.A., et al. (1997). Risk factors for bulimia nervosa: a community-based case-control study. *Archives of General Psychiatry*, 54, 509–517.

Fairburn, C.G., Welch, S.L., Doll, H.A., et al. (1998). Risk factors for binge eating disorder: a community-based, case control study. *Archives of General Psychiatry*, 55, 425–432.

Fassino, S., Piero, A., Tomba, E. and Abbate-Daga, C. (2009). Factors associated with dropout from treatment of eating disorders: a comprehensive literature review. *BioMed Central (BMC) Psychiatry*, 9(67) (www.biomedcentral.com/1471-244X/9/67 on 25.08.2016).

Herzog, D.B. and Eddy, K.T. (2007). Diagnosis, epidemiology and clinical course of eating disorders. In J. Yager and P.S. Powers (Eds.), *Clinical Manual of Eating Disorders* (pp. 1–30). Washington, DC: American Psychiatric Publishing.

Hoek, H.W. (2006). Incidence, prevalence and mortality of anorexia nervosa and other eating disorders. *Current Opinion in Psychiatry*, 19(4), 389–394.

Kaye, W.H., Gwirtsman, H.E., George, D.T. and Ebert, M.H. (1991). Altered serotonin activity in anorexia nervosa after long-term weight restoration. *Archives of General Psychiatry*, 48(6), 556–562.

Lilenfeld, L.R., Kaye, W.H., Greeno, C.G., et al. (1998). A controlled family study of anorexia nervosa and bulimia nervosa. *Archives of General Psychiatry*, 55, 603–610.

Lock, J. (2011). Evaluation of family treatment models for eating disorders. *Current Opinion in Psychiatry*, 24(4), 274–279.

Lock, J. and Le Grange, D. (2012). *Treatment Manual for Anorexia Nervosa: A Family-based Approach* (2nd ed.). New York and London: Guilford Press.

Lock, J., Le Grange, D., Agras, W.S., Moye, A. and Jo, B. (2010). A randomised clinical trial comparing family-based treatment to adolescent-focussed individual therapy for adolescents with anorexia nervosa. *Archives of General Psychiatry*, 67(10), 1025–1032.

Mitchell, J.E., Pomeroy, C. and Adson, D.E. (1997). Managing medical complications. In D.M. Garner and P.E. Garfinkel (Eds.), *Handbook of Treatment for Eating Disorders* (2nd ed., pp. 383–393). New York and London: Guilford Press.

National Collaborating Centre for Mental Health (NCCMH) (2004). *Eating Disorders: Core Interventions in the Treatment and Management of Aanorexia Nervosa, Bulimia Nervosa and Related Eating Disorders*. National Clinical Guideline No. CG9. London: BPS and Gaskell.

NHS England and NCCMH (2015). *Access and Waiting Time Standard for Children and Young People with an Eating Disorder*. London: National Health Service. (www.england.nhs.uk/wp-content/uploads/2015/07/cyp-eating-disorders-access-waiting-time-standard-comm-guid.pdf).

Roerig, J., Steffen, K., Mitchell, J. and Zunker, C. (2010). Laxative misuse. *Drugs*, 70(12), 1487–1503.

Southwick, S.M., Vythillingham, M. and Charney, D.S. (2005). The psychobiology of depression and resilience to stress: implications for prevention and treatment. *Annual Review of Clinical Psychology*, 1, 225–291.

Wakefield, A. and Williams, H. (2009). *Practice Recommendations for the Nutritional Management of Anorexia Nervosa in Adults*. Dietitians Association of Australia. Retrieved on 16 May, 2017 from http://cedd.org.au/wordpress/wp-content/uploads/2014/09/Practice-Recommendations-for-the-Nutritional-Assessment-of-Anorexia-Nervosa-in-Adults.pdf

Wooley, S.C. (1994). Sexual abuse and eating disorders: the concealed debate. In P. Fallon, M.A. Katzman and S.C. Wooley (Eds.), *Feminist Perspectives on Eating Disorders* (pp. 171–211). New York and London: Guilford Press.

World Health Organisation (WHO) (2010). Eating disorders (F50). *International Statistical Classification of Diseases and Related Health Problems* (10th ed.). London: Churchill Livingtone (http://apps.who.int/classifications/icd10/browse/2010/en#/F50).

RECOMMENDED READING

1. Fairburn, C.G. (2008). *Cognitive Behaviour Therapy and Eating Disorders*. New York and London: Guilford Press.

This landmark text details the transdiagnostic theory and individual treatment protocol for adults and adolescents with eating disorders.

2. Lock, J. and Le Grange, D. (2012). *Treatment Manual for Anorexia Nervosa: A Family-based Approach* (2nd ed.). New York and London: Guilford Press.

Lock and Le Grange's family therapy model is also known as the 'Maudsley method'.

3. Jordan, J.V., Kaplan, A.G., Miller, J.B., Stiver, I.P. and Surrey, J.L. (1991). *Women's Growth in Connection: Writings from the Stone Center*. New York and London: Guilford Press.

Core reading for therapists interested in relational-cultural developmental perspectives on women's sense of self. First drawn up by the influential American psychiatrist Jean Baker Miller, the relational-cultural theory proposes that 'separation and individuation' theory fails to describe the healthy task of adolescence, which is the continuation and maturation of generative, empathic relationships with significant others into, and across, adulthood.

6.9   HIV/AIDS

JILL BALMONT AND IDA WAKSBERG

OVERVIEW AND KEY POINTS

We describe HIV/AIDS and its treatment, and explore the challenges presented by an HIV diagnosis. Although it is no longer considered a death sentence, people can experience considerable distress. Some need help to cope with the stigma of the disease, manage the demands of medical treatment and make the adjustments necessary to live well with HIV. We present examples of effective psychological interventions in HIV-related psychotherapy, and consider its limitations.

- Early diagnosis and adherence to medical treatment are essential in decreasing the risk of onward transmission and ensuring the best quality of life for those living with HIV.
- Premorbid history and functioning, and social support are significant in determining subsequent psychological adjustment.

- Ethical dilemmas arise in clinical practice, and supervision is essential to avoid compounding the stigma of moral judgement with which many have to live.
- A life-threatening condition brings opportunities as well as threats, and psychological therapy can help people to realise these in purposeful and creative ways.

INTRODUCTION

The human immuno-deficiency virus (HIV) first began to spread among groups of gay men and intravenous drug users in the late 1970s in the United Kingdom (UK). This was followed by the first report of the constellation of symptoms known as acquired immune deficiency syndrome (AIDS) in 1981. AIDS is the disease of the immune system caused by HIV, and individuals are said to have AIDS when they have advanced

HIV infection. Illnesses commonly seen as AIDS defining are pneumonia, tuberculosis and cancer.

In the context of widespread public ignorance and panic, people tended to be blamed on account of their lifestyles and efforts were focused on reducing HIV transmission. It was clear that HIV disproportionately affected the disempowered and poor in society: those growing up marginalised because of their sexuality, mental health difficulties, impoverished social backgrounds and lifestyles. Services were developed in response to the medical, psychological, support and advocacy needs of patients.

By the late 1990s medication had instilled some hope. Today, with early diagnosis and prompt treatment, the majority of those diagnosed with HIV will have a near-normal life expectancy with minimal side-effects. AIDS is uncommon and people are increasingly living into older age. However, many heterosexually acquired infections are diagnosed late as people are unaware of their infected status, and despite better awareness among gay men, new infection rates remain high. Prevention remains a major concern and, sadly, despite better public knowledge, the stigma of the illness has not gone away.

DEFINITION

HIV is a viral infection which is, at present, incurable. The virus uses the cells it has infected to replicate, and as levels of viral infection in the blood increase, the immune system is weakened such that it cannot function effectively. This leaves the HIV-positive person susceptible to developing HIV-related complications, such as renal disease, opportunistic infections and malignancies.

Infection of the central nervous system by the virus results in neurological complications, ranging from subtle cognitive impairments to severe and disabling dementia, infections such as encephalitis and other neurological dysfunctions. The aim of early diagnosis and treatment is to prevent these medical complications.

Since the first AIDS diagnosis 35 years ago, HIV has remained one of the most serious communicable diseases in the UK. While medical advances have improved the efficacy of HIV treatments, and the quality of life of many HIV-infected people, the disease continues to be associated with serious morbidity and early mortality for some, and high costs of treatment and care.

AETIOLOGY

In 2014 there were 103,700 estimated cases of people living with HIV in the UK; 6,151 new cases were reported, with more than half of these accounted for by men who

have sex with men. Among the 40 per cent of heterosexually acquired new infections, more than half were of people with Black African ethnicity. Small numbers of new infections were children infected perinatally from their mothers, and people who were probably infected through receiving infected blood or body tissue abroad. Small but stable rates of infection were reported among intravenous drug users (Public Health England, 2015). The vast majority of people with HIV are, therefore, infected through unprotected vaginal or anal sexual intercourse.

As HIV infection has a prolonged 'silent' period, it can remain undiagnosed and it is estimated that 17 per cent of people are unaware of their HIV-positive status. This increases the risk of onward transmission, and significant numbers of people are still being diagnosed at a late stage of infection. This means that they are missing out on the benefits of starting treatment early.

MEDICAL TREATMENT

Since 1996, HIV has been treated with anti retroviral therapy (ART) – combinations of drugs which suppress viral replication and restore immune functioning. The discontinuation of ART results in the rapid resurgence of viral replication and so, to be optimally effective, ART needs to continue uninterrupted over a person's lifetime. Modern treatments are increasingly easy to take, often a single pill taken daily, but for some, more complex regimes are required.

The drugs themselves need to be carefully monitored as there may be uncommon but serious side-effects. Interaction with other drugs can also be a problem. Common side-effects at the start of treatment are nausea and diarrhoea, insomnia and vivid dreams and mood disturbances. Allergic reactions can occasionally result in serious complications.

With many anti-HIV drugs now available, it is usually possible to find a combination that suits people's lifestyles. When tolerated well, people can manage the demands of treatment. This is, however, just one of the challenges of living with HIV. People are faced not just with the physical impact of a complex, life-threatening, chronic condition and its treatment, but also the profound psychological impact, compounded by fears of strongly negative social reactions.

PSYCHOLOGICAL ASSESSMENT

In assessing the needs of someone presenting for psychological help, we need to consider the psychological tasks they are facing and the internal and external resources available to them.

FACTORS INFLUENCING PSYCHOLOGICAL ADJUSTMENT

Many factors influence the ease or otherwise by which people adjust to living with an HIV diagnosis. A previous history of psychological disturbance is probably the most significant and may have been a factor in increasing a person's vulnerability to becoming infected. Responses to early experiences of deprivation, abuse and traumatic loss can leave someone predisposed to taking sexual risks, failing to negotiate safer sexual relating or being vulnerable to sexual exploitation. Negative reactions to those with HIV can compound earlier deprivations and abuses, undermining the accessibility of support.

Social support can provide a buffer against being overwhelmed by the emotional impact of the diagnosis and its implications. Consequently, those who are more isolated can be particularly at risk of experiencing psychological difficulties. Young people infected at birth and living in areas of low prevalence, may struggle to find a sense of belonging with their peer group. Partners infected within their committed relationships are also vulnerable on account of the breach of trust and consequent loss of support involved.

Those who are members of marginalised groups in society often have limited support. Being gay may mean, for some, accepting or having to conceal a stigmatised identity, and in some cultures, homosexuality is still regarded as a valid reason for persecution. Drug users are another stigmatised group who can be at increased risk of psychological disturbance as a result of their drug use.

People living in exile from home can be vulnerable to experiencing psychological problems, and especially when the underlying reason for their exile is traumatic, and possibly linked to the transmission of the virus. For many refugees, an HIV diagnosis can compound the sense of loss associated with their departure from their own country and community, and their struggle to resettle here. This is all the more traumatic if HIV was acquired as the result of sexual violence, possibly in the context of war or persecution, and if they come from countries where an HIV diagnosis is associated with certain early death.

COMMON PSYCHOLOGICAL CHALLENGES

There are times in the course of HIV infection and disease progression where people are more vulnerable to experiencing distress, providing opportunities for psychological intervention. These include:

- pre- and post-testing, and at the time of diagnosis (the time between initial and confirmatory testing can be a period of great uncertainty)

- after the initial shock has subsided and adjustment to managing the practical demands of the illness has been achieved, or when someone who has been very ill is in a more stable condition
- when faced with disruption to relationships or problems of disclosure, loss of valued social roles or when faced with having to modify personal aspirations
- when viral levels indicate the need to start medication
- when struggling with side-effects of medication, taking medication consistently or having to change medication
- when faced with the onset of symptoms associated with disease progression
- when faced with terminal stages of disease, in preparation for death.

FORMULATION

To understand what might help involves an appreciation of the potential meanings of HIV infection for people, and an evaluation of its emotional significance and implications for them. Common issues include: the prospect of early mortality and associated losses, fears of contamination and trauma.

THE PROSPECT OF EARLY MORTALITY AND ASSOCIATED LOSSES

Although HIV no longer carries a 'death sentence', an HIV diagnosis confronts someone with the long-term presence of a life-threatening infection. Feared associated losses can include the loss of a valued sense of identity and dignity; increasing dependence on others; loss of trust and security in the world; a reduction or loss of sexual potency and its impact on relationships; and perhaps the growing realisation that some of their personal goals may no longer be attainable.

Premorbid history and functioning determine how well a person's adjustment will facilitate their coping with the losses, both real and anticipated, that follow a positive diagnosis. A sense of psychic integrity is achieved through being able to value and hold on to the positive aspects of oneself and one's experiences. Having had their own dependency needs met well in the past, they are more likely to have confidence that they will continue to be looked after well in the future.

Those more likely to be overwhelmed may be unconsciously anticipating a repeat of failures of dependency in the past. The prospect of life-threatening illness can then be dreaded as a state of continued lonely suffering and neglect, of being rejected, humiliated and hated. Powerful defensive measures can be drawn on to manage such overwhelming dread and anxiety.

The emotional impact may be averted by denying and neglecting the realities of the illness, which may include the need for medication to keep them alive, for sexual partners at risk to be protected and for consent for dependent children at risk to be tested. This can raise difficult ethical dilemmas for the clinical team, including the therapist, on becoming aware of the ways in which a person might be putting themselves or others at risk. See, for example, the case of Mrs M. There can be a pressure to act, especially when the risks are high and confidence in being able to help them understand and manage their risky behaviour is low.

Mrs M, who came to the UK after imprisonment and rape by boy soldiers in her country, was advised to be tested for HIV by her solicitor, who thought this might have a bearing on her asylum case. Mrs M tested positive but refused to know the result of the test, putting the team looking after her under considerable strain as she needed treatment. She was referred to the psychotherapist and for many meetings she sat shivering, wearing a coat and hat, although it was a warm summer.

FEARS OF CONTAMINATION

HIV, as an infectious disease which is easily transmitted, means that people can feel dangerous to themselves and others, and intimacy can become troublesome and unsafe. Since the virus was acquired as a result of the desire for intimacy, and this need does not diminish, sex becomes linked with death. Intimacy can thus become associated with fears of contamination and dread.

The fear and discomfort generated by HIV and the manner of its transmission often becomes attached to the person suffering it so that others can distance themselves from its emotional significance and impact. This is stigma – an isolating mark of shame and disgrace which reminds the infected person of their social unacceptability. This can become internalised as self-reproach if they struggle to accept themselves, and the choices or decisions they have made in the past, which might have contributed to their becoming infected.

Mrs G, in her early 50s and a member of the bourgeoisie in her country of origin, was referred two years after her HIV diagnosis, as distressed as she had been when first diagnosed. She gave a false name in the clinic, and found it very painful to sit in the reception area in case she was recognised. No one knew she was HIV positive, and she felt isolated, remembering how she had previously pitied those with HIV. She had felt that they were contagious and untouchable, and now she felt horrified to feel the same. She was deeply religious and had heard that in her country, where HIV was a sign of promiscuity, someone with HIV had been stoned to death. She often wished she was dead, and thought she would die soon, although she was responding well to medication.

TRAUMA

For many, becoming infected with HIV is traumatic. People can variously feel aggrieved, deeply wounded, guilty and complicit in their own suffering, and furious or ashamed at having this confirmed by the attitudes of others. Facing such feelings is painful and can uncover deeper layers of hurt, isolation and loss (Ratigan, 1991).

Mr S, a 30-year-old white gay man, was referred for psychotherapy for his problems with depression and difficulties with tolerating the side-effects of his HIV medication. After his first appointment, he complained that the meeting had upset him too much. After talking about this, he continued to come but less frequently, then he decided to stop his HIV medication altogether. In his therapy, he disclosed in a detached way a history of sexual abuse as a child by a male teacher, at a time when his home life had been unpredictable and violent.

INTERVENTION

The main therapeutic modalities of practice have all been reported to be helpful (DeRoche and Citron, 2005; Pobuda et al., 2008). If we take an integrative stance, focusing on what tends to take place in a therapy, we identify three main components: the creation of a safe relationship, the exploration of meanings to arrive at an understanding and the

promotion of change. These components can be expressed in different ways, in different theoretical languages, placing a different emphasis on each (Holmes, 2010).

We would suggest that many psychological therapies with people infected with HIV explore, within a safe relationship, themes of mortality, trauma, stigma, shame and guilt in order to achieve changes in areas such as disclosure of HIV status, adherence to medication, negotiating safe sex in relationships and working towards finding an increased investment in life and purpose in living. A life-threatening illness brings opportunities as well as threats, and therapy can help people find or reconnect with their own inner resources, re-evaluate their priorities and live more creatively. We now return to the three case examples introduced already to consider such therapeutic processes.

MRS M

Mrs M talked about the awful things that had happened to her, focusing on her various physical complaints. The therapist listened, and sometimes talked with her about how she protected herself by not wanting to know about things, to which Mrs M quietly agreed. After several weeks she decided to find out the results of the test, and later she told the therapist that she felt strengthened by her understanding and support. She wanted to join a woman's HIV support group, started to take antiretroviral medications and did well in her treatment despite many setbacks in her asylum application.

MRS G

Therapy provided a setting in which Mrs G did not have to pretend that everything was alright. Talking openly and reflecting upon her concerns challenged her sense of isolation and shame. She gradually started to consider a less catastrophic view of HIV, and began to take in some of the positive messages she read in the self-help literature.

She looked forward to her sessions, started to feel better, and after about eight weeks, with great trepidation about the prospect of disclosing her status, she applied for a job. Her success proved to have great therapeutic potential and she later acknowledged that HIV had given her something important: it had brought her down to earth.

MR S

Mr S often seemed to struggle to feel safe with his therapist, equating help with abuse. They explored together whether a helping activity could have other meanings for him, and the frequency of the sessions gradually increased at his request. He appeared to be enjoying her attention, and she wondered if he was feeling a little safer with her. A few weeks later he decided to start another antiretroviral regimen after discussing possible side-effects with his consultant, and this time he seemed to tolerate it better.

In the vignettes, feeling safe and understood allowed Mrs M to face her diagnosis. The therapeutic attachment and opportunity to explore the meanings of her experiences helped Mrs G to feel less isolated, ashamed and untouchable, such that she could participate in life again more fully. With Mr S, it was not until the meanings of help were linked to his previous trauma that he felt able to take medication again.

These are people who engaged in the process, yet therapists must also be prepared for the possibility that many can struggle to engage in therapy, and for some it may not be appropriate.

EVALUATION

Having described the positive outcomes of enhanced well-being and self-care in HIV-related psychotherapy, and reduced risks to others, we now briefly address potential limitations and contra-indications.

Therapy often involves participating in a partial identification with the person seeking help. For example, therapists' capacity to imagine and experience their own vulnerability and fears of mortality can help in understanding and sharing to some extent the other's experience. Therapists can, however, be prone to over-identification and wish to rescue the other from their predicament, blaming or devaluing themselves when they are unable to do so.

Reacting against these feelings can lead to an emotional detachment. This is similar to a stigmatising process whereby the therapist's reactions imply 'the problem is in you'. For example, therapists' personal beliefs about homosexuality, injection use or unsafe sex practices may prevent an empathic relationship developing. The importance of supervision cannot be underestimated in helping therapists to deepen their understanding of the issues facing the people they are trying to help.

A careful assessment is necessary if therapy is to be of benefit. Resistance to exploring problems in psychological terms is self-protective, and we need to respect this when the stakes for unsettling someone's psychological equilibrium are high. Much needed social, self-help or practical support might be more appropriate.

We need to recognise when someone may be heading towards a suicidal crisis or developing serious psychiatric symptoms which might require the skilled intervention of colleagues in mental health services. We also need to ask ourselves if cognitive impairments might be influencing the problems with which someone is presenting, and whether or not a neuropsychometric assessment might be helpful.

CONCLUSIONS

People often minimise the risks of unprotected sex against what they hope to gain, and it only takes one exposure to become infected. This is why HIV continues to be a challenging public health concern which is not helped by the stigma and secrecy which still surround it. The aim for psychological therapy that stands out most strongly for us is to help change the meanings of the HIV virus from something toxic and contagious that resides in certain people from certain social groups, into something more acceptable and reflective of universal risks and the vulnerability of us all.

REFERENCES

DeRoche, P. and Citron, K. (2005) Psychotherapy. In K. Citron, M.J. Brouillette and A.Beckett (Eds), *HIV and Psychiatry: A Training and Resource Manual* (2nd ed., pp. 153–169). Cambridge: Cambridge University Press.

Holmes, J. (2010) Integration in psychoanalytic psychotherapy: an attachment meta-perspective. *Psychoanalytic Psychotherapy*, 24(3), 183–201.

Pobuda, T., Crothers, L., Goldblum, P., Dilley, J.W. and Koopman, C. (2008) Effects of time-limited dynamic psychotherapy on distress among HIV-seropositive men who have sex with men. *AIDS Patient Care and STDs*, 22(7), 1–7.

Public Health England (2015) *HIV in the UK – Situation Report 2015. Incidence, Prevalence and Prevention*. London: Public Health England. (www.gov.uk/government/uploads/system/uploads/attachment_data/file/477702/HIV_in_the_UK_2015_report.pdf).

Ratigan, B. (1991) On not traumatizing the traumatised: the contribution of psychodynamic psychotherapy to work with people with HIV and AIDS. *British Journal of Psychotherapy*, 8(1), 39–47.

RECOMMENDED READING

1. Barret, B., Anderson, J. and Barret, R. (2001) *Ethics in HIV-Related Psychotherapy: Clinical Decision-making in Complex Cases*. New York: American Psychological Association.

Using case examples, this book presents the most common ethical dilemmas encountered in HIV-related psychotherapy and provides a decision-making model for reducing risks in clinical practice.

2.   Citron, K., Brouillette, M.J. and Beckett, A. (Eds) (2005) *HIV and Psychiatry: Training and Resource Manual* (2nd ed.). Cambridge: Cambridge University Press.

Using case studies throughout, this handbook addresses all of the mental health issues involved in caring for HIV and AIDS patients: psychotherapy, cognitive and mood disorders, suicide, work with gay men and couples, etc.

3.   Silverstein, C. (Ed.) (2011) *The Initial Psychotherapy Interview: A Gay Man Seeks Treatment*. London: Elsevier.

Clinicians from a range of theoretical perspectives reflect upon an assessment for therapy with an HIV-negative gay man who is engaging in unsafe sex and has recently lost his gay brother through AIDS.

6.10   LOW SELF-ESTEEM

CHRISTINE WILDING

OVERVIEW AND KEY POINTS

Many people suffer from some element of low self-esteem. Problems develop when self-esteem plummets so low that it starts preventing people from doing things: 'I'm not going to try for the job promotion – I'll never get it anyway', 'I didn't ask so-and-so to go out with me: they'd be sure to say "No" and then I'd feel even worse about myself'. We can understand low self-esteem from a number of perspectives, and numerous options for counselling interventions exist. This chapter comes specifically from the perspective of a cognitive-behavioural understanding. The areas covered in the chapter are:

- What low self-esteem is
- How we measure it
- Where it comes from
- How we can help clients defeat it using cognitive-behavioural therapy (CBT) as the treatment protocol.

DEFINITION

Low self-esteem is, in essence, a measurement. We rate ourselves against a variety of criteria and the result is an estimate of our personal view of our value, or worth. Low self-esteem isn't transitory: it tends to hang around long term. Therefore, low self-esteem can be defined as a longstanding negative self-evaluation or feelings about one's own self or self-capabilities. 'Good self-esteem is essential for psychological survival' (McKay and Fanning, 2016: 1).

AETIOLOGY

Where do these feelings of low self-worth come from? The problem is that some people tend to rate themselves very inaccurately and very harshly. This, in turn, leads to low self-esteem since, based on their negative perceptions, they continue to undervalue themselves. Worse is to come – once a person believes something to be true, he or she will start to act as if it were. The person will start to gather evidence to support the erroneous belief while at the same time discounting evidence that fails to support it, so strengthening the negative view of his or her personal value.

'Most bad feelings come from illogical thoughts' (Burns, 2000: 49). Low esteem is like a rickety bicycle in that it wobbles a lot. If a person's mood drops, so can his thinking and thus his self-esteem – and vice versa. It can also develop in just some areas of people's lives and not all. For example, a person might say, 'I'm extremely confident in the workplace but not in personal relationships'. The cause of this may well be, for example, that the individual was encouraged at home to excel academically but at the expense of socializing with their friends.

Low self-esteem can be caused by a succession of failures for which the person blames themselves, or by a chronic 'drip, drip' of being told that they are not up to much (often perceiving such comments as critical even when that is not the case). An individual may also see these perceptions not as possibilities but as certainties. So low self-esteem can be generalized, where a person has always 'felt that way' or it could come from a specific time, period or event in their lives when they first lost their natural self-confidence. For example:

- Two years ago (a time frame)
- When a relationship broke up (an event)
- Being up at university (a time period).

ASSESSMENT

If an individual has good self-esteem, how would they know? How would they feel? For most people, good self-esteem involves the ability to think of themselves as 'OK' and to believe that others think they are OK as well. It also involves not being too hard on ourselves when we say or do things that are not OK. Not expecting the worst to happen and also believing that if things do go wrong, the adversity will be coped with in the best way possible, accepting that life isn't fair all the time.

Clients will present to you with a great many 'life' issues that seem to have their own harsh realities. However, the task is to measure and recognize not what bad things are happening to the person sitting in front of you, but how does that person feel about these crises? Where the individual cannot cope, while it may be that the task they need to undertake is impossible, it is most likely the lack of personal belief in their capability that is the problem.

So the individual's belief system needs to be checked. Beliefs tend to be hard to shift without work, and they masquerade as facts or truths that block individuals from making any effort at change. How does the person view himself? What does he see as his weaknesses? How does he believe others perceive him? How does he cope with problems and crises? The chances are that the answers to these questions will come back down, time and time again, to low self-esteem.

An individual's beliefs tend to be more deeply ingrained than their thoughts. For example, thoughts tend to be event-specific: 'I won't know what to say to people when I go to the party' is an event-specific thought. It is important in any psychological assessment to look at the belief beneath this thought – perhaps, 'I am dull and boring'. Beliefs tend to be fairly unshakable, no matter what the situation.

FORMULATION

One lens through which we can understand low self-esteem is through cognitive-behavioural therapy (see Mytton and Sequeira – Chapter 5.10, this volume). In this approach we are focused on understanding and adjusting negative thinking patterns which can cause low self-esteem. We can achieve this through understanding the connections between thoughts (also assumptions and beliefs), feelings and behaviours. It is helpful for both therapists and their clients to understand these connections (Padesky and Greenberger, 2015).

Activating Event
Getting turned down for a job

Thoughts
'I'll never get a job'
'I'm unemployable'

Outcome
Sense of hopelessness
Lose motivation
Feel ashamed
Do badly at any interviews
Stop applying for jobs altogether

Figure 6.10.1 Possible effects of negative thinking accompanying low self-esteem

So let's bring all these thoughts, feelings and behaviours together so that we understand what maintains someone's low self-esteem. Look at Figure 6.10.1, which offers an explanation of the possible effects of the negative thinking that can accompany low self-esteem.

As you can see from Figure 6.10.1 (described in CBT terms as a conceptualization or formulation), thoughts, feelings and behaviour are all linked. This linking is what maintains the problem and keeps a person's self-esteem low. As you will see from this formulation, there is nothing here that is going to break this cycle of despair and hopelessness. It is feeding on itself so nothing changes. Yet the sad fact is that the negative thoughts that are causing this may be untrue.

The good news is that we can tap into any of these areas, make a few small changes, and those changes will have a knock-on effect on the other areas. Figure 6.10.2 shows this.

Study the two formulations in Figures 6.10.1 and 6.10.2. Note how the event was the same in each. Yet it created thoughts which generated emotional responses and actions that either maintained and consolidated the problem or drove a way forward out of the problem. Understanding the importance of this formulation will ensure that the low self-esteem sufferer is helped towards good self-esteem.

Activating Event

Getting turned down for a job

Thoughts

'Getting turned down for this job doesn't mean
I will be turned down for all jobs'
'There are other jobs out there and if I keep trying I
will succeed eventually'

Outcome

Keeps determined and focused

Stays calm

Network with friends in jobs I might like

Redouble job applications

Finally get a job offer: not quite what I want but it is a start.

Figure 6.10.2 Possible effects of positive thinking

INTERVENTIONS

MOVING TOWARDS A HEALTHIER SELF-ESTEEM

Appreciating the basic relationship between thoughts, feelings, actions and outcomes is an essential first step as it helps a person identify where they may be going wrong. Now we will move on to look at how these changes can be made, to defeat low self-esteem and replace it with a strong and healthy balanced view of themselves.

REPLACING SELF-DEFEATING THOUGHTS AND BELIEFS

The best way for someone to challenge their negative beliefs is by writing down their negative thoughts and emotions and then asking themselves how they might look at their thoughts more optimistically. Writing things down in this way is called a *Thought Record*. This gives more rational and balanced thoughts a much greater impact than simply trying to challenge the thought mentally. Writing things down can be a chore: 'It takes so much time', 'I can never find a pen', 'Can't I just do this in my head?' No! Writing things down is far more powerful than just trying to think things through. A useful tool here is Burns' (2000) Daily Mood Log, which sets out the process clearly.

This may not come easily at first but that's fine. This is just a start and here are some tips and ideas to turn this into a really useful tool.

Ask your clients to do and consider the following:

1. **Rate your thoughts and emotions.**

How strongly do you believe your negative thoughts and emotions? Also rate how strongly you believe your alternative responses.

2. **Find alternative responses.**

You may initially find it hard to come up with alternative responses. This is simply due to your natural tendency to be self-critical and believe these self-critical thoughts to be true. Be very firm with your rebuttals.

3. **Lack of belief in the alternative.**

You may initially find that although you have come up with some alternative thoughts, you don't really believe them. This will gradually change and you will learn further skills to help you to reinforce your beliefs in a more positive outlook.

Once your clients become good at identifying negative thoughts they can examine how unrealistic or unhelpful they are and whether they are useful to them.

When they are familiar with and are using the tool of the Thought Record, they can move on to **checking for evidence**. When using a Thought Record, many people write diligently but the thought in their mind is 'I don't really believe this – what I really still believe are my negative thoughts'.

How can clients strengthen their belief in their alternative views? One extremely helpful tool, considered by many to be the most important 'thought shifter' around, is to ask the simple question: 'If this is really so, where's the evidence?'

CASE EXAMPLE

Jenny was concerned about her job. She had heard that some redundancies were possible at her firm and she started thinking about her own performance and whether her boss might find a reason to get rid of her. The more she thought about it, the more weaknesses she came up with – being late for an important meeting last week, failing to sign up a new client company that had looked promising. Was she losing her grip?

Over lunch with her colleague Sue, Jenny voiced her concerns. Her friend of course asked Jenny why she was coming to this negative conclusion and Jenny cited what had happened – her 'evidence' for her pessimistic thinking. Sue expressed surprise. 'But Jenny, several people were late for that meeting due to the Tube strike – it couldn't be helped. And although it was disappointing to lose the client, that may not have been your fault at all. You made an excellent presentation and there were many possible reasons why the client may not have gone ahead. Now think of all the new business you have brought into the firm this year. You seem to be discounting that.'

In essence, Sue was presenting Jenny with evidence to contradict Jenny's self-defeating thoughts. But Jenny had not thought of this herself as she was too focused on her negative views of her abilities. This is what can happen to us when our self-esteem is low. We focus on the negative and ignore the helpful evidence.

As mentioned previously, writing down one's thoughts is an essential skill. So, with clients, you can also draw some columns on a sheet of paper and label each column (1) My negative thoughts and emotions (2) What evidence do I have that this thought is true? (3) How can I look at this more optimistically? (4) What evidence do I have that these alternative thoughts are true? You have now made a four-column Thought Record that your clients can use not just to record their thinking but also to validate (or invalidate) it.

For example, if they have looked in the mirror just before going out and thought 'I look dreadful', where is their evidence?

- Is your hair a mess?
- Are your clothes wrong?
- Or do you just feel low about yourself?

Encourage your clients to start with the evidence to support their self-critical thoughts. They will usually find it harder than they think to come up with solid reasoning. For example:

- Would 'Oh, I just do' stand up in a court of law?
- What would a judge think of the evidence?
- Would the judge accept it or throw it out?

When a client comes to the column which asks them to find evidence to support their more optimistic thinking, they may put:

- My partner always tells me I look nice when I get dressed up.
- My best friend has asked to borrow this dress next Saturday.

As they get used to finding evidence for their alternative thinking, the tangible, logical arguments will loosen their hold on their minds in a way that simply repeating optimistic alternatives that they don't really believe will not. This is a very powerful tool.

OVERCOMING THE TYRANNY OF 'SHOULD', 'MUST' AND 'OUGHT'

A lot of negative, self-defeating thinking comes from using the words 'should', 'must' and 'ought'. These words imply personal failure almost every time we use them. They cause us to make demands on individuals and suggest that they cannot meet those demands:

- I should have known better.
- I ought to be able to achieve this.
- I must have made some silly mistakes.

This is *not* positive thinking. We may think this is positive self-talk and that we are motivating ourselves by telling ourselves these things. In fact, it is the opposite: 'I should be … (polite, charming, clever, etc.) and since I am not, I feel badly about myself.'

When self-esteem is low and we feel sorry for ourselves, these 'should', 'musts' and 'oughts' extend to others: people 'should' be nicer to us; others 'must' consider us when making their plans; colleagues 'ought' to take into account how busy we are before giving us extra work. A possible intervention here is to ask your client to visualize themselves gathering all these words up and dropping them into the nearest rubbish bin.

What can we put in their place? Options include:

- Acceptance – adopting the idea that it is OK to be fallible ourselves and that others also make mistakes.

- Replacing 'should', 'must' and 'ought' with softer, less absolute and critical language: 'It would be great if I can achieve this but it's not the end of the world if I don't', 'It would have been better if I'd remembered to … but I am as fallible as the next person'.

STARTING TO UNDERMINE NEGATIVE BELIEFS

We have already looked at personal beliefs and learned how they can almost slip by unnoticed when we make observations about ourselves. This is because we tend not to question their validity. Now this needs to be done.

What beliefs might your clients have that may contribute to their low self-esteem? Try the following:

- Ask your client to think back to early experiences that encouraged them to think badly about themselves. What conclusions did they come to about themselves?
- Ask them to think about the things they may do to keep themselves 'safe'. For example, the thought 'I don't socialize much' may help them to discover a belief, e.g., 'I am boring', 'I can't talk to people'.

Now your clients can use their Thought Records to challenge these assumptions and beliefs.

Clients who remain unsure about what is really going on for themselves can try the excellent **downward arrow technique**. Take any thought from the Thought Record and apply the downward arrow technique to it. See Figure 6.10.3 for an example.

Using this skill, the individual uncovers two core beliefs that they have about themselves ('I'm unattractive and boring') which they can now work on. They can also ask themselves other questions, such as 'What is the personal meaning to me if this does or does not occur?' Their answer might be, 'I'm totally unlikeable'.

Does this make sense as a useful, probing technique? It needs to be practised a great deal. It is a vital component in ensuring that the individual is working on the 'causal' thought or belief (i.e., the thought or belief that is truly responsible for how you are feeling) and not on some superficial idea that won't be relevant to helping them to feel better.

HOW TO THINK LIKE AN OPTIMIST

Optimism is good for us. It is a nicer way to be and the thoughts in our minds from moment to moment are more pleasant. Most importantly, it increases our self-esteem. When we start to think that things might turn out well or that they aren't that bad, we are taking the edge off our negative, self-critical thinking.

Someone has accepted an invitation to a party and is beginning to feel very nervous …

The first thought is

'I'll have a horrible time'

The first question is

'Why?'

The answer is

'I will feel embarrassed'

The second question is

'Why?'

The answer is

'People will judge me and find me boring'

The third question is

'Why?'

The answer is

'Because I'm unattractive and boring'

Figure 6.10.3   Example of the downward arrow technique

CASE EXAMPLE

Jane and Tim worked for the same company as graphic designers. When the company lost a major client it was forced to make redundancies and Jane and Tim both lost their jobs. Although they were both devastated and their self-esteem was dented, Jane recovered far more quickly than Tim and soon found alternative work. Tim, on the other hand, lost interest in everything and put very little effort into applying for new jobs.

These outcomes were due entirely to Jane and Tim's thinking styles:

- When they were made redundant, Jane's view was that her redundancy was a specific event that reflected the company's poor performance at the time.
- Tim's view was that his redundancy reflected his poor abilities as an employee and that he was obviously no good at anything.

When individuals' thinking becomes pervasive like Tim's, they move from the specific to the all-embracing. Instead of seeing one error as an isolated incident (as an optimist would), a pessimist sees the error as an indication of total incapability. In other words, they generalize the specific.

Encourage your clients to 'think like an optimist' and they will find that their self-esteem increases enormously. See Table 6.10.1 for some examples.

Table 6.10.1   Thinking like an optimist

Pessimist	Optimist
I'm unattractive	I'm unattractive to her
I'm a hopeless driver	I didn't drive well on the motorway
Exercise machines are a waste of money	This exercise machine doesn't perform as I'd hoped

EVALUATION

Using the above interventions in counselling can help your clients to develop a set of tools to help them overcome and replace their low self-esteem thinking. What CBT aims to create is *movement*. To feel differently about ourselves, about others, to act differently, to achieve different outcomes, all require us to move away from often long-held beliefs and actions and to be willing to test reality. Most importantly, we need to become curious as to outcomes, which usually involve how we feel. By working through these exercises, individuals will hopefully be able to:

- Challenge self-critical thinking by asking 'Where's the evidence?'
- Bring their positive qualities more into focus, instead of discounting or dismissing them
- Look for evidence to support their more balanced, optimistic alternative thoughts and beliefs.

Whatever happens, people want to feel better about themselves and I suggest that CBT is a wonderful mechanism for achieving this. Nevertheless, while I have written the above from a CBT perspective, there are other therapeutic approaches that offer sound help to those with low self-esteem, but these are beyond the scope of this chapter.

REFERENCES

Burns, D. (2000). *Ten Days to Great Self Esteem*. London: Vermilion.
McKay, M. and Fanning, P. (2016). *Self Esteem* (4th ed.). Oakland, CA: New Harbinger.
Padesky C. and Greenberger, D. (2015). *Mind over Mood* (2nd ed.). New York: Guilford Press.

RECOMMENDED READING

1. Burns, D. (1999). *The Feeling Good Handbook*. New York: Penguin.

This is a bestseller of its genre and a guide for therapists and individuals.

2. Padesky C. and Greenberger, D. (2015). *Mind over Mood* (2nd ed.). New York: Guilford Press.

This book has been updated to provide easy learning about challenging unhelpful thoughts .

3. Fennel, M. (2009). *Overcoming Low Self Esteem*. Oxford: Robinson.

A classic book that uses CBT techniques.

6.11 MEDICALLY UNEXPLAINED SYMPTOMS (MUS)

DANIEL ZAHL

OVERVIEW AND KEY POINTS

As many as half of people attending general practitioner and medical outpatient clinics have symptoms which cannot be clearly medically diagnosed. The majority find these symptoms transient, are reassured that there is nothing seriously wrong and one way or another find their own solutions. However, a proportion continue to believe that there is something seriously wrong, and remain worried and concerned. They may experience considerable impairment in functioning due to symptoms and seek medical help numerous times. Healthcare professionals (HCPs) are often perplexed by the severity and persistence of symptoms, while patients may lose faith in traditional medicine and seek explanation and treatment elsewhere.

Patients are often apprehensive about a referral to psychotherapy services, where issues of engagement and case complexity are common.

- The causes of medically unexplained symptoms (MUS) are poorly understood, with no clear consensus on aetiology.
- The clinical presentation of MUS is highly variable, requiring careful assessment and treatment.
- Psychological treatments can be effective, but are not appropriate for all patients.

DEFINITION

The terminology used to refer to the presentation of unexplained somatic symptoms continues to evolve and be hotly debated. Historically, the terms *somatization* and *psychosomatic* were commonly used to indicate that symptoms were due to an underlying psychological problem. Considered less pejorative by patients, the more

descriptive and aetiologically impartial terms *medically unexplained symptoms* (MUS) and *functional somatic symptoms* (FSS) have been widely adopted. The term MUS acknowledges that medicine is currently unable to explain symptoms, and leaves open the possibility that it may do in the future. The term FSS is used to describe a group of syndromes that people with MUS may be diagnosed with. Recently, the terms 'persistent physical symptoms' and 'complex physical symptoms' have been suggested as more accurate and acceptable to patients (Picariello et al., 2015).

The range of symptoms that are commonly found to be medically unexplained (see Table 6.11.1) includes very common symptoms which many people have experienced, such as headaches, aches and pains and tiredness. Each of the functional somatic syndromes has specific diagnostic criteria, and includes many of these common symptoms; it is the number, severity and duration of symptoms and the exclusion of a medical cause that typically constitutes the diagnosis. Diagnoses of FSS do not require the presence or suspicion of a psychological problem, and can be a reason for excluding a diagnosis. The diagnosis of specific FSS is usually made in specialist medical outpatient clinics without the consultation of a mental health practitioner. Following diagnosis, patients are sometimes referred to multi-disciplinary rehabilitative services.

Table 6.11.1 Symptoms, syndromes and diagnoses that may be medically unexplained

Somatic symptoms	Associated diagnoses and syndromes	Medical speciality
Breathlessness	Dysmorphophobia	Infectious diseases
Diarrhoea	Factitious syndromes	Neurology
Dizziness	Hyperventilation syndrome	Cardiology
Dysphagia (difficulty swallowing)	Post-traumatic syndromes	Ear nose and throat
Dysphonia, aphonia (vocal impairments)	Premenstrual syndrome	Gastroenterology
Fatigue	Somatization disorder	Rheumatology, anaesthetics
Incontinence and urgency	Chronic fatigue syndrome or myalgic encephelomyletis (CFS/ME)	
Nausea		
Pain (abdominal, chest, muscle and joint, low back, headache, facial, pelvic, neuropathic)	Chronic headache, dizziness	
Palpitations	Non-cardiac chest pain	
Pruritis (itching)	Globus pharyngis, dysphonia	
Tinnitus	Irritable bowel syndrome (IBS)	
Tremor	Chronic pain syndromes/fibromyalgia	
Worry about benign tissue lumps and inconsistencies		

Source: adapted from Sanders (1996)

AETIOLOGY

MUS continues to be a controversial area of research and speculation, marked by vigorous debate about the role of biological, environmental and psychological factors. The frequent association of MUS with physical illness, either temporally or contemporaneously, understandably fuels motivation for research into biological causes of MUS. Certainly, many people with chronic fatigue syndrome (CFS) experience a viral illness such as glandular fever prior to diagnosis, and in irritable bowel syndrome (IBS) bacterial gastroenteritis is a common precursor to diagnosis. Observational research focusing on MUS populations has, however, yielded many clinically useful insights.

Elevated rates of mental health problems among those with MUS are frequently observed. Adverse life events, childhood experience of parental illness and physical and sexual abuse have been found to be risk factors for developing MUS in later life. Some have postulated that these experiences can lead to the development of MUS due to the psychological and physiological impact of chronic stress and anxiety, which have well-documented effects on cardiovascular and gastroenterological systems, and on immunity and cognitive function (Shoenberg, 2007), and can generate many of the symptoms commonly observed.

The psychoanalytic idea that particular somatic symptoms have symbolic meaning continues to hold currency in this field, although it lacks an evidence base. Somatization is generally defined as the process whereby people with psychosocial and emotional distress articulate their problems primarily through physical symptoms (Hotopf, 2004). The concept of alexithymia can be seen as a development of the idea that physical symptoms are an outward sign of psychological distress driven by a deficit in the ability to describe emotions. Others have suggested that difficulties in appropriately regulating emotion, rather than describing it, are important in understanding MUS (Woolfolk and Allen, 2007).

Social learning theorists believe that when unwell, we can fall into a 'sick role', which may provide rewards and exemptions often referred to as secondary gain. Fishbain (1994) lists some of these, which include financial compensation, avoidance of unsatisfactory life roles or activity. Furthermore, the 'sick role' itself may induce physical and psychological symptoms and enhance disability through withdrawal.

There is broad consensus that fixed organic illness beliefs, unhelpful responses to symptoms, such as excessive rest and avoidance, coupled with high estimates of personal vulnerability, contribute to the perpetuation of symptoms.

Specific multifactorial models have been developed for FSS, such as CFS (Suraway et al., 1995), IBS (Toner et al., 2000), and fibromyalgia (Bennett and Nelson, 2006). The CFS model suggests that for those who are vulnerable, life events (or a virus) can lead to a self-perpetuating cycle in which illness beliefs, physiological changes, reduced/inconsistent activity, medical uncertainty and lack of guidance interact to maintain symptoms. Specific models can be enormously helpful in clinical practice, when faced with a patient with an array of presenting problems, as they draw attention to specific cognitive and behavioural elements that may otherwise be overlooked. However, on a theoretical level it continues to be hotly debated whether FSS really represent discrete phenomena (Wesseley et al., 1999; White, 2010).

A detailed overarching cognitive-behavioural therapy (CBT) model of MUS, which integrates much of the above research, has been proposed by Deary et al. (2007), which provides a useful reminder of the factors that ought to be considered in any conceptualization.

ASSESSMENT

Many patients report feeling misunderstood or having their symptoms ignored by health professionals. During assessment, time is always well spent building a strong therapeutic alliance; it is likely to be a key factor in determining the outcome of therapy. During this phase, the practitioner must endeavour to engage the client actively in a way that does not threaten the individual's view of the self, takes account of misgivings about therapy and offers an understanding of the problems without either colluding with or rejecting the client's beliefs.

A useful initial approach is to take a very full assessment of the physical symptoms and medical problems, gain an understanding of the clients' medical treatment and finally broaden the agenda to look at psychological factors. Many patients will have been used to short medical appointments, and feel that no one has ever taken the time to listen to and understand the whole story; thus careful listening and the appropriate expression of empathy can help to quickly build a good therapeutic relationship and a place where the patient feels safe to discuss psychosocial variables.

During assessment, beliefs about symptoms can be explored by eliciting the client's explanation of symptoms, such as abdominal pain caused by a food allergy or virus, or chest pain caused by spasm in the heart. Rather than attempting to challenge this assumption directly, it is more helpful to build on the client's view and work on the idea that precipitating factors, causing the symptoms in the first place, may differ from maintaining factors. Therefore, an illness or a disease may have caused symptoms in the first place, but are no longer responsible for keeping it going.

During assessment it is useful to keep in mind that there is a high incidence of anxiety disorders and depression in this client group (and in family members) and careful evaluation of these problems should be made. A proportion of this client group will have experienced physical, emotional or sexual abuse in earlier years, and illness may be one means the individual has developed to cope with such trauma. One will need to proceed with care and caution, only exploring these areas as and when the client is ready.

FORMULATION

The complexity of presentation can leave the therapist unsure about how and when to share a formulation effectively without threatening what may be a fragile level of rapport built up during assessment. Providing at a minimum a basic provisional formulation during a first appointment can help the patient develop confidence in therapy.

Where specific treatment protocols and models exist (e.g., for somatization disorder, fibromyalgia and CFS), much can be gained. The biopsychosocial model provides a template to map relevant physiological, cognitive, affective and behavioural components that may precipitate and/or perpetuate the problem (see Abramowitz and Braddock, 2008). Modification to include specific maintaining factors can be useful, such as 'boom and bust' in fatigue and pain, or reduced activity and mood. It is important that the formulation is jointly owned and drawn up with the patient, and copies shared. This starting formulation is likely to be revised multiple times as the exploration of symptoms evolves.

INTERVENTION

Working with perhaps a very tentative formulation, the therapist will need to consider the extent to which the patient is open to considering the range of intervention strategies at their disposal. Moving too rapidly with approaches the patient is unable or unwilling to try can quickly undo the work done during the assessment stage, leading to a significant rupture in the therapeutic relationship.

Most protocols begin treatment by gaining more specific and detailed information about symptoms through monitoring. This information is used to gradually make behavioural modifications to key areas, such as sleep, activity and rest.

Often the therapist will want to determine if there is benefit to strengthening non-medical explanations for symptoms. One technique commonly used in CBT treatment for health anxiety is the use of hypothesis-testing to introduce the idea that there may be an alternative explanation for symptoms. This can be introduced by proposing that there are two ways of seeing the situation (theory A and theory B): the first is that the client does indeed have a serious physical illness, and that the doctors so far have not been able to diagnose or treat it; the second is that the individual is *concerned and anxious* about the possibility of illness, and that the anxiety is the central problem. The evidence for and against and the usefulness of each hypothesis are reviewed with the client. The therapist then proposes that they work together for a set time on the alternative theory; after that time, if they have had a good try at a psychological approach and the problem has not improved, then it would be reasonable to review their original hypothesis. This can be a useful way of avoiding 'getting into an argument' about the cause of the symptoms, and the client's beliefs are respected.

For other MUS this approach may need to be carefully adapted based on a particular presentation; for those who do not report being anxious, discussion of 'stress' or other unhelpful coping behaviour, such as excessive rest in response to symptoms, may be more relevant. Being clear that therapy is principally concerned with helping people to overcome or better manage their problems rather than with understanding the origin of their symptoms can help avert unproductive discussions about the cause of symptoms.

People with MUS may say they understand that symptoms are not caused by serious disease, and may be keen to explore the possibility that there are links between physical symptoms and psychological factors. Diary-keeping of symptoms and stress can help demonstrate how stress or paying attention to symptoms can make them appear worse (Sanders and Wills, 2003; Sanders et al., 2010). In addition, the client can be encouraged to experiment with discovering alternative explanations by using 'behavioural experiments' devised in cognitive therapy.

MAINTAINING FACTORS

Symptoms can be exacerbated and maintained by a range of activities which the client uses to attempt to cope, such as seeking medical reassurance and further tests, illness behaviour, avoiding exercise and checking or poking sore areas. It is important to identify what kind of unhelpful coping strategies the client may have evolved, and carefully negotiate with the client to reduce or stop, and to monitor how helpful this is. Again, behavioural experiments enable the client to discover the role of maintenance factors, and to experiment with alternative ways of dealing with the symptoms (Sanders et al., 2010; Silver et al., 2004). For example, the client can be encouraged to exercise gradually rather than rest, or to stop seeking reassurance or checking the internet, and monitor the impact on how he or she feels. Taking a systemic approach, looking at the role of the client's family and wider social context, is important. For example, while a client may be trying to get better, the spouse may be inadvertently reinforcing the sick role, or encouraging the individual to seek medical reassurance to allay their own fears.

COPING STRATEGIES

For some clients, learning appropriate ways of coping with symptoms and other factors, such as stress, may be helpful, for example breathing and relaxation exercises, learning to distract from symptoms rather than pay attention to them, and dealing with low mood, stress or anxiety. Mindfulness meditation has been shown to help clients with physical health problems as well as stress, anxiety and depression (see Kabat-Zinn, 2005; Williams et al., 2007), and may be a valuable adjunct to psychological therapies.

WORKING WITH OTHER ISSUES AND DIFFICULTIES

Once the client has acknowledged that psychological factors may be important, therapy can move on to focus on other difficulties. Life difficulties and stress may well be involved; problem-solving and solution-focused therapy can be helpful, enabling the client to look for solutions to the issues which may underlie and maintain difficulties.

CASE EXAMPLE

Penny was a 40-year-old lady referred with an 8-year history of severe chronic fatigue syndrome. She was unable to work due to her symptoms, and rarely left her flat. She presented with co-morbid anxiety and depression. She lived alone, was single and was in receipt of benefits due to the impact of her symptoms. Her mother lived nearby and provided care when needed. She was keen to return to work. She had attended an NHS mindfulness group and CBT in the past, which she had found helpful at the time, but was no better. She reported long periods where she was bed-bound, and other periods where she was able to be functional. She was able to walk less than 100 yards. In regard to her past, Penny's father had died suddenly following a divorce, and she had moved schools multiple times. Following a detailed assessment involving recording of activity and sleep levels, and provisional formulation of the role of behavioural and cognitive factors, Penny began to stabilize activity and sleep. Following this, she started gradually to increase activity levels and reduce sleep. A range of CBT techniques were used to identify and manage distressing and unhelpful thoughts. Through a series of behavioural experiments Penny was able to challenge fears about work and activity, she gradually introduced small elements of work into her day, and over the course of six months was able to start volunteering work.

EVALUATION

There is a growing evidence base for the use of psychological therapies for a range of medically unexplained problems (Hotopf, 2004; Kleinstäuber et al., 2011). Reviews of the literature suggest that CBT is moderately beneficial for MUS in general (e.g., Martin et al., 2007), with stronger support found in randomized controlled trials (RCTs) of CFS and fibromyalgia than in IBS (Deary et al., 2007). CBT has also been found to be beneficial for somatization disorder (Kroenke, 2007). Brief dynamic therapy, group psychotherapy and cognitive-behavioural therapy have been shown to be effective for a range of psychosomatic problems, chronic pain and health anxiety (Kroenke and Swindle, 2000; Lidbeck, 2003).

From a clinical perspective it is also important to consider when psychological approaches might not be helpful. One danger is that the therapist becomes yet another 'expert' who has not been able to help the client. Psychological therapies are more likely to be helpful if the client accepts or is open to the possibility that psychosocial factors affect their somatic problems, such as symptoms being aggravated by stress or emotion.

Factors which may indicate a poor response to treatment include an attempt by the client to claim compensation for the symptoms, an inability to see any link with psychological difficulties or stresses and the presence of persistent dysfunctional beliefs about illness. In many cases it is helpful for the therapist to work closely with those involved in the client's medical treatment, and for some clients a structured, long-term medical management plan is most appropriate. Counsellors and psychologists working in medical settings have a great deal to offer in helping medical professionals to manage such clients.

REFERENCES

Abramowitz, J.S. and Braddock, A.E. (2008) *Psychological Treatment of Health Anxiety and Hypochondriasis: A Biopsychosocial Approach*. Cambridge, MA: Hogrefe.

Bennett, R. and Nelson, D. (2006) Cognitive behavioural therapy for fibromyalgia. *Nature Clinical Practice*, 2: 416–424.

Deary, V., Chalder, T. and Sharpe, M. (2007) The cognitive behavioural model of medically unexplained symptoms: a theoretical and empirical review. *Clinical Psychology Review*, 27: 781–797.

Fishbain, D.A. (1994) Secondary gain concept: definition problems and its abuse in medical practice. *American Pain Society Journal*, 3: 264–273.

Hotopf, M. (2004) Preventing somatization. *Psychological Medicine*, 34: 195–198.

Kabat-Zinn, J. (2005) *Coming to Our Senses: Healing Ourselves and the World through Mindfulness*. London: Piatkus.

Kleinstäuber, M., Witthöft, M. and Hiller, W. (2011) Efficacy of short-term psychotherapy for multiple medically unexplained symptoms: a meta-analysis. *Clinical Psychology Review*, 31(1): 146–160.

Kroenke, K. (2007) Efficacy of treatment for somatoform disorders: a review of randomized controlled trials. *Psychosomatic Medicine*, 69: 881–888.

Kroenke, K. and Swindle, R. (2000) Cognitive behavioral therapy for somatization and symptom syndromes: a critical review of controlled clinical trials. *Psychotherapy and Psychosomatics*, 69(4): 205–215.

Lidbeck, J. (2003) Group therapy for somatization disorders in primary care: maintenance of treatment goals of short cognitive-behavioural treatment one and a half year follow-up. *Acta Psychiatrica Scandinavica*, 107(6): 449–456.

Martin, A., Rauh, E., Fichter, M. and Rief, W. (2007) A one-session treatment for patients suffering from medically unexplained symptoms in primary care: a randomized clinical trial. *Psychosomatics*, 48: 294–303.

Picariello, F., Ali, A., Moss-Morris, R. and Chalder, T. (2015) The most popular terms for medically unexplained symptoms: the views of CFS patients. *Journal of Psychosomatic Research*, 78(5): 420–426.

Sanders, D. (1996) *Counselling for Psychosomatic Problems*. London: Sage.

Sanders, D., Surawy, C., Zahl, D. and Salt, H. (2010) Physical health settings. In M. Mueller et al. (eds), *Oxford Guide to Surviving as a CBT Therapist* (pp. 253–273). Oxford: Oxford University Press.

Sanders, D. and Wills, F. (2003) *Counselling for Anxiety Problems*. London: Sage.

Shoenberg, P. (2007) *The Effects of Stress in Psychosomatics: The Uses of Psychotherapy*. Basingstoke: Palgrave Macmillan.

Silver, A., Sanders, D., Morrison, N. and Cowie, C. (2004) Health anxiety. In J. Bennett-Levy et al. (eds), *The Oxford Guide to Behavioural Experiments in Cognitive Therapy* (pp. 87–105). Oxford: Oxford University Press.

Suraway, C., Hackmann, A., Hawton, K. and Sharpe, M. (1995) Chronic fatigue syndrome: a cognitive approach. *Behavioural Research Therapy*, 33(5): 535–544.

Toner, B.B., Segal, Z.V., Emmott, S.D. and Myran, D. (2000) *Cognitive-Behavioral Treatment of Irritable Bowel Syndrome: The Brain–Gut Connection*. New York: Guilford Press.

Wesseley, S., Nimnuan, C. and Sharpe, M. (1999) Functional somatic syndromes: one or many? *Lancet*, 354: 935–936.

White, P.D. (2010) Chronic fatigue syndrome: is it one discrete syndrome or many? Implications for the 'one vs. many' functional somatic syndromes debate. *Journal of Psychosomatic Research*, 68: 455–459.

Williams, M., Teasdale, J., Segal, Z.V. and Kabat-Zinn, J. (2007) *The Mindful Way through Depression*. New York: Guilford Press.

Woolfolk, R.L. and Allen, L.A. (2007) *Treating Somatization: A Cognitive Behavioural Approach*. New York: Guilford Press.

6.12   OBSESSIVE COMPULSIVE DISORDER

TOM RICKETTS AND GILL DONOHOE

OVERVIEW AND KEY POINTS

This chapter will first outline the clinical features of obsessive compulsive disorder (OCD), exploring the range of common presentations. A behavioural model will then be introduced, and the link between this model and the approaches deriving from it outlined. A case study will be used to illustrate the approaches. Finally, research regarding cognitive-behavioural approaches to OCD will be briefly reviewed. Key points are:

- OCD is a serious mental health problem that tends to follow a chronic course in the absence of treatment.
- Cognitive-behaviour therapy (CBT), including exposure with response prevention, is an effective treatment, more effective than antidepressant medication.
- Client engagement and self-managed exposure with response prevention are central to effective therapy.
- Self-managed and computer-aided approaches show promise in the delivery of CBT for OCD.

DEFINITIONS

OCD is a serious mental health problem whose defining features are the presence of obsessions and/or compulsions. These features are defined and described below.

OBSESSIONS

Obsessions are defined in the *Diagnostic and Statistical Manual of Mental Disorders* (DSM-V) (American Psychiatric Association, 2013) as recurrent and persistent thoughts, urges or images. These are experienced (at least at some point during the disorder) as intrusive and unwanted, and do not represent excessive worries about real-life problems. The person attempts to ignore or suppress such thoughts, urges or images with another thought or action. Table 6.12.1 gives some examples of obsessions.

COMPULSIONS

Compulsions are defined as repetitive and intentional behaviours or mental acts (American Psychiatric

Table 6.12.1   Examples of obsessional thoughts and linked behaviours

Content of obsessional thought	Nature of compulsive behaviour	Avoidances	Behavioural excesses
I may have come into contact with faeces or other contamination	Repeated handwashing Showering for several hours at a time	Avoids crowded areas, touching 'dirty people', touching door handles	Scanning others for indications of cleanliness Wearing gloves Covering mouth
Have I made a mistake which may harm others?	Repeated checking of items in home or at work, e.g., gas taps, switches, door locks	Avoids switching on/off high-risk items	Repeatedly requests reassurance from others Engages others in checking
Sexual, aggressive or blasphemous content	Mental neutralizing by repeated praying and efforts to 'put a good thought' in place	Avoids being alone with children	Scanning environment for evidence of own evil

Association, 2013). These are performed in response to an obsessional thought, according to idiosyncratic rules that have to be applied rigidly, and which aim to reduce distress or prevent a dreadful event or situation. However, the behaviour is not connected in a realistic way to the outcome they are designed to neutralize or prevent, or it is clearly excessive. The act is performed with a sense of subjective compulsion. Table 6.12.1 gives some examples of compulsions and how they link to obsessional thoughts.

INSIGHT

Most people experiencing OCD recognize that their obsessions are senseless or unrealistic, and their actions excessive. However, at the point of assessment there may be wide variability in the degree to which the individual recognizes the inappropriateness of the extent of their behaviour. DSM-V reflects this in distinguishing between three levels of insight in people with OCD. People are grouped into those with (a) 'good or fair insight', who recognize that their OCD fears are probably or definitely not true; (b) 'poor insight', who think that their fears are probably true; and (c) 'absent insight/delusional beliefs', who appear completely convinced that their fears are true.

While the different types of obsessive compulsive presentation can usefully be outlined (as in Table 6.12.1), there is much evidence of overlap between the different types, indicating common pathways to their development.

CATEGORIZATION OF OCD

The most significant change for OCD in DSM-V was the removal of the disorder from the anxiety disorders and

the creation of a new classification of disorders termed 'obsessive-compulsive and related disorders'. This grouped OCD with disorders such as body dysmorphic disorder, hair-pulling disorder and hoarding disorder, on the basis of a number of common features. The removal of OCD from the anxiety disorders classification has been contentious (Abramowitz and Jacoby, 2014), particularly with regard to the different mechanisms underpinning repetitive behaviours with apparent similarity of form.

COMORBIDITY

OCD often coexists with other disorders, with a majority of OCD sufferers reporting another anxiety or mood disorder (American Psychiatric Association, 2013). Comorbidity with specific phobia, generalized anxiety disorder or panic disorder is common. OCD is also commonly complicated by depression, with studies identifying concurrent major depression in one-quarter to one-third of OCD sufferers. However, suicidal ideation or attempts among clients with OCD is reported to be rare (Steketee and Barlow, 2002). Assessing for depression is important, as severe depression has consistently been found to be a predictor of poorer treatment outcome (Keeley et al., 2008).

AETIOLOGY

Until recently, OCD was considered to be relatively uncommon, but this appears to have been due to the large extent of under-reporting by sufferers. Approximately 1.1–1.8% of the population will meet criteria for OCD each year (American Psychiatric Association, 2013), with an average age of onset in the mid-20s. OCD commonly has a chronic course, with untreated individuals suffering difficulties for decades. Developments in understanding, and particularly behavioural and cognitive-behavioural treatment models, have improved the prognosis for sufferers. Therefore, a priority is for the early identification of sufferers and the offering of appropriate therapy.

ASSESSMENT

Assessment of OCD is similar to that for other disorders in that the aim is to obtain as full a picture as possible, utilizing a range of data collection techniques. Assessment is guided by the model, so that at the end of assessment a clear formulation of the development and maintenance of the disorder is possible, this being the basis of the individualized therapeutic plan. Data collection techniques include clinical interviews, self-monitoring of thoughts, emotions and behaviour, and, where possible, direct observation of the client undertaking their compulsive behaviours.

FORMULATION

Behavioural models of OCD have been very helpful in enabling effective treatments to be developed. Figure 6.12.1 shows a behavioural model.

Within the model, intrusive thoughts are viewed as normal phenomena which, due to association with fear-inducing stimuli, have become fear-inducing themselves. This fear is neutralized through the undertaking of voluntary behaviours (compulsions), either overt or covert, to prevent harm ensuing. For example, an obsessional thought regarding being responsible for harm coming to others through carelessness may be followed by a checking behaviour. The undertaking of compulsive behaviours has a number of effects. First, it prevents the anxiety associated with the intrusive thought spontaneously reducing, a process termed extinction. Second, it increases the perceived importance of the intrusive thought. Because the thought is acted upon, the range of situations that will trigger it are increased, and it occurs more often. Third, as the compulsive behaviours are followed by a reduction in anxiety, they are more likely to occur again in similar situations. For example, an obsessional thought about having come into contact with faeces may initially only occur in the vicinity of public toilets. Where the individual repeatedly responds to the thought by washing themselves thoroughly, an increasing range of situations come to be associated with the perceived contamination risk. Eventually any public setting where there are toilets, touching door handles or even being in the same room with others may be sufficient to trigger the obsessional thought, with the individual responding

by repeated handwashing or other extensive decontamination activities.

In contrast, if the obsessional thought, discomfort and urge to engage in the compulsive behaviour are provoked but the individual refrains from carrying out the behaviour, the urge and discomfort will dissipate naturally, but more slowly than if the urges had been acted upon. With repeated induction there is a cumulative effect, with progressively less discomfort, and less urge to engage in the compulsive behaviour, and progressively more rapid reduction in the urge to do so.

The process through which intrusive thoughts come to elicit anxiety and discomfort is the subject of some debate, with acquisition through a process of classical conditioning not finding general support (Jones and Menzies, 1997). However, the model of the maintenance of OCD has proved clinically fruitful, particularly in underpinning exposure and response prevention, which remains the treatment of choice, and is explained in the next section.

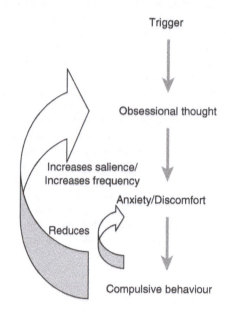

Figure 6.12.1 A behavioural model of OCD

INTERVENTION

CLIENT EDUCATION

Prior to undertaking exposure and response prevention the client is informed of the outcome of the assessment, as a means of making sense of symptoms that they may previously have found incomprehensible. They are also informed about the beneficial impact of experiencing obsessional thoughts in the absence of undertaking compulsive behaviours. This process should enable them to understand the rationale for the therapeutic plan and enhance the collaborative relationship with the therapist. As they will be undertaking what may be frightening procedures, it is important that they understand the purpose and process of therapy.

EXPOSURE AND RESPONSE PREVENTION

The key elements of exposure and response prevention are that the client is enabled to re-enter previously avoided situations while resisting the urge to undertake behaviours which would rapidly reduce subjective discomfort. This process is most effective when the exposure tasks are challenging but achievable, when the tasks are undertaken for an hour or more, and on a daily basis if possible. Specific details linked to a case example are provided below:

- Joe reported obsessional thoughts associated with causing harm to others. These commonly took the form of thoughts doubting that he had completed a critical action correctly, and also included mental images of his children having been injured as a result of his carelessness. He experienced distress and anxiety in response to these thoughts and images, and would often repeat actions or undertake checks in response to them. Specific trigger situations to the obsessional thoughts would include being at home alone with his children when his partner went out, taking his children to school and when driving. Checks would often be repeated multiple times and could take 30 minutes or more. He tended to avoid the trigger situations when possible, which was causing a strain on his relationship. His goal for therapy was to be able to transport his children by car independently to their various social activities without undue discomfort.
- A list of trigger situations/tasks is developed with the client and graded according to difficulty. Tasks to be undertaken with the therapist should be as difficult as the client is willing to undertake. Working with the therapist initially, the client is enabled to engage in contact with the previously avoided triggers for a prolonged period, preferably over an hour. Throughout exposure, the urge to undertake the compulsive behaviour should be monitored, while the client is assisted not to undertake the behaviour. This subjective urge or discomfort should have reduced substantially (by at least 50%) before the exposure session is terminated. For Joe, the initial tasks with

the therapist focused upon his car. Joe practised locking his car and leaving it without checking it. He then practised similar tasks related to the security of his home and driving alone. In each instance the therapist assisted Joe to not check or repeat actions, and discouraged the use of mental neutralizing through self-reassurance.

- A high frequency of exposure sessions is associated with more rapid processing of fear. In practice, the implications of this are that enabling clients to undertake self-managed exposure with response prevention between therapy sessions is essential. Encouraging the client to repeat what has been achieved within the therapy session is often sufficient, but clear written guidance is helpful. For Joe, exposure tasks undertaken with the therapist were practised each day through the week, initially focusing on triggers and checks that were not directly related to his children. As he became more confident that the process of habituation would result in both a reduction in anxiety and subsequently the frequency of obsessional thoughts, Joe became willing to undertake small tasks related to his repeated checking of his children's safety. Eventually he was able to achieve his goal of taking his children to various social activities unaccompanied by his partner, and with minimal anxiety. When mental images did occur, he was able to notice them without feeling the need to check his children's safety or seek reassurance from his partner.

COGNITIVE APPROACHES

Cognitive theories of OCD emphasize the importance of faulty appraisals regarding mental intrusions as a core feature (Clark, 2004). Specific appraisals may relate to inflated responsibility for the prevention of harm (Salkovskis, 1985), or the overestimation of the significance of mental events (Rachman, 1997). Cognitive approaches aim primarily to alter these appraisals through addressing thoughts evaluating the content of the obsessions, rather than the obsessions themselves. Studies investigating this approach indicate that cognitive therapy along these lines can be as effective as exposure and response prevention (Ost et al., 2015).

DRUG TREATMENT

The National Institute for Health and Care Excellence (NICE, 2005) recommends that the initial intervention for people suffering from OCD is CBT as described above. Where the client refuses or is unable to engage with therapy, the use of a serotonergic compound (SSRI) such as fluoxetine and fluvoxamine is recommended. As SSRIs may increase the risk of suicidal thoughts and self-harm in people suffering from depression and young people, careful monitoring is recommended following their commencement. This is particularly important for the large group of clients suffering from OCD who will also be suffering from depression, and those under age 30. The combining of medication with CBT appears to convey few additional benefits over CBT alone, and should only be considered if there is inadequate response to initial intervention or the client is experiencing severe functional impairment (NICE, 2005).

EVALUATION

In a meta-analysis of randomized controlled trials of CBT for OCD, Ost et al. (2015) identified that exposure with response prevention and cognitive therapy were broadly equivalent in their effects, and more effective than antidepressant medication. The addition of cognitive approaches to exposure with response prevention appeared to result in no greater effects than exposure with response prevention alone. However, despite these positive results, a majority of clients continue to suffer significant symptoms following treatment; that is, they improve but do not recover. Eddy et al. (2004) analysed the outcomes of randomized controlled trials using a threshold of 12 or below on the commonly used Yale–Brown Obsessive Compulsive Scale (Goodman et al., 1989) as a definition of recovery. In doing so they identified that approximately two-thirds of clients completing the therapies improved, but only one-third 'recovered'.

There is also a subgroup of clients who refuse or do not complete therapy.

Two other issues have been the focus of recent research. The first is whether the results from research trials can be transferred into routine practice. The second is evaluating delivery approaches to CBT for OCD.

The difficulty of generalizing results from research clinics to routine practice settings has been cited as a reason to ignore the evidence for cognitive-behaviour therapy as summarized in practice guidelines such as those produced by the National Institute for Health and Care Excellence (Holmes, 2002; NICE, 2005). Studies of what outcomes are achieved in routine practice settings are required. When such studies have been undertaken (Houghton et al., 2010) the results have been encouraging, with the routine delivery of cognitive-behaviour therapy for OCD resulting in effects equivalent to those found in research trials.

Self-management and computer-aided approaches to anxiety disorders and specifically OCD have been implemented as part of the Improving Access to Psychological Therapies initiative in the United Kingdom (Clark et al., 2009). The OCD guideline from the National Institute for Health and Care Excellence (NICE, 2005) recommends low-intensity exposure with response prevention supported by self-help materials, or group-delivered cognitive-behaviour therapy as the first intervention for people suffering from milder forms of OCD. Results of the national evaluation are that, for at least a percentage of people suffering from milder forms of OCD, guided self-help delivered by a psychological wellbeing practitioner (Clark et al., 2009) can be sufficient to reduce the functional impact of OCD.

REFERENCES

Abramowitz, J.S. and Jocoby, R.J. (2014) Obsessive-compulsive disorder in the DSM-5. *Clinical Psychology: Science and Practice*, 21: 221–235.

American Psychiatric Association (2013) *Diagnostic and Statistical Manual of Mental Disorders* (5th ed.). Washington, DC: American Psychiatric Association.

Clark, D.A. (2004) *Cognitive-Behavioral Therapy for OCD*. New York: Guilford Press.

Clark, D.M., Layard, R., Smithies, R., Richards, D.A., Suckling, R. and Wright, B. (2009) Improving Access to Psychological Therapies: initial evaluation of two UK demonstration sites. *Behaviour Research and Therapy*, 47: 910–920.

Eddy, K.T., Dutra, L., Bradley, R. and Westen, D. (2004) A multidimensional meta-analysis of psychotherapy and pharmacotherapy for obsessive-compulsive disorder. *Clinical Psychology Review*, 24(8): 1011–1030.

(Continued)

(Continued)

Goodman, W.K., Price, L.H., Rasmussen, S.A., Mazure, C., Fleischmann, R.L., Hill, C.L., Heninger, G.R. and Charney, D.S. (1989) The Yale–Brown Obsessive Compulsive Scale I: development, use and reliability. *Archives of General Psychiatry*, 46: 1006–1011.

Holmes, J. (2002) All you need is cognitive behaviour therapy? *British Medical Journal*, 324: 288–294.

Houghton, S., Saxon, D., Bradburn, M., Ricketts, T. and Hardy, G. (2010) The effectiveness of routinely delivered cognitive behavioural therapy for obsessive-compulsive disorder: a benchmarking study. *British Journal of Clinical Psychology*, 49: 473–489.

Jones, M.K. and Menzies, R.G. (1997) The relevance of associative learning pathways in the development of obsessive-compulsive washing. *Behaviour Research and Therapy*, 36: 273–283.

Keeley, M.L., Storch, E.A., Merlo, L.J. and Geffken, G.R. (2008) Clinical predictors of response to cognitive-behavioral therapy for obsessive-compulsive disorder. *Clinical Psychology Review*, 28(1): 118–130.

NICE (2005) *Obsessive-Compulsive Disorder: Core Interventions in the Treatment of Obsessive-Compulsive Disorder and Body Dysmorphic Disorder*. London: NICE.

Ost, L.-G., Havnen, A., Hansen, B. and Kvale, G. (2015). Cognitive behavioral treatments of obsessive-compulsive disorder: a systematic review and meta-analysis of studies published 1993–2014. *Clinical Psychology Review*, 40: 156–169.

Rachman, S. (1997) A cognitive theory of obsessions. *Behaviour Research and Therapy*, 35: 793–802.

Salkovskis, P.M. (1985) Obsessive-compulsive problems: a cognitive-behavioural analysis. *Behaviour Research and Therapy*, 25: 571–583.

Steketee, G. and Barlow, D.H. (2002) Obsessive-compulsive disorder. In D.H. Barlow (Ed.), *Anxiety and Its Disorders: The Nature and Treatment of Anxiety and Panic* (2nd ed.). New York: Guilford Press.

RECOMMENDED READING

1. Barlow, D.H. (Ed.) (2002) *Anxiety and Its Disorders: The Nature and Treatment of Anxiety and Panic* (2nd ed.). New York: Guildford Press.

This is a thorough and extensive book covering the full range of theories relevant to the understanding and management of obsessive compulsive disorder and other anxiety disorders.

2. Abramowitz, J.S., Deacon, B.J. and Whiteside, S.P.H. (2013) *Exposure Therapy for Anxiety: Principles and Practice*. New York: Guildford Press.

This book provides a detailed overview of the assessment and treatment of a range of anxiety disorders using exposure.

3. Steketee, G.S. and Wilhelm, S. (2006) *Cognitive Therapy for Obsessive-Compulsive Disorder: A Guide for Professionals*. Oakland, CA: Newharbinger.

This book is an excellent manual relating to cognitive approaches to obsessive compulsive disorder. There are clear models, case formulations and treatment interventions described in an accessible way for health professionals.

PERSONALITY DISORDERS

JULIA NOBLE

OVERVIEW AND KEY POINTS

Personality disorders are common, with a prevalence of 4–15% in the general population (Coid, Yang, Tyrer, Roberts and Ullrich, 2006), and every counsellor or psychotherapist is likely to encounter individuals with personality difficulties in their work. Research has shown that individuals with personality disorders have poor treatment outcomes (Hasin et al., 2011), and therefore it is important practitioners have an understanding of personality disorders, in order to inform counselling and psychotherapy. The key points addressed in this chapter are:

- Personality disorders represent one of the most controversial topics within medical and mental health settings due to problems with the diagnosis and concerns over associated stigma.
- Personality disorders represent a core difficulty in how individuals relate to themselves and others.
- The field of personality disorders is in a state of flux. There is a strong pull from practitioners and the research community to move away from a categorical diagnostic view to a more dimensional one, in which maladaptive traits are on a continuum.
- Research indicates there is still far to go before effective interventions are developed for personality

disorders. Long-term approaches incorporating whole-team perspectives are currently recommended.

DEFINITION

The *Diagnostic and Statistical Manual of Mental Disorders* (DSM-5) (American Psychiatric Association, 2013) defines individuals with personality disorders to have significant impairment in self and interpersonal functioning, and one or more pathological personality traits. These impairments are relatively stable across time and consistent across situations, and are not better understood as normal within individuals' culture or environment, or due to the effects of a substance or general medical condition. Although this definition captures the core features of personality disorder, it has been criticised as having a strong subjective element, assuming there is a clear differentiation between 'normal' and 'abnormal' personality. In recent years, this definition has also been criticised for locating individuals' difficulties within themselves rather than as a reflection of wider circumstances. Most researchers now acknowledge personality disorders do not represent solely a biological abnormality, but a natural consequence arising from previous events, such as trauma or deprivation (Van der Hart, Nijenhuis and Steele, 2006).

HISTORY

Personality disorder was not regarded as a diagnosis until the nineteenth century when Schneider (1923) described a group of psychopathic personalities. In his writings he alluded to a core aspect of personality disorders, the inability to form and sustain functional and healthy interpersonal relationships. Schneider (1923) described nine personality types using only his clinical experience. Surprisingly, these nine categories have changed little up the present day.

PERSONALITY DISORDER CATEGORIES

The current version of the DSM-5 (American Psychiatric Association, 2013) contains ten categories of personality

disorders divided into three clusters. Cluster A (odd or eccentric) includes the paranoid, schizoid and schizotypal categories. Cluster B (dramatic, emotional or erratic) contains the anti-social, borderline, histrionic and narcissistic categories. Cluster C (anxious or fearful) covers the avoidant, dependent and obsessive-compulsive categories. The other main diagnostic system, the *International Classification of Diseases* (ICD-10) (World Health Organisation, 1992) includes personality disorder categories very similar to DSM-5 types. The main differences being schizotypal personality is classified instead within the spectrum of schizophrenia, narcissistic personality disorder is not acknowledged, and borderline is considered to a sub-category of emotionally unstable personality disorder.

PREVALENCE

Research has indicated personality disorders are not gender-specific or more prevalent in particular ethnic or cultural groups (Crawford, Rushwaya, Bajaj, Tyrer and Yang, 2012). The prevalence increases when looking at the percentage of people meeting criteria for personality disorders within services: 4–15% of the community meet criteria for personality disorder (Coid et al., 2006), 25% of people within primary care (Moran, Jenkins, Tylee, Blizard and Mann, 2000) 50% of those within outpatient psychiatric settings (Beckwith, Moran and Reilly, 2014) and 66% of prisoners within the criminal justice system meet criteria (Fazel and Danesh, 2002).

OUTCOMES OF PERSONALITY DISORDER

Individuals with a diagnosis of personality disorder have high rates of mortality (Fok et al., 2012). These high rates of mortality are partially accounted for by increased rates of suicide (Hiroeh, Appleby, Mortensen and Dunn, 2001), with rates of attempted suicide reported to be around 5–10%. However, individuals with personality disorder are also at increased risk for physical health conditions, such as heart disease, which might be contributed to by difficulties in interpersonal interactions, preventing effective communication with healthcare professionals. Furthermore, lifestyle choices commonly associated with personality disorders, such as alcohol and drug misuse, and smoking may also increase mortality (Frankenburg and Zanarini, 2004).

AETIOLOGY

The causes of personality disorders are not fully known, although it is accepted by many that a bio-psychosocial model is likely to be the most informative given the pervasive, heterogeneous and developmental nature of the disorder. Cicchetti (2014) proposes equifinality in the development of personality disorders, meaning that a number of pathways, rather than a single trajectory, can lead to a personality disorder. This model suggests a complex interplay of biological predispositions to particular temperaments in association with developmental experiences in early life activate in response to adverse life events, and consequently manifest in personal and interactional difficulties (Bateman, Gunderson and Mulder, 2015).

There is some agreement in the field that personality disorder has its roots in childhood and adolescence (Newton-Howes, Clark and Chanen, 2015), although the evidence for specific risk factors in the development of personality disorder is sparse. Research (Cohen, 2008) indicates adverse childhood experiences, and maternal anxiety, depression and interpersonal difficulties predict personality disorder 10 years later. However, this is not the case for all individuals, so why these experiences result in personality disordered traits in some individuals and not in others is not fully understood. Personality disorder usually becomes clinically recognisable in the transition between childhood to adulthood, yet it is not usually diagnosed before the age of 18 years, due to a lack of a method to differentiate between personality disorder traits and turbulent, yet common, adolescent behaviour. It is important to note that research has found that similar to 'normal' personality, personality disorder traits continue to develop and change throughout life, at least until the age of 60 years (Lenzenweger and Willett, 2007).

ASSESSMENT

Assessment of personality disorder is usually completed using an assessment instrument for personality disorders and/or a semi-structured interview typically taking between one and two hours. A review by Clark et al. (in press) identified 23 validated instruments for the diagnosis of personality disorder, and it has been highlighted that the absence of fast and reliable assessment methods may be one of the reasons why few individuals with personality disorder receive a formal diagnosis. Two widely used screening tools have been developed to address these problems, the Standardised Assessment of Personality – Abbreviated Scale (Moran et al., 2003) and the Iowa Personality Disorder Screen (Langbehn et al., 1999), but research has shown they tend to over-diagnose (Clark and Harrison, 2001). Bateman et al. (2015) pointed out a lack of a standardised assessment procedure results in stereotyped thinking by practitioners, where individuals who self-harm are automatically given a diagnosis of borderline personality disorder, and those who have a history of aggression or with a criminal record are assigned with anti-social personality disorder.

Difficulties in assessment have also led some practitioners to be reluctant to diagnose individuals with personality disorders, regarding it as a diagnosis of exclusion, whereby individuals are beyond help or extremely difficult to work with. There is a growing body of practitioners who prefer to use other terms, such as complex trauma, to acknowledge individuals' previous history and wider context (Van der Hart et al., 2006). Tyrer, Reed and Crawford (2015) suggest that practitioners reluctant to diagnose tend to fall into one of two camps: either practitioners dismiss personality disorders as a non-diagnosis which has no firm underlying construct, or they believe personality disorders should be dealt with by specialist services. Part of the difficulty in assessment is that no one questions the existence of personality but the line between 'normal personality' and 'personality disorders' is not clearly defined. In addition, the core relational deficit as a central feature of the disorder means that assessment of personality disorder is partly through interaction, rather than any individual symptom.

FORMULATION

Many see formulation as an essential element of working with individuals with personality disorders, as it provides a way of conceptualising an individual's difficulties within their unique life experiences, moves away from the associated stigma and bridges across diagnosis. The British Psychological Society recommends practitioners conduct a needs-based formulation (Jarrett, 2006). This process involves placing the individual's experiences in a contextual and explanatory framework that can help the individual and others around them to develop awareness of their behaviours, thoughts and emotions. This tool can then be used to inform any subsequent interventions.

INTERVENTION

Individuals diagnosed with personality disorders often present to practitioners as requesting help from clinical symptoms (such as chronic depression or self-harm) rather than looking for an intervention for their personality difficulties (Tyrer et al., 2015). This can mean there is often a reoccurrence of symptoms, as Tyrer et al. (2015) suggest personality disorders underlie the development and maintenance of co-morbid mental health and social difficulties. Furthermore, improvement in symptoms following an intervention is difficult to distinguish from core personality change. Research looking at effective interventions has been hampered by a lack of consensus on agreed outcomes, therefore making it difficult to draw comparisons across studies (Bateman et al., 2015).

The interventions offered are usually therapeutic and pharmacological. Therapeutic interventions have traditionally included a broad range of approaches, from more structured behavioural approaches, such as dialectical behaviour therapy, to more unstructured approaches, such as long-term psychoanalytic psychotherapies. Personality disorder interventions were typically given in long-term intensive therapeutic community inpatient centres. However, a lack of robust outcomes together with the changing structure of healthcare services, in response to resource constraints, has led to many of these services being revised. Currently, the United Kingdom National Institute for Health and Care Excellence (NICE) guidance recommends a combination of individual and group approaches, alongside other services, such as social services and drug and alcohol rehabilitation (NICE, 2009). An array of interventions has been developed from each of the main paradigm models specifically for personality disorders. These include dialectical behaviour therapy (from the behaviourist paradigm) (Linehan, 1993), mentalisation-based treatment and transference-focused psychotherapy (from the psychodynamic paradigm) (Bateman and Fonagy, 1999; Clarkin et al., 2001), and schema-focused therapy (from the cognitive paradigm) (Young, Klosko and Weishaar, 2003). However, despite the creation of these specialist interventions, problems with providing them remain. Specialist interventions require trained specialists to deliver them, and often much commitment from the individual. In addition, research has shown that these interventions impact on symptoms but do not significantly improve interpersonal functioning (Bateman et al., 2015). Furthermore, when these interventions are compared with each other, and other therapies that are planned with personality disorders in mind, then there is little difference in the effectiveness between them (Noble, 2015). The case example below outlines one particular approach with someone who has been given the label 'borderline personality disorder'.

CASE EXAMPLE: BORDERLINE PERSONALITY DISORDER

Sarah is 27 years old and has a diagnosis of borderline personality disorder. She experienced a chaotic childhood and started self-harming at the age of 11. She has had several intense friendships and romantic partners, but these have not lasted long term, and usually end suddenly, after which she has felt overwhelming emotions and has attempted suicide on four occasions.

PSYCHOLOGICAL INTERVENTION

A practitioner providing an intervention for Sarah could start by developing a shared formulation with her, which acknowledges the traumatic experiences that led to the diagnosis of a personality disorder and the current impact this is having on Sarah's life. This could then lead to working through Sarah's difficulties and her desired outcomes using a specialised intervention (see an example below). During this process, a practitioner would pay close attention to the relational dynamics occurring in the therapeutic relationship, as this could give an indication of Sarah's interpersonal patterns and be a useful opportunity to develop new ways of communicating.

SPECIALIST INTERVENTION EXAMPLE: DIALECTICAL BEHAVIOUR THERAPY (DBT)

CONCEPTUALISATION OF DISTRESS. DBT views borderline personality disorder as a biosocial disorder, citing that there is biological evidence to suggest some individuals have a heightened sensitivity to emotion, experience emotions more intensely and have a slower return to emotional baseline. This is paired with a social environment in which the individual's coping mechanisms and responses to this emotional dysregulation are invalidated. As a result, individuals experience intense emotional states, which they feel unable to regulate.

WHAT DOES THE APPROACH DO? DBT is a structured, manualised method combining behavioural change and acceptance-based approaches in four areas: distress tolerance, emotion regulation, interpersonal effectiveness and mindfulness. This is implemented through an intensive programme of group skills training, individual therapy and immediate telephone support. Typically, dialectical behaviour therapy programmes last for 12–18 months. See Swales and Dunkley (Chapter 5.12, this volume) for a discussion of DBT.

EVALUATION

Due to practitioners and researchers raising concerns over the overlapping nature of the personality disorder categories and the difficulties in defining pathological personality, there is a growing consensus that personality disorder classification should be based on a trait-based dimensional system. DSM-5 tentatively introduced a new dimensional approach within a section entitled 'Emerging Measures and Models' (American Psychiatric Association, 2013), and the proposed ICD-11 abolishes all type-specific categories of personality disorder. Instead ICD-11 emphasises the severity of personality disturbance and the fluctuations over time (Tyrer et al., 2011).

These new approaches acknowledge that individuals fall on a spectrum of universal personality traits, a theory well established in personality research (Matthews, Deary and Whiteman, 2009). Hengartner, Ajdacic-Gross, Rodgers, Müller and Rössler (2014) have evaluated personality disorder literature and propose four dimensions. These are emotional dysregulation versus stability, extraversion versus introversion, antagonism versus compliance and constraint versus impulsivity. Within such an approach, all individuals (including those within the general population) have degrees of these traits, and individuals diagnosed with personality disorder may fall towards the extremes of these traits.

Similarly, interventions for individuals with personality disorders are moving towards looking at the common factors within interventions rather than advocating for particular approaches (Weinberg, Ronningstam, Goldblatt, Schechter and Maltsberger, 2011), since most approaches demonstrate similar outcomes. Bateman et al. (2015) highlight one of the main unanswered questions for the future of interventions for personality disorder, given the high prevalence rates in the population and need for services, is whether interventions should be given by all practitioners who receive training to become personality disorder informed, or whether it remains the domain of specialist practitioners.

After a long history of stagnation in diagnostic and intervention approaches in regards to personality disorder, these debates and questions highlight that the field has moved into a dynamic and exciting era of development.

REFERENCES

American Psychiatric Association (2013). *Diagnostic and statistical manual of mental disorders* (5th ed.). Washington, DC: American Psychiatric Publishing.

Bateman, A. and Fonagy, P. (1999). Effectiveness of partial hospitalization in the treatment of borderline personality disorder: a randomized controlled trial. *American Journal of Psychiatry*, 156, 1563–1569.

Bateman, A. W., Gunderson, J. and Mulder, R. (2015). Treatment of personality disorder. *The Lancet*, 385, 735–743.

Beckwith, H., Moran, P. F. and Reilly, J. (2014). Personality disorder prevalence in psychiatric outpatients: a systematic literature review. *Personality and Mental Health*, 8(2), 91–101.

Cicchetti, D. (2014). Illustrative developmental psychopathology perspectives on precursors and pathways to personality disorder: commentary on the special issue. *Journal of Personality Disorders*, 28(1), 172–179.

Clark, L.-A. and Harrison, J. A. (2001). Assessment instruments. In W. J. Livesley (Ed.), *Handbook of personality disorders* (pp. 277–306). New York: Guildford Press.

Clark, L.-A., Shapiro, J. L., Daly, E., Vanderbleek, E. N., Oiler, M. R. and Harrison, J. (in press). Empirically validated diagnostic and assessment methods. In W. J. Livesley (Ed.), *Handbook of personality disorders* (2nd ed.). New York: Guildford Press.

Clarkin, J. F., Foelsch, P. A., Levy, K. N., Hull, J. W., Delaney, J. C. and Kernberg, O. F. (2001). The development of a psychodynamic treatment for patients with borderline personality disorder: a preliminary study of behavioral change. *Journal of Personality Disorders*, 15, 487–495.

Cohen, P. (2008). Child development and personality disorder. *Psychiatric Clinics of North America*, 31, 477–493.

Coid, J., Yang, M., Tyrer, P., Roberts, A. and Ullrich, S. (2006). Prevalence and correlates of personality disorder in Great Britain. *The British Journal of Psychiatry*, 188, 423–431.

Crawford, M. J., Rushwaya, T., Bajaj, P., Tyrer, P. and Yang, M. (2012). The prevalence of personality disorder among ethnic minorities: findings from a national household survey. *Personality and Mental Health*, 6, 175–182.

Fazel, S. and Danesh, J. (2002). Serious mental disorder in 23,000 prisoners: a systematic review of 62 surveys. *The Lancet*, 359, 545–550.

Fok, M. L.-Y., Hayes, R. D., Chang, C.-K., Stewart, R., Callard, F. J. and Moran, P. (2012). Life expectancy at birth and all-cause mortality among people with personality disorder. *Journal of Psychosomatic Research*, 73(2), 104–107.

Frankenburg, F. R. and Zanarini, M. C. (2004). The association between borderline personality disorder and chronic medical illnesses, poor health-related lifestyle choices, and costly forms of health care utilization. *The Journal of Clinical Psychiatry*, 65, 1478–1665.

Hasin, D., Fenton, M. C., Skodol, A., Krueger, R., Keyes, K., Geier, T., Greenstein, E., Blanco C. and Grant, B. (2011). Personality disorders and the 3-year course of alcohol, drug and nicotine use disorders. *Archives of General Psychiatry*, 68, 1158–1167.

Hengartner, M. P., Ajdacic-Gross, V., Rodgers, S., Müller, M. and Rössler, W. (2014). The joint structure of normal and pathological personality: further evidence for a dimensional model. *Comprehensive Psychiatry*, 55, 667–674.

Hiroeh, U., Appleby, L., Mortensen, P. B. and Dunn, G. (2001). Death by homicide, suicide, and other unnatural causes in people with mental illness: a population-based study. *The Lancet*, 358, 2110–2112.

Jarrett, C. (2006). Understanding personality disorder. *The Psychologist*, 19, 402–404.

Langbehn, D. R., Pfohl, B. M., Reynolds, S., Clark, L.-A., Battaglia, M., Bellodi, L., Cadoret, R., Grove, W., Pilkonis, P. and Links, P. (1999). The Iowa Personality Disorder Screen: development and preliminary validation of a brief screening interview. *Journal of Personality Disorders*, 13(1), 75–89.

Lenzenweger, M. F. and Willett, J. B. (2007). Predicting individual change in personality disorder features by simultaneous individual change in personality dimensions linked to neurobehavioral systems: the longitudinal study of personality disorders. *Journal of Abnormal Psychology*, 116, 684–700.

(Continued)

(Continued)

Linehan, M. M. (1993). *Skills training manual for treating borderline personality disorder*. New York: Guilford Press.

Matthews, G., Deary, I. J. and Whiteman, M. C. (2009). *Personality traits* (3rd ed.). Cambridge: Cambridge University Press.

Moran, P., Jenkins, R., Tylee, A., Blizard, R. and Mann, A. (2000). The prevalence of personality disorder among UK primary care attenders. *Acta Psychiatrica Scandinavica*, 102(1), 52–57.

Moran, P., Leese, M., Lee, T., Walters, P., Thornicroft, G. and Mann, A. (2003). Standardised Assessment of Personality–Abbreviated Scale (SAPAS): preliminary validation of a brief screen for personality disorder. *The British Journal of Psychiatry*, 183, 228–232.

Newton-Howes, G., Clark, L.-A. and Chanen, A. (2015). Personality disorder across the life course. *The Lancet*, 385, 727–734.

NICE (2009). *Borderline personality disorder: The NICE guideline on treatment and management*. Clinical Guidelines 78. London: National Colloborating Centre for Mental Health. (www.nice.org.uk/guidance/CG78/).

Noble, J. (2015). A systematic review of interventions and their effectiveness to prevent recurrent self-harm in individuals diagnosed with borderline personality disorder using quantitative primary research. Paper presented at the International Society for the Study of Personality Disorders, Montreal, Canada.

Schneider, K. (1923). *Die psychopathischen Persönlichkeiten*. Berlin: Springer.

Tyrer, P., Crawford, M., Mulder, R., Blashfield, R., Farnam, A., Fossati, A., Kim, Y.-R., Koldobsky, N., Lecic-Tosevski, D., Ndetei, D., Swales, M., Clark, L.-A. and Reed, G. M. (2011). The rationale for the reclassification of personality disorder in the 11th revision of the international classification of diseases (ICD-11). *Personality and Mental Health*, 5, 246–259.

Tyrer, P., Reed, G. M. and Crawford, M. J. (2015). Classification, assessment, prevalence, and effect of personality disorder. *The Lancet*, 385, 717–726.

Van der Hart, O., Nijenhuis, E. R. and Steele, K. (2006). *The haunted self: Structural dissociation and the treatment of chronic traumatization*. New York: W.W. Norton.

Weinberg, I., Ronningstam, E., Goldblatt, M. J., Schechter, M. and Maltsberger, J. T. (2011). Common factors in empirically supported treatments of borderline personality disorder. *Current Psychiatry Reports*, 13(1), 60–68.

World Health Organisation (1992). *The ICD-10 classification of mental and behavioural disorders: Clinical descriptions and diagnostic guidelines*. London: Churchill Livingstone.

Young, J. E., Klosko, J. S. and Weishaar, M. E. (2003). *Schema therapy: A practitioner's guide*. New York: Guilford Press.

RECOMMENDED READING

1. Paris, J. (2015). *A concise guide to personality disorders*. Washington, DC: American Psychological Association.

This book reviews what is known and unknown about personality disorders, and its applications to clinical practice.

2. Van der Hart, O., Nijenhuis, E. R. and Steele, K. (2006). *The haunted self: Structural dissociation and the treatment of chronic traumatization*. New York: W.W. Norton.

This book acknowledges the wider context surrounding an individual, and presents an alternative understanding and conceptualisation of the difficulties associated with personality disorders.

3. Weinberg, I., Ronningstam, E., Goldblatt, M. J., Schechter, M. and Maltsberger, J. T. (2011). Common factors in empirically supported treatments of borderline personality disorder. *Current Psychiatry Reports*, 13(1), 60–68.

This paper summarises a large body of research on interventions and identifies the common factors which appear to be effective across approaches. Although this paper focuses specifically on borderline personality disorder, it has implications for all personality disorders.

6.14 PHOBIAS

TOM RICKETTS AND GILL DONOHOE

OVERVIEW AND KEY POINTS

The aims of this chapter are to introduce readers to the various phobic disorders, focusing upon shared and specific clinical features. A conceptual base for understanding phobias will be provided. The main treatment approaches will be outlined, with an emphasis on cognitive-behavioural methods, as indicated by research and current clinical practice. The key points addressed in the chapter are:

- Three types of phobia can be identified – specific phobia, agoraphobia and social phobia.
- Phobias are frequent in the general population and may be highly debilitating.
- The learning theory of phobias incorporates the principles of classical and operant conditioning to explain the development and maintenance of phobias.
- The learning theory of phobias has supported the development of exposure therapy approaches that are highly effective.
- Cognitive approaches may be particularly useful in social phobia.

DEFINITIONS

A phobia can be described as a marked and persistent fear that is excessive or unreasonable, cued by the presence or anticipation of a specific object or situation (American Psychiatric Association, 2013). There is a strong desire to avoid the feared situation.

Phobic disorders can be broadly categorized into three main groups: specific phobias, agoraphobia and social phobia (also known as social anxiety disorder). Although in theory an individual can become phobic about any stimulus, and rare cases do exist, the list of five categories for specific phobias, as indicated later, addresses all types seen in clinical practice.

Phobic disorders all share the central feature of anxiety, which is experienced in anticipation of and/or upon confrontation with the feared situation or stimulus. Anxiety responses are intense and extreme and can present in the form of panic. Although symptoms are often negligible when the feared objects or situations are not encountered,

some anxiety may occur at other times, for example in association with anticipation of confrontation. In addition, it is common for individuals with a phobic disorder to have at least one other anxiety disorder, with generalized anxiety being particularly common (Roth and Fonagy, 2005).

Individuals with phobic disorders may also experience panic attacks. These may only occur when faced with the phobic situation, and are referred to as situationally bound panic attacks. Panic attacks are more common in the case of agoraphobia, and panic disorder may also be present, and should be treated. Reference will therefore be made to panic attacks in this chapter, although for a more comprehensive account readers should refer to the chapter on anxiety and panic (Donohoe and Ricketts – Chapter 6.3, this volume).

In order to satisfy diagnostic criteria for a phobic disorder, symptoms must have been present for at least six months and the individual must experience clinically significant distress or difficulties carrying out social, occupational or other important activities. If the person is able to avoid the feared stimulus, for example snakes or plane travel, then treatment may not be warranted or sought.

Individuals with phobic conditions commonly suffer difficulties for many years, with little evidence of spontaneous remission. At the same time, with current behavioural and cognitive-behavioural approaches, they are readily treated. Identification and the offer of intervention for sufferers is therefore a priority.

SPECIFIC PHOBIAS

Specific phobias have in the past been referred to as simple phobias as the fear is confined to one main stimulus. Specific phobias can be further categorized according to the following types:

- animal type, including mammals, insects and reptiles
- natural environment type, for example, storms, water, heights
- blood/injection/injury type
- situational type, for example, aeroplanes, lifts
- other type, for example, situations that may lead to choking or vomiting (American Psychiatric Association, 2013).

In the case of specific phobias, the extreme fear is experienced immediately upon contact with the feared stimulus and is usually proportionate to the proximity.

The symptoms of anxiety experienced upon anticipation or actual contact with the phobic stimulus include the usual range of autonomic symptoms. However, the pattern of arousal seems to differ in one particular type of specific phobia, namely, blood/injection/injury. These individual sufferers commonly experience a vasovagal response whereby the blood pressure may rise as usual initially, but then drops rapidly causing a fainting response (American Psychiatric Association, 2013).

AGORAPHOBIA

Agoraphobia is a complex phobia as it involves a wide range of feared situations. Anxiety symptoms occur on entering a variety of public situations, for example, crowded places such as shops, queues, public transport; open spaces; confined places; and any situations from which escape may be difficult or embarrassing and help is unavailable. Distance from home or other places of safety and being alone are often key factors.

Agoraphobia is a separate disorder from panic disorder (American Psychiatric Association, 2013), but is often closely linked. Where panic attacks are a central feature a diagnosis of both panic disorder and agoraphobia may be appropriate. Panic attacks are characterized by the sudden onset of intense symptoms along with fears associated with the symptoms, for example, of dying or losing control. Symptoms include palpitations, sweating, trembling or shaking, shortness of breath or choking sensations, dizziness or feeling faint, numbness or tingling sensations, derealization (feelings of unreality) or depersonalization (feeling detached from self). See Chapter 6.3 for a detailed outline of the nature and treatment of panic disorder (Donohoe and Ricketts – this volume).

SOCIAL PHOBIA (SOCIAL ANXIETY DISORDER)

Social phobia is another more complex type of phobia, although some individuals present with more specific social performance fears, for instance, only experiencing difficulties when speaking in front of an audience. Although triggered by social interaction, the nature of the fear is associated with prediction of less observable events, such as being rejected or viewed negatively by others. Thoughts regarding social evaluation can themselves be disruptive, as they may distract the person from the tasks involved in social interaction.

AETIOLOGY

There has been, and remains, much debate about how and why phobias develop. Although one single theory does not appear to account for the acquisition and maintenance of all phobias, most of the progress in understanding has arisen from conditioning and learning theory accounts. Learning theories suggest that emotional responses, such as fear, can be learnt in a similar way to other aspects of human development.

The learning theory of phobias incorporates the principles of classical and operant conditioning. Pavlov and other Russian physiologists conducted animal experiments in the early to middle part of the last century which demonstrated that dogs, for example, could be conditioned to salivate at the sound of a bell. It was shown that by repeatedly pairing food (an unconditioned stimulus resulting in the unconditioned response of salivation) with the sound of a bell, the bell eventually became a conditioned stimulus resulting in salivation (conditioned response) even in the absence of food. Thus, the principles are based upon the notion that previously neutral stimuli can develop stimulating properties and provoke new responses if repeatedly presented with another stimulus. In the case of phobias, the new or conditioned response is fear.

The second learning principle is based upon operant conditioning, whereby learning is dependent upon the consequences following the behaviour. For example, if a behaviour is rewarded, then it is more likely to occur in the future. Similarly, a behaviour which is followed by the removal of something the individual finds unpleasant is also rewarded, and is also more likely to occur again in future. These examples are termed positive and negative reinforcement respectively.

In applying these principles to the development and maintenance of phobias, they can be understood to be acquired through the process of classical conditioning and maintained by the effects of negative reinforcement, specifically the rapid reduction of anxiety which follows escape from or avoidance of the phobic situation.

To acquire a phobia through the above process, the individual must experience and associate traumatic or aversive stimuli with the phobic object until the latter develops these properties. While this is reportedly the case for many individuals suffering from phobias, there are cases where such conditioning events have not occurred. This has prompted the suggestion that phobic anxiety may also arise simply through the observation of fearful others, or through being told about potentially fear-invoking stimuli or circumstances. This 'three pathways to fear' model (Rachman, 1977) has found good empirical support, suggesting that the acquisition of phobic anxiety may come about through multiple routes (Lissek et al., 2005).

Maintenance of phobias through negative reinforcement of escape and avoidance is best understood as preventing the spontaneous reduction of fear. In the absence of escape and avoidance, repeated contact with the phobic stimulus reduces the link between the situation and fear. After repeated contact, the previously fearful stimulus becomes neutral, no longer triggering an anxiety response.

Table 6.14.1 gives details of the prevalence, course and gender distributions of the different types of phobic disorder.

Table 6.14.1 Epidemiological data for phobias

Phobic disorder	Prevalence	Onset and course	Gender and distribution
Specific phobia	7–9%	Childhood	Depends upon subtype but generally higher proportion of women
Agoraphobia	1.7%	Late adolescence to mid-thirties	Twice as likely in women
Social phobia	2–7%	Mid to late teens	More frequent in women in epidemiological samples but equal in clinical samples

Source: American Psychiatric Association (2013)

ASSESSMENT

Assessment of phobias is similar to that for other disorders in that the aim is to obtain as full a picture as possible, utilizing a range of data collection techniques. Assessment is guided by the model, so that at the end of assessment a clear formulation of the development and maintenance of the disorder is possible, this being the basis of the individualized therapeutic plan. Data collection techniques include clinical interviews, self-monitoring of thoughts, emotions and behaviour and, where possible, direct observation of the client engaging with the phobic object or situation.

FORMULATION

The behavioural formulation of the development and maintenance of phobias proposes that they can be understood to be acquired through the process of classical conditioning and maintained by the effects of negative reinforcement, specifically the rapid reduction of anxiety which follows escape from or avoidance of the phobic situation. The escape and avoidance behaviours are proposed to prevent the spontaneous reduction in fear that would otherwise occur through prolonged contact.

INTERVENTION

Research studies and reviews on the effectiveness of therapies for phobic disorders have found exposure therapy to be the primary treatment of choice, with the incorporation of cognitive approaches and other strategies such as applied tension in some cases (see below). There seems to be no indication and little evidence for the use of non-directive counselling approaches or for the use of medication as the main approach (Roth and Fonagy, 2005).

Treatment is based upon a detailed assessment and analysis of the presenting difficulty along with any other associated problems. This includes a history of the development of the problem. The assessment information is then discussed with the client within a cognitive-behavioural framework. This forms the first stage of therapy, the main purpose of which is to educate the client on the principles of the approach and the rationale for the treatment plan based upon their difficulties.

EXPOSURE THERAPY

Exposure therapy involves repeated, prolonged confrontation with the feared stimuli until the discomfort reduces and is no longer evoked by further contact. Exposure therapy should be *in vivo* (live) wherever possible and also should be graded, prolonged and repeated regularly (Marks, 1981). To achieve this, exposure tasks should be practised by the client as homework, either with or without the help of a partner or spouse.

The components of exposure will be described below through a case example, Tom:

1. *Assessment and engagement*. Tom reported severe anxiety in crowded situations such as busy supermarkets, buses, trains and other situations where leaving

the situation rapidly would be difficult or embarrassing. He reported that he had experienced anxiety with severe tension, breathlessness and concern that he might faint while on a crowded bus ten years previously. He had got off the bus at the first available stop and had experienced a reduction in symptoms. He had subsequently avoided buses, preferring to walk and drive everywhere. Over the years he had experienced anxiety in other enclosed places, gradually increasing the range of situations he avoids. He has recently begun to feel anxious within his work setting, and this has prompted his treatment seeking. Tom's goals for therapy were to be able to use trains to visit relatives, and to visit the town centre at busy times.

2. *Education and instruction on the nature and principles of exposure therapy.* As homework practice is essential for successful therapy, the client's full understanding and active involvement are required. In Tom's case, the nature of fear acquisition through classical conditioning, and negative reinforcement of escape and avoidance behaviours, was outlined, followed by a description of the habituation of fear through graded exposure. Personally relevant examples from Tom's own experience of habituation were sought and used to illustrate the processes described.

3. *Construction of a hierarchy for graded tasks.* Based on Tom's overall goals for therapy, a hierarchy of exposure tasks was developed that represented the range of avoided situations. Tom estimated how fearful he would be in each situation according to the anxiety evoked or degree of avoidance (on a 0–8 scale). Early steps were then agreed that were practical and realistic to achieve. The hierarchy included equal spacing between steps where possible.

4. *Exposure tasks.* Exposure therapy may be therapist-assisted or self-directed. It can be conducted in a group or with a friend or spouse. If therapist-assisted exposure is the chosen method, it is important to consider the effects of the therapist's (or relevant other's) presence and plan to phase this out. Ultimately, the client must be able to manage phobic situations alone and not have to depend on the presence of others. Whether alone or accompanied, within each session, the client monitors his/her level of anxiety and remains within the situation until this has reduced (at least two points on a 0–8 scale). Tom undertook the first item on his hierarchy, going into a small local supermarket at a quiet time, on each day between two therapy sessions, allowing his anxiety to reduce before entering, and then taking his time to browse the shelves until his anxiety

had reduced again. He noticed habituation between sessions, with the fourth visit to undertake the task much easier than the first.

5. *Homework tasks.* If the exposure task has been conducted within a treatment session, whether accompanied or alone, this should be followed by further practice, which must be specified and agreed between client and therapist along with any relevant others. It is preferable that the task is based upon that which has already been completed so that the client can consolidate their learning. As Tom was undertaking self-managed exposure, this stage was already built into the plan.

6. *Homework review and planning.* After the first and subsequent week of self-managed exposure Tom was encouraged to review the process in the therapy session, identifying any behaviours that had slowed or blocked habituation of anxiety (such as distracting himself). He then agreed further tasks for the subsequent week, gradually working up his hierarchy. Because of the range of phobic situations in which he experienced fear, these situations included crowded public settings as well as different forms of public transport.

ADDITIONAL AND ALTERNATIVE STRATEGIES

Although some form of exposure therapy should be the first treatment of choice in the majority of cases, some individuals and types of phobia may require additional strategies or a focus on cognitive approaches.

APPLIED TENSION

Individuals with blood/injection/injury phobias frequently experience fainting when presented with blood- or injury-associated stimuli due to the unique physiological response. Applied tension is a technique developed specifically for these individuals in order to control the fainting response and is therefore used in conjunction with exposure therapy. Individuals are taught to tense key muscle groups, which in turn increases cerebral blood flow and helps to control fainting (see Ost and Sterner, 1987).

COGNITIVE THERAPY

Cognitive factors are clearly implicated in the maintenance of certain phobias and, in the case of social phobia, specific cognitive models have been developed (Clark, 2005; Clark and Beck, 2009). Whether cognitive approaches are superior to or enhance traditional exposure therapy programmes for phobias has been the focus of research, but so far real benefit has only been shown in the case of social phobia (Clark et al., 2006). Cognitive therapy has demonstrated significant benefits for depression (see Beck et al., 1979) and therefore should be considered if this is a major difficulty.

Cognitive strategies, as initially developed by Beck, focus upon identification and modification of faulty thinking styles by a variety of means, including verbal disputation and behavioural experimentation.

USE OF VIDEOTAPED FEEDBACK

The self-focused attention that is a central feature of social phobia has been linked to poor assessment of social performance by the individual. The wide availability of video recording facilities has enabled the use of feedback on performance to the individual to provide them with information to correct such evaluations within a cognitive approach (Wells, 1997). The use of video feedback can be understood as a behavioural experiment.

DRUG TREATMENT

Antidepressant and anxiolytic drugs have been utilized, although they have only demonstrated short-term benefits and have not been found to be superior to cognitive-behavioural therapy programmes. Medication is certainly not indicated for specific phobias and most of the research has focused upon agoraphobia. This research has found that medication is not as effective as cognitive-behavioural approaches and relapse is more likely. There is some suggestion, however, that antidepressants may have some slight benefits when combined with psychological methods (Roth and Fonagy, 2005).

EVALUATION

The efficacy of exposure-based approaches is well established, but there is increasing recognition of the insufficiency of conditioning theories alone to explain fear processes (Barlow, 2004). Developments in cognitive psychology and cognitive therapy have led to models and interventions to help clients who have not benefited from purely exposure-based methods. In practice, the majority of clinicians now claim to be utilizing cognitive-behavioural methods, demonstrating how well these approaches have been integrated. However, research is still required to determine which aspects of therapy have what effect on which symptoms. For example, although we know that in the majority of cases exposure works, how does it work? Is it through the deconditioning process or is it as a result of the client's reappraisal of the stimulus? Research has focused on the differences between specific approaches (e.g., cognitive versus exposure therapy) in order to determine which has more potency with which type of difficulty or symptom. As cognitive therapy would normally incorporate some aspect of fear confrontation, it has not always been easy to achieve. As suggested previously, for those with a diagnosis of social phobia cognitive models have been developed (Wells, 1997) and have received good research support (Clark, 2005).

The emphasis on tailoring treatment to individual clients has developed in conjunction with the need to investigate more efficient and client-led approaches. In the UK, the Improving Access to Psychological Therapies programme (Clark et al., 2009) has enhanced access to 'low-intensity' cognitive behavioural approaches (Richards and Whyte, 2009) such as guided self-help, telephone interventions, computerized cognitive-behaviour therapy (NICE, 2011) and large-group interventions (Delgadillo et al., 2016; White, 1995) for clients with phobias. Results indicate that large numbers of people with phobic conditions can be assisted through the implementation of such approaches, when the outcomes for individuals are closely monitored (Clark et al., 2009). Further evaluation of these approaches is being undertaken as they are being implemented.

REFERENCES

American Psychiatric Association (2013) *Diagnostic and Statistical Manual of Mental Disorders* (5th ed.). Washington, DC: American Psychiatric Association.
Barlow, D.H. (2004) *Anxiety and Its Disorders: The Nature and Treatment of Anxiety and Panic*. New York: Guilford Press.
Beck, A.T., Rush, A.J., Shaw, B.F. and Emery, G. (1979) *Cognitive Therapy of Depression*. New York: Guilford Press.
Clark, D.M. (2005) A cognitive perspective on social phobia. In W.R. Crozier and L.F. Alden (Eds), *The Essential Handbook of Social Anxiety for Clinicians*. Chichester: Wiley.

(Continued)

(Continued)

Clark, D.M. and Beck, A.T. (2009) *Cognitive Therapy of Anxiety Disorders*. New York: Guilford Press.

Clark, D.M., Ehlers, A., McManus, F., Fennell, M., Grey, N., Waddington, L. and Wild, J. (2006) Cognitive therapy versus exposure and applied relaxation in social phobia: a randomised controlled trial. *Journal of Consulting and Clinical Psychology*, 74: 568–578.

Clark, D.M., Layard, R., Smithies, R., Richards, D.A., Suckling, R. and Wright, B. (2009) Improving Access to Psychological Therapy: initial evaluation of two UK demonstration sites. *Behaviour Research and Therapy*, 47: 910–920.

Delgadillo, J., Kellett, S., Ali, S., MacMillan, D., Barkham, M., Saxon, D., Donohoe, G., Stonebank, H., Mullaney, S., Eschoe, P., Thwaites, R. and Lucock, M. (2016) A multi service practice research network study of large group psychoeducational cognitive behavioural therapy. *Behaviour Research and Therapy*, 67: 155–161.

Lissek, S., Powers, A.S., McClure, E.B., Phelps, E.A., Woldehawariat, G., Grillon, C. and Pine, D.S. (2005) Classical fear conditioning in the anxiety disorders: a meta-analysis. *Behaviour Research and Therapy*, 43: 1391–1424.

Marks, I.M. (1981) *Cure and Care of Neurosis*. Chichester: Wiley.

NICE (2011) *Common Mental Health Problems: Identification and Pathways to Care*. Clinical Guideline 123. London: NICE.

Ost, L.-G. and Sterner, U. (1987) Applied tension: a specific behavioural method for treatment of blood phobia. *Behaviour Research and Therapy*, 25(1): 25–29.

Rachman, S. (1977) The conditioning theory of fear acquisition: a critical examination. *Behaviour Research and Therapy*, 22: 109–117.

Richards, D. and Whyte, M. (2009) *Reach Out: National Programme: Student Materials to Support the Delivery of Training for Psychosociological Wellbeing Practitioners Delivering Low Intensity Interventions* (2nd ed.). London: Rethink.

Roth, A. and Fonagy, P. (2005) *What Works for Whom? A Critical Review of Psychotherapy Research* (2nd ed.). New York: Guilford Press.

Wells, A. (1997) *Cognitive Therapy of Anxiety Disorders: A Practice Manual and Conceptual Guide*. Chichester: Wiley.

White, J. (1995) Stresspac: a controlled trial of a self-help package for the anxiety disorders. *Behavioural and Cognitive Psychotherapy*, 23: 89–107.

RECOMMENDED READING

1. Barlow, D.H. (2002) *Anxiety and Its Disorders. The Nature and Treatment of Anxiety and Panic* (2nd ed.). New York: Guilford Press.

This is a thorough and extensive book covering the full range of theories relevant to the understanding and management of phobias and other anxiety disorders.

2. Abramowitz, J.S., Deacon, B.J. and Whiteside, S.P.H. (2013) *Exposure Therapy for Anxiety: Principles and Practice*. New York: Guilford Press.

This book provides a detailed overview of the assessment and treatment of a range of anxiety disorders using exposure.

3. Wells, A. (1997) *Cognitive Therapy of Anxiety Disorder: A Practice and Conceptual Guide*. Chichester: Wiley.

This book is an excellent manual relating to cognitive approaches to anxiety disorders with particular relevance to social phobia. There are clear models, case formulations and treatment interventions delivered in a way which clearly connects with cognitive theory and the skills required to deliver therapy.

6.15 POST-TRAUMATIC STRESS DISORDER

CLAUDIA HERBERT

OVERVIEW AND KEY POINTS

Trauma can shatter lives. Of people experiencing a traumatic event, 25–30% may go on to develop post-traumatic stress disorder (PTSD) (NICE, 2005). Although awareness of PTSD has significantly increased in recent years and scientific research has flourished, assessing, diagnosing and treating trauma-related problems remains a challenge for many therapists, and clients can go unnoticed, misdiagnosed or untreated for their PTSD for many years. This chapter proposes the following:

- PTSD is caused by the psycho-neurobiological responses to experiences of extreme danger, threat or fear.
- PTSD is made up of symptoms falling into four diverse cluster groups.
- Safe PTSD assessment and treatment requires significant knowledge, skill, time and sensitive attunement to each client's needs.
- Several PTSD therapies have been developed, but currently, only trauma-focused cognitive-behavioural therapy (TF-CBT) and Eye Movement Desensitization and Reprocessing (EMDR) have been trialled as effective and are the two treatments of choice recommended by the National Institute for Health and Care Excellence (NICE).
- PTSD can be a very debilitating and complex condition, especially if linked to multiple, prolonged or developmental trauma which requires a multimodal, longer-term treatment approach.

DEFINITION

PTSD has been around for centuries under different names, but only officially recognized as an emotional disorder since 1980 (DSM-III, American Psychiatric Association, 1980). PTSD was initially mainly associated with soldiers, but increasingly it was recognized that it can develop in any person at any age in response to overwhelming and threatening life events. In the last decade neuroscientific research has advanced understanding of PTSD further; it is increasingly being recognized as a psycho-neurobiological condition, largely determined by the responses of the autonomic nervous system in the body.

Two different systems are used for the diagnosis of PTSD: the *International Classification of Diseases* (ICD-10) (World Health Organization, 1993), which is often used by psychiatrists within the National Health Service, and the *Diagnostic and Statistical Manual of Mental Disorders* classification system, currently in its fifth edition (DSM-V) (American Psychiatric Association (APA), 2013). Due to the more stringent standards, the APA's DSM classification system is preferred in PTSD research and will guide the PTSD diagnostic criteria referred to in this chapter. DSM-V categorizes PTSD under a newly created category 'trauma- and stressor-related disorders', rather than as part of the 'anxiety disorders', as it had been in previous editions (DSM-IV-TR: APA, 2000). This has been heavily criticized on the basis that (1) fear is a critical component for developing PTSD, (2) treating trauma-related fear and avoidance is central to PTSD, and (3) lack of evidence for a stressor meta-construct separate from the anxiety disorders (Zoellner et al., 2011).

AETIOLOGY

DSM-V states in Criterion A that for a diagnosis of PTSD, a person has to have been exposed to death or threatened death, actual or threatened serious injury, or actual or threatened sexual violence, either through direct exposure; witnessing of the event(s); indirectly learning that such event(s) occurred to close others, in which case actual or threatened death must have been violent or accidental; or extreme or repeated exposure to aversive details of such an event(s), usually as part of professional duties.

Criterion A has been described as the 'so-called' gatekeeper criterion (Levin et al., 2014) as it determines the prevalence of PTSD in the general population. This throws up the question as to whether PTSD can develop in response to other stressful life events. Research has found that PTSD symptoms are as likely to develop in response to events that do not involve serious threat to bodily integrity, such as severe conflict in relationships, separation or divorce, loss of a job, loss of a home, serious financial stress (Anders et al., 2011). Although DSM-V attempted to reduce ambiguity about the distinction between 'traumatic' and 'non-traumatic' events, Criterion A has been criticized (Brewin et al., 2009) as inadequate on the grounds that what really matters is whether individuals exhibit PTSD symptoms regardless as to whether or not they were exposed to Criterion A events (Friedman, 2014).

DSM-V does not make provision for Complex PTSD (C-PTSD) as a separate disorder, and diagnostically this has to be accounted for within the specified criteria for PTSD. However, these fail to capture some of the core characteristics of C-PTSD, which arise out of (1) situations of prolonged and repeated severe threat or danger, often spanning months or years, from which the victim cannot escape, for example, torture, hostage taking or living in war zones and conflict-ridden territories or having to flee from these, loss of family, friends, home and belongings and being displaced in camps and/or dictatorships; and/or (2) pervasive relational- or attachment-based trauma, for example, domestic, institutional, child hostage taking, such as in bunkers, ritual and/or childhood sexual, physical or emotional abuse.

ASSESSMENT

Clinical assessment of PTSD involves a person fulfilling the requisite number and severity of symptoms specified by the diagnostic system used, obtained either during clinical interview, often combined with administration of standardized questionnaires, or through self-administered questionnaire measures taken on their own. These measures are also used to evaluate treatment progress and outcome of therapeutic interventions.

However, this widely accepted PTSD assessment practice does not automatically ensure accuracy, and many trauma clients remain misdiagnosed or are not recognized as suffering from PTSD. Therapists need to be able to distinguish between PTSD and C-PTSD and they need to be able to recognize the symptoms of avoidance and those falling into the spectrum of dissociation. Further, therapists need to be able to establish a therapeutic environment of safety and trust, including allowing sufficient assessment time (sometimes over several sessions), in order for a trauma client to feel secure enough to report their symptoms without feeling re-traumatized by the assessment.

SYMPTOMS

If a person meets conditions for trauma under Criterion A, seven further criteria have to be met in order to qualify for a DSM-V diagnosis of PTSD. Four of these criteria (B, C, D and E) describe four different symptom clusters out of which a particular number of symptoms have to be met,

and three criteria state additional requirements which have to be fulfilled.

CRITERION B: INTRUSION SYMPTOMS

Evidenced by one or more symptoms (1/5 required) of the following:

B1 recurrent, involuntary and intrusive memories (children may express these in repetitive play)

B2 traumatic nightmares (children may have frightening dreams without recognizable trauma content)

B3 dissociative reactions (e.g., flashbacks) which may occur on a continuum from brief episodes to complete loss of consciousness (children may re-enact the event in play)

B4 intense or prolonged distress at exposure to traumatic reminders

B5 marked physiological reactivity after exposure to trauma-related stimuli.

CRITERION C: PERSISTENT AVOIDANCE

Persistent effortful avoidance of distressing trauma-related stimuli after the event (1/2 required):

C1 trauma-related thoughts or feelings

C2 trauma-related external reminders (people, places, conversations, activities, objects, situations).

CRITERION D: NEGATIVE ALTERATIONS IN COGNITIONS AND MOOD

These began or worsened after the traumatic event(s) (2/7 required):

D1 inability to remember key features of the traumatic event(s) (typically due to dissociative amnesia; not due to head injury, alcohol or drugs)

D2 persistent (and often distorted) negative beliefs or expectations about oneself, others or the world (e.g., 'I am bad', 'no one can be trusted', 'the world is completely dangerous')

D3 persistent distorted blame of self or others for causing the traumatic event or for resulting consequences

D4 persistent negative trauma-related emotions (e.g., fear, horror, anger, guilt or shame)

D5 markedly diminished interest or participation in (pre-traumatic) significant activities

D6 feeling alienated from others (e.g., detachment or estrangement)

D7 constricted affect: persistent inability to experience positive emotions.

CRITERION E: ALTERATIONS IN AROUSAL AND REACTIVITY

These began or worsened after the traumatic event(s) (2/6 required):

E1 irritable or aggressive behaviour

E2 reckless or self-destructive behaviour

E3 hypervigilance

E4 exaggerated startle response

E5 problems in concentration

E6 sleep disturbance (e.g., difficulty falling or staying asleep or restless sleep).

ADDITIONAL REQUIREMENTS

CRITERION F: DURATION

Persistance of symptoms (in Criteria B, C, D and E) for more than one month.

CRITERION G: FUNCTIONAL SIGNIFICANCE

Significant symptom-related distress or functional impairment in social, occupational or other important areas of functioning.

CRITERION H: EXCLUSION

Disturbance is not due to medication, substance use or other illness. Criterion H also incorporates assessment of two dissociative symptoms: depersonalization and derealization. If either of these are detected, this is classified as PTSD with dissociative symptoms.

If the above symptoms and requirements are not fully met until at least six months or more after the traumatic event(s), a diagnosis of PTSD 'with delayed expression' has to be made.

The DSM-V aims to offer improvement on earlier DSM-IV versions for PTSD. However, they still fail to address one of the greatest areas of confusion from the perspective of a practising clinician (Herbert, 2006), which is the distinction between the psychological effects of a single isolated traumatic event (type I) or multiple such events (type II) and those of long-term, enduring trauma during early childhood, critical stages of development or adult situations of extreme duress (type III). While all of these groups may meet diagnostic criteria for PTSD, the assessment needs of the third group differ and require extensive therapeutic skill and knowledge of additional symptoms (see Herbert, 2006, for a more extensive review).

COMORBIDITY

Research has indicated that PTSD shows a severe and diverse pattern of comorbidity (Keane et al., 2007). Of individuals diagnosed with PTSD, 92% met criteria for another, current axis I disorder, most frequently major depressive disorder (77%), generalized anxiety disorder (38%) and alcohol abuse/dependence (31%). Studies examining veterans diagnosed with PTSD (Dunn et al., 2004) found high comorbidity with an axis II disorder (between 50% and 79%). It is not uncommon in clinical practice that clients are initially referred by their general practitioner (GP) to a therapist for help with their comorbid symptoms and, depending on the level of the treating therapist's knowledge of PTSD, this gets diagnosed during the assessment stage or remains undiagnosed and untreated.

FORMULATION

When an experience is registered as overwhelming and possibly life-threatening, this is registered and stored by arousal structures in the upper brain stem (the Recticular Thalamic Activating system, including the Periaqueductal Grey (PAG), is one). These, together with other brain systems, stimulate the release of specific neurochemicals which prepare the body initially for 'fight' or 'flight' reactions; if this is not possible in a particular situation, it initiates a 'freeze' or '*flop*' response, the most disabling of all trauma-related responses. The rise in sympathetic nervous system activity releases specific neurochemicals which close down activity of the frontal lobes (part of the neocortex), and cortisol shuts down the hippocampus (another part of the limbic system) (Lanius et al., 2006).

While arrest of higher-order brain structures, which operate more slowly and are not necessary for the immediate survival of the organism, is a highly adaptive solution to situations of threat in evolutionary terms, it hinders processing and integration of the emotional, sensory and bodily responses attached to the traumatic event(s) into a person's conscious memory system, and instead these stay stored as 'fragmentary snapshots' in non-verbal body memory systems. They become 'timeless', which means that although an event may have happened a long time ago, a person re-experiencing these 'snapshots' feels as if they were happening in the here-and-now despite the memory's actual content belonging to the past. While unprocessed, retriggering of these memories and associated emotional, sensory and somatic arousal symptoms can occur through external and internal stimuli that resemble aspects of the original traumatic experience. Retriggering is controlled by autonomic nervous system functioning and thus takes place outside a person's conscious control, and can feel overwhelmingly strong and significantly interfere with day-to-day life.

Lanius et al. (2006) outline the importance of the hypothalamus as the primary sensory gateway for all information reaching the neocortex. All sensory information, except olfaction, is routed through the hypothalamus to the neocortex. This enables the resonance between lower brain structures (reptilian brain complex and limbic system) and top brain structures (neocortex) and integrates top-down and bottom-up processing.

In order to protect a person's chances of survival from the emotional and/or physical pain of traumatic experiences, a split in consciousness takes place in a person, whereby the traumatic material becomes disconnected (dissociated) from active consciousness (disconnected from or only partially connected to certain neocortical structures of the brain). Research indicates decreased hypothalamic activity in sufferers of PTSD and complete shutdown of hypothalamic activity in complex trauma sufferers (Lanius et al., 2010). The hypothalamic shutdown would explain why traditional talking therapies or cognitive approaches, which rely on change through rational, top-down processing, cannot tackle the trauma memories that are held in the body.

INTERVENTIONS AND EVALUATION

This chapter highlights how complex the work with PTSD and trauma-related problems is. This stands in the face of currently promoted 'so-called' effectiveness- and cost-driven fast fixes for PTSD, which if applied incorrectly could do more damage than good. Due to the underlying psycho-neurobiological nature of PTSD, the resulting arousal and survival responses driven by the structures of the so-called 'emotional motor system' of the brain, such as the PAG, and the increased sensitivity to threat, specific therapeutic factors must be adhered to in order to ensure safe and successful PTSD assessment and therapy.

THERAPEUTIC SKILLS

Successful assessment and therapy for PTSD can only take place under conditions that feel safe, as anything else will immediately retrigger uncomfortable autonomic arousal reactions and survival-based coping responses (not usually immediately apparent to the therapist), which maintain or even increase PTSD severity and block the possibility of processing and integrating the traumatic content held in fragmented, incomplete, implicit memories. Safety in this context will be determined both by factors in the therapeutic environment and by factors relating to the therapist and the therapeutic relationship.

In order to determine factors in the therapeutic environment, each client's particular needs have to be understood. For example, a PTSD client who survived torture may not feel very safe in a small therapy room without a window, in which the door is shut; or a PTSD client who has experienced medical trauma may not feel very safe being assessed and treated in a hospital setting or rooms that have a sterile medical feel to them. It is important that careful planning goes into the environment in which trauma assessment and therapy are offered, that the needs of individual PTSD clients are considered and that adverse client reactions are validated as indicators of something feeling unsafe that may need to be changed, rather than being dismissed as a client's unreasonable 'acting-out' behaviour. It is advised that once assessment is completed and a PTSD diagnosis has been confirmed that therapy is offered promptly rather than a client being put on another waiting list. Trust has often been violated as part of clients' traumatic experiences and once they have found the courage to reach out for professional help it is advised that they should be assessed and treated by the same therapist, therefore continuity of care is a fundamental factor to consider.

Another factor determining safety relates to session length and pacing. Due to the high levels of autonomic arousal in PTSD, clients often require considerable time before their autonomic nervous system feels calm enough to engage safely in any assessment or therapeutic work. PTSD clients frequently report that the traditional 50- to 60-minute session time framework doesn't work for them, as it does not give them enough time to safely open up, process and then safely close and contain some of the painful content they are bringing to therapy. It is important that session length is individually tailored to each client's needs (rather than the therapist's or service's convenience) in order for therapy to have a positive therapeutic effect and not to re-traumatize.

Lastly, therapists must also be aware of helping each of their clients during assessment and therapy to stay within their individual 'window of tolerance' (Ogden and Minton, 2000), which describes the level of autonomic and emotional arousal that is most effective for the creation of wellbeing and good functioning. This requires significant therapist skill, because of PTSD clients' tendency to experience too much arousal (hyperarousal) or too little (hypoarousal) or to swing erratically between the two.

THERAPEUTIC APPROACHES

Since 2005, national guidelines developed by the National Institute for Health and Care Excellence (NICE) have existed in Britain for the care and treatment of people suffering from PTSD. These recommend that people at risk should be screened one month after a traumatic event and that trauma-focused psychological therapy is offered to all with PTSD in preference to drug treatments, which should not be the routine first-line approach. All clients suffering from single-event PTSD should be offered a course of 8–12 sessions initially (longer sessions of at least 90 minutes are recommended when the trauma is discussed) of either TF-CBT or EMDR on an individual outpatient basis regardless of the time that has elapsed since the trauma. TF-CBT (Friedman et al., 2007) and EMDR (Shapiro, 1989, 2001) are the only two therapies currently shown as effective in randomized controlled trials (RCTs) to specifically address PTSD.

If several problems need to be addressed, particularly after multiple traumas, traumatic bereavement or chronic disability resulting from the trauma, or if significant comorbid disorders or social problems are present, the duration of treatment should be extended beyond the recommended 12 sessions. For PTSD sufferers who find disclosure of their trauma overwhelming or difficult, healthcare professionals are recommended to devote time to establishing a trusting relationship and emotional stabilization before addressing the trauma.

It moves beyond the scope of this chapter to give a detailed outline of the elements entailed in TF-CBT and EMDR. Both forms of therapy aim to reconnect the client with traumatic material which has been so distressing that the client's system has been unable to integrate it and had to shut it out, resulting in fragmented and incomplete memory consolidation. TF-CBT utilizes a collaborative approach with clients, which includes an element of psycho-education about common reactions to trauma, and a rationale for the interventions. Additionally, TF-CBT includes one or more of the following groups of treatment

techniques: exposure, cognitive therapy and stress management. When clients are deemed ready to reconnect with the traumatic material, either imaginal or *in vivo* exposure to the traumatic event(s) or the most distressing aspects of it is used. Negative thoughts, beliefs and assumptions in relation to the trauma and the client's PTSD responses are noted, and therapist and client aim to work together to modify and restructure these during the course of treatment. EMDR employs an eight-stage protocol using an information processing approach which is aligned with the neurobiological processes related to PTSD and allows for top-down and bottom-up processing, enabling processing of trauma-related body memories. Several EMDR treatment protocols are available (Luber, 2009) that can be utilized to work with more complex PTSD presentations.

Whatever the treatment approach, it does require considerable sensitivity, pacing and clinical skill on behalf of the therapist to help a PTSD client reconnect with the traumatic material safely. Such reconnection is achieved through the client's internal feelings of safety in the here-and-now of the therapeutic relationship. For some single-event PTSD clients, it is relatively easy to experience safety in their relationship with the therapist; however, for those who have experienced sudden traumatic loss or experienced multiple traumatic events, and also for C-PTSD clients, this can be very difficult to achieve. In both TF-CBT and EMDR, a client can be re-traumatized if the above described conditions for safety are not met during treatment, which is usually recognized by either a worsening in PTSD symptoms and failure to progress or the client's premature termination of therapy.

Despite the existence of several other models of trauma therapy, according to NICE guidelines (NICE, 2005), PTSD sufferers should be informed that there is as yet no convincing evidence for a clinically important effect of any other treatments for PTSD. While scientific research and examination of therapies for their effectiveness in the treatment of PTSD should be welcomed, current emphasis on RCTs as the only perceived gold standard for an evidence base makes it very difficult for other newer and potentially also effective psychotherapies to be established and validated. Further, measuring therapies' effectiveness with single-event PTSD is misleading, because in clinical practice it is rarely found that clients suffer from a single-event trauma only. Frequently, although referred as a result of having experienced a single-event trauma, for example an accident, a much more multifaceted and complex trauma picture emerges in the course of therapy.

In light of the actual complexity of PTSD-related trauma work, Herbert (2006) suggested in her therapeutic spectrum for trauma and positive growth therapy (Herbert, 2002, revised 2017) that rather than measuring individual therapeutic modalities with each other for comparative effectiveness, it could be far more useful to design a phase-oriented model which incorporated different therapeutic factors, based on current psycho-neurobiological understanding of trauma and PTSD, which should be part of all effective trauma therapies. These factors need to be tailored to each PTSD client's individual needs and requirements, depending on the complexity of their traumatic experiences and PTSD. Such a model moves away from the assumption that any singular modality can serve all PTSD clients and allows for a more holistic and integrative approach to the treatment of trauma, which for many clients provides the stepping stone towards recovery and positive growth.

REFERENCES

American Psychiatric Association (1980, 2000, 2013, 2016). *Diagnostic and Statistical Manual of Mental Disorders* (DSM-III, DSM-IV-TR, DSM-V, DSM-V update). Washington, DC: American Psychiatric Association.

Anders, S.L., Frazier, P. and Frankfurt, S. (2011). Variations in Criterion A and PTSD rates in a community sample of women. *Journal of Anxiety Disorders*, 25(2), 176–184.

Brewin, C.R., Lanius, R.A., Novac, A., Schnyder, U. and Galea, S. (2009). Reformulating PTSD for *DSM-V*: life after Criterion A. *Journal of Traumatic Stress*, 22(5), 366–373.

Dunn, N.J., Yanasak, E., Schilaci, J., Simotas, S., Rehm, L., Souchek, J., et al. (2004). Personality disorders in veterans with posttraumatic stress disorder and depression. *Journal of Traumatic Stress*, 17, 75–82.

Friedman, M.J. (2014). Literature on DSM-V and ICD-11. *PTSD Research Quarterly*, 25(2), 1–10.

Friedman, M.J., Resick, P.A. and Keane, T.M. (2007). PTSD: Twenty-five years of progress and challenges. In M.J. Friedman, T.M. Keane and P.A. Resick (eds), *Handbook of PTSD, Science and Practice*. New York: Guilford Press.

Herbert, C. (2002). A CBT-based therapeutic alternative to working with complex client problems. *European Journal of Psychotherapy, Counselling and Health*, 5(2), 135–144.

Herbert, C. (2006). Healing from complex trauma: an integrated 3-systems' approach. In J. Corrigal, H. Payne and H. Wilkinson (eds), *About a Body: Working with the Embodied Mind in Psychotherapy*. London: Taylor and Francis.

Herbert, C. (2017). *Understanding Your Reactions to Trauma: A Guide for Survivors of Trauma and Their Families* (3rd ed.). Oxford: Merkaba Publications.

Keane, T.M., Brief, D.J., Pratt, E.M. and Miller, M.W. (2007). Assessment of PTSD and its comorbidity in adults. In M.J. Friedman, T.M. Keane and P.A. Resick (eds), *Handbook of PTSD, Science and Practice*. New York: Guilford Press.

Lanius, R., Lanius, U., Fisher, J. and Ogden, P. (2006). Psychological trauma and the brain: toward a neurobiological treatment model. In P. Ogden, K. Minton and C. Pain (eds), *Trauma and the Body*. New York: W.W. Norton.

Lanius, R.A., Vermetten, E., Loewenstein, R.J., Brand, B., Schmahl, C., Bremner, J.D. and Spiegel, D. (2010). Emotion modulation in PTSD: clinical and neurobiological evidence for a dissociative subtype. *American Journal of Psychiatry*, 167(6), 640–647.

Levin, A.P., Kleinman, S.B. and Adler, J.S. (2014). DSM-5 and posttraumatic stress disorder. *The Journal of the American Academy of Psychiatry and the Law*, 42, 146–158.

Luber, M. (ed.) (2009). *Eye Movement Desensitization and Reprocessing (EMDR) Scripted Protocols: Basic and Special Situations*. New York: Springer.

NICE (2005). *Post-Traumatic Stress Disorder (PTSD): The Management of PTSD in Adults and Children in Primary and Secondary Care*. National Clinical Practice Guideline 26. London: National Collaborating Centre for Mental Health, commissioned by the National Institute for Health and Clinical Excellence (NICE), The Royal College of Psychiatrists and The British Psychological Society.

Ogden, P. and Minton, K. (2000). Sensorimotor psychotherapy: one method for processing traumatic memory. *Traumatology*, 6, 1–20.

Shapiro, F. (1989). Eye movement desensitization: a new treatment for post-traumatic stress disorder. *Journal of Behavior Therapy and Experimental Psychiatry*, 20, 211–217.

Shapiro, F. (2001). *Eye Movement Desensitization and Reprocessing: Basic Principles, Protocols and Procedures* (2nd ed.). New York: Guilford Press.

World Health Organization (1993). *The ICD-10 Classification of Mental and Behavioural Disorders: Diagnostic Research Criteria*. Geneva: World Health Organization.

Zoellner, L.A., Rothbaum, B.O. and Feeny, N.C. (2011). PTSD not an anxiety disorder? DSM committee proposal turns back the hands of time. *Depression and Anxiety*, 28, 853–856.

RECOMMENDED READING

1. Friedman, M.J., Keane, T.M. and Resick, P.A. (eds) (2014). *Handbook of PTSD, Science and Practice*. New York: Guilford Press.

Probably the most comprehensive reference book on PTSD for those wishing to understand in depth the diagnostic, conceptual and treatment issues involved.

2. Schwarz, L., Corrigan, F., Hull, A. and Raju, R. (2016). *Comprehensive Resource Model: Effective Healing Techniques for Complex PTSD*. New York: Routledge.

Invaluable reference book presenting a clinically tested treatment model for complex PTSD, thoroughly underpinned by latest neuroscientific research.

3. Herbert, C. and Wetmore, A. (2017). *Overcoming Traumatic Stress: A Self-Help Guide Using Cognitive Behavioural Techniques*. London: Little Brown Books.

Self-help guide and workbook on PTSD, filled with practical strategies and techniques derived from clinical practice.

6.16   SEXUAL VIOLENCE: RAPE AND SEXUAL ASSAULT

BERNIE RYAN

OVERVIEW AND KEY POINTS

Sexual violence encompasses any kind of sexual violation on a person and is a worldwide problem. This chapter will focus on rape and sexual assault, although it is important that the therapist takes into account the client's own classification and experience of sexual violence.

- There are many people who are attempting to recover from the psychological impact of such a traumatic event. Some seek help in the early aftermath while others do not seek support until many years after the assault. Some may never access support.

- Therapists will encounter clients where sexual violence is the primary presentation or where sexual violence surfaces as part of the therapeutic process.

- It is important that the therapist does not make assumptions about a client's experience of sexual violence and is aware of key issues when it presents.

Therapists need to understand what sexual violence is, the potential psychological response and the context in which therapy may be offered.

DEFINITION

Defining the status of someone who has experienced sexual violence is problematic in that clients may not identify with the following terms 'victim' or 'survivor'. A therapist can determine what name the client prefers to use and can avoid the term 'victim' or 'survivor' in the therapy room. For the purposes of this chapter, the terms will be used interchangeably depending on context but is not intended to assume as status for all.

Sexual violence may be defined as:

Any sexual act, attempt to obtain a sexual act, unwanted sexual comments or advances, or acts to traffic, or otherwise directed, against a person's sexuality using coercion, by any person regardless of their relationship to the victim, in any setting, including but not limited to home and work. (World Health Organisation, 2002)

The Sexual Offences Act (2003) outlines the offences of rape:

1. A person (A) commits an offence if ——

   a) He intentionally penetrates the vagina, anus or mouth of another person (B) with his penis,
   b) (B) does not consent to the penetration, and
   c) (A) does not reasonably believe that (B) consents.

2. Whether a belief is reasonable is to be determined having regard to all the circumstances, including any steps A has taken to ascertain whether B consents.

It is important for the therapist to listen to the client's own description and not try to fit the 'story' into the definitions above. Determining whether a crime has taken place or not is a matter for the courts to decide.

AETIOLOGY

Sexual violence or assault can happen to anyone of any age: men, women and children. The extent of the sexual assault is no indication of how distressing the victim may find it, or how violated they feel. Burgess and Holstrom (1974) describe a cognitive, behavioural and emotional response to rape. Often victims feel that their lives are shattered, that they have been invaded and humiliated psychologically and physically.

Understanding an individual's response to sexual violence is complex. Much is dependent on pre-existing coping strategies, the impact of societal attitudes to sexual violence, previous or subsequent exposure to trauma and the client's sense of self. For some, disclosing that a crime has occurred involves a greater degree of exposure than they feel they can cope with initially.

Due to the nature of sexual violence, some of the immediate needs relate to physical and sexual health safety. Further protection from harm is particularly important if the victim knew the perpetrator. Longer-term emotional or therapeutic support becomes important due to the wide range of emotional responses arising from sexual violence. These include (but are not limited to) disbelief, isolation, anxiety, flashbacks, stress, low self-esteem, self-blame and self-harm (Skinner and Taylor, 2004).

Early responses or symptoms can be considered as a normal/understandable response to an abnormal event. For example, the client may describe a feeling of violation, which is common given the intimate nature of rape and therefore can be explained as a normal response. These feelings can become more problematic where they are prolonged and interfere with usual daily living activities. Some victims (not all) may develop long-standing symptoms and possibly post-traumatic stress disorder (PTSD) (Bisson and Andrew, 2007). Some appear to recover quickly only for the psychological trauma to resurface following another significant event. Others suffer immediately after the assault and require support and therapy at an early stage.

While it is acknowledged that sexual violence is under-reported and people do not seek out help, ultimately few are ever offered crucial support. Historically, services have been developed to address the issue of violence against women and girls, and while females are by far the largest group that experience sexual violence, under-reporting in men is significant. Lisak (1994) considers the psychological impact on men and identified the following issues – anger, fear, helplessness, isolation, problems surrounding sexuality, self-blame and shame, among others. Males might be reluctant to involve the police or to access support due to feelings of shame, or the perception that they are expected to be physically and emotionally resilient.

Recovery is an individual journey and can be influenced either positively or negatively by the response of professionals and agencies from which the client seeks help. This is dependent on the therapist and agency understanding the misconceptions around sexual violence, the impact that societal views may have on the client, the psychological impact of sexual violence and the provision of therapeutic interventions in the context of the criminal justice process.

The media, culture and social context all have an impact on an individual's decision either to tell someone or make a report to the police. It follows that the therapist will be influenced by these aspects and may harbour some stereotypes in relation to sexual violence.

Specialist sexual violence counselling services exist to provide specific therapeutic interventions to address the trauma experienced by victims of sexual violence, challenge the client's own misconceptions and stereotypes about rape and support recovery and provide therapeutic interventions which comply with the pre-trial therapy guidance (Crown Prosecution Service, 2011). Therapists will come across sexual abuse/assault in the context of generic therapeutic services.

ASSESSMENT

As discussed, the psychological impact of sexual violence is complex and an individual's experience is based on a wide variety of predisposing factors. It follows that the psychological impact will vary from individual to individual, making a 'one-size-fits-all' response not only inappropriate, but also potentially more harmful.

Due to the potential for reporting to the police at different stages of the process (e.g., either at an early stage or many years later, after therapy), it is often provided in the context of a criminal investigation, which may lead to a criminal prosecution and trial. Consideration should be given to the implications this may have not only on the therapeutic process, but also on the therapist and the therapeutic organisation.

The therapist must make an assessment not only for the client's suitability for treatment, but also to establish other factors, such as safety and if the therapy is pre-trial (i.e., before a court case). In some circumstances this may be difficult to determine, given that the client may not wish to seek justice for the crime committed, but change their mind in years to come. Additionally, the therapist must determine that the organisation/therapist has the requisite skills to provide a safe therapeutic relationship for the client.

Assessment should also take into account the very intimate nature of sexual violence and issues which may arise. Trust, hypervigilance and self-judgement may all be affected. The therapist should have an understanding of mental health issues, such as moderate anxiety, depression and trauma. Therapists should also understand the basic principles of safeguarding children and vulnerable adults, and to manage the lower levels of client risk to self and others.

Family relationships and dynamics are important and may be protective factors that help the client to be understood in their world outside the therapy room. Often sexual violence can be stigmatised and misconceptions can damage close relationships for the person reporting, so usually supportive factors do not always work in these circumstances. Some specialist services offer support and therapy for significant others. It is worth seeking out such services if necessary.

The nature of sexual violence dictates that power and control is removed from the victim at the time of the assault. Assessment should factor this into discussions with the client, in particular ensuring that the client begins to feel empowered and able to make informed choices for themselves. To enable informed choices to be made, the therapist should be knowledgeable and honest about what type of therapies might be suitable and how they can be employed in a pre-trial period, including the implications for disclosure.

FORMULATION

Formulation will assist the therapist to determine what the priorities are for the client. It may be management of the symptoms associated with the aftermath of sexual violence or understanding the impact of the violence on themselves, their sense of the world and their relationships. In cases of PTSD, the priority may be undertaking therapy to improve the wellbeing of the client.

There are a number of practical interventions that may be helpful to the client, such as:

- providing practical care and support, which responds to their concerns, but does not intrude on the client's autonomy,
- grounding and relaxation techniques to manage potential flashbacks and intrusive thoughts, and
- mindfulness.

There is no evidence to suggest that one therapeutic approach is more effective than another for victims of sexual violence. However, some approaches are more popular in managing the trauma response to sexual violence or those experiencing PTSD as a result of the sexual violence, for instance trauma-focused therapy and Eye Movement Desensitisation and Reprocessing (EMDR).

Consideration about the current or potential future legal status of the case should be considered. Why is this so important? Given the previous discussions regarding empowerment, it would be unfortunate if the therapy was deemed prejudicial should the client make a report in the future and therefore negate their choice and be unable to proceed.

It is perfectly acceptable to provide therapeutic treatment pre-trial, taking into account the Crown Prosecution Service's (CPS) *Provision of Therapy to Vulnerable or Intimidated Witnesses prior to Criminal Trial: Practical Guidance* (2011). It should be noted that these are only guidelines and the best treatment for the client and their presenting issues should take precedence. Decisions about the progress of therapy should be effectively communicated with the criminal justice professionals to avoid any adverse impact on the client's ability to provide evidence to the court.

The Crown Prosecution Service (2011) guidance suggests that the least problematic aspect of therapy will focus on improving self-esteem and self-confidence, often using cognitive-behavioural techniques. Other issues, which might be addressed, include:

- the reduction of distress about the impending legal proceedings, and
- the treatment of associated emotional and behavioural disturbance that does not require the rehearsal of abusive events.

Therefore, the case formulation should focus on the presenting factors, which would usually be the psychological responses of sexual violence rather than the story itself.

The CPS guidance (CPS, 2011) recognises that maintaining trust is central to the provision of therapy. As such, it will usually only be appropriate to breach confidentiality in compliance with a court order. To avoid confusion, and ensure clarity between the therapist and client, local protocols can be established between counselling organisations and the CPS.

Other factors to consider are any predisposing life events or stressors, such as the extent of previous violence/trauma. If the client has experienced previous abuse, then other factors are to be considered:

- What is the length of time since the assault?
- What were the responses of others?
- What are the core beliefs of the client?
- What did they tell themselves about the sexual violence?

INTERVENTION

Mary presented as a 17-year-old student reporting sexual abuse by a neighbour from the age of 10 to 15. Mary had found it difficult to tell anyone what was going on. Her father had recently been diagnosed with a life-threatening illness and there was a lot of stress at home.

Mary presented to a specialist sexual violence counselling service, having made a report to the police and the police making a recommendation that Mary seek support.

At assessment it was noted that the case would be going to trial but a date had not yet been set. The therapist discussed the provision of therapy, including the limits of confidentiality, any potential safeguarding issues, confidentiality and access to records in the context of the criminal justice system. This was explained with reference to local protocols and the control that Mary would have, should a request be made.

The therapist advised Mary that due to the pending trial that evidential material would not be discussed during the course of therapy. The therapist suggested that the particular circumstances of the abuse were not discussed, such as what happened, where and how. The therapist explained that the focus of the therapy would be how the abuse impacted on everyday living, psychologically and practically. Mary expressed relief that she did not have to retell her 'story' again as she had already given a full statement to the police.

Mary described feeling responsible for everyone else, as the disclosure had had an impact on her relationship with her younger siblings and also her parents' relationships with each other, but also with Mary. Mary described that her mother was feeling guilty for not having protected Mary from the abuse, but her father had feelings of anger towards the perpetrator to the extent that Mary was afraid that he would intervene outside the police case. Mary felt that she was walking on eggshells around her closer family members and felt that they expected her to want to stay in and behave in a particular way.

The therapist discussed the misconceptions about rape and sexual assault and the impact that may have on others' responses. The therapist also explained that Mary's recovery was the primary concern, although her parents and/or siblings may benefit from support to help them manage and understand their own responses and reactions in light of the disclosure.

On the basis of the discussion, Mary agreed to attend six sessions in the first instance. The therapist explained that at the fifth session a joint review would take place to consider progress, but further sessions could be contracted for if required. The contract for therapy was jointly agreed between Mary and the therapist.

Mary dismissed the impact of the assault on herself and preferred to channel her discussion about feelings through her parents and significant others. She had recently begun a new relationship and was unsure if she wished to disclose her abuse to her new partner.

The therapist worked using integrative techniques (Woolfe and Palmer, 2000). Here the therapist brought together different elements to both develop the therapeutic relationship and help provide a problem-solving approach to the work undertaken. Given that the act of sexual violence and the response/impact is a very individual one, this makes an integrative approach appropriate when working with victims of sexual violence. The client is considered as a whole person rather than focusing on solely the presenting issues, and the therapy is tailored to Mary's individual needs and personal circumstances.

In working in this way the therapist was able initially to focus on Mary's reaction and feelings towards the alleged perpetrator, but also on the assault itself.

Questions/comments that presented themselves in the work with Mary included:

- Why me?
- What did I do to make him (the alleged perpetrator) think it was OK to do that?
- Why didn't anyone stop it?
- It's my fault.

These comments/questions often fit the stereotypical misconceptions people have about sexual violence. In order for Mary to deter from self-blame and shame it is important to counterbalance some of these statements with challenge, which helped Mary to reassess and reframe her experience so that she no longer felt responsible and that she focused on the unacceptability of sexual violence in its wider context.

As the case was due to go to trial, the therapist agreed with Mary that the police and CPS be aware of therapy. By advising this at an early stage, then any application for records and subsequent management could be addressed efficiently and with least disruption to the therapeutic process.

The development of the therapeutic alliance is key to re-establishing relationships of trust. However, the therapist also must manage any move towards a co-dependent relationship, which such cases are prone to given the intimate nature of the crime and the need to be heard and understood.

As the therapy progressed Mary began to feel empowered and took control of her environment. For example, she decided when she would agree to discuss her thoughts and feeling with her parents, rather than it being the focus of all conversation. She felt better able to discuss her needs in the run up to the trail and her anxieties of potentially meeting the perpetrator again. This was supported by the introduction to an Independent Sexual Violence Adviser (ISVA), whose role is to support victims of crime through the criminal justice process.

Towards the end of the six sessions Mary reported feeling more confident and less anxious about socialising and meeting new people. She had told her new partner of the assault and had been assured of his support. This went against her expectations, which had been influenced by her own expectations of how others would perceive her.

The trial was set for six months' time and Mary felt that she was coping well and had met her goals from therapy. An ending was agreed, with continued support from the ISVA and the understanding that she could re-access therapy at any point in the future.

Mary contacted the therapist at the conclusion of the trial to communicate the outcome that the perpetrator had been convicted. She reported a feeling of relief and the belief that she could progress with her future study plans and move on with her life.

Six months after the court case Mary re-accessed counselling as her relationship had come to an end and she had overwhelming feelings of responsibility towards the perpetrator due to his age at conviction. Additionally, she was experiencing some trauma symptoms directly related to the abuse.

Another 12 sessions were offered and contracted for, in order to explore these feelings using a psychodynamic approach (Jacobs, 2012). This approach helps the client understand and resolve their problems by increasing awareness of their inner world and its influence on relationships with significant others, but also with the perpetrator. Additionally, trauma-focused CBT (Foa et al., 2006) was used to support understanding and management of her anxiety symptoms and reoccurring flashbacks.

EVALUATION

Mary responded well to treatment and recovered significantly. It is not unusual for clients to re-experience symptoms on the approach to the anniversary of events and Mary contacted the therapist 12 months after the court case, which in some cases can be a re-experiencing of the feelings associated with the abuse/assault. The therapist talked through some of the coping strategies discussed during the course of therapy and Mary was able to effectively manage these feelings/symptoms without attending therapy sessions, although this was an option if Mary felt that was what she needed.

It is very difficult to say in such cases if recovery is ever complete. The evidence in Mary's case is that she is now employed full-time in a professional role. She and her parents have resolved the feelings of blame and shame which impacted on them all at some point post-disclosure and she feels that she is able to provide challenge and support to her peers around the issues of sexual violence.

Life events may trigger another response. This often occurs during childbirth or the end or start of an intimate relationship, which is why an open-access approach for therapy is important.

REFERENCES

Bisson, J. and Andrew, M. (2007). *Psychological Treatments for Post Traumatic Stress Disorder*. Chichester: Wiley.

Burgess, A.W. and Holmstrom, L.L. (1974). Rape trauma syndrome. *American Journal of Psychiatry*, 131(9): 981–986.

Crown Prosecution Service (2011). *Provision of Therapy to Vulnerable or Intimidated Witnesses prior to Criminal Trial: Practice Guidance*. London: CPS. (www.cps.gov.uk/publications/prosecution/pretrialadult.html).

Foa, E.B., Zoellner, L.A. et al. (2006). An evaluation of three brief programs for facilitating recovery after assault. *Journal of Traumatic Stress*, 19(1): 29–43.

Jacobs, M. (2012). *The Presenting Past: The Core of Psychodynamic Counselling and Therapy: The Core of Psychodynamic Counselling and Therapy*. London: Open University Press.

Lisak, D. (1994). The psychological impact of sexual abuse: content analysis of interviews with male survivors. *Journal of Traumatic Stress*, 7: 525–548.

Sexual Offences Act (2003). *Sexual Offences Act*. London: HMSO. (www.legislation.gov.uk/ukpga/2003/42/contents).

Skinner, T. and Taylor, H. (2004). *Providing Counselling, Support and Information to Survivors of Rape: An Evaluation of the 'STAR' Young Persons' Project*. Home Office Online Report 51/04. London: Home Office.

Woolfe, R. and Palmer, S. (2000). *Integrative and Eclectic Counselling and Psychotherapy*. London: Sage.

World Health Organisation (2002). *World Report on Violence and Health*. Geneva: WHO.

RECOMMENDED READING

1. Hedge, B. (2002). The impact of sexual violence on health care workers. In J. Petrak and B. Hedge (Eds.), *The Trauma of Sexual Assault: Treatment, Prevention and Practice*. Chichester: Wiley.

The potential impact of this work on the therapist cannot be underestimated. Hedge discusses the potential signs which may indicate that the worker is experiencing secondary traumatisation (Vicarious trauma).

2. Jenkins, P. (2013). Pre trial therapy. *Therapy Today*, 24(4): 14–17.

Jenkins outlines the issues relating to pre-trial therapy and the reforms needed to ensure witnesses and victims of crime have access to expert pre-trial therapy.

3. Ryan, B. (2013). The work of a sexual assault referral centre. In J. Pritchard (Ed.), *Good Practice Guide in Promoting Recovery and Healing for Abused Adults*. London: Jessica Kingsley Publishers.

Ryan discusses the services available to victims who experience acute sexual violence, including the role of the ISVA, which could support the therapeutic relationship and provide vital support to the victim during the criminal justice process.

6.17 THE PSYCHOSES

BRIAN MARTINDALE

OVERVIEW AND KEY POINTS

The psychoses are a spectrum of disorders mostly caused by the interaction of overwhelming stresses in a vulnerable person. The distinguishing and defining features are an altered relationship to reality. In recent years there has been a questioning of narrow diagnostic concepts. This chapter suggests:

- there is a lessening of reductionist concepts of the aetiology of psychosis
- there is a questioning of the too-exclusive focus on medication as treatment
- a broad range of psychological and social approaches are developing
- the concept of early intervention is becoming widespread.

DEFINITIONS

For this chapter, I define psychoses as disturbances in which aspects of reality testing have been lost, thereby distinguishing psychoses from non-psychotic conditions where people suffer but *remain in connection* with the realities of their lives. The phenomena that most usually lead to a diagnosis of psychosis are the presence of a combination of delusions, hallucinations and thought disorder. In non-organic psychoses the hallucinations are usually auditory, though any sensory modality may be involved.

The definitions of the broader concepts of psychosis and narrower concepts such as schizophrenia and bipolar disorder (with psychotic features) continue to shift according to culture, context and research. Contemporary debate focuses on whether classifications should be based on categories or dimensions or on putative causes.

The epidemiological work of Van Os et al. (2009) has shown the considerable incidence of 'psychotic' phenomena in the general public and that the categorisation into distinct sub-disorders has little scientific validity (Van Os, 2010). Some contemporary commentators are concerned that classifying a disorder as schizophrenia has led to an erroneous association with an inevitable lifelong brain disease (Van Os, 2016), fuelling therapeutic nihilism.

Manic-depressive states (more commonly called bipolar disorders), extend from *non-psychotic* affective states of mind to *psychotic* states, where voice hearing and delusional beliefs about oneself or one's environment are seemingly driven by and are *congruent with* the positive or negative mood, whereas in the schizophrenias mood is not necessarily congruent with the psychotic phenomena.

AETIOLOGY

THE STRESS-VULNERABILITY MODEL

Developments within the fields of traumatology, cognitive psychology, depth psychologies, neuropsychology, genetics, neurochemistry and neuroimaging fields have contributed to the utility of the *stress-vulnerability* aetiological model of the psychoses (Zubin and Spring, 1977); if this is used in a sophisticated way, it helps avoid reductionist ideologies and explanations. It is a most useful framework for formulating an individualised understanding of aetiology and then developing a personalised therapeutic approach to psychoses.

The stress-vulnerability model implies that, as a result of a potential mixture of constitutional givens, negative developmental and earlier traumatic experiences, a person is vulnerable to psychosis under particular stresses that connect with the earlier difficulties. For example, psychosis often has its onset at a time when a young person is struggling to manage the stress of individuating from their family because a host of earlier developmental issues necessary for this phase have not been mastered.

ORGANIC CAUSES

Street substances are common precipitants of psychosis, but people often also use these to try to dampen down their psychotic experiences. Uncommonly, an organic condition is the primary cause of psychosis, such as hormonal disturbances or certain medications such as steroids. Other brain disorders, including dementias, commonly lead to psychotic phenomena. These conditions are classified separately according to the primary aetiological agent or disorder, for example steroid-induced psychosis, myxoedema psychosis or Alzheimer's disease, and will not be further considered here.

ASSESSMENT

THE PHENOMENOLOGY OF PSYCHOSIS

The phenomena are the consequence of the mind, for whatever reason, being unable to synthesise or integrate the many realities needed to function in life. The phenomena can be primary manifestations of disintegration or secondary attempts to reconstitute the mind, creating a new 'false' reality to avoid a too painful one. A simple example would be the primary psychotic experience of falling apart of the self (akin to annihilation), say, after a belittling rejection, followed by a secondary grandiose delusional false restitutive solution to the annihilation and rejection, such as believing oneself to be the king.

HALLUCINATIONS

Hallucinations in various perceptual modalities (most commonly auditory) are frequent experiences in psychosis. These vary from vague sounds to hearing the clear speech of other persons in external space. Some experience a number of voices. Sometimes the voices are pleasant or soothing or emotionally neutral, but more often they are unpleasant and denigratory and are talking about the person or to the person, sometimes giving commands. They are experienced as real without an 'as if' quality.

DELUSIONS

Delusional beliefs are fixed beliefs that have a minimal basis in objective reality and are out of keeping with cultural beliefs. More bizarre delusions are easy to identify, but some are difficult to differentiate from non-psychotic phenomena, especially if other features of psychosis are not elicited: for example, the person who lives in a violent area and believes that people are trying to break into their house. The fact that *the clinician* can see the symbolic significance or personal origins of the delusion does not necessarily mean that it is not a delusion.

LOSS OF SELF/OTHER BOUNDARIES

A common phenomenon is the loss of normal boundaries between self and others. This usually refers to the mind of the person and others, but can apply to the body as well. The individual experiencing psychosis may feel that they are able to read other people's minds or that others can read their own mind, and this can be very distressing. Likewise, there can be the belief that others are putting ideas into one's mind.

THOUGHT DISORDER

Thoughts can be disordered in a number of ways; thoughts can feel blocked; sentences are not strung together with normal syntax; non-existent words (neologisms) may be used. Especially in affective disorders, the flow of words is more dictated by linkages of sound or similarity than by coherence of a theme in conversation.

AFFECTIVE PSYCHOSES

In bipolar psychoses (also called manic-depressive psychoses), the affect of hallucinatory and other delusional experiences is *in keeping* with their content. For example, the person with a depressive psychosis may experience voices telling them they don't deserve to live or to have positive experiences, whereas the euphoric patient may experience themselves as having physical and sexual energy and be told they have special powers or a sense of entitlement.

DENIAL AND RATIONALISATION

Unconscious denial and rationalisation are the most common phenomena in psychosis and are commonly expressed in clinical interviews. The latter are, therefore, only one tool in ascertaining the diagnosis. Diagnostic evidence may need to be gathered from other sources, such as family, friends or others who are well known to the patient.

'NEGATIVE' SYMPTOMS

These are quieter but lead to major problems in facing life. They are not specific to the psychoses but may be prominent, manifesting as a lack of drive and motivation, a flatness of emotions, apathy, a lack of pleasure and sometimes as a slowing of thought and communications.

PSYCHOTIC AND NON-PSYCHOTIC FUNCTIONING

A person with a psychosis will have aspects of mental functioning which are completely normal and reality-oriented alongside the psychosis. Insight will vary greatly from person to person and from time to time. In some patients there may be quite a struggle going on between the reality-oriented functioning of the patient who 'knows' (has some insight) that they have a psychotic part and the psychotic who tries to convince the patient that the psychotic phenomenon is reality.

FORMULATION

It is important in helping persons with psychosis to develop a formulation that best makes sense of that person and their psychosis and of their interaction with others, including therapists. The stress-vulnerability model (Johnstone and Dallos, 2013) is a useful framework for such formulations. They will need to be modified with increasing understanding of the patient and may well benefit from information collected from a number of sources, bearing in mind that the person's psychotic state may continue to change as well as the person disguising or denying the reality of their current difficult circumstances and painful aspects of their past. The formulation aids the making of realistic shorter- and longer-term interventions and the development of an effective individualised relapse prevention plan.

SIMPLE EXAMPLE OF A FORMULATION

Harry believes that negative information about him is being spread on the national news and that he is being influenced by a microchip implanted behind his eye during an X-ray years ago. He rarely reveals these beliefs, fearing he would be labelled 'mad'. He constantly disengages from services, believing (and convincing others) that he would have no trouble going to college, finding somewhere nice to live and settling down to a family life. In reality, he has declined over the years and can barely manage basic care of himself.

Harry's father had always had great expectations of him, hoping Harry would make up for his own resentments at the little help he had had himself as a child and expecting Harry to fulfil his own dreams. Father was always very abusive of Harry when he did not meet these expectations. Harry was reasonably competent as a wrestler and father would tell us how famous and wealthy Harry would now be if he had followed this career. Mother feared father and was unable to stand up for her son's actual capacities and against father's abuse of Harry; likewise, Harry could not oppose father without being rejected.

It was formulated that as a result Harry had little capacity to develop a sense of realistic self-identity in his formative years and attend to himself realistically. He continues to be mentally governed and driven by concrete representations of two aspects of father: his unrealistic (delusional) expectations or the condemning and publicly shaming authority figures (the national news and staff who would call him mad if he was in trouble). He therefore cannot readily use the help of the mental health services because of the denial that protects him from being open with them, as he believes this would only lead to repetition of the condemnation if he revealed his struggles or staff would be ineffective, as was his experience of his mother.

INTERVENTIONS

MEDICATION

In the United Kingdom there continues to be a dominance of the biological approach to psychoses, with pharmacological interventions forming the mainstay of treatment. Medications are certainly effective for many, but for substantial numbers the effects are limited and side effects remain very problematic (Lieberman et al., 2005) and many patients soon stop taking medication. Medications called neuroleptics may be directed at the psychotic symptoms, or different medications may be used for secondary phenomena such as sleep disturbance, anxiety or depression. It should be noted that the so-called anti-psychotic medications are not specific for psychosis in the way that an antibiotic is for bacteria.

For patients who are on medication and have had a single episode of psychosis and have full symptomatic recovery, it can be a difficult decision how long to continue anti-psychotic medication. Consideration of the circumstances of the onset of psychosis will help evaluate whether there is now evidence that in similar circumstances they would be or have been able to manage better. Withdrawal of medication should always be very slow and in the context of a trusting personal and/or professional relationship that will pick up early signs of relapse before insight is lost.

There is also increasing worrying evidence that medication may cause some reduction in brain volume

(Fusar-Poli et al., 2013) and important preliminary research indicating that patients withdrawn from medication with neuroleptics have better outcomes in the longer term (Wunderink et al., 2013).

Patients with a bipolar psychotic disorder can benefit (as well as be harmed) from the same kind of medications as used in other psychoses. In addition, there are medications that have mood-stabilising qualities that for many will reduce the frequency and severity of either pole of the disorder.

Other approaches to people with psychosis are becoming incorporated in National Institute for Health and Care Excellence (NICE) guidelines (NICE, 2014). Besides medications, supportive therapies, cognitive-behavioural therapy (CBT) and family interventions are those that have been most evaluated in randomised controlled trials and there has also been a resurgence of the recovery movement.

World Health Organisation studies consistently demonstrate better outcomes where neuroleptics were little used. It is important to know of the cohort studies from Alanen (1997) and Seikkula et al. (2006), both from Finland. The latter reports on 'Open Dialogue', a specific family-oriented approach offering immediate and, where necessary, protracted engagement, usually in the patient's home. Their research found that only 30% with a schizophrenic-like psychosis needed anti-psychotic medication in the course of five years, and recovery outcomes were far superior to a traditional approach in which neuroleptics were central to treatment. Some question the ethics of randomised controlled trials (RCTs) as they eliminate the different interventions needed between one individual and another.

For example, a psychosis occurring in the context of a young person unable to separate from his family when he starts at college may first benefit from a family intervention, move on to a therapeutic milieu to allow for better capacities to form peer relationships, and later still use an individual therapy to attend to remaining issues related to his sensitive sense of self. Medication may be needed at times to support the psychological help. This approach requires the careful development and retention of staff so that they have a range of skills relevant to patients' needs – in contrast to an all-too-common situation where the patient has to fit the limited service.

COORDINATION OF CARE AND THERAPEUTIC RELATIONSHIPS

In the British National Health Service, patients should have a care coordinator whose task is to form a reliable, durable and trusting relationship with the patient, and ideally also with his family and friends.

Some general principles are important to bear in mind. Historically, large percentages of patients drop out of services and often then lead very limited, isolated lives. The priority of the team is therefore to develop and sustain sufficient trusting relationships and be the link to more specialist interventions when needed. The establishment of an enduring relationship is much more important than rushing into treatment if the patient is not in imminent danger to themselves or others. Engagement is aided by attending closely to what is most troubling to the patient and the family.

THE SETTING

Quiet respite housing can contribute greatly to recovery for a good percentage of patients (Bola et al., 2009). The general principle here is that in an acute psychotic crisis the patient needs a calm environment and the hectic atmosphere of inpatient wards may be counter-productive for some.

EARLY DETECTION

Many people with psychosis only get help after being psychotic for more than a year or two. Early detection and involvement with quality services reduces suicidality, reduces the secondary psychosocial deterioration stemming from psychosis (loss of relationships, capacity for work, tendency to use substances, involvement in crime, etc.) and improves outcomes.

RELAPSE PREVENTION

It can take a long time for a person to fully recover from a psychosis and a major relapse is a most serious event. The prevention or mitigation of relapse therefore needs considerable attention. Both medication and psychological interventions and combinations can be effective in reducing relapses.

The best chances of success are when there is active cooperation of the patient and those closest to them in the process of recovery. Going back over the sequence of events leading up to previous episodes is very helpful in jointly identifying the stressful factors, the personal warning signs and the factors that either exacerbated or alleviated these. Discussion and education are needed as to what could be more effective in the face of the beginning of new signs of relapse, in removing stress, other psychological techniques and the role of appropriate medication.

COGNITIVE-BEHAVIOURAL THERAPY

Many patients with psychosis will also have problems common to those who do not suffer from psychosis and will benefit from the indications for CBT, such as depression, anxiety, phobias and self-esteem issues, and the same considerations should apply. However, some of these symptoms may relate to their psychotic problems: for example, anxiety about leaving the house could be related to a belief that the government has a hit squad waiting for the patient in the trees behind the nearby park.

CBT has been shown to be useful in residual positive symptoms, such as hallucinations, and to some extent in delusions and in depression, but less useful in those with other negative symptoms. CBT obviously involves engagement with the non-psychotic aspects of a patient's mind to help them reflect and challenge the power of the psychotic experiences. CBT is especially directed at distressing symptoms and disabling social functioning. CBT for psychosis is becoming increasingly sophisticated (Hagen et al., 2011).

LONGER-TERM INTERVENTIONS

In the longer term it is important to assist the person to strengthen their inner capacities and/or to help them develop techniques in dealing with adverse situations and feelings. Here, accurate formulation is essential in identifying the particular vulnerabilities that vary so much from one person to another. For example, for one it could be feelings of attachment that provoked psychosis stemming from *fears* of being let down; for another it could be the opposite, i.e., the actual experiences of separation; for yet another person, psychosis could arise in the face of any potential aggression or name calling or 'failure'. Psychodynamic interventions have a long history in some countries in assisting with developing a more robust sense of self and reducing tendencies to give in to psychotic processes. Here, the formulation may be of immense help. Rosenbaum et al. (2012) have demonstrated evidence of the effectiveness of supportive psychodynamic therapy in a two-year controlled trial.

FAMILY INTERVENTIONS

Family interventions have robust evidence for effectiveness, especially when family circumstances lead to 'high expressed emotion' or 'high EE' (associated with high relapse rates). High EE means either a high frequency of critical comments directed at the patient, a hostile atmosphere or family members spending 'too much time' with the patient. Altering these factors reduces relapse rates. Under-stimulation can be equally undesirable. Nearly all family members will find aspects of living with someone who has psychosis stressful, and NICE (2014) guidelines make extensive recommendations for family interventions.

GROUP INTERVENTIONS

Many patients with psychoses have had poor peer relationships, either preceding the psychosis or as consequence of prolonged psychotic states. Being able to function in groups is a very important part of recovery, opening the doors to many aspects of a richer life. A good number of patients with low self-esteem and poor verbal skills will benefit from simple structured activity groups with people of similar age, doing things they may have little previous experience of, such as playing pool, bicycle rides, bowling, cinema outings, perhaps ending with a low-key meeting in a café or burger bar. Others may become ready for residential therapeutic communities (Gale et al., 2008). Skilled evaluation by a vocational specialist may help people back into college, training or a manageable work environment. Gathering families together in groups and offering education and/or problem-solving techniques can be beneficial and may also reduce the sense of isolation or stigmatisation that many families experience.

SUBSTANCE MISUSE TREATMENT

A significant number of young people with psychosis use substances. It is now well established that: (1) a range of street substances can lead to psychosis; (2) young people will use substances to try to deal with the troubling symptoms of psychosis and often get transient relief; (3) substances can exacerbate pre-existing psychosis. Amphetamines will give rise to a psychosis indistinguishable from non-drug-induced psychosis. Many patients who have used substances will reluctantly come to accept that, unlike their peers, they cannot continue to indulge without putting themselves at severe risk; others may need more specialist help in coming to terms with this and adjusting their way of life. Outcomes are better if such expertise is contained within psychosis services (Copello et al., 2007).

EVALUATION

In recent years the research summarised in this chapter is pointing to the potential effectiveness of a wider range of interventions for people with psychosis than the current too-exclusive focus on medication. There is a major need to create stable mental health systems that allow for such approaches and the development of staff with a wider range of skills and for further real-world research in psychosocial interventions.

REFERENCES

Alanen, Y. (1997) *Schizophrenia: Its Origins and Need-adapted Treatment*. London: Karnac.

Bola, J., Lehtinen, K., Cullberg, J. and Ciompi, L. (2009) Psychosocial treatment, antipsychotic postponement, and low-dose medication: a review of the literature. *Psychosis*, 1(1): 4–18.

Copello, A., Graham, H., Mueser, K. and Birchwood, M. (2007) *Substance Misuse in Psychosis*. Chichester: Wiley.

Fusar-Poli, P., Smieskova, R., Kempton, M.J., Ho, B.C., Andreasen, N.C. and Borgwardt, S. (2013) Progressive brain changes in schizophrenia related to antipsychotic treatment? A meta-analysis of longitudinal MRI studies. *Neuroscience and Biobehavioral Review*, 37(8): 1680–1691.

Gale, J., Realpe, A. and Pedriali, E. (2008) *Therapeutic Communities for Psychosis: Philosophy, History and Clinical Practice*. London: Routledge.

Hagen, R., Turkington, D., Berge, T. and Gråwe, R.W. (2011) *CBT for Psychosis: A Symptom-based Approach*. London and New York: Routledge.

Johnstone, L. and Dallos, R. (2013) *Formulation in Psychology and Psychotherapy* (2nd ed.). Hove and New York: Routledge.

Lieberman, J.A., Stroup, T.S., McEvoy, J.P., Swartz, M.S., Rosenheck, R.A., Perkins, D.O., Keefe, R.S.E., Davis, S.M., Davis, C.E., Lebowitz, B.D., Severe, J. and Hsiao, J.K. (2005) Effectiveness of antipsychotic drugs in patients with chronic schizophrenia. *New England Journal of Medicine*, 353: 1209–1223.

NICE (2014) *Psychosis and Schizophrenia in Adults: Prevention and Management*. Clinical Guidelines 178. London: NICE. (www.nice.org.uk).

Rosenbaum, B., Harder, S., Knudsen, P., Koester, A., Lindhardt, A., Valbak, K. and Winther, G. (2012) Supportive psychodynamic psychotherapy versus treatment as usual for first episode psychosis: two-year outcome. *Psychiatry: Interpersonal and Biological Processes*, 75(4): 331–341.

Seikkula, J., Aaltonen, J., Alakare, B., Haarakangas, K., Keranen, J. and Lehtinen, K. (2006) Five-year experience of first-episode nonaffective psychosis in open-dialogue approach: treatment principles, follow-up outcomes. *Psychotherapy Research*, 16(2): 214–228.

Van Os, J. (2010) Are psychiatric diagnoses of psychosis scientific and useful? The case of schizophrenia. *Journal of Mental Health*, 19(4): 305–317.

Van Os, J. (2016) 'Schizophrenia' does not exist. *British Medical Journal*, 352: i375.

Van Os, J., Linscott, R.J., Myin-Germeys, I., Delespaul, P. and Krabbendam, L. (2009) A systematic review and meta-analysis of the psychosis continuum: evidence for a psychosis proneness–persistence–impairment model of psychotic disorder. *Psychological Medicine*, 39(2): 179–195.

Wunderink, L., Nieboer, R. M., Wiersma, D., Sytema, S., and Nienhuis, F. J. (2013) Recovery in remitted first-episode psychosis at 7 years of follow-up of an early dose reduction/discontinuation or maintenance treatment strategy: long-term follow-up of a 2-year randomized clinical trial. *Journal American Medical Association: Psychiatry*, 70(9): 913–920.

Zubin, J. and Spring, B. (1977) Vulnerability: a new view of schizophrenia. *Journal of Abnormal Psychology*, 86(2): 103–126.

RECOMMENDED READING

1. Alanen, Y., González de Chavez, M., Silver, A.-L. and Martindale, B. (2009) *Psychotherapeutic Approaches to Schizophrenic Psychoses*. London: Routledge.

Takes a historical and multidimensional perspective on interventions for psychosis from different parts of the world and looks to possibilities in the future.

2.   Cooke, A. (Ed.) (2015) *Understanding Psychosis and Schizophrenia*. Leicester: British Psychological Society.

Provides a resource on contemporary psycho social aspects of psychosis and advocates for a fundamental change in services. Many contributions are from service users.

3.   Hagen, R., Turkington, D., Berge, T. and Gråwe, R. (Eds.) (2011) *CBT for Psychosis. A symptom based approach*. London: Routledge

A useful introduction to CBT for psychosis.

6.18   RELATIONSHIP AND SEX PROBLEMS

GAIL EVANS

OVERVIEW AND KEY POINTS

It is useful to read about adult relationships even if you are not intending to be a relationship therapist. All clients (and you yourself) are influenced by close relationships. This chapter considers the following:

- Definitions: What constitutes a couple relationship?
- Aetiology: What makes a good relationship and what goes wrong?
- Assessment: Why clients come for relationship counselling
- Formulation: What approaches could be helpful?
- Resources.

Issues related to practice are considered separately in my chapter in Part VII (Evans – Chapter 7.22, this volume), therefore in contrast to other chapters in this section, I do not include reference to 'intervention' or 'evaluation'.

DEFINITIONS

When I began to write, the attempt to determine clear definitions threatened to stall progress. For example, what is a relationship in this context? A fairly safe starting point is that we are talking about adults. It seems most adults desire to have at least one adult relationship that is primary or 'special' – different from other relationships.

A primary relationship is often referred to as an intimate relationship. What exactly is intimacy? Does this intimacy have to involve sex or some other defining principle, such as emotional closeness or shared home life? Expectations and definitions are affected by gender, orientation, socio-economic environment, education, culture, among many other potential influences.

How many adults are involved? Most people's preconception in this culture is likely to be two individuals and sexual exclusivity as defining an intimate relationship. This is reflected in an (edited) definition of intimacy below.

Communicating openly

Responding with empathy

Negotiating conflicts by accommodating and compromising

Affirming each other's vulnerabilities

Enjoying physical contact

Creating a unique identity… from shared experiences

Respect and support for each other as individuals… by accepting differences

Providing support for each other in a crisis

Contributing to shared goals and responsibilities

Playing together

Remaining monogamous and faithful to each other.

(Mills and Turnbull, 2004)

However, we have *ménage a trois*, *polyamory*, '*open*' marriage/relationship and celibate partnerships in Western culture as well as instances of polygamy, and occasionally polyandry, elsewhere. I cannot deal with these questions here, but invite you to bear them in mind. An issue for therapists is to examine and challenge their own pre-conceptions about what *constitutes* an adult intimate relationship and how it should function; and which clients they feel able to work with.

From within a love relationship it seems unlikely that choices are shaped by wider socio-economic, spiritual, political and technological forces. Yet these do impact on the function, dynamics, aspirations and even necessity of couple relationships as well as on potential availability and choice of partners. In the industrialised world, expectations and the legal status of relationships have changed and continue to evolve, with greater emancipation, economic independence and fertility control available to women, greater tolerance and legal recognition of same-sex relationships, and increased visibility of sexual and gender diversity. Availability of information and open discussion about alternatives to traditional models of couple, family and sexual relationships is modifying expectations, life choices and influences on individuals. All affect what defines a 'normal' relationship and what is perceived to be a problem; and also influence what issues are labelled problematic, what might legitimise the end of a relationship and whether to seek help.

I will not consider why most of us wish to be in a relationship – a complex array of explanations ranging from metaphysical, romantic, biological, evolutionary, socio-economic and political, to psychosexual and intra-psychic. Rather, I will highlight issues that may lead someone to decide they have 'a relationship problem', theoretical understanding of issues and how a relationship may be helped. Counselling theories that are helpful for understanding individual problems and guiding one-to-one practice may be applied to adult relationships, but some are more commonly used. In terms of practice there are significant differences when working with relationships that are addressed in Evans (Chapter 7.22, this volume).

I use *relationship* throughout to denote all adult intimate relationships, and occasionally *couple*, for simplicity: not all relationships are pairings, nor subject to the same pressures – *any* that are considered by prevailing powerful opinions as being transgressive face prejudice, abuse, internalised oppression, ostracism and lack of recognition and support, and often also experience practical obstacles and consequences. There is a lack of role-models for alternatives to the still-prevailing hetero-normative. Sometimes this lends strength and an alternative community bond and culture, but can exert more stress than the individual or relationship can hold. Minority communities may experience difficulty in finding appropriate, sympathetic, confidential and unbiased help.

AETIOLOGY: WHAT MAKES A GOOD RELATIONSHIP?

It is worth thinking about what brings people together, what needs to be in place, or happen, to build resilient relationships, and potential strengths and pressure points. It is useful to reflect on your ideas about what makes for a good relationship and where these come from, as well as consulting relevant research. As with any branch of therapy, your assumptions may adversely affect work with clients.

An early psychotherapeutic attempt to consider relationships in depth was made by Henry Dicks (Dicks, 1993). He suggested three levels of influence on couple relationships:

1. The social – opportunities to meet, shared cultural norms.
2. The personal – personal norms, role expectations.
3. The unconscious – drives, introjections, splits.

Informed by psychoanalytic and attachment ideas, he was interested in the unconscious. However, we should not overlook the very real impact of the first two (the focus of marriage and dating agency questionnaires). Shared values and expectations cement the relationship and perhaps explain how arranged marriages are as likely to be as successful as so-called 'love marriages'. Unconscious drivers help when considering problematic relationships and how to assist them (see later in this chapter).

Research identifies *tasks* that should be successfully negotiated to build a lasting couple relationship, for example:

Separation from family of origin

Becoming a couple: creating togetherness, autonomy

Coping with crises

Making a safe place for conflict

Exploring sexual love and intimacy

Sharing laughter and keeping interests alive

Providing emotional nurturance

Preserving a double vision: holding onto past positive experiences and present realities.

(Wallerstein and Blakeslee, 1996)

Largely based on white, Western examples (and cultural criticism might be levelled against the first in the above list), nevertheless such ideas are endorsed by research from non-Western cultures (e.g., Rabin, 1996). Another finding is that *fairness* is a key principle (Rabin, 1996), regardless of whether the relationship adopts traditional or other role separations.

Other models suggest *stages* of relationship development. The following is suggested as one that may help normalisation and threat-reduction for gay relationships:

A Developmental Model of Gay Relationships:

- Blending (first year)
- Nesting (1–3 years)
- Maintaining (3–5 years)
- Collaborating (5–10 years)
- Trusting (10–20 years)
- Repartnering (20 years)

(McWhirter and Mattison, 1990)

If you deviate from what society defines as 'normal', or if you did not experience a positive parental relationship, the lack of role models for your own relationship is a potential obstacle to:

- identifying and building your own positive relationship ingredients
- defining shared expectations of what should be 'normal' in your own relationship
- knowing how to resolve difficulties or differences.

Some research identifies *elements* needed for creating and maintaining an enduring relationship. For example:

Protective love:	Needs for protection and dependence are normal impulses
Focus:	Couples who do things together and talk to each other are happier
Gratitude:	Consistent demonstration of this makes you feel special and supported

Balance:	The above three provide *balance*, reinforcing protection because it is about mutual support
Pleasure:	Happy couples experience pleasure, which is the glue maintaining mutual protection.

(Reibstein, 1997)

This may be compared with the Mills and Turnbull (2004) suggestions about intimacy mentioned above, and other similar ideas put forward by Erskine et al. (1999) or Gottman (2000) on relationship needs:

Build Love Maps

Share Fondness and Admiration

Turn Towards

The Positive Perspective

Manage Conflict

Make Life Dreams Come True

Create Shared Meaning

(Gottman, 2000)

Security

Validation

Acceptance

Confirmation (of personal experience)

Self-definition

To have an impact

To have the other initiate

Expression of love

(Erskine et al., 1999)

SOME STATISTICAL INFORMATION

The following comes from the Office for National Statistics (www.ons.gov.uk), which compiles information about relationship status and future trends in the United Kingdom.

Since 1979 there has been a steady decline in numbers of married people, with a commensurate rise in divorce and cohabitation. However, since 2004 divorce has been falling, cohabitation is believed to have levelled off and the number of single households has been rising. Remarriage of divorcees has also declined. Civil Partnerships began in December 2005 with a peak and have declined – and dissolutions risen – since then (although numbers are small compared with heterosexual figures), but this may be linked to the rise in same-sex marriage, introduced in 2014.

Relationships are most stressed when children are dependent, but tend to stay together when children are young. By contrast, couples caring for a child with a disability are at greater risk of marital problems and divorce. The presence of children in second and subsequent relationships also heightens the likelihood of relationship breakdown.

Longitudinal studies are scarce, particularly for 'non-standard' relationships, but suggest that socio-political factors, such as childcare provision, are equally important as interpersonal and subjective factors in relationship breakdown. This chapter cannot offer a comprehensive literature review, but examples are offered in Karney and Bradbury's review of 115 studies. (Karney and Bradbury, 1995).

WHAT GOES WRONG?

Indicators of potential for relationships to go wrong can be spotted in the research and models cited above. Most of us have met couples showing clear signs: public arguments, sniping, negative body language. Often, though, it is a surprise to others. The privacy of a relationship, hurt, pride, humiliation, loyalty, not wanting to acknowledge the truth, not having a language to discuss it, are among many factors contributing to secrecy and a tendency to wait too long before addressing issues.

Some baseline factors influence the ability to create a resilient relationship and underlie the development of problems, including:

- Individual capacity to tolerate difference, anxiety and frustration
- Respect and acceptance for self and others
- Interlocking communication and defence patterns
- Shared problem-solving skills
- Shared versus mismatched expectations, attitudes or values
- Attachment patterns
- Gender myths and assumptions – e.g., about differences (heterosexual couples) and similarities (same-sex couples)
- Hidden or unacknowledged traits or wishes.

Even assuming strength in the above areas, stress-points impact relationships, and have greater effect when a secure foundation is lacking. Often, stresses are minimised or overlooked. Focus is on the obvious, typically the prevalence of arguments, and clients can be very surprised when other issues are highlighted as relevant and significant, for example:

- Health
- Financial changes (negative *and* positive)
- Life stages and transitions
- Life and family events (e.g., house moves, pregnancies, terminations, losses, bereavement)
- Wider family relationships, including step-family, previous partners, etc.
- The presence, absence or intrusiveness of support networks
- Other external factors (e.g., work stresses, bullying at work, traumatic incidents)
- Sexual issues, including (increasingly) sexual addiction and influence of pornography
- Triangular relationships intruding (e.g., affairs, but also other intense friendships or family relationships, including with children).

Individual consequences of stress, for example, affairs and other 'acting out', depression and other mental health issues, substance misuse, violence and domestic abuse, and somatic problems, can exacerbate relationship difficulties. Often clients will report a string of stressful events and experiences but fail to have made the connection between these and current difficulties.

There are many ways clients present for relationship help. Commonly, a precipitating event highlights things have not been right for some time. Typically, communication is fraught, either because it is beset by misunderstanding and argument or paralysed by fear of speaking, or it may have ceased due to lack of interest and shared existence. The interactive nature of personalities and issues creates circular and polarised behaviours, for example, the more one partner retreats the more the other pursues, and this pushes the retreating partner further away.

Underlying the presenting issues are often deeper ones. I have worked with many couples where differences in intra-psychic needs, values, role and life expectations or sexual orientation only emerged at a later stage of the relationship, often disastrously and usually when negotiating a transition, for example, from coupledom to family. Systems-behavioural theory and concepts (e.g., Crowe and Ridley, 2000) can illuminate such issues with attention to rules, roles and inter-relationships.

The idea of 'unconscious fit', referred to above, has been developed by writers in psychodynamic and attachment traditions, such as Scarf (2008), Clulow (2000) and Clulow and Mattinson (1989). Potentially destructive pairings are identified and denoted by evocative titles: 'Carer and Wounded Bird', 'Cat and Dog', 'Babes in the Wood' (Scarf, 2008). These capture the interactivity of unconscious processes of two partners and the nature of their relationship dynamics. These could be described in Transactional Analysis terms using the Parent–Adult–Child matrix. Relationships fall into patterns such as Parent (nurturing) and Child (compliant); Parent (critical) and Child (free or rebellious); and Child–Child (where one or both are free, compliant or rebellious).

Most of us can recognise such pairings in our families, friends, selves and clients. It is argued that we tend to seek familiar relationships to replay dramas of our childhood (perhaps with the hope of a more positive outcome). Recognising these interactive patterns can lead to healthier ways of meeting their own and each other's psychological needs for intimacy or distance.

ASSESSMENT: WHY DO CLIENTS COME FOR RELATIONSHIP COUNSELLING?

Some people present for therapy to rescue their partnership; others to discover whether there is anything worth rescuing; and some for help to find a way to part. For some the agenda is not shared or fully owned and therapy is a way of demonstrating 'at least we tried before throwing in the towel'. Sometimes the initiator has brought their partner to be told off, or to be 'dumped' with the therapist so they can leave with a clear conscience. Warring relationships may be overtly looking for a 'referee' and covertly seeking an ally in the war.

Occasionally clients wish to explore an aspect of their relationship, for example the impact of becoming a family, because they are aware of their own adverse history, or to improve their sexual relationship. More often, they recognise they have reached some impasse that their own resources seem unable to dislodge, and frequently one partner is the initiator. Sadly, this is often at a point of crisis, either following an event or when disagreements have reached intolerable intensity. Some are able to give a coherent account of how they reached this point and know what they need to do (although they may disagree about it); others are mystified how it got that bad.

Precipitating factors are usually to do with problematic communication (verbal or sexual, crossed or absent communication), 'acting out' behaviours, such as affairs or excessive energy in non-relational activities, or another precipitating non-containable event, such as a death in the family or other trauma.

Some clients initially avoid discussing their sexual relationship in therapy, although it is likely to be implicated in some way – either as cause or casualty. They may need permission and encouragement to explore this aspect. Others present with a sexual issue at the forefront, either because it genuinely is the key problem, but sometimes because it is easier to acknowledge this contained aspect – it is much more threatening to acknowledge a more general relationship problem. Either way, it is important for the relationship therapist to have a good understanding, and to be comfortable in discussing sexual issues, to recognise limits of their own competence and when specialist help will be more useful. In our psychologically biased theorising about a couple's difficulties we can mis-attribute sexual problems to a relationship problem when it may be medical.

FORMULATION: WHAT APPROACHES COULD BE HELPFUL?

You may hold allegiance to particular theories and these will influence how you approach thinking about and working with relationship issues. Although there is no reliable evidence that any one modality is more effective than another, there is good evidence of the effectiveness of couple therapy (Gurman and Frankel, 2002). Gurman (2008) gives an overview of different possible therapeutic approaches to relationship therapy. Often approaches are integrative (Bobes and Rothman, 2002; Butler and Joyce, 1998; Payne, 2010). Arguably, the most common, currently applied theories are attachment, emotionally focused, narrative, psychodynamic and systemic, with some cognitive-behavioural (particularly for psychosexual therapy) and solution-focused elements.

Predictors of responsiveness to therapy include relationships that are younger, less distressed and polarised, and where there is commitment and active collaboration, with early 'softening' of interaction (Gurman and Frankel, 2002). The nature and duration of the work is likely to reflect the degree to which the inner world needs addressing. Some relationships are readily helped by a neutral, safe space to talk with minimal guidance. Others need a mediator using positive interventions to interrupt unhelpful patterns, to teach communication and problem-solving skills, and to offer exercises and creative means of exploring issues. My own observation from practice is that the therapeutic alliance and the therapist's ability to work openly with (and between) the couple's values, aims, communication and attachment patterns and personality styles are key. Alongside this are some well-tried ideas, techniques and skills for managing relational work and these are discussed in a separate chapter in this volume (Evans – Chapter 7.22).

Care should be taken over decisions to undertake relationship work when one or both partners are in individual therapy elsewhere and there are contra-indicators to relationship work, for example, where there are:

- Court hearings (thus clients are conscripts not volunteers)
- Lack of shared goals
- Serious individual issues
- Ongoing domestic abuse/violence episodes
- Serious mental health issues
- Very heightened, uncontainable emotions.

When clients present with a sexual problem careful assessment is needed to ascertain whether referral to sex therapy would be the most effective form of help. It can be tricky to decide whether the sexual problem caused, or is caused by, relationship difficulties. Two general rules-of-thumb are, first, to ask the client(s) which *they* believe to be most important, and second, if in doubt discuss with, or refer to, a sex therapist for advice.

Occasionally the focus of therapy is on what it would mean to separate. Even if clients are intent on *not* separating, this can be helpful to consider, as it can lead to recognising positive reasons for staying in the relationship and renewed commitment. Some clients seem unable to make use of therapy to progress their relationship (towards commitment or separation) and one may speculate about reasons for this, using different available theories. For example: in behavioural terms, there may be less to gain and more to lose by changing the dynamics of the relationship; in systemic terms, the homeostasis of the system may hold them in place. For some, the struggles of everyday life militate against finding time, energy and money to make productive use of therapy.

What clients discover from therapy is a different explanation, a new and shared narrative, about their relationship and its difficulties. Often there are incomplete stories, laden with blame. Therapy facilitates the creation of another, fuller and more balanced, explanation, which can help rebuild trust, for example by understanding that an affair (blame apportioned to one party) was a symptom of other issues (leading to shared responsibility). Therapy frequently uncovers previously hidden or undiscussed issues and the impact of the history of both partners. This increased understanding may lead to greater mutual acceptance and empathy, even if the outcome is a decision to part.

REFERENCES

Bobes, T. and Rothman, B. (2002). *Doing Couple Therapy: Integrating Theory with Practice.* New York: W.W. Norton.

Butler, C. and Joyce, V. (1998). *Counselling Couples in Relationships: An Introduction to the Relate Approach.* Chichester: Wiley.

Clulow, C. (2000). *Adult Attachment and Couple Psychotherapy: The 'Secure Base' in Practice and Research.* London: Brunner-Routledge.

Clulow C. and Mattinson J. (1989). *Marriage Inside Out.* London: Penguin.

Crowe, M. and Ridley, J. (2000). *Therapy with Couples: A Behavioural-systems Approach to Marital and Sexual Problems.* Oxford: Blackwell Science.

Dicks, H.V. (1993). *Marital Tensions: Clinical Studies towards a Psychological Theory of Interaction.* London: Karnac Books.

Erskine, R., Moursand, J. and Trautmann, R. (1999). *Beyond Empathy: A Therapy of Contact-in Relationships.* London: Brunner/Mazel.

Gottman, J.M. (2000). *The Seven Principles for Making Marriage Work.* London: Orion Books.

Gurman A.S. (ed.) (2008). *Clinical Handbook of Couple Therapy.* London: Guilford Press.

Gurman A.S. and Frankel, P. (2002). The history of couple therapy: a millennial review. *Family Process,* 41(2): 199–260.

Karney, Benjamin R. and Bradbury, Thomas N. (1995) The longitudinal course of marital quality and stability: A review of theory, methods, and research. *Psychological Bulletin,* Vol 118(1): 3–34.

McWhirter, D.P. and Mattison, A.M. (1990). *The Male Couple: How Relationships Develop*. Englewood Cliffs, NJ: Prentice-Hall.

Mills, B. and Turnbull, G. (2004). Broken hearts and mending bodies: the impact of trauma on intimacy. *Sexual and Relationship Therapy*, 19(3): 265–291.

Payne, M. (2010). *Couple Counselling: A Practical Guide*. London: Sage.

Rabin, C. (1996). *Equal Partners, Good Friends: Empowering Couples through Therapy*. London: Routledge.

Reibstein, J. (1997). *Love Life: How to Make Your Relationship Work*. London: Fourth Estate.

Scarf, M. (2008). *Intimate Partners: Patterns in Love and Marriage*. New York: Ballantine.

Wallerstein, J.S. and Blakeslee, S. (1996). *The Good Marriage*. London: Transworld.

RECOMMENDED READING

1. Bobes, T. and Rothman, B. (2002). *Doing Couple Therapy: Integrating Theory with Practice*. New York: W.W. Norton.

A good introduction to working with relationships in therapy.

2. Butler, C. and Joyce, V. (1998). *Counselling Couples in Relationships: An Introduction to the Relate Approach*. Chichester: Wiley.

Another good introduction to working with relationships in therapy. This text specifically introduces the approach adopted by Relate services.

3. Greenberg, L.S. and Johnson, S.M. (1988). *Emotionally Focused Therapy for Couples*. New York: Guilford Press.

This book stresses the importance of paying attention to emotions and gives guidance on how to manage this process.

6.19

SEXUAL ABUSE IN CHILDHOOD

ROSALEEN MCELVANEY

OVERVIEW AND KEY POINTS

This chapter will discuss child sexual abuse and how it impacts on the individual across the lifespan. I will use a fictitious client, Julie, to illustrate how one might work with a client in counselling or psychotherapy. The chapter covers:

- Examples of sexual abuse
- Assessment and formulation of impact of abuse
- An illustration of working with a female client, Julie
- A discussion of intervention, based on a range of theoretical models.

DEFINITION

Most definitions of child sexual abuse refer to sexual activity in the context of a relationship where there is an imbalance of power and coercion is used to engage a child in sexually inappropriate behaviour. Examples include:

- Exposing children intentionally to others' sexual organs or to sexual activity
- Touching children, having children touch themselves or others in a sexual manner, taking pictures or recordings of a child for the purpose of sexual gratification
- Attempted or actual sexual intercourse with children
- Sexual exploitation
- Showing sexually explicit material to a child.

AETIOLOGY

It is widely accepted that abuse in childhood has potentially long-term consequences. These can continue into adulthood and may include anxiety, depression, eating difficulties, substance misuse and dependency, personality difficulties, heart disease, liver disease, cancer and acute stress (Toth and Cicchetti, 2013). Not all children experience negative psychological outcomes. Indeed, there is a growing body of literature indicating that many adults report post-traumatic growth arising from experiences of abuse (Tedeschi and Calhoun, 2004). Some children do not show short-term effects but experience difficulties later, in adolescence or adulthood. Many manage to 'block it out' either consciously or unconsciously but, over time, come to understand that what happened to them was wrong, and question the origins of current difficulties. We know that most people who have been abused do not tell until adulthood, depriving them of the opportunity to reflect with others on what happened; to be reassured that it was not their fault; and to come to terms with the impact of such experiences.

It is important to bear in mind that psychological impact is cumulative – subsequent experiences of trauma will exacerbate earlier difficulties. Sexual abuse does not happen in isolation; often children experience some form of physical abuse, sometimes neglect and always emotional abuse. In addition, childhood abuse is a significant risk factor for later victimization – thus it is important to enquire about all experiences of victimization when meeting a client with a history of child abuse. Finally, early child abuse can impact both the structure and function of the brain, that is, the size and shape of specific areas of the brain and how these parts of the brain work in terms of emotional and cognitive functioning, evidenced through the use of neuroimaging technology (van der Kolk, 2014). The abused child may experience difficulties encoding emotionally overwhelming information, affecting the amygdala (the part of the brain that facilitates emotional processing), leading to later difficulties in emotional experiencing. Parts of the frontal lobe of the brain can be impaired from chronic abuse, resulting in difficulties with problem-solving and decision-making when faced with a conflict.

Although assessment and formulation are interlinked activities, these will be addressed below under distinct headings.

ASSESSMENT

Assessing the psychological impact of any adverse childhood experience is complex, as this depends to a large extent on the individual's existing vulnerabilities and other difficult experiences the person may have had, and certain protective factors that can mediate the psychological fallout from experiences of abuse (Toth and Cicchetti, 2013). Intrapersonal factors may include temperament, personality, self-esteem, sense of efficacy and agency, intelligence and problem-solving skills and attachment style. Interpersonal factors may include relationships with family or peers, supportive or conflictual. Family factors may include poverty, parental mental health or family stability. At the community or social level, involvement in co-curricular activities, such as sports or social clubs, can mediate the impact, while living in a volatile neighbourhood may exacerbate the child's difficulties. At a societal level, how a nation protects its children through legislation and national policy impacts on children's and families' experiences of coping with the aftermath of abuse.

It can be useful to use psychometric tests, such as the Trauma Symptom Inventory (TSI) (Briere, 1995) in gathering information about difficulties that clients bring to therapy. The TSI is a self-report measure that consists of 100 questions about a range of difficulties that are typically associated with trauma. Clients are asked to indicate whether, and the degree to which, they experienced these difficulties in the previous six months. Standardized norms are available so that clients' scores can be compared with populations of individuals who have experienced trauma. The 10 clinical scales measure difficulties such as anxiety, depression, anger/irritability, intrusive experiences (such as flashbacks), avoidance and dissociation, sexual difficulties and self-identity difficulties, and tension-reduction behaviours that attempt to reduce internal tension (self-harm, angry outbursts, suicidal feelings). The results can provide a useful focus for therapy and an opportunity to talk about some of the more painful and embarrassing difficulties that clients experience.

Each individual is unique and will respond to life adversities in their own unique way. The extent of support they have to draw on, both intrapersonally and interpersonally, will strongly determine how they have been impacted by such experiences and the extent to which they will benefit from therapy.

FORMULATION

Formulation in counselling and psychotherapy helps us develop ideas about what the client's presenting difficulties are, what may have contributed to these difficulties and how we might help the client overcome these difficulties. Each client is unique, their experiences are unique and so the psychological, social and physical impact of their childhood experiences is unique. The formulation takes account of the client's developmental and family history, to build a picture of the individual's protective and risk factors that may help us understand the client, what the client needs now and how we might best help this unique individual in resolving their unique difficulties.

The psychological impact of childhood sexual abuse can be understood in terms of three key domains of functioning: interpersonal relatedness, self-identity and emotion regulation.

Interpersonal relatedness: Child sexual abuse occurs in an interpersonal context, and so there is potential fallout for the child in terms of their capacity for relatedness. This can take the form of difficulties with trust and expectations of others that can lead to difficulties with forming and maintaining healthy, meaningful relationships, difficulties with assertiveness or conflict in relationships and managing interpersonal boundaries. For those who experience abuse within the family, it can significantly alter the child's internal working model of others, whether they can be trusted, and how the child manages relationships. Difficulties with trust can be experienced in peer relationships, friendships, work relationships and intimate and sexual relationships.

Sense of self: The experience of abuse is one where the child often feels powerless. This can impact on a child's sense of agency and autonomy, important processes for the development of a sense of self. The stigmatization associated with abuse may result in the child feeling ashamed and embarrassed, which may be exacerbated by many years of keeping silent about the experience. Trauma shatters a child's assumptions about themselves and the world around them; in particular the assumption that they are intrinsically good, that adults are to be trusted and that they deserve to be treated with respect. Adults who have experienced childhood abuse engage in more negative thinking about themselves and about the world than individuals who have not experienced childhood trauma.

Affect regulation: The emotionally overwhelming nature of child sexual abuse, the difficulty in making sense of the experience, presents a challenge to a developing child's capacity for regulating their feelings, in particular their capacity to tolerate negative emotional states. This may manifest itself along a spectrum from extreme avoidance of strong feelings to emotional outburst, reflecting extreme sensitivity (hypervigilance and hyperarousal). Avoiding talking about or thinking about what happened can be a coping strategy that works well for many. In the extreme, this is manifested as dissociation, an unconscious protective mechanism to help us avoid having to confront intolerable emotional pain. However, this avoidance results in a narrowing of emotional repertoire, preventing many from engaging in a meaningful way in life and relationships. An over-attentiveness to others can represent an intense need for predictability and control in order to feel safe. This continuous state of alertness can impact on the individual's physical wellbeing. Individuals struggle to find ways to manage their emotions, to self soothe, which can result in them numbing themselves to avoid feeling anything. To reduce tension, they may resort to self-harming behaviour, such as cutting, eating difficulties, substance abuse or aggressive behaviour.

INTERVENTION

I will now discuss work with Julie, a fictional client, to illustrate how the above formulation framework might apply to the therapeutic process.

CASE EXAMPLE

Julie (28 years) presents for therapy following a series of arguments with her fiancé. Julie is ambivalent about getting married, constantly postponing the decision. She and her fiancé are experiencing difficulties with intimacy in that Julie has become avoidant in recent months. She describes not having any inhibition in engaging

(Continued)

(Continued)

in sexual activity since she was 14. Having been sexually abused when she was 8 years old by an uncle over a period of two years, she said 'it didn't matter' – if a boyfriend wanted sex, they met no resistance from her. Julie presents with significant low self-esteem issues; she sees herself as fundamentally flawed. She copes with emotional pain by avoidance. Julie has recently begun to suffer from panic attacks and has been encouraged to attend therapy, although she is ambivalent about how this could help.

In my first meeting with Julie, I will begin the process of developing a formulation from simply giving her the space to tell me about herself, what brought her to therapy. I will be listening out for information that helps me make sense of her story and why she may be experiencing her current difficulties and I will be listening to how she tells her story. I will also be focusing on my own experience of Julie, how it is to be with her and what emotions she evokes in me – how I respond to her and her story.

I draw on a range of theoretical models in my work. The humanistic approach offers a basis for developing a strong therapeutic relationship, while the cognitive-behavioural approach helps me focus on our collaborative working relationship. A psychodynamic approach will encourage Julie to be curious about herself, to reflect on her experiences, fostering her reflective capacity and enabling her to process and work through her feelings about what happened. Given Julie's reported difficulties with self-esteem and her struggle with intimacy and commitment, I am interested in particular on attachment style and interpersonal functioning. While it is often the symptoms (anxiety, relationship difficulties) that bring clients for help, focusing on the presenting difficulties may not be enough to lead to longer-lasting change. Julie's recent panic attacks and her ambivalence about therapy suggest that we need to focus on helping her develop skills to manage these attacks. If I can help Julie gain more mastery over her anxious feelings, this may result in her feeling more empowered and give her more hope that therapy will help her – important predictors of successful outcome in therapy. I will draw on emotion-focused therapy to help Julie experience her emotions and help her transform painful maladaptive emotions into more adaptive life-affirming emotions. I will try to give Julie the opportunity to re-experience unconscious internal conflicts through the transference with me, thus providing her with an opportunity to work through such conflicts in the here and now, through the vehicle of the therapeutic relationship.

My aim is for therapy to be a corrective emotional experience for Julie. I may offer interpretations that help her gain insight into how her early relationships and early trauma get re-enacted in her current life and current relationships. This may help Julie gain insight into interpersonal communication styles that are unhelpful. I will help her identify her defence mechanisms that she uses to protect herself from the overwhelming anxiety that threatens to overcome her.

Therapeutic relationship: While the therapeutic relationship is important for all clients, it takes on a particular significance for those who have experienced childhood abuse as theirs is an interpersonal wound. The client's capacity to trust is often significantly impaired and so the initial task of the therapist is to find a way to provide healing through the relationship. Depending on Julie's personality and emotional processing style, this may require providing a warm, caring, authentic and non-judgemental presence; a safe place within which Julie can share and explore difficult thoughts and feelings. Julie may find such an approach threatening and unbearable to tolerate. A cognitive-behavioural focus on the working relationship may suit better, where the attention is on shared goal setting, transparency and collaboration. I will want to create the right environment, where Julie will learn to trust me so that she can share her innermost thoughts and feelings, feel understood and met in an authentic encounter where she is not judged, no matter how abhorrent her story. At some point it will be important for me to take a neutral stance, to enable her to project onto me those intolerable feelings, such as shame and being judged, to experience the negative transference. Julie may then experience me as the withholding therapist, the abuser or the neglectful parent. I will need to pay attention to my countertransference, how it makes me feel to be experienced as withholding or abusive, if I am to help Julie work through unresolved conflicts as I try to hold the limits of the therapeutic frame and provide a safe and containing experience for Julie. I will need to use my own supervision to keep me on the right path, both inviting Julie's transference reactions and acknowledging whatever strong emotions get triggered in me through this relationship to ensure that I can stay present and bear witness to her intense emotional pain. I may fall into a trap of being the 'rescuer', wanting to protect Julie from her own pain. My own emotional processing style will impact on my ability to facilitate her in expressing her emotions.

Developing a sense of self: The experience of being valued and respected will hopefully help Julie to feel a greater sense of self-worth. After all, this is how we develop our sense of self, through being loved and cared for by our primary caregivers. I may ask Julie to perform 'homework' exercises that will boost her experience of herself as competent, capable of experiencing pleasure and being cared for. Trauma-focused cognitive-behaviour therapy (TF-CBT) can be useful to help the client understand the connections between thoughts, feelings and behaviours (Lowe and Murray, 2014). I will explore with Julie her automatic thoughts and negative self-statements that serve to reinforce her negative self-image. I will help her identify unhelpful beliefs and assumptions (schema) about herself and the world. Through processes of gradual exposure, talking about and processing the trauma, I can facilitate Julie to modify these unhelpful beliefs and assumptions, to gain self-mastery over her psychological difficulties, to build her repertoire of coping skills and to reduce the symptoms of trauma. CBT can foster empowerment and a sense of agency for Julie – aspects of self that are essential components of self-esteem.

Exploring Julie's story may also reveal issues of self-blame and shame, giving me an opportunity to challenge her beliefs about herself and the abuse. I will try to help Julie make sense of what has happened, drawing on my own knowledge and experience of working in this field – why it happens, how it happens, how common it is, how it can impact on people. This may bring some comfort to her, knowing that she is not alone in having these difficult thoughts and feelings. It may help her understand that sexual abuse is never a child's fault; that no matter what a child does, the responsibility lies with the abuser. Knowing that others have been through these experiences, have felt the same way, have had the same crazy thoughts and have gone on to experience healing may give hope to Julie who may feel stuck in repeated patterns.

Managing feelings: Most trauma literature indicates that emotional processing of the traumatic experience is necessary to enable clients to overcome many of their psychological difficulties. The coping mechanisms that children use to manage overwhelming emotions may work for a period of time but result in later difficulties. In addition, the manner in which experiences are encoded into the memory systems results in visceral patchy memories that are fragmented and difficult to make sense of. This may be due to a combination of the child being emotionally overwhelmed at the time and a lack of ability to understand what is happening (van der Kolk, 2014). Memories can be activated or triggered by innocuous events or experiences. Julie's pending marriage may have triggered some fears that have been out of her awareness and now demand attention.

Emotion-focused therapy for trauma (Paivio and Pascual Leone, 2010) aims to reduce intrusive symptoms (such as nightmares or flashbacks), change maladaptive perceptions of self and others and reduce avoidance. It is through engagement with our experiences that we are able to address our unresolved emotions and find better, more adaptive ways of being in the world. Change processes in emotion-focused therapy focus on developing and maintaining a safe therapeutic relationship and working actively with memories, bringing them into the here and now so that the associated emotions can be experienced and worked with to transform painful emotions into more productive and constructive ones (Timulak, 2015). Work that facilitates Julie in expressing her anxieties, learning to moderate them will, I hope, lead to an expansion in her emotional repertoire and help her to engage more fully in her life.

It is important in any therapeutic work to consider the client's environment outside the therapeutic space, how current relationships or family issues impact on the change process and what social supports can be harnessed to support Julie. It may also be necessary for Julie and her fiancé to consider couples therapy work.

EVALUATION

There is a substantial body of evidence for the efficacy of cognitive-behaviour therapy, emotion-focused therapy and psychodynamic therapy with both young people and adults who have experienced childhood sexual abuse (see Lalor and McElvaney, 2010, for a review). More research is needed on how these approaches can be integrated and tailored to the complex needs of individual clients.

Of utmost importance is that we monitor our work with clients, constantly checking in with them as to what they find helpful and what they find unhelpful. The TSI can be useful in tracking progress with specific difficulties, but inviting feedback on a regular basis is even more important.

Recovering from the impact of childhood sexual abuse can be a long and difficult journey for many clients. The task of the therapist is to share that journey; sometimes to lead, sometimes to follow and sometimes to travel alongside, but always to be present.

REFERENCES

Briere, J. (1995). *Trauma Symptom Inventory (TSI) Professional Manual*, Lutz, FL: Psychological Assessment Resources, Inc.

Briere, J. and Hodges, M. (2010). Assessing the effects of early and later childhood trauma in adults. In E. Vermetten, R. Lanius and C. Palin (eds), *The Impact of Early Life Trauma on Health and Disease*. Cambridge: Cambridge University Press.

Lalor, K. and McElvaney, R. (2010). A review of the literature on child sexual abuse, links to sexual exploitation and prevention/treatment programmes. *Trauma, Violence and Abuse*, 11, 159–177.

Lowe, C. and Murray, C. (2014). Adult service-users' experiences of trauma-focused cognitive behavioural therapy. *Journal of Contemporary Psychotherapy*, 44, 223–231. DOI 10.1007/s10879-014-9272-1.

Paivio, S. C. and Pascual-Leone, A. (2010). *Emotion-focused therapy for complex trauma: An integrative approach*. Washington, DC: American Psychological Association.

Tedeschi, R.G. and Calhoun, L.G. (2004). Target article: 'Posttraumatic growth': Conceptual foundations and empirical evidence. *Psychological Inquiry*, 15(1), 1–18.

Timulak, L. (2015). *Transforming Emotional Pain in Psychotherapy*. London: Routledge.

Toth, S.L. and Cicchetti, D. (2013). A developmental psychopathology perspective on child maltreatment. *Child Maltreatment*, 18(3), 135–139.

van der Kolk, B. (2014). *The Body Keeps the Score: Brain, Mind, and Body in the Healing of Trauma*. New York: Viking.

RECOMMENDED READING

1. Sanderson, C. (2013). *Counselling Skills for Trauma*. London: Jessica Kingsley Publishers.

A rich resource of knowledge and skills essential for practitioners, written in an accessible style.

2. Paivo, S. and Pascual-Leone, A. (2010). *Emotion-focused Therapy for Complex Trauma: An Integrative Approach*. Washington, DC: American Psychological Association.

Part One provides the theoretical and research base for the EFTT model, while Part Two outlines how the model is put into practice.

3. Van der Kolk, B. (2014). *The Body Bears the Score: Brain, Mind, and Body in the Healing of Trauma*. New York: Viking.

A review of neuroscience research and ways of working with traumatised clients, taking account of the physiological and psychological impact of trauma.

6.20 MANAGING STRESS

ROWAN BAYNE

OVERVIEW AND KEY POINTS

Personality differences are central to understanding and managing stress. They explain major causes of stress and provide rationales for choices of intervention. Two causes of negative stress are discussed: (1) everyday pressures and their interactions with personality, and (2) not expressing core aspects of one's personality sufficiently (the opposite of self-actualization or authenticity). The main personality concepts applied in this chapter to managing stress are preference and preference development from Myers' psychological type theory (in the Myers-Briggs Type Indicator sense). These concepts can be used in stress counselling without assessing counsellors' or clients' personalities.

- Two causes of negative stress are everyday pressures (with personality a central factor) and people not expressing core aspects of their personalities sufficiently.
- Four levels of applying personality differences to managing stress are distinguished, one of which is useful without using a test or assessing your clients' personalities.
- The main personality concepts applied to stress in this chapter are preference and preference development.
- The preferences and their development also provide rationales for choice of interventions to manage stress, for modifications of standard interventions and for different styles of relating to clients.

DEFINITIONS

The term 'stress' is generally used to mean feeling strained and sometimes used to describe having too little to do, or too little that's engaging or fulfilling. 'Managing stress' is similar in meaning to developing resilience, which has been defined as 'the capacity to persist in the face of challenges and to bounce back from adversity' (Reivich et al., 2011: 25). Indeed, most of the interventions in Reivich et al.'s ambitious resilience training might well appear in a stress management course, for example, developing self-awareness and empathy, discovering and changing thinking traps and 'icebergs' (deeply held and undermining beliefs, such as 'asking for help shows weakness'), improving 'energy management', increasing assertiveness and identifying strengths.

A more formal definition of stress is 'a perceived mismatch between pressures and resources which leads to feeling stretched, strained or overwhelmed'. In this definition:

- pressures refers to, for example, a remark, a task, a misunderstanding, a personality clash, a loss, the cumulative effect of smaller losses, not expressing aspects of one's personality enough
- resources refers to circumstances, personality, personality development, strengths and abilities
- perceived recognizes that the pressure may be less formidable or the resources more adequate than they seem
- stretched refers to a stimulating effect of stress
- strained or overwhelmed refers to the numerous potential effects of negative stress, from being irritable to serious illness.

AETIOLOGY

Current approaches to managing stress generally emphasize the role of individuals, rather than their organizations, social contexts or cultures, in creating stress. However, if, for example, an organization tolerates bullying, then the organization is arguably the main source of stress and the most effective interventions are most likely to be made at that level. Providing courses that focus on individuals managing their own stress won't tackle the real source. On the other hand, we generally do contribute significantly to our own stress and this chapter, having acknowledged the wider context, focuses on personality, drawing on the most widely used theory of normal personality: preference or psychological type theory in its Myers–Briggs Type Indicator (MBTI) sense.

Preference can be defined as 'feeling most natural, energized and comfortable with particular ways of behaving and experiencing'. For example, someone who prefers Extraversion to Introversion and who has experienced an upbringing which supported or at least did not unduly discourage extraverted behaviour, will probably talk socially more and with less effort than most introverts. They will also, according to the theory, be more likely as a result to feel fulfilled and less likely to feel negatively stressed.

Conversely, the theory assumes that people who don't express their preferences sufficiently become 'frustrated, inferior copies of other people' (Myers with Myers, 1980: 181). This idea is consistent with several personality theories, for example, those of Rogers, Maslow, Jung and Jourard, and concepts such as self-actualization and authenticity. Isabel Myers' contribution was to clarify ideas about central elements of the content of the real self, which she called preferences, and to add two new preferences, those for Judging and Perceiving.

In its standard form, preference theory suggests eight preferences, organized in pairs. The theory assumes that each of us prefers one preference in each pair. They are all matters of degree and make most sense when contrasted with their opposing preference (hence the term 'versus' in the next paragraph). For example, almost everyone is outgoing sometimes (part of Extraversion) and reflective sometimes (part of Introversion) but each of these ways of behaving is *more* characteristic of some of us than others.

With a brief indication of their meanings, the pairs of preferences in Myers' theory are:

- Extraversion – more outgoing and active – versus Introversion – more reflective and reserved
- Sensing – more practical and interested in facts and details – versus Intuition – more interested in possibilities and an overview
- Thinking – more logical and reasoned – versus Feeling – more agreeable and appreciative
- Judging – more planning and coming to conclusions – versus Perceiving – more flexible and easy-going.

A further pair of preferences has recently been suggested (Bayne, 2013). This became possible when Nettle (2007) described high anxiety in much more positive terms than is usual in personality research. He argued that, for example, worrying about the worst possible effects of an action can be a valuable balance to people who are low in anxiety and who therefore tend to be optimistic and take risks (often unjustified ones from a high anxiety viewpoint). High anxiety is still generally regarded in personality theory as a problem and burden when preferences by definition are strengths to develop, but there seems to be enough in Nettle's interpretation to support the case for preferences for Calm (low anxiety) versus Worrying (high anxiety).

Examples of likely causes of stress for people with each preference are as follows:

Extraversion – Not much happening, not enough contact with people

Introversion – Not enough time alone

Sensing – Vagueness and unrealistic speculation, abstract theory, not enough action

Intuition – Routine, repetition, lots of detail, not enough novelty

Thinking – Lack of logic, intense emotions, loss of control

Feeling – Conflict, criticism, a core value being ignored

Judging – Lack of plans and organization, sudden changes of plan, lack of closure

Perceiving – Restrictions on autonomy, few or no options

Calm – Not much! (Because very stable emotionally). Caution and 'fussing'

Worrying – Risks, the unknown.

ASSESSMENT

Four levels of applying preference theory in stress counselling are:

1. Using preference theory as a source of a wider range of options. This level can increase empathy and acceptance by showing how opposite people can be: some people's pleasures are others' causes of negative stress. Moreover, it counteracts the human tendencies to be biased in favour of interventions that work for us or that fit our own preferences and biased against those that don't. Thus the theory questions assumptions about what is healthy and what is odd. It says there are several radically different ways of being a fulfilled and effective person. This level of use does not require assessment of clients' personalities, either with a psychometric test or through questioning or observation.
2. Observing the client's preferences formally or informally during counselling sessions. With some clients, none of the preferences will be relevant; with others, one preference may be useful, and so on.
3. Using the MBTI or other appropriate psychometric measure. There are many tests that claim to be valid

measures of the preferences in the MBTI sense but which lack its careful development and evidence base, and therefore are less likely to be accurate. Two limitations of the MBTI are that it doesn't measure how developed preferences are (though this can have the advantage of making it less threatening to complete) and that specialized training is required to use it (see www.opp.eu.com).

4. Discussing whether your client wishes to develop one or more of their preferences and non-preferences.

Assessment of your client involves, first, listening for signs of stress both in themselves and as possible clues to causes. Feeling 'tired all the time', aches, irritability, sleeping difficulties and lack of concentration are among the most common signs. Another, unfortunately, is ignoring them. Ideally, *early* signs of negative stress will be noticed and action to reduce them considered. Signs of negative stress may be symptoms of illness, so referral to a doctor or other health professional should also be considered.

A second area often worth exploring is the interventions your client has tried and how effective or ineffective they were. This information is useful in itself and, if appropriate, about your client's preferences.

Third, you may choose to assess your client's preferences, especially those which seem most relevant. This assessment can be (or seem) straightforward but should always be done provisionally. When the assessment is explicit it should always be collaborative and it is the client who decides on their preferences, however compelling your own assessments feel.

The ideal approach to measuring preferences is the Myers–Briggs Type Indicator with expert one-to-one feedback on the results, or experiential training in which groups of people with opposite preferences take part in exercises which (usually) illustrate those preferences in action. The ethics and practicalities of assessing the preferences in counselling sessions by observation or using the MBTI or other properly validated measure are discussed in Bayne (2013).

FORMULATION

There are numerous models, theories and research findings to draw on in stress counselling, including those on the basic physiology underlying many of the signs of stress and on problems associated with stress, such as alcohol problems and depression. For example, an early decision is whether to describe the stress response, for example, the see-saw interactions between the sympathetic and parasympathetic nervous systems, the fight-or-flight response and the power of stress hormones like cortisol and adrenaline (Sapolsky, 2004). For some clients such information is a great relief – 'I'm not going mad' – and provides a reassuring rationale for trying out relaxation techniques. (In preference theory, people who prefer both Intuition and Thinking tend to want rationales and evidence most.)

Another early decision is how much emphasis to put on managing signs of stress and how much on managing causes. For example, John was disgusted with himself for checking up on his girlfriend and for getting drunk more often, which seemed to be a result. He wanted to stop his obsessive thoughts as quickly and efficiently as possible. Taking a collaborative approach (Tryon and Winograd, 2011), we agreed to try thought stopping and that he'd try exploring the source of his obsession and/or his current relationship if it didn't work.

INTERVENTIONS

Generally effective methods of managing stress include counselling, relaxation, some of the many and varied forms of meditation, assertiveness, exercise and expressive writing (Lynn et al., 2015; Nicolson and Bayne, 2014; Walsh, 2011). However, choosing which interventions to try is still largely a matter of trial and error.

Lyubomirsky (2010) suggested a systematic way of matching clients and interventions (in her case for increasing happiness) which is consistent with the concept of preference. In modified form, it is to reflect on what it would be like to do an intervention for, say, several days and to rate it on criteria of feeling natural, enjoyment and doing it to please others or because it's fashionable. Obviously, the first two criteria indicate trying that intervention and the second two are warning signs.

The following list is of preferences and examples of interventions that, given normal development, will meet the criteria. In the list, X refers to a source of stress. These interventions and others are also ways of developing preferences and non-preferences (Bayne, 2013; Myers and Kirby, 1994). Two important assumptions in preference theory are that each person's preferences have a higher ceiling for development than their opposed non-preferences, and thus, in a good enough environment, develop more than them, and that this is desirable.

Extraversion – Talking about X

Introversion – Quiet reflection about X

Sensing – Check details relevant to X, e.g., what was actually said or happened

Intuition – Brainstorm about X or an aspect of X, summarize the main issues

Thinking – Analyse X, do a cost–benefit analysis, create a flow chart

Feeling – Empathize with other people involved (if any), clarify if any of your core values are relevant to X

Judging – Make a plan about X or an aspect of X, do it as a list of actions and consider doing one of them

Perceiving – Gather more information relevant to X

Calm – Stay relaxed, think of all the potential benefits of a decision you may take about X

Worrying – Think of more worries and risks relating to X and precautions and preparation to reduce them.

If those interventions which fit your client's preferences don't work well enough, Kroeger et al. (2002: 252–253) suggest a 'good stretch', by which they mean a brief switch to using your non-preferences. Obviously, this approach could be attacked as not falsifiable, as 'having it both ways'. However, trying interventions consistent with preferences first and usually, and the emphasis on brevity in trying 'a good stretch', are sound counter-arguments.

Preference theory sometimes explains, in a constructive way, why generally effective interventions fail. Thus, for exercise, the brief quiz on Brue's website (www. the8colors.com) indicates those forms of exercise most and least likely to suit people with each set of preferences. For example, some people enjoy a calm, familiar and pleasing setting, and letting their minds drift – exercise as 'a moving meditation' – while others want lots of stimulation, variety and speed – exercise as 'absorbing action' (Brue, 2008).

Similarly, counsellors may choose to try using preference theory to refine something that happens naturally: varying their way of relating to clients with different personalities, for example, being more organized and detailed with clients who prefer both Sensing and Judging, showing their expertise through rationales and explicit use of theory with people who prefer both Intuition and Thinking, being warmer with clients who prefer Feeling, more playful (but still professional) with clients who prefer both Sensing and Perceiving and more patient with clients who prefer Worrying.

This is not asking counsellors to be inauthentic. Rather, it offers the beginnings of a clearer account of how to be what Lazarus (1993: 404–407) called an 'authentic chameleon'. Dryden has also commented helpfully on this concept: that counsellors 'cannot be all things to all clients … your personality and temperament limit how much you can vary' and that he tends to be referred clients 'whom the referrer thinks need a robust and no nonsense counsellor, rather than clients who need a lot of gentle coaxing' (Dryden, 2011: 41). In other words, use your preferences most but non-preferences sometimes, including when being empathic with clients whose personality is very different from your own and when your own development allows. If not, referral is a positive and ethical option.

CASE EXAMPLE

Blossom was sleeping badly. She was worried about her brother's imminent wedding and anticipating a stressful day that she would make worse just by being there. She'd decided that poor sleep was making everything else worse so she'd searched the internet and two authoritative books, Rosenberg (2014) and Wiseman (2014), for ideas. She'd tried walking more, increasing speed and distance gradually, but found it boring and too regimented, and no computer later in the evening, but found that frustrating.

In counselling, she identified three aspects of 'the wedding problem': that she was boring (because introverts are boring); that because she finds small talk 'excruciatingly tedious' people give up on her and walk away; and that in order to be healthy and well balanced she'd have to change her personality, but she didn't know how to.

Blossom challenged and replaced each of these beliefs and found that appreciating herself as an introvert also meant that she felt more confident socially: less worried about other people's reactions to her and more interested in how she felt in them. She said: 'It's such a relief to learn that I'm not antisocial and that I don't have some deep personality defect – I just need more time to myself than some people and lots of peace and quiet!' Thus, Blossom became much more accepting of an element of her real self (not always so easy to do) and, more subtly, no longer criticized herself for not having the opposite quality, for being an 'unsuccessful extravert'.

She took a further step: assertively expressing her needs by giving herself time to recover from periods of being sociable. Thus, at her brother's wedding, she escaped (her term) and read for an hour between dinner and dancing, and even enjoyed the social part more as a result. And, before the wedding day, she'd explained to her brother what she was doing and why. This direct talk with her brother was unusual for Blossom and she rehearsed it first, following the guidelines in Dickson (2012). The image of a tree bending in the wind, then coming upright again – part of the skill of persisting with a key phrase in the face of strong pleas and emotional requests – proved particularly helpful.

Blossom decided to work more on directly developing her non-preference for extraversion with a friend who was a socially skilled introvert (or possibly an extravert).

EVALUATION

Quite a lot is known about the causes and effects (especially on health) of stress, and about effective interventions. However, there are still many questions about even the interventions with the strongest empirical support, such as exercise, relaxation, expressive writing and mindfulness, for example, about how they work, if there are risks, how long positive effects last and whether they are less effective with some groups of people in terms of, say, age or certain personality characteristics. On the other hand, the interventions are usually inexpensive, have few or no side effects and generally don't have negative outcomes.

The validity of preference theory is supported by the close relationship between the main measures of the preferences and of the factors in Big Five Theory. Big Five Theory has been the most studied and widely accepted trait personality theory since the 1980s. The applications of preference theory to stress counselling discussed in this chapter are consistent with the theory but need to be tested in their own right.

REFERENCES

Bayne, R. (2013) *The Counsellor's Guide to Personality: Understanding Preferences, Motives and Life Stories*. Basingstoke: Palgrave Macmillan.

Brue, S. (2008) *The 8 Colors of Fitness*. Delroy Beach, FL: Oakledge Press.

Dickson, A. (2012) *A Woman in Your Own Right: Assertiveness and You* (2nd ed.). London: Quartet.

Dryden, W. (2011) *Counselling in a Nutshell* (2nd ed.). London: Sage

Kroeger, O. with Thuesen, J.M. and Rutledge, H. (2002) *Type Talk at Work*. New York: Dell Publishing.

Lazarus, A.A. (1993) Tailoring the therapeutic relationship, or being an authentic chameleon. *Psychotherapy*, 30: 404–407.

Lynn, S.J., O' Donohue, W.T and Lilienfeld, S.O. (eds) (2015) *Health, Happiness, and Well-Being: Better Living through Psychological Science*. London: Sage.

Lyubomirsky, S. (2010) *The How of Happiness: A Practical Guide to Getting the Life You Want*. London: Piatkus.

Myers, I.B. with Myers, P.B. (1980) *Gifts Differing*. Palo Alto, CA: CPP.

Myers, K.D. and Kirby, L.K. (1994) *Introduction to Type Dynamics and Type Development*. Palo Alto, CA: CPP.

Nettle, D. (2007) *Personality*. Oxford: Oxford University Press.

Nicolson, P. and Bayne, R. (2014) *Psychology for Social Work Theory and Practice* (4th ed.). Basingstoke: Palgrave Macmillan.

Reivich, K.J., Seligman, M.E.P. and McBride, S. (2011) Master resilience training in the US army. *American Psychologist*, 66: 25–34.

Rosenberg, R.S. (2014) *Sleep Soundly Every Night, Feel Fantastic Every Day: A Doctor's Guide to Solving Your Sleep Problems*. New York: Demos Health.

Sapolsky, R. (2004) *Why Zebras Don't Get Ulcers* (3rd ed.). New York: Holt.

Tryon, G.S. and Winograd, G. (2011) Goal consensus and collaboration. *Psychotherapy*, 48: 50–57.

Walsh, R. (2011) Lifestyle and mental health. *American Psychologist*, 66: 579–592.

Wiseman, R. (2014) *Nightschool: The Life-changing Science of Sleep*. London: Pan Books.

RECOMMENDED READING

1.   Dickson, A. (2012) *A Woman in Your Own Right: Assertiveness and You* (2nd ed.). London: Quartet.

The best practical book on assertiveness, for both sexes.

2.   Lynn, S.J., O' Donohue, W.T. and Lilienfeld, S.O. (eds) (2015) *Health, Happiness, and Well-Being: Better Living through Psychological Science*. London: Sage.

Literature reviews, with some attention to applications, by leading researchers on 'chilling out' (meditation, relaxation and yoga), sleep, exercise, happiness and other areas of psychology relevant to managing stress.

3.   Nicolson, P. and Bayne, R. (2014) *Psychology for Social Work Theory and Practice* (4th ed.). Basingstoke: Palgrave Macmillan.

Includes detailed practical guidelines for some generally effective methods of managing stress: assertiveness, strengths, expressive writing and preference theory.

6.21   SUICIDE AND SELF-HARM

ANDREW REEVES

OVERVIEW AND KEY POINTS

Working with suicide and self-harm in therapy can be both challenging and demanding. The demands of organisational working, meeting the requirements of procedural or policy expectations, in addition to responding empathically and appropriately to a potentially highly distressed client, require commensurate skill. Knowing how best to respond to a client's potential suicidal intent or self-harm, or helping a client to begin to explore these potentially highly shameful aspects of their experience, require that the therapist is aware of both their client's process and their own.

- Suicide and self-ham, while relatively simply defined, represent complex responses to life difficulties and crisis.
- The risk of suicide, or the presence of self-harm, can easily become the focus for therapy. Instead, the therapeutic encounter should provide clients with opportunities to understand the meaning of their thoughts and actions in the context of their difficulties.

- While an assessment of the risk and protective factors is important, a therapeutic exploration of those factors is more likely to provide insight for the therapist and client alike into levels of risk.

DEFINITIONS

SUICIDE

The World Health Organisation (WHO) defines suicide simply as: 'Suicide is the act of deliberately killing oneself' (World Health Organisation, 2016a). For a coroner in the United Kingdom (UK) to classify a death as suicide, they must be beyond reasonable doubt that:

- The event which caused the deceased's death must have been self-inflicted, self-enacted and self-administered.
- The intention of the deceased in initiating the fatal event must unequivocally have been to bring about his or her own death (McCarthy and Walsh, 1975; cited in O'Connor and Sheehy, 2000: 15).

Suicide itself is not a single process of deciding to end one's life with subsequent action, but rather can present in different ways. For some, suicide is a response to unimaginable emotional turmoil or life crisis (e.g., terminal illness), where a plan is considered and moved towards. For others, suicide is an ever-present consideration; some clients say that knowing they can end their life is the only way in which they manage to live. Whereas for others, often young people particularly, suicide can be an impulsive act in response to a situation, where there had been no previous thoughts about suicide, but with the person then propelled quickly and unexpectedly to a suicidal crisis. Therapists can helpfully reflect on these differences when working with suicide risk.

SELF-HARM

Babiker and Arnold (1997: 2) define self-harm as: 'an act which involves deliberately inflicting pain and/or injury to one's body, but without suicidal intent', while the National Institute for Health and Care Excellence (NICE) states that self-harm is 'self-poisoning or injury, irrespective of the apparent purpose of the act' and that 'self-harm is an expression of personal distress, not an illness, and there are many varied reasons for a person to harm him or herself' (NICE, 2004: 7).

Babiker and Arnold's definition draws out a distinction between self-harm and suicidal ideation when they state 'but without suicidal intent'. A generally held view is that self-harm is usually used as a coping strategy against profound or overwhelming feelings of distress (anger, hurt, rage, low self-esteem) and is a means of living rather than dying. In the UK, a report by the Royal College of Psychiatrists (2010: 6) stated, 'an act of self-harm is not necessarily an attempt or even indicator of suicide, indeed it can sometimes be a bizarre form of self-preservation'.

It can be helpful therapeutically to consider differences between self-harm and self-injury (Reeves, 2015).

Self-harm can include behaviours with indirect and deferred consequence, such as over-exercise, eating disorders, smoking, alcohol and drug use, and sexual risk-taking, for example.

Self-injury can include behaviours with direct and immediate consequence, such as cutting, burning, banging, ingesting dangerous substances (including of medication), for example.

This is not simply a semantic difference, but rather focuses on the differences in *communication* of the action – with immediate or deferred impact – and also the potential understanding and insight of the client into the nature of the behaviour. For example, while a client may understand for themselves that cutting is a form of self-injury, they may not necessarily think of over-exercise as a potentially equally damaging behaviour.

AETIOLOGY

It is impossible to provide a simple, single explanation as to why someone might decide to end their own life through suicide, nor indeed inflict injury or harm onto their body. While much of the literature surrounding suicide offers a strong correlation between suicidal thought and mental disorder (Appleby et al., 2015), many commentators have historically challenged this link, arguing that suicide can equally be a carefully thought-through response to a set of particular circumstances, for example, chronic or terminal illness (Szasz, 2002).

One of the helpful aspects of differentiating between self-injury and self-harm is that it provides us all with an opportunity to understand the motivating factors. We may not all cut ourselves at times of distress, but I have asserted elsewhere (Reeves, 2015) that, at times, we will all self-harm: through over-work, excessive spending, over- or under-eating, disregarding physical ill-health and pushing on regardless. In terms of self-harm, the behaviour itself is an unhelpful defining criterion, but rather than driver behind the behaviour (e.g., anxiety, rage, hurt, powerlessness, etc.).

The World Health Organisation (2016b) states that internationally: 'Every year, an estimated 900,000 people die [through] suicide. This represents one death every 40 seconds. Worldwide, suicide ranks among the three leading causes of death among those aged 15–44 years.' It also states that suicide rates have increased by 60 per cent over the last 45 years. Bertolote and Fleischmann (2002) estimated that approximately 1.53 million people will die from suicide in 2020.

The National Inquiry into Self-Harm (Mental Health Foundation, 2004) is cautious about offering detailed statistics regarding the number of people who self-harm. This is because the many people who self-harm very probably never present to agencies; self-harm is often hidden and self-treated. Statistics can therefore only be the tip of an iceberg. However, various studies have estimated that one in 10 young people have self-harmed at some point in their lives. If the findings of another study were extrapolated to the wider population, estimates would be that more than 1 million adolescents have considered self-harm, with 800,000 of those actually having inflicted injuries. Full details of these studies, with a discussion, can be found in the National Inquiry document (Mental Health Foundation, 2004).

ASSESSMENT

While some clients may talk openly about their suicidal thoughts or self-harming, many will not talk about them at all, or will perhaps allude to them through metaphor or imagery (Reeves et al., 2004). Likewise, contrary to the myths of self-harm being 'attention-seeking', the overwhelming majority of self-harm is hidden and masked, often not coming to the attention of treating or helping organisations.

Assessment approaches will be strongly informed by working context and the theoretical orientation of the therapist, as has been discussed in other chapters.

Fundamentally, however, the therapist must attend to two critical considerations when working with risk, which an assessment can help inform:

1. The level of risk the client is currently experiencing and whether they are able to work in therapy safely.
2. The nature of the risk (whether that be through suicidal ideation, self-harm or both) and the meaning that might have for the client. This is the central therapeutic premise in working with risk, but can only be undertaken if the therapist (and client) are satisfied with the answer to (1), above.

Table 6.21.1 Factors associated with higher risk

Gender, e.g., males generally present with greater risk across age groups

Age, e.g., males across the age span, but particularly 15–59, and the over 75 years

Relationships: single, widowed, divorced, separated

Social isolation

Psychopathology including:

schizophrenia

mood disorders, including depression

psychosis

post-traumatic stress disorder

affective disorders, including bipolar

affective disorder

organic disorders

personality disorders, e.g., sociopathy, aggression

Alcohol and drug use

Hopelessness

Occupational factors, e.g., unemployment, retirement

History of childhood sexual or physical abuse

Adult sexual assault

Specific suicide plan formulated

Prior suicide attempt and/or family history of suicide or suicide attempts

Physical illness, e.g., terminal illness, biochemical, hormonal

Bereavement or recent trauma

Significant and unexplained mood change

Self-harm

(Reeves, 2010; and based on Appleby et al., 2015; Battle, 1991; Battle et al., 1993; Bernhard and Bernhard, 1985; Gilliland, 1985; Hazell and Lewin, 1993; Hersh, 1985; Ruddell and Curwen, 2008; Williams and Morgan, 1994)

ASSESSING (AND EXPLORING) RISK

Assessing risk demands psychological contact and a willingness and ability to remain connected with the client. The predominant approach to assessing risk in the UK continues to be informed by risk factors (factors that make risk more likely), and the research evidence is heavily weighted to this information (see Table 6.21.1).

Understanding factors associated with a higher risk can help contextualise the presentation of the individual's experience. However, is important that therapists engage openly with their clients about suicide, asking such questions as:

- Have you ever thought about harming yourself or killing yourself in response to how you are feeling?
- Have you made any plans about how you might kill yourself?
- What has helped you not kill or harm yourself? How do you support yourself at difficult times?
- On a scale of 1–10, with 1 being the best and 10 being the worst, how would you rate your feelings and thoughts about suicide or self-harm at the moment?

I would argue that this approach most effectively locates risk assessment in the dialogue with the client. As Shneidman (1998: 6) states:

> Our best route to understanding suicide is not through the study of the structure of the brain, nor the study of social statistics, nor the study of mental diseases, but directly through the study of human emotions described in plain English, in the words of the suicidal person. The most important question to a potentially suicidal person is not an inquiry about family history or laboratory tests of blood or spinal fluid, but 'where do you hurt?' and 'how can I help you?'

Shneidman's assertion here superbly articulates the primary focus for working with risk: 'where do you hurt?' and 'how can I help you?'. Once satisfied the client is able to work safely in therapy, the focus of therapy should be an exploration of the distress underpinning and informing the risk, rather than simply a continuation of a two-dimensional risk management strategy.

FORMULATION

Much is written about how suicide might present in therapy, with less written about how therapists might respond to suicide potential or self-harm. The majority of what has been written focuses only on the client's risk; the therapist apparently should have the capacity to leave their own responses 'at the door' (as it is often said) and meet the client in some form of *tabula rasa* encounter. Of course, the reality of therapy is that the therapist's response to their client or their counter-transferential response – a complex interplay of different responses and experiences – is equally important in determining the formulation of therapy. The same is true when working with suicide potential or self-harm.

How a therapist responds to the disclosure of self-harm, or the possibility of suicide, can profoundly shape the formulation and understanding of the focus of therapy. The therapist will, in virtue of the fact that they are human too, already have a 'position' on suicide and self-harm: it is a subject that rarely leaves people feeling neutral. Likewise, therapists may intellectually understand why an individual may self-harm, but then may experience a very different response in therapy with a client perhaps showing a cut or burn, or providing a description of their self-harming behaviour. The intellectual niceties around suicide and self-harm evaporate quickly when contextualised by a client with whom we have developed an intimate relationship. The potential for therapists to feel angry, hurt, rejected, attacked or undermined by their client's suicide potential or self-harm is high.

THERAPEUTIC CHALLENGES IN FORMULATION

There are many ways in which counsellors and psychotherapists might 'act out' their otherwise unacknowledged responses to risk in a therapy session. Most commonly, of course, is therapists denying they have a 'response' at all: 'I am fine in working with self-harm, it really doesn't bother me', or perhaps 'I believe that every client has a right to kill themselves if they wish, so it is not for me to get involved'. Both of these examples on the surface might appear to be acceptable. However, I would argue that it is essential for us as therapists to be impacted by our client's potential suicide or self-harm. Anaesthetising ourselves against such pain has the potential to parallel the client's experience of themselves, and potentially undermines the empathy and insight required to offer emotional support.

Leenaars (2004: 101–102) outlines a number of ways 'unacknowledged counter-transference' might hinder a formulation with clients at risk, particularly when the therapist's response includes guilt, anger, anxiety or fear. For example:

- Underestimation of the seriousness of the suicidal action (or intent)
- Absence of a discussion of suicidal thoughts (or intent)
- Allowing oneself to be lulled into a false sense of security by the client's promise not to repeat a suicide attempt (or act on suicidal thoughts)
- Disregard of the 'cry for help' aspect of the suicidal attempt (or thoughts), and concentration exclusively on its manipulative character
- Exaggeration of the client's provocative, infantile and aggressive sides
- Denial of one's own importance to the client
- Failure to persuade the client to undergo (or continue with) counselling or psychotherapy
- Feeling of lacking the resources for the evaluation required by a particular client
- Exaggerated sense of hopelessness in response to the client's social situation and abuse of drugs/alcohol
- Being pleased with the client's claims to have all problems solved after only a brief period of time
- Feeling upset when the client shows resistance after only a brief course of inquiry, despite the therapist's initial profound commitment.

Perhaps, however, unacknowledged counter-transferential responses are most often seen in the minutiae of the therapeutic discourse. Regardless of length of post-qualifying experience or therapeutic orientation, therapists can be silenced by suicide potential, not exploring with the client the meaning of their suicidal thoughts and thus not considering, again with the client, the degree of intent and thus the level of risk (Reeves et al., 2004).

The same is true when working with self-harm. In some instances, therapists will only focus on the self-destructive aspect of self-harm (as opposed to that part of the behaviour that facilitates coping), and view this as contra-indicatory to growth and development. Self-harm can often provoke powerful responses in the therapist, including anger, a sense of being attacked by it, revulsion and hopelessness. The more insight a therapist can have into their own process, the more they will be able to connect with their client's.

The feelings and responses outlined above to both suicide potential and self-harm are not wrong: they are understandable human reactions to another's profound distress. However, they become potentially harmful when they are unacknowledged and unsupported. The more a therapist is able to reflect on their own process – their feelings, thoughts, reactions and behaviours in response to suicide potential or self-harm – the clearer and more collaborative the therapeutic formulation will be.

INTERVENTION

Unlike some other client presentations, suicide potential and self-harm demand the therapist not only *works with* these issues from a therapeutic position, but also *responds to* these issues in virtue of the risk that may be present. The task is therefore two-fold: providing space for meaning-making and change, and ensuring the client's safety. Consider the client Sam, below.

CASE EXAMPLE: SAM

Sam is a 52-year-old male client. He attends for counselling because of depression, but on further exploration Sam talks of sometimes 'wanting to be out of the way', as well as punching walls when angry. He is socially isolated but is a member of a local faith group, with whom is spends time during the week. When he feels particularly lonely he drinks but recognises this is not helpful. He experienced a close bereavement 12 months previously.

The therapist faces an immediate challenge here, regarding the ambiguous nature of Sam's statement 'wanting to be out of the way', and whether this refers to suicidal thinking. At some stage it will be important for the therapist to ask Sam about this, perhaps by saying, '…when you say you "want to get out of the way", Sam, I wonder if you mean finding space for yourself, or if these are thoughts about ending your life…?' If Sam's thoughts are about suicide, these need to be contextualised by the other risk factors present in this scenario:

- Gender (male is a high-risk group)
- Age (52 sits in the highest-risk age group for suicide in men)
- Self-injury (punching the wall when angry)
- Social isolation
- Use of alcohol
- Bereavement
- Stated ideation ('I want to be out of the way').

There are protective factors (that make suicide less likely) too, however, which also need to be considered:

- Attending counselling
- Some social contact
- Attending a community group (faith group)
- Self-injury (paradoxically, it helps provide an outlet for feelings, albeit self-destructively)
- Some insight (awareness of the impact of alcohol).

A judgement as to Sam's level of risk needs to be made, informed by the protective and risk factors but, most importantly, through dialogue with Sam directly about how he takes care of himself and how he has managed not to try to end his life up to this point. In such a situation, a crisis plan, or 'keep safe' plan, might be collaboratively developed, which provides Sam with a structured way of thinking about his risk and how he can respond to that when away from sessions. I have written more about such plans elsewhere (Reeves, 2015: 53–54), but they might include:

- The actual risk being considered (e.g., thoughts of taking an overdose)
- The times when the risks are likely to be at their highest (e.g., at night)
- 'Red flags' the client might be aware of that could trigger such thoughts (e.g., when they are alone)
- Factors that make the feelings worse, being as specific as possible (e.g., alcohol or drugs)
- Factors that make the feelings better, being as specific as possible (e.g., being around people)
- Who is available to offer informal support (e.g., family, friends)
- Who is available to offer formal support (e.g., a crisis team, accident and emergency, a telephone helpline),

and ensuring details such as telephone numbers are recorded on the plan

- What might make accessing support less likely (e.g., not wanting to wake someone up)
- What might make accessing support more likely (e.g., agreeing contact with someone in advance)
- Intrapersonal mechanisms for self-care (e.g., meditation, breathing techniques, distraction, etc.)
- A date for review (which will usually be the next session).

SELF-HARM

Many clients who self-harm do not necessarily wish to talk about their harm specifically, but rather concentrate on the factors that shape how their feel – as is the case for suicidal potential. If clients do wish to focus on their self-harm, exploration on the meaning of their self-harming behaviour, rather than spending time on the behaviour itself, can be helpful. I have written in more detail elsewhere (Reeves, 2013) about the important of a relational approach in helping the client to find words for feelings that are otherwise expressed through injury. Different approaches all have something to offer here: I have given a specific example using a narrative approach to help in meaning-making (Reeves, 2013). Likewise, in the same text, I have also offered an overview of a more cognitive-behavioural approach when clients wish to find strategies to stop self-harming, including alternatives to self-harm.

EVALUATION

There is a strong temptation when working with risk for the therapist to determine a 'good outcome' based on the mitigation of risk. Likewise, with self-harm, therapists can be inadvertently drawn into using the behaviour of self-harm as a barometer of 'success', that is, a reduction in self-harm = effective therapy; an increase in self-harm = ineffective therapy; things are never that binary. Undoubtedly, and as has been discussed here, responding to risk is a critical consideration in ensuring the client's capacity to make use of therapy safely. However, a client's sense of a 'good outcome' for them might not necessarily include the eradication of suicidal ideation or the elimination of self-harm.

The use of process and outcome measures can help both investigate the client's experience of therapy and whether, according to the agreed goals and tasks set at the outset, there is any change. Additionally, enabling the client to be able to consider their experience of therapy – and of the therapeutic relationship – will help ensure therapy remains client-focused rather than risk-driven.

REFERENCES

Appleby, L., Kapur, N., Shaw, J., Windfuhr, K., Hunt, I.M., Flynn, S., While, D., Roscoe, A., Rodway, C., Ibrahim, S. and Tham, S. (2015) *National Confidential Inquiry into Suicide and Homicide by People with Mental Illness.* Manchester: Centre for Mental Health and Safety, University of Manchester.

Babiker, G. and Arnold, L. (1997) *The Language of Injury: Comprehending Self-Mutilation.* Leicester: British Psychological Society.

Battle, A.O. (1991) Factors in assessing suicidal lethality. Paper presented at the Crisis Center Preservice Volunteer Training, University of Tennessee College of Medicine, Department of Psychiatry, Memphis, TN.

Battle, A.O., Battle, M.V. and Trolley, E.A. (1993) Potential for suicide and aggression in delinquents at juvenile court in a southern city. *Suicide and Life Threatening Behaviour,* 23(3): 230–243.

Bernhard, J.L. and Bernhard, M.L. (1985) Suicide on campus: response to the problem. In E.S. Zinner (ed.), *Coping with Death on Campus* (pp. 69–83). San Francisco, CA: Jossey-Bass.

Bertolote, J.M. and Fleischmann, A. (2002) Suicide and psychiatric diagnosis: a worldwide perspective. *World Psychiatry,* 1(3): 181–185.

Gilligand, B.E. (1985) Surviving college: teaching college students to cope. Paper presented at the Symposium on Suicide in Teenagers and Young Adults, University of Tennessee College of Medicine, Department of Psychiatry, Memphis, TN.

Hazell, P. and Lewin, T. (1993) An evaluation of postvention following adolescent suicide. *Suicide and Life Threatening Behaviour,* 23(2): 101–109.

Hersh, J.B. (1985) Interviewing college students in crisis. *Journal of Counseling and Development,* 63: 286–289.

Leenaars, A.A. (2004) *Psychotherapy with Suicidal People: A Person-centred Approach.* Chichester: Wiley.

McCarthy, P. and Walsh, D. (1975) Suicide in Dublin: under-reporting of suicide and the consequences for national statistics. *British Journal of Psychiatry,* 126: 301–308.

Mental Health Foundation (2004) *Truth Hurts: A Report on the National Inquiry into Self-Harm among Young People.* London: Mental Health Foundation.

NICE (2004) *Self-Harm: The Short-term Physical and Psychological Management and Secondary Prevention of Self-harm in Primary and Secondary Care.* London: National Institute for Health and Clinical Excellence.

O'Connor, R. and Sheehy, N. (2000) *Understanding Suicidal Behaviour.* Oxford: Blackwells.

Reeves, A. (2010) *Counselling Suicidal Clients.* London: Sage.

Reeves, A. (2013) *Challenges in Counselling: Self-harm.* London: Hodder Education.

Reeves, A. (2015) *Working with Risk in Counselling and Psychotherapy.* London: Sage.

Reeves, A., Bowl, R., Wheeler, S. and Guthrie, E. (2004) The hardest words: exploring the dialogue of suicide in the counselling process: a discourse analysis. *Counselling and Psychotherapy Research,* 4(1): 62–71.

Royal College of Psychiatrists (2010) *Self-harm, Suicide and Risk: Helping People Who Self-harm.* College Report CR158. London: Royal College of Psychiatrists.

Ruddell, P. and Curwen, B. (2008) Understanding suicidal ideation and assessing for risk. In S. Palmer (ed.), *Suicide: Strategies and Interventions for Reduction and Prevention* (pp. 84–99). London: Routledge.

Shneidman, E.S. (1998) *The Suicidal Mind.* Oxford: Oxford University Press.

Szasz, T. (2002) *Fatal Freedom: The Ethics and Politics of Suicide.* Syracuse, NY: Syracuse University Press.

Williams, R. and Morgan, H.G. (eds) (1994) *Suicide Prevention: The Challenge Confronted.* London: HMSO.

World Health Organisation (2016a) *Suicide.* Geneva: World Health Organisation. (www.who.int/topics/suicide/en/).

World Health Organization (2016b) *How Can Suicide be Prevented?* Geneva: World Health Organisation. www.who.int/features/qa/24/en/).

RECOMMENDED READING

1.   Leenaars, A. (2004) *Psychotherapy with Suicidal People: A Person-centred Approach*. Chichester: Wiley.

A broad account of the range of issues therapists face when working with suicidal clients; additionally including explanations for suicidal thinking.

2.   Reeves, A. (2015) *Working with Risk in Counselling and Psychotherapy*. London: Sage.

Discusses therapeutic work with suicide risk and self-harm, as well and other areas of risk, e.g., violence to others and safeguarding. Looks at the concept of positive risk-taking in therapy.

3.   Shneidman, E.S. (1998) *The Suicidal Mind*. Oxford: Oxford University Press.

A seminal text from a key suicidologist, providing a critical evaluation of our understanding of suicide, as well as challenging preconceived ideas and intervention approaches.

PART VII

THERAPEUTIC SPECIALISMS

7.1 INTRODUCING THERAPEUTIC SPECIALISMS: CONTINUING PERSONAL AND PROFESSIONAL DEVELOPMENT

TERRY HANLEY

OVERVIEW OF THIS SECTION

The final section of this *Handbook* is another large and multifaceted one. It includes a further 25 chapters for individuals to get their teeth into, and this introductory chapter provides a brief reflection on the five subsections that they are broken up into. In doing so, the section builds upon the 'specialisms' that might be viewed as inherent in section VI, which focused upon client presenting issues, and purposefully slices the issue from a different angle. Specifically, this section might be viewed as focusing more upon therapist factors rather than the client ones previously discussed.

The five subdivisions of this section are (1) Diversity and difference in therapy, (2) Therapy settings, (3) Lifespan issues, (4) Therapeutic modalities, and (5) Technology and therapy. Although there are numerous ways that therapeutic specialisms can be divided up, and we do not claim to cover all potential specialisms, these topics help us to harness some of the major areas that therapists are likely to encounter throughout their careers.

To cater for the variety on offer in this section, each chapter is framed around a relatively open brief. In addition to providing the usual *Overview and Key Points*, authors have been asked to provide reflections upon the *Background and Context* for the particular specialism being discussed and any specific *Ways of Working* that the reader should be aware of. At the end of each chapter, there is a *Recommended Reading* section in which the authors suggest titles for those who wish to continue learning about the area in question.

CONTINUING PERSONAL AND PROFESSIONAL DEVELOPMENT

There are numerous reasons for getting into the therapeutic professions. When interviewing people for training programmes it is not uncommon for people to list wide varieties of personal and professional motivations (e.g., 'to learn about myself' and 'to get a job', respectively). Most likely, there are as many reasons as there are therapists, and

the personal nature of the decision ripples down into the specific arenas and specialisms that people focus on. For instance, individuals might be intellectually stimulated by a specific presenting issue or have a personal connection with a subject area.

Throughout the career of a therapist, the focus of their work might evolve or change into something completely different. In my case, I initially worked with young people as a therapist in a variety of educational settings and via the internet. I now work as a volunteer football therapist supporting a group of men who are survivors of torture and have fled their home countries. My choices have been influenced by events that have been personal (e.g., having children, liking playing football and considering how particular therapeutic work fits with my value system) and professional (e.g., working in academia and seeing a wide variety of opportunities that appealed to me). Even in this one case, the abundance of possibilities for counsellors and psychotherapists to diversify in the work that they do is clear. I have worked in settings where I have encountered people from different cultural backgrounds and life stages, offered individual and group therapy, and developed online therapeutic provision. Who knows where this part of my career may lead next.

When considering the wide variety of areas that people might specialise in, the stage of career development is important to consider. Rønnestad and Skovholt (2003) describe six phases that therapists go through. These are: (1) the lay helper, (2) the beginning student, (3) the advanced student, (4) the novice professional, (5) the experienced professional, and (6) the senior professional. Across each of these phases some key processes were observed. Therapists reported their own shifts in attentional focus and emotional functioning, changes in how they perceived the importance of continuous reflection for professional growth, and how they viewed their therapeutic career as a life-long personal/profession integration process. It is with these processes in mind that this section brings to the fore the issue of continuing professional development (CPD).

When considering CPD, the British Association for Counselling and Psychotherapy notes on its website:

'Your learning does not finish when you qualify as a counsellor or psychotherapist'. It goes on to reflect that therapists need to 'continually seek learning experiences to maintain, improve and broaden their competence, knowledge and skills, ensuring they can practise safely, effectively and legally within an evolving scope of practice'. Such sentiments are echoed by all of the major professional bodies in the United Kingdom (UK). In continuing this development, there are plenty of opportunities for therapists to develop into different arenas. For instance, therapists might shadow the work of colleagues, attend training sessions, discuss issues in supervision, watch videos, create a discussion group or read books (such as this one). Further, they might conduct research, publish their findings and attend or present at conferences (see Hanley, O'Hara and Steffen, 2016). The list goes on.

With the above in mind, this section introduces numerous areas that therapists might decide to specialise in. Below, I reflect briefly upon the areas covered in the chapters that follow.

DIVERSITY AND DIFFERENCE IN THERAPY

It can be argued that all therapeutic work involves encountering difference and diversity (see section II for more consideration of this). Whereas some of this work might be relatively subtle and on a surface level, in this subsection we introduce a number of areas where this topic might be viewed as more of a foreground issue for the work. Here we discuss issues of disability, gender, homelessness, working with refugees and asylum seekers and delivering therapeutic interventions while working with interpreters. Each area can be construed as specialist in its own right, with professionals in these fields being greatly attuned to the nuances of the topic, and needs to be sensitively navigated to ensure that those accessing services are treated with the appropriate levels of care and respect.

THERAPY SETTINGS

The second subsection focuses on the type of setting. As with all of the sections within this book, these settings can be incredibly rich and varied in nature. Here, the authors introduce working in primary care, further and higher education, private practice and workplace therapy. These settings are briefly introduced by Winter, Feltham and Hanley (Chapter 1.4 – this volume), but these additional chapters provide the opportunity to describe them in more detail. The chapters also outline specific roles that therapists take on, such as working as a coach and working with the media, and focus on specific issues that therapists might

encounter, such as working in a short-term way or liaising with neuroscience and neuropsychological services.

LIFESPAN ISSUES

Therapists might be keen to work with a specific age group. For instance, in watching trainees select placements for over a decade, it is not uncommon for younger therapists to work in settings with children and young people and older therapists to work in older adult settings. This is an interesting phenomenon, and by no means all encompassing, but one that warrants further exploration. The chapters here introduce work in three key periods of life where demand continues to grow, notably, work with children, young people and older adults. At the younger end of the spectrum, numerous reports highlight the vast potential need for support (e.g., Green, McGinnity, Meltzer, Ford and Goodman, 2005) and the projected impact upon society if provision is not forthcoming (e.g., Suhrcke, Pillas and Selai, 2008). Further, as populations in countries such as the UK continue to get older (e.g., United Nations, 2015), the need to provide specialist support for older adults becomes increasingly acute.

THERAPEUTIC MODALITIES

A majority of therapeutic training focuses upon the development of skills for working one-to-one with clients. As the issue of cost-effectiveness of therapy becomes ever more common, group interventions have great potential to be offered at a lower cost per person and to reach a wider audience. Outside the financial aspect of therapy, work with more than one client can have distinct therapeutic benefits. The introduction of peers, like-minded others, family members, or a partner in couple therapy, can prove fruitful in engaging the broader systems in which people live.

TECHNOLOGY AND THERAPY

The final subsection discusses technology and therapy. Douglas Adams, citing the computer scientist Bran Ferren, said that 'technology is stuff that doesn't work yet' (Adams, 1999: no page). These sentiments reflect the challenges that counsellors and psychotherapists have encountered when working in new frontiers. More recently, however, therapy via the telephone or internet has become increasingly commonplace and more reliable. Although this territory is hostile and alien to some therapists, to others it is a land rife with opportunity. Wherever you position yourself on this spectrum, such developments have become almost impossible to ignore and technology has a habit of entering into therapeutic spaces whether we are expecting them or not (e.g., when a client asked to meet via the telephone while they are on holiday or when a client brings in photos of his recently deceased father into face-to-face therapy). With this in mind, these chapters become essential introductions for all therapists (for further discussion about where technology and therapy meet in face-to-face work, see also Pattison, Hanley, Pykhtina and Ersahin (2015)).

After this point we come to the end of the section on specialities. Indeed, we come to the end of the book. We hope that throughout the text you have found the contents thought-provoking and useful in your work. Further, we hope we have provided you with much food for thought and sparked areas of interest that will support you in your journey as a therapist. Whether at the start of a journey or towards the end, we believe there is plenty in here for everyone.

QUESTIONS

1. What drives you to learn more about therapy/work as a therapist? Do you believe certain environments or ways of working resonate more with who you are as a person?
2. How competent do you feel at working (i) with diversity and difference, (ii) in different settings, (iii) with different age groups, (iv) with groups, families or couples, or (v) using a telephone or computer?
3. If you project five years into the future, how do you see your career developing? Is there a specialism that you want to develop? How might you do that?

REFERENCES

Adams, D. (1999). How to stop worrying and learn to love the internet. *Sunday Times*, 29 September.
Green, H., McGinnity, A., Meltzer, H., Ford, T. and Goodman, R. (2005). *Mental health of children and young people in Great Britain 2004*. London: Palgrave.
Hanley, T., O'Hara, D. and Steffen, E. (2016). Research: from consumer to producer. In B. Douglas, R. Woolfe, S. Strawbridge, E. Kasket and V. Galbraith (Eds.), *The handbook for counselling psychology* (4th ed., pp. 530–546). London: Sage.
Pattison, S., Hanley, T., Pykhtina, O. and Ersahin, Z. (2015). Extending practice: new horizons and contexts. In M. Robson, S. Pattison and A. Benyon (Eds.), *The Sage handbook for counselling children and young people* (pp. 427–441). London: Sage.
Rønnestad, M. H. and Skovholt, T. M. (2003). The journey of the counselor and therapist: research findings and perspectives on professional development. *Journal of Career Development*, 30(1), 5–44.
Suhrcke, M., Pillas, D. and Selai, C. (2008). Economic aspects of mental health in children and adolescents. In *Social cohesion for mental well-being among adolescents* (pp. 43–64). Copenhagen: World Health Organisation, Regional Office for Europe.
United Nations. (2015). *World population ageing 2015 (ST/ESA/SER.A/390)*. New York: United Nations.

THERAPEUTIC SPECIALISMS: DIVERSITY AND DIFFERENCE IN THERAPY

7.2 COUNSELLING PEOPLE LABELLED WITH ASPERGER SYNDROME

NICK HODGE AND ANJA RUTTEN

OVERVIEW AND KEY POINTS

This chapter conceptualises Asperger Syndrome (AS) before considering associated issues that might appear within the counselling room. An argument is made that many of these concerns arise from a misfit between a person's mode of being and the ways in which the social world is constructed. Counselling can be an effective tool for helping a client to understand and resist the effects of disabling practices.

- AS arises from a misfit between particular modes of being and the social world.
- Experiencing disabling environments and practices can inflict significant emotional damage on individuals.
- Counselling can help clients to identify and resist these effects.
- Counsellors may need to embrace different ways of working to best support clients with AS.

BACKGROUND AND CONTEXT

DEFINING AND RECOGNISING ASPERGER SYNDROME

Asperger Syndrome is one of the 'conditions' that come within the umbrella title of the autism spectrum. While diagnostic labelling of autism has changed with the latest version of the *Diagnostic Statistical Manual of Mental Disorders* (DSM-5) (American Psychiatric Association, 2013), the term Asperger Syndrome is still used. Dominant modes of communication and social engagement can result in profound and fundamental difficulties for people who identify with the label of AS. Modes of being identified as AS result from a misfit between physiology and the environment and not from developmental experience (Rutter, 2005). These difficulties are said to occur in three key areas: social communication, social interaction and flexibility of thinking (Wing, 1996). People with AS can find it problematic to understand themselves and non-autistic ways of being. They can experience difficulty

with understanding and employing expected social rules and etiquette; predicting or monitoring how others might react to social exchanges; and identifying, and fitting in with, social and cultural trends that differ from their own. Other common characteristics are said to include very strong but narrow and dominating interests and unusual sensory experiences that can make environments highly challenging and stressful. However, people are of course individuals with their own distinct profile of interests, abilities and challenges. In addition, majority constructions of experience impose certain ways of being on people while often not understanding or accepting that differences are not pathological. Therefore, understandings of people with AS by non-autistic people can be deeply problematic too. This is what Milton (2012) describes as the double empathy problem. Ways of experiencing the world are rich and varied and it should not be assumed that all people with AS will have a prescribed set of concerns or will demonstrate similar responses to counselling approaches.

Estimates of incidence of AS vary widely, but generally, a figure of around 1 per cent of the population is now commonly referred to (Brugha et al., 2011). Although it still appears that significantly more males than females are claimed to have AS, this is partly due to under-recognition of AS in women (Gill, 2016). There is no medical test for AS: it is identified by observation of behaviour and accounts of development and experience.

ACCESSING COUNSELLING

To receive a diagnosis, people with AS have average or above average intellectual abilities and they are often articulate. These strengths can mask the extent of the difficulties that they experience. Clients with AS may arrive at counselling because of years of being bullied and ostracised for being perceived as 'different'; because of trying to manage environments that are overwhelmingly stressful; and/or because partners are seeking help with relationship difficulties arising from different priorities and perspectives. So significant are the tensions of trying to exist in a socially-oriented world that these are often demonstrated in people with AS through forms such as extreme anxiety and depression. Other associated conditions include eating disorders, substance abuse and bipolar disorder (Mannion et al., 2014; Matson and Nebel-Schwalm, 2007).

Clients may or may not have a diagnosis of AS at the time of seeing a counsellor or may not disclose it. Indeed, many counsellors will have encountered AS without either the counsellor or the client realising it. For those who have acquired a diagnosis, identifying to others as having AS is something that is often tightly controlled by individuals who have internalised a view of AS as a negative and lesser way of being (Davidson and Henderson, 2010). They may have learned to fear how association with this label might impact on how others perceive and respond to them. Clients are likely to have established different positions in relation to this, from embracing and promoting the label to trying to 'pass' as non-autistic. Counsellors, therefore, may need to recognise the AS modes of thinking and experiencing from how a client expresses his or her life account. Likely signposts will include difficulties in understanding the viewpoints of others in relationships. People with AS may experience feelings of (and actual) marginalisation and rejection. Some clients with AS will experience fundamental difficulty with reflecting on their own behaviour, emotions and thoughts in a way that makes sense to a non-autistic counsellor. A further signpost may be that the client does not use a typical range of body and facial gestures: counsellors may find it harder to 'read' the client with AS or may feel that their own gestural communications are not being responded to.

BARRIERS TO ACCESSING COUNSELLING

People with AS may experience a number of barriers to accessing counselling services. Generally, they will have fewer financial resources than those who are non-disabled and so the cost of counselling is frequently prohibitive (Reeve, 2000). Professionals or carers may assume that anxiety and depression are characteristic of AS, rather than a response to stressful environments, and so then do not support people with AS in accessing counselling services. Some are also excluded from mainstream psychological and psychiatric services on the basis of their autism.

Additional barriers may include a lack of awareness of the availability and purpose of counselling, or inaccessible information about this; a perspective that the problem *always* lies 'out there' in society and it is that which needs to change rather than the individual with AS; and difficulty with pragmatic processes, such as locating a counsellor, making an appointment and finding a venue (Tantam, 2003). Counsellors' perceptions of their own competence can also lead them to reject potential clients because they have a label signifying a 'condition' that the counsellor feels needs specialist help (Raffensperger, 2009). Unfortunately, there are very few specialist services available and so this position can then leave people with AS without any access to counselling services.

WAYS OF WORKING

There are a number of principles that counsellors can use to help to remove some of these barriers. These include promoting their services through AS support networks, identifying potential sources of funding, reporting on how counselling has supported clients with AS, and being flexible about where sessions might take place and in what form. For example, some clients need more frequent, shorter sessions; others need a high level of consistency around room layout, dates and times.

CASE EXAMPLE – JACOB

Jacob is a 28-year-old man with AS. He is excellent at his job as a software engineer but has been passed over for promotion several times due to his strained relationships with other staff. Jacob has been told by his manager to 'sort himself out'. When Jacob arrives, he questions the counsellor at length about her qualifications and he wants to know what he needs to do to achieve 'being sorted'. Rather than seeing Jacob as controlling or inappropriate, the counsellor explains in detail how counselling works and what Jacob can expect. This includes a discussion about how they will know whether counselling is working for Jacob and what they will do if Jacob finds counselling unhelpful.

Counsellors may help the person with AS to identify and articulate the barriers to their personal wellbeing but enabling solutions might well require help from outside the counselling relationship. Counsellors could consider working as part of a team with someone who knows the client well. This raises ethical issues for counsellors, including confidentiality and client consent, but research has shown that this type of teamworking is likely to make a positive contribution to counselling outcomes for people with AS (Raffensperger, 2009).

CASE EXAMPLE – ROSE

Rose is 17 years old and attends college where she is taking a catering course. She is highly anxious and her parents are concerned about her frequent difficulties managing her emotions. Rose often has 'meltdowns', where her environment feels overwhelming, and these experiences leave her exhausted and low. As part of counselling Rose and her therapist write notes at the end of the session in a book that Rose takes home to share with her parents. Sometimes Rose or her parents will write notes in the book for Rose to take back to therapy. This enables Rose's family to support her outside the sessions and helps Rose connect what she is working on in sessions to daily life.

Counsellors should not be discouraged from engaging with people with AS if access to a support team is not immediately apparent. People with AS often experience a very limited number of positive relationships; the act of regular and predictable engagement with another person that enables being heard, feeling understood and being reminded of skills and capabilities might go a long way to raising self-esteem and improving quality of life.

Working with people with less expected modes of thinking, experiencing and engagement can challenge and enrich the practice of counselling (Hodge, 2013). Counsellors may well need to act differently to meet the requirements of clients with AS. People with AS often rely upon clearly expressed expectations from others and the boundaries around particular relationships being made explicit. This is good counselling practice anyway but it may help to record this agreement – to make a visual account that the client can revisit, as required, until sure of what is expected. An assessment of the client's needs may also lead to the counsellor needing to learn to work with approaches that might feel outside her/his immediate comfort zone, such as using technology in sessions (Abney and Maddux, 2004) or even conducting the whole process over the internet (Barak et al., 2009): engagement via computers is reported frequently as especially suited to the communicative and processing style of people with AS, particularly because unpredictability and inconsistency can be reduced. Linking people with AS into internet or local support groups where they might be able to share interests and life management strategies can also make significant differences to levels of wellbeing. A word of caution remains to negotiate this with clients,

as individual preferences may of course be different from global stereotypes.

RESEARCH EVIDENCE

There have been relatively few research studies and accounts of counselling with clients who have AS, although this is changing. More claims are made within the academic literature for the effectiveness of cognitive-behavioural and mindfulness approaches, alongside evaluation of psycho-education in the form of social skills training (Spain et al., 2015). There are also emerging accounts of other approaches, for example, systemic therapy (Haydon-Laurelut, 2016). While studies of counselling show general trends towards improvement of emotional distress, it is not possible to draw population-based conclusions from this.

Many people with AS are dismissive of psychotherapy, viewing their difficulties with social understanding and engagement as unconnected to psychological causation rooted in the past (Singer, 1999). Many have therapeutic experiences that have not met their needs and have become sceptical about therapists and therapy, as the principles of counselling are predicated on normative functioning. However, psychotherapy might have something to offer people with AS if it uses their particular strengths to identify and understand how environments and relationships with others might have disabled and disempowered them. Psychotherapy, if based upon an acceptance of the nature of autistic development, does have the potential to help people with AS live more satisfying lives.

Attwood (2004) suggests a number of useful, practical and accessible strategies that can support some people with AS by presenting abstract concepts in more visual, concrete forms. Information that is visual is said to be much more accessible to people with AS, because it can be referred to, and processed, over time.

It can be helpful to support a client with formulating practical strategies for managing breakdowns in communication. These might include identifying whom to go to for guidance or using a phrase to 'buy processing time', such as 'let me think about that and I will get back to you'. Selecting appropriate forms of support will depend upon a counsellor being able to understand the client's unique individual perspective and to position this in relation to the person's capacity for empathy and reflection. Distress caused by unwanted isolation, lack of meaningful occupation, living on benefits, being subject to current or past victimisation is not easily resolved unless there is a realistic chance of improving the underlying environmental factors.

The value of therapy as a general practice is well established and there is no reason to think that these benefits cannot apply equally to clients with AS. For clients with AS, successful counselling is likely to involve validating the experience of the client and collaborating on what the client may wish to work on. This may also require a focus on changing disabling environments rather than the client. Counsellors may need to seek support for this process from those who know the client well, so that therapeutic gains transfer to the client's life outside therapy. Organisations that can inform about AS will also be a useful resource.

Counsellors may need to adapt their style of communication and engage with a wider range of approaches than they are used to; many such developments in their practice may well benefit all clients, not just those with AS. Specialist counselling services for people with AS are rare and it is not helpful if lack of access denies people with AS the benefits of counselling. Counsellors embracing working with clients who have AS are likely to find this an enriching and personally developing experience. The ability to identify, appreciate, learn about and accommodate different ways of being in the world is really the essential requirement for effective counselling with people with AS.

REFERENCES

Abney, P.C. and Maddux, C.D. (2004) Counseling and technology: some thoughts about the controversy. *Journal of Technology in Human Services*, 22(3): 1–24.

American Psychiatric Association (2013) *Diagnostic and Statistical Manual of Mental Disorders* (5th ed.). Washington, DC: American Psychiatric Association.

Attwood, T. (2004) Cognitive behaviour therapy for children and adults with Asperger's syndrome. *Behaviour Change*, 21(3): 147–161.

Barak, A., Klein, B. and Proudfoot, J.G. (2009) Defining internet-supported therapeutic interventions. *Annals of Behavioral Medicine*, 38: 4–17.

Brugha, T.S., McManus, S., Bankart, J., Scott, F., Purdon, S., Smith, J., Bebbington, P., Jenkins, R. and Meltzer, H. (2011) Epidemiology of autism spectrum disorders in adults in the community in England. *Archive of General Psychiatry*, 68(5): 459–465.

Davidson, J. and Henderson, V.L. (2010) 'Coming out' on the autism spectrum: autism, identity and disclosure. *Social & Cultural Geography*, 11(2): 155–170.

Gill, M. (2016) The other 25%: autistic girls and women. *European Psychiatry*, 33(Suppl): S351–S352.

Haydon-Laurelut, M. (2016) Autism stories and disabled people with learning difficulties. In K. Runswick-Cole, R. Mallett and S. Timimi (eds), *Re-thinking Autism: Diagnosis, Identity and Equality* (pp. 221–238). London: Jessica Kingsley Publishers.

Hodge, N. (2013) Counselling, autism and the problem of empathy. *British Journal of Guidance & Counselling*, 41(2): 105–116.

Mannion, A., Brahm, M. and Leader, G., (2014) Comorbid psychopathology in autism spectrum disorder. *Review Journal of Autism and Developmental Disorders*, 1(2): 124–134.

Matson, J.L. and Nebel-Schwalm, M.S. (2007) Comorbid psychopathology with autism spectrum disorder in children: an overview. *Research in Developmental Disabilities*, 28(4): 341–352.

Milton, D. (2012) On the ontological status of autism: the 'double empathy problem'. *Disability and Society*, 27(6): 883–887.

(Continued)

(Continued)

Raffensperger, M. (2009) Factors that influence outcomes for clients with an intellectual disability. *British Journal of Guidance & Counselling*, 37(4): 495–509.

Reeve, D. (2000) Oppression within the counselling room. *Disability & Society*, 15(4): 669–682.

Rutter, M. (2005) Aetiology of autism: findings and questions. *Journal of Intellectual Disability Research*, 49(4) 231–238.

Singer, J. (1999) 'Why can't you be normal for once in your life?' From a 'problem with no name' to the emergence of a new category of difference. In M. Corker and S. French (eds), *Disability Discourse* (pp. 59–66). Buckingham: Open University Press.

Spain, D., Sin, J., Chalder, T., Murphy, D. and Happé, F. (2015) Cognitive behaviour therapy for adults with autism spectrum disorders and psychiatric co-morbidity: A review. *Research in Autism Spectrum Disorders*, 9: 151–162.

Tantam, D. (2003) The challenge of adolescents and adults with Asperger Syndrome. *Child & Adolescent Psychiatric Clinics of North America*, 12: 143–163.

Wing, L. (1996) *The Autistic Spectrum*. London: Constable & Robinson.

RECOMMENDED READING

1.   Attwood, T. (2007) *The Complete Guide to Asperger's Syndrome*. London: Jessica Kingsley Publishers.

An excellent introduction for anyone wanting to know more about AS.

2.   Runswick-Cole, K., Mallett, R. and Timimi, S. (eds) (2016) *Re-thinking Autism: Disability, Identity and Equality*. London: Jessica Kingsley Publishers.

A text exploring the ways in which autism is currently conceptualised and practised. Includes a chapter by Mark Haydon-Laurelut on the use of critical systemic therapy.

3.   Sutton, M. (ed.) (2015) *The Real Experts: Readings for Parents of Autistic Children*. Fort Worth, TX: Autonomous Press.

This book represents the most critical source of information on autistic experience: people with autism themselves. The contributors to this book all identify with the label of autism and explore what they feel it means to be autistic in the world.

7.3   WORKING WITH DISABILITY

SIMON PARRITT

OVERVIEW AND KEY POINTS

Working with disability requires the same skills and awareness when working with difference and diversity in other groups. However, this chapter will address the particular differences of working with disabled people, of whom 17% (Papworth Trust, 2013) are born with their impairments but the majority are acquired later in life. A key element is the interaction between impairment, identity, life stage and the socio-cultural environment. Accessibility, not only environmental and attitudinal but the therapeutic model, service provider and the counsellor will be explored as well as the role the internet plays in offering some disabled clients access to counselling and psychotherapy. It will also address the importance of identity, autonomy and choice when working with disabled people.

The key points to consider include:

- As the population ages, disabled people represent an increasing proportion of clients. It is therefore essential that all counsellors and psychotherapists examine their attitudes, practices and understanding of disability.
- Disability continues to be associated with stigma, low status and/or tragedy. As such, disabled clients may present by hiding, minimizing or denying the impact disability has on their emotional and social lives.
- Autonomy, choice and identity are all at risk for disabled people. Distinguishing between what is a result of society and what is a consequence of impairment itself are often at the heart of what therapy can offer.
- It is important to acknowledge the wide diversity within disability and understand the differences between illness, disability and impairment.

BACKGROUND AND CONTEXT

While 17% of people are born with impairments, most acquire them later in life and struggle to identify positively as 'disabled', preferring terms such as 'being ill' or 'suffering from' particular conditions, such as epilepsy, arthritis or even multiple sclerosis. Despite improved attitudes, government initiatives and greater awareness, including media and sports events such as the paralympics, 'disability' continues to be associated with dependency and benefits, and therefore being seen as belonging to this group can be problematic. Working with what disability means in everyday life for the client, yourself and society is central both within the therapeutic relationship and in the wider world. For a more extensive exploration of the social and cultural context in which disability can be placed, and how this can be reflected within the therapeutic relationship and the wider society, see Parritt (Chapter 2.3, this volume).

It is important to consider that for a client who has had many previous encounters where they have been subject to assessment, treatment and judgement by the health and social care system, you may be seen as just another professional. The power differential in these encounters is quite different from the therapeutic encounter you can offer and therefore paying special attention to the lived experience of the disabled client is particularly important. Never assume the client understands the meaning of confidentiality or trusts you easily, as compliance or even resistance may be a habitual and adapted way of responding. As a result, the therapeutic relationship, confidentiality and consent should be explored, as they may be unique concepts and a particularly powerful and valuable a part of what you offer.

PRIVACY AND AUTONOMY

The first casualties of becoming a disabled person are privacy and autonomy. Experiencing 'public' access to body and person is something few of us experience beyond infancy. Medical interventions and personal assistance in day-to-day activities only increases the stressors on disabled people's lives as they negotiate their autonomy and privacy in intimate and sexual relationships, family, friends and the wider community. While never diminishing the actual impact of impairment, pain and fatigue, what brings people to therapy is largely distress in relationship to others and their social environment. The therapeutic relationship with a disabled client will therefore reflect the two dimensions of disability and impairment which disrupt and distort all relationships. We must be brave enough to listen and learn about the disabled client's lived experience and never be afraid to ask questions, as the client is the expert. Exploring the tensions between social attitudes, behaviour and prejudice with a positive identity as a disabled person is a task that can be undertaken collaboratively within an empowering empathic therapeutic relationship.

THE WIDER CONTEXT

It is regrettable that disability remains under-represented or invisible within the profession, but not because, as some have suggested, therapy for disabled people should be by disabled people, as this is unrealistic and uneconomic, but because it is also 'ghettoizing'. Disabled counsellors and psychotherapists may share something of the same, but this can mislead and it ignores the wide diversity that exists within the disabled community. Being non-disabled is therefore no reason not to enjoy and embrace working in this area effectively. Indeed, employing the relationship itself between yourself and your disabled client offers a safe space in which difference and otherness can be explored.

SUPERVISION

Disability is not well covered within training and in a study by a disabled counsellor, 75% of trainees were surprised, following awareness exposure, that they viewed disability in terms of tragedy and loss (Parkinson, 2006). There seem fewer opportunities to work with disability *per se*, let alone from an empowerment perspective, and therefore less opportunity to develop these skills and confidence once qualified.

A client who presents with an obvious physical difference or impairment that is a result of a violent or traumatic event may be unsettling and evoke personal feelings or memories within the counsellor. Because aspects of disabled people's lives, such as the constant presence of assistants and carers, are alien for those with no experience, reactions are best explored with a supervisor. It is therefore useful to have some access to a supervisor experienced in working with disability from an empowerment perspective, even if they are not a disabled person, where also the wider socio-cultural issues can be discussed. Evidence suggests that exposure to disability, either professionally or sometimes through personal experiences, will mitigate some of the pitfalls enabling a more open, empowering and constructive approach (Parritt and O'Callaghan, 2000).

VENUE AND ACCESSIBILITY

The Disability Discrimination Act 1995, now largely superseded by the Equalities Act 2010, makes it illegal to discriminate against disabled people in the provision of goods and services. You are therefore expected to make 'reasonable adjustment' to accommodate your clients, but what is 'reasonable' is not always clear. Many counselling services are still difficult to access because of stairs, transport or other barriers, including cost. While you cannot be expected to anticipate all access requirements, it is good practice to enquire prior to the initial session what adjustments or assistance might be needed to access your service. For instance, arranging a ground-floor room, disabled parking, accessible toilets and amenities or even flexible session times to take account of the unpredictability of accessible transport or physical fatigue or pain.

WAYS OF WORKING

ONLINE COUNSELLING

The role of social media and the internet, with all its pros and cons, has given freedom of access to the outside world and become an integral part of many disabled people's lives in the twenty-first century. The use of online counselling and psychotherapy is therefore particularly relevant to the disabled people and having some experience in and

possible training in this area and the issues of the internet is therefore becoming increasingly valuable.

However, for some already socially isolated disabled people, the essentially remote aspect of online counselling can be a double-edged sword. It offers access by overcoming some communication impairments and distance, environmental and transport problems. The price to pay is loss of human physical presence and the holistic nature of 'being in the room', and the virtual world is real only in as far as it has relation to the physical world. For this reason, the very medium of online therapy can reinforce a distance already existing between disability and the non-disabled world. Indeed, for many with more impairment, or isolation, travelling to and being in the room with another person, who is there for them as a whole person, is one of the most beneficial and valuable aspects of the therapeutic experience.

ASSESSMENT: INITIAL SESSION

There is nothing essentially different in assessing disabled clients and the general rule is to follow your own theoretical and practical training and practice experience. However, the social and cultural context is of particular importance in reconciling an individual's internalized attitude to disability and their identity now with their previous non-disabled identity and beliefs.

The tension between past and present can be stark and accompanied and reinforced by loss of friends, work and social integration. Understanding and working with what it means to be 'different' is central to working with marginalized and disadvantaged groups, but unlike others, such as Black, Minority Ethnic (BME), Lesbian, Gay, Bisexual and Transgendered (LGBT) or gender, adopting a positive identity as a disabled person has the added challenge of being defined by actual physical or cognitive impairment, not social and cultural discrimination alone. Indeed, the dynamics within the client's own identity group as the family or a couple are always disrupted by the onset of impairment, whether slow and progressive, as with some neurological conditions, or sudden, such as traumatic injury.

A client's age, socio-cultural context as well as sexual and emotional life are all influencing factors at the time of onset and when seeking counselling. A disabled child is rarely expected or desired and experiencing any positive mirroring or finding a peer group in which to develop and mature as a whole disabled person is therefore difficult at best, impossible at worst. The usual learning opportunities to experiment and form close intimate relationships may have been disrupted or as disabled people are seen as asexual. This can lead to an over-abundance of platonic friendships accompanied with a delay in gaining full social integration, despite living independently.

THE DISABLED CLIENT

Disabled people come to counselling and psychotherapy for the same reasons as anyone else, and not necessarily because of impairment or because they are a disabled person. Often, psychotherapy has relied upon a model of loss and bereavement when dealing with disabled people. While there may be a place for this, counsellors need to be aware that concentrating on loss with disabled people may be inappropriate. Disability remains a low-status and negative identity and many clients hold internalized negative beliefs echoing the wider socio-cultural perception of disability. This goes some way to explain the resistance to accepting the term 'disabled', preferring to be seen as 'ill' or be 'suffering' from a 'condition'. While pain, fatigue and physical impairment may be foreground for the client, it is often the interactions and experiences of living in a non-disabled world that is the origin of distress. This is challenging for all disabled people but, for many, reconciling who they are and can be now with who they once were and hoped to be creates an ongoing dissonance between the real world out there, its reactions, and the new self. Integrating a positive identity as a disabled person alongside the reality of impairment within a society that is at best ambivalent and often rejecting is the core issue.

CASE EXAMPLE: JOHN

John is in his late 30s. Following changes at work, he is feeling stressed and relationships with his wife and family have become increasingly difficult. He wants help dealing with his anxiety, low mood and what he calls his 'short fuse'. He was diagnosed with multiple sclerosis (MS) last year. After enquiring if the changes at work were related to the MS diagnosis, he says yes, only his wife and work know. He says he isn't disabled and can work and manage fine at present, though his voice tails off on the words 'at present'. When asked about others knowing about his MS, he says that he doesn't want people to look at him differently, avoid or pity him.

It becomes clear that John has a strong work ethic and beliefs about being 'a man' and his role as 'a provider' for his family. While the progressive nature of his condition will require constant psychological and physical re-adaption, issues around male identity and the stigma of disability underlie his rejection of help and sharing with others. Challenging at this point may undermine the therapeutic alliance, but ignoring it or adopting a cognitive and coping paradigm may collude and potentially reinforce a view of disability as a negative identity and individual dysfunction. Exploring the differences between impairment, illness and disability as and when he is ready offers a chance to deal with each more clearly. Impairments are real restrictions and the loss of the former 'embodied self' is quite different from being ill, while disability is a social construction and different again from impairment. Reframing disability as a new identity, separate and different from his, and society's, concept of it as loss and dependency is potentially a powerful option. This can allow the exploration of feelings around others' comments and prejudices towards disability which may also have echoes within past life and relationships experiences. This can enable thoughts, cognitions and coping strategies to be more effectively worked on alongside a new socio-cultural context for his life.

There is a difficult balancing act for both counsellor and client as the real impact of physical impairment cannot, and should not, be dismissed or ignored during the therapeutic process. An understanding and empathy for the amount of mental and physical energy required in living life as a disabled person is essential. There may be less energy, however accessible, for social and leisure activities due to fatigue and/or pain, and others will not necessarily understand the impact or the physical support and assistance required for daily tasks. The quantity of different factors and the extent to which any of them are applicable to the particular client's experiences are part of the collaborative discovery that must take place.

Naturally, helping a client with the trauma or an accident will be part of working with this client group, but the underlying work may lie in helping to integrate a new self-affirming identity, of which being a disabled person and coping with social reactions to them are part. This can be an ongoing struggle, and offering a space where it can be explored, moving beyond but not ignoring the trauma and loss, can be the most rewarding aspect of this work for both client and counsellor.

RESEARCH EVIDENCE

There is a paucity of coherent and valid research into counselling, psychotherapy and disability, and where it does exist, it largely addresses particular conditions, with a focus on coping skills and strategies using cognitive and behavioural approaches. In recent years the Improving Access to Psychological Therapies (IAPT) initiative has favoured cognitive-behavioural therapy (CBT) as the model to make counselling more widely available, particularly for anxiety and depression. However, many psychotherapists and counsellors come from a tradition that involves a more relational and person-centred approach. This is not to say that CBT does not recognize that the therapeutic relationship as important, but it was not originally prioritized within the core competencies (Roth and Pilling, 2007). For disabled clients, this bias towards a 'medical and systemized' approach, while effective within certain limits, may collude with a 'cure' or 'coping' paradigm. This can reinforce disability as dysfunction at the individual level, without encorporating the socio-cultural perspective or the oppression and prejudice that is the everyday experience of disabled people. Indeed, recently the level of reported 'hate crime' against disabled people is on the increase (Home Office, 2015).

The number and demographic of disabled people who have sought counselling is unknown, although it has accepted that disabled people are more likely than the general population to experience co-morbidities, such as anxiety and depression. Public Health England (2015) has found that those using social care services are around seven times more likely to feel moderately or extremely anxious or depressed compared with the general population.

Whatever your approach, there is nothing essentially different about working with disabled people, whether born with this identity or whether it is acquired later in life. We live, love and work within a diverse world and few, if any, impairments prevent or remove sexual identity and the need for sexual expression and intimacy. This is often a silent and overlooked aspect of disability and professionals, as well as society, can find it difficult to address, even in themselves. However, without incorporating this aspect of a client's identity and life we can fail to address and meet with the whole person, and, as such, ultimately diminish the full humanity of the client and society.

REFERENCES

Home Office (2015) *Hate Crime, England and Wales, 2014 to 2015*. London: HMSO. (www.gov.uk/government/statistics/hate-crime-england-and-wales-2014-to-2015).

Papworth Trust (2013) *Disability in the United Kingdom 2013: Facts and Figures*. (www.papworthtrust.org.uk/sites/default/files/Facts%20and%20Figures%202013%20web.pdf).

Parkinson, G. (2006) Counsellors' attitudes towards Disability Equality Training (DET) *British Journal of Guidance & Counselling*, 34(1): 93–105.

Parritt, S. and O'Callaghan, J. (2000) Splitting the difference: an exploratory study of therapists' work with sexuality, relationships and disability. *Sexual and Relationship Therapy*, 15(2): 151–169.

Public Health England (2015) *Common Mental Health Disorders 2013/2014*. (http://fingertips.phe.org.uk/profile-group/mental-health/profile/common-mentaldisorders/data#page/0/gid/8000026/pat/6/par/E12000007/ati/102/are/E09000024/iid/90535/age/168/sex/4).

Roth, D.A. and Pilling, S. (2007) *The Competences Required to Deliver Effective Cognitive and Behavioural Therapy for People with Depression and with Anxiety Disorders*. London: Department of Health.

RECOMMENDED READING

1.   Barnes, C. and Mercer, G. (2010) *Exploring Disability.* Cambridge: Polity Press.

This book is a good overview of the social model and the context in which disability is placed within society, providing a good background for those working with a wider perspective with disabled people.

2. Olkin, R. (1999) *What Psychotherapists Should Know about Disability*. New York: Guilford Press.

Written by a disabled psychologist from the USA, it covers a great deal of ground and is both practical and useful whatever your model of working. It is also valuable in that it addresses many relationship issues.

3. Wilson, S. (2003) *Disability, Counselling and Psychotherapy: Challenges and Opportunities*. Basingstoke: Palgrave Macmillan.

Wilson takes a psychodynamic approach while maintaining a positive view of disability and the social context in which disabled people experience life and its challenges. It includes a section on sexuality.

7.4 FEMINIST THERAPY

LIZ BALLINGER

OVERVIEW AND KEY POINTS

This chapter describes the emergence of feminist therapy as a grassroots movement that emerged out of the Women's Liberation Movement of the 1960s. Its central contribution to fourth-wave therapy is described as well as its wider influence on therapeutic practice. While its divergent nature is highlighted, its broad tenets and therapeutic strategies are summarised. Its underdeveloped research profile is sketched and potentially problematised.

- Feminist therapy provides a radical critique of the power imbalance and pathologisation that characterises orthodox therapeutic approaches.
- 'The personal is political' reflects its belief in the all-encompassing role of the patriarchy, or society built upon male power, in shaping female lives and creating their distress.
- The central aim of feminist therapy is the empowerment of clients and both personal and social change.
- The call for evidence-based practice provides a potential challenge to its future development.

BACKGROUND AND CONTEXT

Feminist therapy started out as a grassroots movement among female practitioners who rejected the therapeutic orthodoxies of the time and sought ways of practising that were both relevant and respectful to the needs of women. As its name implies, this movement was inspired

and continues to be shaped by feminism, a movement dedicated to the empowerment of individual women and the achievement of political, economic, personal and social rights for all women equal to those of men.

THE RISE OF FEMINISM

Focused initially within the United States of America (USA) and Europe, feminism has a history spanning three centuries and antecedents that reach back further. While it remains characterised by diversity, 'waves' in its development have been identified. The first wave, from the 1840s to the 1920s, focused on the gaining of specific property, educational and political rights for women. The second wave, emerging from the 1960s, sought to highlight and challenge inequality across a wide range of fronts. Its clarion call 'the personal is political' reflected its emphasis on patriarchy's all-pervasive impact on women's lives. The third wave, dated from the 1980s to the present, marked a shift to a more self-critical and diverse feminism. The divisions within, rather than the unity of, women's experiences were emphasised, alongside the intersectionality of oppressions relating to gender, class, sexuality, age, race and disability. The focus of concern is described as shifting from collective social activism towards individual emancipation and micro-politics. An emergent fourth wave has been more recently identified and is connected with, on the one hand, an increased focus on spirituality and community and, on the other, a new surge of global feminist activity stimulated and enabled by the rise of social media.

DEVELOPMENTS WITHIN COUNSELLING AND PSYCHOTHERAPY

Developmental waves have similarly been identified within counselling and psychotherapy. Jones-Smith (2016) identifies five. The first two were characterised by psychoanalysis and behaviourism respectively, and the third, from the 1960s, by the rise of humanistic therapies. A fourth wave, gaining momentum from the 1970s, reflected the rise of approaches reflecting social constructionist and postmodern understandings. A fifth emergent wave is identified, connected with the rise of neuroscience and neuropsychotherapy.

The roots of feminist counselling practice are located within the third wave, during which some practitioners turned to humanistic approaches in reaction against 'the determinism and misogyny of psychoanalysis and the mechanistic view of humans that then defined behaviorism' (Brown, 2010: 9). However, it was the fourth wave that saw feminist therapy emerging as a distinct approach, stimulated by practitioners' involvement in the feminist conscious-raising groups that characterised second-wave feminism of the 1960s. Feminist therapy proved to be a key constituent of the therapeutic fourth wave, and went on to influence theory and practice across the therapeutic field.

THE DEVELOPING NATURE OF FEMINIST THERAPY

As has been widely observed, feminist therapy lacks unity and cohesion. Feminist therapists assume divergent standpoints within the modality. There are identifiable national differences in its developmental trajectory. In Britain, while many feminists remain critical of psychoanalysis, a feminist psychoanalytic approach gained ground, developed and spearheaded by Eichenbaum and Orbach (1982). Another British variant is the rhythm model associated with Chaplin (1999), which embraces feminine values and ways of thinking. In America, feminist therapy became more closely associated with an empowerment model, shaped by humanistic and cognitive-behavioural understandings (Worell and Remer, 2003). On a wider front, in Britain and elsewhere, feminist principles became integrated into the practice of therapists working across a range of theoretical perspectives, making variety in its application inevitable.

Again, as with feminism and psychotherapy, and with the same danger of oversimplification, phases in the development of feminist therapy have been picked out. Brown (2010) identifies four. The first, dating from the 1960s to the early 1980s, emphasised the unity of female experience and denied any inherent difference between the sexes that could justify social inequality. The second stage, from the mid-1980s to the mid-1990s, saw a shift of emphasis towards difference. Some therapists emphasised the innate differences between men and women, and the consistent devaluing of particularly feminine qualities, priorities and values under the patriarchy. In parallel, the diversity-awareness of third-wave feminism was leading to an increased emphasis on the differences between women. This ultimately paved the way for the third stage of development, which emerged from the mid-1990s and embraced these differences. A feminist multicultural approach to counselling developed from the intersection of feminist and multicultural perspectives and continues to grow in significance, particularly within the field of counselling psychology. Patriarchy's destructive effect on both sexes was also recognised, leading to an argument for the relevance of feminist therapy for men (e.g., Mintz and Tager, 2013). The period also marked attempts to further develop the theoretical and practical underpinnings of feminist counselling. One product was the empowerment feminist therapy model (Worell and Remer, 1996, 2003). Reflecting recent shifts in feminism, an emergent fourth stage has been identified, which incorporates a more global and multicultural analysis as well as a greater concern with the spiritual dimension.

WAYS OF WORKING

As emphasised, diversity marks feminist practice. This has stimulated attempts to identify core principles that cut across this diversity. Evans et al. (2011) provide a useful synthesis of these, under four core tenets, which help provide a good sense of the key 'structural elements' of feminist practice.

The personal is political. A feminist analysis of society informs practice, with an emphasis placed on the central role played by society in shaping women's psychological wellbeing. Women's distress is seen as a product of patriarchal society rather than of individual pathology, with personal experience understood as the 'lived version of political reality' (Brown, 1994: 50). The role of power in diagnosis is highlighted and orthodox diagnosis problematised as oppressive due to its focus on individual pathology. Pathology is redefined to include wider environmental causes. Rather than signifying 'illness', symptoms are reframed as potentially creative ways of coping with socially induced damage.

An egalitarian relationship. The focus is on serving a client rather than treating a patient. While acknowledging the power invested in the therapist's role, the aim is one of equality between therapist and client. Attempts are made to dismantle power imbalances by openness about therapeutic processes and procedures, the use of jargon-free language and therapist transparency. Cooperative goal-setting and ongoing negotiation are key, as is the valuing of client viewpoints, concerns and agency.

The privileging of women's experiences. Feminist therapy aims to provide an experience antithetical to societal norms by normalising and valuing women's experiences rather than problematising and/or devaluing them. Women's experiences are centrally placed rather than side-lined. The commonality of experience is acknowledged, as well as its complexity and diversity. Respect for clients' priorities, frames of reference and lived experience is central. As McLellan (1995) argues, listening to and facilitating clients in the telling of their stories is central to feminist therapy.

Empowerment. Feminist therapy concerns change rather than adjustment, growth and development rather than symptom reduction and retrenchment. The aim of therapy is to empower clients to make positive changes in their world. The focus, therefore, is both personal and social transformation. Client strengths, achievements and potential are emphasised rather than client weaknesses or deficits. The ability to accord care and respect to self as well as to be instrumental in enacting change is recognised and valorised.

While these tenets reflect feminist therapy's value-driven nature and manifest themselves somewhat as 'mission statements', there have been attempts to put 'flesh on the bone' via the provision of practical guidelines (e.g., Chaplin, 1999; McLellan, 1995). Ironically, such attempts can provide further evidence of therapy's divided nature. With this caveat in mind, Evans et al. (2011) provide some useful guidelines on how such tenets might further translate into practice. It is useful to note how a number of these strategies and techniques have become absorbed into mainstream practice, reflecting feminist therapy's wider influence.

1. INITIAL ASSESSMENT AND CONCEPTUALISATION

Evans et al. (2011) describe a five-stage process. The first stage describes how the therapist focuses on her feminist awareness and on any conditioned beliefs that might impact negatively on her work with the client. The next two stages involve the collaborative construction of a client history and generation of possible hypotheses, both processes informed by feminist analysis. In the fourth

stage, a conceptualisation of the client's distress is, again, collaboratively produced. A fifth stage might be invoked where a referral and/or medical diagnosis is necessary. Here, care would be taken to explore the meaning and potential implications of this and the content of any report negotiated.

2. ESTABLISHING AND MAINTAINING THE EGALITARIAN RELATIONSHIP

While the feminist therapeutic relationship bears many hallmarks of the person-centred one, an area of potential difference in practice lies in the willingness of feminist therapists to direct the process in the pursuit of client empowerment and equalisation of power. McLellan (1995) directly refers to the therapist's educative role. Strategies focus on the letting go of ownership of the norms, values and understandings that underpin therapy. Clients are encouraged to identify and own their strengths. Selective self-disclosure may be used by the therapist as a means of equalising power. Transparency, information-giving, negotiation and collaboration are key strategies throughout.

3. GENDER-ROLE AND POWER ANALYSIS

These are described by Evans et al. (2011) as unique to feminist therapy. Gender-role analysis involves encouraging clients to explore the gender-related messages they grew up with and how they continue to impact on their thoughts, feelings and behaviour in their adult life. Power analysis involves an exploration of clients' understanding of and relationship with power – their own and others'. In helping clients identify the effects of gender and power on their lives, the client is enabled to identify areas for change.

4. SOCIAL CHANGE AND EMPOWERMENT

A key goal of therapy is the empowerment of clients to enact change in their lives across the personal, interpersonal and social realms. The role of therapist is to 'help clients gain the awareness, knowledge and skills to address their life issues' (Evans et al., 2011: 171). A key task is to enable clients to apply feminist lenses to a reflection on their lives and present experiencing, and to utilise their developed understanding to help identify goals that will help them effect meaningful change. Although there is arguably a greater emphasis in contemporary feminist therapy on the personal and interpersonal realm, the importance of social action is reinforced.

CASE EXAMPLE

Jane is a young, white childcare worker who has been diagnosed as suffering from stress and anxiety. A friend has suggested she try counselling at a local centre that offers low-cost therapy. Jane has been referred to Anna, a white lecturer in her 50s, who works at the centre on a voluntary basis.

Anna begins by explaining to Jane what feminist therapy entails and their mutual roles within it. She introduces herself, talks about her personal values and her recognition of the social differences between them. She invites Jane to tell her how she feels about all of this and to decide whether she wants to move forward with the therapy. Jane agrees to go ahead and they negotiate an initial 10-week contract. Anna helps Jane to start to tell her story on her own terms, which forms the basis of the collaborative process of assessment and conceptualisation. At this early stage, her understandings of the external context for her distress focus on the demanding nature of her work, its long hours, and the lack of support from her male partner – all things she regards as unchangeable.

As the work progresses, while the focus remains on Jane telling her story, Anna encourages her to start to explore her experiences and distress in the light of feminist understandings. Anna introduces literature which connects the low pay and status of childcare work with its devaluation as unskilled 'women's work'. Jane expresses her anger at her partner's dismissal of her work as 'babysitting'. She expresses her sense of her limited power in her relationship linked to her low pay. She starts to link her low self-esteem with the low social status she is accorded, her sense of personal powerlessness with her lack of social power. She starts to understand her distress as rooted both within her gender and class-based experiences.

In further sessions, work continues on connecting the personal and the political. Jane's focus shifts to the past, to how she felt treated differently from her brothers by her parents and how at school she felt ignored and invisible. Anna shares her similar childhood experiences but tells how as an adult she went on to return to study. She is open about the internal and external obstacles she faced, and the resources she called on to help her. This leads into the initial stages of exploration of what Jane might want and feel able to change and the resources she might call on. These resources include her personal strengths, which Anna encourages her to identify.

In the final sessions, the focus is on change. Jane has a more highly developed sense of her own strengths and entitlements and of the changes that she can make to enhance her wellbeing. One priority is reconnecting with her own friendship groups and leisure interests separate from her partner. A second priority is a renegotiation of the sharing of housework, enabled by her growing self-confidence and support network. At work, she decides to talk with her supervisor about ways in which the nursery might promote the professional profile of all of its childcare workers. She also looks at ways of creating a clear divide between home and work.

In the tenth session, they together review and applaud her progress. Jane decides that it is time to end. She has returned to work and 'feels much better'. Anna, while feeling that there is scope for further work together, respects her decision and wishes her well.

RESEARCH EVIDENCE

There is a paucity of research demonstrating the effectiveness of feminist therapy. This makes it vulnerable in the new evidence-based practice climate, which is acting to favour more socially and politically conservative approaches, geared to maintaining the status quo rather than stimulating social change.

The nature and goals of feminist therapy are in many ways opposed to the production of statistical evidence of its effectiveness, and many feminist therapists are reluctant to 'buy into' the assumptions underpinning such research. Moreover, any attempts to so engage are hampered by feminist therapy's diverse composition, as well as lack of funding and opportunity (Brown, 2010).

Feminists argue generally that a multiplicity of evidence should be utilised in any assessment of effectiveness. There have been studies which demonstrate clients' experience of its positive impact (e.g., McLeod, 1994). The bulk of support for its effectiveness, however, comes from common factors literature, which does indeed utilise a wide range of evidence. Feminist therapy's focus on empowerment and the quality of the therapeutic relationship is viewed as generating therapy alliance variables consistently identified with positive outcomes in psychotherapy research (Norcross and Lambert, 2005). Other variables associated with the egalitarian relationship, such as collaborative goal-setting, tailoring the therapy to the client, and the client's active engagement in the process have all been similarly linked to positive outcome. While these are all positive indications of feminist therapy's worth, further research is needed to strengthen its position.

REFERENCES

Brown, L.S. (1994) *Subversive Dialogues*. New York: Basic Books.

Brown, L.S. (2010) *Feminist Therapy*. Washington, DC: American Psychological Association.

Chaplin, J. (1999) *Feminist Counselling in Action* (2nd ed.). London: Sage.

Eichenbaum, L. and Orbach, S. (1982) *Outside In Inside Out. Women's Psychology: A Feminist Psychoanalytic Approach*. Harmondsworth: Pelican.

Evans, K.M., Kincade, A.E. and Seem, S.R. (2011) *Introduction to Feminist Therapy: Strategies for Social and Individual Change*. Thousand Oaks, CA: Sage.

Jones-Smith, E. (2016) *Theories of Counseling and Psychotherapy* (2nd ed.). Thousand Oaks, CA: Sage.

McLellan, B. (1995) *Beyond Psychoppression: A Feminist Alternative Therapy*. North Melbourne, Vic.: Spinifex Press.

McLeod, E. (1994) *Women's Experience of Feminist Therapy and Counselling*. Buckingham: Open University Press.

Mintz, L.B. and Tager, D. (2013) Feminist therapy with male clients: empowering men to be their whole selves. In C.Z. Enns and E.N. Williams (Eds.), *The Oxford Handbook of Feminist Multicultural Counseling Psychology* (pp. 322–338). New York: Oxford University Press.

Norcross, J.C. and Lambert, M.J. (2005) The therapy relationship. In J. Norcross, L. Beutler and R. Levant (Eds.), *Evidence-based Practices in Mental Health: Debate and Dialogue on Fundamental Questions* (pp. 208–218). Washington, DC: American Psychological Association.

Worell, J. and Remer, P. (1996) *Feminist Perspectives in Therapy: An Empowerment Model for Women*. New York: Wiley.

Worell, J. and Remer, P. (2003) *Feminist Perspectives in Therapy: Empowering Diverse Women* (2nd ed.). New York: Wiley.

RECOMMENDED READING

1. Enns, C.Z. and E.N. Williams, E.N. (Eds.) (2013) *The Oxford Handbook of Feminist Multicultural Counseling Psychology*. New York: Oxford University Press.

While heavily oriented to the USA, this provides a comprehensive and authoritative introduction to the theory and practice of feminist multicultural counselling. It is an invaluable reference book.

2. Evans, K.M., Kincade, A.E. and Seem, S.R. (2011) *Introduction to Feminist Therapy: Strategies for Social and Individual Change*. Thousand Oaks, CA: Sage.

An accessible introduction to feminist therapy which incorporates useful discussion of specific skills and techniques.

3. Seu, I.B. and Heenan, M.C. (Eds.) (1998) *Feminism and Psychotherapy: Reflections on Contemporary Theories and Practices*. London: Sage.

An informative introduction to different aspects of feminist therapy which includes contributions from British theorists and practitioners.

GENDER, SEXUALITY AND RELATIONSHIP DIVERSITY THERAPY

OLIVIER CORMIER-OTAÑO AND DOMINIC DAVIES

OVERVIEW AND KEY POINTS

Gender, sexuality and relationship diversity (GSRD) therapy is at the forefront of current thinking on working with the more traditionally known LGBT(IQ) (lesbian, gay, bisexual, transgender/sexual, intersex, questioning). GSRD also encompasses a wider range of gender and sexual minority identities, including, but not restricted to, asexuals, celibates, people who either engage in Kink/BDSM (bondage, dominance, discipline, submission, sadism and masochism) practices or as a lifestyle – irrespective of sexual orientation (Langridge and Barker, 2007) – as well as people who may identify anywhere across the gender spectrum and not simply intersex or transsexual (including non-binary or agender identities, for instance). GSRD is also opening up the debate on different possibilities in relationship styles, such as the many forms of consensual non-monogamy (Barker and Langdridge, 2010), and thus is challenging patriarchal and heteronormative views of intimate relationships. The core theoretical concepts of this approach, which are discussed in this chapter, include:

- Minority stress accounts for the elevated levels of mental health problems among lesbians, gay men, bisexuals and gender variant people.
- The high frequency of microaggressions contribute to an unconscious understanding that the microaggressed identity is unacceptable.
- Hypervigilance against pathologisation, discrimination and criminalisation.
- Shame is compounded by the oppressive power of the heteronormative and bi-, homo- and transphobic, patriarchal society and communities.
- Understanding intersectionality is essential to comprehending and working with the multiple identities of GSRD clients.

BACKGROUND AND CONTEXT

Since the declassification of homosexuality by the American Psychiatric Association (APA) in 1973, and particularly since the mid-1990s, the field of counselling and psychotherapy with 'homosexual' clients has gone through many iterations in parallel with gay liberation movements of the 1970s morphing into LGBT (lesbian, gay, bisexual, transgender) social movements. From 'gay affirmative therapy' (Maylon, 1982) to sexual minority therapy to sexual diversity therapy to gender and sexual diversity therapy – the authors and associated colleagues are now using gender, sexuality and relationship diversity (GSRD) therapy. This theoretical approach encompasses and support all forms, aspects and issues around gender and sexual and relationship diversities. It is a trans-theoretical approach where all theoretical models (psychodynamic, humanistic, cognitive-behavioural, etc.) can operate within their central organising principles and tenets (Davies and Neal, 2000).

MINORITY STRESS

Meyer (2003) demonstrated via a meta-analysis that minority stress accounts for the elevated levels of mental health problems among lesbians, gay men and bisexuals (LGB), with depression and self-harm, anxiety and substance misuse affecting LGB people. Meyer distinguished between distal and proximal processes. Distal processes would include knowledge of the risk of anti-gay violence and harassment, discrimination in employment, goods and services. One doesn't have to have directly experienced these stresses to develop a hypervigilance to and expectations of prejudice and discrimination. He contrasts distal stress with proximal stress, where concealment of sexuality for fear of rejection can lead to internalised homo-/bi- phobia and the development of shame. We would extend his theory to gender variant people and others who are open about their GSRD identities.

MICROAGGRESSIONS

The concept of microaggressions was coined by Chester M. Pierce in 1970 and applied to a racial context. It has since been further developed by Derald Sue (2010) and applied to other identities, such as sexuality and gender. Microaggressions can be defined as highly frequent, brief, subtle and 'ordinary' messages that convey discrimination, hostility or negative connotations whether consciously or unconsciously expressed. They are discriminations and insults often at a homeopathic dosage, so low that they can often be unnoticed by others or people try to ignore them because they appear too insignificant to challenge. The difficulty resides in their high frequency as they permeate everyday life and contribute to an unconscious understanding that the microaggressed identity is unacceptable. An obvious example is the expression 'That is so gay'. Other ambiguous messages can be 'you gay guys are so sexually liberated'. These external messages will compound into internalised oppression, shame, distress, anxiety and minority stress.

HYPERVIGILANCE

GSRD's have a long history of being considered 'mad, bad or dangerous to know', in other words pathologised, criminalised or considered as contagious, toxic or of bad influence. This results in hypervigilance against pathologisation, discrimination, deviancy and criminalisation. GSRDs will scan their environment for signs of hostility or safety: am I going to be (mis)read? Am I going to be accepted or understood? Is it safe to reveal myself? (Carroll, 2010). This very sensitive state of constant alert is a source of anxiety and distress that will also be present in the counselling room. Clients may often unconsciously or directly question their therapists around their understanding of gender, sexual or relationship differences. Consequently, some clients may benefit from or request to work with a therapist who is also from a gender or sexual minority; others may benefit from, and prefer to work with, someone from outside their community. The client's choice of therapist is charged with meaning and it is well worth exploring the assumptions that lie behind the request for a minority therapist or, indeed, a non-minority therapist. However, the client's wishes need to be respected and accommodated where possible. This issue also raises the question of whether GSRD therapists are comfortable and willing to reveal their sexual orientation or gender history. This is doubly challenging when the therapist has been basted in their own toxic marinade of minority stress and microaggressions, alongside outdated notions of therapeutic 'neutrality'. Hypervigilance should be seen and understood as a unique strategy for survival and a coping mechanism against aggressions.

SHAME

GSRD clients may well come to therapy with issues not so different from those presented by all clients, but the social context will bring an extra dimension and different layers to their narrative. The social context specific to each GSRD identity (although many such identities share some similar social contexts) can be compared to a pair of 3D glasses, where, if viewed through a heteronormative lens, one won't see the nuances and alternative values and perspectives of lived experience for those people of the other 'tribe'.

It is important to consider the oppressive power of the heteronormative and bi-, homo- and transphobic, patriarchal society and communities in which our clients grow and evolve. External oppression and negative messages around sexual orientation, gender, relationship style and ethnicity lead to internalised oppression. Society is highly structured into believing there are only two genders, and certain norms and expectations are placed upon people as soon as they are born. It is becoming clear that these often do not fit the gender identity of the person assigned that gender at birth. Similarly, messages that sex and its expression should be limited to heterosexual, procreative activities only within the context of a committed relationship and remote from consensual experimentation can lead to feelings of guilt and shame. This kind of internalised oppression can result in self-loathing, low self-esteem, isolation, fear of rejection and other psychological difficulties.

Isolation, hiding and shame are common among GSRD clients and are exacerbated by a lack of access to accurate information. This means that the therapist may need to employ psycho-educational methods and bibliotherapy, homework and so on to help with relationship skills, sex education and other issues. In cases where the therapist's sexual orientation matches the client's and is disclosed, the therapist can sometimes be seen as a role model (whether they want that or not). Therapist's self disclosure should be thoroughly explored before and only happen in the interest of the client's therapy. There is increasing evidence that therapists self-disclosure of sexuality is beneficial to clients, the therapeutic relationship and to the ability of the therapist to make best use of the therapeutic relationship (Jeffery and Tweed, 2015; Satterly, 2006). This, of course, is one of the dynamics to be discussed in supervision.

INTERSECTIONALITY

The concept of intersectionality refers to the interaction of social identity structures such as race, class, and gender and sexuality in fostering life experiences, especially experiences of privilege and oppression. Originally coined by black feminist scholar Crenshaw (1989), GSRD clients belong to many communities (ethnic, cultural, spiritual, professional, political, family, gender, etc.) and may experience the impact of conflicting beliefs or ideologies. Most religions or faiths do not tolerate same-sex relationships or non-monogamies. Similarly, within the various GSRD communities, not all individualities, ethnicities, sexual practices or gender identities are embraced. Ableism, ageism and racism are just some of the very real discriminations operating from within a broadly GSRD culture (das Nair and Butler, 2012).

RESILIENCE

More recently, researchers (Colpitts and Gagahan, 2016; Ritter et al., 2012; Shilo et al., 2015) have sought to investigate what protective factors might promote resilience among GSRD people to hostile environments and which protective factors might be involved in maintaining resilience. Individuals carrying such strongly internalised self-oppressive thoughts may well question their own identity and sense of belonging. Only by exploring their own narratives or in finding kindred spirits does the client experience an integration of these different parts. The GSRD-aware therapist can help to empower clients to find the words to describe and make sense of their own sexuality and sexual expression. Having gained a sense of their own sexual identity, clients will often move to a position where the need to belong to a community then becomes more important. However, difficulties can arise when the pressure to embrace cultural norms within the GSRD communities is very strong and oppressive (fashion, lifestyle, peer pressure) and lead to the development of a false self where the client again feels only conditionally accepted.

WAYS OF WORKING

WORK GUIDELINES

Good practice in GSRD therapy requires a subtle curiosity and interest in the client's life, and an ability to work sensitively with their hypervigilance. It is not the client's place to educate the therapist with regard to the social context of their lives. However, the client's own perspective on that social context is, of course, entirely relevant and appropriate. This requires therapists to have a wide understanding of the social context in which gender, sexuality and relationship diverse people are living their lives, as well as how intersecting identities can overlap, interact and sometimes conflict. There are a wealth of books and information online that deal with gender, sexuality and relationship diverse clients. Much of the current literature is American, although the UK is making a good contribution to the field (for a good recent example, see especially Richards and Barker, 2013).

It is also paramount for any therapist to develop their awareness of their own prejudices, beliefs and assumptions about what is 'healthy' and 'normal' in terms of sex, gender role, relationships, etc. All of us have been socialised within mainstream culture, in which heteronormative beliefs are an inherent and perpetuated given, and therefore none of us is entirely free of heterosexism, cisgenderism and homo- bi- and transphobia – in the same way as it is hard to be free of racist or sexist attitudes.

UK therapy trainings rarely offer adequate training around gender and sexual minority issues. Often these issues are included in a single lecture on diversity and rarely exceed a day's teaching. A common training experience is that teaching is only included at the request of LGBT trainees and, more often than not, these students are expected to facilitate their peers' learning. This can result in their own learning needs (to know more about how to work effectively within their own communities) remaining unattended to, and they are forced to seek post-qualification specialist training elsewhere (Davies, 2007; Davies and Barker, 2015).

CASE EXAMPLE: UNDERSTANDING THE SOCIAL CONTEXT – CHEMSEX

David is a 43-year-old gay professional working in a very demanding job in the City. He often pulls 60–70-hour working weeks and his recent history of days 'off sick' and poor attention to detail have been noticed by his manager and by HR. Three years ago, his partner of ten years left him for another man and since then he's quietly gone to pieces. Since his partner left him, he has re-entered the world of dating via online apps like Grindr (a geolocation dating app which helps men find others local to them for sex and relationships). Very early on in this unfamiliar dating world he was offered drugs and started to participate in 'Chemsex' (the intentional sexualised use of three or four specific drugs, such as crystal methamphetamine, mephedrone, GBL/GHB and ketamine, to enhance long, intense sex sessions), both one-to-one and at Chillouts (sex parties normally held at people's homes and often involving several men and going on for several days with different men coming and going fairly frequently). His drug use has included 'slamming' (intravenous injecting) crystal methamphetamine, which is a powerful stimulant and can keep people awake and sexually aroused for days at a time. He can't remember the last time he had sober sex (without any drugs) and spent most weekends having sex with minimal sleep. He presented for help after he was recently diagnosed with Hepatitis C. He has avoided HIV infection by buying PrEP online (PrEP (Pre-Exposure Prophylaxis) is an anti-retroviral medication which, if taken regularly, prevents HIV infection. The NHS are at the current time resisting the decision to make it available for people at highest risk (i.e., gay men who have a history of condomless sex) and so many gay men are purchasing generic PrEP online from overseas pharmacies. For more information: http://prepster.info).

Utilising principles of Motivational Interviewing, we focused on client-identified goal-setting, initially risk reduction strategies to moderate drug use, rebuilding social support from his friends, and the loss of his significant other, and exploring the impact of the Hepatitis C. David was profoundly depressed and realised he has been self-medicating with powerful sex-enhancing drugs to ameliorate the loneliness and isolation and to give him greater confidence. We explored how to date in the age of social media and fast connections and avoid the temptations of drug use. We also explored his work/life balance and he found a less demanding job which significantly lowered his stress levels and gave him time to rebuild his life.

GENDER IDENTITY: TRANS VERSUS NON-BINARY IDENTITY

An increasing number of clients are coming to therapy with questions around their gender identity. Philosophy student Jaq, 25, is presenting as non-binary: neither man nor woman, and uses 'they' as their preferred pronoun. Jaq doesn't identify with the gender assigned to them at birth or with the notion of 'opposite gender', and they are coming to therapy to explore their sense of self. Within non-binary identities there are a multitude of identities and narratives, from gender fluidity to being genderless or agender.

Gender can be seen as a combination of physiological traits, a social construct and a sense of self. Exploring with Jaq their sense of self and how they want to be perceived by others allowed for the expression of the complexity of their gender beyond the binary male–female. Jaq also feels distressed by the presence of their breasts and is considering a double mastectomy. They are exploring the idea of being androgynous-looking. They have been in a relationship with a cisgender (a term for people who have a gender identity that matches their assigned sex at birth) woman for the last three years and they struggle to define their sexual orientation, neither gay nor heterosexual (which is another binary construct) and wonder who this definition will be for.

The construction of male or female identity can be oppressive to everyone. Cisgender and transgender alike find their identity within the binary as either man or woman. Whereas non-binary people may present distressed at the lack of understanding of their experience and the difficulty to express their narrative and the limitation of belonging/identifying to a gender, transgender people may want to transition from one gender to another and therefore fit within the binary of gender identity. The changes non-binary people wish to achieve (be it physical treatments or social goals of acceptance) will therefore be more often met with lack of understanding and pathologisation.

RESEARCH EVIDENCE

GSRD is fast becoming an area of great research interest. Richards and Barker (2015) have managed to pull an impressive array of authors to review the latest research in gender and sexuality and notably include both heterosexuality and cisgender as areas under research. Whereas previously research has focused on minority identities and 'othering' or pathologising, we are now seeing research into mainstream, majority identities from a critical perspective. This book will be invaluable for people wishing to dig deeper into this subject.

REFERENCES

Barker, M. and Langdridge, D. (2010) *Understanding Non-Monogamies*. Abingdon: Routledge.

Carroll, L. (2010) *Counseling Sexual and Gender Minorities*. Upper Saddle River, NJ: Merrill.

Colpitts, E. and Gahagan, J. (2016) The utility of resilience as a conceptual framework for understanding and measuring LGBTQ health. *International Journal of Equity Health*, 15: 60, 1–8.

Crenshaw, K.W. (1989) Demarginalizing the Intersection of Race and Sex: A Black Feminist Critique of Antidiscrimination Doctrine, Feminist Theory and Antiracist Politics. Chicago, IL: *University of Chicago Legal Forum* (pp. 138–167).

das Nair, R. and Butler, C. (eds) (2012) *Intersectionality, Sexuality and Psychological Therapies: Working with Lesbian, Gay and Bisexual Diversity*. Oxford: British Psychological Society/Blackwell.

Davies, D. (2007) Not in front of the students. *Therapy Today*, 18(1).

Davies, D. and Barker, M.J. (2015) How gender and sexually diverse-friendly is your therapy training? *The Psychotherapist*, 61, 8–10.

Davies, D. and Neal, C. (eds) (2000) *Therapeutic Perspectives on Working with Lesbian, Gay and Bisexual Clients* (Pink Therapy, Vol. 2). Buckingham: Open University Press.

Jeffery, M.K. and Tweed, A.E. (2015) Clinician self-disclosure or clinician self-concealment? Lesbian, gay and bisexual mental health practitioners' experiences of disclosure in therapeutic relationships. *Counselling and Psychotherapy Research*, 15(1), 41–49.

Langdridge, D. and Barker, M. (eds) (2007) *Safe, Sane and Consensual*. Basingstoke: Palgrave.

Maylon, A. (1982) Psychotherapeutic implications of internalized homophobia in gay men. In J. Gonsiorek (ed.), *Homosexuality and Psychotherapy* (pp. 59–69). New York: Haworth Press.

Meyer, I.H. (2003) Prejudice, social stress, and mental health in lesbian, gay, and bisexual populations: conceptual issues and research evidence. *Psychological Bulletin*, 129(5), 674–697.

Richards, C. and Barker, M.J. (2013) *Sexuality and Gender for Mental Health Professionals: A Practical Guide*. London: Sage.

Richards, C. and Barker, M.J. (2015) *The Palgrave Handbook of the Psychology of Sexuality and Gender*. Basingstoke: Palgrave Macmillan.

Ritter, A., Matthew-Simmons, F. and Carragher, N. (2012) *Prevalence of and Interventions for Mental Health and Alcohol and Other Drug Problems amongst the Gay, Lesbian, Bisexual and Transgender Communities: A Review of the Literature*. London: National Drug and Alcohol Research Centre. (https://ndarc.med.unsw.edu.au/resource/23-prevalence-and-interventions-mental-health-and-alcohol-and-other-drug-problems-amongst, accessed 1 August 2016).

Satterly, B.A. (2006) Therapist self-disclosure from a gay male perspective. *Families in Society: The Journal of Contemporary Social Services*, 87(2), 240–247.

Shilo, G., Antebi, N. and Mor, Z. (2015) Individual and community resilience factors among lesbian, gay, bisexual, queer and questioning youth and adults in Israel. *American Journal of Community Psychology*, 55(1–2), 215–222. (www.ncbi.nlm.nih.gov/pubmed/25510593).

Sue, D.W. (2010) *Microaggressions in Everyday Life: Race, Gender and Sexual Orientation*. Hoboken, NJ: Wiley.

RECOMMENDED READING

1. Richards, C. and Barker, M.J. (2013) *Sexuality and Gender for Mental Health Professionals: A Practical Guide*. London: Sage.

One of the most recent and extensive books on working with gender, sexual and relationship diversity clients.

2.   das Nair, R. and Butler, C. (eds) (2012) *Intersectionality, Sexuality and Psychological Therapies: Working with Lesbian, Gay and Bisexual Diversity*. Oxford: British Psychological Society/Blackwell.

Though this book does not include transgender identities, it is the best textbook in print for understanding best practice with intersectionalities as applied to LGB identities.

3.   National LGBTI Health Alliance (2014) *Working Therapeutically with LGBTI Clients: A Practice Wisdom Resource*. Newtown: National LGBTI Health Alliance.

A useful resource document for counsellors and psychotherapists. Free to download at: www.beyondblue.org.au/docs/default-source/default-document-library/bw0256-practice-wisdom-guide-online.pdf.

7.6   WORKING WITH HOMELESS PEOPLE

EMMA WILLIAMSON

OVERVIEW AND KEY POINTS

If – to borrow a Winnicott (1986) title – **'home is where we start from'** – then we can't be surprised to find enormous challenges working with those for whom home and its meanings have been so ruinous. (Luepnitz, 2005: 329, emphasis added)

This chapter will explore the prevalence of mental health needs in the homeless population and provide an explanation of the underlying psychological difficulties which can lead to and maintain homelessness. This will include recognition of how histories of complex trauma, and difficulty trusting and engaging with services, can result in multiple social exclusions beginning with the challenge of sustaining safe stable accommodation. By holding these psychological needs centrally, the current evidence base will be explored revealing the creative adaptations felt to be needed to reach homeless people – on their terms and their turf – in a range of settings beyond the traditional consulting room.

The key points addressed in this chapter are:

- Homeless people have significantly poorer physical and mental health than the general population, which commonly leads to a lower quality of life and premature death.
- These multiple comobidites can impact on their ability to access and make use of services in a planned and sustainable way.

- The psychological mechanisms, complex trauma and disrupted attachments that underlie homelessness crucially need to inform treatment approaches.
- 'Psychologically Informed Environments' are a current United Kingdom (UK)-based best practice approach for working with homeless people that are able to address these multiple needs through tailored treatment design and creative onsite service integration.

BACKGROUND AND CONTEXT

The term 'homeless' has been used to describe a group of people living in a range of unsatisfactory housing situations from rough sleepers to those living in squats, bed and breakfasts, hostels, sofa surfing or insecurely housed with friends and family. After years of decline, the numbers of homeless people in the UK are on the rise as a result of government policies, housing shortages and economic recession. This is a wide-scale societal problem with double the number of people recorded rough sleeping in 2015 compared to 2010, one in ten people in the UK reporting that they have been homeless at some point and a fifth having been homeless in the last five years (Crisis, 2016). Within this group, some people have a more transient experience of homelessness, but it is the chronic, 'revolving door' homeless population who struggle to sustain accommodation or take up available support that are of interest in this chapter.

Homelessness has been argued to have its origins in childhood adversity, complex trauma and to be significantly affected by serious ongoing mental health problems (Maguire, Johnson, Vostanis, Keats and Remington, 2009; Roos et al., 2013). This group suffers from major health inequalities arising from the complex interaction between housing, income, education, social isolation and disabilities, which impact on their economic and social status (Marmot, 2010). It is reported that up to 70% of homeless people have experienced mental health problems, with high levels of comorbid substance misuse (MH Network NHS Confederation, 2012); 70% also meet the criteria for a personality disorder, with high rates of complex trauma preceding and further compounded by the experience of homelessness (Maguire et al., 2009). This group commonly engages in high-risk behaviours such as crime, substance misuse, prostitution and risky sexual activity, violence and deliberate self-harm. They are over nine times more likely to commit suicide than the general population and have a life expectancy of 47 years compared to 70 years in the general population (St Mungo's, 2013). These multiple and complex needs aggravate recovery and lead to marginalisation and deterioration (Fazel, Khosla, Doll and Geddes, 2008). As Cockersell (2011: 89) cautions, 'if the psychological root causes do not get treated, the multiple social interventions [e.g., housing] are ineffective, not as effective as they might be, or are sometimes even detrimental, and the homeless person becomes "entrenched"'.

WAYS OF WORKING

There have been numerous debates about how health and mental health services can meet the needs of homeless people (Essali, Tarboush and Awad, 2012; Zerger, 2002). A full review of the literature on psychotherapy with homeless people is beyond the scope of this chapter. However, there is a great deal of creative and inspiring 'community psychology' oriented work with this population that should be acknowledged. To reach this group, counselling and psychotherapy have been offered in a range of settings from street-based therapy, GP practices, homeless community mental health teams and day centres to hostel-based interventions and modified therapeutic communities. A range of psychological models have also proven useful, including, among others, cognitive-behavioural therapy (CBT), dialectical behaviour therapy (DBT), psychoanalytic psychotherapy, mentalisation-based treatment (Cockersell, 2011; Maguire et al., 2009).

Sadly, this work can occur in isolated pockets of good practice with the government commitment to improving equity of access to psychological therapies routinely failing to reach homeless people (Mind, 2013). Barriers are perpetuated by service exclusion criteria and the lack of provision for integrated substance misuse and mental health treatment. Homeless people's chaotic lifestyles can negatively impact on regular appointment attendance and engagement can be defeated by 'Did Not Attend' (DNA) discharge policies and professional assessment of treatment 'readiness'. There are prevailing myths that homeless people are 'treatment resistant', have poor coping mechanisms for managing psychosocial interventions, and do not want or engage in treatment when offered. However, Dykeman (2011) counters that homeless people readily take up support when it is specifically tailored to meet their needs.

Certain features appear more consistently in the most successful therapeutic interventions, such as offering a degree of flexibility, individualisation, a slower period of initial engagement and open on-site access (see Dykeman, 2011). The psychological and emotional needs of the client group also need to be at the forefront of interventions by recognising the levels of trauma that accompany homelessness. It is with this in mind that the 'Psychologically Informed Environments' (PIEs) initiative, first introduced by Johnson and Haigh (2011), rose to prominence as a best practice recommendation from the Communities and Local Government and the National Mental Health Development Unit (Keats, Maguire, Johnson and Cockersell, 2012; Maguire, Johnson, Vostanis and Keats, 2010). PIEs advocate that a shared psychological understanding among staff within a settled environment, such as a hostel, is the best way to facilitate growth, recovery and enablement. There is national variation in PIE models and the degree of formal direct and indirect psychological therapy on offer. Nevertheless this is an approach that appears able to deliver many of the mutative ingredients recommended by Dykeman (2011).

The Lambeth Psychology in Hostels (PIH) Project, which spans several homeless hostels across this central London borough, delivers the principles of a 'PIE' in a multi-agency partnership between Thames Reach, a homeless charity accommodation provider, Lambeth Council hostel commissioner and South London and Maudsley NHS Foundation Trust (Williamson and Taylor, 2015). The fully integrated National Health Service (NHS) Clinical Psychology and Psychiatry team work full-time in the hostel, delivering flexible on-site, individual, group and arts-based therapies. This happens alongside specialist hostel staff-based support interventions, consistent team approaches and integrated psychologically-informed housing management, risk assessment and resettlement interventions. Regular specialist training, group reflective practice meetings, clinical supervision and consultation are offered to all hostel staff, and psychologists have developed a shared psychological framework for understanding and working with the residents.

Psychoanalytic theory has been helpful in understanding the challenge that hostel residents have in taking up care. Offering help to someone who has never been cared for can be experienced, as Winnicott described, as an 'impingement', or something coming at them (Luepnitz, 2005: 331). Winnicott (1945) felt that newborn babies came into the world in an 'unintegrated' state, where their first developmental task involved progression towards ego(self) development, psychological integration and coherence. Here the primary caregiver plays a crucial role in supporting the infant to make sense of their experiences and master primitive psychological processes to become strong and stable. When, on the other hand, caregiving fails, the undeveloped infant can be overwhelmed by uncontained primitive anxieties, as commonly seen with homeless people whose childhoods have been populated by frightened, frightening or absent caregivers. As Luepnitz (n.d.) describes:

> Disruptions at this early stage make it difficult for the individual to ever really inhabit his or her own body – which makes it impossible to inhabit other spaces. Many homeless people end up sleeping in doorways, i.e., unable to exist either inside or outside a dwelling. (Conference Paper, unknown date)

These individuals are not able to understand separateness and boundaries, resultantly having trouble managing the distance between themselves and others. There is an intense longing for, yet a profound fear of attachment, and an ambivalent pattern of desperately seeking and then rejecting care. This is why homeless people can find forming safe, reliable relationships so challenging and why care can feel threatening and overwhelming. Individuals resultantly bounce in and out of contact with accommodation and care services, never finding a place where they can feel comfortable and settle.

CASE EXAMPLE

When Ben, a Black British man in his early 40s, moved into the PIH hostel he had been circling round the homeless and prison network for 20 years, unable to sustain hostel accommodation or a flat of his own. He had been repeatedly pursuing, obtaining, abandoning or destroying places. From the age of five he had moved from institution to institution and experienced some form of abuse in almost every setting. In search of a way to cope, he began drinking and taking drugs from 10 years old, and when he came to the hostel he was dependant on the daily use of alcohol, heroin and crack cocaine. He had a history of impulsivity, violence, self-harm, suicide attempts and difficulties in sustaining relationships.

Ben was discussed in a reflective practice meeting and the team described his desperate attempts to please – bringing gifts for staff and residents, helping with chores and wanting to spend time in the office seeking support – but that this could so easily switch to a state of anxiety where he felt controlled, intruded upon or that his life was literally in danger. He would seek multiple mental and physical health treatments from providers in different regions, preventing a full or coherent picture of him and his needs developing and acting out a repetition of failed caregiving. As Adshead (2001) appreciates, this group is 'longing for a secure attachment that would reduce their distress, but have no idea either how to elicit care productively, or how to use it when it is offered by a competent caregiver' (cited in Cockersell, 2016: 224). Early work with the hostel team and psychologist focused on risk management and shared care planning to redirect and contain Ben's chaotic multi-service use. Once his physical health had been cohered, he was offered hostel-based psychology sessions but requested an external referral, fearing a lack of privacy and boundaries. However, as soon as he was referred, he felt rejected and changed his mind, wanting to meet with the PIH psychologist after all. The first months of contact were marked by ongoing ambivalence. He would check the session time, appear keen to attend, but would then miss the planned appointment, arriving as the psychologist was going into another meeting or leaving for the day. It was important to hold the boundary, resist being pulled to action and

(Continued)

(Continued)

stay attentive to potential impingements that would be too much for Ben and cause him to retreat. The work was slow, flexible, with open contact that aimed to facilitate a new experience of available, containing yet non-violating interpersonal contact. The sessions were also conducted in the park, which reduced the 'intensity' of the contact. As Ben began to trust in the psychologist's dependability, he would attend more regularly and stay for longer. Using a mentalisation-based treatment (MBT) approach (Bateman and Fonagy, 2010), they focused on improving affect regulation, the oscillating interpersonal pattern of feeling that others were attacking/overwhelming or abandoning him and the use of substances to manage this. Mentalising is a form of *imaginative* mental activity about oneself and others in which you perceive and interpret human behaviour in terms of *intentional* mental states (e.g., needs, desires, feelings, beliefs). This therapy, first developed for work with personality disorder, works with the significant impairments in mentalising that impact on people's struggle to understand and manage themselves and their relationships.

The work took in the moment-to-moment fluctuations in the psychological proximity Ben could manage and adapted accordingly. There were times when this balance couldn't be right and Ben would storm from the contact, but this was understood as part of the process, allowing Ben to see the psychologist survive and not retaliate. Ben would also regulate his contact by jumping from topic to topic to avoid emotional states that could not be tolerated. This was reflective of his underlying fragmented psychic state, which can be seen in the incoherent narratives and scattered memories of those with complex trauma. After two years, his narrative became more coherent and it was noted that there were fewer extreme fluctuations in his emotional state, with self-harm and drug-taking all but stopping. Alongside development in the stability of his therapeutic relationship, he developed a stable romantic relationship and there were noted improvements in peer relationships and general health service engagement. Following decades spent in prison and on the streets, Ben moved into his own flat after finally having been able to settle and stabilise in the Lambeth PIH. He began volunteering and four years on was proud to have spent the longest period without criminal justice contact in his adult life.

RESEARCH EVIDENCE

Empirical research into the efficacy of psychotherapy with homeless people is in its infancy, with most published work arising from practice-generated evidence and case study design. Several therapeutic models have been highlighted as useful, including: family therapy, behavioural contingency programmes, CBT, mentalisation-based treatment, psychodynamic psychotherapy, 12-step programmes and generic counselling in the context of supported housing (Cockersell, 2011; Maguire et al., 2009). However, the evidence base suffers from poor research methodology and study design, few controlled trials and only one randomised control trial to date (Maguire et al., 2009; Maguire et al., in preparation). Most of the research has been conducted in the United States of America, with generalisability to the UK homeless population yet to be established (Maguire et al., 2009). Treatment research in the main focuses on individual therapy, with some suggesting group work is unsustainable with homeless people due to the relational difficulties that predominate (Cockersell, 2011). However, others have found modest success in therapeutic group work when offered as part of a wider treatment programme (Williamson and Taylor, 2015). Integrated residential interventions, such as PIEs (Cockersell, 2016) and Modified Therapeutic Communities (Sacks, McKendrick, Sacks and Clelan, 2010), also show promise. There is an ongoing drive to strengthen research in this area and improved treatment descriptions and intervention standards would contribute to this, as long as a degree of flexibility and individualisation is maintained (Dykeman, 2011).

CONCLUSION

Homelessness is a multifaceted issue: an 'internal state of unhousedness' (Henderson Hospital, cited in Campbell, 2006) where interwoven traumas, relational anxieties and arising functional difficulties demand more than a housing solution. In recent years, there has been a consolidation and refocusing of psychological practice in homelessness. However, what remains clear is that homelessness will likely repeat unless the underlying psychological factors preceding and perpetuating it are addressed.

REFERENCES

Bateman, A.W. and Fonagy, P. (2010). Mentalization-based treatment for borderline personality disorder. *World Psychiatry*, 9, 11–15.

Campbell, J. (2006). Homelessness and containment: a psychotherapy project with homeless people and workers in the homeless field. *Psychoanalytic Psychotherapy*, 20(3), 157–174.

Cockersell, P. (2011). Homelessness and mental health: adding clinical mental health interventions to existing social ones can greatly enhance positive outcomes. *Journal of Public Mental Health*, 10(2), 88–98.

Cockersell, P. (2016). PIEs five years on. *Mental Health and Social Inclusion*, 20(4), 221–230.

Crisis (2016). *About Homelessness: Briefing on Key Homelessness Facts and Statistics England.* (www.crisis.org.uk/data/files/publications/Homelessness%20briefing%202016%20EXTERNAL.pdf).

Dykeman, B. (2011). Interventions strategies with the homeless population. *Journal of Instructional Psychology*, 38(1), 32–39.

Essali, A., Tarboush, M. and Awad, M. (2012). Specialist interventions for homeless people with severe mental illness (protocol). *The Cochrane Library*, 12.

Fazel, S., Khosla, V., Doll, H. and Geddes, J. (2008). The prevalence of mental disorders among the homeless in western countries: systematic review and meta-regression analysis. *PLoS Medicine*, 5(12), e225.

Johnson, R. and Haigh, R. (2011). Social psychiatry and social policy for the 21st century: new concepts for new needs – the 'Enabling Environments' initiative. *Mental Health and Social Inclusion*, 15(1), 17–23.

Keats, H., Maguire, N.J., Johnson, R. and Cockersell, P. (2012) *Psychologically-informed Services for Homeless People: Good Practice Guide.* London: Department of Communities and Local Government.

Luepnitz, D.A. (n.d.). Psychoanalytic work with homeless adults. Conference paper. Division 39 Meeting, San Antonio, TX. (www.scribd.com/document/183472607/Deborah-Luepnitz-Interview-pdf).

Luepnitz, D.A. (2005). Orwell, Winnicott, and Lacan: notes of a psychoanalyst from Project HOME. *Psychoanalysis, Culture & Society*, 10(3), 328–334.

Maguire, N.J., Fulcher-Cornah, D., Phiri, P., Hughes, V., Davies, E., Hulland, D. & Kingdon, D. (In prep). *The Effectiveness of a Cognitive-Behavioural Intervention for Homeless People: An RCT Feasibility Study.*

Maguire, N.J., Johnson, R., Vostanis, P., Keats, H. and Remington, R.E. (2009). *Homelessness and Complex Trauma: A Review of the Literature.* Southampton, UK: University of Southampton.

Maguire, N.J., Johnson, R., Vostanis, P. and Keats, H. (2010). *Meeting the Psychological and Emotional Needs of the Homeless.* London: Communities and Local Government/National Mental Health Development Unit. (www.nmhdu.org.uk/complextrauma).

Marmot, M. (2010). *Fair Society, Healthy Lives.* The Marmot Review. London: University College London. (www.instituteofhealthequity.org/resources-reports/fair-society-healthy-lives-the-marmot-review).

MH Network NHS Confederation (2012). *Mental Health and Homelessness: Planning and Delivering Mental Health Services for Homeless People.* London: MH Network NHS Confederation. (www.nhsconfed.org/~/media/Confederation/Files/Publications/Documents/mental_health_homelessness.pdf)

Mind (2013). *We Still Need to Talk.* London: Mind. (www.mind.org.uk/media/494424/we-still-need-to-talk_report.pdf).

Roos, L.E., Mota, N., Afifi, T.A., Katz, L.Y., Distasio, J. and Sareen, J. (2013). Relationship between adverse childhood experiences and homelessness and the impact of Axis I and II disorders. *American Journal of Public Health*, 103(2), 275–281.

Sacks, S., McKendrick, K., Sacks, J.Y. and Clelan, C.M. (2010). Modified therapeutic community for co-occuring disorders: single investigator meta-analysis. *Substance Abuse*, 31(3), 146–161.

St Mungo's (2013). Health and Homelessness: Understanding the Costs and Role of Primary Care Services for Homeless People. London: St Mungo's. (www.mungos.org/documents/4153/4153.pdf).

Williamson, E. and Taylor, K. (2015). Minding the margins: an innovation to integrate psychology in a homeless hostel environment. *DCP Clinical Psychology Forum*, 265, 33–37.

Winnicott, D.W. (1945). Primitive emotional development. In D.W. Winnicott, *Through Paediatrics to Psychoanalysis: Collected Papers* (Chapter 12). London: Tavistock.

Zerger, S. (2002). *Substance Abuse Treatment: What works for homeless people? A Review of the Literature.* Nashville, TN: National Health Care for the Homeless Council (https://www.nhchc.org/wp-content/uploads/2012/02/SubstanceAbuseTreatmentLitReview.pdf)

RECOMMENDED READING

1. Clinical Psychology Forum (2015). Special Edition: Homelessness – The Extreme of Social Exclusion. *Clinical Psychology Forum*, Vol. 265.

    A selection of papers written by UK clinicians currently working with homeless people.

2. Campbell, J. (2006). Homelessness and containment: a psychotherapy project with homeless people and workers in the homeless field. *Psychoanalytic Psychotherapy*, 20(3), 157–174.

    Exploration of homeless through psychoanalyst Henri Rey's theory of the claustro-agoraphobic dilemma.

3. Keats, H., Maguire, N.J., Johnson, R. and Cockersell, P. (2012) *Psychologically-informed Services for Homeless People: Good Practice Guide*. London: Department of Communities and Local Government. (https://eprints.soton.ac.uk/340022/).

    Practical guidance on creating psychologically-informed environments.

7.7 WORKING WITH INTERPRETERS

RACHEL TRIBE AND ANETA TUNARIU

OVERVIEW AND KEY POINTS

'I felt I was living in darkness and having an interpreter helped bring me light' (Lola – an expert by experience). The inability to speak fluently in English does not preclude the need to access psychotherapeutic services. It follows that an appreciation of the intertwined relationship between culture, language and experience is crucial if counselling and psychotherapy in Britain are to address issues of inclusion, social justice and provide equality of meaningful access to psychotherapeutic services. The rich multicultural tapestry of contemporary Britain means that there will always be residents who are not fluent in the English language, but who may require access to psychotherapy. Key points include:

- In the United Kingdom (UK), recent data estimates that 7.7% of the population is non-native English speakers (Statista, 2016).
- Approximately 100 languages are reportedly spoken in almost every London borough (2011 Census; Office for National Statistics, 2011).
- A reduced fluency in the use of English may be due to migration, lack of opportunities, gender politics or a range of other reasons (Bhugra and Gupta, 2010). It may also be related to some forms of cognitive decline affecting an individual that may occur in later life; someone who was previously fluent in English may lose this skill (Shah, 2017).
- Clinicians' readiness and skill in working with interpreters in a clinical setting are therefore necessary.

BACKGROUND AND CONTEXT

THERAPEUTIC DISCOURSE

The role of interpreters in mental health is a sophisticated and multilayered task (Kuay et al., 2015; Resera et al., 2015). With the introduction of an interpreter/cultural broker into the session, the psychotherapist needs to adopt deliberate language and a cultural awareness to their work. Working with an interpreter and across language and culture may initially be seen as challenging, and it certainly requires re/adjustments, but may lead to a number of positive outcomes. It ensures that potential service users who are not fluent English speakers are not denied access to a meaningful service (Tribe and Tunariu, 2009). Additional outcomes may include adopting a questioning stance to one's work, encouraging reflective practice and may ultimately lead to an expansion and enriching of many aspects of therapeutic practice and an enlarged clinical repertoire for the psychotherapist. Psychotherapists may be reminded of the central role of language in creating versions of selves, of ill-health and of 'recovery', and the ways in which wellbeing and mental health are linguistically and culturally located. Attention to language-in-action helps make clearer the opportunities and restrictions within the therapeutic discourse.

The socially constructed nature of the therapeutic discourse in itself contains power differentials (Harper and Speed, 2014) wherein dominant, expert-led perceptions may come to define the process. The clients' reduced access to articulating for themselves, because they are not fluent in English, adds a further layer to these dynamics. Guidelines on working with interpreters in mental health have been published by the British Association for Counselling and Psychotherapy (BACP) (Trivasse, 2005) and the British Psychological Society (BPS) (2008).

QUALITY OF CARE WHEN WORKING WITH AN INTERPRETER

It has been demonstrated that quality of care is negatively affected when patients with limited English proficiency (LEP) are not provided with interpreters (Karliner et al., 2007). Legislation in Britain, including the Equality Act 2010, requires equity of service provision, while the Mental Health Act 1983 (amended 2007) guidance recommends that qualified interpreters should be used in this context. Moreover, a wide range of benefits of working with a professional interpreter have been reported, including that clients reported feeling understood and experienced improved clinical care (Angelelli, 2004). Karliner et al. (2007), in a systematic review, noted that using a professional interpreter can improve care to a point that approaches or equals that for patients without language barriers. Similarly, outcome measures of therapeutic intervention conducted with intermediated communication (when working with asylum seekers and refugees who have experienced trauma) indicates that it is as effective as therapy conducted with direct language communication (d'Ardenne et al., 2007).

The ambivalence of clinicians in working with interpreters has been acknowledged by practitioners in the UK (Tribe and Tunariu, 2009). Reasons for this may include anxiety at having a third person in the room, which can give rise to feelings of being observed and possibly judged, as well as changes in the experience of a therapeutic space being altered and the dynamics being changed. This is in addition to concerns about payment and the availability of interpreters (Tribe and Thompson, 2009).

MODELS OF INTERPRETATION

Tribe (1999) distinguishes four modes of interpretation:

1. Linguistic mode
2. Psychotherapeutic/constructionist mode
3. Advocate mode
4. Cultural broker mode

Each mode of working lends itself better to different contexts. In the *Psychotherapeutic/Constructionist mode*, the interpreter is primarily concerned with interpreting the intended meaning and feeling-content being conveyed rather than word-for-word (Tribe and Raval, 2003). Similarly, in the *Cultural broker mode*, the interpreter interprets not only the spoken word but also relevant cultural and contextual variables. *These two modes are the most relevant for psychotherapists and counsellors. The advocate mode is when an interpreter has a wider role and is there to advocate not only for the individual client but also for a specific section of the community, the term link worker or health advocate has also been used to describe this mode. Whilst the linguistic mode* is used when (as far as is possible) word for word interpretation is required, for example in a police statement. Interpreters make a substantial contribution in enabling the consultation/intervention to actually take place. In alliance with the clinician, they also play a key role in building trust, facilitating mutual respect, communicating affect as well as interpreting the words over and over often negotiating complex system-of-meanings between two cultural worlds (Angelelli, 2004). The contribution interpreters make to providing health and care, and services such as counselling and psychotherapy often goes unrecognised. Interpreters have voiced concerns and dissatisfaction with clinicians for not acknowledging their professional skills and status (Granger and Baker, 2003). Acknowledgement by the clinicians of interpreters' role as complex and pivotal would reinforce a positive and collaborative attitude towards working together, which in turn may also safeguard from incidental misunderstandings (Resera et al., 2015).

WAYS OF WORKING

Language represents one of the fundamental components of psychotherapeutic work, not only in terms of the cathartic effect of talking and being listened to, as well as of conveying meanings and having these witnessed by a skilled practitioner, but also in the sense that language actively constructs realities – of what is possible and what is marginalised or denied, and of modes of relating (McNamee and Gergen, 1992). Language and culture stand in a mutual, reciprocal and interactive relationship with one another. Working with an interpreter concentrates attention on this.

Culture shapes the delivery of our spoken language as well as a range of non-verbal behaviours, including facial expressions, gestures, distance, gaze, including appropriate eye contact and postures. All of these form part of psychotherapeutic practice. The interpreter may be able to assist the clinician to engage with the intended message behind gestures or expressions, so adding nuance and minimising misunderstandings.

Languages are not directly interchangeable, and what may be said in a few words in one language may take several sentences for the meaning to be accurately conveyed in another language. For example, there is no word which defines the gender of a cousin in English, no equivalent word for 'mind' in Swiss German, and no words for 'please' and 'thank you' in Finnish. Similarly, the term 'burn-out' does not exist in either of the Sri Lankan languages and there is no word for 'menopause' in Somali. When these words are used, interpreters will have to think carefully about how to convey the corresponding meaning of a 'missing' word. Many of the words used within mental health settings in Britain will be drawn from a western or ethnocentric perspective. (The debate about the appropriateness of using this model uncritically and indiscriminately across cultures is outside the scope of this chapter. The interested reader is referred to Fernando (2014) and Tribe (2016).)

THE ROLE OF LANGUAGE AND THE MOTHER TONGUE

Research relating to how we process emotions through a mother tongue versus a subsequent language is beginning to be better understood (de Zuleta et al., 2001; Taylor, 2016; Tribe and Keefe, 2009). One of the emerging agreements is that emotions that were laid down or stored in a first language tend to only become fully and deeply accessible when that language is deployed. However subjectively concrete and privately located they may be perceived and experienced, emotions are in some way culturally and linguistically mediated (Tsai, 2007). The necessity for the clinician to grasp the cultural context in which such memories have been initially represented adds further impetus for working with an interpreter when language poses a barrier.

CHANGED DYNAMICS

The inability to communicate effectively can isolate people and prevent them from access to or meaningful engagement with talking therapy. The need to seek support in itself is often accompanied by vulnerability. Sometimes this means a retreat into self and a strong reliance on habitual, individualised ways of dealing with anxiety as well as accepting or resisting 'help'. The combined contribution of these two aspects highlights the crucial importance of working with interpreters/cultural brokers.

The presence of an interpreter in the clinical session will shape the dynamics of the therapeutic encounter. This can be beneficial, although at times it can generate challenges. For example, some clinicians have argued that the presence of interpreters:

- adds to the complexity of the therapy process (Leanza et al., 2014)
- can contribute to clinicians feeling a greater detachment from the service users, as well as feeling less powerful and less effective in their work (Raval, 1996).

Working with interpreters has at the same time been reported as crucial for the depth, quality and outcome of therapy (e.g., Tribe and Tunariu, 2009). It has also been shown to increase clients' understanding of their situation and the care options offered, and lead to enhanced trust in the process and improved rapport with the health professional (Raval, 1996).

CASE STUDY

Ali has been referred to you by his general practitioner (GP), who says that he is suffering from post-traumatic stress disorder having arrived from Syria and having experienced multiple traumatic events prior to leaving his country and during his flight, by land, across a number of countries. Ali mentions that he came to the UK via the 'Jungle' in Calais six months ago and would benefit from 'talking therapy'. Ali now has full refugee status and is legally entitled to live and work in the UK. He is attending English classes. He previously worked as an architect in Syria. The GP notes that Ali will require an interpreter for the work. What preparations might you need to make before meeting Ali? How would you go about preparing yourself for working with Ali through an interpreter? Why did you select these preparations?

KEY PRACTICE ISSUES

- If you have not been trained in working with interpreters, undertake a training course. If this is not feasible, as you will be working with an interpreter unexpectedly, read the relevant guidelines and allocate time to consider the issues or discuss them with a more experienced colleague in advance of your first session with an interpreter. Psychotherapists should consider attending a deaf awareness training course in advance of working with a British Sign Language Interpreter (BSLI).
- Check that the interpreter is qualified, appropriate for the consultation/meeting and speaks the mother tongue of the service user rather than a second or third language.
- Allocate 10–15 minutes in advance of the meeting to enable the interpreter to brief you on any cultural issues which may have bearing on the session.
- Interpreters may not have had experience of psychotherapy before and it may be useful to clarify the purpose of the meeting.
- Be mindful of issues of confidentiality and trust when working with someone from a small language community (including the Deaf community) as the client may be anxious about being identifiable and mistrustful of an interpreter's professionalism.
- State clearly that you alone hold clinical responsibility for the meeting.
- Create a good atmosphere where each member of the triad feels able to ask for clarification if anything is unclear.
- Be respectful to your interpreter; they are an important member of the team who makes your work possible.
- Match, when appropriate, for gender and age, do not use a relative and never use a child as an interpreter.
- Be aware of the wellbeing of your interpreter and the possibility of your interpreter suffering from vicarious traumatisation. Consider what support they will be offered.

- At the end of the session allocate 10–15 minutes to debrief the interpreter about the session and offer support and supervision, as appropriate.

With thanks to the British Psychological Society for permission to adapt the above from the BPS guidelines for *Working with Interpreters in Health Settings* (British Psychological Society, 2008).

RESEARCH EVIDENCE

Most interpreters have not undergone comprehensive training in mental health care or clinical supervision in order to minimise susceptibility to vicarious trauma (Splevins et al., 2010). In their study on the emotional impact of interpreting in mental health, Doherty et al. (2010) noted that of the 18 participating interpreters:

- 67% reported experiencing difficulties putting their service users out of their minds
- 33% recounted that interpreting for service users with mental health problems had an impact on their personal lives.

The value of undertaking specialist professional training and related continuing professional development (CPD) for personal resourcing and development by interpreters remains a live issue.

Establishing a good working alliance between client, interpreter and clinician is paramount. Shared similarities in terms of gender, culture, history may be helpful (Tribe and Thompson, 2009). In addition, interpreters as cultural brokers are expected to be fluent and demonstrate an adequate understanding of the languages they interpret (Kuay et al., 2015; Tribe and Raval, 2003). Preferably, interpreters should undergo language testing to ensure that they have the requisite experience and expertise to handle the interpreting task. Children, family members and bilingual staff who are *not* professional interpreters should never be used as interpreters (British Psychological Society, 2008).

Some service users may insist on using family members. If so, it is important to explore with service users that using family members and other unqualified interpreters may present risks, such as breaking confidentiality or that the family member may have a different agenda from the service user (Tribe and Thompson, 2009). Doherty et al. (2010) and Miller et al. (2005) highlight common difficulties associated with mental health care interpreting, including a range of powerful emotions, such as sadness, anger, and feeling powerless and helpless.

REFERENCES

Angelelli, C.V. (2004). *Medical Interpreting and Cross-cultural Communication*. Cambridge: Cambridge University Press.

Bhugra, D. and Gupta, S. (Eds.) (2010). *Migration and Mental Health*. Cambridge: Cambridge University Press.

British Psychological Society (2008). *Working with Interpreters in Health Settings: Guidelines for Psychologists*. Leicester: BPS. (www.bps.org.uk/content/working-interpreters-health-settings).

d'Ardenne, P., Ruaro, L., Cestari, L., Fakhoury, W. and Priebe, S. (2007). Does interpreter-mediated CBT with traumatized refugee people work? A comparison of patient outcomes in East London. *Behavioural and Cognitive Psychotherapy*, 35(3), 293–301.

de Zuleta, F., Gene-Cos, N. and Grachev, S. (2001). Differential psychotic symptomatology in polygot patients: case reports and their implications. *British Journal of Medical Psychology*, 74(3), 277–292.

Doherty, S.M., MacIntyre, A.M. and Wyne, T. (2010). How does it feel for you? The emotional impact and specific challenges of mental health interpreting. *Mental Health Review Journal*, 15(3), 31–44.

Equality Act (2010). *Equality Act 2010*. London: HMSO. (www.legislation.gov.uk).

Fernando, S. (2014). *Mental Health Worldwide: Culture, Globalization and Development*. Basingstoke: Palgrave Macmillan.

Granger, E. and Baker, M. (2003). The role and experience of interpreters. In R. Tribe and H. Raval (Eds.), *Working with Interpreters in Mental Health* (pp. 99–121). London: Routledge.

Harper, D. and Speed, E. (2014). Uncovering recovery: the resistible rise of recovery and resilience. In J. Moncrieff, M. Rapley and E. Speed (Eds.), *De-medicalizing Misery II: Society, Politics and the Mental Health Industry* (pp. 40–57). Basingstoke: Palgrave.

Karliner, L.S., Jacobs, E.A., Chen, A.H. and Mutha, S. (2007). Do professional interpreters improve clinical care for patients with limited English proficiency? A systematic review of the literature. *Health Service Research*, 42(2), 726–754.

Kuay, J., Chopra, P., Kaplan, I. and Szwarc, J. (2015). Conducting psychotherapy with an interpreter. *Australasian Psychiatry*, 23(3), 282–286.

Leanza, Y., Miklavcic, A., Boivin, I. and Rosenberg, E. (2014). Working with interpreters. In L.J. Kirmayer, J. Guzder and C. Rousseau (Eds.), *Cultural Consultation: Encountering the Other in Mental Health Care*. New York: Springer.

McNamee, S. and Gergen, K. (Eds.) (1992). *Therapy as a Social Construction*. London: Sage.

Mental Health Act (1983 amended 2007). *The Mental Health Act 1983 (as amended 2007)*. London: HMSO. (www.mentalhealthcare.org.uk/mentalhealthact).

Miller, K., Martell, Z., Pazdirek, L., Carruth, M. and Lopez, D. (2005). The role of interpreters in psychotherapy with refugees: an exploratory study. *American Journal of Orthopsychiatry*, 75(1), 27–39.

Office for National Statistics (2011). *Census (2011)*. London: Office for National Statistics. (www.ons.gov.uk/census/2011 census).

Raval, H. (1996). A systemic perspective on working with interpreters. *Clinical Child Psychology and Psychiatry*, 1, 29–43.

Resera, E., Tribe, R. and Lane, P. (2015). An introductory study into the experiences of interpreters and counsellors working with refugees and asylum seekers. *International Journal of Culture and Mental Health*, 8(2), 192–206.

Shah, A. (2017). Mental capacity and ageing. In P. Lane and R. Tribe (Eds.), *Anti-discriminatory Practice in Mental Health for Older People*. London: Jessica Kingsley Publishers.

Splevins, K., Cohen, K., Joseph, S., Murray, C. and Bowley, J. (2010). Vicarious post traumatic growth amongst interpreters. *Qualitative Health Research*, 20(12), 1705–1715.

Statista (2016). (www.statista.com).

Taylor, C. (2016) *The Language Animal, the Full Shape of the Human Linguistic Capacity*. Cambridge: Harvard University Press.

Tribe, R. (2016). Commentary on 'Case studies of innovative practice and policy' section. In R. White et al. (Eds.), *The Palgrave Handbook of Sociocultural Perspectives on Global Mental Health*. Basingstoke: Macmillan-Palgrave.

Tribe, R. (1999) Bridging the gap or damming the flow? Some observations on using interpreters/bicultural workers when working with refugee clients, many of whom have been tortured. *British Journal of Medical Psychology*, 72, 567–576.

Tribe, R., & Keefe, A. (2009). Issues in using interpreters in therapeutic work with refugees. What is not being expressed? *European Journal of Psychotherapy and Counselling*, 11(4) 409–424.

Tribe, R. and Raval, H. (Eds.) (2003). *Working with Interpreters in Mental Health*. London: Brunner-Routledge.

Tribe, R. and Thompson, K. (2009). Exploring the three way relationship in therapeutic work with interpreters. *International Journal of Migration, Health and Social Care*, 5(2), 13–21.

Tribe, R. and Tunariu, A.D. (2009). Mind your language? Working with interpreters in health care settings and therapeutic encounters. *Sexual and Relationship Therapy*, 24, 74–84.

Trivasse, M. (2005). *An Interpreter in the Therapy Room: Guidelines on Working with an Interpreter*. BACP Information Sheet. Lutterworth: British Association for Counselling and Psychotherapy (www.bacp.co.uk/members/info_sheets).

Tsai, J.L. (2007). Ideal affect: cultural causes and behavioural consequences. *Perspectives on Psychological Science*, 2(3), 242–259.

RECOMMENDED READING

1. British Psychological Society (Tribe, R. and Thompson, K.) (2016). *Guidelines for Working with Interpreters in Health Settings*. Leicester: BPS. (www.bps.org.uk/content/working-interpreters-health-settings).

These guidelines provide a range of information about working with interpreters, including the relevant legislation, conducting a language needs assessment, training and related issues, preparation, written translations, psychometric assessment and recommendations for improvements in the future.

2. Tribe, R. and Raval, H. (Eds.) (2014[2003]). *Working with Interpreters in Mental Health* (2nd ed.). London: Brunner-Routledge.

This edited book provides an insight into the issues and challenges facing interpreters and professionals working with interpreters. It is informed by theoretical, research and clinical considerations, and helps practitioners to develop better ways of working in partnership with interpreters to assist service users who require an interpreter.

3. *Interpretation in Mental Health Settings: A Quick Guide*. (Film).

A 10-minute film on working with interpreters in mental health, which was made for the Department of Health. It is available from the UEL website (www.uel.ac.uk/psychology/staff/racheltribe.htm) or on YouTube (www.youtube.com/watch?v=k0wzhakyjck).

7.8 WORKING WITH REFUGEES

JUDE BOYLES

OVERVIEW AND KEY POINTS

> The feeling of trust in the world, both human and natural, which is essential to ordinary life, has been broken apart and people describe living in a meaningless void. (Bracken, 2002: 142)

The office of the United Nations High Commissioner for Refugees (UNHCR) estimates that there are 59.5 million forcibly displaced people in the world, and women and girls make up 50% of these populations (UNHCR, 2016). Refugees flee torture, war, oppression, persecution and genocide. Women flee gender-based abuses, such as female genital mutilation (FGM), honour violence, domestic abuse and forced marriage: 'Many States exhibit a societal acceptance of widespread and systematic violence perpetrated against women where abuse forms part of women's daily lives' (Smith and Boyles, 2009: 8).

I have chosen to refer to individuals who have left their country of origin to seek asylum as *refugees* in this chapter; the term encompasses both those seeking asylum and individuals who have been recognised as refugees. The term most commonly used in the United Kingdom (UK) media is 'asylum seeker', which defines individuals by a legal process. Under the 1951 United Nations Convention Relating to the Status of Refugees and the 1967 Protocol, a refugee is:

> A person who owing to a well founded fear of being persecuted for reasons of race, religion, nationality, membership of a particular social group or political opinion, is outside the country of his nationality and is unable or, owing to such fear, is unwilling to avail himself of the protection of that country; or who, not having a nationality and being outside the country of his former habitual residence as a result of such events, is unable or, owing to such fear, is unwilling to return to it.

Therapists have reported on diverse approaches to working with traumatised refugees from across the globe, but there is no model that has emerged in the field as the most effective. A holistic and flexible approach is helpful 'given the diversity of refugees and asylum seekers as a group and the variety of clinical presentations encountered' (Aroche and Coello, 2004: 70).

- Herman's three-stage model transfers well to working with refugees: 'The fundamental stages of recovery are establishing safety, reconstructing the trauma story, and restoring the connection between survivors and their community' (Herman, 1992: 3).
- Claiming asylum is experienced by most individuals and families as a stressful and dehumanising process that can last for many years.
- Most therapists are working with refugees who have a different racial and ethnic background. The task of any therapist is to be self-reflexive: dynamically self-aware about the impact of our reflections on ourselves as therapists, and on our clients, both in session and afterwards.

BACKGROUND AND CONTEXT

Refugees will be referred for therapy at various stages of seeking asylum. Individuals may be newly arrived, relieved to be safe but anxious about family members left behind, others will be referred as destitute and hopeless, with complex post-traumatic stress disorder (PTSD). A comprehensive assessment is required, ensuring that therapists are mindful that not all refugees are traumatised, but may be experiencing what Papadopoulos (2002) refers to as distressing psychological reactions or the 'ordinary human suffering' that accompanies the refugee experience. Many will require therapeutic assistance for trauma. Critics of PTSD argue that the 'diagnosis cannot take account of the magnitude, depth and complexity of refugee peoples experience in its entirety' (Afuape, 2011: 53). In my experience, naming and developing a shared and culturally congruent framework for understanding an individual's overwhelming reactions to traumatic life events has brought relief and enabled refugees to understand and learn to manage their responses.

When working with refugees it is important to ensure that time is taken to contextualise what therapy is and why it might help. The dynamic of seeking relief from distress through talking to a trained professional may be familiar to some, but may be disconcerting and uncomfortable for many. Attend to the whole person and ensure that you engage with the range of difficulties an individual brings.

The approach at assessment has the potential to re-victimise survivors of human rights abuses; find opportunities to validate positive strategies for coping and facilitate access to community and social support.

Refugees come to therapy with profound feelings of loss, and many feel defeated by the scale of their difficulties and describe the agony of not being believed by the authorities. Individuals describe living in constant fear of detention and/or removal to their own or a transit country. This is exacerbated by a requirement to report to the authorities on a regular basis.

Many refugees will have long histories of conflict, oppression and/or abuse, and have lived in societies where there was poor access to healthcare and basic needs were not met. Others will have left behind homes and businesses and find themselves living in poverty in deprived areas, facing hostility from local communities.

Refugees describe experiences of racism and multiple barriers to accessing advice, support and information. It can be appropriate to undertake practical tasks, such as making telephone calls or writing letters of support, particularly at assessment and in the early stages of therapy. 'Torture survivors living in exile in the United Kingdom are pushed into poverty by government systems' (Mendez, 2013: 2). Thoughtful negotiation about when you can provide practical assistance and why is crucial, as well as recognising that asking for assistance can be seen as a strength: 'their perception that the therapists' intervention will enable greater access for them is (also) reasonable, especially given the current political climate, with its consequent growth of prejudice. By using what they know and asking for help they are not relinquishing autonomy but acting with autonomy (West, 2006: 12).

Many therapists are anxious about processing traumatic experiences with refugees who face such uncertainty. It is my experience that, following a thorough assessment and a period of engagement and stabilising work, individuals can and do process traumatic experiences effectively. The 'assumption that asylum seekers should "survive" migration and a long application procedure before treatment is potentially pathogenic' (Drozdek and Wilson, 2004: 245).

Therapy with refugees inevitably requires working with qualified interpreters. Fully preparing both the therapist and interpreter to work effectively in the partnership requires training and preparation. Mothertongue (www.mothertongue.org.uk), a cross-cultural psychotherapy service in London, has produced a 'Code of Practice and Ethics for Interpreters and Practitioners in Joint Work'. The British Psychological Society (www.bps.org.uk) has published its own *set of guidelines, Working with Interpreters in Health Settings* (British Psychological Society, 2016). See also Chapter 7.7 (Tribe and Tunariu – this volume).

Therapists should record therapeutic work comprehensively, mindful that they are bearing witness to human rights abuses and may be required to write a report to document the impact of an individual's experience of torture or abuse. For guidance on writing clinical letters or psychological therapy reports for survivors of torture, refer to the Istanbul Protocol (1999).

In all settings, there are cultural and racial differences and issues of power that require further exploration. The power of the therapist's position is likely to be amplified in refugee work.

WAYS OF WORKING – MOHSEN

Mohsen was a Kurdish survivor of torture. He had been an activist, and his entire life and identity was rooted in the Kurdish struggle. At assessment he told me that 'his visa [asylum claim] had been turned down' and that his two brothers were in prison and his father was forcibly *disappeared*. He was physically injured following torture, and had a chronic pain condition.

He had no concept of therapy and did not know why his general practitioner (GP) had referred him to our crisis service. He was suspicious of the interpreter and shocked by his recent refusal by the Home Office. He described nightmares, sleeplessness, anxiety, intrusive thoughts, waves of panic and flashbacks. He described a long family history of oppression and exclusion. His earliest memory was as an 8-year-old of watching his father being beaten in front of him. He was not in contact with his family and felt humiliated by the asylum process. In our first session together, I contacted his legal representative to make him an appointment so that the refusal could be appealed. Mohsen had not been able to face contacting his lawyer; his relief was palpable.

Time was taken at assessment to help Mohsen understand what therapy was. Vague descriptions of how talking is helpful would not have given therapy any credibility and could easily have alienated him. I described myself as a trained helper who was familiar with torture and explained how I could assist. I reassured him about the confidentiality of both myself and the interpreter in a culturally accessible way.

I took a family and cultural history, so that I could begin to understand the person he was before he was imprisoned.

Mohsen was isolated and living on the top floor of a large house. He rarely left his room as it involved climbing several flights of stairs and his left knee was badly injured.

Our early work included undertaking practical tasks that would provide some relief and support our engagement, as well as assisting him with his difficulties around disturbed sleep, anxiety and recovering from nightmares. I wrote letters to assist with a move to a smaller property where his room was on the ground floor, and applied for a bus pass so he could freely travel. As he gained some physical strength, I gave him details of local English classes at a community college.

I carefully introduced some basic psycho-education so that we reached a shared understanding of his difficulties. He found some basic grounding and breathing techniques helpful, and began to pay a little more attention to his needs though some basic self care. He bought a low light for his room so he was not sleeping in the dark and kept a picture from his country by his bed to help him recover from nightmares. I liaised with his GP about a referral to the Pain Clinic.

He became less fearful that he was going mad, and began to understand his responses as a normal consequence to his horrific experiences. He described feeling less ashamed of being weak, especially in front of a woman. As our relationship developed, he readily brought his fears and problems into the clinical space, having been quite baffled by the process of therapy at first. We explored his sense of alienation, grief and anger: 'It is recommended [to take] an existential approach to catastrophic stress or brutality... therapists [should] assist clients to relate their symptoms to life events' (Bemak et al., 2003: 50).

Mohsen clearly felt estranged from the political struggle that had defined him and so we began to explore how he could find a way to be active in his community. He began to consider phoning his family.

We were able to identify aspects of his torture history that created the most distress and processed them together. This narrative work was disrupted by Home Office letters, micro assaults, bad news from home and other crises. Mohsen began to engage in conversations with other refugees at college, and found that despite his fears, his memory and concentration were not irreparably damaged.

Mohsen was waiting for an Asylum Tribunal appeal date as we ended, but he had become an active participant in his asylum claim. He had a structure to his day and had met some Kurdish men that he would socialise with occasionally. His trauma symptoms were significantly reduced. He missed his family terribly, but telephoned his mother and mostly felt reassured by these calls. His early life, though unpredictable and harsh at times, had been loving. He was able to identify some good memories from growing up, especially time spent with his younger brother and mother. He had a little hope that he could build the future he wanted in the UK, but he was less afraid and was seeking connections. 'Restoring relationships and community is central to restoring well being' (van der Kolk, 2014: 38).

Herman writes that in working with survivors of trauma, the 'single most common therapeutic error is avoidance of the traumatic material', but she argues that the 'second most common error is premature or precipitate engagement in exploratory work, without sufficient attention to the tasks of establishing safety and securing a therapeutic alliance' (Herman, 1992: 155–156).

SEEKING SAFETY...

At closure, I asked Mohsen what had been helpful. His response reflected his activism, and our connection as two activists from very different worlds: 'don't keep what happened to me quiet [confidential], people should know. I don't mean what happened to me in prison, I mean how I have been treated here [in the UK]. I have been treated like a liar and a criminal. This is not a safe country for me. But I feel safe when I am here'. What Mohsen summarised so eloquently is the therapist's role in bearing witness and our responsibility to use that knowledge responsibly to further human rights.

Mohsen also shows how, despite living in a frightening and insecure world, therapy can still provide a safe and containing space, where a connection is made, injustices are named and distress can be alleviated. The experience of being a refugee in the UK is harsh and uncertain. Refugees and refugee therapists/interpreters are profoundly impacted by the anti-migrant feeling in the West and the rise of racism.

It is important for therapists to remember that our clients bring such fears into the therapy room whatever our cultural background. We must be explicit that we are not neutral and believe in the legal right of refugees to seek safety and be welcomed into a fair system. In the absence of this, we must welcome refugees into our clinical spaces, ensuring we are flexible, accessible and do all we can to assist with the skills, information and power at our disposal.

However this war may end, we have won the war against you; none of you will be left to bear witness, but even if someone were to survive, the world would not believe him. (Wiesenthal, 1968: 293)

RESEARCH EVIDENCE

Depression, anxiety and PTSD are higher for those seeking asylum in the UK than the general population (e.g., Turner and Gorst-Unsworth 1990; van der Veer, 1998). Fazel et al. (2005), in their study of over 7,000 cases, identified that refugees in exile in the West are ten times more likely than the host population to have PTSD. A lack of social support has been shown to exacerbate mental health distress in refugees (Gorst-Unsworth and Goldenberg, 1998).

Despite what we know about the mental health of refugees, there remains less research about what types of intervention assist. In the torture rehabilitation movement, therapists deliver within a multidisciplinary setting that attends to the psychological and physical impact of torture as well as meeting the legal, welfare and social needs of survivors. Often such centres are provided from a community setting (Kira, 2002).

REFERENCES

Afuape, T. (2011) *Power, Resistance and Liberation in Therapy with Survivors of Trauma: To Have Our Hearts Broken*. London and New York: Routledge.

Aroche, J. and Coello, M.J. (2004) Ethnocultural considerations in the treatment of refugees and asylum seekers. In J.P. Wilson and B. Drozdek (eds), *Broken Spirits: The Treatment of Traumatised Asylum Seekers, Refugees, War and Torture Victims* (pp. 53–80). New York: Brunner-Routledge.

Bemak, F., Chi-Ying Chung, R. and Pedersen, P.B. (2003) *Counselling Refugees: A Psychosocial Approach to Innovative Multicultural Interventions*. Westport, CT: Greenwood Press.

Bracken, P. (2002) *Trauma: Culture, Meaning and Philosophy*. London: Whurr Publishers.

British Psychological Society (2016). *Working with Interpreters in Health Settings: Guidelines for Psychologists*. Leicester: BPS. (www.bps.org.uk/content/working-interpreters-health-settings).

Drozdek, B. and Wilson, J.P. (2004) Uncovering: trauma-focused treatment techniques with asylum seekers. In J.P. Wilson and B. Drozdek (eds), *Broken Spirits: The Treatment of Traumatised Asylum Seekers, Refugees, War and Torture Victims* (pp. 243–276). New York: Brunner-Routledge.

Fazel, M., Wheeler, J. and Danesh, J. (2005) Prevalence of serious mental disorder in 7000 refugees. *The Lancet*, 365 (9467, April), 1309–1314.

Gorst-Unsworth, C. and Goldenberg, E. (1998) Psychological sequelae of torture and organised violence suffered by refugees from Iraq. *British Journal of Psychiatry*, 172: 90–94.

Herman, J.L. (1992) *Trauma and Recovery: From Domestic Abuse to Political Terror*. London: Pandora.

Istanbul Protocol (1999) The UN Manual on the Effective Investigation and Documentation of Torture and other Cruel, Inhuman or Degrading Treatment or Punishment. New York: United Nations. (www.ohchr.org).

Kira, I.A. (2002) Torture assessment and treatment: the wraparound approach. *Traumatology*, 8(2): 54–86.

Mendez, J.E. (2013) Foreword. In J. Pettitt (ed.), *The Poverty Barrier: The Right to Rehabilitation for Survivors of Torture in the UK*. London: Freedom from Torture.

Papadopoulos, R.K. (2002) *Therapeutic Care for Refugees: No Place Like Home*. The Tavistock Clinic Series. London: Karnac.

Smith, E. and Boyles, J. (2009) *Justice Denied: The Experiences of 100 Torture Surviving Women of Seeking Justice and Rehabilitation*. London: Medical Foundation for the Care of Victims of Torture.

Turner, S. and Gorst-Unsworth, C. (1990) Psychological sequelae of torture: a descriptive model. *British Journal of Psychiatry*, 157(4): 475–480.

UNHCR (1951) *Convention and Protocol Relating to the Status of Refugees*. New York: UNHCR. (http://www.unhcr.org/protect/PROTECTION/3b66c2aa10.pdf)

UNHCR (2016) *Key Facts and Figures*. New York: UNHCR. (www.unhcr.org.uk/about-us/key-facts-and-figures.html).

(Continued)

(Continued)

van der Kolk, B. (2014) *The Body Keeps the Score: Brain, Mind, and Body in the Healing of Trauma*. London: Penguin.
van der Veer, G. (1998) *Counselling and Therapy with Refugees and Victims of Torture: Psychological Problems of Victims of War, Torture and Repression* (2nd ed.). Chichester, UK: Wiley.
West, A. (2006) To do or not to do – is that the question? *Therapy Today*, 17(6): 10–13.
Wiesenthal, S. (1968) *The Murderers among Us*. London: Bantam.

RECOMMENDED READING

1. Web resources: The Refugee Council, UK. (www.refugeecouncil.org.uk), Amnesty International (www.amnesty.org.uk), and Human Rights Watch (www.hrw.org).

Visit the Refugee Council website for translated information about the asylum process and Home Office support arrangements in the UK. For country profiles, see the Amnesty International and Human Rights Watch websites.

2. Wilson, J.P. and Drozdek, B. (eds) (2004) *Broken Spirits: The Treatment of Traumatised Asylum Seekers, Refugees, War and Torture Victims*. New York: Brunner-Routledge.

This is a comprehensive manual that gives theoretical and practical insight into working with refugees across a range of settings by leading practitioners in the field. It includes chapters for those working with refugees in affected areas as well as for therapists working with refugees in exile.

3. Herman, J.L. (1994) *Trauma and Recovery: From Domestic Abuse to Political Terror*. London: Pandora.

Herman's three-phase approach to recovery from traumatic events emphasizes the task of establishing safety and securing a therapeutic alliance with survivors of atrocities before engaging with traumatic material.

THERAPEUTIC SPECIALISMS: THERAPY SETTINGS

7.9 COACHING

ZSÓFIA ANNA UTRY AND STEPHEN PALMER

OVERVIEW AND KEY POINTS

When living and working conditions are becoming more challenging for both individuals and organisations, coaching seems to have the potential to provide a helpful service for the non-clinical population during difficult times. Coaching is becoming widely recognised in society and this growth is paralleled with increased professionalisation and increased academic research in the area. There are still existing issues regarding the definition of coaching and its relation to therapy. However, robust evidence suggests now that coaching does work for individuals and organisations and enhances people's wellbeing and performance. In the future, research needs to explain how coaching works and how individual differences effect the process of coaching. This chapter will cover:

- Coaching offers a much needed reflective and developmental space for everyday people.
- Coaching's interdisciplinary nature presents challenges but aims for positive behavioural change in all cases.
- A common life transition: returning to work from maternity leave with coaching support.
- A new research approach required to understand how coaching works and with whom.

BACKGROUND AND CONTEXT

It has been widely recognised that our living and working circumstances in globalised societies are increasingly becoming more and more challenging and unpredictable. These living conditions are often associated with the military acronym VUCA in leadership literature, which stands for volatile, uncertain, complex and ambiguous (Hall, 2015). With globalisation, there is increased diversity in all domains of life, and there are no working, clear-cut rules available but only locally created, context-based ones (Stelter, 2014).

People and organisations face more changes and transitions and they are required to process new information at an ongoing basis. Reflection and adaptation became generally necessary skills to be able to navigate through life. Giddens argues (1991) that conversation-based helping professions are necessary in our late modern society to increase self-reflexivity. It may not be a surprise, then, that people seek out more professional guidance now (Theeboom, 2016).

Coaching is arguably filling in the empty space where therapy and counselling did not go (Western, 2012). Coaching offers a dialogue-based service which aims to facilitate a coachee's personal development and support them to achieve their personal and professional goals. The caveat is that coaching services are not generally offered to people who are suffering from high levels of distress or clinical disorders such as anxiety or depression.

The International Coach Federation's (ICF) global survey indicates that the number of organisations using coaching and its market value is on the rise (ICF, 2012). Also, the number of people who identify themselves as coaches has dramatically increased (ICF, 2012).

Coaching is generally considered to originate from the United States of America in the 1960s, so essentially has been a western cultural phenomenon, embedded in an individualised, democratic-capitalist value-system (Western, 2012). However, one of the first academic papers was published much earlier by Gorby (1937), describing how employees were coached to reduce waste and thereby increase profits and their own profit-sharing programme bonuses. Now coaching is aiming to be a truly global phenomenon, setting foot in China and Far East countries as well (Einzig, 2016).

While the first decades of coaching were more like 'the wild west of coaching' (Sherman and Freas, 2004) in terms of lack of professionalisation, currently professional certification and evidence of experience is expected from practitioners in general on the market.

As opposed to the early years, people in organisations often perceive having a coach as an achievement, and is not a service exclusive to senior-level leaders now (ICF, 2013). Organisations are the biggest buyers of coaching, and to manage the costs of coaching, more and more companies invest in internal coaches' training instead of using independent practitioners (ICF, 2013).

WAYS OF WORKING

From a cultural perspective, Western (2012: 10) describes coaching as 'a hybrid expertise, that adapted brilliantly to the complex and competing demands of contemporary society'. Coaching draws on a wide range of branches, including philosophy, sociology, anthropology, sports, communication science and even natural sciences (Brock, 2008), and coaches have therefore various backgrounds (Sherman and Freas, 2004). A global survey (Newnham-Kanas et al., 2012) found that most practising coaches have a business background (49.1%), followed by educators (20.8%) and helping professionals (15.6%). Coaches also tend to have an integrative or eclectic approach to practice (Lai and McDowall, 2014).

Given the cross-disciplinary nature of coaching, there is no professional consensus on what exactly constitutes coaching and what does not (Jones, 2015; Theeboom, 2016). Research also suggests that clients have different and limited understandings of coaching which can be problematic in practice not only in research (Jones, 2015).

Typical coachees want to work on different transitions in their lives (such as career or personal life changes), improve in executive or leadership roles, and/or they experience dissatisfaction with one or more aspects of their lives (for example, with work–life imbalance or unhealthy lifestyle). However, the topics of coaching are less intimidating than therapy and require a less close relationship between coach and coachee (Gessnitzer and Kauffeld, 2015). It is also different from training and mentoring because it does not aim to transfer pre-defined knowledge or skills, and different from therapy because its target audience is the non-clinical population (Theeboom, 2016).

Day et al. (2008) argue that coaching has many similar characteristics with therapy. Coaching is also an essentially client-centred, positive and collaborative relationship that is mostly associated with successful outcomes (Gessnitzer and Kauffeld, 2015), and coaching involves the understanding of cognitive and emotional reactions in relation to coachees' wellbeing and performance as well (Day et al., 2008).

There is evidence to suggest that people during periods of significant stress may seek less stigmatising forms of help, such as coaching, when therapy would be a more appropriate intervention. Studies found that in one screening process seeking a non-clinical population for the research programme, 52% of applicants reported a clinical level of stress (Green et al., 2006), and in another case the rate was 25% (Spence and Grant, 2007).

Regarding the obvious issues about boundaries between coaching and therapy, there is a debate about whether coaches should have a background in psychological training (as cited in Lai and McDowall, 2014). Assessing coachees' mental health state can be critical and reacting to coachees' challenging emotional states appropriately is also fundamental (Day et al., 2008; Lai and McDowall, 2014). Passmore and Fillery-Travis (2011), in their research review, identify that client readiness is a major contributor for coaching success. If a coachee is not ready to change, coaching may not be a suitable intervention.

Lai and McDowall (2014: 124) define coaching as 'a reflective process between coaches and coachees which helps or facilitates coachees to experience positive behavioural changes through continuous dialogue and negotiations with coaches to meet coachees' personal or work goals'. This definition suggests that successful coaching should result in positive behavioural change.

CASE EXAMPLE

Emma, aged 33, had been on maternity leave for two years when she decided to go back to work in six months' time. She wanted a career change this time, and a more fulfilling new job that aligned with her internal values and circle of real interests. Because she was unsure about the specific practices she needed to undertake for this change (CV writing, job searching in a new sector, networking) and also because she wanted feedback and reassurance on her plans and the level of rationality of her desires, she sought out a career coach's support.

Upon assessment, Emma identified two goals. First, she wanted to build a practical career plan and to start realising practical steps to advance her career. Second, Emma stated that she tended to stress out and lose confidence in herself when she thought about this change, so she also wanted help to manage her stress.

(Continued)

Emma had strengths to enhance her goals: she had an excellent professional track record of five years' employment at a multinational company, and she was communicative, open and excited to work with a coach on her career dreams. They contracted for six sessions with a possible extension to eight sessions on a weekly or biweekly basis, depending on circumstances.

Emma was actively contemplating change (Prochaska et al., 1992) when she started the coaching process. Career options were drafted and evaluated and intersessional tasks were set. Meanwhile Emma thought about and defined her tasks, she simultaneously discussed with the coach the emerging negative or unhelpful thoughts she had about herself (e.g., 'I don't have what it takes to have a creative career'). The coach aimed to provide a non-judgemental space so Emma could verbalise, explore and eventually demystify her self-doubts.

The coach also kept in touch via email between sessions, and they spoke on the phone when Emma had opportunities to take the initiative in her career but needed technical (e.g., getting feedback on written applications) or emotional support to make that move (e.g., calling the 'dream' employer).

While they eventually met on a three-weekly basis, by the fourth session Emma was actively looking for opportunities and was inquiring about and applying for positions she preferred. The coach's main role was to help Emma to realise what she could actually do to achieve her career goal through active listening, open and challenging questions and dialoguing with Emma about the meaning of optimism and pessimism related to her goals. Additionally, the coach shared online career-related practical articles and mindfulness materials to help her to regulate stress between sessions. Emma was an active and motivated coachee and used this to experiment with new ways of thinking. So she started to manage her unhelpful thoughts by assessing the level of rationality of her self-deprecating beliefs when those occurred more often, so those would not stop her from achieving her goals.

RESEARCH EVIDENCE

There is now strong evidence to show that coaching does indeed work. However, we know much less about how it actually works and with whom. For people who want to exploit their potential and be successful, there is a plethora of approaches, models and techniques out there, but much more rigorous research is needed to find the most effective ways to really support them in their efforts.

There are certain factors that prompted more research in coaching in the past 20 years. Organisations – the largest buyers of coaching services – now expect to see evidence of their return on investment (Passmore and Fillery-Travis, 2011). From a training and development aspect, Passmore and Fillery-Travis argue (2011) that coach trainings need to be based on evidence-based practices to give the best to clients.

Coaching research before 2001 was found to be limited in quality (Kampa-Kokesch and Anderson, 2001). Even though there are still methodological and theoretical issues in coaching research, there have been an increased number of formal qualitative studies and randomised controlled trials since then (Passmore and Fillery-Travis, 2011).

The coaching relationship started to emerge as possibly the most significant factor in coaching success (e.g., Baron and Morin, 2009; Gyllensten and Palmer, 2007; O'Broin and Palmer, 2010). This was supported in a meta-study as well (De Haan et al., 2013) and now the research focus seems to have shifted towards the common factors instead of models and techniques (Jones, 2015).

Randomised controlled trials contributed to coaching research considerably. Green et al. (2007) investigated the effect of cognitive-behavioural, solution-focused life coaching on senior high school students. As a result of 10 sessions with trained teachers over two terms, a significant increase was found in cognitive hardiness and hope, and a decrease in depression in the participants compared to those in control group. Grant et al. (2009) found that short-term coaching enhanced the performance and wellbeing of executives in the health sector. Their cognitive-behavioural, solution-focused approach helped participants to increase goal-attainment, resilience, workplace wellbeing and reduced depression and stress.

Gessnitzer and Kauffeld (2015), instead of relying on retrospective subjective ratings only (as most relationship research does), added observational data to their analysis of the working alliance in the case of short-term career coaching dyads at a German university. They found in the observed behaviour that agreement on the goals and tasks of coaching was only associated with goal attainment when these were initiated by the coachee. The effect was reversed when the coach initiated the goals and tasks, even if the coachee agreed with them. This highlights the importance of an active coachee in the process. Interestingly, they found no impact of the working alliance ratings of the coachee on the results in this case.

Theeboom et al.'s (2014) meta-analysis integrates quantitative findings from the literature related to the effectiveness of coaching in an organisational context. The study concludes that coaching is an effective tool in organisations for improving individuals' performance and skills, wellbeing, coping, work attitudes, and goal-directed self-regulation (Theeboom et al., 2014).

Regarding the future of coaching research, Lai and McDowall (2014) point out that methods and evaluation approaches should aim for more rigorous and replicable results. In their systematic literature review, 65% of the studies they examined used only data based on coachees' personal satisfaction and attitude changes. They suggest that behavioural and performance improvement measures should be applied much more often. Furthermore, 70% of the studies applied a qualitative approach, which made the outcomes less reliable (Lai and McDowall, 2014).

Coaching research follows the trends of therapy and counselling research (Passmore and Fillery-Travis, 2011). A recent development in systematic case study research is the adjudicated case study method (McLeod et al., 2015; Thurston et al., 2015), which may have the potential to demonstrate reliably how coaching works and to build theory. The protocol not only requires the collection of a wide range of data, but eliminates the sole researcher's bias towards the case by analysing it in a group from many different perspectives. As a result, analyses and conclusions of cases can be much more rigorous and credible, and details of the coaching process can be better understood than from randomised controlled trials.

REFERENCES

Baron, L. and Morin, L. (2009) The coach–coachee relationship in executive coaching: a field study. *Human Resource Development Quarterly*, 20(1): 85–106.

Brock, V.G. (2008) *Grounded Theory of the Roots and Emergence of Coaching*. PhD dissertation, International University of Professional Studies, Hawaii. (http:// libraryofprofessionalcoaching.com).

Day, A., De Haan, E., Sills, C., Bertie, C. and Blass, E. (2008) Coaches' experience of critical moments in the coaching. *International Coaching Psychology Review*, 3(3): 207–218.

De Haan, E., Duckworth, A., Birch, D. and Jones, C. (2013) Executive coaching outcome research: the contribution of common factors such as relationship, personality match, and self-efficacy. *Consulting Psychology Journal: Practice and Research*, 65(1): 40–57.

Einzig, H. (2016) Editorial – Special edition on China and the Far East. *Global Coaching Perspectives*, 9: 1–2.

Gessnitzer, S. and Kauffeld, S. (2015) The working alliance in coaching: why behavior is the key to success. *The Journal of Applied Behavioral Science*, 51(2): 177–197.

Giddens, A. (1991) *Modernity and Self-identity: Self and Society in the Late Modern Age*. Stanford, CA: Stanford University Press.

Gorby, C.B. (1937) Everyone gets a share of the profits. *Factory Management and Maintenance*, 95: 82–83.

Grant, A.M., Curtayne, L. and Burton, G. (2009) Executive coaching enhances goal attainment, resilience and workplace well-being: a randomised controlled study. *The Journal of Positive Psychology*, 4(5): 396–407.

Green, L.S., Grant, A.M. and Rynsaardt, J. (2007) Evidence-based life coaching for senior high school students: Building hardiness and hope. *International Coaching Psychology Review*, 2(1): 24–32.

Green, L.S., Oades, L., and Grant, A. (2006) Cognitive-behavioral, solution-focused life coaching: Enhancing goal striving, wellbeing, and hope. *The Journal of Positive Psychology*, 1(3): 142–149.

Gyllensten, K. and Palmer, S. (2007) The coaching relationship: an interpretative phenomenological analysis. *International Coaching Psychology Review*, 2(2): 168–177.

Hall, L. (2015) Definitions. In L. Hall (ed.), *Coaching in Times of Crisis and Transformation* (pp. 5–11). London: Kogan Page.

(Continued)

(Continued)

International Coach Federation (2012) *Global Coaching Study: Executive Summary*. (http://coachfederation.org/files/ FileDownloads/2012GlobalCoachingStudy.pdf).

International Coach Federation (2013) *Organizational Coaching Study: Executive Summary* (http://coachfederation. org/files/FileDownloads/2013OrgCoachingStudy.pdf).

Jones, C.W. (2015) *Choosing your Coach: What Matters and When. An Interpretative Phenomenological Exploration of the Voice of the Coachee*. PhD dissertation, Oxford Brookes University, Oxford.

Kampa-Kokesch, S. and Anderson, M. Z. (2001) Executive coaching: a comprehensive review of the literature. *Consulting Psychology Journal: Practice and Research*, 53(4): 205–228.

Lai, Y.L. and McDowall, A. (2014) A systematic review (SR) of coaching psychology: focusing on the attributes of effective coaching. *International Coaching Psychology Review*, 9(2): 120–136.

McLeod, J., Thurston, M. and McLeod, J. (2015) Case study methodologies. In A. Vossler and N. Moller (eds), *The Counselling and Psychotherapy Research Handbook* (pp. 198–211). London: Sage.

Newnham-Kanas, C., Morrow, D. and Irwin, J.D. (2012) Certified professional co-active coaches: why they enjoy coaching. *International Journal of Evidence-based Coaching and Mentoring*, 10(1): 48–56.

O'Broin, A. and Palmer, S. (2010) Exploring key aspects in the formation of coaching relationships: initial indicators from the perspective of the coachee and the coach. *Coaching: An International Journal of Theory, Research and Practice*, 3(2): 124–143.

Passmore, J. and Fillery-Travis, A. (2011) A critical review of executive coaching research: a decade of progress and what's to come. *Coaching: An International Journal of Theory, Research and Practice*, 4(2): 70–88.

Prochaska, J. Q, & DiClemente, C. C. (1992). Stages of change in the modification of problem behaviors. In M. Hersen, R. M. Eisler, & P. M. Miller (Eds.), *Progress in Behavior Modification* (pp. 184–214). Sycamore, IL: Sycamore Press.

Sherman, S. and Freas, A. (2004) The wild west of executive coaching. *Harvard Business Review*, November. (https:// hbr.org/2004/11/the-wild-west-of-executive-coaching). Retrieved on 31/05/2016.

Spence, G. B. and Grant, A. (2007) Professional and peer life coaching and the enhancement of goal striving and well-being: An exploratory study. *The Journal of Positive Psychology*, 2(3): 185–194.

Stelter, R. (2014) *A Guide to Third Generation Coaching*. London: Springer.

Theeboom, T. (2016) *Workplace Coaching: Processes and Effect*. PhD dissertation, University of Amsterdam, Amsterdam.

Theeboom, T., Beersma, B. and van Vianen, A.E.M. (2014) Does coaching work? A meta-analysis on the effects of coaching on individual level outcomes in an organizational context. *The Journal of Positive Psychology*, 9(1): 1–18.

Thurston, M., McLeod, J. and McLeod, J. (2015) How to use case study methodology with single client therapy data. In A. Vossler and N. Moller (eds), *The Counselling and Psychotherapy Research Handbook* (pp. 212–224). London: Sage.

Western, S. (2012) *Coaching and Mentoring: A Critical Text*. London: Sage.

RECOMMENDED READING

1.   Palmer, S. and Whybrow, A. (2007) *Handbook of Coaching Psychology: A Guide for Practitioners*. Hove: Routledge.

This is a comprehensive read for professionals interested in coaching.

2.   Western, S. (2012) *Coaching and Mentoring: A Critical Text*. London: Sage.

Western's book challenges common assumptions about coaching and investigates coaching from a broader, macro perspective.

3.   Stelter, R. (2014) *A Guide to Third Generation Coaching*. London: Springer.

Stelter argues that coaching needs to be reconceptualised to better serve people in the twenty-first century.

7.10 WORKING IN FURTHER AND HIGHER EDUCATION

ANDREW REEVES

OVERVIEW AND KEY POINTS

Counselling services have been long established in further and higher education settings in the United Kingdom (UK) and typically sit within a wider student support network of services. Early professional standards of the Association for Student Counselling helped inform the early work of the British Association for Counselling (later, with Psychotherapy added) and, as such, student counselling has been an important influencing factor in the wider development of counselling the UK.

- Counselling services can range from single-person services through to larger teams of counsellors and other related professionals (e.g., mental health advisers).
- Students present with a range of difficulties that fall beyond problems with academic work, including depression, anxiety, risk and eating-related problems.
- Counsellors will use a range of theoretical interventions to help meet a student's need. As such, many will work from integrative or increasingly pluralistic approaches to practice.

BACKGROUND AND CONTEXT

A HISTORICAL OVERVIEW

Bell (1996: 1) notes the difficulty in identifying the point at which student counselling developed, stating that 'searching for the source of student counselling is a little like searching for the source of a river with many tributaries'. However, Bell (2006: 555) suggested three main influences on the formation of the Association for Student Counselling (ASC) (later the Association for University and College Counsellors (AUCC) and then the British Association for Counselling and Psychotherapy: Universities and Colleges division (BACP: UC)):

- the work of psychodynamic/psychoanalytic counsellors such as Mary Swainson, whose work in education helped develop the service at the University of Leicesterchanges in North America

with the development of person-centred counselling and the provision of counselling in US colleges and universities
- the work of specific individuals in the UK (e.g., Nick Malleson).

The early professional standards developed by the ASC helped inform the early work of the then British Association for Counselling (now the British Association for Counselling and Pychotherapy (BACP)). As a division of BACP, BACP:UC has always retained its own strong identity, taking responsibility for the development of counselling in student settings. For the purposes of this chapter, 'students' refers to those post primary and secondary education (ages 5–16 years), that is, tertiary education in further or higher educational settings, such as colleges and universities.

THE INSTITUTIONAL SETTING

Like students themselves, there is no such thing as a 'typical' education institution. Broadly speaking, in the UK such institutions can be divided into two categories: further education and higher education. Further education traditionally has offered non-graduate programmes, including A levels and a range of diplomas, while higher education has offered graduate and postgraduate programmes. These areas of demarcation are no longer as clear, with both settings offering a range of educational opportunities that sometimes overlap.

Further education settings have traditionally attracted 16–18 year-olds looking for an alternative to a school setting to complete their non-graduate education (although again this demographic is changing). As such, counsellors and psychotherapists in these institutions have to be familiar with key legislative directives that inform practice, such as safeguarding, capacity and consent.

STUDENT SUPPORT STRUCTURES

The nature and form of student support services within education institutions will be dependent on the available funding and the culture and size of the institution, for example. In addition to counselling services, some institutions employ allied staff, such as clinical psychologists or sessional psychiatrists, to assess students with more complex mental health problems. Additionally, a number of institutions also employ 'mental health advisers', often qualified in social work, mental health nursing or an allied field, offering mental health-specific interventions to students, such as crisis intervention, liaison and assessment.

The wider task of any counselling service is to understand the nature of the institution it is serving: the culture of learning, the profile of other staff (e.g., academics, support staff, administrative staff), the profile of students (e.g., age, culture, diversity), the community in which it is located, the socio-economic climate of the area, competitor institutions, and so on. By understanding these issues, the counselling service will be well placed to develop a service that is a 'best match' for the institution and the clients it supports, as well as increasing the potential for supporting the institution in ways beyond the delivery of individual or group work (e.g., consultative support to staff, delivery of training, etc.) (May, 1999). It will also be able to develop policies and procedures (e.g., around referral, assessment and confidentiality) that appropriately complement other available services, avoiding duplication.

WAYS OF WORKING

Many services in smaller institutions are staffed by 'lone counsellors', that is, where there is only one counsellor employed to deliver counselling. In larger institutions the counselling team may be much larger, often constituting a mix of full-time and part-time staff. Often working in a dedicated counselling service, therapists may also be situated in a larger, generic student services team.

Twenty years ago Bell (1996) noted that the working orientation of counsellors in education settings tended to divide between psychodynamic and person-centred. However, the resurgence of other models over the last two decades in the UK, such as cognitive-behavioural therapy (CBT) or cognitive analytic therapy (CAT), is now reflected in education counselling services. The majority of services that employ a number of counsellors now have the capacity to offer a variety of interventions, which might additionally include transactional analysis (TA), gestalt therapy, etc. Many services in reality work to an integrative model of practice or, latterly, are developing pluralistic ways of working with students (Cooper and Dryden, 2016).

Training placements in education settings can often be popular due to the diversity of client work and the range of working approaches used. Additionally, a proportion of qualified practitioners in such settings are also educators, who are familiar with current thinking and research. Bell (2006: 559), citing Butcher et al. (1998), identified the following areas of competence for student counsellors:

- general management
- information management
- information giving
- facilitating self-help groups
- advising
- liaison with, and giving feedback to, providers
- teaching and training
- advocacy
- supporting other key pastoral workers in the institution.

I would add: supporting and advising parents; crisis response; consultative support regarding individual or institutional dynamics; supervision; writing; and research.

A PROFILE OF CLIENT WORK: SUSIE AND CHENG

Counselling in education settings demands a range of different responses, including *functional duties* (i.e., contextual factors to be responded to) and *therapeutic interventions* (i.e., the specific therapeutic response to the student). Susie and Cheng provide a little insight into the types of client student counsellors may work with.

SUSIE

Susie is a 17-year-old student studying for her 'A' levels. Susie has self-injured for some years and was, for a short time, seen by the Child and Adolescent Mental Health Service (CAMHS) team. Her parents separated when she was 12 and she has little contact with her father and has a difficult relationship with her mother. Susie feels angry a lot of the time and is struggling to make and maintain friendships.

CHENG

Cheng is a 19-year-old Chinese student studying medicine. He has experienced anxiety and panic attacks for some years, but has never sought help previously. He is due to begin his clinical placement as part of his degree and his panic attacks have increased in severity and frequency and has started to fall behind with his work. He feels great pressure to succeed due to the fact that his family is funding his degree, at a significant financial sacrifice. His family is unaware of his problems and he feels greatly ashamed at having to seek out help.

RESPONDING TO SUSIE AND CHENG

Susie and Cheng's difficulties are common in education settings, in that they are sometimes complex, long-standing, and are not directly related to their academic studies but do impact on their capacity to study. The counsellors here would need to undertake a number of important functions, as well as considering with Susie and Cheng the best sort of interventions to offer. The functional duties to be considered might include:

- assessing risk
- contracting and confirming the nature and extent of confidentiality offered
- whether additional support is required to support their studies, and referring to specialist teams, if necessary
- keeping in mind fitness to practise issues (for Cheng)
- potential liaison with other teams, if consent is given and it is deemed necessary (e.g., CAMHS)
- supporting mitigation applications.

The therapeutic interventions might include:

- time for Susie and Cheng to name their problems
- assessing the degree to which they feel impaired by their problems (e.g., appetite, sleep, sex, concentration, etc.)
- meditation and relaxation strategies (e.g., mindfulness)
- psycho-education regarding anxiety and self-injury
- anxiety management strategies (e.g., breathing, 'grounding' (see Reeves, 2015))
- facilitating self-exploration to encourage self-care and further self-insight.

These are some of the issues Susie and Cheng's therapists might need to consider, but more are likely to emerge as the counselling progresses. Other presentations seen in student counselling might include:

- eating disorders
- low self-esteem and low self-confidence
- trauma
- abuse
- body dysmorphia
- other mental health problems (e.g., bipolar affective disorder, other mood disorders)
- panic attacks
- obsessive compulsive disorder (OCD)
- early onset psychosis
- attachment issues
- family breakdown
- relationship problems

- pregnancy and termination
- sexual problems
- sexuality and identity
- self-harm
- suicide potential
- bereavement
- procrastination and academic issues.

Alongside the variety of presenting issues will be the differences in demographic: males and females (although female students are more regularly seen); a range of ages (there is no longer a 'typical' school leaver undergraduate, with many people returning to education later on in life, or studying at postgraduate levels); diversity around culture (many international students choose to study in the UK); and diversity around sexuality, disability, etc.

The challenge for a therapist in the education setting is therefore competency and flexibility in thinking when responding appropriately to such different presentations. For example, in a drop-in service (often available in education settings, where students can attend for short sessions without an appointment), a practitioner might offer techniques and support around procrastination to one student, then support another following a sexual assault, and then see a student with deteriorating mental health or possible early onset psychosis. The Royal College of Psychiatrists' report into student mental health concluded that, 'University counselling services are, in effect, the primary mental health care option for many students' (2011: 41).

ETHICAL AND PROFESSIONAL CHALLENGES

ASSESSMENT

The demand for a timely assessment of a client's needs is a particular problem in education settings where the population is much more transient than the 'static' population found in primary or secondary care services, for example. In higher education (HE) settings, students may only be in the area for a number of weeks, before often returning home some distance away for extended periods. A vulnerable or distressed client self-referring to a counselling service midway through term may only be available for five or six more weeks. The problem becomes more acute towards the end of an academic year in May or June, when students who have presented at risk may be leaving the area permanently, and in the meantime are facing end-of-year examinations. The imperative to see clients quickly then transcends targets, and is driven more by urgency of time and availability.

The majority of counselling services assess students in a first-appointment face-to-face interview before deciding with the student the best form of support, or by telephone. Such assessments are often supplemented by the use of self-report assessment or benchmarking questionnaires. For example, the Clinical Outcomes in Routine Evaluation Outcome Measure (CORE-OM) is widely used in the UK (Barkham et al., 2006). More specifically, such tools may be used to help determine levels of priority for assessment, particularly around risk. A fuller discussion of the factors that might inform a therapeutic assessment can be found in Reeves (2008).

WORKING BRIEFLY

Working briefly (e.g., to a time-limited model of six sessions or fewer) is a requirement of many agencies managing high demands for counselling. For many counsellors and psychotherapists, working briefly is not an imposition but instead is a preferred way of working. Many counselling services within education settings offer brief contracts for therapy for several reasons, including: management of high demand for counselling; availability of students for counselling within the context of academic terms/semesters; high numbers of part-time staff employed within counselling services; and the fact that many students, regardless of age, opt into counselling for help with a specific problem, or at a time of transition or change as well as personal and professional development.

Counsellors and psychotherapists can sometimes maintain a small caseload of longer-term work (because most counselling is offered briefly), but increasingly services are opting exclusively for a brief model as well as delivering some therapy in groups (e.g, for anxiety). These models vary, ranging from assessment plus four to 10 sessions, through to some single-session or dual-session models. Many services see their role as triage: assessing needs, meeting them where appropriate and possible, but typically referring on to other internal or community support services.

CONFIDENTIALITY

Traditionally, counsellors and psychotherapists have agreed a very exclusive contract of confidentiality with their clients, limited only by risk to self and others, together with statutory limitations in the UK (e.g., terrorism, notes subpoenaed in court hearings). As counsellors and psychotherapists have found themselves increasingly working in multidisciplinary settings (e.g., in health-care settings), the agreements made around confidentiality have evolved. The challenge for practitioners working in education settings is achieving the correct balance of confidentiality: where the client's autonomy and privacy are respected, but where a wider student support system can also be taken into account.

FITNESS TO PRACTISE/STUDY

Educators are tasked with the responsibility of determining the fitness of any given student to undertake professional training (e.g., medicine), and to determine whether they are 'fit to practise'. This is crucial given that the majority of health-care students will undertake a practice placement during their study.

The pressures of training and the demands of practice will bring many such students to counselling services. There is often a tension for counsellors in working with such students between the confidentiality of counselling – respecting the individual student's right to explore their mental health distress in the privacy of therapy – and the institution's duty of care in determining fitness to practise.

Aligned with fitness to practise are concerns around fitness to study. All students have the potential to experience, at some point in their studies, a crisis or deterioration in their mental health that significantly impairs their capacity to study effectively. For most students these impairments may be short-term and transient, but for others, their capability to study over a longer period can become seriously jeopardised.

Counsellors are usually very clear that they do not see themselves as having a role in assessing, and therefore determining, an individual student's fitness to study or practise. However, increasingly, services or individual counsellors are being approached for their professional opinion. The role of professional organisations and associations, such as the British Association for Counselling and Psychotherapy (BACP), is key in offering advice and guidance in such situations, such as through their *Ethical Framework* (BACP, 2016), or through the BACP:UC Division. Through the latter's advisory service, regular updated guidance is offered to services to help in such situations (Lawton et al., 2010).

DUAL ROLES

Ethical requirements for the provision of counselling and psychotherapy typically warn against the dangers of dual roles, that is, where a therapist has contact with their client in a capacity other than therapy. While colleges and universities can be large institutions, sometimes with many thousands of students, they also have the potential to become surprisingly small communities in which the potential for dual roles is high.

Many counselling services engage with the institution in ways beyond the provision of individual or group therapy. Counsellors can often be found on key institutional committees (e.g., student welfare, international students), and meet with the students to whom they are offering counselling. It is essential, therefore, that counselling services pay particular attention to how counselling is contracted initially with clients so that, when such a scenario arises, it is not necessarily a shock, and practitioner and client can explore the implications in a way that protects the therapeutic relationship and the autonomy of both the client and the therapist.

RESEARCH EVIDENCE

Beyond the wider evidence base for counselling *per se* (see Cooper, 2008, for a good overview of this), counsellors in education settings have typically been very active in evaluating and researching their own work. Evidence suggests an increase in the severity of mental health distress in the student population (BACP, 1999; Royal College of Psychiatrists, 2011).

The use of CORE-OM is widespread in such services, and this provides valuable insight into the efficacy of interventions. For example, McKenzie et al. (2015: 288) noted that, 'counselling was found to result in reliable change for 67% of [students] and an equivalent level of clinically significant change to those without identified academic issues'.

BACP (2012: 3) additionally found that, 'Based on the quantitative findings, we can conclude that over 75 per cent of students who completed counselling within the 2011/12 academic year at the 65 institutions involved in the research found that counselling:

- helped them stay at university or college
- improved their academic achievement
- improved their overall experience of being a student
- helped them develop employability skills'.

The evidence base for counselling in further and higher education continues to grow, further supporting the value of it as a student provision.

REFERENCES

BACP (1999) *Degrees of Disturbance: The Impact of Increasing Levels of Psychological Disturbance amongst Students in Higher Education*. Lutterworth: British Association for Counselling and Psychotherapy.

BACP (2012) *The Impact of Counselling on Academic Outcomes in Further and Higher Education: The Student Perspective: Final Research Findings*. Lutterworth: British Association for Counselling and Psychotherapy.

BACP (2016) *Ethical Framework for the Counselling Professions*. Lutterworth: British Association for Counselling and Psychotherapy.

Barkham, M., Mellor-Clark, J., Connell, J. and Cahill, J. (2006) A CORE approach to practice-based evidence: a brief history of the origins and applications of the CORE-OM and CORE System. *Counselling and Psychotherapy Research*, 6(1): 3–15.

Bell, E. (1996) *Counselling in Further and Higher Education*. Buckingham: Open University Press.

Bell, E. (2006) Student counselling. In C. Feltham and I. Horton (eds), *The Sage Handbook of Counselling and Psychotherapy* (2nd ed., pp. 554–560). London: Sage.

Butcher, V., Bell, E., Hurst, A. and Mortensen, R. (1998) *New Skills for New Futures: Higher Education Guidance and Counselling Services in the UK*. Cambridge: Careers Research and Advisory Centre.

Cooper, M. (2008) Counselling in UK secondary schools: a comprehensive review of audit and evaluation data. *Counselling and Psychotherapy Research*, 9(3): 137–150.

Cooper, M. and Dryden, W. (eds) (2016) *The Handbook of Pluralistic Counselling and Psychotherapy*. London: Sage.

Lawton, B., Bradley, A.M., Collins, J., Holt, C. and Kelley, F. (2010) *AUCC Guidelines for University and College Counselling Services*. Lutterworth: British Association for Counselling and Psychotherapy.

McKenzie, K., Murray, K.R., Murray, A.L. and Richelieu, M. (2015) The effectiveness of university counselling for students with academic issues. *Counselling and Psychotherapy Research*, 15(4): 284–288.

May, R. (1999) Doing clinical work in a college or university: how does the context matter? In J. Lees and A. Vaspe (eds), *Clinical Counselling and Further and Higher Education* (pp. 13–25). London: Routledge.

(Continued)

(Continued)

Reeves, A. (2008) Assessment. In W. Dryden and A. Reeves (eds), *Key Issues for Counselling in Action* (2nd ed, pp. 61–75.). London: Sage.

Reeves, A. (2015) *Working with Risk in Counselling and Psychotherapy*. London: Sage.

Royal College of Psychiatrists (2011) *The Mental Health of Students in Higher Education*. Council Report CR166. London: RCP.

RECOMMENDED READING

1. Lawton, B., Bradley, A.M., Collins, J., Holt, C. and Kelley, F. (2010) *AUCC Guidelines for University and College Counselling Services*. Lutterworth: British Association for Counselling and Psychotherapy.

Provides an excellent overview of the work of student counselling, including an outline of key standards for service provision.

2. BACP (2012) *The Impact of Counselling on Academic Outcomes in Further and Higher Education: The Student Perspective: Final Research Findings*. Lutterworth: British Association for Counselling and Psychotherapy.

The BACP's short report offers an excellent insight into a key research study of the work of counselling in further and higher education.

3. Mair, D. (ed.) (2016) *Short-term Counselling in Higher Education: Context, Theory and Practice*. London: Routledge.

Offers a contemporary view of counselling in higher education, looking at the particular implications of short-term work, the principles of which can be transferable into a further education context.

7.11 WORKING WITH THE MEDIA

ELAINE KASKET

OVERVIEW AND KEY POINTS

Not so long ago, the opportunities for psychotherapists or counsellors to offer their knowledge and expertise to the public were relatively limited. If you did not publish self-help books, author or contribute to articles in the popular press, or appear on radio or television, you would likely live out your professional life free from mass media attention. With the advent of the digital age, however, our media contributions are likely to be stored and accessible online over the longer term, and we can also utilise blogging, social media, and other internet platforms to directly reach the public. These developments increase the need for practitioners to understand both the benefits and vicissitudes of media work, and to act ethically and responsibly. To that end, this chapter covers the following key points:

- Reflections on the media landscape for practitioners
- Classification of media work from 'high control' to 'low control' scenarios
- Ethical guidance for media work

- Decision-making guidelines for engaging in media work
- Research on psychotherapy and the media
- Useful recommended readings.

BACKGROUND AND CONTEXT

Most psychotherapists and counsellors carry out the bulk of their therapeutic activities in the private sphere, behind the closed door of the consulting room, one client at a time. The confidential quietude of that space stands in stark contrast to the exposing, sometimes sensationalist world of mass media, in which a comment on Twitter, a quote for a news story, or a sound bite from a live broadcast can flash around the world in an instant and be received by an audience of millions. When practitioners use the media to extend their therapeutic reach and to influence the wider world, they need a particular set of skills, a hefty measure of caution, and an awareness of the potential ethical pitfalls. Done well, however, media work can inform, educate and assist the public; destigmatise mental health issues; and demystify and promote psychotherapy.

Over the last couple of decades, the media landscape has changed in ways that are highly relevant for psychotherapy. The reality-television explosion has seen programmes such as *Big Brother* subjecting contestants to psychologically stressful conditions and employing psychologists for onscreen commentary as well as off-screen care of participants. Other formats, exemplified by programmes like *Hoarders* and *House of Agoraphobics*, focus on real individuals suffering from particular psychological difficulties and blur the lines between education, psychotherapeutic intervention and entertainment, perhaps risking exploitation in the process. Long-running talk shows such as *Dr. Phil* in the United States have shaped the public's perception of how psychotherapy works and what mental health professionals do, as have popular fictional programmes that portray 'shrinks' in action, such as *The Sopranos* and *In Treatment*. As mental health issues have become more acceptable to discuss and as the psychological/psychotherapeutic perspective has become more valued, practitioners are more frequently approached for 'expert contributions' across all types of media. Nor is a journalist or a publisher a necessary player, of course; practitioners can now disseminate information to the public directly, using the internet as their vehicle.

In short, therefore, there is no shortage of opportunity for the willing psychotherapeutic practitioner to step outside the confines of the consulting room and to engage in media work. So what are the different ways of doing this, and are they right for you? If so, how can you proceed ethically and responsibly?

WAYS OF WORKING

When thinking about a particular media opportunity, first think about its *purpose*: What is your involvement and contribution in service of? Educating your audience in some way, or providing a psychological perspective on a particular issue or incident? Shedding light on someone's behaviour – for example, a public figure (something that is warned against in most ethical codes)? Providing treatment or caring for participants in a programme? Promoting yourself? Advancing the reputation and/or accessibility of psychology or psychotherapy? Entertaining people? Unsurprisingly, the wisdom of proceeding depends a lot on these considerations of purpose. You might also wish to think about media opportunities as ranging across a 'control spectrum'.

High control. Any situation where you retain maximum editorial power over your words is a relatively 'high control' scenario. Imagine, for example, that you have expertise and experience in working with conflictual couples; there is a number of ways you could use mass media to disseminate your wisdom. You could pitch a proposal for a regular column to *Psychologies* magazine, for example; if they buy it, although they will provide some editorial input, you could insist upon final approval of the column before it goes to press. Alternatively, you could publish a book on couples work, and although your publisher or editor may push for certain changes, you would likely largely retain your authorial voice. Independent of any editorial input at all, you could write a regular online blog, record a series of podcasts, or launch an educational video series on YouTube or Vimeo. You could also create a professional profile on a social media platform such as Twitter, composing tweets about your research or linking to relevant academic or news articles.

Even in all of these relatively high-control scenarios, however, there are caveats. For example, while you might retain control over the content of your book, your publisher could try to sell more books by insisting on a sensationalist cover that makes overly extravagant claims, such as 'Cure Your Anxiety for Good!!' You may craft the material on your blog or your Twitter feed carefully, but if comments are enabled, readers could post undermining remarks. Even if your psychoeducational videos are helpful and informative, an internet 'troll' could still link to them from his or her blog and say, 'Can you believe this idiot?!' Inevitably, whenever you enter the public forum in the modern world, you invite interaction and comment, and thus your control is never absolute.

Medium control. Medium-control media work includes live interviews or call-in programmes broadcast via television, radio or the web. In live broadcasts you need not fear the distorting potential of others' editing, but this does not mean you will end up communicating what and how you want. Even when questions have been provided in advance, making preparation possible, limitations of the format and the involvement of other people – interviewers, fellow interviewees, callers or audience members – can influence your input significantly. Before appearing live on BBC television, for example, I was advised that I should get my core message across clearly within the first 20 seconds, and should keep it 'upbeat' as it was breakfast television. I had not had my coffee, the line of questioning was unexpected, my topic was complex, and the fact that I was speaking about death made 'upbeat' a challenge. While I could choose my responses, ultimately I did not feel fully in control of my message.

Pre-recorded audio or video interviews are another example of medium-control scenarios. After recording sometimes quite long conversations, decisions will be made about which segments to use, and these decisions will virtually always occur without you. For example, I have done two hours of recording from which a 10-second segment was used, and I have never been able to control or predict the contexts into which my pre-recorded contributions would be placed. Even when one collaborates closely with producers, directors and/or editors – for example, in a television series where a psychotherapeutic practitioner is a central player – other people will ultimately decide precisely how the practitioner and their views are portrayed.

Low control. Based on long experience, I would classify any situation in which a print journalist translates your words as 'low control'. Imagine a newspaper journalist interviews you on the phone, tapping away in the background as you speak. Even if the journalist transcribes your words exactly, in the finished piece you may discover rampant paraphrasing, rigorous editing, decontextualised comments, and innocent errors or misunderstandings. Other examples of low-control scenarios include the (relatively uncommon) 'ambush' interview, in which you are neither prepared for the interview situation nor the questions asked, and the more frequent instance of the media piece or other public commentary that references your ideas without consulting you.

The first time there was a press release about one of my conference papers, I thought I had complete control; I had, after all, approved the text of the release as being accurate. What I did not realise at the time is that journalists worldwide would take the release and write articles implying that they had interviewed me directly, most of which were rife with misunderstandings and misrepresentations of my research findings and their implications. While I could control my conference presentation and the text in the press release, I lost the reins from there. To try to restore a sense of ownership over my work, I began maintaining

my own research blog so that the public could get more accurate information 'from the horse's mouth'.

ETHICAL DECISION-MAKING ABOUT MEDIA WORK

For those practitioners who decide to dip their toes into the potentially murky waters of media work, there are multiple sources of guidance, some of which are listed in the 'Recommended Reading' section of this chapter. The 'meta-code' of media ethics compiled by the European Federation of Psychologists' Association (EFPA) lists eight elements that should form the basis of any ethical guidance around media work, and these could be argued to apply to any type of mental health professional. They are:

1. Show respect for all persons involved.
2. Avoid giving professional opinions about any person in public.
3. Be very careful not to bring into the public domain any personal data about persons with whom the [practitioner] has, or has had, a professional relationship.
4. Be careful not to go beyond your range and level of competence.
5. Aim at empowering your audience.
6. Be aware that you are representing a community of [practitioners].
7. Be sensitive to the potential effects on third parties, like relatives and other acquaintances.
8. Be sensitive to negative effects of self-promotion.

(European Federation of Psychologists' Associations, 2011)

The principles above are critical if one is to handle media contact and communication ethically, but a decision-making system is also extremely useful. Shahid (n.d.) suggests considering the following three areas when deciding whether to pursue a media invitation:

1. Competence: Do you have research and/or clinical competence in the area you are being requested to speak about?
2. Time constraints: Do you have sufficient time to review the literature, gain background on the relevant players, and gather your thoughts on the topic?
3. Control over final product: Do you have the ability to review and/or edit the piece before it is disseminated?

If you decide to accept an opportunity, Shahid further recommends that you consider the goals, motivations, and psychological 'savviness' of the interviewer, production company, or journalist; the intended and/or likely audience; what you will do if you are asked to provide examples from your own clinical experience or comment upon a public figure; and whether you can get questions or other parameters in advance.

Even when you follow the above guidance, it can be difficult to discern the risks and to proceed in a savvy fashion, particularly if you are inexperienced. Remember that the Media Centre of the British Association for Counselling and Psychotherapy (BACP) (www.bacp. co.uk/media/) and the British Psychological Society's (BPS) Press Centre (www.bps.org.uk/what-we-do/bps/press-centre/press-centre) stand ready and willing to respond to members about potential interactions with the press, and can provide support and advice on specific situations as well as signposting to appropriate media training.

To illustrate the ethical considerations and decision-making process, here is an example from my own experience of being approached about a well-known 'structured reality' television series. In the next season, one of the main characters would be seeking therapy for his relationship issues. While this would purportedly be an actual therapeutic process, a camera crew would sometimes be in the consulting room, and segments of his recorded therapy sessions would weave through the show. In her attempts to persuade, the producer repeatedly emphasised the 'exposure' and 'free advertising' that I would get if I served as therapist.

I certainly have clinical competence to see people with relationship issues, but I spotted several problems. This was clearly a 'low control' scenario, in which I would be pulled into a 'structured reality' format with no say over editing. The production company had no concept that recording and broadcasting therapy might be unethical. Despite suggestions that it would educate a million viewers about psychotherapy, their motivations were purely entertainment-driven, and guidance from the BACP's Media Centre identifies that 'filming of any genuine "live" therapeutic session is a particularly high-risk enterprise which raises several serious ethical questions and should not be embarked on without careful consideration' (www.bacp. co.uk/media). The BACP's additional warning that filming can 'interfere with the natural course of the treatment' was amply illustrated in my example. In contrast with the producer's claims, the star in question said in several published interviews later on that therapy was the production company's idea, not his. The producer also described that she was selecting a therapist for him based on the 'telegenic' qualities of the practitioner and consulting room. From the start, therefore, therapy was inextricably bound up with entertainment and considerations of plot and character. Unable to see how this enterprise could be accomplished ethically or to the advancement of the profession, I declined, and ever since I have limited myself to expert contributions within my areas of research and scholarship.

RESEARCH EVIDENCE

Research indicates that media portrayals can significantly affect viewers' perceptions of psychology and psychotherapy. For example, one study found that people's perceptions of actual psychotherapy were significantly constructed by its portrayals on fictional comedy and drama programmes, and that these portrayals were associated with negative attitudes towards psychotherapy, lower intentions to seek services, and greater reluctance to disclose to a therapist (Vogel, Gentile and Kaplan, 2008). The researchers remark that '[when] portrayals [of psychotherapy] are inaccurate or misleading, they could have direct and indirect implications on people's mental health' (p. 292), and remember that they were studying people's attitudes in response to *fictional* comedy and drama. Imagine how much more damaging it can be when *real* practitioners are untrustworthy, unethical, misleading, and/or self-promoting in the media.

In addition, remember that psychotherapeutic practitioners who work with the media or take a public stance on various issues will inevitably see this reflected in their general online presence, which incorporates contributions to news and other media stories, postings on social media platforms, blogs and other websites, and various other disclosures both inadvertent and intentional, personal and professional. Of the 332 psychotherapist clients who participated in one study, nearly half used online information about their therapist to decide whether to move forward with treatment (Kolmes and Taube, 2016) – all the more reason to acknowledge and consider the potential effects of our public pronouncements on the private therapeutic work we do.

Psychotherapeutic practitioners who choose to do media work shoulder a fourfold burden of responsibility: they are accountable to themselves, their clients, the public and the profession. In this era of mass data storage and easy retrieval, the public commentary we make proliferates and persists in various online locations, for better or for worse. That errant tweet or that interview segment for which you were drastically unprepared may be perpetually linked to your name on internet search engines. On the flip side, while you may only see hundreds of face-to-face psychotherapy clients in the course of your career, you may help thousands of suffering people through that blog post you wrote or through what you said on that radio programme. As a psychotherapist, counsellor or psychologist, there is much you can do outside the consulting room to heal, help, and be a force for good in the world. With ethical awareness, education, preparation and media training, you can undertake that mission confidently, safely and well.

REFERENCES

European Federation of Psychologists' Association (2011). Guidelines for psychologists who contribute to the media. Available on: http://ethics.efpa.eu/guidelines/ [accessed 2 June 2017].

Kolmes, K. and Taube, D. O. (2016). Client discovery of psychotherapist personal information online. *Professional Psychology: Research and Practice*, 47(2), 147–154.

Shahid, S. (n.d.). The nuts and bolts of media involvement. In *The ethics of psychology and the media: Print, internet and TV* [open access PowerPoint presentation]. Available at: www.adaa.org/sites/default/files/McGrath%20348.pdf. [accessed 3 July 2016].

Vogel, D. L., Gentile, D. A. and Kaplan, S. A. (2008). The influence of television on willingness to seek therapy. *Journal of Clinical Psychology*, 64(3), 276–295.

RECOMMENDED READING

1. Atcheson, L. (2010). Counselling psychology and the media: the highs and lows. In M. Milton (Ed.), *Therapy and beyond: Counselling psychology contributions to therapeutic and social issues* (pp. 277–292). Chichester, West Sussex: Wiley Blackwell.

This chapter highlights critical considerations when working with print media, and with live and pre-recorded radio and television. It also features a helpful list of 'dos and don'ts'.

2. Clowes, R. (2015). Demystifying the media. *Private Practice*, Summer, 16–19.

Authored by the Media and Communications Manager for the BACP, this article gives a summary of the key issues in media work and signposts to BACP resources.

3. McGarrah, N. A., Alvord, M. K., Martin, J. N. and Haldenman, D. C. (2009). In the public eye: the ethical practice of media psychology. *Professional Psychology: Research and Practice*, 40(2), 172–180.

This series of pieces on working with the media will help you think clearly through the ethical pitfalls and how to avoid them.

7.12 WORKING WITH NEUROSCIENCE AND NEUROPSYCHOLOGY

DAVID GOSS

OVERVIEW AND KEY POINTS

Neuroscience, subsequently neuropsychology, has undergone rapid developments of the last few decades and has been labelled 'the newest force' in counselling and psychotherapy (Ivey, D'Andrea, & Ivey, 2012). In this chapter, I present a number of ideas and reflections for psychotherapists to consider when working with neuropsychology information and client populations. Key points for the chapter include:

- Neuropsychology integrates neuroscience and psychology to develop theory and interventions which can serve a range of client populations, particularly people affected by neurological conditions.
- Neuropsychological research can be used to support and develop the role of empathy in psychotherapy, to help psychoeducate clients and to provide an evidence base for interventions.
- Psychotherapists may benefit from being mindful of the challenges involved when utilising neuropsychological information, including the risk of losing sight of a client's subjective sense of self through biological pathology, as well as ensuring they work within ethical knowledge and competency boundaries.
- A range of psychotherapeutic models can be used when working with a neurological client population.

BACKGROUND AND CONTEXT

DEFINING NEUROPSYCHOLOGY

Given the *neuro* connection, the fields of neuropsychology and neuroscience can be referred to as one of the same. However, there is also a distinction between them. Neuropsychology is a profession which serves people with neurological conditions (British Psychological Society, n.d.). The World Health Organisation (WHO) defines a neurological condition as:

> [D]iseases of the central and peripheral nervous system. … These disorders [conditions] include epilepsy, Alzheimer disease and other dementias, cerebrovascular diseases including stroke, migraine and other headache disorders, multiple sclerosis, Parkinson's disease, neuroinfections, brain tumours, traumatic disorders of the nervous system such as brain trauma, and neurological disorders as a result of malnutrition. (World Health Organisation, 2014)

This somewhat differs from neuroscience, a general branch of scientific enquiry, which can be related to all research and client populations (Bear, Connors and Paradiso, 2007; Cozolino, 2010). However, there are people who define neuropsychology in a looser sense, as a discipline which bridges psychology (emotion, cognition, perception and behaviour) and neuroscience (chemical, electrical, structural and cellular underpinnings of the central nervous system) (Hallett, 1993), thus making neuropsychology applicable to all client populations.

Given the discussions above, the working definition of neuropsychology for this chapter is a discipline which integrates neuroscience and psychology to develop theory and interventions which can serve a range of client populations, particularly those affected by neurological conditions. As such, this chapter will present information on how integrating information from neuroscience and psychology can support counsellors and psychotherapists in all aspects of their work, with a case example for those working with neurological populations.

THE ARRIVAL OF NEUROPSYCHOTHERAPY

The development of research techniques has led to a neuroscience revolution these last few decades and psychotherapy has subsequently increased its integration with neuroscience during this time. *Neuropsychotherapy* (Grawe, 2007), *interpersonal neurobiology* (Siegel, 2011, 2015) and *neuropsychoanalysis* (Solms and Turnbull, 2011) are disciplines geared towards understanding and integrating the mechanisms of biology, neurology, psychology and social interaction, to develop holistic therapeutic practices and understanding of our species.

THE BENEFIT OF NEUROPSYCHOLOGY TO PSYCHOTHERAPY

Neuroimaging technologies such as functional magnetic resonance imaging (fMRI) and electroencephalogram (EEG) (for more details see Eysenck and Keane, 2010: 7–14) allow us to obtain information about the brain's structure and functioning. This information can be used to support and enhance psychotherapeutic interventions. For example, neuroimaging has demonstrated the brain's ability to reproduce new neurons (neurogenesis) and reorganise neural networks throughout its lifetime, a concept known as *neuroplasticity* (Begley, 2007). This restructuring is at the heart of learning and memory development (Clark and Beck, 2010). Additional research demonstrates that the expression (activation) of many genes depends on a person's environment and social experiences (Szyf, McGowan and Meaney, 2008), a concept known as *epigenetics*. The concepts of neuroplasticity and epigenetics provide scientific evidence for the long-held psychotherapeutic notions that a person's environment contributes greatly to their personality, and that psychotherapy can help restructure maladaptive brain networks. Neuroimaging has been used to demonstrate the effects of different psychotherapies on areas of the brain related to symptoms such as depression, obsessive-compulsive disorder and social phobia (Peres and Nasello, 2008).

WAYS OF WORKING

ADVANTAGES

In addition to harnessing support for the profession, practitioners can use neuropsychological theory to support and enhance a variety of interventions. Examples of how neuropsychology can be used for interventions include:

- *Developing empathy for clients* – One of the tenets of psychotherapy is promoting a safe and empathic therapeutic relationship. Neuroscience has provided neural evidence of empathy (Gallese, 2001; Gallese, Fadiga, Fogassi and Rizzolatti, 1996). Armed with evidence that we each have neurons which attempt to mirror that of another person, a therapist can not only build security and support for a client by empathising with them, but they can also model emotional regulation within the therapy setting, which the client can in turn attempt to mirror. This advocates the importance of therapists continually working on understanding their own internal processes, aiding their own ability to feel and self-regulate distressing emotions, which can in turn help their clients (Coutinho, Silva and Decety, 2014).
- *Psychoeducation for clients* – Neuropsychological information can be used to psychoeducate clients as to why they may be experiencing certain changes in their personality and functioning. This can help the client make sense of their experience and may also help carers, friends and family develop increased understanding and empathy for the client.
- *Evidence base for intervention* – Neuropsychology has helped provide support for individual modalities of therapy. For example, efforts have been made to develop models of the brain that help provide information on psychodynamic phenomena such as repression (Bazan and Snodgrass, 2012), dreaming (Zellner, 2013) and the dynamic unconscious (Berlin, 2011; Solms and Zellner, 2012). The existence of unconscious processes such as repression has been supported through studies with neurological patients suffering with anosognosia, a condition in which people deny the existence of impairment (Vuilleumier, 2004). Further evidence exists for numerous counselling and psychotherapy models.

CHALLENGES

- *Losing the self through biological pathology* – Fuchs (2004: 483) proposed that 'a reductionist biological concept of mental life may gradually lead to a

self-alienation … we are beginning to regard ourselves not as persons having wishes, motives or reasons, but as agents of our genes, hormones and neurones'. Ivey (2011) suggested that many psychotherapists worry about the medical model and that by focusing on neuroscience, we focus on pathology. However, Ivey et al. (2012) argue that neuroscience places a high value on environmental impacts and therefore reinforces psychotherapy's psychosocial wellness model. The majority of therapeutic models focus on client empowerment and motivation for change (Ryan, Lynch, Vansteenkiste and Deci, 2011). The psychotherapist should be cautious of clients becoming overly dependent and/or downhearted about biological issues, as they may lose the motivation and self-autonomy required for change. This is where competency and integrity is crucial. If a therapist is attuned to concepts such a brain plasticity and other elements which demonstrate how a client can overcome certain deficits, they will then be better placed to use neurobiological information to help and psychoeducate a client's development, while also recognising the realistic limits as to what can be achieved (Goss, 2015).

- *Therapist competency and ethics* – Ivey et al. (2012) suggest that psychotherapists often are not aware of the positive neurological impact of the client relationships they form (Goleman, 2007; Siegel, 2011), largely due to the lack of training and theoretical textbooks on offer for integrating neuropsychology and psychotherapy. Developing more theory and training around neuropsychology is vital to ensuring that therapists practice in a safe and ethical manner.

CASE EXAMPLE

Below is a case example which outlines some of the factors which psychotherapists may consider when working with a client in a neuropsychological setting. I have used a client with an acquired brain injury (ABI) as this can often be a complex neurological presentation, due to the extent and location variability of brain injuries. However, the reflections discussed below can be applied to many neurological presentations, although it is important to note that each client will differ in how they respond to a condition and individual formulations are vital.

Client – Casey is a 30-year-old woman who suffered an ABI as a result of a car crash. Casey sometimes struggles to speak, has difficulty concentrating and often displays sudden bursts of emotion.

Psychotherapist considerations – By consulting with neurologist reports and through the client's narrative, it appeared that Casey suffered an ABI to the front and left-hand side of her brain. The areas effected correlate with Casey's presentation. Broca's area is located towards the front of the left-hand side of the brain and has been shown to be involved in speech production and comprehension (Wallentina, Gravholtc and Skakkebæk, 2015); therefore, damage to this area would understandably affect speech. Adjacent to this area of the brain is the dorsolateral pre-frontal cortex. This area of the brain has been shown to be involved in selective attention (Forster, Elizalde, Castle and Bishop, 2015); therefore, damage to this area would understandably affect concentration. The front part of the brain, particularly the prefrontal cortex (the very front of the brain) consists of a number of areas which are involved in emotion regulation (Wager, Davidson, Hughes, Lindquist, Ochsner, 2008); therefore, damage to this area would understandably affect emotion display.

POTENTIAL INTERVENTIONS

Person-centred: A common first step in this type of work is allowing Casey to vent/grieve/mourn what has happened to her, processing the things she has lost (which may include her job, partner, friends, independence, etc.). Casey may have thought about what has happened, but it is only by voicing these thoughts out loud and connecting them with the deeper emotions within, that she may be able to fully acknowledge what has happened – this is one of the key benefits of psychotherapy.

Cognitive-behaviour therapy (CBT): A first step in CBT could be normalising Casey's symptoms, providing psychoeducation on her injury and subsequent difficulties. It is likely that one or all of Casey's symptoms (i.e., speech, attention, emotion) will be causing her distress, leading to feelings of anxiety and depression. For example, her speech difficulties may lead her to feel embarrassed and anxious of social situations in case people judge her, so she avoids going out and talking to people, which leads to her feeling isolated and depressed without an outlet to discuss these emotions. In Casey's situation, CBT allows us to formulate that she is embarrassed about her speech difficulties for the reasons outlined above. In this instance, CBT can be used for multiple purposes, including understanding and working on her social anxiety and developing her social skills. This type of work can be undertaken through gradual exposure, using therapy as a catalyst for Casey to begin feeling comfortable talking about her difficulties, which can then in turn be extended to her engaging in social groups with friends, ABI support groups or groups related to her hobbies and interests. Socialising and developing a sense of purpose in life are two things

which have been shown to be neurologically relevant in reducing depression (Panksepp and Biven, 2012). Third-wave CBT interventions, such as mindfulness, can also be used. Mindfulness has been shown to develop emotional and attentional brain regions, including the frontal lobe (Santarnecchi et al., 2014). Through the notion of plasticity, Casey can begin to redevelop these areas of her brain and recruit additional brain networks to help with her emotion and attention regulation.

Psychodynamic: Some clients may respond to an ABI or neurological condition in an overly maladaptive response in comparison to other people. For example, I have worked with clients who experience a neurological condition which leads to them having issues regulating their emotion, but they are not overly affected by this and they grow accustomed to the change. However, for some clients, an inability to control emotions can cause them high levels of distress. In the example of Casey, she explains that she never used to really show emotion, so she finds it extremely embarrassing when she starts crying all of a sudden, leading to isolation, anxiety and depression. This information may come about through Casey's explanation, or it may first be spotted in transference and unconscious processes. For example, the therapist may notice that Casey demonstrates defences when becoming emotional, even cancelling sessions following displays of emotion in front of the therapist. When this is explored, it materialises that Casey was not allowed to demonstrate any emotion when she was younger, as her parents told her this was a sign of weakness. As such, the psychotherapist and Casey may then work on this, exploring past and present to allow Casey to feel more comfortable with displaying emotion.

RESEARCH EVIDENCE

Research supporting the use of psychotherapy within neuropsychological populations is often tailored to specific conditions. For example, mindfulness-based therapy and acceptance and commitment therapy have been shown to improve wellbeing for people with epilepsy (Dewhurst, Novakova and Reuber, 2015; Tang, Poon and Kwan, 2015). Psychotherapy has also been shown to be beneficial in patient outcome and cost-effectiveness for people presenting with functional neurological disorders, that is, symptoms which resemble manifestations of organic disorders of the nervous system but are medically unexplained (Reuber, Burness, Howlett, Brazier and Grünewald, 2007). Klonoff (2010) presents a range of evidence and discussion for undertaking psychotherapy with clients who have experienced a brain injury, as well as how to support family members (Klonoff, 2014).

REFERENCES

Bazan A. and Snodgrass M. (2012). On unconscious inhibition: instantiating repression in the brain. In A. Fotopoulou, D. Pfaff and M. A. Conway (Eds.), *From the couch to the lab: Trends in psychodynamic neuroscience* (pp. 307–337). New York: Oxford University Press.

Bear, M. F., Connors, B.W. and Paradiso, M. A. (Eds.) (2007). *Neuroscience: Exploring the* (3rd ed.). Baltimore, MD: Lippincott Williams & Wilkins.

Begley, S. (2007). *The plastic mind.* London: Constable & Robinson.

Berlin, H. A. (2011). The neural basis of the dynamic unconscious. *Neuropsychoanalysis, 13,* 5–31.

British Psychological Society (BPS) (n.d.). *Careers: Neuropsychology* [web page]. (http://careers.bps.org.uk/area/neuro).

Clark, D. A. and Beck, A. T. (2010). Cognitive theory and therapy of anxiety and depression: convergence with neurobiological findings. *Trends in Cognitive Sciences, 14*(9), 418–424.

Coutinho, J. F., Silva, P. O. and Decety, J. (2014). Neurosciences, empathy, and healthy interpersonal relationships: recent findings and implications for counseling psychology. *Journal of Counseling Psychology, 61*(4), 541–548.

Cozolino, L. (2010). *The neuroscience of psychotherapy: Healing the social brain* (2nd ed.). New York: W.W. Norton.

Dewhurst, E., Novakova, B. and Reuber, M. (2015). A prospective service evaluation of acceptance and commitment therapy for patients with refractory epilepsy. *Epilepsy & Behavior, 46,* 234–241.

Eysenck, M. W. and Keane, M. T. (2010). *Cognitive psychology: A student's handbook* (6th ed.). Brighton: Psychology Press.

Forster, S., Elizalde, A. O. N., Castle, E. and Bishop, S. J. (2015). Unraveling the anxious mind: anxiety, worry, and frontal engagement in sustained attention versus off-task processing. *Cerebral Cortex, 25*(3), 609–618.

Fuchs, T. (2004). Neurobiology and psychotherapy: an emerging dialogue. *Current Opinion in Psychiatry,* 17(6), 479–485.

Gallese, V. (2001). The 'shared manifold' hypothesis: from mirror neurons to empathy. *Journal of Consciousness Studies, 8*(5–7), 33–50.

Gallese, V., Fadiga, L., Fogassi, L. and Rizzolatti, G. (1996). Action recognition in the premotor cortex. *Brain, 119*(2), 593–609.

Goleman, D. (2007). *Social Intelligence.* London: Arrow Books.

Goss, D. (2015). The importance of incorporating neuroscientific knowledge into counselling psychology: an introduction to affective neuroscience. *Counselling Psychology Review, 30,* 52–63.

Grawe, K. (2007). *Neuropsychotherapy: How the neurosciences inform effective psychotherapy.* New York: Psychology Press.

Hallett, S. (1993). Neuropsychology. In G. Morgan and S. Butler (Eds.), *Seminars in basic neurosciences* (pp. 151–186). The Royal College of Psychiatrists. (www.rcpsych.ac.uk/pdf/semBasNeuro_chapter5.pdf).

Ivey, A. E. (2011). Neuroscience and counseling: central issue for social justice leaders. *Journal for Social Action in Counseling and Psychology, 3,* 103–116.

Ivey, A. E., D'Andrea, M. J. and Ivey, M. B. (2012). *Theories of counseling and psychotherapy: A multicultural perspective.* (www.sagepub.com/upm-data/40557_2.pdf).

Klonoff, P. S. (2010). *Psychotherapy after brain injury: Principles and techniques.* New York: Guilford Press.

Klonoff, P. S. (2014). *Psychotherapy for families after brain injury.* New York: Springer.

Panksepp, J. and Biven, L. (2012). *The archaeology of mind: Neuroevolutionary origins of human emotions.* New York: W.W. Norton.

Peres, J. and Nasello, A. (2008). Psychotherapy and neuroscience: towards closer integration. *International Journal of Psychology, 43*(6), 943–957.

Reuber, M., Burness, C., Howlett, S., Brazier, J., Grünewald, R. (2007). Tailored psychotherapy for patients with functional neurological symptoms: a pilot study. *Journal of Psychosomatic Research, 63*(6), 625–632.

Ryan, R. M., Lynch, M. F., Vansteenkiste, M. and Deci, E. L. (2011). Motivation and autonomy in counseling, psychotherapy, and behavior change: a look at theory and practice. *The Counseling Psychologist, 39*(2), 193–260.

Santarnecchi, E., D'Arista, S., Egiziano, E., Gardi, C., Petrosino, R., Vatti, G., Reda, M. and Rossi, A. (2014). Interaction between neuroanatomical and psychological changes after mindfulness based training. *PLoS ONE, 9*(10), 1–9.

Siegel, D. J. (2011). *Mindsight: Transform your brain with the new science of kindness.* London: One World Publications.

Siegel, D. J. (2015). The developing mind: How relationships and the brain interact to shape who we are (2nd ed.). New York: Guilford Press.

Solms, M. and Turnbull, O. H. (2011). What is neuropsychoanalysis? *Neuropsychoanalysis, 13*(2), 1–13.

Solms, M. and Zellner, M. R. (2012). The Freudian unconscious today. In A. Fotopoulou, D. Pfaff and M. A. Conway (Eds.), *From the couch to the lab: Trends in psychodynamic neuroscience* (pp. 209–218). New York: Oxford University Press.

Szyf, M., McGowan, P. and Meaney, M. (2008). The social environment and the epigenome. *Environmental and Molecular Mutagenesis, 49*, 46–60.

Tang, V., Poon, W. S. and Kwan, P. (2015). Mindfulness-based therapy for drug resistant epilepsy: an assessor-blinded randomized trial. *Neurology, 85*(13), 1100–1107.

Vuilleumier, P. (2004). Anosognosia: the neurology of beliefs and uncertainties. *Cortex, 40*, 9–17.

Wager, T. D., Davidson, M. L., Hughes, B. L., Lindquist, M. A. and Ochsner, K. N. (2008). Prefrontal-subcortical pathways mediating successful emotion regulation. *Neuron, 59*(6), 1037–1050.

Wallentina, M., Gravholtc, C. H. and Skakkebæk, A. (2015). Broca's region and Visual Word Form Area activation differ during a predictive stroop task. *Cortex, 73*, 257–270.

World Health Organisation (WHO). (February 2014). *What are neurological disorders?* [web page]. (www.who.int/features/qa/55/en/).

Zellner, M. R. (2013). Dreaming and the default mode network: some psychoanalytic notes. *Contemporary Psychoanalysis, 49*(2), 226–232.

RECOMMENDED READING

1. McHenry, B., Sikorski, A. M. and McHenry, J. (2014). *A counselor's introduction to neuroscience*. New York: Routledge.

Provides an introduction to neuroscience information that may be relevant to counsellors.

2. Cozolino, L. (2010). *The neuroscience of psychotherapy: Healing the social brain* (2nd ed.). New York: W.W. Norton.

A thorough exploration of how neuroscience can be used by psychotherapists across a variety of contexts and methods.

3. Klonoff, P. S. (2010). *Psychotherapy after brain injury: Principles and techniques*. New York: Guilford Press.

Presents a range of evidence and discussion for undertaking psychotherapy with clients who have experienced a brain injury.

7.13 PRIVATE PRACTICE

GARETH WILLIAMS

OVERVIEW AND KEY POINTS

This chapter's aim is to support people who are interested in developing a sustainable private practice – one that is rewarding, inspiring, and in alignment with their values. The approach here rests on an understanding of the importance of core values in our work; how they infuse it with a sense of purpose, and how purpose naturally motivates us, can make our goals more attainable and protect us from demoralisation and burnout (Deci and Ryan, 2002).

Towards the end of the chapter, we consider a series of practical matters relevant to anyone working in private practice. Our approach will not be to provide answers but to encourage practitioners to respond to these matters from a grounding in their values and sense of purpose.

The key points of the chapter are:

- Consciously aligning our work with our values brings a greater sense of purpose and motivation.
- Purposefulness enhances resilience, commitment and the likelihood of achieving one's goals.
- Explicitly formulating a vision and mission statement for our work provides a compass for navigating the inevitable challenges we will encounter.
- A number of significant challenges to working in private practice, both inner and outer, are presented.

INTRODUCTION

If you have your why … then you can get along with almost any how. (Nietzsche)

The British Association for Counselling and Psychotherapy's (BACP) *Ethical Framework* (2015) outlines the fundamental values of the profession, as listed in Figure 7.13.1.

Respecting human rights and dignity

Alleviating symptoms of personal distress and suffering

Enhancing people's wellbeing and capabilities

Improving the quality of relationships between people

Increasing personal resilience and effectiveness

Facilitating a sense of self that is meaningful to the person(s) concerned within their personal and cultural context

Appreciating the variety of human experience and culture

Protecting the safety of clients

Ensuring the integrity of practitioner–client relationships

Enhancing the quality of professional knowledge and its application

Striving for the fair and adequate provision of services

Figure 7.13.1   BACP professional values

Source: British Psychological Society Press Centre: www.bps.org.uk/what-we-do/bps/press-centre/press-centre

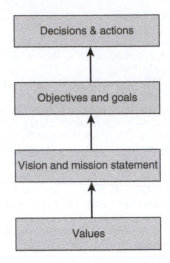

Figure 7.13.2   A values-based approach to practice

Against the background of this professional commitment, we are going to put our focus on our personal values – the ones that feel most important to us. There may be areas of overlap with the values expressed by the BACP, but the point here is to clarify our core values, what really matters most to us, in a way that feels authentic and alive.

A visual overview of this approach is shown in Figure 7.13.2: values inform the vision of our work and guide us to a mission statement; vision and mission lead us to goals and objectives; goals and objectives shape our decisions and give rise to actions.

This chapter is intended to be useful to practitioners whatever their therapeutic orientations. What follows constitutes an extended reflection on how our core values, along with the unique configuration of our interests, experience and training, can guide us in establishing a private practice.

VALUES

Principles or standards of behaviour; one's judgement of what is important in life. (*Oxford English Dictionary*)

What makes life meaningful are the connections with closely held values through daily life actions. (Hayes, Strosahl and Wilson, 2012: 92)

This chapter proceeds from the hypothesis that living your life in alignment with your core values will bring inevitable enrichment and success. To live your life in a way that truly matters to you is its own reward – financial gain and social status may accompany it, but these will be incidental, not defining features. Clarity about our values can enhance our sense of purpose (Dahl, Plumb, Stewart and Lundgren, 2009) and 'purpose provides a bedrock foundation that allows a person to be more resilient to obstacles, stress, and strain' (Kashdan and McKnight, 2009: 303).

How are we to recognise what really matters to us? Can we be honest and clear enough with ourselves?

Many schools of therapy have recognised how mixed and multiple we can be (Rowan, 1990). One part of me wants 'x', while another part wants 'y', and yet another 'z'! Our motivations can be equally mixed, with some of them less than congruent with the intention to facilitate growth and healing. Gandhi is commonly paraphrased as saying 'be the change you want to see in the world'. So the point here is *what do we really want to stand for? What do we deeply wish our lives to contribute to?*

Though the process of knowing oneself is endless, mindfulness, inner work, personal therapy and supervision can enable us to venture into the world of private practice, with a relatively clear sense of why and what we want to do.

CLARIFYING VALUES

There are a number of ways to help clarify one's values. One exercise involves imagining you are approaching the end of your life and, looking back, you feel contentment that you lived your life in tune with what really mattered to you. Next, you reflect upon what you prioritised – what you took a stand on throughout your life – that led to this sense of contentment.

Another means of clarification involves sorting through a list of cards, each one labelled with a particular value. The cards can be sorted into piles: 'those that really matter to me' (core values); 'those that somewhat matter'; and 'those that are less important to me'. A list of example values is shown in Figure 7.13.3.

This kind of reflection calls for time and focus. Rather than constituting a purely cognitive exercise, it calls for a holistic approach, involving attention to what Gendlin (1981) described as the 'felt sense'.

From a position of clarity about what really matters to us, we can then proceed to reflect upon how these values could be expressed through our work. We can do this by formulating a vision and a personal mission statement.

VISION AND PERSONAL MISSION STATEMENT

Creating a vision and a personal mission statement makes one's sense of purpose explicit. Mission and vision express our values and the direction we are committed to proceeding in.

Acceptance	Fairness	Learning
Authenticity	Faith	Love
Appreciation of beauty	Friendship	Nature
	Fun	Open mindedness
Bravery	Generosity	
Citizenship	Gratitude	Optimism
Compassion	Growth	Patience
Community	Happiness	Peace
Contribution	Health	Pleasure
Cooperation	Humility	Respect
Creativity	Humour	Responsibility
Duty	Independence	Service
Doing your best	Integrity	Spirituality
Diversity	Justice	Trust
Equality	Kindness	Wisdom

Figure 7.13.3   *Examples of values*

PERSONAL MISSION STATEMENT

It is common practice for organisations to have a mission statement and, over the past few decades, it has become frequent for leaders and entrepreneurs to formulate a personal one. As Covey (2004: 137) points out, writing and/or reviewing your personal mission statement 'forces you to think through your priorities deeply, carefully, and to align your behaviour with your beliefs'. An example of the values and personal mission statement of a particularly well-known businessman, Richard Branson, is illustrated in Figure 7.13.4.

The process of formulating a mission statement can take a few days, a few weeks or even months. Essentially, it requires us to ask 'what really fits for me, what is my mission?' We can live this inquiry by intentionally being receptive to what touches or inspires us as we go through our days. Gathering a collection of notes, quotes and ideas may prove useful as resource material in composing the statement.

Metaphorically, we gather ingredients for a 'mission soup', out of which a statement is crafted. A good mix includes core values, passionate interests, talents and experience (we might reflect on past successes and/or ask peers and supervisors for feedback), and any particular

What values … did your parents pass on to you that you still follow today?

My parents are extremely kind, thoughtful, and loving people. They believe you should treat others as you would wish to be treated yourself. My mum taught me never to be afraid of failure – it's just a learning curve. My wonderful dad taught me to listen and to value other people's advice and opinions.

Do you have a personal mission statement?

Have fun in your journey through life and learn from your mistakes.

In business, know how to be a good leader and always try to bring out the best in people. It's very simple: listen to them, trust in them, believe in them, respect them, and let them have a go!

Figure 7.13.4 An example of values and a personal mission statement (excerpted from *Motivated Magazine*, 2011)

client groups with whom we are particularly drawn to working (e.g., people suffering with anxiety, the elderly, young people, etc.).

The more authentic and honest we can be with ourselves, the more potent the process and the product promises to be. Once we have gathered our ingredients, we can experiment with different wordings, once again attending to the 'felt sense' of fit (Gendlin, 1981).

VISION

Our vision describes what we want to achieve in the long term. It expresses our dreams for how our values, put into action, can come to fruition.

Some questions we can ask ourselves include the following: If my core values were free to express themselves through me, what would they do? If they were free to make the best use of my abilities, experience, knowledge and so on, to what would they lead me? Contemplating such questions reveals aspirations and generates values-congruent ideas.

From a standpoint of vision we can generate values-congruent goals and objectives.

OBJECTIVES AND GOALS

Objectives and goals that emerge from vision and mission are fuelled by intrinsic motivation. Such motivation arises from within, rather than being driven by external rewards such as money. Intrinsic motivation is more likely to be sustainable; values-congruent goals are more likely to be achieved (see the work of Ryan and Deci, for example, Deci and Ryan, 2002; Ryan and Deci, 2008).

As we use the terms here, goals express the outcomes we are aiming for, usually in the longer term. Objectives are steps on the path to achieving these goals. Objectives and goals shape our day-to-day decisions and actions.

SMARTNESS

SMART is an acronym meaning specific, measurable, achievable, realistic and timeframe – the five guides to setting goals and objectives. Rather than holding tight to SMART as a formula and insisting that all goals must satisfy all the criteria, we can remain creative and flexible, both in terms of formulation and implementation.

For example, I might formulate a goal to become a provider of online counselling services, with the specific objectives of: (1) raising my profile in the internet search engines, (2) working with more online clients in the coming year, and (3) giving my website a makeover. My goal and objectives seem realistic and achievable to me, but I could probably use some help with goal (1). I could also be more specific about a timetable for goals (1) and (2). Although I can easily measure goal (2), with my current skill set, it is not easy to do so with goal (1). For goal (3), measurement is not really an issue, as I am going to use my own subjectivity to guide me in designing the new look of my website.

'THE PATH'

Once we have clarity related to our values, vision and mission to give us a sense of direction and a set of goals and objectives, we can set to work putting it into action. This can be envisaged as setting out on what Castaneda (1968) described as 'a path with heart'.

Traditionally, in Yogic teachings, the symbol of the heart was two overlapping triangles – one pointing up, the other pointing down (Figure 7.13.5). Mythologist Joseph

Campbell (1991) taught that the upward triangle represents the direction of our values and vision, and the download triangle represents inertia, difficulties and life challenges. The path with heart is the meeting of these two. Likewise, with any creative endeavour – painting, music, cooking a meal, a relationship, a project – there is the inevitable meeting of the inspiration with the limitations of the materials, skills or the actual situation.

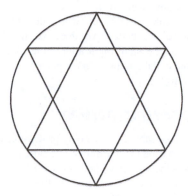

Figure 7.13.5   Yogic symbol of the heart

For example, making a work of art, there's an innate constraint on the creative impulse due to the materials themselves: the canvas has a particular size, only certain brushes and paints are available. These limitations, however, are not only obstructions; they are also the very medium for the expression of the vision.

Rather than situational, economic and psychological difficulties being nothing more than impediments, the meeting of our vision with the challenges *is* the path. Willingness to travel this path, with its inevitable hardships, requires courage. 'Courage' derives from the Latin 'cor', meaning heart.

INNER CHALLENGES

Life is characterised by ups and downs and, sooner or later, anyone who travels the path of private practice will meet obstacles.

Many of these obstacles are internal. Common ones include:

1. *Expectations and the inner critic* – A frequent source of difficulty for practitioners are expectations that we should be 'sorted out', be paragons of health and wellbeing. 'You're not good enough', says the inner critic. Getting caught up in such narratives can feel very demoralising.

2. *Fear of failure* – This can be an obstacle at any point on the path: it can arise when we try to clarify our values, when we begin the process of envisioning a mission statement, or when we think about objectives and implementing a plan. It can take the form of avoidance, procrastination and self-doubt.

3. *Assumptions and inflexibility* – Knowing 'how it should be' and attachment to doing things the 'right way' can place a significant limit on our potential for creativity and responsiveness.

4. *Ambition* – If we are too invested in achievement, we can overlook the small steps taken in line with our core values, gradual change may be missed, and small victories unnoticed.

5. *Impatience* – Setting up and developing a private practice usually takes considerable time. Setbacks, as we have already considered, are inevitable. This calls for patience.

OUTER CHALLENGES

What follows is a list of areas particularly relevant to setting up a private practice. Each area is presented as a collection of questions for consideration.

1. PROMOTION

How can I promote myself in line with my vision and mission? Do I want certain images to represent my work? Do I promote myself as an individual, a service, a project? What do I call myself? What kind of words am I going to use on any promotional material? Do I want a logo? Are there certain client groups I want to reach out to? What message do I hope to convey? Which of my colleagues, peers or mentors might I consult for feedback?

Is it worth paying a web designer to design a site for me or might it be better to register with an established online counselling directory? Perhaps I could do both?

How are potential clients going to contact me?

2. INSURANCE AND TAX

What insurance do I need? Public liability? Public indemnity? Are there special packages available? Might I be eligible for a discount based on BACP or United Kingdom Council for Psychotherapy (UKCP) membership? Do I want to shop around for the best offer or take whatever I can find?

Do I feel confident to take care of my own taxes? Am I able to be sufficiently organised? Perhaps I could pay someone to take care of my accounts?

3. PREMISES

If I am planning to work from home, am I insured for this? Are there any health and safety issues? Does it feel OK for me to have my work take place in my home? Do I have a space that is confidential? Is it welcoming enough? Warm enough? Does it have the right kind of decor to fit my practice?

Do I want to work online? If so, have I got sufficient information technology (IT) skills?

Is there a therapy centre nearby where I could hire a room? Might I benefit from the centre's presence and publicity?

4. RECORD KEEPING

What records will I keep? Where will I store them? For how long? Are there current legal and/or professional requirements that I need to be aware of?

5. PROVISION FOR ILLNESS OR DEATH

What if become incapacitated in an accident or due to illness? What if I die? If I work in an agency, there are colleagues who can step into the vacuum and help the situation? Working privately, what provision can I make for this?

6. ASSESSMENTS

What kind of assessments am I going to use? Are they congruent with my approach to therapy? What purpose will assessment serve? How much time am I going to spend on these measures?

7. CONTRACTS

Am I going to have a printed pro forma? What will it say? Will I want a signature? Or would I prefer a verbal contract?

8. TIME MANAGEMENT

Am I well enough able to manage my time? Can I balance my work and personal life in a way that works for me?

Do I want to work full-time in private practice? Part-time? Perhaps it is better for me to develop a portfolio approach – working privately as well as for a local organisation, employee assistance scheme, general practitioner (GP) surgery, etc.

What other opportunities might there be for me besides working as a counsellor? Teaching? Supervision? Could I write something for the local newspaper about an issue I care about? Am I open to creative possibilities?

9. ISOLATION

How will I be, working in relative isolation? Would it suit me better to work in a team? Is my supervision supportive enough? Is there a peer group I could join? Would some personal therapy be helpful?

Is it possible to team up with other practitioners? Would that suit me better? Are there like-minded people out there whose vision might align with mine? Would I benefit from collaborating with people who have complementary skills?

10. PROFESSIONAL DEVELOPMENT

How will I take care of my ongoing professional development? Supervision? What training could I benefit from? Shall I try something new, perhaps something I'm really interested in? What will help me stay fresh?

How will I keep informed of developments in the field? What areas of research will I attend to?

11. FEES

What am I going to charge people for my services? Is there some kind of standard charge locally? Will I operate a sliding scale? Will I accept donations, or work for free with clients who have no or very little financial income?

12. IS PRIVATE PRACTICE FOR ME?

Are my values and strengths best served by working in private practice? Do I have enough experience at this time? Could I benefit from being part of an organisation for a while, and then gradually start building up something private?

SUMMARY

Our core values can steer us through the complexities and the inevitable ups and downs of private practice. Creating a vision and a mission statement for one's practice enables the generation of values-congruent goals and objectives which, in turn, lead to actions and decisions in alignment with purpose. Working purposefully, we can be more resilient and our practices can be more sustainable and rewarding.

REFERENCES

British Association for Counselling and Psychotherapy (2015) *Ethical Framework for the Counselling Professions*. Lutterworth: British Association for Counselling and Psychotherapy.

Campbell, J. (1991) *A Joseph Campbell Companion*. New York: Harper Collins.

Castaneda, C. (1968) *The Teachings of Don Juan: A Yaqui Way of Knowledge*. Berkeley, CA: University of California Press.

Covey, S. (2004) *The 7 Habits of Highly Effective People*. London: Simon & Schuster.

Dahl, J.C., Plumb, J.C., Stewart, I. and Lundgren, T. (2009) *The Art and Science of Valuing in Psychotherapy: Helping Clients Discover, Explore, and Commit to Valued Action Using Acceptance and Commitment Therapy*. Oakland, CA: New Harbinger.

Deci, E.L. and Ryan, R.M. (2002) *Handbook of Self-determination Research*. New York: The University of Rochester Press.

Gendlin, E.T. (1981) *Focusing*. New York: Bantam.

Hayes, S., Strosahl, K. and Wilson, K. (2012) *Acceptance and Commitment Therapy: The Process and Practice of Mindful Change*. New York: Guilford Press.

Kashdan, T.B. and McKnight, P.E. (2009) Origins of purpose in life: Refining our understanding of a life well lived. *Psychological Topics*, 18(2), 303–316.

Motivated Magazine (2011) Sir Richard Branson: On a mission to mentor. *Motivated Magazine*. (http://motivated online.com/sir-richard-branson-on-a-mission-to-mentor/).

Rowan, J. (1990) *Subpersonalities: The People Inside Us*. London: Routledge.

Ryan, R.M. and Deci, E.L. (2008) A self-determination theory approach to psychotherapy: The motivational basis for effective change. *Canadian Psychology*, 49(3), 186–193.

RECOMMENDED READING

1. Bor, R. and Stokes, A. (2011) *Setting Up in Independent Practice: A Handbook for Counsellors, Therapists and Psychologists*. Basingstoke: Palgrave Macmillan.

2. Thistle, R. (1998) *Counselling and Psychotherapy in Private Practice*. London: Sage.

These books both offer a comprehensive resource about the nuts and bolts of establishing a private practice.

3. The British Association for Counselling and Psychotherapy (www.bacppp.org.uk).

The BACP's private practice division produces a quarterly journal for for counsellors and psychotherapists working independently.

7.14   WORKING IN PRIMARY CARE

SARAH HOVINGTON AND ZUBEIDA ALI

OVERVIEW AND KEY POINTS

Counselling in primary care is influenced by the specific setting in which it takes place – that of healthcare funded by the National Health Service (NHS). It thus retains the core elements of counselling as a modality while being carried out in a fast-changing arena driven by government policy. This chapter covers the distinctive features of counselling in primary care, with particular reference to:

- The context of primary care counselling and how it has changed over the past few years as governments across the four nations have striven to make psychological therapies more accessible and evidence-based.
- The development of the evidence-based psychological intervention, Counselling for Depression (CfD) in NHS England's Improving Access to Psychological Therapies (IAPT) services.
- What a primary care counsellor's job involves, and how the role is influenced by policies, guidelines and targets.
- The training and experience required to become a primary care counsellor.
- Elements that might influence the future for counselling in NHS-funded services.

BACKGROUND AND CONTEXT

The first challenge we had in writing this chapter was defining counselling in primary care, not least because both 'counselling' and 'primary care' require their own definitions.

Counselling, along with psychotherapy, has been defined as an umbrella term that covers a range of talking therapies, with counsellors helping people to talk about their choices or behaviour, and make positive changes in their lives (British Association for Counselling and Psychotherapy, 2017). 'Primary care' in the NHS is described by the National Association of Primary Care (2015) as having four central features: the first point of contact for all new health needs; person-centred, continuous lifetime care; comprehensive care provided for all needs that are common in a population; and coordination and integration of care when a person's need is sufficiently uncommon as to require special services from another sector (secondary or tertiary care). As many people's first point of contact with the NHS, around 90 per cent of patient interaction is with primary care services, general practitioner (GP) practices in particular (Health and Social Care Information Centre, 2016).

Put together, counselling *in* primary care means something unique: a specialism that retains the core purpose of 'enhancing wellbeing' while being shaped, and therefore changed, by the specific setting in which it takes place. Counselling in primary care, therefore, has distinctive features that relate specifically to the healthcare arena in which it is carried out.

We will detail those features later in this chapter, but to start, it is important to mention the historical context of counselling in primary care, and how this has evolved, especially over the past few years.

This brings us to our second challenge in writing this chapter: how to adequately cover, and do justice to, the differing contexts of primary care counselling in each of the four nations. We decided to concentrate here mainly on developments in NHS England, not because we wish to exclude our colleagues in Scotland, Wales and Northern Ireland, but because we both work in NHS-funded services in England and this is where our experience and knowledge lies. We do so in the recognition that services in each of the four nations are being developed along the same lines, and so the information is broadly generalisable.

Historically, counselling has been the most widely available primary care psychological therapy, with practitioners working in a range of modalities, including person-centred, psychodynamic and cognitive-behavioural – often in an integrative way. In the past, provision across the United Kingdom (UK) was patchy, and while some primary care counselling services existed, counsellors often worked in isolation, mainly employed by fund-holding GPs.

The move over the past few years to make psychological therapies more accessible, accountable, cost-efficient and equitable has led to a massive change in provision. This change has occurred particularly in NHS England with the introduction of the Improving Access to Psychological Therapies (IAPT) programme, which supports the NHS in implementing National Institute for Health and Care Excellence (NICE), guidelines for anxiety disorders and depression (NICE, 2005a, 2005b, 2009, 2011, 2013). These guidelines, which correspond to specific diagnoses, make recommendations on psychological treatments combined, where appropriate, with recommendations on medication – traditionally the only treatment available for health problems, including psychological health. To be included in the guidelines, psychological therapies need to be supported by positive findings in randomised controlled trials (RCTs), the research design commonly viewed as providing the 'gold standard' of evidence.

Similarly, in Scotland, national policy and guidance are placing increasing emphasis on the provision of therapies supported by RCTs. The development of *The Matrix: A Guide for the Delivery of Psychological Therapies in Scotland* (NHS Education for Scotland, 2011), in parallel with Scottish Intercollegiate Guidelines Network's (SIGN) *Guidelines for the Non-pharmaceutical Management of Depression* (SIGN, 2010), signalled the intention of the Scottish Executive Health Department (SEHD) to prioritise provision of SIGN-recommended therapies for specific diagnoses.

The devolved governments in Northern Ireland and Wales have also published strategies for the development of psychological therapy provision (Department of Health,

Social Services and Public Safety (Northern Ireland), 2010; Welsh Government, 2012), and although the implementation of these strategies is not yet as advanced, a move towards the use of specific therapies for specific diagnoses seems to be echoed across the four nations.

These developments are important to counselling in primary care as such guidance is largely dictating which services are commissioned and which therapy modalities are funded. (Commissioning is basically a decision-making process as to who pays to provide what services, and arrangements can be different in each of the four UK nations because of political devolution.)

As commissioners are increasingly led by national guidance, they are largely commissioning psychological therapies with the best RCT evidence. Further, because this guidance is organised into diagnoses, there is a focus on psychological therapies for the specific diagnoses of depression and the anxiety disorders (generalised anxiety disorder (GAD) and panic disorder, obsessive compulsive disorder (OCD), post-traumatic stress disorder (PTSD), social phobia). The effect on counselling provision has been enormous because the guidelines make distinctions between different modalities of therapy, according to which one has the best evidence for a particular diagnosis, and commissioners have been reluctant to commission counselling as it does not feature strongly enough in the clinical guidelines.

Although RCTs into the effectiveness of counselling exist, research into humanistic/person-centred counselling has predominantly focused on qualitative research to gain an understanding of underlying motivations, rather than the quantitative research used in large-scale RCTs. Historically, RCTs have been used for medication trials and counselling has not allied itself to the design due to its reductive nature. As a result, counselling does not feature strongly in the NICE guideline for depression (NICE, 2009), which recommends counselling only for people with persistent sub-threshold depressive symptoms or mild to moderate depression who decline another first-line form of treatment. The recommended modality for all anxiety disorders is CBT. Eye-Movement Desensitization and Reprocessing (EMDR) is additionally recommended for PTSD, and Applied Relaxation is additionally recommended for GAD.

WAYS OF WORKING

The IAPT programme in England originally focused on training in CBT interventions to address the shortage of CBT-qualified workers. However, following the publication of *Talking Therapies: A Four-year Plan*

of Action (Department of Health, 2011b) to support the cross-governmental mental health strategy *No Health without Mental Health* (Department of Health, 2011a), the focus broadened to offering continuing professional development (CPD) to therapists from other modalities recommended by NICE for treating depression and the anxiety disorders.

This resulted in the development, by BACP and partners in higher education, of the humanistic/person-centred Counselling for Depression (CfD) training for counsellors wishing to access IAPT-compliant training. Counselling for Depression is now recognised as a form of evidence-based psychological therapy within the IAPT programme, with its own framework of competences (Roth, Hill and Pilling, 2010) and a CfD textbook – a manualised model of practice – which supports the training programme. The therapy itself – intended as an 'add-on' for qualified counsellors – addresses emotions underlying depression and intrapersonal processes such as low self-esteem and self-criticism that maintain depressed mood (Sanders and Hill, 2014).

It is important to remember that counsellors who were already working in the NHS when the running of services transferred to IAPT (which follows a very specific model) remained non-IAPT compliant. Therefore, the introduction of CfD was welcomed by the profession as it ensured the place of counselling in the NHS via an evidence-based intervention, ensuring that counselling is provided free at the point of access to NHS patients and that the status of counsellors in IAPT is recognised (Pearce et al., 2013).

CfD is now widely used in IAPT services to treat depression, along with a range of other modalities, including CBT, interpersonal therapy (IPT), dynamic interpersonal therapy (DIT), and couple therapy for depression (CTfD).

Significantly for counselling in primary care, the advent of clinical guidelines has changed the definition of counselling in NHS-funded services. Instead of counselling being an covering a range of talking therapies, as in BACP's generic description cited earlier, it is now widely used in NHS healthcare to describe humanistic/person-centred counselling, as distinct from other therapies, such as CBT or IPT.

The job title of 'counsellor' is now largely treated as distinct from other roles within primary care psychological services, and counsellors now find themselves in multi-modality teams which include psychological wellbeing practitioners (PWPs) trained in the use of CBT skills for brief interventions, CBT therapists, IPT therapists, CTfD therapists, and DIT therapists. And although primary care counselling does still take place in GP surgeries, the variety of settings has enlarged, with counsellors now found in a range of community settings, or offering therapy via groups, by telephone or online rather than just face to face (one-to-one).

One of the biggest changes to structure, and one which is recommended by both NICE in England and SIGN in Scotland, is the advent of 'stepped care'. This is a tiered approach, with the lowest intensity psychological interventions being provided to people with less severe difficulties, the idea being that the client receives the minimum input compatible with effective treatment. Subsequent 'steps' are defined by increasing levels of problem complexity and increasingly intensive forms of treatment. For example, someone with mild depression may benefit from guided self-help ('low intensity'), whereas someone with severe depression may need more intensive help ('high intensity'). Individual cases are usually considered and, in line with clinical guidance, there are exceptions for specific diagnoses. For example, clients with PTSD would always receive more intensive treatment. As a modality, counselling is most usually placed at 'high-intensity level', along with CBT, IPT, DIT and CTfD, whereas guided CBT-based self-help is found at the 'low-intensity' step.

Taking all the above into consideration, what makes a primary care counsellor's role different from that of counsellors working in non NHS-funded settings?

As in other settings, their roles involve providing talking therapy to people to enhance their emotional well-being. However, their day-to-day jobs are more likely to be defined by a governance framework which includes adherence to policies, guidelines and/or commissioned targets that relate to population needs and cost-effectiveness.

In IAPT services in England, where, due to NICE guidance, counselling is used only to treat depression, counsellors are likely to see clients with mild, moderate or severe depression as a primary diagnosis. This incorporates clients with a range of presenting problems, including relationships difficulties, problems with adjustment (bereavement, parenthood, retirement, illness diagnosis, unresolved grief), sexual abuse, or people for whom another form of therapy hasn't been successful for them (based on Clark, Layard and Smithies, 2008) or who opt for counselling as an informed choice.

While BACP guidelines suggest no more than 20 actual client contacts a week for a full-time member of staff (depending on the experience of the counsellor and the complexity of the work), some counsellors are likely to offer five to six appointments a day (to make up for attrition rates) in order to meet the required number of actual face-to-face contacts. In some IAPT services,

counsellors may also undertake telephone assessments in the time clients do not attend appointments. The course of face-to-face therapy is time-limited, and session numbers are likely to be between six and ten over 8–12 weeks (NICE, 2009).

Collecting therapy outcome data is a requirement in any NHS-funded service – to indicate to commissioners what they are paying for – and so measurement is part of a primary care counsellor's role on a day-to-day basis. In IAPT services, each client is asked to complete the minimum data set (MDS) of outcome questionnaires at each appointment (IAPT, 2008). The rationale for asking the client to complete these at each appointment is that data will be lost if a client drops out of treatment unplanned as it affects data completeness and recovery measures (see below). Among others, the MDS contains outcome measures for depression and generalised anxiety disorder, the PHQ9 and GAD7 respectively. Services aim to meet the target of a 50 per cent recovery rate, and clients are deemed to have reached recovery if their scores in each have reduced from above to below a certain threshold – this relies on having scores at the start and end of therapy.

In addition, all therapists, including counsellors, are now increasingly expected to 'cluster' patient problems. These clusters focus mainly on severity and level of need (as opposed to the types of problems experienced) and form the basis of the mental health payment by results (PbR) national tariff payment system, whereby provider services are allocated a certain amount of money to treat each patient (tariff) depending on their cluster. The system used in IAPT services in England is HoNOS (Health of the Nation Outcome Scales) and therapists are required to assign people at first assessment to a 'care cluster' that indicates their need for care. There are 21 care clusters which group psychiatric diagnoses that have comparable levels of severity and treatment. The clusters cover 'non-psychotic' (numbered 1 to 9), 'psychosis' (10 to 17) and 'organic', the latter indicating cognitive impairment (18 to 21). Primary care counsellors work with clients in the non-psychotic cluster groups, usually clusters 1 to 4, which cover the mild, moderate and severe range of common mental health problems.

Public protection and patient safety play a part in counselling services whether they are NHS-funded or not. However, this may be intensified when working in NHS-funded psychological services. Counsellors in primary care are expected to be familiar with carrying out a mental health assessment, including a risk assessment and management plan. As a consequence, they are required to have a good knowledge of onward referral pathways, particularly in crisis management and secondary care, and to work with other agencies for the benefit of the client and the wider public. This includes adherence to procedures regarding confidentiality, and corresponding knowledge of social care agencies (for example, child protection) and they have a statutory duty to disclose issues surrounding the protection of children and vulnerable adults.

Counsellors will receive clinical supervision for their work, and this is generally provided in-house by a supervisor who is a trained counsellor. In healthcare, and particularly in IAPT services, supervision can also take the form of case management, focusing on changes in outcome measurements (an IAPT target) and risk management. Frequency of supervision varies across services: in some, supervision is weekly. All services, however, should provide the BACP-recommended minimum of 1.5 hours per month.

In addition, counsellors attend team meetings and undertake mandatory training in elements such as safeguarding and information governance.

What training and experience is required for a counsellor in primary care?

In NHS England, jobs in counselling are banded through Agenda for Change (A4C), which means they are scored against national job profiles. Entry-level counselling posts are banded at 5, progressing to band 6 post-entry level and on to band 7 for a specialist counsellor.

As essential criteria, an IAPT entry-level counsellor generally requires diploma-level training in counselling (BACP-accredited course or equivalent); experience within a mental health setting; a commitment to CPD; and an understanding of IAPT and stepped care. Desirable criteria can include knowledge of policies such as NICE guidelines and mental health legislation, and experience of clinical outcome measures and assessments. Jobs are advertised on the BACP website (www.bacp.co.uk) (members only) and the NHS job site (www.jobs.nhs.uk).

Nearly all person specifications for NHS counsellor posts cite 'working towards BACP accreditation' or 'actively seeking BACP accreditation'. Implicit is the expectation that counsellors working in primary care NHS services will maintain membership of a professional body. Primary care counsellors can also choose to belong to a specialist organisation such as BACP Healthcare, a division of BACP for practitioners who work in healthcare settings, either within the public, private and/or third sector across the UK (www.bacphealthcare.org. uk). We expect that it will be soon be a requirement for a counsellor employed in primary care to be on the BACP Register (www.bacpregister.org.uk), an accredited voluntary register for public protection which provides access to professionals who are committed to high standards.

Training as part of the diploma qualification tends to be non-specific in terms of primary care counselling. In addition, the person specification requirements can make it difficult for newly-trained counsellors to acquire the specific experience relevant to the job. CfD training is usually only provided for those already in post: IAPT has provided some funding for this and employers are expected to fund the rest of the amount. However, this has become an issue within the current financial climate. More recently, training providers have started to offer places to anyone wishing to fund their own training, which is helping to increase the numbers of counsellors trained in an IAPT-compliant modality.

While there is graduate training available in the form of university modules, and some trained counsellors gain employment in another role, such as a PWP, before applying for a counselling job, it is more common that trainee counsellors look to acquire healthcare experience training and development while on counselling placements.

Placements in primary care counselling can, however, be hard to come by, and their quality varies. This is mainly because there isn't a formal national workforce planning programme for the training of counsellors, unlike that provided for IAPT trainee PWPs and CBT therapists, and for trainee clinical psychologists. The lack of this strategy has meant that any placements provided within NHS-funded services impact on existing resources that have been carefully commissioned to meet outcome targets, often leading to a reluctance on the part of services to offer opportunities to trainee counsellors.

If fortunate to be offered a placement in the NHS, trainee counsellors should expect a qualified counsellor on site, appropriate mentorship, case management supervision, clear referral pathways with good recording systems, screening for appropriate referral, and information regarding policies. All trainee placements should include a formal end of placement review, in alignment with the standards set within BACP's *Accreditation of Training Courses* (BACP, 2016), unofficially known as the '*Gold Book*'.

RESEARCH EVIDENCE

In England, all NICE guidelines are periodically reviewed so that fresh evidence can be taken into account: the presence of humanistic counselling in the guidance is seen as important to the future commissioning of counselling in NHS-funded services.

The advantages of evaluating humanistic counselling are evident in terms of feeding into the next phases of guideline development and informing commissioners. More evidence is needed if counselling is going to feature more strongly in future NICE and SIGN guidance and also be part of psychological therapy provision strategy in Northern Ireland and Wales.

As a result, BACP has been working to generate such evidence. In addition to analysing a large IAPT routine dataset, the BACP Research Foundation has funded an RCT to compare CfD to a CBT treatment for depression (originated by Beck, Rush, Shaw and Emery, 1987) to see whether CfD has equivalent outcomes to Beckian cognitive therapy (University of Sheffield, 2016).

REFERENCES

Beck, A.T., Rush A. J., Shaw B.F. and Emery, G. (1987) *Cognitive Therapy of Depression*. New York and Oxford: Guilford Press.

British Association for Counselling and Psychotherapy (BACP) (2016) *Accreditation of Training Courses*. Lutterworth: BACP. (www.bacp.co.uk/accreditation/COURSE%20ACCREDITATION%20SCHEME/)

British Association for Counselling and Psychotherapy (BACP) (2017) (www.bacp.co.uk/crs/Training/whatis counselling.php).

Clark, D.M., Layard, R. and Smithies, R. (2008) *Improving Access to Psychological Therapy: Initial Evaluation of the Two Demonstration Sites*. LSE Centre for Economic Performance Working Paper no. 1648. London: LSE Centre for Economic Performance.

Department of Health (DH) (2011a) *No Health without Mental Health. A Cross-Government Mental Health Outcomes Strategy for People of All Ages: A Call to Action*. London: Department of Health.

Department of Health (DH) (2011b) *Talking Therapies: A Four-year Plan of Action*. London: Department of Health.

Department of Health, Social Services and Public Safety (Northern Ireland) (2010) *A Strategy for the Development of Psychological Therapy Service*. Belfast: Department of Health (Northern Ireland).

Health and Social Care Information Centre (2016) (www.hscic.gov.uk/primary-care).

Improving Access to Psychological Therapies (IAPT) (2008) (https://www.england.nhs.uk/mental-health/adults/iapt/).

National Association of Primary Care (2015) (www.napc.co.uk/primary-care-home).

National Institute for Health and Clinical Excellence (NICE) (2005a) *Post-traumatic Stress Disorder: Management*. NICE Guidelines CG26. London: NICE.

National Institute for Health and Clinical Excellence (NICE) (2005b) *Obsessive-compulsive Disorder and Body Dysmorphic Disorder: Treatment*. NICE Guidelines CG31. London: NICE.

National Institute for Health and Clinical Excellence (NICE) (2009) *Depression in Adults (update). Depression: The Treatment and Management of Depression in Adults*. NICE Guidelines CG 90. London: NICE/National Collaborating Centre for Mental Health.

National Institute for Health and Clinical Excellence (NICE) (2011) *Generalised Anxiety Disorder and Panic Disorder in Adults: Management*. NICE Guidelines CG113. London: NICE.

National Institute for Health and Clinical Excellence (NICE) (2013) *Social Anxiety Disorder: Recognition, Assessment and Treatment*. NICE Guidelines CG159. London: NICE.

NHS Education for Scotland (2011) The Matrix: A Guide for the Delivery of Psychological Therapies in Scotland. Edinburgh: NHS Education for Scotland.

Pearce, P., Sewell, R., Hill, A., Coles, H., Pybis, J., Hunt, J., et al. (2013) Counselling for Depression: the perceptions of trainees. *Healthcare Counsellng and Psychotherapy Journal*, 13(1), 8–13.

Roth, A.D., Hill, A. and Pilling S. (2010) *The Competences Required to Deliver Effective Humanistic Psychological Therapies*. London: Research Department of Clinical, Educational and Health Psychology, University College London.

Sanders, P. and Hill, A. (2014) *Counselling for Depression: A Person-centred and Experiential Approach to Practice*. London: Sage, in association with the British Association for Counselling and Psychotherapy.

Scottish Intercollegiate Guidelines Network (SIGN) (2010) *Non-pharmaceutical Management of Depression in Adults*. Edinburgh: SIGN/Healthcare Improvement Scotland.

University of Sheffield (2016) (www.shef.ac.uk/scharr/sections/hsr/mh/mhresearch/practiced/info)

Welsh Government (2012) *A Strategy for Mental Health and Wellbeing in Wales*. Cardiff: Welsh Government.

RECOMMENDED READING

1. Sanders, P. and Hill, A. (2014) *Counselling for Depression: A Person-centred and Experiential Approach to Practice*. London: Sage, in association with the British Association for Counselling and Psychotherapy.

The textbook for Counselling for Depression (CfD) – essential for counsellors undertaking the training and also useful for trainees on Diploma courses who would like to know what is involved in the approach.

2. NHS England's IAPT programme (www.england.nhs.uk/mental-health/adults/iapt).

The website of NHS England's IAPT programme, featuring guidance documents, learning resources and examples of materials.

3. Hill, A., Brettle, A., Jenkins, P. and Hulme, C. (2008) *Counselling in Primary Care: A Systematic Review of the Evidence*. Lutterworth: British Association for Counselling and Psychotherapy.

BACP publication reviewing a range of UK and international studies on the effectiveness of counselling in primary care settings, providing an overview of effectiveness, cost-effectiveness and acceptability.

7.15   SHORT-TERM THERAPY

ALEX COREN

OVERVIEW AND KEY POINTS

The majority of clinical encounters today are brief. Frequently this is by default rather than design due to factors such as managerial, as opposed to clinical, decisions on the length of therapy, and client drop-out. Problems of definition occur when brief therapy is defined by the number of sessions offered. It is perhaps more helpful to view short-term therapy as a modality which operates to a specific time frame – is time-aware and time-limited – and places time as the central organising factor of the work. Some time-limited therapies are not particularly brief but what distinguishes them is the open acknowledgement that the therapeutic frame needs to incorporate, and use, time as a therapeutic resource. Rather than conceptualising the issue in terms of brief or long-term therapies, it is more helpful to distinguish between time-limited and open-ended therapies.

General features of short-term therapy would include:

*   Short-term therapy is time-limited – has a mutually agreed ending – as opposed to being open-ended.
*   It is helpful to distinguish between what can be termed a short-term consultation or conversation, which may be in the region of four to six sessions, or even a single session, and planned, focal short-term therapy, which can involve treatments which stretch over some months. Anything from one to 40 or 50 sessions has been put forward as 'brief', depending on modality. Typically, 12–16 sessions are considered optimal for short-term interventions, depending on assessment variables.
*   Activity – short-term therapy involves an active and collaborative therapist.
*   Most short-term therapies will involve the collaborative articulation of a focus which will assist in providing a therapeutic framework or scaffolding to the intervention.
*   Many short-term approaches will include a relational approach, where the therapeutic relationship, the client's relational history and current relational patterns can be used to facilitate therapeutic change.
*   Short-term therapies range on a continuum from manualised, protocol-driven interventions to process relational-led approaches, depending on therapeutic modality.

BACKGROUND AND CONTEXT

It is significant that originally most psychological interventions were brief and highly focused. Over time these were supplanted in favour of the increasing length of treatments, making therapy longer and the clinician more passive and less time-sensitive (see Coren (2010) for a description of the history of brief interventions).

Contemporary short-term therapists (see Coren, 2010, 2014, 2016; Della Selva, 2004; Lemma et al., 2011; Levenson, 2012; Mander, 2000; Messer and Warren, 1998; Smith, 2006; Stadter, 2004) advocate that the therapist is active, establishes a therapeutic focus, and has a confidence in outcome – albeit with limited goals – which is conveyed to the client. Material is proactively elicited and a mutually empowering therapeutic relationship forms the basis of the work. This is not dissimilar to the early psychological, including Freudian, clinical interventions.

It was through the work of Davanloo (1980), Malan (1979), and the behavioural and humanistic modalities of the mid-twentieth century, that shorter-term therapies became more widespread. The work of Horowitz (1997), Budman and Gurman's Interpersonal, Developmental, Existential (IDE) therapy (1988), James Mann (1992), Klerman's inter personal therapy (Klerman et al., 1994), as well as cognitive analytic therapy (Ryle and Kerr, 2001) and more recent developments in cognitive-behavioural therapy (Bor et al., 2003; Brosnan and Westerbrook, 2015; Curwen and Palmer, 2000; Wills and Sanders, 1997) have all contributed to short-term interventions. Humanistic or client-centred approaches have also addressed the issue of short-term interventions (Tudor, 2008), as has Systems Theory (Gustafson, 2005). Solution-focused therapy (de Shazer, 1985; Macdonald, 2007), a very brief intervention, rather than focusing on pathology, looks at how clients solve problems and attempts to generalise these successful strategies to other areas of their lives. Single-session interventions (Talmon, 1993), the Two Plus One Model (Barkham, 1989) and the Cardiff Model (Cowley and Groves, 2016) have also provided the framework for many time-limited approaches. These theories have all had an impact on the practice of integrative time-aware therapy. Existential therapy (Strasser and Strasser, 1997), Transactional Analysis (Berne et al., 2011) and Art Therapy (Hughes, 2016) are among modalities which have articulated discrete short-term models, and short-term models have been applied to, among others, attachment theory (Wake, 2010) and narrative therapy (White, 2011.)

The progressively more widespread acceptance of psychological interventions, and the increasing demand for them, has led to a variety of therapeutic modalities articulating short-term models of practice. Developments in public, private and voluntary sectors, employment assistance programmes (EAPs), general practice (GP), education and coaching have all contributed to their popularity. The rise of both an evidence base which suggests the efficacy of short-term approaches (and the suggestion that major therapeutic change happens early in therapy) and the increasing influence of the managed care, insurance and employer-led approach, has led to the increasing popularity of short-term interventions. New technology (email, Skype counselling, etc.) has also contributed to the growth of short-term therapies, as has the impact of Improving Access to Psychological Therapy (IAPT) programme and the National Institute for Health and Care Excellence (NICE) guidelines. It is worth noting, however, that the NICE guidelines suggest that 12–16 sessions are the optimum number of sessions for many clinical populations, which contrasts with many contemporary clinical contexts where 4–6 sessions are frequently the maximum offered. The danger then exists that short-term interventions are seen in response to managing clinical demands, or practised at the behest of management diktats, rather than being the treatment of choice for many populations. We are seeing this in the increasingly 'one size fits all' approach to the number of sessions offered in many contexts.

MODELS

There are a variety of modality-led models of short-term therapy but they can grouped into two different categories:

- Those that use the time frame as non-negotiable and offer a specific number of sessions (either by number or by date). Examples would include Mann's 12-session model, cognitive analytic therapy's 16 sessions and dynamic interpersonal therapy's 16 sessions.
- Therapies that use time more flexibly either by spreading a number of sessions over time, offering reviews at the end of a time-limited course of counselling or offering blocks of therapy – often referred to as 'life span', 'intermittent' or 'top up' therapy – which may suit the clients' developmental needs over time.

Within these categories, modalities also differ between more structured, protocol- or manual-led, short-term therapies and those that are more unstructured and process-led.

Clinical assessment is important in guiding the clinician as to length of treatment and the number of sessions offered. Increasingly, clinicians are agreeing on the assessment criteria which are indicated for short-term approaches. In general these are clients presenting with mild to moderate problems, motivation, psychological readiness and the ability to form a therapeutic alliance. While it has been assumed that clients with long-standing personality issues, multiple problems, substance and alcohol abuse, developmentally early deprivation and reluctant attenders would be contra-indicated for time-limited approaches, it is now thought that these clients might need more sessions than the former group but could still benefit from a time-aware approach. Increasingly, attachment style (see Holmes, 2014) is also likely to have a bearing on the number of sessions offered and the length of treatment, with those securely attached needing fewer sessions than those exhibiting more insecure attachment patterns. Clinicians also need to be mindful in distinguishing between those clients who would benefit from an emotionally expressive approach and those who require a more supportive therapeutic intervention.

WAYS OF WORKING

KEY PRINCIPLES

The clinician has to have a commitment to, and belief in, short-term therapy. In cases where there is a profound ambivalence towards short-term work on behalf of the clinician for whatever reason (e.g., management, or context, prescription of session numbers), a brief approach is unlikely to be successful. The clinician needs to believe that something of real value can be achieved in limited time. Equally, a joint clinician/client agreement on time and focus is important for short-term therapy to be helpful. Short-term therapy is collaborative and relational and in this sense empowering for the client. The establishment of an early working/therapeutic alliance is central to short-term approaches. This can involve therapeutic hope, the early identification of resistances (relational obstacles) and any transferential material (often in the 'here and now' which makes it very accessible) that need to be promptly identified and addressed. While working in the transference, as traditionally defined, is often not applicable to brief work, the 'here and now' relational experience assumes greater significance and the use of symbols and metaphors can be of major importance. Therapeutic collaboration is the basis for the establishment of a sound working alliance in short-term work.

The establishment of a central organising focus provides the framework for many short-term therapies. This involves high levels of therapeutic activity on the part of the therapist and a collaborative agreement on a therapeutic focus to be articulated and worked with from the beginning of counselling. Some modalities may find this easier than others to implement. Frequently, the focus is an interpersonal one and is apparent in the client's history, present(ing) problem and, interestingly, in the therapeutic alliance (see Malan's Therapeutic Triangle (Malan, 1979) and Coren's Concept of Idiom (Coren, 2010)). The focus can be related to therapeutic content (an issue or difficulty) or process (relational history, self-regulation, affects, etc.). It can also be in evidence in the client's transference to time (too short or too long) and become a 'navigational beacon' (Stadter, 2004) for the counselling.

The establishment of a focal framework for the work will inevitably lead to 'selective attention' and 'benign neglect' of some therapeutic material on behalf of the clinician. One of the functions of the focus is to prevent the clinician being overwhelmed by clinical material and enable both client and clinician to identify core issues which are marbled throughout the sessions and recur over time.

Working with time, especially in relation to endings, assumes great significance in brief work. Therapist resistance to ending can contribute to termination difficulties and needs to be acknowledged and addressed. The end needs to be kept in mind from the beginning of therapy – often used by counting down sessions – and the client's feelings about limited time needs to be constantly kept in mind. However, clinicians need to be led by their clients – some client's may consider 4–6 sessions long term. Realism needs to be factored into endings, which need to give space for a therapeutic review and the articulation of both successes and disappointments. Modalities differ as to whether follow-up sessions are offered or not.

Some short-term models are applications of existing open-ended therapeutic modalities, while others are specifically geared to brief interventions. This means that traditional theoretical models may need to be adapted or even sometimes abandoned, and that the brief intervention needs to be suited to the client's problem rather than the client's difficulty being shoehorned into a favoured theoretical model.

A certain flexibility based on a pragmatic approach may be required and the therapist may need to use techniques from other modalities in the service of the client. Examples would include the 'miracle question' (de Shazer, 1985) where clients are asked how things would be different if they were magically transformed. Asking clients for exceptions to the presenting problem can be helpful in providing the hope of generalising from the positive to more problematic areas of their lives, as can paradoxical injunctions where clients are asked to escalate a problem.

Since the goals of short-term therapy are modest and not generic to personality or characterlogical change – although one can be surprised by the ripple effect of brief interventions – different clinical paradigms and therapeutic techniques are required and the clinician needs to develop a short-term state of mind. This can be very different from their trainings. It is a source of some debate currently whether discrete short-term therapy training alone can suffice for time-limited work (and might be advantageous) or whether the counsellor's experience of, and comfort with, open-ended therapies are a necessary prerequisite to be able to work effectively with a brief therapeutic alliance. Binder (2010) has written about the competencies needed by the clinician for successful short-term work.

CASE STUDY

Bill was referred to a counsellor by his GP, having been depressed and on antidepressant medication for some time. He was bewildered by this suggestion and thought he would be seen for a few minutes and given advice, not unlike his experience of consulting his GP. He was a somewhat withdrawn and hostile young man, suspicious of the motives of others and had limited, and unsatisfactory, relationships since his childhood, which he described as uneventful but unhappy. In answer to the magic question, Bill said he would be sociable, with lots of friends, happy and in a relationship. A short-term, process-led contract of six sessions was agreed with Bill. It involved:

- initial psycho-education about the counselling process – that they would meet at the same time for 50 minutes for six weeks to try to shed some light on the reasons Bill was feeling as he was and what was preventing him being able to live a life more in line with what the answer to his magic question suggested.
- an agreed focus of Bill's depression. This was broken down into sub-foci, including its association with his sadness and anger at the lack of satisfying relationships, and their possible origins in the past, but, most importantly, their current manifestations in Bill's life. As became evident, they were to be replicated in the therapeutic relationship and were thus able to be expressed in the 'here and now'. ('Here and now' tends to assume greater importance in short-term work than the 'there and then'. The past tends only to be important to the extent in which it casts a shadow over the present difficulties.)
- the counsellor explaining that he would expect Bill to talk about the things he felt were important to him as well as anything that came into his mind in the context of the general focus, while the counsellor would help Bill to think about them by commenting on Bill's thoughts and adding some of his own. More protocol-led therapies may have approached this issue differently.
- the counsellor maintaining an active and collaborative stance with Bill, frequently linking therapeutic material to the focus and asking for Bill's comments and reflections while continually ensuring that both parties were aware of the time frame and how that might affect the therapeutic alliance and process.
- sessions being counted down at the end of each one. Bill was relieved and felt safe that the length of therapy was clear and transparent. Both felt that more regular sessions were not indicated, although a follow-up was arranged two months after ending.

RESEARCH EVIDENCE

Short-term work is often the treatment of choice for clients. Evidence suggests that clients tend to have rather more limited temporal expectations of counselling than their clinicians. Top-up/intermittent therapy is also claimed to be more efficacious than open-ended therapy and deals with one of the concerns about brief work, which is the danger of relapse, particularly in relation to more severe and long-standing difficulties.

There are a considerable number of time-limited therapies that are developing a sound and rigorous evidence base. These include intensive short term dynamic psychotherapy (ISTDP) (Abbass et al.; Abbass et al., 2012; Della Selva, 2004; Malan and Della Selva, 2006; Neborsky et al., 2012), accelerated experiential dynamic psychotherapy (AEDP) (Fosha, 2000), time-limited dynamic psychotherapy (Levenson, 1995, 2002, 2012), and interpersonal therapy (IPT) (Klerman et al., 1994). Short-term therapies originating in the UK with a sound evidence base include psychodynamic interpersonal therapy (PIT, Barkham, Guthrie, Hardy, Margison 2017), based on the seminal work of Hobson (1982) and Guthrie (1999), dynamic interpersonal therapy (DIT) (Lemma, Target and Fonagy, 2011) and brief psychoanalytic therapy (Hobson, 2016). The increasing use of structured therapies, including IAPT, are also contributing to this, and there is growing evidence that many clients who have received short-term counselling have experienced considerable benefit from it (Roth and Fonagy, 2005).

REFERENCES

Abbass, A., et al. (2012) ISTDP: Systematic review and meta-analysis of outcome research. *Harvard Review of Psychiatry*, 20(2), 97–108.

Abbass, A., et al. (2008) Short term psychodynamic psychotherapy for common mental disorders. *Cochrane Database of Systematic Reviews*.

Barkham, M. (1989) Exploratory therapy in 21 sessions: rationale for a brief psychotherapy model. *British Journal of Psychiatry*, 6(1), 81–88.

Barkham M., Guthrie E., Hardy G., and Margison, F. (2017). '*Psychodynamic Interpersonal Therapy: A Conversational Model*'. Sage

Berne, E. (2011) *Games People Play: Basic Handbook of Transactional Analysis*. Tantor ebooks.

Binder, J. (2010) *Key Competencies in Brief Dynamic Psychotherapy*. New York: Guilford Press.

Bor, R., et al. (2003) *Doing Therapy Briefly*. London: Palgrave.

Brosnan, L. and Westerbrook, D. (2015) *The Complete CBT Guide to Depression and Low Mood*. London: Constable & Robinson.

Budman, S.H., & Gurman, A.S. (1988). *Theory and Practice of Brief Therapy*. New York: Guilford Press.

Coren, A. (2010) *Short Term Psychotherapy: A Psychodynamic Approach*. London: Palgrave.

Coren, A. (2014) Learning and teaching (briefly). *Psychodynamic Practice*, 20(1), 40–53.

Coren, A. (2016) Short-term therapy: therapy lite? In D. Mair (ed.), *Short-term Counselling in Higher Education: Context Theory and Practice* (pp. 29–44). London: Routledge.

Cowley, J. and Groves, V. (2016) The Cardiff Model of short-term engagement. In D. Mair (ed.), *Short-term Counselling in Higher Education: Context Theory and Practice* (pp. 108–126). London: Routledge.

Curwen, B., Palmer, S. and Ruddell, P. (2000) *Brief CBT*. London: Sage.

Davanloo, H. (Ed.). (1980). *Short-term Dynamic Psychotherapy*. New York: Jason Aronson.

Della Selva, P. (2004) *Intensive Dynamic Short-term Therapy*. London: Karnac.

de Shazer, S. (1985) *Keys to Solution in Brief Therapy*. New York: W.W. Norton.

Fosha, D. (2000) *The Transforming Power of Affect: A Model for Accelerated Change*. New York: Basic Books.

Gustafson, J.P. (2005) *Very Brief Psychotherapy*. New York: W.W. Norton.

Guthrie, E. (1999) Psychodynamic interpersonal therapy. *Advances in Psychiatric Treatment*, 5, 135–145.

Hobson, R.F. (1982) *A Conversational Model of Psychotherapy: A Training Method*. London: Tavistock.

Hobson, R.P. (2016) *Brief Psychoanalytic Therapy*. Oxford: Oxford University Press.

Holmes, J. (2014) *The Search for the Secure Base: Attachment Theory and Psychotherapy*. London: Routledge.

Horowitz, M.J. (1997) *Stress Response Syndromes: PTSD Grief and Adjustment Disorders*. New York: Aronson.

Hughes, R. (2016) *Time Limited Art Psychotherapy: Developments in Theory and Practice*. London: Routledge.

Klerman, G.L. et al. (1994) *Interpersonal Psychotherapy of Depression*. New York: Aronson.

Lemma, A., Target, M. and Fonagy, P. (2011) *Brief Dynamic Interpersonal Therapy: A Clinician's Guide*. Oxford: Oxford University Press.

(Continued)

(Continued)

Levenson, H. (1995) *Time Limited Dynamic Psychotherapy*. New York: Basic Books.

Levenson, H. (2002) *Brief Dynamic Therapy*. New York: American Psychiatric Association.

Levenson, H. (2012) Time limited dynamic psychotherapy: an integrative perspective. In M. Dewan, B. Steenbarger and R. Greenberg (eds), *The Art and Science of Brief Psycotherapies*. New York: American Psychiatric Association.

Macdonald, A. (2007) *Solution Focused Therapy: Theory, Research and Practice*. London: Sage.

Malan, D. (1979) *Individual Psychotherapy and the Science of Psychodynamics*. London: Butterworth.

Malan, D. and Della Selva, P. (2006) *Lives Transformed: A Revolutionary Method of Dynamic Psychotherapy*. London: Karnac.

Mander, G. (2000) *A Psychodynamic Approach to Brief Therapy*. London: Sage.

Mann, J. (1992) Time limited psychotherapy. In P. Crits-Cristoph and J. Barber (eds), *Handbook of Short Term Dynamic Psychotherapy*. New York: Basic Books.

Messer, S. and Warren, C. (1998) *Models of Brief Psychodynamic Therapy: A Comparative Approach*. New York and London: Guilford Press.

Neborsky, R. et al. (2012) *Mastering Intensive Short-term Dynamic Therapy: A Road Map to the Unconscious*. London: Karnac.

Roth, A. and Fonagy, P. (2005) *What Works for Whom? A Critical Review of Psychotherapy Research* (2nd ed.). New York and London: Guilford Press.

Ryle, A. and Kerr, I. (2001) *Introducing Cognitive Analytic Therapy*. London: Wiley.

Smith, J.D. (2006) Form and forming a focus in brief dynamic psychotherapy. *Psychodynamic Practice*, 12(3), 261–280.

Stadter, M. (2004) *Object Relations Brief Therapy: The Therapeutic Relationship in Short-term Work*. New York: Aronson.

Strasser, F. and Strasser, A. (1997) *Existential Time Limited Therapy: The Wheel of Existence*. London: Wiley.

Talmon, M. (1993) *Single Session Solutions*. Reading, MA: Addison-Wesley.

Tudor, K. (2008) *Brief Person Centered Therapies*. London: Sage.

Wake, L. (2010) *The Role of Brief Therapy in Attachment Disorders*. London: Karnac.

White, M. (2011) *Narrative Practice: Continuing the Conversations*. New York and London: W.W. Norton.

Wills, F. and Sanders, D. (1997) *Cognitive Therapy: Transforming the Image*. London: Sage.

RECOMMENDED READING

1. Coren, A. (2010) *Short-Term Psychotherapy: A Psychodynamic Approach*. London: Palgrave.

A generic overview of the field of brief interventions which includes a time-specific model for short-term work and a discussion of the strengths and limitations of the approach in contemporary therapeutic contexts and settings.

2. Feltham, C. and Dryden, W. (2006) *Brief Counselling: A Practical Integrative Approach*. London: Sage.

A detailed and practical introduction to brief interventions with a step-by-step guide for the clinician on how to arrange and conduct short-term therapy in different contexts.

3. Lemma, A., Target, M. and Fonagy, P. (2011) *Brief Dynamic Interpersonal Therapy: A Clinician's Guide*. Oxford: Oxford University Press.

This book outlines a brief model of therapy which seeks to integrate both process- and protocol-based interventions in an approachable and practical fashion.

7.16

WORKPLACE THERAPY

KEVIN FRIERY

OVERVIEW AND KEY POINTS

This section looks specifically at the provision of therapy to employees and explores the different contexts within which this may be offered. Key points include:

- At a time when there is a political drive to make work a health outcome, the role of the workplace counsellor has come into sharp focus in the arenas of engagement, performance, productivity and wellbeing. These are rarely features of a basic therapy training course and the argument is made that workplace therapy is a specialism within the profession.
- With over 50% of the working population in the United Kingdom (UK) having access to Employee Assistance Programmes, there are other delivery models that support many more workers so that, in the last few decades, access to therapy via an employer-provided service has become the norm for employees.
- Workplace therapy calls on therapists to engage beyond the 'I and Thou', and introduces multiple stakeholders into the relationship.
- This section enlarges on this and looks at the science and evidence behind different approaches, posing some challenges for those who want to work in this field.

BACKGROUND AND CONTEXT

Workplace Counselling has a long and complex history. Its origins are hard to pin down precisely. Industrialists like the Lever family and the great Quaker chocolate firms of Cadbury, Rowntree and Fry were certainly at the forefront of recognising the need to treat workers well and to meet their social needs, to such an extent that communities such as Port Sunlight and Bournville were created not only to house the workers, but also to provide a social infrastructure, including education and economic activity beyond the workplace. This was in contrast to employment norms at the time that simply saw employees as units of production. Fast forward from that to the First World War of 1914–18 and, with men going to fight, more women entered the workplace. They

brought with them needs and demands that employers had not previously addressed, including welfare needs, and it became clear that it would be impossible to sustain a high-performing workforce with limited amounts of absence and unrest without a different approach to the employer/employee relationship. Thus, the first seeds of workplace wellbeing were sown.

From then, several strands developed. In post-Prohibition America there was great concern about the extent of alcohol use among workers, so some employers developed Alcohol Prevention programmes. It has been said (perhaps apocryphally) that today's Employee Assistance Programmes (EAPs) first started in the United States of America as Employee Alcohol Programmes. Whether this is true or not, the fact remains that for some workers this was their first opportunity to access help for psychological and behavioural problems funded by their employer. The health insurance regime in the United States also played a significant part. Insurance companies there picked up the cost of treatment programmes and consequently the insurance premium for a specific employer can be directly affected by the extent to which the workforce experiences problems. An employer who funds an Employee Assistance Programme that supports wellbeing will find itself paying significantly lower health insurance premiums – often at a reduction that more than compensates for the cost of the EAP – hence, the emergence and prevalence of such services.

Increased employment legislation in the UK put more pressure on employers to consider the psychological hazards that their workers may face at work, and for over 40 years the Health and Safety at Work etc. Act 1974 has been in place to put a legal obligation on employers to think and act in this arena. Eventually, the all-embracing role of 'Personnel Management' gave way to separate activities of welfare, occupational health, counselling and advice. 'Personnel' became 'Human Relations – HR', which was more involved with strategic organisational issues rather than the nitty-gritty of individual problems, which were now dealt with by other professionals. It was in this context that Workplace Counselling emerged as a recognised professional activity.

Alongside changes in workplace legislation, there have also been social and cultural changes that have created a new engagement between employee and employer. Employers have recognised that wellbeing, as a holistic concept, is a significant indicator of economic performance and employees have recognised that it is possible and acceptable to access help and support to bring about desired change. Concepts like 'Corporate Social Responsibility', through which employers demonstrate their commitment to a larger constituency, have led to improved boardroom commitment to psychological health, while the work of MacKay et al. (2004) has highlighted the evidence linking workplace and stress, at the same time giving pointers to employers about the ways in which they can mitigate this.

All of this provides a backdrop and context for today's workplace therapy.

The other major factor that influences the provision and delivery of workplace therapy is the reasons that lie behind the commissioning of such a service.

Research published as long ago as 1998 showed the direct link between stress and employee absence (Borrill et al., 1998). This helped to strengthen the argument in favour of workplace therapy for those employers who recognised this link and wanted to make a difference. The National Health Service (NHS), for example, responded by setting out the case for counselling for NHS staff (Greenwood, 2001) and citing the 1998 work as part of the argument. For some employers, as we will see below, absence management is a key commissioning driver, but this is not the only driver. As we mentioned above, changes in the workplace have led to a shift in the way people management is achieved. Increasingly, line managers are responsible for a wider range of employee support and they are expected to address the psychological health of their direct reports as well as what might be called task fulfilment – the historic role of managers. To support people in this new world of work, workplace therapy is seen as an asset that aids managers while meeting the needs of employees.

Inherent in all of this discussion is the acceptance that workplace therapy introduces a new level of complexity because there can be two different 'customers' – the employer with a workforce management need and the employee with a personal wellbeing need. Sometimes these coincide, but more often they don't.

WAYS OF WORKING

Counsellors can be involved in workplace therapy in a host of ways. Many people will immediately think of EAPs as the primary touch point, but in fact there are a number of workplace therapy activities in the UK that do not follow this route. Let us start, though, with EAPs and consider how and why they bring therapy to the workforce.

In brief, an EAP contracts with the employer to make its services available to the workforce. Normally this is built around a 24-hour self-referral confidential service, but there are other models. One thing for the counsellor to be aware of is the range of non-therapy services also available under the EAP scheme, because she or he may find it of benefit to refer a client back to these services. For instance, it is not unusual to find legal and financial information available to support an employee who is accessing help to cope with a divorce. Different EAPs have different ways of working, but approximately one third of employees who access a service will have formal session-based therapy, and this introduces a third 'customer' into the picture, so that the counsellor can have the employer, the EAP and the employee all within scope. It can be important for the counsellor to know under what model the client (employee) has been referred. An employer will receive Management Information (MI) regularly, data that show the level of usage along with information about the sorts of reasons for which people have used the service. This MI is presented in a manner that protects the privacy and confidentiality of individuals yet draws a picture for the employer to help with strategic workforce management. The variations to this may have an impact on the level of reporting, hence confidentiality, and other factors. The key thing for the EAP counsellor is to be aware of the parameters and constraints at the outset. The following two hypothetical case examples may help clarify some of the different ways of working.

CASE EXAMPLE 1

John is an employee of a manufacturing company which provides an EAP for its staff. He rings the service and says he is struggling because his children have all grown up and left home and he feels very isolated. His wife died five years ago and he can't cope. He would like therapy.

In this case, the EAP contract allows for a maximum of six sessions per employee per year, so John is referred to a local counsellor to deliver these sessions on behalf of the EAP. The EAP will require some information from the counsellor so that they can case-manage the referral and this will typically involve some form of pre- and post-therapy assessment. The counsellor will work with John for up to six sessions and will then close the case and complete any necessary records for the EAP before ending the engagement. Sometimes the counsellor delivering this service will be an employee of the EAP, but in the great majority of cases the counsellor will be a private practitioner, so will invoice the EAP at the completion of the case. The employer will never know that John used the service (unless he tells them) and the details of his therapy remain confidential between him, the counsellor and the EAP company.

CASE EXAMPLE 2

Mary works for a large bank. She has been facing a number of challenges in her role and her attendance and performance has deteriorated. At a performance review meeting she told her manager she was suffering from some mental health problems and felt out of her depth. The manager referred her to Occupational Health and they met with her to discuss the problems she was facing. With her agreement, Occupational Health contacted the EAP and asked them to provide therapy for Mary. They asked for an assessment and report, outlining the obstacles to better attendance and performance, and also required an end-of-therapy report highlighting any steps the employer could take to support Mary in the future.

Obviously, in this case the confidentiality parameters are quite different, and the employer (through Occupational Health) is setting the agenda for the therapy. It is quite possible to provide ethical, professional therapy in this case so long as all parties are clear that there will be reporting, are clear about who will see any reports and agree that the work will focus on the issues as set out by Occupational Health.

In almost all cases the therapy will be conducted within a handful of sessions. This can pose a challenge for counsellors whose core training has revolved around an open-ended model, and it brings to the fore a key professional ethical issue.

The British Association for Counselling and Psychotherapy (BACP) *Ethical Framework* (2016) sets out the commitment to clients that members and registrants of BACP make to the people they work with. This includes a commitment to:

Work to professional standards by:

a. working within our competence

b. keeping our skills and knowledge up to date....

Counsellors working in short-term therapy need to be competent and skilled in this type of work. It is quite different from open-ended therapy and two of the differences can be highlighted at the outset. First, it starts with an ending – the available maximum number of sessions tell both the counsellor and the client that the work will end no later than a fixed future date or number of sessions. The question for the counsellor is 'What can we do in order to enable us to finish in the available time?' rather than 'Where can we go in this open-ended work?' Second, it requires both counsellor and client to agree on a focus, to acknowledge that there may well be multiple factors at play in the client's life, but that short-term therapy requires some of these to be acknowledged yet set aside during the therapy in order to focus on more achievable outcomes.

Almost 50% of the UK workforce has access to an EAP. More can be found about EAPs from the UK Employee Assistance Professionals Association (www.eapa.org.uk/wp-content/uploads/2014/02/UK-EAPA-GUIDELINES-DOCUMENT.pdf).

Some employers do not use the services of an EAP. In some cases, local counsellors have arrangements with an employer to allow for either self-referral or organisational referral on a case-by-case basis. In such situations, the counsellor needs to have clear and transparent contracting arrangements in place with the referrer. The degree of feedback, for instance, can vary from none at all through to attendance reports and, in some cases, to details of the therapy along with outcome reports. Forging an ethical path through this sometimes requires good use of supervision.

When referrals come from Occupational Health professionals, for instance, the feedback loop may be quite different from when the referral comes from a manager or trades union representative. Feedback from some counsellors has been that becoming the local therapy provider can have mixed outcomes. It is clearly a good strand in building a professional practice, but the problems of being the main provider of therapy means the counsellor hears a lot from different clients who may be moving in the same circles. Cases where a counsellor works with an employee complaining about a difficult workplace relationship and then takes on a client who turns out to be the other party in the workplace issues are not uncommon. Clear boundaries that protect the confidentiality and respect the individuality of each client are essential components of the workplace counsellor toolkit.

In a small number of workplaces, counsellors can be found directly employed by the organisation. There are examples of this in some NHS hospitals. Greenwood (2001) explores this further. Staff therapy services typically are managed by an experienced Therapy Manager, who provides a mixture of line management, case management and supervision. One of the hazards in this situation is that both counsellor and client have the same employer. There is a risk of collusion if they both have similar experiences of the employer, for instance, and counsellors need to work carefully to retain professional detachment without becoming enmeshed in workplace politics. This is not to suggest it always works this way, just that it is a risk to be aware of. There are many very effective staff therapy services and this can be a route into the profession of workplace therapy.

RESEARCH EVIDENCE

Research into workplace therapy has been conducted over the last few decades but it has not always applied the most rigorous methodologies. McLeod (2010: 238) reported that 'the results of research suggest that counselling is generally effective in alleviating psychological problems, has a significant impact on sickness absence, and has a moderate effect on attitudes to work'. Chan (2011) conducted a meta-analysis and found that:

studies indicate that workplace counselling improves employee well-being; the intervention helps employees in alleviating symptoms of workplace stress, burnout and depression. However, workplace counselling seems to have neutral effect on employee performance, although some studies reported reduction in absenteeism and positive impact on work performance. Regardless of the outcome to the organisation, employees almost unanimously reported satisfaction with the workplace counselling sessions and found them to be helpful, personally and professionally.

Chan's research highlights an important point in workplace therapy – it is not all about an obvious return for the organisation; the psychological benefits for an individual employee may be entirely about her or his own internal world, without having a measurable workplace impact. Of course, we would expect to find that one impacts the other, but the primary measurement may well be about individual wellbeing rather than about performance, productivity or engagement.

Collins et al. (2012) compared a treatment group with a non-treatment control group over a number of months, with the treatment group receiving an average of seven sessions of counselling. They found that the provision of time-limited therapy by employers is an effective support for personal difficulties affecting work.

In considering the research, and research design, one of the important questions to ask is 'What is the objective of the therapy on offer?' In the workplace this has added dimensions because, as mentioned earlier, different people may have different expectations of the same piece of work. The employer may be hoping for better attendance or engagement, whereas the individual may have different priorities. Using standardised validated assessment tools is an essential element but the different tools have a different focus. They can be split roughly into measures of symptom reduction and measures of qualitative improvement. Increasingly, the Warwick and Edinburgh Mental Wellbeing Scale (WEMWBS) is being used to demonstrate improvements in subjective wellbeing, and this was the tool used in the Cambridge study reported by Collins et al. (2012).

REFERENCES

Borrill, C.S. et al. (1998) *Stress among Staff in NHS Trusts: Final Report*. Sheffield: Institute of Work Psychology, University of Sheffield.
British Association for Counselling and Psychotherapy (2016) *Ethical Framework for the Counselling Professions*. Lutterworth: BACP.

Chan, Y.K. (2011) *How Effective is Workplace Counselling in Improving Employee Well-Being and Performance?* Master's dissertation, University of Leicester.

Collins, J. et al. (2012) Counselling in the workplace: how time-limited counselling can effect change in well-being. *Counselling & Psychotherapy Research*, 12(2): 84–92.

Greenwood, A. (2001) *Counselling for Staff in Health Care Settings*. London: Royal College of Nursing (amendments 2006 by Shane Buckeridge).

MacKay, C.J. et al. (2004) 'Management Standards' and work-related stress in the UK: policy background and science. *Work & Stress*, 18(2): 91–112.

McLeod, J. (2010) The effectiveness of workplace counselling: a systematic review. *Counselling and Psychotherapy Research*, 10(4): 238–248.

RECOMMENDED READING

1. Coles, A. (2003) *Counselling in the Workplace*. London: McGraw-Hill Education.

This is an excellent primer for those who want to understand this counselling context in more detail. Coles has an extensive understanding of the issues and brings his experience to the fore to help readers understand more.

2. Hughes, R. and Kinder, A. (2007) *Guidelines for Counselling in the Workplace*. Lutterworth: British Association for Counselling and Psychotherapy.

These helpful guidelines are essential reading today. Both authors have worked in the field for a long time and are considered among the leading practitioners in the UK. The booklet can be accessed for free at http://bacpworkplace.or.uk.

3. Feltham, C. (1997) *Time-limited Counselling* (Vol. 1). London: Sage.

This book is part of an essential library for someone wishing to understand and work in this way. Feltham takes a professional skills approach and helps the counsellor to marry the two key components – effectiveness and efficiency – by exploring the evidence with helpful examples.

THERAPEUTIC SPECIALISMS: LIFESPAN ISSUES

7.17 COUNSELLING CHILDREN

KATHRYN GELDARD, DAVID GELDARD AND REBECCA YIN FOO

OVERVIEW AND KEY POINTS

An introduction to counselling children is provided in this chapter. First, differences between counselling children and counselling young people or adults are highlighted before different approaches to counselling children are identified. An integrative model of counselling children is then introduced to provide a framework for drawing on different approaches that best fit a particular stage of the counselling process. The chapter concludes with an exploration of the research base for counselling children.

- Counselling children is different from counselling young people or adults, therefore a different approach is required.
- Approaches to counselling children include non-directive play therapy, creative and expressive therapies, gestalt therapy, time-limited play therapy, cognitive-behavioural therapy and family therapy.
- The integrative 'sequentially planned integrative counselling for children' (SPICC) model is designed to draw on various approaches that best fit each stage of the counselling process.
- There is a growing research base for the effectiveness of counselling children.

BACKGROUND AND CONTEXT

Counselling children is different from counselling young people or adults. Whereas many young people and most adults seek counselling of their own volition, children are usually brought by their parents or significant other adults. The adults involved likely have agendas of their own, therefore are also involved in the therapeutic process in some way. Additionally, children live in families and their emotional and behavioural problems occur within, and likely result in some consequences for, the family system. Therefore, a counsellor usually needs to address the intrapersonal issues of the child in individual counselling, along with systemic issues involving parents and/or family which may be causing, maintaining and/or a consequence of the child's problems.

Adults are generally comfortable and able to explore and resolve their issues in a conversational relationship with a counsellor. Although some children are able to do this, many cannot share troubling issues using only conversational strategies. Media and activity can, therefore, be used to engage the child, enable them to talk about troubling issues and help the child find resolution of their issues.

Although many children engaging in counselling have underlying emotional problems, they are commonly brought to counselling only after adults notice behavioural problems. For successful therapeutic outcomes, counsellors need to address both emotional and behavioural issues.

While usual limitations imposed by ethical considerations apply to confidentiality with adults, confidentiality with children is confounded by the rights of the parents' access to information also. If a child is to talk freely, they must have some confidence that the information they share is treated respectfully and not disclosed without good reason (Fox and Butler, 2007; Jenkins, 2010).

In light of the differences highlighted above, specialist skills are required to be developed under a counselling supervisor who is trained and experienced in working with children. Additionally, ongoing supervision is essential to ensure good practice.

WAYS OF WORKING

Several therapeutic approaches can be used when counselling children, including:

- non-directive play therapy
- creative and expressive therapy
- gestalt therapy
- time-limited play therapy
- cognitive-behavioural therapy
- family therapy.

Each of these approaches has advantages and limitations. The literature suggests that there is not one preferred way of working appropriate for all children. Some counsellors practise flexibly, selecting a method of working suitable for a particular child and their issues. This 'prescriptive approach' was proposed by Millman and Schaefer (1977). An alternative is an integrative approach incorporating ideas from a number of therapeutic frameworks. The counsellor, for example, selects and makes use of strategies from multiple therapeutic approaches with the goal of meeting a child's needs as they arise. Whatever approach is used, a number of goals can usefully be achieved when counselling children. These include:

- To help the child gain mastery over issues and events.
- To enable the child to feel empowered.
- To help the child develop problem-solving and decision-making skills.
- To build the child's self-concept and self-esteem.
- To improve the child's communication skills.
- To help the child develop insight.

NON-DIRECTIVE PLAY THERAPY

Non-directive play therapy is one means of assisting children with self-expression, when facilitated by the therapist (Axline, 1989 [1947]; Landreth, 2002; Ray et al., 2001). Non-directive approaches to therapeutic play are used to support the child's developing self within the safe boundaries provided by the setting and the counsellor's emotional holding and containment (McMahon, 2009). The counsellor observes the child as they play without direction with media including children's toys, toy furniture, and materials such as clay, paint and crayons. The counsellor's observations might include mood or affect, intellectual functioning, thinking processes, speech and language, motor skills, play, and the relationship with the counsellor.

CREATIVE AND EXPRESSIVE THERAPY

Through their emotional reactions to internal needs, children develop internal working models (IWMs) of their social world (Johnson et al., 2007). As children mature they further develop their emotional understanding, expression and regulation by building on their IWMs. Strategies which address the physiology of emotional processing, and hence target unconscious IWMs, may be useful when working with children (Wright et al., 2009). Literature provides evidence that creative techniques can be used to access and modify unconscious aspects of self, such as implicit emotional memories and IWMs (Gantt and Tinnin, 2009; Glover, 1999; Harris, 2009; Herman, 1997; Walker, 1998). Sand play and symbol work are creative therapeutic tools that can access and allow expression of the child's inner world, hence reveal unconscious processes and dilemmas, bringing them into a representational form that allows resolution. Margaret Lowenfeld pioneered this approach with the aim of helping children communicate without the use of language (Schaefer and O'Connor, 1994). She used objects as symbols in a sand tray to encourage non-verbal expression less influenced by rational thinking (Ryce-Menuhin, 1992). Many counsellors use sand tray to engage the child and enable them to talk openly and explore their issues (Sweeney et al., 2009). Sand tray work is useful in helping children to tell their story, explore issues and express emotions.

GESTALT THERAPY

Oaklander (1988, 2011) and Blom (2006) combine the use of gestalt therapy principles and practice with media when working with children. Oaklander uses fantasy and/or metaphor, and believes that usually the fantasy process will be the same as the life process in the child. She therefore works indirectly in bringing out what is hidden or avoided, relying on a projective process. Although this works well for some children, others may have difficulty making the connection between fantasy and real life. Other counsellors use gestalt therapy in a more direct way. As the child engages with media and/or activity, they will use gestalt techniques to raise awareness while the child tells their story. For example, Blom (2006) uses a stage-related process to build a relationship and assess and develop a treatment plan followed by contact-making and building self-support in children, emotional expression, self-nurturing, addressing inappropriate processes and termination.

TIME-LIMITED PLAY THERAPY

This approach uses ideas from brief psychodynamic therapy (Sloves and Belinger-Peterlin, 1986). A brief assessment of the child's issues is made before the counsellor selects a central theme to work with. Counselling focuses on empowerment, adaptation, strengthening the ego and the future rather than the past. Generally, work with the child is limited to 12 sessions. This form of therapy is directive and interpretative. It is effective for some children and not others (Schaefer and O'Connor, 1994). It is particularly effective for children with recent post-traumatic stress disorder and adjustment disorders, and for children who have lost a parent to a chronic medical condition (Christ et al., 1991).

COGNITIVE-BEHAVIOURAL THERAPY

An educational model described by Beck (1995) and developed more recently (Friedberg et al., 2009), cognitive-behavioural therapy (CBT) describes the connection between thoughts, emotions and behaviours. Current thoughts, which are driving the child's emotions and behaviours, are explored. The goal is to enable the child to replace unhelpful thoughts with more adaptive ones. When working with children using CBT, media and activity are useful. Worksheets, drawing and role-playing might be used to help the child explore their current thoughts and behaviours and practise new ways of thinking and behaving.

CBT tends to be popular with health services which have limited financial resources as the process is short term, involving a few counselling sessions. CBT is useful in enabling many children to gain a level of control over emotions and behaviours. One limitation is that it does not directly target emotions or encourage emotional release. Also, the approach requires reasonably good language skills, and a level of cognitive development and emotional maturity. Without this, the child will not understand the educational model, and may not be able to interrupt emotional outbursts by making changes to their thinking. Consequently, it is not suitable for very young children.

CBT is often used with behavioural psychotherapy where incentives are used to reinforce positive behaviour, and there are consequences for undesirable behaviour. Behaviour therapy can be used with children of all ages.

FAMILY THERAPY

This approach is discussed in Chapter 7.20 in this volume. Some counsellors believe it is sufficient to explore and resolve a child's emotional and behavioural problems within the context of the family system. This can be very effective for some children. However, many children who attend counselling are troubled by emotional issues and/or thoughts which are highly personal and which they may not be able to talk about in the family context.

ECLECTIC AND INTEGRATIVE COUNSELLING

Some counsellors like to use a particular therapeutic approach, but others prefer to work in an integrative or eclectic way by using, for example, the prescriptive (Millman and Schaefer, 1977) and integrative approaches described earlier in this chapter. Both approaches can have positive outcomes. However, there is a risk that the process of counselling might be compromised by the inappropriate selection and/or sequence of strategies used. An alternative is an integrative model where strategies from particular therapeutic approaches are intentionally used at particular points in the therapeutic process.

THE SPICC MODEL

The 'sequentially planned integrative counselling for children' model (the SPICC model) is an integrative approach which we developed and use ourselves (Geldard, Geldard and Yin Foo, 2017). This model divides the counselling process into a sequence of stages.

Before using the SPICC model, we try to engage the family in family therapy to gain a full understanding of family dynamics and the child in the context of the family system. Sometimes after family therapy we discover that the problem has been resolved and no further therapeutic work is required. At other times, the child with the presenting problem, or another child in the family, may experience emotional distress requiring individual counselling using the SPICC model.

The SPICC model involves the following sequence: joining with the child, enabling the child to tell their story, raising the child's awareness so they get in touch with and express emotions, helping the child to cognitively restructure, helping the child to look into options and choices, and enabling the child to rehearse and experiment with new behaviours.

SAND PLAY WORK

In the initial stage the counsellor joins with and engages the child using media and/or activity. A counsellor might use symbols in the sand tray, or with older children, who are cognitively able to use a projective technique, miniature animals to represent family members. In the sand tray, the child can be encouraged to use objects as symbols to make a picture in the sand of their world and/or family as they perceive it. The activity component enables the child to feel relaxed rather than pressured to talk. As the picture in the sand tray develops, the counsellor can explore its meaning with the child and help the child talk about their life.

USE OF GESTALT THERAPY

Once a trusting relationship has been established, the counsellor can use media and/or activity together with gestalt therapy awareness-raising techniques to help the child connect with troubling emotions. The use of media and/or activity maintains the child's interest, allows them to anchor their story, and ensures the child has time to process thoughts rather than feel pressured to talk.

As the child's awareness is raised, the counsellor might encourage the release of troubling emotions through the use of media such as clay, or an activity such as painting and drawing.

USE OF COGNITIVE-BEHAVIOURAL THERAPY AND BEHAVIOUR THERAPY

The next stage is to target any unhelpful and/or maladaptive thoughts and behaviours in order to restructure unhelpful thinking patterns using CBT. Change is unlikely and emotional distress will probably recur if this stage is overlooked. Similarly, the child needs to be encouraged to explore their options and choices regarding current and future behaviour. The new behaviour can be reinforced using a behaviour therapy approach with the parents' cooperation.

INTEGRATION OF INDIVIDUAL AND FAMILY WORK

During the individual counselling process with the child there may be times when it is useful for the child to share information with their parents or family. Towards the end of the therapeutic process it can be useful to re-engage the whole family in family therapy so that any changes can be reinforced and supported and remaining problems can be addressed.

RESEARCH EVIDENCE

A number of review articles and books have now been published summarising the research into the effectiveness of counselling children (e.g., Lin and Bratton, 2015; Midgley et al., 2009). As counsellors, familiarising ourselves with this research can enhance our practice. Review studies have found moderate to large effect sizes supporting the effectiveness of counselling children across behavioural, cognitive-behavioural and play therapy approaches. Furthermore, counselling children is effective across a range of challenges that children may face, including 'global behavioral problems, internalizing behavior problems, externalizing behavioral problems, caregiver-child relationship stress, self-efficacy, academic performance, and other presenting issues' (Lin and Bratton, 2015: 52).

REFERENCES

Axline, V.M. (1989 [1947]) *Play Therapy*. London: Ballantine Books.

Beck, J.S. (1995) *Cognitive Therapy: Basics and Beyond*. New York: Guilford Press.

Blom, R. (2006) *The Handbook of Gestalt Play Therapy: Practical Guidelines for Child Therapists*. London: Jessica Kingsley Publishers.

Christ, G.H., Siegel, K., Mesagno, F. and Langosch, D. (1991) A preventative intervention program for bereaved children: problems of implementation. *Journal of Orthopsychiatry*, 61(2): 168–178.

Fox, C. and Butler, I. (2007) 'If you don't want to tell anyone else, you can tell her': young people's views on school counselling. *British Journal of Guidance & Counselling*, 35(1): 97–114.

Friedberg, R.D., McClure, J. and Garcia, J.H. (2009) *Cognitive Therapy Techniques for Children and Adolescents: Tools for Enhancing Practice*. New York: Guilford Press.

Gantt, L. and Tinnin, L.W. (2009) Support for a neurobiological view of trauma with implications for art therapy. *The Arts in Psychotherapy*, 36(3): 148–153.

Geldard, K., Geldard, D. and Yin Foo, R. (2017) *Counselling Children: A Practical Introduction* (5th ed.). London: Sage.

Glover, N.M. (1999) Play therapy and art therapy for substance abuse clients who have a history of incest victimization. *Journal of Substance Abuse Treatment*, 16(4): 281–287.

Harris, D.A. (2009) The paradox of expressing speechless terror: ritual liminality in the creative arts therapies' treatment of posttraumatic distress. *The Arts in Psychotherapy*, 36(2): 94–104.

Herman, L. (1997) Good enough fairy tales for resolving sexual abuse trauma. *The Arts in Psychotherapy*, 24(5): 439–445.

(Continued)

(Continued)

Jenkins, P. (2010) Having confidence in therapeutic work with young people: constraints and challenges to confidentiality. *British Journal of Guidance & Counselling*, 38(3): 263–274.

Johnson, S.C., Dweck, C.S. and Chen, F.S. (2007) Evidence for infants' internal working models of attachment. *Psychological Science*, 18(6): 501–502.

Landreth, G.L. (2002) *Play Therapy: The Art of the Relationship* (2nd ed.). New York: Bruner-Routledge.

Lin, Y.-W. and Bratton, S.C. (2015) A meta-analytic review of child-centered play therapy approaches. *Journal of Counseling & Development*, 93(1): 45–58.

McMahon, L. (2009) *The Handbook of Play Therapy and Therapeutic Play* (2nd ed.). New York: Routledge/Taylor.

Midgley, N., Anderson, J., Grainger, E., Nesic-Vuckovic, T. and Urwin, C. (eds) (2009) *Child Psychotherapy and Research: New Approaches, Emerging Findings*. London: Routledge.

Millman, H.L. and Schaefer, C.E. (1977) *Therapies for Children*. San Francisco, CA: Jossey-Bass.

Oaklander, V. (1988) *Windows to Our Children*. New York: Center for Gestalt Development.

Oaklander, V. (2011) Gestalt play therapy. In C.E. Schaefer (ed.), *Foundations of Play Therapy* (2nd ed., pp. 171–186). Hoboken, NJ: Wiley.

Ray, D., Bratton, S., Rhine, T. and Jones, L. (2001) The effectiveness of play therapy: responding to the critics. *International Journal of Play Therapy*, 10(1): 85–108.

Ryce-Menuhin, J. (1992) *Jungian Sandplay: The Wonderful Therapy*. New York: Routledge/Chapman and Hall.

Schaefer, C.E. and O'Connor, K.J. (eds) (1994) *Handbook of Play Therapy*. Vol. 2: *Advances and Innovations*. New York: Wiley.

Sloves, R. and Belinger-Peterlin, K. (1986) The process of time-limited psychotherapy with latency-aged children. *Journal of the American Academy of Child Psychiatry*, 25(6): 847–851.

Sweeney, D.S., Homeyer, L.E. and Drewes, A. (2009) Blending play therapy with cognitive behavioral therapy: evidence-based and other effective treatments and techniques. In D. Sweeney and L. Homeyer (eds), *Sandtray Therapy* (pp. 297–318). Hoboken, NJ: Wiley.

Walker, S.C. (1998) Stories of two children: making sense of children's therapeutic work. *The Arts in Psychotherapy*, 25(4): 263–275.

Wright, M.O., Crawford, E. and Del Castillo, D. (2009) Childhood emotional maltreatment and later psychological distress among college students: the mediating role of maladaptive schemas. *Child Abuse & Neglect*, 33: 59–68.

RECOMMENDED READING

1. Geldard, K., Geldard, D. and Yin Foo, R. (2013) *Counselling Children: A Practical Introduction* (4th ed.). London: Sage.

The book outlines an integrative and practical approach to working with children.

2. Geldard, K. and Geldard, D. (2001) *Working with Children in Groups: A Handbook for Counsellors, Educators and Community Workers*. New York: Palgrave Macmillian.

For those wanting to extend their skills to supporting children in a group environment, this book is a useful introduction.

3. Midgley, N., Anderson, J., Grainger, E., Nesic-Vuckovic, T. and Urwin, C. (eds) (2009) *Child Psychotherapy and Research: New Approaches, Emerging Findings*. London: Routledge.

This book provides an overview of the current research into counselling children.

7.18

7.18 COUNSELLING YOUNG PEOPLE

KATHRYN GELDARD, DAVID GELDARD AND REBECCA YIN FOO

OVERVIEW AND KEY POINTS

This chapter describes the principles and practices for counselling young people in the adolescent stage. To help young people effectively, a counselling approach designed to fit with their developmental stage and take account of their typical communication processes is required. This approach enables a collaborative working relationship to be developed with the young person. The chapter concludes by exploring the evidence base for counselling young people.

- Two major challenges young people face are the process of individuation and developing a personal identity, and re-evaluating constructs about their world.
- Using typical adolescent communication processes is important when counselling young people.
- A proactive counselling approach draws on symbolic, creative, behavioural and psycho-educational strategies to create an effective environment and counselling relationship.
- There is growing research evidence for the effectiveness of counselling young people.

BACKGROUND AND CONTEXT

THE ADOLESCENT STAGE OF DEVELOPMENT

Young people experience biological, cognitive, psychological, social, moral and spiritual challenges during adolescence. Two major challenges are the need for young people to individuate and establish a personal identity, and the struggle to re-evaluate constructs about their world.

INDIVIDUATION AND THE ESTABLISHMENT OF A PERSONAL IDENTITY

Whereas a child is primarily joined with parents and family, during adolescence a young person develops a level of relative independence and increased capacity to assume a functional role in adult society (Nelson and Nelson, 2010). This process of socialisation balances individuation

together with formation of personal identity, and integration with society (Fadjukoff and Pulkkinen, 2006). Unless balance is achieved, personal crises which may require counselling are likely.

CONTINUAL RE-EVALUATION OF CONSTRUCTS

According to Piaget (1966 [1948]), during the early adolescent stage young people typically move from concrete thinking to being able to deal cognitively with ideas, concepts and abstract theories, becoming able to discern what is real from what is ideal.

Constructivist theory explains how we try to make sense of the world by forming constructs (Fransella et al., 2007). Young people use personal experiences to develop ideas or beliefs, thereby forming constructs, about their world. These personal constructs will be revised and replaced as new information emerges via new, previously unmet experiences during adolescence (Kelly, 1955; Winter, 2003).

Because young people are continually revising their constructs, a counsellor needs to actively listen in order to explore, understand and respect the constructs underlying the young person's personal narrative. The counsellor can then select therapeutic strategies which fit with the young person's constructs. The narrative therapy work of White and Epston (Becvar, 2008) highlights the value of this process when working with young people.

WAYS OF WORKING

ESTABLISHING AND MAINTAINING A THERAPEUTIC ALLIANCE

The quality of the therapeutic relationship is critical in influencing outcomes and client satisfaction (Safran and Muran, 2000). It is desirable that the counselling relationship be an authentic person-to-person relationship, accepting and understanding, and warm and empathic.

Acceptance and understanding are particularly important because young people can feel judged and criticised by adults. They are unlikely to talk freely if they believe negative judgements are being made. Counsellors need, as far as possible, to accept and validate the young person's story and constructs without judgement.

A counsellor can enhance their opportunity to establish and maintain a positive working relationship with a young person by:

- making use of typical adolescent communication processes
- using a proactive approach.

MAKING USE OF TYPICAL ADOLESCENT COMMUNICATION PROCESSES

Many counsellors find it difficult to join with young people in a way that enables them to talk freely. Indeed, young people are generally reluctant to talk to adults about sensitive issues (Boldero and Fallon, 1995; Gibson-Cline, 1996). Making use of strategies commonly employed by young people when they communicate can be helpful.

When young people meet with peers they usually engage in some of the following behaviours (Seiffge-Krenke et al., 2010):

- positively connote the other person's presentation, including appearance, behaviours and adornments or possessions
- use direct closed questions to get information
- disclose information about themselves and assume others will self-disclose
- validate other's views, if possible
- use praise when relevant
- be very direct about what they like and do not like
- match and exaggerate other's emotional expressions.

Additionally, we have noticed that many young people tend to:

- frequently digress, move away from a topic, then return to it
- take the lead in conversation and feel in control of it
- give and receive advice.

As counsellors, we can learn from, and use, these communication processes when appropriate.

BELIEVING AND ACCEPTING THE YOUNG PERSON'S CONSTRUCTS

Generally, young people will validate each other's points of view by sharing their beliefs, attitudes and constructs, examining these together, and possibly revising them

(Geldard, 2006). Even if we do not agree, we can validate and accept a young person by letting them know we understand their beliefs, attitudes and constructs. This creates the opportunity to collaboratively help them explore, review and revise their constructs within a genuine, open and honest relationship.

POSITIVELY JOINING IN DIGRESSIONS

Young people tend to frequently digress from a topic and talk about something else, before returning to it. We believe this digression and then return to a topic has useful purposes.

Because young people are continually revising their constructs, they are often trying to grapple with many different ideas. Digression allows them to deal with new thoughts without putting them on hold.

Digression also allows a young person some respite from discussing troubling issues. After a less intense conversation, they may feel ready to return to distressing issues. Similarly, young people often experience powerful emotions as they confront new and challenging experiences. During counselling, they may worry about getting in touch with, or feeling overwhelmed by, emotion. Allowing young people to digress away from intense emotions when needed can foster safety in the counselling environment.

Sometimes a young person will become distracted and withdraw from the counselling process. This distraction may serve the same purpose as digression, allowing an escape from talking about important but troubling issues. Alternatively, they may have lost the desire to continue talking, and consequently have become distracted.

In response to distraction, the counsellor can introduce a digression. If the young person starts to play with their shoes, the counsellor might say, 'I had some shoes like those, but mine weren't very comfortable. What are yours like?' While the conversation will no longer involve addressing issues, a low-key conversation will develop likely helping the young person relax, regain energy and develop a closer connection with the counsellor. The counsellor can then help the young person return to important issues by using, for example, a transitional question such as, 'Earlier we were talking about … would you like to tell me more about that?'

APPROPRIATE USE OF SELF-DISCLOSURE

Most counsellors working with adults believe counsellor self-disclosure should be strictly limited or non-existent. However, we believe there are good reasons for appropriate self-disclosure when working with young people.

Appropriate counsellor self-disclosure enables young people to more comfortably self-disclose to us. When a counsellor shares personal information, the young person is implicitly invited to relate as an equal to another real person with feelings and experiences potentially similar to their own. However, it is not appropriate or ethical for self-disclosure to lead to undesirable closeness and over-involvement by the counsellor.

Generally, counsellor self-disclosure should not include the counsellor's own problems, unless these are minor, resolved, and useful for joining or demonstrating depth of understanding. For example, if a young person is discussing their parents' separation, and if the counsellor has had a similar experience, then disclosure might be appropriate. Self-disclosure may normalise the grief experience and encourage the young person to disclose more information. When using self-disclosure, the focus must always remain on the young person's problems.

Counsellors need to acknowledge that full understanding is impossible because two experiences will never be identical. This acknowledgement invites the young person to talk more about their own personal experience and to avoid matching their responses inappropriately to the counsellor's.

BEING DIRECT

Most young people are direct about what they like and what they don't. To foster a counselling relationship, young people need to see us as real people who are open about who we are. It can therefore be useful to be more direct about our values and beliefs compared to working with adults. However, we need to respect the young person by letting them know we accept their values and beliefs, even though they may be different.

Young people typically make use of direct closed questions during peer conversations. Similarly, many young people like a direct approach from the counsellor. In contrast, adults prefer more circumspect questioning, allowing them to reveal the information they choose.

MATCHING AND EXAGGERATING

Young people typically match and exaggerate each other's emotional expressions. As counsellors, we can learn from the lively, energetic and dynamic communication of young people and ourselves be energised when communicating with them.

USE OF PRAISE

Most young people use praise naturally when communicating with peers. Similarly, counsellors can endorse a young person's beliefs or behaviour using positive feedback in a genuine, not patronising, way.

GIVING ADVICE

Typically, when young people are uncertain about what to do, they ask peers for advice to gain another point of view. They are less likely to approach a parent because they want to make their own decisions without parental direction. When asking for advice, it is unlikely they, or their friend, will expect the advice to be followed (Geldard, 2006), whereas adults usually expect their advice to be taken. Advice-giving, then, for young people, involves sharing ideas about possible solutions rather than giving advice to be adopted.

Empowering adult clients to find their own solutions is generally preferred to advice-giving. This is also true for young people who don't want to be told what to do. However, young people also expect counsellors to give advice (Gibson-Cline, 1996) and have experience and knowledge they do not, that may be useful for construct formation. When a young person seeks advice, we believe it is helpful to join with them and offer to explore their situation, possible solutions and consequences. Hence, the young person is invited into a collaborative process of mutual sharing of ideas and information.

USING A PROACTIVE APPROACH

When compared with counselling children or adults, counselling young people needs to be more flexible. Young people are generally less engaged in a counselling process which follows sequentially through stages. They may have difficulty articulating their challenges, possibly moving between subjects and exploring seemingly disconnected parts of their world. Counsellors can therefore use strategies that enable young people to draw their ideas and beliefs together to form constructs, helping them make sense of their world.

The counsellor also needs to use ways to explore that are similar to those young people generally use. They need to be proactively spontaneous, creative, flexible and opportunistic, while continually attending to the counselling relationship. Being proactive involves taking responsibility for responding to the young person by introducing new direction and counselling strategies when appropriate. However, the young person must understand they have *choice* about what they say and do, to avoid feeling controlled when the counsellor takes the initiative by focusing the process.

Preferably, the counselling relationship is not predominantly intense or serious. There should be balance between serious matters and pleasant times involving friendly conversation and/or humour. Indeed, humour can be a useful treatment technique when working with young people (Radomska, 2007; Yuan et al., 2008).

Figure 7.18.1 illustrates a proactive process for counselling young people. The central feature involves supporting the therapeutic alliance by attending to the relationship, and collaboratively addressing the issues presented. While focusing on these primary counselling functions, the counsellor can proactively introduce counselling skills, as described in Geldard and Geldard (2005, 2016a, b) and parallel typical adolescent communication processes. Additionally, the counsellor can introduce, at appropriate times, symbolic, creative, behavioural, or psycho-educational strategies as described in Geldard, Geldard and Yin Foo (2016a, b).

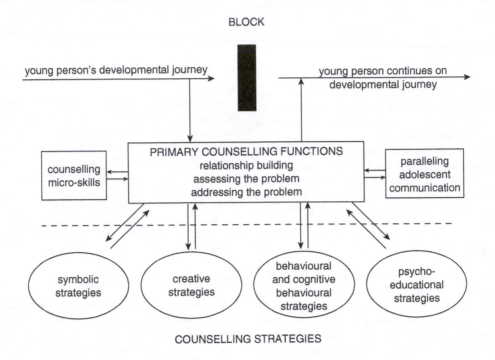

Figure 7.18.1 The proactive counselling process

SYMBOLIC, CREATIVE, BEHAVIOURAL AND PSYCHO-EDUCATIONAL STRATEGIES

Symbolic strategies include metaphor, ritual, symbols, sand tray and miniature animals. These strategies can support a young person to talk about sensitive issues in a non-threatening way. Additionally, they may enable a young person to get more fully in touch with their experience and therefore re-evaluate their constructs. Creative strategies involve art, role-play, journals, relaxation, imagination and dream work. These strategies appeal to many young people who like using artistic expression. Behavioural strategies are useful for addressing issues involving self-regulation, unhelpful beliefs, anger management, assertiveness training, lifestyle goals and decision-making. Psycho-educational strategies can be used to enable the young person to share

information, explain relationships and/or behaviour, and examine ways to change behaviour.

During a counselling session, one or more strategies may be utilised. The counsellor can proactively select and introduce relevant strategies at particular times. Being proactive involves taking responsibility for orchestrating the counselling process to fulfil the primary counselling functions, while allowing the young person freedom to explore and resolve issues. Counselling strategies are selected in response to the young person's cognitive, emotional, somatic, verbal and non-verbal behaviours and the presenting issues.

MAKING EACH SESSION COMPLETE IN ITSELF

Many young people come to see a counsellor during a crisis but do not believe it is helpful to continue following the crisis. Young people often return when a new crisis occurs, particularly if they had a positive experience of counselling previously. Furthermore, because of their developmental stage, young people may be unreliable with keeping appointments. Hence, it is useful to assume each appointment with a young person may be the last. Achieving a level of completion in single-session therapy (SST) is, therefore, a useful goal when counselling young people. Indeed, SST appears to be an empirically supported and cost-effective therapy for children and adolescents with a range of mental health problems (e.g., Perkins and Scarlett, 2008).

RESEARCH EVIDENCE

There is a large and growing research base for the effectiveness of counselling young people (e.g., Midgley, Hayes and Cooper, 2017; Pattison and Harris, 2006). The research covers multiple approaches, including 'cognitive-behavioural; psychoanalytic; humanistic; and creative therapies', and presenting issues, including 'behavioural problems and conduct disorders; emotional problems including anxiety, depression and post-traumatic stress; medical illness; school-related issues; self-harming practices and sexual abuse' (Pattison and Harris, 2006: 233). While there is evidence for the effectiveness of all counselling approaches for young people, this evidence varied according to presenting issue. For example, there was a larger body of research supporting cognitive-behaviour therapy. Therefore, this approach was found to be effective across a range of issues. This doesn't mean other approaches are less effective, just that more research is needed to build the evidence base.

REFERENCES

Becvar, D.S. (ed.) (2008) The legacy of Michael White. *Contemporary Family Therapy: An International Journal*, 30(3): 139–140.

Boldero, J. and Fallon, B. (1995) Adolescent help-seeking: what do they get help for and from whom? *Journal of Adolescence*, 18(2): 193–209.

Fadjukoff, P. and Pulkkinen, L. (2006) Identity formation, personal control over development, and well-being. In L. Pulkkinen, J. Kaprio and R. Rose (eds), *Socioemotional Development and Health from Adolescence to Adulthood* (pp. 265–285). New York and Cambridge: Cambridge University Press.

Fransella, F., Dalton, P., Weselby, G. and Dryden, W. (2007) Personal construct therapy. In W. Dryden (ed.), *Handbook of Individual Therapy* (5th ed., pp. 173–194). Thousand Oaks, CA: Sage.

Geldard, K. (2006) *Adolescent Peer Counselling*. Doctoral dissertation, Queensland University of Technology, Brisbane, Australia.

Geldard, K. and Geldard, D. (2005) *Practical Counselling Skills: An Integrative Approach*. Basingstoke: Palgrave Macmillan.

Geldard, K., Geldard, D. and Yin Foo, R. (2016a) *Basic Personal Counselling: A Training Manual for Counsellors* (8th ed.). South Melbourne, Vic: Cengage.

Geldard, K., Geldard, D. and Yin Foo, R. (2016b) *Counselling Adolescents: The Proactive Approach for Young People* (4th ed.). London: Sage.

Gibson-Cline, J. (1996) *Adolescence: From Crisis to Coping. A Thirteen Nation Study*. Oxford: Butterworth-Heinemann.

Kelly, G.A. (1955) *The Psychology of Personal Constructs*. New York: W.W. Norton.

Midgley, N., Hayes, J. and Cooper, M. (2017) *Essential Research Findings in Child and Adolescent Counselling and Psychotherapy*. London: Sage.

Nelson, T. and Nelson, J.M. (2010) Evidence-based practice and the culture of adolescence. *Professional Psychology: Research and Practice*, 41(4): 305–311.

Pattison, S. and Harris, B. (2006) Counselling children and young people: a review of the evidence for its effectiveness. *Counselling and Psychotherapy Research*, 6(4): 233–237.

Perkins, R. and Scarlett, G. (2008) The effectiveness of single session therapy in child and adolescent mental health. Part 2: An 18-month follow-up study. *Psychology and Psychotherapy: Theory, Research and Practice*, 81(2): 143–156.

Piaget, J. (1966 [1948]) *Psychology of Intelligence*. New York: Harcourt.

(Continued)

(Continued)

Radomska, A. (2007) Understanding and appreciating humour in late childhood and adolescence. *Polish Psychological Bulletin*, 38(4): 189–197.

Safran, J.D. and Muran, J.C. (2000) *Negotiating the Therapeutic Alliance: A Relational Treatment Guide*. New York: Guilford Press.

Seiffge-Krenke, I., Kiuru, N. and Nurmi, J.-E. (2010) Adolescents as 'producers of their own development': correlates and consequences of the importance and attainment of developmental tasks. *European Journal of Developmental Psychology*, 7(4): 479–510.

Winter, D.A. (2003) The constructivist paradigm. In R. Woolfe and W. Dryden (eds), *Handbook of Counselling Psychology* (2nd ed., pp. 241–259). London: Sage.

Yuan, L., Zhang, J. and Chen, M. (2008) Moderating role of sense of humor to the relationship between stressful events and mental health. *Chinese Journal of Clinical Psychology*, 16(6): 576–578.

RECOMMENDED READING

1. Geldard, K., Geldard, D. and Yin Foo, R. (2016) *Counselling Adolescents: The Proactive Approach for Young People* (4th ed.). London: Sage.

This book provides an overview of working with young people within an integrative counselling framework.

2. Geldard, K. (ed.) (2009) *Practical Interventions for Young People at Risk*. London: Sage.

This book provides more specific information about supporting young people with a range of presenting issues.

3. Midgley, N., Hayes, J. and Cooper, M. (2017) *Essential Research Findings in Child and Adolescent Counselling and Psychotherapy*. London: Sage.

For an overview of the research base when counselling young people, readers are directed to this book.

7.19   COUNSELLING OLDER PEOPLE

NAOKO KISHITA AND KEN LAIDLAW

OVERVIEW AND KEY POINTS

Common psychological conditions of older people may be experienced qualitatively differently from those of younger generations due to the types of challenges people face as they age (e.g., physical comorbidity, chronicity, loss experiences, living with decisions made earlier in life that may impact on their wellbeing in future years). As such, understanding an appropriate developmental context and frame of reference is important for therapists working with older clients. This chapter will introduce theories about aging that will improve engagement and understanding between client and counsellor. Psychological interventions derived from theories about aging, such as wisdom, socio-emotional selectivity theory, stereotype embodiment theory (attitudes to aging), selective, optimisation with compensation (SOC), can be useful to bring about an enhanced treatment outcome in older adults where non-age-appropriate counselling has been ineffectual.

- Psychotherapy is an efficacious treatment for late-life depression and anxiety but the application of theories about aging (gerontology) has the potential to improve outcome.
- The therapeutic alliance between counsellor and older client may be enhanced if the different attitudes, beliefs and culture experienced by different generations (cohort values) are appreciated and understood.
- The therapeutic alliance may be enhanced further if familial values that shape generational (cohort) beliefs are explicitly examined in the early stages of therapy.
- Older clients may possess 'lifeskills' that can be drawn upon in therapy to enhance treatment outcome. A timeline exercise (a specific means of asking a client to provide an autobiographical account of their life experiences) can help clients in using their own experiences of overcoming adversity in the past to manage current presenting problems more effectively.
- SOC helps clients purposefully and proactively allocate their resources to prevent the loss of function. SOC can be used in psychotherapy when older clients have realistic age-related challenges that require adjustment and adaptation (e.g., loss of physical function).

BACKGROUND AND CONTEXT

The prevalence of affective disorders, such as depression and anxiety, appear to be lower in older adults compared to younger adults. A recent systematic review on the global prevalence of anxiety disorders (Baxter et al., 2013) demonstrated that older adults (55 years plus) were 20% less likely to have anxiety disorders compared with younger adults (35–54 years). The data from the World Health Organisation (WHO) World Mental survey, a series of community epidemiological surveys, showed that major depressive episodes were significantly less prevalent among respondents aged 65+ than adults of working age (Kessler et al., 2010). Although the majority of older people stay psychologically well into late life, certain subgroups of older people, such as those with chronic medical conditions (e.g., Ballard et al., 2000; Pontone et al., 2009), or residents of long-term aged care facilities are at greater risk of developing mental health disorders (e.g., Seitz et al., 2010). Given the known potential risks associated with psychotropic medications in older people (e.g., Kerse et al., 2008), psychological approaches such as counselling and psychotherapy have a lot to offer in improving the health and wellbeing of this population.

The number of older people aged 60 and over have increased substantially in recent years in most countries, and that growth is projected to accelerate in the coming decades and exponentially amongt the oldest-old (see United Nations, 2015). Due to increased levels of life expectancy, counsellors and therapists are more likely to come into contact with older people seeking help, and in many cases these clients will be substantially older than they will have experienced previously. The common psychological conditions of such older clients may be qualitatively different from those of younger generations due to the types of challenges people face as they age (Laidlaw and Kishita, 2015). Consequently, psychological approaches such as cognitive-behaviour therapy (CBT), which currently report strong evidence for its efficacy with older people, may be augmented further if therapists adopt a developmentally appropriate approach.

The application of gerontological theories to counselling is such an example. Gerontology is the science of aging. It is a multidisciplinary research exploring the physical, cognitive, emotional and social changes associated with the process of aging and ways of managing such age-related changes. Combining theories about aging, such as wisdom, socio-emotional selectivity theory, stereotype embodiment theory (attitudes to aging) and SOC, with person-centred approaches in counselling and psychotherapy can bring about an enhanced treatment outcome where other non-age-appropriate approaches have proven ineffectual. If counsellors and therapists wish to improve their work with older clients, it is important that they educate themselves and invest in the development of their competencies in geropsychology practice (Karel et al., 2012).

In the next section we will demonstrate how an intervention derived from a theoretical gerontological concept of wisdom can be used within traditional CBT as 'vehicles for change' (Laidlaw, 2015) to illustrate the usefulness of such age-appropriate approach. Baltes and Staudinger (2000) state that wisdom can be adjudged by how an individual deals with the recognition and management of uncertainty. As such, wisdom may be used to suggest to clients that they can manage uncertainty and deal with ambiguity of decisions by focusing on past experience as a teacher in CBT (Laidlaw and Kishita, 2015). This is the basis of our approach, termed 'wisdom enhancement', that is, the process of using lifeskills to enhance psychological wellbeing. In this approach, developed by Laidlaw (2015), timelines are the means by which wisdom enhancement is enacted in person-centred psychological approaches.

WAYS OF WORKING

Mr Ellis, aged 83 years, presented in our clinic because of low mood and agitation. At the time he was the primary caregiver of his wife Alice, who had developed vascular dementia. Mr Ellis found it exceptionally stressful looking after his wife as he was anxious about what the future held for his wife and for them as a couple. They had been married for over 53 years and had always been close. He was losing his friend and confidant to a terrible disease that terrified him, but he nevertheless refused to read any information about the condition from his carer support nurse. As a result, his fantasies about dementia were never fully addressed before attending for therapy, resulting in an escalating sense of agitation. As a carer Mr Ellis was devoted to his wife's comfort, and like many dementia caregivers he spent all his time looking after his wife's needs, neglecting his interests of cycling, painting and swimming. Early in therapy, Alice died, quite suddenly, from a stroke. Mr Ellis coped well with his loss, although this was a time of loneliness and grief.

Mr Ellis is a very fit man who regularly swims and attends his local gym. Until very recently he was cycling with a club two or three times per week. He has been cycling for many years and can travel far distances in one day. A 40-mile round trip was not beyond his physical capabilities.

Mr Ellis recently developed strange pains and sensations in the backs of his legs, and after consulting his family doctor he was apparently advised that this was 'wear and tear' and perhaps a result of overdoing cycling. Mr Ellis was eventually referred for a number of specialist assessments but no physical cause was found for his sensations in his legs. This caused much distress for Mr Ellis: 'Personally I think the symptoms suggest some kind of nerve problem yet to be diagnosed'.

A typical pattern developed following consultations and assessments where each serious condition was assessed for and discounted. Mr Ellis expressed great relief, but this was followed by equally great confusion and alarm as the sensations continued to be experienced, leaving Mr Ellis to conclude: 'No one has told me what is wrong. Somebody has missed something, as my legs are getting worse'. As a result he spends a lot of time worrying about physical sensations and he avoids participating in exercise in case he 'aggravates whatever is causing my pains'. When he does attempt to exercise, he notices that he gets fatigued more quickly than before, misinterpreting this as evidence of physical deterioration as a result of his leg sensations. Thus a self-defeating vicious cycle is set up, as detailed in Figure 7.19.1.

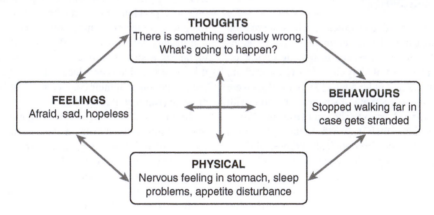

Figure 7.19.1 The hot cross bun model for CBT

Source: adapted from Padesky and Mooney (1990)

One could reasonably conclude that this is a fairly typical presentation of health anxiety. However, there was a rigidity with which Mr Ellis was convinced that a catastrophic event was occurring and he was quite fixed in his belief that he would end up in a wheelchair, having lost the power of his legs. As was evident from assessments, no deteriorating condition was ever found by the numerous specialists he had consulted.

While standard approaches within CBT using behavioural experiments and cognitive restructuring were reducing acute affect, progress was slow as Mr Ellis clung on to his belief that a diagnosis had been missed as 'So far no one had come up with any ideas what could be causing my legs not to function properly!'

The therapist used a timeline with Mr Ellis to gain an enhanced sense of understanding and to help the client to see how he had managed to deal with challenging and ambiguous situations in the past. As noted by Laidlaw (2015), this is a useful technique to employ when understanding an individual's personal narrative in order to use events from the past to help the client manage better in the 'here and now'. The timeline is simple to employ in therapy. 'The therapist can ask the client to put all notable events from life on this timeline. The completion of the timeline is left to the client, although they can be based on overall life events, adverse life events, turning points (high or low), or a combination of all three' (Laidlaw, 2015: 149). Figure 7.19.2 is an example of a blank timeline.

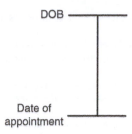

Figure 7.19.2 Timeline

Mr Ellis is very resilient and probably has been all his life. His father was killed during the Second World War and he had to leave school to work to support his mother and younger sister. In his mid-20s he enrolled at a local university. Academically able, he progressed quickly in his chosen career, eventually becoming a partner in an engineering consultancy firm.

It became evident when looking at his timeline that he had overcome a number of challenges in the past. When we examined each experience factually (by asking: What did you do? How confident did you feel tackling this problem then? Are there any lessons you can take from the past to help you cope better in the here and now?), a timeline of negative experiences of aging were evident. He had neatly, methodologically and chronologically charted his wife's demise over the years. The therapist used this information to ask Mr Ellis whether what happened to his wife was relevant to his current experiences. Mr Ellis noted that his wife's experience of decline had frightened him and he had always been anxious about growing older. He had kept up his physical exercise in part to delay the start of aging. He saw aging as a time

of declining strength. Hence his sensations were the start of a 'slippery slope' of decline into old age. Levy (2008) notes that negative stereotypes of old people can become self-stereotypes that act much like a self-fulfilling prophecy. Thus he had assumed his sensations were evidence that what occurred to Alice prior to her eventual death was now happening to him; the feared process of aging was here now and his decline was inevitable. The therapist and client were able to focus on the erroneous cognitions beyond anxiety about health that were maintaining his distress.

Mr Ellis was eventually able to distance himself from searching for a definitive diagnosis for the sensation in his legs. As he noted, '[If you] keep searching [for answers] makes you pretty depressed'. He was also able to self-manage his anxiety by reintroducing watercolour painting into his routine, and had started to increase his behavioural activity. At the same time, scores on anxiety and depression measures had declined sharply by the end of therapy.

RESEARCH EVIDENCE

Evidence suggests that psychosocial approaches such as CBT are an efficacious treatment approach for late-life depression (e.g., Gould et al., 2012a) and anxiety (e.g., Gould et al., 2012b). However, the efficacy of psychotherapy with older adults seems to be significantly larger when compared with a non-active control condition (e.g., being on a waiting list), but the group difference becomes smaller when compared with an active control condition (e.g., a discussion group) or another type of psychological treatment. Greater research into factors that may augment positive outcomes in counselling and psychotherapy with older people is therefore needed.

Kishita and Laidlaw (2016) conducted a content analysis of treatment protocols used in CBT studies with older people experiencing generalised anxiety disorder and demonstrated that the majority of previous research used a standard CBT protocol or standard CBT with some procedural modifications, such as the use of mnemonic aids and simplifying homework forms and terminology used. Although these modifications are primarily procedural and appear to be sensible, the evidence suggests these add little to improving treatment outcome (Kishita and Laidlaw, 2016). As such, a more conceptual and age-appropriate approach to enhancing treatment for late-life depression and anxiety is required.

In addition, many studies exploring CBT with older people recruited relatively healthy older adults (i.e., individuals without multimorbidity) and did not include the oldest-old age group into the trial. Therefore, participants from these controlled trials may not demographically represent the groups of clients seen in the psychological services today.

Although older adults benefit from psychotherapy and appear to do so at least in comparison to outcomes with adults of working age, research suggests that efficacy gains can be made with regards to treatment outcomes, and especially so as working with older people may present therapists with unique challenges. Future studies that use an age-appropriate frame of reference based upon gerontological theories may augment treatment outcome. With the change in demographics, the new cohorts of older people will likely demand more from counselling and psychotherapy and have a reasonable expectation that their current needs and concerns will be met with evidence-based, age-appropriate psychological treatments.

REFERENCES

Ballard, C., Neill, D., O'Brien, J., McKeith, I.G., Ince, P., and Perry, R. (2000) Anxiety, depression and psychosis in vascular dementia: prevalence and associations. *Journal of Affective Disorders*, 59(2): 97–106.

Baltes, P.B. and Staudinger, U.M. (2000) Wisdom: a metaheuristic (pragmatic) to orchestrate mind and virtue toward excellence. *American Psychologist*, 55: 122–136.

Baxter, A.J., Scott, K.M., Vos, T., and Whiteford, H.A. (2013) Global prevalence of anxiety disorders: a systematic review and meta-regression. *Psychological Medicine*, 43(5): 897–910.

Gould, R.L., Coulson, M.C., and Howard, R.J. (2012a) Cognitive behavioral therapy for depression in older people: a meta-analysis and meta-regression of randomized controlled trials. *Journal of the American Geriatrics Society*, 60(10): 1817–1830.

Gould, R.L., Coulson, M.C., and Howard, R.J. (2012b) Cognitive behavioral therapy for anxiety disorders in older people: a meta-analysis and meta-regression of randomized controlled trials. *Journal of the American Geriatrics Society*, 60(2): 218–229.

Karel, M.J., Gatz, M., and Smyer, M.A. (2012) Aging and mental health in the decade ahead: what psychologists need to know. *American Psychologist*, 67(3): 184–198.

Kerse, N., Flicker, L., Pfaff, J.J., et al. (2008) Falls, depression and antidepressants in later life: a large primary care appraisal. *PLoS ONE*, 3(6): e2423.

Kessler, R.C., Birnbaum, H., Shahly, V., et al. (2010) Age differences in the prevalence and comorbidity of DSM-IV major depressive episodes: results from the WHO World Mental Health Survey Initiative. *Depression and Anxiety*, 27(4): 351–364.

Kishita, N. and Laidlaw, K. (2016, June) Cognitive behaviour therapy for generalised anxiety disorder: is CBT equally effective in adults of working age and older people? Paper presented at the 8th World Congress of Behavioural and Cognitive Therapies, Melbourne.

Laidlaw, K. (2015) *Cognitive Behaviour Therapy for Older People: An Introduction*. London: Sage.

Laidlaw, K. and Kishita, N. (2015) Age-appropriate augmented cognitive behavior therapy to enhance treatment outcome for late-life depression and anxiety disorders. *The Journal of Gerontopsychology and Geriatric Psychiatry*, 28: 57–66.

Levy. B. R. (2008) Rigidity as a predictor of older person's aging stereotypes and aging self-perceptions. *Social Behavior and Personality*, 36(4): 559–70.

Padesky, C.A. & Mooney, K.A. (1990) Presenting the cognitive model to clients. *International Cognitive Therapy Newsletter*, 6: 13–14. Retrieved from https://padesky.com/newpad/wp-content/uploads/2016/02/v6no_1_2_present_model_currentweb.pdf

Pontone, G.M., Williams, J.R., Anderson, K.E., Chase, G., Goldstein, S.A., Grill, S., Hirsch, E.S., Lehmann, S., Little, J.T., Margolis, R.L., Rabins, P.V., Weiss, H.D., and Marsh, L. (2009). Prevalence of anxiety disorders and anxiety subtypes in patients with Parkinson's disease. *Movement Disorders*, 24(9): 1333–1338.

Seitz, D., Purandare, N., and Conn, D. (2010) Prevalence of psychiatric disorders among older adults in long-term care homes: a systematic review. *International Psychogeriatrics*, 22(7): 1025–1039.

United Nations, Department of Economic and Social Affairs, Population Division (2015) *World Population Ageing 2015 (ST/ESA/SER.A/390)*. New York: United Nations.

RECOMMENDED READING

1. Laidlaw, K. (2015) *Cognitive Behaviour Therapy for Older People: An Introduction.* London: Sage.

This 'Counselling older people' chapter demonstrated how the gerontological theory of wisdom can be used within traditional CBT to augment treatment outcome. For the readers who wish to learn more about this topic, we recommend reading this book. It provides more in-depth and comprehensive coverage of the application of gerontological theories to CBT practice and how such age-appropriate approaches can enhance treatment outcomes among older clients.

2. Karel, M.J., Gatz, M., and Smyer, M.A. (2012) Aging and mental health in the decade ahead: what psychologists need to know. *American Psychologist,* 67(3): 184–198.

This article provides an overview of demographic and epidemiological trends and their implications for therapists working with older people. It also reviews major contextual trends (e.g., health care policy) that will likely affect psychological practice with older adults.

3. United Nations Population Fund and HelpAge International (UNFPA) (2012) *Ageing in the Twenty-first Century: A Celebration and a Challenge.* New York: UNFPA and HelpAge International.

This is a landmark report on aging published by UNFPA and HelpAge. It will help readers obtain an overview of population aging and its social and economic implications as well as policies and legislation on aging across the world.

THERAPEUTIC SPECIALISMS: THERAPEUTIC MODALITIES

7.20 SYSTEMIC FAMILY THERAPY

RUDI DALLOS

OVERVIEW AND KEY POINTS

Family therapy embraces a variety of therapeutic approaches devoted to promoting changes in the dynamics of families, but the most prevalent and influential of these models is 'systemic' family therapy. The founding conceptual framework for family therapy derived from cybernetics and systems theories developed in the 1950s. The distinguishing feature of this approach is the view that problems typically displayed by individuals are seen to arise from the transactional processes in the family or other intimate relational system in which the person is immersed (Dallos and Draper, 2015). Systemic family therapy includes the idea that not only family dynamics but relationships, for example between the family members and the school situation, processes within therapeutic/clinical teams, mental health units (e.g., residential therapeutic settings), dynamics between organisations (e.g., social services) and mental health, may also play a significant role in the development and maintenance of problems.

- Family therapy sees problems as caused by and maintained by relational processes.
- Family therapy involves working with family members and not just individuals.
- 'Family' is used in a broad sense and can include all significant relationships.
- Family therapy is usually, but not invariably, conducted by teams.
- The founding conceptual ideas of family therapy drew on cybernetic and systems theory.

BACKGROUND AND CONTEXT

There have been extensive debates about whether this implies that families are seen to 'cause' problems and many family therapists prefer to by-pass this debate and instead adopt a pragmatic view that promoting changes in family dynamics can help ameliorate problems, such as anorexia, self-harm, depressions, anxiety and psychosis. The most obvious difference between family therapy and other forms of therapy is that the target interventions are aimed predominantly at altering family relationships rather than individuals. Consistent with this, family therapists spend most of their time working with groups of people rather than individuals. Of course, some other forms of therapy, such as group therapies, also involve working with groups of people. However, family therapy aims to focus on natural groups of people, such as families, who have spent considerable time with each other. This exposure to each other over time is seen as leading to the development of patterned, repetitive and predictable forms of interaction, and it is these patterns – what goes on between rather than what goes on within people – that are the focus of interest.

THERAPEUTIC ASSUMPTIONS AND PRACTICE

Systemic family therapy was one of the first of the therapeutic approaches to employ live supervision of the therapeutic work. Originally this was done with a team observing the session from behind an observation screen or on video. Alternatively, there could be an ongoing process (in-room consultation) with a colleague in the room with the family regularly offering advice. This emphasis on live supervision was based on the recognition of the complexity of working with the whole family at the same time, and also on the idea that there needed to be some removal from the interaction in the room to be able to detect some of the family patterns maintaining the problems. The therapist would be consulted regularly by the team via telephone or an earpiece, and given suggestions, for example, to ask the family to enact how the problems occur at home, to change seats, to engage in role-play or sculpt, for one person to speak more or less, to explore certain areas more, such as their attempted solutions to the problems, and so on. After about 40 minutes, the therapist generally took a break to talk with the team and then returned with some substantive interventions, such as a reframe, for example, describing their intentions in a more positive way or suggesting 'homework' tasks, such as the parents changing roles in relation to a child – who puts her to bed, or gets her up for school, etc.

FROM PATTERNS AND PROCESSES TO BELIEFS AND NARRATIVES

The central concept of systemic family therapy is that family members are mutually influencing each other. Over time families are seen to develop predictable patterns of interaction and this is necessary for them to be able to coordinate their activities and manage the demands of life, education, work, leisure and intimacy. They also need to be able to change and adapt to challenges and unexpected demand and crises. One guiding idea has been that the demands for change escalate at critical transitional points in the life of a family, such as the birth of a child, the death of a member, marriages, starting school, and so on (Carter and McGoldrick, 1988). This may coincide with a family experiencing some distress and crises such that they cannot manage the transition and instead it becomes avoided by developing a symptom. For example, illness in a parent at a point when a child is about to leave home may mean that the child feels unable to go and may subsequently become depressed or withdrawn. Unfortunately, this may become embedded into the family dynamic such that it becomes increasingly difficult for the child to manage the transition and the focus becomes more and more on 'their' depression rather than the difficulty the family was facing in making the changes. This had been described as the family becoming 'stuck', and perversely the dynamics serve to maintain a symptom.

Family therapy has seen a gradual shift from an emphasis on patterns of actions to an emphasis on the construction of meanings and their creation in families and between the family and the therapist. Inherent in this was a change in the perceived role of the therapist as less of an expert and more of a collaborative explorer who works alongside a family to co-create some new, more productive ways of the family seeing their situation. Furthermore, this represented a move towards an increased sensitivity to therapeutic relationships. Rather than trying to adopt an 'objective' stance, the therapist is encouraged to be continually reflective – to monitor their perceptions, beliefs, expectations, needs and feelings, especially in terms of how these may in turn have an influence on the family. Earlier approaches largely adopted a *functionalist* view of problems: families were seen as interacting systems in which symptoms functioned to preserve stability (Minuchin, 1974). In a perverse way, painful and distressing symptoms rather than threatening family life and stability were often seen as holding families together: symptoms were seen as distracting from or diverting conflicts, anxieties and fears (often unconsciously held) from other areas of the family's experience. This view was challenged on the grounds that the function of a symptom was not there to be 'discovered', but was the therapist's hypothesis. In turn, how difficulties were handled – the attempted solutions – was seen as linked to the wider belief system of the family.

A typical view in families is that the source of their problems lies in one member and may represent a form of diagnosable condition, similar to a form of 'illness', for example anorexia, attention deficit disorder, psychosis, depression, and so on. Once established, such assumptions can become increasingly painful to confront. For example, if the child's symptoms become severe, the parents may feel guilty and blameworthy when the therapist attempts to focus on their relationships. This may be perceived by parents to suggest the implication that their conflicts have in a sense been the cause of the problems. Other processes can also be seen to operate in families, for example, young children may discover the power that a symptom of illness confers, such as being able to avoid school and unpleasant duties, and gaining sympathy and attention. Therefore, a child may start to collude with this state of affairs and continue to display symptoms, in part because of the apparent advantages he or she gains (Haley, 1976). This in turn can serve to confirm for the whole family, including the child, the beliefs that the child is the source of the problems. A frequent dynamic is also that the parents hold different beliefs and disagree on how to treat the child (e.g., discipline versus sympathy), which leads to contradictory stances towards their child or to a position where they feel frozen and unable to make decisions regarding how to solve the problems.

CONTEMPORARY PRACTICE OF FAMILY THERAPY

Most family therapists and teams now adopt a less directive and expert stance to the early pioneers. Although teams and observation screens are still used, there are attempts to be much more transparent in the process of family therapy. A key feature of contemporary practice is the use of *reflecting teams* (Andersen, 1987; White and Epston, 1990). Instead of consulting in relative secret with an anonymous supervision team, the discussions between the therapist and the team are held openly in front of the family, so that the team members share their thoughts and concerns with the family and also voice any personal connections that team members have with what they have heard about the family. Through the team's discussion, the family is invited to consider alternative stories and explanations regarding their lives together. This may allow different family members who are holding opposing views to feel understood and perhaps enable them to move on to more constructive stories. Importantly, the reflecting team enables family members to hear and perhaps internalise a different conversation rather than simply different explanations. In turn, the family members are invited to reflect back on the reflecting team discussion regarding what they found helpful, interesting, useful and less helpful. The guiding idea is that family members may connect with the stories in different ways and be able to choose what they found to be helpful. More implicitly, it communicates the idea that there are multiple ways of seeing events, helping to free up some of the family's more rigid ways of thinking that they may have developed as a result of their sense of anxiety, failure and desperation.

ATTACHMENT THEORY

Although ideas from attachment theory were an early influence on family therapy, they have resurfaced as being relevant. It has been argued that Bolwby (1969, 1988) was one of the innovators of family therapy in that he was one of the first to suggest that therapy should involve working jointly with members of a family. In addition, attachment theory incorporates concepts from systems theory in describing the bond between a parent and a child as a self-corrective feedback system. Although clearly relevant to family therapy, it is only relatively recently that attachment-based family therapies have come to hold a significant place in the family therapy movement. Some key contributions it offers are to consider how family difficulties may have been prompted by attachment disruptions, parents separating, a child losing a bond with her father following a divorce. Alongside a consideration of current attachment dynamics in the family, there is a focus on trans-generational processes, for example, the parents own childhood attachment disruptions. Importantly, the emphasis is also on how life events, such as a bereavement, illness or accident, may have temporarily unbalanced the family attachment system, but that this has become stuck around the anxiety and insecurity that has been experienced (Dallos, 2006; Marvin and Stewart, 1990).

Attachment-based family therapies emphasise that these attachment issues drive relational patterns. A core theme in assisting families is to help them to feel secure and safe in the therapeutic situation. This involves the family therapist becoming a transitional attachment figure, like a parent or uncle to the family. From this 'secure base' they are more able to understand and be able to manage the emotional conflicts and stresses that may adversely shape their interactions and disrupt their attempts to solve their problems (Bowlby, 1988). This includes parents becoming aware of how their own attachment experiences may be shaping their parenting, marital dynamics and emotional coping strategies. Key to this is the idea that parents' attempts to apply 'corrective scripts' – to do things differently and better than their parents had with them – may, despite their best intentions, be causing problems (Byng-Hall, 1995). For example, a father may attempt to be more emotionally available for his daughter than his own parents had been for him, but this may unfortunately serve to make it difficult for his daughter to also stay emotionally connected to her mother after their divorce.

FAMILIES AND WIDER SYSTEMS

Systemic family therapy adopts a broader focus than on the dynamics of the immediate family (Campbell and Draper, 1985; Dallos and Draper, 2016). A central idea is that families are involved in and influenced by a variety of different contexts. Importantly, this includes a consideration of wider cultural contexts in terms of differences in cultural values about family life, gender roles and expectations about the relationships across the generations. What may initially appear to be family problems may, for example, be helpfully seen as confusions and conflicts related to cultural values and expectations. As an example, second-generation Asian children may feel powerful conflicts between adopting the values of western, British culture and maintaining a connection and loyalty to their Asian cultures. The parents may feel a sense of betrayal or disloyalty to a child who appears to have rejected their values, and this can be played out as an interpersonal conflict in the family. The young person may, in turn, be critical and disappointed that their parents do not understand or try to help them with their dilemmas.

WAYS OF WORKING

A consideration of wider systems is also related to thinking about the various external systems that a family is involved with and the relationships and processes between these systems. For example, a family may be concerned about how a child is experiencing school, their relationships with other children and the staff. Likewise, the school staff may have concerns about the family, and wish or need to involve them in decisions that need to be made about a child in the school situation. In some cases some difficulties in communication may occur between a family and a school, with misunderstandings possibly aggravating difficulties that a child is displaying. A common scenario is where a child displays significant problems at home. For example, Jonathan, aged 13, was reported by his parents to show frequent outbursts of anger at home but appeared to be well-behaved at school. His teachers noticed that at times he seemed pre-occupied and upset about things at home, so they contacted his parents. However, this had the unfortunate consequence of making the parents feel inadequate and to blame, and had an effect of aggravating the situation. One consequence of this escalating process was that they turned to child mental health services to try to gain a diagnosis of attention deficit hyperactivity disorder (ADHD) for their son. They also became angry with what they felt were accusations from the school which in turn generated concern in the school. School staff eventually contacted social services because they feared that Jonathan might be at 'risk' or harm. Consequently,

the involvement of social services further fuelled the problems and led the parents to feel as though they were being blamed more by the school and social services and to become more angry and committed to seeking a diagnosis.

A systemic perspective can assist in considering how various systems interact and how processes are escalating in unhelpful ways. In the example above, it might be that family therapy is at the centre of initiating some change in how these various systems are interacting. However, it might also be the case that social services or the school are able to apply such a perspective and initiate some changes. A starting point can be to develop a multi-context systemic formulation. This can include a visual mapping of the various professional and family systems that are involved (see Figure 7.20.1 for an example).

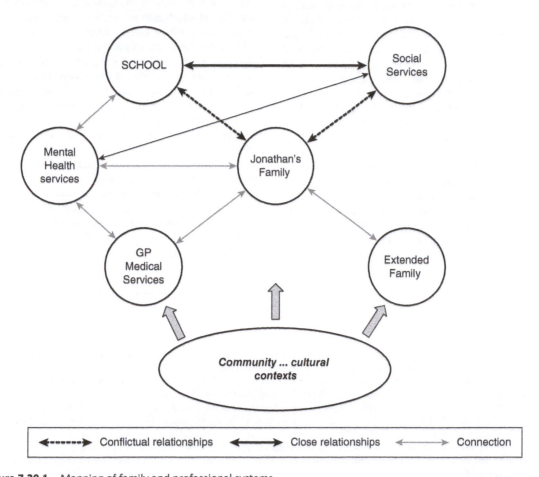

Figure 7.20.1 Mapping of family and professional systems

An initial mapping can start to reveal which systems are involved and also to consider the relationships between them. For example, that the school and social services have started to develop frequent communication and the school and family have a more difficult conflictual relationship. It also became apparent in this example that the extended family has little communication with any of the professional systems. In this case, the maternal grandparents were closely involved with Jonathan and his parents, and when they were invited to attend for a family session it transpired that they were strongly advising the parents to seek a diagnosis of ADHD. The parents in fact were concerned about their own parenting abilities, but also about some bullying at school which they felt Jonathan had kept a secret from the school and which they felt the school was not taking seriously enough.

Pursuing an analysis of the interplay of different systems can start to reveal that there are potential difficulties in various parts of such a network of systems and also in misunderstandings that have led to an escalation of negative processes between the different parties. Here the social services agency had recently received a critical report of their work, and were anxious to avoid the 'risk' of child abuse and possible further negative allegations. Partly as a consequence of this, their communication with the school was fuelled by some anxiety and concerns about the parents, which escalated rather than contained and resolved the situation. The role of a family therapy team in such a multiple system may be to help contain anxieties, as much in the professional systems as within the family. In some cases this can involve initiating a meeting with representatives from the various agencies, such as school staff, social services and colleagues in mental health services. This is an increasingly important role that family therapy teams hold. At the same time, they need to be skilful in reassuring the family so that they are not seen, as in this example, simply to be colluding with other professional to further blame the family.

RESEARCH EVIDENCE

Systemic family therapy has developed in various ways from a focus on family patterns to a consideration of beliefs and the influence on families of wider cultural ideas. The developments have been supported by research evidence, which has established the effectiveness of family therapy. For example, it is the recommended treatment for young people suffering with a range of problems, including eating disorders, depression, couples problems and psychosis, and a recent major trial has shown its electiveness in helping families with a young person who is self-harming (Dallos and Draper, 2016). We are conducting a major study to examine the effectives of an integration of attachment and systemic family therapy for families with a child who has a diagnosis of autism.

There has been considerable integration and assimilation across various forms of therapy, so, for example, systemic ideas are included in some individual therapies and, likewise, systemic therapy has continually drawn on ideas from attachment theory and psychodynamic theory. Systemic therapy has also expanded to consider not only family dynamics but also the relationships between and within services. Not infrequently, work with families has shown that confusions and conflicts between the professionals with whom they are involved can contribute significantly to 'stuckness' or even the escalation of their problems. Thinking about problems in such a multilevel way in terms of complex interacting systems continues to be an important area of development in systemic family therapy.

REFERENCES

Andersen, T. (1987) The reflecting team: dialogue and meta-dialogue in clinical work. *Family Process*, 26(4): 415–428.
Bowlby, J. (1969) *Attachment and Loss* (Vol. 1). London: Hogarth Press.
Bowlby, J. (1988) *A Secure Base: Parent-Child Attachment and Healthy Human Development*. New York: Basic Books.
Byng-Hall, J. (1995) *Rewriting Family Scripts*. New York and London: Guilford Press.
Campbell, D. and Draper, R. (eds) (1985) *Applications of Systemic Family Therapy*. London: Grune & Stratton.
Carter, E. and McGoldrick, M. (1988) *The Changing Family Life Cycle: A Framework for Family Therapy* (2nd ed.). New York: Gardner.
Dallos, R. (2006) *Attachment Narrative Therapy*. Maidenhead: Open University Press/ McGraw-Hill.
Dallos, R. and Draper, R. (2015) *An Introduction to Family Therapy* (3rd ed.). Maidenhead: Open University Press/ McGraw-Hill.

Haley, J. (1976) *Problem Solving Therapy*. San Francisco, CA: Jossey-Bass.

Marvin, R. and Stewart, R. (1990) A family systems framework for the study of attachment. In M. Greenberg, D. Cicchetti and E. Cummings (eds), *Attachment in the Pre-school Years*. Chicago, IL: University of Chicago Press.

Minuchin, S. (1974) *Families and Family Therapy*. Cambridge, MA: Harvard University Press.

White, M. and Epston, D. (1990) *Narrative Means to Therapeutic Ends*. New York: W.W. Norton.

RECOMMENDED READING

1. Byng-Hall, J. (1995) *Rewriting Family Scripts*. New York and London: Guilford Press.

This is seminal text that offers an interesting integration of systemic family therapy concepts and the idea of stories/scripts across the generations. It has powerful and clear illustrations of practice.

2. Dallos, R. and Vetere, A. (2009) *Working Systemically with Attachment Narratives*. London: Routledge.

This is the author's own integration of systemic family with concepts from attachment theory. This approach adds the important dimension of emotional connections and attachment across the generations.

3. Dallos, R. and Draper, R. (2015) *An Introduction to Family Therapy* (3rd ed.). Maidenhead: Open University Press/McGraw-Hill.

This book offers a comprehensive overview of the field of family therapy. It offers a history of the movement, which is summarised in terms of four key phases of developments. The main techniques are illustrated with case examples. There is also an extensive overview of the evidence base for family therapy.

7.21   GROUP THERAPY

STEPHEN PAUL

OVERVIEW AND KEY POINTS

We live in relation to others and our external environment. Our self-concept is formed and develops through our experiences with others. We learn to value ourselves in relation with others.

Many of the life problems people bring to therapy evolve from trauma experienced in relation to others. People play out their relational patterns, often developed from childhood, in relation to others. Group therapy provides an environment to explore and heal the trauma of our interpersonal relations in a setting which can mirror the dynamics of the original. A skilled group therapist can help group members to work through issues and patterns, as they arise, in a safe and securely boundaried setting.

Group therapy can be particularly helpful for:

- those whose problems are interpersonal in nature and/or rooted in relations to a number of others
- those who are able to give and receive feedback and be empathic to others
- those who are isolated and/or experiencing something missing in their lives
- those who are not helped by the dynamic of the one-to-one relationship.

BACKGROUND AND CONTEXT

Group therapy developed from the beginning of the twentieth century. Initially, it was the only therapy available for those people who could not afford individual therapy. The foundation of group work is credited to Pratt (see Paul, 2008, 2012). He established an outpatient tuberculosis therapy programme for those who could not afford individual treatment. He used encouragement, support and the didactic delivery of practical information to help attendees (a formula now developed in modern Weight Watchers programmes).

After the First World War, Marsh developed group methods for the first time in a residential psychiatric setting. Concurrently, Lazell worked with groups of mentally disturbed combatants using a didactic-instructional approach.

Freudian insights into the human psyche led to the understanding of transference (Wender, 1936) and free association (Schilder, 1936) in groups. Burrow (1927) coined the term 'group analysis', noting that in groups individuals behaved as they believed others wanted them to. Maintaining these social images impeded spontaneity and maintained rigid ways of behaving.

Around the same time, Moreno (1958) developed psychodrama. He introduced role-playing, working with group members to re-enact past experiences and resolve repressed feelings. Moreno introduced the term 'group psychotherapy' in 1932.

In the United Kingdom (UK), Bion (1959) formulated classical group analysis. Foulkes (1964) worked under Goldstein alongside Perls, the founder of gestalt therapy (Perls et al., 1959). Goldstein (1939) discovered that individual neurones always functioned as part of a network. This led Foulkes to postulate that the individual is a nodal point within the network of relationships in any group and that psychoanalysis needs to view all the relationships in which the individual is involved. There are no rigid delineations between the individual and the environment, the inner and the outer.

During the 1950s, Rogers (1970) developed encounter groups. He criticised the psychoanalytic concept of 'homeostasis' – that is, that the person is a closed adaptive system with no potential for growth. He believed that the desire for change and growth is the healthy result of inner sickness. Maslow (1964) introduced 'synergy': the idea that an individual has more potential for development in a healthy group than alone.

The 1960s saw the development of family therapy (Slipp, 1993): the 'disturbed' family member was a symptom of a dysfunction in the family unit as a whole. Laing (1985) popularised the therapeutic community approach based on existential philosophy and family systems theory as an alternative to psychiatric treatment. It was not an individual's perception of the world that was faulty, but that social pressure led to the falsification of the self. Psychotic behaviour was, literally, a sane response to an insane situation.

Yalom (1981) initially explored existential approaches to group work. His later writings are now considered within an interpersonal, relational frame.

Cognitive and behavioural groups have been mostly developed in mental health settings. Task-focused group work has been used. The outcomes of such groups were more measurable quantitatively and thus lend themselves to research. A mushrooming of evidence-based practice research in this field and the development of wide-ranging group approaches for a variety of psychological problems have greatly enhanced the use of CBT in health service practice.

In the modern era, a more theoretically generic interpersonal approach to group therapy has also developed (Paul and Charura 2014; Yalom with Leszcz, 2005). This approach is often used by therapists from different disciplines who work relationally and are not explicitly trained within a traditional core model of group therapy.

A PERSONAL REFLECTION

Through over 40 years' practice as a therapist and trainer, I have noticed that many competent individual therapists:

- have trouble relating in therapeutic groups
- have difficulty with 360° perception
- are often fearful or hesitant about communicating in a group.

Considering that so many life problems evolve from trauma experienced in relation to others, it is paradoxical that many practitioners struggle with group dynamics. Of course this may be partly due to the training of individual therapists, which is focused on one-to-one dynamics.

There are significant differences between individual and group therapies (see Table 7.21.1). These include:

1. The therapist client relationship is not central in group therapy. Therapist training, with its focus on the unidimensional therapeutic relationship, may lead the therapist to be blind to other communications that take place in a group.
2. The group has a unique pattern of dynamics related exponentially to the number of members. Complex process issues may predominate and the group

therapist needs to be able to work with process issues at an individual and group level.

3. There may be different levels of intrapsychic, interpersonal and intragroup relationships in play at any one time. The therapist needs to be aware of and competent to work with them.

4. Boundary issues are often of added importance as the therapist works with the group. Clients often test boundaries and challenge the therapist in quite different ways to individual therapy.

5. Social phenomena occur in groups which are not necessarily pathological or interpretable psychotherapeutically (e.g., groupthink, conformity, influence, cognitive dissonance, etc.) (summarised in Paul, 2008). There is a real potential for stereotyping to take place in groups, which a therapist needs to be aware of and able to work with.

6. There are a number of 'experts' who may question the therapist or offer their own therapeutic insights and support to each other.

Table 7.21.1 Summary of differences for therapists between individual and group therapy

Individual	Group
Therapist–client relationship central	Variety of relationships possible
Content issues may predominate	Process issues may be more central in activating live material in the group
One relationship processes all outside material	Group can replicate outside experiences
Therapist trained typically in self-focused therapy	Therapist trained in interpersonal dynamics
Therapist may hold more expert power and have more influence over interactions	Plethora of interactions that the therapist has to work with. Therapist may have less personal influence or power as expert
Feedback to therapist only from one person	Therapist open to feedback at any time from any member about any things
Research indicates *Therapeutic Relationship* most important in-therapy factor	Research indicates *Cohesiveness* most important factor

The group context, therefore, is often a challenging one for individually trained therapists who find themselves working with groups.

WAYS OF WORKING

The role and functions of the therapist may be very different, depending on the therapeutic model used. I summarise some of the key ways of working here using an example of a group for people suffering from depression.

All prospective group members have been referred via medical services. They report having significant debilitating depression. Optimum group size is 8–12 members with two therapists. A group session will be one and a half hours and the group is contracted for 10 weeks. All members will have been met before the group starts to determine suitability and to agree contracts.

PSYCHOANALYTIC THERAPY

Modern psychoanalytic group therapy is based on the work of Foulkes (1964), who saw the individual as a social being whose psychological disturbances have their roots in relationships. In different situations people behave in ways which seek to reduce their anxieties based on self-perceptions they believe to be true. In a group there is a 'group tension', the conflict between the individual's and the group's needs. Individuals take up roles in groups as a result of this. Foulkes believed that, unlike classical psychoanalysis, interpretation was not to be used by the leader alone but that group members could have important insights to make about others in the group. The role of the therapist is as a conductor, who makes subtle, informing contributions. Foulkes believed in working with the healthy functioning of group members which enables the group to move towards maturation and gradually lessens the influence of what he called 'neurotic' forces (after Lewin, 1939). The conductor encourages free-floating group discussion. As the culture of the group develops through open personal communications between members, the group matrix is formed. Group members respond in their own subjective ways, sharing their feelings with the group. The open sharing of all feelings creates a resonance in the group, each member resonating to the content. The conductor's role is to help identify underlying causes of disturbance and to make links for members of the processes in the group and their own personal material.

> In our therapy group, the conductor will facilitate the building up of cohesiveness in the group and help members explore common themes. Sharing by members of their own struggles will help other members to resonate with their own issues and enable some release of tensions. In some cases the causes of the problems, such as abandonment, may have to be visited again and again in the group for the underlying conflicts to be released.

EXISTENTIAL THERAPY

In the existential approach the subjective experience of the individual is at its core. The freedom of each individual to choose how to respond to life's limitations, the inter-subjectivity of living, and the focus on authenticity are all underlying themes.

There can be said to be three aims of group therapy

1. enabling members to become authentic with themselves,
2. broadening members' perspectives on themselves and their environment, and
3. enabling members to find meaning for their lives (van Deurzen-Smith, 1990).

The therapeutic relationship is a focus for corrective emotional experiences and therapy is a partnership (Corey, 2003).

Change comes through relationship with others. The therapist works to foster meaningful interpersonal relationships. S/he will also work with members in confronting and working through existential life issues, common in some way to all members, and to help find meaning and authenticity (Yalom with Leszcz, 2005).

> In our therapeutic group, the therapist encourages open and frank sharing between members to help them accept the causes of the depressive states they find themselves in, to realise that such states are common reactions to life's events and, through the group, to see and understand that we all have to face up to such limits and challenges. Through realising this, and the realisation that all members are in the same situation, members are helped to find more helpful ways of responding to the challenges they face.

PERSON-CENTRED THERAPY

The work of Rogers (1970) is central to the development of humanistic group therapy. The facilitative conditions are seen as central to the development of the group. The therapist models congruence, unconditional positive regard and empathy, and communicates them through her/his interactions with group members. The therapist is present in the group, is willing to take part as an equal member of the group and to share his/her struggles with group issues as appropriate (Paul, 2008). When growthful opportunities are present, members of the group choose these opportunities. Obstacles as previously experienced will dissolve away or be overcome. The group becomes a safe place to explore personal incongruities in relationship with others (see Paul, 2016).

> In our therapeutic group, the therapist models the therapeutic conditions in his/her relations to others and this helps create an environment in which members can communicate authentically with each other. Feelings of depression are caused by an inner disempowerment and distortion of innate motivation. As personal incongruities are revealed, explored and resolved, members are able to be more accessing of their inner motivation and make growthful and enhancing life choices.

COGNITIVE-BEHAVIOURAL APPROACHES

Cognitive-behavioural therapy (CBT) group therapy was originally developed to facilitate the treatment of individual in groups. Group processes and dynamics were not considered important or helpful to the task in hand. However, the importance of establishing a climate of trust and respect is indicated and particular therapist characteristics are linked with successful outcomes: respect for others, a non-judgemental attitude, warmth, humour, congruence and authenticity (Lazarus, 1989). A key component of CBT approaches is modelling (Bandura, 1986). The behaviour of the therapist is therefore an important element. More recently, CBT group therapists recognise and work with group dynamic processes in their work (White, 2000). Many CBT programmes are psycho-educational and didactic in nature. CBT programmes are therefore concerned with working with individuals in the group with a focus on individual targets. Members may take part in role-plays, exercises and collaborative problem-solving.

> Members of our therapeutic group will have agreed goals and will be encouraged to challenge and change unhealthy thinking and behaviour patterns. A typical group session will include a warm-up, introduction of new material, practice, review and setting of homework tasks. Members may take part in role-plays, exercises and collaborative problem-solving.

INTERPERSONAL/RELATIONAL APPROACHES

The prolific contributions of Yalom (with Leszcz, 2005) have been important in the development of interpersonal and relational approaches to group therapy. Therapy works through *interpersonal learning* (see Yalom's curative factors – Table 7.21.3 below), the group as *social microcosm* and the *here-and-now* focus of the group. The therapist works with the relationships between members and the therapist, relationships between group members themselves

and relationships between group members and the group. The therapist processes individual (intrapsychic), interpersonal and group as a whole phenomena.

With the flourishing research on the importance of the therapeutic relationship, a relational paradigm has developed (see Paul and Charura, 2014) in which the focus of therapy is relational and that a range of theoretical perspectives can assist the therapist in the task of working with the individual in making sense of the individual in her/his social relationships. The therapeutic relationship itself is considered 'central to change' (Paul and Pelham 2000: 110).

RESEARCH EVIDENCE

A comprehensive summary of research into group therapies can be found in Burlingame et al. (2013).

Research tends to fall into two approaches to group therapy. First, interpersonal group therapy, as exemplified by Yalom (with Leszcz, 2005), Rogers (1970) and relational approaches. Many practitioners with no formal group therapy training work in this way. It is probably the case that it is generally the most practised approach to group therapy overall. The focus is more on the process and interpersonal relationships in the here-and-now. The second type of group therapy is the more structured kind, with a focus on goals. This approach lends itself more to quantifiable research than the first by its very nature, which compounds the problem researchers have in comparing effectiveness.

Table 7.21.2 summarises Johnson's (2008) review of effective group therapy treatments.

Table 7.21.2 Effective group therapy treatments (updated from Johnson, 2008)

Type of approach	Methods	Success
Alcohol abuse and dependence		
Community reinforcement approach	Social groupwork using CBT	Some evidence of general success
Cue exposure treatment	Desensitisation to stimuli	Well-established
Project CALM (treating alcoholism in the family unit)	Groupwork with couples	Some evidence of general success
Social skills training	Developing communication skills	Probably proven effective
Anxiety disorders		
CBT for generalised anxiety disorder	CBT in groups	Too few studies to indicate generalised success
Exposure and response prevention for obsessive compulsive disorder	Behaviour therapy in groups	Probably proven effective
CBT for panic disorder and agoraphobia	CBT in groups	Probably proven effective

(Continued)

Table 7.21.2 (Continued)

Type of approach	Methods	Success
Depression		
Cognitive therapy	Includes CBT	Well-established
Behaviour therapy	In groups	Too few studies to indicate generalised probability
Interpersonal therapy		Well-established
Eating disorders		
CBT for binge eating disorder	In groups	Well-established
Interpersonal therapy for binge eating disorder		Probably proven effective
CBT for bulimia nervosa	In groups	Too few studies to indicate generalised probability

Yalom questions those approaches which rely on technique and are driven by goals of efficiency rather than effectiveness. For him, the 'interactional focus is the engine of group therapy' (Yalom with Leszcz, 2005: xvi).

The therapeutic factors developed by Yalom have been recognised as a benchmark in group therapy research (Bednar and Kaul, 1994; Burlingame et al., 2004). Variously described, these are outlined in Table 7.21.3.

Table 7.21.3 Yalom's curative factors

Interpersonal input	Learning through the input of others in the group
Catharsis	Letting out feelings in the group
Cohesiveness	A sense of belonging and feeling accepted in the group
Self-understanding	Linking past experiences to present thoughts and feelings
Interpersonal output	Learning how to behave in relation to helpful advice from others in the group
Existential factors	Coming to terms with the fact that some things cannot be changed but have to be faced up to and that literally we are all in the same life situation and can find mutual support in this
Instillation of hope	The realisation that as others in the group can improve so the group member can
Altruism	The gains to self-esteem through helping others in the group
Family re-enactment	The group somehow recreates the family experience and can help members to understand behaviour patterns from their past
Guidance identification	Getting helpful advice from others in the group

Cohesiveness is identified by Burlingame et al. (2004: 683) in their summary of group therapy research as 'the therapeutic relationship in group psychotherapy':

- Cohesion is positively associated with reductions in symptom distress and/or improvement in interpersonal functioning.
- All therapists need to foster cohesiveness in all its elements in the group.
- Cohesion is positively associated with outcome in groups of different theoretical orientations.

- Group leaders who focus on member interaction, irrespective of theoretical orientation, achieve higher cohesiveness-outcome links versus groups without this focus. It is important to encourage member interaction.
- Group cohesiveness builds over time.

Burlingame et al. (2002) consider that group therapy is blighted with too many models. Meta-summaries of research do concur that group members who experience acceptance, belonging and support, *regardless of therapeutic model*, typically report more improvement (Burlingame et al., 2002). Attributes such as warmth, openness and empathy have been associated with increased cohesion and better outcomes.

Apart from these findings it is difficult to quantify other significant findings. We can summarise thus:

- Group therapy works as a whole.
- There is no significant evidence to suggest that one modality is better than any other.
- Modality-based intervention may pathologise normal behaviours.

- Therapists should check recent research into group therapy with the client group they are working with.
- Therapists may be more effective working in a way which they are comfortable with rather than trying to 'fit' into a modality.
- Cohesiveness is central to group therapy and the therapeutic relationship is central to outcome.
- Many social factors may affect group members. Therapists should not pathologise them and be mindful of the human rights of members of therapy groups.
- A group leader is in a position of power and needs be mindful of this.

REFERENCES

Bandura, A. (1986) *Social Foundations of Thought and Action: A Social Cognitive Theory*. Englewood Cliffs, NJ: Prentice-Hall.

Bednar, R.L. and Kaul, T. (1994) Experiential group research. In A.E. Bergin and S.L. Garfield (eds), *Handbook of Psychotherapy and Behavior Change* (pp. 631–663). New York: Wiley.

Bion, W.R. (1959) *Experiences in Groups*. New York: Basic Books.

Burlingame, G.M., Fuhriman, A. and Johnson, J. (2002) Cohesion in group psychotherapy. In J. Norcross (ed.), *A Guide to Psychotherapy Relationships that Work* (pp. 71–88). Oxford: Oxford University Press.

Burlingame, G.M., Mackenzie, K.R. and Strauss, B. (2004) Small-group treatment: evidence for effectiveness and mechanisms of change. In M.J. Lambert (ed.), *Bergin and Garfield's Handbook of Psychotherapy and Behaviour Change* (5th ed., pp. 647–696). New York: Wiley.

Burlingame, G.M., Strauss B. and Joyce, A.S. (2013) Change mechanisms and effectiveness of small group treatments. In M.J. Lambert (ed.), *Bergin and Garfield's Handbook of Psychotherapy and Behavior Change* (5th ed., pp. 640–689). New York: Wiley.

Burrow, T. (1927) *The Social Basis of Consciousness*. New York: Harcourt Brace and World.

Corey, G. (2003) *Theory and Practice of Group Counseling* (6th ed.). Belmont, CA: Wadsworth.

Foulkes, S.H. (1964) *Therapeutic Group Analysis*. New York: International Universities Press.

Goldstein, K. (1939) *The Organism: A Holistic Approach to Biology Derived from Pathological Data in Man*. New York: American Book Company.

Johnson, J. (2008) Using research-supported group treatments. *Journal of Clinical Psychology: In Session*, 64(11): 1206–1224.

Laing, R.D. (1985) *Wisdom, Madness and Folly: The Making of a Psychiatrist*. London: Macmillan.

Lazarus, A.A. (1989) Multimodal therapy. In R.J. Corsini and D. Wedding (eds), *Current Psychotherapies* (4th ed.). Itasca, IL: Peacock.

Lewin, K. (1939) Field theory and experiment in social psychology: concepts and methods. *American Journal of Sociology*, 44(6): 868–896.

Maslow, A.H. (1964) Synergy in society and the individual. *Journal of Individual Psychology*, 20: 153–164.

Moreno, J.L. (1958) Fundamental rules and techniques of psychodrama. In J.H. Masserman and J.L. Moreno (eds), *Progress in Psychotherapy*. New York: Grune and Stratton.

Paul, S. (2008) The relationship in group therapy. In S. Haugh and S. Paul (eds), *The Therapeutic Relationship: Perspectives and Themes* (pp. 230–246). Ross-on-Wye: PCCS Books.

Paul, S. (2012) Group counselling and therapy. In C. Feltham and I. Horton (eds.) *The Sage Handbook of Counselling and Psychotherapy* (3rd ed., (pp. 617–625). London: Sage.

(Continued)

(Continued)

Paul, S. (2016) Group therapy and therapeutic groups. In C. Lago and D. Charura (eds), *Person-centred Counselling and Psychotherapy Handbook: Origins, Developments and Contemporary Considerations*. Maidenhead: Open University/McGraw-Hill.

Paul, S. and Charura D. (2014) The relationship in group therapy. In D. Charura and S. Paul (eds), *The Therapeutic Relationship Handbook* (pp. 131–145). Maidenhead: Open University Press.

Paul, S. and Pelham, G. (2000) A relational approach to therapy. In S. Palmer and R. Woolfe (eds), *Integrative and Eclectic Counselling and Psychotherapy* (pp. 110–126). London: Sage.

Perls, F., Hefferline, R. and Goodman, P. (1959) *Gestalt Therapy: Excitement and Growth in the Human Personality*. Harmondsworth: Penguin.

Rogers, C. (1970) *Carl Rogers on Encounter Groups*. New York: Harper & Row.

Schilder, P. (1936) The analysis of ideologies as a psychotherapeutic method, especially in group treatment. *American Journal of Psychiatry*, 93(3): 601–617.

Slipp, S. (1993) Family therapy and multiple family therapy. In H. Kaplan and B. Sadock (eds), *Comprehensive Group Psychotherapy* (3rd ed., pp. 270–283). Baltimore, MD: Williams and Wilkins.

van Deurzen-Smith, E. (1990) *Existential Therapy*. London: Society for Existential Analysis Publications.

Wender, L. (1936) The dynamics of group psychotherapy and its application. *Journal of Nervous and Mental Disease*, 84: 55.

White, J. (2000) Introduction. In J. White and A. Freeman (eds), *Cognitive-behavioural Group Therapy for Specific Problems and Populations*. Washington, DC: American Psychological Association.

Yalom, I.D. (1981) *Existential Psychotherapy*. New York: Basic Books.

Yalom, I.D. with Leszcz, M. (2005) *The Theory and Practice of Group Psychotherapy* (5th ed.). New York: Basic Books.

RECOMMENDED READING

1. Corey, G. (2008) *Theory and Practice of Group Counseling* (7th ed.) Belmont, CA: Wadsworth/Thomson.

A generic text that reviews the theory and practice of the different modalities. This is useful in helping understand the different ways of working.

2. Tudor, K. (1999) *Group Counselling*. London: Sage.

Tudor covers key considerations in the practice of group therapy. A useful reference guide.

3. Yalom, I.D. with Leszcz, M. (2005) *The Theory and Practice of Group Psychotherapy* (5th ed.). New York: Basic Books.

A classic exposition. Every group therapist should have a copy.

7.22   RELATIONSHIP THERAPY

GAIL EVANS

OVERVIEW AND KEY POINTS

This chapter intends to be a practical introduction to work-ing with more than one adult client. Mainly these are adult intimate relationships but the techniques are relevant for other pairings (e.g., adult siblings, adult child–parent). The chapter discusses:

- issues of context and preparation
- assessment and referral considerations
- particular aspects of ethics and safety in this work
- the tasks and characteristics of relationship therapy
- the research evidence.

BACKGROUND AND CONTEXT

Therapy with more than one client can be draining and challenging, but also liberating. Because it is different from working with individuals, specialised training and supervision is beneficial. This supports development of knowledge and skills, and challenges self-awareness, especially for work with non-traditional relationships.

Whatever context you work in, consider how the service is publicised and to whom it appeals. Disadvantaged groups need encouragement that their needs will be understood. Certain groups retain fears that their lifestyle or orientation will be judged or not understood, and may justifiably ask about therapist sexual orientation, experience and attitudes. Organisations should train staff to respond sensitively to enquiries, taking into account this issue and others men-tioned below. If sexual therapy or another specialised service is offered, clients should be openly asked which type of help they are seeking, as they may feel reticent to ask.

WHO CONTACTS?

One person usually arranges an appointment, but the fol-lowing should be considered:

- How has your service been selected?
- Has the decision been motivated and taken jointly and equally?
- Has one client 'brought' the other, perhaps to be changed or abandoned to the therapist's care?

It is useful to think through how referrals are taken and what information is asked for because the freer one is from internal conversations and concerns the better one is able to notice clues to relationship dynamics.

THE THERAPY ENVIRONMENT

Consider the therapy room and its layout for working with two clients:

- What messages and choices do seating and surround-ings convey?
- Do clients have free choice of seat? What if one takes the only chair and you are left to share a sofa with the other?

Power and relationship dynamics in the pair, and the ther-apeutic triad, are played out. Whatever your therapeutic orientation, this means that working with two clients is likely to involve more direction from you – a key differ-ence from most one-to-one therapies.

THE ROLE OF THE THERAPIST

From the moment of first communication, much is inferred about your position in the triad, for example:

- Whose side are you on?
- What is your role: parent (nurturing, critical), friend, sibling, expert, collaborator?

As far as possible, and explicitly, you need to engage both clients equally (don't forget about body language). However, when there is a power imbalance, by maintain-ing neutrality, do you *de facto* collude with the stronger party (Rabin, 1996)? Whether your role is collegial or par-ent-like may depend on the attachment patterns of each client – the more secure the attachment style, the better able they are to engage with you as adult problem-solvers.

ASSESSMENT

Assessment resembles the beginnings of other therapy rela-tionships. Here, though, you aim to establish a relationship with *two* people and discover whether both are willing and able to work well enough *together*, albeit there may be hurt, animosity and differences. Without a shared agenda useful therapy may be impossible. Part of *my* agenda as a relationship therapist is that *the relationship is the client*, which impacts the nature of the contract and interaction.

In short-term settings it must be decided whether it is in the clients' interests to offer therapy or refer. There are short-term couple therapy models (e.g., Gilbert and Shmukler, 1996; Payne, 2010). As in one-to-one work, some clients are on the cusp of change. Arranging and coming to therapy galvanises their own resources. Airing issues in a supportive environment launches them into working together to find their own resolution, sometimes one session being enough. However, there are many instances where issues are complex, long-standing and less easily resolved. When only short-term work can be offered, you should note signs that clients can quickly respond to facilitation of effective communication and engage in cooperative work (where both parties lower defences to hear and respect each other's point of view, taking shared responsibility for change). One indicator is that their narratives are broadly similar, or adapt during dialogue, to create shared goals.

Assessment should uncover whether they need a specific approach, like sexual therapy, or both require one-to-one work. Anxiety or depression in one partner often causes relationship difficulties. General difficulties may be caused by, or be the cause of, sexual problems and this needs to be teased out. While it may appear from the media that there is openness about sex, in practice many adult couples need explicit invitation and encouragement to discuss this aspect. Conversely, some discuss sexual difficulties freely but are reluctant to examine their general relationship: to acknowledge the whole relationship is in trouble is more disturbing than identifying a part for blame.

With specific sexual difficulties it is advisable to:

- recommend consultation with a general practitioner (GP) or sexual health clinic to rule out physical causes. Sexual problems can be the first sign of an *underlying* medical condition.
- consult with a sexual therapist about the appropriateness of referral.

Sexual issues that are likely to benefit from specialised knowledge include:

- pain (either partner) at, during or preventing penetration
- desire and arousal problems (including erectile)

- orgasmic problems, including inability to orgasm (either partner), premature and retarded ejaculation
- fetishes and addictions
- gender dysphoria.

ETHICS

Working with more than one client poses different ethical challenges from one-to-one therapy. Being clear about your role, purpose, skills and values is key. Some issues emerge on contact or during assessment. Examples from my own practice include:

- being asked to work with 'affair couples' (e.g., a couple engaged in an affair for 20 years)
- information being offered or asked for by one partner (e.g., being told about an affair with a request not to reveal this to their partner)
- one partner arrives without the other: do you see them? what implications are there for future shared sessions?
- being asked to offer separate individual sessions
- one partner is also having individual therapy
- lawyers and other professionals involved in divorce and custody cases wanting information, supporting letters or asking for notes.

As with many ethical dilemmas, these can take you unawares, so it is wise to defer decisions until you can think them through. Supervision with an experienced relationship supervisor is recommended.

THE CONTRACT

The contract, therefore, requires negotiation around confidentiality and its limits, being clear about your attitude to different permutations of working. Will you insist that both partners attend all appointments *together*, as some relationship therapists do? If you and the couple think some separate appointments would help, an agreement is needed about what can be shared back into the triad. The impact of developing a relationship with one client while the other client is more distant from the therapeutic process is an issue. Being clear about principles and rationales will aid you to handle situations sensitively and calmly when put on the spot.

SAFETY

Domestic abuse crosses class, gender and orientation boundaries and is commonplace. Domestic violence is more likely when the relationship is strained and when the victim leaves, or threatens to leave, the relationship. Threatening behaviour may be deployed; one partner may relentlessly pursue the other for a response, culminating in the pursued partner lashing out. People are frequently unaware of *how* behaviour escalates, how intimidating their actions may be to their partner and the impact on children (often wrongly thought to be unaware). Therapists must be alert for signs and should ascertain, *routinely*, whether incidents are, or have ever been, happening. It takes confidence to 'hold' the couple, to convey acceptance but also firmness that continued abuse is not acceptable, and (with good supervision) to know when proceeding may be dangerous.

Many relationship therapists refuse to work on relationship issues until a domestic abuse contract is in place, even when incidents seem 'minor' or not recent. Therapy may inflame emotions. A client subjected to abuse is unlikely to speak openly without risk of assault outside therapy. The contract identifies a workable plan of action for situations of potential abuse so both parties take responsibility for safety, and sets out expectations of behaviour within the therapy room and possible safeguarding action.

WAYS OF WORKING

TASKS OF THERAPY

While a therapist's approach to relationship issues will be influenced by their theoretical allegiance, common therapeutic goals may be summed up as follows:

- Exploring compatibility of goals, values, beliefs, frames of reference
- Developing shared awareness of the nature of the problem and how each client *experiences* it, including any impact of societal attitudes and internalised oppression, to create a different narrative

- Encouraging *relational* communication to improve emotional intimacy, catharsis, fun and shared sexual gratification (where appropriate)
- Improving problem-solving and conflict resolution
- Strengthening relational bonds, care and support for each other by developing mutual empathy and acceptance.

In several ways, couple therapy has a different and unfamiliar feel compared with many one-to-one approaches. From the outset the message is that *both* clients will be heard and this requires more management by the therapist. One consideration is power in the room, which may be influenced by a number of factors, for example:

- Who pays, and the symbolism of money in the relationship
- How appointments are negotiated with multiple commitments, issues of childcare, etc.
- The therapist's gender and/or sexuality
- Ensuring engagement and feedback from *both* clients (e.g., one partner's lack of proficiency in English meaning the other acts as translator)
- Negotiating tasks, homework, etc., so that *both* parties have the same information and both understand and agree to tasks
- The therapist's power (e.g., the attitude to difference and varied relationship styles).

You may need to take charge of interaction, as in the case example below: enabling each to speak; to show they have been heard; preventing negative patterns being established (e.g., one speaks for both, one speaks most) or time wasted on repeated arguments; and to maintain a *relational* focus (rather than individual issues or third parties), encouraging the couple to develop their relationship *with each other*. This sounds obvious but can be tricky because as a one-to-one therapist you are used to clients relating to *you*. It is more important that they understand each other than be understood by you.

CASE EXAMPLE

A couple self-referred having become increasingly isolated from each other and angry, despite being best friends for years before they became a couple. At first meeting they were so angry, mutually blaming and unable to empathise with each other that they wondered if the only solution was separation. I actively managed the interaction to curtail argument and give each partner air time. We attempted a communication exercise,

(Continued)

which was too difficult for them, so I recommended we practise again in our next session. The second session sought to understand more about how they had reached this point and a tragic tale emerged. The session was cathartic, enabling them to recognise, through telling the shared story, they had *both* been through a prolonged and extremely difficult series of life events. It was amazing that their relationship had endured. The third session found a different atmosphere between them: they had been able to talk between sessions using the communication exercise 'rules'; they were ready to cooperate and rebuild.

Asking a pair to face and speak to each other allows you to observe interaction. *Decentring* subtly influences the conversation: when one client speaks, direct your gaze downwards, or towards the other. This encourages the speaker also to address their partner. When the conversational turn passes to the partner, switch your attention back. This will feel odd, running counter to normal conversational 'rules'!

When clients cannot listen to each other they may be too fearful. Explicitly building a relationship with *each* may help, before they can empathise with each other, for example dividing a session between them, offering separate sessions, working with one client at a time, with the other as witness.

STRENGTHENING RELATIONAL BONDS

Mutual empathy is a relational need (Erskine, 2015). Relational therapy fosters mutual understanding and acceptance (e.g., Greenberg and Johnson, 2010). The therapist can model, and deliberately encourage this, for example, highlighting *shared emotional experiences and values*. This supports reconnection with an earlier, more positive, shared history, which in turn engenders hope and motivation.

NORMALISING

Contextualising difficulties is helpful: many challenges come with life changes or stages. History exploration assists clients to understand their situation and develop self and mutual empathy, and is one way to distract from damaging exchanges and identify strengths.

A tool from family therapy, the genogram (e.g., McGoldrick et al., 2008), can be used for such exploration. Using a large piece of paper and marker pens, working together facilitates common purpose in making a family tree. Actors in family history, relationships between them, repeating patterns across generations, expectations, rules, roles, conflicts and boundaries, and how these are similar

or different between the clients, are identified. Clients are often surprised, enlightened and develop mutual empathy, strengthening the relational bond.

DEVELOPING RELATIONAL COMMUNICATION

When partners are in distress, a major cause and casualty is communication. Some never establish helpful communication patterns, while others lose the capacity to communicate constructively, allowing projections and assumptions to develop and exacerbate issues. The model of the therapist demonstrating careful listening is helpful, but teaching can actively assist *them* to establish constructive communication. A step-by-step listening and reflecting back exercise, similar to skills exercises in counselling training, is simple to teach, but it is important to explain carefully, explore specific times to do it and potential pitfalls, and try it in the therapy room first. If a couple cannot do it with you as referee, they will certainly not manage it elsewhere.

This is an example of how liberating relationship counselling can be. The emphasis is not all on the interaction between client and therapist. While clients talk to each other, you can observe relational patterns.

One common pattern is a repeating loop of interactions (see Figure 7.22.1, showing partners A and B) that replays earlier attachment wounds. Clients find it illuminating to see this on paper. Attachment theory holds useful insights and may also be explored through the genogram. See also Chapter 6.18 (Evans – this volume) for more information about working with relationships and sex problems.

Thus, relationship therapy may be more directive and psycho-educational than some individual therapies. For instance, Wile (1993) advocates teaching couples how to argue effectively; sex therapy includes psychosexual education and specific tasks.

As with individual therapy, once emotive issues are ventilated clients' own resourcefulness re-emerges and they may find their own solutions to fit their values. Some relationship therapies focus on emotional ventilation (e.g., Greenberg and Johnson, 2010).

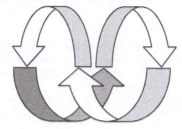

A. When I
experience attack
I get scared

When I get
scared I
withdraw

B. When I experience
withdrawal I feel
rejected

When I feel
rejected I
get angry (attack)

Figure 7.22.1   Figure of eight pattern of interaction

SEXUAL ISSUES

Depending on knowledge and experience you might help with general sexual problems (e.g., sexual ignorance, doubts about orientation). Relate's PLISSIT model can been used as a guide:

P – Permission Many clients merely need invitation and support to discuss sexual matters, including familiarisation with language and normalisation

L – Limited Basic education in sexuality and sexual functioning

I – Information may be within your knowledge and comfort

S – Specific With some knowledge and training you may

S – Sexual tasks negotiate specific tasks to reduce anxiety and enhance their sexual relationship

I – Intensive Referral to a sexual therapist is indicated because of a

T – Therapy specific sexual dysfunction.

In all instances, you should facilitate a free and frank exchange. There are many publications available to expand knowledge and understanding, and numerous television programmes (e.g., *Embarrassing Bodies*, Channel 4

Television Corporation) and documentaries on sexuality are informative and challenging of attitudes.

RESEARCH EVIDENCE

There are few longitudinal studies of successful, long-term relationships. Many publications cite Noller and Fitzpatrick (1990) that communication is key to successful long-term relationship satisfaction. Rabin (1996) cites fairness as a key principle. Wallerstein and Blakeslee (1996) identified tasks that need to be successfully negotiated. Other writers have, from observation and interviews, identified key features of happy relationships (e.g., Moursund and Erskine, 2003; Reibstein, 1997).

There is evidence for the effectiveness of relationship therapy (e.g., Lebow, 2012; Cowan and Cowan, 2014; Spielhofer et al., 2014), but most research is hetero-normative and role-models for other forms of adult intimate relationship are sparse.

Video has been used and researched as an effective relationship-building tool (e.g., a National Society for the Prevention of Cruelty to Children (NSPCC) project to strengthen parent–child interactions: Whalley and Williams, 2015). Documentaries about relationships have demonstrated how powerful video is to highlight interaction patterns, and suggest that it may be advantageous to take the work outside the therapy room. With modern easy-to-use video technology, therapists can incorporate this into work with clients, so clients see their interactions for themselves.

REFERENCES

Cowan, P.A. and Cowan, C.P. (2014) Controversies in couple relationship education (CRE): Overlooked evidence and implications for research and policy. *Psychology, Public Policy, and Law,* 20(4): 361–383
Erskine, R.G. (2015) *Relational Patterns, Therapeutic Presence.* London: Karnac.

(Continued)

(Continued)

Gilbert, M. and Shmukler, D. (1996) *Brief Therapy with Couples: An Integrative Approach*. Chichester: Wiley.

Greenberg, L.S. and Johnson, S.M. (2010). *Emotionally Focused Therapy for Couples*. New York: Guilford Press.

Lebow, J.L., Chambers, A.L., Christensen, A. and Johnson, S.M. (2012) Research on the treatment of couple distress. *Journal of Marital and Family Therapy*, 38(1): 145–168.

McGoldrick, M., Gerson, R. and Petry, S. (2008) *Genograms: Assessment and Intervention*. New York: W.W. Norton.

McWhirter, D.P. and Mattison, A.M. (1990) *The Male Couple: How Relationships Develop*. Englewood Cliffs, NJ: Prentice-Hall.

Moursund, J.P. and Erskine, R.G. (2003) *Integrative Psychotherapy: The Art and Science of Relationship*. Belmont, CA: Wadsworth.

Noller, P. and Fitzpatrick, M.A. (1990) Marital communication in the eighties. *Journal of Marriage and the Family*, 52(4): 832–843.

Payne, M. (2010) *Couple Counselling: A Practical Guide*. London: Sage.

Rabin, C. (1996) *Equal Partners, Good Friends: Empowering Couples through Therapy*. London: Routledge.

Reibstein, J. (1997) *Love Life: How to Make Your Relationship Work*. London: Fourth Estate.

Spielhofer, T., Corlyon, J., Durbin, B., Smith, M., Stock, L. and Gieve, M. (2014) *Relationship Support Interventions Evaluation*. London: Department for Education.

Wallerstein, J.S. and Blakeslee, S. (1996) *The Good Marriage*. London: Transworld.

Whalley, P. and Williams, M. (2015) *Child Neglect and Video Interaction Guidance*. London: NSPCC.

Wile, D.B. (1993) *Couples Therapy: A Nontraditional Approach*. Chichester: Wiley.

RECOMMENDED READING

1. Relate website (www.relate.org.uk).

Relate offers training and relevant books on relationships. See www.relate.org.uk/about-us/work-us/train-be-counsellor and www.relate.org.uk/relationship-help/self-help-tools/book-shop.

2. Richards, C. and Barker, M. (2013) *Sexuality and Gender for Mental Health Professionals: A Practical Guide*. London: Sage.

An excellent, challenging and modern guide to the complexities of gender, sexuality, culture and relationships.

3. Sue Johnson's website (www.drsuejohnson.com).

A number of publications about emotionally-focused therapy (a structured model) are authored by Sue Johnson. See this website for information and videos.

THERAPEUTIC SPECIALISMS: TECHNOLOGY AND THERAPY

OVERVIEW AND KEY POINTS

Since the last edition of this *Handbook*, there has been a substantial increase in the use of mobile phones. Counselling by phone is sometimes considered 'old technology', yet more people use phones every day and clients are able to access counselling wherever they might be and at times to suit them. The skills required to work effectively by phone are among the highest order skills a counsellor can attain:

- Counselling effectively with a stranger with no visual cues
- Counselling with no background knowledge, except perhaps a brief referral
- Counselling skilfully, aware of and appropriately responding to nuances, silences, slight audible changes in voice tone or pitch, words used that might be at odds with information provided
- Holding a clear contract and its inherent boundaries negotiated by voice alone, though a written final version must be signed by the client before sessions commence.

BACKGROUND AND CONTEXT

Smartphones have become the hub of many people's daily lives and are now used by two-thirds (66%) of United Kingdom (UK) adults, up from 39% in 2012. A majority (90%) of 16–24 year-olds own one; but 55–64 year olds are also joining the smartphone revolution, with ownership in this age group more than doubling since 2012, from 19% to 50% (Ofcom, 2015).

As this chapter will highlight, working as a counsellor by telephone is significantly different from face-to-face and internet-based work. Also examined are the standards and ethical considerations that should be taken into account to ensure that clients receive the best possible service from their counsellors and that the counsellors develop high-quality practice.

Telephone counselling is not the same as one-off crisis interventions on a helpline; nor is it the same as an education-based programme such as one for quitting smoking or tackling gambling problems. While these programmes might teach a modified cognitive-behavioural therapy (CBT) approach, this is not considered true telephone counselling in the context of working with a range of issues requiring a deeper exploration of the client's past and present challenges. It is holding this depth of relationship that necessitates the highly specialised skill base and clear contracts that keep both parties safe (Rosenfield, 2013: 47–65).

WAYS OF WORKING

Telephone counselling has many advantages over face-to-face or visual internet counselling. The lack of the impact of any visual impressions and assumptions or prejudices that occur when client and counsellor see each other in a formal counselling room causes both parties to focus on each other's voice tones and words. The anonymity of the medium is liberating for many clients (and counsellors!). The intensity of the interaction further enhances the development of the relationship, because there is less opportunity for distractions during the session while both parties are focused on words and voice tone alone. This usually enables a deeper therapeutic relationship to be established sooner than would occur in much face-to-face work. Silences are nuanced and form an essential part of the process.

The entire process of counselling in this medium is generally accelerated so that fewer sessions are indicated for the client to gain insight, awareness, understanding and/or empowerment. In my contracts, I suggest a maximum of six sessions, with a review often at session four, as clients reach their most emotionally challenging sessions during session two and perhaps continuing into session three.

Telephone counselling is an excellent example of an integrative approach to counselling. It can utilise aspects of psychodynamic orientations, person-centred approaches, brief therapeutic interventions and other humanistic methods of working. Cognitive-behavioural techniques may be used alongside interpretative psycho-therapeutic disciplines.

There is no doubt that transference and countertransference occur, triggered by language, subject matter and by voice tones, pitch and accents. Psycho-education, goal-setting and action-planning may be as much a part of some sessions as exploring the emotional aspects of the client's situation. Much effective work by telephone can focus on helping the client to draw on their own strengths or on the client's 'self-healing potential'.

When someone contracts for telephone counselling sessions, they lose some of their anonymity and confidentiality. As with helpline work, a point of crisis may be the trigger for the person to seek counselling but, unlike talking to someone on a helpline, the client is not anonymous. The client has to agree a contract for the work and therefore provide some personal details which they might not reveal if they are calling a helpline for a one-off call. Telephone counselling is an excellent medium for challenging the inherent power relationship between counsellor and client. Both parties have to work with the unknown in ways that face-to-face counselling does not present. Further, it could be argued that the ultimate power lies with the client, who can choose to hang up at any time. Of course the counsellor who has completed a degree or equivalent is going to have the theoretical knowledge and therefore likely hold 'academic' power in the relationship, but in practice, the client and counsellor work more 'collegially' than in any other counselling mode.

ACCESSIBILITY AND FINANCIAL CONSIDERATIONS OF TELEPHONE COUNSELLING

Many people have relatively easy access to a telephone, but for a one-hour counselling session finding a place that is private, quiet and uninterrupted is more difficult. As the statistics mentioned earlier demonstrate, many people now use mobile phones for their counselling. These are as reliable in sound quality as fixed phone lines and make the mobile the choice of phone for many clients. It is good for the counsellor to discuss the likely choice of phone with the client at the assessment session so that the client can plan to be in a suitable safe space for their sessions. Headsets or earpieces attached to the phone provide good quality audio and voice quality.

The cost of calls between a private counsellor and client, whether on a landline or mobile, can impact on the consideration of both parties to enter into a therapeutic relationship, although many mobile phone plans include 'unlimited' calls. Technology has also come to the aid of this potential financial constraint. The use of voice over internet protocol (VOIP) enables people to talk at low cost over internet networks, although there may be data limitations for heavy usage. Software such as Skype enables users to make voice calls over the internet. Skype calls are free to other Skype users but calls can be made to both landlines and mobiles for a fee.

Telephone counselling makes it unnecessary for the client to travel to see a counsellor; when the client has access to a phone and a quiet room, the session can take place without the client or counsellor having to be in the same location for each session. It is therefore a very accessible medium for people who travel, for someone who has limited mobility, or who has limited time in their schedule.

Where illness can result in face-to-face sessions being cancelled, it does not always prevent telephone counselling sessions from taking place. People who are terminally ill or limited in mobility can still receive counselling. Carers who might wish to attend counselling sessions, but cannot guarantee the availability of regular respite care at a specific time for an appointment, can also benefit from telephone counselling.

The cost of any phone call is likely to be less than the cost in time and travel to visit a counsellor, making telephone work more financially accessible in many cases. Clients can choose to work by telephone with counsellors who are not geographically accessible to them. This enables people to find a specific counsellor for a specific purpose. Some counsellors and clients work together when one party is outside their own country.

From the counsellor's perspective, the telephone can be liberating, enabling them to operate from any environment that is quiet and where they are uninterrupted. It may also mean that the counsellor can work with a wider variety of clients at a greater range of times.

For telephone group work, the teleconference can bring together people from all over the country, or indeed the world, as long as each individual can be in a quiet, private place. This can lead to groups being created for people who are linked through rarer situations, specific illnesses, age or any other common theme.

CONTRACTING

Some of the issues to be considered for contracting have already been addressed, such as location and time.

A contract must be agreed at an initial assessment session which may be free of charge except, perhaps, for the cost of the phone call, and can last for up to an hour. Sometimes the core elements of the contract are agreed in a first conversation prior to a formal session. The core elements of a contract should include:

- the goals or aims of the sessions
- the length of each session, which should be fixed at no longer than an hour and no less than 30 minutes
- the likely time interval between sessions, ideally a week or two

- the number of sessions before a review – a block of six with a review during the fourth or fifth is suggested. Further blocks of four to six sessions can be agreed as desired.
- who calls whom and therefore pays if there is any cost for the call
- methods of payment – how much, when and how it will be received?
- the terms for the cancellation of a session
- what is considered a late start or no-show and what happens in these instances?
- what types of notes or other means of recording the sessions would be acceptable? If recording is to happen, both parties must give overt consent.
- what the client might do to 'leave the room' in a practical sense after the session ends, given there is no travelling which helps the session to 'end' or 'close' psychologically?
- what would constitute a breach of confidentiality and why?
- how confidentiality relates to technological issues for both parties
- what happens if the technology fails – if the phone lines drop out or, if using VOIP, the internet crashes?
- what happens if the client makes contact between sessions?

ETHICAL ISSUES

Ethical issues include the counsellor explicitly adhering to existing codes of conduct, such as those published by professional counselling associations. There is also an ethical consideration regarding payment. It is possible for a counsellor to purchase a premium rate tariff telephone line. In this case, the client calling the counsellor pays more than the cost of a regular phone call and the 'profit' could constitute all or part of the counsellor's fee. If this is the case, the counsellor must inform the client or the potential client of the likely cost per session in advance. Ethically, it is inappropriate for the counsellor to use this premium rate telephone line for the assessment session. In addition, such a tariff does not permit any discretionary rate for clients.

Mixing face-to-face sessions and telephone sessions is not acceptable for telephone counselling. This is because the mixing of the media will affect the transference issues/ power relationship/dynamics of the relationship, with visual assumptions or judgements or prejudices changing the phone relationship thereafter. When a counselling relationship is being established, this could have an impact on the trust and the development of the partnership.

Confidentiality comes into both contracting and ethics. If the counsellor who operates anything other than a freephone service, calls the client, the counsellor's phone number will be itemised on the client's telephone bill, unless the counsellor applies the 'one off' block code prior to dialling or has their number permanently blocked.

SETTLING IN TO A SESSION

It is important to have some 'settling in' comments to enable the client to feel as comfortable as possible to start talking in session. The counsellor needs to take responsibility for leading this so that the client is welcomed and encouraged to talk if they want to. Often a welcome followed by a pause then a simple open question such as 'what is it that has brought you to counselling?' or 'what's been happening since last time we spoke?' is enough. For a first session, it can be useful to start with a few 'safe' comments, perhaps about the sessions, reiterating parts of the contract, and including a reminder of how long each session will last. I also make explicit any strategies for re-contacting if technology fails for any reason, taking responsibility for trying to re-contact the client. The reason I take this role is so that I have some control over this. I have scheduled an hour and can only re-try for that time period. If for some reason we were not able to get back in contact during the hour, I would call, text, email or get in touch by post later in the day to re-establish contact and suggest another time to talk.

The first few minutes of any session are crucial for establishing the bond between client and counsellor and particular attention needs to be paid to the sounds, the tone and pitch of voice, the way the client presents. This indicates where they are, emotionally speaking, at that time and enables the counsellor to respond empathically and appropriately, following the client's agenda, which might not be overt to them.

IN PRACTICE: WORKING WITH OLIVIA

Session 1:

Me: 'Hello Olivia'.

Olivia: 'Hello I'm a bit unsure how to begin…'

Me: 'Well, just before we start talking today, I want to remind you that we have up to an hour to talk and if we get cut off for any reason, we will try to re-connect with me calling you again or texting your mobile if I cannot get through to the landline that we are using just now'.

At the end of the first session Olivia decided to try to talk to her mother about one of the big issues she thought blocked their conversations – how her mother seemed to tell Olivia's sister everything they ever discussed.

Session 2:

Starting session 2, Olivia sounded quieter than I had remembered and her voice was almost childlike. It is usual to make explicit what is heard, so after she had been talking about what had happened in the past week, I commented on her voice:

> Me: 'Olivia, as you've been talking, I've noticed that you sound quite different from how you sounded in our last session…'

I always pause after such a comment, just for a couple of seconds to see if the client wishes to respond. If not, I would ask an open question seeking to explore this further or to open up the session in any other way the client wanted. In this case, the pause provided the space for Olivia to open up.

Intense emotions can be expressed freely in a phone session and the counsellor role is to sit and attend, making non-verbal sounds which the client may not even hear, but if they do, it is reassurance that the counsellor is still there.

The importance of such subtleties cannot be underestimated.

TRAINING AND SUPERVISION

One assumption throughout this section is that the counsellor should hold at least a full Graduate Diploma or Degree in Counselling and have at least a year's experience of face-to-face counselling practice before they commence telephone work. This ensures their core skills are adequately developed to adapt to the non-visual medium.

It is not enough to assume that a good face-to-face counsellor will have, or be able to develop, the necessary skills for telephone counselling and there is a worrying trend in trained counsellors or therapists developing a telephone practice without ever receiving qualitative feedback about their voice, style and manner, which would be assessed during a telephone counselling training course.

Telephone Group Counselling requires additional skills, usually learned 'on the job'. Counsellors with previous experience of running face-to-face therapy groups should have the necessary core skills and could adapt these to the non-visual medium.

A SKILLS CHECKLIST FOR THE TRAINED COUNSELLOR/ THERAPIST STARTING TELEPHONE WORK

- How do you sound?
- Is your accent pronounced or could it be off-putting to the client group you seek to attract?
- Are you able to work with silence on the phone? Be aware that a silence of a few seconds on the phone often seems like minutes and the usual counselling/ therapeutic interpretations of silence and methods of responding to silence need to be adapted for successful work on the phone.
- How skilled would you be at handling distress with no visual clues?
- Are you confident at interrupting the client's flow if needs be because the session is almost over?

SUPERVISION BY TELEPHONE

This form of supervision is growing as counsellors seek out supervisors for specific reasons. The issues relating to skills transfer and voice tones are the same as for the client–counsellor relationship, and not all supervisors can or should adapt to the phone. At the very least, a supervisor might ask a fellow supervisor to do an objective assessment for voice tone, manner and style before offering themselves to work in this medium.

RESEARCH EVIDENCE

There is limited published research into telephone counselling; there is plenty about helpline work and plenty about specific CBT-based programmes, such as to help quit smoking, but these are not true phone counselling and are excluded here.

Often the research will contrast phone and internet counselling, such as King, Bambling, Reid and Thomas (2006: 175), who concluded that the phone was more beneficial: 'thought to be due to the greater communication efficiency of the phone enabling more counselling to be undertaken in the time available'.

Countertransference during telephone counselling is discussed by Christogiorgos et al. (2010). The paper considers countertransference phenomena, which may become apparent when working by phone, originating from the same factors that are experienced in a traditional psychotherapeutic framework.

REFERENCES

Christogiorgos, S., Vassilopoulou, V., Florou, A., Xydou, V., Douvou, M., Vgenopoulou, S. and Tsiantis, J. (2010) Telephone counselling with adolescents and countertransference phenomena: particularities and challenges. *British Journal of Guidance & Counselling*, 38(3): 313–325.

King, R., Bambling, M., Reid, W. and Thomas, I. (2006) Telephone and online counselling for young people: a naturalistic comparison of session outcome, session impact and therapeutic alliance. *Counselling and Psychotherapy Research*, 6(3): 175–181.

Ofcom (2015) Percentage of households with landline telephones in the United Kingdom (UK) from 1970 to 2014. Ofcom's 12th Annual Communications Market Report. (www.statista.com/statistics/289158/telephone-presence-in-households-in-the-uk/).

Rosenfield, M. (2013) *Telephone Counselling*: *A Handbook for Practitioners*. Basingstoke: Palgrave Macmillan.

RECOMMENDED READING

1. Rosenfield, M. (1997) *Counselling by Telephone*. London: Sage.

An introductory text for those counselling by telephone.

2. Rosenfield, M. (2013) *Telephone Counselling*: *A Handbook for Practitioners*. Basingstoke: Palgrave Macmillan.

A practitioner-focused text aimed at developing skills in telephone counselling.

3. King, R., Bambling, M., Reid, W. and Thomas, I. (2006) Telephone and online counselling for young people: a naturalistic comparison of session outcome, session impact and therapeutic alliance. *Counselling and Psychotherapy Research*, 6(3): 175–181.

An interesting research article comparing telephone and online counselling for young people.

7.24 ELECTRONICALLY DELIVERED TEXT THERAPIES

KATE ANTHONY

OVERVIEW AND KEY POINTS

This chapter describes the most essential elements that practitioners need to be aware of before considering an online presence. It will concentrate on the use of *text* (via email, chat, forums and mobile phone texting (Short Message Service: SMS)) for conducting an individual client–practitioner therapeutic relationship. Key points include:

- Text-based therapies have become an established part of the therapy world.
- There are specific skills, such as enhanced writing techniques, that are needed to work online with clients.
- Research in this area commonly demonstrates the effectiveness of working through text-based media.

BACKGROUND AND CONTEXT

The concept of delivering psychotherapeutic services via technology has traditionally been a controversial one. However, the body of evidence that was slowly increasing when previous editions of this *Handbook* were published is now established, and it is increasingly rare to find a mental health service that does not have an internet presence in some form – from a simple website or directory listing to a fully developed e-clinic or presence in a virtual environment.

Twenty years on from the first appearance of commercial websites that offered email and chat for therapeutic communication, many publications have provided a wealth of information and literature around the topic. Perhaps the most comprehensive of these, for further textbook reading, are Hsiung (2002), Goss and Anthony (2003), Kraus, Zack and Stricker (2004), Derrig-Palumbo and Zeine (2005), Evans (2009), Jones and Stokes (2009), Anthony and Nagel (2010) and Anthony and Goss (2009; Goss, Anthony, Stretch and Nagel, 2016), Kraus, Stricker and Speyer (2010), and see Chapter 7.25 (Anthony, Goss and Nagel – this volume).

As well as the work of international experts in the field, publishing literature and collaborating on research projects, the area of electronically delivered therapy (and in particular the ethical and legal side of it) has been addressed by mental health organizations worldwide. Professional bodies such as the British Association for Counselling and Psychotherapy (Anthony and Goss, 2009; Anthony and Jamieson, 2005; Goss, Anthony, Palmer and Jamieson, 2001; Hill and Roth, 2014), the National Board of Certified Counselors (2001), and the American Counseling Association (1999) have addressed and published guidelines for their members who wish to offer an online presence. The International Society for Mental Health Online (www.acto-org.uk) was formed in 1997 and offers suggested principles for working online; the Association for Counselling and Therapy Online (www.acto-uk.org) was formed in 2006 for UK practitioners and offers a code of ethics; and in 2008, the formation of the Online Therapy Institute (www.onlinetherapyinstitute.com) in 2008 led to the *Ethical Framework for the Use of Technology in Mental Health* (Nagel and Anthony, 2009), a framework designed to be applicable to as many areas of mental health provision as possible. Online mental health clinics are increasingly turning to developing their own ethical frameworks in light of the lack of concrete advice from professional organizations (see PlusGuidance.com, for example).

WAYS OF WORKING

TYPES OF ELECTRONICALLY DELIVERED THERAPY

USING BLOCK-TEXT EMAIL (ASYNCHRONOUS) FOR THERAPY. This is most people's perception of using email for therapeutic use: the exchanging back and forth of emails between two people within a contract, which is (usually) short term and (usually) weekly, and which utilizes encryption software for privacy and confidentiality.

USING NARRATIVE DYNAMIC EMAIL (ASYNCHRONOUS) FOR THERAPY. This type of email is where the practitioner inserts his/her responses *within* the client's email using different fonts and/or colours, and the client reciprocates in the same way, usually for a small number of exchanges before the dynamic text becomes too unwieldy and a new narrative is required. Again, it is (usually) short term and (usually) weekly, and utilizes encryption software for privacy and confidentiality.

USING CHAT ROOMS (SYNCHRONOUS) FOR THERAPY. This method involves a dialogue between client and practitioner in real time, using an encrypted internet chat room or encrypted instant messaging software. The contracted sessions are usually weekly, and often incorporate a weekly exchange of asynchronous email (this is a useful function to allow the client to expand upon actual descriptive situations that would otherwise take up valuable time within the sessions).

USING FORUMS (ASYNCHRONOUS) FOR THERAPY. More secure than any other form of electronically delivered therapy within this context, forums are held on the internet itself behind a password protected access system so that client and therapist visit a website to view and post responses to each other.

USING MOBILE PHONE TEXTING (ASYNCHRONOUS) FOR THERAPY. Mobile phone texting (SMS) is often reserved for making and cancelling face-to-face appointments, but is increasingly used as part of the therapeutic process and is useful if used with care within a boundaried relationship. It is increasingly also used for crisis intervention by organizations such as Samaritans (Goss and Ferns, 2016).

THE ESSENTIAL CONCEPTS OF ONLINE TEXTUAL THERAPY

The first aspect of working with text that may seem obvious but bears clarifying is that it is a distance method of communication. There are obvious benefits to those who cannot access therapy, for example because of disability or geographical reasons, but apart from practical reasons it is important to understand the 'disinhibition effect' (Suler, 2004) that often makes for a more open and honest relationship. The ability for the client to reveal much more when working at a certain perceived distance (the one with which they feel comfortable) is significant. It also means that the level of disclosure occurs at a much faster pace than it usually does in a face-to-face relationship or even within other methods of distance therapy, such as the telephone. This intensity of disinhibition is peculiar to using typed text over the internet for communication, and should not be underestimated, particularly when taking care of the self and the client. Many clients find that a one-off outpouring of emotion and narrative, due to the disinhibition that affords a cathartic experience, means that they feel better and can disappear into cyberspace – a particularly distressing experience for the practitioner (also known as a black hole experience). For the most part, though, the disinhibition effect is a positive empowering experience, and one that is important to clients who cannot reveal sensitive information due to shame, embarrassment or being unable to 'look someone in the eye' while doing so.

The distance of the client also means that self-revelation of practitioner material, where appropriate within the work, can be a useful tool to facilitate a second aspect of working online – the concept of presence, described by Lombard and Ditton (1997) as 'the perceptual illusion of non-mediation'. This is described in my original research as occurring when 'the media used (in this case the computer and keyboard) is unimportant and you are interacting with another person in a separate space' (Anthony, 2000: 626). In this way, the medium used to conduct a therapeutic relationship is secondary to the therapeutic relationship actually taking place as a mutual journey towards the client's recovery. Despite the lack of any body language, so often cited as the reason that online work via text can never be 'real' therapy, the practitioner is able to enter the client's mental constructs of their world through their text, respond in a similar manner, and so develop a rapport that transcends the hardware used to support the communication as *well* as the 'white noise' that a physical presence can induce.

The white noise of the physical presence, which can introduce bias and judgement into a face-to-face therapeutic relationship, is bypassed when working online. Rather than seeing this as a negative part of the method, many online practitioners believe that it is not only positive, but also essential to the development of the therapeutic relationship to encourage a fantasy of the other person via a visual, auditory and kinaesthetic representation system. In this way, the client can build an overall sense of their counsellor or psychotherapist and develop that fantasy to fit their perception of the person they are most able to work with. It can be argued that the person behind each other's defences is found and the therapeutic relationship becomes stronger much more quickly.

Finally, we must consider how all this building of the therapeutic relationship can occur without the gestures, vocal interventions and eye contact that make up the traditional face-to-face relationship. The quality of the practitioner's written communication and their ability to convey the nuances of body language that facilitate the client's growth (empathic facial gestures, for example) are paramount when working online. However, it should be noted that respect for the client means that their ability to communicate in this way need not be expert (although the practitioner's work is made much easier if it is). The use of text to replicate body language takes many forms online, as does the use of netiquette (a combination of 'net' and 'etiquette'), but both aspects are integral to the success of the communication and therefore the client's recovery. Both of these aspects are also sometimes considered facile within the conventional profession, and yet their contributions to the online therapeutic relationship being established, developed and maintained are vital. While in no way exhaustive, the following should give the reader some insight into what is possible within the remit of using typed text:

- There are different ways of communicating in an appropriate manner, depending on the context of that communication. Danet (2001) identified two types of textual communication: business and personal. However, in Goss and Anthony (2003) I explain how a third definition is necessary because the 'therapeutic textual communication' is at once both a business transaction (contracted between therapist and client) and a personal communication (because of the nature of the content).
- One rule of netiquette that it is essential to be aware of is that the use of CAPITALIZATION for an entire sentence or block of text is considered to be shouting and is usually disrespectful and rude.
- There are many ways of emphasizing certain words where necessary, such as *italicizing*, **bold**, underlining, _underscoring_, and *asterisks*.

- Overuse of exclamation marks generally makes the text difficult to read and is considered poor form.
- There are thousands of emoticons that are used to convey facial expressions. Most are supplied in email and chat software and some have to be (or are preferred to be) created using keyboard characters and read by holding the head to the left (this does not apply in Asian countries – a cultural issue practitioners need to be aware of). Some of the more frequently used in online therapeutic work are:

☺ or :o) or :)   smiles (smileys)

☹ or :o(or >:o{   frowns

;) or ;o)   winks (winkies)

The winky, in particular, is essential to indicate irony or a non-serious statement.

- Abbreviations and acronyms are also widely used. Some of the more frequently used in online therapeutic work (and more generally) are:

LOL   laugh out loud

BTW   by the way

PFT, k?   pause for thought, OK?

The latter is particularly useful for the client to use silence within a synchronous text session.

- Emotional bracketing is also used to clarify emotion. As well as being able to hug your client by using parentheses, as in ((((Kate)))), some other uses are:

<<crying>>

[[sigh]]

- Automatic signature files, greetings and sign-offs also need careful consideration and the use of personal style *within the appropriate context of the communication.*

As well as the above facets of using typed text for therapeutic communication, there is, of course, a wealth of both practical and ethical considerations that need to be taken into account when setting up an online presence to work with clients. In-depth analysis of these facets is available in Anthony and Goss (2009) and Anthony and Nagel (2010), but some of the more obvious considerations are:

- confidentiality and data protection
- limitations of the method
- contracting and informed consent
- encryption
- fee structure
- assessment skills, suitability of client and referring on
- verification of parties (identity management)
- practitioner competence (both within IT and online clinical work)
- boundaries
- licensing, regulation and quality control
- virus, worm and trojan management
- crisis intervention and the suicidal client
- cultural differences
- technical breakdown.

Training in online work is now considered essential (Anthony and Goss, 2009; Anthony and Nagel, 2010; Gehl et al., 2016), and there are now a variety of online trainings available in the form of long or modular courses, such as those of the Online Therapy Institute (www.onlinetherapyinstitute.com).

The world of technological development is one that moves and develops extremely quickly, and it is well known that the counselling and psychotherapy profession in particular has been playing catch-up with the arrival of technology for therapeutic use over the last 20 years. What is certain, however, is that the profession has had to come to terms with the idea that sometimes the client is in a situation that means that they not only *cannot* sit with us face to face, but also that *they don't want to*. It is these clients that practitioners can now stop excluding from our services, ensuring that the world of counselling and psychotherapy becomes more accessible to our potential clients worldwide.

RESEARCH EVIDENCE

Barak et al. (2008) offer 'A comprehensive review and a meta-analysis of the effectiveness of internet-based psychotherapeutic interventions', which concludes that on average online therapy is as effective as face-to-face intervention. They also conclude that 'Psychotherapy and counseling should adjust to this changing world and adopt new, innovative tools accordingly to fit into the world of today and tomorrow so as to better meet clients' expectations and needs. The current review shows that this is not only theoretically possible but actually a developing professional reality' (p. 148).

REFERENCES

American Counseling Association (1999) *Ethical Standards for Internet Online Counselling*. Alexandria, VA: ACM. (http://ct.counseling.org/2006/12/ct-online-ethics-update-)

Anthony, K. (2000) Counselling in cyberspace. *Counselling Journal*, 11(10), 625–627.

Anthony, K. and Goss, S. (2009) *Guidelines for Online Counselling and Psychotherapy* (3rd ed.). Lutterworth: British Association for Counselling and Psychotherapy.

Anthony, K. and Jamieson, A. (2005) *Guidelines for Online Counselling and Psychotherapy* (2nd ed.). Rugby: British Association for Counselling and Psychotherapy.

Anthony, K. and Nagel, D.M. (2010) *Therapy Online: A Practical Guide*. London: Sage.

Barak, A., Hen, L., Boniel-Nissim, M. and Shapira, N. (2008) A comprehensive review and a meta-analysis of the effectiveness of internet-based psychotherapeutic interventions. *Journal of Technology in Human Services*, 26(2–4), 109–160.

Danet, B. (2001) *Cyberpl@y*. London: Berg.

Derrig-Palumbo, K. and Zeine, F. (2005) *Online Therapy: A Therapist's Guide to Expanding Your Practice*. New York: W.W. Norton.

Evans, J. (2009) *Online Counselling and Guidance Skills: A Practical Resource for Trainees and Practitioners*. London: Sage.

Gehl, N., Anthony, K. and Nagel, D.M. (2016) Online training for online mental health. In S. Goss, K. Anthony, L. Stretch and D.M. Nagel (eds), *Technology in Mental Health: Applications in Practice, Supervision and Training* (2nd ed.). Springfield, IL: CC Thomas.

Goss, S. and Anthony, K. (2003) *Technology in Counselling and Psychotherapy: A Practitioner's Guide*. Basingstoke: Palgrave Macmillan.

Goss, S., Anthony, K., Palmer, S. and Jamieson, A. (2001) *Guidelines for Online Counselling and Psychotherapy*. Rugby: British Association for Counselling and Psychotherapy.

Goss, S., Anthony, K., Stretch, L. and Nagel, D.M. (eds) (2016) *Technology in Mental Health: Applications in Practice, Supervision and Training* (2nd ed.). Springfield, IL: CC Thomas.

Goss, S. and Ferns, J. (2016) Using cell/mobile phone SMS to enhance client crisis and peer support. In S. Goss, K. Anthony, L. Stretch and D.M. Nagel (eds), *Technology in Mental Health: Applications in Practice, Supervision and Training* (2nd ed.). Springfield, IL: CC Thomas.

Hill, A. and Roth, A. (2014) *The Competences Required to Deliver Psychological Therapies 'at a Distance'*. Lutterworth: British Association for Counselling and Psychotherapy.

Hsiung, R.C. (ed.) (2002) *e-Therapy*. New York: W.W. Norton.

Jones, G. and Stokes, A. (2009) *Online Counselling: A Handbook for Practitioners*. Basingstoke: Palgrave Macmillan.

Kraus, R., Stricker, G. and Speyer, C. (eds) (2010) *Online Counseling* (2nd ed.). San Diego, CA: Elsevier.

Kraus, R., Zack, J. and Stricker, G. (eds) (2004) *Online Counseling*. San Diego, CA: Elsevier.

Lombard, M. and Ditton, T. (1997) At the heart of it all: the concept of presence. *Journal of Computer-Mediated Communication*, 3(2). (http://onlinelibrary.wiley.com/doi/10.1111/j.1083-6101.1997.tb00072.x/abstract).

Nagel, D.M. and Anthony, K. (2009) *Ethical Framework for the Use of Technology in Mental Health*. Online Therapy Institute. (www.onlinetherapyinstitute.com/ethical-training).

National Board of Certified Counselors (2001) *The Practice of Internet Counseling*. Greensboro, NC: NBCC. (www.nbcc.org/Assets/Ethics/nbcccodeofethics.pdf).

Suler, J. (2004) The online disinhibition effect. (http://users.rider.edu/~suler/psycyber/disinhibit.html).

RECOMMENDED READING

1. Goss, S., Anthony, K., Stretch, L. and Nagel, D.M. (eds) (2016) *Technology in Mental Health: Applications in Practice, Supervision and Training* (2nd ed.). Springfield, IL: CC Thomas.

The second edition of this 2010 edited textbook includes 40 updated chapters on all available technologies used in the profession in 2016. It also includes a new section on clinical supervision and training. Authors are selected from experts worldwide, giving a true international flavour to the book.

2. Anthony, K. and Nagel, D.M. (2010) *Therapy Online: A Practical Guide*. London: Sage.

This textbook focuses on the use of text in online work and is written by the two leading experts in online therapy and counselling. It also includes a full case study between a counsellor and a client from online assessment, through email, mobile SMS, chat, telephone and videoconferencing to closure of the therapeutic online relationship.

3. Anthony, K. (2014) Training therapists to work effectively online and offline within digital culture. *British Journal of Guidance & Counselling*, 43(1), 36–42.

A peer-reviewed paper analysing the author's considerable experience in the training of practitioners to use online methods of delivery.

7.25 WIDER USES OF TECHNOLOGIES IN THERAPY

KATE ANTHONY, STEPHEN GOSS, AND DEEANNA MERZ NAGEL

OVERVIEW AND KEY POINTS

This chapter briefly considers a small sampling of technologies of relevance to therapy, either as an adjunct to it or to support client development and self-help, such as:

- Computerized cognitive-behavioural therapy (CCBT)
- Videoconferencing
- Blogging
- Virtual worlds and avatar therapy
- Web 2.0, social media and health 2.0

BACKGROUND AND CONTEXT

Every therapist now needs to be able, *at least*, to understand the ramifications of technologically mediated relationships for their clients, lest they fail to appreciate that such things are real and not merely 'virtual' (Anthony, 2001), and to be able to utilize the opportunities technologies now afford.

Use of technology is not for every client or every therapist. Dangers exist – such as touching deeply sensitive parts of a client's life while not physically being present to help contain the experience – and are evident in the specialist ethical guidance (Anthony and Goss, 2009; Nagel and Anthony, 2009a) and competencies (Hill and Roth, 2014) that are required.

Developments in technologically mediated psychological support have, in the past, frequently been led by clients rather than therapists, who often have strongly polarized reactions to the concept (Goss and Anthony, 2003; Goss and Hooley, 2015), although this may change as central organizations, such as the United Kingdom's (UK) National Health Service, increasingly adopt technological means of delivering services. These services are particularly relevant for those who are unable or reluctant to access services face to face or for specific or acute needs, as in suicide prevention (Goss and Ferns, 2016).

This chapter briefly considers a small sampling of technologies of assistance in providing therapy, either as an adjunct to it or to support client development and self-help. Telephones, email and internet chat are considered in other chapters in this volume.

WAYS OF WORKING

COMPUTERIZED COGNITIVE-BEHAVIOURAL THERAPY

Computerized cognitive-behavioural therapy (CCBT) has been one of the most successful psychotherapeutic applications of technology, with a strong and growing evidence base (Cavanagh and Grist, 2016; Kaltenthaler et al., 2016).

CCBT distils key elements of cognitive-behavioural therapy (CBT) into software for clients previously screened by a professional. Clients undertake tasks to identify, monitor and evaluate negative thought patterns and are guided through strategies such as graded exposure, problem solving and behavioural experiments.

CCBT varies from single-session anonymous use software to complex systems facilitating sophisticated relationships with the user. CCBT may require no therapist input, be designed as an adjunct to therapy or be provided with support by telephone, email or in person. Good programs will monitor risk (such as suicidality) and provide appropriate alerts to the user, the responsible practitioner or both.

Among numerous others, examples of CCBT include *Beating the Blues* and *FearFighter*. CCBT received 'class approval' from the UK National Institute for Health and Care Excellence since 2006 (NICE, 2006; see also NICE 2009), although variable outcomes across different packages suggest this may be premature and caution is still warranted (Cavanagh and Grist, 2016).

MOBILE/SMS TEXT MESSAGING

Also noted in Chapter 7.24 (Anthony – this volume), despite being restricted to just 160 characters per message, anecdotal and growing research evidence suggests that it is possible to create helpful therapeutic services based on short message service (SMS) interactions (Blake-Buffini and Gordon, 2015), commonly referred to as mobile phone text messages or texts. This is a popular means of communication with many clients, especially younger populations (Haxell, 2015; Ling, 2007). The UK Samaritans' SMS service, for example, received 413,000 messages from over 7,500 unique mobile numbers in its first 36 months alone (Goss and Ferns, 2016).

In addition to providing ready access to professional interventions, text messaging offers a psychologically and physically involving activity, itself of value, for example for people who self-harm. Mobile devices can also act as a platform for other interventions (Preziosa et al., 2009), are accessible during peak stress periods (e.g., during a suicide attempt), or can be well suited to semi-automated interventions, such as post-therapy follow-up (e.g., Bauer et al., 2003), symptom monitoring (e.g., Elliott, 2008) or reinforcing treatment protocol adherence or health information (e.g., Bertrand, 2006). Mobile-phone-based services are of particular relevance for emerging economies, typified by poor mental health care provision but burgeoning mobile phone availability (e.g., Hoefman and Apunyu, 2010).

BLOGGING AND PODCASTING

A web log or 'blog' contains a series of entries somewhat like an online diary. Most are interactive to some degree, allowing responses to posts that facilitate conversations between readers and authors, and potentially fostering the development of distinctive communities focused around the blog's themes (Nagel and Anthony, 2009b). Podcasting is a similarly used means of self-publishing recorded items (usually audio or video) and often centred on recurrent interests and topics.

Some blogs are overtly psycho-educational or designed to keep practitioners informed of developments in the field (e.g., http://onlinetherapyinstitute.com/blog/ or www.psychcentral.com/blog). Others are far more personally oriented, and may be none the worse, or less useful, for that. Writing about one's experiences has long been known to have therapeutic potential (Pennebaker, 1997; Thompson, 2004). Writing in electronic formats, like blogging, may offer specific additional advantages (Hyland et al., 1993), if done with sufficient attention to self-protection. Tan (2008) reported that around 50 per cent of blogs are kept at least in part for the therapeutic effects experienced by the author.

Privacy issues can easily arise, however, and practitioners should be aware of the potential for clients to blog or create podcasts or other forms of public discussion about their therapy. Whether practising via technology or not, it is wise to include discussion of these kinds of issues in contracting with clients to ensure adequate protection of privacy for both parties (Anthony and Goss, 2009; Grohol, 2016; see also www.onlinetherapyinstitute.com/ethical-training/).

VIDEOCONFERENCING

Videoconferencing (sometimes referred to as voice over internet protocol, VOIP) is effectively an extension of familiar audio telephony (see Anthony – Chapter 7.24, this volume; Simpson, 2009) and has been used effectively to extend the reach of mental health services in many parts of the world. Simpson et al. (2016) note evidence supporting video therapy and examine factors associated with the quality of the therapeutic alliance and also give extensive recommendations for enhancing the quality. Like many therapeutic technologies, privacy is an important issue. Practitioners should beware services that retain ownership of the data transmitted (such as, at the time of writing, Skype, despite its ubiquity) even if they are otherwise well encrypted. Increasingly, specialist platforms such as PlusGuidance.com are designed specifically for mental health care and offer secure private means of communicating with clients with a focus on videoconferencing.

VIRTUAL REALITY, VIRTUAL EXPOSURE THERAPY AND AVATAR THERAPY

Virtual reality environments allow users to experience synthetically created environments with which they can interact and, often, communicate with other users.

A virtual world may be limited, like a single room or set of objects, or extensive, like the infinitely expandable world of Second Life, within which relationships, businesses – and therapy – can all flourish. Virtual worlds have tens of millions of users (Schwartz, 2008) and are expected to exceed a billion by 2018, with real clients paying for real services worth billions each year (Gilbert, 2008).

Virtual worlds with a community of users – massively multiplayer online (MMO) environments – can offer vastly increased social opportunities (Deeley, 2008; Live2Give, 2005) with an equality not restricted by the users' gender, race or disability, including social skills deficits (Nagel, 2009).

Avatars – the digital representation of the user – can express one's actual or ideal self or different 'configurations of self' (Mearns and Thorne, 2000) – a child, a different gender or even an animal – in what has been termed 'avatar therapy' (Anthony and Lawson, 2002). It is possible to construct conversations with deceased family members (Nagel and Anthony, 2010), allowing clients to process 'unfinished business', or to address other parts of their selves, extending familiar 'empty chair' techniques (Ivey and Ivey, 1999).

While security issues may require virtual worlds, including Second Life, to be combined with more thoroughly encrypted services to allow properly private conversations, some, such as NeuroVR Editor (Riva and Repetto, 2016) or EMMA's World (Baños et al., 2009), have been created with therapeutic levels of safety and benefit in mind (Riva, 2005; Riva and Repetto, 2016).

Clinical applications include virtual exposure therapy, in which clients address problematic situations within the safety of a virtual environment. Sexual disorders (Optale, 2003), stress management (Villani et al., 2007), fear of spiders (Emmelkamp et al., 2001) or fear of public speaking can be addressed by placing the client – or an avatar representing them – in a simulation of the feared situation. Behavioural rehearsal, it should be noted, has potential for negative effects when conducted outwith a safe therapeutic frame: examples have been noted of suicidal behaviours being rehearsed in Second Life, leading to increased suicidality in the everyday physical world.

WEB 2.0, SOCIAL MEDIA AND HEALTH 2.0

Web 2.0 marked a shift in internet use (rather than a new technology as such) away from central control of web-based information towards shared control among communities of users, and they are changing the way mental health practitioners do their work even further. McDonald (2010) describes the hallmarks of Web 2.0 as interactive applications, independent from specific operating systems that facilitate information sharing and, importantly, relationships and interaction between people with common interests. 'Social media' refers to the increasingly open and social nature of web-based communications – an essential feature of Web 2.0.

Health 2.0 (Landro, 2006) is the social networking revolution applied in health care, such that consumers locate personalized health information, often with discussion groups and user communities, enabling information sharing and personal networking. Traditional websites that once only offered static data are developing blogs, podcasts and customized search engines to deliver the most relevant and timely information on health topics. Health 2.0 and its social networking represents a new wave of health care (Porter, 2009).

CONCLUSION

Proper training and preparation are prerequisites to ensure client safety and optimal use as new technologies emerge (Nagel and Anthony, 2009a; Anthony, 2015). More extensive discussion of these technologies, and others, such as social networking, telehealth, the use of film and media and technologically facilitated training and supervision, can be found in Goss et al. (2016), Goss and Anthony (2009) and Anthony and Nagel (2010). Additional up-to-date discussion can also be found at www.onlinetherapyinstitute/blog.

REFERENCES

Anthony, K. (2001) Online relationships and cyberinfidelity. *Counselling Journal*, 12(9): 38–39. (http://onlinetherapy institute.com/2011/03/14/from-the-archives-online-relationships-and-cyberinfidelity/).
Anthony, K. (2015) Training therapists to work effectively online and offline within digital culture. *British Journal of Guidance & Counselling*, 43(1): 36–42.

(Continued)

(Continued)

Anthony, K. and Goss, S. (2009) *Guidelines for Online Counselling and Psychotherapy Including Guidelines for Online Supervision* (3rd ed.). Lutterworth: British Association for Counselling and Psychotherapy.

Anthony, K. and Lawson, M. (2002) The use of innovative avatar and virtual environment technology for counselling and psychotherapy. (http://onlinetherapyinstitute.com/wp-content/uploads/2012/08/BTexact.avatar.pdf).

Anthony, K. and Nagel, D.M. (2010) *Therapy Online: A Practical Guide*. London: Sage.

Baños, R.M., Botella, C., Guillen, V., García-Palacios, A., Quero, S., Bretón-López, J. and Alcañiz, M. (2009) An adaptive display to treat stress-related disorders: EMMA's World. *British Journal of Guidance & Counselling*, 37(3): 347–356.

Bauer, S., Percevic, R., Okon, E., Meerman, R. and Kordy, H. (2003) The use of text messaging in the aftercare of patients with bulimia nervosa. *European Eating Disorders Review*, 11(3): 279–290.

Bertrand, J.T., O'Reilly, K., Denison, J., Anhang, R. and Sweat, M. (2006) Systematic review of the effectiveness of mass communication programs to change HIV/AIDS related behaviors in developing countries. *Health Education Research*, 21(4): 567–597.

Blake-Buffini, K. and Gordon, M. (2015) One-to-one support for crisis intervention using online synchronous instant messaging: evaluating working alliance and client satisfaction. *British Journal of Guidance & Counselling*, 43(1): 105–116.

Cavanagh, K. and Grist, R. (2016) The use of computer-aided cognitive behavioural therapy (CCBT) in therapeutic settings. In S. Goss, K. Anthony, L. Stretch and D.M. Nagel (eds), *Technology in Mental Health: Applications in Practice, Supervision and Training* (2nd ed.). Springfield, IL: CC Thomas.

Deeley, L. (2008) Is this a real life, is this just fantasy? *TimesOnline* 24 March. (women.timesonline.co.uk/tol/life_and_style/women/body_and_soul/article1557980.ece).

Elliott, J. (2008) Monitoring mental health by text. *BBC WorldNews America*, 31 December. (news.bbc.co.uk/2/hi/health/7797155.stm).

Emmelkamp, P.M., Bruynzeel, M., Drost, L. and van der Mast, C.A.P.G. (2001) Virtual reality treatment in acrophobia: a comparison with exposure *in vivo*. *CyberPsychology & Behavior*, 4(3): 335–340.

Gilbert, B. (2008) Virtual worlds projected to mushroom to nearly one billion users. *Strategy Analytics*. (www4.strategyanalytics.com/default.aspx?mod=PressReleaseViewer&a0=3983).

Goss, S. and Anthony, K. (eds) (2003) *Technology in Counselling and Psychotherapy: A Practitioner's Guide*. London: Palgrave Macmillan.

Goss, S. and Anthony, K. (2009) Developments in the use of technology in counselling and psychotherapy. *British Journal of Guidance & Counselling*, 37(3): 223–230.

Goss, S., Anthony, K., Stretch, L. and Nagel, D.M. (eds) (2016) *Technology in Mental Health: Applications in Practice, Supervision and Training* (2nd ed.). Springfield, IL: CC Thomas.

Goss, S. and Ferns, J. (2016) Using cell/mobile phone SMS to enhance client crisis and peer support. In S. Goss, K. Anthony, L. Stretch and D.M. Nagel (eds), *Technology in Mental Health: Applications in Practice, Supervision and Training* (2nd ed.). Springfield, IL: CC Thomas.

Goss, S. and Hooley, T. (2015) Symposium on online practice in counselling and guidance. *British Journal of Guidance & Counselling*, 43(1): 1–7.

Grohol, J. (2016) Using websites, blogs and wikis within mental health. In S. Goss, K. Anthony, L. Stretch and D.M. Nagel (eds), *Technology in Mental Health: Applications in Practice, Supervision and Training* (2nd ed.). Springfield, IL: CC Thomas.

Haxell, A. (2015) On becoming textually active at Youthline, New Zealand. *British Journal of Guidance & Counselling*, 43(1): 144–155.

Hill, A. and Roth, A. (2014) *The Competencies Required to Deliver Psychological Therapies 'at a Distance'*. Lutterworth: British Association for Counselling and Psychotherapy.

Hoefman, B.A.S. and Apunyu, B. (2010) Using SMS for HIV/AIDS education and to expand the use of HIV testing and counseling services at the AIDS Information Centre (AIC) Uganda. *M4D 2010: Proceedings of the 2nd International Conference on M4D Mobile Communication Technology for Development*. Kampala, Uganda, November, pp. 40–48.

Hyland, M., Kenyon, C.A., Allen, R. and Howarth, P. (1993) Diary keeping in asthma: comparison of written and electronic methods. *British Medical Journal*, 306(6876): 487–489.

Ivey, A.E. and Ivey, M.B. (1999) *Intentional Interviewing and Counseling*. Pacific Grove, CA: Brooks/Cole.

Kaltenthaler, E., Cavanagh, K. and McCrone, P. (2016) Evaluating the role of electronic and web-based (e-CBT) CBT in mental health. In S. Goss, K. Anthony, L. Stretch and D.M. Nagel (eds), *Technology in Mental Health: Applications in Practice, Supervision and Training* (2nd ed.). Springfield, IL: CC Thomas.

Landro, L. (2006) Social networking comes to health care: online tools give patients better access to information and help build communities. *Wall Street Journal Digital Network*. (online.wsj.com/article/SB116717686202159961.html).

Ling, R. (2007) Children, youth and mobile communication. *Journal of Children and Media*, 1(1): 60–67.

Live2Give (2005) *All About Live2Give*. (braintalk.blogs.com/live2give/2005/01/all_about_live2.html).

McDonald, D.D. (2010) On attempting an updated definition of 'Web 2.0'. (socialmediatoday.com/dennismcdonald/139517/attempting-updated-definition-web-20).

Mearns, D. and Thorne, B. (2000) *Person-centred Therapy Today*. London: Sage.

Nagel, D.M. (2009) People with Asperger's syndrome learn social skills in Second Life. *Telehealth World*, 2(1): 1–8. (www.telehealthworld.com/images/Spring09.pdf).

Nagel, D.M. and Anthony, K. (2009a) *Ethical Framework for the Use of Technology in Mental Health*. Online Therapy Institute. (www.onlinetherapyinstitute.com/id43.html).

Nagel, D.M. and Anthony, K. (2009b) Writing therapies using new technologies: the art of blogging. *Journal of Poetry Therapy*, 22(1): 41–45.

Nagel, D.M. and Anthony, K. (2010) Conclusion: innovation and the future of technology in mental health. In K. Anthony, D.M. Nagel and S. Goss (eds), *The Use of Technology in Mental Health: Applications, Ethics and Practice*. Springfield, IL: CC Thomas.

NICE (2006) *Guidance on the Use of Computerised Cognitive Behavioural Therapy for Anxiety and Depression*. Technology Appraisal no. 97. London: National Institute for Health and Clinical Excellence.

NICE (2009) *Depression: Management of Depression in Primary and Secondary Care*. Guidance CG90. London: National Institute for Health and Clinical Excellence.

Optale, G. (2003) Male sexual dysfunctions and multimedia immersion therapy. *CyberPsychology & Behavior*, 6(3): 289–294.

Pennebaker, J.W. (1997) Writing about emotional experiences as a therapeutic process. *Psychological Science*, 8(3): 162–166.

Porter, M.E. (2009) A strategy for health care reform: toward a value-based system. *New England Journal of Medicine*, 361: 109–112. (www. nejm.org/doi/full/10.1056/NEJMp0904131).

Preziosa, A., Grassi, A., Gaggioli, A. and Riva, G. (2009) Therapeutic applications of the mobile phone. *British Journal of Guidance & Counselling*, 37(3): 313–325.

Riva, G. (2005) Virtual reality in psychotherapy: review. *CyberPsychology & Behavior*, 8(3): 220–240.

Riva, G. and Repetto, C. (2016) Using virtual reality immersion therapeutically. In S. Goss, K. Anthony, L. Stretch and D.M. Nagel (eds), *Technology in Mental Health: Applications in Practice, Supervision and Training* (2nd ed.). Springfield, IL: CC Thomas.

Schwartz, D. (2008) Noted Gartner analyst Steven Prentice updates his predictions on virtual worlds. *Fast Company*. (www.fastcompany.com/954954/noted-gartner-analyst-steven-prentice-updates-his-predictions-virtual-worlds).

Simpson, S. (2009) Psychotherapy via videoconferencing: a review. *British Journal of Guidance & Counselling*, 37(3): 271–286.

Simpson, S., Richardson, L. and Reid, C. (2016) Therapeutic alliance in videoconferencing-based psychotherapy. In S. Goss, K. Anthony, L. Stretch and D.M. Nagel (eds), *Technology in Mental Health: Applications in Practice, Supervision and Training* (2nd ed.). Springfield, IL: CC Thomas.

Tan, L. (2008) Psychotherapy 2.0: MySpace® blogging as self-therapy. *American Journal of Psychotherapy*, 62(2): 143–163.

Thompson, K. (2004) Journal writing as a therapeutic tool. In G. Bolton, S. Howlett, C. Lago and J.K. Wright (eds), *Writing Cures*. Hove: Brunner-Routledge.

Villani, D., Riva, F. and Riva, G. (2007) New technologies for relaxation: the role of presence. *International Journal of Stress Management*, 14(3): 260–274.

RECOMMENDED READING

1. Goss, S., Anthony, K., Stretch L. and Nagel, D.M. (eds) (2016) *Technology in Mental Health: Applications in Practice, Supervision and Training* (2nd ed.). Springfield, IL: CC Thomas.

The second edition of this wide-ranging edited textbook includes 40 updated chapters on all available technologies used in the profession in 2016, including a new section on clinical supervision and training.

2. Anthony, K. and Nagel, D.M. (2010) *Therapy Online: A Practical Guide*. London: Sage.

This textbook focuses on the use of text in online work and is written by the two leading experts in online therapy and counselling. It also includes a full case study between a counsellor and a client from online assessment through email, mobile SMS, chat, telephone and videoconferencing to closure of the therapeutic online relationship.

3. *Therapeutic Innovations in Light of Technology* (*TILT*) Archives (https://issuu.com/onlinetherapyinstitute/docs).

TILT magazine was a quarterly publication from the Online Therapy Institute provided free of charge to all readers. It focuses on the use of technology in mental health and coaching. Archives of the online magazine are available for free download, including features, articles, book reviews and a regular research digest.

INDEX

Note: Page numbers in **bold** indicate a more comprehensive coverage of the topic. Page numbers in *italic* refer to figures and tables.